Mar 28
ap 21
May 30

accounting principles

10th EDITION

C. Rollin Niswonger, PhD, CPA
Professor of Accountancy
Miami University, Oxford, Ohio

Philip E. Fess, PhD, CPA
Professor of Accountancy
University of Illinois, Urbana

published by South-Western Publishing Co.
Cincinnati • Chicago • Dallas • New Rochelle, N.Y. and Burlingame, California

4 5 6 7 8 9 K 3 2 1 0 9   Printed in the United States of America

In its various editions, *Accounting Principles* has been studied by several million students. During nearly four decades it has kept pace with the accelerating rate of change in business operations and the increasing competence of college students. The tenth edition continues to stress basic concepts, presented clearly and concisely. More use has been made of diagrams, charts, and other illustrative devices, and their effectiveness has been enhanced by greater use of color and contrasting type faces.

As in earlier editions, the selection and development of subject matter has been designed to fulfill the needs of college students planning a career in accounting, as

Preface

well as of those studying business administration, the liberal arts, law, or other disciplines. Attention to procedural aspects of accounting has been reduced but there remains sufficient coverage of data processing to impart an understanding of the sources of financial information.

Although the tenth is a more thoroughgoing revision than any preceding edition, those familiar with the book will recognize the continuance of many successful features. Numerous rearrangements have been made to improve the sequential order of subject matter. Presentation of the accounting cycle, heretofore requiring four chapters, is now completed within the first three chap-

ters. Receivables and payables, including interest, discount, and provision for uncollectibles, have been combined into one chapter (Chapter 7). The chapter now confined exclusively to merchandise inventory (Chapter 8) includes coverage of perpetual inventory. Materials on intangible assets and depletion have been added to the chapter (Chapter 10) hitherto limited to long-lived depreciable assets. A new chapter on systems design and automated data processing (Chapter 13) has been added, in recognition of the increasing importance and the curricular emphasis on these subjects.

The four chapters heretofore devoted to corporation accounting concepts and practices have been extensively rewritten and condensed into three chapters (Chapters 16–18). The procedural and other peripheral matters deleted in the condensation process were partially replaced by discussions of current practices in such subjects as interperiod income tax allocation, prior period adjustments and extraordinary items, and presentation of earnings per share.

Much of the material on process and job order cost accounting systems, budgetary controls, and standard costs (Chapters 20–22) has been rewritten, with increased emphasis on reports for management. Most of the detailed descriptions of deductions allowed in determining taxable income have been replaced (Chapter 23) by explanations of tax minimization through selection of the form of organization, timing of transactions, and equalization among taxable entities. Other chapters emphasizing management decisions (Chapters 24–25) include various applications of variable costing, differential analysis, and cost-volume-profit analysis.

In response to the increasing attention to funds flow and cash flow in financial reporting, an entire chapter (Chapter 26) is now devoted to the subject. Similarly, in recognition of the heightened activity in corporate combinations and the continued concern about inflation, basic materials on application of the pooling of interests concept, and recognition of price-level changes, have been introduced (Chapter 27).

As in the preceding edition, the variety and quantity of questions, exercises, and problems presented at the end of each chapter provide a wide choice of subject matter and range of difficulty. An additional series of problems is provided in Appendix C. The working papers correlating with the problems are designed to relieve students of the burden of repetitive details in order that attention may be more effectively directed to mastery of the underlying concepts.

Four short practice sets, each requiring the recording, analysis, interpretation, and reporting of accounting data for a single month, are available for use in developing greater student proficiency or for review purposes. Workbooks of study guides, student check sheets, transparencies of solutions to problems, objective tests, and other teaching aids are also available.

The authors acknowledge with gratitude the helpful suggestions received from many teachers who have used earlier editions. Although space limitations prohibit a listing of all of those who have made significant contributions, we acknowledge with sincere thanks the detailed suggestions and recommendations submitted by Professors James B. Bower, The University of Wisconsin; Emmett W. Boyd, Kent State University; John E. Field, University of Auckland, New Zealand; L. H. Gilles, Jr., Wichita State University; Dennis Gordon, University of Akron; Harold E. Griffin, Jr., The University of Connecticut; William H. Hartzell, University of Pennsylvania; Wayne M. Higley, University of Nebraska at Omaha; Rudolph Malandro, Kent State University; Arthur G. Mehl, Bradley University; Harry R. Price, University of Miami; and Mervyn W. Wingfield, University of South Carolina. Our special thanks go to Professor Harold Q. Langenderfer, The University of North Carolina; Dean James H. MacNeill, Fordham University; and Professor Robert W. Vanasse, The Ohio State University, for their assistance in preparing specific portions of the manuscript.

We are also grateful to the American Accounting Association and to the American Institute of Certified Public Accountants for permission to use materials from their publications.

C. Rollin Niswonger
Philip E. Fess

Contents

Practice Set 1   Wilcox Supply Company

The narrative accompanies the set, which is available both with and without business papers. This set provides practice in accounting for a sole proprietorship that uses five journals, a general ledger, and two subsidiary ledgers.

Practice Set   2   Central Appliance Company

The narrative accompanies the set, which is available both with and without business papers. This set provides practice in accounting for a sole proprietorship using the voucher system.

Contents

Chapter 24 Cost and revenue relationships for management
613

Chapter 25 Management reports and special analyses
636

part Ten • Additional statements and analyses

Chapter 26 Funds statement and cash flow
657

Chapter 27 Consolidated statements and other statements
683

Chapter 28 Financial statement analysis
708

part Eleven • Appendixes

part One | Accounting processes for a
service enterprise

1

Basic structure
of accounting

Accounting defined

Accounting is often characterized as "the language of business." Because of the wide range of accounting activity, a concise yet all-inclusive description of accounting is difficult to devise. Accounting is concerned with processes of recording, sorting, and summarizing data resulting from business transactions and events. The data are to a large extent but not exclusively of a financial nature, and are frequently but not always stated in monetary terms. Accounting is more than this, however; its involvement with preparation of reports and interpretations of the data is of even greater significance.

Accounting has been defined rather broadly as:

> . . . the process of identifying, measuring, and communicating economic information to permit informed judgments and decisions by users of the information.[1]

Implicit in this definition is the necessity of recording the economic information that is to be measured. An understanding of the kinds of information to be accounted for and their manner of recording must be

---

[1]*A Statement of Basic Accounting Theory* (Evanston, Illinois: American Accounting Association, 1966), p. 1.

acquired before the student can advance very far into the area of effective communication.

Without exploring in detail the characteristics of economic information, it is sufficient at this point to indicate that it includes financial information about business transactions. Much of the "raw-material" with which accounting deals is composed of business transaction data, expressed in terms of money. The recording of such data may take various forms, such as pen or pencil markings made by hand, printing by various mechanical and electronic devices, or holes or magnetic impressions in cards or tape.

The mere records of transactions are of little use in making "informed judgments and decisions." The recorded data must be sorted and summarized before significant reports and analyses can be prepared. It is not the single business act but the sum of all the operations of a day, week, month, or year that has significance. Some of the reports to enterprise managers and to others who need economic information may be made frequently; other reports are issued only at longer intervals. The usefulness of reports is often enhanced by analyses, such as percentages and ratios, and comparisons between different dates or periods of time. The trends and other significant developments in the affairs of an organization set forth in various reports are, in a general sense, the "end-product" of accounting.

2

Need for accounting

Accounting is the "language" employed to communicate financial information. Such information is sought for a variety of reasons. Owners and prospective owners of a business enterprise need to know about its financial status and its prospects for the future. Bankers and suppliers appraise the financial soundness of a business organization and weigh the risks involved before making loans or granting credit. Government agencies are concerned with the financial activities of business organizations for purposes of taxation and regulation. Employees are also vitally interested in the stability and the profitability of the organization that employs them.

The managers of business enterprises need a wide range of data about every facet of operations, much of which is made available through accounting. The manager of a small business may be thoroughly familiar with all operating and financial details and hence need relatively little accounting information. As the size of a business unit increases, however, the manager becomes farther and farther removed from direct contact with day-to-day operations. He must be supplied with timely financial information about various aspects of the business. The growth of large business units and of the importance of accounting in such organizations has given rise to the expression that accounting provides the "eyes and ears of management."

The accountant has the responsibility of keeping track of the essential dollar information affecting the organization, of interpreting the information in terms of relative success or failure, and of helping to plan the course of future action.

Relationship to other fields

Individuals engaged in such areas of business as finance, production, marketing, personnel, and general management need not be expert accountants, but their usefulness is enhanced and their advancement is more assured if they have a good understanding of accounting principles. Everyone engaged in business activity, from the youngest employee to the manager and owner, comes into contact with accounting. The higher the level of authority and responsibility, the greater is the need for an understanding of accounting concepts and terminology.

Many other persons with specialized training in nonbusiness areas who are employed by business organizations also make use of accounting data and need to understand accounting principles. For example, an engineer responsible for selecting the most desirable solution to a technical manufacturing problem may consider cost accounting data to be the decisive factor. Lawyers use accounting data in tax cases and in lawsuits involving property ownership and damages from breach of contract. Governmental agencies rely on accounting data in evaluating the efficiency of government operations and for appraising the feasibility of proposed taxation and spending programs. Finally, every adult engages in business transactions and must necessarily be concerned with the financial aspects of his own life, and perhaps of others. Accounting plays an important role in modern society and, broadly speaking, it can be said that all citizens are affected by accounting. The closer the contact with financial activity, of course, the greater the need for an understanding of accounting concepts and terminology.

Profession of accountancy

Accountancy is a profession with stature comparable to that of law or engineering. The tremendous development of accounting theory and technique during the current century has been accompanied by an ever-increasing number of professionally trained accountants. Among the factors contributing to this growth have been the increase in number, size, and complexity of business corporations; the imposition of new and increasingly complex taxes, particularly the federal income tax; and other restrictions imposed on business operations by governmental regulations.

Accountants who render accounting services on a fee basis, and staff accountants employed by them, are said to be engaged in *public accounting*. Accountants employed by a particular business firm or nonprofit organization, perhaps as chief accountant, controller, or financial vice president, are said to be engaged in *private accounting*.

Recognizing the need for reliable professional accounting service, all the states have enacted laws providing for the licensing of certified public accountants, commonly called CPAs. Only those individuals who have met the qualifications and received a license may engage in public practice as CPAs.

The qualifications required for the CPA certificate differ among the various states. A specified level of education is required, often the completion of a collegiate course of study in accounting. All states require that a candidate pass an examination prepared by the American Institute of Certified Public Accountants. Most states give the examination twice a year, in May and November, and many permit candidates to take the examination upon graduation from college or during the term in which they will complete the educational requirements. The examination, which occupies one afternoon and two all-day sessions, is divided into four parts: Accounting Practice, Theory of Accounts, Auditing, and Commercial Law. Some states also require an examination in an additional subject, such as Rules of Professional Conduct. Most states do not permit successful candidates to practice as CPAs until they have had from one to three years' experience in public accounting or in employment considered equivalent.

Some states do not restrict the practice of public accounting to those licensed as CPAs. In the absence of express statutory prohibition, any person may style himself as a public accountant, or PA. Details regarding requirements for practice as a CPA or PA in any particular state can be obtained from the respective state Board of Accountancy.

The scope of activities and responsibilities of private accountants varies quite widely. They are frequently referred to as administrative or executive accountants, or, if they are employed by a manufacturing concern, as industrial accountants. Various branches of federal, state, and local governments also employ accountants in increasing numbers.

Both public and private accounting have long been recognized as excellent training for top managerial responsibilities. Many executive positions in government and in industry are held by CPAs and others with education and experience in accounting.

Specialized accounting fields

As in many other areas of human activity in the twentieth century, a number of specialized fields in accounting have evolved. This tendency toward specialization has been caused in large measure by growth in size of business units, mounting taxes, and increasing regulation of business by law and by governmental agencies. These influences, together with rapid technological advances and accelerated economic growth, have created the need for accountants to acquire a high degree of expertness in various specialties.

The term *general accounting* or *financial accounting* applies to the overall accounting for an economic unit. It is concerned with the recording of transactions for a business or other economic unit and the periodic preparation of statements from these records. The various general purpose and special purpose reports and statements prepared from the accounting records are used to impart useful information to managers, owners, creditors, governmental agencies, and the general public. The accounting principles and techniques that will be developed in this book are in large part included in general accounting.

Auditing represents a field of accounting activity that independently reviews general accounting. Auditing was the first service rendered by public accountants and is still one of their principal activities. These accountants examine records supporting the financial statements and express an opinion regarding the fairness and accuracy of such statements. Large corporations with widely dispersed operations frequently employ their own staffs of *internal auditors*. One of the most important duties of internal auditors is to determine the extent to which the various operating divisions observe the policies and procedures prescribed by management.

Cost accounting emphasizes the determination and the control of costs. It is concerned primarily with the costs of manufacturing processes and of manufactured products, but increasing attention is being given to distribution costs. In addition, one of the principal functions of the cost accountant is to assemble and interpret cost data, both actual and prospective, for the use of management in controlling current operations and in planning for the future.

Management accounting employs both historical and estimated data in assisting management in day-to-day operations and in planning future operations. It deals with specific problems that confront enterprise managers at various organizational levels. The management accountant is frequently concerned with identifying alternative courses of action and then helping to select the best one. For example, he may assist the company treasurer in preparing plans for future financing, or he may develop data for the use of the sales manager in determining the selling price to be placed on a new product. In recent years, public accounting firms have come to realize that their training and experience uniquely qualify them to advise management personnel on policies and administration, even in matters which might seem to have little relationship to accounting. This rapidly growing field of specialization by CPAs is frequently called *management services* or *administrative services.*

Tax accounting encompasses the preparation of tax returns and the consideration of the tax consequences of proposed business transactions or alternative courses of action. Accountants specializing in this field must be familiar with the tax statutes affecting their employer or clients and also must keep up-to-date on administrative regulations and court decisions on tax cases.

Accounting systems is the special field concerned with the creation of procedures for the accumulation and the reporting of financial data. The systems accountant must devise appropriate "checks and balances" to safeguard business assets and, to the fullest possible extent, provide for information flow that will be helpful to management. It is essential that he also be knowledgeable about the uses and relative merits of available mechanical and electronic data processing equipment.

Budgetary accounting presents the plan of financial operations for a period and, through accounts and summaries, provides comparisons of actual operations with the predetermined plan. It is a combination of planning, coordinating, and controlling future operations.

Governmental accounting specializes in the transactions of political units, such as states and municipalities. It seeks to provide useful accounting information regarding the business aspects of public administration and helps to control the expenditure of public funds in accordance with statutory requirements.

Accounting instruction, as a field of specialization, requires no explanation. However, in addition to teaching, accounting professors often engage in research, auditing, tax accounting, or other areas of accounting on a part-time or consulting basis.

There is some overlapping among the various specialized fields, and leaders in any particular field are likely to be well versed in related areas. There is also a considerable degree of specialization within particular specialties. For example, within the field of auditing one may become an expert in a particular classification such as department stores or public utilities; in tax accounting one may specialize in the problems of oil and gas producing companies; or in systems one may become an expert in electronic data processing equipment.

Bookkeeping and accounting

There is some confusion over the distinction between "bookkeeping" and "accounting." This is due in part to the fact that the two are related and that there is no universally accepted line of demarcation between bookkeeping and accounting.

In general, *bookkeeping* is the recording of business data in a prescribed manner. A bookkeeper may be responsible for keeping all of the records of a business or only a minor segment, such as a portion of the customers' accounts in a department store. Much of the work of the bookkeeper is clerical in nature and is increasingly being accomplished through the use of mechanical and electronic equipment.

Accounting is primarily concerned with the design of the system of records, the preparation of reports based on the recorded data, and the interpretation of the reports. Accountants often direct and review the work of bookkeepers. The larger the firm, the greater is the number of gradations in responsibility and authority. The work of accountants at the beginning levels may include some bookkeeping. In any event, the accountant must possess a much higher level of knowledge, conceptual understanding, and analytical skill than is required of the bookkeeper.

Principles and practice

In accounting, as in the physical and biological sciences, experimentation, development, and change are never-ending. Capable scholars devote their lives and their intellectual energies to analyzing accounting phenomena. Experienced professional accountants contribute their best thinking to the solution of problems forever confronting their clients or employers. The several professional accounting associations regard research as a major activity. It is from such research that accounting principles evolve to form the underlying basis for accounting practice.

This book is devoted both to explanations of accounting principles and to demonstrations of related practices or procedures. It is through this duality of emphasis on the "why" of accounting as well as on the "how" that the full significance of accounting is learned.

Business entity

Accounting always applies to an economic organization or unit in society. Economic units include profit-making enterprises; governmental units, such as states, cities, and school districts; consumers, such as families and individuals; and nonprofit organizations, such as churches, hospitals, and clubs. Each economic unit has business transactions that must be recorded, sorted, summarized, and reported. The accounting must therefore apply to each unit. For example, it is each particular automobile manufacturer, not the automobile industry as a whole, that has business transactions.

The *business entity* concept does not mean, however, that accounting data for a particular unit cannot be combined with data for other similar units to obtain an overall picture. For example, accounting data accumulated by each airline in the country may be assembled to provide financial information about the entire airline industry. Similarly, figures for national income may be developed from the accounting records of many separate economic units.

Although accounting principles and techniques have been developed for all types of economic units, this textbook emphasizes those applicable to profit-making business enterprises. Such enterprises may be organized in a variety of ways. The principal forms of organization are sole proprietorship, partnership, and corporation. A *sole proprietorship* is a business that is owned entirely by one individual. A *partnership* is an enterprise owned by two or more individuals in accordance with a contractual arrangement among them. A *corporation* is a separate legal entity, organized in accordance with state or federal statutes, in which ownership is divided into shares of stock. The principal difference among the three types of organization, from the standpoint of accounting, lies in the nature of the ownership and in the legal rights and responsibilities related to it.

The accounting principles developed in the early chapters of this textbook are based on the sole proprietorship form of organization. It is the simplest type of business organization and by far the most common. Later chapters will be devoted to variations in accounting related to partnerships and corporations.

8   Basic business operations

The use of property is essential to the conduct of business. A place for the business must be provided in a building that is owned or rented; equipment adapted to the activities of the business must be owned or leased; if commodities are sold, they must be purchased or manufactured and stored prior to sale; if services are rendered, the equipment and the supplies needed to render the services must be available for use. Wherever there is business, property is found.

Through the sale of commodities or services at a profit, a business enterprise increases its property. Such increases, a part of which is ordinarily in the form of cash, may be retained in the business and used for business expansion or reduction of indebtedness, or the property increases may be withdrawn from the business by the owners. Those who organize a new business venture or invest in established business firms do so with the expectation that operations will yield a profit, or net income. There is always the risk, of course, that the business will be unsuccessful, and the owners may lose all or part of their investment.

Role of accounting in business decisions

Knowledge of the past performance of an enterprise is of additional value beyond its historical aspects; it is useful in planning future operations. By comparing summaries of the most recent month with the preceding month and with the comparable month of the preceding year, trends become apparent. Further study and analysis may develop the contributory causes of the trends and point the way to accelerating those that are favorable and to halting those that are undesirable. For example, an increase in the volume of services or merchandise sold is a favorable indication. If the increase is accompanied by increases in costs and expenses of such magnitude that net income is decreased, the end result is, of course, unfavorable. Questions such as the following should be answered: Was the increased volume of sales attributable to excessive reductions in selling price? Did the cost of the merchandise increase without a comparable adjustment in selling price? What types of expenses increased and what were the causes of the increases? Which of the increases were unavoidable and which ones can be reduced in the future without adverse effects?

A business that is contemplating expansion needs to give careful consideration to the probable effect of the added facilities on the future volume of business and expenses. Will the return on the additional investment justify the expansion? There may also be problems of financing. If money is to be borrowed, when can it be repaid? These are illustrations of the many problems that constantly confront owners and managers in planning future operations. Business records do not supply all of the answers, nor do they take the place of good judgment. The data obtainable from the records are essential, however, as a partial basis for making decisions.

There are many other needs of a more routine nature served by records. For example, it is necessary to know the amount owed to each creditor and by each customer and the date each payment is due. Records of property are necessary in determining the amount and type of insurance that should be carried and in ascertaining the amount of any insured loss that may occur. Knowing when to place orders for merchandise and supplies, granting credit to customers, anticipating the amount of cash required at any particular time — these and many other essential items of information can be obtained in a timely and orderly fashion only if adequate records are maintained.

In addition to managers and owners, there are others who must be supplied with reports based on the business records. Banks customarily require periodic financial statements from businesses that owe them money. It is customary to submit annual reports to credit-rating companies. Various branches of federal, state, and local governments require reports in connection with income, property, sales, social security, and other taxes. One of the prerequisites to the issuance of securities by corporations is the filing of detailed reports on business operations and

9

financial position with governmental agencies. Stock exchanges also require periodic reports from corporations whose stocks are listed. The foregoing reasons for preparing accounting reports for outsiders are merely illustrative; there are many others.

Thus far attention has been focused on business enterprises. Records are also needed by those engaged in professional pursuits and even by persons who have retired from active participation in a business or profession. Governmental units must maintain records of their transactions; they are required to report to other agencies at a higher level of authority and also to the citizenry. Records of past performance also serve as background in planning for the future. For similar reasons, churches, educational institutions, labor unions, and other organizations must maintain records and report on their financial transactions.

Business transactions

A *business transaction* is the occurrence of an event or of a condition that must be recorded. For example, the payment of a monthly telephone bill of $25, the purchase of $500 of merchandise on credit, and the acquisition of land and a store building for $100,000 are illustrative of the variety of business transactions.

The first two transactions are relatively simple: a payment of money in exchange for a service, and a promise to pay within a short time in exchange for commodities. The purchase of a building and the land on which it is situated is usually a more complex transaction. The total price agreed upon must be allocated between the land and the building, and the agreement usually provides for spreading the payment of a substantial part of the price over a period of years and for the payment of interest on the unpaid balance. There may be other provisions designed to safeguard the seller until the full price has been paid.

It can readily be seen that a particular business transaction may lead to an event or a condition that constitutes another transaction. For example, the purchase of merchandise on credit described above will be followed by payment to the creditor, which is another transaction; and each time a portion of the merchandise is sold, another transaction occurs. Each of these events needs to be recorded. Each payment to the seller of the land and the building is a transaction, as is the payment of interest. The fact that the life of the building is limited must also be given recognition in the records.

The wearing-out of the building is not an exchange of goods or services between the business and an outsider, but it is nevertheless a significant event that must be recorded. Transactions of this type, as well as others not directly related to outsiders, are sometimes referred to as *internal* transactions.

The system of records begins with the recording of each transaction. There are many different methods of recording transactions. For example, a sale of a service for cash may be recorded by a handwritten sales ticket, or it may be recorded by merely depressing the appropriate keys of a cash register. Regardless of the recording system used, the historical data thus accumulated provide the basis for the preparation of various summarizing reports. In addition, the supporting documents and other forms of evidence furnish a basis for subsequent review and verification by internal auditors, independent CPAs, and others.

Business transactions and monetary amounts

When properties or services are purchased by a business, the monetary amount at which they are recorded is the price agreed upon in the business transaction. For example, if a business building is purchased for $50,000, that amount is used in the buyer's accounting records. The seller may have been asking $60,000 for the building up to the time of sale; the buyer may have initially offered $40,000 for it; the building may have been assessed at $35,000 for property tax purposes and insured for $45,000; and the buyer may have received an offer of $75,000 for the building the day after he acquired it. These latter amounts have no effect on the accounting records because they do not originate from an exchange transaction. The transaction price, or cost, of $50,000 determines the basis at which the building is recorded. Cost results from the actions of an informed buyer and an informed seller who are each attempting to obtain the most favorable price. It is an objective fact that can be verified from the evidence created by an exchange transaction; it is not a mere subjective opinion.

The offer of $75,000 for the building is an indication that it was a bargain at $50,000, but to record the building at $75,000 would give recognition to an illusory or unrealized profit. If the offer should be accepted and the building sold, the seller would realize a profit of $25,000 and, of course, the cost to the new owner would be $75,000.

Accounting is fundamentally a process of accounting for costs and revenues; it is not a process of valuation. Only the amount agreed upon between buyer and seller in a transaction is sufficiently objective for accounting purposes. If upward and downward adjustments to properties were made on the basis of mere offers, appraisals, and opinions, accounting records would soon become so unstable and unreliable as to be meaningless.

Assets, liabilities, and capital

The use of property in the operation of a business has been emphasized. It has also been pointed out that accounting deals with property and rights to property. For every business enterprise, the sum of the properties owned is equal to the sum of the rights to the properties.

The properties owned by a business are called *assets*. The rights to the properties are called *equities*. The relationship between assets and equities may therefore be stated in the equation:

$$\text{Assets} = \text{Equities}$$

Equities may be subdivided into two principal types: the rights of creditors and the rights of owners. The equities of creditors represent *debts* of the business and are called *liabilities*. The equity of the owners is called *capital, proprietorship*, or *owner's equity*. Expansion of the equation to give recognition to the two basic types of equities yields the following, which is known as the *accounting equation*:

$$\text{Assets} = \text{Liabilities} + \text{Capital}$$

It is customary to place "Liabilities" before "Capital" in the accounting equation because creditors have preferential rights to the assets. The residual claim of the owner or owners is sometimes given greater emphasis by transposing liabilities to the other side of the equation, yielding:

$$\text{Assets} - \text{Liabilities} = \text{Capital}$$

All business transactions, from the simplest to the most complex, can be stated in terms of their effect on the three basic elements of the accounting equation.

12

Transactions and the accounting equation

The effect of changes in assets, liabilities, and capital on the accounting equation can be demonstrated by studying some typical transactions. As the basis of the illustration, assume that Lee Holt establishes a new business under the name of Holt Taxi. Each transaction or group of similar transactions during the first month of operations is described and the effect on the accounting equation shown.

Transaction (a)

Holt's first transaction is to deposit $9,000 in a bank account in the name of Holt Taxi. The effect of this transaction is to increase the asset cash by $9,000 and to increase capital, on the other side of the equation, by the same amount. After the transaction the equation for Holt Taxi will appear as follows:

Assets		Capital
Cash	=	Lee Holt, Capital
(a) 9,000		9,000

It should be noted that the equation relates only to the business enterprise. Holt's personal assets, such as his home and his personal

bank account, and his personal liabilities are excluded from consideration. The business is treated as a distinct entity apart from the owner.

Transaction (b)

Holt's next transaction in establishing his business is to purchase
automobiles and other equipment, for which he pays $7,400 in cash.
This transaction changes the composition of the assets but does not
change the total. The items in the equation prior to this transaction,
the effects of this transaction, and the new balances after the transaction
are as follows:

	Assets			Capital
	Cash	+	Equipment	Lee Holt, Capital
Bal.	9,000			9,000
(b)	−7,400		+7,400	
Bal.	1,600		7,400	9,000

Transaction (c)

During the month Holt purchases $650 of gasoline, oil, and other
supplies from various suppliers, agreeing to pay in the near future. This
type of transaction is called a purchase *on account* and the liability created
is termed an *account payable*. In actual practice each purchase would be
recorded as it occurred and a separate record would be maintained for
each creditor. The effect of this group of transactions is to increase assets
and liabilities by $650, as indicated below:

13

	Assets					Liabilities	+	Capital
						Accounts		Lee Holt,
	Cash	+	Supplies	+	Equipment	Payable	+	Capital
Bal.	1,600				7,400			9,000
(c)			+650			+650		
Bal.	1,600		650		7,400	650		9,000

Transaction (d)

During the month Holt pays $300 to his creditors on account,
thereby reducing both assets and liabilities. The effect on the equation
is as follows:

	Assets					Liabilities	+	Capital
						Accounts		Lee Holt,
	Cash	+	Supplies	+	Equipment	Payable	+	Capital
Bal.	1,600		650		7,400	650		9,000
(d)	− 300					−300		
Bal.	1,300		650		7,400	350		9,000

The principal objective of the owner of a business enterprise is to
increase his capital by earning a net income. For Lee Holt this means
that the assets he acquires from the sale of services must exceed the cost
of supplies used, salaries incurred, and all other expenses of operating

the business. In general, the amount charged to customers for goods or services sold to them is called *revenue*.[2] Alternative terms may be used for particular types of revenue, such as *sales* for the sale of merchandise or business services, *fees earned* for charges by a physician to his patient, *rent earned* for the use of real estate or other property, and *fares earned* for Holt's business.

The excess of the revenue over the expenses incurred in earning the revenue is called *net income*. If the expenses of the enterprise exceed the revenue, the excess is a *net loss*. As it is ordinarily impossible to determine the exact amount of expense incurred in connection with each revenue transaction, it is considered satisfactory to determine the net income or the net loss for a specified period of time, such as a month or a year, rather than for each sale or small group of sales.

Transaction (e)

During the first month of operations Holt earned taxi fares of $2,000, for which he received cash. The total effect of these transactions is to increase cash by $2,000 and to yield revenue in the same amount. The revenue can be viewed as though it effected a $2,000 increase in capital. At the time expenses of the business are incurred, they are treated as offsets against revenue and hence as reductions in capital. In terms of the accounting equation, the effect of the receipt of cash for services performed is as follows:

	Assets				Liabilities +	Capital
					Accounts +	Lee Holt,
	Cash +	Supplies +	Equipment	=	Payable	Capital
Bal.	1,300	650	7,400		350	9,000
(e)	+2,000					+ 2,000 Fares earned
Bal.	3,300	650	7,400		350	11,000

Instead of requiring the payment of cash at the time goods or services are sold, a business may make sales *on account*, allowing the customer to pay later. In such cases the firm acquires a claim against the customer called an *account receivable*. It is as much an asset as cash, and the revenue is realized in exactly the same manner as if cash had been immediately received. At a later date, when the money is collected, there is only an exchange of one asset for another, cash increasing and accounts receivable decreasing.

Transaction (f)

Various business expenses incurred and paid during the month were as follows: wages, $550; rent, $50; utilities, $25; miscellaneous, $75.

---

[2] *Accounting Research and Terminology Bulletins*, "No. 2, Proceeds, Revenue, Income, Profit, and Earnings" (New York: American Institute of Certified Public Accountants, 1961), p. 34.

The effect of this group of transactions is to reduce cash and to reduce capital, as indicated in the following manner:

	Assets				Liabilities +	Capital	
	Cash	+ Supplies	+ Equipment		Accounts Payable	+	Lee Holt, Capital	
Bal.	3,300	650	7,400		350		11,000	
(f)	− 700			=			−	550 Wages exp.
							−	50 Rent expense
							−	25 Utilities exp.
							−	75 Misc. expense
Bal.	2,600	650	7,400		350		10,300	

Transaction (g)

At the end of the month Holt determines that the cost of the supplies on hand is $250, the remainder ($650 − $250) having been used in the operations of the business. This reduction of $400 in supplies and capital may be shown as follows:

	Assets				Liabilities +	Capital	
	Cash	+ Supplies	+ Equipment		Accounts Payable	+	Lee Holt, Capital	
Bal.	2,600	650	7,400	=	350		10,300	
(g)		−400					−	400 Supplies exp.
Bal.	2,600	250	7,400		350		9,900	

Transaction (h)

Although Holt has used the automobile and other equipment throughout the month, there is no apparent reduction in the amount on hand as was the case with the supplies. It is obvious, however, that the equipment does gradually lose its usefulness with the passage of time. This expiration of usefulness represents a business expense, which is called *depreciation*. It has the effect of decreasing both assets and capital. For reasons that will become apparent in a later chapter, it is customary to keep a cumulative record of the recognized depreciation rather than to deduct it directly from the equipment. The effect on the equation of the depreciation expense, estimated at $200, is as follows:

	Assets					Liabilities +	Capital	
	Cash	+ Sup- plies	+ Equip- ment	− Accumu- lated Depre- ciation		Accounts Payable	+	Lee Holt, Capital	
Bal.	2,600	250	7,400		=	350		9,900	
(h)				+200				−	200 Depr. exp.
Bal.	2,600	250	7,400	200		350		9,700	

Although the equipment balance of $7,400 is unchanged, the remaining unexpired cost of the asset after recognition of the depreciation expense is clearly only $7,200, shown as follows:

Equipment $7,400
Less accumulated depreciation 200 $7,200

It should be noted that the accumulated depreciation is presented on the left side of the equation as a reduction in assets. Hence the $200 increase in the item, which is in effect a decrease in assets, is matched by the $200 decrease in capital on the right side of the equation.

Transaction (i)

At the end of the month Holt withdraws from the business $500 in cash for his personal use. This transaction, which effects a decrease in cash and a decrease in capital, is the exact opposite of an investment in the business by the owner. The withdrawal is not a business expense, and it should be excluded from consideration in determining the net income from operations of the enterprise. The balances in the equation, the effect of the $500 withdrawal, and the new balances are as follows:

		Assets			=	Liabilities +	Capital
	Cash +	Sup-plies +	Equip-ment −	Accumu-lated Depre-ciation	=	Accounts Payable +	Lee Holt, Capital
Bal.	2,600	250	7,400	200		350	9,700
(i)	− 500						− 500 Drawing
Bal.	2,100	250	7,400	200		350	9,200

Summary of illustration

The business transactions of Lee Holt are summarized in tabular form below. The transactions are identified by letter, and the balance of each item is shown after each transaction. The following observations,

		Assets			=	Liabilities +	Capital	
	Cash +	Sup-plies +	Equip-ment −	Accumu-lated Depre-ciation	=	Accounts Payable +	Lee Holt, Capital	
(a)	+9,000						+ 9,000	
(b)	−7,400		+7,400					
	1,600		7,400				9,000	
(c)		+650				+650		
	1,600	650	7,400			650	9,000	
(d)	− 300					−300		
	1,300	650	7,400			350	9,000	
(e)	+2,000						+ 2,000	Fares earned
	3,300	650	7,400			350	11,000	
(f)	− 700						− 550	Wages exp.
							− 50	Rent expense
							− 25	Utilities exp.
							− 75	Misc. expense
	2,600	650	7,400			350	10,300	
(g)		−400					− 400	Supplies exp.
	2,600	250	7,400			350	9,900	
(h)				+200			− 200	Depr. expense
	2,600	250	7,400	200		350	9,700	
(i)	− 500						− 500	Drawing
	2,100	250	7,400	200		350	9,200	

which apply equally to all types of business enterprises, should be particularly noted:

1. The effect of every transaction can be stated in terms of increases and/or decreases in one or more of the elements of the accounting equation.
2. The equality of the two sides of the accounting equation is always maintained.

Accounting statements

The principal accounting statements are the *balance sheet* and the *income statement*. They are usually accompanied by a less important, but nevertheless useful, statement called the *capital statement*. The nature of the data presented in each statement, in general terms, is as follows:

Balance sheet

A list of the assets, liabilities, and capital of a business entity as of a specific date, usually at the close of the last day of a month.

Income statement

A summary of the revenue and the expenses of a business entity for a specific period of time, such as a month or a year.

Capital statement

A summary of the changes in capital of a business entity that have occurred during a specific period of time, such as a month or a year.

The basic features of the three statements and their interrelationships are illustrated on page 18. The data for the statements were taken from the summary of transactions of Holt Taxi presented in the preceding section.

All financial statements should be identified by the name of the business, the title of the statement, and the date or period of time. The data presented in the balance sheet are for a specific date; the data presented in the income statement and the capital statement are for a period of time.

The use of indentions, captions, dollar signs, and rulings in the financial statements should be noted. They are employed to accentuate the several distinct sections of the various statements.

Balance sheet. The amounts of Holt Taxi's assets, liabilities, and capital at the end of the first month of operations appear on the last line of the summary on page 16. Minor rearrangements of these data and the addition of a heading yield the balance sheet illustrated on page 18. This form of balance sheet, with the liability and capital sections presented below the asset section, is called the *report form*. Another arrangement in common use lists the assets on the left and the liabilities and capital on the right. Because of its similarity to the account, a basic accounting device described in the next chapter, it is referred to as the *account form* of balance sheet.

Holt Taxi
Balance Sheet
August 31, 1969

Assets		
Cash		$2 100 00
Supplies		25 00
Equipment	$7 400 00	
Less accumulated depreciation	200 00	7 200 00
Total assets		$9 550 00
Liabilities		
Accounts payable		$ 350 00
Capital		
Lee Holt, capital		9 200 00
Total liabilities and capital		$9 550 00

Balance sheet — report form

Holt Taxi
Income Statement
For Month Ended August 31, 1969

Fares earned		$2 000 00
Operating expenses:		
Wages expense	$ 550 00	
Supplies expense	400 00	
Depreciation expense	200 00	
Rent expense	50 00	
Utilities expense	25 00	
Miscellaneous expense	75 00	
Total operating expenses		1 300 00
Net income from operations		$ 700 00

Income statement

Holt Taxi
Capital Statement
For Month Ended August 31, 1969

Capital, August 1, 1969		$9 000 00
Net income for the month	$ 700 00	
Less withdrawals	500 00	
Increase in capital		200 00
Capital, August 31, 1969		$9 200 00

Capital statement

It is customary to begin the asset section with cash, which is followed by receivables, supplies, and other assets, such as prepaid expenses, that will be converted into cash or consumed in the near future. The assets of a relatively permanent nature, such as equipment, buildings, and land, follow in that order.

In the liabilities and capital section of the balance sheet, it is customary to present the liabilities first, followed by capital. In the illustration on page 18 the liabilities are composed entirely of accounts payable. When there are two or more categories of liabilities, each should be listed and the total amount of liabilities shown as follows:

LIABILITIES

Notes payable.............	$ 600	
Accounts payable.........	1,500	
Salaries payable...........	100	
Total liabilities...........		$ 2,200

Income statement. Revenue earned and expenses incurred during the month were recorded in the equation as increases and decreases in capital, respectively. The details, together with net income in the amount of $700, are reported in the income statement on page 18.

The order in which the operating expenses are presented in the income statement varies among businesses. One of the arrangements commonly followed is to list them approximately in the order of size, beginning with the larger items. Miscellaneous expense is usually shown as the last item regardless of the relative magnitude of the item.

Capital statement. Comparison of the original investment of $9,000 at the beginning of the month with the $9,200 of capital reported in the balance sheet at the end of the month reveals an increase in capital of $200. This net increase is composed of two significant changes in capital that occurred during the period: (1) net income of $700 and (2) withdrawals of $500 by the owner. This information is presented in the capital statement on page 18, which serves as a connecting link between the two principal statements.

Accounting periods

There is no standard time interval between accounting statements. The maximum length of the accounting period is ordinarily one year, which includes a complete cycle of the seasons and of business activities. Income and property taxes are also based on yearly periods and thus require that annual reckonings be made.

The shortest accounting period is customarily one month. The practice of preparing financial statements at the end of each month is followed by many business firms. Such monthly statements are invaluable to management in assessing current performance, in detecting trends, and for future planning. In addition to the balance sheet as of the last day of the month and an income statement for the month then ended, it is common practice to prepare a cumulative income statement for the year to date. The accompanying capital statements may then report details either for the most recent month only or for the year to date. Assuming adoption of the latter alternative, the following statements would be prepared covering the first three months of a business year beginning on January 1:

As of the close of January:

Balance sheet dated January 31
Income statement for period January 1–January 31
Capital statement for period January 1–January 31

As of the close of February:

Balance sheet dated February 28
Income statement for period February 1–February 28
Income statement for period January 1–February 28
Capital statement for period January 1–February 28

As of the close of March:

Balance sheet dated March 31
Income statement for period March 1–March 31
Income statement for period January 1–March 31
Capital statement for period January 1–March 31

The annual accounting period adopted by an enterprise is known as its *fiscal year*. Fiscal years ordinarily begin with the first day of the particular month selected and end on the last day of the twelfth month hence. The period most commonly adopted is the calendar year, beginning on January 1 and ending on December 31, but other periods are not infrequently elected, particularly by incorporated businesses.

The long-term financial history of a business enterprise may be depicted by a succession of balance sheets, prepared at yearly intervals. The history of operations for the intervening periods is presented in a series of income statements. Serving as a connecting link between these two principal statements is the capital statement. If the life of a business enterprise is represented by a line moving from left to right, a series of accounting statements may be diagrammed as follows:

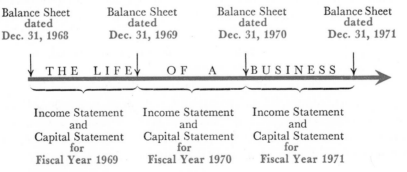

QUESTIONS

1. Why is a knowledge of accounting concepts and terminology useful to all individuals engaged in business activities?

2. Distinguish between public accounting and private accounting.

3. Describe in general terms the requirements that an individual must meet to become a CPA.

4. Name some of the specialized fields of accounting activity.

5. What is meant by the *business entity* concept?

6. What are the three principal forms of profit-making business organizations and in what principal respect do they differ, so far as accounting is concerned?

7. Discuss the meanings of the terms *business transaction* and *internal transaction*.

8. In what way are accounting reports of past performance useful to the owner or manager in making plans for the future?

9. Distinguish between *cost* and *value* and explain their relative significance in accounting.

10. Land with an assessed value of $20,000 for property tax purposes was acquired by a business enterprise two years ago for $32,000. At the present time the assessed valuation is $24,000 and the enterprise has received an offer of $45,000 for the land. (a) At what amount should the land have been recorded when acquired? (b) Should recognition be given in the accounting records to today's values? Discuss.

11. (a) If the assets and the capital of an enterprise amount to $30,000 and $20,000 respectively, what is the total amount of the liabilities?
(b) If the liabilities and the capital of an enterprise amount to $10,000 and $30,000 respectively, what is the total amount of the assets?
(c) If the assets and the liabilities of an enterprise amount to $40,000 and $10,000 respectively, what is the amount of the capital?

12. State the possible effects on the three elements in the accounting equation of (a) a transaction that increases an asset and (b) a transaction that increases a liability.

13. During the month of June, Ace Decorators fulfilled a contract to clean and paint the exterior of Superior Supply Company's buildings. The contract price was $4,000, with payment to be made in July. (a) In which month did Ace Decorators earn the $4,000 of revenue? (b) In which month did Superior Supply Company incur $4,000 of maintenance expense? (c) What was the effect, in terms of the accounting equation, of Superior Supply Company's payment of the $4,000 in July? (d) What was the effect, in terms of the accounting equation, of the receipt of the $4,000 by Ace Decorators in July?

14. Assume that some time ago you acquired a vacant lot at a price of $10,000, and that you still owe the seller $4,000. Assume also that you now sell the lot for $15,000 in cash, and pay the $4,000 you owed. (a) What is the effect of the sale of the lot on the total amount of your (1) assets, (2) liabilities, (3) capital? (b) What is the effect of the payment of $4,000 to the original seller on the total amount of your (1) assets, (2) liabilities, (3) capital?

15. Operations of a service enterprise for a particular month are summarized as follows:

Service sales: on account, $6,000; for cash, $8,000
Expenses incurred: on account, $4,000; for cash, $5,000

What was the amount of the enterprise's (a) revenue, (b) expenses, and (c) net income from operations?

16. Indicate for each of the following annual statements, prepared for the fiscal year ended September 30, whether the information reported is as of September 30 or for the period October 1–September 30: (a) income statement, (b) balance sheet, (c) capital statement.

17. What particular item of financial or operating data, for a service enterprise, appears on (a) both the income statement and the capital statement, and (b) both the balance sheet and the capital statement?

18. Selected data applicable to a particular business enterprise for the fiscal year just ended are:

Net income from operations. . . . . $ 45,000
Withdrawals by owner. 18,000
Additional investments by owner. None
Total assets at beginning of year . 150,000
Total assets at end of year. 162,000

What was the amount and direction (increase or decrease) of the year's change in (a) capital and (b) total liabilities?

19. What are the usual minimum and maximum lengths of accounting periods?

20. The income statement of a business enterprise for the month of November indicates a net income of $2,000. During the same period the owner withdrew $2,300 in cash from the business for personal use. Would it be correct to say that the owner incurred a *net loss* of $300 during the month? Discuss.

21. If the total liabilities of the enterprise in Question 20 increased by $4,000 during the same month, and the owner made no additional investments in the business, what was the amount and direction of change (increase or decrease) in total assets during the month?

EXERCISES

1-1. The following selected transactions were completed by Paragon Cleaners during the month of July.

(1) Paid rent for July, $120.
(2) Purchased supplies for cash, $140.
(3) Purchased cleaning equipment on account, $2,000.
(4) Received cash from cash customers, $340.
(5) Paid miscellaneous expenses, $40.
(6) Paid creditors on account, $700.
(7) Charged customers for services sold on account, $290.
(8) Paid cash to owner for personal use, $200.
(9) Received cash on account from charge customers, $250.
(10) Determined by taking an inventory that $95 of supplies had been used during the month.

List the numbers identifying the transactions (1) through (10) in a vertical column and indicate their effect on the accounting equation by inserting at the right of each number the appropriate letter from the following:

(a) Increase in one asset, decrease in another asset.
(b) Increase in an asset, increase in a liability.
(c) Increase in an asset, increase in capital.
(d) Decrease in an asset, decrease in a liability.
(e) Decrease in an asset, decrease in capital.

1-2. A list of transactions completed by R. D. Cooper Co. is presented below. Indicate the increase or the decrease ($+$ or $-$) in assets, liabilities, and capital resulting from each transaction. Tabulate your answers, identifying each by number, using Assets, Liabilities, and Capital as column headings.

(1) Paid advertising expense.
(2) Charged customers for services rendered on account.
(3) The owner, R. D. Cooper, withdrew cash.
(4) Returned defective equipment originally purchased on account and not yet paid for.
(5) Paid a liability.
(6) The owner, R. D. Cooper, invested additional cash in the business.
(7) Purchased equipment on account.
(8) Purchased a car on account for personal use of the owner, R. D. Cooper.

1-3. Summary financial data of Hamilton Co. (a service business) for June are presented in equation form below. Each line designated by a number indicates the effect of a transaction on the equation. All changes in capital are revenue or expense except transactions (1) and (9).

(a) Describe each transaction.
(b) What is the amount of net increase in cash during the month?
(c) What is the amount of net increase in capital during the month?
(d) What is the amount of the net income for the month?
(e) How much of the net income of the month was retained in the business?

	Cash +	Supplies +	Equipment −	Accumulated Depreciation =	Liabilities +	Capital
Bal.	2,000	1,000	6,000	1,500 =	1,200	6,300
(1)	+ 500					+ 500
(2)	− 400		+ 400			
(3)		+ 100			+ 100	
(4)	+1,800					+1,800
(5)	− 700				− 700	
(6)	− 500					− 500
(7)		− 350				− 350
(8)				+ 100		− 100
(9)	− 250					− 250
Bal.	2,450	750	6,400	1,600	600	7,400

1-4. The total assets and the total liabilities of each of four different companies, A, B, C, and D, at the beginning and the end of a year were as follows:

	Assets	Liabilities
Beginning of year ..	$25,000	$10,000
End of year	50,000	15,000

On the basis of the above data and the additional information for the year presented at the top of the next page, determine the net income (or loss) from operations of each company for the year.

23

Company A: The owner had made no additional investments in the business and no withdrawals from the business.

Company B: The owner had made no additional investments in the business but had withdrawn $12,000.

Company C: The owner had made an additional investment of $22,000 but had made no withdrawals.

Company D: The owner had made an additional investment of $11,000 and had withdrawn $18,000.

1-5. Belton Co. manufactures a product at a unit cost of 55 cents and sells it at a unit price of $1. Annual sales have averaged 1,000,000 units and total annual operating expenses have been approximately $230,000. On the basis of a study of markets, costs, and expenses it is concluded that (1) reduction of the selling price to 90 cents would result in a 60% increase in the number of units sold, (2) a 60% increase in production would result in a cost reduction of 5 cents a unit, (3) a 60% increase in volume would be accompanied by a 30% increase in operating expenses, and (4) the increased volume would not necessitate the investment of additional funds in the business.

Assuming the correctness of the study, determine whether the reduction in price would increase or decrease net income from operations, and the amount, presenting your report in tabular form in good order.

PROBLEMS

The following additional problems for this chapter are located in Appendix C: 1-2B, 1-3B.

1-1A. On September 1 of the current year Henry Ross established an enterprise under the name Ross Realty. Transactions completed during the month were as follows:

(a) Opened a business bank account with a deposit of $1,500.
(b) Paid office rent for the month, $150.
(c) Purchased supplies (stationery, stamps, pencils, ink, etc.) for cash, $60.
(d) Purchased equipment (desk, chairs, filing cabinet, etc.) for $1,400, paying cash of $800, with the balance on account.
(e) Earned sales commissions, receiving cash, $800.
(f) Paid cash to Ross for personal use, $400.
(g) Paid automobile expenses (including rental charge) for month, $95, and miscellaneous expenses, $50.
(h) Paid creditor on account, $100.
(i) Estimated depreciation on the equipment to be $25.
(j) Determined by taking an inventory that the cost of supplies used was $5.

Instructions:

(1) Record the transactions and the balances after each transaction, using the following tabular headings:

Assets				Liabilities		Capital
			Accumulated	= Accounts	+	Henry Ross,
Cash +	Supplies +	Equipment −	Depreciation	Payable		Capital

Indicate the nature of each increase and decrease in capital subsequent to the initial investment by appropriate notations at the right of each change.

(2) Prepare an income statement for September, a capital statement for September, and a balance sheet as of September 30.

24

1-2A. On July 1, the beginning of the current fiscal year, the amount of M. G. Murphy's capital in Murphy Co. was $32,430. During the year he made weekly cash withdrawals of $250 (total of $13,000). The amounts of the enterprise's assets and liabilities at June 30, the close of the current fiscal year, and of its revenue and expense for the year ended on that date are listed below.

Accounts payable.......................	$ 4,620
Accounts receivable....................	6,910
Advertising expense....................	2,860
Building..............................	41,700
Accumulated depreciation — building. . .	19,250
Cash..................................	7,450
Depreciation expense — building........	970
Depreciation expense — equipment......	1,430
Equipment............................	16,380
Accumulated depreciation — equipment.	7,120
Insurance expense	880
Land	3,500
Miscellaneous expense.................	1,690
Prepaid insurance.....................	2,230
Sales.................................	65,460
Salaries payable	210
Salary expense	22,340
Supplies..............................	1,740
Supplies expense......................	1,750
Taxes expense........................	3,410
Taxes payable........................	1,470
Utilities expense.....................	2,320

Instructions:

(1) Prepare an income statement for the current fiscal year ending June 30, exercising care to include each item of expense listed.
(2) Prepare a capital statement for the current fiscal year ending June 30.
(3) Prepare a balance sheet as of June 30 of the current fiscal year.

1-3A. R. L. Logan operates a business known as Model Dry Cleaners. The actual work of dry cleaning is done by another company at wholesale rates. The assets and the liabilities of the business on May 1 of the current year are as follows: Cash, $1,500; Accounts Receivable, $200; Supplies, $90; Equipment, $4,800; Accumulated Depreciation, $900; Accounts Payable, $1,120. Business transactions during May are summarized below.

(a) Paid rent for the month, $160.
(b) Purchased supplies on account, $40.
(c) Paid creditors on account, $890.
(d) Received cash from cash customers for dry cleaning sales, $1,200.
(e) Charged customers for dry cleaning sales on account, $570.
(f) Received monthly invoice for dry cleaning expense for May (to be paid on June 10), $850.
(g) Received cash from customers on account, $510.
(h) Reimbursed a customer $15 for a garment lost by the cleaning company, which agreed to deduct the amount from the invoice received in transaction (f).
(i) Paid the following: wages expense, $140; truck expense, $45; utilities expense, $25; miscellaneous expense, $30.
(j) Purchased an item of equipment on account, $70.

(k) Paid personal expenses by checks drawn on the business, $280, and withdrew $100 in cash for personal use.
(l) Determined by taking an inventory the cost of supplies used during the month, $10.
(m) Estimated depreciation of truck and other equipment for the month, $80.

Instructions:

(1) State the assets, liabilities, and capital as of May 1 in equation form similar to that shown in this chapter.
(2) Record, in tabular form below the equation, the increases and decreases resulting from each transaction, indicating the new balances after each transaction. Explain the nature of each increase and decrease in capital by an appropriate notation at the right of the amount.
(3) Prepare an income statement, a capital statement, and a balance sheet.

1-4A. On October 1 of the current year David Shaw established a business enterprise. The transactions of the business for the three months ending on December 31 are summarized below.

(a) Deposited cash in a business bank account.		$14,000
(b) Purchased a going business operating under the name of Ace Delivery Service.		
Assets acquired:		
Accounts receivable..................	$ 3,200	
Truck supplies.....................	750	
Office supplies.....................	50	
Trucks...........................	16,000	$20,000
Liabilities assumed:		
Accounts payable...................		1,500
Terms of payment to be made:		
Cash.............................	$10,500	
Four non-interest-bearing notes payable of $2,000 each, due at three-month intervals........................	8,000	$18,500
(c) Charged delivery service sales to customers on account.........................		$13,000
(d) Purchased truck supplies on account.......		1,400
(e) Purchased office supplies for cash.........		60
(f) Received cash from customers on account..		12,900
(g) Paid creditors on account...............		2,300
(h) Paid first of the four notes payable........		2,000
(i) Paid license taxes in advance............		480
(j) Paid insurance premiums in advance......		1,360
(k) Purchased truck supplies on account.......		140
(l) Paid drivers' wages....................		4,700
(m) Paid rent expense.....................		330
(n) Paid utilities expense..................		105
(o) Paid repairs expense...................		250
(p) Paid miscellaneous expenses.............		90
(q) Paid to Shaw as personal withdrawals.....		1,800
(r) Truck supplies used...................		1,350
(s) Office supplies used...................		15
(t) Depreciation of trucks.................		810

26

(u) Insurance expired........................ 290
(v) Taxes expired........................... 120

Instructions:

(1) List the following captions in a single line at the top of a sheet turned sideways.

Cash + Accounts Receivable + Truck Supplies + Office Supplies + Prepaid Insurance + Prepaid Taxes + Trucks

− Accumulated Depreciation = Notes Payable + Accounts Payable + David Shaw, Capital   Capital Notations

(2) Record Shaw's original investment and the remaining transactions in the appropriate columns, identifying each by letter. Indicate increases by + and decreases by −. *Do not determine the new balances of the items after each transaction.* In the space for capital notations, identify each revenue and expense item and withdrawals by the owner.

(3) Insert the final balances in each column and determine that the equation is in balance at December 31, the end of the period.

(4) Prepare the following: (a) income statement for the three months, (b) capital statement for the three months, and (c) balance sheet as of December 31. (The name of the business was not changed.)

27

2
Journal, ledger, and trial balance

Recording transactions

The nature of transactions and their effect on business enterprises were illustrated in the preceding chapter by the use of the accounting equation, Assets = Liabilities + Capital (+ Revenues − Expenses). Although transactions can be analyzed and recorded in terms of their effect on the equation, such a format is not practicable as a design for actual accounting systems.

The transactions completed by an enterprise during a fiscal period may effect increases and decreases in a great many different asset, liability, capital, revenue, and expense items. In order to have day-to-day information available when needed and to be able to prepare timely periodic financial statements, it is necessary to maintain a separate record for each different item. For example, it is necessary to have a form devoted solely to recording increases and decreases in cash, another form devoted exclusively to recording increases and decreases in supplies, another devoted to equipment, etc. The form traditionally used for this purpose is called an *account.* A group of related accounts that comprise a complete unit, such as all of the accounts of a specific business enterprise, is referred to as a *ledger.*

Familiarity with the manner in which increases and decreases are recorded in accounts is prerequisite to an understanding of the system known as double-entry accounting.

Nature of an account

The simplest form of an account has three parts: (1) a title, which is the name of the item recorded in the account; (2) a space for recording increases in the amount of the item, in terms of money; and (3) a space for recording decreases in the amount of the item, also in monetary terms. This form of an account, illustrated below, is known as a *T account* because of its similarity to the letter T. Other account forms that provide spaces for recording additional information are illustrated later. Regardless of form, however, the three basic parts of an account are a title, a section for increases, and a section for decreases.

TITLE	
Left	Right
or	or
debit	*credit*

T account

The left side of the account is called the *debit* side and the right side is called the *credit* side. The word *charge* is sometimes used as a synonym for debit. Amounts entered on the left side of an account, regardless of the account title, are called *debits* or *charges* to the account, and the account is said to be *debited* or *charged*. Amounts entered on the right side of an account are called *credits*, and the account is said to be *credited*.

CASH	
	3,000	500
	2,500	1,000
	4,000	2,500
4,300 *9,500*	300
	900
	5,200

In the illustration at the left, receipts of cash during a period of time have been listed vertically on the debit side of the cash account. The cash payments for the same period have been listed in similar fashion on the credit side of the account. A memorandum total of the cash receipts for the period to date may be inserted below the last debit at any time the information is desired. The figures should be small, and written in pencil, in order to avoid mistaking the amount for an additional debit. (The procedure is sometimes referred to as *pencil footing*.) The total of the cash payments may be inserted on the credit side in a similar manner. Subtraction of the smaller sum from the larger, $9,500 − $5,200, in the illustration, yields the amount of cash on hand, which is called the *balance* of the account. The cash account in the illustration has a balance of $4,300, which may be inserted in pencil figures next to the larger pencil footing, which identifies it as a *debit balance*. If a balance sheet were to be prepared at this time, the amount of cash reported thereon would be $4,300.

Relationship of accounts to the balance sheet

The manner of recording transactions in the accounts, and the relationship of accounts to the balance sheet are presented on pages 30–31.

Assume that R. B. Knox establishes a business venture, to be known as Knox TV Service, by initially depositing $3,200 cash in a bank account for the use of the enterprise. Immediately after the deposit, the balance sheet for the business, in account form, would contain the following information:

Assets		Capital	
Cash......................	$3,200	R. B. Knox, capital...........	$3,200

The effect of the transaction on accounts in the ledger can be described as a $3,200 debit to Cash and a $3,200 credit to R. B. Knox, Capital. The information can also be stated in a formalized manner by listing the title of the account and the amount to be debited, followed by a similar listing, below and to the right of the debit, of the title of the account and the amount to be credited. This form of presentation is called a *journal entry*, and is illustrated as follows:

Cash...	3,200
R. B. Knox, Capital.................................	3,200

The data in the journal entry are transferred to the appropriate accounts by a process known as *posting*. The accounts after posting the above journal entry appear as follows:

CASH		R. B. KNOX, CAPITAL	
3,200			3,200

Note that the amount of the cash, which is reported on the left side of the account form of balance sheet, is posted to the left (debit) side of Cash. The owner's equity in the business, which is reported on the right side of the balance sheet is posted to the right (credit) side of R. B. Knox, Capital. When other assets are acquired the increase will be recorded as debits to the appropriate accounts; and as capital is increased or liabilities are incurred the increases will be recorded as credits.

For the second illustration assume that after opening the checking account Knox purchased equipment and tools at a cost of $2,400. He paid $1,400 in cash and agreed to pay the remaining $1,000 within thirty days. After this transaction the data reported in the balance sheet would be as follows:

Assets		Liabilities	
Cash......................	$1,800	Accounts payable............	$1,000
Equipment.................	2,400	Capital	
		R. B. Knox, capital...........	3,200
Total assets..............	$4,200	Total liabilities and capital.....	$4,200

The effect of the transaction can be described as a $2,400 debit (increase) to Equipment, a $1,400 credit (decrease) to Cash and a $1,000 credit (increase) to Accounts Payable. The same information can be presented in the form of the journal entry appearing below. (An entry composed of more than two items is called a *compound journal entry*.)

Equipment...	2,400	
Cash...		1,400
Accounts Payable..................................		1,000

After the journal entry for the second transaction has been posted, the accounts of Knox TV Service appear as follows:

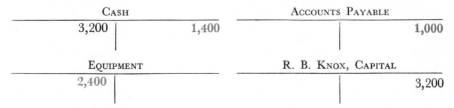

CASH		ACCOUNTS PAYABLE	
3,200	1,400		1,000

EQUIPMENT		R. B. KNOX, CAPITAL	
2,400			3,200

Note that the effect of the transaction was to increase one asset account, decrease another asset account, and increase a liability account. Note also that although each of the amounts, $2,400, $1,400, and $1,000, differed, the equality of debits and credits was maintained.

Classification of accounts

Before proceeding with the debit-credit analysis of additional types of transactions, consideration will be given to the customary categories or classes of accounts that comprise a ledger. The exact nature and composition of the most common accounts will also be explained.

31

ASSETS. Any physical thing (tangible) or right (intangible) owned that has a money value is an asset. Assets are frequently presented on the balance sheet as two distinct groups: (1) *current assets* and (2) *plant assets*. These two categories and the most common individual accounts in each are discussed in the paragraphs that follow.

Current assets. Cash and other assets that may reasonably be expected to be realized in cash or sold or consumed usually within a year or less through the normal operations of the business are called *current assets*. In addition to cash, the assets in this group usually owned by a service business are notes receivable and accounts receivable, and supplies and other prepaid expenses.

Cash is any medium of exchange that a bank will accept at face value; it includes bank deposits, currency, checks, bank drafts, and money orders. *Notes receivable* are claims against debtors evidenced by a written promise to pay a certain sum in money at a definite time to the order of a specified person or to bearer. *Accounts receivable* are claims against debtors, less formal than notes, that arise from sales of services or merchandise on account. *Prepaid expenses* include supplies on hand and advance payments of expenses such as insurance and property taxes.

Plant assets. Tangible assets used in the business that are of a relatively fixed or permanent nature are called *plant assets* or *fixed assets.* Such assets, with the exception of land, wear out or *depreciate* with the passage of time. The amount of *depreciation* for an accounting period cannot be determined with the same degree of certainty that applies to the expiration of insurance or of other prepaid expenses; consequently the cost of the plant assets is recorded in one account and the accumulated depreciation is recorded in another account.

Typical titles of plant asset accounts are Equipment, Buildings, and Land. Equipment may be classified by functions, with separate accounts entitled Delivery Equipment, Store Equipment, and Office Equipment.

LIABILITIES. Liabilities are amounts owed to outsiders (creditors) and are customarily described in the balance sheet by titles that include the word *payable.* They are divided into two principal classes: (1) *current liabilities* and (2) *long-term liabilities.*

Current liabilities. Liabilities that will be due within a short time (usually one year or less) and that are to be paid out of current assets are called *current liabilities.* The most common liabilities in this group are *notes payable* and *accounts payable*, which are exactly like their receivable counterparts except that the debtor-creditor relationship is reversed. Other current liability accounts commonly found in the ledger are Salaries Payable, Interest Payable, and Taxes Payable.

Long-term liabilities. Liabilities that will not be due for a comparatively long time (usually more than one year) are called *long-term liabilities* or *fixed liabilities.* As they come within the one-year range and are to be paid, such liabilities become current. If the obligation is to be renewed rather than paid at maturity, however, it would continue to be classed as long-term. When payment of a long-term debt is to be spread over a number of years, the installment due within one year from a balance sheet date is classed as a current liability.

Long-term liabilities are usually evidenced by *notes payable.* When notes are accompanied by security in the form of a mortgage, the obligation may be referred to as *mortgage notes payable* or *mortgage payable.*

CAPITAL. *Capital* is the term applied to the owner's equity in the business. It is a residual claim against the assets of the business after the total liabilities are deducted. Other commonly used terms for capital are *owner's equity, proprietorship*, and *net worth.*

REVENUE. *Revenue* is the gross increase in capital attributable to business activities. It results from the sale of merchandise, the performance of services for a customer or a client, the rental of property, the lending of money, and other business and professional activities entered into for the purpose of earning income. More specific terms employed to identify the source of revenue include *sales, fees, commissions revenue, fares earned,* and *interest income.* If an enterprise has several different types of revenue, a separate account should be maintained for each.

EXPENSES. Costs that have been consumed in the process of producing revenue are *expired* costs or *expenses.* The number of expense categories and individual expense accounts maintained in the ledger varies with the nature and the size of an enterprise. A large business with authority and responsibility spread among many employees may use an elaborate classification and hundreds of accounts as an aid in controlling expenses. For a small service business of the type assumed here for illustrative purposes, a modest number of expense accounts is satisfactory.

Debit and credit

Balance sheet accounts. Earlier in the chapter it was observed that the left side of asset accounts is used for recording increases and the right side is used for recording decreases. It was also observed that the right side of liability and capital accounts is used to record increases. It naturally follows that the left side of such accounts is used to record decreases. The left side of all accounts, whether asset, liability, or capital, is called *debit* and the right side is called *credit.* Consequently, a debit may signify either an increase or a decrease, depending on the nature of the account, and a credit may likewise signify either increase or decrease, depending on the nature of the account. The rules of debit and credit may therefore be stated as follows:

33

DEBIT may signify:	CREDIT may signify:
Increase in asset accounts	Decrease in asset accounts
Decrease in liability accounts	Increase in liability accounts
Decrease in capital accounts	Increase in capital accounts

The rules of debit and credit may also be stated in relationship to the accounting equation and the account form of balance sheet as in the diagram at the top of the next page.

Every business transaction affects a minimum of two accounts. Regardless of the complexity of a transaction or the number of accounts affected, the sum of the debits is always equal to the sum of the credits. This equality of debit and credit for each transaction is inherent in the equation A = L + C. It is also because of this duality that the system is known as "double-entry accounting."

Income statement accounts. The theory of debit and credit in its application to revenue and expense accounts is based on the relationship

ASSETS		LIABILITIES	
ASSET ACCOUNTS		LIABILITY ACCOUNTS	
Debit for increases	Credit for decreases	Debit for decreases	Credit for increases

CAPITAL	
CAPITAL ACCOUNTS	
Debit for decreases	Credit for increases

of these accounts to capital. The net income or the net loss for a period, as reported on the income statement, is the net increase or the net decrease in capital resulting from operations.

Revenue increases capital; and just as increases in capital are recorded as credits, increases in revenues during an accounting period are recorded as credits.

34 Expenses have the effect of decreasing capital; and just as decreases in capital are recorded as debits, increases in expense accounts are recorded as debits. Although debits to expense accounts signify *decreases in capital*, they may also be referred to as *increases in expense*. The usual practice is to consider debits to expense accounts in the positive sense (increases in expense) rather than in the negative sense (decreases in capital). The rules of debit and credit as applied to revenue and expense accounts are shown in the diagram below.

CAPITAL ACCOUNTS

DEBIT *Decreases in capital* EXPENSE ACCOUNTS		CREDIT *Increases in capital* REVENUE ACCOUNTS	
Debit for increases	Credit for decreases	Debit for decreases	Credit for increases

At the end of the fiscal period, the balances of the revenue and expense accounts are reported in the income statement. The account balances are then transferred to a summary account, after which the revenue accounts are said to be *closed*. The summary account, which represents the net income or the net loss for the period, is then closed by transferring the balance to the capital account. Because of this periodic closing of the revenue, expense, and summary accounts, they are sometimes called *temporary capital* or *nominal* accounts. The balance of each asset and each liability account and the balance of the capital account are carried forward to succeeding fiscal periods. They are more permanent in nature and are sometimes referred to as *real* accounts.

Drawing account. The owner of a sole proprietorship may from time to time withdraw cash from the business for his personal use. It is customary for the owner to do so if he devotes full time to the business or if the business is his principal source of income. Although such withdrawals reduce capital, they do not represent an operating expense. The usual practice is to record withdrawals in an account bearing the owner's name followed by *Drawing* or *Personal*.

Debits to the drawing account may be considered either as decreases in capital (negative sense) or as increases in drawings (positive sense). Ordinarily the periodic withdrawals of the owner are made in anticipation that the enterprise is operating profitably and that the total amount withdrawn during the period will not exceed the net income.

Normal balances. The sum of the increases recorded in an account is customarily equal to or greater than the sum of the decreases recorded in the account; consequently, the normal balances of all accounts are positive rather than negative. For example, the total debits (increases) in an asset account will ordinarily be greater than the total credits (decreases); thus, asset accounts normally have debit balances. It is entirely possible, of course, for the debits and the credits in an account to be equal, in which case the account is said to be *in balance*.

The rules of debit and credit, and the normal balances of the various types of accounts, are summarized below. Note that drawing and expense accounts are considered in the positive sense. Increases in both types of accounts, which represent decreases in capital, are recorded as debits.

TYPE OF ACCOUNT	INCREASE	DECREASE	NORMAL BALANCE
Asset	Debit	Credit	Debit
Liability	Credit	Debit	Credit
Capital			
Capital	Credit	Debit	Credit
Drawing	Debit	Credit	Debit
Revenue	Credit	Debit	Credit
Expense	Debit	Credit	Debit

When an account that normally has a debit balance actually has a credit balance, or vice versa, it is an indication of an accounting error or of an unusual transaction. For example, a credit balance in the office equipment account could result only from an accounting error. On the other hand, a debit balance in an account payable account could result from an overpayment.

Flow of accounting data

The sources of transaction data and their subsequent flow into the ledger are considered before the presentation of a more detailed description of recording processes. In practice, an initial record of each transaction, or of a group of similar transactions, is evidenced by a business document such as a sales ticket, a check stub, or a cash register tape. On the basis of the evidence provided by the business document, the transactions are entered in chronological order in a journal. The amounts of the debits and the credits in the journal are then transferred or posted to the accounts in the ledger. The sequence of events leading to postings to the ledger may be diagrammed as follows:

		Entry recorded in	Entry posted to
Business TRANSACTION → occurs	Business DOCUMENT → prepared	JOURNAL →	LEDGER

Two-column journal

The basic features of a journal entry were illustrated earlier when introducing the use of debit and credit. There is great variety in both the design of journals and the number of different journals that can be employed by an enterprise. The standard form of two-column journal is illustrated below. Instead of such a single all-purpose two-column journal, a business may use many multicolumn journals, restricting each to a single type of transaction. Examples of more sophisticated journal systems are discussed and illustrated in later chapters. Means by which business documents or automated processing devices may entirely supplant journals is also discussed. However, the two-column journal is still widely used. It also serves as a valuable device in analyzing transactions.

JOURNAL   PAGE 6

	DATE		DESCRIPTION	POST. REF.	DEBIT	CREDIT	
1	1969 July 1		Salary Expense		3 1 0 00		1
2			Cash			3 1 0 00	2
3			Paid salaries for week.				3
4							4
5		1	Accounts Payable		3 5 0 00		5
6			Cash			3 5 0 00	6
7			Paid Sims Supply Co. on				7
8			account.				8
9							9
10		1	Cash		2 8 6 00		10
11			Sales			2 8 6 00	11
12			Cash sales for the day.				12
13							13

Standard form of the two-column journal

The process of recording a transaction in a journal is called *journalizing.* The procedures employed for the two-column journal are as follows:

1. Recording the date:
   a. Year is inserted at top only of date column, except when the year date changes.
   b. Month is inserted on first line only of date column, except when the month date changes.
   c. Day is inserted in date column on first line used for each transaction, regardless of number of transactions during the day.
2. Recording the debit:
   Title of account to be debited is inserted at extreme left of the description column and amount is entered in the debit column.
3. Recording the credit:
   Title of account to be credited is inserted below the account debited, moderately indented, and the amount is entered in the credit column.
4. Writing explanation:
   Brief explanations may be written below each entry, moderately indented. Some accountants prefer that the explanation be omitted if the nature of the transaction is obvious. It is also permissible to omit a lengthy explanation of a complex transaction if it is feasible to substitute a reference to the related business document.

It should be noted that all transactions are recorded only in terms of debits and credits to specific accounts. The titles used in the entries should correspond exactly to the titles of the accounts in the ledger. For example, a desk purchased for use in the office should be entered as a debit to Office Equipment, not to "desks purchased," and cash received should be entered as a debit to Cash, not to "cash received."

The line following an entry is left blank in order to clearly separate each entry. The column headed Post. Ref. (posting reference) is not used until the debits and credits are posted to the appropriate accounts in the ledger.

37

Two-column account

Accounts in the simple T form are used primarily for illustrative purposes. The addition of special rulings to the T form yields the standard two-column form illustrated below.

ACCOUNT *Cash* ACCOUNT NO. *11*

DATE	ITEM	POST. REF.	DEBIT	DATE	ITEM	POST. REF.	CREDIT
1969 July 1	Balance	✓	2 1 1 5 00	1969 July 1		6	3 1 0 00
1		6	2 8 6 00	1		6	3 5 0 00
3		6	3 1 9 00	3		6	1 1 0 00
3		6	2 6 0 00	3		6	1 9 00
				3		7	1 2 5 00

Standard form of the two-column account

The two sides of the account are identical in form; the left side is used for debit postings and the right side is used for credit postings.

Journal and ledger forms similar to the foregoing illustrations are readily available, either with or without printed columnar headings.

Posting

In many accounting systems much or all of the posting to the ledger is done by the use of mechanical or electronic equipment designed for the purpose. When the posting is performed manually, the debits and credits in the journal may be posted sequentially as they occur or, if a considerable number of items is to be posted at one time, all of the debits may be posted first, followed by the credits. The use of the latter procedure lessens the likelihood of posting items to the wrong side of accounts. Details of the procedure for posting a debit or a credit are as follows:

1. Recording the amount and the date in the *account:*
   The amount and the date are recorded as a debit if the item appears as a debit in the journal; if it appears as a credit, the posting is to the credit side of the account. The system of inserting dates (year, month, day) is similar to that employed in the journal.

2. Recording the posting reference in the *account:*
   The number of the journal page from which the posting is made is entered in the posting reference column of the *account.*

3. Recording the posting reference in the *journal:*
   The number of the account to which the posting has been made is entered in the posting reference column of the *journal,* completing the cross-reference between the journal and the ledger.

The foregoing procedures are illustrated by the diagrams appearing below and on page 39.

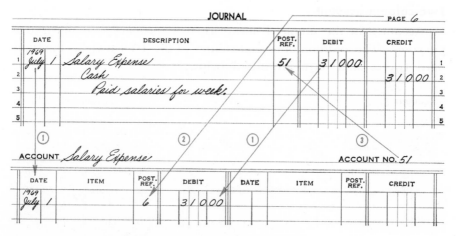

Diagram of the posting of a debit

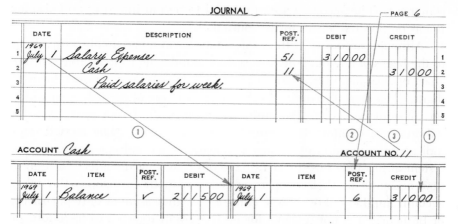

DATE		DESCRIPTION	POST. REF.	DEBIT	CREDIT	
1969 July	1	Salary Expense	51	3 1 0 00		1
		Cash	11		3 1 0 00	2
		Paid salaries for week.				3
						4
						5

ACCOUNT Cash   ACCOUNT NO. 11

DATE		ITEM	POST. REF.	DEBIT	DATE		ITEM	POST. REF.	CREDIT
1969 July	1	Balance	✓	2 1 1 5 00	1969 July	1		6	3 1 0 00

Diagram of the posting of a credit

Chart of accounts

The number of accounts maintained by a particular business is affected by the nature of its operations, its volume of business, and the extent to which details are needed for taxing authorities, managerial decisions, credit purposes, etc. For example, one particular enterprise may have separate accounts for Executive Salaries, Office Salaries, and Sales Salaries, while another may find it satisfactory to record all types of salaries in a single salary expense account.

Insofar as possible, the order of the accounts in the ledger should agree with the order of the items in the balance sheet and the income

39

BALANCE SHEET ACCOUNTS

1. *Assets*

11 Cash
12 Accounts Receivable
14 Supplies
15 Prepaid Rent
18 Printing Equipment
19 Accumulated Depreciation

2. *Liabilities*

21 Accounts Payable
22 Salaries Payable

3. *Capital*

31 Charles Bell, Capital
32 Charles Bell, Drawing
33 Expense and Revenue Summary

INCOME STATEMENT ACCOUNTS

4. *Revenue*

41 Sales

5. *Expenses*

51 Salary Expense
52 Supplies Expense
53 Rent Expense
54 Depreciation Expense
59 Miscellaneous Expense

Chart of accounts for Bell Print Shop

statement. The accounts are numbered to permit indexing and also for use as posting references in the journal.

Although accounts in the ledger may be numbered consecutively as in the pages of a book, a flexible system of indexing is preferable. In the chart of accounts illustrated on page 39, each account number has two digits. The first digit indicates the major division of the ledger in which the account is placed. Accounts beginning with 1 represent assets; 2, liabilities; 3, capital; 4, revenue; and 5, expenses. The second digit indicates the position of the account within its division. A numbering system of this type has the advantage of permitting the later insertion of new accounts in their proper sequence without disturbing the other account numbers. For a large enterprise with a number of departments or branches, it is not unusual for each account number to have four or more digits.

Illustrative problem

The transactions of a hypothetical business enterprise for a month are used to illustrate the recording process. The sequence of the analysis and recording of each element in a transaction is as follows:

1. Determine the type of item affected (i.e. asset, liability, capital, revenue, or expense).
2. Determine the nature of the effect (i.e. increase or decrease).
3. Determine how the effect is recorded (i.e. debit or credit).
4. Record the entry in the journal.
5. Post the entry to the ledger. (The entire ledger is presented on pages 45 and 46.)

In order to restrict the length of the illustration and to reduce repetition, some of the transactions are stated as a summary. For example, sales of services for cash are ordinarily recorded on a daily basis, but in the illustration summary totals are given only at the middle and end of the month. Similarly, all sales of services on account during the month are summarized as a single transaction; in practice each sale would be recorded separately.

Oct 2. Charles Bell operated a printing business in his home workshop on a part-time basis. He decided to move to rented quarters as of October 2 and to devote full time to the business, which was to be known as Bell Print Shop. The following assets were invested in the enterprise: cash, $1,100; accounts receivable, $600; supplies, $400; and printing equipment, $4,200. There were no liabilities transferred to the business.

Analysis: The four asset accounts Cash, Accounts Receivable, Supplies, and Printing Equipment increase and are debited for $1,100, $600, $400, and $4,200 respectively. The owner's equity in these assets is equal to the sum of the assets, or $6,300; hence Charles Bell, Capital is credited for that amount. (The manner in which individual accounts for customers are maintained is considered in a later chapter.)

	DATE	DESCRIPTION	POST. REF.	DEBIT	CREDIT	
1	1969 Oct. 2	Cash	11	1 1 0 0 00		1
2		Accounts Receivable	12	6 0 0 00		2
3		Supplies	14	4 0 0 00		3
4		Printing Equipment	18	4 2 0 0 00		4
5		Charles Bell, Capital	31		6 3 0 0 00	5
6		Invested assets in Bell				6
7		Print Shop.				7

Oct. 2. Paid $600 on a lease rental contract, the payment representing three months' rental.

Analysis: The asset acquired in exchange for the cash payment is the right to use the property for three months. The asset Prepaid Rent increases and is debited for $600; the asset Cash decreases and is credited for $600. (When rent for a single month is prepaid it is customarily debited to the rent expense account at the time of payment, thus avoiding the necessity of transferring the amount from Prepaid Rent to Rent Expense at the close of the fiscal period.)

8						8
9	2	Prepaid Rent	15	6 0 0 00		9
10		Cash	11		6 0 0 00	10
11		Paid three months' rent.				11

Oct. 3. Purchased additional printing equipment on account from Miller Equipment Co. for $1,800.

41

Analysis: The asset Printing Equipment increases and is therefore debited for $1,800. The liability Accounts Payable increases and is credited for $1,800. (The manner in which individual accounts for creditors are maintained is considered in a later chapter.)

12						12
13	3	Printing Equipment	18	1 8 0 0 00		13
14		Accounts Payable	21		1 8 0 0 00	14
15		On account from Miller				15
16		Equipment Co.				16

Oct. 4. Received $525 from customers in payment of their accounts.

Analysis: The asset Cash increases and is debited for $525; the asset Accounts Receivable decreases and is credited for $525.

17						17
18	4	Cash	11	5 2 5 00		18
19		Accounts Receivable	12		5 2 5 00	19
20		Received cash on account.				20

Oct. 6. Paid $38 for a newspaper advertisement.

Analysis: Expense accounts are subdivisions of capital. Increases in expense are decreases in capital; hence an expense account is debited for $38. The asset Cash was decreased by the transaction; therefore that account is credited for $38. (Miscellaneous Expense is debited because total expenditures for advertising during a fiscal period are expected to be relatively minor.)

21						21
22	6	Miscellaneous Expense	59	3 8 00		22
23		Cash	11		3 8 00	23
24		Newspaper advertisement.				24

Oct. 10. Paid $400 to Miller Equipment Co. to apply on the $1,800 debt owed them.

Analysis: This payment decreases the liability Accounts Payable, so that account is debited for $400. It also decreases the asset Cash, which is credited for $400.

25						25
26	10	Accounts Payable	21	4 0 0 00		26
27		Cash	11		4 0 0 00	27
28		Miller Equipment Co.				28

Oct. 13. Paid part-time assistants $320 for two weeks' salary.

Analysis: Similar to transaction of October 6.

29						29
30	13	Salary Expense	51	3 2 0 00		30
31		Cash	11		3 2 0 00	31
32		Biweekly salaries.				32

Oct. 16. Received $960 cash from sales for the first half of October.

Analysis: Cash increases and is debited for $960. The revenue account Sales, which is a subdivision of capital, increases and is credited for $960.

33						33
34	16	Cash	11	9 6 0 00		34
35		Sales	41		9 6 0 00	35
36		Cash sales for first half				36
37		of month.				37

Oct. 20. Paid $350 for supplies.

Analysis: The asset Supplies increases and is debited for $350; the asset Cash decreases and is credited for $350.

38						38
39	20	Supplies	14	3 5 0 00		39
40		Cash	11		3 5 0 00	40
41		Cash purchase of supplies.				41

42

Oct. 27. Paid part-time assistants $320 for two weeks' salary.

Analysis: Similar to transaction of October 6.

JOURNAL   PAGE 2

	DATE	DESCRIPTION	POST. REF.	DEBIT	CREDIT	
1	1969 Oct. 27	Salary Expense	51	320 00		1
2		Cash	11		320 00	2
3		Biweekly salaries.				3

Oct. 31. Paid $20 for telephone bill for the month.

Analysis: Similar to transaction of October 6.

4						4
5	31	Miscellaneous Expense	59	20 00		5
6		Cash	11		20 00	6
7		October telephone bill.				7

Oct. 31. Paid $45 for electric bill for the month.

Analysis: Similar to transaction of October 6.

8						8
9	31	Miscellaneous Expense	59	45 00		9
10		Cash	11		45 00	10
11		October electric bill.				11

43

Oct. 31. Received $1,070 from sales for the second half of October.

Analysis: Similar to transaction of October 16.

12						12
13	31	Cash	11	1070 00		13
14		Sales	41		1070 00	14
15		Cash sales for second half				15
16		of month.				16

Oct. 31. Sales on account totaled $510 for the month.

Analysis: The asset Accounts Receivable increases and is debited for $510. The revenue account Sales increases and is credited for $510. (Note that the revenue is earned even though no cash is received; the claim against the customers is as much an asset as cash. As customers pay their accounts later, Cash will be debited and Accounts Receivable will be credited.)

17						17
18	31	Accounts Receivable	12	510 00		18
19		Sales	41		510 00	19
20		Charge sales for month				20

Oct. 31. Bell withdrew $500 for his personal use.

Analysis: The transaction resulted in a decrease in the amount of capital invested in the business and is recorded by a $500 debit to Charles Bell, Drawing; the decrease in business cash is recorded by a $500 credit to Cash.

21					21
22	31 Charles Bell, Drawing	32	500 00		22
23	Cash	11		500 00	23
24	Withdrew cash.				24

After all of the entries for the month have been posted, the ledger will appear as shown on pages 45 and 46. Tracing each entry from the journal to the accounts in the ledger will give a clear understanding of the posting process.

In practice, each account would appear on a separate page in the ledger. They are numbered in accordance with the chart shown on page 39. However, some of the accounts listed in the chart are excluded from the illustrative ledger. The additional accounts will be used later when completing the work of the accounting cycle.

Trial balance

From time to time the equality of debits and credits in the ledger should be verified. In any event the verification should be performed at the end of each fiscal period. Such a verification, which is called a *trial balance*, may be in the form of an adding machine tape or in the form illustrated on page 47. The summary listing of both the balances and titles of the accounts is also useful in preparing the income statement and balance sheet.

As the first step in preparing the trial balance, all accounts having two or more debits or credits are pencil footed. For accounts having both debits and credits, the memorandum balance is also indicated. These procedures are illustrated by the account Cash, appearing on page 45. The total debits of $3,655 minus the total credits of $2,593 yields a balance of $1,062, which is inserted on the debit side of the account.

The Bell Print Shop accounts Supplies, Printing Equipment, Sales, Salary Expense, and Miscellaneous Expense are also pencil footed. However, inasmuch as each of them contains entries on one side only, the footing is the same as the balance, and there is no need to insert the balance in the item section.

Accounts containing only a single debit and a single credit, such as Accounts Payable on page 45, need no pencil footings; the memorandum balance is entered in the item section of the account.

Accounts that contain a single entry only, such as Prepaid Rent on page 45, need neither a pencil footing nor a memorandum balance.

ACCOUNT *Cash*   ACCOUNT NO. 11

DATE	ITEM	POST. REF.	DEBIT	DATE	ITEM	POST. REF.	CREDIT
1969 Oct. 2		1	1 100 00	1969 Oct. 2		1	600 00
4		1	525 00	6		1	38 00
16		1	960 00	10		1	400 00
31	1,062.00	2	1 070 00	13		1	320 00
			3 655 00	20		1	350 00
				27		2	320 00
				31		2	20 00
				31		2	45 00
				31		2	500 00
							2 593 00

ACCOUNT *Accounts Receivable*   ACCOUNT NO. 12

DATE	ITEM	POST. REF.	DEBIT	DATE	ITEM	POST. REF.	CREDIT
1969 Oct. 2		1	600 00	1969 Oct. 4		1	525 00
31	585.00	2	510 00				
			1 110 00				

ACCOUNT *Supplies*   ACCOUNT NO. 14

DATE	ITEM	POST. REF.	DEBIT	DATE	ITEM	POST. REF.	CREDIT
1969 Oct. 2		1	400 00				
20		1	350 00				
			750 00				

ACCOUNT *Prepaid Rent*   ACCOUNT NO. 15

DATE	ITEM	POST. REF.	DEBIT	DATE	ITEM	POST. REF.	CREDIT
1969 Oct. 2		1	600 00				

ACCOUNT *Printing Equipment*   ACCOUNT NO. 18

DATE	ITEM	POST. REF.	DEBIT	DATE	ITEM	POST. REF.	CREDIT
1969 Oct. 2		1	4 200 00				
3		1	1 800 00				
			6 000 00				

ACCOUNT *Accounts Payable*   ACCOUNT NO. 21

DATE	ITEM	POST. REF.	DEBIT	DATE	ITEM	POST. REF.	CREDIT
1969 Oct. 10		1	400 00	1969 Oct. 3	1,400.00	1	1 800 00

45

Ledger — Bell Print Shop

ACCOUNT *Charles Bell, Capital*   ACCOUNT NO. 31

DATE	ITEM	POST. REF.	DEBIT	DATE	ITEM	POST. REF.	CREDIT
				1969 Oct. 2		1	6 3 0 0 00

ACCOUNT *Charles Bell, Drawing*   ACCOUNT NO. 32

DATE	ITEM	POST. REF.	DEBIT	DATE	ITEM	POST. REF.	CREDIT
1969 Oct. 31		2	5 0 0 00				

ACCOUNT *Sales*   ACCOUNT NO. 41

DATE	ITEM	POST. REF.	DEBIT	DATE	ITEM	POST. REF.	CREDIT
				1969 Oct. 16		1	9 6 0 00
				31		2	1 0 7 0 00
				31		2	5 1 0 00
							2 5 4 0 00

ACCOUNT *Salary Expense*   ACCOUNT NO. 51

DATE	ITEM	POST. REF.	DEBIT	DATE	ITEM	POST. REF.	CREDIT
1969 Oct. 13		1	3 2 0 00				
27		2	3 2 0 00				
			6 4 0 00				

ACCOUNT *Miscellaneous Expense*   ACCOUNT NO. 59

DATE	ITEM	POST. REF.	DEBIT	DATE	ITEM	POST. REF.	CREDIT
1969 Oct. 6		1	3 8 00				
31		2	2 0 00				
31		2	4 5 00				
			1 0 3 00				

Ledger — Bell Print Shop (concluded)

Proof provided by the trial balance

The trial balance does not provide complete proof of the accuracy of the ledger. It indicates only that the *debits* and the *credits* are *equal*. This proof is of value, however, because errors frequently affect the equality of debits and credits. If the two totals of a trial balance are not equal, it is probably due to one or more of the following types of errors:

1. Error in preparing the trial balance, such as:
    a. One of the columns of the trial balance was incorrectly added.

Bell Print Shop
Trial Balance
October 31, 1969

	Debit	Credit
Cash	1062 00	
Accounts Receivable	585 00	
Supplies	750 00	
Prepaid Rent	600 00	
Printing Equipment	6000 00	
Accounts Payable		1400 00
Charles Bell, Capital		6300 00
Charles Bell, Drawing	500 00	
Sales		2540 00
Salary Expense	640 00	
Miscellaneous Expense	103 00	
	10240 00	10240 00

Trial balance — Bell Print Shop

b. The amount of an account balance was incorrectly recorded on the trial balance.

c. A debit balance was recorded on the trial balance as a credit, or vice versa, or a balance was omitted entirely.

2. Error in determining the account balances, such as:
   a. A balance was incorrectly computed.
   b. A balance was entered on the wrong side of an account.
   c. One side of an account was incorrectly computed.
3. Error in recording a transaction in the ledger, such as:
   a. An erroneous amount was posted to the account.
   b. A debit entry was posted as a credit, or vice versa.
   c. A debit or a credit posting was omitted.

Among the types of errors that will not cause an inequality in the trial balance totals are the following:

1. Failure to record a transaction or to post a transaction.
2. Recording the same erroneous amount for both the debit and the credit parts of a transaction.
3. Recording the same transaction more than once.
4. Posting a part of a transaction to the wrong account.

It is readily apparent that care should be exercised both in recording transactions in the journal and in posting to the accounts. The desirability of accuracy in determining account balances and reporting them on the trial balance is equally obvious.

Discovery of errors

The existence of errors in the accounts may be ascertained in a variety of ways: through audit procedures, through chance discovery, or through the medium of the trial balance. If the debit and the credit totals of the trial balance are unequal, the reason for the discrepancy must be found and the error must be corrected.

The amount of the difference between the two totals of the trial balance sometimes gives a clue to the type or the location of the error. For example, a difference of 10, 100, or 1,000 in two totals is frequently the result of an error in addition. A difference between totals can also be due to the omission of a debit or a credit posting or, if it is divisible evenly by 2, to the posting of a debit as a credit, or vice versa. For example, if the debit and the credit totals of a trial balance are $20,640 and $20,236 respectively, the difference of $404 may indicate that a credit posting of that amount was omitted or that a credit of $202 was erroneously posted as a debit.

Two other common types of errors are known as *transpositions* and *slides*. A transposition is the erroneous rearrangement of digits, such as writing $542 as $452 or $524. In a slide the entire number is erroneously moved one or more spaces to the right or the left, such as writing $542.00 as $54.20 or $5,420.00. If a single error of either type has occurred, the discrepancy between the trial balance totals will be evenly divisible by 9.

A preliminary examination along the lines suggested by the preceding paragraphs will frequently disclose the error. If it does not, the general procedure is to retrace the various steps in the accounting process, beginning with the last step and working back to the original entries in the journal. While there are no rigid rules governing this check or audit, the following plan is suggested:

1. Double check the totals that were obtained for the trial balance by re-adding the columns.
2. Compare the listings in the trial balance with the balances shown in the ledger, making certain that no accounts have been omitted.
3. Verify the accuracy of the account footings and balances by recomputing them.
4. Trace the postings in the ledger back to the journal, placing a small check mark by the item in the ledger and also in the journal. If the error is not found, scrutinize each account to see if there is an entry without a check mark; do the same with the entries in the journal.
5. Verify the equality of the debits and the credits in the journal.

Ordinarily, errors that affect the trial balance will be revealed before the foregoing procedures have been completed.

QUESTIONS

1. Differentiate between an account and a ledger.
2. Name the three parts of an account.

3. Do the terms *debit* and *credit* signify increase or decrease, or may they signify either? Explain.

4. Describe the assets that compose the current assets category.

5. As of the close of the current fiscal year there is owed a mortgage note payable of $15,000, the terms of which provide for monthly payments of $500. How should the liability be classified on the balance sheet prepared at this time?

6. Identify each of the following accounts as asset, liability, capital, revenue, or expense, and state in each case whether the normal balance is a debit or a credit: (a) Accounts Receivable, (b) Advertising Expense, (c) A. L. Blake, Capital, (d) Cash, (e) A. L. Blake, Drawing, (f) Equipment, (g) Interest Income, (h) Notes Payable, (i) Supplies.

7. What is the effect (increase or decrease) of debits to expense accounts, (a) in terms of capital, (b) in terms of expense?

8. Differentiate between real accounts and temporary capital accounts.

9. Rearrange the following in proper sequence: (a) business document prepared, (b) entry posted to ledger, (c) entry recorded in journal, (d) business transaction occurs.

10. Indicate whether the following items of information could be determined more efficiently by referring to the journal or to the ledger: (a) details of a specific transaction, (b) amount of the cash balance on the last day of the preceding month, (c) amount of service sales for a preceding month, (d) amount of cash paid in connection with a trade-in of equipment that occurred the preceding day.

11. Assuming that during a fiscal period a business has a substantial number of transactions affecting each of the accounts listed below, state for each account whether it is likely to have (a) debit entries only, (b) credit entries only, or (c) both debit and credit entries.

(1) Cash	(4) Sales
(2) John Baker, Drawing	(5) Accounts Payable
(3) Notes Receivable	(6) Miscellaneous Expense

49

12. A particular business enterprise deposits all cash receipts in a bank account and makes all payments by check. The cash account at the end of the current fiscal period has a credit balance of $190 and there is no undeposited cash on hand. (a) Assuming that there were no errors in recording, what is the explanation of this unusual balance? (b) At this particular time is the cash account an asset, a liability, capital, a revenue, or an expense?

13. Describe the three steps involved in posting the credit portion of the following journal entry (Accounts Payable is Account No. 21):

		JOURNAL		PAGE 18
19—				
May	15	Supplies.............................	76	
		Accounts Payable....................		76

14. What is the general sequence of accounts in the ledger?

15. A business enterprise renders services to a customer for $300 in one fiscal period and receives payment from the customer in the following period. What accounts should be debited and credited in the period in which (a) the service was rendered and (b) the cash was received?

16. At the beginning of the fiscal period the account C. D. Gordon, Capital had a credit balance of $8,000. During the period the owner's withdrawals totaled $7,000 and the business incurred a net loss of $1,500; there were no additional investments in the business. Assuming that there have been no recording errors, will the balance sheet prepared at this time balance? Explain.

17. During the month Triumph Service Station received $8,400 in cash and paid out $7,000 in cash. (a) How were the receipts and the disbursements entered in the cash account? (b) Do these data indicate that there was a net income of $1,400 for the month? Explain.

18. What is a trial balance and what does it prove?

19. Does the amount listed for Cash in the trial balance represent (a) the cash at the beginning of the period, (b) the receipts during the period, (c) the disbursements during the period, (d) the receipts minus the disbursements during the period, or (e) the balance of cash on the trial balance date?

20. Give an example of (a) a transposition and (b) a slide.

21. In journalizing a purchase of supplies of $74.56 for cash, both amounts were recorded and posted as $47.56. (a) Would this error cause the trial balance to be out of balance? (b) Would the answer be the same if the entry had been journalized correctly but the credit to Cash had been posted as $47.56?

22. Indicate which of the following errors, each considered individually, would cause the trial balance totals to be unequal:

(a) A receipt of $75 from an account receivable was recorded as a debit of $75 to Cash and a credit of $75 to Sales.
(b) A payment of $120 for equipment was recorded as a debit of $100 to Equipment and a credit of $120 to Cash.
(c) A fee of $150 due from a client was not debited to Accounts Receivable or credited to a revenue account because the cash had not been received.
(d) A payment of $140 to a creditor was recorded as a credit of $140 to Accounts Payable and a credit of $140 to Cash.
(e) A withdrawal of $200 by the owner was recorded as a debit of $20 to Salary Expense and a credit of $20 to Cash.

EXERCISES

2-1. The City Telephone Answering Service has the following accounts in its ledger: Cash; Accounts Receivable; Supplies; Office Equipment; Accounts Payable; Alice Carter, Capital; Alice Carter, Drawing; Fees Earned; Rent Expense; Advertising Expense; Utilities Expense; Miscellaneous Expense.

Record the following transactions completed during the month of April of the current year in a two-column journal:

April 1. Paid rent for the month, $120.
    4. Purchased office equipment on account, $410.
    11. Paid cash for supplies, $13.
    15. Collected accounts receivable, $225.
    22. Paid creditor on account, $240.
    26. Paid advertising expense, $25.
    28. Withdrew cash for personal use, $300.
    29. Paid telephone bill for the month, $22.
    30. Fees earned and billed to customers for month, $715.

30. Paid for repairs to typewriter, $10.
30. Paid electricity bill for the month, $18.

2-2. List the following accounts in the order in which they should appear in the ledger of Black's Realty:

(1) Accounts Payable	(7) Miscellaneous Expense
(2) Accounts Receivable	(8) Prepaid Insurance
(3) Marvin Black, Capital	(9) Interest Payable
(4) Cash	(10) Salary Expense
(5) Marvin Black, Drawing	(11) Sales
(6) Equipment	(12) Mortgage Note Payable

2-3. Eight transactions are recorded in the T accounts presented below. Indicate for each debit and each credit: (a) the type of account affected (asset, liability, capital, revenue, or expense) and (b) whether the account was increased ($+$) or decreased ($-$). Answers should be presented in the following form; transaction (1) is given as an example:

Transaction	Account Debited		Account Credited	
	Type	Effect	Type	Effect
(1)	asset	$+$	capital	$+$

	CASH					EQUIPMENT			HENRY COHEN, DRAWING	
(1)	7,000	(2)	800		(2)	2,300		(5)	300	
(8)	900	(3)	100							
		(5)	300							
		(6)	600							
		(7)	500							

	ACCOUNTS RECEIVABLE					ACCOUNTS PAYABLE			SERVICE REVENUE	
(4)	1,800	(8)	900		(7)	500	(2)	1,500	(4)	1,800

	SUPPLIES			HENRY COHEN, CAPITAL			OPERATING EXPENSES	
(3)	100				(1)	7,000	(6)	600

2-4. The accounts (all normal balances) in the ledger of Jeffrey Clinic as of June 30 of the current year are listed below, in alphabetical order. The balance of the cash account has been intentionally omitted. Prepare a trial balance, listing the accounts in proper sequence, inserting the missing figure for cash.

Accounts Payable	1,700	H. L. Jeffrey, Drawing	6,000
Accounts Receivable	4,100	Land	4,000
Buildings	10,000	Miscellaneous Expense	900
Cash	X	Mortgage Note Payable	
Cleaning Expense	600	(due 1980)	5,100
Equipment	25,000	Prepaid Insurance	1,700
Fees Earned	25,000	Salary Expense	3,400
H. L. Jeffrey, Capital	27,500	Supplies	800
		Utilities Expense	1,100

2-5. The preliminary trial balance of Stuart Company presented below does not balance. In reviewing the ledger and other records you discover the following: (1) the debits and the credits in the cash account total $15,560 and $11,360 respectively; (2) a payment of $600 to a creditor on account was not posted to the cash account; (3) a receipt of $400 from a customer on account was not posted to the accounts receivable account; (4) the balance of the equipment account is $2,400; (5) each account had a normal balance. Prepare a corrected trial balance.

Stuart Company
Trial Balance
May 31, 19—

Cash	4,300	
Accounts Receivable . . .	3,400	
Prepaid Insurance		500
Equipment	4,200	
Accounts Payable		2,600
Salaries Payable	300	
M. B. Stuart, Capital . .		5,400
Service Revenue		4,500
Salary Expense	2,500	
Advertising Expense . . .		200
Miscellaneous Expense .	600	
	15,300	13,200

2-6. Errors in posting from a two-column journal are described as follows:

(1) A debit of $300 to Equipment was posted twice.
(2) A debit of $642 to Supplies was posted as $462.
(3) An entry debiting Salary Expense and crediting Cash for $200 was not posted.
(4) A credit of $200 to Accounts Payable was not posted.
(5) A credit of $90 to Cash was posted as $900.
(6) A credit of $400 to Accounts Receivable was posted to Sales.
(7) A debit of $80 to Accounts Receivable was posted as a credit.

Considering each case individually (i.e. assuming that no other errors had occurred) indicate: (a) by "yes" or "no" whether the trial balance would be out of balance; (b) if answer to (a) is "yes," the amount by which the trial balance totals would differ; and (c) which column of the trial balance would have the larger total. Answers should be presented in the following form; error (1) is given as an example:

Error	(a) Out of Balance	(b) Difference	(c) Larger Total
(1)	yes	$300	Dr.

PROBLEMS

The following additional problems for this chapter are located in Appendix C: 2-1B, 2-3B, 2-4B, 2-6B.

2-1A. Paul B. Ryan established an enterprise to be known as Ryan Decorators, on September 16 of the current year. During the remainder of the month he completed the following business transactions:

Sept. 16. Ryan transferred cash from a personal bank account to an account to be used for the business, $2,400.

52

16. Purchased supplies for cash, $80.
16. Purchased a truck for $3,600, paying $1,000 cash and giving a note payable for the remainder.
17. Purchased equipment on account, $320.
18. Paid rent for period of September 16 to end of month, $70.
19. Received cash for job completed, $140.
22. Purchased supplies on account, $210.
23. Paid wages of employees, $425.
25. Paid premiums on property and casualty insurance, $304.
26. Paid creditor for equipment purchased on Sept. 17, $320.
27. Recorded sales on account and sent invoices to customers, $2,050.
28. Received cash for job completed, $118. This sale had not been recorded previously.
29. Received an invoice for truck expenses, to be paid in October, $43.
29. Paid utilities expense, $17.
29. Paid miscellaneous expenses, $31.
30. Received cash from customers on account, $1,320.
30. Paid wages of employees, $450.
30. Withdrew cash for personal use, $325.

Instructions:

(1) Prepare a ledger for Ryan Decorators, using the following titles and account numbers: Cash, 11; Accounts Receivable, 12; Supplies, 13; Prepaid Insurance, 14; Truck, 16; Equipment, 18; Notes Payable, 21; Accounts Payable, 22; Paul B. Ryan, Capital, 31; Paul B. Ryan, Drawing, 32; Sales, 41; Wages Expense, 51; Rent Expense, 53; Truck Expense, 54; Utilities Expense, 55; Miscellaneous Expense, 59.
(2) Record each transaction in a two-column journal, referring to the above list of accounts or to the ledger in selecting appropriate account titles. (Do *not* insert the account numbers in the journal at this time.)
(3) Post the journal to the ledger, inserting appropriate posting references as each item is posted.
(4) Insert pencil footings and balances in the accounts where appropriate, and prepare a trial balance as of September 30.

2-2A. John L. Nolan, M.D., completed the following transactions in the practice of his profession during March of the current year:

Mar. 2. Paid office rent for March, $500.
    4. Purchased equipment on account, $1,300.
    5. Received cash on account from patients, $3,100.
    9. Purchased X-ray film and other supplies on account, $75.
   11. One of the items of equipment purchased on March 4 was defective. It was returned, with the permission of the supplier, who agreed to reduce the account for the amount charged for the item, $80.
   12. Paid cash for renewal of property insurance policy, $160.
   16. Sold X-ray film to another doctor at cost, as an accommodation, receiving cash, $32.
   17. Paid cash to creditors on account, $1,400.
   20. Discovered that the balance of the cash account and of the accounts payable account as of March 1 were overstated by $25. A payment of that amount to a creditor in February had not been recorded. Journalize the $25 payment as of March 20.
   23. Received cash in payment of services rendered to patients during March, $2,850.

25. Paid invoice for laboratory analyses, $175.
27. Paid cash from business bank account for personal and family expenses, $900.
30. Paid salaries of receptionist and nurses, $1,600.
30. Paid gas and electricity expense, $128.
30. Paid water expense, $19.
31. Recorded fees charged to customers on account for services rendered in March, $1,750.
31. Paid telephone expense, $41.
31. Paid miscellaneous expenses, $80.

Instructions:

(1) Prepare a ledger for Dr. Nolan as of March 1 of the current year. The accounts and their balances (all normal balances) as of March 1 are listed below. Identify the balances by writing "Balance" to the left of the amount and place a check mark ($\sqrt{}$) in the posting reference column. Cash, 11, $2,650; Accounts Receivable, 12, $5,900; Supplies, 13, $260; Prepaid Insurance, 14, $365; Equipment, 18, $14,500; Accounts Payable, 22, $610; John L. Nolan, Capital, 31, $23,065; John L. Nolan, Drawing, 32; Professional Fees, 41; Salary Expense, 51; Rent Expense, 53; Laboratory Expense, 55; Utilities Expense, 56; Miscellaneous Expense, 59. (It is advisable to verify the equality of the debits and credits in the ledger before proceeding with the next instruction.)
(2) Record each transaction in a two-column journal.
(3) Post the journal to the ledger.
(4) Prepare a trial balance as of March 31.
(5) Assuming that the supplies expense, insurance expense, and depreciation expense (which have not been recorded) amount to a total of $245 for the month, determine the following amounts:

(a) Net income for the month of March.
(b) Increase or decrease in capital during the month of March.
(c) Capital as of March 31.

If the working papers correlating with the textbook are not used, omit Problem 2-3A.

2-3A. The following records of Speedy TV Service are presented in the working papers:

> Two-column journal for the month of January
> Ledger as of January 31
> Preliminary trial balance as of January 31

Locate the errors, supply the information requested, and prepare a corrected trial balance, proceeding in accordance with the detailed instructions presented below. The balances recorded in the accounts as of January 1 and the entries in the journal are correctly stated. If it is necessary to correct any posted amounts in the ledger, a line should be drawn through the erroneous figure and the correct amount inserted above. Although corrections to memorandum pencil footings and balances are ordinarily accomplished through erasures, any such errors discovered may be corrected by crossing out the erroneous amount and substituting the correct figure. Corrections or other notations may be inserted on the preliminary trial balance in any manner desired. It is not necessary to complete all of the instructions if equal trial balance totals can be obtained earlier. However, the requirements of instructions (9) and (10) should be completed in any event.

Instructions:

(1) Verify the totals of the preliminary trial balance, inserting the amounts obtained in the schedule provided.
(2) Compute the difference between the trial balance totals.
(3) Determine whether the amount obtained in (2) is evenly divisible by 9.
(4) If the amount obtained in (2) is an even number, determine half the amount.
(5) Scan the amounts in the ledger to determine whether a posting has been omitted or erroneously posted to the wrong side of an account.
(6) Compare the listings in the trial balance with the balances shown in the ledger.
(7) Verify the accuracy of the memorandum footings and balances in the ledger.
(8) Trace the postings in the ledger back to the journal, using small check marks to identify items traced. (Correct any memorandum amounts in the ledger that may be necessitated by errors in posting.)
(9) Journalize as of January 31 the payment of $9.30 for telephone service. The bill had been paid on January 31 but was inadvertently omitted from the journal. Post to the ledger. (Revise any memorandum amounts necessitated by posting.)
(10) Prepare a new trial balance.

2-4A. The following business transactions were completed by James C. Hunt during June of the current year:

June 3. Deposited $17,000 in a bank account for use in acquiring and operating Sunset Drive-In Theatre.
4. Purchased the Sunset Drive-In Theatre for $28,000, allocated as follows: equipment, $5,000; buildings, $11,000; land, $12,000. Paid $10,000 in cash and gave a mortgage note for the remainder.
5. Paid premiums for property and casualty insurance policies, $1,160.
7. Paid for June billboard and newspaper advertising, $350.
8. Purchased supplies, $220, and equipment, $1,100, on account.
9. Cash received from admissions for the week, $1,400.
11. Paid miscellaneous expense, $75.
15. Paid semimonthly wages, $1,500.
16. Cash received from admissions for the week, $1,980.
16. Entered into a contract for the operation of the refreshment stand at a rental of 10% of the concessionaire's sales, with a monthly minimum of $250, payable in advance. Received cash of $125 as the advance payment for the period June 16, the effective date of the contract, to June 30.
18. Paid miscellaneous expenses, $47.
20. Returned portion of equipment purchased on June 8 to the supplier, receiving full credit for its cost, $175.
22. Paid cash to creditors on account, $1,145.
23. Cash received from admissions for the week, $2,100.
24. Purchased supplies for cash, $28.
25. Paid for advertising leaflets for June, $36.
27. Paid cash to owner for his personal use, $850.
28. Recorded invoice of $1,850 for rental of film for June. Payment is due on July 5.
29. Paid electricity and water bills, $245.
30. Paid semimonthly wages, $1,800.
30. Cash received from admissions for remainder of the month, $2,530.

55

30. Recorded additional amount owed by the concessionaire for June, whose sales for June 16–30 totaled $1,850. Rental charges in excess of the advance payment are not due and payable until the tenth of the following month.

Instructions:

(1) Prepare a ledger for Sunset Drive-In Theatre, using the following account titles and numbers: Cash, 11; Accounts Receivable, 12; Prepaid Insurance, 13; Supplies, 14; Equipment, 17; Buildings, 18; Land, 19; Accounts Payable, 21; Mortgage Note Payable, 24; James C. Hunt, Capital, 31; James C. Hunt, Drawing, 32; Admissions Income, 41; Concession Income, 42; Wages Expense, 51; Film Rental Expense, 52; Advertising Expense, 53; Electricity & Water Expense, 54; Miscellaneous Expense, 59.

(2) Record the transactions in a two-column journal.

(3) Post the journal to the ledger.

(4) Prepare a trial balance as of June 30.

(5) Determine the following:

   (a) Amount of total revenue recorded in the ledger.

   (b) Amount of total expenses recorded in the ledger.

   (c) Amount of net income for June, assuming that additional unrecorded expenses were as follows: Supplies expense, $40; Insurance expense, $30; Depreciation expense—equipment, $50; Depreciation expense—buildings, $60; Interest expense (on mortgage note), $90.

   (d) Based on the assumptions in (c), the amount of increase or decrease in capital subsequent to the initial investment on June 3.

   (e) Based on the assumptions in (c), the amount of capital as of June 30.

   (f) The understatement or overstatement of net income for June that would have resulted from failure to record the invoice for film rental until it was paid in July. (See transaction of June 28.)

   (g) The understatement or overstatement of liabilities as of June 30 that would have resulted from failure to record the invoice for film rental in June.

2-5A. Gordon Lang owns and manages Lang Realty, which acts as an agent in buying, selling, renting, and managing real estate. The account balances at the end of June of the current year are presented below.

Account Balances, June 30

11	Cash	2,794	
12	Accounts Receivable	5,163	
13	Prepaid Insurance	306	
14	Office Supplies	90	
16	Automobile	4,750	
17	Accumulated Depr. — Automobile		2,400
18	Office Equipment	2,960	
19	Accumulated Depr. — Office Equip.		845
21	Accounts Payable		138
31	Gordon Lang, Capital		6,504
32	Gordon Lang, Drawing	6,000	
41	Revenue from Fees		29,815
51	Salary and Commission Expense	15,100	
52	Rent Expense	1,200	
53	Advertising Expense	810	
54	Automobile Expense	318	
59	Miscellaneous Expense	211	

The following business transactions were completed by Gordon Long during July of the current year.

July 1. Paid rent for month, $200.
2. Purchased office supplies on account, $75.
4. Purchased office equipment on account, $610.
10. Received cash from clients on account, $3,418.
12. Paid premium on automobile insurance, $256.
15. Paid salaries and commissions, $1,310.
15. Recorded revenue earned and billed to clients during first half of month, $2,418.
16. Discovered an error in computing a commission; received cash from the salesman for the overpayment, $20.
18. Paid creditors on account, $823.
20. Received cash from clients on account, $2,130.
23. Paid advertising expense, $135.
24. Returned an item of office equipment purchased on May 4, receiving full credit for its cost, $55.
28. Paid automobile expenses, $63.
29. Paid miscellaneous expenses, $46.
30. Lang withdrew cash for personal use, $1,000.
31. Recorded revenue earned and billed to clients during second half of month, $2,174.
31. Paid salaries and commissions, $1,248.

Instructions:

(1) Prepare a ledger for the accounts listed; record the balances as of July 1, write "Balance" in the item section, and place a check mark (√) in the posting reference column.
(2) Record the transactions for July in a two-column journal.
(3) Post to the ledger.
(4) Prepare a trial balance of the ledger as of July 31.
(5) What is the nature of the balance in Accounts Payable?

2-6A. The following trial balance for Ace Household Services as of November 30 of the current year does not balance because of a number of errors.

Cash............................	2,490	
Accounts Receivable..............	2,440	
Supplies........................	1,315	
Prepaid Insurance................	174	
Equipment.......................	7,860	
Notes Payable...................		1,300
Accounts Payable................		720
Robert Davis, Capital............		6,130
Robert Davis, Drawing...........	450	
Sales...........................		9,600
Wages Expense..................	2,100	
Rent Expense....................	550	
Advertising Expense.............	22	
Gas, Electricity, and Water Expense .	97	
	17,498	17,750

In the process of comparing the amounts in the trial balance with the ledger, recomputing the balances of the accounts, and comparing the postings with the journal entries, the errors described on the next page were discovered.

(a) The pencil footing of the credits to Cash was understated by $100.
(b) A cash receipt of $190 was posted as a debit to Cash of $910.
(c) A debit of $80 to Accounts Receivable was not posted.
(d) A return of $15 of defective supplies was erroneously posted as a $150 credit to Supplies.
(e) An insurance policy acquired at a cost of $72 was posted as a credit to Prepaid Insurance.
(f) A debit of $100 in Notes Payable was overlooked when determining the balance of the account.
(g) The pencil footings of $1,610 debit and $2,430 credit in Accounts Payable were correct but the balance was computed incorrectly.
(h) A debit of $150 for a withdrawal by the owner was posted as a credit to the capital account.
(i) The balance of $220 in Advertising Expense was entered as $22 in the trial balance.
(j) Miscellaneous Expense, with a balance of $215, was omitted from the trial balance.

Instructions:

Prepare a corrected trial balance as of November 30 of the current year.

58

3
Completion of the accounting cycle

Trial balance and accounting statements

The summary of the ledger at the end of an accounting period, as set forth in the trial balance, is a convenient starting point in the preparation of financial statements. Assuming no errors in journalizing or posting, many of the amounts listed are acceptable for presentation on the income statement, balance sheet, and capital statement respectively. For example, the balance of the cash account probably represents the amount of that asset owned by the enterprise on the last day of the accounting period. Similarly, the balance in Accounts Payable is likely to represent the total amount of that type of liability owed by the enterprise on the last day of the accounting period.

The assumption of correctness of trial balance amounts is not necessarily applicable to every account listed on the trial balance. The amounts listed on the trial balance for prepaid assets are ordinarily overstated. The reason for the overstatement is that the day-to-day usage or expiration of such assets has, for reasons of practicability, not been recorded. For example, the balance in the supplies account represents the cost of the supplies on hand at the beginning of the period plus the cost of those acquired during the period. Some of the supplies would inevitably have been consumed during the period, hence the balance listed on the trial balance is overstated. In the same manner, the balance in Prepaid Insurance represents the beginning balance plus the cost of policies acquired during the period, and no entries were made for the premiums as they expired. The effect of not recording the reduction in prepaid assets is twofold: (1) asset accounts are overstated and (2) expense accounts are understated.

Other data needed for the financial statements may be entirely omitted from the trial balance because of revenue or expense applicable to the period that has not been recorded. For example, salary expense incurred between the last payday and the end of the fiscal period would not ordinarily be recorded in the accounts because salaries are customarily recorded only when they are paid. Such salaries are an expense of the period, however, because the services were rendered during the period; they also represent a liability as of the last day of the period because they are owed to the employees.

Mixed accounts and business operations

An account with a balance that is partly a balance sheet amount and partly an income statement amount is called a *mixed account*. Again using supplies as an example, the balance reported on the trial balance is composed of two elements, the supplies on hand at the end of the period, which is an unexpired cost or asset, and the supplies used during the period, which is an expired cost or expense. Before financial statements are prepared, it is necessary to determine the amount allocable to the asset and the amount allocable to the expense.

The amount of the asset can be determined by counting the quantity of each of the various commodities, multiplying each quantity by the unit cost of that particular commodity, and totaling the dollar amounts thus obtained. The resulting figure represents the amount of the supplies inventory (asset). The cost of the supplies consumed (expense) is then determined by deducting the amount of the inventory from the balance of the supplies account. On the basis of this information, the cost of the supplies used can be transferred from the asset account to the supplies expense account.

An alternative to initially recording the cost of supplies and other prepaid expenses as assets is to record them as expenses. When this procedure is adopted, Supplies Expense and other expense accounts would be mixed accounts at the end of the period, and it would be necessary to transfer the unexpired cost from the expense accounts to appropriate asset accounts. Further consideration will be given to this alternative procedure in a later chapter. In the meantime all expenditures that include prepayments of expense for future periods will be initially recorded as assets. It is important to note that, before preparing financial statements, it is always necessary to determine the portion of mixed accounts allocable to assets and the portion allocable to expenses, regardless of the recording procedure employed.

Prepayments of expenses applicable solely to a particular accounting period are sometimes made at the beginning of the period to which they apply. When this is the case, the expenditure is ordinarily recorded as an expense rather than as an asset. The expense account debited will be a mixed account during the accounting period, but it will be wholly expense at the end of the period. For example, if rent for March is paid on March 1, it is almost entirely an asset at the time of payment. The asset expires gradually from day to day, and at the end of the month the entire amount has become an expense. Therefore, if the expenditure is initially recorded as a debit to Rent Expense, no additional attention need be given to the matter at the close of the period.

Adjusting process

The entries required at the end of a fiscal period to record internal transactions are called *adjusting entries*. In a broad sense they may be said to be corrections to the ledger. But the necessity for bringing the ledger up-to-date is a planned part of the accounting procedure; it is not caused by errors. The term "adjusting entries" is therefore more appropriate than "correcting entries."

The illustrations of adjusting entries that follow are based on the ledger of Bell Print Shop. T accounts are used for illustrative purposes and the adjusting entries, which are presented directly in the accounts, appear in bold face type to differentiate them from items that were posted during the month.

Prepaid expenses. According to Bell's trial balance appearing on page 47, the balance in the supplies account on October 31 is $750. Some of these supplies (paper, ink, etc.) have been used during the past month and some are still in stock. If the amount of either is known, the other can be readily determined. It is more economical to determine the cost of the supplies on hand at the end of the month and to assume that the remainder have been used than it is to keep a record of those used from day to day. Assuming that the inventory of supplies on October 31 is determined to be $230, the amount to be transferred from the asset account to the expense account is computed as follows:

Supplies available (balance of account).........	$750
Supplies on hand (inventory).................	230
Supplies used (amount of adjustment).........	$520

Increases in expense accounts are recorded as debits and decreases in asset accounts are recorded as credits. Hence the adjusting entry required is a debit to Supplies Expense of $520 and a credit to Supplies of $520. After the adjustment, the asset account has a debit balance of $230 and the expense account has a debit balance of $520.

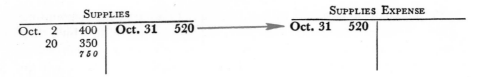

	SUPPLIES			SUPPLIES EXPENSE
Oct. 2	400	Oct. 31	520 ⟶	**Oct. 31** 520
20	350			
	750			

Prepaid Rent is another mixed account that needs to be adjusted at the end of the accounting period. The debit balance in this account represents in part an expense of the current period and in part a prepayment of expense of future periods. The portion that is expense should be transferred to the expense account, Rent Expense.

The debit of $600 in the prepaid rent account illustrated below represents payment of rent for three months, October, November, and December. At the end of October, the rent expense account should be increased (debited) and the prepaid rent account should be decreased (credited) for $200, the rental for one month. The two accounts appear as follows after the adjusting entry has been recorded:

	PREPAID RENT			RENT EXPENSE
Oct. 2	600	Oct. 31	200 ⟶	**Oct. 31** 200

The prepaid rent account now has a debit balance of $400, which is an asset; the rent expense account has a debit balance of $200, which is an expense.

If adjustments for these prepayments were not made, assets and capital would be overstated on the balance sheet for October 31 and net income would be overstated on the income statement for the month of October.

Plant assets. As was explained earlier, all plant assets except land depreciate. The adjusting entry to record depreciation is similar to those illustrated in the preceding section in that there is a transfer from an asset account to an expense account. The amount to be transferred to expense, however, must be based on estimate rather than on verifiable facts, as in the case of expiration of rent and other prepaid expenses. Because of this and the desire to present both the original cost and the accumulated depreciation on the balance sheet, the reduction of the asset is credited to an account titled Accumulated Depreciation.

The adjusting entry to record depreciation for October is illustrated in the T accounts on page 63. The estimated amount of depreciation[1] for the month is $50.

The accumulated depreciation account is called a *contra* asset account. The $50 increase in the account represents a subtraction from the cost

---

[1]Methods of estimating depreciation will be presented in a later chapter.

PRINTING EQUIPMENT		ACCUMULATED DEPRECIATION	
Oct. 2 4,200			Oct. 31 50
3 1,800			
6,000			

DEPRECIATION EXPENSE	
Oct. 31 50	

recorded in the corresponding asset account. The asset account and the related contra account are component parts of the asset, the difference between the two balances being customarily referred to as the *book value* of the asset.

The balances in both the asset and contra asset accounts, together with the book value, may be presented on the balance sheet in the following manner.

Plant assets:
Printing equipment. $6,000
   Less accumulated depreciation. . .   50 $5,950

Accrued expenses (liabilities). As has been explained, it is customary to pay for some types of services and commodities, such as insurance and supplies, before they are used. It is also not unusual for services or commodities to be used before payment has been made for them. An example of this type of situation, which is known as an *accrual*, is service performed by an employee. The salary expense accrues day by day but payment is made only at the end of the week or other regular time period.

If the last day of a pay period does not coincide with the last day of the fiscal period, there is an expense and a liability that must be recorded in the accounts by an adjusting entry.

The data in the T accounts below were taken from the ledger of Bell Print Shop. The debits of $320 on October 13 and 27 in the salary expense account were biweekly payments on alternate Fridays for the payroll periods ended on those days. The salaries earned on Monday and Tuesday, October 30 and 31, amount to $68. This amount is an additional expense of October and it is therefore debited to the salary expense account. It is also a liability as of October 31 and it is therefore credited to Salaries Payable.

SALARIES PAYABLE		SALARY EXPENSE	
	Oct. 31 68	Oct. 13 320	
		27 320	
		640	
		31 68	

After the adjustment, the debit balance of the salary expense account is $708, which is the actual expense for the month; the credit balance of

$68 in Salaries Payable is the liability for salaries owed as of October 31. If the accrual is overlooked when preparing financial statements as of the end of October, the net income reported on the income statement would be overstated; and on the balance sheet, liabilities would be understated and capital overstated.

Work sheet for financial statements

Before journalizing and posting adjustments similar to those just described, it is necessary to determine and assemble the relevant data. For example, it is necessary to determine the cost of supplies on hand and the salaries accrued at the end of the period. Such details, as well as other compilations of data, preliminary drafts of financial statements, and other facilitating analyses prepared by accountants are characterized generally as *working papers*.

A particular type of working paper frequently employed by accountants as a preliminary to the preparation of financial statements has come to be called a *work sheet*. Its use reduces the possibility of overlooking the need for an adjustment, it provides a convenient means of verifying arithmetical accuracy, and it provides for the arrangement of data in a logical form.

The work sheet for Bell Print Shop is presented on page 65. Note that there are three parts to the heading: (1) the name of the enterprise, (2) the title, and (3) the period of time covered. It has a column for account titles and eight money columns, arranged in four pairs of debit and credit columns. The principal headings of the four sets of money columns are as follows:

1. Trial Balance
2. Adjustments
3. Income Statement
4. Balance Sheet

Trial Balance columns. The trial balance data may be assembled directly on the work sheet form or it may be prepared on another sheet first and then copied on the work sheet form.

Adjustments columns. Both the debit and the credit portions of an adjustment should be inserted on the appropriate lines before proceeding to another adjustment. Cross-referencing the related debit and credit of each adjustment by letters is useful to anyone who may have occasion to review the work sheet; it is also helpful later when recording the adjusting entries in the journal. The sequence of adjustments is immaterial except that there is a time and accuracy advantage in following the order in which the adjustment data are assembled. If titles of accounts to be adjusted do not appear in the trial balance, they should be inserted below the trial balance totals as needed.

Bell Print Shop
Work Sheet
For Month Ended October 31, 1969

	ACCOUNT TITLE	TRIAL BALANCE DEBIT	TRIAL BALANCE CREDIT	ADJUSTMENTS DEBIT	ADJUSTMENTS CREDIT	INCOME STATEMENT DEBIT	INCOME STATEMENT CREDIT	BALANCE SHEET DEBIT	BALANCE SHEET CREDIT	
1	Cash	106200						106200		1
2	Accounts Receivable	58500						58500		2
3	Supplies	75000			(a)52000			23000		3
4	Prepaid Rent	60000			(b)20000			40000		4
5	Printing Equipment	600000						600000		5
6	Accounts Payable		140000						140000	6
7	Charles Bell, Capital		630000						630000	7
8	Charles Bell, Drawing	50000						50000		8
9	Sales		254000				254000			9
10	Salary Expense	64000		(d) 6800		70800				10
11	Miscellaneous Expense	10300				10300				11
12		1024000	1024000							12
13	Supplies Expense			(a)52000		52000				13
14	Rent Expense			(b)20000		20000				14
15	Depreciation Expense			(c) 5000		5000				15
16	Accumulated Depreciation				(c) 5000				5000	16
17	Salaries Payable				(d) 6800				6800	17
18				83800	83800	158100	254000	877700	781800	18
19	Net Income					95900			95900	19
20						254000	254000	877700	877700	20

Eight-column work sheet

65

The adjusting entries for Bell Print Shop were explained and illustrated by T accounts earlier in the chapter. In practice the adjustments are inserted directly on the work sheet on the basis of the data assembled by the accounting department.

Explanatory notes for the entries in the adjustments columns of the work sheet on page 65 follow.

(a) *Supplies.* The supplies account has a debit balance of $750; the cost of the supplies on hand at the end of the period is $230; therefore, the supplies expense for October is the difference between the two amounts, or $520. The adjustment is entered by writing (1) *Supplies Expense* in the Account Title column, (2) *$520* in the Adjustments Debit column on the same line, and (3) *$520* in the Adjustments Credit column on the line with Supplies.

(b) *Rent.* The prepaid rent account has a debit balance of $600, which represents a payment for three months beginning with October; therefore, the rent expense for October is $200. The adjustment is entered by writing (1) *Rent Expense* in the Account Title column, (2) *$200* in the Adjustments Debit column on the same line, and (3) *$200* in the Adjustments Credit column on the line with Prepaid Rent.

(c) *Depreciation.* Depreciation of the printing equipment for the month is estimated at $50. This expired portion of the cost of the equipment is both an expense and a reduction in the asset. The adjustment is entered by writing (1) *Depreciation Expense* in the Account Title column, (2) *$50* in the Adjustments Debit column on the same line, (3) *Accumulated Depreciation* in the Account Title column, and (4) *$50* in the Adjustments Credit column on the same line.

(d) *Salaries.* Salaries accrued but not paid at the end of October amount to $68. This is an increase in expense and an increase in liabilities. The adjustment is entered by writing (1) *$68* in the Adjustments Debit column on the same line with Salary Expense, (2) *Salaries Payable* in the Account Title column, and (3) *$68* in the Adjustments Credit column on the same line.

The final step in completing the Adjustments columns is to prove the equality of debits and credits by totaling and ruling the two columns.

Income Statement and Balance Sheet columns. The data in the trial balance columns are combined with the adjustments data and extended to one of the remaining four columns. The amounts of assets, liabilities, capital, and drawing are extended to the balance sheet columns, and the revenues and expenses are extended to the income statement columns.

This procedure must be applied to the balance of each account listed, beginning at the top and proceeding down the page in sequential order.

In the illustrative work sheet, the first account listed is Cash and the balance appearing in the trial balance is $1,062. Since there are no adjustments to Cash, the trial balance amount is to be extended to the appropriate column. Cash is an asset, it is listed on the balance sheet, and it has a debit balance. Accordingly, the $1,062 amount is extended to the debit column of the balance sheet section. The balance of Accounts Receivable is extended in similar fashion. Supplies has an initial debit balance of $750 and a credit adjustment (decrease) of $520. The amount to be extended is therefore the remaining debit balance of $230. The same procedure is continued until all account balances, with or without adjustment as the case may be, have been extended to the appropriate columns. The balances of the capital and drawing accounts are extended to the balance sheet section, even though they are reported on the capital statement. Note that for accounts listed below the trial balance totals, the account balance is the amount of the adjustment. For example, Supplies Expense has no initial balance and a debit adjustment of $520, which is the amount extended to the debit column of the income statement section.

After all of the balances have been extended, each of the four columns is totaled. The amount of the net income or the net loss for the period is then determined by ascertaining the amount of the difference between the totals of the two income statement columns. If the credit column total is greater than the debit column total, the excess is the net income. For the work sheet presented on page 65, the computation of net income is as follows:

Total of credit column (revenue)............	$2,540
Total of debit column (expenses)............	1,581
Net income (excess of revenue over expenses).	$ 959

Revenue and expense accounts, which are in reality subdivisions of the capital account, are temporary in nature. They are used during the fiscal period to facilitate the accumulation of detailed operating data. After they have served their purpose, the net balance, which in the illustration is a credit of $959, will be transferred to the capital account in the ledger. This transfer is accomplished on the work sheet by entries in the income statement debit column and the balance sheet credit column, as illustrated on page 65. If there had been a net loss instead of a net income, the amount would have been entered in the income statement credit column and the balance sheet debit column.

After the final entry on the work sheet, each of the four statement columns is totaled to verify the arithmetic accuracy of the amount of net income or net loss transferred from the income statement to the balance sheet. The totals of the two income statement columns must be equal, as must the totals of the two balance sheet columns. The form of work sheet illustrated may be expanded by the addition of a pair of columns solely for capital statement data. However, because of the very few items involved, this variation is not illustrated.[2]

Financial statements

The income statement, capital statement, and balance sheet prepared from the work sheet of Bell Print Shop appear on the next page. The form of the statements corresponds to those presented in Chapter 1, with the exception of the balance sheet, which has been expanded by the addition of subcaptions for current assets, plant assets, and current liabilities. Additional variations in the format of the balance sheet, as well as variations in the other statements, will be presented at times.

The work sheet is the source of all of the data reported on the income statement. Similarly, it is the source of all basic data reported on the balance sheet, with the exception of the amount of the owner's capital which can be obtained from the capital statement.

In preparing the capital statement it is necessary to refer to the capital account in the ledger to determine the balance at the beginning of the period and the amount of any additional investments that may have been made during the period. The amounts of net income and withdrawals for the period are taken from the Balance Sheet columns of the work sheet, and the balance of capital at the end of the period is determined arithmetically.

The form of the capital statement can be modified to meet the circumstances of any particular case. In the illustration on the next page, the amount withdrawn by the owner was less than the net income. If the withdrawals had exceeded the net income, the order of the two items could have been reversed and the difference between the two deducted from the beginning capital.

Other factors, such as additional investments or a net loss, also necessitate modifications in form, as in the following example:

Capital, January 1, 19--	$35,000.00	
Additional investment during the year.	6,000.00	
Total...........................		$41,000.00
Net loss for the year.................	$ 8,000.00	
Withdrawals.......................	3,600.00	
Decrease in capital..................		11,600.00
Capital, December 31, 19--		$29,400.00

[2]If there are a great many adjustments, it may be advisable to insert a section entitled Adjusted Trial Balance between the trial balance section and the income statement section. The arithmetic of combining the data may then be verified before extending balances to the statement sections. Other variations in form may be introduced to meet special requirements or to accord with the preferences of the particular user.

```
                        Bell Print Shop
                       Income Statement
              For Month Ended October 31, 1969

Sales . . . . . . . . . . . . . . .              $2,540.00

Operating expenses:
   Salary expense. . . . . . . . . . .  $708.00
   Supplies expense. . . . . . . . . .   520.00
   Rent expense. . . . . . . . . . . .   200.00
   Depreciation expense. . . . . . . .    50.00
   Miscellaneous expense . . . . . . .   103.00
      Total operating expenses. . . . .           1,581.00

Net income from operations. . . . . .             $  959.00
```

Income statement

```
                        Bell Print Shop
                       Capital Statement
              For Month Ended October 31, 1969

Capital, October 2, 1969. . . . . . .             $6,300.00
Net income for the month. . . . . . .  $959.00
Less withdrawals. . . . . . . . . . .   500.00
Increase in capital . . . . . . . . .               459.00
Capital, October 31, 1969 . . . . . .             $6,759.00
```

Capital statement

69

```
                        Bell Print Shop
                        Balance Sheet
                       October 31, 1969

                            Assets
Current assets:
   Cash. . . . . . . . . . . . . . . .  $1,062.00
   Accounts receivable . . . . . . . .     585.00
   Supplies. . . . . . . . . . . . . .     230.00
   Prepaid rent. . . . . . . . . . . .     400.00
      Total current assets. . . . . . .           $2,277.00
Plant assets:
   Printing equipment. . . . . . . . .  $6,000.00
      Less accumulated depreciation . .     50.00   5,950.00
Total assets. . . . . . . . . . . . .             $8,227.00

                          Liabilities
Current liabilities:
   Accounts payable. . . . . . . . . .  $1,400.00
   Salaries payable. . . . . . . . . .      68.00
Total liabilities . . . . . . . . . .             $1,468.00

                            Capital
Charles Bell, capital . . . . . . . .               6,759.00
Total liabilities and capital . . . .             $8,227.00
```

Balance sheet

Journalizing and posting adjusting entries

At the end of the fiscal period the adjusting entries appearing in the work sheet are recorded in the journal and posted to the ledger, bringing the ledger into agreement with the data reported on the financial statements. The adjusting entries are dated as of the last day of the accounting period, even though they are usually recorded some time later. Each entry may be supported by an explanation, but a suitable caption above the first adjusting entry, as in the illustration below, is sufficient. A brief explanation of each separate entry serves no useful purpose and, on the other hand, a detailed explanation would needlessly duplicate working papers and other basic documents available in the files.

The adjusting entries in the journal of Bell Print Shop are presented below. The accounts to which they have been posted appear in the ledger beginning on page 74. To facilitate identification, each adjusting entry is identified in the item section of the accounts. It is not necessary that this be done in actual practice.

JOURNAL   PAGE 2

	DATE	DESCRIPTION	POST. REF.	DEBIT	CREDIT	
26		Adjusting Entries				26
27	31	Supplies Expense	52	52000		27
28		Supplies	14		52000	28
29						29
30	31	Rent Expense	53	20000		30
31		Prepaid Rent	15		20000	31
32						32
33	31	Depreciation Expense	54	5000		33
34		Accumulated Depreciation	19		5000	34
35						35
36	31	Salary Expense	51	6800		36
37		Salaries Payable	22		6800	37
38						38

Adjusting entries

Closing entries

As was explained earlier, the revenue, expense, and drawing accounts are temporary accounts employed in classifying and summarizing changes in capital during the accounting period. At the end of the period the net effect of the balances in these accounts must be recorded in the permanent capital account. The balances must also be removed so that the accounts will be ready for use in accumulating data for the ensuing accounting period. Both of these objectives are accomplished by a series of entries called *closing entries*.

An account titled Expense and Revenue Summary is used for summarizing the data in the revenue and expense accounts. It is employed only at the end of the accounting period and is both opened and closed during the closing process. Various other titles are used for the account, including Profit and Loss Summary, Income and Expense Summary, and Income Summary.

Four entries are required to close the temporary accounts at the end of the period. They are as follows:

1. Each revenue account is debited for the amount of its balance, and Expense and Revenue Summary is credited for the total revenue.
2. Each expense account is credited for the amount of its balance, and Expense and Revenue Summary is debited for the total expense.
3. Expense and Revenue Summary is debited for the amount of its balance (net income), and the capital account is credited for the same amount. (Debit and credit are reversed if there is a net loss.)
4. The drawing account is credited for the amount of its balance, and the capital account is debited for the same amount.

After the closing entries have been journalized, as illustrated below, and posted to the ledger, the balance in the capital account will correspond to the amounts reported on the capital statement and balance sheet. In addition, the revenue, expense, and drawing accounts will be closed (in balance). The process of closing is illustrated by the flow chart presented on page 72.

The account titles and amounts needed in journalizing the closing entries may be obtained from any one of three sources: (1) work sheet,

JOURNAL   PAGE 3

	DATE	DESCRIPTION	POST. REF.	DEBIT	CREDIT	
1	1969	Closing Entries				1
2	Oct. 31	Sales	41	2540 00		2
3		Expense and Revenue Summary	33		2540 00	3
4						4
5	31	Expense and Revenue Summary	33	1581 00		5
6		Salary Expense	51		708 00	6
7		Miscellaneous Expense	59		103 00	7
8		Supplies Expense	52		520 00	8
9		Rent Expense	53		200 00	9
10		Depreciation Expense	54		50 00	10
11						11
12	31	Expense and Revenue Summary	33	959 00		12
13		Charles Bell, Capital	31		959 00	13
14						14
15	31	Charles Bell, Capital	31	500 00		15
16		Charles Bell, Drawing	32		500 00	16
17						17

Closing entries

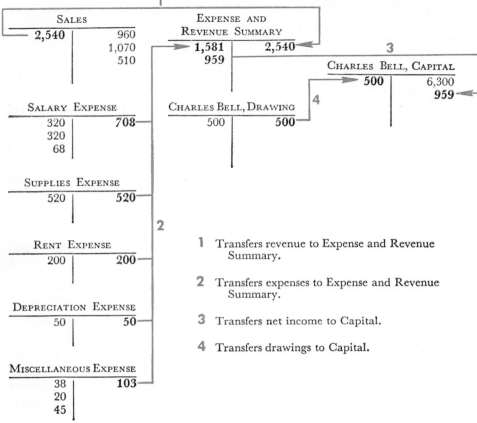

1 Transfers revenue to Expense and Revenue Summary.

2 Transfers expenses to Expense and Revenue Summary.

3 Transfers net income to Capital.

4 Transfers drawings to Capital.

72

(2) income and capital statements, and (3) ledger. When the work sheet is used, the data for the first two entries are taken from the income statement columns; the amount for the third entry is the net income or net loss appearing at the bottom of the work sheet; and reference to the drawing account balance appearing in the balance sheet column of the work sheet supplies the information for the fourth, and final, entry.

Flow of data in closing entries

Data for the closing entries appearing in the journal on page 71 are taken from the work sheet on page 65. A caption above the first closing entry in the series, as in the illustration, is sufficient to identify them; explanations are unnecessary. The entries are dated as of the last day of the accounting period even though they are actually recorded at a later date. The accounts to which they have been posted appear in the ledger beginning on page 74. Each posting of a closing entry is identified in the item section of the accounts as an aid to the student. It is not necessary that this be done in actual practice.

Instead of transferring net income from the expense and revenue summary account to the capital account, some accountants prefer that it be closed to the drawing account. In terms of the Bell Print Shop illustration, the drawing account would then have a credit balance of $459 (net income of $959 minus drawing of $500). The balance in the drawing account would then be closed to the capital account. The final result of both methods is the same, of course.

Ruling and balancing the accounts

After the closing entries have been posted, the accounts in the ledger must be prepared to receive entries for the ensuing fiscal period. This is done by ruling them in such a manner as to segregate entries of the old period just ended from entries of the new period just beginning. Each of the procedures described in the paragraphs that follow is illustrated in the ledger beginning on page 74. The parenthetical references are to accounts appearing in that ledger.

Temporary capital accounts. After the revenue, expense, and drawing accounts have been closed, the debits in each account are equal to the credits in each account. To avoid the possibility of erroneously combining any of these entries with entries of the ensuing period, it is necessary to proceed as follows (see Sales):

1. A single ruling is drawn across the amount columns beneath the last figure in the longer of the two columns and on the same line of the shorter column.
2. The total of each column is written beneath the single rulings.
3. Double rulings are drawn beneath the totals, across all columns except the item sections.

If an account has only one debit and one credit (see Supplies Expense), there is no need to repeat the same figures as totals; the double rulings are drawn beneath the entries.

Asset, liability, and capital accounts. The entries in each of the permanent accounts may be summarized and the balance recorded in the account as the first item for the new period. The procedure is optional and in any case would be omitted for an account with only one entry (see Accumulated Depreciation). The sequence of procedures to rule and balance an account is as follows (see Cash):

1. The balance of the account is written in the amount column of the first available line of the smaller of the two sides. *Balance* is written in the item section, a check mark is placed in the posting reference column to differentiate it from posted entries, and the last day of the period is written in the date column.
2. A single ruling is drawn across the amount columns beneath the last

ACCOUNT Cash   ACCOUNT NO. 11

DATE	ITEM	POST. REF.	DEBIT	DATE	ITEM	POST. REF.	CREDIT
1969 Oct. 2		/	1 1 0 0 00	1969 Oct. 2		/	6 0 0 00
4		/	5 2 5 00	6		/	3 8 00
16		/	9 6 0 00	10		/	4 0 0 00
31		2	1 0 7 0 00	13		/	3 2 0 00
	1,062.00		3 6 5 5 00	20		/	3 5 0 00
				27		2	3 2 0 00
				31		2	2 0 00
				31		2	4 5 00
				31		2	5 0 0 00
							2 5 9 3 00
				31	Balance	✓	1 0 6 2 00
			3 6 5 5 00				3 6 5 5 00
Nov. 1	Balance	✓	1 0 6 2 00				

ACCOUNT Accounts Receivable   ACCOUNT NO. 12

DATE	ITEM	POST. REF.	DEBIT	DATE	ITEM	POST. REF.	CREDIT
1969 Oct. 2		/	6 0 0 00	1969 Oct. 4		/	5 2 5 00
31		2	5 1 0 00	31	Balance	✓	5 8 5 00
	585.00		1 1 1 0 00				1 1 1 0 00
			1 1 1 0 00				
Nov. 1	Balance	✓	5 8 5 00				

ACCOUNT Supplies   ACCOUNT NO. 14

DATE	ITEM	POST. REF.	DEBIT	DATE	ITEM	POST. REF.	CREDIT
1969 Oct. 2		/	4 0 0 00	1969 Oct. 31	Adjusting	2	5 2 0 00
20		/	3 5 0 00	31	Balance	✓	2 3 0 00
			7 5 0 00				7 5 0 00
			7 5 0 00				
Nov. 1	Balance	✓	2 3 0 00				

ACCOUNT Prepaid Rent   ACCOUNT NO. 15

DATE	ITEM	POST. REF.	DEBIT	DATE	ITEM	POST. REF.	CREDIT
1969 Oct. 2		/	6 0 0 00	1969 Oct. 31	Adjusting	2	2 0 0 00
				31	Balance	✓	4 0 0 00
			6 0 0 00				6 0 0 00
Nov. 1	Balance	✓	4 0 0 00				

ACCOUNT Printing Equipment   ACCOUNT NO. 18

DATE	ITEM	POST. REF.	DEBIT	DATE	ITEM	POST. REF.	CREDIT
1969 Oct. 2		/	4 2 0 0 00	1969 Oct. 31	Balance	✓	6 0 0 0 00
3		/	1 8 0 0 00				
			6 0 0 0 00				
			6 0 0 0 00				6 0 0 0 00
Nov. 1	Balance	✓	6 0 0 0 00				

Ledger after the accounts have been adjusted, closed, ruled, and balanced

part one ● Accounting processes for a service enterprise

ACCOUNT *Accumulated Depreciation*   ACCOUNT NO. 19

DATE	ITEM	POST. REF.	DEBIT	DATE	ITEM	POST. REF.	CREDIT
				1969 Oct. 31	Adjusting	2	50 00

ACCOUNT *Accounts Payable*   ACCOUNT NO. 21

DATE	ITEM	POST. REF.	DEBIT	DATE	ITEM	POST. REF.	CREDIT
1969 Oct. 10		1	40 00 00	1969 Oct. 3		1	1 80 00 00
31	Balance	✓	1 40 00 00		1,400.00		
			1 80 00 00				1 80 00 00
				Nov. 1	Balance	✓	1 40 00 00

ACCOUNT *Salaries Payable*   ACCOUNT NO. 22

DATE	ITEM	POST. REF.	DEBIT	DATE	ITEM	POST. REF.	CREDIT
				1969 Oct. 31	Adjusting	2	6 8 00

ACCOUNT *Charles Bell, Capital*   ACCOUNT NO. 31

DATE	ITEM	POST. REF.	DEBIT	DATE	ITEM	POST. REF.	CREDIT
1969 Oct. 31	Closing	3	50 00 00	1969 Oct. 2		1	6 30 00 00
31	Balance	✓	6 75 9 00	31	Closing	3	9 5 9 00
			7 25 9 00				7 25 9 00
				Nov. 1	Balance	✓	6 75 9 00

ACCOUNT *Charles Bell, Drawing*   ACCOUNT NO. 32

DATE	ITEM	POST. REF.	DEBIT	DATE	ITEM	POST. REF.	CREDIT
1969 Oct. 31		2	50 00 00	1969 Oct. 31	Closing	3	50 00 00

ACCOUNT *Expense and Revenue Summary*   ACCOUNT NO. 33

DATE	ITEM	POST. REF.	DEBIT	DATE	ITEM	POST. REF.	CREDIT
1969 Oct. 31	Closing	3	1 58 1 00	1969 Oct. 31	Closing	3	2 54 0 00
31	Closing	3	9 5 9 00				
			2 54 0 00				2 54 0 00

**Ledger after the accounts have been adjusted, closed,
ruled, and balanced — continued**

ACCOUNT *Sales*   ACCOUNT NO. 41

DATE	ITEM	POST. REF.	DEBIT	DATE	ITEM	POST. REF.	CREDIT
1969 Oct. 31	Closing	3	2 5 4 0 00	1969 Oct. 16		1	9 6 0 00
				31		2	1 0 7 0 00
				31		2	5 1 0 00
							2 5 4 0 00
			2 5 4 0 00				2 5 4 0 00

ACCOUNT *Salary Expense*   ACCOUNT NO. 51

DATE	ITEM	POST. REF.	DEBIT	DATE	ITEM	POST. REF.	CREDIT
1969 Oct. 13		1	3 2 0 00	1969 Oct. 31	Closing	3	7 0 8 00
27		2	3 2 0 00				
			6 4 0 00				
31	Adjusting	2	6 8 00				
			7 0 8 00				7 0 8 00

ACCOUNT *Supplies Expense*   ACCOUNT NO. 52

DATE	ITEM	POST. REF.	DEBIT	DATE	ITEM	POST. REF.	CREDIT
1969 Oct. 31	Adjusting	2	5 2 0 00	1969 Oct. 31	Closing	3	5 2 0 00

76

ACCOUNT *Rent Expense*   ACCOUNT NO. 53

DATE	ITEM	POST. REF.	DEBIT	DATE	ITEM	POST. REF.	CREDIT
1969 Oct. 31	Adjusting	2	2 0 0 00	1969 Oct. 31	Closing	3	2 0 0 00

ACCOUNT *Depreciation Expense*   ACCOUNT NO. 54

DATE	ITEM	POST. REF.	DEBIT.	DATE	ITEM	POST. REF.	CREDIT
1969 Oct. 31	Adjusting	2	5 0 00	1969 Oct. 31	Closing	3	5 0 00

ACCOUNT *Miscellaneous Expense*   ACCOUNT NO. 59

DATE	ITEM	POST. REF.	DEBIT	DATE	ITEM	POST. REF.	CREDIT
1969 Oct. 6		1	3 8 00	1969 Oct. 31	Closing	3	1 0 3 00
31		2	2 0 00				
31		2	4 5 00				
			1 0 3 00				
			1 0 3 00				1 0 3 00

**Ledger after the accounts have been adjusted, closed,
ruled, and balanced — concluded**

figure in the longer of the two columns and on the same line of the shorter column.

3. The total of each column is written beneath the single rulings.
4. Double rulings are drawn beneath the totals, across all columns except the item sections.
5. The balance is written in the amount column of the side that was originally the larger, *Balance* is written in the item section, a check mark is placed in the posting reference column, and the first day of the new period is written in the date column.

Post-closing trial balance

The final procedure of the accounting cycle is the preparation of a post-closing trial balance. Its purpose is to assure that the ledger is in balance at the beginning of the new accounting period. The items on the post-closing trial balance should correspond exactly with those reported on the balance sheet.

A post-closing trial balance is illustrated below. A common practice is to proceed directly from the ledger to the preparation of adding machine listings, omitting the more formalized procedure. The adding machine tapes then become the post-closing trial balance.

Bell Print Shop
Post-Closing Trial Balance
October 31, 1969

Cash	1062 00	
Accounts Receivable	585 00	
Supplies	230 00	
Prepaid Rent	400 00	
Printing Equipment	6000 00	
Accumulated Depreciation		50 00
Accounts Payable		1400 00
Salaries Payable		68 00
Charles Bell, Capital		6759 00
	8277 00	8277 00

Post-closing trial balance

Accounting cycle

The principal accounting procedures of a fiscal period have been presented in this and the preceding chapter. The sequence of procedures is frequently called the *accounting cycle*. It begins with the analysis and the journalizing of transactions and ends with the post-closing trial balance. The most significant output of the cycle is, of course, the financial statements.

An understanding of all phases of the accounting cycle is essential as a foundation for further study of accounting principles and the uses of accounting data by management. The following outline summarizes the basic phases of the cycle:

1. The transactions are analyzed.
2. The transactions are journalized.
3. The journal entries are posted to the ledger.
4. A trial balance is prepared.
5. The data needed to adjust the accounts are assembled.
6. A work sheet is prepared.
7. The financial statements are prepared.
8. The adjusting entries are journalized and posted.
9. The closing entries are journalized and posted.
10. The ledger accounts are ruled and balanced.
11. A post-closing trial balance is prepared.

Interim statements

In the illustrative case of Bell Print Shop a complete accounting cycle occupied only a single month. Most business enterprises close the temporary capital accounts annually rather than at the end of each month. Regardless of the length of the period, the closing procedures are identical. A short period was used in the illustration to minimize the number of transactions and the physical space requirements.

When the books are closed annually, only phases 1 through 4 of the accounting cycle need to be repeated monthly. The completion of posting and the preparation of a trial balance at the end of each month is customary regardless of whether or not the accounts are closed. When interim financial statements are prepared monthly, phases 5 through 7 of the accounting cycle, ending with the financial statements, are also completed monthly.

When the temporary accounts are closed annually, the revenue and expense data for the interim income statements will be cumulative. For example, assuming a fiscal year that begins on January 1, the amounts in the income statement columns of the February work sheet will be the cumulative totals for January and February; the revenue and expenses on the March work sheet will be the cumulative totals for January, February, and March; and so on. An income statement for each individual month may be prepared, however, by subtracting from the current cumulative amount of each revenue and expense the amount of the corresponding items on the preceding cumulative statement. Thus the sales figure reported on the cumulative statement for January 1 to March 31 minus the sales figure reported on the cumulative statement for January 1 to February 28 will be the sales figure for the month of March, and so on.

Correction of errors

Occasional errors in journalizing and posting transactions are inevitable. Procedures employed to correct errors in the journal and ledger vary according to the nature of the error and the phase of the accounting cycle in which it is discovered.

When an error in an account title or amount in the journal is discovered before the entry is posted, the correction may be effected by drawing a line through the error and inserting the correct title or amount immediately above. If a debit journal entry is erroneously posted as a credit, or vice versa, or if the amount of the posting is in error, the correction may be accomplished in a similar manner. If there is any likelihood of questions arising later, the person responsible may initial the correction as in the illustration below.

ACCOUNT *Miscellaneous Expense*   ACCOUNT NO. 59

DATE	ITEM	POST. REF.	DEBIT		DATE	ITEM	POST. REF.	CREDIT
1969 Oct. 6		DC 1	~~3 8 0 00~~ 3 8 00					

Account with corrected posting

When an account has been erroneously debited or credited in the journal and the item has been posted, the correction should be made by means of a correcting entry. For example, if at the end of March it is discovered that a cash purchase of office equipment for $500 on March 5 had been journalized as a debit to Office Supplies and a credit to Cash, the error should be corrected by an additional entry in the journal. Before attempting to formulate a correcting entry, it is advisable to establish clearly both (1) the debit(s) and credit(s) of the entry in which the error(s) occurred and (2) the debit(s) and credit(s) that should have been recorded. T accounts may be helpful in making this analysis, as in the example below.

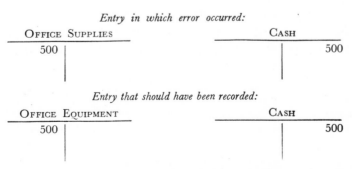

Entry in which error occurred:

OFFICE SUPPLIES   CASH

500   500

Entry that should have been recorded:

OFFICE EQUIPMENT   CASH

500   500

Comparison of the two sets of T accounts reveals that the erroneous debit of $500 to Office Supplies may be corrected by a $500 credit to that

79

account and that Office Equipment should be debited for $500. The following correcting entry is then journalized and posted:

	DATE	DESCRIPTION	POST. REF.	DEBIT		CREDIT		
JOURNAL						PAGE *18*		
1	1969 Mar. 31	Office Equipment	18	500 00				1
2		Office Supplies	15			500 00		2
3		To correct erroneous debit to						3
4		Office Supplies on March 5.						4
5		See invoice from Allen						5
6		Supply Company. C.R.N.						6
7								7

Correcting entry

Although there is some latitude in the techniques employed to correct errors, the explanations should be sufficiently clear to be readily understood by anyone examining the records.

QUESTIONS

1. What is the nature of the balance in the supplies account at the end of the accounting period (a) before adjustment? (b) after adjustment?

2. What is the term usually employed in referring to (a) unexpired costs? (b) expired costs?

3. State whether each of the following assets and services is customarily paid for in advance of its use or after it has been consumed: (a) rent, (b) supplies, (c) services of office employees, (d) property insurance, (e) office equipment, (f) electric power, (g) water.

4. If the effect of the credit portion of an adjusting entry is to decrease the balance of an asset account, which of the following statements describes the effect of the debit portion of the entry: (a) decrease the balance of a liability account? (b) increase the balance of an expense account? (c) decrease the balance of an expense account?

5. Does every adjusting entry have an effect on the determination of the amount of net income for a period? Explain.

6. On October 1, an enterprise pays the October rent on the building that it occupies. (a) Do the rights acquired at October 1 represent an asset or an expense? (b) What is the justification for debiting Rent Expense at the time of payment?

7. (a) Explain the purpose of the two accounts: Depreciation Expense and Accumulated Depreciation. (b) What is the normal balance of each account? (c) Is it customary for the balances of the two accounts to be equal in amount? (d) In what financial statements, if any, will each account appear?

8. How is the *book value* of a plant asset determined?

9. At the end of January, the first month of the fiscal year, the usual adjusting entry transferring expired insurance to an expense account is inadvertently omitted. Which items will be erroneously stated, because of the error, on (a) the income statement for January and (b) the balance sheet as of January 31? Also indicate whether the items in error will be overstated or understated.

10. Accrued salaries of $800 owed to employees for December 30 and 31 are not taken into consideration in preparing the financial statements for the fiscal year ended December 31. Which items will be erroneously stated, because of the error, on (a) the income statement for the year and (b) the balance sheet as of December 31? Also indicate whether the items in error will be overstated or understated.

11. Assume that the error in question 10 was not corrected and that the $800 of accrued salaries was included in the first salary payment in January. Which items will be erroneously stated, because of failure to correct the initial error, on (a) the income statement for January and (b) the balance sheet as of January 31?

12. Is the work sheet a substitute for the financial statements? Discuss.

13. What is the purpose of the expense and revenue summary account?

14. Identify the accounts in the following list that should be closed to Expense and Revenue Summary at the end of the fiscal year: (a) Accounts Receivable, (b) Accumulated Depreciation, (c) Advertising Expense, (d) Cash, (e) D. Davis, Drawing, (f) Depreciation Expense, (g) Insurance Expense, (h) Office Equipment, (i) Prepaid Insurance, (j) Sales, (k) Supplies.

15. Are adjusting and closing entries in the journal dated as of the last day of the fiscal period or as of the day the entries are actually made? Explain.

16. Which of the following accounts in the ledger will ordinarily appear in the post-closing trial balance: (a) Accounts Payable, (b) Accumulated Depreciation, (c) Cash, (d) Depreciation Expense, (e) Equipment, (f) E. E. Evans, Capital, (g) E. E. Evans, Drawing, (h) Prepaid Insurance, (i) Sales, (j) Utilities Expense.

17. At what time intervals are the temporary capital accounts ordinarily closed and a new cycle begun?

18. For an enterprise that closes its temporary capital accounts annually as of June 30, the end of its fiscal year, what period will be covered by the income statement prepared from the work sheet as of November 30?

EXERCISES

3-1. The balance in the prepaid insurance account before adjustment at the end of the year is $1,730. Journalize the adjusting entry required under each of the following alternatives: (a) the amount of insurance expired during the year is $620; (b) the amount of unexpired insurance applicable to future periods is $1,240.

3-2. A business enterprise pays weekly salaries of $5,500 on Friday for a five-day week ending on that day. Journalize the necessary adjusting entry at the end of the fiscal period, assuming that the fiscal period ends (a) on Monday, (b) on Thursday.

3-3. On January 2 of the current year a business enterprise pays $960 to the city for license fees for the coming calendar year. The same enterprise is also required to pay an annual property tax at the end of the year. The estimated amount of the current year's property tax allocable to January is $110. (a) Journalize the two adjusting entries required to bring the accounts affected by the taxes up-to-date as of January 31. (b) What is the amount of tax expense for the month of January?

3-4. After all revenues and expenses have been closed at the end of the fiscal year, Expense and Revenue Summary has a debit of $180,000 and a credit of $210,000. As of the same date R. J. Porter, Capital has a credit balance of $72,000 and R. J. Porter, Drawing has a debit balance of $18,000. (a) Journalize the entries required to complete the closing of the accounts. (b) State the amount of Porter's capital at the end of the period.

3-5. Selected accounts from a ledger are presented below. (a) Journalize the adjusting entries that have been posted to the accounts. (b) Journalize the closing entries that have been posted to the accounts. (c) List any open accounts that should have been closed.

SUPPLIES		SALARY EXPENSE	
320	70	2,960	6,200
10		2,840	
30		400	

PREPAID INSURANCE		SUPPLIES EXPENSE	
720	110	70	
160			

ACCUMULATED DEPRECIATION		INSURANCE EXPENSE	
	1,200	110	110
	450		

SALARIES PAYABLE		DEPRECIATION EXPENSE	
	400	450	450

EXPENSE AND REVENUE SUMMARY	
6,760	

3-6. The capital, drawing, and expense and revenue summary accounts of Barlow & Co. for the current year ended December 31 are presented in T form at the top of the next page. Prepare a capital statement for the year.

John Barlow, Capital				John Barlow, Drawing		
Dec. 31	9,000	Jan. 1	35,000	June 30	3,000	Dec. 31	9,000
		Dec. 31	8,000	Sept. 30	3,000		
				Dec. 30	3,000		

Expense and Revenue Summary			
Dec. 31	82,000	Dec. 31	90,000
31	8,000		

3-7. A number of errors in journalizing and posting transactions are described below. Present the journal entries to correct the errors.

(a) A $40 cash payment for supplies was recorded as a debit to Utilities Expense and a credit to Cash.

(b) Cash of $240 received from a customer on account was recorded as a $420 debit to Cash and credit to Accounts Receivable.

(c) Equipment of $1,000 purchased for cash was recorded as a debit to Buildings and a credit to Accounts Payable.

(d) Rent of $200 for the current month was recorded as a debit to Prepaid Insurance and a credit to Cash.

(e) Payment of $350 cash for personal use to R. M. Scott, owner of the enterprise, was recorded as a debit to Salary Expense and a credit to Cash.

PROBLEMS

The following additional problems for this chapter are located in Appendix C: 3-1B, 3-2B, 3-3B.

3-1A. The trial balance of Colfax Laundromat at December 31, the end of the current fiscal year, and data needed for year-end adjustments are presented below.

Colfax Laundromat
Trial Balance
December 31, 19—

Cash......................	1,160	
Laundry Supplies............	1,930	
Prepaid Insurance...........	516	
Laundry Equipment..........	20,600	
Accumulated Depreciation......		5,400
Accounts Payable............		325
Mary Turner, Capital........		11,126
Mary Turner, Drawing........	4,800	
Laundry Revenue............		21,720
Wages Expense..............	6,920	
Rent Expense...............	1,200	
Utilities Expense.............	950	
Miscellaneous Expense........	495	
	38,571	38,571

Adjustment data:

(a) Laundry supplies on hand at December 31. $ 180

(b) Insurance expired during the year 270

(c) Depreciation for the year 1,690
(d) Wages accrued at December 31 68

Instructions:
(1) Record the trial balance on an eight-column work sheet.
(2) Complete the work sheet.
(3) Prepare an income statement, a capital statement (no additional investments were made during the year), and a balance sheet in report form.
(4) Record the adjusting entries in a two-column journal.
(5) Record the closing entries in a two-column journal.
(6) Compute the following:
    (a) Percent of net income to sales.
    (b) Percent of net income to the capital balance at the beginning of the year.

3-2A. As of September 30, the end of the current fiscal year, the accountant for Williams Company prepared a trial balance, journalized and posted the adjusting entries, prepared an adjusted trial balance, prepared the statements, and completed the other procedures required at the end of the accounting cycle. The two trial balances as of September 30, one before adjustments and the other after adjustments, are presented below.

Williams Company
Trial Balance
September 30, 19—

	Unadjusted		Adjusted	
Cash	1,630		1,630	
Supplies	2,250		500	
Prepaid Rent....................	3,270		1,440	
Prepaid Insurance...............	395		235	
Automobile.....................	4,800		4,800	
Accumulated Depr. — Automobile..		750		1,750
Equipment......................	11,500		11,500	
Accumulated Depr. — Equipment...		3,600		4,820
Accounts Payable................		430		495
Salaries Payable.................		—		115
Taxes Payable...................		—		40
Joseph Williams, Capital..........		10,065		10,065
Joseph Williams, Drawing.........	9,000		9,000	
Service Fees Earned..............		32,700		32,700
Salaries Expense.................	13,410		13,525	
Rent Expense....................	—		1,830	
Supplies Expense.................	—		1,750	
Depreciation Expense — Equipment.	—		1,220	
Depreciation Expense — Automobile.	—		1,000	
Utilities Expense.................	520		585	
Taxes Expense...................	390		430	
Insurance Expense...............	—		160	
Miscellaneous Expense............	380		380	
	47,545	47,545	49,985	49,985

Instructions:
(1) Present the eight journal entries that were required to adjust the accounts at September 30. None of the accounts was

affected by more than one adjusting entry.
(2) Present the journal entries that were required to close the books at September 30.
(3) Prepare a capital statement for the fiscal year ended September 30. There were no additional investments during the year.

If the working papers correlating with this textbook are not used, omit Problem 3-3A.

3-3A. The ledger of Scott Machine Repairs as of October 31, the end of the first month of its current fiscal year, is presented in the working papers. The books had been closed on September 30.

Instructions:
(1) Prepare a trial balance of the ledger, listing only the accounts with balances, on an eight-column work sheet.
(2) Complete the eight-column work sheet. Data for the adjustments are as follows:

Supplies on hand at October 31.......	$324.00
Insurance expired during the month...	29.85
Truck depreciation for the month......	120.00
Equipment depreciation for the month.	55.00
Wages accrued at October 31.........	124.00

(3) Prepare an income statement, a capital statement, and a balance sheet.
(4) Record the adjusting entries in a two-column journal and post.
(5) Record the closing entries in a two-column journal and post.
(6) Rule the closed accounts and balance and rule the remaining accounts that contain more than one entry.
(7) Prepare a post-closing trial balance.

3-4A. Midway Bowling Lanes prepares interim statements at the end of each month and closes its books annually as of December 31. The trial balance at

Midway Bowling Lanes
Trial Balance
April 30, 19—

Cash...............................	1,470	
Prepaid Insurance....................	845	
Supplies............................	1,160	
Equipment..........................	82,600	
Accumulated Depreciation — Equipment.		13,200
Building............................	45,700	
Accumulated Depreciation — Building...		2,800
Land...............................	10,000	
Accounts Payable....................		1,220
Mortgage Note Payable (Due 1979).....		40,000
Howard Foley, Capital................		75,846
Howard Foley, Drawing...............	2,400	
Bowling Fees Earned..................		17,947
Salaries and Wages Expense...........	3,800	
Advertising Expense..................	1,065	
Utilities Expense.....................	860	
Repairs Expense.....................	654	
Miscellaneous Expense................	459	
	151,013	151,013

April 30 of the current year, the adjustment data needed at April 30, and the income statement for the three months ended March 31 of the current year are presented on page 85 and below.

Adjustment data at April 30 are:

(a) Insurance expired for the period January 1–April 30........ $ 128
(b) Inventory of supplies................................... 850
(c) Depreciation of equipment for the period January 1–April 30. 2,400
(d) Depreciation of building for the period January 1–April 30.. 600
(e) Accrued salaries and wages............................. 115

Midway Bowling Lanes
Income Statement
For Three Months Ended March 31, 19—

Bowling fees earned..................		$14,126
Operating expenses:		
Salaries and wages expense..........	$2,970	
Depreciation expense — equipment...	1,800	
Advertising expense................	795	
Utilities expense...................	650	
Repairs expense....................	485	
Depreciation expense — building.....	450	
Supplies expense...................	240	
Insurance expense..................	96	
Miscellaneous expense..............	357	
Total operating expenses..........		7,843
Net income from operations..........		$ 6,283

Instructions:
(1) Record the trial balance on an eight-column work sheet.
(2) Complete the work sheet.
(3) Prepare an interim income statement for the four months ended April 30.
(4) Prepare a capital statement for the four months ended April 30.
(5) Prepare a balance sheet as of April 30.
(6) Prepare an income statement for the month of April.
(7) Compute the percent of net income to revenue for:

    (a) The three-month period ended March 31.
    (b) The four-month period ended April 30.
    (c) The month of April.

3-5A. The selected transactions and errors described below relate to the accounts of Emerald Hills Co. during the current fiscal year:

May 20. Ralph B. Kline established the business with the investment of $15,000 in cash and $900 in equipment, on which there was a balance owed of $300. The account payable is to be recorded on the books of the enterprise.

June 10. Discovered that $25 of supplies returned to the supplier for credit had been journalized and posted as a debit to Accounts Receivable and a credit to Equipment. Payment had not been made for the supplies.

July 25. Discovered that cash of $350, received from a customer on account, had been journalized and posted as a debit to Cash and a credit to Commissions Earned.

Aug. 10. Received $510 as payment on a note receivable ($500) and interest income ($10).

Sept. 20. Acquired land and a building to be used as an office at a contract price of $22,000, of which $1,000 was allocated to the land. The property was encumbered by a mortgage of $10,000. Paid the seller $12,000 in cash and agreed to assume the responsibility for paying the mortgage note.

Oct. 10. Discovered that a withdrawal of $700 by the owner had been debited to Salary Expense.

Nov. 15. Discovered that a cash payment of $63 for prepaid insurance had been journalized and posted as a debit to Supplies of $36 and a credit to Cash of $36.

Dec. 19. Paid the installment due on the mortgage note, $500, and interest expense, $150.

Instructions:

Journalize the transactions and the corrections in a two-column journal. When there are more than two items in an entry, present the entry in compound form.

4

Processing sales and cash receipts media

Special Journals

As was explained in Chapters 2 and 3, it is customary to initially journalize all transactions, adjustments, corrections, and closing entries before posting the data to accounts in the ledger. The discerning student quickly realizes that, in actual practice, the use of a two-column journal for recording each individual transaction of a repetitive nature would be inordinately time-consuming. Furthermore, it is readily apparent that the multiplicity of postings necessitated by such a procedure would be an unnecessary duplication and hence uneconomic in terms of both time and expense.

There are many ways in which transactions may be recorded and summarized more efficiently than by the sole use of a two-column journal. One of the simplest is to add more money columns to the journal, restricting each additional column to the recording of transactions affecting a specific account. For example, the addition of a special column for recording debits to cash and another special column for recording credits to cash would save the time of writing "Cash" in the journal for each entry affecting that account. In addition, the Cash Dr. and Cash Cr. columns could be totaled periodically and only the sums posted to the cash account, which would yield additional economies. Similarly, special columns could be added for recording credits to sales, debits and credits to accounts receivable and accounts payable, and for other entries of a repetitive nature. Although the maximum number of columns that may be effectively used in a single journal is not subject to exact determination, there is an optimum beyond which the journal would become unwieldy. Also, the possibilities of errors in recording become greater as the number of columns and width of the page increases.

An all-purpose multicolumn journal is frequently satisfactory for a small business enterprise that requires the services of only one bookkeeper. If the volume of transactions is sufficient to require two or more bookkeepers, the use of a single journal is usually not practicable. The next logical development in expanding the recording, classifying, and summarizing phases is to replace an all-purpose journal with a number of special journals, each designed to record a single type of transaction. Of course, special journals would be needed only for the types of transactions that occur frequently. For example, most enterprises have many transactions in which cash is received and many in which cash is paid out; hence, it is common practice to employ a special journal for recording cash receipts and another special journal for recording cash payments. A business that extends credit to its customers might advantageously use a special journal to record sales of services or merchandise on account. Conversely, a business that does not extend credit would have no need for such a journal.

In addition to variations among enterprises in the number and type of special journals employed, there are also many possible variations in the design of any particular journal. For example, the sources of revenue of a bank are quite different from those of an establishment that buys and sells merchandise. The accounting systems of both businesses would need to provide for the expeditious recording of all cash receipts, but their cash receipts journals would be dissimilar in many respects.

The recording and posting of transactions may be done manually or by the use of mechanical, electrical, or electronic devices. Manually operated systems are easier to understand and more adaptable to learning through practice; therefore, special journals designed for manual operation will be described and illustrated in this and the following chapter. Other methods of maintaining the financial records will be explored in later chapters.

Merchandising

The special journals to be illustrated are those designed for use by a business engaged primarily in the buying and selling of merchandise.

Although the accounting procedures applicable to a merchandising business differ in some respects from those employed by a business that sells services, there are also many similarities. Therefore much of the discussion will apply to both types of business activity. In order to fully understand the accounting for an enterprise, it is also necessary to be familiar with the nature of its operations. Accordingly some of the discussion will be devoted to business customs and practices of general applicability to merchandising.

Merchandising activities may ordinarily be classified as *wholesale* or *retail*. Manufacturers, producers, and importers usually sell their goods to wholesalers, to brokers, or directly to retailers. Wholesale merchants sell to retailers and sometimes to large consumers, such as schools and hospitals. Retail merchants sell to consumers.

The number, purpose, and design of the special journals used in merchandising will of necessity vary, depending upon the needs of the particular enterprise. In the typical firm of moderate size the transactions that occur most frequently and the special journals in which they are recorded are as follows:

TRANSACTION:	RECORDED IN:
Sale of merchandise *on account*	Sales journal
Receipt of cash from *any* source	Cash receipts journal
Purchase of merchandise or other item *on account*	Purchases journal
Payment of cash for *any* purpose	Cash payments journal

Although most of the transactions of a typical merchandising business fit one of the four categories listed above, there are always some that do not. Provision must also be made for the recording of correcting, adjusting, and closing entries. All such miscellaneous entries that cannot be accommodated readily in a special journal may be recorded in a two-column journal like the one illustrated in Chapter 2. To differentiate it from the special journals it is commonly referred to as the *general journal*.

Sales

Sales of merchandise by a merchandising business are typically identified merely as *Sales*. The number of individual sales transactions completed is typically quite large in relationship to other transactions. Some businesses sell merchandise for cash only, others sell only on a credit basis, and still others have many transactions of both types.

Sales of merchandise for cash result in a debit to Cash and a credit to Sales. The customary practice is to record *cash sales* in the cash receipts journal. Sales of merchandise *on account* result in a debit to Accounts Receivable and a credit to Sales and should be recorded in the sales journal. A sale of supplies, plant assets, or other items acquired for use in the business (i.e. not as merchandise for resale) must be recorded by a debit to the Cash or appropriate receivable account and a credit to the supplies account or other account for the asset that is being sold. Such transactions should be recorded in the cash receipts journal or the general journal, depending upon the terms of sale.

Trade discounts

Manufacturers and wholesalers of certain types of commodities frequently grant substantial reductions from the *list price* quoted in their catalogs. Such reductions in price are called *trade discounts*. Trade discounts are a convenient method of making revisions in prices without the necessity of reprinting catalogs. As prices fluctuate, new schedules of discounts may be issued. Trade discounts may also be used to make price differentials among different classes of customers. For example, a manufacturer may use two different schedules of discounts, one of which applies to wholesalers and the other to retailers.

There is no need to record list prices and their related trade discounts in the books of account. For example, the seller of an article listed at $100 with a trade discount of $40 would record the transaction as a sale of $60. Similarly, the buyer would record the transaction as a purchase of $60. For accounting purposes it is only the agreed price, which in the example is $60, that is significant. Trade discounts have been described here in order to more readily distinguish between them and another type of discount discussed in later paragraphs.

Procedures for sales on account

Every sale is made in response to an order received from a customer. An order given a retail store is usually oral; an order given a manufacturing, a wholesale, or a mail-order business is ordinarily written. There are many methods of handling orders and of recording sales, the routines varying with the type and the size of the business.

In a retail business a *sales ticket* is usually prepared for a sale on account. Sales tickets are usually prepared in duplicate or triplicate. One copy is given to the customer, one copy is sent to the accounting department for use as the basis of an entry in the sales journal, and one copy may be used as the salesman's personal record of his sales or for such other purposes as the organization of the business requires.

In a manufacturing, a wholesale, or a mail-order business, a written order is received from a customer or from the salesman who obtained the order from the customer. After the order has been approved by the credit department, it is sent to the billing department, where the invoice is prepared. At least two copies of a *sales invoice* are made by the billing department. The original is sent to the customer, and the carbon copy is sent to the accounting department for use as the basis of an entry in the sales journal. Sometimes additional copies of the invoice are made for the use of different departments of the business. For example, the credit department may desire a copy for use in following up the payment of the invoice, or the shipping department may need a copy as authorization to pack and ship the goods.

One of the sales invoices used by Preston Electrical Supplies is illustrated below.

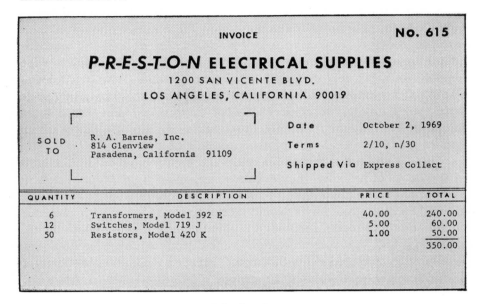

Sales invoice

Controlling accounts and subsidiary ledgers

When illustrating credit transactions with customers in earlier chapters, the debits and credits to the customer were recorded in the single account "Accounts Receivable." Consideration of procedures associated with maintaining an individual account receivable for each credit customer was purposely postponed until this point.

It is possible to delete from the ledger the single account for accounts receivable and substitute a separate account for each individual credit customer. However, when there is a substantial number of credit customers, such an arrangement is not satisfactory. The inclusion of a large number of accounts with customers would delay the preparation of the trial balance, make the ledger cumbersome, complicate posting, and make errors more difficult to find. When a business has a large number of accounts that have a common characteristic, it is customary to maintain them separately in a special ledger called a *subsidiary ledger*. When one or more subsidiary ledgers is used, the principal ledger that contains all of the balance sheet and income statement accounts is then referred to as the *general ledger*. In order to detect errors and facilitate the preparation of a trial balance, each subsidiary ledger is represented in the general ledger by a single summarizing account which is called a *controlling account*. Each controlling account may be said to *control* its related subsidiary ledger.

The controlling account for customers to whom sales are made on account is Accounts Receivable, which is located in the general ledger. The individual accounts with such customers comprise a subsidiary ledger called the *accounts receivable ledger* or *customers ledger*.

The special journals in which numerous transactions affecting customers are to be recorded are designed in such a way as to facilitate the posting of monthly totals to the controlling account, Accounts Receivable, and the posting of the individual transactions to the accounts receivable ledger. The basic techniques of posting a sales journal are depicted in the following flow chart.

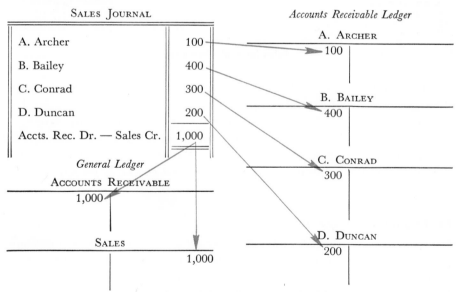

Flow of data from sales journal to ledgers

The total of the sales journal is posted both as a $1,000 debit to Accounts Receivable and a $1,000 credit to Sales in the general ledger. In addition, the charges to Archer, Bailey, Conrad, and Duncan recorded in the sales journal are posted to their respective individual accounts in the accounts receivable ledger. It is evident that the sum of the debits to the four individual accounts in the subsidiary ledger is equal to the single $1,000 debit to the controlling account in the general ledger.

Sales journal

The sales journal is used solely for recording *sales of merchandise on account*. As was indicated earlier, sales of merchandise for cash are recorded in the cash receipts journal. Sales of assets not a part of the stock in trade are recorded in the cash receipts journal or the general journal.

SALES JOURNAL   PAGE   35

	DATE		INVOICE NO.	ACCOUNT DEBITED	POST. REF.	ACCTS. REC. DR. SALES CR.	
1	1969 Oct.	2	615	R. A. Barnes, Inc.	✓	3 5 0 00	1
2		3	616	Standard Supply Co.	✓	1 6 0 4 00	2
3		5	617	David T. Mattox	✓	3 0 5 00	3
4		9	618	R. A. Barnes, Inc.	✓	1 3 9 6 00	4
5		10	619	Adler Company	✓	7 5 0 00	5
6		17	620	R. E. Hamilton, Inc.	✓	8 6 5 00	6
7		23	621	Cooper & Co.	✓	1 5 0 2 00	7
8		26	622	Tracy & Lee, Inc.	✓	2 6 0 00	8
9		27	623	Standard Supply Co.	✓	1 9 0 8 00	9
10		31				8 9 4 0 00	10
11						(1 13) (4 11)	11
12							12

Sales journal after posting

The sales journal of Preston Electrical Supplies is illustrated above. The sales invoice illustrated on page 92 is recorded on the first line. The invoice number (615) is recorded in order to facilitate future reference to the supporting document if questions concerning the transaction should arise. The customer's name (R. A. Barnes, Inc.) is recorded in the Account Debited column, and the invoice total ($350) is recorded in the amount column.

Posting the sales journal

Each entry in the sales journal is posted as a debit to the appropriate account in the accounts receivable ledger. The postings should be made at frequent intervals, preferably daily, so that the status of all customers' accounts can be readily determined at all times. The source of the entries is indicated by inserting "S" and the appropriate page number in the posting reference column of the accounts.

Customers' accounts are ordinarily arranged in alphabetical sequence to provide ready availability. New accounts may be inserted and inactive accounts may be removed without disturbing the arrangement. At the time a debit is posted to a customer's account, a check mark ($\checkmark$) is placed in the posting reference column of the sales journal to indicate that the item has been posted.

A customer's account with a single posting is illustrated by the account with Adler Company, which appears below. Instead of the T form presented in earlier chapters, it is a three-column form designed to display at all times the current balance of the account. Inasmuch as the balances in customers' accounts are normally debits, it is not necessary to identify normal balances as debits. When an occasional credit balance does occur, it should be identified by an asterisk, parentheses, or other notation. When a customer's account is in balance, a line may be drawn in the Balance column, as illustrated on page 105.

NAME   Adler Company
ADDRESS   7608 Melton Ave., Los Angeles, California 90025

DATE	ITEM	POST. REF.	DEBIT	CREDIT	BALANCE
1969 Oct. 10		S35	7 5 0 00		7 5 0 00

An account in the accounts receivable ledger

At the end of each month the sales journal is totaled, and the total is posted as a debit to Accounts Receivable and a credit to Sales. The respective account numbers are then inserted below the total to indicate that the posting has been completed. The procedure is illustrated by the sales journal appearing on page 94 and the two general ledger accounts presented on page 96.

The general ledger account forms illustrated differ from both the three-column form used in the accounts receivable ledger and the T form heretofore used in the general ledger. The traditional T form emphasizes to the greatest possible extent the difference between debit entries and credit entries. It is primarily because of this feature that it is customarily used at the beginning of the introductory course in accounting. In actual practice there has been a tendency for the four-column form to displace the simpler T form, though the latter is still widely used.

The principal advantage of the four-column form lies in its provision for clearly displaying the amount and the debit-credit nature of account balances, reducing possible confusion and errors in preparing a trial balance. The single date column and the contiguity of the debit and credit columns also facilitate both the scanning of an account and the careful examination of its details. Finally, the four-column form permits a marked simplification of the periodic ruling and balancing procedures that are employed with the T form. These features will be illustrated in a later chapter.

When posting machines are used with the four-column form, the new balance of an account is automatically computed and printed in the

95

Accounts Receivable

DATE	ITEM	POST. REF.	DEBIT	CREDIT	BALANCE DEBIT	BALANCE CREDIT
1969 Oct. 1	Balance	✓			5 2 6 0 00	
31		S35	8 9 4 0 00		14 2 0 0 00	

Sales   ACCOUNT NO. 411

DATE	ITEM	POST. REF.	DEBIT	CREDIT	BALANCE DEBIT	BALANCE CREDIT
1969 Oct. 1	Balance	✓				108 2 3 6 00
31		S35		8 9 4 0 00		117 1 7 6 00

Accounts receivable account and sales account in the general ledger after the sales journal has been posted

proper column after each posting. The account balance is thus always readily available. The same procedure may be followed when the posting is done manually. An alternative is to postpone the computation of the balance until all postings for the month have been completed. When this is done, only the final month-end balance is inserted in the appropriate balance column, usually at the time the trial balance is being prepared. The exact procedure adopted in a particular situation will depend upon such factors as the accessibility of adding machines and the desirability of having current balances readily available at all times.

Sales returns and allowances

Merchandise sold on account may be returned by the customer (*sales return*) or, because of defects or for other reasons, the customer may be allowed a reduction from the original price at which the goods were sold (*sales allowance*). In such cases the seller usually issues to the customer a *credit memorandum* indicating the amount for which the customer is to be credited and the reason therefor. A typical credit memorandum is illustrated at the top of the next page.

The effect of a sales return or allowance is a reduction in sales revenue and a reduction in accounts receivable. If the sales account is debited, however, the balance of the account at the end of the period will represent net sales, and the volume of returns and allowances will not be disclosed. Because of the loss in revenue resulting from allowances, and the various expenses (transportation, unpacking, repairing, etc.) related to returns, it is advisable that management be informed of the magnitude of such transactions. It is therefore preferable to debit an account entitled Sales Returns and Allowances. The remainder of the transaction is recorded by a credit to the accounts receivable (controlling) account in the general ledger and to the customer's account in the accounts receivable (subsidiary) ledger.

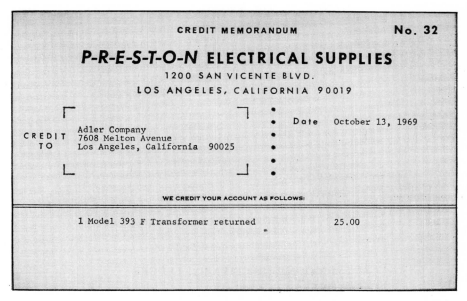

Credit memorandum

Preston Electrical Supplies issued two credit memorandums during the month. They were recorded in the general journal as shown below.

	DATE		DESCRIPTION	POST. REF.	DEBIT	CREDIT	
1	1969 Oct.	13	Sales Returns and Allowances	412	2 5 00		1
2			Accounts Receivable - Adler Company	113 ✓		2 5 00	2
3			Credit Memo No. 32.				3
33		28	Sales Returns and Allowances	412	6 5 00		33
34			Accounts Receivable - Cooper & Co.	113 ✓		6 5 00	34
35			Credit Memo No. 33.				35

JOURNAL   PAGE 18

General journal entries for sales returns

Note that in each transaction both the controlling account and the customer's account are credited. As an indication that the amount must be posted to both the general ledger and the subsidiary ledger, a diagonal line should be placed in the posting reference column *at the time the entry is recorded in the general journal.* When the credit is posted to the customer's account, a check mark is inserted at the right of the diagonal line. The number of the accounts receivable controlling account is inserted at the left in accordance with the usual routine of posting to that account in the general ledger. After the posting has been completed, the accounts affected appear as reproduced on the following page.

GENERAL LEDGER

Accounts Receivable   ACCOUNT NO. 113

DATE	ITEM	POST. REF.	DEBIT	CREDIT	BALANCE DEBIT	BALANCE CREDIT
1969 Oct. 1	Balance	✓			5 2 6 0 00	
13		J18		2 5 00	5 2 3 5 00	
28		J18		6 5 00	5 1 7 0 00	

Sales Returns and Allowances   ACCOUNT NO. 412

DATE	ITEM	POST. REF.	DEBIT	CREDIT	BALANCE DEBIT	BALANCE CREDIT
1969 Oct. 1	Balance	✓			2 3 6 5 00	
13		J18	2 5 00		2 3 9 0 00	
28		J18	6 5 00		2 4 5 5 00	

ACCOUNTS RECEIVABLE LEDGER

NAME   Adler Company

ADDRESS   7608 Melton Ave., Los Angeles, California 90025

DATE	ITEM	POST. REF.	DEBIT	CREDIT	BALANCE
1969 Oct. 10		S35	7 5 0 00		7 5 0 00
13		J18		2 5 00	7 2 5 00

NAME   Cooper & Co.

ADDRESS   57 LaBrea Ave., Los Angeles, California 90036

DATE	ITEM	POST. REF.	DEBIT	CREDIT	BALANCE
1969 Oct. 23		S35	1 5 0 2 00		1 5 0 2 00
28		J18		6 5 00	1 4 3 7 00

Accounts receivable account, sales returns and allowances account, and customers' accounts after the posting of sales returns and allowances

If the volume of credit memorandums issued is substantial, the general journal may be expanded by inserting special columns to record debits to Sales Returns and Allowances and credits to Accounts Receivable. Alternatively, an additional journal such as the one illustrated at the top of the next page may be employed. The recording and posting routines for this special journal are the same as those that apply to the sales journal.

It should be noted that in each of the foregoing illustrations the amount of the credit memorandums was credited both to Accounts Receivable and to the customer's account. If merchandise is returned or an allowance is granted after the customer has made full payment of his account, the seller may make a cash refund instead of crediting the

DATE		CR. MEMO. NO.	ACCOUNT CREDITED	POST. REF.	SALES RET. & ALLOW. DR. ACCTS. REC. CR.
1969 Nov.	2	12	Ralph Boyer	√	142 00
	6	13	Morrow & Co.	√	150 00
	29	26	J. R. Field Co.	√	13 00
	30				1,762 50
					(412) (113)

Sales returns and allowances journal

customer's account. In such cases the transaction is recorded in the cash payments journal, which is considered in Chapter 5.

Business documents as journals

Instead of recording each merchandise sale on account in a sales journal, many businesses use carbon copies of sales invoices as the posting medium. Postings to the customers' accounts are made directly from each carbon copy, and the total amount for the month is determined from an adding machine listing of all of the duplicate invoices. The total amount thus obtained provides the basis for an entry in the general journal debiting Accounts Receivable and crediting Sales.

The use of duplicate sales invoices as a journal may effect a material savings in bookkeeping expenses, particularly if the volume of sales transactions is substantial. Not only is the necessity of copying the name of the customer and other details in the sales journal avoided, but the elimination of this intermediate step also reduces the number of errors and the amount of time devoted to their detection and correction. In addition, posting to customers' accounts can be facilitated by dividing invoices into a number of alphabetical groupings and assigning each segment to a particular posting clerk.

The same system can be employed with equal effectiveness in accounting for returns and allowances, carbon copies of the credit memorandums becoming in effect the sales returns and allowances journal.

Cash receipts

All transactions that increase the amount of cash are recorded in a cash receipts journal. Cash may be received from a variety of sources, such as investments in the business by the owner, receipts from cash sales, collections from customers to whom sales have been made on account, and collections of principal and interest on notes receivable. In a typical merchandising business the most frequent sources of cash receipts are likely to be cash sales and collections from customers on account.

Before describing the form and the use of the cash receipts journal, it is desirable that consideration be given to the nature of the agreement between a business enterprise and its customers.

Credit terms

The arrangements agreed upon by the seller and the buyer as to when payments for commodities are to be made are called the *credit terms*. If payment is required immediately upon delivery, the terms are said to be "cash" or "net cash." Otherwise, the buyer is allowed a specified time, known as the *credit period*, in which to pay.

There is considerable variation in credit periods. Retailers may require that all purchases by customers in one month be paid for by a particular date in the succeeding month. They sometimes stipulate that purchases made after a particular date, such as the 25th, will not be included in the billing for that month but will be carried over to the succeeding month. They may also have special "budget" and "lay-away" terms.

Among manufacturers and wholesalers it is usual for the credit period to begin with the date of the sale as evidenced by the date of the invoice. If payment is due within a stated number of days after the date of the invoice, for example 30 days, the terms are said to be "net 30 days," which may be written as "n/30." If payment is due by the end of the month in which the sale was made, it may be expressed as "n/eom."

Cash discounts

As a means of encouraging payment before the expiration of the credit period, a discount may be offered for the early payment of cash. Thus the expression "2/10, n/30" means that, while the credit period is 30 days, the debtor may deduct 2% of the amount of the bill if payment is made in 10 days from the date of the invoice. This deduction is known as a *cash discount*.

For example, assume a sales invoice totaling $500 dated July 6, with credit terms of 2/10, n/30. If the buyer mails his check on or before July 16, he may deduct $10 from the invoice and pay $490. If he wishes to wait the full credit term, he should mail his check for $500, or otherwise deliver it, not later than August 5.

From the seller's point of view, cash discounts are known as *sales discounts;* the purchaser refers to them as *purchases discounts*. At one time cash discounts were considered to be similar to interest for the use of money and were accordingly treated as an expense by the seller and as revenue by the buyer. Today, however, when cash discounts are offered by the seller, it is with the expectation that the customer will pay within the discount period. In effect the seller is offering to make the sale for the invoice price reduced by the amount of the cash discount. Therefore, it is customary for the seller to view cash discounts as a reduction of sales revenue and for the buyer to consider them as a deduction from the quoted price of the commodity purchased.

Cash receipts journal

Inasmuch as the cash receipts journal is designed for the recording of all incoming cash, it obviously should contain a special column entitled Cash Dr. The number and titles of the other columns will be governed by the frequency of the various types of transactions by which cash is received. Receipts of cash by Preston Electrical Supplies that occur most frequently are from cash sales and collections from retailers to whom sales have been made on 2/10, n/30 terms. There are also occasional receipts of cash from various other sources. Accordingly, the cash receipts journal illustrated below has the following columns:

For credits — Sundry Accounts, Sales, Accounts Receivable
For debits — Sales Discount, Cash

CASH RECEIPTS JOURNAL — PAGE 14

Sales made for Cash

	DATE	ACCOUNT CREDITED	POST. REF.	SUNDRY ACCOUNTS CR.	SALES CR.	ACCOUNTS RECEIVABLE CR.	SALES DISCOUNT DR.	CASH DR.	
1	1969 Oct. 2	Notes Receivable	112	400 00				412 00	1
2		Interest Income	811	12 00					2
3	5	R. A. Barnes, Inc.	✓			800 00	16 00	784 00	3
4	6	Fogarty & Jacobs	✓			625 00	12 50	612 50	4
5	7	Sales	✓		1700 00			1700 00	5
6	10	David T. Mattox	✓			600 00	12 00	588 00	6
7	13	Standard Supply Co.	✓			1604 00	32 08	1571 92	7
8	14	Sales	✓		1632 00			1632 00	8
9	17	Adler Company	✓			725 00	14 50	710 50	9
10	19	R. E. Hamilton, Inc.	✓			1850 00		1850 00	10
11	21	Sales	✓		1920 30			1920 30	11
12	23	Purchases	511	36 20				36 20	12
13	24	B. C. Wallace Corporation	✓			200 00		200 00	13
14	27	R. E. Hamilton, Inc.	✓			865 00	17 30	847 70	14
15	28	Sales	✓		2086 00			2086 00	15
16	31	Sales	✓		423 40			423 40	16
17	31			448 20	7761 70	7269 00	104 38	15374 52	17
18				(✓)	(411)	(113)	(413)	(111)	18
19									19

Cash receipts journal after posting

The Sundry Accounts Cr. column is used for recording credits to any account for which there is no special column. For example, as of October 2, in the illustration, the receipt of $412 in payment of an interest-bearing note[1] was recorded by a credit to Notes Receivable of $400

---

[1]It is not necessary to maintain a subsidiary ledger for notes receivable, the note itself containing all essential information. Detailed consideration of notes is postponed to later chapters.

101

and a credit to Interest Income of $12, both amounts being entered in the Sundry Accounts Cr. column. The posting references for the notes receivable and interest income accounts were inserted later, at the time the amounts were posted.

The Sales Cr. column is used for recording sales of merchandise for cash. Each individual sale is recorded on a cash register, and the totals thus accumulated are recorded in the cash receipts journal daily, weekly, or at other regular intervals. This is illustrated by the entry of October 7 recording weekly sales and cash receipts of $1,700. Inasmuch as the total of the Sales Cr. column will be posted at the end of the month, a check mark was inserted in the posting reference column to indicate that the $1,700 item needed no further attention.

Credits to customers' accounts for payments of invoices are recorded in the Accounts Receivable Cr. column. The amount of the cash discount granted, if any, is recorded in the Sales Discount Dr. column, and the amount of cash actually received is recorded in the Cash Dr. column. The entry on October 5 illustrates the use of these columns. Cash in the amount of $784 was received from R. A. Barnes, Inc. in payment of their account of $800, the cash discount being 2% of $800 or $16. The Post. Ref. column was left blank until the credit of $800 was posted to the account, at which time a check mark was inserted.

It should be noted that when a debtor has returned merchandise or has been granted an allowance, the discount should be computed on the amount of the invoice reduced by the amount of the credit memorandum. For example, on October 17 a check for $710.50 was received from Adler Company. Reference to the account receivable, reproduced on page 105, reveals a debit of $750 (sale), a credit of $25 (sales return), and a balance of $725. Deduction of the cash discount of $14.50 (2% of $725) from the account balance yields cash of $710.50.

Posting the cash receipts journal

Each amount in the Sundry Accounts Cr. column of the cash receipts journal is posted to the appropriate account in the general ledger at any time during the month, and the posting is indicated by writing the account number in the posting reference column. At regular intervals the amounts in the Accounts Receivable Cr. column are posted to the customers' accounts in the subsidiary ledger and check marks are placed in the posting reference column to indicate that they have been posted and need no further attention. None of the individual amounts in the remaining three columns of the cash receipts journal is posted.

At the end of the month all the amount columns are footed and ruled as shown in the illustration. To check the accuracy of the footings, the equality of debits and credits should be proved by use of an adding machine or a listing similar to that shown on the next page.

DEBIT TOTALS		CREDIT TOTALS	
Sales Discount......	$ 104.38	Sundry Accounts.....	$ 448.20
Cash...............	15,374.52	Sales..............	7 761.70
		Accounts Receivable.	7,269.00
	$15,478.90		$15,478.90

Inasmuch as each amount in the Sundry Accounts Cr. column has been posted individually to general ledger accounts, the total of the column is not posted. A check mark may be inserted below this column total to indicate that no further action is necessary. The totals of the other four columns are posted to the appropriate accounts in the general ledger and their account numbers are inserted below the totals to indicate that the posting has been completed.

In terms of posting procedures, there are three distinct types of columns in the cash receipts journal. They may be described as follows:

1. Individual entries posted to general ledger accounts, column total not posted:

    Sundry Accounts Cr. column

2. Individual entries not posted, column total posted to a general ledger account:

    Sales Cr. column
    Sales Discount Dr. column
    Cash Dr. column

3. Individual entries posted to subsidiary ledger accounts, column total posted to the corresponding general ledger controlling account:

    Accounts Receivable Cr. column

The relationship between the cash receipts journal and the ledgers of Preston Electrical Supplies is presented in the flow diagram below.

CASH RECEIPTS JOURNAL

ACCOUNT CREDITED	P. R.	SUNDRY ACCOUNTS CR.	SALES CR.	ACCOUNTS RECEIVABLE CR.	SALES DISCOUNT DR.	CASH DR.
Notes Receivable	112	400.00				412.00
Interest Income	811	12.00				
R. A. Barnes, Inc.	√			800.00	16.00	784.00
Fogarty & Jacobs	√			625.00	12.50	612.50
Sales	√		1,700.00			1,700.00
David T. Mattox	√			600.00	12.00	588.00
Sales	√		423.40			423.40
		448.20	7,761.70	7,269.00	104.38	15,374.52

Accounts Receivable Ledger

Each individual entry is posted to the credit of an account in the accounts receivable ledger, making a total of $7,269.00.	

General Ledger

Notes Receivable
400.00

Interest Income
12.00

Accounts Receivable
7,269.00

Sales
7,761.70 15,374.52

Sales Discount
104.38

Cash

Relationship between the cash receipts journal and the ledgers

Accounts receivable control and subsidiary ledger

During October the following postings were made to Accounts Receivable in the general ledger of Preston Electrical Supplies:

DEBITS

Oct. 31 (Total sales on account, from sales journal)............ $8,940.00

CREDITS

Oct. 13 (A sales return, from general journal)................. 25.00
Oct. 28 (A sales return, from general journal)................. 65.00
Oct. 31 (Total credits resulting from cash received on account, from cash receipts journal)......................... 7,269.00

The controlling account with its opening balance, the foregoing postings, and the balances is shown below.

Accounts Receivable   ACCOUNT NO. 113

DATE	ITEM	POST. REF.	DEBIT	CREDIT	BALANCE DEBIT	BALANCE CREDIT
1969 Oct. 1	Balance	✓			5 2 6 0 00	
13		J18		2 5 00	5 2 3 5 00	
28		J18		6 5 00	5 1 7 0 00	
31		S35	8 9 4 0 00		14 1 1 0 00	
31		CR14		7 2 6 9 00	6 8 4 1 00	

Accounts receivable account in the general ledger at the end of the month

It is the usual practice to post to customers' accounts in the subsidiary ledger at frequent intervals, preferably daily. If the accounts are kept up-to-date they can be relied upon in deciding whether to grant additional credit, and inquiries from customers about the status of their accounts can be answered promptly. There is also an obvious advantage in spreading the posting over the month rather than allowing it to accumulate until the end of the month.

The accounts receivable ledger of Preston Electrical Supplies after the posting of all entries for the month is shown on the following pages.

The sum of the balances of the accounts in the customers ledger should be compared periodically with the balance of the accounts receivable account in the general ledger. This is customarily done at the end of each month at the same time that the trial balance is prepared. If the subsidiary ledger and the controlling account are not in agreement, the error must be found and corrected. As in the case of the trial balance, however, arithmetic equality is not an absolute guarantee of correctness. For example, the erroneous posting of a credit for cash received from a particular customer as a credit to another customer's account would not be revealed by this comparison.

NAME   Adler Company

ADDRESS   7608 Melton Ave., Los Angeles, California   90025

DATE	ITEM	POST. REF.	DEBIT	CREDIT	BALANCE
1969 Oct. 10		S35	7 5 0 00		7 5 0 00
13		J18		2 5 00	7 2 5 00
17		CR14		7 2 5 00	——

NAME   R. A. Barnes, Inc.

ADDRESS   814 Glenview, Pasadena, California   91109

DATE	ITEM	POST. REF.	DEBIT	CREDIT	BALANCE
1969 Sept. 27		S34	8 0 0 00		8 0 0 00
Oct. 2		S35	3 5 0 00		1 1 5 0 00
5		CR14		8 0 0 00	3 5 0 00
9		S35	1 3 9 6 00		1 7 4 6 00

NAME   Cooper & Co.

ADDRESS   57 LaBrea Ave., Los Angeles, California   90036

DATE	ITEM	POST. REF.	DEBIT	CREDIT	BALANCE
1969 Oct. 23		S35	1 5 0 2 00		1 5 0 2 00
28		J18		6 5 00	1 4 3 7 00

NAME   Fogarty & Jacobs

ADDRESS   1001 State Street, Burbank, California   91503

DATE	ITEM	POST. REF.	DEBIT	CREDIT	BALANCE
1969 Sept. 28		S34	6 2 5 00		6 2 5 00
Oct. 6		CR14		6 2 5 00	——

NAME   R. E. Hamilton, Inc.

ADDRESS   91 S. Spring, Los Angeles, California   90012

DATE	ITEM	POST. REF.	DEBIT	CREDIT	BALANCE
1969 Sept. 19		S34	1 8 5 0 00		1 8 5 0 00
Oct. 17		S35	8 6 5 00		2 7 1 5 00
19		CR14		1 8 5 0 00	8 6 5 00
27		CR14		8 6 5 00	——

NAME   David T. Mattox

ADDRESS   8050 Broadway, Burbank, Califorana   91503

DATE	ITEM	POST. REF.	DEBIT	CREDIT	BALANCE
1969 Sept. 29		S34	6 0 0 00		6 0 0 00
Oct. 5		S35	3 0 5 00		9 0 5 00
10		CR14		6 0 0 00	3 0 5 00

Accounts receivable ledger at the end of the month

NAME   Standard Supply Co.

ADDRESS   40 West Fourth Street, Los Angeles, California 90019

DATE	ITEM	POST. REF.	DEBIT	CREDIT	BALANCE
1969 Oct. 3		S35	1 6 0 4 00		1 6 0 4 00
13		CR14		1 6 0 4 00	
27		S35	1 9 0 8 00		1 9 0 8 00

NAME   Tracy & Lee, Inc.

ADDRESS   1500 Santa Ana Blvd., Los Angeles, California 90002

DATE	ITEM	POST. REF.	DEBIT	CREDIT	BALANCE
1969 Oct. 26		S35	2 6 0 00		2 6 0 00

NAME   B. C. Wallace Corporation

ADDRESS   412 Maple Ave., Los Angeles, California 90013

DATE	ITEM	POST. REF.	DEBIT	CREDIT	BALANCE
1969 Aug. 24		S33	1 3 8 5 00		1 3 8 5 00
Oct. 24		CR14		2 0 0 00	1 1 8 5 00

Accounts receivable ledger at the end of the month — concluded

The balances in the subsidiary ledger accounts may be summarized by use of an adding machine, or a schedule of accounts receivable similar to the one illustrated below may be prepared. Note that the total of the schedule, $6,841, is in agreement with the balance of the accounts receivable account appearing on page 104.

Preston Electrical Supplies
Schedule of Accounts Receivable
October 31, 1969

R. A. Barnes, Inc.	$1,746
Cooper & Co.	1,437
David T. Mattox	305
Standard Supply Co.	1,908
Tracy & Lee, Inc.	260
B. C. Wallace Corporation	1,185
Total accounts receivable	$6,841

Schedule of accounts receivable

Delivery of merchandise sold

The terms of a sales agreement include an implied or expressed provision concerning the cost of delivering the goods to the buyer. If the seller is to assume the cost of transportation, the terms are said to be *FOB* (free on board) *destination;* if the buyer is to absorb the cost, the terms are stated as *FOB shipping point.*

If the agreement provides that the seller is to bear the delivery costs, the payments to airlines, trucking companies, and other carriers are debited to Delivery Expense, Transportation Out, or a similarly titled account. The total of such costs incurred during a period is reported on the seller's income statement as a selling expense.

On the other hand, if the agreement provides that the buyer is to bear the delivery costs and the buyer pays the carrier upon delivery, the seller's responsibility ceases when the carrier takes custody of the merchandise.

Prepayment of delivery charges

It is not unusual for the seller to prepay transportation charges on merchandise sold even though the terms are FOB shipping point. The seller may do so as an accommodation to the customer, or it may be the only procedure practicable, as in the case of postage charges on goods shipped by parcel post. In all such situations the postage or other delivery costs to be borne by the purchaser should be listed on the sales invoice as a separate item and the invoice total (sale plus transportation) debited to the customer's account.

A sales journal designed to accommodate such transactions is illustrated below. The amount recorded in the Accounts Receivable Dr. column and posted to the customer's account is the sum of the sale plus the prepaid delivery charges.

SALES JOURNAL
PAGE 43

DATE	IN-VOICE NO.	ACCOUNT DEBITED	POST. REF.	ACCOUNTS RECEIV-ABLE DR.	DELIVERY EXPENSE CR.	SALES CR.
1969 Nov. 1	2477	Reed Corporation	√	820 00	20 00	800 00
30				26,925 00	525 00	26,400 00
				(113)	(615)	(411)

Sales journal designed for charging
prepaid transportation costs to customers

The amount of the delivery charge is recorded in the sales journal as a *credit* to Delivery Expense rather than as a credit to Sales. The actual payment of cash to the carrier by the seller is a separate transaction; it will be recorded in the cash payments journal as a *debit* to Delivery Expense and a credit to the cash account. If the sale terms are uniformly FOB shipping point, all of the prepaid delivery costs will be passed on to customers. Consequently, the amount paid to carriers will be exactly the same as the total delivery costs charged to customers, and the amount of the debits and the credits to Delivery Expense will be equal. However, if some of the sales are on an FOB destination basis, the delivery expense account will have a debit balance after all related transactions have been recorded and posted. To illustrate, assume that the policy of the business whose partial sales journal appears on page 107 is to absorb the delivery costs on sales to customers located within a relatively short radius. In addition, assume that during November the debits to Delivery Expense for charges on outgoing shipments totaled $657. The excess of the $657 of delivery costs (debit to Delivery Expense) over the $525 of such costs passed on to customers (credit to Delivery Expense) yields a debit balance of $132 of delivery expense for the month. It is an operating expense of the business.

When delivery costs are prepaid as an accommodation on sales subject to a cash discount, the discount should be computed on the sale price only; it does not apply to the transportation charges advanced by the seller. For example, assuming that the sale to Reed Corporation recorded in the sales journal on page 107 is subject to a 2% discount, the amount of the discount would be 2% of $800 (sale) or $16. The amount to be paid within the discount period would be $800 (sale) — $16 (discount) + $20 (prepaid transportation), or $804.

In order to facilitate computation of the discount, a memorandum notation of the amount of transportation added to the invoice should be inserted in the item section of the customer's account when posting the sales journal.

Sales taxes

Many business enterprises are required by state or city statute to collect sales taxes from their customers and remit to the taxing authority. Such taxes may be levied only on the sale of commodities or they may also apply to the sale of specified services, such as dry cleaning, shoe repairs, and property rentals. Such taxes are usually imposed only upon retail sales or sales to consumers, with sales of certain commodities exempted from tax. For example, in some jurisdictions there is no tax on the sale of food for consumption off the premises of the seller. Sales of gasoline, cigarettes, and other commodities subject to a special tax by the state may also be exempted from the general sales tax.

Sales taxes are levied as a percent of all sales except those specifically exempted. The tax may be assessed against the seller, who may in turn charge it to his customers, or the statutes may specifically impose the tax upon the purchaser but require the seller to collect it. In either case, procedures should be adopted to assure collection of the tax and the timely transmittal of tax returns accompanied by remittances.

Collection of sales taxes

Liability for the tax is ordinarily incurred at the time the sale is made, regardless of the terms of payment. The seller therefore collects the tax at the time of a cash sale and charges the customer's account for the tax when credit is granted. The sales account should be credited only for the amount of the sale, the tax being credited to Sales Tax Payable. For example, a sale of $100 on account subject to a tax of 3% would be recorded as a debit of $103 to Accounts Receivable and credits of $100 to Sales and $3 to Sales Tax Payable.

In preparing sales invoices the sales tax should be listed as a separate item. If a sales journal is employed for sales on account, a special column should be provided for recording the credit to Sales Tax Payable. Provision for differentiating between taxable sales and exempt sales may also be made if necessary. Arrangements for recording decreases in the tax liability account attributable to sales returns and allowances can be made in a similar manner.

The sales tax collected on a cash sale is ordinarily recorded separately in the cash register. When this is not possible, the money received for the tax may be physically separated until the close of the day and then counted. Special columns for recording the amount of exempt sales and the sales tax liability can be added to the cash receipts journal.

Variations from the system outlined above can be made where necessary to provide all data needed in preparing periodic tax returns. As payments of the tax are made, usually on a monthly, quarterly, or semiannual basis, they are recorded as debits to Sales Tax Payable and credits to Cash.

109

QUESTIONS

1. In recording 1,000 sales on account during a single month, how many times will it be necessary to write "Sales" (a) if each sale is recorded, together with all other transactions, in a two-column general journal; (b) if each sale is recorded in a sales journal?

2. How many postings to Sales would be required in Question 1 if the journal described in (a) had been used; if the journal described in (b) had been used?

3. If an item of merchandise with a list price of $150 is subject to a trade discount of 40%, at what amount should the sale of the item be recorded?

4. (a) What term is applied to an account in the general ledger that summarizes the details of all accounts in a related special ledger?
   (b) What term is applied to the special ledger?

5. The following errors were made in recording transactions in a single-column sales journal or in posting therefrom. How will each error be discovered other than by chance?

   (a) A sale of $15 to L. J. Marsh was recorded in the sales journal as $51 and posted to Marsh's account as $51.

(b) A sale of $60 to Barron Co. was recorded correctly in the sales journal but was posted to Barron Co.'s account as $6.

(c) A sale of $200 to A. J. Adams was recorded in the sales journal and posted as a debit to the account of B. J. Adams.

(d) The $46,900 total of the sales journal was posted correctly but the column had been incorrectly footed. The correct amount was $47,900.

6. Why is it advisable to maintain an account for sales returns and allowances when the same net result may be obtained by debiting returns and allowances directly to the sales account?

7. Describe the two related transactions recorded in the T accounts below.

Cash	Accounts Receivable	Sales	Sales Discount
(2) 2,940	(1) 3,000 (2) 3,000	(1) 3,000 (2)	60

8. A customer who has paid his account in full returns merchandise for credit. A credit memorandum for $40 is issued, recorded, and posted. (a) Is the $40 balance of the customer's account a debit or a credit balance? (b) Is the balance of the account an asset, liability, revenue, or expense?

9. Assuming the use of the sales journal and the cash receipts journal described in this chapter and a two-column general journal, indicate the journal in which each of the following should be recorded:

(a) Investment of additional cash in the business by the owner.
(b) Sale of supplies on account, at cost, to a competitor.
(c) Receipt of cash refund for an overcharge on an insurance premium.
(d) Issuance of a credit memorandum to a customer.
(e) Adjustment of Salaries Payable at the end of the year.
(f) Sale of merchandise on account.
(g) Sale of merchandise for cash.
(h) Closing of the owner's drawing account at the end of the year.
(i) Receipt of cash in payment of principal and interest on a note.

10. In posting the general journal entry appearing below the bookkeeper posted correctly to Shaw's account but failed to post to the controlling account.

Nov.	12	Sales Returns and Allowances...............	412	76	
		Accounts Receivable — M. L. Shaw........	✓		76

(a) How will the error be discovered? (b) Describe the procedure that is designed to prevent oversights of this type.

11. What is the meaning of (a) 2/10, n/30; (b) n/eom; (c) n/30?

12. What is the term applied to cash discounts by (a) the seller, (b) the buyer?

13. What is the amount of the cash discount allowable on a sale of $1,100, terms 1/10, n/30, on which a credit memo for $100 was issued prior to payment?

14. (a) What is the normal balance of Sales Discount? (b) Is it an asset, expense, or contra revenue account?

15. After receiving payment from a customer, within the discount period, of the amount due on a sale of $500, terms 2/10, n/30, the seller consents to the return of the entire shipment. (a) What is the amount of the refund owed to the customer? (b) What entries should be made to record the return and the refund.

16. Who bears the transportation costs when the terms of sale are (a) FOB destination, (b) FOB shipping point?

17. Merchandise is sold on account to a customer for $1,000, terms FOB shipping point, 2/10, n/30. The seller prepays the transportation costs of $30. (a) What entries should be made to record the sale? (b) What is the amount of the cash discount? (c) What is the correct amount of the remittance if payment is made within the discount period?

18. A business that sells to in-state customers on FOB destination terms and to out-of-state customers on FOB shipping point terms prepays the delivery charges on all sales. (a) What is the normal balance of the delivery expense account before closing at the end of the period? (b) Is the balance of the account related to the in-state customers or to the out-of-state customers? (c) Is the balance of the account an asset, liability, revenue, or expense?

19. Is the buyer entitled to a discount on prepaid freight, assuming that the terms are FOB shipping point and that he pays the invoice within the discount period? Explain.

20. A $200 sale of merchandise on account is subject to a 3% sales tax. (a) When should the sales tax be recorded, at the time of sale or when payment is received? (b) What entries should be made at the time of sale?

21. It is discovered that a cash sale subject to a sales tax of 4% was recorded in the cash register as a sale of $131.56, which included the correct amount of sales tax. (a) Was the amount of the sales tax $5.26, which is 4% of $131.56? (b) If the answer to (a) is "no," how can the amount of the sales tax be determined?

EXERCISES

4-1. For each of the following sales on account determine (a) the amount to be recorded for the sale, and (b) the correct amount of the remittance.

	Invoice Date	List Price	Trade Discount	Credit Terms	Payment Date
(1)	April 6	$1,500	30%	2/10, n/30	April 16
(2)	April 10	1,000	40%	1/10, n/30	April 20
(3)	April 17	900	—	2/10, n/30	April 26
(4)	April 23	600	50%	1/10, n/30	May 23

4-2. Determine for each sale described below, all of which are subject to terms of 2/10, n/30, (a) the amount of the cash discount and (b) the correct amount of the remittance if the account is paid within the discount period. Assume that all credit memorandums were received by the buyer before payment was made.

	Amount of Sale	Transportation Terms	Prepaid Transportation	Credit Memorandum
(1)	$ 600	FOB shipping point	$—	$50
(2)	800	FOB destination	25	30
(3)	1,100	FOB shipping point	40	—
(4)	1,500	FOB shipping point	50	40

4-3. A business uses carbon copies of business documents in place of journals to record sales on account and related returns and allowances. During August, 932 invoices for $146,200 and 26 credit memorandums for $473 were issued. Present the general journal entries necessary to record the foregoing data as of August 31.

4-4. Record the following transactions in the form of general journal entries:

Oct. 8. Sold merchandise to a customer for $800, terms FOB shipping point, 2/10, n/30, charging the customer an additional $30 for delivery costs to be prepaid.

14. Issued a credit memorandum for $75 to the customer for merchandise returned.

18. Received a check for the amount due from the sale to the customer.

4-5. Present the general journal entries necessary to correct each of the errors described below. Assume that the incorrect entries had been posted and that the errors are discovered in the same fiscal period in which they occurred.

(a) A cash sale of $40 was recorded as a sale to H. S. Hunt on account.

(b) Cash refund of $25 received for an overcharge on a purchase of office equipment was recorded as a sale of merchandise for cash.

(c) A $350 sale to Robert Jackson on account, FOB shipping point, with prepaid delivery expense of $20, was recorded as a $370 debit to Jackson (and Accounts Receivable) and a $370 credit to Sales.

(d) A cash receipt of $792 ($800 less 1% discount) from Miller Corp. was recorded as a $792 debit to Cash and a $792 credit to Miller Corp. (and Accounts Receivable).

4-6. In recording sales during its first three months of operations, Harmony Appliance Co. failed to differentiate between the amount of its sales and the amount of a 2% sales tax charged on all sales. All credits to the sales account and debits to the sales returns and allowances account included the sales tax. Permission is granted by the state tax department to estimate the net amount of tax charged to customers during the quarter. Balances in the sales account and the sales returns and allowances account at the end of the three-month period are $99,293.48 and $864.38 respectively. (a) Determine as accurately as possible the net amount of sales tax charged to customers. (b) Present the general journal entry necessary to record the liability for sales tax and to correct other accounts affected by the transactions.

PROBLEMS

The following additional problems for this chapter are located in Appendix C: 4-1B, 4-2B, 4-3B, 4-4B.

4-1A. Maynard Trading Co. was established in August of the current year. Its sales of merchandise on account and related returns and allowances during the remainder of the month are described below. Terms of all sales were n/30, FOB destination.

Aug. 17. Sold merchandise on account to Reliable Corp., Invoice No. 1, $580.

18. Sold merchandise on account to Lyle & Mason, Invoice No. 2, $670.

20. Sold merchandise on account to Barker & Co., Invoice No. 3, $1,420.

22. Issued Credit Memorandum No. 1 for $50 to Lyle & Mason for merchandise returned.

22. Sold merchandise on account to A. R. Taylor Co., Invoice No. 4, $240.

25. Sold merchandise on account to L. G. Henry, Inc., Invoice No. 5, $950.

26. Issued Credit Memorandum No. 2 for $70 to Reliable Corp. for merchandise returned.

27. Sold merchandise on account to Lyle & Mason, Invoice No. 6, $1,120.

28. Issued Credit Memorandum No. 3 for $20 to A. R. Taylor Co. for damages to merchandise caused by faulty packing.

30. Sold merchandise on account to Barker & Co., Invoice No. 7, $190.

Instructions:

(1) Open the following accounts in the general ledger, using the account numbers indicated: Accounts Receivable, 113; Sales, 411; Sales Returns and Allowances, 412.

(2) Open the following accounts in the accounts receivable ledger: Barker & Co.; L. G. Henry, Inc.; Lyle & Mason; Reliable Corp.; A. R. Taylor Co.

(3) Record the transactions for August, posting to the customers' accounts in the accounts receivable ledger *immediately* after recording each entry. Use a sales journal similar to the one illustrated on page 94 and a two-column general journal.

(4) Post the general journal and the sales journal to the three accounts in the general ledger, inserting the account balances only after the last postings.

(5) (a) What is the sum of the balances of the accounts in the subsidiary ledger?
    (b) What is the balance of the controlling account?

If the working papers correlating with the textbook are not used, omit Problem 4-2A.

4-2A. Three journals, the accounts receivable ledger, and portions of the general ledger of Randall Company are presented in the working papers. Sales invoices and credit memorandums were entered in the journals by an assistant. Terms of sales on account are 2/10, n/30, FOB shipping point. Transactions in which cash and notes receivable were received during June of the current year are as follows:

June 1. Received $1,029 cash from George Ives & Co. in payment of May 22 invoice, less discount.

      2. Received $1,530 cash in payment of a $1,500 note receivable and interest of $30.

      Post transactions of June 1, 3, and 4 to customers' accounts.

      8. Received $686 cash from Paul M. Vincent in payment of May 29 invoice, less discount.

      9. Received $1,600 cash from John T. Porter Corp. in payment of May 9 invoice, no discount.

      Post transactions of June 8, 9, 10, 12, and 15 to customers' accounts.

    15. Cash sales for first half of June totaled $7,842.

    17. Received $420 cash refund for return of defective equipment purchased for cash in May.

    19. Received $1,323 cash from George Ives & Co. in payment of balance due on June 10 invoice, less discount.

    22. Received $735 cash from John T. Porter Corp. in payment of June 12 invoice, less discount.

      Post transactions of June 18, 19, 22, 23, 24, 25, and 26 to customers' accounts.

    29. Received $8 cash for sale of store supplies at cost.

    30. Received $259 cash and a $600 note receivable from R. J. Cole, Inc. in settlement of the balance due on the invoice of May 3, no discount. (Record receipt of note in the general journal.)

    30. Cash sales for second half of June totaled $8,117.

      Post transactions of June 30 to the customer's account.

Instructions:

(1) Record the cash and notes received in June and post all three journals to the customers' accounts, in date sequence, at the points indicated in the narrative of transactions.

(2) Post the appropriate individual entries from the cash receipts journal and the general journal to the general ledger.

(3) Add the columns of the sales journal and the cash receipts journal and post the appropriate totals to the general ledger. Insert the balance of each account after the last posting.

(4) Prepare a schedule of accounts receivable and compare the total with the balance of the controlling account.

4-3A. Transactions related to sales and cash receipts completed by Camden Company during January of the current year are described below. The terms of all sales on account are 2/10, n/30, FOB shipping point. All delivery charges are prepaid and charged to the customer.

Jan. 2. Received cash from Allen & Beeler for the balance due on its account, less discount.
3. Issued Invoice No. 537 to Henry Morrow Co., $1,400; delivery, $28; total, $1,428.
6. Received cash from Stone & Co. for the balance due on their account, less discount.

Post all journals to the accounts receivable ledger.

8. Issued Invoice No. 538 to R. M. Hart, $1,242; delivery, $31; total, $1,273.
11. Issued Invoice No. 539 to Henry Morrow Co., $1,850; delivery, $36; total, $1,886.
12. Received cash refund for return of office supplies, $17.
13. Received cash from Henry Morrow Co. for invoice of January 3, less discount.

Post all journals to the accounts receivable ledger.

16. Recorded cash sales for first half of the month, $5,230.
17. Received cash from R. M. Hart for the balance owed on January 1; no discount.
17. Issued Invoice No. 540 to Stone & Co., $2,193; delivery, $38; total, $2,231.
21. Received cash from Henry Morrow Co. for invoice of January 11, less discount.
24. Issued Credit Memo No. 27 to Stone & Co., $43.

Post all journals to the accounts receivable ledger.

24. Issued Invoice No. 541 to Henry Morrow Co., $1,317; delivery, $25; total $1,342.
26. Received $707 cash in payment of a $700 note receivable and interest of $7.
27. Received cash from Stone & Co. for the balance due on invoice of January 17, less discount.
29. Issued Invoice No. 542 to Allen & Beeler, $2,100; delivery, $51; total, $2,151.
31. Recorded cash sales for the second half of the month, $4,810.
31. Issued Credit Memo No. 28 to Allen & Beeler, $65.

Post all journals to the accounts receivable ledger.

Instructions:

(1) Open the following accounts in the general ledger, inserting the balances indicated, as of January 1:

111 Cash	$2,437	412 Sales Returns and Allowances. ―――
112 Notes Receivable . . .	1,900	413 Sales Discount . . . . ―――
113 Accounts Receivable	3,668	615 Delivery Expense . . . . ―――
115 Office Supplies	174	811 Interest Income . . . . ―――
411 Sales	―――	

(2) Open the following accounts in the accounts receivable ledger, inserting the balances indicated, as of January 1: Allen & Beeler, $1,193, including a delivery charge of $43; R. M. Hart, $1,651, including a delivery charge of $51; Henry Morrow Co.; Stone & Co., $824, including a delivery charge of $24. Make a notation of the amount of the delivery charges in the item section of each account.

(3) Record the transactions for the month in a sales journal similar to the one illustrated on page 107, a sales returns and allowances journal similar to the one illustrated on page 99, and a cash receipts journal similar to the one illustrated on page 101. Post to the accounts receivable ledger at the points indicated in the narrative of transactions.

(4) Add the columns of the journals and post the individual entries and totals to the general ledger. Insert account balances after the last posting.

(5) Determine that the subsidiary ledger agrees with the controlling account.

4-4A. The statutes of the state in which Talbert Markets Co. is located require that retailers collect a sales tax of 4% on all sales to consumers except on certain items, such as seeds and fertilizers, and on sales to governmental units, such as public schools, cities, and counties. They provide further that in the event the amount charged to customers is less than 4% of net taxable sales, the deficiency must be borne by the retailer. Payments for each calendar quarter are payable by the end of the month following the quarter.

The balances in certain accounts of Talbert Markets Co. as of March 31, after adjustments had been made for the additional tax liability for the period January 1–March 31, and balances of the same accounts as of June 30, before adjustments for the additional tax liability for the period April 1–June 30, are presented below. The company closes its books on December 31.

	March 31	June 30
Sales Tax Payable	3,876.82	4,705.35
Sales	102,420.10	226,815.40
Sales Returns and Allowances.	1,574.80	3,428.60
Sales Tax Expense	24.18	24.18

Supplementary records indicate that sales for the period April 1 through June 30 included nontaxable sales of $4,316.30 and that returns and allowances on nontaxable sales for the same period amounted to $207.70.

Instructions:

(1) Determine the amount of the total liability for sales tax for the period April 1–June 30, identifying all figures and presenting them in good order.

(2) Determine the sales tax expense (deficiency in amount of tax charged to customers) for the period April 1–June 30.

(3) Present the entry as of June 30 to record the sales tax expense and the additional liability for sales taxes for the period April 1–June 30.

(4) On the basis of the ledger information presented above, determine the amount of the net taxable sales for the *first* quarter of the year.

5

Processing purchases
and
cash payments media

Purchasing procedures

The procedures followed in purchasing activities vary considerably among different types of business enterprises, and in accordance with the volume of such activities. The owner of a small retail store may do all of the buying, in many cases placing orders with salesmen who periodically call at his place of business. In large enterprises all procedures related to buying commodities are usually centralized in a separate department. The purchasing department maintains catalogs and other data on quality and prices, on reliability of various suppliers, on current price trends, and other information which promotes the efficient operation of all buying activities.

To avoid misunderstanding, all orders for merchandise, equipment, supplies, or other assets should be in writing. An order may be written on a form supplied by the vendor, or the buyer may use his own forms. The original of the purchase order is sent to the supplier; it is his authorization to deliver the items listed at the prices specified. A duplicate copy of the order should be retained as evidence of what was ordered and of the other terms stipulated.

The seller usually mails an invoice to the buyer at about the time the goods are shipped. From the viewpoint of the seller, the invoice is a *sales invoice*; the buyer refers to it as a *purchase invoice*. An invoice should contain the names and the addresses of both the buyer and the seller; the date of the transaction; the terms; the method of shipment; and the quantities, descriptions, and prices of the goods. An invoice from Arnold Electronics Supply in response to a purchase order of Preston Electrical Supplies is shown below.

The invoice form illustrated is a standard form recommended by the National Association of Purchasing Agents. It is divided into three distinct sections: (1) upper left section for miscellaneous details of the terms of the transaction; (2) lower section for quantity, description, unit price, and amount; and (3) upper right section for use by the purchaser as a record that various comparisons and verifications have been made.

ARNOLD ELECTRONICS SUPPLY

7900 MARKET STREET
SAN FRANCISCO, CALIFORNIA 94131

FOR CUSTOMER'S USE ONLY

Register No.	Voucher No.
F. O. B. Checked	

Terms Approved	Price Approved
	ℋ. T.
Calculations Checked	
C. R. S.	

Customer's Order No. & Date 412 Oct. 9, 1969 Refer to Invoice No. 106-8

Requisition No.

Contract No. Invoice Date Oct. 11, 1969   Transportation

Vendor's Nos.   Freight Bill No.   Amount

SOLD TO Preston Electrical Supplies
1200 San Vicente Blvd.
Los Angeles, California 90019

Material Received
10/13 19 69 m.a.s. Rec. Cl.
Date Signature Title

Shipped to and Destination Same   Satisfactory and Approved

Date Shipped Oct. 11, 1969 From San Francisco Prepaid or Collect?   Adjustments

Car Initials and No.   F. O. B. Los Angeles Prepaid   Accounting Distribution
How Shipped and Route Western Trucking Co.

Terms 2/10, n/30   Made in U. S. A.   Audited J H C   Final Approval

QUANTITY	DESCRIPTION	UNIT PRICE	AMOUNT
20	392E Transformers	30.00	600.00
43	719J Switches	2.50	107.50
7	824L Switches	2.50	17.50
25	406P Capacitors	4.00	100.00
10	215J Reactors	15.00	150.00
10	115R Chassis	40.00	400.00
4	274T Turntables	45.00	180.00
			1,555.00

Invoice

The invoice usually arrives in advance of the goods, and it is sometimes recorded in the journal before the shipment is received. Terms, quantities, prices, and other details on the invoice should be compared with the corresponding items on the copy of the purchase order.

Upon arrival, the shipment should be inspected for possible damage, and the quantities should be determined. This verification function is ordinarily the responsibility of the receiving department. The purchase invoice may be routed to the receiving department where the quantities received are compared with those billed. A preferable alternative is to issue to the receiving department a partial carbon copy of the purchase order, with quantities and dollar amounts omitted. As quantities are determined, the amounts are inserted in the carbon copy, which becomes the *receiving report*. It is then sent to the purchasing department, where it is compared with the invoice. Discrepancies between the two are investigated and appropriate action taken. Such independent verification is an important element of internal control over purchasing activities.

In summary, the following verifications should be completed and appropriate actions taken before a purchase invoice is approved for payment:

1. Determine that the invoice details conform to the details of the purchase order.
2. Ascertain that commodities listed on the invoice have been received.
3. Determine that all arithmetic details, such as price extensions and amount of discount, are correct.

Purchases journal

A wide variety of assets may be purchased by a business enterprise. Property most frequently purchased on account by a trading concern is of the following types: (1) merchandise for resale to customers, (2) supplies for use in conducting the business, and (3) plant assets. Because of the variety of assets acquired on credit terms, the purchases journal should be designed to accommodate the recording of everything purchased on account. The number and the purpose of the special col-

PAGE 19   PURCHASES JOURNAL

	DATE		ACCOUNT CREDITED	POST. REF.	ACCOUNTS PAYABLE CR.	
1	1969 Oct.	2	Video-Audio Co.	✓	7 2 4 00	1
2		3	Marsh Electronics, Inc.	✓	4 0 6 00	2
3		7	Parker Supply Co.	✓	5 7 00	3
4		9	Marsh Electronics, Inc.	✓	2 0 8 00	4
5		11	Dunlap Electric Corp.	✓	6 2 3 00	5
6		13	Arnold Electronics Supply	✓	1 5 5 5 00	6
7		14	Walton Manufacturing Co.	✓	9 1 0 00	7
8		16	Office Equipment Distributors	✓	9 7 0 00	8
9		19	Tri-State Distributors	✓	1 0 0 0 00	9
10		21	Walton Manufacturing Co.	✓	1 6 5 00	10
11		25	Parker Supply Co.	✓	3 2 00	11
12		27	Dunlap Electric Corp.	✓	3 7 5 00	12
13		31			7 0 2 5 00	13
14					(211)	14

Purchases journal, left page

umns provided in the journal depend upon the nature of the business and the frequency of purchases of the various assets. The form of purchases journal used by Preston Electrical Supplies is illustrated below and on page 118.

For each transaction recorded in the purchases journal, the credit is entered in the Accounts Payable Cr. column. The next three columns are used in accumulating debits to the particular accounts most frequently affected.

The Purchases Dr. column is for merchandise bought for resale. A more exact title for the column and the account to which the total is posted would be Merchandise Purchases. It is customary, however, to employ the shorter account title, Purchases. The purpose of the Store Supplies Dr. and Office Supplies Dr. columns is readily apparent. If supplies of these two categories were bought only infrequently, the two columns could be omitted from the journal.

The final set of columns, under the principal heading Sundry Accounts Dr., is used to record acquisitions, on account, of items not provided for in the special debit columns. The title of the account to be debited is entered in the Account column and the amount is entered in the Amount column; the account number is inserted in the Post. Ref. column at the time of posting.

Controlling account and subsidiary ledger

The necessity for maintaining a separate account for each creditor is evident. Although it would be possible to keep these accounts in the general ledger, it is ordinarily preferable, for convenience and control

PURCHASES JOURNAL   PAGE 19

	PURCHASES DR.	STORE SUPPLIES DR.	OFFICE SUPPLIES DR.	SUNDRY ACCOUNTS DR.			
				ACCOUNT	POST. REF.	AMOUNT	
1	7 2 4 00						1
2	4 0 6 00						2
3		3 1 00	2 6 00				3
4	2 0 8 00						4
5	6 2 3 00						5
6	1 5 5 5 00						6
7	9 1 0 00						7
8				Office Equipment	122	9 7 0 00	8
9	1 0 0 0 00						9
10				Store Equipment	121	1 6 5 00	10
11		2 5 00	7 00				11
12	3 7 5 00						12
13	5 8 0 1 00	5 6 00	3 3 00			1 1 3 5 00	13
14	(511)	(115)	(116)			(✓)	14

Purchases journal, right page

purposes, to segregate them in a subsidiary ledger. The account in the general ledger that summarizes the debits and the credits to the individual accounts in the subsidiary ledger is entitled Accounts Payable. It is a controlling account. The subsidiary ledger may be referred to as the *accounts payable ledger* or *creditors ledger*.

Posting the purchases journal

At frequent intervals, usually daily, throughout the month the amounts in the Accounts Payable Cr. column are posted to the creditors' accounts in the subsidiary ledger. As each posting is completed, a check mark is placed in the posting reference column of the purchases journal at the left of the amount posted.

The three-column account form ordinarily used for the accounts payable ledger is designed to disclose at all times the balance owed each creditor. The accounts are arranged alphabetically so as to permit easy access. A loose-leaf binder is used to facilitate the insertion of new accounts and the withdrawal of pages that have been completely filled.

As each item is posted to a creditor's account, the source of the entry is recorded in the posting reference column of the account by the letter "P" and the page number of the purchases journal. The account with Arnold Electronics Supply, taken from the accounts payable ledger of Preston Electrical Supplies, is presented below as an example.

NAME   Arnold Electronics Supply

ADDRESS   7900 Market Street, San Francisco 94131

DATE	ITEM	POST. REF.	DEBIT	CREDIT	BALANCE
1969 Oct. 13		P19		1 5 5 5 00	1 5 5 5 00

An account in the accounts payable ledger

At the end of the month, the purchases journal is totaled and ruled in the manner illustrated on pages 118 and 119. Before it is posted to the general ledger, the equality of the debits and the credits should be verified. This may be done on an adding machine tape or by a listing similar to the following:

DEBIT TOTALS		CREDIT TOTALS	
Purchases............	$5,801.00	Accounts Payable....	$7,025.00
Store Supplies........	56.00		
Office Supplies.......	33.00		
Sundry Accounts.....	1,135.00		
	$7,025.00		$7,025.00

The total of the Accounts Payable Cr. column is posted to the accounts payable account in the general ledger and the posting reference is indicated below the column total. The totals of the Purchases Dr.,

Store Supplies Dr., and Office Supplies Dr. columns are posted in a similar manner. Each individual amount in the Sundry Accounts Dr. section is posted to the appropriate account in the general ledger, the posting reference being entered at the left of the amount. The total of the column is not posted. A check mark is therefore placed below the $1,135 total to indicate that no action is required.

Postings were made to six accounts in the general ledger of Preston Electrical Supplies. Three of the accounts are presented below. The debit of $970 to Office Equipment was posted from the Sundry Accounts Dr. column of the purchases journal; the credit of $7,025 to Accounts Payable and the debit of $5,801 to Purchases were posted as totals from the Accounts Payable Cr. and Purchases Dr. columns respectively.

Office Equipment   ACCOUNT NO. 122

DATE		ITEM	POST. REF.	DEBIT	CREDIT	BALANCE	
						DEBIT	CREDIT
1969 Oct.	1	Balance	✓			4 6 0 0 00	
	16		P19	9 7 0 00		5 5 7 0 00	

Accounts Payable   ACCOUNT NO. 211

DATE		ITEM	POST. REF.	DEBIT	CREDIT	BALANCE	
						DEBIT	CREDIT
1969 Oct.	1	Balance	✓				6 2 7 5 00
	31		P19		7 0 2 5 00		13 3 0 0 00

121

Purchases   ACCOUNT NO. 511

DATE		ITEM	POST. REF.	DEBIT	CREDIT	BALANCE	
						DEBIT	CREDIT
1969 Oct.	1	Balance	✓			89 1 2 8 00	
	31		P19	5 8 0 1 00		94 9 2 9 00	

General ledger accounts after posting from purchases journal

The relationship between the purchases journal and the ledgers is presented graphically in a flow diagram on the following page.

Two procedures revealed by the flow diagram should be particularly emphasized:

1. Postings are made from the purchases journal to (a) accounts in the subsidiary ledger and (b) accounts in the general ledger.
2. The sum of the postings to individual accounts in the subsidiary ledger equals the columnar total posted to the controlling account in the general ledger.

Returns and allowances

When merchandise or other commodities purchased are returned or a price adjustment is requested, the purchaser usually communicates

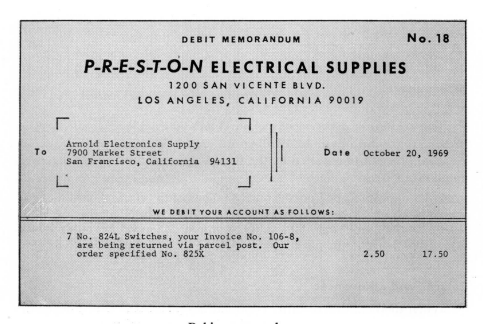

PURCHASES JOURNAL

ACCOUNT CREDITED	P. R.	ACCTS. PAYABLE CR.	PUR- CHASES DR.	STORE SUP. DR.	OFFICE SUP. DR.	SUNDRY ACCOUNTS DEBIT		
						ACCOUNT	P. R.	AMOUNT
Video-Audio Co.	√	724	724					
Marsh Electronics	√	406	406					
Parker Supply Co.	√	57		31	26			
Walton Mfg. Co.	√	165				Store Equip.	121	165
Parker Supply Co.	√	32		25	7			
Dunlap Electric Corp.	√	375	375					
		7,025	5,801	56	33			1,135

Accounts Payable Ledger

Each individual entry is posted to the credit of an account in the accounts payable ledger, making a total of $7,025.

General Ledger

Accounts Payable
7,025

Store Supplies
56

Office Supplies
33

Purchases
5,801

Store Equipment
165

Flow of data from the purchases journal to the ledgers

with the seller in writing. The details may be stated in a letter or the debtor may use his own *debit memorandum* form. This form, illustrated below, is a convenient medium for informing the creditor of the amount to be debited to his account on the buyer's books and the reasons for the return or price adjustment.

122

DEBIT MEMORANDUM   No. 18

P-R-E-S-T-O-N ELECTRICAL SUPPLIES

1200 SAN VICENTE BLVD.
LOS ANGELES, CALIFORNIA 90019

To   Arnold Electronics Supply
     7900 Market Street
     San Francisco, California 94131

Date   October 20, 1969

WE DEBIT YOUR ACCOUNT AS FOLLOWS:

7 No. 824L Switches, your Invoice No. 106-8,
are being returned via parcel post. Our
order specified No. 825X   2.50   17.50

Debit memorandum

part two ● Accounting processes for a merchandising enterprise

The debtor may use a copy of the debit memorandum as the basis for an entry or he may await confirmation from the creditor, which is usually in the form of a *credit memorandum*. In either event, both the creditor's account and the controlling account must be debited and the account to which the commodities were originally debited must be credited. For example, if the return or the allowance relates to merchandise purchased for resale to customers, the amount of the cost reduction is credited to Purchases. On the other hand, if the reduction is in the cost of some other commodity, such as office equipment, the credit is made to Office Equipment.

During October, Preston Electrical Supplies issued two debit memorandums, one for a return of merchandise and the other for an allowance granted on office equipment that deviated somewhat from the stipulated specifications. The entries may be recorded in a two-column general journal as follows:

JOURNAL   PAGE   18

	DATE		DESCRIPTION	POST. REF.	DEBIT	CREDIT	
17	Oct.	20	Accounts Payable - Arnold Electronics Supply	211 ✓	1 7 50		17
18			Purchases	511		1 7 50	18
19			Debit Memo No. 18.				19
37		29	Accounts Payable - Office Equip. Distributors	211 ✓	2 0 00		37
38			Office Equipment	122		2 0 00	38
39			Debit Memo No. 19.				39

General journal entries for returns and allowances on commodities purchased

It should be noted that the debit portions of the entries are posted to the accounts payable account in the general ledger (No. 211), and also to the respective creditors' accounts in the subsidiary ledger (✓). The necessity for posting the debits to two different accounts is indicated, at the time these entries are journalized, by drawing a diagonal line in the posting reference column. The account numbers and check marks are inserted, in the usual manner, at the time the entries are posted.

In both of the examples above the creditors' accounts were debited for the amount of the debit memorandums. When the return or the allowance is granted after the invoice has been paid, the settlement may be made in cash. In such cases the transaction is recorded in the cash receipts journal as a debit to Cash and a credit to the appropriate account.

Significant losses in revenue and additional operating expenses caused by returns and allowances usually affect the seller rather than

123

the buyer. Hence, there is ordinarily no need for accumulating separately the amount of reductions in purchases attributable to returns and allowances. However, if the total dollar volume of merchandise purchase returns and allowances is thought to be significant, a separate account, Purchases Returns and Allowances, can be maintained.

Purchases invoices as a journal

Many business enterprises dispense with a formal purchases journal, replacing it with the invoices themselves. When this system is used, the original invoices become the basis for posting credits to the individual accounts in the subsidiary ledger. As each credit is posted, an appropriate notation of the fact is stamped or written on the invoice. At the end of each month, the data on all invoices received during that month are summarized and an entry is made in the general journal debiting the appropriate general ledger accounts and crediting the accounts payable account. For example, if the summary lists purchases of merchandise, $8,612, office supplies, $340, store supplies, $218, and office equipment, $670, the general journal entry would be as follows:

Nov.	30	Purchases........................	8,612	
		Office Supplies...................	340	
		Store Supplies....................	218	
		Office Equipment.................	670	
		Accounts Payable................		9,840

124

Credit terms and cash discounts

Purchases on account from some suppliers may be on what is termed a *net cash* basis, which means that payment is to be made immediately following delivery of the commodities. Other suppliers may grant credit for varying lengths of time, sometimes with a cash discount allowed for early payment. The payment of accounts as they come due is an important determinant of credit ratings. It is also important that advantage be taken of all available cash discounts, even though it may be necessary to borrow the money with which to make the payment. For example, assume that an invoice for $1,000, with terms of 2/10, n/30, is to be paid within the discount period with funds borrowed for the remaining 20 days of the credit period. If an annual interest rate of 6% is assumed, the net savings to the purchaser is $16.73, determined as follows:

Discount of 2% on $1,000................	$20.00
Interest for 20 days, at rate of 6%, on $980.	3.27
Savings effected by borrowing...........	$16.73

Payments on account are ordinarily made by use of the mails. For purposes of determining timeliness of payment, the customary business practice is to consider the date of the postmark as the date of payment. The possible time lag of as much as several days for delivery of the remittance is likely to be no more than the time lag between the date of the invoice and the date of its receipt by the purchaser.

There are various systems designed to assure payment within the discount period or on the last day of the credit period. A simple but effective method is to file each unpaid invoice according to the earliest date that consideration should be given to its payment. The file may be composed of a group of folders, numbered from 1 to 31, the numbers representing days of a month.

To illustrate the foregoing, assume that a purchase invoice dated October 10, with terms of 2/10, n/30, is received on October 12. After the appropriate verifications are completed, the invoice is placed in File No. 20 so that it will be considered for payment on October 20, the last day of the discount period.

On October 20 this invoice, together with all other invoices requiring consideration on that date, will be taken from File No. 20 by the treasurer or other person responsible for making disbursements. Each invoice in the folder will then either be paid or be refiled in the appropriate folder. If the October 10 invoice is not paid on October 20, consideration should again be given to its payment on November 9, which is the last day of the credit period. Accordingly, it should be refiled in File No. 9. The maintenance of such a system is also helpful in determining the amount of cash that should be available each day in the near future. This control feature may in turn yield benefits in the form of increased revenue from investments or reductions in the amount of interest incurred on short term loans.

Cash payments journal

The criteria for determining the special columns to be provided in the cash payments journal are the same as for other journals illustrated earlier, namely, the nature of the transactions to be recorded and the frequency of their occurrence. It is necessary, of course, to have a Cash Cr. column. Payments to creditors on account are usually sufficiently frequent to require columns for Accounts Payable Dr. and Purchases Discount Cr. The cash payments journal illustrated on page 126 has these three columns and an additional column for Sundry Accounts Dr. If payments for one or more specific operating expenses were sufficiently numerous, other special columns could be added to the journal.

All payments by Preston Electrical Supplies are made by check and the check stubs serve as the written evidence of the transactions. As each transaction is recorded in the cash payments journal, the related check number is entered in the column at the right of the Date column. The check numbers provide a convenient cross-reference, and their use also is helpful in controlling cash payments. A review of the Check No. column from time to time will disclose any failure to record a payment.

125

DATE	CK. NO.	ACCOUNT DEBITED	POST. REF.	SUNDRY ACCOUNTS DR.	ACCOUNTS PAYABLE DR.	PURCHASES DISCOUNT CR.	CASH CR.	
1969 Oct. 2	312	Purchases	511	275 00			275 00	1
4	313	Store Equipment	121	350 00			350 00	2
12	314	Marsh Electronics, Inc.	✓		406 00	4 06	401 94	3
12	315	Sales Salaries	611	560 00			560 00	4
12	316	Office Salaries	711	180 00			180 00	5
14	317	Misc. General Expense	715	26 40			26 40	6
16	318	Prepaid Insurance	117	84 00			84 00	7
18	319	Marsh Electronics, Inc.	✓		208 00	2 08	205 92	8
20	320	M. B. Heath Co.	✓		1850 00		1850 00	9
21	321	Sales Returns and Allowances	412	62 00			62 00	10
23	322	Video-Audio Co.	✓		1600 00		1600 00	11
23	323	Purchases	511	89 20			89 20	12
24	324	Tri-State Distributors	✓		2300 00		2300 00	13
24	325	Walton Manufacturing Co.	✓		525 00		525 00	14
26	326	Sales Salaries	611	560 00			560 00	15
26	327	Office Salaries	711	180 00			180 00	16
26	328	Arnold Electronics Supply	✓		1537 50	30 75	1506 75	17
26	329	Advertising Expense	613	86 00			86 00	18
27	330	Misc. Selling Expense	617	41 50			41 50	19
28	331	T. J. Preston, Drawing	312	900 00			900 00	20
31				3394 10	8426 50	36 89	11783 71	21
				(✓)	(211)	(512)	(111)	22
								23

126

Cash payments journal after posting

The Sundry Accounts Dr. column is used to record debits to any account for which there is no special column. For example, on October 2 Preston Electrical Supplies paid $275 for a cash purchase of merchandise. The transaction was recorded by writing "Purchases" in the space provided and $275 in the Sundry Accounts Dr. and the Cash Cr. columns. The posting reference was inserted later, at the time the debit was posted.

Debits to creditors' accounts for invoices paid are recorded in the Accounts Payable Dr. column. If there is no cash discount, the amount recorded in the Cash Cr. column will be the same as the debit to the creditor. If a discount is allowed, the credit to Cash will be correspondingly less. Cash discounts taken on merchandise purchased for resale are recorded in the Purchases Discount Cr. column. For example, the payment to Marsh Electronics, Inc. on October 12 was recorded as a debit to Accounts Payable of $406, a credit to Purchases Discount of $4.06, and a credit to Cash of $401.94.

At frequent intervals during the month, the amounts entered in the Accounts Payable Dr. column are posted to the creditors' accounts in the accounts payable ledger. The source of the entries is indicated by inserting "CP" and the appropriate journal page number in the posting reference column of the accounts. Check marks are placed in the posting reference column of the cash payments journal to indicate that the amounts have been posted. The items in the Sundry Accounts Dr. column are also posted to the appropriate accounts in the general ledger at frequent intervals and the posting is indicated by writing the account numbers in the posting reference column of the cash payments journal.

At the end of the month the cash payments journal is ruled, each of the money columns is footed, and the equality of debits and credits is determined as follows:

DEBIT TOTALS		CREDIT TOTALS	
Sundry Accounts...	$ 3,394.10	Purchases Discount.	$ 36.89
Accounts Payable..	8,426.50	Cash.............	11,783.71
	$11,820.60		$11,820.60

A check mark is placed below the total of the Sundry Accounts Dr. column to indicate that it is not posted. As each of the totals of the other three columns is posted to a general ledger account, the appropriate posting references are inserted below the column totals.

Accounts payable control and subsidiary ledger

During October the following postings were made to Accounts Payable in the general ledger of Preston Electrical Supplies:

CREDITS TO ACCOUNTS PAYABLE

Oct. 31 (Total purchases on account, from purchases journal)... $7,025.00

DEBITS TO ACCOUNTS PAYABLE

Oct. 20	(A return of merchandise, from general journal)........	17.50
29	(An allowance on office equipment, from general journal).	20.00
31	(Total debits resulting from payments on account, from cash payments journal).........................	8,426.50

The controlling account with its opening balance, the foregoing postings, and the resulting balances is shown below.

Accounts Payable   ACCOUNT NO. 211

DATE	ITEM	POST. REF.	DEBIT	CREDIT	BALANCE DEBIT	BALANCE CREDIT
1969 Oct. 1	Balance	✓				6 2 7 5 00
20		J18	1 7 50			6 2 5 7 50
29		J18	2 0 00			6 2 3 7 50
31		P19		7 0 2 5 00		13 2 6 2 50
31		CP16	8 4 2 6 50			4 8 3 6 00

Accounts payable account in the general ledger at the end of the month

The accounts payable ledger of Preston Electrical Supplies, after posting all entries for the month, is shown on the following pages.

NAME   Arnold Electronics Supply

ADDRESS   7900 Market Street, San Francisco, California   94131

DATE		ITEM	POST. REF.	DEBIT	CREDIT	BALANCE
1969 Oct.	13		P19		1 5 5 5 00	1 5 5 5 00
	20		J18	1 7 50		1 5 3 7 50
	26		CP16	1 5 3 7 50		

NAME   Dunlap Electric Corporation

ADDRESS   521 Scottsdale Blvd., Phoenix, Arizona   85004

DATE		ITEM	POST. REF.	DEBIT	CREDIT	BALANCE
1969 Oct.	11		P19		6 2 3 00	6 2 3 00
	27		P19		3 7 5 00	9 9 8 00

NAME   M. B. Heath Co.

ADDRESS   9950 Ridge Ave., Los Angeles, California   90048

DATE		ITEM	POST. REF.	DEBIT	CREDIT	BALANCE
1969 Sept.	21		P18		1 8 5 0 00	1 8 5 0 00
Oct.	20		CP16	1 8 5 0 00		

NAME   Marsh Electronics, Inc.

ADDRESS   650 Wilson, Portland, Oregon   97209

128

DATE		ITEM	POST. REF.	DEBIT	CREDIT	BALANCE
1969 Oct.	3		P19		4 0 6 00	4 0 6 00
	9		P19		2 0 8 00	6 1 4 00
	12		CP16	4 0 6 00		2 0 8 00
	18		CP16	2 0 8 00		

NAME   Office Equipment Distributors

ADDRESS   4872 Webster, Oakland, California   94609

DATE		ITEM	POST. REF.	DEBIT	CREDIT	BALANCE
1969 Oct.	16		P19		9 7 0 00	9 7 0 00
	29		J18	2 0 00		9 5 0 00

NAME   Parker Supply Co.

ADDRESS   142 West 8th, Los Angeles, California   90014

DATE		ITEM	POST. REF.	DEBIT	CREDIT	BALANCE
1969 Oct.	7		P19		5 7 00	5 7 00
	25		P19		3 2 00	8 9 00

Accounts payable ledger at the end of the month

NAME   Tri-State Distributors
ADDRESS   8876 Montgomery, San Francisco, California 94111

DATE	ITEM	POST. REF.	DEBIT	CREDIT	BALANCE
1969 Sept. 26		P18		2 3 0 0 00	2 3 0 0 00
Oct. 19		P19		1 0 0 0 00	3 3 0 0 00
24		CP16	2 3 0 0 00		1 0 0 0 00

NAME   Video-Audio Co.
ADDRESS   1200 Capitol Ave., Sacramento, California 95814

DATE	ITEM	POST. REF.	DEBIT	CREDIT	BALANCE
1969 Sept. 25		P18		1 6 0 0 00	1 6 0 0 00
Oct. 2		P19		7 2 4 00	2 3 2 4 00
23		CP16	1 6 0 0 00		7 2 4 00

NAME   Walton Manufacturing Co.
ADDRESS   9554 W. Colorado Blvd., Pasadena, California 91107

DATE	ITEM	POST. REF.	DEBIT	CREDIT	BALANCE
1969 Sept. 28		P18		5 2 5 00	5 2 5 00
Oct. 14		P19		9 1 0 00	1 4 3 5 00
21		P19		1 6 5 00	1 6 0 0 00
24		CP16	5 2 5 00		1 0 7 5 00

Accounts payable ledger at the end of the month — concluded

After all posting has been completed for the month, the sum of the balances in the creditors ledger should be compared with the balance of the accounts payable account in the general ledger. If the controlling account and the subsidiary ledger are not in agreement, the error or errors must be located and corrected. The balances of the individual creditors' accounts may be summarized on an adding machine tape, or a schedule like the one below may be prepared. The total of the schedule, $4,836, agrees with the balance of the accounts payable account shown on page 127.

```
                     Preston Electrical Supplies
                     Schedule of Accounts Payable
                          October 31, 1969
```

Dunlap Electric Corporation	$ 998
Office Equipment Distributors	950
Parker Supply Co.	89
Tri-State Distributors.	1,000
Video-Audio Co.	724
Walton Manufacturing Co.	1,075
Total accounts payable.	$4,836

Schedule of accounts payable

Transportation on incoming shipments

The cost of merchandise acquired for resale includes the transportation charges for delivery of the goods. Similarly, the cost of plant assets, supplies, and other items purchased includes the cost of transporting them from the seller to the buyer. This is true, in a general sense, regardless of the agreement as to who shall pay the transportation company. Businesses that quote prices FOB destination, making no specific charge for delivery, must of necessity provide for recoupment of transportation costs when establishing their schedule of selling prices.

When assets are purchased on FOB shipping point terms, the related freight, express, postage, or other transportation costs borne by the buyer should be debited to the same account to which the commodities are debited. Thus, transportation charges on merchandise purchased for resale should be debited to Purchases, transportation charges on store equipment should be debited to Store Equipment, etc. If the shipper pays the delivery costs and adds them to the invoice, the entire amount of the invoice, including transportation, is debited by the buyer to the appropriate account. If the buyer pays the transportation company directly, the delivery charges are recorded when such payment is made.

Some enterprises maintain an account titled Freight In or Transportation In for accumulating all separately charged delivery costs on merchandise purchased for resale to customers. If such merchandise is invariably purchased on an FOB shipping point basis, the data thus accumulated may be useful in determining the amount of transportation cost allocable to the merchandise inventory at the end of the accounting period. On the other hand, if much of the merchandise is purchased on FOB destination terms, the percentage relationship of the balance of the freight-in account to the balance of the purchases account at the end of the period is not significant. The important consideration, in this regard, is that every reasonable effort be made to buy at the lowest possible delivered price. This can be accomplished only through efficient management of the purchasing department. Each time a purchase order is to be issued, consideration must be given not only to the quoted price but also to the transportation and discount terms.

QUESTIONS

1. (a) Name two commonly used business forms described in this chapter that are the basis for accounting entries. (b) Name a business form that facilitates but does not represent a completed business transaction.

2. How can an invoice be both a purchase invoice and a sales invoice?

3. What is the title of the account to which each of the purchases on account described below should be charged by a men's clothing store:

(a) Six dozen shirts
(b) Pads of sales tickets
(c) One gross neckties
(d) New typewriter for the office
(e) A three-year fire insurance policy on merchandise
(f) Fifteen ski jackets
(g) Printed letterheads for the office

4. Three related transactions are recorded in the T accounts below. (a) Describe each transaction. (b) What is the rate of the cash discount and on what amount was it computed?

CASH		
	(3)	1,372

ACCOUNTS PAYABLE		
(2)	100	(1)	1,500
(3)	1,400		

PURCHASES		
(1) 1,500	(2)	100

PURCHASES DISCOUNT		
	(3)	28

5. Comment on the relative merits of the two systems described below of reporting the receipt of merchandise purchased.

(a) The purchase invoice is sent to the receiving department. The receiving department indicates quantities received by inserting a check mark or actual quantities opposite each item on the invoice.

(b) A carbon copy of the purchase order, on which quantities and prices do not appear, is sent to the receiving department. The receiving department inserts the actual quantities received opposite each description on the purchase order.

131

6. Which is more likely to cause the greater amount of expense to be incurred by an enterprise, merchandise returned to it by customers (sales returns) or merchandise returned by it to suppliers (purchases returns)? Discuss.

7. The following errors were made in recording transactions in the purchases journal or in posting therefrom. How will each error come to the attention of the bookkeeper other than by chance discovery?

(a) An invoice for merchandise of $300 from Procter Corp. was recorded as having been received from Proctor, Inc., another supplier.
(b) A credit of $500 to M. J. Carter, Inc. was posted as $50.
(c) The accounts payable column of the purchases journal was overadded by $100.
(d) An invoice for office equipment of $200 was recorded as $20.

8. The accounts payable and cash columns in the cash payments journal were unknowingly underadded by $1,000 at the end of the month. (a) Assuming no other errors in recording or posting, will the error cause the trial balance totals to be unequal? (b) Will the creditors ledger agree with the accounts payable controlling account?

9. (a) Under what circumstances is a diagonal line inserted in the posting reference column opposite an entry in a two-column general journal? (b) Should the diagonal line be inserted when the entry is recorded in the general journal or at the time the entry is posted?

10. Prices and terms quoted by two companies for the sale of 100 units of a particular commodity are as follows:

Supplier A: 100 at $10 a unit, FOB shipping point, 2/10, n/30
(Transportation costs will amount to $50)
Supplier B: 100 at $10.40 a unit, FOB destination, n/30

Which offer yields the lower price? Discuss.

11. Name the accounts that would be credited in recording the following returns of commodities purchased on account assuming that there is not an account in the ledger for purchases returns and allowances: (a) Merchandise purchased for resale. (b) Supplies purchased for use in the business.

12. Is the normal balance of Purchases Discount a debit or a credit?

13. In recording a cash payment the bookkeeper enters the correct amount of $700 in the Accounts Payable Dr. column and the correct amount of $693 in the Cash Cr. column but omits the entry for Purchases Discount. How will this error come to his attention other than by chance discovery?

14. An appliance company purchases 10 identical television sets at $200 each, FOB shipping point, 2/10, n/30. Transportation charges on the shipment amount to $30. Assuming payment within the discount period, what is the net unit cost of the sets?

EXERCISES

5-1. Determine the amount to be paid in full settlement of each of the following invoices, assuming that credit for returns and allowances was received prior to payment and that all invoices were paid within the discount period.

| | Purchase Invoice | | | Returns and |
	Merchandise	Transportation	Terms	Allowances
(a)	$1,000	—	FOB shipping point, 2/10, n/30	$ 50
(b)	1,600	$70	FOB shipping point, 1/10, n/30	—
(c)	900	—	FOB destination, n/30	60
(d)	1,300	40	FOB shipping point, 1/10, n/30	100
(e)	580	—	FOB destination, 2/10, n/30	30

5-2. Mabley & Co. uses its purchase invoices as its purchases journal. Summarization of the invoices for August yields the following totals for the various categories of commodities purchased on account: merchandise for resale, $50,496; store supplies, $353; office supplies, $72; office equipment, $675. Prepare the general journal entry that should be made on the basis of this information.

5-3. Hadley Corp. purchases $900 of merchandise from Bascom Co., FOB shipping point, 2/10, n/30. Bascom Co. adds transportation charges of $40 to the invoice. Hadley Corp. returns some of the merchandise, receiving a credit memorandum for $60, and then pays the amount due within the discount period. Present Hadley Corp.'s entries, in general journal form, to record (a) the purchase, (b) the merchandise return, and (c) the payment. (Hadley Corp. does not maintain a separate account for the recording of purchases returns and allowances.)

5-4. Present entries in general journal form for the following related transactions of Randolph Decorators, recording merchandise purchases returns and allowances in the purchases account:

  (a) Purchased $800 of fabrics from Priscilla Mills on account, terms 2/10, n/30.
  (b) Paid the amount owed on the invoice within the discount period.
  (c) Discovered that many of the fabrics were not color fast and returned items with an invoice price of $450, receiving credit.
  (d) Purchased $350 of fabrics from Priscilla Mills on account, terms 2/10, n/30.
  (e) Received a check for the balance owed from the return in (c), after deducting for the purchase in (d).

5-5. Present the general journal entries necessary to correct each of the errors described below, assuming that the incorrect entries had been posted and that the corrections are recorded in the same fiscal period in which the errors occurred.

  (a) Transportation costs of $50 incurred on office equipment purchased for use in the business were charged to Purchases.
  (b) A $75 cash purchase of merchandise from W. R. Brock Co. was recorded as a purchase on account.
  (c) The $110 cost of faulty store equipment returned to the supplier was credited to Purchases.
  (d) The payment of a $2,000 invoice for merchandise, less 2% discount, to R. T. Able Co. was recorded as a $1,960 debit to R. T. Able Co. (and Accounts Payable) and a $1,960 credit to Cash.

PROBLEMS

The following additional problems for this chapter are located in Appendix C: 5-2B, 5-3B, 5-4B.

5-1A. Purchases on account and related returns and allowances completed by Summit Book Shop during June of the current year are described below.

June 3. Purchased merchandise on account from Custom Card Co., $126.10.
  4. Purchased merchandise on account from Gregory Publishing Co., $672.
  6. Received a credit memorandum from Custom Card Co. for merchandise returned, $10.80.
  10. Purchased office supplies on account from Parker Supply, Inc., $27.40.
  12. Purchased office equipment on account from Milton Equipment Co., $397.30.
  13. Purchased merchandise on account from Custom Card Co., $289.60.
  18. Purchased merchandise on account from Wabash Publishers, $415.50.
  19. Received a credit memorandum from Parker Supply, Inc. for office supplies returned, $4.60.
  20. Purchased merchandise on account from Stuart Press, Inc., $510.
  24. Received a credit memorandum from Gregory Publishing Co. as an allowance for damaged merchandise, $65.
  25. Purchased store supplies on account from Parker Supply, Inc., $35.70.
  27. Purchased merchandise on account from Wabash Publishers, $218.20.
  28. Purchased office supplies on account from Parker Supply, Inc., $19.30.

Instructions:

(1) Open the following accounts in the general ledger and enter the balances as of June 1:

114 Store Supplies...... $ 124.50   211 Accounts Payable.. $ 1,432.50
115 Office Supplies.....   74.10   511 Purchases.........   19,632.60
122 Office Equipment... 3,970.00

(2) Open the following accounts in the accounts payable ledger and enter the balances in the balance columns as of June 1: Custom Card Co., $196.30; Gregory Publishing Co., $542; Milton Equipment Co.; Parker Supply, Inc.; Stuart Press, Inc.; Wabash Publishers, $694.20.

(3) Record the transactions for June, posting to the creditors' accounts in the accounts payable ledger immediately after each entry. Use a purchases journal similar to the one illustrated on pages 118 and 119 and a two-column general journal.

(4) Post the general journal and the purchases journal to the accounts in the general ledger.

(5) (a) What is the sum of the balances in the subsidiary ledger?
    (b) What is the balance of the controlling account?

5-2A. Glendale Men's Wear was established in October of the current year. Transactions related to purchases, returns and allowances, and cash payments during the remainder of the month are described below.

Oct. 16. Purchased store equipment on account from Reed Supply Corp., $7,400.
16. Issued Check No. 1 in payment of rent for October, $350.
17. Purchased merchandise on account from Smart Clothes, Inc., $2,650.
17. Issued Check No. 2 in payment of store supplies, $47, and office supplies, $26.
19. Purchased merchandise on account from Norris Clothing Co., $1,923.
20. Purchased merchandise on account from Damon & Co., $1,300.
21. Received a credit memorandum from Norris Clothing Co. for returned merchandise, $73.

Post the journals to the accounts payable ledger.

24. Issued Check No. 3 to Reed Supply Corp. in payment of invoice of $7,400.
25. Received a credit memorandum from Damon & Co. for defective merchandise, $38.
26. Issued Check No. 4 to Smart Clothes, Inc. in payment of invoice of $2,650, less 2% discount.
27. Issued Check No. 5 to a cash customer for merchandise returned, $17.
28. Issued Check No. 6 to Norris Clothing Co. in payment of the balance owed, less 2% discount.
28. Purchased merchandise on account from Damon & Co., $2,118.

Post the journals to the accounts payable ledger.

29. Purchased the following from Reed Supply Corp. on account: store supplies, $32; office supplies, $45; office equipment, $1,100.
30. Issued Check No. 7 to Damon & Co. in payment of the invoice of $1,300 less the credit of $38.
30. Purchased merchandise on account from Smart Clothes, Inc., $1,760.
31. Issued Check No. 8 in payment of incoming transportation charges on merchandise delivered during October, $135.
31. Issued Check No. 9 in payment of sales salaries, $965.
31. Received a credit memorandum from Reed Supply Corp. for defect in office equipment, $50.

Post the journals to the accounts payable ledger.

Instructions:

(1) Open the following accounts in the general ledger, using the account numbers indicated.

111 Cash	412 Sales Returns and Allowances
116 Store Supplies	511 Purchases
117 Office Supplies	512 Purchases Discount
121 Store Equipment	611 Sales Salaries
122 Office Equipment	712 Rent Expense
211 Accounts Payable	

(2) Open the following accounts in the accounts payable ledger: Damon & Co.; Norris Clothing Co.; Reed Supply Corp.; Smart Clothes, Inc.

(3) Record the transactions for October, using a purchases journal similar to the one illustrated on pages 118 and 119, a cash payments journal similar to the one illustrated on page 126, and a two-column general journal. Post to the *accounts payable ledger* at the points indicated in the narrative of transactions.

(4) Post the appropriate individual entries to the *general ledger.*

(5) Add the columns of the purchases journal and the cash payments journal, and post the appropriate totals to the general ledger. (Because of omission from the problem of transactions related to cash receipts, the cash account in the ledger will have a credit balance.)

(6) Prepare a schedule of accounts payable.

If the working papers correlating with the textbook are not used, omit Problem 5-3A.

5-3A. Western Specialty Co. uses carbon copies of its sales invoices as a sales journal, posting to the accounts receivable ledger directly from the invoices. At the end of the month the invoices are totaled and the appropriate entry is recorded in the general journal. Purchases on account are recorded in a similar manner, the invoices being used as a purchases journal. Sales and purchases on account during May of the current year were as follows:

Sales

May	4. James Oliver Corp.	$2,100
	6. Vincent & Yost	765
	10. Howard Alden & Co.	1,340
	16. C. A. Harris	936
	17. Howard Alden & Co.	2,648
	22. Vincent & Yost	1,830

Purchases

May	2. M. J. Barton & Co.: store supplies, $95; office supplies, $25	$ 120
	3. Lee Corp., merchandise	2,630
	11. Fisher-Jordan, Inc., merchandise	2,100
	18. Potter Manufacturing Co., store equipment	1,500
	19. R. B. Warren, Inc., merchandise	748
	29. M. J. Barton & Co., store supplies	42
	31. Fisher-Jordan, Inc., merchandise	918

Other transactions completed during the month were recorded in a 4-column general journal, a cash receipts journal, and a cash payments journal, all of which are presented in the working papers. The subsidiary ledgers and the general ledger accounts affected by transactions of the month are also presented in the working papers.

Instructions:
(1) Summarize the sales invoices and the purchases invoices listed above and record the appropriate entries in the 4-column general journal.
(2) Post all items affecting the subsidiary ledgers in the following order: (a) sales invoices, (b) purchases invoices, (c) general journal, (d) cash receipts journal, (e) cash payments journal. When postings are made daily, which is the usual practice, the entries in customers' and creditors' accounts will appear in chronological order. The fact that in this problem postings to some of the accounts will not be in perfect date sequence is immaterial.
(3) Post all items recorded in the Sundry Accounts Dr. and Sundry Accounts Cr. columns of the journals in the following order: (a) general journal, (b) cash receipts journal, (c) cash payments journal.
(4) Add the columns of the general journal. Post the appropriate columnar totals of the journals in the following order: (a) general journal, (b) cash receipts journal, (c) cash payments journal.
(5) Prepare a trial balance.
(6) Determine the sum of the balances in the:
(a) Accounts receivable ledger (compare with balance of controlling account).
(b) Accounts payable ledger (compare with balance of controlling account).

5-4A. The transactions completed by Trump's during September, the first month of the current fiscal year, were as follows:

Sept. 1. Issued Check No. 497 for September rent, $500.
  2. Purchased merchandise on account from Sloan-Wiley Corp., $2,335.
  3. Purchased equipment on account from Foster Supply Corp., $1,490.
  3. Issued Invoice No. 721 to S. R. Riggs, Inc., $980.
  5. Received check for $2,744 from Ames & Marlowe in payment of $2,800 invoice, less discount.
  5. Issued Check No. 498 for miscellaneous selling expense, $125.
  5. Received credit memorandum from Sloan-Wiley Corp. for merchandise returned to them, $85.
  8. Issued Invoice No. 722 to West & Co., $1,700.
  9. Issued Check No. 499 for $3,626 to Beck Manufacturing Co. in payment of $3,700 balance, less 2% discount.
  9. Received check for $931 from James Hoyt Corp. in payment of $950 invoice, less discount.
  10. Issued Check No. 500 to L. A. Mitchell & Co. in payment of invoice of $631, no discount.
  Post all journals to the accounts receivable ledger and accounts payable ledger.
  10. Issued Invoice No. 723 to Ames & Marlowe, $2,720.
  11. Issued Check No. 501 to W. J. Zimmer, Inc. in payment of account, $1,273, no discount.
  12. Received check from S. R. Riggs, Inc. on account, $776, no discount.
  14. Issued credit memorandum to Ames & Marlowe for damaged merchandise, $120.
  15. Issued Check No. 502 for $2,205 to Sloan-Wiley Corp. in payment of $2,250 balance, less 2% discount.
  15. Issued Check No. 503 for $475 for cash purchase of merchandise.
  15. Cash sales for September 1–15, $3,745.
  17. Purchased merchandise on account from L. A. Mitchell & Co., $2,430.
  18. Received check for return of merchandise that had been purchased for cash, $27.
  18. Issued Check No. 504 for miscellaneous general expense, $168.

22. Purchased the following on account from Foster Supply Corp.: store supplies, $19; office supplies, $31.
22. Issued Check No. 505 in payment of advertising expense, $350.
   Post all journals to the accounts receivable ledger and accounts payable ledger.
23. Issued Invoice No. 724 to James Hoyt Corp., $2,368.
24. Purchased the following on account from Beck Manufacturing Co.: merchandise, $840; store supplies, $22.
25. Issued Invoice No. 725 to West & Co., $1,970.
25. Received check for $2,548 from Ames & Marlowe in payment of $2,600 balance, less discount.
26. Issued Check No. 506 to Foster Supply Corp. in payment of invoice of September 3, $1,490, no discount.
29. Issued Check No. 507 to David Trump as a personal withdrawal, $700.
30. Issued Check No. 508 for monthly salaries as follows: sales salaries, $1,250; office salaries, $550.
30. Cash sales for September 16–30, $4,215.
30. Issued Check No. 509 for transportation on commodities purchased during the month as follows: merchandise, $109; equipment, $29.
   Post all journals to the accounts receivable ledger and accounts payable ledger.

Instructions:

(1) Open the following accounts in the general ledger, entering the balances indicated as of September 1:

111	Cash	$ 6,370	411	Sales
113	Accounts Receivable	4,526	412	Sales Returns and Allow.
114	Merchandise Inventory	24,720	413	Sales Discount
115	Store Supplies	280	511	Purchases
116	Office Supplies	165	512	Purchases Discount
117	Prepaid Insurance	839	611	Sales Salaries
121	Equipment	16,417	612	Advertising Expense
121.1	Accumulated Depreciation	4,680	619	Miscellaneous Selling Exp.
211	Accounts Payable	5.604	711	Office Salaries
311	David Trump, Capital	43,033	712	Rent Expense
312	David Trump, Drawing		719	Miscellaneous General Exp.

(2) Open the following accounts in the accounts receivable ledger, entering the balances as of September 1 in the balance columns: Ames & Marlowe, $2,800; James Hoyt Corp., $950; S. R. Riggs, Inc., $776; West & Co.
(3) Open the following accounts in the accounts payable ledger, entering the balances as of September 1 in the balance columns: Beck Manufacturing Co., $3,700; Foster Supply Corp.; L. A. Mitchell & Co., $631; Sloan-Wiley Corp.; W. J. Zimmer, Inc., $1,273.
(4) Record the transactions for September, using a sales journal (as on page 94), a purchases journal (as on pages 118 and 119), a cash receipts journal (as on page 101), a cash payments journal (as on page 126), and a 2-column general journal. The terms of all sales on account are FOB shipping point, 2/15, n/60. Post to the subsidiary ledgers at the points indicated in the narrative of transactions.
(5) Post to the appropriate individual entries to the *general ledger*.
(6) Add the columns of the special journals and post the appropriate totals to the general ledger.
(7) Prepare a trial balance.
(8) Prepare a schedule of accounts receivable and a schedule of accounts payable. (Compare totals with balances of related controlling accounts.)

6

Summarizing
and reporting

Year-end summarization

Although many business enterprises prepare interim statements on a monthly or quarterly basis, a complete cycle of business operations is usually assumed to recur every twelve months. At yearly intervals throughout the life of a business enterprise the operating data for the fiscal year must be summarized and reported for the use of managers, owners, creditors, various governmental agencies, and other interested persons. Summaries of the various assets of the enterprise on the last day of the fiscal year, together with the status of the equities of creditors and owners, must also be reported. The ledger, which contains the basic data for the reports, must then be brought up-to-date through appropriate adjusting entries. Finally, the accounts must be prepared to receive entries for transactions that will occur in the following year. The sequence of year-end procedures may be varied to a minor extent but in general the following outline is typical:

1. Prepare a trial balance of the general ledger.
2. Determine that each subsidiary ledger is in agreement with the related controlling account in the general ledger.
3. Review the accounts to determine which ones should be adjusted, and compile the data necessary for making the adjustments.
4. Prepare a work sheet from the unadjusted trial balance and the data for the adjustments.

5. Prepare financial statements from the data in the work sheet.
6. Journalize and post the adjusting entries.
7. Journalize and post the closing entries.
8. Prepare a post-closing trial balance of the general ledger.
9. Journalize and post the reversing entries required to facilitate the recording of transactions in the following year.

Although the summarizing and reporting procedures that are presented in this chapter are similar, in broad outline, to those discussed in an earlier chapter, there are a number of differences. For businesses that purchase and sell merchandise, consideration must be given to the inventory of commodities on hand at the beginning and at the end of the year. In addition, the use of subsidiary ledgers for accounts receivable and accounts payable necessitate verifications that were not required in the less complex situations discussed in earlier chapters. The relationship between certain adjusting entries at the close of a year and entries for transactions in the following year is also considered in this chapter, as well as variations in trial balance preparation and the ruling of accounts.

Merchandise inventory adjustments

Purchases of merchandise during a period and the inventory adjustment at the end of the period could be recorded in much the same manner as purchases of supplies and the related year-end adjustment. If such a procedure were followed, the balance in the account Merchandise at the beginning of the period would represent the cost of the merchandise on hand at that time; during the period the cost of merchandise purchased would be debited to the same account. At the end of the period an adjusting entry would be made to transfer the cost of the merchandise sold to an account so named, leaving the ending inventory of merchandise as the balance of the asset account. Because of the greater significance of merchandise transactions, however, it is customary to accumulate more detailed data about the cost of merchandise sold than about supplies expense. Such details may be presented on the income statement in the following manner:

Cost of merchandise sold:		
Merchandise inventory, January 1, 1969........		$ 19,700
Purchases....................................	$105,280	
Less purchases discount.....................	1,525	
Net purchases...............................		103,755
Merchandise available for sale...............		$123,455
Less merchandise inventory, December 31, 1969.		22,150
Cost of merchandise sold...................		$101,305

The most efficient method of making the foregoing data readily available is to maintain a separate account in the ledger entitled Merchandise Inventory. Purchases of merchandise during the period are then debited to the account entitled Purchases. Related cash discounts, transportation in, and returns and allowances may also be recorded directly in the purchases account or in separate accounts, in accordance with the principles and procedures presented in the preceding chapter.

At the end of the period it is necessary to remove from Merchandise Inventory the amount representing the inventory at the beginning of the period and to replace it with the amount representing the inventory at the end of the period. This is accomplished by two adjusting entries. The first entry transfers the beginning inventory to Expense and Revenue Summary. Inasmuch as this beginning inventory is part of the cost of merchandise sold, it is debited to Expense and Revenue Summary. It is also a subtraction from the asset account Merchandise Inventory and hence is credited to that account. The first adjusting entry is as follows:

Dec.	31	Expense and Revenue Summary........	19,700	
		Merchandise Inventory.............		19,700

The second of the two adjusting entries debits the cost of the merchandise inventory at the end of the fiscal period to the asset account Merchandise Inventory. The credit portion of the entry effects a deduction of the unsold merchandise from the total cost of the merchandise available for sale during the period. In terms of the illustration of the partial income statement on page 139, the credit portion of the entry accomplishes the subtraction of $22,150 from $123,455 to yield the $101,305 cost of merchandise sold. The second adjusting entry is as follows:

Dec.	31	Merchandise Inventory...............	22,150	
		Expense and Revenue Summary......		22,150

The effect of the two inventory adjustments is indicated by the following T accounts, Merchandise Inventory and Expense and Revenue Summary:

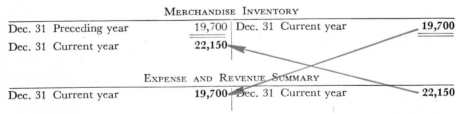

MERCHANDISE INVENTORY

Dec. 31 Preceding year	19,700	Dec. 31 Current year	19,700
Dec. 31 Current year	22,150		

EXPENSE AND REVENUE SUMMARY

Dec. 31 Current year	19,700	Dec. 31 Current year	22,150

In the accounts, the inventory of $19,700 at the end of the preceding year (beginning of current year) has been transferred to Expense and Revenue Summary as a part of the cost of merchandise available for sale. It is replaced by a debit of $22,150, the merchandise inventory at the end of the current year; the credit of the same amount to Expense and Revenue Summary is a deduction from the cost of merchandise available for sale.

Trial balance and adjustments on the work sheet

After year-end posting of the various journals has been completed, a trial balance of the general ledger is taken and conformity between each subsidiary ledger and its related controlling account verified. Any discrepancies should of course be corrected before proceeding with the adjusting entries.

The trial balance for Preston Electrical Supplies as of December 31, 1969, appears on the work sheet presented on pages 142 and 143. It differs slightly from trial balances illustrated earlier. All of the accounts in the ledger are listed in sequential order, including titles of accounts that have no balances. This variation in format has the advantage of listing accounts in the order in which they will be used when the statements are prepared. If additional accounts are needed in making the necessary adjustments, their titles can be inserted below the trial balance totals, as illustrated earlier.

The data needed for adjusting the accounts of Preston Electrical Supplies are summarized as follows:

Merchandise inventory as of December 31, 1969............		$22,150
Inventories of supplies as of December 31, 1969:		
Store supplies......................................		550
Office supplies.....................................		280
Insurance expired during 1969 on:		
Merchandise and store equipment.....................	$580	
Office equipment and building.......................	330	910
Depreciation during 1969 on:		
Store equipment....................................		1,100
Office equipment...................................		490
Building..		1,500
Salaries accrued on December 31, 1969:		
Sales salaries.....................................	$224	
Office salaries....................................	72	296

141

Explanations of the adjusting entries in the work sheet appearing on pages 142 and 143 are given in the paragraphs that follow.

Merchandise inventory. The $19,700 balance of merchandise inventory appearing in the trial balance represents the amount of the inventory at the end of the preceding year (beginning of the current year). It is a part of the merchandise available for sale during the year and is hence transferred to Expense and Revenue Summary, where it will be combined with the net cost of merchandise purchased during the year. (Entry (a) on the work sheet.)

The merchandise on hand at the end of the current year, as determined by a physical inventory, amounts to $22,150. It is an asset and must be debited to the asset account Merchandise Inventory. It must also be deducted from the cost of merchandise available for sale (beginning inventory plus net purchases) to yield the cost of the merchandise

Preston Electrical Supplies
Work Sheet
For Year Ended December 31, 1969

	TRIAL BALANCE		ADJUSTMENTS		INCOME STATEMENT		BALANCE SHEET	
ACCOUNT TITLE	DEBIT	CREDIT	DEBIT	CREDIT	DEBIT	CREDIT	DEBIT	CREDIT
1 Cash	8590 00						8590 00	
2 Accounts Receivable	6880 00						6880 00	
3 Merchandise Inventory	19700 00		(b) 22150 00	(a) 19700 00			22150 00	
4 Store Supplies	970 00			(c) 420 00			550 00	
5 Office Supplies	480 00			(d) 200 00			280 00	
6 Prepaid Insurance	1560 00			(e) 910 00			650 00	
7 Store Equipment	10200 00						10200 00	
8 Accumulated Depreciation - Store Equipment		4600 00		(f) 1100 00				5700 00
9 Office Equipment	5570 00						5570 00	
10 Accumulated Depreciation - Office Equipment		2230 00		(g) 490 00				2720 00
11 Building	41000 00						41000 00	
12 Accumulated Depreciation - Building		9400 00		(h) 1500 00				10900 00
13 Land	3000 00						3000 00	
14 Accounts Payable		7420 00						7420 00
15 Salaries Payable				(i) 296 00				296 00
16 Mortgage Note Payable		9000 00						9000 00
17 T. J. Preston, Capital		48256 00						48256 00
18 T. J. Preston, Drawing	12000 00						12000 00	
19 Expense and Revenue Summary			(a) 19700 00	(b) 22150 00	19700 00	22150 00		
20 Sales		162736 00				162736 00		
21 Sales Returns and Allowances	2140 00				2140 00			
22 Sales Discount	1822 00				1822 00			

	Trial Balance Dr	Trial Balance Cr	Adjustments Dr	Adjustments Cr	Income Statement Dr	Income Statement Cr	Balance Sheet Dr	Balance Sheet Cr
23 Purchases	105280 00				105280 00			
24 Purchases Discount		1525 00				1525 00		
25 Sales Salaries	15820 00		(i) 224 00		16044 00			
26 Advertising Expense	3460 00				3460 00			
27 Depreciation Expense - Store Equipment			(f) 1100 00		1100 00			
28 Insurance Expense - Selling			(e) 580 00		580 00			
29 Store Supplies Expense			(c) 420 00		420 00			
30 Miscellaneous Selling Expense	230 00				230 00			
31 Office Salaries	4960 00		(i) 72 00		5032 00			
32 Taxes Expense	1810 00				1810 00			
33 Depreciation Expense - Building			(h) 1500 00		1500 00			
34 Depreciation Expense - Office Equipment			(g) 490 00		490 00			
35 Insurance Expense - General			(e) 330 00		330 00			
36 Office Supplies Expense			(d) 200 00		200 00			
37 Miscellaneous General Expense	310 00				310 00			
38 Rent Income		1200 00				1200 00		
39 Interest Expense	585 00				585 00			
40	246367 00	246367 00	4766 00	4766 00	161033 00	187611 00	110870 00	84292 00
41 Net Income					26578 00			26578 00
42					187611 00	187611 00	110870 00	110870 00

Work sheet

sold. These objectives are accomplished by debiting Merchandise Inventory and crediting Expense and Revenue Summary. (Entry (b) on the work sheet.)

Supplies. The $970 balance of the store supplies account in the trial balance is the aggregate cost of supplies on hand at the beginning of the year plus store supplies purchased during the year. The physical inventory at the end of the year indicates store supplies on hand totaling $550. The excess of $970 over the inventory of $550 is $420, which is the cost of the store supplies consumed during the period. The accounts are adjusted by debiting Store Supplies Expense and crediting Store Supplies for $420. (Entry (c) on the work sheet.) The adjustment for office supplies consumed is determined in the same manner. (Entry (d) on the work sheet.)

Prepaid insurance. The adjustment for insurance expired is similar to the adjustment for supplies consumed. The balance in Prepaid Insurance is the amount prepaid at the beginning of the year plus the additional premium costs incurred during the year. Analysis of the various insurance policies reveals that a total of $910 in premiums has expired, of which $580 is applicable to merchandise and store equipment and $330 is applicable to office equipment and building. Insurance Expense — Selling is debited for $580, Insurance Expense — General is debited for $330, and Prepaid Insurance is credited for $910. (Entry (e) on the work sheet.)

Depreciation of plant assets. The expired cost of a plant asset is debited to a depreciation expense account and credited to an accumulated depreciation account. A separate account for the expense and for the accumulation is maintained for each plant asset account. Thus, the adjustment for $1,100 depreciation of the store equipment is recorded by a debit to Depreciation Expense — Store Equipment and a credit to Accumulated Depreciation — Store Equipment for $1,100. The adjustments for depreciation of the office equipment and for depreciation of the building are recorded in a similar manner. (Entries (f), (g), and (h) on the work sheet.)

Salaries payable. The liability for the salaries earned by employees but not yet paid is recorded by a credit of $296 to Salaries Payable and debits to Sales Salaries and Office Salaries of $224 and $72 respectively. (Entry (i) on the work sheet.)

Completing the work sheet

After all necessary adjustments are entered on the work sheet, the two Adjustments columns are totaled to prove the equality of debits and credits.

The process of extending the balances to the statement columns is accomplished most expeditiously by beginning with Cash at the top of the work sheet and proceeding down the sheet, item by item, in sequential order. An exception to the usual practice of extending only the account balances should be noted. Both the debit and credit amounts for Expense and Revenue Summary are extended to the Income Statement columns. Inasmuch as both the amount of the debit adjustment (beginning inventory of $19,700) and the amount of the credit adjustment (ending inventory of $22,150) are needed in preparing the income statement, no purpose would be served by determining and extending only the single balancing amount ($22,150 − $19,700).[1]

After all of the items have been extended into the statement sections of the work sheet, the four columns are totaled and the net income or net loss is determined. In the illustration the difference between the credit and the debit columns of the Income Statement section is $26,578, the amount of the net income. The difference between the debit and the credit columns of the Balance Sheet section is also $26,578, which is the increase in capital resulting from net income. Agreement between the two balancing amounts is evidence of debit-credit equality and arithmetical accuracy.

Preparation of statements and supporting schedules

The income statement, the capital statement, and the balance sheet are prepared from the account titles and the data in the statement sections of the work sheet. For the capital statement it is also necessary to refer to the capital account in the general ledger to determine whether the amount listed in the trial balance is in fact the balance at the beginning of the year. If the account had been credited for additional investments by the owner, or debited for reductions in investment, such details appearing in the account should be summarized in the capital statement.

Formal schedules of accounts receivable and accounts payable are sometimes prepared from the respective subsidiary ledgers. They may be useful to management in reviewing customer accounts for credit purposes and in preparing statements for credit-rating agencies.

Income statement

The accompanying income statement for Preston Electrical Supplies, a merchandising business, is somewhat more complex than the income statements illustrated in earlier chapters. Because of its numerous subsections and intermediate summary figures, it is sometimes called the *multiple-step* form. The *single-step* form, in which the total of all expired

---

[1]An alternative method of recording merchandise inventories on the work sheet is presented in Appendix A.

Revenue from sales:			
Sales		$162,736	
Less: Sales returns and allowances.	$ 2,140		
Sales discount.	1,822	3,962	
Net sales			$158,774
Cost of merchandise sold:			
Merchandise inventory, January 1, 1969.		$ 19,700	
Purchases	$105,280		
Less purchases discount	1,525		
Net purchases		103,755	
Merchandise available for sale.		$123,455	
Less merchandise inventory, Dec. 31, 1969		22,150	
Cost of merchandise sold.			101,305
Gross profit on sales			$ 57,469
Operating expenses:			
Selling expenses:			
Sales salaries.	$ 16,044		
Advertising expense	3,460		
Depreciation expense--store equipment.	1,100		
Insurance expense--selling.	580		
Store supplies expense.	420		
Miscellaneous selling expense	230		
Total selling expenses.		$ 21,834	
General expenses:			
Office salaries	$ 5,032		
Taxes expense	1,810		
Depreciation expense--building.	1,500		
Depreciation expense--office equipment.	490		
Insurance expense--general.	330		
Office supplies expense	200		
Miscellaneous general expense	310		
Total general expenses.		9,672	
Total operating expenses.			31,506
Net income from operations.			$ 25,963
Other income:			
Rent income		$ 1,200	
Other expense:			
Interest expense.		585	615
Net income.			$ 26,578

Income statement

costs is deducted as a single figure from the total of all revenues, is illustrated in a later chapter.

In practice, there is considerable variation in the amount of detail presented in income statements. For example, instead of reporting separately gross sales and the related returns, allowances, and discounts, the statement may begin with net sales. Similarly, the supporting data for the determination of the cost of merchandise sold may be omitted from the statement. The various sections of a conventional multiple-step income statement for a mercantile enterprise are discussed briefly in the paragraphs that follow.

Revenue from sales. The total of all charges to customers for merchandise sold, both for cash and on account, is reported in this section. Sales returns and allowances and sales discounts are deducted from the gross amount to yield net sales.

Cost of merchandise sold. The determination of this important figure was explained and illustrated earlier in the chapter. Other descriptive terms frequently employed are *cost of goods sold* and *cost of sales*.

Gross profit on sales. The excess of the net revenue from sales over the cost of merchandise sold is called *gross profit on sales* or *gross margin*. It is termed *gross* because all other expenses for the period must be deducted from it to obtain the *net* profit or *net* income of the business.

Operating expenses. The operating expenses of a business may be classified under any desired number of headings and subheadings. In a small retail business of the kind that has been used for illustrative purposes, it is usually satisfactory to classify operating expenses as either *selling* or *general*.

Expenses that are incurred directly and entirely in connection with the sale of merchandise are known as *selling expenses*. They include such expenses as salaries of the sales force, store supplies used, depreciation of store equipment, and advertising.

Expenses incurred in the general operations of the business are known as *general expenses* or *administrative expenses*. Examples of these expenses are office salaries, depreciation of office equipment, and office supplies used. Expenses that are partly connected with selling and partly connected with the general operations of the business may be divided between the two categories. In a small business, however, mixed expenses such as rent, insurance, and taxes are commonly reported as general expenses.

Expenses of relatively small amount that cannot be identified with the principal accounts are usually accumulated in accounts entitled Miscellaneous Selling Expense and Miscellaneous General Expense respectively.

Net income from operations. The excess of gross profit on sales over total operating expenses is called *net income from operations*. The amount of the net operating income and its relationship to capital investment and to net sales are important factors in judging the efficiency of management and the degree of profitability of an enterprise. If operating expenses should exceed gross profit, the excess is designated *net loss from operations*.

Other income. Minor sources of revenue are classified as *other income*, or *nonoperating income*. In a merchandising business this category often

Preston Electrical Supplies
Balance Sheet
December 31, 1969

Assets

Current assets:
Cash	$ 8,590	
Accounts receivable.	6,880	
Merchandise inventory.	22,150	
Store supplies	550	
Office supplies.	280	
Prepaid insurance.	650	
Total current assets		$39,100

Plant assets:
Store equipment.	$10,200		
Less accumulated depreciation.	5,700	$ 4,500	
Office equipment	$ 5,570		
Less accumulated depreciation.	2,720	2,850	
Building	$41,000		
Less accumulated depreciation.	10,900	30,100	
Land		3,000	
Total plant assets			40,450

Total assets $79,550

Liabilities

Current liabilities:
Accounts payable	$ 7,420	
Mortgage note payable (current portion). .	1,500	
Salaries payable	296	
Total current liabilities.		$ 9,216

148

Long-term liabilities:
Mortgage note payable (last payment, 1975)	7,500

Total liabilities. $16,716

Capital

T. J. Preston, capital   62,834

Total liabilities and capital. $79,550

Balance sheet

Preston Electrical Supplies
Schedule of Accounts Receivable
December 31, 1969

Adler Company	$ 320
R. A. Barnes, Inc.	1,280
Cooper & Co.	516
Fogarty & Jacobs.	402
R. E. Hamilton, Inc.	1,310
David T. Mattox	745
Standard Supply Co.	97
Tracy & Lee, Inc.	1,883
B. C. Wallace Corporation	327
Total accounts receivable	$6,880

Schedule of accounts receivable

Arnold Electronics Supply	$2,316
Dunlap Electric Corporation	1,193
Marsh Electronics, Inc.	975
Office Equipment Distributors	210
Parker Supply Co.	55
Tri-State Distributors.	2,114
Walton Manufacturing Co.	557
Total accounts payable.	$7,420

Schedule of accounts payable

includes income from interest, rent, dividends, and gains resulting from the sale of plant assets.

Other expense. Expenses that cannot be associated definitely with operations are identified as *other expense*, or *nonoperating expense*. Interest expense that results from financing activities and losses incurred in the disposal of plant assets are examples of items reported in this section.

The two categories of nonoperating items are offset against each other on the income statement. If the total of other income exceeds the total of other expense, the excess is added to net income from operations; if the reverse is true, the difference is subtracted from net income from operations.

Net income. The final figure on the income statement of an unincorporated enterprise is labeled *net income* (or *net loss*). It is the net increase in capital resulting from profit-making activities.

Balance sheet and capital statement

The form of the balance sheet for a merchandising business is basically the same as that for a service enterprise illustrated in an earlier chapter. There may be a larger number of both assets and liabilities to report, as in the accompanying balance sheet for Preston Electrical Supplies. The manner in which the mortgage note payable is reported should be noted. The $9,000 balance of this account in the ledger is divided between the $1,500 installment due within a year, which is classified as a current liability, and the remaining $7,500, which is classified as a long-term liability.

The form of the capital statement is not affected by the nature of the business operations. The statement summarizes the changes in the owner's capital during the fiscal period and serves as a connecting link between the income statement and the balance sheet. The net income of $26,578, reported on the accompanying income statement, is also reported on the capital statement where it is combined with the withdrawals to yield a capital increase of $14,578. This sum is then added to

149

the capital balance at the beginning of the year to yield a capital balance of $62,834 at the end of the year, which is the amount reported as capital on the balance sheet.

Preston Electrical Supplies
Capital Statement
For Year Ended December 31, 1969

Capital, January 1, 1969		$48,256
Net income for the year.	$26,578	
Less withdrawals	12,000	
Increase in capital.		14,578
Capital, December 31, 1969		$62,834

Capital statement

JOURNAL   PAGE 28

	DATE		DESCRIPTION	POST. REF.	DEBIT	CREDIT	
1			Adjusting Entries				1
2	1969 Dec.	31	Expense and Revenue Summary	313	19 7 0 0 00		2
3			Merchandise Inventory	114		19 7 0 0 00	3
4							4
5		31	Merchandise Inventory	114	22 1 5 0 00		5
6			Expense and Revenue Summary	313		22 1 5 0 00	6
7							7
8		31	Store Supplies Expense	615	4 2 0 00		8
9			Store Supplies	115		4 2 0 00	9
10							10
11		31	Office Supplies Expense	716	2 0 0 00		11
12			Office Supplies	116		2 0 0 00	12
13							13
14		31	Insurance Expense - Selling	614	5 8 0 00		14
15			Insurance Expense - General	715	3 3 0 00		15
16			Prepaid Insurance	117		9 1 0 00	16
17							17
18		31	Depreciation Expense - Store Equipment	613	1 1 0 0 00		18
19			Accumulated Depreciation - Store Equip.	122		1 1 0 0 00	19
20							20
21		31	Depreciation Expense - Office Equipment	714	4 9 0 00		21
22			Accumulated Depreciation - Office Equip.	124		4 9 0 00	22
23							23
24		31	Depreciation Expense - Building	713	1 5 0 0 00		24
25			Accumulated Depreciation - Building	126		1 5 0 0 00	25
26							26
27		31	Sales Salaries	611	2 2 4 00		27
28			Office Salaries	711	7 2 00		28
29			Salaries Payable	213		2 9 6 00	29

Adjusting entries

Adjusting entries

The analyses required to formulate the adjustments were completed during the process of preparing the work sheet. It is therefore unnecessary to refer again to the basic data when recording the adjusting entries in the general journal. After the entries are posted, the balances of all asset, liability, revenue, and expense accounts correspond exactly to the amounts reported in the financial statements. The adjusting entries for Preston Electrical Supplies are presented on the preceding page.

Closing entries

The closing entries are recorded in the general journal immediately following the adjusting entries. All of the temporary capital accounts are cleared of their balances, reducing them to zero. The final effect of closing out such balances is a net increase or a net decrease in the capital account. The closing entries for Preston Electrical Supplies follow:

JOURNAL

PAGE 29

	DATE		DESCRIPTION	POST. REF.	DEBIT	CREDIT	
1	1969		Closing Entries				1
2	Dec.	31	Sales	411	162 7 3 6 00		2
3			Purchases Discount	512	1 5 2 5 00		3
4			Rent Income	812	1 2 0 0 00		4
5			Expense and Revenue Summary	313		165 4 6 1 00	5
6							6
7		31	Expense and Revenue Summary	313	141 3 3 3 00		7
8			Sales Returns and Allowances	412		2 1 4 0 00	8
9			Sales Discount	413		1 8 2 2 00	9
10			Purchases	511		105 2 8 0 00	10
11			Sales Salaries	611		16 0 4 4 00	11
12			Advertising Expense	612		3 4 6 0 00	12
13			Depreciation Expense - Store Equipment	613		1 1 0 0 00	13
14			Insurance Expense - Selling	614		5 8 0 00	14
15			Store Supplies Expense	615		4 2 0 00	15
16			Miscellaneous Selling Expense	619		2 3 0 00	16
17			Office Salaries	711		5 0 3 2 00	17
18			Taxes Expense	712		1 8 1 0 00	18
19			Depreciation Expense - Building	713		1 5 0 0 00	19
20			Depreciation Expense - Office Equip.	714		4 9 0 00	20
21			Insurance Expense - General	715		3 3 0 00	21
22			Office Supplies Expense	716		2 0 0 00	22
23			Miscellaneous General Expense	719		3 1 0 00	23
24			Interest Expense	911		5 8 5 00	24
25							25
26		31	Expense and Revenue Summary	313	26 5 7 8 00		26
27			T. J. Preston, Capital	311		26 5 7 8 00	27
28							28
29		31	T. J. Preston, Capital	311	12 0 0 0 00		29
30			T. J. Preston, Drawing	312		12 0 0 0 00	30

Closing entries

151

The effect of each of the four closing entries journalized on the preceding page may be described as follows:

1. The first entry closes all income statement accounts with *credit* balances by transferring the total to the *credit* side of Expense and Revenue Summary.
2. The second entry closes all income statement accounts with *debit* balances by transferring the total to the *debit* side of Expense and Revenue Summary.
3. The third entry closes Expense and Revenue Summary by transferring its balance to T. J. Preston, Capital.
4. The fourth entry closes T. J. Preston, Drawing by transferring its balance to T. J. Preston, Capital.

The expense and revenue summary account, as it will appear after the merchandise inventory adjustments and the closing entries have been posted, is presented below. Each item in the account is identified as an aid to understanding; such notations are not an essential part of the posting procedure.

Expense and Revenue Summary   ACCOUNT NO.   313

DATE	ITEM	POST. REF.	DEBIT	CREDIT	BALANCE DEBIT	BALANCE CREDIT
1969 Dec. 31	Mer. inv., Jan. 1	J28	19 7 0 0 00		19 7 0 0 00	
31	Mer. inv., Dec. 31	J28		22 1 5 0 00		2 4 5 0 00
31	Revenue, etc.	J29		165 4 6 1 00		167 9 1 1 00
31	Expense, etc.	J29	141 3 3 3 00			26 5 7 8 00
31	Net income	J29	26 5 7 8 00			

Expense and revenue summary account

After the closing of all temporary capital accounts, only the accounts for assets, contra assets, liabilities, and owner's capital remain with balances. The balances of these accounts in the ledger will correspond exactly with the amounts appearing on the balance sheet presented on page 148.

Post-closing trial balance

As indicated at the beginning of this chapter, the first step in the year-end summarizing procedures is the taking of a trial balance of the general ledger. After the adjusting and closing entries have been recorded, it is advisable to take another trial balance to verify the debit-credit equality of the ledger at the beginning of the following year. This post-closing trial balance may be composed of two adding machine listings, one for the debit balances and the other for the credit balances, or its details may be set forth in a more formal fashion, as the trial balance reproduced at the top of the next page.

Cash	8	5	9	0	00						
Accounts Receivable	6	8	8	0	00						
Merchandise Inventory	22	1	5	0	00						
Store Supplies		5	5	0	00						
Office Supplies		2	8	0	00						
Prepaid Insurance		6	5	0	00						
Store Equipment	10	2	0	0	00						
Accumulated Depreciation - Store Equipment						5	7	0	0	00	
Office Equipment	5	5	7	0	00						
Accumulated Depreciation - Office Equipment						2	7	2	0	00	
Building	41	0	0	0	00						
Accumulated Depreciation - Building						10	9	0	0	00	
Land	3	0	0	0	00						
Accounts Payable						7	4	2	0	00	
Salaries Payable							2	9	6	00	
Mortgage Note Payable						9	0	0	0	00	
T. J. Preston, Capital						62	8	3	4	00	
	98	8	7	0	00	98	8	7	0	00	

Post-closing trial balance

Reversing entries

153

Some of the adjusting entries recorded at the close of a fiscal year have a significant effect on otherwise routine transactions that occur in the following year. A typical example is the adjusting entry for accrued salaries owed to employees at the end of the year. The wage or salary expense of an enterprise and the accompanying liability to employees actually accumulates or accrues day by day, or even hour by hour, during any part of the fiscal year. Nevertheless, the customary practice of recording the expense only at the time of payment is more efficient. When salaries are paid weekly, an entry debiting Salary Expense and crediting Cash will be recorded 52 or 53 times during the year. If there has been an adjusting entry for accrued salaries at the end of the year, however, the first payment of salaries in the following year will include such year-end accrual. In the absence of some special provision, it would be necessary to debit Salaries Payable for the amount owed for the earlier year and Salary Expense for the portion of the payroll that represents expense for the later year.

In order to illustrate the situation, assume the following four facts for an enterprise that pays salaries weekly and ends its fiscal year on December 31:

1. Salaries are paid on Friday for the five-day week ending on Friday.
2. The balance in Salary Expense as of Friday, December 27, is $62,500.

3. Salaries accrued for Monday and Tuesday, December 30 and 31, total $500.
4. Salaries paid on Friday, January 3, of the following year total $1,200.

The foregoing data may be presented in diagrammatic form as follows:

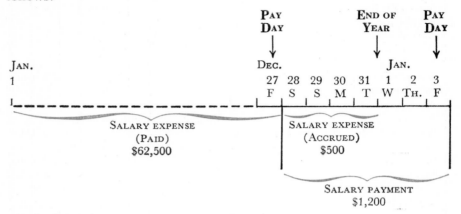

The adjusting entry to record the accrued salary expense and salaries payable for Monday and Tuesday, December 30 and 31, is as follows:

| Dec. | 31 | Salary Expense...................... | 611 | 500 | |
| | | Salaries Payable.................. | 213 | | 500 |

After the adjusting entry has been posted, Salary Expense will have a debit balance of $63,000 ($62,500 + $500) and Salaries Payable will have a credit balance of $500. After the closing process is completed, the account Salary Expense is in balance and ready for entries of the following year, but Salaries Payable continues to have a credit balance of $500. As matters now stand it would be necessary to record the $1,200 payroll on January 3 as a debit of $500 to Salaries Payable and a debit of $700 to Salary Expense. This means that the employee who records payroll entries must not only record this particular payroll in a different manner from all other weekly payrolls for the year, but that he must also refer back to the adjusting entries in the journal or the ledger to determine the amount of the $1,200 payment to be debited to each of the two accounts.

The need to refer to earlier entries and to divide the debit between two accounts can be avoided by recording a *reversing* entry as of the first day of the following fiscal period. As the term implies, such an entry is the exact reverse of the adjusting entry to which it relates. The amounts are the same and the accounts debited and credited are the same; they are merely reversed. Continuing with the illustration, the reversing entry for the accrued salaries is as follows:

Jan.	1	Salaries Payable....................	213	500			
		Salary Expense....................	611			500	

The effect of the reversing entry is to transfer the $500 liability from Salaries Payable to the credit side of Salary Expense. The real nature of the $500 balance is unchanged; it remains a liability. When the payroll is paid on January 3, Salary Expense will be debited and Cash will be credited for $1,200, the entire amount of the weekly salaries. After the entry is posted, Salary Expense will have a debit balance of $700, which is the amount of expense incurred in January. The sequence of entries, including adjusting, closing, and reversing entries, may be traced in the accounts reproduced below.

SALARY EXPENSE   ACCOUNT No. 611

DATE		ITEM	POST. REF.	DEBIT	CREDIT	BALANCE DEBIT	BALANCE CREDIT
1969 Jan.	5		CP36	1,240		1,240	
Dec.	6		CP80	1,300		58,440	
	13		CP81	1,450		59,890	
	20		CP83	1,260		61,150	
	27		CP84	1,350		62,500	
	31	Adjusting	J8	500		63,000	
	31	Closing	J9		63,000	—	—
1970 Jan.	1	Reversing	J9		500		500
	3		CP85	1,200		700	

155

SALARIES PAYABLE   ACCOUNT No. 213

DATE		ITEM	POST. REF.	DEBIT	CREDIT	BALANCE DEBIT	BALANCE CREDIT
1969 Dec.	31	Adjusting	J8		500		500
1970 Jan.	1	Reversing	J9	500		—	—

The adjusting entry for salaries recorded on the books of Preston Electrical Supplies is reversed as of January 1 so that at the time of payment the entire amount may be charged to the appropriate expense account. The reversing entry is illustrated on the next page.

After the reversing entry has been posted, the account Salaries Payable will be in balance. The liability for salaries will now appear as a credit in the salary expense account. As salaries are paid in the new period, the entire amount will be debited to the salary expense account. The balance of the salary expense account will then automatically represent the expense of the new period.

	DATE	DESCRIPTION	POST. REF.	DEBIT	CREDIT	
32		Reversing Entry				32
33	1970 Jan. 1	Salaries Payable	213	2 9 6 00		33
34		Sales Salaries	611		2 2 4 00	34
35		Office Salaries	711		7 2 00	35
36						36

Reversing entry

Prior period corrections

Various techniques employed to correct errors in journal and ledger entries were described in Chapter 3, the discussion being limited to corrections in the same fiscal period in which the errors had occurred. In such situations the financial statements for the period are not affected by the error; the data reported are the same as though the error had not occurred.

When an error in the determination of net income is not discovered until after the statements for the period have been issued, the resolution of the problem is less simple. The misstatement could be rectified by correcting the balance of the capital account and presenting it on the capital statement for the following period. Another possibility is to make the correction in the same manner as though the error had occurred in the current period. To illustrate, assume that an arithmetical error in computing depreciation at the end of a fiscal year resulted in an understatement of $10,000 in depreciation expense for the year, and that the error was not discovered until financial statements had been issued. If the correction were to be made through the capital account, a reduction of $10,000 in the opening balance would be shown on the capital statement of the following year. Alternatively, the correction could be made by increasing the depreciation expense for the following year by $10,000, the amount of the earlier understatement.

Although at one time opinion was divided as to which of the foregoing alternatives was superior in terms of fairness and usefulness, the second of the alternatives is now recognized as being preferable in most circumstances.[2] Thus the generally accepted practice is to report all items of revenue or expense on the income statement for the period in which the revenue or expense is *recognized*, regardless of whether the events occurred in an earlier period. Adherence to this principle assures that the aggregate of the periodic amounts of net income reported over the entire life of an enterprise will constitute the total net income of the enterprise.

156

---

[2] *Opinions of the Accounting Principles Board*, *No. 9*, "Reporting the Results of Operations" (New York: American Institute of Certified Public Accountants, December, 1966).

Under certain unusual circumstances, a prior period adjustment of major significance may properly be reported as a correction to the capital account.[3] The subject will be discussed in greater detail later in relationship to corporate enterprises. Meanwhile, all corrections of net income of prior periods will be assumed to be of the type that should be treated as if they were current transactions or adjustments to income of the current period.

QUESTIONS

1. Does the fact that the trial balance is in balance at the end of the year prove that all transactions for the year have been recorded correctly? Discuss.

2. In the following equations identify the items designated by X:

(a) Purchases $-$ X $=$ Net purchases.
(b) Merchandise inventory (beginning) $+$ X $=$ Merchandise available for sale.
(c) Merchandise available for sale $-$ X $=$ Cost of merchandise sold.
(d) Sales $-$ (X $+$ X) $=$ Net sales.
(e) Net sales $-$ cost of merchandise sold $=$ X.

3. The account Merchandise Inventory is listed at $40,000 on the trial balance (before adjustments) as of June 30, the end of the current fiscal year. Which of the following phrases describes the item correctly?

(a) Inventory of merchandise at June 30, end of the current fiscal year.
(b) Purchases of merchandise during the current fiscal year.
(c) Merchandise available for sale during the current fiscal year.
(d) Inventory of merchandise at July 1, beginning of the current fiscal year.
(e) Cost of merchandise sold during the current fiscal year.

4. What accounts, if any, should be debited and credited for the $40,000 in question 3, as a part of the adjusting process?

5. In adjusting for the ending merchandise inventory, what is the effect of (a) the debit portion of the entry, (b) the credit portion of the entry?

6. The merchandise inventory at the beginning of the fiscal year was $30,000, and at the end of the year it was $20,000. Net purchases for the year were $250,000 and net sales were $350,000. Determine the following amounts:

(a) Merchandise available for sale.
(b) Cost of merchandise sold.
(c) Gross profit on sales.
(d) Merchandise inventory listed on the balance sheet as of the end of the year.

7. The amounts extended into the Income Statement columns of a work sheet for Expense and Revenue Summary are $15,000 debit and $10,000 credit. (a) Which of the two amounts represents the inventory at the beginning of the period? (b) Would the amount determined to be net income be affected by extending only the net amount of $5,000 ($15,000 debit $-$ $10,000 credit) into the Income Statement debit column?

---

[3] *Ibid.*

8. Salary Expense before adjustment at September 30, the end of the fiscal year, has a balance of $150,000. The amount accrued on September 30 is $2,100. Give the required (a) adjusting entry, (b) closing entry, and (c) reversing entry.

9. At the end of the current fiscal year there is a balance of $32,000 in Mortgage Note Payable. Terms of the note require monthly payments of $1,000. How should the liability be reported on the balance sheet at this time?

10. The expenses described below were incurred by a merchandising enterprise during the year. In which of the following expense sections of the income statement should each be reported: (a) selling, (b) general, (c) other?

    (1) Depreciation of office equipment.
    (2) Gasoline and oil used in delivery truck.
    (3) Advertising materials.
    (4) Fire insurance premiums on store equipment.
    (5) Interest on notes payable.
    (6) Salary of the general manager.
    (7) Salary of the salesmen.
    (8) Heating and lighting expense.

11. On what two financial statements are each of the following items reported: (a) net income for the period and (b) capital balance at the end of the period?

12. What is the effect of closing the temporary accounts at the end of the fiscal period?

13. Immediately after the year-end entries have been recorded, the account Salary Expense has a credit balance of $1,380. Assuming that there have been no errors, does the balance represent an asset, expense, revenue, liability, contra asset, or contra revenue?

14. On August 1, the first day of the fiscal year, Office Salary Expense has a credit balance of $700. On August 4, the first payday in the year, office salaries of $1,900 are paid. (a) Is the office salary expense thus far in the new fiscal year $700, $1,200, $1,900, or $2,600? (b) What entry should be made to record the payment on August 4?

15. What purpose is served by the use of reversing entries?

16. After the closing entries have been recorded in the ledger, it is discovered that an expenditure of $100 for building repairs has been erroneously debited to Utilities Expense. (a) Should an entry be made to correct this error or would presentation of the correct amounts of the two expense items in the income statement be sufficient? (b) If the income statement had been issued before the error was discovered, should a correcting entry be made for the prior period error? Discuss.

17. At the close of fiscal year A, accrued taxes of $1,100 were overlooked and no adjusting entry was made. Early in the following year, fiscal year B, payment of the tax bill of $1,200, which included the accrual, was recorded by a $1,200 debit to Taxes Expense and a credit of the same amount to Cash. What was the effect of the error, in terms of (a) amount and (b) under-or-over-statement in each of the following, assuming that no corrections were made:

    (1) Net income for fiscal year A.
    (2) Net income for fiscal year B.
    (3) Total assets, total liabilities, or capital at end of fiscal year A.
    (4) Total assets, total liabilities, or capital at end of fiscal year B.

18. Early in the fiscal year, after the accounts are closed and statements issued for the preceding year, it is discovered that a purchase invoice for merchandise, in the amount of $700, had never been recorded. The invoice is now being paid. What entry should be made to record the payment?

EXERCISES

6-1. On the basis of the following data, journalize the necessary adjusting entries at March 31, the close of the current fiscal year.

(a) Merchandise inventory: April 1, $22,500; March 31, $24,700.
(b) Office supplies physical inventory, March 31, $70; office supplies account balance before adjustment, $200.
(c) The prepaid insurance account before adjustments on March 31 has a balance of $1,450. An analysis of the policies indicates that $520 has expired during the year.
(d) Sales salaries are uniformly $2,000 for a five-day work week, ending on Friday. The last payday of the year was Friday, March 26.

6-2. At the beginning of the year the merchandise inventory was $32,000; during the year net purchases of merchandise amounted to $165,000; the inventory of merchandise at the end of the year is $35,500. Determine the following:

(a) Merchandise available for sale.
(b) Cost of merchandise sold.

6-3. Selected account titles and related amounts appearing in the Income Statement and Balance Sheet columns of the work sheet of the L. J. Reid Co. for December 31 are listed in alphabetical order below.

159

Accum. Depreciation —		L. J. Reid, Capital........	$ 65,400
Building..............	$ 17,700	L. J. Reid, Drawing......	18,000
General Expenses (total)...	25,500	Rent Income............	1,500
Merchandise Inv. (1/1)....	50,000	Salaries Payable.........	850
Merchandise Inv. (12/31)..	53,300	Sales..................	300,000
Prepaid Insurance........	1,100	Sales Discount...........	1,900
Purchases...............	198,000	Sales Returns and Allow....	2,200
Purchases Discount........	1,600	Selling Expenses (total)....	49,600

(a) Prepare an income statement for the year.
(b) Determine the amount of capital to be reported in the balance sheet at the end of the year.
(c) Journalize the entries to adjust the merchandise inventory.
(d) Journalize the closing entries. Controlling accounts are maintained in the general ledger for selling expenses and general expenses.

6-4. Two or more items are omitted in each of the following tabulations of income statement data. Determine the amounts of the missing items, identifying them by letter.

Sales	Sales Returns	Net Sales	Beginning Inventory	Net Purchases	Ending Inventory	Cost of Merchandise Sold	Gross Profit on Sales
$50,000	$2,000	(a)	$12,000	$42,000	(b)	$35,000	(c)
42,000	(d)	$41,000	8,000	24,000	$ 6,000	(e)	(f)
82,000	(g)	82,000	(h)	64,000	12,000	(i)	$14,000
71,000	3,000	68,000	20,000	51,000	(j)	(k)	11,000

6-5. Portions of the salary expense account of an enterprise are presented below.
(a) Describe the nature of the transaction or adjusting, closing, or reversing

entry that resulted in each of the postings identified by number. (b) Present in general journal form the complete entry from which each of the items identified by number was posted.

SALARY EXPENSE

19—					19—				
Jan.	6		CP15	1,600	Dec.	31	(3)	J11	84,300

	27	(1)	CP35	1,900					
	31	(2)	J10	800					
				84,300					84,300
19—					19—				
Jan.	3	(5)	CP36	1,700	Jan.	1	(4)	J11	800

6-6. Present in general journal form the entries required in the current fiscal year to record the following transactions, corrections, and adjustments for A. J. Cooper & Associates:

(a) Discovered that an expenditure of $5,000 made late in the current year for new store equipment had been erroneously debited to Equipment Repairs.

(b) Discovered that $200 received on account from M. L. Benton near the close of the preceding year had been credited erroneously to Benton Corp.

(c) Received and paid a $620 invoice for an additional property tax assessment applicable to the preceding year. There had been no indication of such action at the close of the preceding year, hence there had been no recognition in the accounts of the liability for the deficiency.

(d) At the close of the current year the balance in Office Supplies before adjustment is $510; the year-end inventory is $110. No entry had been made at the close of the preceding year to adjust the account, at which time its balance had been $230.

PROBLEMS

The following additional problems for this chapter are located in Appendix C: 6-1B, 6-2B, 6-3B.

6-1A. The accounts in the ledger of the Newman Company, with the balances on June 30, the end of the current fiscal year, are as follows:

Cash.....................	$ 3,900	Sales....................	$160,000
Accounts Receivable......	10,400	Purchases................	97,000
Merchandise Inventory....	38,600	Sales Salaries...........	18,000
Store Supplies...........	590	Advertising Expense......	2,110
Prepaid Insurance........	2,170	Depreciation Expense —	
Store Equipment.........	19,100	Store Equipment.......	——
Accum. Depreciation —		Delivery Expense.........	1,400
Store Equipment.......	1,600	Store Supplies Expense....	——
Accounts Payable.........	5,700	Rent Expense............	7,500
Salaries Payable..........	——	Insurance Expense.......	——
Henry Newman, Capital...	50,470	Misc. General Expense....	1,850
Henry Newman, Drawing..	15,000	Loss on Disposal of Equip...	150
Expense and Revenue Sum.	——		

The data needed for year-end adjustments on June 30 are as follows:

Merchandise inventory on June 30.....	$32,500
Store supplies inventory on June 30....	240
Insurance expired during the year......	650
Depreciation for the current year......	1,700
Accrued sales salaries on June 30......	200

Instructions:

(1) Prepare an eight-column work sheet for the fiscal year ended June 30, listing all of the accounts in the order given.
(2) Prepare an income statement.
(3) Prepare a capital statement. There were no additional investments during the year.
(4) Prepare a balance sheet.
(5) Compute the following:
   (a) Percent of the net income from operations to sales.
   (b) Percent of net income to the capital balance at the beginning of the year.

If the working papers correlating with this textbook are not used, omit Problem 6-2A.

6-2A. A. R. Hoyt owns and operates Hoyt Appliances. The general ledger balances at the beginning of the twelfth month and the journals for the twelfth month of the current fiscal year are presented in the working papers.

Instructions:

(1) Post the journals to the general ledger accounts, following the order indicated below. Balances need not be inserted in the balance columns of the accounts until all journals have been posted. Assume that entries to the subsidiary ledgers have been posted by an assistant.

POSTING ORDER

Individual items in Sundry Accounts columns:
   General Journal, Purchases Journal, Cash Receipts Journal, Cash Payments Journal.
Column totals:
   Sales Journal, Purchases Journal, Cash Receipts Journal, Cash Payments Journal.

(2) Take a trial balance at December 31 on an eight-column work sheet, listing all of the accounts in the ledger.
(3) Complete the work sheet. Adjustment data are:

Merchandise inventory at December 31.	$21,430.00
Supplies on hand at December 31......	136.50
Insurance expired during the year......	526.00
Depreciation for the current year on:	
Store equipment....................	1,100.00
Office equipment..................	192.00
Accrued taxes at December 31........	165.00

(4) Prepare an income statement, a capital statement, and a balance sheet. There were no additional investments of capital by the owner during the year.
(5) Journalize and post the adjusting entries.
(6) Journalize and post the closing entries.
   Indicate closed accounts by inserting a line in both balance columns,

as illustrated in the salary expense account on page 155.

(7) Prepare a post-closing trial balance.

(8) Journalize and post the reversing entry or entries as of January 1.

6-3A. A portion of the work sheet of Hansen & Co. for the current year ending September 30 is presented below.

Account Title	Income Statement		Balance Sheet	
	Debit	Credit	Debit	Credit
Cash................................			12,300	
Accounts Receivable...................			45,700	
Merchandise Inventory.................			54.000	
Supplies.............................			370	
Prepaid Rent.........................			1,800	
Prepaid Insurance.....................			1,640	
Store Equipment......................			18,900	
Accumulated Depr. — Store Equip........				5,700
Office Equipment.....................			4,200	
Accumulated Depr. — Office Equip.......				1,850
Accounts Payable.....................				31,600
Sales Salaries Payable..................				320
Mortgage Note Payable				13,000
Arthur G. Hansen, Capital.............				62,830
Arthur G. Hansen, Drawing............			12,000	
Expense and Revenue Summary.........	51,500	54,000		
Sales................................		310,000		
Sales Returns and Allowances...........	9,100			
Purchases............................	210,000			
Purchases Discount....................		2,300		
Sales Salaries........................	22,200			
Delivery Expense......................	10,800			
Supplies Expense......................	1,920			
Depreciation Expense — Store Equip......	1,200			
Miscellaneous Selling Expense..........	760			
Office Salaries........................	12,300			
Rent Expense........................	6,900			
Insurance Expense.....................	2,500			
Depreciation Expense — Office Equip.....	400			
Miscellaneous General Expense..........	1,310			
Interest Income.......................		200		
	330,890	366,500	150,910	115,300

Instructions:

(1) From the partial work sheet presented above, determine the entries that appeared in the adjustments columns and present them in general journal form. The only accounts affected by more than a single adjusting entry were Merchandise Inventory and Expense and Revenue Summary. The balance in Prepaid Rent before adjustment was $8,700, representing a prepayment for the first three months of the past year at $500 a month and for the next twelve months at $600 a month.

(2) Determine the following:
   (a) Amount of net income for the year.
   (b) Amount of the owner's capital at the end of the year.

6-4A. The accounts and their balances in the ledger of Gregory Specialty Co. on March 31 of the current year are as follows:

Cash.................	$ 11,200	Sales.................	$321,400
Accounts Receivable.....	32,500	Sales Ret. and Allow.....	2,100
Merchandise Inventory...	51,700	Purchases..............	232,600
Store Supplies..........	720	Purchases Discount	2,930
Office Supplies..........	390	Sales Salaries...........	25,600
Prepaid Insurance........	2,130	Rent Expense — Selling..	5,400
Store Equipment	18,400	Depreciation Expense —	
Accum. Depreciation —		Store Equipment......	——
Store Equipment......	5,200	Insurance Exp. — Selling.	——
Office Equipment........	6,300	Store Supplies Expense..	——
Accum. Depreciation —		Misc. Selling Expense....	960
Office Equipment......	1,400	Office Salaries..........	12,300
Accounts Payable........	29,700	Rent Expense — General.	1,200
Salaries Payable.........	——	Depreciation Expense —	
Mortgage Note Payable		Office Equipment......	
(due 1978)...........	12,000	Insurance Exp. — General	——
Ralph B. Gregory, Capital	47,210	Office Supplies Exp.......	——
Ralph B. Gregory,		Misc. General Expense....	1,440
Drawing.............	15,000	Gain on Disposal of	
Expense and Revenue		Plant Assets...........	700
Summary	——	Interest Expense........	600

The data for year-end adjustments on March 31 are as follows:

Merchandise inventory on March 31..	$49,300	
Inventory of supplies on March 31:		
Store supplies		310
Office supplies.................		160
Insurance expired during the year:		
Allocable as selling expense..	$870	
Allocable as general expense.	420	1,290
Depreciation for the year:		
Store equipment................		1,650
Office equipment...............		550
Salaries payable on March 31:		
Sales salaries..................		540
Office salaries.................		330

Instructions:
(1) Prepare a work sheet for the fiscal year ended March 31, listing all accounts in the order given.
(2) Prepare an income statement.
(3) Prepare a capital statement. There were no additional investments during the year.
(4) Prepare a balance sheet.
(5) Journalize the adjusting entries.
(6) Journalize the closing entries.
(7) Journalize the reversing entries as of April 1.

| Receivables, payables, and inventories

7

Receivables and payables

Use of credit in business

The extension of credit plays an important role in the operations of many business enterprises. Credit may be granted on open account or on the basis of a formal instrument of credit such as a *promissory note*. The use of the latter is customary for credit periods in excess of sixty days, as in sales of equipment on the installment plan, and for transactions of relatively large dollar amounts. Promissory notes may also be used in settlement of an open account and in borrowing or lending money.

From the point of view of the creditor, a claim evidenced by a note has some advantages over a claim in the form of an account receivable. By signing a note, the debtor acknowledges the debt and agrees to pay it in accordance with the terms specified. It is therefore a stronger legal claim in the event of court action. It is also more liquid than an open account because the holder may transfer it to one of his creditors in settlement of a debt or to a bank in exchange for cash.

When relatively large sums are borrowed for an appreciable period of time, the borrower may be required to furnish some type of security. The practice is also followed when payments for substantial purchases of land, buildings, or equipment are to be spread over a number of years. One of the most frequently employed types of security is a mortgage, which gives the creditor a lien, or claim, on property owned by the debtor. In the event that the debtor (mortgagor) defaults on his obligation, the creditor (mortgagee) may, under certain conditions, take possession of the property or force its sale to satisfy his claim. When a note secured by a mortgage is fully paid, the lien is canceled.

Increased assurance of the payment of individual notes or accounts may also be provided through the pledging of specific assets such as marketable securities, notes and accounts receivable, and inventories. Assets that are pledged may not be disposed of until the related debt has been paid or unless the proceeds from their disposition are used in settlement of the obligation.

Classification of receivables

The term *receivables* includes all money claims against individuals, organizations, or other debtors. They are acquired by a business enterprise in various types of transactions, the most common being the sale of merchandise or services on a credit basis. Accounts and notes receivable originating from sales transactions are sometimes referred to as *trade receivables.* In the absence of other descriptive words or phrases, accounts and notes receivable may be assumed to have originated from sales in the usual course of the business.

Other receivables of not infrequent occurrence include interest receivable, loans to officers or employees, and loans to affiliated companies. Separate accounts should be maintained in the general ledger for each type of receivable.

All receivables that are expected to be realized in cash within a year are presented in the current assets section of the balance sheet. Those that are not currently collectible, such as long-term loans, should be listed under the caption "Investments" below the current assets section.

The importance of accounts and notes receivable to specific enterprises varies with the volume of credit sales and the length of the credit period. For many businesses the revenue from sales of their products on a credit basis is the largest factor influencing the amount of net income. Claims against customers may also represent a substantial percentage of the total amount of their current assets.

Classification of payables

Payables are, of course, the opposite of receivables; they are debts owed by an enterprise to its creditors. Money claims against a firm may originate in numerous ways, such as purchases of merchandise or services on a credit basis, loans from banks, purchases of equipment, and purchases of marketable securities. At any particular moment of time a business may also owe its employees for wages or salaries accrued, banks or other creditors for interest accrued on notes, and governmental agencies for taxes.

Liabilities that are due and payable within a year are presented in the current liability section of the balance sheet. Those that are not payable until a more distant future date are listed as long-term liabilities. If a long-term liability, such as a mortgage note payable, is payable in periodic installments over its term, the portion due within one year should be listed as a current liability.

In addition to known liabilities of a definite or reasonably approximate amount, there may be potential obligations that will materialize only if certain events occur in the future. Such liabilities, which are termed *contingent* liabilities, should be disclosed either on the financial statements or in accompanying notes. The nature of the contingency and, if the events should occur, the magnitude of the obligation, are important considerations in assessing the ability of an enterprise to meet its commitments.

Promissory notes

A promissory note, frequently referred to simply as a *note*, is a written promise to pay a sum certain in money on demand or at a definite time. As in the case of a check, it must be payable to the order of a particular person or firm, or to bearer. It must also be signed by the person or firm that makes the promise. The one to whose order the note is payable is called the *payee*, and the one making the promise is called the *maker*. In the note illustrated below, Connor Equipment Corporation is the payee and H. B. Lane is the maker.

$ 2,500.00	DAYTON, OHIO October 2 19 69
Sixty days	AFTER DATE I PROMISE TO PAY TO
THE ORDER OF Connor Equipment Corporation	
Two thousand five hundred 00/100 - DOLLARS	
PAYABLE AT Merchants National Bank	
VALUE RECEIVED WITH INTEREST AT 6%	
No. 14 DUE December 1, 1969	H. B. Lane

Interest-bearing note

The enterprise owning a note refers to it as a *note receivable* and records it as an asset at its face amount; the maker of a note refers to it as a *note payable* and records it as a liability at its face amount. Thus, the note in the illustration would be recorded in the ledger of Connor Equipment Corporation as a $2,500 debit in Notes Receivable and in the ledger of H. B. Lane Co. as a $2,500 credit in Notes Payable.

A note that provides for the payment of interest for the period between the issuance date and the due date is called an *interest-bearing* note. If a note makes no provision for interest, it is said to be *non-interest bearing*. In such cases, however, interest may be charged at the legal rate for any time that the note remains unpaid after it is due. The interest that a business is obliged to pay is an expense and is called *interest expense*. The interest that a business is entitled to receive is revenue and is called *interest income*.

Determining interest

Rates of interest are usually stated in terms of a period of one year. Thus, the interest on a $1,500, 1-year, 6% note would amount to 6% of $1,500, or $90. If, instead of one year, the term of the note was one-half year, interest at the rate of 6% would amount to one half of $90, or $45.

Notes covering a period of time longer than a year ordinarily provide that the interest be paid annually, semiannually, or at some other stated interval. The time involved in commercial credit transactions is usually less than a year, and the interest provided for by the note is payable at the time the note is paid. In computing interest for a period of less than a year, agencies of the federal government use the actual number of days in the year; for example, 90 days is considered to be 90/365 of a year. The usual commercial practice is to use 360 as the denominator of the fraction; thus 90 days is considered to be 90/360 of a year.

The basic formula for computing interest is as follows:

$$\text{Principle} \times \text{Rate} \times \text{Time} = \text{Interest}$$

To illustrate the application of the formula, assume a note for $800, payable 15 days from date, with interest at 6%. The interest would be $2, computed as follows:

$$\$800 \times \frac{6}{100} \times \frac{15}{360} = \$2 \text{ interest}$$

There are a number of shortcut methods of computing interest. One that is commonly used is called the 60-day, 6% method. It utilizes the fact that interest at the rate of 6% a year for 60 days (1/6 of 360) is equivalent to 1% (1/6 of 6%) of the principal sum. The interest on any amount for 60 days at 6% can be determined, therefore, by moving the decimal point in the principal two places to the left. Thus for 60 days the interest at 6% on $1,342 is $13.42; on $264, the interest is $2.64; and on $982.73, the interest is $9.83. The interest on $1,000 for 93 days at 6% may be determined by the use of this method as shown at the top of the next page.

Principal		Interest
$1,000	60 days (1% of $1,000).......	$10.00
	30 days (1/2 of $10).........	5.00
	3 days (1/20 of $10)........	.50
$1,000	93 days at 6%..............	$15.50

This same method may also be used in computing interest at a rate other than 6%. The interest is first determined at the rate of 6%. The amount thus obtained is then converted to interest at the desired rate. As an example, the various steps in the determination of interest on $940 for 81 days at 7% are illustrated below.

Principal		Interest
$940	60 days at 6% (1% of $940)..	$ 9.40
	15 days at 6% (1/4 of $9.40)..	2.35
	6 days at 6% (1/10 of $9.40)..	.94
	81 days at 6%..............	$12.69
	81 days at 1% (1/6 of $12.69).	2.115
$940	81 days at 7%..............	$14.81

Comprehensive interest tables are available and are commonly used by financial institutions and other enterprises that require frequent interest calculations. Nevertheless, the student of business should be sufficiently conversant with the mechanics of interest computations to employ them with complete accuracy and to recognize significant errors in interest determinations that come to his attention.

When the term of a note is expressed in months, each month may be considered as being 1/12 of a year, or, alternatively, the actual number of days in the term may be counted. For example, the interest on a 3-month note dated June 1 could be computed on the basis of 3/12 of a year or on the basis of 92/360 of a year. It is the usual commercial practice to employ the first method, while banks usually charge interest for the exact number of days. For the sake of uniformity, the commercial practice will be followed here.

Determining due date

The period of time between the issuance date and the maturity date of a short-term note may be expressed in either days or months. When the term of a note is expressed in days, the due date is the specified number of days after its issuance and may be determined as follows:

1. Subtract the date of the note from the number of days in the month in which it is dated.
2. Add as many full months as possible without exceeding the number of days in the note, counting the full number of days in these months.
3. Subtract the sum of the days obtained in *1* and *2* from the number of days in the note.

To illustrate, the due day of a 90-day note dated March 16 may be determined as follows:

Term of the note................ 90	
March (days)............. 31	
Date of note.............. 16	
Remainder................ 15	
April (days)................. 30	
May (days)................. 31	
Total......................... 76	
Due date, June................. 14	

When the term of a note is expressed as a specified number of months after the issuance date, the due date is determined by counting the number of months from the issuance date. Thus, a 3-month note dated June 5 would be due on September 5. In those cases in which there is no date in the month of maturity that corresponds to the issuance date, the due date becomes the last day of the month. For example, a 2-month note dated July 31 would be due on September 30.

Notes payable and interest expense

Notes payable are ordinarily issued to a relatively small number of creditors. When such is the case there is no need for a subsidiary ledger; all transactions involving notes may be recorded in a single account in the general ledger. The details of all notes issued can be made readily available by use of a carbon copy prepared when the note is issued.

Notes may be issued to creditors in temporary satisfaction of an account payable created earlier, or they may be issued at the time merchandise, equipment, or other assets are purchased. To illustrate the former, assume that an enterprise, which owes F. B. Murray Co. $1,000 on account, issues a 30-day, 6% note for $1,000 in settlement. The transaction is recorded by the following entry in the general journal:

June	6	Accounts Payable — F. B. Murray Co........	1,000	
		Notes Payable........................		1,000
		Issued a 30-day, 6% note on account.		

The payee may hold the note until maturity, or he may transfer it by endorsement to his bank or to a creditor. In any event, on the due date the note is ordinarily presented by the holder at the maker's place of business or other designated location. Upon payment, the holder surrenders the note to the maker. The effect of paying the $1,000 note recorded in the entry above may be presented in general journal form as shown at the top of the next page.

July 6	Notes Payable...............................	1,000	
	Interest expense.............................	5	
	Cash.......................................		1,005

In practice, the foregoing transaction would be recorded in the cash payments journal rather than in the general journal. Because of its greater simplicity and clarity, the general journal format will continue to be used to illustrate entries throughout the remainder of the chapter.

There are numerous variations in interest and repayment terms when borrowing money from banks. The most direct procedure is for the borrower to issue an interest-bearing note for the amount of the loan. For example, assuming that on September 19 a firm borrows $5,000 from the First National Bank, the loan being evidenced by its 90-day, 6% note, the effect of the transaction is as follows:

| Sept. 19 | Cash....................................... | 5,000 | |
| | Notes payable.......................... | | 5,000 |

On the due date of the note, ninety days later, the borrower owes $5,000, the face amount of the note, and interest of $75. The accounts affected by the payment are as follows:

Dec. 18	Notes Payable............................	5,000	
	Interest Expense.........................	75	
	Cash.....................................		5,075

Discounting notes payable. A relatively common variant of the bank loan transaction just illustrated is to issue a non-interest-bearing note for the amount that is to be paid at maturity. When this plan is followed, the interest is deducted from the maturity value of the note and the borrower receives the remainder. The deduction of interest from a future value is termed *discounting*. The rate used in computing the interest may be termed the *discount rate*, the deduction may be referred to as the *discount*, and the net amount available to the borrower is called the *proceeds*.

To illustrate the discounting of a note payable, assume that on August 10 an enterprise issues to a bank an $8,000, 90-day, non-interest-bearing note and that the bank discount rate is 6½%. The amount of the discount is $130 and the proceeds $7,870. The debits and credit required to record the transaction follow:

Aug. 10	Cash.......................................	7,870	
	Interest Expense.........................	130	
	Notes Payable..........................		8,000

It should be observed that the above note payable is recorded at its face value, which is also its maturity value, and that the interest expense is recorded at the time the note is issued. When the note is paid, the effect is as follows:

| Nov. 8 | Notes Payable............................ | 8,000 | |
| | Cash..................................... | | 8,000 |

Notes receivable and interest income

The typical retail enterprise makes most of its sales for cash or on account. If the account of a customer becomes delinquent, the creditor may insist that the account be converted into a note. In this way the debtor may be given an extension of time, and if the creditor needs additional funds, he may endorse and transfer the note to his bank. Notes may also be received by retail firms that sell merchandise on long-term credit. For example, a dealer in household appliances may require a down payment at the time of sale and accept a note or a series of notes for the remainder. Such arrangements usually provide for monthly payments. Wholesale firms and manufacturers are likely to receive notes more frequently than retailers, although here, too, much depends upon the nature of the product and the length of the credit period.

When a note is received from a customer to apply on his account, the facts are recorded by debiting the notes receivable account and crediting the accounts receivable controlling account and the account of the customer from whom the note is received. It is not necessary to maintain a subsidiary ledger for notes receivable because the notes themselves provide detailed information.

To illustrate, assume that the account of Norton & Co., which has a debit balance of $600, is past due. A 20-day, 6% note for that amount, dated April 23, is accepted in settlement of the account. The entry to record the transaction is as follows:

Apr.	23	Notes Receivable........................	600	
		Accounts Receivable — Norton & Co......		600
		Received a 20-day, 6% note dated April 23.		

Upon receipt of the principal and interest due on the above note, the following debits and credits are recorded in the cash receipts journal:

May 13	Cash..	602	
	Notes Receivable...........................		600
	Interest Income............................		2

Discounting notes receivable. Instead of being retained by the holder until maturity, notes receivable may be transferred to a bank by endorsement. The discount (interest) charged is computed on the maturity value of the note for the period of time that will elapse between the date of the transfer and the due date of the note. The amount of the proceeds paid to the endorser is the excess of the maturity value over the discount. Two examples will illustrate discounting operations, one for a noninterest-bearing note and the other for an interest-bearing note.

Non-interest-bearing note. Assume that among the notes receivable held by an enterprise is a 90-day non-interest-bearing note for $1,350, dated August 21, and that the note is discounted at a bank on September 20 at the rate of 7%. The data may be tabulated as follows:

Face value of note dated Aug. 21		$1,350.00
Maturity value of note due Nov. 19		$1,350.00
Discount period — Sept. 20 to Nov. 19	60 days	
Discount on maturity value — 60 days at 7%		15.75
Proceeds		$1,334.25

The effect of the transaction, which would be recorded in the cash receipts journal, is as follows:

```
Sept. 20   Cash..............................  1,334.25
           Interest Expense...................     15.75
              Notes Receivable................            1,350.00
```

Interest-bearing note. Assume that a 90-day, 5% note receivable for $1,800, dated November 8, is discounted on December 3 at the rate of 6%. The data used in determining the effect of the transaction are as follows:

Face value of note dated Nov. 8		$1,800.00
Interest on note — 90 days at 5%		22.50
Maturity value of note due Feb. 6		$1,822.50
Discount period — Dec. 3 to Feb. 6	65 days	
Discount on maturity value — 65 days at 6%		19.74
Proceeds		$1,802.76

The same information is presented graphically in the following flow diagram. In reading the data, follow the direction of the arrows.

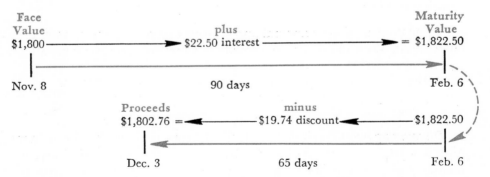

The entry for the discounting transaction, in general journal form, is as follows:

```
Dec.  3   Cash..............................  1,802.76
             Notes Receivable................            1,800.00
             Interest Income.................               2.76
```

It should be observed that the excess of the proceeds over the face amount of the note is recorded as interest income. The proceeds from discounting an interest-bearing note receivable may, of course, be less than the face value. The amount and direction of the difference between the interest rate and the discount rate will affect the result, as will the relationship between the full term of the note and the length of the discount period.

Contingent liability. In the absence of a qualification limiting his responsibility, the endorser of a note is committed to paying the bank or other endorsee if the maker should default. Accordingly, the discounting of a note receivable creates a contingent liability that continues in effect until the due date. If the maker pays the promised amount at maturity, the contingent liability is discharged without any action on the part of the endorser. If, on the other hand, the maker defaults and the endorser is notified in accordance with legal requirements, the liability becomes an actual one.

The nature and amount of the contingency should be disclosed on the balance sheet or in an accompanying notation somewhat as follows: "As of [balance sheet date] the company was contingently liable for notes receivable discounted in the amount of [amount]." It should be noted that it is only the amount of the unmatured notes discounted as of the balance sheet date that is significant. The number of such notes may represent only a minor portion of the total volume of short-term notes that were discounted during the year. The amount of the contingent liability can ordinarily be determined from a memorandum record of amounts, due dates, and other pertinent data for each note.

Dishonored notes receivable

If the maker of a note fails to pay his obligation on the due date, the note is said to be *dishonored*. A dishonored note receivable ceases to be negotiable, and for that reason the holder ordinarily transfers the claim, including any interest due, to the accounts receivable account. For example, if the $600, 20-day, 6% note received and recorded on April 23 (page 171) had been dishonored at maturity, the entry to charge the note back to the customer's account would have been as follows:

May	13	Accounts Receivable — Norton & Co........	602	
		Notes Receivable......................		600
		Interest Income......................		2
		Dishonored note and interest.		

If there had been some assurance that the maker would pay the note within a relatively short time, action could have been postponed until the matter was resolved. However, for future guidance in extending credit it may be desirable that the customer's account in the subsidiary ledger disclose the dishonor of the note.

When a discounted note receivable is dishonored, the holder ordinarily notifies the endorser of such fact and requests payment. If the presentation for payment and notification of dishonor are timely, the endorser is required to pay the note, including any interest due. The entire amount paid by the endorser should be debited to the maker's account. To illustrate, assume that the $1,800, 90-day, 5% note discounted on December 3 (page 172) is dishonored by the maker, W. D. Pryor Co., at maturity. The entry, in general journal form, would be as follows:

Feb. 6	Accounts Receivable — W. D. Pryor Co....	1,822.50
	Cash..............................	1,822.50

In some cases the holder of a dishonored note submits to the endorser a notarized statement of the facts of the dishonor. The fee for this statement, known as a *protest fee*, is charged to the endorser, who in turn charges it to the maker of the note. If there had been a protest fee of $2 in connection with the dishonor and the payment recorded above, the debit to the maker's account and the credit to Cash would have been $1,824.50.

Uncollectible accounts

When merchandise or services are sold without the immediate receipt of cash, a portion of the claims against customers ordinarily proves to be uncollectible. This is usually the case regardless of the care used in granting credit and the efficacy of the collection procedures employed. The operating expense incurred because of the failure to collect receivables is variously termed an expense or a loss from *uncollectible accounts, doubtful accounts,* or *bad debts.*[1]

There is no single general rule for determining when an account or a note becomes uncollectible. The fact that a debtor fails to pay his account in accordance with the sales contract or dishonors a note on the due date does not necessarily indicate uncollectibility. Bankruptcy of the debtor is one of the most positive indications of partial or complete worthlessness of a receivable. Other evidence includes discontinuance of the debtor's business, disappearance of the debtor, failure of repeated attempts to collect, and the barring of collection by the statute of limitations.

There are two generally accepted methods of accounting for receivables that are deemed to be uncollectible. The *allowance* method, which is sometimes referred to as *reserve* method, makes advance provision for uncollectible receivables. The other procedure, called the *direct write-off*

---

[1] If both notes and accounts are involved, both may be included in the title, as in "uncollectible notes and accounts expense," or the general term "uncollectible receivables expense" may be substituted. Because of its wide usage and simplicity, "uncollectible accounts expense" will be used in this book.

or *direct charge-off* method, recognizes the expense only when specific accounts are judged to be worthless.

Allowance method of accounting for uncollectibles

Most large business enterprises provide currently for the amount of their trade receivables estimated to become uncollectible in the future. The advance provision for future uncollectibility is effected by an adjusting entry at the end of the fiscal period. As with all periodic adjustments, the entry serves a dual purpose. In this instance it provides for (1) the reduction of the value of the receivables to the amount of cash expected to be realized from them in the future and (2) the allocation to the current period of the expected expense resulting from such reduction.

Assumed data for a new business firm will be used to explain and illustrate the allowance method. The enterprise began business in August and elected to adopt the calendar year as its fiscal year. The accounts receivable account, which is reproduced below, has a balance of $105,000 at the end of the period.

ACCOUNTS RECEIVABLE   ACCOUNT No. 114

DATE		ITEM	POST. REF.	DEBIT	CREDIT	BALANCE	
						DEBIT	CREDIT
1969							
Aug.	31		S3	20,000		20,000	
Sept.	30		S6	25,000		45,000	
	30		CR4		15,000	30,000	
Oct.	31		S10	40,000		70,000	
	31		CR7		25,000	45,000	
Nov.	30		S13	38,000		83,000	
	30		CR10		23,000	60,000	
Dec.	31		S16	75,000		135,000	
	31		CR13		30,000	105,000	

Among the individual customers' accounts comprising the $105,000 balance in Accounts Receivable are a number of balances which are a varying number of days past due. No specific accounts are determined to be wholly uncollectible at this time, but it appears inevitable that some will be collected only in part and that others are likely to become entirely worthless. Based on a careful study, it is estimated that a total of $3,000 will eventually prove to be uncollectible. The amount expected to be realized from the accounts receivable is accordingly $105,000 — $3,000, or $102,000, and the $3,000 reduction in value is the uncollectible accounts expense for the period.

It is obvious that the $3,000 reduction in accounts receivable cannot be identified with specific customers' accounts in the subsidiary ledger and should therefore not be credited to the controlling account in the general ledger. The customary practice is to employ a *contra asset* account entitled Allowance for Doubtful Accounts. The adjusting entry to record the expense and the reduction in the asset is presented below, followed by the two accounts to which the entry is posted.

			Adjusting entry				
Dec.	31	Uncollectible Accounts Expense.......	717	3,000			
		Allowance for Doubtful Accounts ...	114.1			3,000	

UNCOLLECTIBLE ACCOUNTS EXPENSE — ACCOUNT No. 717

DATE		ITEM	POST. REF.	DEBIT	CREDIT	BALANCE DEBIT	BALANCE CREDIT
1969 Dec.	31	Adjusting	J4	3,000		3,000	

ALLOWANCE FOR DOUBTFUL ACCOUNTS — ACCOUNT No. 114.1

DATE		ITEM	POST. REF.	DEBIT	CREDIT	BALANCE DEBIT	BALANCE CREDIT
1969 Dec.	31	Adjusting	J4		3,000		3,000

The debit balance of $105,000 in Accounts Receivable is the face amount of the total claims against customers on open account, and the credit balance of $3,000 in Allowance for Doubtful Accounts is the amount to be deducted from Accounts Receivable to determine their expected realizable value. The $3,000 reduction in the asset was transferred to uncollectible accounts expense, which will in turn be closed to the expense and revenue summary account.

Uncollectible accounts expense is reported on the income statement as either selling expense or general expense, depending upon the department responsible. Credits and collections may be the responsibility of the sales department or of an independent department within the general administrative framework.

The accounts receivable may be listed on the balance sheet at the net amount of $102,000 with a parenthetical notation disclosing the amount of the allowance, or the details may be presented as shown on the partial balance sheet below.

Richards Company
Balance Sheet
December 31, 1969

Assets

Current assets:

Cash.....		$ 21,600
Accounts receivable.....	$105,000	
Less allowance for doubtful accounts.....	3,000	102,000

When the allowance account includes provision for doubtful notes as well as accounts, it should be deducted from the total of Notes Receivable and Accounts Receivable.

Write-offs to the allowance account. When an account is deemed to be uncollectible, it is written off against the allowance account as in the following entry:

Jan.	21	Allowance for Doubtful Accounts........	110	
		Accounts Receivable — John Parker...		110
		To write off the uncollectible account.		

As additional accounts or portions of accounts are determined during the year to be uncollectible, they are written off against Allowance for Doubtful Accounts in the same manner. Instructions for write-offs should originate with the credit manager or other designated official. The authorizations, which should always be written, serve as objective evidence in support of the accounting entry.

Naturally enough, the total amount written off against the allowance account during the period will rarely be exactly equal to the amount in the account as of the beginning of the period. The allowance account will have a credit balance if the write-offs during the period amount to less than the beginning balance; it will have a debit balance if the write-offs exceed the beginning balance. In any event, the allowance account will have a credit balance after the year-end adjustment is recorded.

An account receivable that has been written off against the allowance account may subsequently be collected. In such cases the account should be reinstated by an entry that is the exact reverse of the write-off entry. For example, assume that the account of $110 written off in the preceding journal entry is later collected. The entry to reinstate the account would be as follows:

June	10	Accounts Receivable — John Parker.....	110	
		Allowance for Doubtful Accounts.....		110
		To reinstate account written off earlier in the year.		

The cash received in payment would be recorded in the cash receipts journal as a receipt on account. Although it is possible to combine the reinstatement and the receipt of cash into a single debit and credit, the entries in the customer's account, with an appropriate notation, provide useful credit information.

Estimating uncollectibles. The estimate of uncollectibles at the end of the fiscal period is based on past experience modified by forecasts of future business activity. When the trend of general sales volume is upward and there is relatively full employment, the magnitude of the expense should ordinarily be less than when the trend is in the opposite direction. The estimate is customarily based on either (1) the amount of sales for the period or (2) the amount and the age of trade receivable accounts at the end of the fiscal period.

Estimate based on sales. Accounts receivable are acquired as a result of sales on account. The volume of such sales during the year may therefore be used as an indication of the probable amount of the accounts that will be uncollectible. For example, if it is known from past experience that about 1% of charge sales will be uncollectible and the charge sales for a particular year amount to $300,000, the adjusting entry for uncollectible accounts at the end of the year would be as follows:

		Adjusting Entry		
Dec.	31	Uncollectible Accounts Expense..........	3,000	
		Allowance for Doubtful Accounts......		3,000

Instead of charge sales, total sales (including those made for cash) may be used in developing the percentage. The total sales figure is obtainable from the ledger without the necessity for the analysis that may be required to determine charge sales. If the ratio of sales on account to cash sales does not change materially from year to year, the results obtained will be equally satisfactory. For example, if in the example above the balance of the sales account at the end of the year is assumed to be $400,000, the application of ¾ of 1% to that amount would also yield an estimate of $3,000.

If it becomes apparent over a period of time that the amount of the write-offs is consistently greater or less than the amount provided by the adjusting entry, the percentage applied to sales data should be revised accordingly. A newly established business enterprise, having no record of credit experience, may obtain data on the probable amount of the expense from trade association journals and other publications containing information on credit and collections.

Estimate based on analysis of trade receivables. The process of analyzing the trade receivable accounts is sometimes called *aging the receivables.* The base point for determining age is the due date of the account. The number and breadth of the time intervals used will vary according to the credit terms granted to customers. A portion of a typical analysis is presented at the top of the next page. Observe that account balances composed of debits of more than one month, as in the second item of the analysis, must be treated as separate components.

CUSTOMER	BALANCE	NOT DUE	0–30	31–60	61–90	91–180	181–365	over 365
				DAYS PAST DUE				
Ashby & Co.....	$ 150			$ 150				
B. T. Barr.......	610					$ 350	$ 260	
Brock Co........	470	$ 470						
J. Zimmer Co....	160							160
Total.........	$86,300	$75,000	$4,000	$3,100	$1,900	$1,200	$ 800	$ 300

Analysis of accounts receivable

The analysis is completed by adding the columns to determine the total amount of receivables in each age group. A sliding scale of percentages, based on experience, is next applied to obtain the estimated amount of uncollectibles in each group. The manner in which the data may be assembled is illustrated below.

		ESTIMATED UNCOLLECTIBLE ACCOUNTS	
AGE INTERVAL	BALANCE	PERCENT	AMOUNT
Not due.........................	$75,000	2%	$1,500
0–30 days past due..............	4,000	5	200
31–60 days past due.............	3,100	10	310
61–90 days past due.............	1,900	20	380
91–180 days past due............	1,200	30	360
181–365 days past due...........	800	50	400
Over 365 days past due..........	300	80	240
Total......................	$86,300		$3,390

Estimate of uncollectible accounts

The estimate of uncollectible accounts, $3,390 in the above example, is the amount to be deducted from accounts receivable in order to yield their expected realizable value. It is thus the amount of the desired balance of the allowance account after adjustment. The excess of this figure over the balance of the allowance account before adjustment is the amount of the current provision to be made for uncollectible accounts expense.

To continue the illustration, assume that the allowance account has a credit balance of $510 before adjustment. The amount to be added to this balance is therefore $3,390 − $510, or $2,880, and the adjusting entry is as follows:

		Adjusting Entry		
Dec.	31	Uncollectible Accounts Expense..............	2,880	
		Allowance for Doubtful Accounts..........		2,880

After the adjusting entry is posted, the balance in the allowance account will be $3,390, which is the desired amount. If the balance of

179

the allowance account before adjustment had been a debit of $300, the amount of the adjustment would have been $3,390 + $300, or $3,690.

The use of the analysis-of-receivables method of determining the uncollectible accounts expense yields a more reasoned estimate of the current realizable value of the receivables and is frequently preferred over the percent of sales method. An inadequate or excessive provision in one period automatically influences the amount of the adjustment for the succeeding period. The percent of sales method lacks this relatively automatic device for keeping the amount of the estimated expense close to the actual net write-offs.

Direct write-off method of accounting for uncollectibles

If an enterprise sells most of its merchandise or services on a cash basis, the amount of its expense from uncollectible accounts is ordinarily minor in relation to its revenue. The amount of its receivables at any time is also likely to represent a relatively small portion of its total current assets. These observations are based on the assumption that the credit period is short, which would be usual if sales are preponderantly on a cash basis, and that credit policies and collection procedures are adequate. The nature of the service or the product sold and the type of clientele may also have an important bearing on collection experience. For example, an enterprise that sells most of its output on account to a small number of companies, all of which are financially strong, will incur little, if any, expense from inability to collect its accounts.

In such situations, as well as in many small business and professional enterprises, it is satisfactory to defer recognition of uncollectibility until the period in which specific accounts are deemed to be worthless and are actually written off. Accordingly, there is no necessity for an allowance account or for an adjusting entry at the end of the period. The entry to write off an account when it is believed to be uncollectible is as follows:

May	10	Uncollectible Accounts Expense	42	
		Accounts Receivable — D. L. Ross		42
		To write off uncollectible account.		

If an account that has been written off is collected later, the account should be reinstated. If the recovery is in the same fiscal year as the write-off, the earlier entry should be reversed to reinstate the account. To illustrate, assume that the account written off in the May 10 entry above is collected in November of the same fiscal year. The entry to reinstate the account would be as follows:

Nov.	21	Accounts Receivable — D. L. Ross	42	
		Uncollectible Accounts Expense		42
		To reinstate account written off		
		earlier in the year.		

The receipt of cash in payment of the reinstated amount would be recorded in the cash receipts journal in the usual manner.

When an account that has been written off is collected in a subsequent fiscal year, it may be reinstated by an entry like that just illustrated. An alternative is to credit some other appropriately titled account, such as Recovery of Uncollectible Accounts Written Off. The credit balance in such an account at the end of the year may then be reported on the income statement as a deduction from Uncollectible Accounts Expense, or the net expense only may be reported. Such amounts are likely to be minor in relationship to net income.

QUESTIONS

1. Under what caption should a loan to an employee due five years hence be listed on the balance sheet?

2. What is meant by the term *trade receivables*?

3. Why are the notes receivable considered to be more liquid than the accounts receivable?

4. The unpaid balance of a mortgage note payable is $40,000 at the close of the current fiscal year. The terms of the note provide for monthly principal payments of $500. How should the liability be presented on the balance sheet as of this date?

5. A business firm is contesting a suit for damages of a substantial amount brought by a supplier for alleged breach of contract. Is this a contingent liability of the defendant? If so, should it be disclosed in financial reports issued during the period of litigation? Discuss.

6. Name the two parties to a promissory note and state the title of the account each would use in recording the note.

7. If a $1,000 note provides for the payment of 6% interest, will the interest amount to $60? Explain.

8. The following questions refer to a 30-day, 6% note for $1,000, dated July 10: (a) What is the face value of the note? (b) What is the amount of interest payable at maturity? (c) What is the maturity value of the note? (d) What is the due date of the note?

9. A business enterprise issues a 60-day, 6% note for $500 to a creditor on account. Give the general journal entries to record (a) the issuance of the note and (b) the payment of the note at maturity.

10. In borrowing money from a bank an enterprise issues a non-interest-bearing note, which the bank discounts at 7%. Does the maker incur a contingent liability? Explain.

11. The payee of a 90-day, 6% note for $2,000, dated May 1, endorses it to his bank on May 16. The bank discounts the note at 6%, paying the endorser $2,004.62. Identify or determine the following, as they relate to the note: (a) face value, (b) maturity value, (c) due date, (d) number of days in the discount period, (e) proceeds, (f) interest income or expense recorded by payee, (g) amount payable to the bank if the maker should default.

12. A discounted note receivable is dishonored by the maker and the endorser pays the bank the face of the note, $800, the interest, $16, and a protest fee of $2. What entry should be made to record the payment?

13. Of the $125,000 of notes receivable discounted to a bank by an enterprise during the year, $110,000 have matured by the end of the year. All matured notes were paid by their makers except one note for $1,000, on which there was accrued interest of $15. What is the amount of the endorser's contingent liability for notes receivable discounted at the close of the year?

14. The series of six transactions recorded in the T accounts below were related to a sale to a customer on account and payment of the amount owed. Describe each transaction briefly.

CASH				NOTES RECEIVABLE				ACCOUNTS RECEIVABLE		
(4)	795	(5)	808	(3)	800	(4)	800	(1)	815	(2)	15
(6)	810							(5)	808	(3)	800
										(6)	808

SALES				INTEREST INCOME				INTEREST EXPENSE		
(2)	15	(1)	815			(6)	2	(4)	5		

15. Which of the two methods of accounting for uncollectible accounts provides for recognition of the expense at the earlier date?

16. What kind of an account (asset, liability, etc.) is Allowance for Doubtful Accounts, and is its normal balance a debit or a credit?

17. Give the adjusting entry to increase Allowance for Doubtful Accounts by $2,800.

18. The $350 balance of an account owed by a customer is considered to be uncollectible and is to be written off. Give the entry to record the write-off in the general ledger (a) assuming that the allowance method is used and (b) assuming that the direct write-off method is used.

19. After accounts are adjusted and closed at the end of the fiscal year, Accounts Receivable has a balance of $170,000 and Allowance for Doubtful Accounts has a balance of $3,000.

   (a) What is the expected realizable value of the accounts receivable?
   (b) If an account receivable of $100 is written off against the allowance account, what will be the expected realizable value of the accounts receivable after the write-off, assuming that no other changes in either account have occurred in the meantime?

20. A firm has consistently adjusted its allowance account at the end of the fiscal year by adding a fixed percent of the period's net sales on account. After six years the balance in Allowance for Doubtful Accounts has become disproportionately large in relationship to the balance in Accounts Receivable. Give two possible explanations.

7-1. Determine the interest on the following notes, using the 60-day, 6% method:

Face Amount	Number of Days	Interest Rate
(a) $ 780.00	34	6%
(b) 1,320.50	75	6½%
(c) 936.10	68	7%
(d) 2,164.00	57	5%

7-2. G. H. Hunt Co. issues a 90-day, 6% note for $1,200, dated March 10, to Mercer & Co. on account.

(a) What is the due date of the note?
(b) What is the amount of interest to be paid on the note at maturity?
(c) Present entries, in general journal form, to record the following:
  (1) Issuance of the note by the maker.
  (2) Receipt of the note by the payee.
  (3) Payment of the note at maturity.
  (4) Receipt of payment of the note at maturity.

7-3. Graham Co. issues a 120-day, non-interest-bearing note for $12,000 to Merchants Bank and Trust Co., which the bank discounts at 7%. Present the maker's entries, in general journal form, to record (a) issuance of the note and (b) payment of the note at maturity.

7-4. In negotiating a 60-day loan, Bargain Appliances had the option of either (1) issuing a $40,000, non-interest-bearing note that will be discounted at the rate of 6%, or (2) issuing a $40,000 note bearing interest at the rate of 6% that will be accepted at face value.

(a) What would be the amount of the interest expense in each case?
(b) What would be the amount of the proceeds in each case?
(c) Which of the two alternatives is more favorable to the borrower?

7-5. On July 1 Kenwood Plaza purchases land for $60,000 and a building for $650,000, paying $110,000 in cash and issuing a 6½% note, secured by a mortgage on the property, for the remainder. The terms of the note provide for twenty-four semiannual payments of $25,000 on the principal plus the interest accrued since the date of the preceding payment. Give the entry, in general journal form, to record (a) the transaction on July 1, (b) payment of the first installment on December 31, and (c) payment of the second installment the following June 30.

7-6. Wagner Co. holds a 60-day, 5% note for $1,800, dated September 8, that was received from a customer on account. On October 8 the note is discounted at the First National Bank at the rate of 6%. (a) What is the maturity value of the note? (b) How many days are there in the discount period? (c) What is the amount of the discount? (d) What is the amount of the proceeds? (e) Give the entry, in general journal form, to record the discounting of the note on October 8.

7-7. Record the following transactions, each in general journal form, in the accounts of M. O. Barrett Company:

Apr. 1. Received a $2,000, 90-day, 5% note dated April 1 from Tru-Valu Co. on account.
May 1. Discounted the note at Citizens State Bank, discount rate 6%.

183

June 30. The note is dishonored; paid the bank the amount due on the note plus a protest fee of $2.

July 30. Received the amount due on the dishonored note plus interest for 30 days at 6% on the total amount debited to Tru-Valu Co. on June 30.

7-8. At the end of the current year, the accounts receivable account has a debit balance of $90,000 and net sales for the year total $800,000. Determine the amount of the adjusting entry to record the provision for doubtful accounts under each of the following assumptions:

    (a) The allowance account before adjustment has a credit balance of $750.
        (1) Uncollectible accounts expense is estimated at ¾ of 1% of net sales.
        (2) Analysis of the accounts in the customers ledger indicates doubtful accounts of $6,100.
    (b) The allowance account before adjustment has a debit balance of $400.
        (1) Uncollectible accounts expense is estimated at ½ of 1% of net sales.
        (2) Analysis of the accounts in the customers ledger indicates doubtful accounts of $4,300.

PROBLEMS

The following additional problems for this chapter are located in Appendix C: 7-1B, 7-2B, 7-3B, 7-4B.

7-1A. The following were selected from among the transactions completed by Hartley Co. during the current year:

Jan. 10. Purchased merchandise on account from B. J. Foley Co., $800.
     20. Paid B. J. Foley Co. for the invoice of January 10, less 2% discount.
Feb. 11. Purchased merchandise on account from Morton & Co., $1,000.
Mar. 13. Issued a 30-day, 6% note for $1,000 to Morton & Co. on account.
Apr. 12. Paid Morton & Co. the amount owed on the note of March 13.
May 23. Issued a 60-day, non-interest-bearing note for $5,000 to Citizens National Bank. The bank discounted the note at the rate of 7%.
July 22. Paid Citizens National Bank the amount due on the note of May 23.
Aug. 5. Borrowed $3,000 from Merchants National Bank, issuing a 60-day, 6½% note for that amount.
Oct. 4. Paid Merchants National Bank the interest due on the note of August 5 and renewed the loan by issuing a new 30-day, 6½% note for $3,000. (Record both the debit and the credit to the notes payable account).
Nov. 3. Paid Merchants National Bank the amount due on the note of October 4.
Dec. 1. Purchased office equipment from Ryan Co. for $5,700, paying $700 and issuing a series of ten 6% notes for $500 each, coming due at 30-day intervals.
     31. Paid the amount due Ryan Co. on the first note in the series issued on December 1.

Instructions:
(1) Record the transactions in general journal form.
(2) Determine the total amount of interest accrued as of December 31 on the nine notes owed to Ryan Co.
(3) Assume that a single note for $5,000 had been issued on December 1 instead of the series of ten notes, and that its terms required principal payments of $500 each 30 days, with interest at 6% on the principal balance before applying the $500 payment. Determine the amount that would have been due and payable on December 31.

7-2A. The following were selected from among the transactions completed by Friedman & Co. during the current year:

Jan. 5. Sold merchandise on account to Daley & Hill, $720.
  15. Accepted a 30-day, 7% note for $720 from Daley & Hill on account.
Feb. 14. Received from Daley & Hill the amount due on the note of January 15.
Mar. 12. Sold merchandise on account to Morgan Co., $1,200, charging an additional $25 for prepaid transportation costs.
  22. Received from Morgan Co. the amount due on the invoice of March 12, less 2% discount.
Apr. 10. Loaned $400 cash to Robert Porter, receiving a 30-day, 6% note.
May 10. Received the interest due from Robert Porter and a new 60-day, 6% note as a renewal of the loan. (Record both the debit and the credit to the notes receivable account.)
July 9. Received from Robert Porter the amount due on his note.
Aug. 23. Sold merchandise on account to R. B. Jenkins, Inc., $1,500.
Sept. 22. Accepted a 60-day, 8% note for $1,500 from R. B. Jenkins, Inc. on account.
Oct. 12. Discounted the note from R. B. Jenkins, Inc. at the Bank of Commerce at 6%.
Nov. 21. Received notice from Bank of Commerce that R. B. Jenkins, Inc. had dishonored its note. Paid the bank the maturity value of the note.
Dec. 11. Received from R. B. Jenkins, Inc. the amount owed on the dishonored note, plus interest computed on the maturity value of the note at 8% for the additional 20 days.

Instructions:
Record the transactions in general journal form.

7-3A. The transactions, adjusting entries, and closing entries described below are related to uncollectible accounts. All were completed during the current fiscal year ended December 31.

Feb. 11. Wrote off the $310 balance owed by Elder Corp., which has no assets.
April 23. Reinstated the account of Roger Scudder that had been written off in the preceding year and received $115 cash in full payment.
July 9. Received 10% of the $800 balance owed by Conley & Co., a bankrupt, and wrote off the remainder as uncollectible.
Oct. 17. Reinstated the account of David Riley that had been written off two years earlier and received $60 cash in full payment.
Dec. 28. Wrote off the following accounts as uncollectible (compound entry): Robert Bowen, $390; Field & Keller, $916; Sanford & Co., $723; Paul M. Yost, Inc., $218.
  31. On the basis of an analysis of the $98,470 of accounts receivable, it was estimated that $3,140 will be uncollectible. Recorded the adjusting entry.
  31. Recorded the entry to close the appropriate account to Expense and Revenue Summary.

Instructions:
(1) Open the following selected accounts, recording the credit balance indicated as of January 1 of the current fiscal year:

  114.1 Allowance for Doubtful Accounts.... $2,750
  313 Expense and Revenue Summary.... ———
  718 Uncollectible Accounts Expense..... ———

(2) Record in general journal form the transactions and the adjusting and closing entries described above. After each

entry, post to the three selected accounts affected and extend the new balances.

(3) Determine the expected realizable value of the accounts receivable as of December 31.

(4) Assuming that, instead of basing the provision for uncollectible accounts on an analysis of receivables, the adjusting entry on December 31 had been based on an estimated loss of ¾ of 1% of net sales for the year of $400,000, determine the following:

    (a) Uncollectible accounts expense for the year.

    (b) Balance in the allowance account after the adjustment of December 31.

    (c) Expected realizable value of the accounts receivable on December 31.

If the working papers correlating with the textbook are not used, omit Problem 7-4A.

7-4A. The following transactions, all of which are related to receivables and payables, were selected from among the transactions completed by Lawson Co. during the current fiscal year.

Jan. 7. Received from Trianon Co. a 90-day, non-interest-bearing note for $5,000, dated January 6, on account.

21. Issued to Davis & Son a 2-month, 7% note for $4,000, on account.

Feb. 20. Discounted at Manufacturers Trust Co. at 6% the note received from Trianon Co., dated January 6.

Mar. 12. Received from A. H. Beck the amount due on a March 2 invoice for $1,600, less 2% discount.

21. Issued Check No. 461 to Davis & Son in payment of the note issued on January 21.

Apr. 10. Wrote off against the allowance account the $325 owed by M. R. Hayden.

25. Borrowed $3,000 from Manufacturers Trust Co., issuing a 7%, 90-day note.

May 6. Received from T. Lang a 90-day, 5% note for $1,000, dated May 4, on account.

18. Purchased land for a building site from Modern Development Co. for $35,000, issuing Check No. 503 for $5,000 and a 7% mortgage note for the balance. The contract provides for payments of $3,000 of principal plus accrued interest at intervals of six months.

June 20. Discounted at First State Bank at 6% the note received from T. Lang dated May 4.

July 10. Received from Eaton's, Inc. on account a 30-day, 6% note for $800, dated July 10.

24. Issued Check No. 598 to Manufacturers Trust Co. for the amount due on the note dated April 25.

Aug. 3. Received notice from First State Bank that T. Lang had dishonored the note due on August 2. Issued Check No. 610 for the amount due on the note, plus a protest fee of $3.

9. Eaton's, Inc. dishonored its note dated July 10. Charged the dishonored note to its account.

Sept. 8. Received from Eaton's, Inc. the amount due on the note dishonored on August 9, including interest at 6% for 30 days on the maturity value of the note.

15. Reinstated the account of Fred Price that had been written off against the allowance account in the preceding year, and received cash in full payment, $95.

Oct. 2. Received from T. Lang the amount due on the note dishonored on August 2, including interest at 6% from August 2 to October 1 on the amount charged to his account on August 3.

Nov. 18. Issued Check No. 721 for principal and interest due on the mortgage note issued on May 18.

Instructions:

(1) Record the selected entries in the three journals provided in the working papers: Cash Receipts, Cash Payments, and a general journal. No posting is required.

(2) At the end of the year, Accounts Receivable has a debit balance of $106,000. The distribution of the accounts, by age intervals, is presented in the working papers, together with the percent of each class estimated to be uncollectible. Determine the amount of the accounts estimated to be uncollectible.

(3) Prior to adjustment at the end of the year, Allowance for Doubtful Accounts has a credit balance of $742. Record the adjusting entry in the general journal as of December 31.

(4) Present the data on accounts receivable as they will appear in the balance sheet as of December 31.

7-5A. Continental Sales Co. has just completed its fourth year of operations. The direct write-off method of recording uncollectible accounts expense has been employed during the entire period. Because of substantial increases in sales volume and amount of uncollectible accounts, the firm is considering the possibility of changing to the allowance method. Information is requested as to the effect that an annual provision of ½ of 1% of sales would have had on the amount of uncollectible accounts expense reported for each of the past four years. It is also considered desirable to know what the balance of Allowance for Doubtful Accounts would have been at the end of each year. The following data have been obtained from the accounts:

Year	Sales	Uncollectible Accounts Written Off	Year in Which Uncollectible Accounts Written Off Were Acquired			
			1st	2nd	3rd	4th
1st	$400,000	$ 300	$ 300			
2nd	600,000	2,300	1,800	$ 500		
3rd	700,000	2,700	100	2,000	$ 600	
4th	900,000	3,500		400	2,300	$ 800

Instructions:

(1) Assemble the desired information, using the following columnar captions:

	Uncollectible Accounts Expense			Balance of
Year	Expense Actually Reported	Expense Based on Estimate	Increase in Amount of Expense	Allowance Account, End of Year

(2) Advise management as to whether the estimate of ½ of 1% of sales appears to be reasonably close to the actual experience with uncollectible accounts, stating the basis for your opinion.

7-6A. The Nelson Co. received the notes described below during the last three months of the current fiscal year. Notes (1), (2), (3), and (4) were discounted on the dates and at the rates indicated.

Date	Face Amount	Term	Interest Rate	Date Discounted	Discount Rate
(1) Oct. 5	$2,400	60 days	—	Oct. 15	6%
(2) Oct. 18	960	30 days	5%	Nov. 7	6%
(3) Nov. 9	740	90 days	6%	Nov. 13	7%
(4) Nov. 23	1,800	30 days	6%	Dec. 8	6%
(5) Dec. 12	2,100	60 days	6%	——	——
(6) Dec. 22	4,200	60 days	7%	——	——

Instructions:

(1) Determine for each note (a) the due date and (b) the amount of interest due at maturity, identifying each note by number.

(2) Determine for each of the first four notes (a) the maturity value, (b) the discount period, (c) the discount, (d) the proceeds, and (e) the interest income or interest expense, identifying each note by number.

(3) Present, in general journal form, the entries to record the discounting of notes (1) and (2) at a bank.

(4) Assuming that notes (5) and (6) are held until maturity, determine for each the amount of interest earned (a) in the current fiscal year and (b) in the following fiscal year.

188

8

Merchandise inventory

Importance of inventories

The term *inventories* is used to designate merchandise held for sale in the normal course of business and also materials in the process of production or held for such use. This chapter is devoted to problems arising in the determination of the inventory of merchandise purchased for resale, commonly called *merchandise inventory*. Consideration will be given in a later chapter to inventories of raw materials and partially processed materials of a manufacturing enterprise.

Merchandise is one of the most active elements in the operation of wholesale and retail businesses, being continuously purchased and sold. The sale of merchandise at a price above cost provides the principal source of revenue for such enterprises. In determining net income, the cost of merchandise sold is the largest deduction from sales; in fact, it is customarily larger than all other deductions combined. In addition, a substantial portion of a merchandising firm's resources is invested in inventory; it is frequently the largest of the current assets.

Inventory determination plays an important role in matching costs with revenues of the period. As was explained and illustrated in Chapter 6, the total cost of merchandise available for sale during a period of time must be divided into two elements at the end of the period. The cost of the merchandise determined to be in the inventory will appear on the balance sheet as a current asset; the other element, which is the cost of the merchandise sold, will be reported on the income statement as a deduction from net sales to yield gross profit on sales. An error in the determination of the inventory figure at the end of the period will cause an equal misstatement of gross profit and net income in the income statement, and the amount reported for both assets and capital in the balance sheet will be incorrect by the same amount. The effects of understatements and overstatements of merchandise inventory at the end of the period are demonstrated below by three sets of severely condensed income statements and balance sheets. The first statements are based on a correct inventory determination, in the second set of statements the inventory has been understated by $8,000, and in the third example the inventory has been overstated by $7,000.

1. Inventory at end of period correctly stated at $20,000.

INCOME STATEMENT FOR THE YEAR		BALANCE SHEET AT END OF YEAR	
Net sales....................	200,000	Merchandise inventory.........	20,000
Cost of merchandise sold.......	120,000	Other assets.................	80,000
Gross profit...............	80,000	Total....................	100,000
Expenses...................	55,000		
Net income...............	25,000	Liabilities....................	30,000
		Capital.....................	70,000
		Total....................	100,000

2. Inventory at end of period incorrectly stated at $12,000.

Net sales....................	200,000	Merchandise inventory.........	12,000
Cost of merchandise sold.......	128,000	Other assets.................	80,000
Gross profit...............	72,000	Total....................	92,000
Expenses...................	55,000		
Net income...............	17,000	Liabilities....................	30,000
		Capital.....................	62,000
		Total....................	92,000

3. Inventory at end of period incorrectly stated at $27,000.

Net sales....................	200,000	Merchandise inventory.........	27,000
Cost of merchandise sold.......	113,000	Other assets.................	80,000
Gross profit...............	87,000	Total....................	107,000
Expenses...................	55,000		
Net income...............	32,000	Liabilities....................	30,000
		Capital.....................	77,000
		Total....................	107,000

Note that in the illustration the total amount of merchandise cost to be accounted for was constant at $140,000; it was the manner in which the cost was allocated that varied. The variations in allocating the $140,000 of merchandise cost are summarized as follows:

	MERCHANDISE AVAILABLE		
	TOTAL	INVENTORY	SOLD
1. Inventory correctly stated..................	$140,000	$20,000	$120,000
2. Inventory understated by $8,000............	140,000	12,000	128,000
3. Inventory overstated by $7,000.............	140,000	27,000	113,000

The effect of the erroneous allocations on net income, assets, and capital may also be summarized. Comparison of the amounts of the items reported on the preceding page in financial statements *2* and *3* with the comparable amounts reported in financial statement *1* yields the following:

	NET INCOME	ASSETS	CAPITAL
2. Inventory understated by $8,000	Understated by $8,000	Understated by $8,000	Understated by $8,000
3. Inventory overstated by $7,000	Overstated by $7,000	Overstated by $7,000	Overstated by $7,000

Elements of the foregoing analyses are closely related to the various inventory systems and methods presented hereinafter. A thorough understanding of the effect of inventories on the determination of net income, as presented in the foregoing examples, will be helpful.

Inventory systems

There are two principal systems of inventory accounting, *periodic* and *perpetual*. When the periodic system is employed, only the revenue from sales is recorded each time a sale is made; no entries are made to credit the inventory account or the purchases account for the cost of the merchandise that has been sold. Consequently, it is only by a detailed listing of the merchandise on hand (called a *physical inventory*) at the close of an accounting period that the cost of the inventory can be determined. It is ordinarily feasible to take a complete physical inventory only at the end of the fiscal year. When the merchandise inventory can be determined only by a physical measurement at specified intervals, the system can be characterized as *periodic*. In earlier chapters dealing with sales and purchases of merchandise, the periodic system has always been assumed.

In contrast to the periodic system, the *perpetual* inventory system employs accounting records that continuously disclose the amount of the inventory. A separate account for each type of merchandise is maintained in a subsidiary ledger. Increases in inventory items are recorded as debits to the appropriate accounts, and decreases are recorded as credits; the balances of the accounts are called the *book* inventories of the items on hand. Regardless of the care with which the perpetual inventory records are maintained, it is necessary to test their accuracy by taking a physical inventory of each type of commodity at least once a year. The records are then compared with the actual quantities and any discrepancies corrected.

The periodic inventory system of accounting is ordinarily used by retail enterprises that sell a great variety of low unit cost merchandise, such as groceries, hardware, and drugs. The expense of maintaining perpetual inventory records is likely to be prohibitive in such cases. Firms selling a relatively small number of high unit cost items, such as

191

office equipment, automobiles, or fur garments, are more likely to employ the perpetual system.

Although much of the discussion that follows is applicable to both inventory systems, the use of the periodic system will be assumed. Later in the chapter, consideration will be given to principles and procedures related exclusively to perpetual inventories.

Determining actual quantities in the inventory

The first stage in the process of "taking" an inventory is the determination of the quantity of each type of merchandise owned by the enterprise. Where the periodic system is used, the counting, weighing, and measuring should be done at the end of the accounting period. In order to accomplish this, the inventory crew may work during the night, or business operations may be suspended until the count is completed.

The details of the specific procedures for determining quantities and assembling the data vary considerably among companies. A common practice is to employ two-man teams; one person counts, weighs, or otherwise determines quantity, and the other lists the description and the quantity on inventory sheets. The quantity indicated for high-cost items should be verified by a third person at some time during the inventory-taking period. It is also advisable to recheck other items selected at random from the inventory sheets.

All of the merchandise owned by the business on the inventory date, and only such merchandise, should be included in the inventory. It may be necessary to examine sales and purchase invoices of the last few days of the accounting period and the first few days of the ensuing period to determine who has legal title to merchandise in transit on the inventory date. When goods are purchased or sold FOB shipping point, title ordinarily passes to the buyer when the goods are shipped. When the terms are FOB destination, title usually does not pass to the buyer until the commodities are delivered. To illustrate, assume that merchandise purchased FOB shipping point is shipped by the seller on the last day of the buyer's fiscal period. The merchandise does not arrive until the following period and hence is not available for "counting" by the inventory crew. Such merchandise should nevertheless be included in the buyer's inventory because title has passed. It is also evident that a debit to Purchases and credit to Accounts Payable should be recorded by the buyer as of the end of the period, rather than recording it as a transaction of the following period.

Another example, although less common, will further emphasize the importance of careful scrutiny of transactions involving shipments of merchandise. Manufacturers sometimes ship merchandise to retailers on a consignment basis, retaining title until the commodities are sold.

192

Obviously, such unsold merchandise is a part of the consignor's inventory even though he does not have physical possession. It is just as obvious that the consignee should not list the consigned merchandise on his inventory sheets.

Determining the cost of inventory

The cost of merchandise inventory is composed of the purchase price and all expenditures incurred in acquiring such merchandise, including transportation, customs duties, and insurance. The purchase price can be readily determined, as may some of the other costs. Those that are difficult to associate with specific inventory items may be prorated on some equitable basis. Minor costs that are difficult to allocate may be excluded entirely from inventory cost and treated as operating expenses of the period.

If purchases discounts are treated as a deduction from purchases on the income statement, they should also be deducted from the purchase price of items in the inventory. If it is not feasible to determine the exact amount of discount applicable to each inventory item, a pro rata amount of the total discount for the period may be deducted instead. For example, if net purchases and purchases discount for the period amount to $200,000 and $3,000 respectively, the discount represents 1½% of net purchases. If the inventory cost, before considering cash discount, is $30,000, the amount may be reduced by 1½%, or $450, to yield an inventory cost of $29,550.

One of the most significant complications encountered in determining inventory cost is related to the fact that identical units of a particular commodity may have been acquired at various unit cost prices during the period. When such is the case, it is necessary to determine the unit prices to be used in valuing the items still on hand. The exact nature of the problem and its relationship to the determination of net income and inventory cost are indicated by the illustration that follows.

Assume that during the fiscal year there have been three identical units of Commodity X available for sale to customers, one of which was on hand at the beginning of the fiscal period. Details are as follows:

COMMODITY X		UNITS	COST
Jan. 1	Inventory......	1	$ 9
Mar. 4	Purchase.......	1	13
May 9	Purchase.......	1	14
	Total	3	$36
	Average cost per unit....		$12

During the period two units of Commodity X were sold, leaving a single unit in the inventory at the end of the period. Information is not available as to which two of the three units were sold and which unit remains. Consequently it becomes necessary to devise an arbitrary assumption as to the *flow of costs* of merchandise through the enterprise. The three most common assumptions employed in determining the cost of merchandise sold are as follows:

1. The merchandise sold is in the order in which the expenditures were made.
2. The merchandise sold is in the reverse order in which the expenditures were made.
3. The merchandise sold is an average of the expenditures for merchandise.

Details of the cost of the two units of Commodity X sold and the cost of the one unit remaining, determined in accordance with each of these assumptions, are presented below.

COMMODITY X COSTS

	UNITS AVAILABLE	UNITS SOLD	UNIT REMAINING
1. In order of expenditures...............	$36	−($ 9 + $13) =	$14
2. In reverse order of expenditures.........	36	−(14 + 13) =	9
3. In accordance with average expenditures..	36	−(12 + 12) =	12

In actual practice it may be possible to identify units with specific expenditures if both the variety of merchandise carried in stock and the volume of sales are relatively small. Ordinarily, however, specific identification procedures are too laborious and costly to justify their use. It is customary, therefore, to adopt one of the three inventory costing methods, each of which is acceptable in determining income subject to the federal income tax.

First-in, first-out method. The first-in, first-out (*fifo*) method of costing inventory is based on the assumption that costs should be charged against revenue in the order in which they were incurred. Hence the inventory remaining is assumed to be composed of the most recent costs. The illustration of the application of this method is based on the following data for a particular commodity:

Jan. 1	Inventory............	200 units at $ 9.....	$ 1,800
Mar. 10	Purchase............	300 units at 10.....	3,000
Sept. 21	Purchase............	400 units at 11.....	4,400
Nov. 18	Purchase............	100 units at 12.....	1,200
	Available for sale during year.	1,000...............	$10,400

The physical count on December 31 indicates that 300 units of the commodity are on hand. In accordance with the assumption that the inventory is composed of the most recent costs, the cost of the 300 units is determined as follows:

Most recent costs, Nov. 18.......100 units at $12.......	$1,200
Next most recent costs, Sept. 21 ..200 units at 11.......	2,200
Inventory, Dec. 31.........300..................	$3,400

Deduction of the inventory of $3,400 from the $10,400 of merchandise available for sale yields $7,000 as the cost of merchandise sold, which represents the earliest costs incurred for this particular commodity.

In most businesses there is a tendency to dispose of commodities in the order of their acquisition. This would be particularly true of perishable merchandise and other goods in which style or model changes are frequent. Thus the fifo method is generally in harmony with the physical movement of merchandise in an enterprise. To the extent that this is the case, the fifo method approximates the results that would be obtained by specific identification of costs.

Last-in, first-out method. The last-in, first-out (*lifo*) method is based on the assumption that the most recent costs incurred should be charged against revenue. Hence the inventory remaining is assumed to be composed of the earliest costs. Based on the illustrative data presented in the preceding section, the cost of the inventory is determined in the following manner:

Earliest costs, Jan. 1............200 units at $ 9.......	$1,800
Next earliest costs, Mar. 10......100 units at 10.......	1,000
Inventory, Dec. 31.........300.................	$2,800

Deduction of the inventory of $2,800 from the $10,400 of merchandise available for sale yields $7,600 as the cost of merchandise sold, which represents the most recent costs incurred for this particular commodity.

The use of the lifo method was originally confined to the relatively rare situations in which the units sold were taken from the most recently acquired stock. It use has greatly increased during the past two decades, and it is now employed without regard to physical flow of commodities.

Weighted average method. The weighted average method is based on the assumption that costs should be charged against revenue on the basis of an average, taking into consideration the number of units acquired at each price. The same average unit cost is employed in computing the cost of the merchandise remaining in the inventory. The weighted average is determined by dividing the total costs of a commodity available for sale by the total number of units of that commodity available for sale. Assuming the same cost data as in the preceding illustrations, the weighted average cost of the 1,000 units and the cost of the inventory are determined as follows:

Weighted average cost. ....$10,400 ÷ 1,000 = $10.40 per unit
Inventory, Dec. 31 ... .300 units at $10.40 .... $3,120

Deduction of the inventory of $3,120 from the $10,400 of merchandise available for sale yields $7,280 as the cost of merchandise sold, which represents the average of the costs incurred for this particular commodity.

For businesses in which various purchases of identical units of a commodity are mingled, the weighted average method has some relationship to the physical flow of commodities.

Comparison of inventory costing methods. Each of the three alternative methods of costing inventories under the periodic system is based on a different assumption as to the flow of costs. If the cost of commodities and the prices at which they were sold remained perfectly stable, all three methods would yield the same results. Prices do fluctuate, however, and as a consequence the three methods will ordinarily yield different amounts for both (1) the inventory at the end of the period and (2) the cost of the merchandise sold and net income during the period. The examples presented in the preceding sections illustrated the effect of rising prices. They may be summarized as follows:

	FIRST-IN, FIRST-OUT	LAST-IN, FIRST-OUT	WEIGHTED AVERAGE
Merchandise available for sale	$10,400	$10,400	$10,400
Merchandise inventory, December 31	3,400	2,800	3,120
Cost of merchandise sold	$ 7,000	$ 7,600	$ 7,280

In comparing and evaluating the results obtained in the illustration, it should be borne in mind that both the amount reported as net income and the amount reported as inventory are affected. The method that yields the lowest figure for the cost of merchandise sold will yield the highest figure for gross profit and net income reported on the income statement; it will also yield the highest figure for inventory reported on the balance sheet. Conversely, the method that yields the highest figure for the cost of merchandise sold will yield the lowest figure for gross profit and net income and the lowest figure for inventory.

During periods of consistently rising prices, the use of first-in, first-out yields the highest possible amount of net income. The reason for this effect is that business enterprises tend to increase their selling prices in accordance with market trends, regardless of the fact that merchandise in stock may have been acquired before the price increase. In periods of declining prices the effect is reversed, and the fifo method yields the lowest possible net income. The principal criticism of the fifo method is this tendency to accentuate the effect of inflationary and deflationary trends on reported income. On the other hand, the amount reported for inventory on the balance sheet will closely approximate its current replacement cost, which is desirable.

During periods of consistently rising prices, the use of last-in, first-out yields the lowest possible amount of net income. The reason for this effect is that the cost of the most recently acquired units most nearly approximates the expenditure required to replace the units sold. In

196

periods of declining prices, the effect is reversed and the lifo method yields the highest possible net income. The principal justification for lifo is this tendency to minimize the effect of price trends on reported net income. A criticism of the general use of lifo is its complete lack of relationship to the physical flow of merchandise in most enterprises. The amount reported for inventory on the balance sheet may also be quite far removed from current replacement cost, which is undesirable. If there is little change in the physical composition of the inventory from year to year, the inventory cost reported remains nearly constant, regardless of extreme changes in price levels.

The weighted average method of inventory costing is, in a sense, a compromise between fifo and lifo. The effect of price trends is averaged, both in the determination of net income and the determination of inventory cost. For any given series of acquisitions, the weighted average cost will be the same regardless of the direction of price trends. For example, a complete reversal of the sequence of acquisitions and unit costs presented in the illustration on page 194 would not affect the reported net income or the inventory cost. The time required to assemble the data is likely to be greater for the weighted average method than for the other two methods. The additional expense incurred could be significant if there are numerous purchases of a wide variety of merchandise items.

The foregoing comparisons indicate the importance attached to the selection of the inventory costing method. The method adopted must be consistently followed from year to year, except where there is a valid reason for a change. The effect of any change in method should be fully disclosed in the financial statements for the fiscal period in which the change occurred.

Throughout the discussion of inventory costing there has been an assumption that the commodities on hand were salable in a normal manner. Because of imperfections, shop wear, style changes or other causes, there may be items that are not salable except at prices below cost. Such merchandise should be valued at estimated selling price less any direct cost of disposition, such as sales commission.

Valuation at the lower of cost or market

An alternative to valuing inventory at cost is to compare cost with market price and use the lower of the two. It should be borne in mind that regardless of the method used it is first necessary to determine the cost of the inventory. "Market," as used in the phrase *lower of cost or market* or *cost or market, whichever is lower*, is interpreted to mean the cost to replace the merchandise on the inventory date. To the extent practicable, the market or replacement price should be based on quantities typically purchased from the usual source of supply. In the discussion that follows, the salability of the merchandise in a normal manner will be assumed. The valuation of articles that have to be sold at a price below cost would be determined by the method described in the preceding paragraph.

If the replacement price of an item in the inventory is lower than its cost, there is almost certain to be an accompanying decline in the selling price. Recognition of the price decline in valuing the item reduces the gross profit (and net income) for the period in which the decline occurred. There is also an inherent presumption that when the item is sold in the following period at a reduced price, the sale should yield a normal gross profit. To illustrate, assume that particular merchandise with a unit cost of $70 has sold during the period at $100, yielding a gross profit of $30 a unit, or 30% of sales. Assume also that there is a single unit of the commodity in the inventory at the end of the year and that meanwhile the replacement price has declined to $63. Under such circumstances it would be reasonable to expect that the selling price would also decline, if indeed it had not already done so. Assuming a reduction in selling price to $90, the gross profit based on replacement cost of $63 would be $27, which is also 30% of selling price. Accordingly, valuation of the unit in the inventory at $63 reduces net income of the past period by $7 and permits a normal gross profit of $27 to be realized on its sale in the following period. If the unit had been valued at its original cost of $70, the net income determined for the past year would have been $7 greater, and the net income attributable to the sale of the item in the following period would have been $7 less.

It would be possible to apply the lower of cost or market rule (1) to each item in the inventory, (2) to major classes or categories, or (3) to the inventory as a whole. The first procedure is the one customarily followed in practice, and it is the only one of the three that is acceptable for federal income tax purposes. To illustrate the application of the lower of cost or market to individual items, assume that there are 400 identical units of Commodity A in the inventory, each acquired at a unit cost of $10.25. If at the inventory date the commodity would cost $10.50 to replace, the cost price of $10.25 would be multiplied by 400 to determine the inventory value. On the other hand, if the commodity could be replaced at $9.50 a unit, the replacement price of $9.50 would be used for valuation purposes. The tabulation at the top of the next page illustrates one of the forms that may be followed in assembling inventory data.

Although the column for total cost is not essential, it permits the measurement of the reduction in inventory attributable to market declines. When the amount of the market decline is known ($450 in the illustration), it may be reported as a separate item on the income statement. Otherwise, the market decline will be included in the amount reported as the cost of merchandise sold and will reduce gross profit by a

198

Description	Quantity	Unit Cost Price	Unit Market Price	Cost	Total Lower of C or M
Commodity A	400	$10.25	$ 9.50	$ 4,100	$ 3,800
Commodity B	120	22.50	24.10	2,700	2,700
Commodity C	600	8.00	7.75	4,800	4,650
Commodity D	280	14.00	14.00	3,920	3,920
Total.....				$15,520	$15,070

corresponding amount. In any event, the amount reported as net income will not be affected; it will be the same regardless of whether or not the amount of the market decline is determined and separately stated.

As with the method elected for the determination of inventory cost (fifo, lifo, or weighted average), the method elected for inventory valuation (cost, or lower of cost or market) must be followed consistently from year to year. Both methods of valuation are acceptable in determining income for federal income tax purposes. When the last-in, first-out procedure is employed, the inventory must be stated at cost. It is not permissible to apply lower of cost or market valuation to a lifo inventory.

Retail method of inventory costing

An additional method of inventory costing that is widely used by retail businesses, particularly department stores, is called the *retail inventory* method. It is employed in connection with the periodic system of inventories and is based on the relationship of the cost of merchandise available for sale to the retail price of the same merchandise. The retail prices of all merchandise acquired are accumulated in supplementary records, and the inventory at retail is determined by deducting sales for the period from the retail price of the goods that were available for sale during the period. The inventory at retail is then converted to cost on the basis of the ratio of the cost of the merchandise available for sale to the selling price of the merchandise available for sale.

Determination of inventory by the retail method is illustrated below.

	Cost	Retail
Merchandise inventory, January 1.......................	$19,400	$ 36,000
Purchases in January (net)...............................	42,600	64,000
Merchandise available for sale...........................	$62,000	$100,000

Ratio of cost to retail price:
$$\frac{\$62,000}{\$100,000} = 62\%$$

Sales for January (net).................................		70,000
Merchandise inventory, January 31, at retail price...........		$ 30,000
Merchandise inventory, January 31, at estimated cost price ($30,000 × 62%).......................................		$ 18,600

There is an inherent assumption in the retail method that the composition or "mix" of the commodities in the ending inventory, in terms of percent of cost to selling price, is comparable to the entire stock of merchandise available for sale. For example, in the illustration above it is unlikely that the retail price of every item was composed of exactly 62% cost and 38% gross profit margin. It is assumed, however, that the weighted average of the cost percentages of the merchandise in the inventory ($30,000) is the same as in the merchandise available for sale ($100,000). Where the inventory is composed of different classes of merchandise with significantly different gross profit rates, the cost percentages and the inventory should be developed separately for each section or department.

The use of the retail method does not eliminate the necessity for taking a physical inventory at the end of the year. The items are recorded on the inventory sheets at their selling prices instead of their cost prices, however. The physical inventory at selling price is then converted to cost by applying the ratio of the cost of merchandise available for sale to the selling price of the same merchandise. To illustrate, assume that the data presented in the example above are for an entire fiscal year rather than for the first month of the year only. If the physical inventory taken on December 31, priced at retail, totaled $29,000, it would be this amount rather than the $30,000 in the illustration that would be converted to cost. Accordingly, the inventory at cost would be $17,980 ($29,000 × 62%) instead of $18,600 ($30,000 × 62%).

200

One of the principal advantages of the retail method is that it provides inventory figures for use in preparing interim statements. Department stores and similar merchandisers customarily determine gross profit and net operating income each month but take a physical inventory only once a year. In addition to facilitating frequent income determinations, a comparison of the computed inventory total with the physical inventory total, both at retail prices, will disclose the extent of inventory shortages and the consequent need for corrective measures.

Perpetual inventory system

The use of a perpetual inventory system for merchandise provides the most effective means of control over this important asset. Although it is possible to maintain a perpetual inventory in memorandum records only or to limit the data to quantities, a complete set of records integrated with the general ledger is preferable. The basic feature of the system is the recording of all merchandise increases and decreases in a manner somewhat similar to the recording of increases and decreases in cash. Just as receipts of cash are debited to Cash so are purchases of merchandise debited to Merchandise Inventory. Similarly, sales or other reductions of merchandise are recorded in a comparable manner to reductions in Cash, that is, by credits to Merchandise Inventory. Thus, just as the balance of the cash account indicates the amount of cash presumed to be on hand, so the balance of the merchandise inventory account represents the amount of merchandise presumed to be on hand.

Unlike cash, merchandise is a heterogeneous mass of commodities. Details of the cost of each type of merchandise purchased and sold, together with such related transactions as returns and allowances, must be maintained in a subsidiary ledger, with a separate account for each type. Thus an enterprise that stocks five hundred types of merchandise would need five hundred accounts in its inventory ledger. The flow of costs through a subsidiary account is illustrated below. There was a beginning inventory, two purchases, and three sales of the particular commodity during the period covered. The number of units on hand after each transaction, together with unit prices and total amounts, appear in the balance section.

	PURCHASES		SALES		BALANCE		
DATE	QUANTITY	AMOUNT	QUANTITY	AMOUNT	QUANTITY	UNIT PRICE	AMOUNT
Jan. 1					2	$20	$ 40
15	8	$160			10	20	200
21			2	$ 40	8	20	160
29			6	120	{ 2	20	40
Feb. 4	15	315			{ 15	21	315
10			4	82	13	21	273

With a perpetual system, as in a periodic system of inventory determination, it is necessary either to identify the items sold with a specific purchase or to employ a cost flow assumption. In the foregoing illustration the first-in, first-out flow method of costing was used. Note that after the sale on January 29 there was a balance remaining of 2 units at $20 each. The 15 units added on February 4 were acquired at a unit cost of $21 instead of $20, and hence could not be combined with the preceding balance. The brace connecting the two quantities in the balance section was inserted as a safeguard against error when pricing out the next sale and determining the new balance. Finally, it should be noted that the February 10 sale of 4 units was composed of the 2 units remaining from the first purchase ($40) plus 2 units from the second purchase ($42), leaving a balance of 13 units at a unit price of $21.

The first-in, first-out cost flow assumption yields the same unit inventory prices for the perpetual system as for the periodic system. The last-in, first-out method of cost flow, as it is generally understood, cannot be applied to a perpetual inventory system because the unit costs of the last purchases of a period cannot be determined until the end of the period. The weighted average method of cost flow can be applied to the perpetual system, though in a somewhat modified form. Instead of determining a weighted average price for each type of commodity at the end of a period, an average unit price is computed each time a purchase is made. The unit price so computed is then used to determine the cost of the items sold until another purchase is made. This averaging technique is called a *moving average*.

In earlier chapters, sales of merchandise were recorded by debits to the cash or accounts receivable account and credits to the sales account. The cost of the merchandise sold was not determined for each sale. It was determined only periodically by means of a physical inventory. In contrast to the periodic system, the perpetual system provides the cost data related to each sale. The cost data for sales on account may be accumulated in a special column inserted in the sales journal. Each time merchandise is sold on account the amount entered in the "cost" column represents a debit to Cost of Merchandise Sold and a credit to Merchandise Inventory. Similar provisions can be made for cash sales. To illustrate sales on account, assume that the monthly total of the cost column of the sales journal is $140,000 and that the monthly total of the sales column is $210,000. The effect on the general ledger accounts is indicated by the two entries below, in general journal form.

Cost of Merchandise Sold........................	140,000	
Merchandise Inventory........................		140,000
Accounts Receivable..........................	210,000	
Sales..		210,000

The control feature is the most important advantage of the perpetual system. The inventory of each class of merchandise is always readily available in the subsidiary ledger, both in terms of number of units and dollar amounts. A physical count of any class of merchandise can be made at any time and compared with the balance of the subsidiary account to determine the existence and seriousness of any shortages. When a shortage is discovered, an entry is made debiting Inventory Shortages and crediting Merchandise Inventory for the cost. If the balance of the inventory shortages account at the end of a fiscal period is relatively minor, it may be included in Miscellaneous General Expense on the income statement. Otherwise it may be separately reported in the general expense section.

Presentation of merchandise inventory on the balance sheet

Merchandise inventory is customarily presented on the balance sheet immediately below receivables. Both the method of determining the cost of the inventory (lifo, fifo, or average) and the method of valuing the inventory (cost, or lower of cost or market) should be disclosed. Both are significant to the reader. The details may be disclosed by a parenthetical notation or a footnote. The use of a parenthetical notation is illustrated by the following partial balance sheet:

Brewster Company
Balance Sheet
December 31, 1969

Assets

Current assets:		
Cash...		$19,400
Accounts receivable............................	$80,000	
Less allowance for doubtful accounts..............	3,000	77,000
Merchandise inventory — at lower of cost (first-in, first-out method) or market.........................		216,300

It is not unusual for large enterprises with diversified activities to use different costing and pricing methods for different segments of their inventories. The following note from the balance sheet of a merchandising chain is illustrative: "Merchandise inventories in stores are stated at the lower of cost or market, as calculated by the retail method of inventory. Merchandise in warehouses and in transit and food products inventories in restaurants are stated at cost."

Gross profit method of estimating inventories

When perpetual inventories are maintained or when the retail inventory method is used, the inventory on hand may be closely approximated at any time without the necessity of a physical count. In the absence of these devices, the inventory may be estimated by the *gross profit* method, which utilizes an estimate of the gross profit realized on sales during the period.

If the rate of gross profit on sales is known, the dollar amount of sales for a period can be divided into its two components: (1) gross profit and (2) cost of merchandise sold. The latter may then be deducted from the cost of merchandise available for sale to yield the inventory of merchandise on hand.

To illustrate this method, assume that the inventory on January 1 is $17,000, that net purchases during the month amount to $9,000, that net sales during the month amount to $15,000, and finally that gross profit is *estimated* to be 30% of net sales. The inventory on January 31 may be estimated as follows:

Merchandise inventory, January 1		$17,000
Purchases in January (net)...................		9,000
Merchandise available for sale...............		$26,000
Sales in January (net).......................	$15,000	
Less estimated gross profit ($15,000 × 30%)....	4,500	
Estimated cost of merchandise sold...........		10,500
Estimated merchandise inventory, January 31 ..		$15,500

The estimate of the rate of gross profit is ordinarily based on the actual rate for the preceding year, adjusted for any known changes in markups during the current period. Inventories estimated in this manner are useful in preparing interim statements. The method may also be employed in establishing an estimate of the cost of merchandise destroyed by fire.

QUESTIONS

1. The merchandise inventory at the end of the year was inadvertently understated by $10,000. (a) Did the error cause an overstatement or an understatement of the net income for the year? (b) Which items on the balance sheet at the end of the year were overstated or understated as a result of the error?

2. The $10,000 inventory error in Question 1 was not discovered and the inventory at the end of the following year was correctly stated. (a) Will the earlier error cause a $10,000 overstatement or understatement of the net income for the following year? (b) Which items on the balance sheet at the end of the following year will be overstated or understated by $10,000 as a result of the error in the earlier year?

3. (a) Differentiate between the periodic system and the perpetual system of inventory determination. (b) Which system ordinarily is more expensive to maintain?

4. What is meant by the term *physical inventory*?

5. When does title to merchandise ordinarily pass from the seller to the buyer if the terms of shipment are (a) FOB destination; (b) FOB shipping point?

6. Purchases of merchandise for the year totaled $500,000 and purchases discounts for the same period, which are considered to be reductions in cost, amounted to $4,800. If the cost of the merchandise inventory at the end of the year, before considering the purchases discount, is $50,000, what would be a reasonable amount of purchases discount to deduct from the purchase price of the inventory?

7. Do the terms *fifo* and *lifo* refer to techniques employed in determining quantities of the various classes of merchandise on hand? Explain.

8. Does the term *first-in* in the fifo method mean that the items in the inventory are assumed to be those that were acquired first? Explain.

9. Under which method of cost flow are (a) the most recent costs assigned to inventory; (b) the earliest costs assigned to inventory; (c) average costs assigned to inventory?

10. The following lots of a particular commodity were available for sale during the year:

Beginning inventory..... 30 units at $4.00
First purchase.......... 50 units at $4.50
Second purchase........100 units at $5.00

The firm uses the periodic system and there are 25 units of the commodity on hand at the end of the year. (a) What is their unit cost according to fifo? (b) What is their unit cost according to lifo? (c) Is the weighted average unit cost $4.50?

11. If merchandise inventory is being valued at cost and the price level is consistently rising, which of the three methods of costing, fifo, lifo, or weighted average, will yield (a) the highest inventory cost, (b) the lowest inventory cost, (c) the largest net income, (d) the smallest net income?

12. An enterprise using "cost" as its method of inventory valuation proposes to value at $600 a group of items having a total cost of $1,000. On what basis could this reduction in value be justified?

13. Which of the three methods of inventory costing, fifo, lifo, or weighted average, will in general yield an inventory cost most nearly approximating current replacement cost?

14. In the phrase *lower of cost or market*, what is meant by market?

15. How should merchandise be valued that is unsalable in the normal manner because of changes in style or other causes?

16. The cost of a particular inventory item is $50, the current replacement cost is $45, and the selling price is $60. At what amount should the item be included in the inventory according to the rule of cost or market, whichever is lower?

17. In which of the following types of businesses would a perpetual inventory system be practicable: (a) retail hardware store, (b) wholesale grocer, (c) retail fur store, (d) retail druggist, (e) restaurant, and (f) dealer in office machines?

18. Under which, if any, of the following systems or methods of inventory determination is a periodic physical inventory unnecessary: (a) retail inventory method, (b) perpetual inventory system, (c) gross profit method, (d) periodic inventory system?

19. An enterprise using a perpetual inventory system sells merchandise to a customer on account for $1,000; the cost of the merchandise was $700. (a) What are the effects of the transaction on general ledger accounts? (b) What is the amount and direction of the net change in the amount of assets and capital resulting from the transaction?

20. When inventory is valued at cost and the periodic system of inventory determination is used, does the amount reported on the income statement as *cost of merchandise sold* ordinarily include an unknown amount of write-downs for shop wear, the cost of stolen merchandise, and costs attributable to other shortages? Discuss.

21. Is it possible that the expense incurred in maintaining a perpetual inventory system might be greater than the benefits derived through reduction of inventory shortages caused by theft, negligence, and other causes? Discuss.

205

EXERCISES

8-1. The beginning inventory and the purchases of Commodity 487A during the year were as follows:

Commodity 487A

Jan. 1	Inventory..................	20 units at	$19.50
Mar. 10	Purchase	30 units at	21.00
July 26	Purchase	16 units at	20.50
Oct. 19	Purchase	14 units at	22.00

There are 23 units of Commodity 487A in the physical inventory at December 31 (the periodic system is used). Determine the inventory cost and the cost of merchandise sold by three methods, presenting your answers in the following form:

	Cost	
Inventory Method	Merchandise Inventory	Merchandise Sold
(1) First-in, first-out	$	$
(2) Last-in, first-out		
(3) Weighted average		

8-2. On the basis of the data presented below, determine the value of the inventory at the lower of cost or market. Assemble the data in the form illustrated on page 199, in order that the inventory reduction attributable to price declines may be ascertained.

Commodity	Inventory Quantity	Unit Cost	Unit Market
1-A	100	$10.50	$11.00
2-B	300	22.00	20.00
3-C	200	35.00	29.00
4-D	400	21.00	26.00
5-E	500	5.50	5.00

8-3. The cost of four categories of merchandise purchased during the month and the markup are given below. Determine the following for each category: (a) selling price, (b) amount of gross profit, (c) percent of gross profit to selling price, and (d) percent of cost to selling price.

Class	Cost	Markup on Cost
11	$12,000	20%
12	20,000	25%
13	15,000	33⅓%
14	10,000	50%

8-4. On the basis of the following data, estimate the cost of the merchandise inventory at July 31 by the retail method:

		Cost	Retail
July 1	Merchandise inventory....	$133,982	$202,900
July 1–31	Purchases (net)..........	64,918	97,100
July 1–31	Sales (net)..............		90,000

8-5. Beginning inventory, purchases, and sales data for Commodity 479-Y are presented below. The enterprise maintains a perpetual inventory system, costing by the first-in, first-out method. Determine the cost of the merchandise sold in each sale and the inventory balance after each sale, presenting the data in the form illustrated on page 201.

March	1	Inventory	10 units at $21
April	10	Sold.	6 units
May	15	Purchased.	20 units at $22
June	8	Sold.	9 units
	25	Sold.	8 units
July	10	Purchased.	5 units at $23

8-6. The merchandise inventory of Taylor Company was destroyed by fire on May 4. The following data were obtained from the accounting records:

Jan. 1	Merchandise inventory.	$30,000
Jan. 1–May 4	Purchases (net).	16,200
	Sales (net).	19,400
	Estimated gross profit rate. . . .	38%

Estimate the cost of the merchandise destroyed.

PROBLEMS

The following additional problems for this chapter are located in Appendix C: 8-1B, 8-2B, 8-3B, 8-4B, 8-5B.

8-1A. Saratoga TV-Radio Co. employs the periodic inventory system. Details regarding their inventory of television sets at January 1, purchase invoices during the year, and the inventory count at December 31 are summarized below.

Model	Inventory Jan. 1	Purchase Invoices 1st	2nd	3rd	Inventory Count Dec. 31
102	4 at $ 62	8 at $ 65	4 at $ 68	——	2
105	7 at 104	8 at 109	5 at 114	6 at $115	8
214	6 at 129	5 at 135	2 at 144	2 at 144	5
317	2 at 282	4 at 294	9 at 294	4 at 300	5
524	——	4 at 173	6 at 178	——	3
630	4 at 347	3 at 347	6 at 352	5 at 359	4
888	6 at 346	4 at 340	5 at 331	3 at 325	7

Instructions:

(1) Determine the cost of the inventory on December 31 by the first-in, first-out method. Present data in columnar form, using the columnar headings indicated at the top of the next page. If the inventory of a particular model is composed of an entire lot plus a portion of another lot acquired at a different unit price, use a separate line for each lot.

Model	Quantity	Unit Cost	Total Cost

(2) Determine the cost of the inventory on December 31 by the last-in, first-out method, following the procedures described in instruction (1).

(3) Determine the cost of the inventory on December 31 by the weighted average method, using the columnar headings prescribed in instruction (1).

8-2A. The beginning inventory of Commodity 477X and data on purchases and sales for a three-month period are presented below.

April	1	Inventory.......	5 units at $14.00	$ 70.00
	15	Purchase.........	10 units at 14.50	145.00
	16	Sale............	8 units at 20.00	160.00
	28	Sale............	4 units at 20.00	80.00
May	4	Purchase.........	12 units at 14.75	177.00
	8	Sale............	4 units at 20.50	82.00
	15	Sale............	7 units at 21.00	147.00
	26	Purchase........	8 units at 14.75	118.00
June	10	Sale............	6 units at 21.00	126.00
	12	Sale............	3 units at 22.00	66.00
	18	Purchase.........	10 units at 15.50	155.00
	30	Sale............	4 units at 22.50	90.00

Instructions:

208

(1) Record the inventory, purchase, and cost of merchandise sold data in a perpetual inventory record similar to the one illustrated on page 201, using the first-in, first-out method.

(2) Determine the total sales and the total cost of Commodity 477X sold for the period, and express their effect on the general ledger by two entries in general journal form. Assume that all sales were on account.

(3) Determine the gross profit from sales of Commodity 477X for the period.

(4) Determine the cost of the inventory at June 30, assuming that the periodic system of inventory had been employed and that the inventory cost had been determined by the last-in, first-out method.

8-3A. Selected data on merchandise inventory, purchases, and sales for the Oxford Co. and the Dayton Co. are presented below and at the top of the next page.

OXFORD CO.

	Cost	Retail
Merchandise inventory, March 1....	$233,388	$364,100
Transactions during March:		
Purchases.....................	75,790⎫	
Purchases discount.............	610⎭	114,300
Sales........................		215,100
Sales returns and allowances......		2,300

Dayton Co.

Merchandise inventory, July 1	$230,600
Transactions during July and August:	
Purchases	310,700
Purchases discount	3,200
Sales	417,000
Sales returns and allowances	4,300
Estimated gross profit rate	33%

Instructions:

(1) Determine the estimated cost of the merchandise inventory of the Oxford Co. on March 31 by the retail method, presenting details of the computations.

(2) Estimate the cost of the merchandise inventory of the Dayton Co. on August 31 by the gross profit method, presenting details of the computations.

If the working papers correlating with the textbook are not used, omit Problem 8-4A.

8-4A. Data on the physical inventory of Jackson & Co. as of September 30, the close of the current fiscal year, are presented in the working papers. The quantity of each commodity on hand has been determined and recorded on the inventory sheet; unit market prices have also been determined as of September 30 and recorded on the sheet. The inventory is to be determined at cost and also at the lower of cost or market, using the first-in, first-out method. Quantity and cost data from the last purchase invoice of the year and the next-to-the-last purchase invoice are summarized below.

	Last Purchase Invoice		Next-to-the-Last Purchase Invoice	
Description	Quantity Purchased	Unit Cost	Quantity Purchased	Unit Cost
1839B	75	$ 17	50	$ 16
FC566	60	75	120	75
OPL14	25	215	25	220
JM482	12	250	24	240
1642A	8	48	10	47
1945D	50	93	35	90
SL416	300	9	300	10
269LB	100	29	100	28
MJ630	300	5	600	5
653ND	500	8	350	6
WD87	60	14	150	13
31VW	40	42	70	40
AAA17	48	50	96	51
666RS	175	9	75	8
E3B1Y	240	15	480	14
CB111	96	20	144	19
XXX75	250	5	100	5
BC243	360	5	120	4

Instructions:

Record the appropriate unit costs on the inventory sheet and complete the pricing of the inventory. When there are two different unit costs applicable to a commodity, proceed as follows:

(1) Draw a line through the quantity and insert the quantity and unit cost of the last purchase.

(2) On the following line insert the quantity and unit cost of the next-to-the-last purchase. The first item on the inventory sheet has been completed as an example.

8-5A. The preliminary income statement of Newman & Co. presented below was prepared before the accounts were adjusted or closed at the end of the fiscal year. The company uses the periodic inventory system.

Newman & Co.
Income Statement
For Year Ended June 30, 19—

Sales (net)		$237,200
Cost of merchandise sold:		
Merchandise inventory, July 1, 19—	$ 46,940	
Purchases (net)	172,630	
Merchandise available for sale	$219,570	
Less merchandise inventory, June 30, 19— . . .	49,460	
Cost of merchandise sold		170,110
Gross profit on sales		$ 67,090
Operating expenses		49,654
Net income		$ 17,436

The following errors in the ledger and on inventory sheets were discovered by the independent accountant retained to conduct the annual audit:

(a) A number of errors were discovered in pricing inventory items, in extending amounts, and in footing inventory sheets. The net effect of the corrections, exclusive of those described below, was to increase by $2,900 the amount stated as the ending inventory on the income statement above.

(b) A purchase invoice for merchandise of $750, dated June 27, was not received until July 1 and had not been recorded by June 30. However, the merchandise, to which title had passed, had arrived and had been included in the June 30 inventory.

(c) A purchase invoice for merchandise of $600, dated June 28, had been received and correctly recorded, but the merchandise was not received until July 3 and had not been included in the June 30 inventory. Title had passed to Newman & Co. on June 28.

(d) A sales order for $1,500, dated June 30, had been recorded as a sale on that date, but title did not pass to the purchaser until shipment was made on July 3. The merchandise, which had cost $1,050, was excluded from the June 30 inventory.

(e) An item of office equipment, received on June 30, was erroneously included in the June 30 merchandise inventory at its cost of $520. The invoice had been recorded correctly.

(f) A sales invoice for $1,800, dated June 30, had not been recorded. The merchandise was shipped on June 30, FOB shipping point, and its cost, $1,250, was excluded from the June 30 inventory.

Instructions:

(1) Journalize the entries necessary to correct the general ledger accounts as of June 30, inserting the identifying letters in the date column. All purchases and sales were made on account.
(2) Determine the correct inventory for June 30, beginning your analysis with the $49,460 shown on the preliminary income statement. Assemble the corrections in two groupings, "Additions" and "Deductions," allowing six lines for each group. Identify each correction by the appropriate letter.
(3) Prepare a revised income statement.

8-6A. The unadjusted trial balance of Nippon Imports, distributor of imported motor bicycles, as of the end of the current fiscal year, is as follows:

Nippon Imports
Trial Balance
November 30, 19—

Cash.................................	12,310	
Accounts Receivable.................	19,250	
Allowance for Doubtful Accounts........		310
Merchandise Inventory...............	47,600	
Accounts Payable.....................		18,470
J. L. Simpson, Capital................		38,250
J. L. Simpson, Drawing...............	12,000	
Sales................................		234,600
Purchases............................	151,300	
Operating Expenses (control account)....	48,600	
Interest Income.......................		350
Interest Expense......................	920	
	291,980	291,980

Data needed for adjustments at November 30:

(a) Merchandise inventory at November 30, at lower of cost (first-in, first-out method) or market, $59,450.
(b) Uncollectible accounts expense is estimated at $\frac{1}{2}$ of 1% of sales.
(c) Accrued wages on November 30, $210.

Instructions:

(1) Journalize the necessary adjusting entries.
(2) Prepare (a) an income statement, (b) a capital statement, and (c) a balance sheet in report form, without the use of a conventional work sheet.

part Four

Deferrals, accruals, and
long-lived assets

9

Deferrals and accruals

Accounting and periodic reports

Data on revenues earned and expenses incurred by a business enterprise are periodically assembled and reported in the form of an income statement. Such statements always cover a definite period of time, such as a specific month, quarter, half-year, or year. The periodic matching of revenues and expenses yields the amount of net income or net loss, which is of great significance to management, owners, creditors, and others who may be interested in the enterprise. In addition, the matching process yields the amounts of assets, liabilities, and capital to be reported on the balance sheet as of the end of the period, which is also significant to interested parties.

When cash is received for a revenue within the same period that the revenue is earned, there is no question about the period to which the revenue relates. Similarly, when an expense is paid during the period in which the benefits from the service are received, there can be no doubt concerning the period to which the expense should be allocated. Problems of allocation are encountered when there are time differentials between the earning of revenues or the occurrence of expenses and the recognition of their respective effects on assets and equities.

The use of adjusting entries in facilitating the allocation of expenses to appropriate periods was demonstrated in earlier chapters. Deferrals and accruals of various expenses, including insurance, supplies, taxes, wages, and uncollectible accounts, have been described and illustrated in some detail. This chapter is devoted to further consideration of deferrals and accruals of expenses and also of revenues. The underlying purpose of their recognition is to achieve a fair statement of all revenues and expenses for a period of time and a fair statement of all assets and equities as of the last day of the period.

Classification and terminology

There are many kinds of revenues and expenses that may require deferral or accrual in particular circumstances. When such is the case they are recorded as adjusting entries on the work sheet used in preparing financial statements. If the work sheet is for the fiscal year, the adjustments are also journalized and posted to the ledger. For interim statements, the adjustments may appear only on the work sheet.

The following characteristic of all adjustments should be noted in the explanations and illustrations of this chapter: Every adjusting entry affects both a balance sheet account and an income statement account. To illustrate, assume that the effect of the credit portion of a particular adjusting entry is to increase a liability account (balance sheet). It follows that the effect of the debit portion of the entry will be either (1) to increase an expense account (income statement) or (2) to decrease a revenue account (income statement). In no case will an adjustment affect only an asset and a liability (both balance sheet) or only an expense and a revenue (both income statement).

213

Deferral. A deferral is a postponement of the recognition of an expense already paid or of a revenue already received.

Deferred expenses may also be described on the balance sheet as *prepaid expenses* or *deferred charges.* They are assets and may be listed among the current assets or, if the deferment encompasses a number of years, they may be presented as a separate category.

Deferred revenues may also be described on the balance sheet as *unearned revenues, revenue received in advance,* or *deferred credits.* They are liabilities and may be listed among the current liabilities or, if a relatively long period of time is involved, they may be presented as a separate category or classification.

Accrual. An accrual is an expense or a revenue that has gradually accumulated but has not yet been recognized in the accounts by a routine entry.

Accrued expenses may also be described on the balance sheet as *accrued liabilities,* or reference to the accrual may be omitted from the title, as in "Wages payable." The liabilities for accrued expenses are ordinarily due within a year and are listed as current liabilities.

Accrued revenue may also be described on the balance sheet as *accrued assets*, or reference to the accrual may be omitted from the title, as in "Interest receivable." The amounts receivable for accrued revenues are usually due within a short time and are classified as current assets.

Prepaid expenses (Deferral)

Prepaid expenses are commodities and services purchased for consumption that are unconsumed at the end of the accounting period. The portion of the asset that has been used during the period has become an expense; the remainder will not become an expense until some time in the future. It is because of this deferral of benefits to the future that prepaid expenses are sometimes termed *deferred expenses* or *deferred charges*. Prepaid expenses include such items as prepaid insurance, prepaid rent, prepaid advertising, prepaid interest, and various types of supplies.

At the time a prepaid expense is acquired, it may be debited either to an asset account or to an expense account. The two alternative systems are explained and illustrated in the paragraphs that follow. It should be understood that in any particular situation either alternative may be elected. The difference between the systems is entirely procedural; their effect on the financial statements is identical.

Prepaid expenses recorded initially as assets. Insurance premiums or other consumable services or supplies may be debited to asset accounts when purchased, even though all or a part of them is expected to be consumed during the accounting period. The amount actually used is then determined at the end of the period and the accounts adjusted accordingly.

To illustrate, assume that the prepaid insurance account has a balance of $1,034 at the close of the year. This amount represents the unexpired insurance at the beginning of the year plus the total of premiums on policies purchased during the year. Assume further that $406 of insurance premiums is ascertained to have expired during the year. The adjusting entry to record the $406 decrease of the asset and the corresponding increase in expense is as follows:

		Adjusting Entry			
Dec.	31	Insurance Expense...................	716	406	
		Prepaid Insurance................	118		406

After this entry has been posted, the two accounts affected appear as shown at the top of the next page.

After the $406 of expired insurance is transferred to the expense account, the balance of $628 remaining in Prepaid Insurance represents the cost of premiums on various policies that apply to future periods.

DATE		ITEM	POST. REF.	DEBIT	CREDIT	BALANCE	
						DEBIT	CREDIT
1969							
Jan.	1	Balance	√			650	
Mar.	18		CP6	110		760	
Aug.	26		CP16	180		940	
Nov.	11		CP21	94		1,034	
Dec.	31	Adjusting	J17		406	628	

DATE		ITEM	POST. REF.	DEBIT	CREDIT	BALANCE	
						DEBIT	CREDIT
1969							
Dec.	31	Adjusting	J17	406		406	

The $406 expense appears on the income statement for the period and the $628 asset appears on the balance sheet as of the end of the period.

Prepaid expenses recorded initially as expenses. The alternative to the system just illustrated is to debit the costs to an appropriate expense account at the time of the expenditure. It may be considered the preferable procedure for recording the discount on notes payable issued to banks, which are ordinarily for a period of from 30 to 90 days. If the interest deducted by the bank is debited to Interest Expense at the time the funds are borrowed and if the notes are paid by the end of the fiscal year, no adjusting entry is necessary. When one or more discounted notes are still outstanding on the last day of the year, however, the portion of the interest applicable to the following period should be deducted from the expense account and transferred to the asset account by means of an adjusting entry.

215

To illustrate this alternative system, assume that during the year four non-interest-bearing notes payable were discounted and that in each case the discount was debited to Interest Expense. Three of the notes became due and were paid during the year. The fourth, a $12,000, 90-day note, had been issued on December 1 at a discount of $180.

As of the last day of the fiscal year, only 30 days of the 90-day term of the $12,000 note have elapsed. Therefore only $60 ($\frac{1}{3}$ of $180) of the discount is an expense of the year; the remaining $120 ($\frac{2}{3}$ of $180) will become an expense during the first 60 days of the following year. The entry to transfer the $120 to the asset account is as follows:

		Adjusting Entry			
Dec.	31	Prepaid Interest......................	117	120	
		Interest Expense....................	911		120

After the adjusting entry has been posted, the asset account and the expense account appear as follows:

PREPAID INTEREST   ACCOUNT No. 117

DATE		ITEM	POST. REF.	DEBIT	CREDIT	BALANCE DEBIT	BALANCE CREDIT
1969 Dec.	31	Adjusting	J17	120		120	

INTEREST EXPENSE   ACCOUNT No. 911

DATE		ITEM	POST. REF.	DEBIT	CREDIT	BALANCE DEBIT	BALANCE CREDIT
1969 Feb.	5		CR3	50		50	
May	15		CR8	144		194	
June	10		CR10	105		299	
Dec.	1		CR20	180		479	
	31	Adjusting	J17		120	359	

The remaining balance of $359 in Interest Expense is the amount of expense for the year. It is reported in the income statement and will be transferred to Expense and Revenue Summary in the process of closing the accounts. The balance of $120 in Prepaid Interest is reported in the balance sheet as a current asset.

During the first 60 days of the following year, the prepaid interest on the loan becomes interest expense at the rate of $2 a day ($120 ÷ 60). It would be possible, though obviously unnecessary, to record a $2 transfer from the asset account to the expense account on each of the 60 days. Another possibility would be to wait until the 60 days had elapsed and then transfer the entire $120 from the asset account to the expense account. If there were additional notes on which interest was prepaid, a similar transfer would be required each time a note became due.

In such situations, the most efficient means of assuring proper allocations in the ensuing period is to add *reversing entries* to the summarizing procedures. Their use eliminates the necessity of referring back to earlier adjustment data and lessens the possibilities of error. The effect of the reversing entry for the prepayment is to transfer the entire balance of the asset account to the expense account immediately after the temporary accounts have been closed for the period. Continuing with the illustration, the reversing entry is as follows:

		Reversing Entry			
Jan.	1	Interest Expense............	911	120	
		Prepaid Interest............	117		120

216

After the reversing entry has been posted, the prepaid interest account and the interest expense account appear as follows:

PREPAID INTEREST   Account No. 117

DATE		ITEM	POST. REF.	DEBIT	CREDIT	BALANCE	
						DEBIT	CREDIT
1969							
Dec.	31	Adjusting	J17	120		120	
1970							
Jan.	1	Reversing	J18		120	—	—

INTEREST EXPENSE   Account No. 911

DATE		ITEM	POST. REF.	DEBIT	CREDIT	BALANCE	
						DEBIT	CREDIT
1969							
Feb.	5		CR3	50		50	
May	15		CR8	144		194	
June	10		CR10	105		299	
Dec.	1		CR20	180		479	
	31	Adjusting	J17		120	359	
	31	Closing	J17		359	—	—
1970							
Jan.	1	Reversing	J18	120		120	

It should be noted that the reversing entry does not change the essential nature of the $120, only its location in the ledger. It is prepaid interest on January 1, just as it was prepaid interest on December 31. However, it will become an expense before the close of the ensuing year, and hence no further attention needs to be given to the item.

Comparison of the two systems. The two systems of recording prepaid expenses and the related entries at the end of an accounting period are summarized below.

Prepaid expense recorded initially as an asset:

Adjusting — Transfers amount *used* to appropriate expense account.
Closing — Closes balance of expense account.
Reversing — Not required.
(Amount prepaid at beginning of new period is in the asset account.)

Prepaid expense recorded initially as an expense:

Adjusting — Transfers amount *unused* to appropriate asset account.
Closing — Closes balance of expense account.
Reversing — Transfers amount *unused* back to expense account.
(Amount prepaid at beginning of new period is in the expense account.)

Either of the two systems may be adopted for all of the prepaid expenses of an enterprise, or one system may be used for prepayment of certain types of expenses and the other system for other types. Initial

217

debits to the asset account appear to be particularly logical for prepayments of insurance, which are typically for periods of from one to five years. On the other hand, interest charges on notes payable are usually for short periods, some charges may be recorded when a note is issued (as in the illustration), other charges may be recorded when a note is paid, and few, if any, of the debits for interest may require adjustment at the end of the period. It therefore seems logical to record all interest charges initially by debiting the expense account rather than the asset account.

As was noted earlier, the amount reported as expense in the income statement and as asset on the balance sheet will not be affected by the system employed. To avoid confusion and consequent inefficiency the system adopted by an enterprise for each particular type of prepaid expense should be followed consistently from year to year.

Unearned revenues (Deferral)

Revenue received during a particular period may be only partly earned by the end of the period. Items of revenue that are received in advance represent a liability that may be termed *unearned revenue*. The portion of the liability that is discharged during the period through delivery of commodities or services has been earned; the remainder will be earned in the future. It is because of this deferment that unearned revenues are frequently called *deferred credits*. For example, magazine publishers ordinarily receive advance payment for subscriptions extending for periods ranging from a few months to a number of years. At the end of an accounting period, the portion of the receipts applicable to future periods has not been earned and should appear in the balance sheet as a liability.

Other examples of unearned revenue are rent received in advance on property owned, interest deducted in advance on notes receivable, premiums received in advance by an insurance company, tuition received in advance by a school, an annual retainer fee received in advance by an attorney, and amounts received in advance by an advertising firm for advertising services to be rendered in the future.

By accepting payment for the commodity or the service in advance, a business renders itself liable to furnish the commodity or the service at some future time. At the end of the accounting period, if some portion of the commodity or the service has been furnished, part of the revenue has been earned. The earned portion appears in the income statement. The unearned portion represents a liability of the business to furnish the commodity or the service in a future period and is reported in the balance sheet as a liability. As in the case of prepaid expenses, two systems of accounting will be explained and illustrated.

Unearned revenues recorded initially as liabilities. When revenue is received in advance, it may be credited to a liability account. To illustrate, assume that on October 1 a business rents a portion of its building for a period of one year, receiving $3,600 in payment for the entire term of the lease. Assume also that the transaction was originally recorded by a debit to Cash and a credit to the liability account Unearned Rent. On December 31, the end of the fiscal year, one fourth of the amount has been earned and three fourths of the amount remains a liability. The entry to record the revenue and reduce the liability appears as follows:

			Adjusting Entry			
Dec.	31	Unearned Rent....................	218	900	
		Rent Income....................	812		900

After this entry has been posted, the unearned rent account and the rent income account appear as follows:

UNEARNED RENT   ACCOUNT No. 218

DATE		ITEM	POST. REF.	DEBIT	CREDIT	BALANCE DEBIT	BALANCE CREDIT
1969							
Oct.	1		CR8		3,600		3,600
Dec.	31	Adjusting	J17	900			2,700

RENT INCOME   ACCOUNT No. 812

DATE		ITEM	POST. REF.	DEBIT	CREDIT	BALANCE DEBIT	BALANCE CREDIT
1969							
Dec.	31	Adjusting	J17		900		900

After the amount earned, $900, is transferred to Rent Income, the balance of $2,700 remaining in Unearned Rent is a liability to render a service in the future, and it therefore appears as a current liability in the balance sheet. Rent Income is reported in the Other Income section of the income statement; the account is closed to the expense and revenue summary account along with other revenue accounts.

Unearned revenues recorded initially as revenues. Instead of being credited to a liability account, unearned revenue may be credited to a revenue account as the cash is received. To illustrate this alternative, assume the same facts as in the preceding illustration, except that the transaction was originally recorded on October 1 by a debit to Cash and a credit to Rent Income. On December 31, the end of the fiscal year, three fourths of the balance in Rent Income is still unearned and the

219

remaining one fourth has been earned. The entry to record the transfer to the liability account appears as follows:

			Adjusting Entry			
Dec.	31	Rent Income..........................	812	2,700		
		Unearned Rent..................	218		2,700	

After this entry has been posted, the unearned rent account and the rent income account appear as follows:

UNEARNED RENT   ACCOUNT No. 218

DATE		ITEM	POST. REF.	DEBIT	CREDIT	BALANCE DEBIT	BALANCE CREDIT
1969 Dec.	31	Adjusting	J17		2,700		2,700

RENT INCOME   ACCOUNT No. 812

DATE		ITEM	POST. REF.	DEBIT	CREDIT	BALANCE DEBIT	BALANCE CREDIT
1969 Oct.	1		CR8		3,600		3,600
Dec.	31	Adjusting	J17	2,700			900

220

The unearned rent of $2,700 is listed as a current liability in the balance sheet, and the rent income of $900 is reported in the income statement. In the process of closing the accounts, the balance of the rent income account is closed to the expense and revenue summary account.

The $2,700 of unearned rent at the end of the year will be earned during the following year. If it is transferred to the income account by a *reversing* entry immediately after the accounts are closed, no further action will be needed either month by month or at the end of the nine-month period. Furthermore, since the $3,600 rent was credited initially to the income account, all such payments received in the following year will presumably be treated in a similar fashion. If a reversing entry is not made, there may be balances in both the liability account and the income account at the end of the following year, necessitating analysis of both accounts and causing possible confusion. The reversing entry for the unearned rent, which is the exact reverse of the adjusting entry, is as follows:

			Reversing Entry			
Jan.	1	Unearned Rent.....................	218	2,700		
		Rent Income......................	812		2,700	

After the foregoing entry is posted to the two accounts, they will appear as follows:

UNEARNED RENT   ACCOUNT No. 218

DATE		ITEM	POST. REF.	DEBIT	CREDIT	BALANCE DEBIT	BALANCE CREDIT
1969 Dec.	31	Adjusting	J17		2,700		2,700
1970 Jan.	1	Reversing	J18	2,700		—	—

RENT INCOME   ACCOUNT No. 812

DATE		ITEM	POST. REF.	DEBIT	CREDIT	BALANCE DEBIT	BALANCE CREDIT
1969 Oct.	1		CR8		3,600		3,600
Dec.	31	Adjusting	J17	2,700			900
	31	Closing	J17	900		—	—
1970 Jan.	1	Reversing	J18		2,700		2,700

At the beginning of the new fiscal year, there is a credit balance of $2,700 in Rent Income. Although the balance is in reality a liability at this time, it will become revenue before the close of the year. Whenever a revenue account needs adjustment for an unearned amount at the end of a period, the adjusting entry should be reversed after the accounts have been closed.

Comparison of the two systems. The two systems of recording unearned revenue and the related entries at the end of the accounting period are summarized below.

Unearned revenue recorded initially as a liability:

> Adjusting — Transfers amount *earned* to appropriate revenue account.
> Closing — Closes balance of revenue account.
> Reversing — Not required.
> (Amount unearned at beginning of new period is in the liability account.)

Unearned revenue recorded initially as revenue:

> Adjusting — Transfers amount *unearned* to appropriate liability account.
> Closing — Closes balance of revenue account.
> Reversing — Transfers amount *unearned* back to revenue account.
> (Amount unearned at beginning of new period is in the revenue account.)

Either of the systems may be adopted for all revenues received in advance, or the first system may be used for advance receipts of certain types of revenue and the second system for other types. The results obtained are the same under both systems, and of course it is not advisable to shift back and forth arbitrarily from one to the other.

221

Accrued liabilities

Some expenses accrue from day to day but for obvious reasons are ordinarily recorded only when they are paid. Examples are salaries paid to employees and interest paid on notes payable. The amounts of such accrued but unpaid items at the end of the fiscal period are both an expense and a liability. It is for this reason that such accruals are referred to variously as *accrued liabilities* or *accrued expenses*.

To illustrate the adjusting entry for an accrued liability, assume that on December 31, the end of the fiscal year, the salary expense account has a debit balance of $32,300. During the year salaries have been paid each Friday for the five-day week then ended. For this particular fiscal year, December 31 falls on Wednesday. Reference to the records of the business reveals that the salary accrued for these last three days of the year amounts to $575. The entry to record the additional expense and the liability is as follows:

			Adjusting Entry			
Dec.	31	Salary Expense.....................	611	575		
		Salaries Payable..................	214		575	

After the adjusting entry has been posted to the two accounts, they appear as follows:

SALARIES PAYABLE ACCOUNT No. 214

DATE		ITEM	POST. REF.	DEBIT	CREDIT	BALANCE DEBIT	BALANCE CREDIT
1969 Dec.	31	Adjusting	J17		575		575

SALARY EXPENSE ACCOUNT No. 611

DATE		ITEM	POST. REF.	DEBIT	CREDIT	BALANCE DEBIT	BALANCE CREDIT
1969 Dec.	31	Balance	√			32,300	
	31	Adjusting	J17	575		32,875	

The accrued salaries of $575 recorded in Salaries Payable will appear in the balance sheet of December 31 as a current liability. The balance of $32,875 now recorded in Salary Expense will appear in the income statement for the year ended December 31, and the account will be closed to the expense and revenue summary account in the usual manner.

When the weekly salaries are paid on January 2 of the following year, part of the payment will discharge the liability of $575 and the remainder will represent salary expense incurred in January. In order to avoid the necessity of analyzing the payment, a reversing entry is made at the beginning of the new year. The effect of the entry, which is illustrated below, is to transfer the credit balance in the salaries payable account to the credit side of the salary expense account.

<table>
<tr><td></td><td></td><td colspan="2" align="center">Reversing Entry</td><td></td><td></td></tr>
<tr><td>Jan.</td><td>1</td><td>Salaries Payable......................</td><td>214</td><td>575</td><td></td></tr>
<tr><td></td><td></td><td>Salary Expense....................</td><td>611</td><td></td><td>575</td></tr>
</table>

After the reversing entry has been posted, the salaries payable account and the salary expense account appear as follows:

SALARIES PAYABLE   ACCOUNT No. 214

DATE		ITEM	POST. REF.	DEBIT	CREDIT	BALANCE DEBIT	BALANCE CREDIT
1969 Dec.	31	Adjusting	J17		575		575
1970 Jan.	1	Reversing	J18	575		—	—

SALARY EXPENSE   ACCOUNT No. 611

DATE		ITEM	POST. REF.	DEBIT	CREDIT	BALANCE DEBIT	BALANCE CREDIT
1969 Dec.	31	Balance	√			32,300	
	31	Adjusting	J17	575		32,875	
	31	Closing	J18		32,875	—	—
1970 Jan.	1	Reversing	J18		575		575

223

The liability for salaries on December 31 now appears as a credit in Salary Expense. Assuming that the salaries paid on Friday, January 2, amount to $710, the debit to Salary Expense will automatically record the discharge of the liability of $575 and an expense of $135 ($710 — $575).

The discussion of the treatment of accrued salary expense is illustrative of the method of handling accrued liabilities in general. If, in addition to accrued salaries, there are other accrued liabilities at the end of a fiscal period, separate liability accounts may be set up for each type. When these liability items are numerous, however, a single liability account entitled Accrued Payables or Accrued Liabilities may be used. All accrued liabilities may then be recorded as credits to this account instead of to separate accounts.

Because of peculiarities in the timing of their accrual and payment, the adjusting process applicable to property taxes is frequently more complicated than it is for salaries and interest. Accounting for property taxes is described and illustrated later in this chapter.

Accrued assets

All assets belonging to the business at the end of an accounting period and all revenues earned during the period should be recorded in the ledger. But during a fiscal period it is the customary practice to record some types of revenue only as the cash is received; consequently, at the end of the period there may be items of revenue that have not been recorded. In such cases it is necessary to record the amount of the accrued revenue by debiting an asset account and crediting a revenue account. Because of the dual nature of such accruals, they are referred to variously as *accrued assets* or *accrued revenues*.

To illustrate the adjusting entry for an accrued asset, assume that on December 31, the end of the fiscal year, the interest income account has a credit balance of $584. Assume further that on the same date the business owns three short-term, interest-bearing notes accepted from customers. The three notes are for varying amounts and have varying due dates in January and February of the succeeding year. The total interest accrued on the three notes from their respective issuance dates to December 31 is determined to be $167. The entry to record this increase in the amount owed by the debtors and the additional revenue earned on the notes is as follows:

		Adjusting Entry			
Dec.	31	Interest Receivable.....................	114	167	
		Interest Income....................	811		167

After this entry has been posted, the interest receivable account and the interest income account appear as follows:

INTEREST RECEIVABLE   Account No. 114

DATE		ITEM	POST. REF.	DEBIT	CREDIT	BALANCE DEBIT	BALANCE CREDIT
1969 Dec.	31	Adjusting	J17	167		167	

INTEREST INCOME   Account No. 811

DATE		ITEM	POST. REF.	DEBIT	CREDIT	BALANCE DEBIT	BALANCE CREDIT
1969 Dec.	31	Balance	√				584
	31	Adjusting	J17		167		751

The accrued interest of $167 recorded in Interest Receivable will appear in the balance sheet of December 31 as a current asset. The credit balance of $751 now recorded in Interest Income will appear in the Other Income section of the income statement for the year ended December 31 and the account will be closed to the expense and revenue summary account in the usual manner.

When the amount due on each of the three notes is collected in the succeeding year, part of the interest received will effect a reduction of the interest receivable and the remainder will represent revenue for the new year. To avoid the inconvenience of analyzing each receipt of interest in the new year, a reversing entry is made immediately after the accounts are closed. The effect of the entry, which is illustrated below, is to transfer the debit balance in the interest receivable account to the debit side of the interest income account.

			Reversing Entry			
Jan.	1	Interest Income....................	811	167		
		Interest Receivable...............	114			167

After this entry has been posted, the interest receivable account and the interest income account appear as follows:

INTEREST RECEIVABLE   ACCOUNT No. 114

DATE		ITEM	POST. REF.	DEBIT	CREDIT	BALANCE DEBIT	BALANCE CREDIT
1969 Dec.	31	Adjusting	J17	167		167	
1970 Jan.	1	Reversing	J18		167	—	—

INTEREST INCOME   ACCOUNT No. 811

DATE		ITEM	POST. REF.	DEBIT	CREDIT	BALANCE DEBIT	BALANCE CREDIT
1969 Dec.	31	Balance	√				584
	31	Adjusting	J17		167		751
	31	Closing	J17	751		—	—
1970 Jan.	1	Reversing	J18		167	167	

The interest accrued on the three notes receivable as of December 31 now appears as a debit in Interest Income. At the time each note matures and the payment is received from the maker, the entire amount of the interest received will be credited to Interest Income. The credit will in part represent a reduction in the receivable of $167 and in part a revenue of the new period. If, for example, one of the three notes held on December 31 is for the face amount of $5,000 with interest at 6% for 90 days, the total amount of interest received at maturity will be $75. The entire

225

$75 will be credited to Interest Income regardless of the amount representing collection of a receivable and the amount representing revenue of the new period.

The treatment of interest accrued on notes receivable illustrates the method of handling accrued assets in general. If, in addition to accrued interest, there are other accrued assets at the end of a fiscal period, separate accounts may be set up. Each of these accounts will be of the same nature as the account with interest receivable. When such items are numerous, a single account entitled Accrued Receivables or Accrued Assets may be used. All accrued assets may then be recorded as debits to this account.

Property taxes

Various types of taxes are levied on businesses by federal, state, and local governments. The total tax expense incurred by an enterprise each year frequently amounts to a substantial portion of its revenues. It is usually the responsibility of the accounting department to prepare the required tax reports, to design the procedure for recording taxes in the accounts, and to prescribe the manner of reporting taxes in the financial statements. The remainder of this chapter is devoted to a discussion of property taxes, with emphasis on their deferral or accrual.

Types of property. In law, all property is either real property or personal property. *Real property*, also called *realty* or *real estate*, includes land and anything permanently attached to the land. Buildings, trees, fences, water lines, sidewalks, and other improvements to land come within the definition of real property.

All property not classified as realty is termed *personal property*, or *personalty*. Such property is subdivided into two major categories, *tangible* and *intangible*. Tangible personalty includes equipment, merchandise, supplies, and other physical assets. Intangible personalty includes investments in stocks and bonds, accounts and notes receivable, prepaid insurance, bank deposits, and other assets having no physical substance.

Tax base. The method of determining the value of property for tax purposes varies among taxing jurisdictions and for different types of property. The value assigned to real estate is frequently determined by the tax assessor without reference to cost, book value, or other evidence provided in the accounts and records of the owner. In general, the assessed value tends to be lower than the fair market value of the property. Personal property may also be appraised by an assessor, or the owner may be required to declare the value of his property. In the latter case the cost of the property is usually the starting point in determining value for tax purposes. Methods of determining the amount of depreciation to be deducted from cost in arriving at the tax base are usually prescribed by statute or administrative regulations.

Tax rates. A governmental unit determines its tax rate each year by dividing the total revenue to be raised from the tax by the total assessed value of the property within its jurisdiction. For example, if the budgeted revenue requirements of a county for the year amount to $2,000,000 and the value of all taxable property in the county is $100,000,000, the county tax rate will be set at 20 mills (2 cents) per $1 of assessed value ($2,000,000 ÷ $100,000,000). A person whose property is assessed at $30,000 will be required to pay a tax of $600 for the year (.02 x $30,000). In some jurisdictions the tax rate on tangible personal property is lower than the tax rate on real property.

Payment of taxes. The time specified for payment of property taxes varies greatly among governmental units. Real estate taxes and personal property taxes may be billed together or they may be billed separately and at different times. Frequently the law provides for payment in two installments. If taxes are not paid on time, they become *delinquent* and the property owner may be charged with an additional sum as a penalty. If the taxes and the penalties are not paid within a specified period of time, the property may be seized by the government and sold. Property taxes become a *lien* against the property, usually from the date of assessment until they are paid. A purchaser of property with unpaid taxes acquires it subject to the lien of the government.

Accounting for property taxes

The liability for annual property taxes is usually incurred on a particular day of the year, sometimes called the lien date, specified by the laws of the taxing jurisdiction. The period covered by the tax may be the year just ended, the year just begun, or some other twelve-month period, depending upon the tax laws applicable. Inasmuch as the governmental services to which the tax relates are received during an entire year, it is logical to allocate the expense equitably over the twelve months benefited.

The selection of the particular twelve-month period for allocation is complicated by the fact that the exact amount of the tax assessment may not be known until several months after the liability attaches to the property. A difference between the fiscal year of the taxpayer and the fiscal year of the taxing authority may also complicate the problem. Various methods of accounting for property taxes are acceptable, provided the method selected is followed consistently from year to year.

The method to be described here provides for monthly allocation over the fiscal year of the taxing authority for which the tax is levied.[1] Two alternative procedural patterns may be followed: (1) interim adjustments may be recorded solely on working papers, with any required year-end adjustments being recorded in the accounts, or (2) adjustments may be recorded in the accounts at the end of each month. Because of the cumulative nature of the adjustments for property taxes, the second alternative is frequently used. It will be used in the illustration that follows. The allocations reported in the interim and year-end financial statements will be the same regardless of which procedure is adopted. The illustration is based on the following assumed facts:

Fiscal year of the business enterprise: January 1, 1969 to December 31, 1969.
Fiscal year of the taxing authority: July 1, 1969 to June 30, 1970.
Tax statement received: October 15, 1969.
Tax paid in equal installments on November 10, 1969 and May 10, 1970.

The adjustments data and related transactions are described below, followed by the related entries, in each case in general journal form.

At the end of July the taxpayer estimates that the property tax assessment for the 1969–70 fiscal year of the taxing authority will be $3,240. The amount to be accrued as of July 31, 1969 is therefore $270 ($3,240 ÷ 12) and the entry to record the accrual in the taxpayer's accounts is as follows:

			Adjusting Entry		
July	31	Property Tax Expense......................	270		
		Property Tax Payable....................		270	

An entry for the same amount is recorded as of the last day of August and again on September 30, by which time there is a balance of $810 (3 × $270) in the property tax payable account.

On October 15 a tax statement for $3,480 is received, half of which is payable on November 10. The correct amount of the accrual apportionable to each of the past three months is therefore $290 ($3,480 ÷ 12) instead of $270. Ordinarily the difference between the actual and the estimated monthly expense is not material. In any event, the underestimate or overestimate is corrected in the adjusting entry for the month in which the actual amount of the tax becomes known. The amount of the accrual to be recorded at the end of October is therefore determined as follows:

Amount of tax allocable to July, Aug., Sept. and Oct., 4×$290	$1,160
Amount of tax allocated to July, Aug. and Sept., 3×$270...	810
Tax allocation for October.............................	$ 350

[1]Recommended by *Accounting Research and Terminology Bulletins*, "No. 43, Restatement and Revision of Accounting Research Bulletins" (New York: American Institute of Certified Public Accountants, 1961), pp. 81–85.

The $350 allocation for October may also be computed by adding the $60 deficiency ($3 \times \$20$) for the first three months to the regular October monthly allocation of $290. The adjusting entry as of October 31 is as follows:

			Adjusting Entry		
Oct.	31	Property Tax Expense......................	350		
		Property Tax Payable....................		350	

One half of the tax bill, $1,740, is paid on November 10. Of this amount, $1,160 is in payment of the accrual and $580 represents a deferral. The entry to record the payment is as follows, in general journal form:

Nov.	10	Property Tax Payable......................	1,160	
		Prepaid Property Tax......................	580	
		Cash..		1,740

At the end of November, and again at the end of December, the following adjusting entry is made:

			Adjusting Entry		
Nov.	30	Property Tax Expense......................	290		
		Prepaid Property Tax.....................		290	

At December 31, the end of the fiscal year for the business enterprise, one half of the 1969–70 property tax has been charged to expense and there is neither a tax accrual nor a tax deferral recorded in the accounts. The legal obligation for the entire tax of 1969–70 was created in 1969, but the usual accounting treatment is to spread the cost ratably over the period to which the tax relates. If it were considered necessary to report the accrual of the second half of the tax bill as a liability on the balance sheet at December 31, 1969, it would also be necessary to report a deferral of equal amount as an asset.

The adjusting entries and the entry for payment of the second half of the tax bill during January through June of the following year would be similar to those presented for the period July through December. There would, however, be no need to estimate the property tax assessment; the monthly charges to expense would be uniformly $290.

229

QUESTIONS

1. During the fiscal year, an enterprise makes advance payment of premiums on five-year property insurance policies. (a) At the close of such fiscal year will there be a deferral or an accrual? (b) Which of the following types of accounts will be affected by the related adjusting entry at the end of the fiscal year: (1) asset, (2) liability, (3) revenue, (4) expense?

2. At the end of the fiscal year an enterprise holds a 90-day interest-bearing note receivable accepted from a customer thirty days earlier. (a) Will the interest on the note as of the end of the year represent a deferral or an accrual? (b) Which of the following types of accounts will be affected by the related adjusting entry at the end of the fiscal year: (1) asset, (2) liability, (3) revenue, (4) expense? (c) Assuming that the note is held until maturity, what fraction of the total interest should be allocated to the year in which the note is collected?

3. On December 31, the end of its fiscal year, an enterprise owes salaries of $1,500 for an incomplete payroll period. On the first payday in January, salaries of $2,100 are paid. (a) Is the $1,500 a deferral or an accrual as of December 31? (b) Which of the following types of accounts will be affected by the related adjusting entry: (1) asset, (2) liability, (3) revenue, (4) expense? (c) How much of the $2,100 salary payment should be allocated to January?

4. On January 5 an enterprise receives $12,000 from a tenant as rent for the current calendar year. The fiscal year of the enterprise is from August 1 to July 31. (a) Will the adjusting entry for the rent as of July 31 of the current year be a deferral or an accrual? (b) Which of the following types of accounts will be affected by the adjusting entry as of July 31: (1) asset, (2) liability, (3) revenue, (4) expense? (c) How much of the $12,000 rent should be allocated to the current fiscal year ending July 31?

5. The debit portion of a particular adjustment is to an asset account. (a) If the adjustment is for a deferral, which of the following types of accounts will be credited: (1) asset, (2) liability, (3) revenue, (4) expense? (b) If the adjustment is for an accrual, which of the following types of accounts will be credited: (1) asset, (2) liability, (3) revenue, (4) expense?

6. Classify the following items as (a) prepaid expense, (b) unearned revenue, (c) accrued asset, or (d) accrued liability.

(1) Interest owed but not yet due.
(2) Supplies on hand.
(3) Receipts from sale of meal tickets by a restaurant.
(4) Interest earned but not received.
(5) Property taxes paid in advance.
(6) A three-year premium paid on a fire insurance policy.
(7) Subscriptions collected in advance by a publisher.
(8) Life insurance premiums received by an insurance company.
(9) Taxes owed but payable in the following period.
(10) Receipts from sale of season tickets for a series of concerts.
(11) Salary owed but not yet due.
(12) Portion of fee earned but not yet received.

7. Each of the following debits and credits represents one half of an adjusting entry. Name the title of the account that would be used for the remaining half of the entry.

(a) Interest Payable is credited.
(b) Supplies is debited.
(c) Unearned Subscriptions is credited.
(d) Prepaid Insurance is credited.
(e) Unearned Rent is debited.
(f) Interest Income is debited.

8. The interest accrued on a $10,000 note payable at the end of the year is $70. In the following year the note is paid, including interest of $150. (a) Give the adjusting entry that should be made at the end of the year. (b) Give the entry for payment of the note and interest, assuming (1) the adjusting entry for $70 had been reversed and (2) the adjusting entry had not been reversed.

9. There are balances in each of the following accounts after adjustments have been made at the end of the fiscal year. Identify each as (a) asset, (b) liability, (c) revenue, or (d) expense.

(1) Salary Expense
(2) Interest Receivable
(3) Prepaid Insurance
(4) Interest Expense
(5) Rent Income
(6) Rent Expense
(7) Prepaid Interest
(8) Insurance Expense
(9) Interest Payable
(10) Supplies
(11) Interest Income
(12) Unearned Rent

10. The accountant for a real estate brokerage and management company adheres to the following uniform procedures in recording certain transactions:
(1) Premiums on fire insurance are debited to Prepaid Insurance.
(2) Supplies purchased are debited to Supplies Expense.
(3) Management fees, which are collected for one year in advance, are credited to Management Fees when received.

Assuming that an adjusting entry is required for each of the foregoing at the end of the fiscal year, (a) give the accounts to be debited and credited for each adjustment and (b) state whether or not each of the adjusting entries should be reversed as of the beginning of the following year.

11. How is it possible to determine from a trial balance before adjustments whether a particular type of prepaid expense has been recorded initially as an asset or as an expense?

12. Explain how the reversing of adjustments for accrued assets and accrued liabilities facilitates the recording of transactions.

13. If a particular type of revenue typically collected in advance is invariably credited to an income account at the time received, why should the year-end adjusting entry be reversed?

14. (a) Is it almost a certainty that a business enterprise will always have prepaid property and casualty insurance at the end of each fiscal year? Explain.

(b) Is it almost a certainty that a business enterprise that occasionally discounts short-term notes payable at its bank will always have prepaid interest at the end of each fiscal year? Explain.

(c) Would it be logical to record prepayments of the type referred to in (a) as assets and prepayments of the type referred to in (b) as expenses? Discuss.

15. The status of the accounts listed below is as of the beginning of the fiscal year, after reversing entries have been posted but before any transactions have occurred. Identify each balance as (a) an asset or (b) a liability.
(1) Interest Income, debit balance of $310.
(2) Unearned Rent, credit balance of $1,200.
(3) Salary Expense, credit balance of $1,420.
(4) Supplies Expense, debit balance of $60.
(5) Prepaid Insurance, debit balance of $850.

16. The real estate tax rate in a certain county is $41.60 per thousand dollars of valuation. (a) What is the tax rate per dollar of valuation? (b) What is the tax rate stated as a percent?

17. Identify the following as (a) realty, (b) tangible personalty, or (c) intangible personalty:

(1) Flood lights around parking lot
(2) Accounts receivable
(3) Adding machine
(4) Cash in bank
(5) Water pipes installed in building

(6) Shares of stock
(7) Office desk
(8) Notes receivable
(9) Building
(10) Vacant land

18. At the end of the first month of the year, the Oasis Company estimates that its property taxes for such year will amount to $6,000. Give the adjusting entry to be recorded by Oasis Company.

19. During the first three months of the year, Parker Co. records accruals of estimated property tax of $300 a month. The tax statement received in the fourth month is for $3,900, which means that the actual tax accrual is $325 a month. Give the adjusting entry to be recorded at the end of the fourth month.

20. At the time of payment of $2,400 for the semiannual property tax, the property tax payable account has a credit balance of $1,600. Give the entry to record the $2,400 payment.

EXERCISES

9-1. The office supplies inventory of the Lakeview Company at the beginning of the fiscal year is $275, purchases of office supplies during the year total $620, and the inventory at the end of the year is $230.

(a) Set up T accounts for Office Supplies and Office Supplies Expense, and record the following directly in the accounts, employing the system of initially recording office supplies as an asset (identify each entry by number): (1) opening balance; (2) purchases for the period; (3) adjusting entry at end of the period; (4) closing entry; (5) reversing entry if appropriate.

(b) Set up T accounts for Office Supplies and Office Supplies Expense, and record the following directly in the accounts, employing the system of initially recording office supplies as an expense (identify each entry by number): (1) opening balance; (2) purchases for the period; (3) adjusting entry at end of the period; (4) closing entry; (5) reversing entry if appropriate.

9-2. (a) Set up T accounts for Salary Expense, Expense and Revenue Summary, and Salaries Payable, and enter a balance of $86,590 in Salary Expense as of October 26.

(b) Record the following entries directly in the T accounts:

(1) Record accrued salaries of $1,420 as of October 31, the end of the fiscal year.
(2) Close the salary expense account as of October 31.
(3) Reverse the adjusting entry as of November 1.
(4) Record the debit for salaries of $1,845 paid on November 2.

(c) Answer the following questions:

(1) Is the balance of the salary expense account on November 1 an asset, a liability, a revenue, or an expense?

(2) What is the balance of the salary expense account on November 2?

(3) Of the $1,845 salary payment on November 2, how much is expense of November?

(4) If there had been no reversing entry on November 1, how should the debit for the salary payment of November 2 have been recorded?

9-3. In their first year of operations, the King Publishing Co. receives $245,000 from advertising contracts and $168,000 from magazine subscriptions, crediting the two amounts to Advertising Revenue and Circulation Revenue respectively. At the end of the year, the deferral of advertising revenue amounts to $70,000 and the deferral of circulation revenue amounts to $51,000. (a) If no adjustments are made at the end of the year, will revenue for the year be overstated or understated, and by what amount? (b) Present the adjusting entries that should be made at the end of the year. (c) Present the entries to close the two revenue accounts. (d) Present the reversing entries, if appropriate.

9-4. (a) Present entries in general journal form for the following:

Nov. 21. Issued to Heath Co., on account, an $11,100, 60-day, 6% note dated November 21.

Dec. 31. Recorded an adjusting entry for accrued interest on the note of November 21.

31. Closed the interest expense account. The only entry in this account originated from the above adjustment.

Jan. 1. Recorded a reversing entry for accrued interest.

20. Paid Heath Co. $11,211 on the note due today.

(b) Set up T accounts for Interest Payable and Interest Expense and post the foregoing entries.

(c) What is the balance in Interest Expense after the entry of January 20?

(d) How many days' interest on $11,100 at 6% does the amount reported in (c) represent?

9-5. Because of a lack of consistency by the bookkeeper in recording the payment of premiums on property and casualty insurance, there are balances in both the asset and expense accounts at the end of the year before adjustments. Prepaid Insurance has a debit balance of $740 and Insurance Expense has a debit balance of $1,020. You ascertain that the total amount of insurance premiums allocable to future periods is $985.

(a) Assuming that you will instruct the bookkeeper to record all future insurance premiums as an expense, present journal entries: (1) to adjust the accounts, (2) to close the appropriate account, and (3) to reverse the adjusting entry if appropriate.

(b) Assuming that you will instruct the bookkeeper to record all future insurance premiums as an asset, present journal entries: (1) to adjust the accounts, (2) to close the appropriate account, and (3) to reverse the adjusting entry if appropriate.

(c) (1) What is the amount of insurance expense for the year?

(2) What is the amount of prepaid insurance at the close of the year?

9-6. The real estate tax rate for Hamilton is $43.76 per thousand dollars of valuation. Equipment used in business is subject to tax at one half of the real estate rate. On tax listing day, the total cost of all equipment recorded in the accounts of Phelps Co. is $120,600; accumulated depreciation determined in accordance with the regulations of the taxing authority totals $36,200. Determine the property tax on the equipment.

9-7. The entries in the following account identified by numbers are related to the summarizing process at the end of the year. (a) Identify each entry as adjusting, closing, or reversing and (b) present for each entry the title of the account to which the related debit or credit was posted.

INTEREST INCOME

DATE		ITEM	DEBIT	CREDIT	BALANCE DEBIT	BALANCE CREDIT
Jan.	1	(1)	120		120	
	1	(2)		75	45	
Jan. to Dec.	1 31	Transactions during the year		660		615
	31	(3)		80		695
	31	(4)	45			650
	31	(5)	650		—	
Jan.	1	(6)	80		80	
	1	(7)		45	35	

PROBLEMS

The following additional problems for this chapter are located in Appendix C: 9-1B, 9-2B, 9-3B, 9-4B, 9-7B.

9-1A. The accounts listed below appear in the ledger of Meadowbrook Realty at December 31, the end of the current fiscal year. None of the year-end adjustments has been recorded.

113	Interest Receivable...... $ —	411	Rental Income.......... $107,600
114	Supplies............... 395	511	Salary and Commissions
115	Prepaid Insurance........ 1,450		Expense.............. 20,300
116	Prepaid Advertising...... —	513	Advertising Expense..... 3,200
117	Prepaid Interest.......... —	514	Insurance Expense...... —
213	Salaries and Commissions	515	Supplies Expense........ —
	Payable.............. —	611	Interest Income......... 410
215	Unearned Rent.......... —	711	Interest Expense........ 1,160
313	Expense and Revenue		
	Summary............. —		

The following information relating to adjustments at December 31 is obtained from physical inventories, supplementary records, and other sources:

(a) Interest accrued on notes receivable at December 31, $84.

(b) Inventory of supplies at December 31, $125.

(c) The insurance record indicates that $510 of insurance has expired during the year.

(d) Of a prepayment of $1,000 for advertising space in a local newspaper, 60% has been used and the remainder will be used in the following year.

(e) A short-term non-interest-bearing note payable was discounted at a bank in December. The amount of the total discount of $200 applicable to December is $75.

(f) Salaries and commissions accrued at December 31, $1,720.

(g) Rent collected in advance that will not be earned until the following year, $6,180.

Instructions:

(1) Open the accounts listed and record the balances in the appropriate balance columns, as of December 31.

(2) Journalize the adjusting entries and post to the appropriate accounts after each entry, extending the balances. Identify the postings by writing "Adjusting" in the items columns.

(3) Prepare a compound journal entry to close the revenue accounts and another compound entry to close the expense accounts.

(4) Post the closing entries, inserting a short line in both balance columns of accounts that are closed. Identify the postings by writing "Closing" in the items columns.

(5) Prepare the reversing journal entries that should be made on January 1 and post to the appropriate accounts after each entry, inserting a short line in both balance columns of accounts that are now in balance. Write "Reversing" in the items columns.

9-2A. Finch Co. closes its accounts annually as of December 31, the end of the fiscal year. All relevant data regarding notes payable and related interest from November 21 through February 14 of the following year are presented below. (All notes are dated as of the day they are issued.)

Nov. 21. Issued a $9,000, 6%, 90-day note on account.
Dec. 1. Issued a $5,000, 6%, 60-day note on account.
     16. Borrowed $6,000 from Second National Bank, issuing an 8%, 60-day note.
     22. Paid principal, $4,000, and interest, $70, on note payable due today.
     31. Recorded an adjusting entry for the interest accrued on the notes dated November 21, December 1, and December 16. There are no other notes outstanding on this date.
     31. Recorded the entry to close the interest expense account.
Jan. 1. Recorded a reversing entry for the accrued interest.
     12. Issued an $8,000, 6%, 30-day note on account.
     30. Paid $5,050 on the note issued on December 1.
Feb. 11. Paid $8,040 on the note issued on January 12.
     14. Paid $6,080 on the note issued on December 16.
     19. Paid $9,135 on the note issued on November 21.

Instructions:

(1) Open accounts for Interest Payable (Account No. 214) and Interest Expense (Account No. 711), and record a debit balance of $731 in the latter account as of November 21 of the current year.

(2) Present entries in general journal form to record the transactions and other data described above, posting to the two accounts after each entry affecting them.

(3) If the reversing entry had not been recorded as of January 1, indicate how each interest payment in January and February should be allocated. Submit the data in the following form:

Note (face amount)	Total Interest Paid	Dr. Interest Payable	Dr. Interest Expense
$5,000	$	$	$
8,000			
6,000			
9,000			
Total	$	$	$

(4) Do the February 19 balances of Interest Payable and Interest Expense obtained by use of the reversing entry technique correspond to the

balances that would have been obtained by the more laborious process of analyzing each payment?

If the working papers correlating with the textbook are not used, omit Problem 9-3A.

9-3A. The Gibson Company prepares interim financial statements at the end of each month and closes its accounts annually on December 31. Its income statement for the two-month period, January and February of the current year, is presented in the working papers. In addition, the trial balance of the ledger as of one month later is presented on an eight-column work sheet in the working papers. Data needed for adjusting entries at March 31, the end of the three-month period, are as follows:

(a) Uncollectible accounts expense is estimated at ½ of 1% of net sales for the three-month period.
(b) Estimated merchandise inventory at March 31, $58,220.
(c) Insurance expired during the three-month period:
  Allocable as selling expense, $215.
  Allocable as general expense, $90.
(d) Estimated inventory of store supplies at March 31, $260.
(e) Depreciation for the three-month period:
  Store equipment, $440.
  Office equipment, $135.
(f) Estimated property tax of $132 a month for January and February was recorded in the accounts. The tax statement, which was received in March, indicates a liability of $1,740 for the calendar year.
(g) Salaries accrued at March 31:
  Sales salaries, $240.
  Office salaries, $45.
(h) The notes payable balance of $14,000 is composed of the following:
  $10,000, 90-day, non-interest-bearing note discounted at Merchants Trust Co. on March 1. The $150 discount was debited to Interest Expense. (Record adjustment in work sheet before considering the other note.)
  $4,000, 6-month, 6% note dated December 1 of the preceding year. (Accrue interest for 4 months.)

Instructions:

(1) Complete the eight-column work sheet for the three-month period ended March 31 of the current year.
(2) Prepare an income statement for the three-month period, using the last three-column group of the nine-column form in the working papers.
(3) Prepare an income statement for the month of March, using the middle three-column group of the nine-column form in the working papers.
(4) Prepare a capital statement for the three-month period. There were no additional investments during the period.
(5) Prepare a balance sheet as of March 31.
(6) Determine the amount of interest expense on each note allocable to the month of March and compare the total with the amount reported as interest expense in the income statement for March.

9-4A. The Reynolds Co. prepares interim statements at the end of each month and closes its accounts annually on December 31. Property taxes are assessed for fiscal years beginning on July 1 and ending on June 30. Selected transactions and property tax allocations for the period July 1 to December 31 of one year and of January 1 to June 30 of the following year are presented below.

July 31. Property tax allocation for July based on estimated property tax of $6,600 for the taxing authority's fiscal year beginning July 1.

Sept. 30. Property tax allocation for September, based on tax statement dated September 20 indicating a tax assessment of $6,144.

Oct. 15. Paid first half of tax assessment, $3,072.
31. Property tax allocation for October.

Dec. 31. Property tax allocation for December.

Jan. 31. Property tax allocation for January.

May 15. Paid second half of tax assessment, $3,072.
31. Property tax allocation for May.

June 30. Property tax allocation for June.

Instructions:

(1) Present in general journal form the entries to record the selected tax allocations and payments, assuming in all cases that appropriate entries have been recorded in the accounts for all intervening months.

(2) Indicate the amount of prepaid property tax and property tax payable that would be reported on the balance sheets prepared as of (a) November 30, (b) December 31, and (c) April 30. In each case list the section in which the item would appear (Current asset, etc.), the account title (Prepaid Property Tax, etc.), and the amount.

9-5A. The following information was obtained from a review of the ledger (before adjustments) and other records of Fielding Company at the close of the current fiscal year ended June 30:

(a) Office Supplies Expense has a debit balance of $320 at June 30. The inventory of supplies on hand at that date totals $140.

(b) Prepaid Advertising has a debit balance of $2,860 at June 30, which represents the advance payment on May 1 of a yearly contract for a uniform amount of space in 52 consecutive issues of a weekly publication. As of June 30, advertisements had appeared in 10 issues.

(c) As advance premiums have been paid on insurance policies during the year they have been debited to Prepaid Insurance, which has a balance of $1,962 at June 30. Details of premium expirations are as follows:

Policy No.	Premium Cost Per Month	Period in Effect During Year
1374B	$15	July 1–June 30
2692Y	10	July 1–April 30
7460	14	May 1–June 30
9137XX	8	July 1–Nov. 30
9731YY	9	Dec. 1–June 30

(d) Notes Receivable has a debit balance of $16,400 at June 30. The two notes on hand, both of which were accepted at face value, are as follows:

Date	Face	Term	Interest Rate
May 16	$8,000	60 days	7%
May 31	8,400	90 days	7%

(e) Rent Expense has a debit balance of $6,500 on June 30, which includes rent of $500 for July of the following year, paid on June 30.

237

(f) Mortgage Note Payable has a credit balance of $30,000 at June 30. Interest at the rate of 6% is payable semiannually on July 31 and January 31. No entry has been made for the interest accrued since the last semiannual payment on January 31.

(g) Unearned Rent has a credit balance of $1,900, composed of the following: (1) July 1 balance of $400, representing rent prepaid for four months, July through October, and (2) a credit of $1,500 representing advance payment for twelve months rent at $125 a month, beginning with November.

Instructions:

(1) Determine the amount of each adjustment, identifying all principal figures used in the computations.

(2) Journalize the adjusting entries as of June 30 of the current fiscal year, identifying each entry by letter.

(3) Journalize the reversing entries that should be made as of July 1 of the succeeding fiscal year, identifying each entry by the corresponding letter used in (2).

9-6A. Transactions related to advertising and rent are presented below. Accounts are adjusted and closed only at December 31, the end of the fiscal year.

ADVERTISING

Jan. 1. Debit balance of $600 (allocable to Jan.–Feb.).

May 1. Payment of $4,800 (allocable at $400 a month, for 12 months beginning May 1).

RENT

Jan. 1. Credit balance of $7,200 ($2,000 allocable to Jan.–Apr.; $5,200 allocable to Jan.–Aug.).

May 1. Receipt of $6,300 (allocable at $525 a month, for 12 months beginning May 1).

Oct. 1. Receipt of $8,400 (allocable at $700 a month, for 12 months beginning October 1).

Instructions:

(1) Open accounts for Prepaid Advertising, Advertising Expense, Unearned Rent, and Rent Income. Employing the system of initially recording prepaid expense as an asset and unearned revenue as a liability, record the following directly in the accounts: (a) opening balances as of January 1; (b) transactions of May 1 and Oct. 1; (c) adjusting entries at December 31; (d) closing entries at December 31; and (e) reversing entries at January 1, if appropriate. Identify the entries in the items section as balance, transaction, adjusting, closing, or reversing, and extend the account balances after each entry.

(2) Open a duplicate set of accounts and follow the remaining instructions in Instruction (1), except to employ the system of initially recording prepaid expense as an expense and unearned revenue as a revenue.

(3) Determine the amounts that would appear in the balance sheet at December 31 as asset and liability respectively, and in the income statement for the year as expense and revenue respectively, according to the system employed in Instruction (1) and the system employed in Instruction (2). Present your answers in the form shown at the top of the next page.

System	Asset	Expense	Liability	Revenue
Instruction (1)	$	$	$	$
Instruction (2)				

9-7 A. Selected accounts from the ledger of Larchmont Co., with the account balances before and after adjustment, at the close of the fiscal year are presented below:

	Un-adjusted Balance	Adjusted Balance		Un-adjusted Balance	Adjusted Balance
Interest Receivable ...	$ —	$ 110	Rent Income........	$ 7,800	$ 7,200
Supplies.............	1,150	470	Wages Expense......	23,420	23,670
Prepaid Insurance....	1,690	1,160	Supplies Expense....	—	680
Prepaid Property Tax.	200	—	Property Tax Expense	2,600	2,800
Prepaid Interest......	—	70	Insurance Expense...	—	530
Wages Payable.......	—	250	Interest Income.....	360	470
Interest Payable......	—	30	Interest Expense.....	400	360
Unearned Rent......	—	600			

Instructions:

(1) Journalize the adjusting entries that were posted to the ledger at the close of the fiscal year.

(2) Insert the letter "R" in the date column opposite each adjusting entry that should be reversed as of the first day of the following fiscal year.

239

10

Plant assets and intangible assets

Nature of plant assets

"Long-lived" is a general term that may be applied to assets of a relatively fixed or permanent nature owned by a business enterprise. Such assets that are tangible in nature, used in the operations of the business, and are not held for sale in the ordinary course of the business are classified on the balance sheet as *plant assets* or *fixed assets*. Other descriptive titles frequently employed are *property*, *plant*, and *equipment*, used either singly or in various combinations. The properties most frequently included in plant assets may be described in more specific terms as equipment, furniture, tools, machinery, buildings, and land. Although there is no standard criterion as to the minimum length of life necessary for classification as plant assets, they must be capable of repeated use and are ordinarily expected to last more than a year. However, the asset need not actually be used continuously or even frequently. Items of standby equipment held for use in the event of a breakdown of regular equipment or for use only during peak periods of activity are included in plant assets.

Assets acquired for purposes of resale in the normal course of business cannot be characterized as plant assets regardless of their durability or the length of time they are held. Thus, undeveloped land or other real estate acquired as a speculation should not be classified as plant assets. When equipment or machines are removed from service and held for sale, they cease to be plant assets.

Initial costs of plant assets

The initial cost of a plant asset includes all expenditures necessary to get it in place and ready for use. Expenditures for sales tax, transportation charges, insurance on the asset while in transit, special foundations, and installation costs should be added to the related plant asset. Similarly, when a secondhand asset is purchased, the initial costs of getting it ready for use, such as expenditures for new parts, repairs, and painting, are properly chargeable to the asset account. On the other hand, expenditures associated with the acquisition of plant assets that result from carelessness, vandalism, or other abnormal causes should be excluded from the asset account. Such costs do not increase the utility of the asset and should be allocated to the period as an expense.

The cost of constructing a building includes the fees paid to architects and engineers for plans and supervision, insurance during construction, and all other necessary expenditures applicable to the project. Interest incurred during the construction period on money borrowed to finance a building project should be treated as an expense. It is a payment for the use of funds rather than an essential cost of the building.

The cost of land includes not only the negotiated price but broker's commissions, title fees, surveying fees, and other expenditures connected with securing title. If delinquent real estate taxes are assumed by the buyer, they also are chargeable to the land account. If unwanted buildings are located on land acquired for a plant site, the cost of their razing or removal, less any salvage recovered, is properly chargeable to the land account. The cost of leveling or otherwise permanently changing the contour is also an additional cost of the land.

Other expenditures related to the land may be charged to Land, Buildings, or Land Improvements, depending upon the circumstances. If the property owner bears the initial cost of paving the public street bordering his land, either by direct payment or by special tax assessment, the paving may be considered to be as permanent as the land. On the other hand, the cost of constructing walkways to and around the building might be added to the building account if both are expected to have the same life span. Expenditures for improvements that are neither as permanent as the land nor directly associated with the building may be segregated in a land improvements account and depreciated in accordance with their varying life spans. Some of the more usual items of this nature are trees and shrubs, fences, outdoor lighting systems, and paved parking areas.

Nature of depreciation

With the passage of time, all plant assets except land[1] lose their capacity to yield services. The several factors that contribute in varying degrees to the inexorable decline in utility are wear, deterioration, inadequacy, and obsolescence. Accordingly, the cost of such assets should be debited to the related expense accounts in a systematic manner during their expected useful life. This periodic cost expiration is called *depreciation*.

The factors contributing to decline in utility may be divided into two categories, *physical* depreciation, which includes wear attributable to use and deterioration from the action of the elements, and *functional* depreciation, which includes inadequacy and obsolescence. A plant asset becomes inadequate if its capacity is not sufficient to meet the demands of increased production. A plant asset is obsolete if the commodity that it produces is no longer in demand or if a newer machine can produce a commodity of superior quality or at a material reduction in cost. The continued acceleration of technological progress during this century has made obsolescence an increasingly important component of depreciation. Although the several factors comprising depreciation can be defined, it is not feasible to identify them when recording depreciation expense.

The meaning of the term "depreciation" as used in accounting is frequently misunderstood because the same term is also commonly used in business to connote a decline in the market value of an asset. Any similarity between the amount of unexpired cost of plant assets reported in the balance sheet and the amount that could be realized from their sale is merely coincidental. Plant assets are held for use rather than for sale, and their current market values are irrelevant. It is assumed that the enterprise will continue indefinitely as a going concern. Consequently the decision to dispose of a plant asset is based primarily on its utility to the enterprise, rather than the amount that could be realized from its sale.

Another common misunderstanding is that depreciation accounting automatically provides the cash required to replace plant assets as they wear out. The cash account is neither increased or decreased by the periodic entries which charge the cost of plant assets to depreciation expense accounts. The misconception is doubtless attributable to the fact that, unlike most expenses, depreciation expense does not require an equivalent outlay of cash in the period in which the expense is recorded.

242

---

[1]Land is here assumed to be used only as a site. Consideration will be given later to land acquired for its mineral deposits or other natural resources.

Recording depreciation

Depreciation may be recorded by an entry at the end of each month, or the adjustment may be postponed until the end of the fiscal year. The portion of the entry that records the decrease in the plant asset is credited to a *contra asset* account entitled Accumulated Depreciation, Allowance for Depreciation, or Reserve for Depreciation. The use of a contra asset account permits the original cost to remain undisturbed in the plant asset account, which facilitates the computation of periodic depreciation, the listing of both cost and accumulated depreciation on the balance sheet, and the reporting required for property tax and income tax purposes.

An exception to the general procedure of recording depreciation monthly or annually is made when a plant asset is sold, traded in, or scrapped. In order to record the disposal properly, it is necessary to know not only the cost of the item but the amount of its related accumulated depreciation. Hence, it is advisable to record the additional depreciation on the item for the current period before recording the transaction disposing of the asset. A further advantage of recording the depreciation at the time the accounts are relieved of the asset is that no additional attention need be given the transaction later when determining the amount of the periodic depreciation adjustment.

Determining depreciation

The first factor to be considered in computing the periodic depreciation of a plant asset is its cost. The other two factors to be considered are the length of life of the asset and its market value at the time it is permanently retired from service. It is evident that neither of these two factors can be accurately determined until the asset is retired; they must be estimated at the time the asset is placed in service.

The estimated market value of a depreciable asset as of the time of its removal from service is variously termed *residual*, *scrap*, *salvage*, or *trade-in* value. The excess of cost over the estimated residual value is the amount that is to be recorded as depreciation expense during the asset's life. When residual value is expected to be insignificant in comparison to the cost of the asset, it is frequently ignored in computing depreciation.

There are no hard-and-fast rules for estimating either the period of usefulness of an asset nor of its residual value at the end of such period. The two factors, which are interrelated, may be affected to a considerable degree by management policies. The estimates of a company that provides its salesmen with a new automobile every year will differ from those of a firm that retains its cars for three years. Such variables as climate, frequency of use, maintenance, and minimum standards of efficiency will also affect the estimates.

Life estimates for depreciable assets are available in various trade association and other publications. Revenue Procedure 62-21, which was issued by the Internal Revenue Service (IRS) in 1962, provides depreciation "guidelines" classified according to the following types of enterprises: (1) business in general, (2) manufacturing, (3) transportation, communication, and public utilities, and (4) other nonmanufacturing. The guideline lives suggested apply to about seventy-five broad classes of assets rather than to explicitly detailed items of depreciable property. An earlier publication of the IRS, known as Bulletin F, provides life estimates of individual assets for more than a hundred industries and, where practicable, estimates for composite groups. For example, the individual life estimates for office equipment vary from 5 years for typewriters to 50 years for safes and vaults; the composite estimate for office equipment as a group is 15 years. The estimates supplied by both of these publications are suggestive rather than mandatory. The Internal Revenue Code (IRC) requires that the amount deducted from revenue as depreciation expense be "reasonable" but does not prescribe life estimates.

In addition to the many factors that may influence the life estimate of an asset, there is considerable latitude in the degree of exactitude used in the computation. A month is frequently the smallest unit of time employed. When this time interval is adopted, all assets placed in service or retired from service during the first half of a month are treated as if the event had occurred on the first day of that month. Similarly, all plant asset additions and reductions during the second half of a month are considered to have occurred on the last day of that month. In the absence of any statement to the contrary, this practice will be assumed throughout this chapter.

It is not necessary that an enterprise employ a single method of computing depreciation for all classes of its depreciable assets. The methods adopted by management for use in the accounts and financial statements may also differ from the methods employed in determining income taxes and property taxes. The four methods used most frequently, *straight-line*, *units-of-production*, *declining-balance*, and *sum-of-the-years-digits*, will be described and illustrated.

Straight-line method. The straight-line method of determining depreciation provides for equal periodic charges to expense over the estimated life of the asset. To illustrate this method, assume the cost of a depreciable asset to be $15,000, its estimated residual value to be $3,000, and its estimated life to be 10 years. The annual depreciation is computed as follows:

$$\frac{\$15,000 - \$3,000}{10 \text{ years}} = \$1,200 \text{ annual depreciation}$$

The annual depreciation of $1,200 would be prorated for the first and the last partial years of use. Assuming a fiscal year ending on December 31 and first use of the asset on September 15, the depreciation for that fiscal year would be $400 (4 months). If usage had begun on September 16, the depreciation for the year would be $300 (3 months).

The estimated life of a plant asset is frequently converted to an annual *depreciation rate* stated in the form of a percentage. It is usually assumed that the rate is applied to the cost of the asset rather than to the depreciable amount (cost less residual value). Thus, in the above example, the annual depreciation rate based on cost is $1,200 ÷ $15,000, or 8%. If the rate were to be applied to the depreciable amount, it would be $1,200 ÷ ($15,000 − $3,000), or 10%. If residual values are nominal in relationship to cost and are to be excluded from consideration, an estimated life can be converted directly to an annual rate. Thus, a life of 50 years can be said to be equivalent to a rate of 2%, 20 years to be equivalent to 5%, 8 years to be equivalent to 12½%, and so on.

The straight-line method is widely used. In addition to its simplicity, it provides a reasonable allocation of costs to periodic revenue when usage is relatively uniform from period to period.

Units-of-production method. The units-of-production method relates depreciation to the estimated productive capacity of the asset. Depreciation is first computed for an appropriate unit of production, such as hours, miles, or number of operations. The depreciation for each period is then determined by multiplication of the unit depreciation by the number of units used during the period. To illustrate, assume that a machine with a cost of $21,000 and estimated residual value of $1,000 is expected to have an estimated life of 40,000 hours. The depreciation for a unit of one hour is computed as follows:

$$\frac{\$21,000 - \$1,000}{40,000 \text{ hours}} = \$.50 \text{ an hour depreciation}$$

Assuming that the machine was in operation for 2,000 hours during a particular year, the depreciation for that year would be $.50 × 2,000, or $1,000.

When the amount of usage of a plant asset varies considerably from year to year, the units-of-production method is more logical than the straight-line method. It may yield fairer allocations of cost against periodic revenue.

Declining-balance method. The declining-balance method provides a steadily declining periodic depreciation charge over the estimated life of the asset. Of several variants in technique, the most common is to apply double the straight-line depreciation rate, computed without regard to residual value, to the cost of the asset less its accumulated depreciation. Thus, for an asset with an estimated life of five years the rate would be double the straight-line rate of 20%, or 40%. The double rate is then applied to the cost of the asset for the first year of its use and thereafter to the declining book value (cost minus accumulated depreciation). The method is illustrated by the following tabulation:

Year	Cost	Accumulated Depreciation at Beginning of Year	Book Value at Beginning of Year	Rate	Depreciation for Year	Book Value at End of Year
1	$10,000	—	$10,000	40%	$4,000.00	$6,000.00
2	10,000	$4,000	6,000	40%	2,400.00	3,600.00
3	10,000	6,400	3,600	40%	1,440.00	2,160.00
4	10,000	7,840	2,160	40%	864.00	1,296.00
5	10,000	8,704	1,296	40%	518.40	777.60

It should be noted that estimated residual value is not considered in determining the depreciation rate. It is also ignored in computing periodic depreciation, except that the asset should not be depreciated below the estimated residual value. In the foregoing example it was assumed that the estimated residual value at the end of the fifth year approximates the book value of $777.60. If the residual value had been estimated at $1,000, the depreciation for the fifth year would have been $296 instead of $518.40.

There was an implicit assumption in the foregoing illustration that the first use of the asset coincided with the beginning of the fiscal year. This would seldom occur in actual practice, however, and would necessitate a slight variation in the computation for the first partial year of use. If the asset in the example had been placed in service at the end of the third month of the fiscal year, only the pro rata portion of the first full year's depreciation, $9/12 \times (40\% \times \$10,000)$, or $3,000, would be allocated to the first fiscal year. The method of computing the depreciation for subsequent years would not be affected. Thus, the depreciation for the second fiscal year, to continue the illustration, would be $40\% \times (\$10,000 - \$3,000)$, or $2,800.

The declining-balance method is widely used in computing depreciation for purposes of the federal income tax. Acceleration of the "write-off" of the asset reduces the income tax expense in the earlier years and correspondingly increases the amount of funds available to pay for the asset or for other purposes. The method is appropriate for accounting and financial reporting purposes in situations in which the decline in productivity or earning power of the asset is proportionately greater in the early years of its use than in later years. Further justification for its use is based on the tendency of repairs to increase with the age of an asset. The reduced amounts of depreciation in later years are therefore offset to some extent by increased maintenance expenses.

Sum-of-the-years-digits method. The sum-of-the-years-digits method yields results similar to those obtained by use of the declining-balance method, the periodic charge for depreciation steadily declining over the estimated life of the asset. This effect is accomplished by applying a successively smaller fraction each year to the original cost of the asset less the estimated residual value. The denominator of the fraction, which remains constant, is the sum of the digits representing the years of life. The numerator of the fraction, which changes each year, is the number of remaining years of life. Thus, for an asset with an estimated life of 5 years the denominator[2] is $5 + 4 + 3 + 2 + 1$, or 15; for the first year the numerator is 5, for the second year 4, and so on. The method is illustrated by the following depreciation schedule for an asset with an assumed cost of $16,000, residual value of $1,000, and life of 5 years:

YEAR	COST LESS RESIDUAL VALUE	RATE	Depreciation for Year	ACCUMULATED DEPRECIATION AT END OF YEAR	BOOK VALUE AT END OF YEAR
1	$15,000	5/15	$5,000	$ 5,000	$11,000
2	15,000	4/15	4,000	9,000	7,000
3	15,000	3/15	3,000	12,000	4,000
4	15,000	2/15	2,000	14,000	2,000
5	15,000	1/15	1,000	15,000	1,000

When the first use of the asset does not coincide with the beginning of a fiscal year, it is necessary to allocate each full year's depreciation between the two fiscal years benefited. Assuming that the asset in the example was placed in service after three months of the fiscal year had elapsed, the depreciation for that fiscal year would be $9/12 \times (5/15 \times \$15,000)$, or $3,750. The depreciation for the second year would be $4,250, computed as follows:

$$3/12 \times (5/15 \times \$15,000)\dots\dots\dots\dots \quad \$1,250$$
$$9/12 \times (4/15 \times \$15,000)\dots\dots\dots\dots \quad \underline{3,000}$$
$$\text{Total, second fiscal year}\dots\dots\dots \quad \underline{\$4,250}$$

Capital and revenue expenditures

In addition to the initial cost of acquiring a plant asset, other costs related to its efficiency or capacity may be incurred from time to time during its service life. It is often difficult to recognize the difference between expenditures that add to the utility of the asset for more than

---

[2]The denominator can also be determined from the following formula where S = sum of the digits and N = number of years of estimated life:

$$S = N\left(\frac{N+1}{2}\right)$$

one accounting period and those that constitute an expense of the period in which they are incurred. Costs that are chargeable to an asset account or its related accumulated depreciation account are termed *capital expenditures;* those that are chargeable to current operations are referred to as *revenue expenditures.*

Expenditures for an addition to a plant asset would clearly constitute capital expenditures. For example, the cost of installing an air conditioning unit in an automobile or of adding a wing to a building should be debited to the respective asset accounts. It is equally clear that expenditures for maintenance and repairs of a recurring nature should be classified as revenue expenditures. Thus, the cost of replacing spark plugs in an automobile or of repainting a building should be debited to appropriate expense accounts. In less obvious situations, several criteria may be considered in classifying the expenditures.

Expenditures that increase operating efficiency or capacity for the remaining useful life of an asset should be capitalized. For example, if the power unit attached to a machine is replaced by one of greater capacity, the cost and the accumulated depreciation applicable to the old motor should be removed from the accounts and the cost of the new one added to the asset account.

Expenditures that increase the useful life of an asset beyond the original estimate are also capital expenditures. They should be debited to the accumulated depreciation account, however, rather than to the asset account. To illustrate, assume that a machine with an estimated life of ten years is substantially rebuilt at the end of its seventh year of use, and that the extraordinary repairs are expected to extend the life of the machine an additional three years beyond the original estimate. In such circumstances the expenditures may be said to restore or "make good" a portion of the depreciation accumulated in prior years, and it is therefore appropriate that they be debited to the accumulated depreciation account.

When the cost of improvements or extraordinary repairs is substantial or when there is a material change in estimated life, the periodic depreciation allocable to future periods should be redetermined on the basis of the new book value of the asset and the new estimate of the remaining useful life.

Expenditures that are minor in amount are usually treated as repair expense even though they may have the characteristics of capital expenditures. The consequent saving in time and accounting expenses justifies the sacrifice of a small degree of accuracy. Some businesses establish a minimum amount required to classify an item as a capital expenditure.

248

Disposal of plant assets

Plant assets that are no longer useful may be discarded, sold, or applied toward the purchase of other plant assets. The details of the entry to record the disposal will vary, but in all cases it is necessary to remove the book value of the asset from the accounts. This is accomplished by debiting the appropriate accumulated depreciation account for the total depreciation to the date of disposal and crediting the asset account for the cost of the asset.

A plant asset should not be removed from the accounts solely because it has been depreciated for the full period of its estimated life. If the asset is still useful to the enterprise, the cost and accumulated depreciation should remain in the ledger. Otherwise the accounts would contain no evidence of the continued existence of such plant assets and the control function of the ledger would be impaired. In addition, the cost and the accumulated depreciation data on such assets are frequently needed in reporting for property tax and income tax purposes.

Discarding plant assets. When plant assets are no longer useful to the business and have no market value, they are discarded. If the asset has been fully depreciated, no loss is realized. To illustrate, assume that an item of equipment acquired at a cost of $1,000 became fully depreciated at December 31, the close of the preceding fiscal year, and is now to be discarded as worthless. The entry to record the disposal would be as follows:

Mar.	24	Accumulated Depreciation — Equipment....	1,000	
		Equipment................................		1,000
		To write off equipment discarded.		

If the accumulated depreciation applicable to the $1,000 of discarded equipment had been less than $1,000, there would have been a loss on its disposal. Furthermore, it would have been necessary to record depreciation for the three months of use in the current period before recording the disposal. To illustrate these variations, assume that depreciation on the equipment is computed at 10% of cost and that the accumulated depreciation balance is $767 after the annual adjusting entry at the end of the preceding year. The entry to record depreciation of $25 for the three months of the current period is as follows:

Mar.	24	Depreciation Expense — Equipment.........	25	
		Accumulated Depreciation — Equipment..		25
		To record current depreciation on equipment discarded.		

The equipment is then removed from the accounts and the loss is recorded by the following entry:

Mar.	24	Accumulated Depreciation — Equipment....	792	
		Loss on Disposal of Plant Assets...........	208	
		Equipment............................		1,000
		To write off equipment discarded.		

Ordinary losses and gains on the disposal of plant assets are non-operating items and may be reported in the Other Expense and Other Income sections, respectively, of the income statement.

Sale of plant assets. The entry to record the sale of a plant asset is similar to the entries illustrated in the preceding section, except that the cash or other asset received must also be recorded. If the selling price exceeds the book value of the asset, the transaction results in a gain; if the selling price is less than the book value, there is a loss. To illustrate various possibilities, assume that equipment acquired at a cost of $10,000 and depreciated at the rate of 10% of cost is sold for cash on October 12 of the eighth year of its use. The accumulated depreciation in the account as of the preceding December 31 is $7,000. The entry to record the depreciation for the nine months of the current year is as follows:

Oct.	12	Depreciation Expense — Equipment.........	750	
		Accumulated Depreciation — Equipment .		750
		To record current depreciation on equip-		
		ment sold.		

After recording the current depreciation, the book value of the asset is $2,250. Entries to record the sale, in general journal form, are presented below, under three different assumptions as to selling price.

Sold for $2,250, book value. **No gain or loss**

Oct. 12	Cash.....................................	2,250	
	Accumulated Depreciation—Equipment........	7,750	
	Equipment.............................		10,000

Sold for $1,000, below book value. **Loss of $1,250**

Oct. 12	Cash.....................................	1,000	
	Accumulated Depreciation—Equipment........	7,750	
	Loss on Disposal of Plant Assets..............	1,250	
	Equipment.............................		10,000

Sold for $3,000, above book value. **Gain of $750**

Oct. 12	Cash.....................................	3,000	
	Accumulated Depreciation—Equipment........	7,750	
	Equipment.............................		10,000
	Gain on Disposal of Plant Assets.............		750

Exchange of plant assets. Old equipment is frequently traded in for new equipment having a similar use. The trade-in allowance is deducted from the price of the new equipment, and the balance owed ("boot") is paid in accordance with the credit terms. If the trade-in allowance granted by the seller is greater than the book value of the asset traded in, there is a gain on disposal; if it is less than the book value, there is a loss.

Notwithstanding the foregoing, the IRC requires that gains and losses from such transactions not be recognized for income tax purposes if (1) the asset acquired by the taxpayer is similar in use to the asset given in exchange and (2) any boot involved is given (rather than received) by the taxpayer. The gain or loss not recognized affects the cost basis of the plant asset acquired and the amount of depreciation expense deductible in subsequent years. Both methods of recording an exchange are illustrated below, based on the following data:

Equipment traded in (old):

Cost of old equipment....................		$4,000
Accumulated depreciation at end of preceding year.	$2,800	
Depreciation for current year (to be recorded)..	400	3,200
Book value at date of exchange.............		$ 800

Equipment acquired (new):

Price of new equipment....................	$5,000
Trade-in allowance on old equipment.........	1,100
Cash paid (boot).........................	$3,900

Current depreciation of $400 would be recorded in the usual manner before proceeding to record the details of the acquisition and trade-in.

251

Gain or loss recognized on exchange. The amount of the gain or loss realized on trading in the old equipment may be determined as follows:

Trade-in allowance on old equipment...........	$1,100
Book value of old equipment at date of exchange.	800
Gain on exchange.........................	$ 300

The compound entry to record the exchange of the old asset for the new, the payment of cash, and the gain realized, in general journal form, is as follows:

June 19 Accumulated Depreciation — Equipment....	3,200	
Equipment............................	5,000	
Equipment............................		4,000
Cash................................		3,900
Gain on Disposal of Plant Assets.........		300

Gain or loss not recognized on exchange. When the gain or loss is not recognized as such, it is given effect in determining the cost basis of the new asset. The computation may be made by either of two methods: (1) deduct the unrecognized gain or add the unrecognized loss to the price of the new asset or (2) add the boot given to the book value of the old asset. The two methods are illustrated at the top of the next page, based on the transaction data presented earlier in this section.

(1) Price of new equipment...........	$5,000	
Less unrecognized gain on exchange.	300	
Cost of new equipment............	$4,700	

(2) Book value of old equipment.......	$ 800	
Boot given (cash paid)............	3,900	
Cost of new equipment............	$4,700	

The compound entry to record the exchange and the payment of cash, in general journal form, is as follows:

```
June 19  Accumulated Depreciation — Equipment.....   3,200
             Equipment...............................   4,700
                 Equipment............................           4,000
                 Cash.................................           3,900
```

The nonrecognition of gain or loss at the time of the exchange is in reality a postponement. The amount of periodic depreciation on the new equipment allowable for federal income tax purposes is based on a cost of $4,700 rather than on the quoted price of $5,000. The unrecognized gain of $300 at the time of the exchange will be matched by a reduction of $300 in the total amount of depreciation expense allowed during the life of the asset.

The complications that arise from having two different cost bases for a plant asset, one in the ledger and the other for income tax purposes, can be avoided by adopting the tax method of recording exchanges. This is frequently done where the effect on data reported in the financial statements is not material.

Subsidiary ledgers for plant assets

When depreciation is to be computed individually on a substantial number of assets comprising a functional group, it is advisable to maintain a subsidiary ledger. To illustrate, assume that an enterprise owns about 200 individual items of office equipment with an aggregate cost of approximately $100,000. Unless the business is newly organized, the equipment would have been acquired over a number of years. The individual cost, estimated residual value, and estimated life would vary in any case, and the composition of the group will continually change as a result of acquisitions and disposals.

There are many variations in the form of subsidiary records for depreciable assets. Multicolumn analysis sheets may be employed, or a separate ledger account may be maintained for each asset. The form should be designed to provide spaces for recording the acquisition and the disposal of the asset, the depreciation charged each period, the accumulated depreciation to date, and any other pertinent data desired. An example of a subsidiary ledger account for a plant asset appears at the top of the next page.

PLANT ASSET RECORD

Account No. __123-215__

Item __Bookkeeping machine__ General Ledger Account __Office Equipment__

Serial No. __AT 47-3926__ Description __Accounts receivable posting__

From Whom Purchased __Hamilton Office Machines Co., Inc.__

Estimated Life __10 years__ Estimated Scrap or Trade-In Value __$500__ Depreciation per Year __$240__

DATE			EXPLANATION	ASSET			ACCUMULATED DEPRECIATION			BOOK
MO.	DAY	YR.		DEBIT	CREDIT	BALANCE	DEBIT	CREDIT	BALANCE	VALUE
4	8	69		2,900		2,900				2,900
12	31	69						180	180	2,720
12	31	70						240	420	2,480

An account in the office equipment ledger

The number assigned to the account illustrated is composed of the number of the office equipment account in the general ledger (123) followed by the sequential number assigned to each item of office equipment purchased (215). An identification tag or plaque with the corresponding account number is attached to the asset. Depreciation for the year in which the asset was acquired, computed for nine months on a straight-line basis, is $180; for the following year it is $240. These amounts, together with the corresponding amounts from all other accounts in the subsidiary ledger, provide the figures for the respective year-end adjusting entries debiting the depreciation expense account and crediting the accumulated depreciation account.

The sum of the asset balances and the sum of the accumulated depreciation balances in all of the accounts should be compared periodically with the balances of their respective controlling accounts in the general ledger. When a particular asset is disposed of, the asset section of the subsidiary account is credited and the accumulated depreciation section is debited, reducing the balances of both sections to zero. The account is then removed from the ledger and filed for possible future reference.

Subsidiary ledgers for plant assets are useful to the accounting department in (1) determining the periodic depreciation expense, (2) recording the disposal of individual items, (3) preparing tax returns, and (4) preparing insurance claims in the event of insured losses. The forms may also be expanded to provide spaces for accumulating data on the operating efficiency of the asset. Such information as frequency of breakdowns, length of time out of service, and cost of repairs is useful in comparing

253

similar equipment produced by different manufacturers. When new equipment is to be purchased, the data are useful to management in deciding upon size, model, and other specifications and the best source of supply.

Regardless of whether subsidiary equipment ledgers are maintained, plant assets should be inspected periodically in order to ascertain whether they are still in use and their state of repair.

Depreciation based on averages

In the preceding illustrations, depreciation has been computed on each individual plant asset and, unless otherwise stated, this procedure will be assumed in the problem materials at the end of the chapter. An alternative procedure is to determine depreciation for entire groups of assets by use of a single rate. The basis for grouping may be similarity in life estimates or other common characteristics, or it may be broadened to include all assets within a functional class, such as office equipment.

When depreciation is computed on the basis of a composite group of assets of differing life spans, it is necessary to develop a rate based on averages. This may be done by (1) computing the annual depreciation for each asset, (2) determining the total annual depreciation, and (3) dividing the sum thus obtained by the total cost of the assets. The procedure is illustrated below.

Asset No.	Cost	Residual Value	Estimated Life	Annual Depreciation
101	$ 20,000	$4,000	10 years	$ 1,600
102	15,600	1,500	15 years	940
147	41,000	1,000	8 years	5,000
Total	$473,400			$49,707

Composite rate: $49,707 ÷ $473,400 = 10.5%

As new assets are added to the group and old assets are retired, it is assumed that the "mix" remains relatively unchanged. No gain or loss should be recognized on the retirement of items within the group. Instead, the asset account is credited for the cost of the asset and the accumulated depreciation account is debited for the excess of cost over the amount realized from the disposal. Any deficiency in the amount of depreciation recorded on the shorter-lived assets is presumed to be balanced by excessive depreciation on the longer-lived assets.

When composite rates are used, they may be applied against total asset cost on a monthly basis, or some reasonable assumption may be made regarding the timing of increases and decreases in the group. A common practice is to assume that all additions and retirements have occurred uniformly throughout the year; the composite rate is then applied to the average of the beginning and the ending balances of the account. Another acceptable averaging technique is to assume that all additions and retirements during the first half of the year occurred as of the first day of the year, and that all additions and retirements during the second half occurred on the last day of the year.

Regardless of whether depreciation is computed for each individual unit or for composite groups, the periodic depreciation charge is based on estimates. The effect of obsolescence and inadequacy on the life of plant assets is particularly difficult to forecast. Any system that provides for the allocation of depreciation in a systematic and rational manner fulfills the requirements of good accounting.

Depreciation of plant assets of low unit cost

Subsidiary ledgers are not ordinarily maintained for classes of plant assets that are composed of numerous individual items of low unit cost. Hand tools and other portable equipment of small size and value are typical examples. Because of hard usage, breakage, and pilferage, such assets may be relatively short-lived and require constant replacement. In such circumstances the usual depreciation methods are impracticable. One common method of determining cost expiration is to take a periodic inventory of the items on hand, estimate their fair value based on original cost, and transfer the remaining amount from the asset account to an appropriately titled account, such as Tools Expense. Other categories to which the same method is often applied are dies, molds, patterns, and spare parts.

Reporting plant assets and depreciation expense in the financial statements

The balance of each major class of depreciable assets should be disclosed in the financial statements or in notes thereto, together with the related accumulated depreciation, either by major class or in total.[3] A more compact arrangement than that employed in earlier chapters is illustrated at the top of the next page.

When the classes of plant assets are too numerous to permit such detailed listing on the balance sheet, a single figure may be presented, supported by a separate schedule.

The amount of depreciation expense for the period should be set forth separately on the income statement or disclosed in some other manner. A general description of the method or methods used in computing depreciation should also accompany the financial statements.[4]

---

[3]*Opinions of the Accounting Principles Board, No. 12*, "Omnibus Opinion—1967" (New York: American Institute of Certified Public Accountants, 1967), p. 188.
[4]*Ibid.*

Dexter Custom Cabinets
Balance Sheet
December 31, 1969

Assets

Total current assets.. $262,500

Plant assets:	Cost	ACCUMULATED DEPRECIATION	BOOK VALUE	
Office equipment..............	$ 20,000	$ 3,000	$ 17,000	
Factory equipment............	250,000	92,000	158,000	
Buildings....................	100,000	26,000	74,000	
Land........................	10,000	—	10,000	
Total plant assets............	$380,000	$121,000		259,000

Depletion

The cost of metal ores and other minerals removed from the earth is called *depletion*. The amount of the periodic cost allocation is based on the relationship of the cost to the estimated magnitude of the mineral deposit, and the quantity extracted during the particular period. To illustrate, assume that the cost of certain mineral rights is $400,000 and that the deposit is estimated at 1,000,000 tons of ore of uniform grade. The depletion rate is accordingly $400,000 ÷ 1,000,000, or $.40 a ton. If 90,000 tons are mined during the year, the depletion, amounting to $36,000, would be recorded by the following entry:

			Adjusting Entry		
Dec.	31	Depletion Expense.......................		36,000	
		Accumulated Depletion..................			36,000

The accumulated depletion account is a contra asset account and is presented in the balance sheet as a deduction from the cost of the mineral deposit.

In determining income subject to the federal income tax, the IRC permits, with certain limitations, a depletion deduction equal to a specified percent of gross income from the extractive operations. Thus for income tax purposes it is possible for aggregate depletion deductions to exceed the cost of the property. The percentage allowance for oil and gas wells is 27½%. Percentage allowances for quarries, coal, sulphur, uranium, and all metal and nonmetal mines range from 5% to 23%. Detailed examination of the tax law and regulations regarding "percentage depletion" is beyond the scope of this discussion. The subject is introduced here because of frequent references, particularly to percentage depletion of oil wells, that appear in the financial press.

Intangible assets

Long-lived assets useful in the operations of an enterprise that are not held for sale and have no physical qualities are usually classified as *intangible assets*. The expected life of an intangible asset may be limited or it may be permanent. Only those in the former category are described in this section; the latter type are discussed in later chapters.

Manufacturers may acquire exclusive rights to produce and sell commodities with one or more unique features. Such rights are evidenced by *patents*, which are issued to inventors by the federal government. They continue in effect for 17 years. An enterprise may obtain patents on new products developed in its own research laboratories or it may purchase patent rights from others. The initial cost of purchased patents should be charged to an asset and then written off, or *amortized*, over the years of its expected usefulness. This period of time may be less than the remaining legal life of the patent, and it is also subject to change in the future.

To illustrate, assume that at the beginning of its fiscal year an enterprise acquires for $100,000 a patent granted six years earlier. Although the patent will not expire for another eleven years it is expected to be of value for only five years. The entry to amortize the patent at the end of the fiscal year is as follows:

		Adjusting Entry		
Dec.	31	Amortization of Patents..................	20,000	
		Patents..............................		20,000

Continuing the illustration, assume that after two years of use it appears that the patent will cease to have value at the end of an additional two years. The cost to be amortized in the third year would be the balance of the asset account, $60,000, divided by the remaining two years, or $30,000.

The cost of obtaining patents from the government is usually nominal. The cost of the experimental work leading to the development of a new product may be substantial and in theory should be treated as an asset in the same manner as patent rights purchased from others. In practice, however, the effort required to obtain a reasonably fair cost figure for each patent may be such as to make it impracticable. A number of research projects may be in process simultaneously, work on some projects may extend over a number of years, and, perhaps most important of all, there is ordinarily no assurance of ultimate success of a project. Accordingly, many enterprises treat their normally recurring expenditures for research and development as current operating expenses.

The exclusive right to publish and sell a literary, artistic, or musical composition is obtained by a *copyright*. Copyrights are issued by the federal government and extend for 28 years with the privilege of renewal for a like term. The costs assigned to a copyright include all costs of creating the work plus the cost of obtaining the copyright. A copyright that is purchased from another should be recorded at the price paid for it. Because of the uncertainty regarding the useful life of a copyright, it is usually amortized over a relatively short period of time.

Intangible assets are ordinarily presented in the balance sheet as a separate section following plant assets.

QUESTIONS

1. Which of the following qualities of an asset are characteristic of *plant assets?*
   (a) Held for sale in normal course of business.
   (b) Tangible.
   (c) Long-lived.
   (d) Capable of repeated use in operations of the business.
   (e) Intangible.
   (f) Used continuously in operations of the business.

2. Indicate which of the following expenditures incurred in connection with the acquisition of a printing press should be charged to the asset account: (a) freight charges, (b) insurance while in transit, (c) interest on funds borrowed to make the purchase, (d) new parts to replace those damaged in unloading, (e) cost of special foundation, (f) fee paid to factory representative for assembling and adjusting.

3. In order to increase its parking area, the Westgate Shopping Center acquired adjoining land for $50,000 and a building located on the land for $10,000. The net cost of razing the building and leveling the land after deducting amounts received from sale of salvaged building materials, was $1,500. What accounts should be debited for (a) the $50,000, (b) the $10,000, (c) the $1,500?

4. What are the four factors that are included in the broad definition of depreciation?

5. Are the amounts at which plant assets are reported on the balance sheet their approximate market values as of the balance sheet date? Discuss.

6. (a) Does the recognition of depreciation in the accounts provide a special cash fund for the replacement of plant assets? (b) Describe the nature of depreciation as the term is used in accounting.

7. (a) What is the nature of the account Accumulated Depreciation? (b) What is the normal balance of the account? (c) Do credits to the account increase or decrease the account balance? (d) What is meant by the term *book value*, as applied to a plant asset? (e) Do credits to Accumulated Depreciation increase or decrease the book value of plant assets?

8. Why is it advisable, when a plant asset is to be sold, traded in, or scrapped, to first record depreciation on the asset for the current period?

9. For which of the following plant assets is the residual value most likely to be significant in determining depreciation: (a) a building to be depreciated over a period of 50 years; (b) an automobile to be depreciated over a period of 3 years?

10. Convert each of the following life estimates to a straight-line depreciation rate, stated as a percent, assuming that residual value of the plant asset is to be ignored: (a) 4 years, (b) 5 years, (c) 6 years, (d) 10 years, (e) 25 years, (f) $33\frac{1}{3}$ years, (g) 40 years.

11. A plant asset with a cost of $10,000 has an estimated residual value of $400 and an estimated life of 10 years. (a) What is the amount of the annual depreciation, computed by the straight-line method? (b) The amount of the annual depreciation is what percent of the cost of the asset?

12. The declining-balance method, at double the straight-line rate, is to be used for an asset with a cost of $5,000, estimated residual value of $300, and estimated life of 10 years. What is the depreciation for the first fiscal year, assuming that the asset was placed in service at the beginning of the year?

13. An asset with a cost of $10,600, an estimated residual value of $600, and an estimated life of 4 years is to be depreciated by the sum-of-the-years-digits method. (a) What is the denominator of the depreciation fraction? (b) What is the amount of depreciation for the first full year of use? (c) What is the amount of depreciation for the second full year of use?

14. For a number of subsidiary plant ledger accounts of an enterprise, the balance in accumulated depreciation is exactly equal to the cost of the asset. (a) Is it permissible to record additional depreciation on the assets if they are still in use? (b) When should an entry be made to remove the cost and accumulated depreciation from the accounts?

15. In what sections of the income statement are gains and losses from the disposal of plant assets presented?

16. Differentiate between capital expenditures and revenue expenditures.

17. Immediately after a used truck is acquired, a new motor is installed and the tires are replaced at a total cost of $750. Is this a capital expenditure or a revenue expenditure?

18. A plant asset priced at $20,000 is acquired by trading in a similar asset and paying cash for the remainder. (a) Assuming the trade-in allowance to be $2,000, what is the amount of "boot" given? (b) Assuming the book value of the asset traded in to be $3,000, what is the amount of gain or loss on the exchange? (c) What is the cost basis of the new asset for the computation of depreciation for federal income tax purposes?

19. The cost of a composite group of equipment is $200,000 and the annual depreciation, computed on the individual items, totals $20,000. (a) What is the composite straight-line depreciation rate? (b) What would the rate be if the total depreciation amounted to $25,000 instead of $20,000?

20. What is the term applied to the periodic charge for ore removed from a mine?

21. For what period of time are (a) patents and (b) copyrights granted?

22. What is the term applied to the periodic write-off of the cost of patents and copyrights?

EXERCISES

10-1. A building acquired on January 12 at a cost of $246,000 has an estimated life of 40 years. Assuming that it will have no residual value, determine the depreciation for each of the first two years (a) by the straight-line method, (b) by the declining-balance method, using twice the straight-line rate, and (c) by the sum-of-the-years-digits method.

10-2. A diesel engine with a cost of $40,000 and estimated salvage value of $3,000 is expected to have a useful operating life of 100,000 hours. During November the generator was operated 540 hours. Determine the depreciation for the month.

10-3. Balances in Trucks and Accumulated Depreciation — Trucks at the end of the year prior to adjustment are $38,480 and $27,150 respectively. Details of the subsidiary ledger are presented below. (a) Determine the depreciation rates per mile and the amount to be credited to the accumulated depreciation section of each of the subsidiary accounts for the current year. (b) Present the general journal entry to record depreciation for the year.

Truck No.	Cost	Residual Value	Useful Life in Miles	Accumulated Depreciation at Beginning of Year	Miles Operated During Year
1	$ 6,840	$ 600	120,000	$ 5,100	14,000
2	4,400	400	100,000	2,600	11,000
3	12,240	900	180,000	6,800	20,000
4	15,000	1,000	200,000	12,650	25,000

10-4. A plant asset acquired at the beginning of the fiscal year at a cost of $14,100 has an estimated trade-in value of $1,500 and an estimated useful life of 8 years. Determine the following: (a) the amount of annual depreciation by the straight-line method, (b) the amount of depreciation for the second year computed by the declining-balance method (at twice the straight-line rate), (c) the amount of depreciation for the second year computed by the sum-of-the-years-digits method.

10-5. A number of major structural repairs completed at the beginning of the current fiscal year at a cost of $40,000 are expected to extend the life of a building ten years beyond the original estimate. The original cost of the building was $300,000 and it has been depreciated by the straight-line method for 30 years. Residual value is expected to be negligible and has been ignored. The related accumulated depreciation account after the depreciation adjustment at the end of the preceding year is $225,000. (a) What has the amount of annual depreciation been in past years? (b) To what account should the $40,000 be debited? (c) What is the book value of the building after the repairs have been recorded? (d) What is the amount of depreciation for the current year, using the straight-line method (assume that the repairs were completed at the very beginning of the year)?

10-6. On August 26 Coleman Co. acquired a new data processing machine with a list price of $31,200, receiving a trade-in allowance of $2,800 on old equipment of a similar type, paying cash of $4,400, and giving a note for the remainder. The following information about the old equipment is obtained from the account in the office equipment ledger: cost, $19,200; accumulated depreciation on December 31, the close of the preceding fiscal year, $13,400; annual depreciation, $1,800. Present entries, in general journal form, to record the following: (a) current depreciation on the old equipment to date of trade-in, (b) the transaction on August 26, assuming that gain or loss is to be recognized, (c) the transaction on August 26, assuming that gain or loss is not to be recognized.

10-7. On the first day of the fiscal year a delivery truck with a list price of $5,800 was acquired in an exchange transaction in which there was a gain of $600. The new truck is to be depreciated over 4 years by the straight-line method, assuming a trade-in value of $400. Determine the following: (a) annual depreciation, assuming that the gain was recognized, (b) annual depreciation assuming that the gain was not recognized, (c) the quantitative effect of the unrecognized gain on the annual depreciation computed in (b).

10-8. An item of equipment acquired at a cost of $20,100 has an estimated residual value of $2,460 and an estimated life of 6 years. It was placed in service on April 19 of the current fiscal year, which ends on December 31. Determine the depreciation for the current fiscal year and for the following fiscal year (a) by the declining-balance method, at twice the straight-line rate, and (b) by the sum-of-the-years-digits method. (Round computations to nearest dollar.)

10-9. Details of a plant asset account are presented below. A composite depreciation rate of 9% is applied annually to the account. Determine the depreciation for the year according to each of the following assumptions: (a) that all additions and retirements have occurred uniformly throughout the year and (b) that additions and retirements during the first half of the year occurred on the first day of the year and those during the second half occurred on the last day of the year.

261

FACTORY MACHINES

Jan. 1	Balance	145,800	Mar. 7		2,300
Mar. 12		5,800	May 10		2,600
Apr. 20		10,700	Aug. 4		10,500
July 22		3,600			
Oct. 19		2,100			

PROBLEMS

The following additional problems for this chapter are located in Appendix C: 10-1B, 10-2B, 10-3B, 10-4B, 10-6B.

10-1A. The following expenditures and receipts are related to land, land improvements, and buildings acquired for use in a business enterprise. The receipts are identified by an asterisk.

(a) Cost of real estate acquired as a plant site: Land........	$ 40,000
Building......	25,000
(b) Delinquent real estate taxes on property, assumed by purchaser.....................................	2,000
(c) Cost of razing and removing the building..............	2,500
(d) Fee paid to attorney for title search....................	375
(e) Architect's and engineer's fees for plans and supervision...	35,000
(f) Premium on 1-year insurance policy during construction..	4,200

(g)	Cost of land fill and grading...........................	1,400
(h)	Paid to building contractor for new building............	600,000
(i)	Cost of paving parking lot to be used by customers.......	1,900
(j)	Cost of trees and shrubbery, planted....................	700
(k)	Cost of repairing windstorm damage during construction..	1,650
(l)	Special assessment paid to city for extension of water main to the property..	500
(m)	Real estate taxes accrued during construction............	1,800
(n)	Interest accrued on building loan during construction....	24,000
(o)	Cost of floodlights on parking lot, installed..............	850
(p)	Cost of repairing vandalism damage during construction..	150
(q)	Proceeds from sale of salvage materials from old building..	400*
(r)	Money borrowed to pay building contractor.............	350,000*
(s)	Proceeds from insurance company for windstorm damage.	1,500*
(t)	Refund of premium on insurance policy (f) canceled after 11 months...	300*
		$389,825

Instructions:

(1) Assign each expenditure and receipt (indicate receipts by an asterisk) to Land, Land Improvements, Building, or "Other Accounts." Identify each item by letter and list the amounts in columnar form, as follows:

Item	Land	Land Improvements	Building	Other Accounts
	$	$	$	$

(2) Total the amount columns.

10-2A. An item of new equipment acquired at a cost of $40,000 at the beginning of a fiscal year has an estimated life of 5 years and an estimated trade-in value of $4,000. The manager requested information (details given in Instruction 1) regarding the effect of alternative methods on the amount of depreciation expense deductible each year for federal income tax purposes.

Upon the basis of the data presented to the manager in accordance with Instruction 1, the sum-of-the-years-digits method was elected. In the first week of the fourth year the equipment was traded in for similar equipment priced at $60,000. The trade-in allowance on the old equipment was $10,000, cash of $5,000 was paid, and a note payable was issued for the balance.

Instructions:

(1) Determine the annual depreciation for each of the estimated 5 years of use, the accumulated depreciation at the end of each year, and the book value of the equipment at the end of each year by (a) the straight-line method, (b) the declining-balance method (at twice the straight-line rate), and (c) the sum-of-the-years-digits method. The following columnar headings are suggested for each schedule:

Year	Depreciation Expense	Accumulated Depreciation End of Year	Book Value End of Year

(2) Present the debits and credits required, in general journal form, to record the exchange at the beginning of the fourth year, assuming that the gain or loss on the disposal is to be recognized.

(3) Present the debits and credits required, in general journal form, to record the exchange at the beginning of the fourth year, assuming that the gain or loss on the disposal is not to be recognized.

(4) What is the cost basis of the new equipment, for purposes of computing the amount of depreciation allowable for income tax purposes?

(5) Assuming that the trade-in allowance had been $15,000 instead of $10,000, determine the cost basis of the new equipment for purposes of computing the amount of depreciation allowable for income tax purposes, solving by two methods.

If the working papers correlating with the textbook are not used, omit Problem 10-3A.

10-3A. Faultless Printing Co. maintains a subsidiary equipment ledger for the printing equipment and accumulated depreciation accounts in the general ledger. A small portion of the subsidiary ledger, the two controlling accounts, and a general journal are presented in the working papers. The company computes depreciation on each individual item of equipment. Transactions and adjusting entries affecting the printing equipment are described below.

1969

Sept. 23. Purchased a power cutter (Marvel Model, Serial No. 64931) from Glendale Typograph Co. on account for $4,128. The estimated life of the asset is 8 years, it is expected to have no residual value, and the straight-line method of depreciation is to be used. (This is the only transaction of the year that directly affected the printing equipment account.)

Dec. 31. Entered depreciation for the year in subsidiary accounts 125-81 to 125-83, and inserted the new balances. (It is assumed that an assistant enters the depreciation and the new balances in accounts 125-1 to 125-80.)

31. Journalized and posted the annual adjusting entry for depreciation on printing equipment. The depreciation for the year entered in subsidiary accounts 125-1 to 125-80 totals $17,468, to which must be added the depreciation entered in accounts 125-81 to 125-83.

1970

Apr. 8. Purchased a Model C8 rotary press from Andersen Press, Inc., priced at $24,490, giving the Model 16 flatbed press (Account No. 125-81) in exchange plus $4,490 cash and a series of twelve $1,000 notes payable, maturing at 6-month intervals. (Record depreciation to date in 1970 on item traded in; gain or loss on the disposal is not to be recognized.)

Instructions:

(1) Record in general journal form the transaction of September 23. Post to Printing Equipment in the general ledger and to Account No. 125-83 in the subsidiary ledger.

(2) Record the adjusting entries required on December 31 and post to Accumulated Depreciation — Printing Equipment in the general ledger.

(3) Record in general journal form the entries required by the purchase of printing equipment on April 8. Post to Printing Equipment and to Accumulated Depreciation — Printing Equipment.

(4) Assuming that the rotary press purchased on April 8 has an estimated residual value of $2,500 and an estimated life of 10 years, determine the depreciation on this press by the declining-balance method, at twice

the straight-line rate, for the fiscal years ending (a) December 31, 1970 and (b) December 31, 1971.

10-4A. The following transactions, adjusting entries, and closing entries were completed by Richards Furniture Co. during a 3-year period. All are related to the use of delivery equipment.

1969
Feb. 26. Purchased a used delivery truck for $2,700, paying cash.
Mar. 5. Paid $220 for major repairs to the truck.
Nov. 11. Paid garage $36 for miscellaneous repairs to the truck.
Dec. 31. Recorded depreciation on the truck for the fiscal year. The estimated life of the truck is 3 years, with a trade-in value of $400. The straight-line method of depreciation is used.
    31. Closed the appropriate accounts to the expense and revenue summary account.

1970
Oct. 13. Traded in the used truck on a new truck priced at $5,160, receiving a trade-in allowance of $1,250 and paying the balance in cash. (Record depreciation to date in 1970; gain or loss on exchange is not to be recognized.)
Dec. 10. Paid garage $53 for repairs to the truck.
    31. Recorded depreciation on the truck. It has an estimated trade-in value of $700 and an estimated life of 5 years. The declining-balance method (twice the straight-line rate) of depreciation is used.
    31. Closed the appropriate accounts to the expense and revenue summary account.

1971
July 8. Purchased a new truck for $5,000, paying cash.
Sept. 29. Sold the truck purchased in 1970 for $2,800 cash. (Record depreciation.)
Dec. 31. Recorded depreciation on the remaining truck. It has an estimated trade-in value of $800 and an estimated life of 4 years. The declining-balance method (twice the straight-line rate) of depreciation is used.
    31. Closed the appropriate accounts to the expense and revenue summary account.

Instructions:
(1) Open the following accounts in the ledger:
       121   Delivery Equipment
       121.1 Accumulated Depreciation — Delivery Equipment
       614   Depreciation Expense — Delivery Equipment
       615   Truck Repair Expense
       912   Loss on Disposal of Plant Assets
(2) Record the transactions and the adjusting and closing entries in general journal form. Post to the accounts and extend the balances after each posting.

10-5A. The recording errors described below occurred and were discovered during the current year.
(a) A $210 charge for incoming transportation on an item of factory equipment was debited to Purchases.
(b) The $450 cost of a major motor overhaul expected to prolong the life of a truck one year beyond the original estimate was debited to Delivery Equipment. The truck was acquired new three years earlier.

(c) The cost of a razed building, $7,000, was charged to Loss on Disposal of Plant Assets. The building and the land on which it was located had been acquired at a total cost of $25,000 ($18,000 debited to Land, $7,000 debited to Building) as a site for a discount store.

(d) The fee of $800 paid to the wrecking contractor to raze the building in (c) was debited to Miscellaneous Expense.

(e) Property taxes of $1,950 on the real estate in (c) paid during the year and debited to Property Tax Expense included $1,150 for taxes that were delinquent at the time the property was acquired.

(f) The $2,000 cost of repainting the interior of a building was debited to Building. The building had been owned and occupied for six years.

(g) The sale of a copying machine for $300 was recorded by a $300 credit to Office Equipment. The original cost of the machine was $2,500 and the related balance in Accumulated Depreciation at the beginning of the current year was $1,800. Depreciation of $180 accrued during the current year, prior to the sale, had not been recorded.

(h) The $125 cost of repairing factory equipment damaged in the process of installation was charged to Factory Equipment.

Instructions:

Journalize the entries necessary to correct the errors during the current year. Identify each entry by letter.

10-6A. The trial balance of Banner Markets at the end of the current fiscal year, before adjustments, is as follows:

Banner Markets
Trial Balance
June 30, 19--

Cash..	18,360	
Merchandise Inventory........................	93,740	
Prepaid Expenses.............................	6,580	
Delivery Equipment..........................	15,450	
Accumulated Depreciation — Delivery Equipment.		6,465
Store Equipment.............................	26,910	
Accumulated Depreciation — Store Equipment....		12,341
Office Equipment............................	7,360	
Accumulated Depreciation — Office Equipment...		2,982
Buildings...................................	97,600	
Accumulated Depreciation — Buildings..........		43,190
Land.......................................	8,400	
Notes Payable (short term)...................		15,000
Accounts Payable............................		21,410
R. B. Curtis, Capital........................		139,447
R. B. Curtis, Drawing........................	18,000	
Sales (net).................................		947,320
Purchases (net).............................	747,320	
Operating Expenses (control account)...........	147,625	
Interest Expense............................	810	
	1,188,155	1,188,155

Data needed for year-end adjustments:

(a) Merchandise inventory at June 30, $102,510.

(b) Insurance and other prepaid operating expenses expired during the year, $2,130.

(c) Depreciation is computed at composite rates on the average of the beginning and the ending balances of the plant asset accounts. The beginning balances and rates are as follows:

Delivery equipment, $13,590; 25%   Office equipment, $8,140; 8%
Store equipment, $23,690; 9%   Buildings, $97,600; 2½%

(d) Accrued liabilities at the end of the year, $1,109, of which $125 is for interest on the notes and $984 is for wages and other operating expenses.

Instructions:

(1) Prepare an income statement for the current year.

(2) Prepare a balance sheet in report form, presenting the plant assets in the manner illustrated in this chapter.

10-7A. In each of the following selected transactions it is assumed that subsidiary equipment ledgers are maintained and that the fiscal year ends on December 31. Depreciation is recorded only at the end of each year, except for depreciation on items disposed of during the year.

(a) Jan. 8. Paid $4,800 for replacing the roof on a building. It is estimated that the new roof will extend the life of the building from an original estimate of 25 years to a total life of 30 years. Details from the subsidiary ledger are as follows: cost, $150,000; accumulated depreciation on preceding December 31, $90,000; age of building, 15 years.

(b) Apr. 22. Sold 10 desks (office equipment) for cash, $110. The desks were identical and had been acquired at the same time. Details from the subsidiary ledger are as follows: total cost, $1,600; total accumulated depreciation on preceding December 31, $1,300; total annual depreciation, $150.

(c) May 10. Discarded a duplicating machine (office equipment), realizing no salvage. Details from the subsidiary ledger are as follows: cost, $310; accumulated depreciation, $310.

(d) June 27. Traded in an old delivery truck for a new one priced at $5,000, receiving a trade-in allowance of $700 and paying the balance in cash. Data on the old truck are as follows: cost, $3,800; accumulated depreciation on preceding December 31, $2,900; annual depreciation, $1,000. Gain or loss is to be recognized.

(e) Sept. 19. Traded in a refrigerated display case (store equipment) for a new one priced at $1,500, receiving a trade-in allowance of $300 and giving a note for the balance. Data on the old equipment are as follows: cost, $1,000; accumulated depreciation on preceding December 31, $728; annual depreciation, $96. Gain or loss is not be to recognized.

(f) Nov. 10. Discarded store equipment, realizing no salvage. Details from the subsidiary ledger are as follows: cost, $600; accumulated depreciation on preceding December 31, $496; annual depreciation, $48.

Instructions:

(1) Present entries, all in general journal form, to record the transactions and, where appropriate, to accrue the depreciation for the partial year preceding the transaction. Identify each entry by letter.

(2) Determine the depreciation on the building affected by entry (a) for the year in which the roof was replaced, using the straight-line method and assuming no residual value.

(3) Determine the depreciation on the new store equipment recorded in entry (e), using the declining-balance method (twice the straight-line rate) for (a) the remainder of the year and (b) the following year. The expected useful life of the display case is 8 years.

part Five | Accounting systems

11

Systems and controls

Accounting systems

One of the areas of specialization in accounting described in Chapter 1 is the design and installation of accounting systems. In developing principles of accounting in the intervening chapters, attention has been focused to a large extent on analysis and recording of accounting data, preparation of financial statements, and uses of accounting data by management. Consideration has also been given, however, to some aspects of accounting systems, such as documentary evidence of transactions, charts of accounts, journals, special journals, ledgers, and subsidiary ledgers. In this chapter, the basic concepts of accounting systems are emphasized.

The accounting system must provide the data for management's use in conducting the affairs of the business and in reporting the results of operations to interested parties such as owners and creditors. A properly designed accounting system therefore provides for (1) efficient accumulation, recording, and reporting of data, (2) measurement of all phases of a firm's operations, (3) assignment of authority and responsibility, and (4) prevention of errors and fraud. Beyond these fundamental requirements there are an infinite number of variations in the details of accounting systems. Each system must be designed to fit the nature of the individual enterprise, the volume of transactions of various types, and the number and the capacities of the personnel.

Internal control

In a small business it is possible for the owner-manager to personally supervise the employees and direct the affairs of the business. As the number of employees and the complexities of an enterprise increase, it becomes more difficult for management to maintain contact with all phases of operations. As a firm grows, management finds it necessary to delegate authority and to place more reliance on the accounting system in controlling operations.

Plans and procedures designed to meet the need for controlling operations are called *internal control*. It comprises the plan of organization and the related methods and procedures adopted within an enterprise to (1) safeguard its assets, (2) produce accurate accounting data, (3) contribute to efficient operation, and (4) encourage adherence to management policies. In a broad sense, internal control also includes such activities as motion and time study, quality control, and statistical analysis. The portion of internal control related to the accounting system is sometimes referred to as *internal check*.

Some degree of internal control is needed in all businesses. For example, the requirement that each cash sale be recorded by depressing the appropriate keys on a cash register is a fundamental part of internal control. The use of sales tickets, sales invoices, and other documentary evidences of transactions is also a part of internal control. The details of a system of internal control will of necessity vary with the nature and the size of a firm. There are, however, a number of broad principles that should be considered.

Competent personnel and rotation of duties. All accounting systems require people to perform prescribed duties. Obviously, a system can be only as good as the people who perform these duties. Therefore, all employees should be adequately trained and supervised in the performance of their duties. Whenever feasible, clerical employees should be rotated from job to job. The knowledge that another employee may perform his duties at a later date tends to discourage deviations from prescribed procedures. Rotation also helps to disclose any irregularities that may occur.

Assignment of responsibility. If employees are to work efficiently, it is essential that their responsibilities be clearly defined. There should be no overlapping or undefined areas of responsibility. For example, if a particular cash register is to be used by two or more sales clerks, each one should be assigned a separate cash drawer and register key. Thus, daily proof of the handling of cash can be obtained for each clerk. Similarly, if several employees are assigned to posting entries to customers' accounts, each employee should be assigned to a particular alphabetical section so that errors can be traced to the person responsible for the error.

Separation of responsibility for related operations. To minimize the possibility of inefficiency, errors, and fraud, responsibility for a sequence of related operations should be divided among different persons. For example, no single individual should be authorized to order merchandise, verify the receipt of the goods, and pay the supplier. To do so would invite such abuses as placing orders on the basis of friendship with a supplier rather than on price, quality, and other objective factors; perfunctory verification of the quantity and the quality of goods received; conversion of goods to the personal use of the employee; carelessness in verifying the validity and the accuracy of invoices; and payment of fictitious invoices. When the responsibility for purchasing, receiving, and paying are divided among three persons or departments, the possibilities of such abuses are minimized. The documentary evidence of the work of each department, including purchase orders, receiving reports, and invoices should be routed to the accounting department for comparison and recording.

It should be noted that the "checks and balances" provided by distributing responsibility among various departments requires no duplication of effort. The work of each department, as evidenced by the business documents that it prepares, must "fit" with those prepared by the other departments.

Separation of operations and accounting. Responsibility for maintaining the accounting records should be separated from the responsibility for operations and custody of assets. In this way the accounting records can serve as an independent check on operations. For example, the cashier who receives remittances from customers on account should not have access to the journals or the ledgers. Separation of the two functions reduces the possibilities of errors and defalcations.

Proofs and security measures. Proofs and security measures should be utilized to safeguard business assets and assure reliable accounting data. This principle applies to a wide variety of techniques and procedures, such as the use of controlling accounts and subsidiary ledgers; the use of a bank account and other safekeeping measures for cash, investments, and other valuable documents; and the use of various types of mechanical equipment. Cash registers are widely employed in making the initial record of cash sales. The conditioning of the public to observe the amount recorded as the sale or to accept a printed receipt from the salesclerk increases the machine's effectiveness as a part of internal control. Other devices with a similar feature include gasoline pumps and automatic counters in city buses.

The use of fidelity insurance is also an aid to internal control. It insures against losses caused by fraud on the part of employees who are

269

entrusted with company assets and serves as a psychological deterrent to the misappropriation of assets.

Independent review. To determine whether the other internal control principles are being effectively applied, the system should be periodically reviewed and evaluated by internal auditors who are independent of the employees responsible for operations. The auditors should report any weaknesses and recommend changes to correct them. For example, a review of cash disbursements may disclose that invoices were not paid within the discount period, even though sufficient cash had been available.

Control over cash

Because of its high value in relation to bulk, and other obvious qualities, cash is the asset most often subject to improper diversion and use. In addition, almost every transaction eventually affects the receipt or the payment of cash. It is therefore desirable to provide special controls over cash. The most important of these controls are discussed in the following sections.

Bank account

Most businesses deposit all cash receipts in a bank and make all payments by checks drawn against the bank account. The forms used by the depositor in connection with a bank account are signature card, deposit ticket, and check.

Signature card. At the time an account is opened, the bank requires that a *signature card* be signed personally by each individual authorized to sign checks drawn on that account. The card is used by the bank to determine the authenticity of the signature on checks presented to it for payment.

Deposit ticket. The details of a deposit are listed by the depositor on a printed form supplied by the bank. *Deposit tickets* are frequently prepared in duplicate. The carbon copy is stamped or initialed by the bank's teller and is given to the depositor as a receipt. When deposits are mailed to the bank or are placed in a night deposit vault, the bank mails the duplicate deposit ticket or other receipt form to the depositor.

Check. A *check* is a written instrument signed by the depositor, ordering the bank to pay a specified sum of money to a designated person or to his order. There are three parties to a check: the *drawer*, the one who signs the check; the *drawee*, the bank on which the check is drawn; and the *payee*, the one to whose order the check is drawn. When checks are issued to pay obligations, they are recorded as credits to Cash even though they are not presented to the drawer's bank until some later time. Conversely, when checks are received from customers, they are recorded as debits to Cash, on the assumption that the customer has sufficient funds on deposit.

Check forms may be obtained in a variety of styles. The name and the address of the depositor may be printed on each check, and the checks may be serially numbered for purposes of internal control. Banks that employ automatic sorting and posting equipment provide check forms on which the bank's identification number and the depositor's account number are printed along the lower margin in magnetic ink. (When the check is presented for payment, the amount for which it is drawn is inserted next to the account number, also in magnetic ink.)

A carbon copy of each check may be prepared for use by the drawer in recording the transaction in the cash payments journal, or the information may be entered on a *stub* such as that illustrated below. The check stub may also be used as a memorandum record of the current bank balance.

	DOLLARS	CENTS
BAL. BRO'T FOR'D	3,182	76
AMT. DEPOSITED	174	50
TOTAL	3,357	26
AMT. THIS CHECK	226	89
BAL. CAR'D FOR'D	3,130	37

NO. 363 $226 89
DATE May 15, 19 69
TO Rowan + Co,
FOR Merchandise

HARTMAN COMPANY
813 Monroe Street

DETROIT, MICHIGAN May 15 19 69 9-42 / 720

PAY TO THE ORDER OF Rowan & Company $ 226.89

The sum of $226 and 89 cts DOLLARS

LINCOLN BANK
OF DETROIT

Earl M. Hartman
Treasurer

⑆0720⑆0042⑆ 1627⑆042⑆

Check and stub

271

A check sent to a creditor for a payment on account is frequently accompanied by a notification of the particular invoice that is being paid. The purpose of such notification, sometimes called a *remittance advice*, is to assure proper credit in the accounts of the creditor. Misunderstandings are less likely to arise and the possible need for exchanges of correspondence is avoided. An alternative procedure is to record the invoice number or other identification on the face of the check or on an attachment to it.

Bank statement

Although there are some variations in procedure, banks ordinarily maintain an original and a carbon copy of all checking accounts. When this is done, the original becomes the statement of account that is mailed to the depositor, usually at the end of each month. Like any account with a customer or a creditor, the bank statement begins with the opening balance, lists debits (deductions by the bank) and credits (additions by the bank), and ends with the balance at the close of the period. Accompanying the bank statement are the depositor's checks received by the bank during the period, arranged in the order of payment. The *paid* or *canceled* checks are perforated or stamped "Paid" together with the date of payment.

Debit or credit memorandums describing other entries on the depositor's account may also be enclosed with the statement. For example, the bank may have debited the depositor's account for service charges or for deposited checks returned because of insufficient funds; or it may have credited the account for receipts from notes receivable left for collection or for bank loans to the depositor. A typical bank statement is illustrated below.

LINCOLN BANK OF DETROIT
DETROIT, MICHIGAN

STATEMENT OF ACCOUNT

Hartman Company
813 Monroe Street
Detroit, Michigan   48206

ACCOUNT NO.
1627-042

STATEMENT DATE
July 31, 1969

CHECKS AND OTHER DEBITS			DEPOSITS	DATE		BALANCE
BALANCE BROUGHT FORWARD →				July	1	4,218.60
819.40	122.54		585.75	July	1	3,862.41
369.50	732.26	20.15	421.53	July	2	3,162.03
600.00	190.70	52.50	781.30	July	3	3,100.13
25.93	160.00		662.50	July	5	3,576.70
36.80	181.02		503.18	July	7	3,862.06
32.26	535.09		932.00	July	29	3,397.40
21.10	126.20		705.21	July	30	3,955.31
		SC 3.00	MS 400.00	July	30	4,352.31
26.12	1,615.13		648.72	July	31	3,359.78

EC—Error Correction	NSF—Not Sufficient Funds	PS—Payment Stopped
MS—Miscellaneous	OD —Overdraft	SC—Service Charge

The reconcilement of this statement with your records is essential. Any error or exception should be reported immediately.

Bank statement

Bank reconciliation

When all cash receipts are deposited in the bank and all payments are made by check, the cash account is often entitled Cash in Bank. This account in the depositor's ledger is the reciprocal of the account with the depositor in the bank's ledger. Cash in Bank in the depositor's ledger is an asset with a debit balance, and the account with the depositor in the bank's ledger is a liability with a credit balance.

It might seem that the two balances should be equal in amount, but they are not likely to be equal on any specific date because of either or both of the following: (1) delay by either party in recording transactions, and (2) errors by either party in recording transactions.

Ordinarily, there is a time lag of one day or more between the date a check is written and the date that it is presented to the bank for payment. If the depositor mails deposits to his bank or uses the night depository, a time lag between the date of the deposit and the date that it is recorded by the bank is also probable. On the other hand, the bank may debit or credit the depositor's account for transactions about which the depositor will not be informed until later. Examples are service or collection fees charged by the bank and the proceeds of notes receivable sent to the bank for collection.

In order to discover the reasons for the difference between book and bank balances and to correct any errors that may have been made by the bank or the depositor, the depositor should *reconcile* the bank statement with his own records. The bank reconciliation is divided into two major sections: one section begins with the balance according to the bank statement and ends with the adjusted balance; the other section begins with the balance according to the depositor's books and also ends with the adjusted balance. The two amounts designated as the adjusted balance must be in exact agreement. The form and the content of the bank reconciliation is outlined below.

Bank balance according to bank statement..............		xx
Add: Additions by depositor not on bank statement........	xx	
Bank errors....................................	xx	xx
		xx
Deduct: Deductions by depositor not on bank statement....	xx	
Bank errors....................................	xx	xx
Adjusted balance...................................		xx
Bank balance according to depositor's books..............		xx
Add: Additions by bank not recorded in books............	xx	
Book errors....................................	xx	xx
		xx
Deduct: Deductions by bank not recorded in books........	xx	
Book errors....................................	xx	xx
Adjusted balance...................................		xx

To achieve a maximum of internal control, the bank reconciliation should be prepared by an employee who does not engage in or record bank transactions. Errors or irregularities discovered should be reported to the chief accountant, controller, or other supervisory official.

The procedures described in the following paragraphs are employed in locating the reconciling items and determining the adjusted balance of Cash in Bank:

1. Individual deposits listed on the bank statement are compared with unrecorded deposits appearing in the preceding reconciliation and with duplicate deposit slips or other records of deposits. Deposits not recorded by the bank are added to the balance according to the bank statement.

2. Paid checks returned by the bank are arranged in numerical order and are compared with outstanding checks appearing on the preceding reconciliation and with checks listed in the cash payments journal. Checks issued that have not been returned by the bank are outstanding and are deducted from the balance according to the bank statement.

3. Bank credit memorandums are traced to the cash receipts journal. Credit memorandums not recorded in the cash receipts journal are added to the balance according to the books.

4. Bank debit memorandums are traced to the cash payments journal. Debit memorandums not recorded in the cash payments journal are deducted from the balance according to the books.

5. Errors discovered during the process of making the foregoing comparisons are listed separately on the reconciliation. For example, if the amount of a cash payment had been erroneously recorded, the amount of the error should be added to or deducted from the balance according to the books. Similarly, errors by the bank should be added to or deducted from the balance according to the bank statement.

Illustration. The bank statement for Hartman Company reproduced on page 272 indicates a balance of $3,359.78 as of July 31. The balance in Cash in Bank in Hartman Company's ledger as of the same date is $2,242.99. Application of the procedures outlined above reveals the following reconciling items:

1. Deposit of July 31 not recorded on bank statement............... $ 816.20
2. Checks outstanding: No. 812, $1,061.00; No. 878, $435.39; No. 883, $48.60... 1,544.99
3. Note collected by bank (credit memorandum) not recorded in cash receipts journal.. 400.00
4. Bank service charges (debit memorandum) not recorded in cash payments journal... 3.00
5. Check No. 879 for $732.26 to Belden Co. on account recorded in cash payments journal as $723.26............................ 9.00

The bank reconciliation based on the bank statement and the reconciling items above is at the top of the next page.

Entries based on bank reconciliation

Unrecorded transactions and errors on the depositor's books revealed by the bank reconciliation must be corrected. The necessary entries may be recorded in the appropriate special journals if they have not already been posted for the month, or they may be recorded in the general journal.

Hartman Company
Bank Reconciliation
July 31, 1969

Balance per bank statement...................................		$3,359.78
Add: Deposit of July 31, not recorded by bank......................		816.20
		$4,175.98
Deduct: Outstanding checks		
No. 812..................................	$1,061.00	
No. 878..................................	435.39	
No. 883..................................	48.60	1,544.99
Adjusted balance...		$2,630.99
Balance per books.......................................		$2,242.99
Add: Note collected by bank.............................		400.00
		$2,642.99
Deduct: Bank service charges...........................	$3.00	
Error in recording Check No. 879.................	9.00	12.00
Adjusted balance...		$2,630.99

Bank reconciliation

The entries for Hartman Company, based on the bank reconciliation above, are as follows:

July	31	Cash in Bank............................	400	
		Notes Receivable.......................		400
		Note collected by bank.		
	31	Miscellaneous General Expense............	3	
		Accounts Payable — Belden Co.............	9	
		Cash in Bank..........................		12
		Bank service charges and error in recording Check No. 879.		

275

It should be noted that the data necessary for these adjustments are provided by the section of the bank reconciliation that begins with the balance per books.

After the foregoing entries are posted, the cash in bank account will have a debit balance of $2,630.99, which agrees with the adjusted balance shown on the bank reconciliation. This is the amount of cash available for use as of July 31 and the amount that would be reported on the balance sheet on that date. If a memorandum record of the bank balance is maintained on the check stubs, the last stub should be revised by adding the net adjustment of $388 ($400 − $12).

Internal control of cash receipts

A bank account is one of the principal devices for maintaining control over cash. To achieve maximum effectiveness, all cash received must be deposited in the bank and all payments must be made by checks drawn on the bank or from special cash funds. When such a system is strictly adhered to, there is a double record of cash, one maintained by the business and the other by the bank.

Department stores and other retail businesses ordinarily receive cash from two principal sources: (1) over the counter from cash customers and (2) by mail from charge customers making payments on account. At the close of the business day each salesclerk counts the cash in his cash drawer and records the amount on a memorandum form. An employee from the cashier's department removes the cash register tapes on which total receipts were recorded for each cash drawer, recounts the cash, and compares the total with the memorandum and the tape, noting any discrepancies. The cash is taken to the cashier's office and the cash register tapes and memorandum forms are forwarded to the accounting department, where they become the basis for entries in the cash receipts journal.

The employees who open the mail compare the amount of cash received with the amount shown on the remittance advice to be certain that the two amounts agree. When no separate remittance advice accompanies the payment, the employees prepare one on a special form designed for the purpose. All cash received, usually in the form of checks and money orders, is sent to the cashier's department where it is combined with the receipts from cash sales and a deposit ticket is prepared. The remittance advices are delivered to the accounting department where they become the basis for entries in the cash receipts journal and for posting to the customers' accounts in the subsidiary ledger.

The duplicate deposit ticket or other bank receipt form obtained by the cashier is forwarded to the controller or other financial officer, who compares the amount with that reported by the accounting department as the total debit to Cash in Bank for the period.

Cash short and over

The amount of cash actually received during a day often does not agree with the record of cash receipts. Whenever there is a difference between the record and the actual cash and no error can be found in the record, it must be assumed that the mistake occurred in making change. The cash shortage or overage is recorded in an account entitled Cash Short and Over. A common method for handling such mistakes is to include in the cash receipts journal a Cash Short and Over Debit column into which all cash shortages are entered, and a Cash Short and Over Credit column into which all cash overages are entered. For example, if the actual cash received from cash sales is less than the amount indicated by the cash register tally, the entry in the cash receipts journal would include a debit to Cash Short and Over. An example of a complete entry, in general journal form, follows:

Cash in Bank...............................	720.10	
Cash Short and Over........................	1.90	
Sales......................................		722.00

If there is a debit balance in the cash short and over account at the end of the fiscal period, it is an expense and may be included in "Miscellaneous general expense" on the income statement. If there is a credit balance, it is revenue and may be listed in the "Other income" section. If the balance becomes larger than may be accounted for by minor errors in making change, the management should take corrective measures.

Cash change funds

Retail stores and other businesses that receive cash directly from customers must maintain a fund of currency and coins in order to make change. The fund may be established by drawing a check for the required amount, debiting the account Cash on Hand and crediting Cash in Bank. No additional charges or credits to the cash on hand account are necessary unless the amount of the fund is to be increased or decreased. At the close of each business day the total receipts are deposited and the change fund is retained. The desired composition of the fund is maintained by exchanging bills or coins for those of other denominations at the bank.

277

Internal control of cash payments

It is common practice for business enterprises to require that every payment of cash be evidenced by a check signed by a designated official. Some firms require two signatures on all checks or on all checks over a certain amount as an additional control. The use of a check protector that produces an indelible and unalterable amount on the check is also common.

When the owner of a business has personal knowledge of all goods and services purchased, he may sign checks with the assurance that the creditors have complied with the terms of their contracts and that he is paying the exact amount of the obligation. Such all-embracing knowledge of affairs by disbursing officials is seldom possible, however. In enterprises of even moderate size the responsibility for issuing purchase orders, inspecting commodities received, and verifying contractual and arithmetical details of invoices is divided among the employees of various departments. It is desirable, therefore, to coordinate these related activities and to link them with the ultimate issuance of checks to creditors. One of the most effective systems employed for this purpose is known as the *voucher system*.

Basic features of the voucher system

A voucher system is composed of records, methods, and procedures employed in (1) verifying and recording liabilities and (2) paying and recording cash payments. As in all areas of accounting systems and internal controls, many variations in detail are possible. The discussion and the illustrations that follow refer to a merchandising enterprise of moderate size with separate departments for purchasing, receiving, accounting, and disbursing.

A voucher system employs (1) vouchers, (2) a voucher register, (3) a file for unpaid vouchers, (4) a check register, and (5) a file for paid vouchers.

Vouchers. The term *voucher* is widely used in accounting. In a general sense it means any document that serves as evidence of authority to pay cash, such as an invoice approved for payment, or as evidence that cash has been paid, such as a canceled check. The term has a narrower meaning when applied to the voucher system: a voucher is a special form on which is recorded pertinent data about a liability and the particulars of its payment.

A voucher form is illustrated on the opposite page. The face of the voucher provides space for the name and the address of the creditor, the date and the number of the voucher, and pertinent details of the invoice or other supporting document, such as the vendor's invoice number and the amount and the terms of the invoice. One half of the back of the voucher is devoted to the account distribution and the other half to summaries of the voucher and the details of payment. Spaces are also provided for the signature or initials of various employees.

Vouchers are customarily prepared by the accounting department on the basis of an invoice or a memorandum that serves as evidence of the expenditure. This is usually done only after the following comparisons and verifications have been completed and noted on the invoice:

1. Comparison with a copy of the purchase order to verify quantities, prices, and terms.
2. Comparison with the receiving report to determine receipt of the items billed.
3. Verification of the arithmetical accuracy of the invoice.

After all data except details of payment have been inserted, the invoice or other supporting evidence is attached to the face of the voucher, which is then folded with the account distribution and summaries on the outside. The voucher is then presented to the designated official or officials for final approval.

Voucher register. After approval by the designated official, each voucher is recorded in a journal known as a *voucher register*. It is similar to and replaces the purchases journal described in Chapter 5.

VOUCHER

JANSEN AUTO SUPPLIES, INC.

Date July 1, 1969   Voucher No.   451

Payee   Allied Manufacturing Company

               683 Fairmont Road

               Chicago, Illinois 60630

DATE	DETAILS	AMOUNT
June 28, 1969	Invoice No. 4693-C FOB Chicago, 2/10, n/30	450.00

Attach Supporting Documents

Voucher — face

ACCOUNT DISTRIBUTION			VOUCHER	No. 451	
Debit	Amount		Date 7-1-69 Due 7-8-69		
			Payee		
Purchases	450	00	Allied Manufacturing Company		
Supplies			683 Fairmont Road		
Advertising Expense			Chicago, Illinois 60630		
Delivery Expense			**Voucher Summary**		
Misc. Selling Expense			Amount	450	00
Misc. General Expense			Adjustment		
			Discount	9	00
			Net	441	00
			Approved R. G. Davis		Controller
			Recorded T. N.		
			Payment Summary		
			Date 7-8-69		
			Amount 441.00		
			Check No. 863		
Credit **Accounts Payable**	450	00	Approved E. S. Reed		Treasurer
Distribution Approved C. B. White			Recorded B. W. RM		

Voucher — back

A typical form of a voucher register is illustrated below and at the bottom of page 281. The vouchers are entered in numerical sequence, each being recorded as a credit to Accounts Payable (sometimes entitled Vouchers Payable) and as a debit to the account or accounts to be charged for the expenditure.

When a voucher is paid, the date of payment and the number of the check are inserted in the appropriate columns in the voucher register. The effect of such notations is to provide a ready means of determining at any time the amount of individual unpaid vouchers. The total amount of the outstanding liability can also be determined at any time by adding the individual amounts of the vouchers indicated by the voucher register as being unpaid.

Unpaid voucher file. An important characteristic of the voucher system is the requirement that a voucher be prepared for each expenditure. In fact, a check may not be issued except in payment of a properly authorized voucher. Vouchers may be paid immediately after they are prepared or at a later date, depending upon the credit terms.

After a voucher has been prepared and has been recorded in the voucher register, it is filed in an unpaid voucher file, where it remains until it is paid. The amount due on each voucher represents the credit balance of an account payable, and the voucher itself is comparable to an individual account in a subsidiary accounts payable ledger; accordingly, a separate subsidiary ledger is unnecessary.

280

PAGE 11   VOUCHER REGISTER

	DATE	VOU. NO.	PAYEE	PAID DATE	CK. NO.	ACCOUNTS PAYABLE CR.	PURCHASES DR.	
	1969							
1	July 1	451	Allied Mfg. Co.	7–8	863	450 00	450 00	1
2	1	452	Adams Realty Co.	7–1	856	600 00		2
3	2	453	Foster Publications	7–2	857	52 50		3
4	3	454	Benson Express Co.	7–3	859	36 80	24 20	4
5	3	455	Office Outfitters			784 20		5
6	3	456	Moore & Co.	7–11	866	1,236 00	1,236 00	6
7	6	457	J. L. Brown Co.	7–6	860	22 50		7
8	6	458	Turner Corp.			395 30	395 30	8
27	31	477	Central Motors			112 20		27
28	31	478	Petty Cash	7–31	883	48 60		28
29	31					15,551 60	11,640 30	29
30						(212)	(511)	30

Voucher register, left page

All voucher systems include some provision for efficiently determining the vouchers to be paid each day. The method of filing invoices by due date described in Chapter 5 is equally acceptable for filing vouchers. It brings to the attention of the disbursing official the vouchers that are to be paid on each day. It also provides management with a convenient means of continuously forecasting the amount of cash needed to meet maturing obligations.

When a voucher is to be paid, it is removed from the unpaid voucher file and a check is issued in payment. The date, the number, and the amount of the check are listed on the back of the voucher for use in recording the payment in the check register. Paid vouchers and the supporting documents are often run through a canceling machine to prevent accidental or intentional reuse.

An exception to the general rule that vouchers be prepared for all expenditures may be made for bank charges evidenced by debit memorandums or notations on the bank statement. For example, such items as bank service charges, safe-deposit box rentals, and returned NSF (Not Sufficient Funds) checks may be charged to the depositor's account without either a formal voucher or a check. For large expenditures, such as the repayment of a bank loan, a supporting voucher may be prepared, if desired, even though a check is not written. The paid note may then be attached to the voucher as evidence of the obligation. All bank debit memorandums are, of course, the equivalent of checks as evidence of payment.

VOUCHER REGISTER

| | STORE SUPPLIES DR. | ADV. EXP. DR. | DEL. EXP. DR. | MISC. SELLING EXP. DR. | MISC. GENERAL EXP. DR. | SUNDRY ACCOUNTS DR. | | | |
						ACCOUNT	POST. REF.	AMOUNT	
1									1
2						Rent Expense	712	600 00	2
3		52 50							3
4			12 60						4
5	34 20					Office Equipment	122	750 00	5
6									6
7					22 50				7
8									8
27			112 20						27
28	4 30		16 20	19 50	8 60				28
29	59 80	176 40	286 10	48 30	64 90			3,275 80	29
30	(116)	(612)	(613)	(618)	(718)			(√)	30

Voucher register, right page

Check register. The payment of a voucher is recorded in a *check register,* an example of which is illustrated below. The check register is a modified form of the cash payments journal and is so called because it is a complete record of all checks. It is customary to record all checks in the check register in sequential order, including occasional checks that are voided because of an error in their preparation.

Each check issued is in payment of a voucher that has previously been recorded as an account payable in the voucher register. The effect of each entry in the check register is consequently a debit to Accounts Payable and a credit to Cash in Bank (and Purchases Discount, when appropriate).

The memorandum columns for Bank Deposits and Bank Balance appearing in the illustration of the check register are optional. Their use eliminates the necessity of recording deposits and bank balances on the check stubs and provides a convenient means of determining the cash available at all times.

CHECK REGISTER   PAGE 11

	DATE	CK. NO.	PAYEE	VOU. NO.	ACCOUNTS PAYABLE DR.	PURCHASES DISCOUNT CR.	CASH IN BANK CR.	BANK DEPOSITS	BANK BALANCE	
	1969								8,743 10	
1	July 1	856	Adams Realty Co.	452	600 00		600 00	1,240 30	9,383 40	1
2	2	857	Foster Publications	453	52 50		52 50		9,330 90	2
3	2	858	Hill and Davis	436	1,420 00	14 20	1,405 80	865 70	8,790 80	3
4	3	859	Benson Exp. Co.	454	36 80		36 80	942 20	9,696 20	4
22	30	879	Voided							22
23	30	880	Stone & Co.	460	14 30		14 30		9,521 80	23
24	30	881	Evans Corp.	448	1,015 00		1,015 00	765 50	9,272 30	24
25	31	882	Graham & Co.	469	830 00	16 60	813 40		8,458 90	25
26	31	883	Petty Cash	478	48 60		48 60	938 10	9,348 40	26
27	31				17,322 90	198 20	17,124 70			27
28					(212)	(513)	(111)			28

Check register

Paid voucher file. After payment, vouchers are customarily filed in numerical sequence in a paid voucher file. They are then readily available for examination by employees or independent auditors requiring information about a specific expenditure. Eventually the paid vouchers are destroyed in accordance with the firm's policies concerning the retention of records.

Voucher system and management. The voucher system not only provides effective accounting controls but also aids management in discharging other responsibilities. For example, the voucher system helps assure that only valid obligations are paid. In addition, continuous information is readily available for use in planning for future cash requirements. This in turn enables management to make the maximum use of cash resources. Invoices on which cash discounts are allowed can be paid within the discount period. Other invoices can be paid in accordance with the credit terms, thus minimizing costs and maintaining a favorable credit standing. Seasonal borrowing for working capital purposes can also be planned more accurately, with a consequent saving in interest costs.

Purchases discount

In preceding chapters, purchases of merchandise were recorded at the invoice price, and cash discounts taken were credited to the purchases discount account at the time of payment. There are two views on how such purchases discounts should be reported in the income statement.

The most widely accepted view, which has been followed in this textbook, is that purchases discounts should be reported as a deduction from purchases. For example, the cost of merchandise with an invoice price of $1,000, subject to terms of 2/10, n/30, is recorded initially at $1,000. If payment is made within the discount period, the discount of $20 reduces the cost to $980. If the invoice is not paid within the discount period, the cost of the merchandise remains $1,000. This treatment of purchases discounts may be attacked on the grounds that the date of payment should not affect the cost of a commodity; the additional payment required beyond the discount period adds nothing to the value of the commodities purchased.

The second view reports discounts taken as "other income." In terms of the example above, the cost of the merchandise is considered to be $1,000 regardless of the time of payment. If payment is made within the discount period, revenue of $20 is realized. The objection to this procedure lies in the recognition of revenue from the act of purchasing a commodity. Theoretically, an enterprise might make no sales of merchandise during an accounting period and yet might report as revenue the amount of cash discounts taken.

A major disadvantage of recording purchases at the invoice price and recognizing purchases discounts at the time of payment is that this method does not measure the cost of failing to take discounts. Efficiently managed enterprises maintain sufficient cash to pay within the discount period all invoices subject to a discount, and view the failure to take a discount as an inefficiency. To measure the cost of this inefficiency, purchases invoices may be recorded at the net amount, assuming that all discounts will be taken. Any discounts not taken are then recorded in an expense account entitled Discounts Lost. This method measures the

283

cost of failure to take cash discounts and gives management an opportunity to take remedial action. Again assuming the same data, the invoice for $1,000 would be recorded as a debit to Purchases of $980 and a credit to Accounts Payable for the same amount. If the invoice is not paid until after the discount period has expired, the entry, in general journal form, would be as follows:

Accounts Payable..	980	
Discounts Lost..	20	
Cash in Bank..		1,000

When this method is employed with the voucher system, all vouchers are prepared and recorded at the net amount. Any discount lost is noted on the related voucher and recorded in a special column in the check register when the voucher is paid.

Another advantage of this treatment of purchases discounts is that all merchandise purchased is recorded initially at the net price and hence no subsequent adjustments to cost are necessary. An objection, however, is that the amount reported as accounts payable in the balance sheet may be less than the amount necessary to discharge the liability.

Petty cash

In most businesses there is a frequent need for the payment of relatively small amounts, such as to the postman for postage due, to a deliveryman for transportation charges, or to an employee for the purchase of urgently needed supplies at a nearby retail store. Payment by check in such cases would result in delay, annoyance, and excessive expense of maintaining the records. It is usual, therefore, to maintain a special cash fund that is designated *petty cash.*

In establishing a petty cash fund, the first step is to estimate the amount of cash needed for disbursements of relatively small amounts during a specified period such as a week or a month. If the voucher system is used, a voucher is then prepared for this amount and it is recorded in the voucher register as a debit to Petty Cash and a credit to Accounts Payable. The check drawn to pay the voucher is recorded in the check register as a debit to Accounts Payable and a credit to Cash in Bank.

The money obtained from "cashing" the check is placed in the custody of a specific employee who is authorized to disburse the fund in accordance with stipulated restrictions as to maximum amount and purpose. Each time a disbursement is made from the fund, the employee records the essential details on a receipt form, obtains the signature of the payee as evidence of the payment, and adds his own signature or initials. A typical petty cash receipt is illustrated on the opposite page.

When the amount of money in the petty cash fund is reduced to the predetermined minimum amount, the fund is replenished. If the voucher

```
PETTY CASH RECEIPT

NO. ___121___                    DATE ___August 1, 1969___

PAID TO _____Metropolitan Times_____        AMOUNT

FOR _____Daily newspaper_____              3 | 70

CHARGE TO _____Miscellaneous General Expense_____

PAYMENT RECEIVED:

_____S. O. Hall_____  APPROVED BY ___N.E.R.___
```

Petty cash receipt

system is used, the accounts debited on the replenishing voucher are
those indicated by a summary of expenditures. The voucher is then
recorded in the voucher register as a debit to the various expense and
asset accounts and a credit to Accounts Payable. The entry is similar to
that on line 28 of the voucher register on pages 280 and 281. The check
in payment of the voucher is recorded in the check register in the usual
manner, as shown on line 26 of the illustration on page 282.

After the petty cash fund has been replenished, the fund will be
restored to its original amount. It should be noted that the sole entry in
the petty cash account will be the initial debit unless at some later time
the standard amount of the fund is increased or decreased.

Because disbursements are not recorded in the accounts until the
fund is replenished, petty cash funds and other special funds that operate
in a similar manner should always be replenished at the close of an accounting period. The amount of money actually in the fund will then
agree with the balance in the related fund account, and the expenses and
the assets for which payment has been made will be recorded in the
proper period.

Other cash funds

Other funds may be established to meet the special needs of a business. For example, money advanced to a salesman for travel expenses
may be accounted for in the same manner as petty cash. A standard
amount is advanced; then upon receipt of expense reports from the salesman, the expenses are recorded and the fund is replenished. A similar
procedure may be used to provide a working fund for a sales office
located in another city. The amount of the fund may be deposited in a
local bank and the sales representative may be authorized to draw checks
for payment of rent, salaries, and other operating expenses. Each

month the representative sends the invoices, bank statement, paid checks, bank reconciliation, and other business documents to the home office. The data are audited, the expenditures are recorded, and a reimbursing check is returned for deposit in the local bank.

Control over noncash items

Earlier chapters have discussed the use of subsidiary records for recording and controlling such items as accounts receivable, equipment, and accounts payable. Perpetual inventory records assist in the management and control of inventory. Two other useful devices that represent an elaboration of the accounting system are described below.

Note registers. The notes receivable and notes payable accounts in the general ledger are primarily summarizing devices. They are not designed for recording detailed information about the terms of each note and its disposition. If numerous notes are received from customers or issued to creditors, it is customary to record the details of each note in a notes receivable register or a notes payable register.

The initial recording is made in the register at the time a note is given or received, showing the details of the note, such as name of maker or payee, place of payment, amount, term, interest rate, and due date. Daily reference to the due date section directs attention to which notes, if any, are due for payment or are to be presented for collection.

Insurance registers. An important means of safeguarding a firm's investment in plant assets is through insurance against losses from fire,

INSURANCE

DATE OF POLICY		POLICY NO.	INSURER	PROPERTY OR PURPOSE	AMOUNT	TERM	EXPIRATION DATE	UNEXPIRED PREMIUM	
1964									
Mar.	5	24983	Midland Fire	Equipment	15,000	5	3/5/69	8	96
Oct.	28	469AC	National Fire	Building	30,000	5	10/28/69	110	00
1966									
June	4	79481	Acme Fire & Cas.	Merchandise	25,000	3	6/4/69	47	75
1968									
Oct.	1	6947	Columbia Fire & Cas.	Public Liability	100,000	1	10/1/69	94	50
1969									
Mar.	5	37468	Midland Fire	Equipment	15,000	5	3/5/74	270	60
May	26	2694Y	Liberty Auto	Delivery Equip.		1	5/26/70	542	40
June	4	96423	Acme Fire & Cas.	Merchandise	25,000	3	6/4/72	346	32
Oct.	1	11731	Columbia Fire & Cas.	Public Liability	100,000	1	10/1/70	129	00
	28	9847	U.S. Fire	Building	25,000	5	10/28/74	594	00

Insurance register, left page

windstorm, and other casualties. Potential losses resulting from injury to customers or employees while on the business premises, from dishonesty of employees, and from business interruptions caused by fire are only a few of the many other risks that may need to be insured against. The responsibility for appropriate insurance coverage ordinarily rests with the treasurer, controller, or other accounting officer. It is also the responsibility of the accounting department to determine and to record the amount of insurance expense applicable to each accounting period.

The contract between the insurer and the insured is called the *insurance policy*, and the amount paid for the contract is called the *insurance premium*. Insurance policies are written for a definite amount and for a definite period of time, most commonly for one, three, or five years. The amount of insurance that should be carried on a particular asset does not necessarily correspond to its original cost or book value. The reproduction cost of the asset less accumulated depreciation thereon is a better criterion of the appropriate coverage. In any event, the insured cannot recover more than the actual loss incurred.

A large firm may have literally hundreds of insurance policies in effect. For even a small business the number may be considerable. The review of insurance coverage and the determination of periodic insurance expense are facilitated by the use of a multicolumn form termed an *insurance register*.

An insurance register for a small business is illustrated below and at the bottom of page 286. The data for the insurance policies in effect at

REGISTER — 1969

| | | | | | EXPIRED PREMIUM | | | | | | | | UNEXPIRED PREMIUM |
JAN.	FEB.	MAR.	APR.	MAY	JUNE	JULY	AUG.	SEPT.	OCT.	NOV.	DEC.	TOTAL	
4 48	4 48											8 96	—
11 00	11 00	11 00	11 00	11 00	11 00	11 00	11 00	11 00	11 00	11 00		110 00	—
9 55	9 55	9 55	9 55	9 55								47 75	—
10 50	10 50	10 50	10 50	10 50	10 50	10 50	10 50	10 50				94 50	—
			4 51	4 51	4 51	4 51	4 51	4 51	4 51	4 51	4 51	45 10	225 50
					45 20	45 20	45 20	45 20	45 20	45 20	45 20	316 40	226 00
					9 62	9 62	9 62	9 62	9 62	9 62	9 62	67 34	278 98
									10 75	10 75	10 75	32 25	96 75
										9 90	9 90	19 80	574 20
35 53	35 53	35 56	35 56	35 56	80 83	80 83	80 83	80 83	81 08	79 98			

Insurance register, right page

the beginning of the year are taken from the register for the preceding year; policies acquired during the year are recorded in the order of their acquisition. At the end of each month the insurance expense for that month is determined by adding the appropriate column. For example, the November expiration column in the illustration is totaled at the end of that month and an adjusting entry debiting Insurance Expense and crediting Prepaid Insurance for $79.98 is recorded in the general journal.

At the end of the year the Total Expired Premium column and the two unexpired premium columns are added. The total of the first Unexpired Premium column should agree with the total debits to Prepaid Insurance, the Total Expired Premium column should agree with the credits to the account, and the total of the second Unexpired Premium column should agree with the balance of Prepaid Insurance after all adjustments have been posted.

QUESTIONS

1. Name four requisites of a properly designed accounting system.

2. (a) What is the meaning of *internal control*? (b) What is *internal check*?

3. Why should the responsibility for a sequence of related operations be divided among different persons?

4. The ticket seller at a motion picture theater doubles as ticket taker for a few minutes each day while the ticket taker is on a "break." Which principle of internal control is violated in this situation?

5. Why should the responsibility for maintaining the accounting records be separated from the responsibility for operations?

6. The bookkeeper has the responsibility of determining the accounts receivable to be written off as uncollectible. Which principle of internal control is violated in this situation?

7. The bookkeeper pays all obligations by prenumbered checks. What are the strengths and the weaknesses in the internal control over cash disbursements in this situation?

8. When checks are received from customers, they are recorded as debits to Cash, the assumption being that the customer has sufficient funds on deposit. What does the accountant do if such a check is returned by the bank for lack of sufficient funds (NSF)?

9. What is the purpose of preparing a bank reconciliation?

10. Identify each of the following reconciling items as: (a) an addition to the balance per bank statement, (b) a deduction from the balance per bank statement, (c) an addition to the balance per books, or (d) a deduction from the balance per books. (None of the transactions reported by bank debit and credit memorandums has been recorded by the depositor.)
    (1) Note collected by bank, $500.
    (2) Bank service charge, $3.90.
    (3) Outstanding checks, $942.20.

(4) Check drawn by depositor for $10 recorded in check register as $100.
(5) Check of a customer returned by bank to depositor because of insufficient funds, $25.
(6) Check for $35 charged by bank as $53.
(7) Deposit in transit, $173.45.

11. Which of the reconciling items listed in Question 10 will require an entry in the depositor's books?

12. The procedures employed by Miller Food Stores for over-the-counter receipts are as follows: Each salesclerk counts the cash in his cash drawer at the close of business. He then removes the cash register tape and prepares the memorandum daily cash form, noting any discrepancies. An employee from the cashier's office recounts the cash, compares the total with the memorandum, and takes the cash to the cashier's office. (a) Indicate the weak link in internal control. (b) How can the weakness be corrected?

13. The procedures employed by Walton Company for mail receipts are as follows: Mailroom employees send all remittances and remittance advices to the cashier. The cashier deposits the cash in the bank and forwards the remittance advices and duplicate deposit slips to the accounting department. (a) Indicate the weak link in internal control. (b) How can the weakness be corrected?

14. What does a debit balance in the account Cash Short and Over indicate?

15. The combined cash count of all cash registers at the close of business is $5.70 more than the cash sales indicated by the cash register tapes. (a) In what account is the cash overage recorded? (b) Are cash overages debited or credited to this account?

16. What is meant by the term "voucher" as applied to the voucher system?

289

17. Before a voucher for the purchase of merchandise is approved for payment, three documents should be compared to verify the accuracy of the liability. Name these three documents.

18. (a) When the voucher system is employed, is the accounts payable account in the general ledger a controlling account? (b) Is there a subsidiary creditors ledger?

19. (a) In what order are vouchers ordinarily filed in the unpaid voucher file? Give a reason for your answer. (b) In what order are vouchers ordinarily filed in the paid voucher file? Give a reason for your answer.

20. Merchandise with an invoice price of $10,000 is purchased subject to terms of 1/10, n/30. What is the cost of the merchandise according to each of the following assumptions:
  (a) Discounts taken are considered to be adjustments to the invoice price.
      (1) The invoice is paid within the discount period.
      (2) The invoice is paid after the discount period has expired.
  (b) Discounts taken are considered to be other income.
      (1) The invoice is paid within the discount period.
      (2) The invoice is paid after the discount period has expired.
  (c) Discounts allowable are considered to be adjustments to the invoice price.
      (1) The invoice is paid within the discount period.
      (2) The invoice is paid after the discount period has expired.

21. What account or accounts are debited when recording the voucher (a) establishing a petty cash fund and (b) replenishing a petty cash fund?

22. The petty cash account has a debit balance of $250. At the end of the accounting period there is $50 in the petty cash fund along with petty cash receipts totaling $200. Should the fund be replenished as of the last day of the period? Discuss.

23. What two purposes are served by an insurance register?

EXERCISES

11-1. The following data are accumulated for use in reconciling the bank account of Murphy Company for March:

    (a) Balance per bank statement at March 31, $2,591.80.
    (b) Balance per books at March 31, $2,245.80.
    (c) Deposit in transit not recorded by bank, $275.40.
    (d) Checks outstanding, $616.55.
    (e) Bank debit memorandum for service charges, $5.15.
    (f) A check for $75 in payment of a voucher was erroneously recorded in the check register as $85.

Prepare a bank reconciliation.

11-2. Using the data presented in Exercise 1, prepare in general journal form the entry or entries that should be made by the depositor.

11-3. Accompanying a bank statement for Curtis Company is a debit memorandum for $208.50 representing the principal ($200), interest ($6), and protest fee ($2.50) on a discounted note that had been dishonored by J. W. Welch Co. The depositor had been notified by the bank at the time of the dishonor but had made no entries. Present the necessary entry by the depositor, in general journal form.

11-4. Record in general journal form the following selected transactions, indicating above each entry the name of the journal in which it should be recorded. Assume the use of a voucher register similar to that illustrated on pages 280 and 281 and a check register similar to that illustrated on page 282. All invoices are recorded at invoice price.

July 1. Recorded Voucher No. 404 for $750, payable to Mann Office Equipment Co., for office equipment purchased on terms n/30.
     3. Recorded Voucher No. 405 for $1,500, payable to Reed Co., for merchandise purchased on terms 2/10, n/30.
     8. Recorded Voucher No. 408 for $78.20 to replenish the petty cash fund for the following disbursements: Store Supplies, $19.50; Office Supplies, $20.42; Miscellaneous Selling Expense, $19.88; and Miscellaneous General Expense, $18.40.
     8. Issued Check No. 520 in payment of Voucher No. 408.
   12. Issued Check No. 525 in payment of Voucher No. 405.
   19. Recorded Voucher No. 416 for $120, payable to *Newport Times*, for advertising appearing in yesterday's newspaper.
   26. Issued Check No. 532 in payment of Voucher No. 416.
   31. Issued Check No. 533 in payment of Voucher No. 404.

11-5. Record in general journal form the following transactions:

(a) Prepared Voucher No. 1 to establish a change fund of $100.

(b) Issued Check No. 1 in payment of Voucher No. 1.

(c) Determined cash sales for the day, according to the cash register tapes, to be $324.60 and cash on hand to be $424.15. A bank deposit ticket was prepared for $324.15.

11-6. Record in general journal form the following related transactions, assuming that invoices for commodities purchased are recorded at their net price after deducting the allowable discount:

June 10. Prepared Voucher No. 711 for the purchase of merchandise from Emery Supply Co., $2,000, terms 2/10, n/30.

11. Prepared Voucher No. 712 for the purchase of merchandise from Pryor Co., $5,000, terms 1/10, n/30.

19. Issued Check No. 901, payable to Emery Supply Co., in payment of Voucher No. 711.

July 10. Issued Check No. 927, payable to Pryor Co., in payment of Voucher No. 712.

11-7. Prepare in general journal form the entries to record the following:

(a) Voucher No. 270 is prepared to establish a petty cash fund of $100.

(b) Check No. 266 is issued in payment of Voucher No. 270.

(c) The amount of cash in the petty cash fund is now $21.10. Voucher No. 294 is prepared to replenish the fund, based on the following summary of petty cash receipts: Office Supplies, $19.25; Miscellaneous Selling Expense, $34.62; Miscellaneous General Expense, $24.73.

(d) Check No. 290 is issued by the disbursing officer in payment of Voucher No. 294. The check is cashed and the money is placed in the fund.

PROBLEMS

The following additional problems for this chapter are located in Appendix C: 11-1B, 11-2B, 11-3B, 11-5B.

11-1A. The cash in bank account for Bailey Company at January 31 of the current year indicated a balance of $6,674.55 after both the cash receipts journal and the check register for January had been posted. The bank statement indicated a balance of $9,966.85 on January 31. Comparison of the bank statement and the accompanying canceled checks and memorandums with the records revealed the following reconciling items:

(a) A deposit of $1,226.16 representing receipts of January 31 had been made too late to appear on the bank statement.

(b) Checks outstanding totaled $4,125.36.

(c) A check for $59 returned with the statement had been recorded in the check register as $95. The check was for the payment of an obligation to Foley Equipment Company on account for the purchase of store equipment.

(d) A check for $150 drawn by Dailey Company had been erroneously charged by the bank to Bailey Company's account.

(e) The bank had collected for Bailey Company $512 on a note left for collection. The face of the note was $500.

(f) Bank service charges for January amounted to $4.90.

Instructions:

(1) Prepare a bank reconciliation.
(2) Journalize the necessary entries. The accounts have not been closed. The voucher system is used.

11-2A. King Company had the following vouchers in its unpaid voucher file at April 30 of the current year:

Due Date	Voucher No.	Creditor	Date of Invoice	Amount	Terms
May 2	713	Reed Co.	April 22	$ 500	2/10, n/30
11	701	Myers Co.	April 11	725	n/30
23	714	Riley, Inc.	April 23	1,100	n/30

The vouchers prepared and the checks issued during the month of May were as follows:

VOUCHERS

Date	Voucher No.	Payee	Amount	Terms	Distribution
May 1	717	Scott Co.	$ 300	1/10, n/30	Purchases
3	718	Hall and Son	70	cash	Office supplies
6	719	Carr, Inc.	450	2/10, n/30	Purchases
6	720	Stern Supply	350	n/30	Store equipment
10	721	Beck Co.	800	2/10, n/30	Purchases
17	722	Harris Trust Co.	1,015		Note payable, $1,000
					Interest, $15
20	723	Cohen Bros.	1,200	1/10, n/30	Purchases
20	724	Keene Co.	1,500	1/10, n/30	Purchases
20	725	Fisher Co.	85	cash	Store supplies
21	726	Stern Supply	425	n/30	Office equipment
22	727	Parks Co.	3,600	2/10, n/30	Purchases
27	728	News Gazette	50	cash	Advertising expense
29	729	Petty Cash	72		Store supplies, $22
					Office supplies, $19
					Delivery expense, $7
					Miscellaneous selling expense, $15
					Miscellaneous general expense, $9

CHECKS

Date	Check No.	Payee	Voucher Paid	Amount
May 2	909	Reed Co.	713	$ 490
3	910	Hall and Son	718	70
11	911	Myers Co.	701	725
11	912	Scott Co.	717	297
16	913	Carr, Inc.	719	441
17	914	Harris Trust Co.	722	1,015
20	915	Beck Co.	721	784
20	916	Fisher Co.	725	85
23	917	Riley, Inc.	714	1,100
27	918	News Gazette	728	50
29	919	Petty Cash	729	72
30	920	Cohen Bros.	723	1,188
30	921	Keene Co.	724	1,485

292

Instructions:

(1) Set up a four-column account for Accounts Payable, Account No. 211, and record the balance of $2,325 as of May 1.

(2) Record the May vouchers in a voucher register similar to the one illustrated in this chapter, with the following amount columns: Accounts Payable Cr., Purchases Dr., Store Supplies Dr., Office Supplies Dr., and Sundry Accounts Dr. Purchases invoices are recorded at the gross amount.

(3) Record the May checks in a check register similar to the one illustrated in this chapter, but omit the Bank Deposits and Balance columns. As each check is recorded in the check register, the check number should be inserted in the appropriate place in the Check No. column of the voucher register. Assume that appropriate notations are made in the Paid column of the voucher register when the April vouchers are paid.

(4) Total and rule the registers and post to the accounts payable account.

(5) Prepare a schedule of unpaid vouchers.

If the working papers correlating with the textbook are not used, omit Problem 11-3A.

11-3A. Portions of the following accounting records of J. W. Gates Co. are presented in the working papers:

Voucher Register	General ledger accounts:
Check Register	Prepaid Insurance
General Journal	Notes Payable
Insurance Register	Accounts Payable
Notes Payable Register	

Expenditures, cash disbursements, and other selected transactions completed during the period March 25–31 of the current year are described below.

Mar. 25. Recorded Voucher No. 815 payable to Gardner Co. for merchandise, $2,650, terms 2/10, n/30. (Purchases invoices are recorded at the gross amount.)

25. Issued Check No. 901 to Eaton Co. in payment of Voucher No. 803 for $3,000, less cash discount of 1%.

26. Issued a 60-day, 6% note (No. 44), dated today to Castle Co. in settlement of Voucher No. 789, $6,000. The note is payable at First National Bank.

27. Recorded Voucher No. 816 payable to United Automobile Insurance Co. for the following insurance policy, dated today: No. 2103D, automobiles, 1 year, $1,110.

27. Issued Check No. 902 in payment of Voucher No. 816.

27. Recorded Voucher No. 817 payable to Urbana County Bank for note payable (No. 43), $12,500.

27. Issued Check No. 903 in payment of Voucher No. 817.

28. Recorded Voucher No. 818 payable to Carson and Roland for merchandise, $4,250, terms n/30.

28. Recorded Voucher No. 819 payable to *Rantoul Courier* for advertising, $475.

28. Issued Check No. 904 in payment of Voucher No. 819.

29. Recorded Voucher No. 820 payable to Petty Cash for $140.60, distributed as follows: Office Supplies, $32.15; Advertising Expense, $11.40; Delivery Expense, $16.85; Miscellaneous Selling Expense, $51.30; Miscellaneous General Expense, $28.90.

29. Issued Check No. 905 in payment of Voucher No. 820.

30. Recorded Voucher No. 821 payable to Sentry Insurance Co. for the following insurance policy, dated today: No. 4205, building, $500,000, 3 years, $6,915.60.
30. Issued Check No. 906 in payment of Voucher No. 821.
31. Issued Check No. 907 to Hamilton Co. in payment of Voucher No. 812 for $1,750, less cash discount of 2%.

After the journals are posted at the end of the month, the cash in bank account has a debit balance of $14,026.50.

The bank statement indicates a March 31 balance of $23,223.80. Comparison of paid checks returned by the bank with the check register reveals that Nos. 904, 906, and 907 are outstanding. Check No. 896 for $232, which appeared on the February reconciliation as outstanding, is still outstanding. A debit memorandum accompanying the bank statement indicates a charge of $140.30 for a check drawn by R. L. Collins, a customer, which was returned because of insufficient funds.

Instructions:

(1) Record the transactions for March 25–31 in the appropriate journals. Immediately after recording a transaction, post individual items, where appropriate, to the three general ledger accounts given.
(2) Enter the necessary notations in the notes payable register and the insurance register, rounding insurance expirations to the nearest month.
(3) Total and rule the voucher register and the check register, and post totals to the accounts payable account.
(4) Complete the schedule of unpaid vouchers. (Compare the total with the balance of the accounts payable account as of March 31.)
(5) Prepare a bank reconciliation and journalize any necessary entries.
(6) Total the Expired Premium column for March in the insurance register, journalize the adjusting entry, and post to the prepaid insurance account. (Determine the balance of prepaid insurance as of March 31 from the columns in the insurance register and compare it with the balance of the prepaid insurance account as of the same date.)
(7) Determine the amount of interest accrued as of March 31 on notes payable (Nos. 42 and 44). (Assume 28 days in February.)
(8) Determine the amount of interest prepaid as of March 31 on notes payable (No. 40). (The non-interest-bearing note was discounted by the bank.)

11-4A. Ellis Company has just adopted the policy of depositing all cash receipts in the bank and of making all payments by check in conjunction with the voucher system. The following transactions were selected from those completed in July of the current year:

July 1. Recorded Voucher No. 1 to establish a petty cash fund of $100 and a change fund of $500.
1. Issued Check No. 960 in payment of Voucher No. 1.
3. Recorded Voucher No. 5 to establish an advances to salesmen fund of $1,000.
3. Issued Check No. 964 in payment of Voucher No. 5.
8. The cash sales for the day according to the cash register tapes totaled $1,412.30. The combined count of all cash on hand (including the change fund) totaled $1,913.55.

22. Recorded Voucher No. 43 to reimburse the petty cash fund for the following disbursements, each evidenced by a petty cash receipt:

July 2. Office supplies, $8.50.
     3. Express charges on merchandise purchased, $12.25.
     8. Store supplies, $11.20.
   11. Postage stamps, $12 (Office Supplies).
   12. Repair to adding machine, $9.50 (Misc. General Expense).
   15. Postage due on special delivery letter, $.35 (Misc. Gen. Exp.).
   16. Telegram charges, $2.70 (Misc. Selling Expense).
   16. Office supplies, $13.
   18. Repair to typewriter, $9.15 (Misc. General Expense).
   19. Express charges on merchandise purchased, $8.20.

22. Issued Check No. 1012 in payment of Voucher No. 43.
25. Recorded Voucher No. 48 to replenish the advances to salesmen fund for the following expenditures for travel: John Clark, $250; Robert Mitchell, $300; James Root, $210.50.
25. Issued Check No. 1017 in payment of Voucher No. 48.
29. The cash sales for the day according to the cash register tapes totaled $1,207.50. The count of all cash on hand totaled $1,705.10.

Instructions:

Record the above transactions in general journal form.

11-5A. Weaver Company employs the voucher system in controlling expenditures and disbursements. All cash receipts are deposited in a night depository after banking hours each Wednesday and Friday. The data required to reconcile their bank statement as of April 30 of the current year have been abstracted from various documents and records and are reproduced below. To facilitate identification the sources of the data are printed in capital letters. **295**

CASH IN BANK ACCOUNT
    Balance as of April 1 . . . . $4,533.29

CASH RECEIPTS JOURNAL
    Total of Cash in Bank Debit column for month of April 5,454.18

DUPLICATE DEPOSIT TICKETS
    Date and amount of each deposit in April:

Date	Amount	Date	Amount	Date	Amount
April 2	$656.20	April 14	$749.98	April 23	$391.69
7	555.52	16	517.25	28	746.22
9	872.22	21	420.85	30	544.25

CHECK REGISTER
    Number and amount of each check issued in April:

Check No.	Amount	Check No.	Amount	Check No.	Amount
610	$277.15	617	$261.22	624	$247.67
611	74.20	618	147.77	625	151.21
612	157.26	619	Void	626	45.20
613	361.12	620	200.50	627	98.94
614	631.40	621	597.26	628	716.65
615	23.00	622	372.78	629	727.10
616	85.14	623	513.40	630	230.31

    Total checks issued in April $5,919.28

BANK STATEMENT FOR APRIL
Balance as of April 1.............................. $4,790.30
Date and amount of each deposit in April:

Date	Amount	Date	Amount	Date	Amount
April 1	$417.25	April 10	$872.22	April 22	$420.85
3	656.20	15	749.98	24	391.69
8	555.52	17	517.25	29	746.22

Balance as of April 30................................ $5,127.22

CHECKS ACCOMPANYING BANK STATEMENT FOR APRIL
Number and amount of each check, rearranged in numerical sequence:

Check No.	Amount	Check No.	Amount	Check No.	Amount
590	$ 89.94	614	$613.40	623	$513.40
605	277.17	615	23.00	624	247.67
609	189.89	616	85.14	625	151.21
610	277.15	618	147.77	627	98.94
611	74.20	620	200.50	629	727.10
612	157.26	621	597.26	630	230.31
613	361.12	622	372.78		

BANK MEMORANDUMS ACCOMPANYING BANK STATEMENT FOR APRIL
Date, description, and amount of each memorandum:

Date	Description	Amount
April 16	Bank credit memo for note collected:	
	Principal..	$ 500.00
	Interest..	7.50
28	Bank debit memo for check returned because of insufficient funds..	60.50
30	Bank debit memo for service charges.................	2.05

BANK RECONCILIATION FOR PRECEDING MONTH

Weaver Company
Bank Reconciliation
March 31, 19--

Balance per bank statement........................		$4,790.30
Add: Deposit of March 31, not recorded by bank.....		417.25
		$5,207.55
Deduct: Outstanding checks:		
No. 590........................	$ 89.94	
605........................	277.17	
608........................	117.26	
609........................	189.89	674.26
Adjusted balance................................		$4,533.29
Balance per books................................		$4,535.24
Deduct: Service charges........................		1.95
Adjusted balance................................		$4,533.29

Instructions:

(1) Prepare a bank reconciliation as of April 30. If errors in recording deposits or checks are discovered, assume that the errors were made by the company.

(2) Journalize the necessary entries. The accounts have not been closed.
(3) What is the amount of cash in bank that should appear on the balance sheet as of April 30?

11-6A. Meyer and Holt was organized on May 1 of the current year. The voucher system is not used. The following transactions are selected from those completed during May:

May 1. Purchased $10,000 of merchandise from Gregory Industries, terms 2/10, n/30. Purchases invoices are recorded at the net price after deducting allowable cash discounts.
  2. Issued a check to Continental Insurance Co. in payment of the premiums on the following insurance policies, all dated May 1:

Policy No.	Property	Amount	Term	Premium
8180	Merchandise	$25,000	5 years	$360
8181	Building	50,000	3 years	648
8182	Delivery Equipment		1 year	480

  3. Issued a check for $186 to the National Insurance Company in payment of Policy No. 6179X, dated May 1, covering public liability for one year in the amount of $200,000.
  17. Purchased $2,500 of merchandise from Warner Co., terms 1/10, n/30.
  18. Issued a check to the Midland Guaranty Insurance Co. for $168 in payment of the premium on Policy No. 417C, dated May 15, covering fidelity insurance for one year in the amount of $15,000.
  26. Paid the amount due Warner Co. for invoice of May 17.
  29. Paid the amount due Gregory Industries for invoice of May 1.
  31. Issued a check for $100 to Hardenbrook's Garage in payment of the balance due on charges of $700 for repair of a delivery truck damaged in a collision earlier in the month. Continental Insurance Co. paid $600 of the charge in accordance with the terms of Policy No. 8182, which has a $100 deductible clause on collision damage.

Instructions:

(1) Record the transactions in general journal form.
(2) Record the relevant data for the current year in an insurance register similar to the one illustrated on pages 286 and 287. In allocating insurance expirations, round all expirations to the nearest one-half month.
(3) Journalize the insurance adjustment as of May 31.
(4) Considering only those insurance policies included above:
  (a) What will be the total amount of insurance expense for the current year ending December 31?
  (b) What will be the amount of unexpired insurance that will appear on the balance sheet at December 31 of the current year?

11-7A. The bank statement for Lambert Bros. for April of the current year indicates a balance of $16,501.39 on April 30. The balance according to the check stubs as of the same date is $12,936.93. The balance of Cash in Bank in the ledger as of April 1 is $17,174.84; pencil footings of the cash receipts journal and the check register for April indicate receipts and disbursements for the month of $20,701.12 and $24,117.61 respectively. Comparison of the bank statement and the accompanying checks and memorandums with the records reveals the following reconciling items:

(a) A deposit of $821.42 on April 17 was not recorded on the check stubs. The cash received was recorded properly in the cash receipts journal.

(b) Proceeds of a bank loan on April 30 were omitted from the cash receipts journal and the check stubs. The note was for $5,000 and was discounted by the bank at 6% for 60 days.

(c) Receipts of $725.25 from cash sales for April 22 were entered in the cash receipts journal and on the check stubs as $752.25. The receipts, all of which were deposited, appeared on the bank statement as $725.25.

(d) A debit memorandum dated April 27 indicated that the bank had deducted the principal of $4,000, the interest of $60, and the protest fee of $5 on a note that had been discounted at the bank by Lambert Bros. Prior notice of the failure of R. W. Evans Co. to pay the note and of the bank's charge had been received by Lambert Bros. but no entry had been made nor had a deduction been recorded on the check stubs.

(e) Canceled check No. 4312 for $12 was erroneously listed on the bank statement as $120.

(f) Checks outstanding: No. 4310, $197.75; No. 4327, $734.00; No. 4352, $97.57; No. 4353, $147.22; No. 4354, $816.50.

Instructions:

(1) Prepare a reconciliation of the bank statement with the cash in bank account after giving effect to the recorded receipts and disbursements.

(2) Determine the net amount of the adjustment to the check stub balance as of April 30, presenting the computations.

(3) Present in general journal form the necessary entries based on the bank reconciliation.

298

12

Payroll systems

Objectives of payroll systems

The volume of expenditures for labor costs and related payroll taxes has a significant effect on the net income of most business enterprises. Although the degree of importance of such expenses varies widely, it is not uncommon for a business to expend nearly a third of its sales revenue for payroll and labor-related expenses. Accordingly, it is important that the payroll segment of the accounting system provide safeguards to insure that payments are in accord with management's general plans and its specific authorizations.

All employees of a firm expect and are entitled to receive their remuneration at regular intervals following the close of each payroll period. Regardless of the number of employees and of intricacies in computing the amounts to be paid, the payroll system must be designed to process the necessary data quickly and accurately and pay the correct amount to each employee. It is essential that the system provide adequate safeguards against overpayments, payments to fictitious persons, and other misappropriations of funds.

Various federal, state, and local laws require that employers accumulate certain specified data in their payroll records of a summary nature not only for payroll periods but also for each individual employee. Periodic reports of such data must be submitted to the appropriate governmental agencies, accompanied by remittances for amounts withheld from employees and for taxes levied on the employer. The records must also be retained for specified periods of time and be available for inspection by those responsible for enforcement of the laws. In addition, payroll data may be useful in negotiations with labor unions, in settling employee grievances, and in determining entitlement to vacations, sick leaves, and retirement pensions.

Employer-employee relationship

Persons who perform remunerative services for a business enterprise may be classified either as employees or as independent contractors. Payroll systems are concerned only with employees and the records, reports, remuneration, taxes, etc., associated with the employer-employee relationship. The relationship of employer and employee generally exists when the person for whom the services are performed has the right to control and direct the individual in the performance of his services. Accordingly, salesclerks and bookkeepers in a retail store are unquestionably employees. Similarly, an accountant occupying the position of controller of a corporation is an employee. On the other hand, a public accountant or CPA engaged to audit the accounting records of a business chooses his own means of performing the services and is not subject to the control and guidance of his client. He is an independent contractor rather than an employee. In similar fashion an attorney working in the tax department of a corporation would be an employee, but an attorney engaged to negotiate a particular contract or defend a particular lawsuit would be an independent contractor.

Payments to independent contractors for services are usually referred to as *fees* or *charges*. Such payments are not part of the payroll system and are not subject to withholding or to the payroll taxes levied on employers.

Types of remuneration of employees

The term *salary* is usually applied to payment for managerial, administrative, or similar services. The rate of salary is ordinarily expressed in terms of a month or a year. Remuneration for manual labor, both skilled and unskilled, is commonly referred to as *wages* and is stated on an hourly, weekly, or piecework basis. In practice, the terms salary and wages are often used interchangeably. The basic salary or wage of an employee may be supplemented by commissions, bonuses, profit sharing, or cost-of-living adjustments. The form in which remuneration is paid generally has no effect on the manner in which it is treated by either the employer or the employee. Although payment is usually in terms of cash, it may be in other media such as securities, notes, lodging, or other property or services.

Measurement of employee earnings

Wage and salary rates are determined, in general, by agreement between the employer and the employees. Enterprises engaged in interstate commerce must also conform to the requirements of the Federal

Fair Labor Standards Act. Employers covered by this legislation, which is commonly known as the "wages and hours law," are required to pay a minimum rate of 1½ times the regular rate for all hours worked in excess of 40 hours per week. Exemptions from the requirements are provided for executive, administrative, and certain supervisory positions. Premium rates for overtime or for working at night or other less desirable times are fairly common, even when not required by law, and the premium rates may be as much as twice the base rate.

The computation of the earnings of an employee is illustrated below. It is assumed that Harold B. Ashton is employed at the rate of $3.60 per hour for the first 40 hours in the weekly pay period and at $5.40 ($3.60 + $1.80) per hour for any additional hours. His time card reveals that he worked 45 hours during the week ended November 21. His earnings for that week are computed as follows:

Earnings at base rate............	40 × $3.60	$144.00
Earnings at overtime rate........	5 × $5.40	27.00
Total earnings.........................		$171.00

The foregoing computations can be stated in generalized arithmetic formulas or *algorithms*. If the hours worked during the week are less than or equal to ($\leq$) 40, the formula may be expressed by the following equation, where E represents total earnings, H represents hours worked, and R represents hourly rate:

$$E = H \times R$$

The foregoing equation cannot be used to determine the earnings of an employee who has worked more than ($>$) 40 hours during the week because the overtime rate differs from the basic rate. The expansion of the equation to incorporate the additional factor of overtime yields the following:

$$E = 40\,R + 1.5\,R\,(H - 40)$$

The two equations can be expressed graphically in the following algorithm:

If	Then
H $\leq$ 40	E = H × R
H $>$ 40	E = 40R + 1.5R(H − 40)

After the value of H and R are known for each employee at the conclusion of a payroll period, the earnings of each employee can be computed accurately and speedily. Application of the standardized procedure of the algorithm to mechanized or electronic processing equipment makes it possible to routinely process a payroll regardless of the number of employees.

Deductions from employee earnings

The total earnings of an employee for a payroll period are frequently referred to as the *gross pay*. From it there is subtracted one or more *deductions* to arrive at the *net pay*, which is the amount the employer is obligated to pay the employee. The deductions of widest applicability and usually of greatest magnitude are for federal taxes. Deductions may also be required for state or local income taxes and for contributions to state unemployment compensation programs.

FICA tax. Most employers are required by the Federal Insurance Contributions Act (FICA) to withhold a portion of the earnings of each of their employees. The amount withheld is the employees' contribution to the combined federal programs for old-age and disability benefits, insurance benefits to survivors, and health insurance for the aged (medicare). With very few exceptions, employers are required to withhold from each employee a tax at a specified rate on earnings up to a specified amount paid in the calendar year.[1] Although both the schedule of future tax rates and the maximum amount subject to tax are revised frequently by Congress, such changes have no effect on the basic outline of the payroll system. For purposes of illustration, a rate of 5% on maximum annual earnings of $7,800, or a maximum annual tax of $390, will be assumed.

Federal income tax. Except for certain types of employment, all employers are required to withhold a portion of the earnings of their employees for payment of the employees' liability for federal income tax. The amount required to be withheld from each employee varies in accordance with the amount of his gross pay, marital status, and the estimated deductions and exemptions to which he will be entitled when filing his annual income tax return. The withholding can be computed in accordance with either the "percentage" method, which necessitates the determination of taxable earnings and multiplication by the appropriate tax rate, or by the "wage-bracket" method, which is a one-step operation utilizing tables of predetermined withholding amounts. Every employee is required to file with his employer an employee's withholding exemption certificate in which he reports the number of his exemptions. An exemption certificate completed by Harold B. Ashton is shown at the top of the next page.

302

---

[1]The Social Security Amendments of 1967 established the following schedule of rates, on maximum earnings of $7,800: 1968, 4.4%; 1969–70, 4.8%; 1971–2, 5.2%; 1973–5, 5.65%; 1976–9, 5.7%; 1980–6, 5.8%; 1987– , 5.9%.

EMPLOYEE'S WITHHOLDING EXEMPTION CERTIFICATE

Type or print full name __Harold B. Ashton__   Social Security Number __259-08-8114__

Home address __1986 Belmont Street__ City __Lakewood__ State __Ohio__ ZIP code __44112__

EMPLOYEE:	**HOW TO CLAIM YOUR WITHHOLDING EXEMPTIONS**	
File this form with your employer. Otherwise, he must withhold U.S. Income tax from your wages without exemption.	1. If SINGLE (or if married and wish withholding as single person), write "1." If you claim no exemptions, write "0".	
	2. If MARRIED, one exemption each is allowable for husband and wife if not claimed on another certificate.	
	(a) If you claim both of these exemptions, write "2"; (b) If you claim one of these exemptions, write "1"; (c) If you claim neither of these exemptions, write "0"	2
EMPLOYER: Keep this certificate with your records. If the employee is believed to have claimed too many exemptions, the District Director should be so advised.	3. Exemptions for age and blindness (applicable only to your and your wife but not to dependents):	
	(a) If you or your wife will be 65 years of age or older at the end of the year, and you claim this exemption, write "1"; if both will be 65 or older, and you claim both of these exemptions, write "2"	
	(b) If you or your wife are blind, and you claim this exemption, write "1"; if both are blind, and you claim both of these exemptions, write "2".	
	4. If you claim exemptions for one or more dependents, write the number of such exemptions. (Do not claim exemption for a dependent unless you are qualified under Instruction 4 on other side.).	2
	5. If you claim additional withholding allowances for itemized deductions fill out and attach Schedule A (Form W–4), and enter the number of allowances claimed (if claimed file new Form W–4 each year)	
	6. Add the exemptions and allowances (if any) which you have claimed above and write total	4
	7. Additional withholding per pay period under agreement with employer. (See Instruction 1.) $	

I CERTIFY that the number of withholding exemptions claimed on this certificate does not exceed the number to which I am entitled.

(Date) __July 15__, 19 __68__   (Signed) __Harold B. Ashton__   o48—16—79061–1

Employee's withholding exemption certificate

Other deductions. Deductions from gross earnings for payment of taxes are compulsory; neither the employer nor the employee has any choice in the matter. In addition, however, there may be other deductions authorized by individual employees or by the union representing them. For example, an employee may authorize deductions of specified amounts for the purchase of United States savings bonds, for contributions to a Community Chest or other charitable organization, for payment of premiums on various types of employee insurance, or for the purchase of a retirement annuity. The union contract may also require the deduction of union dues or other deductions for group benefits.

303

Computation of employee net pay

Gross earnings for a payroll period less the payroll deductions yields the amount to be paid to the employee, which is frequently called the *net* or *take home* pay. The amount to be paid Harold B. Ashton is $135.40, based on the following summary:

Gross earnings for the week		$171.00
Deductions:		
FICA tax	$ 4.20	
Federal income tax	19.90	
U.S. savings bonds	6.50	
Community Chest	5.00	
Total deductions		35.60
Net pay		$135.40

As has been indicated, there is a ceiling on the annual earnings subject to the FICA tax, and consequently the amount of the annual tax is also limited. Therefore when computing the amount of FICA tax to withhold from an employee, it is necessary to take into consideration either the amount of (1) cumulative gross earnings for the year prior to the present payroll period or (2) total tax withheld for the year prior to the present payroll period. To continue with the above illustration, reference to the cumulative record maintained for Ashton indicates earnings of $7,716 prior to the current week. The amount of the current week's earnings subject to tax is therefore $7,800 (maximum) — $7,716, or $84, and the amount of tax to be withheld is 5% of $84, or $390.00 (maximum) — $385.80 (amount withheld prior to the current week), both of which yield $4.20.

The amount of federal income tax withheld, $19.90, was determined by the wage-bracket method for a married taxpayer claiming four exemptions (see Employee's Withholding Exemption Certificate, page 303). Unlike the FICA tax, there is no ceiling on the amount of earnings subject to withholding for income taxes, and hence no need to consider the cumulative earnings. The deductions for the purchase of bonds and for the charitable contribution were in accordance with Ashton's specific authorizations.

As in the determination of gross earnings where overtime rates are a factor, the computation of deductions can be generalized in the form of algorithms. The algorithm for the determination of the FICA tax deduction, based on the maximum deduction approach, is presented below, where E represents current period's earnings, F represents current period's FICA deduction, and f represents cumulative FICA deductions prior to the current period.

If	Then
$f + (.05E) \leq \$390$	$F = .05E$
$f + (.05E) > \$390$	$F = \$390 - f$

An alternative generalization of the method of determining FICA deductions, based on the maximum taxable earnings approach, is illustrated below in the form of a *decision diagram*. The additional symbol "e" represents cumulative earnings prior to the current period.

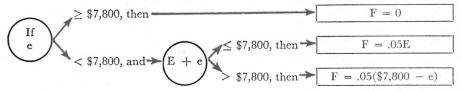

The foregoing are merely examples of standardized instructions that can be applied to computations involving numerous variables. They are employed in many situations as an aid to routine processing of repetitive data, regardless of whether the processing is performed manually, mechanically, or electronically.

Components of payroll systems

The objectives of payroll systems having been explained, basic terms and concepts described, and common factors and relationships explored, attention is now directed toward the major components of a payroll system. Although complex organizational structures may necessitate the use of detailed subsystems, the major components common to most payroll systems are the *payroll register, paycheck,* and *employee's earnings record.* The framework for the illustrations and discussion will be relatively uncomplicated; in actual practice many modifications might be introduced.

Payroll register

The term *payroll* may be used to refer to the total amount paid to employees for a specified period; it is also often applied to the multi-column form used in assembling and summarizing the data needed at the end of each payroll period. This summarizing form is referred to more specifically as the *payroll register.* Its design will vary in accordance with variations in the number and classes of employees, the extent to which automation is employed, and the type of equipment used. A form suitable for a small number of employees is illustrated at the top of pages 306 and 307.

The nature of most of the data appearing in the illustrative payroll register is evident from the columnar headings. Number of hours worked and earnings and deduction data are inserted in the appropriate columns. The sum of the deductions applicable to an employee is then deducted from the total earnings to yield the amount to be paid. Recording the check numbers on the payroll register as the checks are written eliminates any necessity of maintaining check stubs or other detailed records of the payments.

The last two columns of the payroll register are used to accumulate the total wages or salaries to be charged to the expense accounts. This process is usually termed *payroll distribution.* If there is an extensive account classification of labor expense, the charges may be analyzed on a separate payroll distribution sheet.

The two columns under the general heading of Taxable Earnings are used in accumulating data needed to compute the payroll taxes discussed later in the chapter.

The format of the illustrative payroll register and of most variants facilitates the determination of arithmetic accuracy prior to issuance of checks to employees and formal recording of the summary amounts. Specifically, all columnar totals except those in the Taxable Earnings columns should be cross-verified. The miscellaneous deductions must also be summarized by account classification. The tabulation that follows

NAME	TOTAL HOURS	EARNINGS			TAXABLE EARNINGS	
		REGULAR	OVERTIME	TOTAL	UNEMPLOY-MENT COMP.	FICA
ASHTON, HAROLD B.	45	144.00	27.00	171.00		84.00
BALLARD, MARY	40	110.00		110.00		110.00
DAVIS, JOHN T.	41	128.00	4.80	132.80	132.80	132.80
DRAKE, PAUL W.		300.00		300.00		
WILLIAMS, ROSE V.	40	140.00		140.00	60.00	140.00
YORK, HENRY J.		220.00		220.00	220.00	220.00
		5,914.26	320.12	6,234.38	1,763.20	4,881.87

Miscellaneous Deductions: AR — Accounts Receivable

Payroll register, left page

illustrates the method of cross-verification. In practice the amounts
would be listed by means of an adding machine, taking the figures
directly from the payroll register.

306

```
Earnings:
    Regular.......................   $5,914.26
    Overtime......................      320.12
        Total.....................              $6,234.38

Deductions:
    FICA tax......................   $  244.09
    Federal income tax............      691.40
    U.S. savings bonds............      270.50
    Community Chest...............      182.00
    Accounts receivable...........       16.50
        Total.....................              1,404.49
    Paid — net amount.............              $4,829.89

Accounts debited:
    Sales Salary Expense..........              $5,370.94
    Office Salary Expense.........                 863.44
        Total (as above)..........              $6,234.38
```

The payroll register may be used as a posting medium in a manner
similar to the voucher register and check register. Alternatively, it may
be used as a supporting record in a manner similar to the insurance
register and the note registers. In the latter case the payroll data will
be posted to the ledger accounts through the medium of a compound

DEDUCTIONS					PAID		ACCOUNTS DEBITED	
FICA TAX	FEDERAL INCOME TAX	U.S. SAVINGS BONDS	MISCEL-LANEOUS	TOTAL	NET AMOUNT	CHECK NO.	SALES SALARY EXPENSE	OFFICE SALARY EXPENSE
4.20	19.90	6.50	CC 5.00	35.60	135.40	1136	171.00	
5.50	13.20	3.25	CC 4.00	25.95	84.05	1137		110.00
6.64	14.40		AR 16.50	37.54	95.26	1138		132.80
	71.30	20.00	CC 25.00	116.30	183.70	1139	300.00	
7.00	18.90	5.00		30.90	109.10	1170	140.00	
11.00	41.20	10.00	CC 15.00	77.20	142.80	1171		220.00
244.09	691.40	270.50	CC 182.00 AR 16.50	1,404.49	4,829.89		5,370.94	863.44

CC — Community Chest

Payroll register, right page

journal entry such as the following, which is based on the payroll register appearing above and at the top of page 306.

Nov.	21	Sales Salary Expense...................	5,370	94		
		Office Salary Expense.................	863	44		
		FICA Tax Payable..................			244	09
		Employees Income Tax Payable.......			691	40
		Bond Deductions Payable............			270	50
		Community Chest Deductions Payable..			182	00
		Accounts Receivable — John T. Davis..			16	50
		Salaries Payable....................			4,829	89
		Payroll for week ended November 21..			

307

The total expense incurred for the services of employees is recorded by the debits to the salary accounts. Amounts withheld from employees' earnings have no effect on the debits to the salary expense accounts. Of the six credits in the compound entry, five represent increases in specific liability accounts and one represents a decrease in the accounts receivable account.

Paycheck

One of the principal outputs of the system is a series of payroll checks at the conclusion of each payroll period. The data needed for this purpose are provided by the payroll register, each line of which applies to an individual employee. It is possible to prepare the checks solely by reference to the net amount column of the register. However, the customary practice is to provide each employee with a statement of the details of the computation. Employers are required to do so in some states. The statement may be entirely separate from the check or it may be in the form of a removable stub attached to the check.

Employee's earnings record

The necessity of having the cumulative amount of each employee's earnings readily available at the close of each payroll period was discussed earlier. Without such information or the related data on the cumulative amount of FICA tax previously withheld there would be no

NAME **Ashton, Harold B.**

ADDRESS **1986 Belmont Street**   PHONE **531-1149**

Lakewood, Ohio, 44112

MALE √   MARRIED √   PER DAY ____

FEMALE __   SINGLE ____   NUMBER OF EXEMPTIONS **4**   PAY RATE **$144.00**   WEEK √

                                                         MONTH ____

OCCUPATION **Salesman**   EQUIVALENT HOURLY RATE **$3.60**

LINE NO.	PERIOD ENDED	TOTAL HOURS	EARNINGS			
			REGULAR	OVERTIME	TOTAL	CUMULATIVE TOTAL
39	Sept. 26	42	144.00	10.80	154.80	6,470.60
THIRD QUARTER			1,872.00	387.50	2,259.50	
40	Oct. 3	44	144.00	21.60	165.60	6,636.20
46	Nov. 14	47	144.00	37.80	181.80	7,716.00
47	Nov. 21	45	144.00	27.00	171.00	7,887.00
48	Nov. 28	46	144.00	32.40	176.40	8,063.40
49	Dec. 5	44	144.00	21.60	165.60	8,229.00
50	Dec. 12	45	144.00	27.00	171.00	8,400.00
51	Dec. 19	42	144.00	10.80	154.80	8,554.80
52	Dec. 26	40	144.00		144.00	8,698.80
FOURTH QUARTER			1,872.00	354.20	2,226.20	
YEARLY TOTAL			7,488.00	1,210.80	8,698.80	

308

Employee's earnings record, left page

means of determining the appropriate amount to withhold from current earnings. It is essential therefore that detailed records be maintained for each employee.

A portion of an employee's earnings record is illustrated at the bottom of this page and page 308. The relationship between this record and the payroll register can be readily observed by tracing the amounts entered on Ashton's earnings record for November 21 back to its source, which is the first line of the payroll register illustrated at the top of pages 306 and 307.

EARNINGS RECORD

SOC. SEC. NO. 259-08-8114   EMPLOYEE NO. 15

DATE EMPLOYED June 15, 1966

DATE OF BIRTH April 22, 1940

DATE EMPLOYMENT TERMINATED

| | DEDUCTIONS | | | | | PAID | | LINE NO. |
FICA TAX	FEDERAL INCOME TAX	U.S. BONDS	OTHER		TOTAL	NET AMOUNT	CHECK NO.	
7.74	16.10	6.50			30.34	124.46	866	39
112.98	254.90	84.50	AR	22.50	474.88	1,784.62		
8.28	18.00	6.50	CC	5.00	37.78	127.82	901	40
9.09	21.80	6.50			37.39	144.41	1101	46
4.20	19.90	6.50	CC	5.00	35.60	135.40	1136	47
	19.90	6.50			26.40	150.00	1172	48
	18.00	6.50	CC	5.00	29.50	136.10	1220	49
	19.90	6.50			26.40	144.60	1254	50
	16.10	6.50			22.60	132.20	1285	51
	13.80	6.50			20.30	123.70	1323	52
66.47	243.30	84.50	CC	15.00	409.27	1,816.93		
390.00	1,026.80	338.00	AR CC	22.50 15.00	1,792.30	6,906.50		

Employee's earnings record, right page

In addition to spaces for recording data for each payroll period and the cumulative total of earnings, there are spaces for quarterly totals and the yearly total. These totals are used in various reports for tax, insurance, and other purposes. Copies of one such annual report, known as Form W-2, Wage and Tax Statement, must be submitted to each employee as well as to the Internal Revenue Service. The source of the amounts inserted in the statement illustrated below was the employee's earnings record on pages 308 and 309.

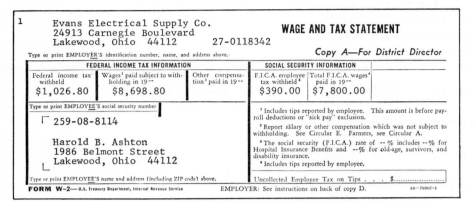

Wage and tax statement

Characteristics of input data

Attention thus far has been directed to the end product or *output* of a payroll system, namely the payroll register, the checks payable to individual employees, the earnings records for each employee, and reports for tax and other purposes. The basic data entering the payroll system are sometimes called the *input* of the system. Input data that remain relatively unchanged and do not need to be reintroduced into the system for each payroll period are characterized as *constants*; those that differ from period to period are *variables*.

Constants include such data for each employee as name and social security number, marital status, number of income tax exemptions claimed, rate of pay, functional category (office, sales, etc.), and department where employed. The FICA tax rate, maximum earnings subject to tax, and various tax tables are also constants which apply to all employees. The variable data for each employee include the number of hours or days worked during each payroll period, days of sick leave with pay, vacation credits, and cumulative amounts of earnings and taxes withheld. If salespersons are employed on a commission basis, the amount of their sales would also vary from period to period. The forms used in initially recording both the constant and the variable data vary widely according to the complexities of the payroll system and the processing methods employed. Perhaps the most basic and widely used records are "In and Out" cards whereby employees indicate, often by "punching" a time clock, their time of arrival and departure.

Payroll system diagram

The flow of data within segments of an accounting system may be shown by diagrams such as the one illustrated below. It depicts the interrelationships of the principal components of the payroll system described in this chapter. The requirement of constant updating of the employee's earnings record is indicated by the dotted line.

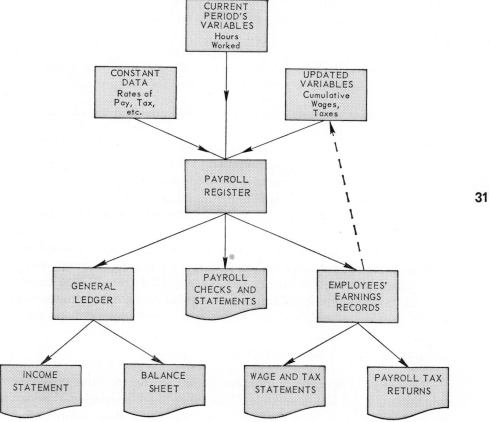

Flow diagram of a payroll system

Internal controls for payroll systems

The considerable volume of data required and the computations necessary to determine the amount of each paycheck is evident. As the number of employees and the mass of data increase, the number of individuals required to manage and process payroll data likewise increases.

Such characteristics, together with the relative magnitude of labor costs in most businesses, are indicative of the need for controls that will assure the reliability of the data and minimize the opportunity for misappropriation of funds.

The expenditure and cash disbursement controls discussed in the preceding chapter are of course applicable to payrolls. Thus the use of the voucher system and the requirement that all payments be supported by vouchers are desirable. The addition or deletion of names on the payroll should be supported by written authorizations from the personnel department. It is also essential that employees' attendance records be controlled in such a manner as to prevent errors and abuses. Employee identification cards or badges are widely used in this connection. They are also useful in assuring that all salaries and wages paid are paid to the proper individuals.

Employees may be paid (1) by checks drawn on the regular bank account, (2) by the use of currency, or (3) by special payroll checks drawn on a special bank account designated for this purpose.

Regular bank account. When employees are paid by checks drawn on the regular bank account and the voucher system is employed, it is necessary to prepare a voucher for the net amount to be paid the employees. The voucher is then recorded in the voucher register as a debit to Salaries Payable and a credit to Accounts Payable, and payment is recorded in the check register in the usual manner. If the voucher system is not used, the payment would be recorded merely by a debit to Salaries Payable and a credit to Cash.

It should be understood, of course, that the general journal entry derived from the payroll register, which is illustrated on pages 306 and 307, would precede the entries just described. It should also be noted that the entire amount paid may be recorded as a single item regardless of the number of employees. There is no need to record each check separately in the check register because all of the details are available in the payroll register for future reference.

Currency. Currency is sometimes used as the medium of payment when the payroll is paid each week or when the business location or the time of payment are such that banking or check-cashing facilities are not readily available to employees. In such cases a single check, payable to Payroll, is drawn for the entire amount to be paid. The check is then cashed at the bank and the money is inserted in individual payroll envelopes. The procedures for recording the payment correspond to those outlined in the preceding section.

When payment is made in currency, each employee should be required to sign a receipt as otherwise there is no evidence of payment.

Special bank account. Most employers with a large number of employees use a special bank account and payroll checks designed specifically for the purpose. After the data for the payroll period have been recorded and summarized in the payroll register, a single check for the total amount to be paid is drawn on the firm's regular bank account and deposited in a special account. The individual payroll checks are then drawn against the special payroll account, and the numbers of the payroll checks are inserted in the payroll register.

The use of special payroll checks makes it possible to relieve the treasurer or other executives of the task of signing a large number of regular checks each payday. The responsibility for signing payroll checks may be assigned to the paymaster, or mechanical means of signing the checks may be employed. Another advantage of this system is that the task of reconciling the regular bank statement is simplified. The paid payroll checks are returned by the bank separately from regular checks and are accompanied by a statement of the special bank account. Any balance shown on the bank's statement will correspond to the sum of the payroll checks outstanding because the amount of each deposit is exactly the same as the total amount of checks drawn. The recording procedures are the same as when checks on the regular bank account are used.

Employer's payroll taxes

Thus far the discussion of taxes has been confined to those levied against employees and withheld by employers. Most employers are subject to federal and state taxes based on the amount of remuneration earned by their employees. Such taxes constitute an operating expense of the business and may in the aggregate amount to a relatively substantial sum.

FICA tax. Employers are required to contribute to the Federal Insurance Contributions Act program for each employee. The tax rate and the maximum amount of remuneration of an employee entering into an employer's tax base correspond to those applicable to employees, which for purposes of illustration are assumed to be 5% and $7,800 respectively.

Federal unemployment compensation tax. Unemployment insurance provides temporary relief to those who become unemployed as a result of economic forces beyond their control and also tends to encourage full employment. Types of employment subject to the unemployment insurance program are similar to those covered by the FICA tax. The tax is levied on employers only, rather than on both employers and employees, and is applicable only to the first $3,000 of remuneration of each covered employee during a calendar year. The funds collected by the federal government are not paid out as benefits to the unemployed but are allocated among the states for use in administering state programs.

State unemployment compensation tax. The amounts paid as benefits to unemployed persons are obtained, for the most part, by taxes levied upon employers only. A very few states also require employee contributions. The most common tax base is the first $3,000 of earnings paid to each employee during the calendar year. The rates of tax vary, and in most states all employers who provide steady employment for their employees are awarded reduced rates. The employment experience and the status of each employer's tax account is reviewed annually, and the merit ratings and tax rates are revised accordingly. Generally, tax rates vary from .1% to 2.7% but in some states a zero tax rate can be achieved, and emergency tax rates in excess of 5% are possible.

Recording and paying payroll taxes

Each time the payroll register is prepared, the amounts of each employee's current earnings entering the tax base are listed in the respective taxable earnings columns. As explained earlier, the cumulative amounts of each employee's earnings just prior to the current period is available in the employee's earnings record.

314   According to the payroll register illustrated on pages 306 and 307, for the week ended November 21, the amount of remuneration subject to FICA tax was $4,881.87 and the amount subject to state and federal unemployment compensation taxes was $1,763.20. Multiplication by the respective tax rates assumed to be applicable yields the following amounts:

FICA tax...............................	$244.09
State unemployment compensation tax.....	31.74
Federal unemployment compensation tax...	7.05
Total payroll tax expense..............	$282.88

The general journal entry to record the payroll tax expense for the week and the liability for the taxes accrued is as follows:

Nov.	21	Payroll Tax Expense...................	282 88		
		FICA Tax Payable..................		244 09	
		State Unemployment Tax Payable.....		31 74	
		Federal Unemployment Tax Payable...		7 05	
		Payroll taxes for the week ended November 21.			

Payment of the liability for each of the taxes is recorded in the same manner as the payment of other liabilities. Employers are required to compute and report all payroll taxes on the calendar year basis regardless of the fiscal year they may employ for financial reporting and income tax purposes. Details of the federal income tax and FICA tax withheld from employees are combined with the employer's FICA tax on a single return filed each quarter, accompanied by the amount of tax due. Earlier payments, on a semimonthly or monthly basis, are required when the combined taxes exceed certain specified minimums. Unemployment compensation tax returns and payments are required by the states on a quarterly basis and by the federal government on an annual basis. The required forms and amounts owed are generally due by the end of the month following the period covered by the return.

Accrual of payroll taxes

All payroll taxes levied against employers become liabilities only at the time the related remuneration is *paid* to employees, rather than at the time the liability to the employees is incurred. Observance of this requirement may create a problem of expense allocation among periods of time. To illustrate the situation, assume that an enterprise using the calendar year as its fiscal year pays its employees on Friday for a weekly payroll period ending the preceding Wednesday, the two-day lag between Wednesday and Friday being required to process the payroll. Regardless of the day of the week on which the year ends, there will be some accrued wages; if it ends on a Thursday, the accrual will cover a full week plus an extra day. Logically, the unpaid wages and the related payroll taxes should both be charged to the period that benefited from the services performed by the employees. On the other hand, there is legally no liability for the payroll taxes until the wages are paid in January, when a new cycle of earnings subject to tax is begun. The distortion of net income that would result from failure to accrue the payroll taxes might well be inconsequential. The practice adopted should, of course, be consistently followed.

315

QUESTIONS

1. What is the distinction between an employee and an independent contractor? Why is it necessary to make this distinction?

2. (a) Identify the federal taxes that most employers are required to withhold from employees. (b) Give the titles of the accounts to which the amounts withheld are credited.

3. What is the purpose of the Employee's Withholding Exemption Certificate?

4. What is *net* or *take home* pay?

5. Why is salary expense measured by the gross amount of the payroll rather than the net amount actually paid to employees?

6. Name the major components common to most payroll systems.

7. Indicate the principal functions served by the employee's earnings record.

8. What is the source of the information needed to prepare the Wage and Tax Statements (Form W-2) that must be distributed to employees after the close of the calendar year?

9. The following questions are based on the assumption that the employer pays his employees in currency and that the pay envelopes are prepared by an employee rather than by the bank: (a) Why would it be advisable to obtain from the bank the exact amount of money needed for a payroll? (b) How could the exact number of each bill and coin denomination needed be determined efficiently in advance?

10. An employer who pays in currency draws a check for $26,413.64 for the payroll of November 21. After the money is inserted in the envelopes for the 125 employees, there remains $14 in currency. Assuming that the arithmetical accuracy of the payroll register has been determined and that the amounts of net pay stated on the pay envelopes agree with the payroll register, what should be done to locate the error?

11. The following questions are based on the assumption of a weekly payroll period and the use of a special bank account for payroll: (a) At what times should deposits be made in the account? (b) How is the amount of the deposit determined? (c) Is it necessary to have in the general ledger an account entitled "Cash in Bank — Special Payroll Account"? Explain. (d) The bank statement for the payroll bank account for the month ended October 31 indicates a bank balance of $527.16. Assuming that the bank has made no errors, what does this amount represent?

12. Identify the payroll taxes levied against employers.

13. The Georgian Company uses the voucher system and for each weekly pay period prepares a voucher for the net amount to be paid to employees. (a) Should this voucher be prepared before the individual payroll checks are distributed to the employees? Explain. (b) At the time the weekly payroll voucher is prepared, should a voucher also be prepared for the liability for taxes withheld from employees? Explain.

14. Prior to the last weekly payroll period of the calendar year, the cumulative earnings of employees A and B are $7,700 and $7,800 respectively. Their earnings for the last completed payroll period of the year, which will be paid in January, are $150 each. If the amount of earnings subject to FICA tax is $7,800 and the tax rate is 5%, (a) what will be the employer's FICA tax on the two salary amounts of $150 each; (b) what is the employer's total FICA tax expense for employees A and B for the calendar year just ended?

15. Explain how a payroll system that is properly designed and operated tends to give assurance (a) that wages paid are based upon hours actually worked, and (b) that payroll checks are not issued to fictitious employees.

16. Do payroll taxes levied against employers become liabilities at the time the liabilities to employees for wages are incurred or at the time the wages are paid?

EXERCISES

12-1. Develop an algorithm, in the form illustrated in this chapter, to compute the amount of each employee's weekly earnings subject to state unemployment compensation tax. Assume that the tax is 1.8% on the first $3,000 of each employee's earnings during the year and that the following symbols are to be used:

e = Cumulative earnings subject to state unemployment compensation tax prior to current week

E = Current week's earnings

S = Amount of current week's earnings subject to state unemployment compensation tax

12-2. Morris Crawford is employed at the rate of $4.70 per hour, with time and a half for all hours in excess of 40 worked during a week. Data to be considered in preparing the payroll register, Crawford's paycheck, and his earnings record for the current week ended September 15 are as follows: hours worked, 44; federal income tax withheld, $30.30; cumulative earnings for year prior to current week, $7,705.60; FICA tax withheld prior to current week, $385.28. Compute the following for the week ended September 15: (a) Crawford's earnings; (b) FICA tax to be withheld (5% on maximum of $7,800); (c) net amount to be paid.

12-3. In the following summary of columnar totals of a payroll register, some amounts have been intentionally omitted:

Earnings:
(1) At regular rate......	____	
(2) At overtime rate....	$ 724.90	
(3) Total earnings......	____	

(7) Medical insurance.	$ 284.34
(8) Total deductions...	1,965.52
(9) Net amount paid..	11,176.64

Deductions:
(4) FICA tax..........	394.26
(5) Income tax withheld.	1,160.92
(6) Union dues........	____

Accounts debited:
(10) Factory Wages....	____
(11) Sales Salaries......	4,110.69
(12) Office Salaries.....	1,145.06

(a) Determine the totals omitted in lines (1), (3), (6), and (10). (b) Present the general journal entry to record the payroll. (c) Present, in general journal form, the entry to record the voucher for the payroll. (d) Present, in general journal form, the entry to record the payment of the payroll. (e) From the data given in this exercise and your answer to part (a), would you conclude that this payroll was paid sometime during the first few weeks of the calendar year? Explain.

12-4. Total wage and salary expense of Dillow Company for the year was $125,000, of which $20,000 was not subject to FICA tax and $35,000 was not subject to state and federal unemployment taxes. Determine the employer's payroll tax expense for the year using the following rates: FICA, 5%; state unemployment, 2.5%; federal unemployment, .4%.

12-5. According to a summary of the payroll register of Madden and Co. for the four weekly payrolls paid in April, the amount of earnings subject to FICA tax is $14,612.93 and the amount subject to unemployment compensation taxes is $8,880.06. Present the general journal entry to record the accrual of payroll taxes for the month, assuming the following rates: FICA, 5%; state unemployment, 1.9%; federal unemployment, .4%.

12-6. The employees' earnings records for the calendar year for the Reliable Optical Service yield the information at the top of the next page.

Employee	Cumulative Earnings
Bressler, John	$ 5,877
Champion, Ernest	10,000
French, Paul	8,500
Jackson, Marie	7,026
Walston, Edith	4,903
Young, Ralph	598
	$36,904

The FICA tax during the year was levied at the rate of 5% on the first $7,800 of wages and salaries, and unemployment insurance rates were 1.8% for the state and .4% for the federal. (a) Calculate the total amount of payroll taxes borne by the employees. (b) Calculate the total amount of payroll taxes borne by the employer. (c) What percentage of the employer's total payroll costs was represented by payroll taxes?

PROBLEMS

The following additional problems for this chapter are located in Appendix C: 12-1B, 12-2B, 12-3B, 12-5B.

12-1A. The Atlas Cleaning Co. has nine employees. They are paid on an hourly basis, receiving time-and-one-half pay for all hours worked in excess of 40 a week. The record of time worked for the week ended December 6 of the current year, together with other relevant information, is summarized below:

Name	Total Hours	Hourly Rate	Income Tax Withheld	Bond Deductions	Cumulative Earnings, November 29
A	40	$2.50	$13.80	$2.50	$2,908
B	38	2.00	10.50	1.50	3,620
C	43	3.00	16.10	3.25	5,960
D	30	2.40	9.70	____	3,400
E	40	2.40	10.20	2.00	2,945
F	40	4.25	14.80	____	7,820
G	45	3.60	12.30	7.50	7,710
H	41	2.20	6.80	1.00	2,965
I	42	2.50	7.30	1.75	4,630

In addition to withholdings for income tax, FICA tax, and bond purchases, $15 is to be withheld from D for partial payment of his account receivable.

B and F are office employees; the others are salesmen. The following tax rates and limitations are assumed: FICA, 5% on maximum of $7,800; state unemployment (employer only), 2.2% on maximum of $3,000; federal unemployment, .4% on maximum of $3,000.

Instructions:
(1) Prepare the payroll register for the week, using a form like the one illustrated on pages 306 and 307.
(2) Journalize the entry to record the payroll for the week.
(3) The company uses a voucher system and pays by regular check. Present the necessary entries in *general journal form* to record the payroll voucher and the issuance of the checks.

(4) Complete the payroll register by inserting the check numbers, beginning with No. 732.

(5) Journalize the entry to record the employer's payroll taxes for the week.

12-2A. The following accounts, with the balances indicated, appear in the ledger of Pelham Service Co. on December 1 of the current year:

214	Salaries Payable....................	—
215.1	FICA Tax Payable.................	$ 376.40
215.2	Employees Income Tax Payable......	843.70
215.3	State Unemployment Tax Payable....	107.64
215.4	Federal Unemployment Tax Payable..	248.38
216.1	Bond Deductions Payable...........	327.50
216.2	Medical Insurance Payable.........	525.00
611	Sales Salary Expense...............	91,632.60
711	Officers Salary Expense.............	37,800.00
712	Office Salary Expense..............	8,690.30
719	Payroll Tax Expense...............	6,118.24

The following transactions relating to payroll, payroll deductions, and payroll taxes occurred during December:

Dec. 1. Prepared Voucher No. 626, payable to First National Bank, for $150 to purchase United States savings bonds for employees.

2. Issued Check No. 707 in payment of Voucher No. 626.

10. Prepared Voucher No. 647 for $1,220.10, payable to First National Bank, for the amount of the combined liability for FICA tax and employees income tax, which is due on December 15.

10. Issued Check No. 728 in payment of Voucher No. 647.

14. Prepared a general journal entry to record the biweekly payroll. A summary of the payroll register follows:

319

> Deductions: FICA tax, $88.30; income tax withheld, $491.10; bond deductions, $71.25; medical insurance deductions, $85.
>
> Salary distribution: sales, $3,470; officers, $1,450; office, $610. Net amount: $4,794.35.

14. Prepared Voucher No. 655, payable to Payroll Bank Account, for the net amount of the biweekly payroll.

14. Issued Check No. 736 in payment of Voucher No. 655.

16. Prepared Voucher No. 658, payable to Reliable Insurance Co., for $525, the semiannual premium on the group medical insurance policy.

17. Issued Check No. 739 in payment of Voucher No. 658.

28. Prepared a general journal entry to record the biweekly payroll. A summary of the payroll record follows:

> Deductions: FICA tax, $76.81; income tax withheld, $497.50; bond deductions, $76.50.
>
> Salary distribution: sales, $3,642; officers, $1,450; office, $610. Net amount: $5,051.19.

28. Prepared Voucher No. 690, payable to Payroll Bank Account, for the net amount of the biweekly payroll.

28. Issued Check No. 772 in payment of Voucher No. 690.

30. Prepared Voucher No. 691 payable to First National Bank, for $112.50 to purchase United States savings bonds for employees.

30. Issued Check No. 774 in payment of Voucher No. 691.

31. Prepared a general journal entry to record the employer's payroll taxes on earnings paid in December. Taxable earnings for the two payrolls, according to the payroll records, are as follows: subject to

FICA tax, $3,302.20, subject to unemployment compensation tax, $942.40. Assume the following tax rates: FICA, 5%; state unemployment, 2.2%; federal unemployment, .4%.

Instructions:

(1) Open the accounts listed and enter the account balances as of December 1.
(2) Record the transactions, using a voucher register, a check register, and a general journal. The only amount columns needed in the voucher register are Accounts Payable Cr. and Sundry Accounts Dr. (subdivided into Account, Post. Ref., and Amount). The only amount columns needed in the check register are Accounts Payable Dr. and Cash in Bank Cr. After each entry, post to the accounts opened in the ledger and extend the new balances to the appropriate balance column.
(3) Journalize the adjusting entry on December 31 to record salaries for the incomplete payroll period. Salaries accrued are as follows: sales salaries, $425; officers salaries, $210; office salaries, $50. Post to the accounts.
(4) Journalize the entry to close the salary expense and payroll tax expense accounts to Expense and Revenue Summary and post to the accounts.
(5) Journalize the entry on January 1 to reverse the adjustment of December 31 and post to the accounts.

12-3A. The following information relative to the payroll for the week ended December 30 was abstracted from the payroll register and other records of Bancroft Enterprises:

Salaries:		Deductions:	
Sales salaries.........	$43,600	Income tax withheld.....	$5,630
Warehouse salaries....	8,100	U. S. savings bonds.......	650
Office salaries........	6,800	Group insurance.........	200
	$58,500	FICA tax withheld is assumed to total the same amount as the employer's tax.	

Tax rates assumed:
FICA, 5%
State unemployment (employer only), 1.8%
Federal unemployment, .4%

Instructions:

(1) Assuming that the payroll for the last week of the year is to be paid on December 31, present the following entries:
  (a) December 30, to record the payroll. Of the total payroll for the last week of the year, $24,300 is subject to FICA tax and $3,420 is subject to unemployment compensation taxes.
  (b) December 30, to record the employer's payroll taxes on the payroll to be paid on December 31.
(2) Assuming that the payroll for the last week of the year is to be paid on January 2 of the following fiscal year, present the following entries:
  (a) December 31, to record the payroll.
  (b) January 2, to record the employer's payroll taxes on the payroll to be paid on January 2.

12-4A. Summary payroll data for Seldin Fixture Co. for the week ended July 25 of the current fiscal year are presented below. Employees on an hourly basis are paid time and a half for hours in excess of 40 a week.

Name	Total Hours	Hourly or Weekly Rate	Income Tax Withheld	Cumulative Earnings, July 18	Classifications
Andrews, R. B.	44	$ 2.80	$10.90	$2,910	Sales
Brown, D. C.	42	2.50	16.60	2,408	Delivery
Cook, Henry H.		160.00	23.20	4,640	Sales
Dunn, Ruth	40	3.10	22.80	3,560	Office
Graham, Joan		140.00	21.40	1,920	Sales
Johnson, James		300.00	41.20	8,100	Sales
Larson, Carl		275.00	43.50	7,975	Office
Taylor, J. R.		120.00	12.50	3,480	Sales
Wagner, M. C.	43	3.30	9.60	2,682	Delivery
Young, R. M.		255.00	42.00	7,650	Sales

Assume the following tax rates: FICA, 5% on maximum of $7,800; state unemployment (employer only), 2.4% on maximum of $3,000; federal unemployment, .4% on maximum of $3,000.

Instructions:

(1) Prepare a payroll register similar in form to the one on pages 306 and 307, deleting the deduction column not needed and adding another column for payroll distribution.

(2) Journalize the entry to record the payroll for the week.

(3) Assuming the use of a voucher system and payment by regular check, present the entries, in *general journal form*, to record the payroll voucher and the issuance of the checks to employees.

(4) Complete the payroll register by inserting the check numbers, beginning with No. 769.

(5) Journalize the entry to record the employer's payroll taxes for the four payroll periods in July. A summary of relevant information taken from the payroll register follows: taxable earnings subject to FICA tax, $6,245; taxable earnings subject to unemployment compensation tax, $2,010.

(6) Present the entries, in *general journal form*, to record the following transactions selected from those completed by Seldin Fixture Co.:

   Aug. 14. Prepared a voucher, payable to Citizens National Bank, for employees income taxes, $1,124.80, and FICA taxes, $549.56, on salaries paid in July.

   14. Issued a check to Citizens National Bank in payment of the above voucher.

12-5A. The Rhodes Company began business on January 2 of last year. Salaries were paid to employees on the 15th and last day of each month, and both FICA tax and federal income tax were withheld in the required amounts. All required payroll tax reports were filed and the correct amount of payroll taxes was remitted by the company for the calendar year. Before the Wage and Tax Statements (Form W-2) could be prepared for distribution to employees and filing with the Internal Revenue Service, the employees' earnings records were inadvertently destroyed.

Data on dates of employment, salary rates, and employees' income tax withheld, which are summarized below, were obtained from personnel records and payroll registers. None of the employees resigned or were discharged during the year and there were no changes in salary rates. The FICA tax was withheld at the rate of 5% on the first $7,800 of salary.

Employee	Date First Employed	Semimonthly Salary	Semimonthly Income Tax Withheld
A	Jan. 2	$250	$40.70
B	Jan. 2	330	39.40
C	Sept. 16	500	81.70
D	Mar. 1	300	30.10
E	Mar. 16	230	36.30
F	Jan. 2	420	73.10
G	Feb. 1	350	43.20

Instructions:

(1) Determine the amounts to be reported on each employee's Wage and Tax Statement (Form W-2) for the year, arranging the data in the following form:

Employee	Gross Earnings	Federal Income Tax Withheld	Earnings Subject to FICA Tax	FICA Tax Withheld

(2) Determine the total FICA tax withheld from employees during the year.
(3) Determine the following payroll taxes for the year paid by the employer; (a) FICA; (b) state unemployment compensation at 2.4% on first $3,000; (c) federal unemployment compensation at .4% on first $3,000; (d) total.
(4) In a manner similar to the illustrations in this chapter, develop four separate algorithms to describe the computations required to determine the four amounts in part (1), using the following symbols:

$$n = \text{Number of payroll periods}$$
$$g = \text{Semimonthly gross earnings}$$
$$f = \text{Semimonthly federal income tax withheld}$$
$$G = \text{Total gross earnings}$$
$$F = \text{Total federal income tax withheld}$$
$$T = \text{Total earnings subject to FICA tax}$$
$$S = \text{Total FICA tax withheld}$$

322

13

Systems design and automated data processing

Accounting system components

In a general sense an accounting system may be said to encompass the entire network of communications employed by a business organization to provide for its informational requirements. Indeed, there are frequent references to accounting systems as the "total informational system" of an enterprise. The variety of types of information collected, summarized, and reported through accounting systems has increased markedly in recent years and will probably continue to increase. Much of the expansion of the role of accounting in this area has been made possible by the development and ever-widening use of automated data processing equipment.

The basic components of an accounting system are the forms, records, procedures, and data processing methods employed to obtain the various reports needed by the enterprise. *Forms* are the media initially used in recording transactions, such as sales invoices, vouchers, and bank checks. *Records* include ledgers, journals, registers, and other media used for compilations of data. Various *procedures* designed to safeguard business assets and control expenditures were described in the two preceding chapters. Although the *data processing methods* described and illustrated in earlier chapters were to a great extent manual in nature, there have been numerous references to data processing equipment. The *reports* to which attention has heretofore been primarily directed have been the principal financial statements. Many other statements and analyses are based on accounting data, a number of which are described and illustrated in later chapters. Reports may be characterized as the end product of the accounting system. It is highly desirable, therefore, that the communications network employed by an enterprise be designed to provide useful information to all interested persons on a timely basis.

Accounting system installation and revision

Prerequisite to designing and installing the accounting system of an enterprise is a thorough knowledge of its operations. At the time a business is first organized, however, there are likely to be many undeterminable factors that will affect such facets of the system as the types and design of the forms needed, the number and titles of the accounts required, and the exact procedures to be employed. It is also quite common for a firm to expand its already successful operations into new areas not originally contemplated, to increase its volume of transactions, to employ additional personnel, and in other ways to "outgrow" its accounting system.

Many large business enterprises maintain an almost continuous review of their accounting system and may constantly be engaged in changing some portion of it. The task of revising an accounting system, either in its entirety or only in part, is composed of three phases: (1) *analysis*, (2) *design*, and (3) *implementation*.

Systems analysis. The objective of systems analysis is the determination of informational needs, the sources of such information, and the deficiencies in procedures and data processing methods presently employed. The analysis ordinarily begins with a review of organizational structure and job descriptions of the personnel affected, followed by a study of the forms, records, procedures, processing methods, and reports used by the enterprise. A detailed description of the system employed by the enterprise, including specific instructions to personnel and minute details of procedures, is of considerable value to the systems analyst in his fact-finding review. Such a compilation is usually referred to as the firm's *Systems Manual.*

In addition to assessing the shortcomings of the current system, the analyst should determine management's plans for changes in operations (volume, products, territories, etc.) in the foreseeable future.

Systems design. Accounting systems are altered as a result of the type of analysis described above. The design of the new system may involve only minor changes from the existing system, such as revision of a particular form and the related procedures and processing methods, or it may constitute a complete revision of the entire system. Systems designers must have a general knowledge of the merits of various types of data processing equipment, and the capacity to evaluate various alternatives.

Although successful systems design depends to a large extent upon the creativity, imagination, and general capabilities of the designer, observance of the following broad principles is essential:

1. The value of the information produced should be at least equal to the cost of obtaining it.
2. The internal control features should be adequate to safeguard assets and assure reliability of data.
3. There should be sufficient flexibility to accommodate increases in volume of data and changes in operating procedures and data processing methods without major disturbances to the existing system.

Systems implementation. The final phase of the creation or revision of an accounting system is to carry out, or implement, the proposals. New or revised forms, records, procedures, and equipment must be installed, and any that are no longer applicable must be withdrawn. All personnel responsible for operating the system must be carefully trained and closely supervised until satisfactory efficiency is achieved.

A major revision for a large organization, such as from manual processing to electronic processing, is customarily accomplished gradually over a protracted period rather than all at once. With such a procedure there is less likelihood that the flow of reliable data will be seriously impeded during the critical phase of implementation. Weaknesses and conflicting or unnecessary elements in the design may also become apparent during the implementation phase. They are more easily detected and remedied when changes in a system are adopted gradually, and the chaos that might otherwise occur is thereby avoided.

Flow charts

One of the principal devices used in systems analysis, design, and implementation is known as a *flow chart*. Such charts depict in graphic form the major data processing operations that are to be performed in accounting for a particular transaction or series of closely related transactions. They are helpful in visualizing the outline of a system and the relationships between the major processes to be performed. The symbols most commonly employed in preparing flow charts are illustrated at the top of the next page. The term "processing," as it is employed in charting, usually refers to procedural matters as well as processing methods.

Flow charts are usually arranged so as to be read from top to bottom, the direction of flow being indicated by arrows. The nature of the process or phase of processing is usually written inside the rectangle. Similarly, when a decision is required at some point in the processing, the factors to

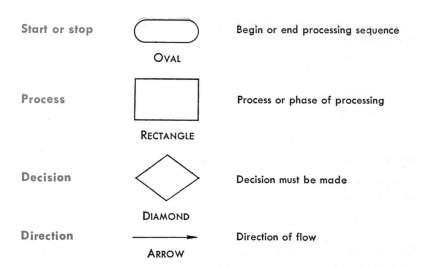

Start or stop	OVAL	Begin or end processing sequence
Process	RECTANGLE	Process or phase of processing
Decision	DIAMOND	Decision must be made
Direction	ARROW	Direction of flow

Flow chart symbols

be considered are described within the diamond symbol. To a large extent, decisions are connected with comparisons of two items of data. If they "match," the decision is to proceed with a particular process; if the desired relationship is lacking, the decision is to proceed in some other manner.

The processes involved in posting debits to accounts receivable in the customers ledger are shown in the flow chart on page 327. The employee begins the process by arranging carbon copies of the sales invoices of the preceding day in alphabetical order by customer. He then looks at the name on the first sales invoice and at the name on the first account in the customers ledger. If the names are the same, he proceeds to post the relevant information to the account. If they are not the same, he looks at the name on each succeeding account until he comes to the right one. After posting the appropriate information to the account, he looks at the name on the next invoice and repeats the process until all invoices have been posted. It was assumed that there was only one invoice per customer and that each time the credit department extended credit to a new customer an account form was prepared and inserted in its proper sequence in the subsidiary ledger. If this were not done, it would be necessary to expand the flow chart to provide for the preparation of ledger forms for new customers.

The amount of detail presented in a flow chart varies in accordance with its purpose and the intricacies of the system. The illustration on the next page provides information about the principal phases of a specific small section of the accounting system. It would be sufficient for purposes of analysis, but for the implementation phase of a revision program it would need to include information concerning the processing

326

equipment to be employed and more minute details about the alphabetization process, removal and restoration of ledger pages, disposition of the sales invoices, etc.

Data processing methods

With pencil, paper, and sufficient time, one or more persons can process all the data needed by an enterprise. If the business requirements for data are few, manually kept records may serve reasonably well. But as businesses become larger and more complex, manual processing becomes too costly and time-consuming. The trend, therefore, is toward replacing manual effort with machines that reduce the cost and speed up the processing of business data.

Some of the more common machines are the typewriter, cash register, adding machine, calculator, and bookkeeping machine. The efficiency of the typewriter is frequently increased merely by using carbon paper. Cash registers can record and accumulate totals for credit sales, cash sales, sales taxes, and receipts on account. The use of adding machines and calculators speeds up processing and minimizes the annoyance and

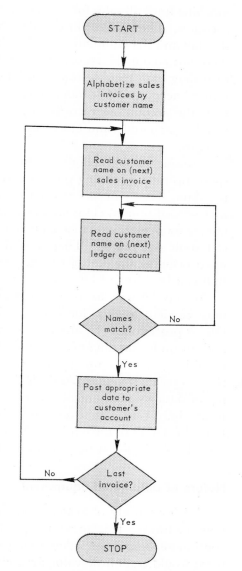

Flow chart — posting debits to customers' accounts

the expense caused by arithmetical errors. Conventional bookkeeping machines, which have movable carriages and keyboards similar to those of a typewriter and accumulating devices similar to adding machines, are commonly used in journalizing transactions and posting to ledger accounts. For example, both a customers ledger account and the sales journal can be placed in the machine together so that sales transactions can be recorded in the sales journal and debits can be posted to the accounts receivable ledger simultaneously. The sales journal remains in the machine until all sales for the day are recorded and posted to customers' accounts. The total credit to Sales and debit to Accounts Receivable for the day and the cumulative total for the month and the year to date are then automatically recorded. Similar techniques are employed for recording cash received on account and posting the credits to the customers' accounts. Additional forms may also be inserted in the machine with the accounting records so that monthly statements for customers can be prepared simultaneously with the recording of sales and cash receipts.

Although bookkeeping machines and other mechanical equipment speed up the accounting process and reduce the clerical costs of processing data, large enterprises need equipment that can process data even more expeditiously. This latent demand has stimulated the development of ever more elaborate mechanical devices and increasingly sophisticated electronic equipment. There has also been an accompanying trend toward bringing the cost of the services of such equipment down to levels that can be afforded by medium or smaller-size enterprises.

It may be well to note that manual processing of data may be the most efficient method for some particular businesses and for some particular procedures. In any event a solid background of basic principles and an understanding of the general framework of accounting are prerequisites to any meaningful consideration of automated data processing. *Automated data processing* (ADP) is the general term applied to the processing of data by mechanical or electronic equipment (sometimes referred to as "hardware") that operates with a minimum of manual intervention. When all of the equipment employed by a processing system operates electronically, it may be termed *electronic data processing* (EDP).

Nature of automated equipment

A wide variety of automation equipment is produced by numerous manufacturers. It is an area noted for rapid technological progress and continuous innovation. Any detailed cataloging of the available equipment would be of little value for our purposes here. There are, however, some characteristics common to all automated systems that should be understood at the outset.

It is customary to subdivide automated data processing systems generally into three major parts: (1) input, (2) processing, and (3) output. *Input* refers to the raw data introduced into the system. The forms used to introduce the data into the system in preparation for processing are called the *input media*. The *processing* portion of a system is concerned largely with the processing equipment that manipulates the data in the desired manner. Information emitted by the system is the *output*. The forms used for various summary figures and reports are the *output media*.

Automated data processing systems may employ various combinations of input media, processing equipment, and output media. Such variables as the nature and the volume of data to be processed, the significance of speed and operating costs, and the type of output desired will influence the type of installation. The relationship of input media, processing equipment, and output media is indicated by the diagram below.

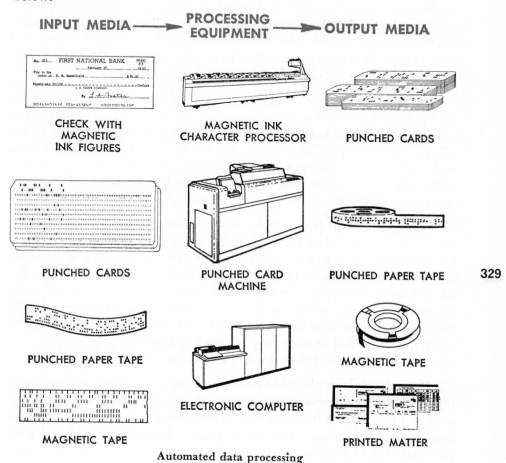

INPUT MEDIA ⟶ PROCESSING EQUIPMENT ⟶ OUTPUT MEDIA

CHECK WITH MAGNETIC INK FIGURES

MAGNETIC INK CHARACTER PROCESSOR

PUNCHED CARDS

PUNCHED CARDS

PUNCHED CARD MACHINE

PUNCHED PAPER TAPE

PUNCHED PAPER TAPE

ELECTRONIC COMPUTER

MAGNETIC TAPE

MAGNETIC TAPE

PRINTED MATTER

Automated data processing

Input media

Data to be processed automatically must be translated into special symbols and transcribed on a medium that can be read by the processing equipment. Input media may be prepared from sales tickets, purchases invoices, and other conventional business documents, or the input for a particular process may be the output media of some other phase of processing. The most common forms of input media are paper with symbols printed in magnetic ink, punched cards, punched paper tape, and magnetic tape.

329

Magnetic ink is usually employed on check forms, particularly those used by individuals and small businesses. The data in magnetic ink appear as numerical symbols printed along the lower margin of the check, as illustrated on page 271. The first set of symbols at the left identifies the Federal Reserve district and the drawee bank. The second set of symbols is the account number assigned to the drawer (depositor). The amount for which the check is drawn is inserted later at the right of the account number by the bank or clearing house first receiving it. Many banks employ a similar system of encoding on their deposit tickets and other memorandums, with additional symbols to designate service charges and other special data.

Punched cards may be prepared for internal use only or they may be used as basic business documents as well as input media for the processing equipment. Checks issued by business firms, particularly those used for payroll or payment of dividends, are frequently of the punched card type. The admonition not to "fold, spindle, or otherwise mutilate" is frequently encountered, not only on checks but on punched card invoices and statements of account designed to be returned to the issuer.

Punched paper tape is employed as an input medium for internal use only, particularly when data must be transmitted from one business location to another, as from a branch to the central office. For example, details of sales orders received at one location may be recorded in the form of holes in the tape, which may then be used to transmit the data, by use of teletype, to one or more other locations. The data at the receiving end may also be produced in the form of punched tape or in other media, which in turn may be used to issue shipping instructions, prepare invoices, and perform other functions.

Magnetic tape is employed in much the same manner as punched paper tape. Data in magnetic form can be compressed into a much smaller area and thus reduce handling and storage expense. The speed of transmission and processing is also much greater than can be achieved with punched tape or punched cards.

Processing equipment

Three of the most common types of processing equipment for automated systems are magnetic ink character processors, punched card machines, and electronic equipment.

Magnetic ink character processors. The most common application of magnetic ink character processors is by commercial banks. The use of magnetic ink on check forms to identify the drawee has increased steadily. Banks that have not yet installed the processing equipment required to

330

utilize the magnetized characters may nevertheless provide such check forms for their depositors. When magnetic ink character processors are fully employed, the recording of all entries to depositors' accounts, computation of service charges, and preparation of monthly statements is completely automated.

Punched card machines. The earliest efforts in the development of large scale mechanization of data processing were based on the use of punched cards. The standard size card contains eighty vertical columns with ten numbers (0 through 9) in each column which may be used for recording numerical data. There are two additional positions in each column which may be used in coding alphabetical information or for other special purposes. The holes are punched in accordance with a predetermined code designed for the particular system, and the various machines are adjusted or "wired" to manipulate the data in the desired manner. An installation of punched card equipment is composed of a series of machines, each of which performs a specific operation. Those most frequently employed, known as key punch, sorter, reproducer, collator, calculator, and tabulator, are briefly described in the paragraphs that follow.

The original data are recorded on the cards by a *key punch* which utilizes a keyboard similar to that of a typewriter. The simplest models punch holes only. Other models are capable of printing both alphabetical and numerical characters along the top of the card simultaneously with the punching operation, thus facilitating the manual reading of the card when the need arises.

One of the commonest processes applied to a group of punched cards is performed by a *sorter*. By successive "passes" through the sorter, cards may be placed in alphabetical or numerical sequence or classified into an almost unlimited number of subgroupings. Cards containing specified data can also be quickly selected without disturbing the sequence of the remaining group. The most efficient sorters can process cards at the rate of 2,000 per minute.

All or portions of data already punched on cards can be automatically transferred to a new set of cards by a *reproducer*. It is also used for converting handwritten marks, made with a special pencil, on a card to punched holes in the same card.

A *collator* is used to insert new cards at the proper point in an already existing group of appropriately arranged cards. Two separate groups of cards may also be merged together into a unified group.

Basic arithmetical operations of addition, subtraction, multiplication, and division are performed on numerical data punched in the cards by a *calculator*. The computation is almost instantaneous and the answer is converted to punched holes in the same cards.

The final stage in a sequence of punched card processes is usually performed by a *tabulator*, which converts to printed matter the data punched in the cards. All or selected portions of the data on a card may be printed in a single horizontal line, with as many as 120 characters to a line. The sequence of the data on the line can differ from the sequence on the punched cards, and it is also possible to obtain subtotals by groups of cards or to omit details and print only subtotals and totals. A typical tabulator prints about 150 lines per minute.

Punched card equipment, arranged in appropriate sequence, can be used to process most accounting data. Human intervention is required only in preparing the punched cards, instructing the equipment, and transferring the cards from one machine to another. "Instructing" the equipment consists of the setting of dials or the wiring of control panels to achieve the proper flow and summarization of data.

Electronic computers. The initial creation and continued development of electronic computers may be subdivided into three periods or "generations," beginning about 1955, 1960, and 1965 respectively. During the first generation the circuitry was composed of vacuum tubes, similar to those used in radio sets. The speed of operations attained during this period was approximately five hundred additions per minute. The second generation was characterized by the replacement of vacuum tubes by transistors. In addition to eliminating the problems caused by the heat generated by vacuum tubes, the space required for the equipment was reduced and the speed of operation was increased approximately tenfold. The circuitry of the present, or third, generation of computers is composed of silicon chips, with a further enhancement of speed and efficiency. Some models are capable of adding two ten-digit numbers in less than a millionth of a second.

Electronic computers are composed of three basic components: (1) storage unit, (2) arithmetic unit, and (3) control unit. The *storage* unit of a computer, also referred to as the *memory*, accepts and retains the data needed to perform an operation. The *arithmetic* unit performs the operations of addition, subtraction, multiplication, and division. In addition, it is capable of performing a logical operation. The usual problem involving logic requires the comparison of one number with another and the determination of whether the two numbers are the same or, if not, which number is the larger. Based upon the results of the comparison, the computer proceeds to the next appropriate processing step. The *control* unit directs the flow of data into, through, and out of the computer in accordance with a set of instructions called a *program*. By following the program, which can be stored within a computer, the electronic computer provides an uninterrupted flow of processing from the input data at the beginning to the output data at the end.

332

Electronic computers employ codes and symbols that are unlike the numerical and alphabetical characters used in ordinary communication. The "machine language" used is not uniform for the various "brands" of computers, causing difficulties in writing programs of broad applicability. The problem was alleviated by the creation of *common* or *symbolic* languages, which enable programmers to write instructions in English and algebraic terms. Two of the widely used common languages are known as FORTRAN (for *FOR*mula *TRAN*slation) and COBOL (for *CO*mmon *B*usiness *O*riented *L*anguage).

After a program is expressed in terms of a common language, it is converted by means of a *compiler* into the machine language of the particular computer employed. For example, an addition operation is designated by FORTRAN as "+" and by COBOL as "ADD." Reference to the compiler for a particular computer model indicates that either of these symbols is translated into the operating code "0400."

Arithmetical symbols and computations are ordinarily based upon Arabic numerals, which employ the decimal system and use ten different symbols, "0" through "9." Multiplication of any whole number by 10 is accomplished by moving the number one space to the left and adding a zero at the right; multiplication by 100 requires movement of two spaces and addition of two zeros, etc. The computations performed by many electronic computers are based upon a *binary* numbering system, which is composed of only two symbols, "0" and "1." The value of 1 depends upon its position in a particular number; if positioned at the extreme right, as in 0001, it has the value of 1; when moved one position to the left, as in 0010, its value is doubled, becoming the equivalent of 2. The process of doubling the value continues with successive positions, moving from right to left, as illustrated at the top of page 334.

It is apparent that a binary number of only four positions severely limits the magnitude of the decimal equivalent. Computers used for processing accounting and business data may employ binary numbers with as many as 60 positions. Despite the seeming disadvantages of the large number of positions required, the binary system is essential in electronics circuitry. The reason is that each circuit in a computer is capable of only two conditions; the current is either "on" or it is "off." Symbolically, the "off" condition can represent "0" in the binary code and the "on" condition can represent "1."

Although punched cards and punched tape can be used as input media for electronic computers, magnetic tape is more commonly used because of the greater speed with which a computer can sense the magnetic signals. Some magnetic tape is capable of an input speed approximately 100 times faster than is possible with punched cards. Various types of equipment can be connected with an electronic computer to produce output media in the form desired. High-speed printers are capable of printing in excess of 1,000 lines per minute.

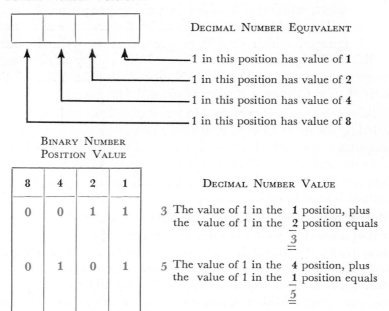

BINARY NUMBER POSITIONS

DECIMAL NUMBER EQUIVALENT

—1 in this position has value of **1**
—1 in this position has value of **2**
—1 in this position has value of **4**
—1 in this position has value of **8**

BINARY NUMBER
POSITION VALUE

8	4	2	1	DECIMAL NUMBER VALUE
0	0	1	1	3 The value of 1 in the **1** position, plus the value of 1 in the **2** position equals $\underline{\underline{3}}$
0	1	0	1	5 The value of 1 in the **4** position, plus the value of 1 in the **1** position equals $\underline{\underline{5}}$
1	0	1	0	10 The value of 1 in the **8** position, plus the value of 1 in the **2** position equals $\underline{\underline{10}}$

The following table compares the decimal numbers 0 through 9 with their counterparts in the binary system.

Decimal	0	1	2	3	4	5	6	7	8	9
Binary	0	1	10	11	100	101	110	111	1000	1001

Output media

The output of processing equipment is ordinarily in the form of punched cards, punched paper tape, magnetic tape, or printed matter, depending upon the use that is to be made of the data. Except for such printed matter as invoices, statements, checks, and other end products of the system, the output media may be used as input at a later date or in other parts of the system. For example, if monthly statements of account for customers are produced by a particular process employing punched cards, the process may simultaneously produce a punched card for the end-of-month balance of each account. At the end of the following month the cards would then be merged with the punched cards for current sales, returns, and cash receipts data, and the month-end processing routine repeated.

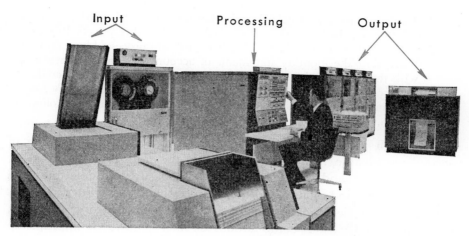

Input   Processing   Output

International Business Machines Corporation

An electronic computer system

Applications of automated equipment

Although in recent years the processing of data has become highly automated for many enterprises, the basic principles and objectives of accounting have not changed. The form of financial statements is not affected, documents to evidence transactions are still essential, and sound principles of internal control and systems design are still relevant. Automation may affect the form of accounting records and the sequence of processing. Less time is required to process accounting data, and additional analyses helpful to management can be produced.

The potential uses of automated equipment in accounting are innumerable. Much of the equipment is quite costly, however, regardless of whether it is purchased or leased. Its use is therefore practical only where there is a considerable mass of data to be processed on a continuous basis. A growing practice is for several firms to acquire and share the equipment on a cooperative basis. In most cities equipment and personnel to operate it are available in data processing service centers which operate on a fee basis. Illustrative uses of automated equipment in accounting systems are briefly described in the paragraphs that follow.

Accounts receivable. A common method of processing accounts receivable is described in the following outline:

1. A master card is prepared for each customer's account, holes being punched for the name, address, and any other desired information.
2. A combination typewriter and card punch is used to prepare simultaneously conventional sales invoices and punched cards, the sales invoices being sent to customers and the cards becoming the input media for additional processing.
3. The punched cards for sales are sorted alphabetically by customer and are merged with the master accounts receivable cards.

335

4. As remittances are received and allowances granted, cards are appropriately punched, sorted, and merged with the other punched cards.
5. At the end of the month, the punched cards are processed by a tabulator that prints the monthly statements of account and punches new cards with the ending balances. The cards representing debits and credits to the accounts during the month are removed and the new balance cards are merged with the master cards, ready for transactions of the following month.

Although the foregoing outline was restricted to the processing of accounts receivable, it should be noted that the cards punched for sales, sales allowances, and cash receipts will also be used to determine the monthly transaction totals. Additional processing of the cards representing sales could yield analyses of sales by product, territory, salesman, magnitude, and various combinations of such factors. If appropriate data regarding the product were recorded on the same cards, they could also be used as a part of a perpetual inventory system.

Perpetual inventories. The use of punched card or electronic equipment in maintaining perpetual inventory records is quite common. The principal processes involved in a punched card system are as follows:

1. A master card is prepared for each commodity, holes being punched to identify the commodity, its color, unit size or weight, or other descriptive data, storage location, and any other information desired.
2. The inventory of each commodity is punched on a separate card as of the date the system is installed, each card being keyed to its related master card. Quantities only may be recorded, or unit cost and total cost may also be punched.
3. Each time the inventory of a commodity increases by purchase or sales return, or decreases by sale or other cause, the data are recorded by punched holes in a card, also keyed to the master card.
4. The cards representing the beginning inventory and the individual transactions are merged with the master cards at appropriate intervals.
5. The inventory of any particular commodity can be determined at any time by passing the master card and its related cards through a tabulator. The tabulator prints only the final inventory quantity and cost, or if desired the details of each transaction can be printed, in sequential order.
6. At the close of each month the entire group of inventory records is tabulated and a complete inventory listing printed. The cards representing the beginning inventory and the increases and decreases for the month are removed and new inventory cards are automatically punched and merged with their master cards.

When an electronic computer is used to process perpetual inventories, the processing phases may vary somewhat from the foregoing outline. The updating of the inventory is more automatic and inventory listings can be obtained more speedily. Either system can be extended to improve control over inventory quantities and thereby minimize investment, reduce losses from obsolescence, and improve ability to fill sales orders without delay. It is first necessary to determine the minimum inventory quantity of each commodity to be maintained and the most economical number to buy or produce at one time. After the data on these factors are merged with the data on actual inventory flow, the equipment is programmed to make the necessary comparisons and initiate purchasing or production activity by preparing purchase orders or other memorandums.

Payrolls. Automation is often applied to payroll systems because of the mass of data to be manipulated, the frequently recurring and routine natures of the processing, and the importance of speed and accuracy. Employees' hourly rates of pay ordinarily remain unchanged for a number of payroll periods, and the withholding structures for FICA tax and income tax usually remain constant for an entire year. Such data can be punched in cards or stored in the memory unit of a computer.

The preceding chapter described and illustrated the computation of gross earnings, computation of tax and other deductions, determination of net pay, preparation of the payroll register, preparation of the payroll check, and updating of each employee's earnings record. All of these processes can be performed mechanically or electronically. In addition, the data needed for determination of the employer's payroll taxes and for reports to governmental agencies and employees can be accumulated automatically by the same equipment.

Integrated data processing

The systematization of processing operations in such a manner as to eliminate retranscriptions of data and to minimize the rehandling and resorting of data from one stage to the next is termed *integrated data processing* (IDP). The term may be applied to a particular segment of the operations of an enterprise or to its entire operations. A totally integrated system, in the strictest sense, would require only the introduction of transaction data and a complete program into the accounting system. All of the processing would then be automatic, and the required business documents, such as checks, sales invoices, and tax reports, and all financial statements and schedules, would be printed without human intervention. It is readily apparent that a high degree of integration requires an exacting coordination of the manual, mechanical, and electronic processing devices employed.

Highly sophisticated data processing systems usually employ an electronic computer with (1) a memory unit of large capacity and (2) the capability of manipulating heterogeneous financial data in random order. Large memory capacity within the computer permits continuous accumulation of new data, comparisons with related data, issuance of the necessary instructions and documents, and restorage for further use.

A hypothetical merchandising enterprise will be assumed in describing the principal features of an integrated data processing system.

When a purchase order is received from a customer, all of the pertinent data, such as name and address, quantity and description of the items ordered, and delivery instructions, are recorded on magnetic tape. This is the input for this part of the system. Acting upon instructions stored in the memory unit, the output unit prints the customer's name and address on a sales invoice and a shipping order. The quantity and description data for each commodity ordered are automatically transmitted to an electronic computer where comparisons are made with the perpetual inventory record, which is also contained in the memory unit. If the supply of a commodity on hand is sufficient to fill the order, its description, quantity, and sales price are printed on the invoice, and the inventory data in the memory unit are adjusted accordingly. The new inventory balance of the item is then compared with the reorder quantity recorded in the memory unit. If a reorder is indicated, a purchase order for disposition by the purchasing department is printed automatically. The sales data and cost of goods sold data for each transaction are also accumulated and stored within the system.

If the quantity of a commodity on hand is not sufficient to fill the customer's order, the lesser quantity and its sales price are recorded on the invoice, the inventory record is modified, and the sales data and the cost of goods sold data are added to the existing balances. In addition, the reason for shipping the smaller quantity is printed on the invoice and a "back order" is printed for the remaining quantity. Later, when the back-ordered goods become available, a sales invoice and a shipping order for the quantity necessary to complete the original order are automatically prepared.

The foregoing processes are repeated for each commodity ordered by the purchaser. After the data for the last item have been processed, the total amount of the sale is printed on the invoice. This amount is then tentatively added to the balance of the appropriate customer's account in the memory unit and the sum compared with the credit limit previously stored in the memory unit. If the credit limit is not exceeded, the addition to the account balance is confirmed and the sales invoice and shipping order are released. All of the required computations and comparisons are accomplished so rapidly that the printing of the invoice and shipping order appear to be uninterrupted.

When a customer's account balance plus the amount of a sale exceeds the credit limit, the invoice and shipping order are routed to the credit department for consideration. If the sale is approved, the documents are released for disposition in the usual manner. If the credit department does not approve the sale, the sales data are reintroduced into the system with instructions to reverse the earlier processes.

The only visible output from the processing of a routine sales transaction are the sales invoice and the shipping order. The updated account receivable and the perpetual inventory records remain in the memory unit. The general ledger accounts affected by the transaction, namely Accounts Receivable, Sales, Merchandise Inventory, and Cost of Merchandise Sold, are also brought up-to-date in the memory unit.

When cash is received on account, the details are introduced into the system by means of magnetic tape. The balances of the individual customers' accounts are automatically revised and the cumulative balances of the general ledger accounts are brought up-to-date.

Details of purchases transactions, cash disbursements, and related data are processed automatically in a similar manner. The individual accounts with creditors are debited and credited, the inventory records are debited for merchandise purchased, and the amounts of assets acquired and expenses incurred are automatically added to the preceding balances of the appropriate general ledger accounts. When a creditor's account is due for payment, the account balances affected by the payment, including purchases discount, are revised and the output unit automatically prints a disbursement check ready for signature. Payrolls are also processed automatically, the output media being payroll checks.

If information is needed at any time about a specific item, such as the balance owed a particular creditor or the inventory of a particular commodity, it can be extracted from the system almost instantly. At the end of the month the general ledger accounts, the trial balance, and the financial statements are printed automatically. Whenever desired, the equipment can produce a printed list of the balances in any of the subsidiary ledgers, the individual withholding tax forms for employees, and analyses of sales and other data in the memory unit.

Computers can also be used to provide data for use by management in controlling current operations and planning for the future. Actual operating results can be compared with predetermined plans and the variances automatically determined. Historical accounting data in the memory unit can also be compared with input data in the memory unit representing various hypothetical future conditions. Output media in the form of reports indicating the expected effect of alternative courses of actions are thus provided for management's use in making decisions.

The most advanced integrated data processing systems for manufacturing enterprises combine engineering and scientific tasks with the processing of financial data. For example, by introducing into the system all data on orders received, job specifications, quantities to be produced, materials required, production priorities, and other relevant factors, the system can be programmed to prepare the production orders for each department. If the results of production are also introduced, the system can monitor the manufacturing operations and prepare up-to-the-minute reports on the progress of production and deviations from the scheduled operations.

Automation has affected requirements for clerical personnel, and its continued development will undoubtedly further reduce the need for manual processing. On the other hand, the demand for accountants needed to assist in the analysis, design, and implementation of automated systems continues to exceed the available supply, and the shortage is expected to continue into the foreseeable future.

QUESTIONS

1. Describe, in general terms, an accounting system.
2. What is the objective of systems analysis?
3. Why should the essential features of internal control be designed into all accounting systems?
4. Discuss how the cash register can be used to strengthen internal control over receipts from cash sales.
5. What is meant by the term *flow chart*?
6. What does the "diamond" flow chart symbol signify?
7. Briefly describe (a) input, (b) processing, and (c) output, as they relate to automated data processing systems.
8. Discuss the primary function performed by each of the following punched card machines: (a) reproducer, (b) collator, (c) tabulator.
9. Name and describe the function of each of the three basic components of electronic computers.
10. Describe the logical operations performed by the arithmetic unit of an electronic computer.
11. What is a computer *program*?
12. Describe the basic function of the *compiler*.
13. Contrast the number of digits in the binary numbering system with the number employed by the decimal system.
14. What is the decimal equivalent of the binary number 1000?
15. What is the binary equivalent of the decimal number 7, assuming that there are four positions?
16. Why is the binary numbering system used to represent numbers being processed by electronic computers?
17. Why is magnetic tape often preferred over punched cards and punched paper tape as input media for electronic computers?
18. Why is the processing of payrolls especially well suited to the use of automated data processing equipment?
19. What do the following initials represent: (a) ADP, (b) EDP, (c) IDP?

EXERCISES

13-1. The Appliance Mart is a wholesaler of major household appliances. Design a form that can be used as a perpetual inventory record to indicate the quantity, unit costs, and total cost of each commodity on hand. The form is also to be used by management as an aid in reordering merchandise, as a check on the storage personnel, and as an aid in taking a physical inventory. Assume that each commodity received is listed on a receiving report prepared by the receiving department and that each commodity sold is listed on a sales invoice.

13-2. A large retail store initiates a procedure requiring that all merchandise purchase orders be issued by its newly created purchasing department. A purchase order is to be prepared upon the receipt of a purchase requisition from the various merchandising departments. All incoming invoices and shipments are to be verified by the receiving department and the merchandise is to be stored or routed to the appropriate sales department. Purchase orders are to be issued in quintuplicate. List the original and each of the four copies and indicate for each its distribution and any special instructions or purpose.

13-3. In reviewing the current income statement of J. W. James and Company, a medium-size merchandising enterprise, the owner noted that the amount of purchases discount was disproportionately small in comparison with earlier periods. Further investigation revealed that in spite of a sufficient bank balance a significant amount of available cash discounts had been lost because of failure to make timely payments. In addition, it was discovered that several purchases invoices had been paid twice.

Outline procedures for the payment of vendors' invoices that will minimize the possibility of losing available cash discounts and of paying an invoice a second time.

13-4. Hamilton Company maintains on magnetic tape a master file of inventory items. The file contains in commodity number sequence the commodity number and unit cost price for each item of merchandise. Another magnetic tape contains the commodity number and number of units sold (sales record) for the current period, also in commodity number sequence.

Construct a flow chart of the following computer operations: read a commodity number from the sales record; read commodity numbers from the master file until the commodity number on the master file is the same as the number from the sales record; multiply the unit cost price obtained from the master file by the number of units sold as indicated by the sales record; print the commodity number, units sold, unit cost price, and total cost price of the sale; and continue the process until the last entry on the sales record has been read and the details of the cost of the sale have been printed.

13-5. (a) Determine the binary equivalents of each of the following decimal numbers, employing five positions: (1) 9, (2) 12, (3) 20.

(b) Determine the decimal equivalents of each of the following binary numbers: (1) 00100, (2) 01010, (3) 10110.

13-6. One of the features of Campbell Wholesale Company's integrated data processing system is automatic approval or rejection of customers' offers to purchase commodities on credit terms.

Accounts receivable and the credit limit established for each customer are stored in the memory unit of an electronic computer. As orders are received from customers, the computer operator actuates the stored program instructing the computer to add the total of the prospective sale to the customer's account balance, compare the resulting total with the credit limit, and print a rejection or approval notice.

Prepare a flow chart of the following computer operations: secure account balance for customer; add amount of sale to account balance; secure credit limit for customer; determine if credit limit is exceeded; and print notice of rejection or approval of credit.

PROBLEMS

The following additional problems for this chapter are located in Appendix C: 13-1B, 13-2B, 13-4B.

13-1A. John Davis Associates is a newly organized enterprise. The list of asset, liability, and capital accounts to be opened in the general ledger is presented below, arranged in alphabetical order. The accounts are to be arranged in balance sheet order and account numbers assigned. Each account number is to be composed of three digits; the first digit is to indicate the major classification ("1" for assets, etc.), the second digit is to indicate the subclassification ("11" for current assets, etc.) and the third digit is to identify the specific account ("111" for Cash in Bank, etc.).

Accounts Payable
Accounts Receivable
Accumulated Depr. — Building
Accumulated Depr. — Office Equip.
Accumulated Depr. — Store Equip.
Allowance for Doubtful Accounts
Building
Cash in Bank
John Davis, Capital
John Davis, Drawing
Interest Payable
Land

Merchandise Inventory
Mortgage Note Payable (long-term)
Office Equipment
Office Supplies
Petty Cash
Prepaid Insurance
Prepaid Taxes
Salaries and Commissions Payable
Store Equipment
Store Supplies
Taxes Payable

Instructions:

Construct a chart of accounts for the accounts listed.

13-2A. Miami Valley Power and Light Co. employs an automated system for billing customers for electric current. There are two rate structures, commercial and residential. A master file of customers is maintained on punched cards, with name, address, and appropriate rate structure indicated. At the end of each billing period the meter readers are given prepunched and printed cards containing the name, address, and last meter reading for each customer on their route. The current meter readings are recorded on the cards by the meter readers with a special pencil. The reproducer converts the pencil markings to holes in the card and the cards are then matched by the collator against the master file to assure that a current billing card has been prepared for each customer. The current billing cards are then processed by an electronic computer that computes the amount of the billing and prints the sales journal. The journal is then subjected to clerical review before processing is continued.

Instructions:

Construct a flow chart of the following computer operations: read a current billing card; compute the amount of billing, including provision to employ the appropriate rate structure; print an entry in the sales journal; and continue the processing until the last current billing card has been processed.

13-3A. Sport Shop is a men's retail clothing store in Middletown, Colorado. The enterprise employs a full-time sales staff of four people, each on a combined salary and commission basis. Sales are made for cash and on account, and are subject to a sales tax.

Instructions:

(1) Identify the various types of data, such as name and address of company, for which provision should be made in the printed sales tickets for the enterprise, and the purpose served by each item. Use the following headings in presenting your recommendations.

<u>Type of Data</u>   <u>Purpose of Data</u>

(2) Design a sales ticket for Sport Shop.

If the working papers correlating with the textbook are not used, omit Problem 13-4A.

13-4A. Martin Supply Company employs punched card machines in processing much of its accounting data. This problem requires the manual processing of a portion of the data normally processed by the machines.

Instructions:

(1) Remove from the working papers and separate the 15 punched cards. Note that the cards numbered 1–3 represent customers' account balances at June 30, the cards numbered 4–6 represent receipts on account from customers at various dates during July, and the cards numbered 7–15 represent sales made to customers on account at various dates in July. Record on the top line of the cards numbered 13–15 the following additional sales data:

	Customer No.	Date	Salesman No.	Invoice No.	Commodity No.	Quantity Sold	Unit Sales Price	Amount
13.	117	7/20	3	17189	212	10	5.00	50.00
14.	117	7/25	3	17190	202	200	.75	150.00
15.	110	7/30	1	17191	208	300	1.25	375.00

(2) Sort the cards into numerical order according to customer number.
(3) Sort the cards for each customer according to date, placing the earliest date on top.
(4) Using the data recorded on the cards, prepare the three customers' statements of account.
(5) Resort cards numbered 7–15 into numerical order according to salesman number. Prepare for the sales manager a report of sales by salesmen during July.
(6) Resort cards numbered 7–15 into numerical order by commodity number. Prepare for the store manager, who also acts as buyer, a report of the quantity of each commodity sold during July.

13-5A. The Nolan Company maintains its customers ledger on magnetic tape. Each day the data for sales, sales returns and allowances, and cash receipts are recorded on the tape. At the end of each month the tape is used in preparing a statement of account for each customer, detailing the beginning balance, debits, credits, and ending balance. In addition to the statement of account, a delinquency letter is prepared for all customers whose ending balance includes sales charges which are more than two months old.

Instructions:

Construct a flow chart of the following computer operations performed at the end of the month: read a customer's beginning balance, debits and credits for the month, and ending balance; determine if the account is delinquent; print a delinquency letter, if appropriate; print a statement of account; and continue the procedure until the last customer's statement of account and delinquency letter have been printed.

13-6A. One of the programming languages designed for use with electronic computers of medium size is called BASIC (**B**eginner's **A**ll-purpose **S**ymbolic **I**nstruction **C**ode). Computer programs expressed in BASIC are composed of a series of instructions, called *statements*, presented in the order in which each operation is to be performed.

To illustrate the format of such a program, assume that the computer is to be instructed to add a series of pairs of numbers, designated as A and B, and print the total of each pair. Assume further that the pairs of numbers are as follows: 7, 9; 15, 105; 1205.2, 3714.4. The six statements required to complete the requisite program are presented below.

Statement 1	READ	A,	B		Statement 4	PRINT	X
Statement 2	DATA	7,	9,	15, 105,	Statement 5	GO	TO 1
		1205.2,	3714.4		Statement 6	END	
Statement 3	LET	X = A + B					

Statement 1 instructs the computer to READ the values of A and B, which are presented in statement 2 as DATA. Statement 3, the LET instruction, indicates the manner in which the data are to be manipulated. Statement 4 instructs the computer to PRINT the results of the computation. After the sum (16) of the first two numbers (7 + 9) is printed, statement 5 instructs the computer to GO TO statement 1 and repeat the process for the next pair of numbers. After the sums 120 (15 + 105) and 4919.6 (1205.2 + 3714.4) are printed, the END of the program is indicated by statement 6.

Instructions:

Construct a program of six statements, in BASIC, to compute and print the net pay for each of the following employees:

Employee No.	Total Hours Worked	Hourly Rate	Income Tax Withheld	FICA Tax Withheld
101	40	$7.50	$47.10	$15.00
102	40	5.55	32.50	11.10
105	20	4.50	13.10	4.50
107	17	5.75	10.20	4.89
108	30	6.75	31.00	10.13

The BASIC symbol used to indicate subtraction is the minus sign (−); multiplication is indicated by an asterisk (*). Although in general the letter designation of the variables in a program is completely arbitrary, the following letters should be used:

A Total hours worked   D FICA tax withheld
B Hourly rate   X Net amount to be paid
C Income tax withheld

14

Concepts and principles

Need for concepts and principles

The historical development of accounting practice has been closely related to the economic development of the country. In the earlier stages of the American economy a business enterprise was very often managed by its owner and the accounting records and reports were used primarily by the owner-manager in conducting the business. Bankers and other lenders often relied more heavily on their personal relationship with the owner than on financial statements as the basis for making loans for business purposes. If a substantial amount was owed to a bank or supplier, the creditor frequently participated in management decisions.

As business organizations grew in size and complexity, a greater demarcation developed between "management" and "outsiders." From the latter group, which includes owners (stockholders), creditors, government, labor unions, customers, and the general public, came the demand for accurate financial information for use in judging the performance of management. In addition, as the size and complexity of the business unit increased, the accounting problems involved in the issuance of financial statements became more and more complex. With these developments came an awareness of the need for a framework of concepts and generally accepted accounting principles.

Development of concepts and principles

Users of financial statements need a basic understanding of the principles underlying the preparation of such statements if they are to interpret them properly. It is equally evident that accountants must have a thorough knowledge of these principles and that they must be in substantial agreement as to the meaning and the importance of the guides and the standards that, collectively, comprise them.

Responsibility for the development of accounting principles has rested primarily on practicing accountants and accounting teachers, working both independently and as groups under the sponsorship of such organizations as the American Accounting Association, the American Institute of Certified Public Accountants, and the Financial Executives Institute. These principles are also influenced by business practices and customs, ideas and beliefs of the users of the financial statements, governmental agencies such as the Securities and Exchange Commission, stock exchanges, and other business groups.

Various terms are employed by accountants in referring to a particular accounting standard. In addition to *principle* and *concept*, the terms *axiom, assumption, postulate, convention, tenet,* and *doctrine* are frequently encountered in accounting literature. An examination of the similarities and the differences in meaning of these terms is not essential to the understanding of the particular principles that will be discussed in this chapter; they are mentioned only for the sake of completeness.

It should be borne in mind that the word "principle" as used in this context does not have the same authoritativeness as universal principles or natural laws employed in the study of astronomy, physics, or the other physical sciences. Accounting principles have been developed by man to enhance the usefulness of accounting data in an ever-changing society. They represent the best possible guides, based on reason, observation, and experimentation, to the achievement of the desired results. The selection of the best single method, or of several equally good methods, among a number of alternatives, has come about gradually, and in some subject matter areas a clear consensus is still lacking. These principles are continually reexamined and revised to keep pace with the increasing complexity of business operations. General acceptance among the members of the accounting profession is the criterion for determining an accounting principle.

Many accounting principles have been introduced and integrated with discussions in earlier chapters. The remainder of this chapter is devoted to the underlying assumptions, concepts, and principles of the greatest importance and the widest applicability. Attention will also be directed to applications of principles to specific situations in order to facilitate better understanding of accounting practices.

Business entity

The *business entity* concept assumes that a business enterprise is separate and distinct from the persons who supply the assets it uses. This is true regardless of the legal form of the business organization. The accounting equation, Assets = Equities, or Assets = Liabilities + Capital, is an expression of the entity concept; it is as if the business itself owns the assets and in turn owes the various claimants. Thus, the accounting process is primarily concerned with the enterprise as a productive economic unit and is only secondarily concerned with the investor as a claimant to the assets.

The business entity concept employed in accounting for a sole proprietorship is distinct from the legal concept of a sole proprietorship. The nonbusiness assets, liabilities, revenues, and expenses of a sole proprietor are excluded from the business accounts. If a sole proprietor owns several different business enterprises, each may be treated as a separate entity for accounting purposes. Legally, however, a sole proprietor is personally liable for his business debts and may be required to use nonbusiness assets to satisfy the business creditors. Conversely, business assets are not immune from claims of the sole proprietor's personal creditors.

Differences between the business entity concept and the legal nature of other forms of business organization will be considered in later chapters. For accounting purposes, however, revenues and expenses of any enterprise are viewed as affecting the business assets and liabilities, not the owners' assets and liabilities.

347

Going concern

Only in rare instances is a business organized with the expectation of remaining in existence for only a specified period of time. In most cases there is no means of foretelling the length of life of an enterprise, and so an assumption must be made. The nature of the assumption will affect the manner of recording some of the business transactions, which in turn will affect the data reported in the financial statements.

It is customary to assume that a business entity has a reasonable expectation of continuing in business at a profit for an indefinite period of time. This assumption that an enterprise is a *going concern* provides much of the justification for recording plant assets at acquisition cost and depreciating them in a systematic manner without reference to their current realizable values. It is pointless to report plant assets on the balance sheet at their estimated realizable values if there is no immediate expectation of selling them. This is true regardless of whether the current market value of the plant assets is less than their book value or greater than their book value. If the firm continues to use the assets, the fluctuation in market value causes no gain or loss, nor does it enhance or diminish the usefulness of the assets. Thus, if the going-concern assumption is a valid concept, the investment in plant assets will serve the purpose for which it was made. In this sense the investment will be recovered even though the assets may be individually marketable only at a loss.

The going-concern assumption similarly supports the treatment of prepaid expenses as assets, even though they may be virtually unsalable. To illustrate, assume that on the last day of its fiscal year a wholesale firm receives from a printer a $20,000 order of sales catalogs. In the absence of the assumption that the firm is to continue in business, the catalogs would be merely scrap paper and the value reported for them on the balance sheet would be negligible.

A less direct effect of the going-concern concept is that it helps to focus attention on the determination of net income rather than on the valuation of assets. The earning power of an enterprise is more significant than the market value of its individual assets in judging the overall worth of a business. Because of this emphasis on earnings, the accountant directs his attention to the proper allocation of revenues and expenses to the current period and needs not be concerned with determining the market value of assets that will not be sold.

Objective evidence

Entries in the accounting records and data reported on financial statements must be based on objectively determined evidence. Without close adherence to this principle, the confidence of the many users of the financial statements could not be maintained. For example, objective evidence such as invoices and vouchers for purchases, bank statements for the amount of cash in bank, and physical counts for merchandise on hand supports much of accounting. Such evidence is completely objective and is subject to verification.

Evidence is not always conclusively objective, for there are numerous occasions in accounting where judgments, estimates, and other subjective factors must be taken into account. In such situations, the most objective evidence available should be used. For example, the provision for doubtful accounts is an estimate of the losses expected from failure to collect sales made on account. Estimation of this amount should be based on such objective factors as past experience in collecting accounts receivable and reliable forecasts of future business activities. To provide accounting reports that can be accepted with confidence, evidence should be developed that will minimize the possibility of error and intentional bias or fraud.

Unit of measurement

All business transactions are recorded in terms of money. Other pertinent information of a nonfinancial nature may also be recorded, such as the description of assets acquired, the terms of purchase and sale contracts, and the purpose, amount, and term of insurance policies. But it is only through the record of dollar amounts that the diverse transactions and activities of a business may be measured, reported, and periodically compared. Money is both the common factor of all business transactions and the only practicable unit of measurement that can be employed to achieve homogeneity of financial data.

The generally accepted use of the monetary unit for accounting for and reporting the activities of an enterprise has two major limitations: (1) it restricts the scope of accounting reports and (2) it assumes a stability of the measurement unit.

Scope of accounting reports. Many factors affecting the activities and the future prospects of an enterprise cannot be expressed in monetary terms. In general, accounting does not attempt to report such factors. For example, information regarding the capabilities of the management, the state of repair of the plant assets, the effectiveness of the employee welfare program, the attitude of the labor union, and the relative strengths and weaknesses of the firm's principal competitors cannot be expressed in monetary terms. Although such information is important to those concerned with the effectiveness of enterprise operations, accountancy assumes no responsibility for providing it.

Stability of monetary unit. The dollar is far inferior, as a unit of measurement, to such quantitative standards as the pound, gallon, or yard, which have remained unchanged for centuries. The instability of the purchasing power of the dollar is well known. The disruptive effects of inflation on accounting reports during the past few decades are acknowledged by accountants, but to date recognition has not been given in the accounts and in the conventional financial statements to the declining value of the unit of measurement.

To indicate the nature of the problem, assume that the plant assets acquired by an enterprise for $100,000 twenty years ago are now to be replaced with similar assets which at present price levels will cost $200,000. The original cost was deducted from revenue as depreciation expense over the twenty-year period, and, assuming that the enterprise has earned an income or at least broken even during the period, the initial outlay of $100,000 has been recovered. The amount recovered represents only one half of the cost of replacing the assets, however, or stated in another manner, the $100,000 recovered is worth only half as much as the sum originally invested. From either point of view, the firm has suffered a loss in purchasing power which, in a sense, is a loss of capital.

Accounting records and the conventional financial statements are based on verifiable objective evidence, and the use of subjective estimates or opinions concerning the effect of price level changes should be avoided. This is the major reason why accountants treat all dollars alike.

Although use of the stable monetary unit in preparing the conventional financial statements insures objectivity, it makes the evaluation of financial position and results of operations difficult in periods when the purchasing power of the dollar fluctuates. Therefore it is generally recognized that information regarding the effects of the fluctuating dollar may be presented in supplementary financial schedules. Additional attention is given to this subject in a later chapter.

Accounting period

A complete and accurate picture of the degree of success achieved by an enterprise cannot be obtained until it discontinues operations, converts its assets into cash, and pays off its debts. Then, and only then, is it possible to determine with finality its net income. But innumerable decisions regarding the business must be made by management and interested outsiders throughout the period of its existence, and it is therefore necessary to prepare periodic reports on operations and financial position.

Reports may be prepared upon the completion of a particular job or project, but more often they are prepared at specified time intervals. For a number of reasons, including custom and various legal requirements, the maximum interval between reports is one year.

This element of periodicity creates many of the problems of accountancy. The fundamental problem is the determination of periodic net income. For example, the necessity for adjusting entries discussed in earlier chapters is directly attributable to the division of an enterprise into arbitrary time periods. Problems of inventory costing, of recognizing the uncollectibility of receivables, and of selecting depreciation methods are also directly related to the periodic measurement process. Furthermore, it should be noted that the amounts of the assets and the equities reported on the balance sheet will also be affected by the methods employed in determining net income. For example, the particular cost flow assumption employed in determining the cost of merchandise sold during the accounting period will have a direct effect on the amount of cost assigned to the remaining inventory.

Matching revenue and expired costs

During the early stages of accounting development, accountants viewed the balance sheet as the principal financial statement. Over the years the emphasis has shifted to the income statement as the users of the financial statements have become more concerned with the results of operations of a business than with its financial position.

The determination of periodic net income is a twofold problem involving (1) the revenue recognized during the period and (2) the expired costs to be allocated to the period. It is thus a problem of matching revenues and expired costs, the residual amount being the provisional net income or net loss for the particular period.

Recognition of revenue

Revenue is measured by the amount charged to customers for merchandise delivered or services rendered to them. The problem created by periodicity is one of timing; at what point is the revenue realized? For any particular accounting period, the question is whether revenue items should be recognized and reported as such in the current period or whether their recognition should be postponed to a future period.

Various criteria are acceptable for determining when revenue is realized. In any case the criteria adopted should be reasonably in accord with the terms of the contractual arrangements with the customer and based insofar as possible on objective evidence. The criteria most frequently used are described in the remaining paragraphs of this section.

Point of sale. It is customary to consider revenue from the sale of commodities as being realized at the time title passes to the buyer. At this point the sale price has been agreed upon, the buyer acquires the right of ownership in the commodity, and the seller has an enforceable claim against the buyer. The realization of revenue from the sale of services may be determined in a somewhat similar manner, although there is frequently a time lag between the time of the initial agreement and the completion of the service. For example, assume that a contract provides that certain repair services be performed, either for a specified price or on a time and materials basis. The price or terms agreed upon in the initial contract does not constitute revenue until the work has been performed.

Theoretically, revenue from the production and sale of commodities and services emerges continuously as effort is expended. As a practical matter, however, it is ordinarily not possible to make an objective determination until both (1) the contract price has been agreed upon and (2) the seller has completed his portion of the contract.

Receipt of payment. The recognition of revenue may be postponed until payment is received. When this criterion is adopted, revenue is considered to be earned at the time the cash is collected, regardless of when the sale was made. The cash basis is widely used by physicians, attorneys, and other enterprises in which professional services are the source of revenue. It has little theoretical justification but has the practical advantage of simplicity of operation and avoidance of the problem of estimating losses from uncollectible accounts. Its acceptability as a fair method of timing the recognition of revenue from personal services is influenced somewhat by the fact that it may be used in determining income subject to the federal income tax. It is not an appropriate method of measuring revenue from the sale of commodities.

Installment method. In some businesses, especially in the retail field, it is common to make sales on the installment plan. In the typical installment sale, the purchaser makes a down payment and agrees to pay the remainder in specified amounts at stated intervals over a period of time. The seller may retain technical title to the goods or may take other means to facilitate repossession in the event the purchaser defaults on his payments. Despite such provisions, installment sales should ordinarily be treated in the same manner as any other sale on account, in which case the revenue is considered to be realized at the point of sale.[1]

In exceptional cases where the circumstances are such that the collection of receivables is not reasonably assured, an alternate method of determining revenues may be used.[2] The alternative is to consider each receipt of cash to be composed of (1) a partial return of cost and (2) gross profit.

As a basis for illustration, assume that in the first year of operations the installment sales of a dealer in household appliances totaled $300,000, that the cost of the merchandise sold on installments totaled $180,000, and that down payments and installment payments received during the year totaled $140,000. The percent of cost of merchandise sold to sales was 60% (180,000 ÷ 300,000) and the percent of gross profit to sales was 40% (120,000 ÷ 300,000). According to the installment method, the $140,000 of cash receipts in the year of sale are assumed to represent a return of cost in the amount of $84,000 (60% × $140,000) and gross profit of $56,000 (40% × $140,000). Collections in future periods from the year's sales would similarly be treated as a pro rata return of cost (60%) and gross profit (40%).

Degree of contract completion. Enterprises engaged in large construction projects may devote several years to the completion of a particular contract. In order to illustrate a situation of this nature, assume that a contractor engages in a project that will require three years to complete, for which he is to receive $50,000,000. Assume also that the total cost to be incurred, which will also be spread over the three-year period, is estimated at $44,000,000. According to the point-of-sale

---

[1]*Opinions of the Accounting Principles Board, No. 10,* "Omnibus Opinion — 1966" (New York: American Institute of Certified Public Accountants, 1966), p. 149.
[2]*Ibid.*

criterion, neither the revenue nor the related costs would be recognized until the project is completed with the result that the entire net income from the contract would be reported in a single year.

Whenever the total cost of a long-term contract and the extent of progress can be reasonably estimated, it is preferable to consider the revenue as being earned over the entire life of the contract. The amount of revenue to be recognized in any particular period is then determined on the basis of the estimated percentage of the contract that has been completed during the period. The estimated percentage of completion can be developed by comparing incurred costs with the most recent estimates of total costs or by estimates by engineers, architects or other qualified personnel of the progress of the work performed. To continue with the illustration, assume that by the close of the first fiscal year the contract is estimated to be one-fourth completed. The amount of revenue recognized for the year would be $\frac{1}{4}$ of $50,000,000, or $12,500,000. The costs actually incurred during the period are then matched against the revenue recognized.

There is, of course, an element of subjectivity, and hence of possible error, in the determination of the amount of revenue earned by the degree-of-contract-completion method. The financial statements may be more useful, however, in spite of estimates, than they would be if none of the revenue were recognized until completion of the contract. Disclosure of the method used should be made on the financial statements.

A situation somewhat comparable to long-term construction contracts arises in connection with revenue from rentals, loans, and other services that are definitely measurable on a time basis. Neither the point of sale, the receipt of payment, nor the installment method is an appropriate criterion for determining the emergence of revenue from such sources. Both the amount of total revenue to be earned and the period over which it is to be earned are readily ascertainable. For example, if a building is leased for a period of 3 years at a rental of $36,000, the revenue is realized at the rate of $1,000 a month. Whether the rent is received in a lump sum at the beginning of the lease, in installments over the life of the lease, or at its termination is irrelevant. In accordance with the concept of the going concern, it is assumed that the owner will supply the use of the building during the term of the lease and that the lessee will fulfill his part of the contract.

Allocation of costs

Properties and services acquired by an enterprise are generally recorded at cost. "Cost" is the amount of cash or equivalent given to acquire the property or the service. If property other than cash is given to acquire properties or services, the cost is the cash equivalent of the

353

property given. When the properties or the services acquired are sold or consumed, the costs are matched with the related revenue to determine the amount of net income or net loss. The costs of properties or services acquired that are on hand at any particular time represent assets. Such costs may also be referred to as "unexpired costs." As the assets are sold or consumed, they become "expired costs" or "expenses."

Theoretically, it is possible to assign all costs to each specific product sold or each service rendered. If this were done, the net income of an enterprise could be measured in terms of units of output. In practice, however, it would be difficult and costly to fragmentize cost allocations to such a degree. As stated earlier in this chapter, the matching of expired revenue and expired costs on a periodic time basis is satisfactory.

The techniques of determining and recording cost expirations have been described and illustrated in earlier chapters. In general, there are two approaches to cost allocations: (1) compute the amount of the expired cost or (2) compute the amount of the unexpired cost. For example, it is customary to determine the portion of plant assets that have expired. After recording the depreciation for the period, the balances of the plant asset accounts minus the balances of the related accumulated depreciation accounts represent the unexpired cost of the assets. The alternative approach must be employed for merchandise and supplies unless perpetual inventory records are maintained. The cost of the merchandise or supplies on hand at the close of the period is ordinarily determined by taking a physical inventory, and the remaining costs in the related accounts are assumed to have expired. It might appear that the first approach emphasizes expired costs and the second emphasizes unexpired costs. This is not the case, however, as the selection of the method is based on convenience or practicability.

Many of the costs allocable to a period are treated as an expense at the time of incurrence because they will be wholly expired at the end of the period. For example, when a monthly rent is paid at the beginning of a month, the cost incurred is unexpired and hence it is an asset; but since the cost incurred will be wholly expired at the end of the month, it is customary to charge the rental directly to the appropriate expense account, thus avoiding the necessity for an additional entry later. The proper allocation of costs among periods is the paramount consideration; any one of a variety of accounting techniques may be employed in achieving this objective.

Consistency

A number of accepted alternative principles affecting the determination of income statement and balance sheet amounts have been presented in earlier sections of the text. Recognizing that different methods may be used under varying circumstances, some guide or standard is needed to assure a high degree of comparability of the periodic financial statements of an enterprise. It is common practice to compare an enterprise's current income statement and balance sheet with the statements of the preceding year.

The amount and the direction of change in net income and financial position from period to period is highly significant to the reader and may greatly influence his decisions. Therefore, interested persons should be able to assume that the successive financial statements of an enterprise are based consistently on the same generally accepted accounting principles. If the principles are not applied consistently, the trends indicated could be the result of changes in accounting methods rather than the result of changes in business conditions or managerial effectiveness.

The concept of consistency does not completely prohibit changes in accounting methods. Changes should be made where changing conditions indicate that another method will more fairly state net income and the financial position. For example, an enterprise that initially adopted the first-in, first-out assumption of cost flow might at some later date decide to change to the last-in, first-out flow assumption. The change in method and its effect upon the financial statements should be clearly disclosed in the financial statements for the period in which the change was made. In this manner, users of financial statements are provided with the data necessary to make the current statements comparable with those of prior periods.

355

Adequate disclosure

Financial statements and their accompanying footnotes or other explanatory materials should contain all of the pertinent data believed essential to the reader's understanding. Criteria for standards of disclosure are of necessity nebulous and indefinite. They are often based on value judgments rather than on objective facts.

The usefulness of financial statements is enhanced by the use of headings and subheadings and by merging items in significant categories. For example, detailed information as to the amount of cash in various special and general funds, the amount on deposit in each of several banks, and the amount invested in a variety of marketable government securities is not needed by the reader of financial statements. Such information displayed on the balance sheet would impede rather than aid understanding. On the other hand, if the terms of significant loan agreements provide for a secured claim through a mortgage on an asset, the details should be disclosed. Some of the less obvious situations that accountants agree should be adequately disclosed on financial statements are briefly described in the following paragraphs.

Accounting methods employed. When there are several acceptable alternative methods that have a significant effect on amounts reported on the statements, the particular method adopted should be disclosed. Examples include inventory cost flow assumptions, inventory pricing methods, depreciation methods, and criteria of revenue recognition.

Changes in accounting methods. When a significant change is made in accounting methods, that fact should be disclosed in the financial statements for the year in which the change is made. The usual practice is to disclose the quantitative effect on the net income and on the balance sheet items.

Contingent liabilities. Contingent liabilities arising from discounted notes receivable, litigation, guarantees of products, possible tax assessments, or other causes should be disclosed.

Events subsequent to date of statements. Events occurring or becoming known after the close of the period that may have a significant effect on the financial statements should be disclosed. For example, if an enterprise should suffer a crippling loss from a fire or other catastrophe between the end of the year and the issuance of the statements, the facts should be disclosed. Similarly, such occurrences as the settlement of pending litigation, the initiation of litigation, or the sale or purchase of plant facilities after the close of the period should be made known if they have a significant effect on the company.

Materiality

In adhering to generally accepted accounting principles, the accountant must consider the relative importance of any event, accounting procedure, or change in procedure that affects items on the financial statements. Absolute accuracy in accounting and full disclosure in reporting are not ends in themselves, and there is no need to exceed the limits of practicability. The determination of what is material and what is unimportant requires the exercise of judgment; precise criteria cannot be applied.

To determine materiality, the size of an item and its nature must be considered in relationship to the size and the nature of other items. The erroneous classification of a $10,000 asset on a balance sheet exhibiting total assets of $10,000,000 would probably be immaterial. If the assets totaled only $100,000, however, it would certainly be material. If the $10,000 represented a loan to an officer of the enterprise, it might well be material even in the first assumption. If the amount of the loan was increased to $100,000 between the close of the period and the issuance of the statements, both the nature of the item at the balance sheet date and the subsequent increase in amount would require disclosure.

The concept of materiality may be applied to procedures employed in recording transactions. As was stated in an earlier chapter, minor expenditures for plant assets may be treated as an expense of the period rather than as an asset. The saving in accounting costs is justified if the practice does not materially affect the financial statements. In establishing a dollar amount as the dividing line between a revenue charge and a capital charge, consideration would need to be given to such factors as: (1) amount of total plant assets, (2) amount of plant assets in relationship to other assets, (3) frequency of occurrence of expenditures for plant assets, (4) nature and expected life of plant assets, and (5) probable effect on the amount of periodic net income reported.

Custom also influences criteria of materiality. In recent years most corporation financial statements omit cents, and some statements round figures to the nearest thousand dollars. For large or medium-size corporations, cents and hundreds of dollars are certainly not material amounts; they tend to imply a degree of accuracy that does not exist.

A technique known as "whole-dollar" accounting has also been developed in recent years. The elimination from accounting entries of the cents amounts wherever possible and at the earliest practicable point in the accounting sequence may effect savings in office costs and improve productivity. There are some accounts, such as those with customers and creditors, in which it is not feasible to round to the nearest dollar. In many of the asset, revenue, and expense accounts, however, the errors introduced by rounding the amounts of individual entries at the time of recording tend to be compensating in nature, and the amount of the final error is not material.

It should not be inferred from the foregoing that whole-dollar accounting encourages or condones errors. The unrecorded cents are not lost; they are merely reported in a manner that reduces bookkeeping costs without materially affecting the accuracy of accounting data.

Conservatism

Periodic statements are of necessity affected to a considerable degree by the selection of accounting procedures and other value judgments. Historically, accountants have tended to be conservative, and in selecting among alternatives they often favored the method or the procedure that yielded the lesser amount of net income or asset value. This attitude of conservatism was frequently expressed in the admonition to "anticipate no profits and provide for all losses." For example, it is acceptable to price merchandise inventory at lower of cost or market. If market price is higher than cost, the higher amount is ignored in the accounts and, if presented in the financial statements, is presented parenthetically. Such an attitude of pessimism has been due in part to the need for an offset to

357

the optimism of business management. It could also be argued that potential future losses to an enterprise from poor management decisions would be lessened if net income and assets were understated.

Current accounting thought has shifted somewhat from this philosophy of conservatism. Conservatism is no longer considered to be a dominant factor in selecting among alternatives. Revenue should be recognized when realized, and expired costs should be matched against revenue in accordance with principles based on reason and logic. The element of conservatism may be considered only when other factors affecting a choice of alternatives are neutral. The concepts of objectivity, consistency, disclosure, and materiality take precedence over conservatism, and the latter should be a factor only where the others do not play a significant role.

Continuing development of accounting principles

Accounting, like most disciplines, has evolved gradually over many years. Accounting principles are continually being examined and refined in an effort to improve accounting practice and to keep it abreast of changes in economic conditions, in the legal environment, and in methods of business operation. Many individual accountants, professional accounting associations, and governmental agencies have contributed to the development of accounting principles.

Among the oldest and most influential organizations of accountants are the American Accounting Association (AAA), the American Institute of Certified Public Accountants (AICPA), the Financial Executives Institute (FEI), and the National Accounting Association (NAA). Each group publishes a periodical journal for its members and other subscribers. They also issue other publications from time to time in the form of research studies, technical opinions, and monographs. There are several additional national organizations of accountants, as well as many state societies and local chapters of the national and state organizations. Each one provides forums for the interchange of ideas and discussion of accounting principles.

One of the earliest attempts by an accounting organization to formulate general principles was published by the AAA in 1936 under the title "A Tentative Statement of Accounting Principles Underlying Corporate Financial Statements."[3] A mere five pages in length, it has been followed by five additional complete statements and thirteen supplements. The latest in the series, entitled *A Statement of Basic Accounting Theory*,[4] was published as a hundred-page volume in 1966.

---

[3] *The Accounting Review* (Evanston, Illinois: American Accounting Association, 1936), Vol. XI, No. 2, pp. 187–191.
[4] *A Statement of Basic Accounting Theory* (Evanston, Illinois: American Accounting Association, 1966).

Another indication of the scope of accounting principles and the importance of their general acceptability is provided by a research study of nearly five hundred pages, published by the AICPA in 1965, under the title "Inventory of Generally Accepted Accounting Principles for Business Enterprises."[5] In addition to presenting discussions of basic concepts and the text of previously published authoritative pronouncements, the "inventory" was intended to

> . . . establish a list or summary of the accounting principles (or practices) now regarded as essential to the fulfillment of fiduciary accountabilities of a business enterprise to persons who have invested in the enterprise or have other bona fide interests in its financial position and results of operations; . . . .[6]

Of the various governmental agencies with an interest in development of accounting principles, the Securities and Exchange Commission (SEC) has undoubtedly been the most influential. Opinions on accounting policies and practices that are to be observed in the preparation of financial statements and the other reports filed with the Commission are published as *Accounting Series Releases*.

QUESTIONS

1. Accounting principles are broad guides to accounting practice. (a) Who has the responsibility for the development of accounting principles? (b) How are accounting principles developed? (c) Of what significance is acceptability in the development of accounting principles? (d) Why must accounting principles be continually reexamined and revised?

2. (a) Would the accountant for a sole proprietorship record in the accounts the personal assets and liabilities of the proprietor? Explain. (b) Would a banker considering a loan to a sole proprietorship have any interest in the amount and the nature of the personal assets and liabilities of the proprietor? Explain.

3. What is the essence of the going-concern concept?

4. Plant assets are reported on the balance sheet of Richmond Brothers at a total cost of $350,000 less accumulated depreciation of $150,000. (a) Is it possible that the assets might realize considerably more or considerably less than $200,000 if the business were discontinued and the assets were sold separately? (b) Why aren't plant assets reported on the balance sheet at their estimated market values?

5. (a) Why are the conventional financial statements based on the assumption of a stable monetary unit? (b) Can the effect of the fluctuating dollar on business operations be presented to users of the financial statements, and if so, by what means?

---

[5]Paul Grady, *Inventory of Generally Accepted Accounting Principles for Business Enterprises*, Accounting Research Study No. 7 (New York: American Institute of Certified Public Accountants, 1965).
[6]*Ibid.*, p. ix.

6. During the current year a mortgage note payable for $100,000 issued by Walker Co. twenty years ago becomes due and is paid. Assuming that the general price level has increased by 50% during the twenty-year period, did the loan result in an increase or decrease in Walker Company's purchasing power? Explain.

7. A machine that had cost $25,000 some time ago will soon need to be replaced by a similar machine that will cost $40,000. (a) At what amount should the machine presently owned be reported on the balance sheet? (b) What amount should management use in planning for the cash required to replace the machine?

8. During June merchandise costing $5,000 was sold for $7,500 in cash. Because the purchasing power of the dollar has declined, it will cost $5,500 to replace the merchandise. (a) What is the gross profit that should be reported on the income statement for June? (b) Assuming that all operating expenses for the month are paid in cash and that the owner withdraws cash for the amount of net income, would there be enough cash remaining from the $7,500 of sales to replace the merchandise sold? Discuss.

9. If it were unnecessary to prepare annual financial statements during the life of a business enterprise, would there be any necessity for recording the annual adjusting entry for depreciation expense?

10. At which point is revenue from sales of merchandise on account more commonly recognized, time of sale or time of cash receipt?

11. Merchandise costing $60,000 was sold on the installment plan for $100,000 during the current year. The down payments and the installment payments received during the current year total $30,000. What is the amount of gross profit considered to be realized in the current year (a) applying the point-of-sale principle of revenue recognition and (b) the installment method of accounting?

12. During the current year, the Simmons Construction Company obtained a contract to build an apartment building. The total contract price was $6,000,000 and the estimated construction costs were $4,500,000. During the current year the project was estimated to be 30% completed and the costs incurred totalled $1,350,000. Under the degree-of-contract-completion method of recognizing revenue, what amount of (a) revenue and (b) net income should be recognized for the current year?

13. The publisher of a new monthly magazine received $30,000 for 5,000 one-year subscriptions, all to begin with the first issue in June. The first issue was published and mailed to all subscribers according to plan. How much revenue should the publisher recognize for June?

14. On January 20 of the current year, Bash Realty acquired a forty-acre tract of land for $120,000. During the year $30,000 was spent in subdividing the tract and in paving streets. The market value of the land at the end of the year was estimated at $170,000. An income statement was prepared for the year indicating revenue of $50,000 less expenses of $30,000 and net income of $20,000. Were generally accepted accounting principles followed? Discuss.

15. Edwards Company constructed a warehouse at a cost of $30,000 after a local contractor had submitted a bid of $36,000. The building was recorded at $36,000 and income of $6,000 was recognized. Were generally accepted accounting principles followed? Discuss.

16. Roberts and Denver purchased equipment for $100,000 at the beginning of a fiscal year. The equipment could be sold for $105,000 at the end of the fiscal year. It was proposed that since the equipment was worth more at the end of the year than at the beginning of the year, (a) no depreciation should be recorded for the current year and (b) the gain of $5,000 should be recorded. Discuss the propriety of the proposals.

17. If significant changes are made in accounting methods from one period to the next, why should the effect of these changes be disclosed in the financial statements?

18. You have just been employed by a relatively small merchandising business that records its revenues only when cash is received and its expenses only when cash is paid. You are aware of the fact that the enterprise should record its revenues and expenses on the accrual basis. Would changing to the accrual basis violate the principle of consistency? Discuss.

19. The Baxter Company has used the straight-line method of computing depreciation for many years. For the current year, the declining-balance method was used and depreciation expense totaled $60,000; net income was $100,000. Depreciation computed on the straight-line method would have been $35,000. (a) What is the quantitative effect of the change in method on the net income for the current year? (b) Is the effect of the change material? (c) Should the effect of the change in method be disclosed in the financial statements?

20. The accountant for a large wholesale firm charged the acquisition of a pencil sharpener to an expense account, even though the asset had an estimated useful life of 10 years. What concept supports this treatment of the expenditure?

21. In 1940 the Champion Corporation acquired a building with a useful life of 40 years, which it depreciated by the sum-of-the-years-digits method. Is this practice conservative (a) for the year 1940 and (b) for the year 1979? Explain.

EXERCISES

14-1. Indicate for each of the following the amount of revenue that should be reported for the current year and the amount that should be postponed to a future period. Give a reason for your answer.

(a) Merchandise on hand at the close of the current fiscal year costing $40,000 is expected to be sold in the following year for $58,500.

(b) Sixty days before the close of the current fiscal year, $40,000 was loaned at 6% for 90 days.

(c) Thirty days before the close of the current fiscal year, a $30,000, 90-day, non-interest-bearing note was accepted at a discount of 6%. Proceeds in the amount of $29,550 were given to the maker of the note.

(d) Season tickets for a series of five concerts were sold for $60,000. Three concerts were played during the current year.

(e) Leased a tract of land on the first day of the second month of the current year, receiving one year's rent of $6,000.

(continued)

(f) Salesman submitted orders in the current year for merchandise for delivery in the following year. The merchandise had a cost of $12,500 and a selling price of $20,500.

(g) Cash of $10,000 was received in the current year on the sale of gift certificates to be redeemed in merchandise in the following year.

(h) The contract price for building a bridge is $5,000,000 and the total costs for construction are estimated at $4,000,000. During the current year, the first year of construction, the bridge is estimated to be 20% completed and the costs incurred totaled $800,000. Revenue is to be recognized by the degree-of-contract-completion method.

14-2. Webert's Furniture makes all sales on the installment plan. Data related to merchandise sold during the current fiscal year are as follows:

Sales...	$360,000
Cash received on the $360,000 of installment contracts.	150,000
Merchandise inventory, beginning of year.............	62,500
Merchandise inventory, end of year.................	65,500
Purchases...	201,000

Determine the amount of gross profit that would be recognized for the current fiscal year according to (a) the point-of-sale method and (b) the installment method of recognizing revenue.

14-3. Properties and services acquired by an enterprise are generally recorded at cost. For each of the following, determine the cost:

(a) A machine was purchased for $5,000 under terms of n/30, FOB shipping point. The freight amounted to $80 and installation costs totaled $110.

(b) A tract of land adjacent to the Mead Department Store was acquired for $15,000 to provide additional parking for customers. The structures on the land were removed at a cost of $800. The salvage from the structures was sold for $400. The cost of grading the land was $250.

(c) McCormack Company purchased $300 of materials and supplies and paid a carpenter $250 to build a showcase. A similar showcase would cost $650 if purchased from a manufacturer.

14-4. The cost of the merchandise inventory at the close of the first fiscal year of operations, according to three different methods, is as follows: fifo, $48,000; average, $46,500; lifo, $45,200. If the average-cost method is employed, the net income reported will be $38,000. (a) What will be the amount of net income reported if the fifo method is adopted? (b) What will be the amount of net income reported if the lifo method is adopted? (c) Which of the three methods is the most conservative? (d) Is the particular method adopted of sufficient materiality to require disclosure in the financial statements?

14-5. Salesmen for the Lamb Company receive a commission of 15% of sales, the amount due on sales of one month being paid in the middle of the following month. At the close of each of the first three years of operations, the accountant failed to record accrued sales commissions expense as follows: first year, $7,500; second year, $12,000; third year, $11,000. In each case the commissions were paid during the first month of the succeeding year and were charged as an expense of that year. Accrued sales commissions expense was properly recorded at the end of the fourth year. (a) Determine the amount by which net income was overstated or understated for each of the four years. (b) What items on the balance sheet would have been overstated or understated as of the end of each of the four years as a result of the errors?

14-6. Of the following matters, considered individually, indicate those that are material and that should be disclosed either on the financial statements or in accompanying explanatory notes:

(a) A manufacturing company employs the last-in, first-out method of pricing inventory.

(b) A change in accounting methods of the current year increased the amount of net income that would otherwise have been reported from $550,000 to $700,000.

(c) Between the end of its fiscal year and the date of publication of the annual reports, a fire destroyed a portion of the plant. The loss is estimated at $10,000 and is fully covered by insurance. The net income for the year is $1,900,000.

(d) The company is facing litigation involving restraint of trade. Damages might amount to $2,000,000. Annual net income reported in the past few years has ranged from $3,500,000 to $5,000,000.

14-7. Wilson Company sells most of its products on a cash basis but extends short-term credit to some of its customers. Invoices for sales on account are placed in a file and are not recorded until cash is received, at which time the sale is recorded in the same manner as a cash sale. The net income reported for the first three years of operations was $40,000, $35,000, and $45,000 respectively. The total amount of the uncollected sales invoices in the file at the end of each of the three years was $4,000, $3,500, and $5,000. In each case the entire amount was collected during the first month of the succeeding year. (a) Determine the amount by which net income was overstated or understated for each of the three years. (b) What items on the balance sheet were overstated or understated as of the end of each year?

14-8. Each of the following represents a decision made by the accountant. State whether or not you agree with his decision. Support your answer with reference to generally accepted accounting principles that are applicable in the circumstances.

(a) A used machine with an estimated four-year life and no salvage value was purchased early in the current fiscal year for $100,000. Since the company planned to purchase a new machine costing $300,000 to replace this machine at the end of four years, depreciation expense of $75,000 was recorded for the current year. The depreciation expense thus provided for one fourth of the cost of the replacement.

(b) A fire destroyed a considerable amount of plant assets on January 10, the tenth day of the current fiscal year. In preparing the balance sheet as of December 31 of the preceding year, the accountant disclosed the facts surrounding the fire in a footnote accompanying the financial statements.

(c) In preparing the balance sheet, detailed information as to the amount of cash on deposit in each of several banks was omitted. Only the total amount of cash under a caption "Cash in banks" was presented.

(d) Merchandise transferred to other parties on a consignment basis and not sold is included in merchandise inventory.

(e) Land, used as a parking lot, was purchased 20 years ago for $20,000. Since its market value is now $50,000, the land account is debited for $30,000 and a gain account is credited for a like amount. The gain is presented as an "Other income" item in the income statement.

(f) All minor expenditures for office equipment are charged to an expense account.

PROBLEMS

The following additional problems for this chapter are located in Appendix C: 14-1B, 14-3B, 14-4B, 14-6B.

14-1A. You are engaged to review the accounting records of Bradshaw Company prior to closing of the expense and revenue accounts as of December 31, the end of the current fiscal year. The following information comes to your attention during the review:

(a) Accounts receivable include $1,200 owed by Blair & Co., a bankrupt. There is no prospect of collecting any of the receivable. The allowance method of accounting for receivables is employed.

(b) No interest has been accrued on a $15,000, 6%, 60-day notes receivable, dated December 1 of the current year.

(c) Merchandise inventory on hand at December 31 of the current year has been recorded in the accounts at cost, $55,000. Current market price of the inventory is $57,500.

(d) The store supplies account has a balance of $1,100. The cost of the store supplies on hand at December 31, as determined by a physical count, was $475.

(e) Land, recorded in the accounts at a cost of $20,000, was appraised at $35,000 by two expert appraisers.

(f) Since net income for the current year is expected to be considerably less than it was for the preceding year, depreciation on equipment has not been recorded. Depreciation for the year on equipment, determined in a manner consistent with the preceding year, amounts to $17,500.

(g) The company is being sued for $100,000 by a customer who is claiming damages for personal injury apparently caused by a defective product. Company attorneys feel extremely confident that the company will have no liability for damages resulting from this case.

Instructions:

Journalize any entries required to adjust or correct the accounts, identifying each entry by letter.

14-2A. Reliable Furniture Company makes all sales on the installment basis and recognizes revenue at the point of sale. Condensed income statements and the amounts collected from customers for each of the first three years of operations are given below.

	First Year	Second Year	Third Year
Sales...........................	$170,000	$220,000	$230,000
Cost of merchandise sold..........	98,600	132,000	128,800
Gross profit on sales..............	$ 71,400	$ 88,000	$101,200
Operating expenses..............	50,000	54,000	59,000
Net income.....................	$ 21,400	$ 34,000	$ 42,200
Collected from sales of first year ...	$ 62,000	$ 55,000	$ 53,000
Collected from sales of second year..........		85,000	75,000
Collected from sales of third year.....................			90,000

Instructions:

Determine the amount of net income that would have been reported in each of the three years if the installment method of recognizing revenue had been employed, ignoring the possible effects of uncollectible accounts on the computation. Present figures in good order.

14-3A. Highland Construction Company began construction on three contracts during 1969. Contract A was completed in 1970 and Contract B in 1971. The contract prices, estimated total costs, and costs incurred are as follows:

	Contract Price	Estimated Cost	1969 Costs	1970 Costs	1971 Costs
Contract A	$2,000,000	$1,600,000	$960,000	$680,000	——
Contract B	2,500,000	1,875,000	468,750	937,500	$ 510,000
Contract C	4,000,000	3,200,000	320,000	960,000	1,600,000

Instructions:

Determine the amount of revenue and the net income to be recognized for each of the following years: 1969, 1970, and 1971. Assume that the recognition of revenue is to be spread over the life of the contract and that the estimated percentage of completion is determined by comparing incurred costs with the estimated total cost. Present computations in good order.

14-4A. Caldwell Company was organized on January 1, 1968. During its first three years of operations, the company determined uncollectible accounts expense by the direct write-off method, the cost of the merchandise inventory at the end of the period by the first-in, first-out method, and depreciation expense by the straight-line method. The amounts of net income reported and the amounts of the foregoing items for each of the three years were as follows:

	First Year	Second Year	Third Year
Net income reported.........	$20,000	$32,000	$40,000
Uncollectible accounts expense.	250	1,200	2,400
Ending merchandise inventory..	35,000	38,000	40,000
Depreciation expense.........	7,000	7,300	7,700

The firm is considering the possibility of changing to the following methods in determining net income for the fourth and subsequent years: provision for doubtful accounts through the use of an allowance account, last-in, first-out inventory, and declining-balance depreciation at twice the straight-line rate. In order to consider the probable future effect of these changes on the determination of net income, the management requests that net income of the past three years be recomputed on the basis of the proposed methods. The uncollectible accounts expense, inventory, and depreciation expense, for the past three years, computed in accordance with the proposed methods, are as follows:

	First Year	Second Year	Third Year
Uncollectible accounts expense.	$ 900	$ 1,300	$ 1,900
Ending merchandise inventory..	33,500	35,500	37,000
Depreciation expense.........	14,000	12,800	11,900

Instructions:

Recompute the net income for each of the three years, presenting the figures in an orderly manner.

14-5A. York Radio and Television Sales employs the installment method of recognizing gross profit for sales made on the installment plan. Details of a particular installment sale, amounts collected from the purchaser, and the repossession of the item sold are presented below.

First year:
Sold for $600 a color television set having a cost of $450 and received a down payment of $100.
Second year:
Received twelve monthly payments of $20 each.
Third year:
The purchaser defaulted on the monthly payments, the set was repossessed, and the remaining 13 installments were canceled. The set was estimated to be worth $250.

Instructions:
(1) Determine the gross profit to be recognized in the first year.
(2) Determine the gross profit to be recognized in the second year.
(3) Determine the gain or the loss to be recognized from the repossession of the set.

14-6A. Glen Wade owns and manages The Art Mart on a full-time basis. He also maintains the accounting records. At the close of the first year of operations, he prepared the following income statement and balance sheet.

The Art Mart
Income Statement
For Year Ended December 31, 19――

Sales........................		$75,000
Purchases..................		68,500
Gross profit on sales.......		$ 6,500
Operating expenses:		
Salary expense.............	$ 8,500	
Rent expense..............	4,550	
Utilities expense..........	1,500	
Miscellaneous expense.....	1,400	
Total operating expenses.		15,950
Net loss....................		$ 9,450

The Art Mart
Balance Sheet
December 31, 19――

Cash.............................	$3,550
Equipment........................	5,000
Glen Wade........................	$8,550

Because of the large net loss reported by the income statement, Wade is considering discontinuing operations. Before making a decision, he asks you to review the accounting methods employed and, if material errors are found, to prepare revised statements. The following information is elicited during the course of the review:

(a) The only transactions recorded have been those in which cash was received or disbursed.

(b) The accounts have not been closed for the year.

(c) The business was established on January 5 by an investment of $15,000 in cash by the owner. An additional investment of $3,000 was made in cash on July 1.

(d) The equipment listed on the balance sheet at $5,000 was purchased for cash on January 6. Equipment purchased July 1 for $1,500 in cash was debited to Purchases. Equipment purchased on December 29 for $2,000, for which a 90-day non-interest-bearing note was issued, was not recorded.

(e) Depreciation on equipment has not been recorded. The equipment is estimated to have a useful life of 15 years and a salvage value of 10% of its original cost. (Use straight-line method.)

(f) Accounts receivable from customers at December 31 total $3,750.

(g) Uncollectible accounts are estimated at $225.

(h) The merchandise inventory at December 31, as nearly as can be determined, has a cost of $15,000.

(i) Insurance premiums of $750 were debited to Miscellaneous Expense during the year. The unexpired portion at December 31 is $300.

(j) Rent Expense includes an advance payment of $350 for the month of January in the subsequent year.

(k) Supplies of $900 purchased during the year were debited to Purchases. An estimated $250 of supplies were on hand at December 31.

(l) A total of $4,700 is owed to merchandise creditors on account at December 31.

(m) Salaries owed but not paid on December 31 total $375.

(n) The classification of operating expenses as "selling" and "general" is not considered to be sufficiently important to justify the cost of the analysis.

(o) The proprietor made no withdrawals during the year.

367

Instructions:

(1) On the basis of the financial statements presented above, prepare an unadjusted trial balance as of December 31, on an eight-column work sheet.

(2) Record the adjustments and the corrections in the Adjustments columns and complete the work sheet.

(3) Prepare an income statement, a capital statement, and a balance sheet.

(4) On the basis of the revised financial statements, evaluate the effectiveness of the first year of operations.

15

Partnerships

Partnership organization and operation

The Uniform Partnership Act, which has been adopted by more than three fourths of the states, defines a partnership as "an association of two or more persons to carry on as co-owners a business for profit." The partnership form of business organization is widely used for comparatively small businesses that wish to take advantage of the combined capital, managerial talent, and experience of two or more persons. In many cases, the alternative to securing the amount of investment required or the various skills needed to operate a business is to adopt the corporate form of organization, which is discussed in later chapters. The corporate form of organization is usually not available, however, to certain professions because of restrictions in state statutes or in professional codes of ethics. Hence, a group of physicians, attorneys, or certified public accountants that wishes to band together to practice a profession ordinarily must do so as a partnership. Medical and legal partnerships composed of 20 or more partners are not unusual, and the number of partners in some CPA firms exceeds 200.

The partnership characteristics that have accounting implications are described in the following paragraphs.

Limited life. Dissolution of a partnership may result from a variety of causes, including death, bankruptcy, incapacity, or expressed will of any one of the partners. In such cases a new partnership must be formed if the operations of the business are to be continued without interruption. This is the usual situation with professional partnerships; their composition may change frequently through admissions of new partners and retirements of others.

Unlimited liability. Each partner is individually liable to creditors for debts incurred by the partnership. Thus, if a partnership becomes insolvent, the partners are required to contribute sufficient personal assets to settle the debts of the partnership.

Co-ownership of property. The property invested in a partnership by a partner becomes the property of all the partners jointly. Upon dissolution of the partnership and distribution of its assets, each member's claim against the assets is measured by the amount of the balance in his capital account.

Participation in income. Net income and net loss are distributed among the partners in accordance with their agreement. In the absence of any agreement, all partners share equally. If the agreement specifies profit distribution but is silent as to losses, the losses are shared in the same manner as profits.

Articles of copartnership. A partnership is created by a voluntary contract containing all the elements essential to any other enforceable contract. It is not necessary that this contract be in writing, nor even that its terms be specifically expressed orally. However, good business practice dictates that the contract should be in writing and should clearly express the intentions of the partners. The contract, known as the *articles of copartnership*, should contain provisions regarding such matters as the amount of investment to be made, limitations on withdrawals of funds, the manner in which net income and net loss are to be divided, and admission and withdrawal of partners.

Accounting for partnerships

Most of the day-to-day accounting for a partnership is the same as the accounting for any other form of business organization. The journals described in earlier chapters may be employed by a partnership without alteration. The chart of accounts, with the exception of drawing and capital accounts for each partner, does not differ from the chart of accounts of a similar business conducted by a single owner. It is in the areas of the formation, income distribution, dissolution, and liquidation of partnerships that transactions peculiar to partnerships arise. The remainder of the chapter is devoted to the accounting principles and procedures applicable in these areas.

Recording investments

A separate entry is made for the investment of each partner in a partnership. The various assets contributed by a partner are debited to the proper asset accounts; if liabilities are assumed by the partnership, the appropriate liability accounts are credited; and the partner's capital account is credited for the net amount.

To illustrate the entry required to record an initial investment, assume that George M. Allen and James D. Barker, who are sole owners of competing hardware stores, agree to combine their enterprises in a partnership. Each is to contribute specified amounts of cash and other business assets. It is also agreed that the partnership is to assume the liabilities of the individual businesses. The entry to record the assets contributed and the liabilities transferred by George M. Allen, in general journal form, is as follows:

Jan. 1	Cash...........................	7,000	
	Accounts Receivable..................	6,300	
	Merchandise Inventory................	18,600	
	Store Equipment.....................	5,400	
	Office Equipment....................	1,500	
	Allowance for Doubtful Accounts.......		1,300
	Accounts Payable....................		2,500
	George M. Allen, Capital.............		35,000

The monetary amounts at which the noncash assets are stated are those agreed upon by the partners. In arriving at an appropriate amount for such assets, particular consideration should be given to their market price at the time of the formation of the partnership. The values agreed upon represent the acquisition cost to the new accounting entity created by the formation of the partnership. These amounts may differ from the balances appearing in the accounts of the separate businesses before the partnership was organized. For example, the store equipment stated at $5,400 in the entry above may have had a book value of $3,500, appearing in Allen's ledger at its original cost of $10,000 with accumulated depreciation of $6,500.

Equipment contributed to the partnership may be recorded at the amount of the original cost to the partner, with a credit to the accumulated depreciation account for the amount necessary to bring the book value into agreement with the value assigned by the partners. For example, the store equipment invested by Allen could have been recorded at $10,000, with an offsetting credit to the accumulated depreciation account for $4,600, effecting a book value of $5,400. But the preferred practice is to record only the net amount agreed upon, as it represents the acquisition cost to the partnership. A similar choice of methods is not available for recording the value ascribed to receivables invested by a partner. It is necessary to debit Accounts Receivable for

370

the face amount of the accounts taken over and to credit Allowance for Doubtful Accounts for the amount estimated to be uncollectible. At the time of organization of the partnership it is not possible to identify the specific accounts in the subsidiary ledger that will eventually become partially or wholly uncollectible.

Division of net income or net loss

As in the case of a sole proprietorship, the net income of a partnership may be said to include a return for the services of the owners, for the capital invested, and for economic or pure profit. A partner is not legally an employee of the partnership, nor is his capital contribution a loan. If each of two partners is to contribute equal services and amounts of capital, an equal sharing in partnership net income would be equitable. But if one partner is to contribute a larger portion of capital than the other, his greater contribution should be taken into consideration in the arrangements for dividing net income. Or, if the services of one partner are much more valuable to the partnership than those of the other, provision for unequal service contributions should be given recognition in their agreement.

To illustrate the division of net income and the accounting for this division, two possible agreements are to be considered. It should be noted that division of the net income or the net loss among the partners in exact accordance with their partnership agreement is of the utmost importance. If the agreement is silent on the matter, the law provides that all partners share equally, regardless of differences in amounts of capital contributed or of time devoted to the business. The partners may, however, make any agreement they wish in regard to the division of net income and net losses.

Income division recognizing services of partners. As a means of recognizing differences in ability and in amount of time devoted to the business, articles of copartnership often provide for the allocation of a portion of net income to the partners in the form of a salary allowance. The articles may also provide for withdrawals of cash by the partners in lieu of salary payments. A clear distinction must therefore be made between the allocation of net income, which is credited to the capital accounts, and payments to the partners, which are debited to the drawing accounts.

As a basis for illustration, assume that the articles of copartnership of Stone and Thomas provide for monthly salary allowances of $600 and $500 respectively, with the balance of the net income to be divided equally, and that the net income for the year is $18,000. A report of the division of net income may be presented as a separate statement accompanying the balance sheet and the income statement, or it may be added at the bottom of the income statement. Assuming that the latter

371

procedure is adopted, the lower part of the income statement would appear as follows:

	J. M. STONE	R. D. THOMAS	TOTAL
Net income			$18,000
Division of net income:			
Salary allowance	$7,200	$6,000	$13,200
Remaining income	2,400	2,400	4,800
Net income	$9,600	$8,400	$18,000

The division of net income is recorded as a closing entry, regardless of whether or not the partners actually withdraw the amounts of their salary allowances. The entry for the division of net income is as follows:

Dec.	31	Expense and Revenue Summary	18,000	
		J. M. Stone, Capital		9,600
		R. D. Thomas, Capital		8,400

If Stone and Thomas had withdrawn their salary allowances monthly, the withdrawals would have accumulated as debits in the drawing accounts during the year. At the end of the year, the debit balances of $7,200 and $6,000 in their respective drawing accounts would be transferred to their respective capital accounts.

Income division recognizing services of partners and investment. Partners may agree that the most equitable plan of income sharing is to allow salaries commensurate with the services rendered and also to allow interest on the capital investments. The remainder is then shared in an arbitrary ratio. To illustrate, assume that Stone and Thomas (1) are allowed monthly salaries of $600 and $500 respectively; (2) are allowed interest at 6% on capital balances at January 1 of the current fiscal year which amounted to $30,000 and $23,000 respectively; and (3) divide the remainder of net income equally. The division of $18,000 net income for the year could then be reported on the income statement as follows:

	J. M. STONE	R. D. THOMAS	TOTAL
Net income			$18,000
Salary allowance	$7,200	$6,000	$13,200
Interest allowance	1,800	1,380	3,180
Remaining income	810	810	1,620
Net income	$9,810	$8,190	$18,000

On the basis of the information in the foregoing income statement, the entry to close the expense and revenue summary account would be recorded in the general journal as follows:

Dec.	31	Expense and Revenue Summary	18,000	
		J. M. Stone, Capital		9,810
		R. D. Thomas, Capital		8,190

In the illustrations presented thus far, the net income has exceeded the sum of the allowances for salary and interest. It is obvious that this may not always be the case. If the net income is less than the total of the special allowances, the "remaining balance" will be a negative figure that must be divided among the partners as though it were a net loss. The effect of this situation may be illustrated by assuming the same salary and interest allowances as in the preceding illustration but changing the amount of net income to $10,000. The salary and interest allowances to Stone total $9,000 and the comparable figure for Thomas is $7,380. The sum of these amounts, $16,380, exceeds the net income of $10,000 by $6,380. It is therefore necessary to deduct $3,190 (½ of $6,380) from each partner's share to arrive at the net income, as indicated below.

	J. M. STONE	R. D. THOMAS	TOTAL
Net income...			$10,000
Salary allowance...................	$7,200	$6,000	$13,200
Interest allowance.................	1,800	1,380	3,180
Total........................	$9,000	$7,380	$16,380
Excess of allowances over income.....	3,190	3,190	6,380
Net income.......................	$5,810	$4,190	$10,000

In closing Expense and Revenue Summary at the end of the year, $5,810 would be credited to J. M. Stone, Capital, and $4,190 would be credited to R. D. Thomas, Capital.

Partners' salaries and interest treated as expenses

Although the traditional view among accountants is to treat salary and interest allowances as allocations of net income, as in the foregoing illustrations, some prefer to treat them as expenses of the enterprise. According to this view, the partnership is treated as a distinct legal entity and the partners are considered to be employees and creditors of the firm. When salaries for partners' services and interest on partners' investments are viewed as expenses of the enterprise, withdrawals of the agreed amount are charged to expense accounts rather than to the partners' drawing accounts. The expense accounts are then closed into the expense and revenue summary account, and the remaining net income is allocated among the partners in the agreed ratio. The amounts paid to partners that are considered to be salary expense and interest expense should be specifically identified as such on the income statement. Regardless of whether partners' salary and interest are treated as expenses of the partnership or as a division of net income, the total amount allocated to each partner will be the same.

Statements for a partnership

Details of the division of net income should be disclosed in the financial statements prepared at the end of the fiscal period. This may be done by adding a section to the income statement, which has been illustrated in the preceding pages, or the data may be presented in a separate statement.

Details of the changes in partnership capital during the period should also be presented in a capital statement. The purposes of the statement and the data included in it correspond to those of the capital statement of a sole proprietorship. There are a number of variations in form, one of which is illustrated as follows.

Stone and Thomas
Capital Statement
For Year Ended December 31, 1969

	J. M. STONE	R. D. THOMAS	TOTAL
Capital, January 1, 1969................	$30,000	$23,000	$53,000
Additional investment during the year.....		3,000	3,000
	$30,000	$26,000	$56,000
Net income for the year................	9,810	8,190	18,000
	$39,810	$34,190	$74,000
Withdrawals during the year.............	9,200	8,000	17,200
Capital, December 31, 1969.............	$30,610	$26,190	$56,800

Capital statement

Under the Internal Revenue Code, enterprises organized as partnerships are not distinct entities and are not required to pay federal income taxes. Instead, the individual partners must report their distributive shares of partnership income on their personal tax returns. However, data on the distributive shares of each partner, as well as a summary of revenue and expense and other financial details of partnership operations, must be reported annually on an "information return." If a partnership provides for payment of salaries or interest to partners without regard to the amount of net income of the enterprise, such payments must be reported on the partnership information return as an expense. The partners are required, in turn, to combine the amounts thus received with their distributive shares of net income so that, despite the method, all income is reported for taxation by the individual partners.

Partnership dissolution

One of the basic characteristics of the partnership form of organization is its limited life. Any change in the personnel of the membership results in the dissolution of the partnership. Thus, admission of a new partner effects the dissolution of the old firm. Similarly, death, bankruptcy, or withdrawal of a partner causes dissolution.

Dissolution of the partnership is not necessarily followed by the winding up of the affairs of the business. For example, a partnership composed of two partners may admit an additional partner. Or if one of three partners in a business withdraws, the remaining two partners may continue to operate the business. In all such cases, a new partnership is formed and new articles of copartnership should be prepared.

Admission of a new partner

A new partner may be admitted to a partnership only with the consent of all the old partners. It does not follow, however, that a partner cannot dispose of part or all of his interest in the firm without the consent of the remaining partners. Under common law, if a partner assigned his interest in the partnership to an outside party, the partnership was automatically dissolved. Under the Uniform Partnership Act, a partner can dispose of part or all of his interest in the firm without the consent of the remaining partners. The person who buys the interest acquires the selling partner's rights to share in net income and to assets upon liquidation. He does not automatically become a partner, however, and has no voice in partnership affairs unless he is admitted to the firm.

A new partner may be admitted to a partnership through either of two procedures:

1. Purchase of an interest from one or more of the old partners.
2. Contribution of assets to the partnership.

375

When the first procedure is followed, the capital interest of the new partner is obtained from the old partners, and neither the total assets nor the total capital of the business is affected. When the second procedure is followed, both the total assets and the total capital of the business are increased.

Admission by purchase of an interest

When a new partner is admitted to a firm by purchasing an interest from one or more of the old partners, he pays the purchase price directly to the old partners. Payment is for partnership equity owned by the partners as individuals, and hence the cash or other consideration paid is not recorded in the accounts of the partnership. The only entry required is the transfer of the appropriate amounts of capital from the capital accounts of the old partners to the capital account established for the new partner.

As an example, assume that partners Abbott and Beck have capital balances of $30,000 each. On June 1, each of them sells one sixth of his capital interest to Carson for $5,000 in cash. The only entry required in the partnership accounts is as shown at the top of the following page.

June	1	John Abbott, Capital...................	5,000	
		Henry Beck, Capital..................	5,000	
		Roger Carson, Capital..............		10,000

The effect of the transaction on the partnership accounts is presented in the following diagram:

PARTNERSHIP ACCOUNTS

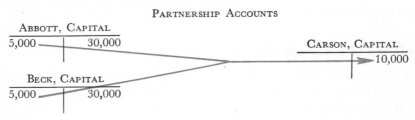

The foregoing entry is made regardless of the amount paid by Carson for the one-sixth interest. If the firm had been earning a high rate of return on the investment and Carson had been very eager to obtain the one-sixth interest, he might have paid considerably more than $10,000. Had other circumstances prevailed, he might have acquired the one-sixth interest for considerably less than $10,000. In either event, the entry to transfer the capital interests would not be affected.

After the admission of Carson, the total capital of the firm is $60,000, in which he has a one-sixth interest, or $10,000. It does not necessarily follow that he will be entitled to a similar share of the partnership net income. Division of net income or net loss will be in accordance with the new partnership agreement.

Admission by contribution of assets

Instead of buying an interest from the former partners, the new partner may contribute assets to the partnership. In this case both the assets and the capital of the firm are increased. To illustrate, assume that Logan and Macy are partners with capital accounts of $18,000 and $12,000 respectively. On June 1, Nichols invests $10,000 cash in the business, for which he is to receive an ownership equity of $10,000. The entry to record this transaction, in general journal form, is:

| June | 1 | Cash..................................... | 10,000 | |
| | | William Nichols, Capital................ | | 10,000 |

The essential difference between the circumstances of the admission of Nichols above and of Carson in the preceding example may be observed by comparing the diagram at the top of the next page with the one above.

With the admission of Nichols, the total capital of the new partnership becomes $40,000, of which he has a one-fourth interest, or $10,000. The extent of his participation in partnership net income will be governed by the articles of copartnership.

376

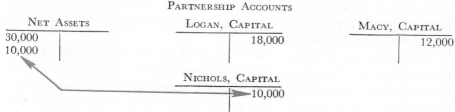

Net Assets		Logan, Capital		Macy, Capital	
30,000			18,000		12,000
10,000					

	Nichols, Capital	
		10,000

Revaluation of assets. In the preceding example, it was assumed that the assets of the Logan and Macy partnership were fairly stated in terms of current market price at the time of the admission of Nichols; hence, no adjustments were made to any of the asset accounts prior to his admission. When the circumstances are otherwise, the book values should be brought into agreement with current prices. The net amount of the revaluation is then allocated to the capital accounts of the old partners in accordance with their income-sharing agreement. For example, if the balance of the merchandise inventory account was $14,000 and the current replacement price was $17,000, the following entry should have been recorded prior to the admission of Nichols, assuming that Logan and Macy share equally in net income:

June	1	Merchandise Inventory..............	3,000		
		George Logan, Capital..............		1,500	
		Thomas Macy, Capital.............		1,500	

If a number of assets are revalued, the adjustments may be debited or credited to a temporary account entitled Asset Revaluations. After all adjustments are made, the net balance of the account is closed to the capital accounts.

It is important that the assets be stated in terms of current prices at the time of admission of a new partner. Failure to recognize current prices will result in participation by the new partner in gains or losses attributable to the period prior to his admission to the partnership.

Goodwill. In the sense that it is used in business, *goodwill* is an intangible asset that attaches to a business as a result of such favorable factors as location, product superiority, reputation, and managerial skill. Its existence is evidenced by the ability of the business to earn a rate of return on the investment that is in excess of the normal rate for other firms in the same line of business.

Accountants are in general agreement that goodwill should be recognized in the accounts only if it can be objectively determined by an event or transaction, such as a purchase or sale. When a new partner is admitted to a partnership, goodwill attributable to either the old partnership or to the incoming partner may be recognized. Although there are various methods of estimating goodwill, such factors as the respective shares owned by the partners and the relative bargaining abilities of the

377

partners will influence the final determination. The amount of goodwill agreed upon is recorded as an asset, with a corresponding addition to the appropriate capital accounts.

To illustrate the recognition of goodwill to the old partners, assume that on March 1 the partnership of Joyce and Keller admits Long, who is to contribute cash of $10,000. After the tangible assets of the old partnership have been adjusted to current market prices, the capital balances of Joyce and Keller are $12,000 and $14,000 respectively. The parties agree, however, that the enterprise is worth $30,000. The excess of $30,000 over the capital balances of $26,000 ($12,000 + $14,000) indicates the existence of $4,000 of goodwill, which should be allocated to the capital accounts of the original partners in accordance with their income-sharing agreement.

The entries to record the goodwill and the admission of the new partner, assuming that the original partners share equally in net income, are as follows, in general journal form:

Mar. 1	Goodwill.................................	4,000	
	F. G. Joyce, Capital....................		2,000
	G. N. Keller, Capital...................		2,000
1	Cash.....................................	10,000	
	W. J. Long, Capital.....................		10,000

If a partnership admits a new partner who is expected to improve the fortunes of the firm, the parties might agree to recognize this high earnings potential. To illustrate, assume that William Evans is to be admitted to the partnership of Cowen and Dodd for an investment of $30,000. If the parties agree to recognize $5,000 of goodwill attributable to Evans, the entry to record his admission is as follows, in general journal form:

July 1	Cash.....................................	30,000	
	Goodwill.................................	5,000	
	William Evans, Capital		35,000

Withdrawal of a partner

When a partner retires or for some other reason wishes to withdraw from the firm, one or more of the remaining partners may purchase his interest and the business may be continued without apparent interruption. In such cases, settlement for the purchase and sale is made between the partners as individuals. The only entry required on the books of the partnership is a debit to the capital account of the partner withdrawing and a credit to the capital account of the partner or partners acquiring the interest.

If the settlement with the withdrawing partner is made by the partnership, the effect is to reduce the assets and the capital of the firm.

In order to determine the ownership equity of the withdrawing partner, the asset accounts should be adjusted to bring them into agreement with current market prices. The net amount of the adjustments should be allocated among the capital accounts of the partners in accordance with the income ratio. In the event that the cash or the other available assets are insufficient to make complete payment at the time of withdrawal, a liability account should be credited for the balance owed to the withdrawing partner.

Death of a partner

The death of a partner effects the dissolution of the partnership. In the absence of any contrary agreement, the accounts should be closed as of the date of death, and the net income for the fractional part of the year should be transferred to the capital accounts. It is not unusual, however, for the partnership agreement to stipulate that the accounts remain open to the end of the fiscal year or until the affairs are wound up, if that should occur earlier. The net income of the entire period is then allocated, as provided by the agreement, to the respective periods occurring before and after dissolution.

The balance in the capital account of the deceased partner is then transferred to a liability account with his estate. The surviving partner or partners may continue the business or the affairs may be wound up. If the former course is followed, the procedures for settling with the estate will conform to those outlined earlier for the withdrawal of a partner from the business.

379

Liquidation of a partnership

When a partnership goes out of business, it customarily sells most of the assets, pays the creditors, and distributes the remaining cash or other assets to the partners in accordance with their claims. The winding-up process may be referred to generally as *liquidation*. Although liquidation refers specifically to the payment of liabilities, it is often used in a broader sense to include the entire winding-up process.

When the ordinary business activities are discontinued preparatory to liquidation, the accounts should be adjusted and closed in accordance with the customary procedures of the periodic summary. The only accounts remaining open will then be the various asset, contra asset, liability, and capital accounts.

The sale of the assets is referred to as *realization*. As cash is realized, it is applied first to the payment of the claims of creditors. After all liabilities have been paid, the remaining cash is distributed to the partners in accordance with their ownership equities as indicated by their capital accounts.

If the assets are sold piecemeal, the liquidation process may extend over a considerable period of time. This creates no special problem, however, if the distribution of cash to the partners is postponed until all of the assets have been sold. As a basis for illustration, assume that Alden, Beeler, and Craig, partners, decide to liquidate their partnership. Their income-sharing ratio is 5:3:2. After discontinuing the ordinary business operations and closing the accounts, the following summary of the general ledger is prepared:

Cash...	$11,000	
All noncash assets................................	64,000	
All liabilities...................................		$ 9,000
J. Alden, Capital.................................		22,000
B. Beeler, Capital................................		22,000
H. Craig, Capital................................		22,000
Total......................................	$75,000	$75,000

Accounting for the liquidation will be illustrated by three examples based on the foregoing statement of facts. In all cases it will be assumed that all noncash assets are disposed of in a single transaction and that all liabilities are paid at one time. This is merely for the sake of brevity. In addition, Assets and Liabilities will be used as account titles in place of the various asset, contra asset, and liability accounts that in actual practice would be affected by the transactions.

Gain on realization. Alden, Beeler, and Craig sell all noncash assets for $72,000, realizing a gain of $8,000 ($72,000 − $64,000). The gain is divided among the capital accounts in the income-sharing ratio of 5:3:2, the liabilities are paid, and the remaining cash is distributed to the partners according to the balances in their capital accounts. A tabular summary of the transactions follows:

					CAPITAL		
		OTHER			J. ALDEN	B. BEELER	H. CRAIG
	CASH	+ ASSETS	= LIABILITIES +	50% +	30% +	20%
Balances before realization......	$11,000	$64,000	$ 9,000	$22,000	$22,000	$22,000
Sale of assets and division of gain.	+72,000	−64,000		+ 4,000	+ 2,400	+ 1,600
Balances after realization.......	$83,000		$ 9,000	$26,000	$24,400	$23,600
Payment of liabilities..........	− 9,000		−9,000			
Balances.....................	$74,000			$26,000	$24,400	$23,600
Distribution of cash to partners..	−74,000			−26,000	−24,400	−23,600

The entries to record the several steps in the liquidation procedure are as follows, in general journal form:

Sale of assets

Cash..	72,000	
Assets....................................		64,000
Loss and Gain on Realization.......................		8,000

Division of gain

Loss and Gain on Realization.......................	8,000	
J. Alden, Capital................................		4,000
B. Beeler, Capital...............................		2,400
H. Craig, Capital................................		1,600

Payment of liabilities

Liabilities......................................	9,000	
Cash..		9,000

Distribution of cash to partners

J. Alden, Capital................................	26,000	
B. Beeler, Capital...............................	24,400	
H. Craig, Capital................................	23,600	
Cash..		74,000

In the foregoing illustration, the distribution of the cash among the partners was determined by reference to the balances of their respective capital accounts after the gain on realization had been allocated. Under no circumstances should the income-sharing ratio be used as a basis for distributing the cash.

Loss on realization; no capital deficiencies. Assume that in the foregoing example Alden, Beeler, and Craig dispose of all noncash assets for $44,000, incurring a loss of $20,000 ($64,000 − $44,000). The various steps in the liquidation of the partnership are summarized as follows:

		OTHER			CAPITAL		
					J. ALDEN	B. BEELER	H. CRAIG
	CASH	+ ASSETS	=	LIABILITIES +	50% +	30% +	20%
Balances before realization......	$11,000	$64,000		$ 9,000	$22,000	$22,000	$ 22,000
Sale of assets and division of loss.	+44,000	−64,000			−10,000	− 6,000	− 4,000
Balances after realization.......	$55,000			$ 9,000	$12,000	$16,000	$18,000
Payment of liabilities..........	− 9,000			− 9,000			
Balances...................	$46,000				$12,000	$16,000	$18,000
Distribution of cash to partners..	−46,000				−12,000	−16,000	−18,000

The entries required to record the liquidation appear at the top of the following page, in general journal form.

Sale of assets

Cash..	44,000	
Loss and Gain on Realization.............................	20,000	
Assets.......................................		64,000

Division of loss

J. Alden, Capital......................................	10,000	
B. Beeler, Capital.....................................	6,000	
H. Craig, Capital.....................................	4,000	
Loss and Gain on Realization.........................		20,000

Payment of liabilities

Liabilities...	9,000	
Cash...		9,000

Distribution of cash to partners

J. Alden, Capital......................................	12,000	
B. Beeler, Capital.....................................	16,000	
H. Craig, Capital.....................................	18,000	
Cash..		46,000

Loss on realization; capital deficiency. In the preceding illustration, the capital account of each partner was more than sufficient to absorb his share of the loss from realization. Each partner shared in the distribution of cash to the extent of the remaining credit balance in his capital account. The share of the loss chargeable to a partner may be such that it exceeds his ownership equity. The resulting debit balance in his capital account, which is referred to as a *deficiency*, is a claim of the partnership against the partner. Pending collection from the deficient partner, the partnership cash will not be sufficient to pay the other partners in full. In such cases the available cash should be distributed in such a manner that, if the claim against the deficient partner cannot be collected, each of the remaining capital balances will be sufficient to absorb the appropriate share of the deficiency.

To illustrate a situation of this type, assume that Alden, Beeler, and Craig sell all of the noncash assets for $10,000, incurring a loss of $54,000 ($64,000 − $10,000). It is readily apparent that the portion of the loss allocable to Alden, which is $27,000 (50% of $54,000), exceeds the $22,000 balance in his capital account. This $5,000 deficiency is a potential loss to Beeler and Craig and must be tentatively divided between them in their income-sharing ratio of 3:2 (3/5 and 2/5). The capital balances remaining represent their claims on the partnership cash. The computations may be summarized in the manner presented at the top of the next page.

	J. Alden 50%	B. Beeler 30%	H. Craig 20%	Total
Balances before realization..........	$ 22,000	$ 22,000	$ 22,000	$ 66,000
Division of loss on realization........	−27,000	−16,200	−10,800	−54,000
Balances after realization...........	$− 5,000	$ 5,800	$ 11,200	$ 12,000
Division of potential additional loss...	5,000	− 3,000	− 2,000	
Claims to partnership cash..........		$ 2,800	$ 9,200	$ 12,000

The complete summary of the various transactions that have occurred thus far in the liquidation may then be reported, in the form illustrated earlier, as follows:

	CASH	+	OTHER ASSETS	=	LIABIL-ITIES	+	J. ALDEN 50%	+	B. BEELER 30%	+	H. CRAIG 20%
Balances before realization......	$11,000		$64,000		$ 9,000		$22,000		$22,000		$22,000
Sale of assets and division of loss.	+10,000		−64,000				−27,000		−16,200		−10,800
Balances after realization.......	$21,000				$ 9,000		$ 5,000 (Dr.)		$ 5,800		$11,200
Payment of liabilities..........	− 9,000				− 9,000						
Balances....................	$12,000						$ 5,000 (Dr.)		$ 5,800		$11,200
Distribution of cash to partners..	−12,000								− 2,800		− 9,200
Balances...................							$ 5,000 (Dr.)		$ 3,000		$ 2,000

The entries to record the liquidation to this point, in general journal form, are as follows:

Sale of assets

```
Cash......................................................  10,000
    Loss and Gain on Realization..........................  54,000
        Assets...........................................           64,000
```

Division of loss

```
J. Alden, Capital....................................  27,000
B. Beeler, Capital....................................  16,200
H. Craig, Capital....................................  10,800
    Loss and Gain on Realization........................           54,000
```

Payment of liabilities

```
Liabilities.............................................   9,000
    Cash...............................................            9,000
```

Distribution of cash to partners

```
B. Beeler, Capital.....................................   2,800
H. Craig, Capital......................................   9,200
    Cash...............................................           12,000
```

The affairs of the partnership are not completely wound up until the claims among the partners are settled. Payments to the firm by the deficient partner are credited to his capital account. Any uncollectible

383

deficiency becomes a loss and is written off against the capital balances of the remaining partners. Finally, the cash received from the deficient partner is distributed to the other partners in accordance with their ownership claims.

To continue with the illustration, the capital balances remaining after the $12,000 cash distribution are as follows: Alden, $5,000 debit; Beeler, $3,000 credit; Craig, $2,000 credit. The entries for the partnership, in general journal form, under three different assumptions as to final settlement are presented below.

If Alden pays the entire amount of his deficiency, $5,000, to the partnership, the final entries will be:

Receipt of deficiency

Cash...	5,000	
J. Alden, Capital.....................................		5,000

Distribution of cash to partners

B. Beeler, Capital.....................................	3,000	
H. Craig, Capital......................................	2,000	
Cash...		5,000

If Alden pays $3,000 of his deficiency to the partnership and the remainder is considered to be uncollectible, the final entries will be:

Receipt of part of deficiency

Cash...	3,000	
J. Alden, Capital.....................................		3,000

Division of loss

B. Beeler, Capital.....................................	1,200	
H. Craig, Capital......................................	800	
J. Alden, Capital.....................................		2,000

Distribution of cash to partners

B. Beeler, Capital.....................................	1,800	
H. Craig, Capital......................................	1,200	
Cash...		3,000

If Alden is unable to pay any part of his $5,000 deficiency, the loss to the other partners will be recorded by the following entry:

Division of loss

B. Beeler, Capital.....................................	3,000	
H. Craig, Capital......................................	2,000	
J. Alden, Capital.....................................		5,000

It should be noted that the type of error most likely to occur in the liquidation of a partnership is improper distribution of cash among the partners. Errors of this type result from confusing the distribution of cash with the division of gains and losses on realization. Gains and losses on realization result from the disposal of assets to outsiders; they represent changes in partnership capital and should be divided among the capital accounts in the same manner as net income or net loss from ordinary business operations, namely, in the income-sharing ratio. Distributions of cash (or other assets) to the partners, on the other hand, are entirely different and have no direct relationship to the income-sharing ratio. Withdrawals of assets by the partners upon dissolution of the partnership are just the reverse of contributions of assets by the partners at the time the partnership was organized. A partner is entitled to receive assets to the extent of the credit balance in his capital account after all potential losses have been taken into consideration.

QUESTIONS

1. Is it possible for a partner to lose a greater amount than the amount of his investment in the partnership enterprise? Explain.

2. Garner, Horn, and Inman are contemplating the formation of a partnership in which Garner is to invest $25,000 and devote one-half time, Horn is to invest $50,000 and devote one-fourth time, and Inman is to make no investment and devote full time. (a) In the absence of a specific agreement on the matter, how should the periodic net income or net loss be divided? (b) Would Inman be correct in assuming that inasmuch as he is not contributing any assets to the firm, he is risking nothing? Explain.

3. As a part of his initial investment, a partner contributes store equipment that had been recorded in his accounts at a cost of $50,000 and on which the accumulated depreciation had totaled $18,000. The partners agree on a valuation of $40,000. How should the store equipment be recorded in the accounts of the partnership?

4. All partners agree that accounts receivable of $10,000 invested by a partner will be collectible to the extent of 85%. How should the accounts receivable be recorded in the general ledger of the partnership?

5. What two principal factors should be considered in arriving at an agreement for the distribution of net income and net loss between the partners?

6. (a) What accounts are debited and credited to record a partner's cash withdrawal in lieu of salary? (b) What accounts are debited and credited to record the division of net income among partners at the end of the fiscal year? (c) The articles of copartnership provide for a salary allowance of $1,000 per month to partner X. If X withdrew only $750 per month, would this affect his share of the partnership net income?

7. (a) What is the purpose of providing for the allocation of a portion of partnership net income to the partners in the form of a salary and/or interest allowance? (b) What is the ultimate effect on the total amount of each partner's equity in the partnership if salary and/or interest allowances are treated as expenses rather than as distributions of net income?

8. Kramer, a partner in the firm of Johnson, Kramer, and Larson, sells his investment (capital balance of $25,000) to Parker. (a) Does the withdrawal of Kramer dissolve the partnership? (b) Are Johnson and Larson required to admit Parker as a partner?

385

9. Differentiate between the admission of a new partner to a partnership (a) by purchase of an interest from another partner and (b) by contribution of assets to the partnership.

10. Barnes and Caldwell are partners who share in net income equally and have capital balances of $20,000 and $10,000 respectively. Barnes, with the consent of Caldwell, sells one half of his interest to Porter. What entry is required on the partnership books if the sale price is (a) $8,000? (b) $12,000?

11. Why is it important to state all partnership assets in terms of current prices at the time of the admission of a new partner?

12. Define goodwill as the term is used in business.

13. (a) Differentiate between "dissolution" and "liquidation" of a partnership. (b) When a partnership is being liquidated, what is the process of realization?

14. In the liquidation process, (a) how are losses and gains on realization divided among the partners, and (b) how is cash distributed among the partners?

15. C and D are partners, sharing gains and losses equally. At the time they decide to terminate the partnership, their capital balances are $25,000 and $35,000 respectively. After all noncash assets are sold and all liabilities are paid, there is a cash balance of $70,000. (a) What is the amount of gain or loss on realization? (b) How should the gain or the loss be divided between C and D? (c) How should the cash be divided between C and D?

16. A, B, and C share equally in net income and net loss. After selling all of the assets for cash, dividing the losses on realization, and paying the liabilities, the balances in the capital accounts are as follows: A, $4,000, Dr.; B, $10,000, Cr.; C, $6,000, Cr. (a) What is the amount of cash on hand? (b) How should the cash be distributed?

17. X, Y, and Z are partners sharing income 2:1:2. After distribution of the firm's loss from liquidation, Z's capital account has a debit balance of $9,000. If Z is personally bankrupt and unable to pay any of the $9,000, how will the loss be distributed to X and Y?

EXERCISES

15-1. John Barton and Robert Grant decide to form a partnership by combining the assets of their separate businesses. Barton contributes the following assets to the partnership: cash $5,000; accounts receivable with a face amount of $20,000 and an allowance for doubtful accounts of $900; inventory with a cost of $17,500; and equipment with a cost of $16,000 and accumulated depreciation of $8,500. The partners agree that $400 of the accounts receivable are completely worthless and are not to be accepted by the partnership, that $700 is a reasonable allowance for the uncollectibility of the remaining accounts, that the inventory is to be recorded at the current market price of $18,250, and that the equipment is to be priced at $5,500. Present the entry, in general journal form, to record Barton's investment in the partnership accounts.

15-2. Mason and Norris form a partnership with investments of $40,000 and $60,000 respectively. Determine their participation in net income of $30,000 for the year under each of the following assumptions: (a) no agreement concerning division of income; (b) income divided in the ratio of their original capital investments; (c) interest at the rate of 6% allowed on original investments and the balance divided in the ratio of 2:1; (d) salary allowances of $5,000 and $9,000 and the balance divided equally; (e) allowance of interest at the rate of 6% on original investments, salary allowances of $5,000 and $9,000 respectively, and the balance divided equally.

15-3. Determine the participation of Mason and Norris in a net income of $9,000 for the year according to each of the five assumptions as to income division listed in Exercise 15-2.

15-4. The capital accounts of R. N. Evans and A. P. Flowers have balances of $17,500 and $22,000 respectively on January 1, the beginning of the current fiscal year. On March 1, Evans invested an additional $2,500. During the year Evans and Flowers withdrew $6,000 and $8,000 respectively, and net income for the year was $18,000. The articles of copartnership make no reference to the division of net income. (a) Present the journal entries to close (1) the expense and revenue summary account and (2) the drawing accounts. (b) Prepare a capital statement for the current year.

15-5. The capital accounts of Raymond Berry and John Callison have balances of $25,000 and $30,000 respectively. James Pence and William Quinn are to be admitted to the partnership. Pence purchases one fifth of Berry's interest for $7,000 and one third of Callison's interest for $14,000. Quinn is admitted to the partnership with an investment of $10,000, for which he is to receive an ownership equity of $10,000. (a) Present the entries in general journal form to record the admission to the partnership of (1) Pence and (2) Quinn. (b) What are the capital balances of each partner after the admission of Pence and Quinn?

15-6. Richard Underwood is to retire from the partnership of Underwood and Associates as of October 31, the end of the current fiscal year. After closing the accounts, the capital balances of the partners are as follows: Richard Underwood, $45,000; Eugene Vance, $30,000; and James Wright, $20,000. They have shared net income and net losses in the ratio of 3:2:2. The partners agree that the merchandise inventory should be decreased by $2,500 and that the allowance for doubtful accounts should be increased by $1,000. Underwood agrees to accept an interest-bearing note for $20,000 in partial settlement of his ownership equity. The remainder of his claim is to be paid in cash. Vance and Wright are to share equally in the net income or net loss of the new partnership. Present entries in general journal form to record (a) the adjustment of the assets to bring them into agreement with current fair prices and (b) the withdrawal of Underwood from the partnership.

387

15-7. Getman and Hiller, with capital balances of $12,000 and $15,000 respectively, decide to liquidate the partnership. After selling the noncash assets and paying the liabilities, there is $6,000 of cash remaining. If the partners share income and losses equally, how should the cash be distributed?

15-8. John Baker, Frank Case, and Harry Downs arrange to import and sell orchid corsages for a university dance. They agree to share the net income or net loss on the venture equally. Baker and Case advance $30 and $20 respectively of their own funds to pay for advertising and other expenses. After collecting for all sales and paying creditors, they have $200 in cash. (a) How should the money be distributed? (b) Assuming that they have only $20 instead of $200, how should the money be distributed? (c) Assuming that the money was distributed as determined in (b), do any of the three have claims against another and, if so, how much?

15-9. After closing the accounts preparatory to liquidating the partnership, the capital accounts of Jackson, Kramer, and Lake are $23,000, $18,000, and $9,000 respectively. Cash and noncash assets total $14,000 and $66,000 respectively. Amounts owing to creditors total $30,000. The partners share income and losses in the ratio of 3:2:1. The noncash assets are sold and sufficient cash is available to pay all of the creditors except one for $4,000. Determine how the claim of the creditors should be settled. Present calculations in good form.

PROBLEMS

The following additional problems for this chapter are located in Appendix C: 15-1B, 15-2B, 15-5B.

15-1A. Alan Kane and Fred Lang have decided to form a partnership. They have agreed that Kane is to invest $25,000 and that Lang is to invest $15,000. Kane is to devote full time to the business and Lang is to devote one-half time. The following plans for the division of income are being considered:

(a) Equal division.
(b) In the ratio of original investments.
(c) In the ratio of time devoted to the business.
(d) Interest of 5% on original investments and the remainder in the ratio of 3:2.
(e) Interest of 5% on original investments, salaries of $10,000 to Kane and $5,000 to Lang, and the remainder equally.
(f) Plan (e), except that Kane is also to be allowed a bonus equal to 10% of the amount by which net income exceeds the salary allowances.

388

Instructions:

Determine the division of net income under each of the following assumptions: net income of $24,000 and net income of $12,000. Present the data in tabular form, using the following columnar headings:

Plan	$24,000		$12,000	
	Kane	Lang	Kane	Lang

15-2A. On September 1 of the current year V. K. Vernon and H. A. Watson form a partnership.

Vernon invests certain business assets at valuations agreed upon, transfers business liabilities, and contributes sufficient cash to bring his total capital to $25,000. Details regarding the book values of the business assets and liabilities, and the agreed valuations, follow:

	Vernon's Ledger Balance	Agreed Valuation
Accounts Receivable....................	$10,600	$10,600
Allowance for Doubtful Accounts.........	500	800
Merchandise Inventory.................	17,000	15,500
Equipment...........................	15,000⎱	8,500
Accumulated Depreciation — Equipment..	8,000⎰	
Accounts Payable.....................	6,200	6,200
Notes Payable.......................	5,000	5,000

Watson agrees to invest merchandise inventory priced at $12,250 and $7,750 in cash.

The articles of copartnership include the following provisions regarding the division of net income: interest on original investment at 6%, salary allowances of $5,000 and $7,500 respectively, and the remainder in the ratio of 3:2.

Instructions:

(1) Give the entries, in general journal form, to record the investments of Vernon and Watson in the partnership accounts.

(2) Prepare a balance sheet as of September 1, the date of formation of the partnership.

(3) After adjustments and the closing of revenue and expense accounts at August 31, the end of the first full year of operations, the expense and revenue summary account has a credit balance of $20,200 and the drawing accounts have debit balances of $5,000 (Vernon) and $7,000 (Watson). Present the journal entries to close the expense and revenue summary account and the drawing accounts at August 31.

15-3 A. The accounts in the ledger of Barnes and Carr, attorneys-at-law, with the balances on December 31, the end of the current fiscal year after adjustments have been recorded, are as follows:

Cash.	$ 3,925
Accounts Receivable	5,200
Supplies.	475
Buildings.	29,000
Accumulated Depreciation — Buildings.	10,050
Office Equipment.	9,900
Accumulated Depreciation — Office Equipment.	1,500
Land.	6,250
Accounts Payable.	750
Salaries Payable.	650
Eugene Barnes, Capital.	20,000
Eugene Barnes, Drawing.	22,000
Frank Carr, Capital.	15,000
Frank Carr, Drawing.	16,000
Professional Fees.	63,975
Salary Expense.	13,950
Depreciation Expense — Buildings.	1,800
Property Tax Expense.	1,200
Heating and Lighting Expense.	700
Depreciation Expense — Office Equipment.	500
Supplies Expense.	450
Miscellaneous Expense.	575

389

Instructions:

(1) Prepare an income statement for the current fiscal year indicating the division of net income. The articles of copartnership provide for salary allowances of $15,000 to Barnes and $12,000 to Carr; that each partner be allowed 6% of his capital balance at the beginning of the fiscal year; and that the remaining net income or net loss be divided equally. An additional investment of $5,000 was made by Carr during the year.

(2) Prepare a capital statement for the current fiscal year.

(3) Prepare a balance sheet as of the end of the current fiscal year.

15-4A. J. L. Johns and B. K. Kemp have operated a successful firm for many years, sharing net income and net losses equally. R. E. Little is to be admitted to the partnership on April 1 of the current year in accordance with the following agreement:

(a) Assets and liabilities of the old partnership are to be valued at their book values as of March 31, except for the following:
   Accounts receivable amounting to $400 are to be written off and the allowance for doubtful accounts is to be increased to 5% of the remaining accounts.
   Merchandise inventory is to be priced at $16,900.
   Equipment is to be priced at $25,000.
(b) Goodwill of $15,000 is to be recognized as attributable to the firm of Johns and Kemp.
(c) Little is to purchase $10,000 of Kemp's ownership interest for $12,500 cash and to invest an additional $5,000 cash in the partnership for an ownership equity of $15,000.
(d) The income-sharing ratio of Johns, Kemp, and Little is to be 2:1:1.

The post-closing trial balance of Johns and Kemp as of March 31 follows:

Johns and Kemp
Post-Closing Trial Balance
March 31, 19 --

Cash.	1,810	
Accounts Receivable.	9,400	
Allowance for Doubtful Accounts.		250
Merchandise Inventory.	16,200	
Prepaid Insurance.	540	
Equipment.	48,750	
Accumulated Depreciation — Equipment.		27,750
Accounts Payable.		4,200
Salaries Payable.		600
J. L. Johns, Capital.		23,450
B. K. Kemp, Capital.		20,450
	76,700	76,700

Instructions:
(1) Present general journal entries as of March 31 to record the revaluations, using a temporary account entitled Asset Revaluations. The balance in the accumulated depreciation account is to be eliminated.
(2) Present the additional entries, in general journal form, to record the remaining transactions relating to the formation of the new partnership. Assume that all transactions occur on April 1.
(3) Present a balance sheet for the new partnership as of April 1.

15-5A. Bell, Carey, and Day decide to discontinue business operations as of July 31 and liquidate their partnership. The firm's post-closing trial balance at that date appears at the top of the next page.

Bell, Carey, and Day
Post-Closing Trial Balance
July 31, 19--

Cash	5,570	
Accounts Receivable	8,200	
Allowance for Doubtful Accounts		800
Notes Receivable	5,000	
Merchandise Inventory	24,700	
Prepaid Insurance	500	
Supplies	450	
Equipment	11,400	
Accumulated Depreciation — Equipment		6,800
Buildings	30,000	
Accumulated Depreciation — Buildings		12,000
Land	5,000	
Accounts Payable		5,500
Mortgage Note Payable		15,000
John Bell, Capital		21,200
Donald Carey, Capital		18,520
Robert Day, Capital		11,000
	90,820	90,820

The partners share net income and losses in the ratio 2:2:1. The realization and liquidation transactions are summarized as follows:

(a) Collected $6,900 of accounts receivable; the remainder are worthless.
(b) Collected $5,000 on notes receivable.
(c) Sold the merchandise for $21,720 cash.
(d) Realized $400 cash from cancellation of the insurance policies.
(e) Sold the supplies for $350 cash.
(f) Sold the equipment for $3,800 cash.
(g) Sold the land and buildings for $25,000, purchaser paying $10,000 cash and assuming the mortgage note. The mortgage holder released the partners from further liability.
(h) Paid miscellaneous expenses in connection with the sale of the assets, $520. (Charge to Loss and Gain on Realization.)
(i) Distributed the loss on realization to the partners' capital accounts.
(j) Paid the accounts payable in full.
(k) Distributed remaining cash to the partners.

Instructions:
(1) Set up T accounts for Cash, Loss and Gain on Realization, and a capital account for each partner.
(2) Record the July 31 balances in the T accounts.
(3) Present entries, in general journal form, to record the liquidation; post to the T accounts as appropriate; rule the accounts.
(4) Assuming that there had been a net loss of $46,300, instead of the amount determined above, prepare a complete summary of the liquidation in the form illustrated in the chapter. No entries are required.
(5) Assuming that there had been a net loss of $49,300, instead of the amount determined above, prepare a complete summary of the liquidation in the form illustrated in the chapter. No entries are required.

391

15-6A. On the date the partners in the firm of May, North, and Owen decide to liquidate the partnership, the partners have capital balances of $60,000, $35,000, and $25,000 respectively. The cash balance is $15,000, the book value of noncash assets totals $125,000, and liabilities total $20,000. The partners share income and losses in the ratio of 3:1:1.

Instructions:
Present the entries, in general journal form, to record the following:
(1) The sale of the assets.
(2) The distribution of the loss or gain on realization.
(3) The payment of creditors.
(4) The distribution of cash to the partners according to each of the assumptions described below.
Use "Assets" as the account title for the noncash assets and "Liabilities" as the account title for creditors' claims. It is suggested that summaries similar to those illustrated in this chapter be prepared as a basis for the entries.

(A) All of the other assets are sold for $150,000 in cash.
(B) All of the other assets are sold for $50,000 in cash.
(C) All of the other assets are sold for $20,000 in cash. After the available cash is paid to the partners:
    (a) The partner with the debit capital balance pays the amount owed to the firm.
    (b) The additional cash is distributed.
(D) All of the other assets are sold for $15,000 in cash. After the available cash is paid to the partners:
    (a) The partner with the debit capital balance pays 50% of his deficiency to the firm.
    (b) The remaining partners absorb the remaining deficiency as a loss.
    (c) The additional cash is distributed.

16

Corporations-- organization and operation

Characteristics of a corporation

In the Dartmouth College Case in 1819, Chief Justice Marshall stated: "A corporation is an artificial being, invisible, intangible, and existing only in contemplation of the law." The concept underlying this definition has become the foundation for the prevailing legal doctrine that a corporation is an artificial person, created by law and having a distinct existence separate and apart from the natural persons who are responsible for its creation and operation. Almost all large business enterprises in the United States are organized as corporations.

Corporations may be classified in a number of ways. For example, the term *public corporation* may refer to a municipality or other political division, and the term *private corporation* may refer to all corporations other than incorporated governmental units. On the other hand, business corporations whose ownership is widely held may be termed *public* or *open corporations*, and those with a relatively small group of owners may be termed *private* or *close corporations*. Corporations may also be classified as profit or nonprofit. *Profit corporations* are organized for the purpose of making a profit. *Nonprofit corporations* include those organized for charitable, educational, or other philanthropic purposes. Regardless of the nature or the purpose of a corporation, it is created in accordance with the statutes and is a separate legal entity.

As a legal entity, the corporation has certain characteristics that distinguish it from other types of business organizations. The most important characteristics with accounting implications are described briefly in the following paragraphs.

Separate legal existence. The corporation may acquire, own, and dispose of property in its corporate name. It may also incur liabilities and enter into other contracts in accordance with the stipulations in the *charter* or *articles of incorporation* received from the state.

Transferable units of ownership. The ownership of a corporation, of which there may be several categories or classes, is divided into transferable units known as *shares of stock*. Each share of stock of a particular class has the same rights and privileges as every other share of the same class. The owners of the corporation, known as *stockholders or shareholders*, may buy and sell their shares without interfering with the activities of the corporation. The millions of transactions that occur daily on stock exchanges are independent transactions between buyers and sellers. Thus, in contrast to the partnership, the life term of the corporation is not affected by the withdrawal of an owner.

Limited liability of stockholders. A corporation is responsible for its own acts and obligations, and therefore its creditors ordinarily may not look beyond the assets of the corporation for satisfaction of their claims. Thus, the financial loss that a stockholder may suffer is limited to the amount of his investment. The phenomenal growth of the corporate form of business would have been impossible without this feature.

Working organization. The stockholders, who are the owners of the corporation, exercise control over the management of corporate affairs indirectly by electing a *board of directors*. The board of directors meets from time to time to determine the corporate policies and to select the officers who manage the corporation. The chart at the right depicts the organizational structure of a corporation.

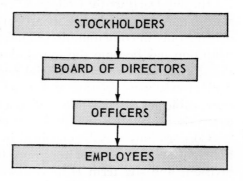

Organizational structure of a corporate enterprise

Additional taxes. A corporation is required to pay a charter fee to the state at the time of its organization and an annual tax thereafter. If the corporation does business in states other than the one in which it is incorporated, it may also be required to pay annual taxes to such states. The earnings of a corporation are subject to the federal income tax. When the remaining earnings are distributed to stockholders as dividends, they are again taxed as income to the individuals receiving them.

Under certain conditions specified in the Internal Revenue Code, corporations with not more than ten stockholders may elect to be treated as a partnership for income tax purposes. The income of a corporation electing this optional treatment must be included in the taxable income of its stockholders, regardless of whether or not the income is distributed to them and the corporation pays no income tax.

Governmental regulation. Being creatures of the state and being owned by stockholders who possess limited liability, corporations have less freedom of action than sole proprietorships and partnerships. They may be restricted in such matters as the amount of real estate they may own, the amount of earnings that they may distribute, and the extent to which they may reacquire their own stock.

Corporate capital

The owners' equity in a corporation is commonly called *stockholders' equity, shareholders' equity, shareholders' investment,* or *capital.* As in the case of sole proprietorships and partnerships, the equity of the owners is equivalent to the excess of assets over liabilities. In a sole proprietorship, the capital is reported in the balance sheet as a single item; in a partnership, the proprietary interest of each partner is stated separately. The amounts reported represent the investment at the balance sheet date, no distinction being made between contributions of capital and net income retained in the business. In contrast, the stockholders' equity section of corporation balance sheets is divided into subsections based on the source of the capital. In addition, the identity of the owners is not disclosed on the balance sheet.

The two principal sources of corporate capital are (1) investments contributed by the stockholders and (2) net income retained in the business. The capital acquired from the stockholders, sometimes referred to as *paid-in capital,* is recorded in accounts maintained for each class of stock. If there is only one class of stock, the account is entitled Common Stock. At the end of each fiscal year, the balance in Expense and Revenue Summary is transferred to an account entitled Retained Earnings. Distributions of net income to the stockholders are debited to Retained Earnings. The stockholders' equity section of the balance sheet presented below illustrates the two principal subdivisions of capital.

Stockholders' Equity

Common stock	$150,000
Retained earnings	30,000
Total stockholders' equity	$180,000

If the retained earnings account has a debit balance, it is termed a *deficit* and is deducted from the common stock to arrive at the total stockholders' equity.

Until recent years, the term customarily applied to retained earnings was *earned surplus*. The meaning of the older term was often misunderstood by readers of financial statements and has to a great extent been supplanted. Other terms frequently employed include *earnings retained for use in the business*, *earnings reinvested in the business*, *earnings employed in the business*, and *accumulated earnings*.

Characteristics of stock

The general term applied to the shares of ownership of a corporation is *capital stock*. The number of shares that a corporation is *authorized* to issue is set forth in its charter. The term *issued* is applied to the shares issued to the stockholders. A corporation may, under various circumstances discussed later in the chapter, reacquire some of the stock that it has issued. The stock remaining in the hands of the stockholders is then referred to as the stock *outstanding*.

The shares of capital stock are commonly assigned an arbitrary amount, known as *par*. The par amount is printed on the *stock certificate*, which is the evidence of ownership issued to the stockholder. Stock may also be issued without par, in which case it is known as *no-par* stock. Many states provide that no-par stock must be assigned a *stated value* by the board of directors, which makes it similar to par stock.

Because of the limited liability feature granted stockholders, the creditors of a corporation have no claim against the personal assets of the stockholders. To afford some protection to the creditors, the law requires that some specific minimum contribution by the stockholders be retained by the corporation for the protection of its creditors. This amount, called *legal capital*, varies among the states but ordinarily includes the par or stated value of the shares.

Classes of stock. The principal basic rights that accompany ownership of a share of stock are (1) the right to vote, (2) the right to share in distributions of earnings, (3) the right to maintain the same fractional interest in the corporation by purchasing a proportionate number of shares of any additional issuances of stock (*preemptive right*), and (4) the right to share in assets upon liquidation.

If a corporation issues only common stock, each share has equal rights. In order to appeal to a broader investment market, a corporation may provide for one or more classes of stock with various preferential rights. The preference usually relates to the right to share in distributions of earnings. Such stock is called *preferred stock* or *preference stock*.

The authority to distribute earnings to the stockholders rests with the board of directors. Distributions of earnings are called *dividends*, and the directors are said to *declare a dividend*. A corporation can make no guarantee that its operations will be profitable, and hence it cannot guarantee dividends to its stockholders. Furthermore, the directors have wide discretionary powers in determining the extent to which earnings should be retained by the corporation to provide for expansion, to offset possible future losses, or to provide for other contingencies.

A corporation with both preferred stock and common stock may declare dividends on the common only after it meets the requirements of the stipulated dividend on the preferred. For example, assume that the Apex Corporation has outstanding 1,000 shares of stock with a preference to a $6 dividend and 4,000 shares of common stock. In its first three years of operation, it earned $12,000, $25,000, and $60,000 respectively and distributed 60% of the earnings each year. The distribution of the dividends among the two classes of stock is tabulated as follows:

	FIRST YEAR	SECOND YEAR	THIRD YEAR
Net income....................	$12,000	$25,000	$60,000
Percent to be distributed..........	60%	60%	60%
Amount of dividend distribution.....	$ 7,200	$15,000	$36,000
Dividends on preferred ($6 per share).	6,000	6,000	6,000
Balance to common (4,000 shares)....	$ 1,200	$ 9,000	$30,000
Dividends per share on common.....	$ .30	$ 2.25	$ 7.50

Participating and nonparticipating preferred stock. In the foregoing illustration the holders of preferred stock received an annual dividend of $6 per share in each of the three years, in contrast to the common stockholders, whose annual per share dividends were $.30, $2.25, and $7.50. It is apparent from the example that holders of preferred stock have relatively greater assurance of receiving dividends but that holders of common stock have the potentiality of receiving larger dividends. The preferred stockholders' preferential right to dividends is ordinarily limited to a specified amount, which was assumed to be the case in the example. Such stock is said to be *nonparticipating*.

Preferred stock which provides for the possibility of dividends in excess of a specified amount is said to be *participating*. Preferred shares may participate with common shares to varying degrees, and the contract must be examined to determine the extent of this participation. To illustrate, assume that the contract covering the preferred stock of the Apex Corporation in the preceding illustration provides that if the total dividends to be distributed exceed the regular preferred dividend and a comparable dividend on common, the preferred shall share ratably with

397

the common in the excess. In accordance with such terms, the $36,000 dividend distribution in the third year would be allocated as follows:

	To PREFERRED	To COMMON	TOTAL
Regular dividend to preferred (1,000 × $6)...	$ 6,000		$ 6,000
Comparable dividend to common (4,000×$6)		$24,000	24,000
Remaining $6,000 to all shares ratably.......	1,200	4,800	6,000
Total dividends......................	$ 7,200	$28,800	$36,000
Dividends per share....................	$ 7.20	$ 7.20	

Cumulative and noncumulative preferred stock. As was indicated in the previous section, most preferred stock is nonparticipating. Provision is usually made, however, to assure the continuation of the preferential dividend right in the event the dividend is *passed* (not declared) in any particular year. This is accomplished by providing that dividends may not be paid on the common stock if any preferred dividends are in arrears. Such preferred stock is known as *cumulative*. To illustrate, assume that a corporation has outstanding 5,000 shares of cumulative preferred 5% stock of $100 par and that dividends have been passed for the preceding two years. In the current year it will be necessary to declare preferred dividends of $50,000 for the past two years and $25,000 for the current year before any dividends can be declared on the common stock. Preferred stock that does not have this cumulative right is called *noncumulative*.

Other preferential rights. Thus far the discussion of preferential rights of preferred stock has related to dividend distributions. Preferred stock may also be given a preference over common stock in its claim to assets upon liquidation of the corporation. If the assets remaining after payment of creditors are not sufficient to return the capital contributions of both classes of stock, payment would first be made to the preferred stockholders and any balance remaining would go to the common stockholders. Another customary difference between preferred stock and common stock is that the former may have no voting rights. It is not unusual for a corporation to have more than one class of preferred stock, with differences as to the amount of dividends, priority of claims upon liquidation, and voting rights. In any particular case the rights of a class of stock may be determined by reference to the charter, the stock certificate, or some other abstract of the agreement.

Issuing stock at par

The entries to record the investment of capital in a corporation are similar to those of other types of business organizations in that cash and other assets received are debited and any liabilities assumed are credited. The credit to capital differs, however, in that there are accounts for each class of stock. To illustrate, assume that the Collins Corporation, organized on June 20 with an authorization of 5,000 shares of preferred stock of $100 par and 50,000 shares of common stock of $20 par, issues one half of each authorization at par for cash on July 1. The entry to record the stockholders' investment and the receipt of the cash, in general journal form, is as follows:

July 1 Cash.................................... 750,000		
Preferred Stock.............................		250,000
Common Stock.............................		500,000

The capital stock accounts (Preferred Stock, Common Stock) are controlling accounts. It is necessary to maintain records of the name and the address of each stockholder and the number of shares held in order to issue dividend checks, proxy forms, and financial reports. The accounts with individual stockholders are kept in a subsidiary ledger known as the *stockholders ledger*.

Issuing stock at a premium or discount

Stock is often issued by a corporation at a price above or below par. When it is issued above par, the excess of the contract price over par is termed a *premium*. When it is issued at a price that is below par, the difference is called a *discount*. Thus, if stock with a par of $50 is issued at $60, the amount of the premium is $10; if the same stock is issued at $45, the amount of the discount is $5.

Theoretically, there is no reason for a newly organized corporation to issue stock at a price other than par. The par designation is merely a part of the plan of dividing capital into a number of units of ownership. Hence, a group of persons investing their funds in a new corporation might all be expected to pay par for the shares. The fortunes of an enterprise do not remain static, however, even when it is still in the process of organizing. The changing prospects for its future success may affect the price per share at which the incorporators can secure additional investors.

After a corporation has become established, a need for additional capital may arise. For example, losses during the early period may have depleted working capital, or the operations may have been successful enough to warrant a substantial expansion of plant and equipment. If the funds are to be obtained by the issuance of additional stock, it is apparent that the current price at which the original stock is selling in the market will affect the price that can be obtained for the new shares.

Generally speaking, the price at which stock can be sold by a corporation is influenced by (1) the financial condition, the earnings record, and the dividend record of the corporation, (2) its potential earning power, (3) the availability of money for investment purposes, and (4) general business and economic conditions and prospects.

399

Premium on stock. When capital stock is issued at a premium, cash or other assets are debited for the amount received, the stock account is credited for par, and a premium account is credited for the premium. For example, if the Wagner Corporation issues 1,000 shares of $100 par preferred stock at $102, the entry to record the transaction would be as follows, in general journal form:

Cash...	102,000	
Preferred Stock.....................................		100,000
Premium on Preferred Stock.........................		2,000

The premium of $2,000 is a part of the investment of the stockholders and is therefore a part of paid-in capital. It is distinguished from the capital stock account because ordinarily it is not a part of legal capital and in many states may be used as a basis for dividends to stockholders. If the premium is returned to stockholders as a dividend at a later date, it should be made quite clear that the dividend is not a distribution of earnings but a return of paid-in capital.

Discount on stock. Some states do not permit the issuance of stock at a discount; in others, it may be done only under specified conditions. When stock is issued at less than its par, it is considered to be fully paid as between the corporation and the stockholder. In some states, however, the stockholders are contingently liable to creditors for the amount of the discount; that is, if the corporation is liquidated and the assets are insufficient to pay creditors in full, the stockholders may be assessed for an additional contribution up to the amount of the discount on their stock.

When capital stock is issued at a discount, cash or other assets are debited for the amount received, a discount account is debited for the amount of the discount, and the capital stock account is credited for par. For example, if the Wagner Corporation issues 20,000 shares of $25 par common stock at $22, the entry to record the transaction would be as follows, in general journal form:

Cash...	440,000	
Discount on Common Stock...........................	60,000	
Common Stock.....................................		500,000

The discount of $60,000 is a contra paid-in capital account and must be offset against Common Stock to arrive at the amount actually invested by the holders of common stock. The discount should not be listed on the balance sheet as an asset, nor should it be amortized against revenue as though it were an expense.

The stockholders' equity section of the balance sheet of the Wagner Corporation, which appears at the top of the next page, illustrates the manner in which discount and premium may be presented on the balance sheet.

Paid-in capital:
Preferred 6% stock, cumulative, $100 par
 (1,000 shares authorized and issued)... $100,000
Premium on preferred stock............   2,000 $102,000

Common stock, $25 par (50,000 shares
 authorized, 20,000 shares issued)...... $500,000
Less discount on common stock........   60,000   440,000
 Total paid-in capital............... $542,000
Retained earnings......................   76,000
Total stockholders' equity............... $618,000

The stockholders' equity section appearing below illustrates the reporting of a deficit and some variations in terminology from that in the foregoing example.

Shareholders' Equity

Paid-in capital:
Preferred 7% stock, cumulative, $50 par
 (5,000 shares authorized and issued).. $ 250,000
Excess of issuance price of stock over par   20,000 $ 270,000

Common stock, $10 par (200,000 shares
 authorized, 100,000 shares issued)..... $1,000,000
Excess of par over issuance price of stock   100,000   900,000
 Total paid in by stockholders........ $1,170,000
Less deficit..........................   55,000
Total shareholders' equity.............. $1,115,000

Issuing stock for assets other than cash

When capital stock is issued in exchange for assets other than cash, such as land, buildings, and equipment, the assets received should be recorded at their fair market price. As a basis for illustration, assume that on December 5 the Powell Corporation acquired buildings and land with a fair market price of $220,000 and $40,000 respectively, in exchange for 2,000 shares of $100 par common stock. The transaction would be recorded as follows:

Dec.	5	Buildings..............................	220,000	
		Land..................................	40,000	
		Common Stock........................		200,000
		Premium on Common Stock...........		60,000

The determination of the fair market price of the assets is the responsibility of the board of directors. It is not always possible to make an objective determination, but if shares of stock are also being issued for cash at about the same time, the price of the stock may provide an indication of the proper valuation of the assets.

No-par stock

In the early days of rapid industrial expansion and increasing use of the corporate form of business organization, it was customary to assign a par of $100 to shares of stock. It is not surprising that unsophisticated investors, mistakenly considering "par value" to be the equivalent of "value," were often induced to invest in mining and other highly speculative enterprises by the simple means of offering $100 par stock at "bargain" prices. Another misleading practice was the use of par in assigning highly inflated values to assets acquired in exchange for stock. For example, stock with a total par of $1,000,000 might be issued in exchange for patents, mineral rights, or other properties with a conservatively estimated value of $50,000. The assets would be recorded at the full par of $1,000,000, whereas in reality the stock had been issued at a discount of $950,000. Balance sheets that were "window-dressed" in this manner were obviously unreliable.

It was to combat such abuses and also to eliminate the troublesome discount liability of stockholders that stock without par was conceived. The issuance of stock without par was first permitted by New York in 1912. At present its use is authorized in nearly all of the states.

The extent to which the expected benefits have materialized is difficult to determine. Over the years questionable practices in the issuance of securities have been eliminated to a considerable degree. Today federal and state laws and rules imposed by organized stock exchanges and governmental agencies such as the Securities and Exchange Commission combine to protect the investor from misrepresentations that were not uncommon in earlier days.

Corporations may issue both preferred and common stock without par. Preferred stock is ordinarily assigned a par, however. When no-par stock is issued, the entire proceeds may be credited to the capital stock account. For example, if the Jackson Corporation issued 1,000 shares of no-par common stock on June 20 at $28 per share and an additional 1,000 shares on July 30 at $26 per share, the entries would be as follows, in general journal form:

June 20 Cash..	28,000	
Common Stock...............................		28,000
July 30 Cash..	26,000	
Common Stock...............................		26,000

The laws of some states require that the entire proceeds from the issuance of no-par stock be regarded as legal capital. The entries above are in conformity with this principle, which also conforms to the original concept of no-par stock. In other states no-par stock may be assigned a stated value per share, and the excess of the proceeds over the stated value may be credited to Paid-in Capital in Excess of Stated Value. Assuming that in the example above the stated value is $10 and the board of directors wishes to credit the common stock for stated value, the transactions would be recorded as follows, in general journal form:

```
June 20  Cash.........................................  28,000
              Common Stock...............................              10,000
              Paid-in Capital in Excess of Stated Value........              18,000

July 30  Cash.........................................  26,000
              Common Stock...............................              10,000
              Paid-in Capital in Excess of Stated Value........              16,000
```

It is readily apparent that the accounting for no-par stock with a stated value may follow the same pattern as the accounting for par stock.

Subscriptions and stock issuance

In some situations involving the initial issue of capital stock or subsequent issuances where the stockholders have waived the preemptive right, a corporation may sell its stock to an *underwriter*. The underwriter then resells the shares to investors at a price high enough to provide him with a profit from the sale. Under these circumstances, the corporation is relieved of the task of marketing the stock; it receives the entire amount of cash without delay and can proceed immediately with its plans for the use of the funds.

In other situations a corporation may sell its stock directly to investors. Ordinarily the investor first enters into an agreement with the corporation to *subscribe* to shares at a specified price per share. The terms may provide for payment in full at some future date or for installment payments over a period of time.

The amount of the subscriptions represents an asset to the corporation. As the subscriptions are received, they are debited to the asset account Stock Subscriptions Receivable and are credited to the capital stock account Stock Subscribed. If there is more than one class of stock, a subscriptions receivable account and a stock subscribed account should be maintained for each class.

When stock is subscribed for at a price above or below par, the stock subscriptions receivable account is debited for the subscription price rather than par. The stock subscribed account is credited at par, and the difference between the subscription price and par is debited to a discount account or credited to a premium account, as the case may be.

The stock subscriptions receivable account is a controlling account. The individual accounts with each subscriber are maintained in a subsidiary ledger known as a *subscribers ledger*. It is used in much the same manner as the accounts receivable ledger.

After a subscriber completes his agreed payments, the corporation issues the stock certificate. The stock subscribed account is then debited for the total par of the shares issued, and the capital stock account is credited for the same amount.

As the basis for illustrating the entries for subscriptions and stock issuance, assume that the newly organized Carson Corporation receives subscriptions, collects cash, and issues stock certificates in accordance with the transactions described below. The required entries, in general journal form, appear after the statement of the transaction.

1. Received subscriptions to 10,000 shares of $20 par common stock from various subscribers at $21 per share, with a down payment of 50% of the subscription price.

March 1	Common Stock Subscriptions Receivable..	210,000	
	Common Stock Subscribed............		200,000
	Premium on Common Stock..........		10,000
1	Cash...............................	105,000	
	Common Stock Subscriptions Receivable		105,000

2. Received 25% of subscription price from all subscribers.

May 1	Cash..............................	52,500	
	Common Stock Subscriptions Receivable		52,500

3. Received final 25% of subscription price from all subscribers and issued the stock certificates.

July 1	Cash..............................	52,500	
	Common Stock Subscriptions Receivable		52,500
1	Common Stock Subscribed.............	200,000	
	Common Stock.....................		200,000

A balance sheet prepared after the transactions of March 1 would list the subscriptions receivable as a current asset and the stock subscribed and the premium as paid-in capital. While it is true that the entire amount has not been "paid-in" in cash, the claim against the subscribers is an asset of equivalent value. The presentation of the items in the balance sheet of the Carson Corporation as of March 1 is illustrated below.

Carson Corporation
Balance Sheet
March 1, 19 ――

Assets		Stockholders' Equity	
Current assets:		Paid-in capital:	
Cash....................	$105,000	Common stock subscribed..	$200,000
Common stock subscriptions		Premium on common stock.	10,000
receivable..............	105,000		
Total assets...............	$210,000	Total stockholders' equity....	$210,000

After all the subscriptions have been collected, the common stock subscriptions receivable account will be in balance. The stock certificates will then be issued and the common stock subscribed account will be in balance. It should be noted that the ultimate effect of the series of transactions is a debit to Cash of $210,000, a credit to Common Stock of $200,000, and a credit to Premium on Common Stock of $10,000.

Treasury stock

A corporation may reacquire some of its own outstanding stock by purchase or by donation from its stockholders. It may also accept shares of its own stock in payment of a debt owed by a stockholder, which in essence is much the same as acquisition by purchase. The term *treasury stock* may be applied only to (1) stock of the issuing corporation, (2) that has been issued as fully paid, (3) that has been subsequently reacquired by the corporation, and (4) that has not been canceled or reissued.

Treasury stock is not an asset. A corporation cannot own a part of itself. Treasury stock has no voting rights, it does not have the preemptive right to participate in additional issuances of stock, nor does it generally participate in dividend distributions. When a corporation purchases its own stock, it is returning capital to the stockholders from whom the purchase was made. If stockholders donate stock to the corporation, the total capital of the corporation is not affected; only the number of shares outstanding is reduced.

Corporations sometimes incorrectly list treasury stock on the balance sheet as a current asset if they expect to sell it in the near future. The justification advanced for such treatment is that the stock is a readily available source of cash and is no different from a temporary investment in stock of another corporation. The same argument might well be extended to authorized but unissued stock, which is obviously indefensible. It is generally agreed among accountants that treasury stock should not be reported as an asset.

405

Purchased treasury stock

Although there are some legal restrictions on the practice, corporations may in general purchase shares of their own stock from stockholders. There are various reasons why a corporation may buy its own stock. For example, it may be to provide shares for resale to employees, for reissuance to employees as a bonus, or to support the market price of the stock. There are several methods of accounting for the purchase and the resale of treasury stock. A commonly used method, known as the *cost basis*, is illustrated in the following paragraphs.

When the stock is purchased, the account Treasury Stock is debited for its cost. The par and the price at which the stock was originally issued are ignored. When the stock is resold, Treasury Stock is credited at the price paid for it, and the difference between the price paid and the selling price is debited or credited to an account entitled Paid-in Capital from Sale of Treasury Stock.

As a basis for illustration, assume that the paid-in capital of the Garner Corporation is composed of common stock and its premium, as shown at the top of the following page.

Common Stock, $25 par (20,000 shares authorized and issued)..... $500,000
Premium on Common Stock.................................... 25,000

The assumed transactions involving treasury stock and the required entries in general journal form are as follows:

1. Purchased 1,000 shares of treasury stock at $40; total $40,000.

Treasury Stock................................... 40,000
    Cash....................................... 40,000

2. Sold 200 shares of treasury stock at $50; total $10,000.

Cash... 10,000
    Treasury Stock............................. 8,000
    Paid-in Capital from Sale of Treasury Stock.......... 2,000

3. Sold 200 shares of treasury stock at $36; total $7,200.

Cash... 7,200
Paid-in Capital from Sale of Treasury Stock........... 800
    Treasury Stock............................. 8,000

The additional capital obtained through the sale of treasury stock is reported in the paid-in capital section of the balance sheet, and the cost of the treasury stock on hand is deducted from the total of the capital accounts. After the three foregoing transactions were completed, the stockholders' equity section of the balance sheet would appear as shown below.

Stockholders' Equity

Paid-in capital:

Common stock, $25 par (20,000 shares authorized and issued)............	$500,000	
Premium on common stock..........	25,000	$525,000
From sale of treasury stock...........		1,200
Total paid-in capital..............		$526,200
Retained earnings....................		120,000
Total......................		$646,200
Deduct treasury stock (600 shares at cost).		24,000
Total stockholders' equity.............		$622,200

The stockholders' equity section of the balance sheet indicates that 20,000 shares of stock were issued, of which 600 are held as treasury stock. The number of shares outstanding is therefore 19,400. If cash dividends were declared at this time, the declaration would apply to 19,400 shares. Similarly, 19,400 shares could be voted at a stockholders' meeting.

If treasury stock transactions result in a shrinkage of capital, the net decrease may be reported as a reduction in paid-in capital, or it may be debited to Retained Earnings.

Donated treasury stock

Stockholders occasionally donate shares of stock to the corporation for resale. This generally happens when a corporation that has issued large blocks of stock in exchange for plant and equipment, an invention, mineral rights, or other noncash assets is in need of working capital and encounters difficulty in finding subscribers willing to invest cash equal to the par of the stock. As a means of avoiding the difficulty of selling new stock at a discount, the original stockholders may donate a portion of their stock to the corporation and the corporation may then resell it at any price without the purchaser incurring a contingent liability to creditors. The donating stockholders may actually incur little financial sacrifice by their action.

One of the acceptable methods of accounting for donated stock requires no entry at the time of the donation, except for a memorandum of the number of shares. As the treasury stock is sold, the proceeds are credited to a paid-in capital account entitled Donated Capital.

As a basis for illustration, assume that the Thomas Corporation originally issued 50,000 shares of $25 par common stock at par for oil properties. The stockholders then donate 10,000 shares to the corporation, which the corporation resells for cash. The entries required, in general journal form, and the paid-in capital section of the balance sheet after each entry are as follows:

1. **Issued 50,000 shares of $25 par common stock for oil properties.**

Oil Properties.	1,250,000	
Common Stock.		1,250,000

   Paid-in capital:
   Common stock, $25 par (200,000 shares authorized, 50,000 shares issued) $1,250,000

2. **Received 10,000 shares of stock from stockholders.**
   (Memo) Received 10,000 shares as a donation.

   Paid-in capital:
   Common stock, $25 par (200,000 shares authorized, 50,000 shares issued less 10,000 shares of treasury stock acquired by donation) $1,250,000

3. **Sold treasury stock at $20 per share for cash.**

Cash.	200,000	
Donated Capital.		200,000

   Paid-in capital:
Common stock, $25 par (200,000 shares authorized, 50,000 shares issued).	$1,250,000
Donated capital.	200,000
Total paid-in capital.	$1,450,000

Equity per share

The amount appearing on the balance sheet as total stockholders' equity can be stated in terms of the equity allocable to a single share of stock. The term frequently used in referring to *equity per share* is *book value.* The latter term is not only less descriptive; it may also be misleading because of its connotation of "worth." It may be said to be an accurate measure of value only to the extent that it represents the amount that would be distributed for a share of stock if the corporation were to liquidate without incurring any expenses, losses, or gains in disposing of its assets and paying its liabilities.

When there is only one class of stock, the equity per share is determined by dividing total stockholders' equity by the number of shares outstanding. For a corporation with both preferred and common stock, it is necessary first to allocate the total equity between the two classes. In making the allocation, consideration must be given to the liquidation rights of the preferred stock, including any participating and cumulative dividend features. After allocating the total to the two classes, the equity per share of each class may then be determined by dividing the respective amounts by the related number of shares outstanding. To illustrate, assume that as of December 31 of the current year the Stuart Corporation has both preferred and common shares outstanding, that there are no preferred dividends in arrears, and that the preferred stock is entitled to receive $105 upon liquidation. The amounts comprising stockholders' equity at the same date and the computation of equity per share are as follows:

STOCKHOLDERS' EQUITY

Preferred 6% stock, cumulative, $100 par (1,000 shares outstanding)......	$100,000
Premium on preferred stock..	2,000
Common stock, $10 par (50,000 shares outstanding).................	500,000
Premium on common stock...	50,000
Retained earnings..	253,000
Total equity..	$905,000

ALLOCATION OF TOTAL EQUITY TO PREFERRED AND COMMON STOCK

Total equity...	$905,000
Allocated to preferred stock:	
Liquidation price...	105,000
Allocated to common stock.......................................	$800,000

EQUITY PER SHARE

Preferred stock: $105,000 ÷ 1,000 shares = $105 per share
Common stock: $800,000 ÷ 50,000 shares = $ 16 per share

If in the foregoing illustration the preferred stock is assumed to be entitled to dividends in arrears in the event of liquidation, and if dividends are in arrears for two years, the computations would be as shown at the top of the next page.

Total equity..		$905,000
Allocated to preferred stock:		
Liquidation price......................................	$105,000	
Dividends in arrears..................................	12,000	117,000
Allocated to common stock.............................		$788,000

EQUITY PER SHARE

Preferred stock: $117,000 ÷ 1,000 shares = $117.00 per share
Common stock: $788,000 ÷ 50,000 shares = $ 15.76 per share

Equity per share, particularly of common stock, is frequently stated in corporation reports to stockholders and quoted in the financial press. It is one of the many factors affecting the *market price*, that is, the price at which a share is bought and sold at a particular moment. However, it should be noted that earning capacity, dividend rates, and prospects for the future usually affect the market price of listed stocks to a much greater extent than does equity per share. So-called "glamour" stocks may at times sell at more than ten times the amount of the equity per share. On the other hand, stock in corporations that have suffered severe declines in earnings or whose future prospects appear to be unfavorable may sell at prices which are substantially less than the equity per share.

409

Organization costs

Expenditures incurred in organizing a corporation, such as legal fees, taxes and fees paid to the state, and promotional costs, are charged to an intangible asset account entitled Organization Costs. Although such costs have no realizable value upon liquidation, they are as essential as plant and equipment and they benefit the corporation as long as it continues its operations. If the life of a corporation is limited to a definite period of time, the organization costs can be amortized over the period by annual charges to an expense account. However, the length of life of most corporations is not determinable in advance.

The Internal Revenue Code permits the amortization of organization costs ratably over a period of not less than sixty months beginning with the month the corporation commences business. Although such a procedure has little theoretical justification, it is generally accepted in accounting practice. The magnitude of such costs is relatively minor in relation to the other assets, and the amount of the periodic amortization ordinarily has an insignificant effect on net income.

QUESTIONS

1. Why are most large business enterprises organized as corporations?

2. Davis is a partner in Davis and Ellis, in which his capital interest is $30,000. He also owns some shares of stock in Lincoln Company acquired at a cost of $7,500. He has other assets worth $50,000. (a) If Lincoln Company fails, what is the maximum loss Davis might have to absorb? (b) If Davis and Ellis fails, what is the maximum loss Davis might have to absorb? (c) If Davis dies, what effect would his death have on Lincoln Company? on the Davis and Ellis partnership?

3. Why is it said that the earnings of a corporation are subject to "double taxation"? Discuss.

4. What are the two principal sources of corporate capital?

5. If the retained earnings account has a debit balance, what is this balance called?

6. The Palmer Insurance Company has been authorized to issue 100,000 shares of $100 par common stock. On May 10, ten years ago, it issued 25,000 shares; on July 20, four years later, it issued 15,000 shares; and on April 2 of the current year, it reacquired 1,000 shares. What is the number of shares (a) authorized, (b) issued, and (c) outstanding after the last transaction?

7. The Dixon Company has issued common stock with a par of $10, while a competitor has issued common stock with a par of $25. Do the pars give any indication as to which stock is preferable as an investment?

8. Differentiate between common stock and preferred stock.

9. What is (a) participating preferred stock and (b) cumulative preferred stock?

10. What are some of the factors that influence the market price of a corporation's stock?

11. When a corporation issues stock at a premium, does the premium constitute income? Explain.

12. A corporation's balance sheet lists: Preferred 7% stock, $300,000; Premium on preferred stock, $40,000; Common stock, $500,000; Discount on common stock, $20,000; and Retained earnings, $120,000. (a) What is the amount of paid-in capital attributable to the preferred stock? (b) What is the amount of paid-in capital attributable to the common stock? (c) What is the amount of earnings retained for use in the business? (d) What is the total stockholders' equity?

13. Land with a fair market price of $52,500 is acquired by a corporation in return for 500 shares of its $100 par, 6% preferred stock. At what figure should the land be recorded by the corporation?

14. Bancraft Corporation acquires machinery from Marshall Corporation in return for 1,000 shares of Bancraft's $25 par common stock. The book value of the machinery in the accounts of Marshall Corporation was $27,500, and the Bancraft common stock is quoted on the stock exchange at $40. At what figure should the machinery be recorded?

15. (a) Define treasury stock. (b) In what way is treasury stock different from unissued stock? (c) Suggest reasons why a corporation might purchase treasury stock.

16. A corporation purchases 100 shares of its own $100 par common stock for $12,500, recording it at cost. (a) What effect does this transaction have on revenue or expense of the period? (b) What effect does it have on stockholders' equity?

17. The treasury stock in Question 16 is resold for $15,000. (a) What is the effect on revenue of the period? (b) What is the effect on stockholders' equity?

18. Nance Company issued 50,000 shares of $20 par common stock and subsequently reacquired 1,000 shares, which it now holds as treasury stock. If the board of directors declares a cash dividend of $1 per share, what will be the total amount of the dividend?

19. Stockholders of Harper Corporation donated 1,000 shares of no-par common stock to the corporation. The corporation resold these shares for cash at $40 per share. What entry is made for (a) the receipt of the stock and (b) the sale of the stock?

20. The par of the common stock of Hill Oil Corporation is $25. The current equity per share and the market price per share are $34.65 and $65.50 respectively. Suggest reasons for the comparatively high market price in relation to par and to equity per share.

21. (a) What type of expenditure is charged to the organization costs account? (b) Give examples of such expenditures.

22. Identify each of the accounts listed below as asset, liability, stockholders' equity, revenue, or expense, and state whether the balance of each is debit or credit.

    (1) Common Stock Subscriptions Receivable
    (2) Common Stock Subscribed
    (3) Retained Earnings
    (4) Paid-in Capital from Sale of Treasury Stock
    (5) Premium on Common Stock
    (6) Common Stock
    (7) Organization Costs
    (8) Preferred Stock
    (9) Discount on Preferred Stock
    (10) Donated Capital
    (11) Treasury Stock

EXERCISES

16-1. Connors, Inc. has stock outstanding as follows: 1,000 shares of 7%, $100 par, cumulative, nonparticipating preferred and 10,000 shares of $20 par common. During its first five years of operations, the following amounts were distributed as dividends: first year, none; second year, $3,500; third year, $17,500; fourth year, $40,000; fifth year, $60,000. Determine the dividends per share on each class of stock for each of the five years.

16-2. The outstanding stock of the Midwest Telephone Company is composed of 5,000 shares of 6%, $100 par, participating preferred stock and 25,000 shares of no-par common stock. The preferred stock is entitled to participate equally with the common, share for share, in any dividend distributions which exceed the regular preferred dividend and a $3 a share common dividend. The directors declare dividends of $135,000 for the current year. What is the amount of the dividend per share on (a) the preferred stock and (b) the common stock?

16-3. On March 15, the Keck Corporation issued for cash 10,000 shares of no-par common stock (with a stated value of $10) at $15, and on March 31 it issued for cash 500 shares of $100 par preferred stock at $105. (a) Give the entries, in general journal form, for March 15 and March 31. (b) What is the total amount invested by all stockholders as of March 31?

16-4. On July 1 the Parks Shoe Company received subscriptions to 20,000 shares of $25 par common stock at $40. Cash for one half of the subscription price accompanied the subscriptions. On September 1 the remaining half was received from all subscribers and the stock was issued. (a) Present entries, in general journal form, to record the transactions of July 1. (b) Present entries, in general journal form, to record the transactions of September 1. (c) Name two controlling accounts used in the transactions above and the related subsidiary ledgers.

16-5. The Wabash Paper Company, with an authorization to issue 5,000 shares of preferred stock and 50,000 shares of common stock, completed several transactions involving its capital stock on June 30, the first day of operations. The trial balance at the end of the day follows:

Cash	65,000	
Common Stock Subscriptions Receivable	325,000	
Buildings	90,000	
Land	20,000	
Preferred 6% Stock, $50 par		100,000
Premium on Preferred Stock		10,000
Common Stock, $25 par		50,000
Premium on Common Stock		90,000
Common Stock Subscribed		250,000
	500,000	500,000

Assuming that all shares within each class of stock were sold or subscribed at the same price, that the preferred stock was issued in exchange for the buildings and the land, and that no cash has been received on the common stock subscribed, prepare (a) the entries, in general journal form, to record the stock transactions and (b) the stockholders' equity section of the balance sheet on June 30.

16-6. J. K. Manning, Inc. was organized on January 2 of the current fiscal year with an authorization of 1,000 shares of cumulative preferred 6% stock, $50 par, and 10,000 shares of $10 par common stock.

(a) Record in general journal form the following selected transactions completed during the first year of operations:

Jan. 2. Sold 2,500 shares of common stock at par for cash.
2. Issued 100 shares of common stock to an attorney in payment for his legal fees for organizing the corporation.

July 15. Issued 3,000 shares of common stock in exchange for land, buildings, and equipment with fair market prices of $3,500, $20,500, and $7,500 respectively.

Oct. 10. Sold 500 shares of preferred stock at $48 for cash.

(b) Prepare the stockholders' equity section of the balance sheet as of December 31, the end of the current fiscal year. The net loss for the year amounted to $2,500.

16-7. The capital accounts of the Wallace Corporation are as follows: Preferred 6% Stock, $100 par, $1,000,000; Common Stock, $25 par, $5,000,000; Premium on Common Stock, $500,000; Retained Earnings, $1,000,000. (a) What is the equity per share of each class of stock, assuming that the preferred stock is entitled to receive $110 upon liquidation. (b) What is the equity per share of each class of stock assuming that the preferred stock is to receive $110 plus dividends in arrears in the event of liquidation, and that only the dividends for the current year are in arrears?

16-8. The following items were listed in the stockholders' equity section of the balance sheet on June 30: Common stock, $50 par (10,000 shares outstanding), $500,000; Discount on common stock, $10,000; Retained earnings, $60,000. On July 1 the corporation purchased 500 shares of its stock at $64.50. (a) Determine the equity per share of stock on June 30. (b) Give the entry, in general journal form, to record the purchase of the stock on July 1. (c) Determine the equity per share on July 1.

16-9. The following items were listed in the stockholders' equity section of the balance sheet on May 31: Preferred stock, $100 par, $100,000; Common stock, $50 par, $400,000; Premium on common stock, $16,000; Deficit, $70,000. On June 1 the board of directors voted to dissolve the corporation immediately. After all noncash assets were sold and liabilities paid, cash of $366,000 remained for distribution to stockholders. (a) Determine the equity per share on May 31 of (1) preferred stock and (2) common stock, assuming that preferred stock is entitled to preference in liquidation to the extent of 110% of par. (b) Determine the amount of the $366,000 that will be distributed for each share of (1) preferred stock and (2) common stock. (c) Explain the reason for the difference between the common stock equity per share on May 31 and the amount of the cash distribution per common share.

413

PROBLEMS

The following additional problems for this chapter are located in Appendix C: 16-2B, 16-3B, 16-5B.

16-1A. Fairmont Motors, Inc. was organized by Barker, Pence, and Wright. The charter authorizes 25,000 shares of common stock with a par of $10. The following transactions affecting stockholders' equity were completed during the first year of operations:

(a) Issued 5,000 shares of stock at par to Barker for cash.
(b) Purchased land and a building from Pence. The building is encumbered by a 6%, 14-year mortgage of $15,000, and there is accrued interest of $300 on the mortgage note at the time of the purchase. It is agreed that the land is to be priced at $8,000 and the building at $37,000, and that

Pence is to accept stock at par for his equity. The corporation agreed to assume responsibility for paying the mortgage note and the accrued interest.

(c) Purchased equipment from Wright for $25,000. Wright accepted a 6-month, non-interest-bearing note for $5,000 and 2,000 shares of stock for the equipment.

(d) Issued 100 shares of stock at par to Wright for promotional services rendered in connection with the organization of the corporation.

(e) Issued 2,000 shares of stock at $11 to various investors for cash.

Instructions:

(1) Prepare entries in general journal form to record the transactions presented above.

(2) Prepare the stockholders' equity section of the balance sheet as of the end of the first year of operations. Net income for the year amounted to $27,300, and no dividends were declared during the year.

16-2A. The annual dividends declared by the North Shore Transit Company during a six-year period are presented in the table below. During the entire period the outstanding stock of the company was composed of 1,000 shares of cumulative, participating, 7% preferred stock, $100 par, and 10,000 shares of common stock, $50 par. The preferred stock contract provides that the preferred stock shall participate in distributions of additional dividends after allowance of a $4 dividend per share on the common stock, the additional dividends to be divided among common and preferred shares on the basis of the total par of the stock outstanding.

Year	Total Dividends	Preferred Dividends Total	Preferred Dividends Per Share	Common Dividends Total	Common Dividends Per Share
1966	$33,500				
1967	3,500				
1968	20,000				
1969	47,000				
1970	53,000				
1971	59,000				

Instructions:

(1) Determine the total dividends and the per share dividends declared on each class of stock for each of the six years, using the headings presented above. There were no dividends in arrears on January 1, 1966.

(2) Determine the average annual dividend per share for each class of stock for the six-year period.

(3) Assuming that the preferred stock was sold at 110 and the common stock was sold at par at the beginning of the six-year period, determine the percentage return on initial shareholders' investment based on the average annual dividend per share (a) for preferred stock, and (b) for common stock.

16-3A. Selected data from the balance sheets of six corporations, identified by letter, are presented at the top of the next page.

A. Common stock, $10 par...... $1,500,000
   Premium on common stock... 50,000
   Deficit.................... 95,000

B. Preferred 6% stock, $100 par. $ 500,000
   Premium on preferred stock .. 25,000
   Common stock, $50 par...... 1,500,000
   Discount on common stock... 75,000
   Deficit.................... 100,000

Preferred stock has prior claim to assets on liquidation to
the extent of par.

C. Preferred 7% stock, $50 par.. $ 200,000
   Common stock, $100 par..... 1,000,000
   Premium on common stock... 20,000
   Retained earnings.......... 180,000

Preferred stock has prior claim to assets on liquidation to the
extent of par.

D. Preferred 6% stock, $100 par. $1,000,000
   Premium on preferred stock .. 30,000
   Common stock, $5 par....... 4,000,000
   Deficit.................... 300,000

Preferred stock has prior claim to assets on liquidation to
extent of 105% of par.

E. Preferred 6% stock, $50 par.. $ 500,000
   Common stock, $25 par...... 1,250,000
   Premium on common stock... 50,000
   Retained earnings.......... 50,000

Dividends on preferred stock are in arrears for 2 years
including the dividend passed during the current year.
Preferred stock is entitled to par plus unpaid cumulative
dividends upon liquidation to the extent of the retained
earnings.

F. Preferred 6% stock, $25 par.. $ 750,000
   Discount on preferred stock... 15,000
   Common stock, $10 par...... 2,000,000
   Retained earnings.......... 70,000

Dividends on preferred stock are in arrears for 3 years
including the dividend passed during the current year.
Preferred stock is entitled to par plus unpaid cumulative
dividends upon liquidation, regardless of the availability of
retained earnings.

Instructions:

Determine for each corporation the equity per share of each
class of stock, presenting the stockholders' equity
allocated to the class and the number of shares outstanding.

16-4A. The following accounts and their balances appear in the ledger of the Windsor Company on June 1 of the current year:

Preferred 6% Stock, par $50 (10,000 shares authorized, 6,000 shares issued)	$ 300,000
Premium on Preferred Stock.	9,000
Common Stock, par $20 (100,000 shares authorized, 80,000 shares issued)	1,600,000
Premium on Common Stock.	80,000
Retained Earnings (debit balance).	150,000

At the annual stockholders meeting on June 10, the chairman of the board of directors presented a plan for modernizing operations at a cost of $600,000. The plan called for the company to borrow $200,000 and for the stockholders to purchase 2,000 shares of the unissued preferred stock at par and to donate one fifth of their common shares to the corporation for resale. The plan which was approved by the stockholders resulted in the following transactions:

July 10. Received 16,000 shares of common stock from stockholders.
20. Issued 2,000 shares of preferred stock at $50, receiving cash.
20. Sold all of the treasury stock for $290,000.
31. Borrowed $200,000 from Oak Park National Bank, giving a 7% mortgage note.

Instructions:

Assuming for the purpose of the problem that no other transactions occurred during June and July:

(1) Prepare, in general journal form, the entries to record the foregoing transactions, recording receipt of the treasury stock by a memorandum entry.
(2) Prepare the stockholders' equity section of the balance sheet as of July 10.
(3) Prepare the stockholders' equity section of the balance sheet as of July 31.

16-5A. The stockholders' equity and related accounts appearing in the ledger of Parker Research and Development Corporation on July 1, the beginning of the current fiscal year, are listed below.

Preferred 6% Stock Subscriptions Receivable. .	$ 260,000
Preferred 6% Stock, $100 par (25,000 shares authorized, 15,000 shares issued)	1,500,000
Preferred 6% Stock Subscribed (5,000 shares).	500,000
Premium on Preferred Stock.	80,000
Common Stock, $20 par (500,000 shares authorized, 300,000 shares issued)	6,000,000
Premium on Common Stock.	1,200,000
Retained Earnings	3,550,000

During the year the corporation completed a number of transactions affecting the stockholders' equity. They are summarized below.

(a) Received balance due on preferred stock subscribed and issued the certificates.
(b) Purchased 4,000 shares of treasury common for $140,000.

(c) Received subscriptions to 2,500 shares of preferred 6% stock at $106, collecting 40% of subscription price.

(d) Sold 2,000 shares of treasury common for $75,000.

(e) Issued 20,000 shares of common stock at $38, receiving cash.

(f) Sold 1,000 shares of treasury common for $32,500.

Instructions:

(1) Prepare entries, in general journal form, to record the transactions listed above. (Use of T accounts for the stockholders' equity accounts is suggested for accumulating balances needed to record particular transactions and for use in remainder of problem.)

(2) Prepare the stockholders' equity section of the balance sheet as of June 30. Net income for the year amounted to $965,000. Dividends charged to Retained Earnings during the year totaled $420,000.

16-6A. Davis Electronics was organized on May 11 of the current year and prepared its first financial statements as of December 31, the date that had been adopted as the end of the fiscal year. The balance sheet prepared by the bookkeeper as of December 31 is presented below. You are retained by the board of directors to audit the accounts and to prepare a revised balance sheet.

Davis Electronics
Balance Sheet
May 11 to December 31, 19—

Assets		Liabilities	
Cash.....................	$ 21,500	Accounts payable.........	$ 38,500
Accounts receivable.......	80,200	Preferred stock...........	50,000
Merchandise inventory....	91,750	Common stock...........	250,000
Prepaid insurance........	350		
Treasury preferred stock...	10,000		
Equipment..............	117,500		
Discount on common stock.	5,000		
Retained earnings (deficit).	12,200		
Total assets.............	$338,500	Total liabilities..........	$338,500

The relevant facts developed during the course of your engagement are:

(a) Stock authorized: 1,000 shares of $100 par, 7% preferred and 50,000 shares of $10 par common.

(b) Stock issued: 500 shares of fully paid preferred at $105 and 20,000 shares of fully paid common at $9.75. The premium on preferred stock was credited to Retained Earnings.

(c) Stock subscribed but not issued: 5,000 shares of common at par, on which all subscribers have paid one half of the subscription price. Unpaid subscriptions are included in accounts receivable.

(d) The company reacquired 100 shares of the issued preferred stock at $102. The difference between par and the price paid was debited to Retained Earnings. (It is decided that the treasury stock is to be recorded at cost.)

(e) Land costing $17,500, which is to be used as a future building site, was charged to Equipment.

(f) No depreciation has been recognized. The equipment is to be depreciated for one-half year by the straight-line method, using an estimated life of 10 years.

(g) Organization costs of $750 were charged to Advertising Expense. (None of the organization costs is to be amortized.)

(h) Included in merchandise inventory is $300 of office supplies.

(i) No dividends have been declared or paid.

(j) In balancing the common stockholders ledger with the common stock control account, it was discovered that the account with William Dixon contained a posting for an issuance of 25 shares, while the carbon copy of the stock certificate indicated that 250 shares had been issued. The stock certificate was found to be correct.

Instructions:

(1) Prepare general journal entries where necessary to record the corrections. Corrections of net income may be recorded as adjustments to retained earnings.

(2) Prepare a six-column work sheet with columns for (a) balances per balance sheet, (b) corrections, and (c) corrected balances. In listing the accounts, leave an extra line blank following the retained earnings account.

(3) Prepare a balance sheet in report form as of the close of the fiscal year.

418

17

Corporations--
stockholders' equity,
earnings, and dividends

Classification of stockholders' equity

The equity of the stockholders is customarily presented on corporate balance sheets in two principal subdivisions, paid-in capital and retained earnings. Although in practice there is considerable variation in the amount of detail presented in describing the various items included in each division, the significant sources of corporate capital should be clearly disclosed.

The stockholders' equity or capital section of corporate balance sheets of earlier days was frequently not very informative. The preferred and common stock accounts were reported at par, which was clear enough, but the remaining stockholders' equity was often described merely as "Surplus." In such cases it was not possible for the reader to determine the sources of capital and, in the absence of such information, to form an intelligent opinion about this section of the balance sheet. For example, a "surplus" of $1,000,000 could represent retained earnings of $1,000,000, or it could be the excess of stock premiums (paid-in capital) of $1,200,000 over an accumulated deficit (losses) of $200,000.

The term "capital surplus" has also been employed in the past to describe paid-in capital in excess of par or stated value of the capital stock. The term "surplus," either alone or with such words as "capital," "paid-in," or "earned," as a descriptive caption in financial statements has been supplanted to a large extent, but it is still encountered, particularly in accounting literature.

Paid-in capital

The principal credits to paid-in capital accounts result from the issuance of stock. If par stock is issued at a price above or below par, the difference is recorded in a separate premium or discount account. It is also not uncommon to employ two accounts in recording the issuance of no-par stock, one for the stated value and the other for the excess over stated value. Other accounts for paid-in capital discussed in the preceding chapter were Paid-in Capital from Sale of Treasury Stock and Donated Capital.

Paid-in capital may also originate from donated real estate and redemptions of a corporation's own stock. Civic organizations sometimes give land or land and buildings to a corporate enterprise as an inducement to locate in the community. In such cases the assets are recorded in the corporate accounts at fair market value, with a credit to Donated Capital. The right to redeem its preferred stock is frequently retained by a corporation when the stock is originally issued. The contract may specify various redemption prices at varying future dates. If the amount paid at the time of redemption is greater than the amount originally received, the excess is considered to be a distribution of retained earnings. On the other hand, if the amount paid is less than the amount originally received by the corporation, the difference is a retention of capital and should be credited to Paid-in Capital from Preferred Stock Redemption or similarly titled account.

As with other sections of the balance sheet, there are numerous variations in terminology and arrangement of the paid-in capital section. The details of each class of stock, including related stock premium or discount, are commonly listed first, followed by the other paid-in capital accounts. Instead of describing the source of each amount in excess of par or stated value, another arrangement combines all such accounts and lists them as a single item below the capital stock accounts. The item is then described as "Additional paid-in capital," "Capital in excess of par (or stated value) of shares," or by a similarly descriptive phrase. Some of the variations in terminology and arrangement are illustrated by the three examples that follow.

Stockholders' Equity

Paid-in capital:		
Common stock, $20 par (50,000 shares authorized, 40,000 shares issued)	$800,000	
Premium on common stock	128,000	$928,000
From stock redemption		30,000
From sale of treasury stock		10,000
Total paid-in capital		$968,000

Capital

Paid-in capital:

Common stock, $20 par (50,000 shares authorized, 40,000 shares issued)			$800,000
Excess of issuance price of stock over par	$128,000		
From donation	30,000		
From transactions in own stock	10,000	168,000	
Total paid-in capital			$968,000

Shareholders' Investment

Contributed capital:

Common stock, $20 par (50,000 shares authorized, 40,000 shares issued)	$800,000	
Additional paid-in capital	168,000	
Total contributed capital		$968,000

Corporate earnings and income taxes

The determination of the net income or net loss of a corporation is comparable, in most respects, to that of other forms of business organization. Unlike sole proprietorships and partnerships, however, corporations are distinct legal entities and in general are subject to the federal income tax and in many cases to income taxes levied by states or other political subdivisions. Our attention will be confined to the income tax levied by the federal government.

Income tax expense should be determined and identified with the fiscal year in which the related income has been earned. In accordance with a pay-as-you-go system first enacted in 1954 and subsequently amended, most corporations are required to make an advance estimate of the amount of their income tax and pay a portion of it, usually in four installments, during the year in which the income is earned.

After the end of the year, the total tax is computed and the amount compared with the payments. If the amount already paid exceeds the tax liability for the year, the amount of the overpayment is credited to the income tax account and debited to a receivable account. If there is an additional amount owed, which is the more usual situation, it may be paid in two equal installments, the first when the tax return is filed 2½ months after the close of the fiscal year and the second installment 3 months later. The entry to record additional tax liability as of the close of a fiscal year coinciding with the calendar year would be as follows:

Dec.	31	Income Tax	26,139	
		Income Tax Payable		26,139

The amount determined by a corporate taxpayer to be its income tax for the year is still provisional rather than final. The tax return and supporting evidence is subject to review and adjustment by the taxing authority, usually for a period of three years after the return is filed.

For this reason the liability for income taxes is sometimes described in the current liability section of the balance sheet as "Estimated income tax payable" or "Provision for income tax."

Because of its close relationship to net income and its materiality, it is customary to report income tax in the income statement in the manner illustrated below.

Ross Corporation
Income Statement
For Year Ended December 31, 19—

Sales..	$920,000
Income before income tax	$180,000
Income tax..	78,500
Net income	$101,500

Income tax allocation

The *taxable income* of a corporation, determined in accordance with the Internal Revenue Code and governmental regulations, frequently differs substantially from the amount reported as net income in the income statement. The difference between the two amounts is usually caused by one or more of the following conditions:

1. A particular revenue earned is excludable or a particular expense incurred is not deductible in determining taxable income. Example: Interest earned on municipal bonds.
2. A deduction allowed in determining taxable income does not constitute an expense. Example: Excess of percentage depletion of oil wells over depletion based on cost.
3. Of various acceptable methods of determining the amount of a particular revenue or expense, one is elected in determining taxable income and another is elected for reporting purposes. Example: Declining-balance depreciation at twice the straight-line rate elected in determining taxable income and straight-line depreciation employed for reporting purposes.
4. The treatment of a particular revenue or expense prescribed for the determination of taxable income is contrary to generally accepted accounting principles. Example: Revenue of future years received in advance must be included in taxable income in the year received, which is contrary to the basic accounting principle that such revenue be allocated among the periods affected.

The specific causes of differences between the amount of a corporation's taxable income and the amount reported in the income statement must be detailed in a section of the income tax return entitled "Reconciliation of Income per Books with Income per Return." Ordinarily the reconciling items are readily identifiable and their quantitative effect determined. However, differences between taxable and reported income caused by the third and fourth conditions described above give rise to an additional problem of financial reporting. The variations are largely attributable to differences in accounting methods, which in turn are related to differences in the timing of revenue and expense recognition. The remainder of this section is devoted to such timing differences and their related effect on the amount of income tax reported in corporate financial statements.

To illustrate the effect of timing differences, assume that a corporation that sells its product on the installment basis considers revenue realized at the time of sale, and maintains its accounts accordingly. At the close of its first year of operations, the income before income tax according to the ledger is $250,000. Recognizing the tax advantage of postponing the recognition of revenue, the corporation elects the installment method, which yields taxable income of only $150,000. Assuming an income tax rate of 50%, the income tax on $250,000 of income would be $125,000, but the actual tax liability for the year would be 50% of taxable income of $150,000, or $75,000. The $50,000 difference between the two amounts is attributable to the timing difference in recognizing revenue. It represents a deferment of $50,000 of income tax to future years. As the installment accounts receivable are collected in subsequent years, the additional $100,000 of income will be included in taxable income and the $50,000 deferment will become a tax liability of those years. The situation may be summarized as follows:

Income (before income tax) according to ledger................	$250,000	
Income tax based on $250,000 of reported income............		$125,000
Income (taxable income) according to tax return..............	$150,000	
Income tax (actual) based on $150,000 of taxable income....		75,000
Income tax deferred to future years........................		$ 50,000

If the effect of the difference in timing of revenue is not recognized in the accounts, the income of the corporation will be reported in its income statement as $250,000 less current income tax of $75,000, or $175,000. Furthermore, the $50,000 of deferred tax liability will not be reported in the balance sheet. In the opinion of many accountants such treatment is erroneous and unacceptable. It is considered preferable to allocate the income tax to the period in which the related income is earned. In accordance with this view, the income tax reported on the financial statements will be the total tax expected to result from the net income of the year regardless of when the tax will become an actual liability.[1]

Application of this viewpoint to the illustrative data yields the results illustrated at the top of the next page, stated in terms of a journal entry:

---

[1]*Opinions of the Accounting Principles Board*, No. 11, "Accounting for Income Taxes" (New York: American Institute of Certified Public Accountants, 1967).

Income Tax	125,000	
Income Tax Payable		75,000
Deferred Income Tax Payable		50,000

Continuing with the illustration, the $50,000 in Deferred Income Tax Payable will be transferred to Income Tax Payable as the remaining $100,000 of income becomes taxable in subsequent years. If, for example, $60,000 of untaxed income of the first year of the corporation's operations becomes taxable in the second year, the effect would be as follows, stated as a journal entry:

Deferred Income Tax Payable	30,000	
Income Tax Payable		30,000

Installment sales of the corporation in succeeding years will continue to result in additional differences between taxable and reported income, and an accompanying deferment of tax liability. Thus the balance in the deferred income tax payable account will fluctuate from year to year.

A substantial number of accountants have challenged the soundness of the income tax allocation principle. One of the objections is that allocation is unrealistic in certain situations where there is considerable doubt that the deferred tax will ever become a current liability. There are many ramifications of interperiod allocations of income tax which go beyond the scope of this discussion.

424   **Current period errors and corrections**

Accounting errors of a fiscal year that are discovered and corrected within the same fiscal year were discussed in Chapter 3. The procedure recommended there for correcting erroneous entries that have been posted to the ledger is summarized as follows: (1) set forth the entire entry in which the error occurred by the use of memorandum T accounts or a journal entry; (2) set forth the entry that should have been made, using a second set of T accounts or a journal entry; and (3) formulate the debits and credits required to bring the erroneous entry in (1) into agreement with the correct entry in (2).

The correction of current errors is entirely a matter of technique, no question of principle being involved. After the correction has been made, the account balances are the same as they would have been in the absence of error, and, more importantly, the information communicated through the income statement and the balance sheet is unaffected.

Prior period adjustments and extraordinary items

The accounting treatment of adjustments or corrections of net income reported for prior fiscal years and of extraordinary items affecting current net income involves matters of principle. The term "extraordinary items" refers to material additions to or deductions from net income resulting from events or transactions of an unusual and nonrecurring nature. Included are such items as gains or losses from the sale of an entire plant or significant segment of a business, gains or losses from the sale of a substantial investment, and losses from floods, earthquakes, or other catastrophes not ordinarily covered by insurance.

For many years there were two conflicting points of view concerning the proper reporting of prior period adjustments and extraordinary items. Proponents of the *current operating performance* viewpoint emphasized the ordinary, normal, recurring operations of an enterprise and held that only such revenues and expenses should be reported in the income statement. To avoid possible misleading implications that might result from distortions of net income, it was considered preferable to report non-recurring items in the retained earnings statement. Supporters of the other viewpoint, designated *all-inclusive*, insisted that all revenue and expense items be reported in the income statement, regardless of source, with significant items of nonrecurring nature appropriately identified. By so doing, it was argued, the aggregate net income of an enterprise during its entire life would be reported in the income statement. Both viewpoints attracted considerable support over the years. There is now substantial agreement as to the appropriate treatment of prior period adjustments and extraordinary items.[2]

Prior period adjustments. Relatively minor amounts of prior period corrections or adjustments to net income necessitated by errors should ordinarily be reported in the income statement. Annual audits by independent accountants, combined with the internal control features of accounting systems, minimize the possibilities of undetected errors of a significant amount. 425

It is considered permissible to present an adjustment in the retained earnings statement only if the adjustment is material in amount and arose from events or transactions of a prior period, the accounting effects of which could not be reasonably determined at that time. The criteria for identifying circumstances of this kind are quoted below. Adjustments that meet such criteria are rare in modern financial accounting.

> . . . material adjustments which (a) can be specifically identified with and directly related to the business activities of particular prior periods, and (b) are not attributable to economic events occurring subsequent to the date of the financial statements for the prior period, and (c) depend primarily on determinations by persons other than management and (d) were not susceptible of reasonable estimation prior to such determination.[3]

Extraordinary items. Extraordinary gains and losses of relatively insignificant amount need not be accorded special treatment; they may

---

[2]*Opinions of the Accounting Principles Board, No. 9,* "Reporting the Results of Operations" (New York: American Institute of Certified Public Accountants, 1966).
[3]*Ibid.,* p. 115.

be reported in the same manner as normally recurring revenues and expenses. Those that are material in amount should be reported in a separate section for extraordinary items which would appear as the last section of the income statement.

Allocation of related income tax. The amount of income tax applicable to a prior period adjustment or to extraordinary items should be disclosed in the appropriate financial statement. Alternatively, the adjustment or extraordinary items may be reported at the net amount and the details presented in a note to the statement.

The manner in which extraordinary items and related income tax effects may be presented on the income statement is presented below.

SRM Corporation
Income Statement
For Year Ended August 31, 1970

Net sales.			$9,600,950
Income before income tax.			$1,310,000
Income tax.			620,000
Net income before extraordinary items.			$ 690,000
Extraordinary items:			
Gain on sale of investments.	$280,000		
Less applicable income tax.	70,000	$210,000	
Loss on sale of branch plant facilities.	$190,000		
Less applicable income tax.	55,000	135,000	75,000
Net income.			$ 765,000

Earnings per share

Data on earnings per share of common stock are ordinarily reported by corporations to their stockholders, by the financial press to the general public, and by various statistical services to their subscribers. For most stockholders, and for investors generally, it is frequently the item of greatest interest contained in corporate annual reports.

There is undoubtedly a tendency among users of financial data to place undue emphasis upon comparisons of quoted earnings per share of current and past periods. The comparisons are sometimes made without regard to the effect of extraordinary items appearing on the income statement. It is recommended that for maximum usefulness earnings per share data should be presented in conjunction with the income statement, and when there are extraordinary items the per share amounts should be presented for (1) net income before extraordinary items, (2) extraordinary items (less applicable income tax), and (3) net income.[4] The per share data may be shown parenthetically or appended at the bottom of the income statement.

[4] *Ibid.*, p. 119.

Appropriation of retained earnings

The amount of a corporation's retained earnings available for distribution to its shareholders may be restricted by action of the board of directors. The amount restricted, which is called an *appropriation* or a *reserve*, remains a part of retained earnings and should be so classified in the financial statements. An appropriation can be effected by transferring the desired amount from Retained Earnings to a special account designating its purpose, such as Appropriation for Plant Expansion.

Appropriations may be initiated by the directors, or they may be required by law or contract. Some states require that a corporation retain earnings equal to the amount paid for treasury stock. For example, if a corporation with accumulated earnings of $100,000 purchases shares of its own issued stock for $40,000, the corporation would not be permitted to pay more than $60,000 in dividends. The restriction is equal to the $40,000 paid for the treasury stock and assures that legal capital will not be impaired by declaration of dividends. The entry to record the appropriation would be:

Apr.	24	Retained Earnings....................	40,000		
		Appropriation for Treasury Stock.....		40,000	

After the corporation sells the treasury stock, the appropriation is no longer needed and it is therefore transferred back to the retained earnings account by the following entry:

Nov.	10	Appropriation for Treasury Stock.......	40,000		
		Retained Earnings.................		40,000	

When a corporation borrows a substantial amount through issuance of bonds or long-term notes, the agreement may provide for restrictions on dividends until the debt is paid. The contract may stipulate that retained earnings equal to the amount borrowed be restricted during the entire period of the loan, or it may require that the restriction be built up by annual appropriations. For example, assume that a corporation borrows $500,000 on ten-year bonds. If equal annual appropriations were to be made over the life of the bonds, there would be a series of ten entries, each in the amount of $50,000, debiting Retained Earnings and crediting an appropriation account entitled Appropriation for Bonded Indebtedness. Even if the bond agreement did not require the restriction on retained earnings, the directors might deem it advisable to establish the appropriation. In that case it would be a *discretionary* rather than a *contractual* appropriation. The entries would be identical in either case.

It must be clearly understood that the appropriation account is not directly related to any particular group of asset accounts. Its existence does not imply that there is an equivalent amount of cash or other assets set aside in a special fund. The appropriation serves the purpose of restricting dividends, but it does not assure that the cash that might otherwise be distributed as dividends will not be invested in additional inventories or other assets, or used to reduce current liabilities.

Appropriations of retained earnings may be accompanied by a segregation of equivalent amounts of cash or marketable securities, in which case the appropriation is said to be *funded.* Accumulation of such funds is discussed in the next chapter.

There are other purposes for which the directors may consider appropriations desirable. Expansion of plant facilities was mentioned earlier. Some companies with properties widely scattered geographically may assume their own risk of losses from fire, windstorm, and other casualties rather than obtain protection from insurance companies. In such cases the appropriation account would be entitled Appropriation for Self-Insurance. An appropriation of this nature is likely to be permanent, although its amount may vary as the total value of properties, the extent of fire protection, etc. fluctuates. If a loss should occur, it should be debited to a special loss account rather than to the appropriation account. It is definitely a loss of the particular period and should be reported in the income statement as an extraordinary item.

A company may also earmark earnings for other specific contingencies, such as inventory price declines or an adverse decision on a pending law suit. A common practice is to establish an appropriation for contingencies to provide for any eventuality.

The details of retained earnings may be presented in the balance sheet in the manner illustrated below. The item designated "Unappropriated" is the balance of the retained earnings account.

Retained earnings:
　Appropriated:
　　For plant expansion. . . . .　$50,000
　　For contingencies. . . . .　10,000　$60,000
　Unappropriated. . . . . 　　　　80,000
　Total retained earnings. . . . . 　　　　　　　$140,000

It is not essential that restrictions on retained earnings be formalized in the ledger. However, compliance with legal requirements and with contractual restrictions is essential, and the nature and the amount of all restrictions should always be disclosed in the balance sheet. For example, the appropriations data appearing in the foregoing illustration could be presented in the form of a note accompanying the balance sheet. Such an alternative might also be employed as a means of simplifying or condensing the balance sheet even though appropriation accounts are maintained in the ledger. The alternative balance sheet presentation, including the note, might appear as shown at the top of the next page.

Retained earnings (see note).. $140,000

Note: Retained earnings in the amount of $50,000 are appropriated for expansion of plant facilities and $10,000 are appropriated for contingencies; the remaining $80,000 is unrestricted.

Nature of dividends

A dividend is a distribution by a corporation to its shareholders. It must be on a pro rata basis for all shares of a particular class. In most cases dividends represent distributions from retained earnings. In many states dividends may be declared from the excess of paid-in capital over par or stated value, but such dividends are unusual. The term *liquidating dividend* is applied to a distribution out of paid-in capital when a corporation permanently contracts its operations or winds up its affairs completely. The discussion that follows will be concerned with dividends based on accumulated earnings.

Dividends may be paid in cash, in stock of the paying company, in scrip, or in other property. The discussion in this chapter will be concerned mainly with the two most common types of dividends — *cash dividends* and *stock dividends* (stock of the paying company).

Ordinarily there are three prerequisites to paying a cash dividend: (1) sufficient unappropriated retained earnings, (2) sufficient cash, and (3) formal action by the board of directors. A substantial amount of accumulated earnings does not necessarily indicate that a corporation is able to pay dividends; there must also be sufficient cash over and above working capital needs. The amount of retained earnings is not directly related to cash; the former represents net income of past periods retained in the business, but the cash provided by the net income may have been used to purchase plant assets, to reduce liabilities, or for other purposes. The directors of a corporation are not compelled by law to declare dividends even when both retained earnings and cash appear to be sufficient. When a dividend has been declared, however, it becomes a liability of the corporation.

Seasoned corporations with a wide distribution of stock usually try to maintain a stable dividend record. They may retain a substantial portion of earnings in good years in order to be able to continue dividend payments in lean years. Dividends may be paid once a year or on a semiannual or quarterly basis. The tendency is to pay quarterly dividends on both common and preferred stock. In particularly good years the directors may declare an "extra" dividend on common stock. It may be paid at one of the usual dividend dates or at some other date. The designation "extra" indicates that the board of directors does not anticipate an increase in the amount of the "regular" dividend.

429

There are three different dates involved in a dividend declaration: (1) the date of declaration, (2) the date of record, and (3) the date of payment. The first is the date the directors take formal action declaring the dividend, the second is the date as of which ownership of shares is to be determined, and the third is the date payment is to be made. For example, on October 11 the board of directors declares a quarterly cash dividend to stockholders of record as of the close of business on October 21, payable on November 15. Notices of dividend declarations are usually reported in financial publications and newspapers.

The liability for the dividend is recorded on the declaration date, as it is incurred when the formal action is taken by the directors. No entry is required on the date of record; it merely fixes the date for determining the identity of the stockholders entitled to receive the dividend. The period of time between the record date and the payment date is provided to permit completion of the postings to the stockholders ledger and preparation of the dividend checks. The liability of the corporation is paid by the mailing of the checks.

Dividends on cumulative preferred stock do not become a liability of the corporation until formal action is taken by the board of directors. However, dividends in arrears at a balance sheet date should be disclosed by a footnote, a parenthetical notation, or a segregation of retained earnings similar to the following:

Retained earnings:

Required to meet dividends in arrears on preferred stock.........	$30,000
Remainder, unrestricted......................................	16,000
Total retained earnings......................................	$46,000

Cash dividends

Dividends payable in cash are by far the most usual form of dividend. Dividends on common stock are usually stated in terms of dollars and cents rather than as a percentage of par. Dividends on preferred stock may be stated either in monetary terms or a percentage of par. For example, the annual dividend rate on a particular $100 par preferred stock may be stated as either $6 or 6%.

Corporations ordinarily follow a fixed pattern of dividend payment dates, such as January 15, April 15, July 15, and October 15, or March 30, June 30, September 30, and December 30. Assuming a sufficient balance in retained earnings, including estimated net income of the current year, the directors ordinarily consider the following factors in determining whether to pass a dividend or declare a particular amount:

1. The company's working capital position.
2. Resources needed for planned expansion or replacement of facilities.
3. Maturity dates of large liabilities.
4. Future business prospects of the company and forecasts for the industry and the economy generally.

To illustrate the entries required in the declaration and the payment of cash dividends, assume that on December 1 the board of directors declares the regular quarterly dividend of $1.50 on the 5,000 shares of $100 par, 6% preferred stock outstanding ($7,500), and a quarterly dividend of 25¢ on the 100,000 shares of $10 par common stock outstanding ($25,000). Both dividends are to stockholders of record on December 10, and checks are to be issued to stockholders on January 2. The entry to record the declaration of the dividends is as follows:

Dec.	1	Retained Earnings....................	32,500	
		Cash Dividends Payable.............		32,500

The cash dividends payable account would be listed as a current liability on the December 31 balance sheet. Payments of the dividends on January 2 would be recorded in the usual manner as a debit to the liability account and a credit to Cash.

Stock dividends

A pro rata distribution of shares of stock to stockholders, accompanied by a transfer of retained earnings to paid-in capital accounts, is called a *stock dividend.* Such distributions are usually in common stock and are issued to holders of common stock. It is possible to issue common stock to preferred stockholders or preferred stock to common stockholders, but such stock dividends are unusual and need not be considered.

Stock dividends are quite unlike cash dividends in that there is no distribution of cash or other corporate assets to the stockholders. They are ordinarily issued by corporations that "plow back" (retain) earnings for use in acquiring new facilities or otherwise expanding their operations.

The effect of a stock dividend on the capital structure of the issuing corporation is to transfer accumulated earnings to paid-in capital. To illustrate, assume the following balances in the stockholders' equity accounts of a hypothetical corporation as of December 15:

Common Stock, $10 par (20,000 shares issued)...	$200,000
Premium on Common Stock................	40,000
Retained Earnings.......................	255,000

On December 15 the board of directors declares a 10% stock dividend (2,000 shares, $20,000 par), to be issued on January 10. The transfer of $20,000 from the retained earnings account to paid-in capital would meet the legal requirements of most states. The preferred treatment, however, is to permanently capitalize an amount equal to the market value (rather than par) of the stock distributed.[5] Assuming the market

------

[5]*Accounting Research and Terminology Bulletins,* "No. 43, Restatement and Revision of Accounting Research Bulletins" (New York: American Institute of Certified Public Accountants, 1961), p. 51.

431

value of the 2,000 shares issued to be $22 per share, the entry to record the declaration of the stock dividend is as follows:

Dec.	15	Retained Earnings.....................	44,000	
		Stock Dividend Distributable........		20,000
		Premium on Common Stock........		24,000

The issuance of the stock certificates is recorded by the following entry:

| Jan. | 10 | Stock Dividend Distributable.......... | 20,000 | |
| | | Common Stock.................... | | 20,000 |

The effect of the stock dividend is to transfer $44,000 from the retained earnings account to paid-in capital accounts and to increase by 2,000 the number of shares outstanding. There is no change in the assets, liabilities, or total stockholders' equity of the corporation. If financial statements are prepared between the date of declaration and the date of issuance, the stock dividend distributable account should be listed in the paid-in capital section of the balance sheet.

A stock dividend is not income to the stockholders. It does not change the amount of their equity nor their proportionate interest in the corporation. The following tabulation of data for the hypothetical corporation and for a stockholder owning one hundred shares demonstrates this point.

THE CORPORATION	BEFORE STOCK DIVIDEND	AFTER STOCK DIVIDEND
Common stock...............	$200,000	$220,000
Premium on common stock....	40,000	64,000
Retained earnings............	255,000	211,000
Total stockholders' equity...	$495,000	$495,000
Number of shares outstanding...	20,000	22,000
Equity per share.............	$24.75	$22.50
A STOCKHOLDER		
Number of shares owned.......	100	110
Total equity...............	$2,475	$2,475
Portion of corporation owned...	.5%	.5%

Stock splits

Corporations sometimes reduce the par or stated value of their common stock and issue a proportionate number of additional shares. Such a procedure is called a *stock split* or *stock split-up*. For example, a corporation with 10,000 shares of $50 par stock outstanding may reduce the par to $25 and increase the number of shares to 20,000. A stockholder who owned 100 shares before the split would own 200 shares after the split. There are no changes in the balances of any of the corporation's accounts, hence no entry is required.

The primary purpose of a stock split is to reduce the selling price of stock when the shares are selling at exceedingly high levels. Such an action will permit more investors to enter the market for this particular security. A stock split is seldom employed by small corporations or by corporations whose stock is not listed on an organized stock exchange.

Dividends and treasury stock

Cash or property dividends are not paid on treasury stock. To do so would place the corporation in the position of earning income through dealing with itself, an obvious fiction. Accordingly, the total amount of a cash (or property) dividend should be based on the number of shares outstanding at the record date. To illustrate, assume the following balances in the stockholders' equity accounts of a corporation:

Common Stock, $10 par (100,000 shares issued).	$1,000,000 cr.
Retained Earnings.	1,600,000 cr.
Treasury Stock (2,000 shares at cost).	42,000 dr.

If the corporation declares a cash dividend of $1 a share, the total amount is computed on the basis of the 98,000 shares outstanding (100,000 − 2,000) and the dividend will be $98,000.

When a corporation holding treasury stock declares a stock dividend, the number of shares to be issued may be determined by either of two methods. The basis for the computation may be (1) the number of shares outstanding or (2) the number of shares issued. If the above hypothetical corporation declares a 5% stock dividend, the issuance will be either 4,900 shares (5% of 98,000) or 5,000 shares (5% of 100,000). If the first alternative is elected, the 2,000 shares in the treasury with a total cost of $42,000 will remain unchanged. If the second alternative is adopted, the number of shares in the treasury will be increased by 100 (5% of 2,000). The total cost of the treasury stock would not be affected, but the average unit cost would become $20 a share ($42,000 ÷ 2,100).

The issuance of stock dividends on treasury stock is theoretically sound because the percentage relationship of the treasury stock to the total issuance remains unchanged. In practice, however, either method of determining the total amount of the dividend is satisfactory. In most cases the number of shares held as treasury stock represents a small percent of the number of shares issued and the rate of dividend is also ordinarily small, so that the difference between the end results is usually not significant.

There is no legal, theoretical, or practical reason for excluding treasury stock when computing the number of shares to be issued in a stock split. The reduction in par or stated value would apply to all shares of the class, including the unissued, issued, and treasury shares. If, for example, the above hypothetical corporation were to reduce the par of its

433

stock from $10 to $5 in a two-for-one split, it would increase the number of its shares by 100,000, of which 98,000 would be issued to stockholders and 2,000 would be added to the treasury shares.

Retained earnings statement

The retained earnings statement is a formal summary of the changes in the retained earnings account during a fiscal period. It is one of the principal statements included in published financial reports.

The retained earnings statement is divided into two major sections: (1) appropriated and (2) unappropriated. The first section is composed of an analysis of all appropriation accounts, beginning with the opening balance, listing the additions or the deductions during the period, and ending with the closing balance. The second section is composed of an analysis of the retained earnings account and is similar in form to the first section. The final figure on the statement is the total retained earnings as of the last day of the period; it corresponds to the amount reported in the balance sheet as of that date.

To illustrate the form of the retained earnings statement and the sources from which the information is obtained, the pertinent accounts of the Douglas Corporation and its retained earnings statement for the year 1969 are given below and on the following page.

APPROPRIATION FOR PLANT EXPANSION   ACCOUNT No. 3202

| DATE | | ITEM | DEBIT | CREDIT | BALANCE | |
					DEBIT	CREDIT
1969						
Jan.	1	Balance				30,000
Dec.	31	Transfer from retained earnings account		25,000		55,000

RETAINED EARNINGS   ACCOUNT No. 3300

| DATE | | ITEM | DEBIT | CREDIT | BALANCE | |
					DEBIT	CREDIT
1969						
Jan.	1	Balance				113,300
Mar.	20	Dividends	9,875			103,425
June	19	Dividends	9,875			93,550
Sept.	18	Dividends	9,875			83,675
Dec.	18	Dividends	17,875			65,800
	31	Net income		100,000		165,800
	31	Appropriation for plant expansion	25,000			140,800

Douglas Corporation
Retained Earnings Statement
For Year Ended December 31, 1969

Appropriated:			
Appropriated for plant expansion, balance January 1, 1969		$ 30,000	
Add appropriation in 1969 (see below)		25,000	
Retained earnings appropriated, December 31, 1969			$ 55,000
Unappropriated:			
Balance, January 1, 1969	$113,300		
Add net income for year	100,000	$213,300	
Deduct: Cash dividends declared	$ 47,500		
Transfer to appropriation for plant expansion (see above)	25,000	72,500	
Retained earnings unappropriated, December 31, 1969			140,800
Total retained earnings, December 31, 1969			$195,800

Retained earnings statement

There are many possible variations in the form of the retained earnings statement. It may also be appended to the income statement to form a combined statement of income and retained earnings, which is illustrated in Chapter 27. If there are significant changes in paid-in capital during the period, they may be presented separately in a paid-in capital statement.[6]

435

QUESTIONS

1. What are the two principal subdivisions of the stockholders' equity section of the corporate balance sheet?

2. Cullen Industries is given land as an inducement to locate in a particular community. (a) How should the amount of the debit to the land account be determined? (b) What is the title of the account that is credited for the same amount?

3. What is the customary manner of presenting income tax in the income statement?

4. How would the amount of "Provision for income tax" be reported on the financial statements?

[6]*Opinions of the Accounting Principles Board, No. 12*, "Omnibus Opinion — 1967" (New York: American Institute of Certified Public Accountants, 1967), p. 190.

5. The income before income tax for the year as reported on the income statement is $200,000, the taxable income for the same year is $150,000. Assuming an income tax rate of 50%, what is the amount of the deferred income tax liability?

6. Classify each of the revenue and expense items listed below as either (a) normally recurring or (b) extraordinary. Assume that the amount of each item is material.

(1) Executive salaries
(2) Loss on sale of an investment not acquired for resale
(3) Depreciation expense on equipment
(4) Bad debt expense
(5) Uninsured flood loss

7. How should extraordinary items of revenue and expense be reported on the income statement?

8. A building owned by the Snyder Company was completely destroyed by a tornado. The building, which had cost $70,000 and had been depreciated in the amount of $30,000, was not covered by insurance. How would the loss, the amount of which is material, be reported in the financial statements?

9. Appropriations of retained earnings may be (a) required by law, (b) required by contract, or (c) made at the discretion of the board of directors. Give an illustration of each type of appropriation.

10. A credit balance in Retained Earnings does not represent cash. Explain.

11. The board of directors of Preston Corporation votes to appropriate $100,000 of retained earnings for plant expansion. What is the effect of their action on (a) cash, (b) total retained earnings, and (c) retained earnings available for dividends?

12. What are the three prerequisites to the declaration and the payment of a cash dividend?

13. The dates in connection with the declaration of a cash dividend are December 30, January 10, and January 30. Identify each date.

14. A corporation with cumulative preferred stock and no-par common stock outstanding has a substantial credit balance in the retained earnings account at the beginning of the current fiscal year. Net income for the current year is estimated at $45,000. The board of directors declares the regular $15,000 dividend on the preferred stock but takes no action on the common stock. Suggest reasons for passing the dividend on the common stock.

15. How should dividends in arrears on cumulative preferred stock be reported on the balance sheet?

16. State the effect of the following on assets, liabilities, and stockholders' equity: (a) declaration of a cash dividend, (b) payment of a cash dividend, (c) declaration of a stock dividend, (d) issuance of a stock dividend, (e) stock split.

17. An owner of 50 shares of Kline Corporation common stock receives a stock dividend of 5 shares. (a) What is the effect of the stock dividend on the equity per share of stock? (b) Is the total equity of the 55 shares greater than, less than, or the same as the total equity of the 50 shares immediately before the dividend?

436

18. A corporation with 25,000 shares of no-par common stock issued, of which 1,000 shares are held as treasury stock, declares a cash dividend of $1 a share. What is the total amount of the dividend?

19. A 10% stock dividend declared by the corporation in Question 18 would amount to what number of shares? Give two alternatives.

20. If a corporation with 1,000 shares of treasury stock has a 3-for-1 stock split (2 additional shares for each share issued), what will be the number of treasury shares after the split?

21. Into what two major sections is the retained earnings statement divided?

EXERCISES

17-1. During its first three years of operations, Barnes Company determined depreciation expense by the straight-line method for book purposes and by the sum-of-the-years-digits method for tax purposes. The amounts of income before income tax and the amounts of taxable income for each of the three years were as follows:

	First Year	Second Year	Third Year
Income before income tax.....	$40,000	$72,000	$85,000
Taxable income..............	34,000	70,000	87,000

Assuming an income tax rate of 50%, determine (a) the amount of income tax that would be reported on the income statement for each year and (b) the amount of deferred income tax payable that would be reported on the balance sheet at the end of each of the three years.

437

17-2. Prior to adjusting and closing the accounts at July 31, the end of the current fiscal year, the accountant discovered the following errors related to such year. Present the entry to correct each error.

(a) A purchase of $750 of merchandise on account was debited to Store Supplies.

(b) In recording a purchase of Office Equipment on July 20 for which a note payable was given, Accounts Payable was credited for $10,000.

(c) Store equipment that had cost $5,000 and on which $3,500 of depreciation had accumulated at the time of sale was sold for $2,000. The transaction was recorded by a debit to Cash and a credit to Sales for $2,000.

17-3. The following data were extracted from the records of Webb Corporation for the current fiscal year ended June 30:

Cost of merchandise sold......................	$322,000
Uninsured flood loss..........................	30,000
Sales..	465,000
Selling expenses..............................	57,500
General expenses.............................	22,500
Income tax applicable to flood loss.............	12,000
Income tax (net of amount applicable to flood loss).	19,400
Interest expense..............................	1,200
Common stock, $10 par.......................	400,000

Prepare an income statement, with earnings per share shown parenthetically for "net income before extraordinary items," "extraordinary items (less applicable income tax)," and "net income."

17-4. Winter Company purchased for cash 2,000 shares of its own $10 par common stock at $20 a share. The equity per share before the purchase was $35. (a) Present the entries in general journal form (1) to record the purchase (treasury stock is recorded at cost) and (2) to provide for the appropriation of retained earnings. (b) One half of the treasury stock was sold at $22 for cash. Present the entries in general journal form (1) to record the sale and (2) to reduce the appropriation.

17-5. The dates in connection with a cash dividend of $50,000 on a corporation's common stock are April 10, April 24, and May 8. Present the entries, in general journal form, required on each date.

17-6. The balance sheet of Tyler Company indicates common stock (20,000 shares authorized), $25 par, $250,000; premium on common stock, $40,000; and retained earnings, $150,000. The board of directors declares a 10% stock dividend when the market price of the stock is $45 a share. (a) Present entries to record (1) the declaration of the dividend and (2) the issuance of the stock certificates. (b) Determine the equity per share (1) before the stock dividend and (2) after the stock dividend. (c) Donald Clark owned 100 shares of the common stock before the stock dividend was declared. Determine the total equity of his holdings (1) before the stock dividend and (2) after the stock dividend.

17-7. The board of directors of the Harris Corporation decided to reduce the par of common shares from $100 to $25. This action will increase the number of outstanding shares to 1,000,000. The market price of the stock immediately before the stock split is $180 a share. (a) Determine the number of outstanding shares prior to the stock split. (b) Present the entries to record the stock split. (c) At approximately what price would a share of stock be expected to sell immediately after the stock split?

17-8. Results of transactions affecting net income and retained earnings for the first complete year of operations for Baxter Corporation are as follows:

Income before income tax........	$151,500
Income tax....................	71,250
Cash dividends declared.........	15,000
Appropriation for plant expansion.	25,000

Prepare a retained earnings statement for the first fiscal year ended October 31.

PROBLEMS

The following additional problems for this chapter are located in Appendix C: 17-1B, 17-3B, 17-4B.

17-1A. Selected transactions completed by the Royer Corporation during the current fiscal year are as follows:

Jan. 20. Purchased 1,000 shares of own common stock at $30, recording the stock at cost. (Prior to the purchase there were 25,000 shares of $10 par common stock outstanding.)

Mar. 2. Discovered that a receipt of $500 cash on account from R. T. Parker had been posted in error to the account of B. T. Barker. The transaction was recorded correctly in the cash receipts journal.

May 15. Declared a semiannual dividend of $1.50 on the 10,000 shares of preferred stock and a 50¢ dividend on the common stock to stockholders of record on May 25, payable on June 10.

June 10. Paid the cash dividends.

Sept. 30. Sold 500 shares of treasury stock at $35, receiving cash.

Nov. 15. Declared semiannual dividends of $1.50 on the preferred stock and 50¢ on the common stock. In addition, a 5% common stock dividend was declared on the common stock outstanding. The fair market value of the common stock to be issued is estimated at $37.

Dec. 10. Paid the cash dividends and issued the certificates for the common stock dividend.

31. Recorded $74,500 additional federal income tax allocable to net income for the year. Of this amount, $68,000 is a current liability and $6,500 is deferred.

31. The board of directors authorized the appropriation necessitated by the holdings of treasury stock.

Instructions:

Record the transactions above in general journal form.

17-2A. The retained earnings accounts of A. B. Moore and Company for the current fiscal year ended December 31 are as follows:

APPROPRIATION FOR PLANT EXPANSION

DATE		ITEM	DEBIT	CREDIT	BALANCE DEBIT	BALANCE CREDIT
Jan.	1	Balance				150,000
Dec.	31	Transfer to retained earnings account	50,000			100,000

APPROPRIATION FOR BONDED INDEBTEDNESS

DATE		ITEM	DEBIT	CREDIT	BALANCE DEBIT	BALANCE CREDIT
Jan.	1	Balance				125,000
Dec.	31	Transfer from retained earnings account		25,000		150,000

RETAINED EARNINGS

DATE		ITEM	DEBIT	CREDIT	BALANCE DEBIT	BALANCE CREDIT
Jan.	1	Balance				361,000
May	30	Cash dividend	40,000			321,000
Nov.	30	Cash dividend	40,000			281,000
	30	Stock dividend	100,000			181,000
Dec.	31	Net income		175,500		356,500
	31	Transfer from appropriation for plant expansion account		50,000		406,500
	31	Transfer to appropriation for bonded indebtedness account	25,000			381,500

Prepare a retained earnings statement for the fiscal
year ended December 31.

17-3A. The following data were selected from the records of Garner, Inc.
for the current fiscal year ended September 30:

Merchandise inventory (October 1)	$ 64,400
Merchandise inventory (September 30)	72,500
Advertising expense	12,100
Depreciation expense — store equipment	4,000
Sales	645,000
Sales salaries	56,400
Sales commissions	28,750
Office salaries	20,500
Purchases	405,900
Rent expense	18,000
Delivery expense	3,650
Store supplies expense	2,000
Office supplies expense	950
Insurance expense	2,700
Depreciation expense — office equipment	1,160
Miscellaneous selling expense	2,300
Miscellaneous general expense	2,850
Interest expense	2,100
Uninsured flood loss	25,000
Gain on sale of investments	40,000
Income tax:	
Net of amounts applicable to extraordinary items	38,370
Applicable to uninsured flood loss	10,500
Applicable to gain on sale of investments	10,000
Common stock, $100 par	1,000,000

Instructions:

Prepare an income statement, with earnings per share shown
parenthetically for "net income before extraordinary items," "extraordinary items (less applicable income tax)," and "net income."

17-4A. The stockholders' equity accounts of Matson Company with balances
on January 1 of the current fiscal year are as follows:

Common Stock, stated value $10 (50,000 shares authorized, 30,000 shares issued)	$300,000
Paid-in Capital in Excess of Stated Value	170,000
Appropriation for Contingencies	50,000
Appropriation for Treasury Stock	19,000
Retained Earnings	128,000
Treasury Stock (1,000 shares, at cost)	19,000

The following selected transactions occurred during the year:

Jan. 15. Paid cash dividends of 50¢ per share on the common stock. The dividend had been properly recorded when declared on December 15 of
the past fiscal year.

Mar. 10. Sold all of the treasury stock for $20,500 cash.

Apr. 2. Issued 5,000 shares of common stock for $100,000 cash.

2. Received land with an estimated fair market value of $12,500 from
the Midwest Industrial Park Council as a donation.

June 15. Declared a 4% stock dividend on common stock. The market price of the stock to be issued is $21 a share.

July 12. Issued the certificates for the dividend declared on June 15.

Nov. 8. Purchased 2,000 shares of treasury stock for $44,000.

Dec. 15. Declared a 50¢ per share dividend on common stock.

15. The board of directors authorized the increase of the appropriation for contingencies by $25,000.

15. Increased the appropriation for treasury stock to $44,000.

31. Closed the credit balance of the expense and revenue summary account, $84,450.

Instructions:

(1) Set up T accounts for the stockholders' equity accounts and enter the balances as of January 1.

(2) Prepare entries in general journal form to record the selected transactions and post to the stockholders' equity accounts. Set up additional stockholders' equity accounts as needed.

(3) Prepare the stockholders' equity section of the balance sheet as of December 31 of the current fiscal year.

17-5A. The stockholders' equity section of the balance sheet of Field Enterprises as of December 31, 1969 is presented below.

Stockholders' Equity

Paid-in capital:

Common stock, $100 par (10,000 shares authorized, 8,000 shares issued less 500 shares of treasury stock acquired by donation)	$800,000	
Premium on common stock	240,000	
Total paid-in capital		$1,040,000
Retained earnings:		
Appropriated for contingencies	$100,000	
Unappropriated	370,000	
Total retained earnings		470,000
Total stockholders' equity		$1,510,000

Selected transactions occurring in 1970 are as follows:

Jan. 30. Sold all of the treasury stock for $75,000.

Mar. 17. Issued 1,000 shares of stock in exchange for land and buildings with an estimated fair market value of $25,000 and $225,000 respectively. The property was encumbered by a mortgage of $100,000 and the company agreed to assume the responsibility for paying the mortgage note.

June 30. Declared a cash dividend of $3 per share to stockholders of record on July 12, payable on July 31.

July 31. Paid the cash dividend declared on June 30.

Aug. 15. Received land for a plant site valued at $20,000 from the Maywood Industrial Development Council as a donation.

Sept. 30. Issued 200 shares of stock to officers as a salary bonus. Market price of the stock, $160. (Debit Officers Salaries.)

Dec. 30. Declared a 5% stock dividend on the stock outstanding to stockholders of record on January 12, to be issued on January 31. The market price of the stock to be issued is $160.

30. Increased the appropriation for contingencies by $25,000.

Dec. 31. After closing all revenue and expense accounts, Expense and Revenue Summary has a credit balance of $150,000. Closed the expense and revenue summary account.

Instructions:

(1) Set up T accounts for the accounts appearing in the stockholders' equity section of the balance sheet and enter the balances as of January 1, 1970.

(2) Prepare entries in general journal form to record the transactions and post to the stockholders' equity accounts. Set up additional stockholders' equity accounts as needed.

(3) Prepare the stockholders' equity section of the balance sheet in good form as of December 31, 1970.

(4) Prepare a retained earnings statement for the year.

442

18

Corporations-- long-term obligations and investments

Financing corporations

Thus far in the discussion of corporations it has been assumed that the funds required for the enterprise are obtained by issuing stock or through the retention of earnings. Those purchasing shares of stock acquire an ownership equity in the corporation and expect to receive income in the form of dividends. Because of the ease of transferring stock and the availability of earnings through dividends, corporations have generally found investors ready to exchange their money for shares of stock. Some corporations have acquired the property of competitors in exchange for shares of their own stock. The great business of investment banking and the huge volume of trading on the stock exchanges give evidence of the present-day interest in corporate stocks.

Corporations may also obtain part of the funds needed for a long period of time by borrowing. They may borrow by selling bonds to many investors, or they may give long-term notes to a few investors or perhaps to a single investor such as an insurance company. In the following discussion reference is made to bonds; but, generally speaking, the accounting principles are the same if long-term notes are used.

When funds are borrowed through the issuance of bonds, there is a definite commitment to pay interest and to repay the principal at some future date. Those buying the bonds are creditors, and their claims for interest and for repayment of principal rank ahead of the claims of stockholders.

Many factors influence the incorporators or the board of directors in deciding upon the best means of obtaining funds. The subject will be limited here to a brief examination of the effect of different financing methods on the income of the corporation and its common stockholders. To illustrate, assume that three different plans for financing a $4,000,000 corporation are under consideration by its organizers. The three plans are as follows, assuming in each case that the securities will be issued at face value:

Plan 1.	Common stock......	$4,000,000
Plan 2.	7% preferred stock..	$2,000,000
	Common stock......	$2,000,000
Plan 3.	6% bonds..........	$2,000,000
	7% preferred stock..	$1,000,000
	Common stock......	$1,000,000

The incorporators estimate that the enterprise will earn $680,000 annually, before deducting interest on the bonds and income tax estimated at 50% of income. The tabulation below indicates the amount of earnings that would be available to common stockholders under each of the three plans.

	PLAN 1	PLAN 2	PLAN 3
6% bonds.........................			$2,000,000
7% preferred stock..................		$2,000,000	1,000,000
Common stock, $100 par.............	$4,000,000	2,000,000	1,000,000
Total.........................	$4,000,000	$4,000,000	$4,000,000
Earnings before interest and income tax..	$ 680,000	$ 680,000	$ 680,000
Deduct interest on bonds.............			120,000
Income before income tax...........	$ 680,000	$ 680,000	$ 560,000
Deduct income tax..................	340,000	340,000	280,000
Net income.......................	$ 340,000	$ 340,000	$ 280,000
Dividends on preferred stock...........		140,000	70,000
Available for dividends on common stock.	$ 340,000	$ 200,000	$ 210,000
Earnings per share on common stock..	$ 8.50	$ 10.00	$ 21.00

If only common stock is issued as in Plan 1, the earnings per share on the common stock would be $8.50 per share. Under Plan 2, the effect of issuing 7% preferred stock for half of the capitalization results in $10 earnings per common share. The issuance of 6% bonds in Plan 3, with the remaining capitalization split between preferred and common, results in a return of $21 per share on common stock.

Obviously, under this set of conditions Plan 3 is the most attractive for common stockholders. If the total of assumed earnings increases beyond $680,000, the spread between the yield to common stockholders under Plan 1 and Plan 3 would become even greater. But if successively smaller amounts of earnings are assumed, the comparative attractiveness of Plan 2 and Plan 3 decreases. This is illustrated by the tabulation below, in which earnings, before deducting interest and income tax, are assumed to be $280,000.

	PLAN 1	PLAN 2	PLAN 3
6% bonds..........................			$2,000,000
7% preferred stock..................		$2,000,000	1,000,000
Common stock, $100 par.............	$4,000,000	2,000,000	1,000,000
Total.......................	$4,000,000	$4,000,000	$4,000,000
Earnings before interest and income tax..	$ 280,000	$ 280,000	$ 280,000
Deduct interest on bonds.............			120,000
Income before income tax..........	$ 280,000	$ 280,000	$ 160,000
Deduct income tax.................	140,000	140,000	80,000
Net income.......................	$ 140,000	$ 140,000	$ 80,000
Dividends on preferred stock..........		140,000	70,000
Available for dividends on common stock.	$ 140,000	—	$ 10,000
Earnings per share on common stock ..	$ 3.50	—	$ 1.00

The preceding analysis of financing methods concentrated on the effect of different plans on earnings per share to the common stockholder. Other factors must be considered in evaluating different methods of financing. For example, the issuance of bonds represents a fixed annual interest charge and an obligation that must be paid. On the other hand, a decision to finance by issuing only common stock will require a large investment by one stockholder or group of stockholders if they are to have control of the corporation.

445

Characteristics of bonds

When a corporation issues bonds, it executes a contract with the bondholders known as a *bond indenture* or *trust indenture.* The bond issue is divided into a number of individual bonds, which may be of varying denominations. Ordinarily the principal of each bond, also referred to as the *face value*, is $1,000 or a multiple thereof. The interest on bonds may be payable at annual, semiannual, or quarterly intervals. Most bonds provide for payment on a semiannual basis.

Registered bonds may be transferred from one owner to another only by proper endorsement on the certificate, and the issuing corporation maintains a record of the name and the address of each bondholder. Interest payments are made by check to the owner of record. Title to *bearer bonds, which are also referred to as coupon bonds*, is transferred by delivery. Interest coupons for the entire term are attached to the bond certificate. They are in the form of checks or drafts payable to bearer, and at each interest date the holder detaches the appropriate coupon and presents it at his bank for collection.

On a Debenture Bond be a serial bond, term bond convertible

When all bonds of an issue mature at the same time, they are called *term bonds*. If the maturities are spread over several dates, they are called *serial bonds*. For example, one tenth of an issue of $1,000,000, or $100,000, may mature eleven years from the issuance date, another $100,000 may mature twelve years from the issuance date, and so on until the final $100,000 matures at the end of the twentieth year. Bonds that may be exchanged for other securities under specified conditions are called *convertible bonds*. If the issuing corporation reserves the right to redeem the bonds before maturity, they are referred to as *callable bonds*.

A *secured bond* is one that gives the bondholder a claim on particular assets in the event that the issuing corporation fails to meet its obligations on the bonds. The properties mortgaged or pledged may be specific buildings and equipment, the entire plant, or stocks and bonds of other companies owned by the debtor corporation. Bonds issued on the basis of the general credit of the corporation are called *debenture bonds*.

Accounting for the issuance of bonds

When bonds are issued at face value, the transaction is recorded by a debit to Cash and a credit to Bonds Payable. If there is more than one bond issue, a separate account should be maintained for each issue. Bonds Payable are reported on the balance sheet as long-term or fixed liabilities. As the maturity date comes within one year of the balance sheet date, they should be transferred to the current liability classification if they are to be paid out of current assets. If they are to be paid with segregated funds or if they are to be replaced with another bond issue, they should remain in the noncurrent category and their disposition should be disclosed by an explanatory note. The listing in the balance sheet should include data as to security, interest rate, and due date.

Bonds issued at a premium. Bonds may be issued at a price above or below face value, depending upon the rate of interest offered and the general credit standing of the corporation. If a corporation offers a rate of interest that is higher than the market rate for similar securities, investors may be willing to pay a premium for the bonds. To illustrate the accounting for bonds sold at a premium, assume that on January 1 a corporation issues $100,000 of 6%, 10-year bonds at 105, with interest payable annually on December 31. The entry for the transaction, in general journal form, is as follows:

Jan. 1	Cash..	105,000	
	Bonds Payable.............................		100,000
	Premium on Bonds Payable.................		5,000

The investors paid the premium because they were willing to lend money to the corporation at less than the contract rate of 6%. The

446

premium represents an advance payment by the investors for the privilege of receiving interest in excess of the prevailing market rate.

The issuing corporation has incurred two liabilities: (1) to repay $100,000, the face amount of the bonds, in 10 years, and (2) to pay annual interest of $6,000 for 10 years. The $5,000 premium is not income to the corporation; rather, it is an advance of interest collected from the bondholders that will be repaid to them over the life of the bonds. This may be demonstrated by determining the movement of cash related to the bond issue. As shown by the following tabulation, the excess of the cash paid during the 10-year period over the cash received from the sale of the bonds is $55,000. This amount represents the total interest expense for the 10-year period.

Cash to be paid:		
Face of the bonds....................................	$100,000	
Interest — 10 payments of $6,000 each (6% of $100,000)	60,000	$160,000
Cash received:		
Face of the bonds................................	$100,000	
Premium on the bonds...........................	5,000	105,000
Total interest expense for 10 years...................		$ 55,000
Interest expense per year..........................		$ 5,500

The total interest expense for the life of the bonds is spread ratably over the 10 years by amortizing $1/10$ of the premium against interest expense each year. The entry for the payment of the annual interest and the annual entry to amortize the premium are as follows, in general journal form:

447

Dec. 31	Interest Expense...............................	6,000	
	Cash...		6,000
31	Premium on Bonds Payable......................	500	
	Interest Expense.............................		500

The debit of $6,000 to the expense account in the first entry is partially offset by the $500 credit to the expense account in the second entry, leaving a net interest expense of $5,500 for the year. At the time the bonds mature, the premium account will be completely written off.

Bonds issued at a discount. When the contract rate of interest on a bond issue is less than the prevailing market rate for comparable bonds, the bonds can be issued only at a discount. For example, assume that on January 1 a corporation issues 5%, 10-year bonds with a face value of $100,000. The prevailing rate of interest on similar securities being somewhat in excess of 5%, the bonds are sold at 95. The entry for the transaction, in general journal form, is:

Jan. 1	Cash...	95,000	
	Discount on Bonds Payable....................	5,000	
	Bonds Payable...............................		100,000

The bond discount is not an immediate loss or expense to the corporation. Rather, it represents a deferred charge to interest expense. The corporation has contracted to repay at maturity an amount greater than it received from the issuance of the bonds. As a compensating factor, however, it will pay interest at a rate lower than the prevailing rate. The discount may be considered analogous to interest deducted in advance when a note is discounted.

The corporation contracts to pay: (1) $100,000, the face amount of the bonds, in 10 years, and (2) annual interest of $5,000 for 10 years. The total interest cost for the 10 years, as indicated in the tabulation below, will be $55,000, or $5,500 per year on a straight-line basis.

Cash to be paid:		
Face of the bonds..................................	$100,000	
Interest — 10 payments of $5,000 each (5% of $100,000)	50,000	$150,000
Cash received:		
Face of the bonds.................................	$100,000	
Less discount on the bonds........................	5,000	95,000
Total interest expense for 10 years..................		$ 55,000
Interest expense per year...........................		$ 5,500

The entry for the payment of the annual interest and the annual entry to amortize the discount, in general journal form, are:

448

Dec. 31	Interest Expense..............................		5,000	
	Cash.......................................			5,000
31	Interest Expense.............................		500	
	Discount on Bonds Payable....................			500

Over the life of the bonds the charges to the interest expense account will total $55,000 and the bond discount account will be in balance when the bonds mature.

Another system of amortizing bond premium and discount, called the *compound-interest* method, yields a *uniform periodic rate* of interest on the carrying value of the bonds rather than an equal periodic amount of interest. *Carrying value* is the face value of the bonds plus the unamortized premium or minus the unamortized discount. The entries to record the periodic amortization by the compound-interest method are the same as those presented in the preceding illustrations, except that the amounts are different.

Bond discount and bond premium on the balance sheet

The balance of the bond discount account is viewed as deferred interest that will be gradually added to interest expense over the life of the bonds. It is ordinarily reported in the balance sheet as an asset under the caption "Deferred expenses" or "Deferred charges."

Premium on bonds is considered to be an advance of interest that is returned to bondholders as a part of the periodic interest payments. It is ordinarily reported in the balance sheet as a liability under the caption "Deferred credits."

There is good theoretical justification for treating bond discount as a deduction from Bonds Payable and bond premium as an addition to Bonds Payable. According to this view, a $100,000 bond issue sold at 95 would be reported as bonds payable of $100,000 less discount of $5,000, or a net liability of $95,000. With the amortization of the discount, the net amount of the liability would gradually increase until it became equal to $100,000 at maturity. An objection to this approach is that the bond indenture agreement requires the payment of face value, and it is that amount for which the corporation is liable during the entire period that the bonds are outstanding.

Bond sinking fund

The bond indenture may provide that funds for the payment of bonds at maturity be accumulated over the life of the issue. The amounts set aside are kept separate from other assets in a special fund called a *sinking fund*. Cash deposited in the fund is ordinarily invested in income-producing securities. The periodic deposits plus the earnings on the investments should approximately equal the face amount of the bonds at maturity. Control over the fund may be exercised by the corporation or it may be in the hands of a *trustee*, which is usually a bank or trust company.

When cash is transferred to the sinking fund, an account called Sinking Fund Cash is debited and Cash is credited. The purchase of investments is recorded by a debit to Sinking Fund Investments and a credit to Sinking Fund Cash. As interest or dividends on the investments are received, the cash is debited to Sinking Fund Cash and Sinking Fund Income is credited.

To illustrate the accounting for a bond sinking fund, assume that a corporation issues $100,000 of 10-year bonds dated January 1, with the provision that equal annual deposits be made in the bond sinking fund at the end of each of the 10 years. The fund is expected to be invested in securities that will yield approximately 4½% per year. Reference to compound interest tables indicates that an annual deposit of $8,150 is sufficient to provide a fund of approximately $100,000 at the end of 10 years. Typical transactions and the related entries affecting a sinking fund are illustrated on the next page in general journal form. It should be noted that they represent only a few of the numerous transactions that might occur during the 10-year period.

449

Deposit of cash in the fund

A deposit is made at the end of each of the 10 years.

Entry: Sinking Fund Cash.......................... 8,150

Cash..................................... 8,150

Purchase of investments

The time of purchase and the amount invested at one time vary, depending upon market conditions and the unit price of securities purchased.

Entry: Sinking Fund Investments.................... 8,100

Sinking Fund Cash...................... 8,100

Receipt of income from investments

Interest and dividends are received at different times during the year. The amount earned per year increases as the fund increases. The entry below summarizes the receipt of income for the year on the securities purchased with the first deposit.

Entry: Sinking Fund Cash.......................... 360

Sinking Fund Income...................... 360

Sale of investments

Investments may be sold from time to time and the proceeds reinvested. Prior to maturity, all investments are converted into cash. The entry below records the sale of securities at the end of the tenth year.

Entry: Sinking Fund Cash.......................... 88,225

Sinking Fund Investments................. 87,750

Gain on Sale of Investments.............. 475

Payments of bonds

The cash available in the fund at the end of the tenth year is composed of the following:

Proceeds from sale of investments (above)........	$ 88,225
Income earned in tenth year..................	3,950
Last annual deposit..........................	8,150
Total.....................................	$100,325

The entry below records the payment of the bonds and the transfer of the excess cash to the regular cash account.

Entry: Bonds Payable........................... 100,000

Cash....................................... 325

Sinking Fund Cash........................ 100,325

In the illustration the amount of the fund exceeded the amount of the liability by $325. This excess was transferred to the regular cash account. If the fund had been less than the amount of the liability, for example $99,500, the regular cash account would have been drawn upon for the $500 deficiency.

Sinking fund income represents earnings of the corporation and is reported in the income statement as "Other income." The cash and the securities comprising the sinking fund are classified in the balance sheet as "Investments." The investments section ordinarily appears immediately below the current assets section.

Restriction of dividends

The restriction of dividends during the life of a bond issue is another means of increasing the assurance that the obligation will be paid at maturity. Assuming that the corporation in the preceding example is required by the bond indenture to appropriate $10,000 of retained earnings each year for the 10-year life of the bonds, the following entry would be made annually:

Dec. 31	Retained Earnings..........................	10,000	
	Appropriation for Bonded Indebtedness......		10,000

As was indicated in the preceding chapter, an appropriation has no direct relationship to a sinking fund; each is independent of the other. When there is both a fund and an appropriation for the same purpose, the appropriation may be said to be *funded*.

Bond redemption

Callable bonds are redeemable by the issuing corporation within the period of time and at the price specified in the bond indenture. Ordinarily the call price is above face value. If the market rate of interest declines subsequent to issuance of the bonds, the corporation may sell new bonds at a lower interest rate and use the funds to redeem the original issue. The reduction of future interest expense is, of course, always an incentive to bond redemption. A corporation may also redeem all or a portion of its bonds before maturity by purchasing them on the open market.

When a corporation redeems bonds at a price below their carrying value, the corporation realizes a gain; if the price is in excess of carrying value, a loss is incurred. To illustrate redemption, assume that on June 30 a corporation has a bond issue of $100,000 outstanding, on which there is an unamortized premium of $4,000. The corporation has the option of calling the bonds at 105, which it exercises on this date. The entry to record the redemption, in general journal form, is:

June 30	Bonds Payable..........................	100,000	
	Premium on Bonds Payable...............	4,000	
	Loss on Redemption of Bonds.............	1,000	
	Cash....................................		105,000

If the bonds were not callable, the corporation might purchase a portion on the open market. Assuming that the corporation purchases $25,000 of bonds at 96 on June 30, the entry to record the redemption would be as follows, in general journal form:

June 30	Bonds Payable..........................	25,000	
	Premium on Bonds Payable...............	1,000	
	Cash....................................		24,000
	Gain on Redemption of Bonds............		2,000

It should be noted that only the portion of the premium relating to the bonds redeemed is written off. The excess of the carrying value of the liability, $26,000, over the cash paid, $24,000, is recognized as a gain.

Investments in stocks and bonds

The issuance of stocks and bonds, the declaration and the payment of dividends, and other related transactions have thus far been discussed from the standpoint of the issuing corporation. Whenever a corporation records a transaction between itself and the owners of its stock or bonds, there is a reciprocal entry in the accounts of the investor. In this and the following sections of the chapter, attention will be given to the principles underlying the accounting for investments in stocks and bonds.

Investments in corporate securities may be made by individuals, partnerships, industrial corporations, financial corporations such as banks and life insurance companies, and other types of organizations. Some investors are attracted to stocks because of the ownership equity and the expectation of large dividends, while others prefer the greater safety of principal and certainty as to income (even though often of a lesser amount) that bonds afford.

Corporate securities may be purchased directly from the issuing corporation or from other investors. Stocks and bonds may be *listed* on an organized exchange, or they may be *unlisted*, in which case they are said to be bought and sold *over the counter*. The services of a broker are usually employed in buying and selling both listed and unlisted securities. The record of transactions on stock exchanges is reported daily in the financial pages of newspapers. This record usually includes data on the volume of sales and the high, low, and closing prices for each security traded during the day. Prices for stocks are quoted in terms of fractional dollars, $1/8$ of a dollar being the usual minimum fraction. Some low-priced stocks are sold in lower fractions of a dollar, such as $1/16$ or $1/32$. A price of $40^3/8$ per share means $40.375; a price of $40^1/2$ means $40.50; and so on. As indicated earlier, prices for bonds are quoted as a percentage of face value; thus the price of a $1,000 bond quoted at $104^1/2$ would be $1,045.

The cost of securities purchased includes not only the price paid but also other costs incident to the purchase, such as broker's commission and postage charges for delivery. When bonds are purchased between interest dates, the purchaser pays the seller the interest accrued from the last interest payment date to the date of purchase. The amount of the interest paid should be debited to Interest Income, as it is an offset against the amount that will be received at the next interest date. To illustrate, assume that a $1,000 bond is purchased at 102 plus brokerage fees of $5.30 and accrued interest of $10.20. The entry to record the transaction, in general journal form, is as follows:

452

Apr. 2	Investment in Taylor Co. Bonds.............	1,025.30	
	Interest Income..........................	10.20	
	Cash....................................		1,035.50

When stocks are purchased between dividend dates, there is no separate charge for the pro rata amount of the dividend. Dividends do not accrue from day to day, since they become an obligation of the issuing corporation only as they are declared by the directors. The price of stocks may be affected by the anticipated dividend as the usual declaration date approaches, but this anticipated dividend is only one of many factors that influence stock prices.

Temporary investments

A corporation may have on hand an amount of cash considerably in excess of its immediate requirements, but it may believe that this cash will be needed in operating the business, possibly within the coming year. Rather than allow this excess cash to lie idle until it is actually needed, the corporation may invest all or a portion of it in income-yielding securities. Such securities are known as *temporary investments* or *marketable securities*. These investments may actually be held by the corporation for several years, but they are still considered to be temporary if (1) they can be turned into cash readily at any time and (2) management intends to make them available for sale when the business needs additional cash in its normal operations.

453

Securities representing a temporary investment are classified in the balance sheet as current assets and are shown immediately below cash. They are usually valued at cost or at the lower of cost or market. If they are carried at cost, their market value at the balance sheet date may be disclosed by a footnote or a parenthetical statement.

Although temporary investments are often carried in the accounts at the lower of cost or market, minor declines in their market value need not be given recognition in the accounts. If their market value declines substantially below cost and there is evidence that the fluctuation is not temporary, the securities should be stated at market value. The reduction in value is treated as a loss of the period. If the same securities are still owned at subsequent balance sheet dates, adjustments are made only for the later declines in market price. If their market price has increased, the current market value should be disclosed parenthetically on the balance sheet.

Declines in the market value of securities are not recognized as losses for income tax purposes regardless of whether they are recorded in the accounts. When the securities are sold, the gain or the loss to be recognized for tax purposes is determined by comparing the proceeds from the sale with the original cost.

Long-term investments

Investments that are not intended as a ready source of cash in the normal operations of the business are known as *long-term investments*. A business may make long-term investments simply because it has cash that it cannot use in its normal operations; but a corporation is more likely to make long-term investments for other reasons.

It is not unusual for a corporation to purchase stocks or bonds as a means of establishing or maintaining business relations with the issuing company. Such investments are ordinarily held for an indefinite period and are not sold so long as the relationship remains satisfactory. Corporations may also acquire all or a substantial portion of the voting stock of another corporation in order to control its activities. Similarly, a corporation may organize a new corporation for the purpose of marketing a new product or for some other business reason, receiving stock in exchange for the assets transferred to the new corporation. Cash and securities in bond sinking funds are also considered long-term investments, as they are accumulated for the purpose of paying the bond liability.

Investments in long-term securities are recorded in the accounts at cost and are so shown on the balance sheet. Fluctuations in price subsequent to acquisition are ordinarily ignored except when there has been a permanent and material decline, in which case the recorded amount may be reduced or the facts may be disclosed by a parenthetical notation on the balance sheet. Long-term investments are listed in the balance sheet under the caption "Investments."

Income from investments in stocks

Cash dividends declared on stock owned either as temporary investments or as long-term investments may be recorded by a debit to Dividends Receivable and a credit to Dividend Income. The receivable account is then credited when the cash is received. For federal income tax purposes, however, dividends are not considered to be income until the cash is made available to the stockholder. For this reason a common practice is to ignore the receivable and to record the income when the cash is received. Although this is a deviation from accrual accounting, the practice ordinarily causes no material distortion of income when followed consistently.

A dividend in the form of additional shares of stock is ordinarily not income and hence no entry is necessary beyond a notation as to the additional number of shares now owned. The receipt of a stock dividend does, however, affect the cost basis of each share of stock. Thus, if a 5-share common stock dividend is received on 100 shares of common stock originally purchased for $4,200 ($42 per share), the unit cost basis of the 105 shares becomes $4,200 ÷ 105, or $40 per share.

Income from investments in bonds

Interest on bonds held either as temporary investments or as long-term investments is recorded in the same manner as interest on notes receivable. Interest received during a fiscal period is recorded as a debit to Cash and a credit to Interest Income. At the end of a fiscal period, an adjusting entry debiting Interest Receivable and crediting Interest Income is made for interest accrued. After the accounts are closed, the entry is reversed in order that all receipts of bond interest during the year may be credited to the interest income account.

When interest is recorded on temporary bond investments, the fact that these investments may have been purchased for more or less than their face value is ignored. But when the cost of bonds purchased for long-term investments is greater or less than the face value, the amount of the premium or the discount should be written off over the remaining life of the bonds in much the same manner in which the debtor corporation accounts for a premium or a discount on the original issuance of the bonds. To illustrate, assume that twenty $1,000, 6% bonds are purchased on July 1 for $21,155, including commission, plus accrued interest. Interest on the bonds is payable semiannually on April 1 and October 1 and the bonds are due 8¾ years (105 months) from the date of purchase. Entries in the accounts of the purchaser at the time of purchase and for the remainder of the fiscal year, ending December 31, are presented below, in general journal form.

455

Purchase of bonds and payment of accrued interest on July 1

Cost of $20,000 Reid Corp. bonds..............		$21,155
Interest accrued from April 1 on $20,000 (3 months)..		300
Cash payment....................		$21,455

Entry: Investment in Reid Corp. Bonds.............. 21,155
Interest Income........................... 300
Cash.................................. 21,455

Receipt of semiannual interest on October 1

Interest from April 1 on $20,000 (6 months)........		$600

Entry: Cash..................................... 600
Interest Income....................... 600

Adjustment for interest accrual on December 31

Interest accrued from October 1 on $20,000 (3 months).		$300

Entry: Interest Receivable.......................... 300
Interest Income....................... 300

Adjustment for premium amortization on December 31

Premium of $1,155 ÷ 105 months.................		$11
Number of months from date of purchase...........		6
Premium amortization.........................		$66

Entry: Interest Income......................... 66
Investment in Reid Corp. Bonds............. 66

Ch. 18 • Corporations — long-term obligations and investments

The net effect of the four entries in the interest income account is a credit of $534, which represents interest at 6% for 6 months ($600) less amortization of premium for 6 months ($66). By following the foregoing procedures, the premium of $1,155 will be amortized against interest income over the life of the bonds, and the investment account will be reduced to $20,000 at the maturity date.

A similar procedure may be applied to bonds purchased at a price below face value. The amount of the discount is accumulated by periodic entries debiting the investment account and crediting Interest Income. It may be noted that when speculative bonds are purchased at a substantial discount, it would be imprudent to accumulate the discount because of the uncertainty of payment at maturity.

Sale of investments

When shares of stock that have been held as either temporary or long-term investments are sold, the cash account is debited for the proceeds (selling price less commission and other costs) and the investment account is credited for the cost of the shares sold. If there is a gain, it is credited to an account entitled Gain on Sale of Investments; if there is a loss, it is debited to an account entitled Loss on Sale of Investments.

A sale of bonds held as temporary investments is recorded in the same manner as a sale of stocks. A sale of bonds held as a long-term investment is also recorded in the same manner, provided there has been no amortization of premium or discount during the period of ownership.

The periodic amortization of premium on bonds held as long-term investments tends to reduce the book value of the investment from its original cost to its face value. Conversely, the amortization of discount tends to increase the book value of the investment from original cost to face value. When the bonds are sold before maturity, the gain or loss is the difference between their book value and the proceeds of the sale. To illustrate, assume that the bonds of the Reid Corporation in the preceding example are sold at 99 plus accrued interest on June 30, 1971, which is two years after they were purchased. The entries to record the amortization of premium and the other debits and credits incident to the sale are presented below, in general journal form.

Amortization of premium for current year to June 30

Monthly premium (determined previously)...........	$11
Number of months in fiscal year to date.............	6
Premium amortization.............................	$66

Entry: Interest Income............................. 66
           Investment in Reid Corp. Bonds..............   66

Receipt of accrued interest and sale of bonds on June 30

Interest accrued from April 1 on $20,000 (3 months)..	$300

```
Cost of bonds purchased two years earlier............      $21,155
Premium amortization, 24 months at $11............           264
                                                          --------
Book value of bonds on date of sale, June 30........      $20,891
Proceeds from sale, $20,000 face value at 99.........      19,800
                                                          --------
    Loss on sale..............................             $1,091
                                                          ========
Entry:  Cash.......................................  20,100
        Loss on Sale of Investments.................   1,091
        Interest Income.............................               300
        Investment in Reid Corp. Bonds.............             20,891  Book Value
```

Corporation financial statements

Examples of retained earnings statements, the stockholders' equity section of balance sheets, and sections of income statements affected by the corporate form of organization have been presented in preceding chapters. A complete balance sheet of a corporation, containing items discussed in this and preceding chapters, is illustrated on page 458.

Some of the many variations in the form of corporation financial statements have been described and illustrated; additional possibilities will be presented in later chapters. Attention has also been directed to many of the alternatives in terminology used to describe items in the statements. Although accountants and others engaged in various business pursuits are likely to prefer certain forms and terms over other alternatives, it is important that they understand the import of the alternatives. Selected statements from the annual reports of a number of corporations are presented in Appendix B.

Auditors' report

Responsibility for the form and content of financial statements issued to stockholders and creditors rests primarily with the principal officers of a corporation. Before issuing the annual statements all publicly held corporations, as well as many closed corporations, engage independent public accountants, usually CPAs, to conduct an *examination*. Upon completion of the examination, which for large corporations may engage the time of scores of accountants for several weeks or longer, the auditors prepare a *report* (at one time called *certificate*) which then accompanies the financial statements. A typical report briefly describes the scope of the auditors' examination and their opinion as to the fairness of the statements. The phraseology used in the report illustrated at the top of page 459 conforms with general usage.[1]

In most instances the auditors can render a report such as the one illustrated, which may be said to be "unqualified." However, it is

[1]*Statements on Auditing Procedure, No. 33,* "Auditing Standards and Procedures" (New York: American Institute of Certified Public Accountants, 1963), p. 57.

Logan Corporation
Balance Sheet
December 31, 1969

Assets

Current assets:

Cash..................................		$ 51,379	
Marketable securities, at cost (market price, $78,000).		70,000	
Accounts and notes receivable....................	$156,000		
Less allowance for doubtful receivables..........	6,000	150,000	
Inventories, at lower of cost (first-in, first-out) or market......		192,880	
Prepaid expenses..........................		12,000	
Total current assets..........................			$ 476,259

Investments:

Bond sinking fund............................		$ 53,962	
Investment in affiliated company.................		140,000	
Total investments...........................			193,962

	Cost	Accumulated Depreciation	Book Value	
Plant assets:				
Machinery and equipment............	$ 764,400	$166,200	$598,200	
Buildings..........................	220,000	79,955	140,045	
Land..............................	50,000	——	50,000	
Total plant assets.................	$1,034,400	$246,155		788,245

Intangible assets:

Goodwill.............................	$100,000	
Organization costs.....................	18,000	
Total intangible assets.................		118,000

Deferred expenses:

Discount on bonds payable......................	5,600
Total assets...................................	$1,582,066

Liabilities

Current liabilities:

Accounts payable............................	$108,810	
Income tax payable..........................	30,500	
Dividends payable...........................	24,000	
Accrued liabilities..........................	11,400	
Total current liabilities.....................		$ 174,710

Long-term liabilities:

Debenture 6% bonds payable, due December 31, 1977.	250,000

Deferred credits:

Deferred income tax payable....................	25,500
Total liabilities...............................	$ 450,210

Stockholders' Equity

Paid-in capital:

Common stock, $20 par (50,000 shares authorized, 20,000 shares issued)......................	$400,000	
Premium on common stock......................	320,000	
Total paid-in capital......................		$720,000

Retained earnings:

Appropriated:			
For bonded indebtedness.............	$ 60,000		
For plant expansion................	150,000	$210,000	
Unappropriated.......................		201,856	
Total retained earnings.............		411,856	
Total stockholders' equity...............			1,131,856
Total liabilities and stockholders' equity.............			$1,582,066

Balance sheet of a corporation

To the Stockholders of Logan Corporation:

We have examined the balance sheet of Logan Corporation as of December 31, 1969 and the related statements of income and retained earnings for the year then ended. Our examination was made in accordance with generally accepted auditing standards, and accordingly included such tests of the accounting records and such other auditing procedures as we considered necessary in the circumstances.

In our opinion, the accompanying balance sheet and statements of income and retained earnings present fairly the financial position of Logan Corporation at December 31, 1969 and the results of its operations for the year then ended, in conformity with generally accepted accounting principles applied on a basis consistent with that of the preceding year.

Cincinnati, Ohio
January 28, 1970

Allen & White
Certified Public Accountants

Auditors' report

possible that accounting methods employed by a client do not conform with generally accepted accounting principles or that a client has not been consistent in the application of principles. In such cases a "qualified" opinion may be rendered, in which case the exception is briefly described and sometimes presented in greater detail in a separate note. If the effect of the departure from accepted principles or change in principles is sufficiently material, the opinion may be "adverse."

The reporting responsibilities of independent CPAs in attesting to the fairness of financial statements is described as follows:

459

The report shall either contain an expression of opinion regarding the financial statements, taken as a whole, or an assertion to the effect that an opinion cannot be expressed. When an over-all opinion cannot be expressed, the reasons therefor should be stated. In all cases where an auditor's name is associated with financial statements the report should contain a clear-cut indication of the character of the auditor's examination, if any, and the degree of responsibility he is taking.[2]

Professional accountants cannot disregard the foregoing auditing standard without seriously jeopardizing their reputations. Indeed, they also risk legal action by persons who may suffer loss from reliance on erroneous statements for which they have rendered an unqualified opinion.

QUESTIONS

1. Contrast the status of interest on bonds payable and cash dividends on stock in determining the income tax of corporations making such payments.

2. How are interest payments made to holders of (a) registered bonds and (b) bearer or coupon bonds?

---

[2]*Ibid.*, p. 56.

3. Differentiate between term bonds and serial bonds.

4. Under what circumstances would Bonds Payable be reported in the balance sheet as a current liability?

5. If a corporation issues 6% bonds at a time when the market rate of interest on securities of this type is lower than 6%, is it likely that the bonds will be sold at face value, at a discount, or at a premium?

6. Casner Corporation sells a $1,000,000 bond issue to an underwriter for $1,035,000. The underwriter resells the bonds to individual investors at 105. What amount of premium on bonds payable would Casner Corporation record in its accounts?

7. What is the purpose of a bond sinking fund?

8. What is the purpose of establishing an appropriation of retained earnings for bonded indebtedness?

9. When there is both a fund and an appropriation for bonded indebtedness, what is the additional descriptive term that may be applied to the appropriation?

10. Under what caption would each of the following accounts be reported on the balance sheet: (a) Discount on Bonds Payable; (b) Premium on Bonds Payable; (c) Sinking Fund Cash; (d) Sinking Fund Investments; (e) Appropriation for Bonded Indebtedness?

11. Bonds Payable has a balance of $100,000 and Premium on Bonds Payable has a balance of $2,000. If the issuing corporation redeems the bonds at 103, what is the amount of gain or loss on redemption?

460   **12.** Compare bonds with stocks as an investment in terms of potential amount of income and safety of principal.

13. What is the cost of the following securities, exclusive of commissions, etc.: (a) bonds with a face value of $10,000 purchased at 101½; (b) 100 shares of $50 par stock purchased at 92¾?

14. Is the interest accrued on bonds at the date of purchase included in the quoted price?

15. When stocks are purchased between dividend dates, does the purchaser pay the seller the dividend accrued since the last dividend payment date? Explain.

16. Under what caption would each of the following be reported on the balance sheet: (a) securities held as a temporary investment; (b) securities held as a long-term investment?

17. Tanner Company purchased $10,000 of Strong Corporation bonds at 103 plus accrued interest of $100 and brokerage commission of $25. For what amount should the investment account be debited?

18. Are brokerage commissions on the sale of securities owned considered to be an expense of the period or a reduction in the sales proceeds?

19. A stockholder owning 100 shares of Wade Co. common stock acquired at a total cost of $5,500 receives a common stock dividend of 10 shares. (a) What is the unit cost basis of the 110 shares? (b) If the stockholder later sells 10 shares at 60, what is the amount of the gain or the loss?

18-1. Two companies are financed as follows:

	Ames Co.	Barr, Inc.
Bonds Payable, 6% (issued at face value)...	$ 250,000	$500,000
Preferred 7% Stock......................	250,000	500,000
Common Stock, $50.....................	1,000,000	500,000

Income tax is estimated at 50% of income. Determine for each company the earnings per share of common stock, assuming the income before bond interest and income tax for each company to be (a) $100,000, (b) $150,000, and (c) $250,000.

18-2. On the first day of the fiscal year, W. S. Eaton Company issued $100,000 of 10-year, 5% bonds at 95. On the same day, also the first day of its fiscal year Stewart Corporation issued $100,000 of 10-year, 6% bonds at 105.

(a) Present the entries, in general journal form, for the W. S. Eaton Company to record:
   (1) The sale of the bonds (the bonds were sold on the date of issue).
   (2) The payment of one year's interest at the end of the first fiscal year.
   (3) The amortization of the premium or the discount at the end of the first fiscal year.
(b) Present the entries, in general journal form, for Stewart Corporation to record the three transactions described in (a).
(c) Determine the amount of the bond interest expense for the year for each company.

18-3. The Graham Corporation issued $500,000 of 20-year bonds on the first day of the fiscal year. The bond indenture provides that a sinking fund be accumulated by 20 annual deposits, beginning at the end of the first year. The corporation expects to earn 5% on the fund and accordingly deposits $16,000 annually.

(a) Present the entry in general journal form to record the first deposit.
(b) Present the entry in general journal form to record the investment of $15,790 from the first deposit in securities.
(c) Assuming that the fund earned a total of $810 during the year following the first deposit, prepare the summary entry in general journal form to record receipt of the income.
(d) Assuming that the cash in the fund totaled $501,210 at the maturity date of the bonds, prepare the entry in general journal form to record the payment of the bonds and the transfer of the excess cash to the regular cash account.

18-4. The bond indenture for the Graham Corporation bonds (Exercise 18-3) also provides that dividends be restricted by equal annual appropriations of retained earnings, which are to total the face value of the bonds at maturity. Give the entry to record the appropriation at the end of the first year.

18-5. The Olson Company issued $1,000,000 of 10-year, 6% bonds dated June 1, 1969. Interest is payable semiannually on June 1 and December 1. Present in general journal form (a) all entries related to the bonds in 1969, assuming that the issue was sold on June 1 for $1,018,000 to an underwriter; (b) the reversing entry to be made on January 1, 1970, the first day of the fiscal year; and (c) the entry to be made on June 1, 1970, for the payment of interest.

18-6. Assuming that on June 1, 1972, the Olson Company (Exercise 18-5) redeems $100,000 of its outstanding bonds at 101, present in general journal form the entries to record (a) the amortization of bond premium for the current year applicable to the bonds redeemed and (b) the redemption.

18-7. On March 8, McGraw Corporation acquired 100 shares of Ellis Chemical Co. common stock at 60¼ plus brokerage commission and postage charges of $25. On July 25, a cash dividend of $1 per share and a 10% stock dividend were received. On November 10, 50 shares were sold for 52½ less brokerage commission and postage charges of $15. Present entries in general journal form to record (a) purchase of the stock, (b) receipt of the dividends, and (c) sale of the 50 shares.

18-8. On the first day of the fiscal year, Miller Corporation purchases $100,000 of 5% bonds of the Oliver Dawson Corporation at 95. The bonds are due 10 years from the date of purchase.

(a) Assuming that the bonds are classified as temporary investments, determine:

(1) The amount of the annual income.

(2) The gain or the loss when the bonds are sold at 97 exactly 2 years from the date purchased.

(3) The total income from the bonds for the entire period held, including gain or loss on sale.

(b) Assuming that the bonds are classified as long-term investments and the discount is amortized, make the three determinations required in (a).

18-9. On the basis of the following data, prepare an income statement for the Sexton Company for the current fiscal year ended June 30, indicating earnings per share for the 10,000 shares of common stock (no preferred stock) outstanding during the year:

Cost of merchandise sold.	$317,500
Loss on sale of investments (no effect on income tax).	6,400
Selling expenses.	81,600
General expenses.	67,100
Gain on sale of branch plant facilities.	40,000
Income tax (including $10,000 applicable to gain on sale of branch plant facilities).	44,100
Sales.	550,000
Interest expense.	2,500

PROBLEMS

The following additional problems for this chapter are located in Appendix C: 18-1B, 18-2B, 18-3B, 18-5B.

18-1A. The following transactions were completed by Garbor Oil Co.:

1969

Sept. 30. Issued $1,000,000 of 20-year, 5% bonds dated September 30, 1969 at 94. Interest is payable semiannually on September 30 and March 31.

Dec. 31. Recorded the adjusting entry for interest payable.

31. Recorded amortization of discount on bonds.

31. Closed the interest expense account.

1970

Jan.   1. Reversed the adjusting entry for interest payable.

Mar. 31. Paid the semiannual interest on the bonds.

Sept. 30. Paid the semiannual interest on the bonds.

Dec. 31. Recorded the adjusting entry for interest payable.

      31. Recorded amortization of discount on bonds.

      31. Closed the interest expense account.

Instructions:

(1) Record the foregoing transactions in general journal form.

(2) State the amount of the interest expense in (a) 1969 and (b) 1970.

(3) What is the effective rate of interest expressed as a percentage of the face value of the bonds?

18-2A. The board of directors of Carey Electronics is planning an expansion of plant facilities expected to cost $2,000,000. The board is undecided about the method of financing this expansion and has two plans under consideration:

Plan A. Issue $2,000,000 of 10-year, 5% bonds at face value.

Plan B. Issue an additional 50,000 shares of no-par common stock at $40 per share.

The condensed balance sheet of Carey Electronics at the end of the most recent fiscal year is presented below.

Carey Electronics
Balance Sheet
December 31, 19--

Assets		Liabilities and Capital	
Current assets..........	$1,170,000	Current liabilities........	$1,020,000
Plant assets............	4,830,000	Common stock (100,000 shares issued).........	3,500,000
		Retained earnings.......	1,480,000
Total assets...........	$6,000,000	Total liabilities and capital	$6,000,000

463

Net income has remained relatively constant over the past several years. The expansion program is expected to increase yearly income before income tax (and before bond interest) from $650,000 to $900,000. Assume a tax rate of 50%.

Instructions:

(1) Prepare a tabulation indicating the expected earnings per share on common stock under each plan.

(2) List factors other than earnings per share that the board should consider in evaluating the two plans.

(3) Which plan offers the greater benefit to the present stockholders? Give reasons for your opinion.

18-3A. During 1969 and 1970 Gray Construction Company completed the transactions, given on the next page, relating to its $6,000,000 issue of 25-year, 6% bonds dated March 31, 1969. Interest is payable on March 31 and September 30. The corporation's fiscal year is the calendar year.

1969

Mar. 31. Sold the bond issue for $6,060,000.

Sept. 30. Paid the semiannual interest on the bonds.

Dec. 31. Recorded the adjusting entry for interest payable.
31. Recorded amortization of bond premium.
31. Deposited $99,000 in a bond sinking fund.
31. Appropriated $180,000 of retained earnings for bonded indebtedness.
31. Closed the interest expense account.

1970

Jan. 1. Reversed the adjustment for interest payable.
8. Purchased various securities with sinking fund cash, cost $97,950.

Mar. 31. Paid the semiannual interest on the bonds.

Sept. 30. Paid the semiannual interest on the bonds.

Dec. 31. Recorded the receipt of $4,525 of income on sinking fund securities, depositing the cash in the sinking fund.
31. Recorded the adjusting entry for interest payable.
31. Recorded amortization of bond premium.
31. Deposited $132,000 cash in the sinking fund.
31. Appropriated $240,000 of retained earnings for bonded indebtedness.
31. Closed the interest expense account.

Instructions:

(1) Record the foregoing transactions in general journal form.

(2) Prepare a columnar table, using the headings presented below, and include the information for each of the two years.

Year	Bond Interest Expense for Year	Sinking Fund Income for Year	Bonds Payable	Premium on Bonds	Cash	Investments	Appropriation for Bonded Indebtedness

The last five columns (Bonds Payable, Premium on Bonds, Cash, Investments, Appropriation for Bonded Indebtedness) fall under the heading "Account Balances at End of Year", with "Cash" and "Investments" grouped under "Sinking Fund".

18-4A. The board of directors of Dunlap Incorporated has asked you to review the rough draft of the balance sheet presented on the next page.

During the course of your review and examination of the accounts and records, you assemble the following pertinent data:

(a) Marketable securities are stated at cost; the market price is $81,500.

(b) Accounts receivable, equipment, buildings, land, goodwill, and investment in affiliated company are stated at cost. Provisions for doubtful accounts and depreciation have been recorded correctly.

(c) Treasury stock is composed of 1,000 shares purchased at 22½ a share.

(d) Inventories are stated at the lower of cost (first-in, first-out) or market.

(e) The stock dividend distributable represents a 3% stock dividend declared on June 30.

(f) Bonds payable (20-year) are due 5 years from the balance sheet date. They are secured by a first mortgage and bear 6% interest.

(g) The common stock is $20 par; 50,000 shares are authorized, 31,000 shares have been issued.

(h) The reserve for income taxes is the balance due on the estimated liability for taxes on income of the current fiscal year ended June 30.

Instructions:

Present a revised balance sheet in good order. Titles of items should be changed where appropriate.

Dunlap Incorporated
Balance Sheet
June 30, 19--

Assets

Current assets:

Cash..................................		$144,500	
Marketable securities..................		80,000	
Investment in affiliated company.......		150,000	
Treasury stock.........................	$ 22,500		
Deduct reserve for treasury stock purchased.........................	22,500	—	
Accounts receivable....................	$157,500		
Deduct accounts payable............	130,500	27,000	
Inventories...........................	$245,000		
Deduct reserve for possible price declines.........................	12,500	232,500	
Discount on bonds payable............		5,000	
Total current assets.................			$ 639,000

Plant assets:

Equipment............................		$475,000	
Buildings..............................	$500,000		
Deduct reserve for plant expansion . . .	100,000	400,000	
Land..................................		80,000	
Goodwill..............................		35,000	
Prepaid expenses......................		12,500	
Total plant assets.................			1,002,500
Total assets............................			$1,641,500

465

Liabilities

Cash dividends payable.................		$ 21,000	
Stock dividend distributable.............		18,000	
Accrued liabilities......................		15,600	
Bonds payable.........................	$500,000		
Deduct bond sinking fund.............	331,500	168,500	
Total liabilities.....................			$ 223,100

Stockholders' Equity

Paid-in capital:

Common stock.......................		$620,000	

Retained earnings and reserves:

Premium on common stock............	$ 84,000		
Reserve for doubtful accounts.........	17,500		
Reserve for depreciation — equipment . .	145,000		
Reserve for depreciation — buildings....	190,000		
Reserve for income taxes..............	80,000		
Retained earnings....................	281,900	798,400	
Total stockholders' equity...........			1,418,400
Total liabilities and stockholders' equity...			$1,641,500

18-5A. The following transactions relate to certain securities acquired by Fitch and Company:

1966

Mar. 10. Purchased as a long-term investment 500 common shares of Root Corporation at 40¾ plus commission and other costs of $250.

May 1. Purchased $100,000 of Curtis Company 10-year, 6% coupon bonds dated March 1, 1966 directly from the issuing company for $98,820 plus accrued interest. It is expected that the bonds will be held as a long-term investment.

July 25. Received the semiannual dividend of $1 per share on Root Corporation stock.

Sept. 1. Deposited the coupons for semiannual interest on Curtis Company bonds.

Dec. 31. Recorded the adjustment for interest receivable on the Curtis Company bonds.

31. Recorded the amortization of discount on the Curtis Company bonds.

(Assume that all intervening transactions and adjustments have been recorded properly, and that the amount of bonds and shares of stocks have not changed from December 31, 1966 to December 31, 1969.)

1970

Jan. 1. Reversed the adjustment for interest receivable.

24. Received the semiannual dividend of $1 per share and a 10% stock dividend on the Root Corporation stock.

Mar. 1. Deposited coupons for semiannual interest on the Curtis Company bonds.

May 1. Sold the Curtis Company bonds at 98½ plus accrued interest. The broker deducted $225, remitting the balance. The amortization of the discount for the year to date was also recorded.

July 27. Received the semiannual dividend of $1 per share on the Root Corporation stock.

Sept. 18. Sold 100 shares of Root Corporation stock at 48½. The broker deducted commission and other costs of $45, remitting the balance.

Instructions:

Record the foregoing transactions in general journal form.

18-6A. The accounts in the ledger of Hall Company, with the balances on December 31, the end of the current fiscal year, are as follows:

Cash	$ 82,500
Accounts Receivable	173,500
Allowance for Doubtful Accounts	1,500
Merchandise Inventory	190,000
Prepaid Insurance	11,000
Store Supplies	6,550
Bond Sinking Fund	78,750
Store Equipment	410,000
Accumulated Depreciation — Store Equipment	190,400
Office Equipment	275,000
Accumulated Depreciation — Office Equipment	141,725
Organization Costs	12,000
Accounts Payable	82,450
Income Tax Payable	

Interest Payable................................	——
Accrued Liabilities.............................	1,975
First Mortgage 6% Bonds Payable.............	200,000
Deferred Income Tax Payable.................	21,500
Premium on Bonds Payable...................	12,000
Common Stock, $10 par.......................	250,000
Premium on Common Stock....................	100,000
Appropriation for Bonded Indebtedness........	100,000
Retained Earnings.............................	30,000
Expense and Revenue Summary...............	——
Sales...	1,800,000
Purchases.....................................	1,340,000
Purchases Discount............................	18,700
Sales Salaries and Commissions...............	110,250
Advertising Expense...........................	60,100
Depreciation Expense — Store Equipment......	——
Store Supplies Expense........................	——
Miscellaneous Selling Expenses................	8,250
Office and Officers' Salaries...................	97,000
Rent Expense.................................	45,000
Uncollectible Accounts Expense...............	——
Depreciation Expense — Office Equipment.....	——
Insurance Expense.............................	——
Miscellaneous General Expenses...............	6,700
Interest Expense..............................	12,000
Sinking Fund Income..........................	4,000
Rent Income..................................	3,350
Uninsured Loss from Vandalism...............	15,000
Income Tax...................................	24,000

The data needed for year-end adjustments on December 31 are as follows:

Merchandise inventory on December 31 (at cost, first-in, first-out).	$205,000
Insurance expired during the year............................	3,250
Store supplies inventory on December 31......................	3,450
Depreciation for the current year on:	
Store equipment...	9,600
Office equipment..	4,750
Bonds payable are due 6 years from the beginning of the current year	——
Interest on bonds is payable on April 30 and October 31.........	——
Uncollectible accounts expense is estimated at ½ of 1% of sales...	——
Balance due on income tax for the current year................	35,550

Instructions:

(1) Prepare an eight-column work sheet for the fiscal year ended December 31.

(2) Prepare an income statement, indicating per share data where appropriate. The reduction in income tax applicable to the uninsured loss from vandalism is $7,000; hence, the income tax applicable to net income before extraordinary items is $66,550.

(3) Prepare a retained earnings statement. The balance of unappropriated retained earnings on January 1 was $80,000, the appropriation for bonded indebtedness was increased by $20,000 on November 30, and cash dividends of $30,000 were declared during the year.

(4) Prepare a balance sheet.

18-7A. Bennett Corporation issued $1,000,000 of 6% debenture bonds on May 1, 1969, at 101½. Interest is payable on May 1 and November 1. The bonds mature on May 1, 1979, but they may be called at 102½ on any interest date after 4 years from the date of issue. The company's fiscal year ends on December 31. The following transactions and adjustments were selected from those relating to the bonds over the 10-year period.

1969

May 1. Issued the bonds for cash.
Nov. 1. Paid semiannual interest.
Dec. 31. Recorded accrual of the interest.
    31. Recorded amortization of the bond premium.
    31. Closed the interest expense account.

1970

Jan. 1. Reversed the adjusting entry for accrued interest.
May 1. Paid semiannual interest.
July 1. Recorded amortization of premium for the year related to bonds purchased. (See next transaction.)
    1. Purchased $200,000 of bonds on the open market at 101 plus accrued interest and retired them.
Nov. 1. Paid semiannual interest.
Dec. 31. Recorded accrual of the interest.
    31. Recorded amortization of the bond premium.
    31. Closed the interest expense account.

(Assume that all intervening transactions and adjustments have been recorded properly, and that the number of bonds outstanding has not changed from January 1, 1971 to December 31, 1973.)

1974

Jan. 1. Reversed the December 31, 1973 adjusting entry for accrued interest.
May 1. Paid semiannual interest.
    1. Recorded amortization of premium for the year related to bonds called. (See next transaction.)
    1. Called and retired $300,000 of the bonds.
Nov. 1. Paid semiannual interest.
Dec. 31. Recorded accrual of the interest.
    31. Recorded amortization of the bond premium.
    31. Closed the interest expense account.

(Assume that all intervening transactions and adjustments have been recorded properly and that the number of bonds outstanding has not changed from January 1, 1975 to December 31, 1978.)

1979

Jan. 1. Reversed the December 31, 1978 adjusting entry for accrued interest.
May 1. Paid semiannual interest.
    1. Recorded amortization of the bond premium.
    1. Paid the bonds at maturity.
Dec. 31. Closed the interest expense account.

Instructions:

Record the foregoing transactions in general journal form.
(It is suggested that memorandum T accounts for Interest Expense, Premium on Bonds Payable, and Bonds Payable be maintained.)

part **Eight** | Control accounting

19

Departments
and branches

Accounting for departmental operations

Management of an enterprise that sells two or more distinct classes
of services or commodities or that is divided into departments needs
accounting reports to evaluate the various segments of the business.
Such reports are needed by management not only to evaluate past operations of each department but also to control costs and to plan future
departmental operations.

Departmental accounting is more likely to be used by a large business
than by a small one. Some degree of departmentalization may be employed by a small enterprise, however. For example, the owner of a one-
man real estate and property insurance agency could account separately
for real estate commissions and for insurance commissions. Analysis of
the division of his time between the two activities and of his revenue and
expenses by type of activity may indicate the desirability of devoting
more time to one department and less to the other.

Departmental accounting for a large enterprise is likely to be both
feasible and desirable. In a modern department store, for example, there
are a number of distinct departments, each under the control of a departmental manager. A departmental breakdown for accounting and

reporting helps place responsibility for the control of a department's operations upon departmental managers. It assists top management both in evaluating the relative operating efficiencies of individual departments and in planning future operations.

Departmental accounting is useful to service, merchandising, and manufacturing concerns. Although subsequent discussions in this chapter deal with merchandising businesses, the fundamental considerations are not affected by the type of operations.

Accounting reports for departmental operations

Accounting reports for departmental operations are generally limited to income statements. Ordinarily they are of concern only to management and are not issued to stockholders or others outside the management group. The degree to which departmental accounting may be adopted for a merchandising enterprise, therefore, varies with the desires of management. Analysis of operations by departments may end with the determination of gross profit on sales or it may extend through the determination of net income. An income statement that includes a departmental breakdown of revenue and expenses categorized by responsibility for the incurrence of costs has been widely used in recent years. The most common departmental income statements are described in the paragraphs that follow.

470

Gross profit by departments

For a merchandising enterprise, the gross profit on sales is one of the most significant figures in the income statement. Since the sales and the cost of merchandise sold are both, to a large extent, controlled by departmental management, the reporting of gross profit by departments is useful in cost analysis and control. In addition, such reports assist management in directing its efforts toward obtaining a mix of sales that will maximize profits. After studying the reports, management may decide to change sales or purchases policies, curtail or expand operations, or shift personnel to achieve a higher gross profit for each department. Caution must be exercised in the use of such reports to insure that proposed changes affecting gross profit do not have an adverse effect on net income. For example, a change that increases gross profit but results in an even greater increase in operating expenses would decrease net income.

In order to determine gross profit on sales by departments, it is necessary to determine by departments each element entering into gross profit. There are two basic methods of doing this: (1) setting up departmental accounts and identifying each element by department at the time of the transaction, or (2) maintaining only one account for the element and then allocating it among the departments at the time the income statement is prepared. Ordinarily, the first method is used unless the time required in analyzing each transaction is too great. Allocation among departments at the end of a period is likely to yield less accurate results than the first method, but some degree of accuracy may be sacrificed to obtain a commensurate saving of time and expense.

The elements that must be departmentalized in order to determine gross profit by departments are merchandise inventory, purchases, sales, and the related cash discounts and returns and allowances. Departmental accounts may be maintained for each element so that the entries may be classified by department at the time the transactions are recorded. This can be accomplished by providing special departmental columns in the appropriate journals. For example, in a furniture store that sells furniture and carpeting, the sales journal may have a credit column for Furniture Sales and a credit column for Carpet Sales. To facilitate the journalizing of departmental transactions, the supporting documents such as sales invoices, vouchers, and cash register readings must identify the department affected by each transaction. Postings to departmental accounts from the special journals follow the procedures described in earlier chapters.

An income statement showing gross profit by departments for the York Company, which has two sales departments, appears on page 472. For illustrative purposes, the operating expenses are shown in condensed form; ordinarily they would be listed in detail.

Net income by departments

Departmental reporting of income may be extended to various points, such as gross profit less selling expenses (gross selling profit), gross profit less all operating expenses (net operating income), income before income tax, or net income. The underlying principle is the same for all degrees of departmentalization, namely, to assign to each department the related revenues and that portion of the expenses incurred for its benefit.

Some expenses may be easily identified with the department benefited. For example, if each salesperson is restricted to a particular sales department, the sales salaries may be assigned to the appropriate departmental salary accounts each time the payroll is prepared. On the other hand, the salaries of company officers, executives, and office personnel are not identifiable with specific sales departments and must therefore be allocated on an equitable basis.

Many accountants prefer to apportion all expenses to departments only at the end of the accounting period. When this is done, there is no need for departmental expense accounts in the general ledger and fewer postings are required. The apportionments may be made on a work sheet, which serves as the basis for preparing the departmental income statement.

York Company
Income Statement
For Year Ended December 31, 19--

	DEPARTMENT A		DEPARTMENT B		TOTAL	
Revenue from sales:						
Sales...................		$280,000		$120,000		$400,000
Less sales returns and allowances.....		7,600		3,100		10,700
Net sales.....		$272,400		$116,900		$389,300
Cost of merchandise sold:						
Merchandise inventory, January 1, 19--..		$ 40,300		$ 30,700		$ 71,000
Purchases........	$152,900		$ 87,300		$240,200	
Less purchases discount.....	2,800	150,100	1,300	86,000	4,100	236,100
Merchandise available for sale.....		$190,400		$116,700		$307,100
Less merchandise inventory, December 31, 19--..		41,900		39,100		81,000
Cost of merchandise sold.....		148,500		77,600		226,100
Gross profit on sales.....		$123,900		$ 39,300		$163,200
Operating expenses:						
Selling expenses.....					$ 54,700	
General expenses.....					53,900	
Total operating expenses.....						108,600
Net income from operations.....						$ 54,600
Other expense:						
Interest expense.....						1,200
Income before income tax.....						$ 53,400
Income tax.....						19,132
Net income.....						$ 34,268

Income statement departmentalized through gross profit

Apportionment of operating expenses

As was indicated in the preceding section, some operating expenses are directly identifiable with particular departments and some are not. When operating expenses are allocated, they should be apportioned to the respective departments as nearly as possible in accordance with the cost of services rendered to them. Determining the amount of an expense chargeable to each department is not always a simple matter. In the first place, it requires the exercise of judgment; and accountants of equal ability may well differ in their opinions as to the proper basis for apportionment. Second, the cost of collecting data for use in making an apportionment must be kept within reasonable bounds; consequently, information that is readily available and is substantially reliable may be used in lieu of more accurate information that would be more costly to collect.

To illustrate the apportionment of operating expenses, assume that the York Company extends its departmentalization through net income from operations. The company's operating expenses for the calendar year and the methods used in apportioning them are presented in the paragraphs that follow.

Sales Salaries is apportioned to the two departments in accordance with the distributions shown in the payroll records. Of the $42,000 total in the account, $27,000 is chargeable to Department A and $15,000 is chargeable to Department B.

Advertising Expense, covering billboard advertising and newspaper advertising, is apportioned according to the amount of advertising incurred for each department. The billboard advertising totaling $2,000 emphasizes the name and the location of the company. This expense is allocated on the basis of sales, the assumption being that this basis represents a fair allocation of billboard advertising to each department. Analysis of the newspaper space costing $7,000 indicates that 65% of the space was devoted to Department A and 35% to Department B. The apportionment of the total advertising expense is indicated in the tabulation below.

	TOTAL		DEPARTMENT A		DEPARTMENT B
Sales — dollars...........	$400,000		$280,000		$120,000
Sales — percent..........	100%		70%		30%
Billboard advertising....		$2,000		$1,400	$ 600
Newspaper space—percent.	100%		65%		35%
Newspaper advertising..		7,000		4,550	2,450
Advertising expense		$9,000		$5,950	$3,050

Depreciation of Store Equipment is apportioned in accordance with the average cost of the equipment in each of the two departments. The computations for the apportionment of the depreciation expense are given below.

	TOTAL	DEPARTMENT A	DEPARTMENT B
Cost of store equipment:			
January 1	$13,600	$ 8,800	$ 4,800
December 31	14,400	8,000	6,400
Total	$28,000	$16,800	$11,200
Average	$14,000	$ 8,400	$ 5,600
Percent	100%	60%	40%
Depreciation expense	$ 1,650	$ 990	$ 660

Officers' Salaries and *Office Salaries* are apportioned on the basis of the relative amount of time devoted to each department by the officers and by the office personnel. Obviously, this can be only an approximation. The number of sales transactions may have some bearing on the matter, as may billing and collection procedures and other factors such as promotional campaigns that might vary from period to period. Of the total officers' salaries of $26,000 and office salaries of $9,000, it is estimated that 60%, or $15,600 and $5,400 respectively, is chargeable to Department A and that 40%, or $10,400 and $3,600 respectively, is chargeable to Department B.

Rent Expense and *Heating and Lighting Expense* are usually apportioned on the basis of the floor space devoted to each department. In apportioning rent expense for a multistory building, differences in the value of the various floors and locations may be taken into account. For example, the space near the main entrance of a department store is more valuable than the same amount of floor space located far from the elevator on the sixth floor. For York Company, rent expense is apportioned on the basis of floor space used because there is no significant difference in the value of the floor areas used by each department. In allocating heating and lighting expense, it is assumed that the number of lights, their wattage, and the extent of use are uniform throughout the sales departments. If there are major variations and the total lighting expense is material, further analysis and separate apportionment may be advisable. The rent expense and the heating and lighting expense are apportioned as follows:

	TOTAL	DEPARTMENT A	DEPARTMENT B
Floor space, square feet	160,000	104,000	56,000
Percent	100%	65%	35%
Rent expense	$7,200	$4,680	$2,520
Heating and lighting expense	$2,400	$1,560	$ 840

Property Tax Expense and *Insurance Expense* are related primarily to the value of the merchandise inventory and the store equipment. Although there are differences between assessed value for tax purposes, value for insurance purposes, and cost, the latter is most readily available and is considered to be satisfactory as a basis for apportioning these expenses. The computation of the apportionment follows:

	TOTAL	DEPARTMENT A	DEPARTMENT B
Merchandise inventory:			
January 1..................	$ 71,000	$40,300	$30,700
December 31..............	81,000	41,900	39,100
Total...................	$152,000	$82,200	$69,800
Average.................	$ 76,000	$41,100	$34,900
Average cost of store equipment (computed previously)......	14,000	8,400	5,600
Total....................	$ 90,000	$49,500	$40,500
Percent.................	100%	55%	45%
Property tax expense........	$ 3,300	$ 1,815	$ 1,485
Insurance expense..........	$ 1,900	$ 1,045	$ 855

Uncollectible Accounts Expense, Miscellaneous Selling Expense, and *Miscellaneous General Expense* are apportioned on the basis of sales. Although the uncollectible accounts expense may be apportioned on the basis of an analysis of accounts receivable written off, it is assumed that the expense varies closely with sales. The miscellaneous selling and general expenses are apportioned on the basis of sales, the assumption being that this is a reasonable measure of the benefit to each department. The computation of the apportionment follows:

475

	TOTAL	DEPARTMENT A	DEPARTMENT B
Sales......................	$400,000	$280,000	$120,000
Percent...................	100%	70%	30%
Uncollectible accounts expense	$ 2,000	$ 1,400	$ 600
Miscellaneous selling expense.	$ 2,050	$ 1,435	$ 615
Miscellaneous general expense	$ 2,100	$ 1,470	$ 630

An income statement presenting net income from operations by departments for York Company appears on page 476. The amounts for sales and cost of merchandise sold are presented in condensed form. Details could be reported, if desired, in the manner illustrated by the income statement on page 472.

Departmental margin approach to income reporting

Many accountants caution against the imprudent use of departmental income statements. They point out that the more the revenue and the expenses must be allocated to departments on an arbitrary basis, the less useful the statements become in evaluating past operations and in planning for the future. In addition, some accountants object to reporting

York Company
Income Statement
For Year Ended December 31, 19––

	DEPARTMENT A		DEPARTMENT B		TOTAL	
Net sales		$272,400		$116,900		$389,300
Cost of merchandise sold		148,500		77,600		226,100
Gross profit on sales		$123,900		$ 39,300		$163,200
Operating expenses:						
Selling expenses:						
Sales salaries	$ 27,000		$ 15,000		$ 42,000	
Advertising expense	5,950		3,050		9,000	
Depreciation expense — store equipment	990		660		1,650	
Miscellaneous selling expense	1,435		615		2,050	
Total selling expenses		$ 35,375		$ 19,325		$ 54,700
General expenses:						
Officers' salaries	$ 15,600		$ 10,400		$ 26,000	
Office salaries	5,400		3,600		9,000	
Rent expense	4,680		2,520		7,200	
Property tax expense	1,815		1,485		3,300	
Heating and lighting expense	1,560		840		2,400	
Uncollectible accounts expense	1,400		600		2,000	
Insurance expense	1,045		855		1,900	
Miscellaneous general expense	1,470		630		2,100	
Total general expenses		32,970		20,930		53,900
Total operating expenses		68,345		40,255		108,600
Net income (loss) from operations		$ 55,555		$ (955)		$ 54,600
Other expense:						
Interest expense						1,200
Income before income tax						$ 53,400
Income tax						19,132
Net income						$ 34,268

Income statement departmentalized through net income from operations

net income by departments on the grounds that departments are not independent operating units but segments of one business and that therefore no single department of a business can earn a profit. For these reasons, accountants often prepare income statements that report the revenue and the expense in a manner that emphasizes the contribution each department makes to the expenses incurred on behalf of the business as a whole. Income statements prepared in such a manner use the *departmental margin* or *contribution margin* approach to income reporting.

In preparing an income statement in the departmental margin format, the operating expenses are generally divided into two classes: (1) *direct expenses*, those incurred for the benefit of and traceable to a specific department and thus generally subject to the control of the department head; and (2) *indirect expenses*, those incurred for the benefit of the business as a whole and not traceable to a specific department and consequently beyond the control of the department head. The direct expenses for each department are deducted from gross profit on sales, also determined for each department, in arriving at the *departmental margin*. The indirect expenses are not allocated to the departments but are deducted in total from the total departmental margin to determine the net income from operations.

Sales salaries for the York Company is a direct expense because it is directly traceable to a specific department. Officers' salaries for the York Company is an indirect expense because it benefits the entire company and cannot be traced to a specific department. Some operating expenses may have to be divided between the two categories. For example, the newspaper advertising portion of advertising expense for the York Company is directly related to each department. The billboard advertising, however, mentions only the name and the location of the company and is therefore an indirect expense. An income statement for the York Company prepared on the departmental margin basis appears on page 478.

The departmental margin income statement can be used advantageously in controlling operating expenses and maximizing net income. The manager of each sales department can be held strictly accountable for the operating expenses directly traceable to his department and hence subject to his control. A reduction in the direct expenses of a department will have a favorable effect on the contribution made by that department to the net income of the enterprise.

The departmental margin income statement may also be useful to management in formulating fundamental plans for future operations. For example, this type of analysis can be employed when the discontinuance of a particular operation or department is being considered. If a sales department yields a departmental margin, it generally should be

	DEPARTMENT A		DEPARTMENT B		TOTAL	
Net sales..........	....	$272,400	....	$116,900	....	$389,300
Cost of merchandise sold ...	....	148,500	....	77,600	....	226,100
Gross profit on sales........	....	$123,900	....	$ 39,300	....	$163,200
Direct departmental expenses:						
Sales salaries............	$27,000	....	$15,000	....	$42,000	....
Advertising expense.......	4,550	....	2,450	....	7,000	....
Property tax expense.....	1,815	....	1,485	....	3,300	....
Uncollectible accounts expense.............	1,400	....	600	....	2,000	....
Insurance expense......	1,045	....	855	....	1,900	....
Depreciation expense — store equipment.......	990	....	660	....	1,650	....
Total direct departmental expenses.....	....	36,800	....	21,050	....	57,850
Departmental margin......	....	$ 87,100	....	$ 18,250	....	$105,350
Indirect expenses:						
Officers' salaries.........					$26,000	....
Office salaries...........					9,000	....
Rent expense..........					7,200	....
Heating and lighting expense...............					2,400	....
Advertising expense.....					2,000	....
Miscellaneous selling expense............					2,050	....
Miscellaneous general expense...............					2,100	....
Total indirect expenses					....	50,750
Net income from operations					....	$ 54,600
Other expense:						
Interest expense........						1,200
Income before income tax					....	$ 53,400
Income tax.............					....	19,132
Net income............					....	$ 34,268

Income statement departmentalized through departmental margin

retained even though the allocation of all of the operating expenses indicates a net loss for the department. This observation is based upon the assumption that the department in question represents a relatively minor segment of the enterprise. Its termination, therefore, would not cause any significant reduction in the volume of indirect expenses. For example, if an enterprise occupying a rented three-story building is divided into twenty departments, each occupying about the same amount of space, termination of the least thriving department would probably not cause any reduction in rent or other occupancy expenses. The space vacated would probably be absorbed by the remaining nineteen departments. On the other hand, if the enterprise were divided into three departments, each occupying approximately equal areas, the discontinuance of one could result in vacating an entire floor and consequently materially reduce occupancy expenses. When the departmental margin analysis is applied to problems of this type, consideration should be given to the organizational structure of the enterprise and to related proposals for the use of released space or productive capacity.

To illustrate the application of the departmental margin approach to long-range planning, assume that an enterprise with six departments has earned $70,000 before income tax during the past year, which is fairly typical of recent operations. Assume also that recent income statements, in which all operating expenses are allocated, indicate that Department F has been incurring losses, the net loss having amounted to $5,000 for the past year. Departmental margin analysis indicates that, in spite of the losses, Department F should not be discontinued unless there is sufficient assurance that a commensurate increase in the gross profit of other departments or a decrease in indirect expenses can be effected. The analysis, considerably condensed, may be presented in the following form:

Proposal to Discontinue Department F
September 20, 19 − −

| | CURRENT OPERATIONS | | | DISCONTINUANCE OF |
	DEPARTMENT F	DEPARTMENTS A–E	TOTAL	DEPARTMENT F
Sales.....................	$100,000	$900,000	$1,000,000	$900,000
Cost of merchandise sold.....	70,000	540,000	610,000	540,000
Gross profit on sales.........	$ 30,000	$360,000	$ 390,000	$360,000
Direct departmental expenses.	20,000	210,000	230,000	210,000
Departmental margin.......	$ 10,000	$150,000	$ 160,000	$150,000
Indirect expenses...........			90,000	90,000
Income before income tax....			$ 70,000	$ 60,000

Departmental analysis — discontinuance of unprofitable department

The analysis indicates a possible reduction of $10,000 in net income if Department F is discontinued. There are also other factors that may need to be considered. For example, there may be problems regarding the displacement of sales personnel. Or customers attracted by the least profitable department may make substantial purchases in other departments, so that discontinuance of that department may adversely affect the sales of other departments.

The foregoing discussion of departmental income statements has suggested various ways in which income data may be made useful to management in making important policy decisions. It should be kept in mind that the format selected for the presentation of income data to management must be that which will be most useful under the circumstances for evaluating, controlling, and planning departmental operations.

Branch operations

Just as a firm may add a new department in an effort to increase its sales and income, it also may open new stores (branches) in different locations with the same objective in mind. Among the types of retail businesses in which branch operations were first successfully developed on a major scale were variety, grocery, and drug stores. There are a number of large corporations with hundreds or thousands of retail branches distributed over a large area. In addition to the national chain store organizations, there are many of a regional or local nature. The growth of suburban shopping centers in recent years has added materially to the number of firms, especially department stores, that have expanded through the opening of branches.

Although commonly associated with retailing, branch operations are also carried on by banking institutions, service organizations, and many types of manufacturing enterprises. Regardless of the nature of the business, each branch ordinarily has a branch manager. Within the framework of general policies set by top management, the branch manager may be given wide latitude in conducting the business of the branch. Data concerning the volume of business handled and the profitability of operations at each location are essential as a basis for decisions by the principal executives. It is also necessary to maintain a record of the assets at the branch locations and of liabilities incurred by each branch.

The remainder of this chapter deals with the central office and the single branch of a merchandising business. The fundamental considerations are not materially affected, however, by a multiplicity of branches or by the particular type of business.

Systems for branch accounting

There are various systems of accounting for branch operations. The system may be highly centralized, with the accounting for the branch done at the home office. Or the system may be almost completely decentralized, with the branch responsible for the detailed accounting and only summary accounts carried for the branch by the home office. Or there may be some variation between these two extremes. Although there are many possible variations, two typical methods of branch accounting will be described.

Centralized system. The branch may prepare only the basic records of its transactions, such as sales invoices, time tickets for employees, and vouchers for liabilities incurred. Copies of all such documents are forwarded to the home office, where they are recorded in appropriate journals in the usual manner. When this system is used, the branch has no journals or ledgers. If the operating results of the branch are to be determined separately, which is normally the case, separate branch accounts for sales, cost of merchandise sold, and expenses must be maintained in the home office ledger. It is apparent that the principles of departmental accounting will apply in such cases, the branch being treated as a department.

One important result of centralizing the bookkeeping activities at one location may be substantial savings in office expense. There is also greater assurance of uniformity in accounting methods employed. On the other hand, there is some likelihood of delays and inaccuracies in submitting data to the home office, with the result that periodic reports on the operations of a branch may not be available when needed.

Decentralized system. When the accounting for branches is decentralized, each branch maintains its own accounting system with journals and ledgers. The account classification for assets, liabilities, revenues, and expenses in the branch ledger conforms to the classification employed by the home office. The accounting processes are comparable to those of an independent business, except that the branch does not have capital accounts. A special account entitled Home Office takes the place of the capital accounts. The process of preparing financial statements and adjusting and closing the books is substantially the same as for an independent enterprise. It is this system of branch accounting to which the remainder of the chapter will be devoted.

Underlying principles of decentralized branch accounting

When the branch has a ledger with a full complement of accounts, except capital accounts, it is apparent that there must be some tie-in between the branch ledger and the general ledger at the home office. The properties at the branch are a part of the assets of the entire enterprise, and liabilities incurred at the branch are similarly liabilities of the enterprise as a whole. Although the accounting system at the branch is much like that of an independent company, the fact remains that the branch is not a separate entity but only a segment of the business.

The tie-in between the home office and the branch is accomplished by the control-account-subsidiary-ledger technique, with an added modification that makes the branch ledger a self-contained unit. The basic features of the system are shown in the chart at the top of page 482. In the home office ledger, the account Branch #1 has a debit balance of

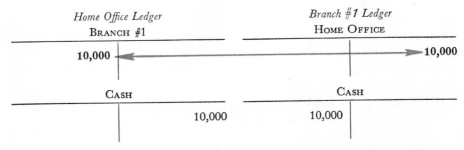

| Home Office Ledger | Branch #1 Ledger |
| BRANCH #1 | VARIOUS ASSET ACCOUNTS |

| 100,000 | 120,000 |

VARIOUS LIABILITY ACCOUNTS

20,000

HOME OFFICE

100,000

Reciprocal Accounts

$100,000. This balance represents the sum of the assets minus the sum of the liabilities recorded in the ledger at the branch. The various asset and liability accounts in the branch ledger are represented in the chart by one account for all assets ($120,000) and one account for all liabilities ($20,000). In order to make the branch ledger self-balancing, an account entitled Home Office is added. It has a credit balance of $100,000. The two accounts, Branch #1 in the home office books and Home Office in the branch books, have equal but opposite balances and are known as *reciprocal accounts*. The home office account in the branch ledger replaces the capital accounts that would be used if the branch were a separate entity. Actually, the account does represent the branch's portion of the entire capital of the home office.

When the home office sends assets to the branch, it debits Branch #1 for the totals and credits the appropriate asset accounts. Upon receiving the assets, the branch debits the appropriate asset accounts and credits Home Office. To illustrate, assume that branch operations are begun by sending $10,000 in cash to the newly appointed branch manager. The entries in the two ledgers are presented in the accounts below:

| Home Office Ledger | Branch #1 Ledger |
| BRANCH #1 | HOME OFFICE |

| 10,000 | 10,000 |

| CASH | CASH |

| 10,000 | 10,000 |

When the branch disburses the cash, it records the transactions as though it were an independent entity. For example, if the branch purchases office equipment for $4,000, paying cash, the transaction is recorded in the branch books by a debit to Office Equipment and a credit

482

to Cash. No entry is required in the home office books because there is no change in the amount of the investment at the branch.

As the branch incurs expenses and earns revenues, the transactions are recorded in its books in the usual manner. Such transactions do affect the amount of the total investment of the home office at the branch, but recognition of the change is postponed until the accounts are closed at the end of the accounting period. At that time the expense and revenue summary account in the branch books is closed to the account Home Office. If operations have resulted in a net income, the account Home Office will be credited. In the home office books a net income at the branch is recorded by a debit to Branch #1 and a credit to Branch Net Income. For a net loss the entries would be just the reverse.

In a merchandising enterprise all or a substantial part of the stock in trade of the branch is usually supplied by the home office. A shipment of merchandise from the home office is recorded in the home office books by a debit to Branch #1 and a credit to Shipments to Branch #1. The branch records the transaction in its books by a debit to Shipments from Home Office and a credit to Home Office. It is evident from the accounts below that the two shipments accounts are also reciprocal accounts.

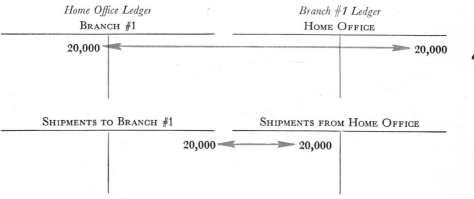

From the point of view of the home office, the account Shipments to Branch #1 is an unallocated reduction of its merchandise inventory and purchases accounts. From the standpoint of the branch, the account Shipments from Home Office is comparable to a purchases account. The final disposition of these accounts is described later in the chapter.

Illustration of decentralized branch accounting

A series of entries illustrating the underlying principles applicable to branch accounting on a decentralized basis is presented on pages 484–485. The illustration begins with the opening of a branch and continues with operations covering a complete accounting period. Typical transactions between the home office and the branch, and between the branch and outsiders, are considered. Transactions between the home office and outsiders are ignored unless they affect the branch. A summary of transactions, together with the entries on the home office books and the branch books, is presented below in general journal form.

Transactions	Home Office Books		Branch Books	
(1) The home office established Branch #1, sending $10,000 in cash and $30,000 in merchandise.	Branch #1........40,000 Cash.......... Shipments to Branch #1......	 10,000 30,000	Cash............10,000 Shipments from Home Office......30,000 Home Office....	 40,000
(2) The branch purchased on account merchandise costing $10,000.			Purchases.........10,000 Accounts Pay...	 10,000
(3) The branch sold merchandise for $16,000 in cash and for $8,000 on account.			Cash............16,000 Accounts Rec...... 8,000 Sales..........	 24,000
(4) The branch paid operating expenses amounting to $3,500.			Operating Exp.... 3,500 Cash..........	 3,500
(5) The branch collected $6,000 on accounts receivable.			Cash............ 6,000 Accounts Rec...	 6,000
(6) The branch paid $1,000 on accounts payable.			Accounts Pay...... 1,000 Cash..........	 1,000
(7) The branch sent $20,000 in cash to the home office.	Cash............20,000 Branch #1......	 20,000	Home Office......20,000 Cash	 20,000

484

The entries to adjust and close the accounts of the branch at the end of the accounting period, together with the entries in the books of the home office to record the net income of the branch, are presented at the top of page 485.

After the foregoing entries have been posted, the home office accounts affected and the branch ledger accounts appear as shown on pages 485–486.

Branch financial statements

Branch financial statements differ from those of a separate business entity in two minor respects. In the branch income statement, shipments

Adjusting & Closing	Home Office Books	Branch Books
(a) To record the ending merchandise inventory of the branch.		Mdse. Inventory...22,000 Expense and Revenue Summary.. 22,000
(b) To close the sales account of the branch.		Sales............24,000 Expense and Revenue Summary.. 24,000
(c) To close the cost and expense accounts of the branch.		Expense and Revenue Summary.....43,500 Shipments from Home Office.... 30,000 Purchases....... 10,000 Operating Exp... 3,500
(d) To close the expense and revenue summary account on the books of the branch and to record the net income of the branch on the books of the home office.	Branch #1........ 2,500 Branch Net Income......... 2,500	Expense and Revenue Summary..... 2,500 Home Office.... 2,500

Home Office Ledger	Branch Ledger	485

CASH (Home Office Ledger)

(7)	20,000	(1)	10,000

Other cash transactions of the home office would also be recorded in the account above.

CASH (Branch Ledger)

(1)	10,000	(4)	3,500
(3)	16,000	(6)	1,000
(5)	6,000	(7)	20,000
		Balance	7,500
	32,000		32,000
Balance	7,500		

ACCOUNTS RECEIVABLE

(3)	8,000	(5)	6,000
		Balance	2,000
	8,000		8,000
Balance	2,000		

MERCHANDISE INVENTORY

(a)	22,000	

	Home Office Ledger		Branch Ledger	

Accounts Payable

(6)	1,000	(2)		10,000
Balance	9,000			
	10,000			10,000
		Balance		9,000

Branch #1 / Home Office

(1)	40,000	(7)	20,000	(7)	20,000	(1)	40,000
(d)	2,500	Balance	22,500	Balance	22,500	(d)	2,500
	42,500		42,500		42,500		42,500
Balance	22,500					Balance	22,500

Branch Net Income / Expense and Revenue Summary

		(d)	2,500	(c)	43,500	(a)	22,000
				(d)	2,500	(b)	24,000
					46,000		46,000

486

Branch Net Income will be closed to the home office expense and revenue summary account.

Sales

		(b)	24,000	(3)	24,000

Shipments to Branch #1 / Shipments from Home Office

	(1)	30,000	(1)	30,000	(c)	30,000

Shipments to Branch #1 is a deduction from purchases. It will be closed to the home office expense and revenue summary account.

Purchases

(2)	10,000	(c)	10,000

Operating Expenses

(4)	3,500	(c)	3,500

from the home office appear in the cost of merchandise sold section following purchases. In the branch balance sheet the account Home Office takes the place of the capital accounts. Actually it is not capital in the usual sense, but merely the balancing amount. Statements for the branches are used only by management and are not published.

Combined statements for home office and branch

The income statement based on the home office ledger reports details of sales, cost of merchandise sold, expenses, and net income or loss from home office operations in the usual manner. The net income or loss of each branch is then listed, and the net operating results for the entire enterprise are reported. The assets section of the balance sheet prepared from the home office ledger will include the controlling accounts for the various branches. The nature and the amounts of the various assets and liabilities at the branch locations will not be disclosed. The home office statements, together with financial statements for each individual branch, serve a useful purpose for management, but they are obviously unsuitable for presentation to stockholders and creditors.

Accordingly, it is necessary to combine the data on the income statements of the home office and the branches to form one overall income statement. The data on the balance sheets of the home office and of the various branches are also combined to form one balance sheet for the **487** enterprise. The preparation of the combined statements is facilitated by the use of work sheets. The work sheets are similar in that each has a column for the home office account balances, a column for the account balances of each branch, a set of columns headed "Eliminations," and a final column to which the combined figures are extended.

The work sheet for the combined income statement and the related income statement, as prepared from the work sheet, of Taylor Corporation are presented on the next page. The account Shipments from Home Office is canceled by a credit in the Eliminations column, and the account Shipments to Branch #1 is canceled by a debit in the Eliminations column. These eliminations are not recorded in either set of accounts, but they are necessary in the preparation of a combined statement that reports the home office and the branch as one operating unit. These two accounts are eliminated because they represent the shipment of goods within the company and not a sale to an outside party.

The work sheet for the combined balance sheet and the related balance sheet, as prepared from the work sheet, of Taylor Corporation are presented on page 489. The reciprocal account Branch #1 is canceled by a credit elimination, and the reciprocal account Home Office is canceled by a debit elimination.

Taylor Corporation
Work Sheet for Combined Income Statement
For Month Ended March 31, 19––

| | HOME OFFICE | BRANCH #1 | ELIMINATIONS | | COMBINED INCOME STATEMENT |
			DEBIT	CREDIT	
Sales......................	47,000	24,000			71,000
Cost of merchandise sold:					
Mdse. inv., March 1..........	41,000				41,000
Purchases.................	52,000	10,000			62,000
	93,000				
Shipments from home office..		30,000		30,000	
Less shipments to branch #1..	30,000		30,000		
Mdse. available for sale......	63,000	40,000			103,000
Less mdse. inv., March 31...	35,000	22,000			57,000
Cost of merchandise sold.....	28,000	18,000			46,000
Gross profit on sales..........	19,000	6,000			25,000
Operating expenses..........	10,500	3,500			14,000
Net income from operations....	8,500	2,500	30,000	30,000	11,000

Taylor Corporation
Income Statement
For Month Ended March 31, 19––

Sales..		$71,000
Cost of merchandise sold:		
Merchandise inventory, March 1, 19––...................	$ 41,000	
Purchases...	62,000	
Merchandise available for sale.........................	$103,000	
Less merchandise inventory, March 31, 19––..............	57,000	
Cost of merchandise sold............................		46,000
Gross profit on sales.....................................		$25,000
Operating expenses......................................		14,000
Net income from operations..............................		$11,000

Shipments to branch billed at selling price

In the foregoing discussion and illustrations, the billing for merchandise shipped to the branch has been assumed to be at cost price. When all or most of the merchandise handled by the branch is supplied by the home office, it is not unusual for billings to be made at selling price. An advantage of this procedure is that it provides a convenient control over inventories at the branch. The branch merchandise inventory at the beginning of a period (at selling price), plus shipments during the period (at selling price), less sales for the period yields the ending inventory (at selling price). Comparison of the physical in-

Taylor Corporation
Work Sheet for Combined Balance Sheet
March 31, 19——

	HOME OFFICE	BRANCH #1	ELIMINATIONS		COMBINED BALANCE SHEET
			DEBIT	CREDIT	
Debit balances:					
Cash.....................	53,000	7,500			60,500
Accounts receivable.........	46,000	2,000			48,000
Merchandise inventory......	35,000	22,000			57,000
Prepaid insurance..........	250				250
Branch #1	22,500			22,500	
Equipment...............	15,000				15,000
Total..............	171,750	31,500			180,750
Credit balances:					
Accumulated depreciation...	3,000				3,000
Accounts payable..........	28,000	9,000			37,000
Home office...............		22,500	22,500		
Common stock............	100,000				100,000
Retained earnings.........	40,750				40,750
Total..............	171,750	31,500	22,500	22,500	180,750

Taylor Corporation
Balance Sheet
March 31, 19——

Assets

Cash........		$ 60,500
Accounts receivable........		48,000
Merchandise inventory........		57,000
Prepaid insurance........		250
Equipment........	$15,000	
Less accumulated depreciation........	3,000	12,000
Total assets........		$177,750

Liabilities and Capital

Accounts payable........		$ 37,000
Common stock........	$100,000	
Retained earnings........	40,750	140,750
Total liabilities and capital........		$177,750

ventory taken at selling prices with the book amount discloses any discrepancies. A significant difference between the physical and the book inventories indicates a need for remedial action by the management.

When shipments to the branch are billed at selling prices, no gross profit on sales will be reported on the branch income statement. The merchandise inventory on the branch balance sheet will also be stated at the billed (selling) price of the merchandise on hand. In combining the branch statements with the home office statements, it is necessary to convert the data back to cost by eliminating the markup from both the shipments accounts and the inventory accounts.

Analyses of operating segments

With the ever-increasing size and diversification of business units, the need for analysis of operations is likewise growing. It is necessary to account separately for the various segments that make up the larger unit. Departments and branches are two such segments. Accounting procedures can also be established for other segments of operations such as sales territories and individual products. The accounting procedures for sales territories would follow the principles of departmental accounting, each territory being treated as a department.

Business operations are often analyzed in terms of individual products. For the merchandising enterprise, accounting procedures similar to those illustrated for departmental operations could be employed. For the manufacturing enterprise the accounting process would be extended to include the various costs that are necessary in the manufacture of the product. Product cost data are essential in the evaluation of past manufacturing operations, in establishing effective control over costs, and in providing the information useful to management in making decisions. The accounting concepts and procedures applicable to manufacturing operations are discussed in subsequent chapters.

490

QUESTIONS

1. Departmental income statements are ordinarily not included in the published annual reports issued to stockholders and other parties outside the business enterprise. For whom are they prepared?

2. The newly appointed general manager of a department store is studying the income statements presenting gross profit by departments in an attempt to adjust operations to achieve the highest possible gross profit for each department. (a) Suggest ways in which an income statement departmentalized through gross profit can be used in achieving this goal. (b) Suggest reasons why caution must be exercised in using such statements.

3. For each of the following types of expenses, select the allocation basis listed that is most appropriate for use in arriving at net income by departments:

Expense:	Basis of allocation:
(a) Property tax expense	(1) Physical space occupied
(b) Uncollectible accounts	(2) Departmental sales
(c) Sales salaries	(3) Cost of inventory and equipment
(d) Rent	(4) Time devoted to department

4. Differentiate between a direct and an indirect operating expense.

5. Indicate whether each of the following operating expenses incurred by Reed Department Store is a direct or an indirect expense:

(a) President's salary	(c) Salesmen's commissions
(b) Rent on building	(d) Office salaries

6. What term is applied to the dollar amount representing the excess of departmental gross profit over direct departmental expenses?

7. The income statement departmentalized through net income from operations for the year just ended is presented below in condensed form.

	Department A	Other Departments
Net sales..........................	$ 65,000	$550,000
Cost of merchandise sold...........	40,000	290,000
Gross profit on sales..............	$ 25,000	$260,000
Operating expenses................	35,000	225,000
Net income (loss) from operations..	$(10,000)	$ 35,000

The operating expenses include $20,000 and $165,000 of direct expenses for Department A and the other departments respectively.

It is estimated that the discontinuance of Department A would not have affected the sales of the other departments nor have reduced the indirect expenses. Assuming the accuracy of these estimates, what would the net income from operations have been if Department A had been discontinued?

8. Where are the journals and ledgers detailing the operations of a branch maintained in (a) a centralized system for branch accounting and (b) a decentralized system?

9. What is the nature of reciprocal accounts employed in branch accounting?

10. For each of the following accounts appearing in the home office ledger, name the reciprocal account in the branch ledger: (a) Dayton Branch; (b) Shipments to Dayton Branch.

11. In the branch ledger, what is the name of the account that takes the place of the capital accounts common to separate accounting entities?

12. What accounts are debited and credited (a) to close the expense and revenue summary account in the accounts of the Westside Branch and (b) to record the net income of the Westside Branch in the home office accounts?

13. Where, in the branch income statement, is the amount of shipments from the home office reported?

14. In the work sheet for a combined income statement for the home office and its Columbus Branch, what item is eliminated as an offset to shipments from home office?

15. In the work sheet for a combined balance sheet for the home office and its Lincoln Square Branch, what item is eliminated as an offset to Lincoln Square Branch?

16. After the accounts are closed, the asset accounts at Branch #1 total $110,000; the contra asset accounts total $10,000; and liabilities to outsiders total $12,000. (a) What is the title of the remaining account in the branch ledger and what is the amount of its balance? (b) What is the title of the reciprocal account in the home office ledger and what is the amount of its balance? (c) Do these reciprocal items appear in the combined balance sheet?

17. At the close of each accounting period Wilson Company charges each of its branches with interest on the net investment in the branch. At the end of the current year the home office debited the branch accounts for various amounts and credited Interest Income for a total of $10,000. The branches make comparable entries, debiting Interest Expense and crediting Home Office. How should the interest expense and the interest income be treated on the work sheet for the combined income statement?

18. During the first year of operations of the Country Fair Branch, the home office shipped merchandise that had cost $156,800 to the branch. The branch was billed at $224,000, which was the selling price of the merchandise. No merchandise was purchased from other suppliers. Branch net sales for the year totaled $180,000 (all sales were at the billed price). (a) What should be the amount of the branch ending physical inventory at billed prices? (b) Assuming that there are no inventory shortages at the branch, what is the cost of the closing inventory? (c) Which of the two amounts should be added to the home office inventory for presentation in the combined balance sheet? (d) How much gross profit will be reported in the branch income statement?

EXERCISES

19-1. J. W. Porter Company occupies a two-story building. The departments and the floor space occupied by each are as follows:

Receiving and Storage...	basement.....	6,000 sq. ft.
Department 1..........	basement.....	6,000 sq. ft.
Department 2..........	first floor......	4,800 sq. ft.
Department 3..........	first floor......	4,800 sq. ft.
Department 4..........	first floor......	2,400 sq. ft.
Department 5..........	second floor ...	9,000 sq. ft.
Department 6..........	second floor ...	3,000 sq. ft.

The building is leased at an annual rental of $40,000, allocated to the floors as follows: basement, 25%; first floor, 45%; second floor, 30%. Determine the amount of rent to be apportioned to each department.

19-2. Baker Company apportions depreciation expense on equipment on the basis of the average cost of the equipment, and apportions insurance expense on the basis of the combined total of average cost of the equipment and average cost of the merchandise inventories. Depreciation expense on equipment amounted to $15,000 and insurance expense amounted to $4,000 for the year. Determine the apportionment of the depreciation expense and the insurance expense based on the following data:

	Average Cost	
Departments	Equipment	Inventories
Service:		
1	$ 45,000	
2	30,000	
Sales:		
A	75,000	$150,000
B	90,000	172,500
C	60,000	127,500
Total	$300,000	$450,000

19-3. Bailey and Harris Sporting Goods is considering eliminating one of its ten departments. If operations in Department A are discontinued, it is estimated that the indirect operating expenses and the level of operations in the other departments will not be affected.

Data from the income statement for the past year ended December 31, which is considered to be a typical year, are presented below.

	Department A		Departments B–J	
Sales		$35,000		$420,000
Cost of merchandise sold		19,500		242,000
Gross profit on sales		$15,500		$178,000
Operating expenses:				
Direct expenses	$12,000		$90,000	
Indirect expenses	6,000	18,000	60,000	150,000
Income (loss) before income tax		$(2,500)		$ 28,000

(a) Prepare an estimated income statement for the current year ending December 31, assuming the elimination of Department A. (b) On the basis of the data presented, would it be advisable to retain Department A?

19-4. Alpha Company maintains sales offices in several cities. The home office provides the sales manager at each office with a working fund of $5,000 with which to meet payrolls and to pay other office expenses. Prepare the entries, in general journal form, for the home office books to record the following:
(a) Sent a check to establish a $5,000 fund for Branch No. 3.
(b) Sent a check to replenish the fund after receiving a report from Branch No. 3 indicating the following disbursements: sales salaries, $2,000; office salaries, $900; rent, $750; utilities expense, $175; miscellaneous general expense, $75. *3900*

493

19-5. Prepare the entries, in general journal form, to record the following selected transactions on the books of the Sidney Branch.

April 1. The home office sent to the branch: cash, $1,500; equipment, $900; merchandise at cost, $3,500.
   3. The branch purchased merchandise on account from an outside firm, $3,000.
   11. The branch sold merchandise as follows: on account, $2,500; for cash $3,500.
   13. The branch paid accounts payable, $3,000.
   17. The branch received merchandise at cost from the home office, $2,000.
   22. The branch collected $2,200 on account.
   28. The branch paid operating expenses of $450.
   30. The branch sent the home office cash, $2,500.
   30. The branch reported a net income of $1,150. *Exp & R DR / HOME OE CR*

19-6. Present the entries, in general journal form, to record the transactions in Exercise 19-5 on the books of the home office.

19-7. Manning Department Store maintains accounts entitled Dover Branch and Gilman Branch. Each branch maintains an account entitled Home Office. The Dover Branch received instructions from the home office to ship to the Gilman Branch merchandise costing $2,500 that had been received from the home office. Give the general journal entry to record the transfer of the merchandise on the books of (a) the home office, (b) the Dover Branch, and (c) the Gilman Branch.

a) G, B 2,500 DR
D, B. 2,500 CR
c) SH 2,500 DR
H.O 2,500 CR
b) H,O 2500 DR
c) SHP 2500 CR

19-8. During the year, the home office shipped merchandise that had cost $250,000 to the branch. The branch was billed for $375,000, which was the selling price of the merchandise. No merchandise was purchased from any outside sources. Branch net sales for the year totaled $390,000. All sales were made at the billed price. Merchandise on hand at the beginning of the period totaled $70,000 at the billed price. Merchandise on hand at the end of the period as determined by physical count was $53,000 at the billed price. Determine the amount, at the billed price, of any discrepancy between the book amount and the physical count of inventory.

12,000

PROBLEMS

The following additional problems for this chapter are located in Appendix C: 19-1B, 19-2B, 19-4B.

19-1A. Hill Radio and TV operates two sales departments: Department R for radios and Department T for television. The following trial balance was prepared at the end of the current fiscal year after all adjustments, including the adjustments for merchandise inventory, were recorded and posted:

Hill Radio and TV
Trial Balance
August 31, 19 – –

Cash	82,400	
Accounts Receivable	42,500	
Merchandise Inventory — Department R	9,700	
Merchandise Inventory — Department T	26,000	
Prepaid Insurance	1,700	
Store Supplies	550	
Store Equipment	48,800	
Accumulated Depreciation — Store Equipment		17,600
Accounts Payable		33,400
Income Tax Payable		6,200
Common Stock		100,000
Retained Earnings		22,050
Expense and Revenue Summary	31,300	35,700
Sales — Department R		150,000
Sales — Department T		450,000
Sales Returns and Allowances — Department R	3,150	
Sales Returns and Allowances — Department T	11,400	
Purchases — Department R	108,500	
Purchases — Department T	360,000	
Sales Salaries	27,750	
Advertising Expense	10,000	
Depreciation Expense — Store Equipment	4,800	
Store Supplies Expense	700	
Miscellaneous Selling Expense	1,000	
Office Salaries	10,000	
Rent Expense	9,600	
Heating and Lighting Expense	3,600	
Property Tax Expense	2,000	
Insurance Expense	900	
Uncollectible Accounts Expense	600	
Miscellaneous General Expense	500	
Interest Expense	1,200	
Income Tax	16,300	
	814,950	814,950

Merchandise inventories at the beginning of the year were as follows: Department R, $9,100; Department T, $22,200.

The bases to be used in apportioning expenses, together with other essential information, are as follows:

Sales salaries — payroll records: Department R, $7,750; Department T, $20,000.

Advertising expense — usage: Department R, $2,000; Department T, $8,000.

Depreciation expense — average cost of equipment: Balances at beginning of year: Department R, $18,200; Department T, $26,000. Balances at end of year: Department R, $19,000; Department T, $29,800.

Store supplies expense — requisitions: Department R, $200; Department T, $500.

Office salaries — Department R, 20%; Department T, 80%.

Rent expense and heating and lighting expense — floor space: Department R, 1,200 sq. ft.; Department T, 6,000 sq. ft.

Property tax expense and insurance expense — average cost of equipment plus average cost of merchandise inventory.

Uncollectible accounts expense, miscellaneous selling expense, and miscellaneous general expense — volume of gross sales.

Instructions:

Prepare an income statement departmentalized through net income from operations.

19-2A. Martin and Company has 15 departments. Those with the least sales volume are Department D and Department L, which were established about a year ago on a trial basis. The board of directors feels that it is now time to consider the retention or the termination of these two departments. The adjusted trial balance, severely condensed, as of July 31, the end of the first month of the current fiscal year, is presented below. July is considered to be a typical month. The income tax accrual has no bearing on the problem and is excluded from consideration.

Martin and Company
Trial Balance
July 31, 19--

Current Assets.	410,000	
Plant Assets	360,000	
Accumulated Depreciation — Plant Assets.		190,000
Current Liabilities.		95,500
Common Stock.		350,000
Retained Earnings.		114,950
Sales — Department D.		17,100
Sales — Department L.		11,250
Sales — Other Departments.		355,000
Cost of Merchandise Sold—Department D.	12,000	
Cost of Merchandise Sold—Department L.	8,350	
Cost of Merchandise Sold—Other Departments.	249,500	
Direct Expenses — Department D.	3,700	
Direct Expenses — Department L.	3,950	
Direct Expenses — Other Departments.	51,200	
Indirect Expenses.	35,000	
Interest Expense.	100	
	1,133,800	1,133,800

Instructions:

(1) Prepare an income statement for July departmentalized through departmental margin.
(2) State your recommendations concerning the retention of Departments D and L, giving reasons.

19-3A. The following data relating to revenue and expenses are obtained from the ledger of Thomas Rug Company on June 30, the end of the current fiscal year.

	Debit	Credit
Sales — Department A		$350,000
Sales — Department B		250,000
Cost of Merchandise Sold — Department A	$227,500	
Cost of Merchandise Sold — Department B	155,000	
Sales Salaries and Commissions	79,000	
Advertising Expense	9,300	
Depreciation Expense — Store Equipment	8,400	
Miscellaneous Selling Expense	950	
Administrative Salaries	22,000	
Rent Expense	10,800	
Utilities Expense	4,400	
Insurance Expense	1,800	
Uncollectible Accounts Expense	1,500	
Miscellaneous General Expense	850	
Interest Expense	600	
Income Tax	31,500	

Other essential data are:

Sales salaries and commissions — Salesmen are paid a basic salary plus 6% of sales. Basic salaries for Department A, $20,000; Department B, $23,000.

Advertising expense — All advertising expense was incurred for brochures distributed within each department advertising specific products. Usages: Department A, $4,595; Department B, $4,705.

Depreciation expense — Average cost of store equipment: Department A, $48,000; Department B, $32,000.

Uncollectible accounts expense — Departmental managers are responsible for the granting of credit on the sales made by their respective departments. Uncollectible accounts expense is estimated at ¼% of sales.

Insurance expense — Based on average cost of store equipment plus average cost of merchandise inventory. Average cost of merchandise inventory was $51,000 for Department A and $49,000 for Department B.

Instructions:

(1) Prepare an income statement departmentalized through departmental margin.
(2) Determine the rate of gross profit on sales for each department.
(3) Determine the rate of departmental margin to sales for each department.

19-4A. Cardwell Brothers opened a branch office in San Diego on March 1 of the current year. Summaries of transactions, adjustments, and year-end closing for branch operations of the current year ended December 31 are described below: *Branch Books*

(a) Received cash advance, $30,000, and merchandise (billed at cost), $100,000, from the home office.

CASH 30,000
Shipment/merch 100,000
Home office 130,000

(b) Purchased merchandise on account, $125,000. *PURCHASES 125,000*
      ACC PAY 125,000
(c) Purchased equipment on account, $25,000.   *EQUIP 25,000*
(d) Sales on account, $120,000; cash sales, $80,000.
(e) Received cash from customers on account, $105,000.
(f) Paid creditors on account, $127,500.
(g) Paid operating expenses, $20,800 (all expenses are charged to Operating Expenses, a controlling account).
(h) Recorded accumulated depreciation, $500, and allowance for doubtful accounts, $400.
(i) Merchandise inventory at December 31, $70,000. *Merch Inventory 7000*
      Shp to Purch
(j) Sent $25,000 cash to home office.
(k) Closed revenue and expense accounts.

Instructions:

(1) Present, in general journal form, the entries on the branch books to record the foregoing. Post to the following T accounts: Cash, Accounts Receivable, Allowance for Doubtful Accounts, Merchandise Inventory, Equipment, Accumulated Depreciation, Accounts Payable, Home Office, Expense and Revenue Summary, Sales, Shipments from Home Office, Purchases, and Operating Expenses.

(2) Prepare an income statement for the year and a balance sheet as of December 31 for the branch.

(3) Present, in general journal form, the entries required on the home office books. Post to a T account entitled San Diego Branch.

19-5A. The board of directors of Wallace Corporation has tentatively decided to discontinue operating Department D, which has incurred a net loss for several years. Condensed revenue and expense data for the most recent year ended June 30 are presented on the following page. Bases used in allocating operating expenses among departments are described below.

Expense	Basis
Sales commissions	Actual: 10% of net sales
Advertising expense	Actual: all advertising consists of brochures distributed by the various departments advertising specific products
Depreciation expense	Average cost of store equipment used
Miscellaneous selling expense	Amount of net sales
Administrative salaries	Each of the 10 departments apportioned an equal share
Rent expense	Floor space occupied
Utilities expense	Floor space occupied
Insurance and property tax expense	Average cost of equipment used plus average cost of inventory
Miscellaneous general expense	Amount of net sales

Instructions:

Prepare a brief statement of your recommendation to the board, supported by such schedule(s) as you think will be helpful to them in reaching a decision.

Wallace Corporation
Income Statement
For Year Ended June 30, 19--

	Department D		Other Departments		Total	
Net sales		$ 61,000		$910,000		$971,000
Cost of merchandise sold		40,500		555,000		595,500
Gross profit on sales		$ 20,500		$355,000		$375,500
Operating expenses:						
Selling expenses:						
Sales commissions	$ 6,100		$ 91,000		$ 97,100	
Advertising expense	2,500		26,000		28,500	
Depreciation expense — store equipment	1,900		21,500		23,400	
Miscellaneous selling expense	915		13,650		14,565	
Total selling expenses		$ 11,415		$152,150		$163,565
General expenses:						
Administrative salaries	$ 8,515		$ 76,635		$ 85,150	
Rent expense	2,880		21,120		24,000	
Utilities expense	2,160		15,840		18,000	
Insurance and property tax expense	1,800		20,100		21,900	
Miscellaneous general expense	610		9,100		9,710	
Total general expenses		15,965		142,795		158,760
Total operating expenses		27,380		294,945		322,325
Net income (loss) from operations		$ (6,880)		$ 60,055		$ 53,175
Other income:						
Interest income						1,000
Income before income tax						$ 54,175
Income tax						19,600
Net income						$ 34,575

19-6A. The adjusted trial balances of the home office of Grant and Co. and of its Toledo Branch as of October 31, the close of the current fiscal year, are given below.

	Home Office		Toledo Branch	
	Debit	Credit	Debit	Credit
Cash..........................	77,700		37,500	
Accounts Receivable.............	79,200		30,200	
Allowance for Doubtful Accounts.		1,100		600
Merchandise Inventory...........	185,000		60,200	
Prepaid Expenses................	950		450	
Toledo Branch..................	111,200			
Equipment......................	89,500		12,500	
Accumulated Depreciation........		49,200		4,100
Accounts Payable................		60,500		3,450
Home Office....................				111,200
Common Stock..................		300,000		
Retained Earnings..............		67,750		
Expense and Revenue Summary..	172,500	185,000	65,500	60,200
Sales..........................		960,000		260,000
Shipments to Branch............		125,000		
Purchases......................	812,500		40,000	
Shipments from Home Office.....			125,000	
Operating Expenses.............	220,000		68,200	
	1,748,550	1,748,550	439,550	439,550

Instructions:
(1) Prepare an income statement and a balance sheet for the branch.
(2) Prepare an income statement for the home office.
(3) Prepare the journal entry to record branch income on the home office books.
(4) Prepare a balance sheet for the home office, giving effect to the journal entry in (3).
(5) Prepare a work sheet for a combined income statement and a work sheet for a combined balance sheet.
(6) Prepare a combined income statement and a combined balance sheet.

499

20

Manufacturing and process cost systems

Manufacturing operations

Manufacturers employ labor and use machinery to convert materials into finished products. In thus changing the form of commodities, their activities differ from those of merchandisers. The furniture manufacturer, for example, converts lumber and other materials into furniture. The furniture dealer in turn purchases the finished goods from the manufacturer and sells them without additional processing.

Some functions of manufacturing companies are similar to those of merchandising organizations, such as selling, administration, and financing. The accounting procedures for these functions are identical for both types of enterprises.

Accounting procedures for a manufacturing business must also provide for the accumulation of the accounting data identified with the production processes. Additional ledger accounts are required and the accounting system must establish internal control over the manufacturing operations. Periodic reports to management and other interested parties must include data that will be useful in measuring the efficiency of manufacturing operations and in guiding future operations.

Concepts of cost and expense

The amount of cash paid or liability incurred for a commodity or service is referred to as the *cost* of the item. As the commodity or service is consumed in the operations of a business enterprise, its cost is said to expire. An expiration of cost is ordinarily called an *expense*. For example, as office equipment is used, the expiration of its cost is periodically recognized in the accounts as depreciation expense. The unexpired portion of its cost is the excess of the balance of the plant asset account over its related accumulated depreciation account. The expenses (expired costs) of an enterprise are reported periodically in the income statement as deductions from revenue.

The cost of merchandise acquired for resale to customers is treated somewhat differently from the cost of commodities and services that will be consumed during operations. The cost of merchandise, which is a composite of invoice prices and various additions and deductions to cover such items as delivery charges, allowances, and cash discounts, does not expire, in the usual sense. The merchandise is sold rather than consumed, and the amount sold is referred to as the "cost of merchandise sold" rather than as an expense.

Determination of the cost of the merchandise available for sale and the cost of the merchandise sold is infinitely more complex for a manufacturing enterprise than for a merchandising business. The cost of manufacturing a commodity is composed not only of the cost of tangible materials but of the many costs incurred in transforming the materials into a finished product ready for sale. This chapter and the next two are concerned principally with the determination and control of the costs incurred in manufacturing operations.

501

Inventories

Manufacturing businesses maintain three inventory accounts instead of a single merchandise inventory account. Separate accounts are maintained for (1) goods in the state in which they are to be sold, (2) goods in the process of manufacture, and (3) goods in the state in which they were acquired. These inventories are called respectively *finished goods*, *work in process*, and *materials*. The balances in the inventory accounts may be presented in the balance sheet in the following manner:

```
Inventories:
  Finished goods...............................   $300,000
  Work in process.............................     55,000
  Materials...................................    123,000   $478,000
```

The finished goods inventory and work in process inventory are composed of three separate catgories of manufacturing costs: *direct materials*, *direct labor*, and *factory overhead*. Direct materials represent the delivered cost of the materials that enter directly into the finished product. Direct labor represents the wages of the workmen who convert the materials into a finished product. Factory overhead includes all of the remaining costs of operating the factory, such as taxes, insurance, depreciation, and maintenance related to factory plant and equipment, supplies used in the factory but not entering directly into the finished product, and wages for factory supervision.

General accounting for manufacturing operations

Although the accounting procedures applicable to manufacturing operations are likely to be more complex than those employed in trading operations, the range in the degree of complexity is quite broad. If only a single product or several similar products are manufactured, and if the manufacturing processes are neither complicated nor numerous, the accounting system may be fairly simple. In such cases the periodic system of inventory accounting employed in merchandising may be extended to the three inventories described in the preceding section, and the manufacturing accounts may be summarized periodically in an account entitled Manufacturing Summary. It is to such a relatively simple situation that attention will first be directed.

Statement of cost of goods manufactured

Inasmuch as manufacturing activities differ materially from selling and general administration activities, it is customary to segregate the two groups of accounts in the summarizing process at the end of the accounting period. In addition, the manufacturing group is usually reported in a separate statement in order to avoid a lengthy and complicated income statement. The data reported in the separate statement are those needed to determine the cost of the goods (merchandise) manufactured during the period. It is therefore comparable to that section of the income statement of a trading concern that presents the net cost of merchandise purchased. The relationship between the statement of cost of goods manufactured and the income statement is illustrated on the next page.

The amount listed for the work in process inventory at the beginning of the period is composed of the estimated cost of the direct materials, the direct labor, and the factory overhead applicable to the inventory of partially processed products in the factory at the close of the preceding period.

The cost of the direct materials placed in production is determined by adding to the beginning inventory the net cost of the direct materials purchased and deducting the ending inventory. The cost of the direct labor for the period is presented as a single item. The factory overhead costs are listed individually either as a part of the statement of cost of goods manufactured or on a separate schedule. The sum of the costs of direct materials placed in production, the direct labor, and the factory overhead represents the total manufacturing costs incurred during the period. Addition of this amount to the beginning inventory of work in process yields the total cost of the work that has been in process during the period. The estimated cost of the ending inventory of work in process is then deducted to yield the cost of goods manufactured.

Perpetual In Periodic

Sullivan Manufacturing Company
Income Statement
For Year Ended December 31, 1970

Sales		$415,100
Cost of goods sold:		
Finished goods inventory, January 1, 1970 . .	$ 38,500	
Cost of goods manufactured.	294,675 ←	
Cost of finished goods available for sale . .	$333,175	
Less finished goods inventory, December 31, 1970.	51,000	
Cost of goods sold.		282,175

Income statement

Sullivan Manufacturing Company
Statement of Cost of Goods Manufactured
For Year Ended December 31, 1970

Periodic Summary Monthly

PERPETUAL COSTS

503

Work in process inventory, January 1, 1970			$ 25,000
Direct materials:			
Direct materials inventory, January 1, 1970.		$ 32,000	
Direct materials purchases		120,800	
Cost of direct materials available for use.		$152,800	
Less direct materials inventory, December 31, 1970.		28,725	
Cost of direct materials placed in production		$124,075	
Direct labor		98,750	
Factory overhead:			
Indirect labor	$19,300		
Depreciation of factory equipment. .	17,600		
Heat, light, and power	11,800		
Factory maintenance.	8,000		
Property taxes	4,000		
Depreciation of buildings.	3,000		
Amortization of patents.	2,500		
Insurance expired.	2,100		
Factory supplies used.	1,000		
Miscellaneous factory costs.	2,050		
Total factory overhead		71,350	
Total manufacturing costs.			294,175
Total work in process during period. .			$319,175
Less work in process inventory, December 31, 1970.			24,500
Cost of goods manufactured			$294,675

Statement of cost of goods manufactured

Periodic procedures

The process of adjusting the periodic inventory and other accounts of a manufacturing business is similar to that for a merchandising enterprise. Adjustments to the merchandise inventory account are replaced by adjusting entries for each of the three inventory accounts, direct materials, work in process, and finished goods. The first two accounts are adjusted through Manufacturing Summary, and the third is adjusted through Expense and Revenue Summary.

In closing the accounts at the end of the accounting period, the temporary accounts that appear in the statement of cost of goods manufactured are closed to Manufacturing Summary. The final balance of this account, which represents the cost of goods manufactured during the period, is then closed to Expense and Revenue Summary. The remaining temporary accounts (sales, expenses, etc.) are then closed to Expense and Revenue Summary in the usual manner.

The relationship of the manufacturing summary account to the expense and revenue summary account is illustrated below. Note that the balance transferred from the manufacturing summary account to the expense and revenue summary account, $294,675, is the same as the final figure reported on the statement of cost of goods manufactured.

MANUFACTURING SUMMARY

1970			1970		
Dec. 31	Work in Pro. Inv., Jan. 1	25,000	Dec. 31	Work in Pro. Inv., Dec. 31	24,500
31	Direct Mat. Inv., Jan. 1	32,000	31	Direct Mat. Inv., Dec. 31	28,725
31	Direct Mat. Purchases	120,800	31	To Exp. and Rev. Sum.	294,675
31	Direct Labor	98,750			
31	Factory Overhead	71,350			
		347,900			347,900

EXPENSE AND REVENUE SUMMARY

1970			1970		
Dec. 31	Fin. Goods Inv., Jan. 1	38,500	Dec. 31	Fin. Goods Inv., Dec. 31	51,000
31	From Manufac. Sum.	294,675			

The work sheet used in preparing financial statements for a merchandising business, which was illustrated in Chapter 6, may be expanded for the manufacturing enterprise to include the addition of a pair of columns for the statement of cost of goods manufactured.

Cost accounting

Cost accounting achieves greater accuracy in the determination of costs than is possible with a general accounting system such as that described in the preceding sections. Cost accounting procedures also permit far more effective control by supplying data on the costs incurred by each factory department and the unit cost of manufacturing each type of product. Such procedures provide not only data useful to management in minimizing costs but also other valuable information about production methods to employ, quantities to produce, product lines to "push," and sales prices to charge. There are two principal types of cost systems, *process cost* and *job order cost*.

Under process cost systems, the costs are accumulated for each of the various departments or processes within the factory. A process system is best utilized by manufacturers of homogeneous units of product that are not distinguishable from each other during a continuous production process.

Job order cost systems provide for a separate record of the cost of each particular quantity of product that passes through the factory. They are best suited to industries that manufacture commodities to fill special orders from customers and to industries that produce heterogeneous lines of products for stock.

Each of the two systems is widely used, and a manufacturer may employ a process cost system for some of its departments or products and a job order cost system for others.

Process cost systems

Companies manufacturing a homogeneous mass such as cement or flour do so on a continuous basis. The manufacturing costs incurred are accumulated for each manufacturing department or process. The cost elements are identified first with the separate processes and then with the physical output of these processes. For example, the cost of producing a ton of cement equals the sum of costs incurred in each separate process divided by the number of tons produced. Other industries that use process cost accounting include ink, paint, soap, and paper manufacturing.

Flow of costs in process cost systems

Perpetual inventory accounts for materials, work in process, and finished goods are requisites of a process cost accounting system. Each of these accounts is debited for all additions and is credited for all deductions. The balance of each account thus represents the inventory on hand.

All expenditures incidental to manufacturing move through the work in process account, the finished goods account, and eventually into the cost of goods sold account. The flow of costs through the perpetual inventory accounts and into the cost of goods sold account is exemplified by the diagram shown on the next page.

Materials and factory labor used in production are classified as direct and indirect. The materials and the factory labor used directly in

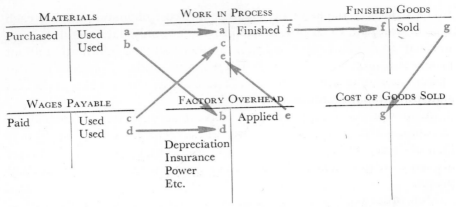

Flow of costs through perpetual inventory accounts

the process of manufacturing are debited to Work in Process (a and c in the diagram). The materials and the factory labor used that do not enter directly into the finished product are debited to Factory Overhead (b and d in the diagram). Examples of indirect materials are oils and greases, abrasives and polishes, cleaning supplies, gloves, molding sand, drilling soap, and brushes. Examples of indirect labor are salaries of supervisors, inspectors, material handlers, watchmen, and janitors. The appropriate amount of factory overhead costs, which include depreciation, insurance, power, taxes, and other indirect manufacturing costs as well as indirect materials and indirect labor, are transferred to Work in Process (e in the diagram). The costs of the goods finished are transferred from Work in Process to Finished Goods when they are finished (f in the diagram) and thence to Cost of Goods Sold when they are sold (g in the diagram).

The number of accounts presented in the flow chart was severely restricted. In practice, separate work in process accounts and factory overhead accounts are maintained for each department or *cost center* in the factory. There is ordinarily a separate account in a subsidiary ledger for each type of material used in manufacturing, controlled by the account Materials. Similarly, if numerous commodities are manufactured, an account for each type may be maintained in a subsidiary ledger, controlled by the account Finished Goods.

Service departments and process costs

In a factory with a number of processes, there may be one or more *service departments* that do not process the materials directly. They assist the processing departments in producing finished goods, and the costs that they incur must be charged to the processing departments. Service departments include such departments as the factory office, the power plant, and the maintenance and repair shop.

The services rendered by a service department give rise to internal transactions between it and the processing departments benefited. These internal transactions are recorded periodically in order to charge the factory overhead accounts of the processing departments with their share of the costs incurred by the service departments. The period usually chosen is a month, although a different period of time may be used. To illustrate, assume that the Power Department produced 300,000 kilowatt-hours during the month at a total cost of $6,000, or 2¢ per kilowatt-hour ($6,000 ÷ 300,000). The factory overhead accounts for the departments that used the power are accordingly charged for power at the 2¢ rate. Assuming that during the month Department 1 used 100,000 kwh and Department 2 used 200,000 kwh, the accounts affected by the interdepartmental transfer of cost would appear as follows:

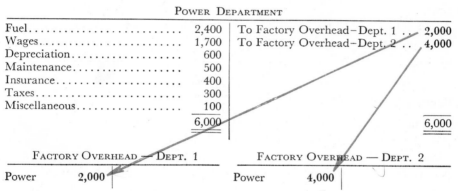

POWER DEPARTMENT

Fuel............................	2,400	To Factory Overhead–Dept. 1 ...	2,000
Wages.........................	1,700	To Factory Overhead–Dept. 2 ...	4,000
Depreciation..................	600		
Maintenance..................	500		
Insurance.....................	400		
Taxes.........................	300		
Miscellaneous.................	100		
	6,000		6,000

FACTORY OVERHEAD — DEPT. 1

| Power | 2,000 | |

FACTORY OVERHEAD — DEPT. 2

| Power | 4,000 | |

Some service departments render services to other service departments. For example, the power department may supply electric current to light the factory office and to operate various bookkeeping and office machines. At the same time the factory office provides general supervision for the power department, maintains its payroll records, buys its fuel, and so on. In such cases the costs of the department rendering the greatest service to other service departments may be distributed first, ignoring the fact that it receives benefits from other service departments.

Processing costs

The accumulated costs transferred from preceding departments and the costs of direct materials and direct labor incurred in each processing department are debited to the related work in process account. Each work in process account is also debited for its portion of the factory overhead. The costs incurred are summarized periodically, usually at the end of the month. The costs applicable to the output of each department during the month are then transferred to the next processing department or to Finished Goods, as the case may be. This flow of costs through a work in process account is illustrated on the next page.

10,000 units at $1.20 from Dept. 1	12,000	To Dept. 3, 10,000 units......	20,000
Direct labor............ 4,600		Cost per unit $\dfrac{\$20,000}{10,000} = \$2.00$	
Factory overhead....... 3,400	8,000		
	20,000		20,000

The three debits in the account above may be grouped into two distinct categories: (1) direct materials or partially processed materials received from another department, which in this case is composed of 10,000 units with a total cost of $12,000, and (2) direct labor and factory overhead applied in Department 2, which in this case totaled $8,000. This second group of costs is called the *processing cost*.

Again referring to the illustration, all of the 10,000 units were completely processed in Department 2 and passed on to Department 3. The $2 unit cost of the product transferred to Department 3 is composed of Department 1 cost of $1.20 ($12,000 ÷ 10,000 units) and processing cost of $.80 ($8,000 ÷ 10,000 units) incurred in Department 2.

Factory overhead

The identification of factory overhead with specific processing departments is usually more difficult than identification of costs of a more direct nature. The cost of the direct materials physically entering a processing department can be determined and recorded on requisition forms. Similarly, the cost of direct labor can be identified with the department in which the labor is performed, and records maintained on time tickets. On the other hand, many items of factory overhead are incurred for the factory as a whole and are only indirectly related to the activity of the processing departments. The problem is further complicated by the fact that some items of cost are relatively fixed in amount, while others tend to vary in accordance with changes in the volume of production.

The factory overhead costs incurred can be accumulated in their respective accounts until the end of the fiscal year and then apportioned among departments on some equitable basis. Such a procedure may be quite acceptable from the standpoint of accuracy, but it is usually highly unsatisfactory in terms of timeliness. Cost data must be available currently throughout the year if they are to be useful to management. If a shorter time period, such as a month, is selected for allocations of overhead, the costs per unit of product manufactured may fluctuate so greatly as to be meaningless. Such fluctuations may be caused by substantial variations in the number of units produced monthly, by the effect of seasonal variation in climatic conditions or other uncontrollable factors, or by a combination of factors.

The difficulties inherent in sole reliance on actual overhead costs can be overcome by the use of estimates. Advance estimates of the magnitude of overhead costs are combined with advance estimates of the volume of factory activity to yield measures called *predetermined factory overhead rates*. The use of such rates permits significant comparisons of unit product costs from month to month. In addition, management is able to make monthly comparisons of the amount of factory overhead actually incurred with the amount charged to processes by use of the predetermined rates.

Predetermined factory overhead rates. Factory overhead rates are determined by relating the estimated amount of factory overhead for each department for the forthcoming year to some common activity base, one that will equitably apply the factory overhead costs to the goods manufactured. The common bases include direct labor costs, direct labor hours, and machine hours. For example, if it is estimated that the total factory overhead costs for a particular department for the year will be $48,000 and that the total direct labor cost for that department will be $60,000, an overhead rate of 80% ($48,000 ÷ $60,000) may be applied to the direct labor cost incurred within the department during the year.

The actual factory overhead costs incurred are debited to the factory overhead accounts. The amounts of factory overhead costs applied to production are credited to the factory overhead accounts and debited to the work in process accounts. Assuming that the direct labor cost in Department 7 during a month is $5,000 and that the predetermined departmental overhead rate is 80%, the entry to apply factory overhead to production is as follows:

Work in Process — Department 7..........................	4,000	
Factory Overhead — Department 7.....................		4,000

Inevitably, factory overhead costs applied and actual factory overhead costs incurred during a particular period will differ. If the amount applied exceeds the actual costs, the factory overhead account will have a credit balance and the overhead is said to be *overapplied* or *overabsorbed;* if the amount applied is less than the actual costs, the account will have a debit balance and the overhead is said to be *underapplied* or *underabsorbed.* Both situations are illustrated in the account presented below.

FACTORY OVERHEAD — DEPARTMENT 7

DATE		ITEM	DEBIT	CREDIT	BALANCE	
					DEBIT	CREDIT
May	1	Balance				300
	31	Costs incurred	4,510			
	31	Costs applied		4,000	210	

The $300 credit balance at the beginning of the month is an over-applied balance. During the month actual costs incurred amounted to $4,510 and factory overhead applied to work in process amounted to $4,000. The $210 debit balance at the end of the month is an under-applied balance.

Disposition of factory overhead balances. The balances in the factory overhead accounts are carried forward from month to month until the end of the year. The net amount of the balances is reported on interim balance sheets as either a deferred charge (net underapplied balance) or a deferred credit (net overapplied balance).

The nature of the balance in the factory overhead account for a particular department (underapplied or overapplied), as well as the amount, will fluctuate during the year. If there is a decided trend in either direction and the amount is substantial, the reason should be determined. If the variation is caused by alterations in manufacturing methods or by substantial changes in production goals, it may be advisable to revise the factory overhead rate. The accumulation of a large underapplied balance is more serious than a trend in the opposite direction and may indicate inefficiencies in production methods, excessive expenditures, or a combination of factors.

Despite any corrective actions that may be taken to avoid an under-application or overapplication of factory overhead, the accounts will ordinarily have balances at the end of the fiscal year. Since the sum of the balances represents the underapplied or overapplied factory overhead applicable to the operations of the year just ended, it is not proper to report it in the year-end balance sheet as a deferred charge or a deferred credit to manufacturing costs of the following year.

There are two principal alternatives for disposing of the balances of factory overhead at the end of the year: (1) by allocation among work in process, finished goods, and cost of goods sold accounts on the basis of the total amounts of applied factory overhead included in those accounts at the end of the year or (2) by transfer of the balances to the cost of goods sold account. Theoretically only the first alternative is sound because it represents a correction of the estimated overhead rates and brings the accounts into agreement with the costs actually incurred. On the other hand, considerable time and expense may be required to make the allocation and to revise the unit costs of the work in process and finished goods inventories. Furthermore, in most manufacturing enterprises a very large proportion of the manufacturing costs for the year pass through the work in process and the finished goods accounts into the cost of goods sold account before the end of the year. Therefore, unless the amount of the underapplied or overapplied balance is substantial, it is satisfactory to transfer it to Cost of Goods Sold.

Inventories of partially processed materials

Preceding illustrations assumed that all materials entering a process were completely processed at the end of the accounting period. In such cases the determination of unit costs is quite simple. The total of costs transferred from other departments, direct materials, direct labor, and factory overhead charged to a department is divided by the number of units completed and passed on to the next department or to finished goods. Frequently, however, some partially processed materials remain in various stages of production in a department at the close of a period. In this case, the processing costs must be allocated between the units that have been completed and transferred to the next process and those that are only partially completed and remain within the department.

To allocate direct material and transferred costs between the output completed and transferred to the next process and inventory of goods within the department, it is necessary to determine the manner in which the materials are placed in production. They may be placed in production at different stages, depending upon the nature of the product being manufactured. For some products, it is necessary to have all materials on hand before any work commences. For other products, materials may be added to production in relatively the same proportion as processing costs are incurred. In still other situations, materials may enter the process at relatively few points, which may or may not be evenly spaced throughout the process.

In order to allocate the processing costs between the output completed and transferred to the next process and the inventory of goods within the process, it is necessary to determine (1) the number of *equivalent units* of production during the period and (2) the *processing cost per equivalent unit* for the same period. The equivalent units of production are the number of units that would have been produced if there had been no inventories within the process either at the beginning or the end of the period. To illustrate, assume that there is no inventory of goods in process in a particular processing department at the beginning of the period, that 1,000 units of materials enter the process during the period, and that at the end of the period all of the units are 75% completed. The equivalent production in the processing department for the period would be 750 units (75% of 1,000). Assuming further that the processing costs incurred during the period totaled $15,000, the processing cost per equivalent unit would be $20 ($15,000 ÷ 750).

Ordinarily there is an inventory of partially processed units in the department at the beginning of the period, some units are completed during the period and transferred to the next department, and other units are partially processed and remain in the inventory at the end of the period. To illustrate the computation of equivalent units under such circumstances, the following data are assumed for Department 5 for the month of March:

Inventory within Department 5 on March 1:   600 units, ⅓ completed.
Completed in Department 5 and transferred
    to finished goods during March: 4,000 units, completed.
Inventory within Department 5 on March 31:   1,000 units, ⅖ completed.

The equivalent units of production in Department 5 for March may be determined as follows:

To process units in inventory on March 1:	600 units × ⅔......	400
To process units started and completed in March:	4,000 units − 600 units	3,400
To process units in inventory on March 31:	1,000 units × ⅖......	400
Equivalent units of production in March........................		4,200

Continuing with the illustration, the next step is to allocate the costs incurred in Department 5 between the units completed during March and those remaining in process at the end of the month. If materials (including transferred costs) were used and processing costs were incurred uniformly throughout the month, the total costs of the process would be divided by 4,200 units to obtain the unit cost. On the other hand, if all materials were introduced at the beginning of the period, the full materials cost per unit must be assigned to the uncompleted units. The processing costs would then be allocated to the finished and the uncompleted units on the basis of equivalent units of production. Entries in the account below are based on the latter assumption.

WORK IN PROCESS — DEPARTMENT 5

Process inventory, March 1:			Goods finished during March:	
600 units, ⅓ completed......		1,160	4,000 units................	14,060
From Department 4:			Process inventory, March 31:	
4,400 units at $1...........		4,400	1,000 units, ⅖ completed.....	2,000
Direct labor...........	6,000			
Factory overhead.......	4,500	10,500		
		16,060		16,060
Process inventory, April 1:				
1,000 units, ⅖ completed.....		2,000		

The processing costs incurred in Department 5 during March total $10,500. The equivalent units of production for March, determined above, is 4,200. The processing cost per equivalent unit is therefore $2.50 ($10,500 ÷ 4,200). Of the $16,060 debited to Department 5, $14,060 was transferred to Finished Goods and $2,000 remained in the account as work in process inventory. The calculation of the allocations to finished goods and to inventory is illustrated at the top of the next page.

Cost of production report

A report is prepared periodically for each processing department, summarizing (1) the units for which the department is accountable and

600 units: Inventory on March 1, ⅓ completed................ $1,160

Processing cost in March:

600 × ⅔, or 400 units at $2.50.................. 1,000

Total... $ 2,160

(Unit cost: $2,160 ÷ 600 = $3.60)

3,400 units: Materials cost in March, at $1 per unit............. $3,400

Processing cost in March:

3,400 at $2.50 per unit........................ 8,500

Total... 11,900

(Unit cost: $11,900 ÷ 3,400 = $3.50)

4,000 units: Goods finished during March........................... $14,060

PROCESS 5 INVENTORY ON MARCH 31

1,000 units: Materials cost in March, at $1 per unit............. $1,000

Processing cost in March:

1,000 × ⅖, or 400 at $2.50.................... 1,000

1,000 units: Department 5 Inventory on March 31.................... $ 2,000

the disposition of these units and (2) the costs charged to the department and the allocation of these costs. This report, termed the *cost of production report*, may be used as the source of the computation of unit production costs and the allocation of the processing costs in the general ledger to the finished and the uncompleted units. More importantly, the report is used as a means of controlling costs. Each department head is held responsible for the units entering production and the costs incurred in his department. Any variations in unit product costs from one month to another are carefully scrutinized and the causes of significant variations are determined.

The cost of production report based on the data presented in the preceding section for Department 5 is illustrated on the next page.

Joint products

When two or more commodities of significant value are produced from a single principal direct material, the products are termed *joint products*. Similarly, the costs incurred in the manufacture of joint products are called *joint costs*. A common example of joint products are gasoline, naphtha, kerosene, paraffine, benzine, and other related commodities, all of which emerge from the processing of crude oil.

In management decisions concerning the production and sale of joint products, only the relationship of the total revenue to be derived from the entire group to their total production cost is relevant. Nothing is to be gained from an allocation of joint costs to each individual product because one product cannot be produced without the others. A decision to produce a joint product is in effect a decision to produce all of the products.

Avery Manufacturing Company
Cost of Production Report — Department 5
For the Month Ended March 31, 19--

Quantities:
  Charged to production:
    In process, March 1 600
    Received from Department 4 4,400
    Total units to be accounted for................... 5,000

  Units accounted for:
    Transferred to finished goods.................... 4,000
    In process, March 31 1,000
    Total units accounted for........................ 5,000

Costs:
  Charged to production:
    In process, March 1 .... $ 1,160

  March costs:
    Direct materials from Department 4 ($1 per unit). 4,400

    Processing costs:
      Direct labor................................. $ 6,000
      Factory overhead 4,500
      Total processing costs ($2.50 per unit).......... 10,500
    Total costs to be accounted for................... $16,060

  Costs allocated as follows:
    Transferred to finished goods:
      600 units at $3.60 .... $ 2,160
      3,400 units at $3.50 11,900
      Total cost of finished goods.................... $14,060

    In process, March 31:
      Direct materials (1,000 units at $1).............. $ 1,000
      Processing costs (1,000 units $\times$ $\frac{2}{5}$ $\times$ $2.50)........ 1,000
      Total cost of inventory in process, March 31 2,000
    Total costs accounted for........................ $16,060

Computations:
  Equivalent units of production:
    To process units in inventory on March 1:
      600 units $\times$ $\frac{2}{3}$ 400
    To process units started and completed in **March**:
      4,000 units − 600 units....................... 3,400
    To process units in inventory on March 31:
      1,000 units $\times$ $\frac{2}{5}$................................ 400
      Equivalent units of production 4,200

  Unit processing cost:
    $10,500 ÷ 4,200 .... $ 2.50

Cost of production report

For one purpose, namely inventory valuation for periodic income statements, it is necessary to make an arbitrary allocation of joint costs among the joint products. One common method of allocation is the *market (sales) value* method. Its essential feature is the assignment of costs to the various products in accordance with their relative sales values. To illustrate, assume that 10,000 units of Product X and 50,000 units of Product Y were produced at a total cost of $63,000. The sales values of the two products and the allocation of the joint costs are presented below.

JOINT PRODUCT	UNITS PRODUCED	JOINT COSTS	SALES VALUE PER UNIT	TOTAL SALES VALUE
X	10,000	$63,000	$3.00	$30,000
Y	50,000		1.20	60,000
Total sales value				$90,000

Allocation of joint costs:

$$X \quad \frac{30,000}{90,000} \times \$63,000. \ldots \ldots \ldots \ldots \ldots \ldots \ldots \ldots \ldots \ldots \quad \$21,000$$

$$Y \quad \frac{60,000}{90,000} \times \$63,000. \ldots \ldots \ldots \ldots \ldots \ldots \ldots \ldots \ldots \quad 42,000$$

Unit cost:

X	$21,000 ÷ 10,000 units.	$2.10
Y	$42,000 ÷ 50,000 units.	.84

Inasmuch as joint products emerge from the processing of a common parent material, the assignment of cost to each separate product cannot be based on actual expenditures. It is impossible to determine the amount of cost incurred in the manufacture of each separate product. By apportioning joint costs on the basis of relative sales values, it is assumed that the cost of producing an item is proportional to its sales value.

515

By-products

If one of the products resulting from a process has little value in relation to the principal product or joint products, it is known as a *by-product*. The emergence of a by-product is only incidental to the manufacture of the principal product or joint products. By-products may be leftover materials, such as sawdust and scraps of wood in a lumber mill; or they may be separated from the material at the beginning of production, as in the case of cottonseed from raw cotton.

The amount of manufacturing cost ordinarily assigned to a by-product is the sales value of the by-product reduced by any additional costs necessary to complete and sell it. The amount of cost thus determined is removed from the appropriate work in process account and transferred to a finished goods inventory account. To illustrate, assume that for a particular period the costs accumulated in Department 4 total

$24,400, and that during the same period of time 1,000 units of by-product B, having an estimated value of $200, emerge from the processing in Department 4. Finished Goods — Product B would be debited for $200 and Work in Process — Department 4 would be credited for the same amount, as illustrated in the accounts below.

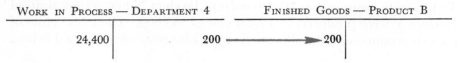

WORK IN PROCESS — DEPARTMENT 4	FINISHED GOODS — PRODUCT B
24,400	200 ⟶ 200

The accounting for the costs remaining in the work in process account and for the sale of the by-product would follow the usual procedures.

Illustration of process cost accounting

To illustrate further the procedures that have been described, the following facts are assumed: The Howell Manufacturing Company manufactures one principal product designated Product A. The manufacturing activity begins in Department 1, where all materials enter production. The materials remain in Department 1 for a relatively short time and there is ordinarily no inventory of work in process in that department at the end of the accounting period. A by-product, designated Product B, is also produced in Department 1. From Department 1 the materials comprising the principal product are transferred to Department 2. In Department 2 there are usually inventories at the end of the accounting period. Separate factory overhead accounts are maintained for Departments 1 and 2. Factory overhead is applied at 80% and 50% of direct labor cost respectively for Departments 1 and 2. There are two service departments, Maintenance and Power.

The trial balance of the general ledger on January 1, the first day of the fiscal year, is presented below.

Howell Manufacturing Company
Trial Balance
January 1, 19--

Cash..	18,500	
Accounts Receivable.......................................	15,000	
Finished Goods — Product A (1,000 units at $11.50)..........	11,500	
Finished Goods — Product B (600 pounds at $.50).............	300	
Work in Process — Department 2 (800 units, ½ completed)....	7,800	
Materials	12,000	
Prepaid Expenses	2,150	
Plant Assets	310,000	
Accumulated Depreciation — Plant Assets....................		95,000
Accounts Payable...		21,180
Wages Payable..		1,400
Common Stock...		200,000
Retained Earnings		59,670
	377,250	377,250

In order to reduce the illustrative entries to a manageable number and to avoid repetition, the transactions and the adjustments for the month of January are stated as summaries. In practice, the transactions would be recorded from day to day in various journals. The descriptions of the transactions, followed in each case by the entry in general journal form, are presented below.

(a) Materials purchased and prepaid expenses incurred on account.

Entry: Materials...	33,500	
Prepaid Expenses..................................	1,100	
Accounts Payable..............................		34,600

(b) Materials requisitioned for use by the various factory departments.

Entry: Maintenance Department.........................	400	
Power Department.................................	2,000	
Factory Overhead — Department 1..................	1,240	
Factory Overhead — Department 2..................	900	
Work in Process — Department 1...................	19,900	
Materials..		24,440

(c) Labor used by the various factory departments.

Entry: Maintenance Department.........................	1,200	
Power Department.................................	1,500	
Factory Overhead — Department 1..................	950	
Factory Overhead — Department 2..................	700	
Work in Process — Department 1...................	8,300	
Work in Process — Department 2...................	12,600	
Wages Payable................................		25,250

(d) Costs and expenses incurred on account by the various factory departments and by the sales and administrative divisions.

Entry: Maintenance Department.........................	200	
Power Department.................................	300	
Factory Overhead — Department 1..................	600	
Factory Overhead — Department 2..................	400	
Selling Expenses..................................	5,000	
General Expenses.................................	4,500	
Accounts Payable..............................		11,000

(e) Expiration of prepaid expenses chargeable to the various factory departments and to the sales and administrative divisions.

Entry: Maintenance Department.........................	100	
Power Department.................................	250	
Factory Overhead — Department 1..................	450	
Factory Overhead — Department 2..................	350	
Selling Expenses..................................	300	
General Expenses.................................	200	
Prepaid Expenses..............................		1,650

(f) Depreciation chargeable to the various factory departments and to the sales and administrative divisions.

Entry: Maintenance Department.........................	100	
Power Department.................................	350	
Factory Overhead — Department 1..................	600	
Factory Overhead — Department 2..................	900	
Selling Expenses..................................	200	
General Expenses.................................	100	
Accumulated Depreciation — Plant Assets..........		2,250

(g) Distribution of Maintenance Department costs to other factory departments on the basis of maintenance services rendered.

Entry: Power Department.............................. 100
Factory Overhead — Department 1.................. 900
Factory Overhead — Department 2................. 1,000
Maintenance Department........................ 2,000

(h) Distribution of Power Department costs to factory processing departments on the basis of kwh supplied.

Entry: Factory Overhead — Department 1.................. 1,800
Factory Overhead — Department 2.................. 2,700
Power Department............................ 4,500

(i) Application of factory overhead costs to work in process accounts at predetermined rates of 80% and 50% of direct labor cost, respectively, for Departments 1 and 2. See transaction (c).

Entry: Work in Process — Department 1.................... 6,640
Work in Process — Department 2.................... 6,300
Factory Overhead — Department 1................ 6,640
Factory Overhead — Department 2................ 6,300

(j) Transfer of production costs from Department 1 to Department 2 and to Product B (by-product). 4,100 units were fully processed and 800 pounds of Product B, valued at 50¢ per pound, were produced. There is no work in process remaining in Department 1 at the end of the month.

Allocation of total costs of $34,840 charged to Department 1:
Product B, 800 × $.50............................. $ 400
Transferred to Department 2......................... 34,440
Total costs...................................... $34,840

Unit cost of product transferred to Department 2:
$34,440 ÷ 4,100.................................. $ 8.40

Entry: Finished Goods — Product B...................... 400
Work in Process — Department 2.................... 34,440
Work in Process — Department 1................ 34,840

(k) Transfer of production costs from Department 2 to Finished Goods. 4,000 units were completed, and the remaining 900 units were ⅔ completed at the end of the month.

Equivalent units of production:
To process units in inventory on January 1:
800 × ½...................................... 400
To process units started and completed in January:
4,000 − 800................................. 3,200
To process units in inventory on January 31:
900 × ⅔..................................... 600
Equivalent units of production in January............... 4,200

Processing costs:
Direct labor (c)................................. $12,600
Factory overhead (i)................................. 6,300
Total processing costs............................. $18,900

Unit processing costs:
$18,900 ÷ 4,200.................................. $ 4.50

518

Allocation of costs of Department 2:

Units started in December, completed in January:

Inventory on January 1, 800 units ½ completed.......	$ 7,800	
Processing costs in January, 400 at $4.50............	1,800	
Total ($9,600 ÷ 800 = $12 unit cost).............		$ 9,600

Units started and completed in January:

From Department 1, 3,200 units at $8.40............	$26,880	
Processing costs, 3,200 at $4.50..................	14,400	
Total ($41,280 ÷ 3,200 = $12.90 unit cost).........		41,280
Total transferred to Product A...................		$50,880

Units started in January, ⅔ completed:

From Department 1, 900 units at $8.40..............	$ 7,560	
Processing costs, 600 at $4.50....................	2,700	
Total work in process — Department 2............		10,260
Total costs charged to Department 2................		$61,140

Entry:

Finished Goods — Product A.....................	50,880	
Work in Process — Department 2................		50,880

(l) Cost of goods sold.

Product A, 3,800 units:

1,000 units at $11.50...........................	$11,500	
800 units at $12.00...........................	9,600	
2,000 units at $12.90...........................	25,800	
Total cost of Product A sold.....................		$46,900

Product B, 1,000 pounds:

1,000 pounds at $.50...........................		500
Total cost of goods sold........................		$47,400

Entry:

Cost of Goods Sold............................	47,400	
Finished Goods — Product A....................		46,900
Finished Goods — Product B....................		500

(m) Sales on account.

Entry:

Accounts Receivable...........................	71,100	
Sales.......................................		71,100

(n) Cash received on account.

Entry:

Cash.......................................	70,000	
Accounts Receivable.........................		70,000

(o) Cash disbursed.

Entry:

Accounts Payable............................	50,000	
Wages Payable..............................	22,000	
Cash.......................................		72,000

A chart of the flow of costs from the service and processing department accounts into the finished goods accounts and thence to the cost of goods sold account is illustrated on page 520. Entries in the accounts are identified by letters to facilitate comparison with the summary journal entries presented above.

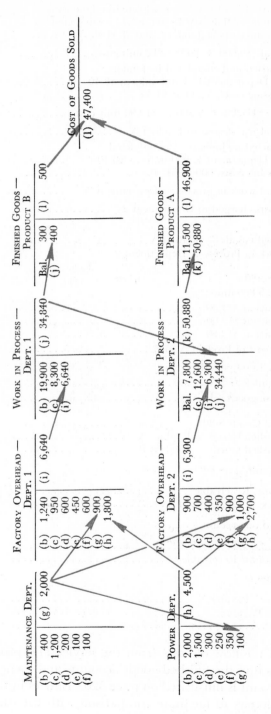

Flow of costs through process cost accounts

After recording and posting the foregoing entries, the trial balance of the ledger is as shown below:

Howell Manufacturing Company
Trial Balance
January 31, 19--

Cash.....	16,500	
Accounts Receivable.....	16,100	
Finished Goods — Product A (1,200 units at $12.90).....	15,480	
Finished Goods — Product B (400 pounds at $.50).....	200	
Work in Process — Department 2 (900 units, ⅔ completed)....	10,260	
Materials.....	21,060	
Prepaid Expenses.....	1,600	
Plant Assets.....	310,000	
Accumulated Depreciation — Plant Assets.....		97,250
Accounts Payable.....		16,780
Wages Payable.....		4,650
Common Stock.....		200,000
Retained Earnings.....		59,670
Sales.....		71,100
Cost of Goods Sold.....	47,400	
Factory Overhead — Department 1.....		100
Factory Overhead — Department 2.....	650	
Selling Expenses.....	5,500	
General Expenses.....	4,800	
	449,550	449,550

On the balance sheet at January 31, the net underapplied factory overhead of $550 would appear as a deferred charge. The balance in the cost of goods sold account would appear on the income statement as a deduction from sales.

521

QUESTIONS

1. Name the three inventory accounts for a manufacturing business and describe what each balance represents at the end of an accounting period.

2. Name and describe the three categories of manufacturing costs included in the cost of finished goods and the cost of work in process.

3. Which of the following would be included in factory overhead cost? (a) depreciation of machinery, (b) direct labor, (c) machinery repairs, (d) factory foreman's salary, (e) advertising, (f) factory rent.

4. (a) Name the two principal types of cost accounting systems. (b) How are the manufacturing costs accumulated under each system?

5. Distinguish between direct and indirect labor used in the process of manufacturing.

6. (a) How does a service department differ from a processing department? (b) Give two examples of a service department.

7. In the manufacture of 13,500 units of a product, direct materials cost incurred was $33,750, direct labor cost incurred was $18,000, and factory over-

head applied was $9,000. (a) What is the total processing cost? (b) What is the processing cost per unit? (c) What is the total manufacturing cost? (d) What is the manufacturing cost per unit? *60,750*

4.50

8. Why do many manufacturing enterprises use predetermined factory overhead rates?

9. (a) How are predetermined factory overhead rates determined? (b) Name three common bases used in determining rates.

10. Factory employees in Department 2 of the Bennett Manufacturing Co. are paid widely varying wage rates. In such circumstances, would direct labor hours or direct labor cost be the more equitable base for applying factory overhead to the production of the department? Explain.

11. (a) What is (1) underapplied factory overhead and (2) overapplied factory overhead? (b) If the factory overhead account for Department 5 has a credit balance, was factory overhead underapplied or overapplied?

12. On interim balance sheets, where would the amount of (a) net overapplied factory overhead or (b) net underapplied factory overhead appear?

13. At the end of a fiscal year there was a relatively minor balance in each of the factory overhead accounts. What is the simplest, yet satisfactory procedure for the disposition of the balances in the accounts?

14. (a) What is meant by the term "equivalent units"? (b) If Department 1 had no work in process at the beginning of the period, 2,000 units were completed during the period, and 1,000 units were 50% completed at the end of the period, what was the number of equivalent units of production for the period? *b) 2,500*

15. The information concerning production in Department 3 for May is presented below. All direct materials are placed in process at the beginning of production. Determine the number of units in work in process inventory at the end of the month.

WORK IN PROCESS — DEPARTMENT 1

		Goods finished during May:	
Process inventory, May 1:			
1,000 units, ½ completed	2,550	3,000 units...............	12,250
Direct material, 3,500 units........	3,850	Process inventory, May 31:	
Direct labor....................	7,400	—— units, ⅘ completed .	5,250
Factory overhead................	3,700		
	17,500		17,500

Beg. Iw = 1,000 ✓
PLACED in Prod 3,500
Process inventory, June 1: *avaiable 4,500*
1,560 units, ⅘ completed ..... 5,250 *Completed 3,000*

16. What is the most important purpose of the cost of production report?

17. Distinguish between a by-product and a joint product.

18. Department 3 produces two products. How should the costs be allocated (a) if the products are joint products and (b) if one of the products is a by-product?

19. Carter Company manufactures Products A and B and By-Product C from Process X. In deciding whether or not to continue producing and selling Products A, B, and C, it is not necessary to allocate the joint costs between the products. Explain.

EXERCISES

20-1. The accounts listed below were selected from the pre-closing trial balance at December 31, the end of the current fiscal year, of Roberts Machine Shop.

Finished Goods Inventory	$ 42,000
Work in Process Inventory	20,000
Direct Materials Inventory	26,000
Direct Materials Purchases	119,500
Direct Labor	142,000
Factory Overhead (control)	81,700
Selling Expense (control)	74,200
General Expense (control)	67,700
Sales	545,500

Inventories at December 31 were as follows:

Finished Goods	$ 40,000
Work in Process	32,100
Direct Materials	27,500

Prepare a statement of cost of goods manufactured.

20-2. On the basis of the data presented in Exercise 1, prepare journal entries on December 31 to:

(a) Adjust the inventory accounts.
(b) Close the appropriate accounts to Manufacturing Summary.
(c) Close Manufacturing Summary.

20-3. The Morgan Manufacturing Company manufactures two products. The entire output of Department 1 is transferred to Department 2. Part of the fully processed goods from Department 2 are sold as Product X and the remainder are transferred to Department 3 for further processing into Product Y. The service department, Factory Office, provides service for each of the processing departments.

Prepare a chart of the flow of costs from the service and processing department accounts into the finished goods accounts and then into the cost of goods sold account. The relevant accounts are presented below.

Factory Office	Work in Process — Department 2
Factory Overhead — Department 1	Work in Process — Department 3
Factory Overhead — Department 2	Finished Goods — Product X
Factory Overhead — Department 3	Finished Goods — Product Y
Work in Process — Department 1	Cost of Goods Sold

20-4. The Carter Company manufactures a single product by a continuous process involving four production departments. The records indicate that $34,500 of direct materials were issued to and $72,700 of direct labor incurred by Department 1 in the manufacture of the product; the factory overhead rate is 80% of direct labor cost; work in process in the department at the beginning of the period totaled $29,400; and work in process at the end of the period totaled $26,300.

Prepare general journal entries to record (a) the flow of costs into Department 1 during the period for (1) direct materials, (2) direct labor, and (3) factory overhead; (b) the transfer of production costs to Department 2.

20-5. The chief cost accountant for Thomas Manufacturing Company estimates total factory overhead cost for Department 2 for the year at $135,000 and total direct labor cost at $90,000. During January, actual direct labor cost totaled $8,200 and factory overhead cost incurred totaled $12,450. (a) What is the factory overhead rate based on direct labor cost? (b) Prepare the entry to apply factory overhead to production for January. (c) What is the balance of the account Factory Overhead — Department 2 at January 31? (d) Does the balance in (c) represent overapplied or underapplied factory overhead?

20-6. The charges to Work in Process — Department 1 for a period, together with information concerning production, are presented below. All direct materials are placed in process at the beginning of production.

Work in Process — Department 1

1,000 units, 60% completed.......	7,600	To Dept. 2, 2,800 units.......	28,660
Direct materials, 1,800 at $4.......	7,200		
Direct labor.....................	9,240		
Factory overhead................	4,620		
	28,660		28,660

Determine the following, presenting your computations: (a) equivalent units of production, (b) processing cost per equivalent unit of production, (c) total and unit cost of product started in prior period and completed in the current period, and (d) total and unit cost of product started and completed in the current period.

20-7. Prepare a cost production report for the Finishing Department of Baldwin Tools, Inc. for the month of August of the current fiscal year, using the following data: *EQUIV. UNITS 5625 PROCESS COST $3.40*

Inventory, August 1, 1,500 units, 1/4 completed	$12,750
Materials from the Plating Department, 5,000 units...............	40,000
Direct labor for August....................... *19,125*	11,250
Factory overhead for August.....................	7,875
Goods finished during August (includes units in process, August 1), 5,500 units....................................... *62,175*	
Inventory August 31, 1,000 units, 1/2 completed................. *9700*	

20-8. The charges to Work in Process — Department 5, together with units of product completed during the period, are indicated in the following account:

Work in Process — Department 5

From Department 4..............	4,660	By-product B, 200 units
Direct labor....................	4,800	Joint product X, 1,000 units
Factory overhead...............	3,840	Joint product Y, 1,500 units

There is no inventory of goods in process at either the beginning or the end of the period. The value of B is $.50 a unit; X sells at $10 a unit and Y sells at $8 a unit.

Allocate the costs to the three products and determine the unit cost of each, presenting your computations.

524

PROBLEMS

The following additional problems for this chapter are located in Appendix C: 20-1B, 20-2B, 20-4B, 20-6B.

If the working papers correlating with the textbook are not used, omit Problem 20-1A.

20-1A. The work sheet for Jenkins Manufacturing Co. for the current year ended December 31 is presented in the working papers. Data concerning account titles, trial balance amounts, and selected adjustments have been entered on the work sheet.

Instructions:

(1) Enter the six adjustments required for the inventories on the work sheet. Additional adjustment data are:

Finished goods inventory at December 31.................	$49,500
Work in process inventory at December 31...............	39,650
Direct materials inventory at December 31...............	32,500

(2) Complete the work sheet.
(3) Prepare a statement of cost of goods manufactured.
(4) Prepare an income statement.

20-2A. The Dunn Company manufactures Product C. Material X is placed in process in Department 1 where it is ground and partially refined. The output of Department 1 is transferred to Department 2, where Material Y is added at the beginning of the process and the refining is completed. On July 1, the Dunn Company had the following inventories:

Finished goods (3,000 units).............................	$26,400
Work in process — Department 1.........................	———
Work in process — Department 2 (1,200 units, 1/2 completed)..	9,000
Materials..	10,500

Departmental accounts are maintained for factory overhead and there is one service department, factory office. Manufacturing operations for the month of July are summarized as follows:

(a) Materials purchased on account........................ $10,500
(b) Materials requisitioned for use:

Material X..	$ 4,000
Material Y..	4,500
Indirect materials — Department 1....................	225
Indirect materials — Department 2....................	190

(c) Labor used:

Direct labor — Department 1.........................	$ 3,000
Direct labor — Department 2.........................	4,000
Indirect labor — Department 1.......................	800
Indirect labor — Department 2.......................	950
Factory office.....................................	150

(d) Miscellaneous costs incurred on account:

Department 1.......................................	$ 560
Department 2.......................................	400
Factory office.....................................	600

(e) Depreciation charged on plant assets:

Department 1.......................................	$ 350
Department 2.......................................	550
Factory office.....................................	175

525

(f) Expiration of prepaid expenses:

Department 1	$	90
Department 2		150
Factory office		75

(g) Distribution of factory office costs:

Department 1 ....40% of total factory office costs
Department 2 ....60% of total factory office costs

(h) Application of factory overhead costs:

Department 1 ....60% of direct labor cost
Department 2 ....80% of direct labor cost

(i) Production costs transferred from Department 1 to Department 2: 2,000 units were fully processed and there was no inventory of work in process in Department 1 at July 31.

(j) Production costs transferred from Department 2 to finished goods: 2,600 units were fully processed including the inventory at July 1. 600 units were 2/3 completed at July 31.

(k) Cost of goods sold during July: 3,200 units (use the first-in, first-out method in crediting the finished goods account).

Instructions:

Prepare entries in general journal form to record the foregoing operations.

20-3A. The trial balance for Edwards Electronics Incorporated at January 31, the end of the first month of the current fiscal year is presented below.

Edwards Electronics Incorporated
Trial Balance
January 31, 19--

Cash	48,750	
Marketable Securities	25,000	
Accounts Receivable	85,500	
Allowance for Doubtful Accounts		5,300
Finished Goods — Product A	47,000	
Finished Goods — Product B	38,500	
Work in Process — Department 1	10,450	
Work in Process — Department 2	8,325	
Work in Process — Department 3	11,100	
Work in Process — Department 4	9,175	
Materials	33,600	
Office Supplies	2,350	
Prepaid Insurance	7,550	
Office Equipment	31,000	
Accumulated Depreciation — Office Equipment		13,700
Machinery and Equipment	172,500	
Accumulated Depreciation — Mach. and Equip.		85,500
Buildings	450,000	
Accumulated Depreciation — Buildings		295,000
Land	70,000	
Patents	22,000	
Accounts Payable		67,500
Wages Payable		8,900
Mortgage Note Payable (due 1980)		150,000
Common Stock ($50 par)		300,000

Retained Earnings........		124,940
Sales.....		212,500
Cost of Goods Sold.....	140,650	
Factory Overhead — Department 1.....		250
Factory Overhead — Department 2.....		100
Factory Overhead — Department 3....	175	
Factory Overhead — Department 4.....	275	
Selling Expenses.....	30,750	
General Expenses.....	18,600	
Interest Expense.....	500	
Interest Income.....		60
	1,263,750	1,263,750

Instructions:

(1) Prepare an income statement.

(2) Prepare a balance sheet.

20-4A. Walker Company manufactures Product M-1 by a series of four processes, all materials being introduced in Department 1. From Department 1 the materials pass through Departments 2, 3, and 4, emerging as finished Product M-1. All inventories are priced at cost by the first-in, first-out method.

The balances in the accounts Work in Process — Department 4 and Finished Goods were as follows on May 1:

Work in Process — Department 4
500 units, 4/5 completed............................ $ 7,400
Finished Goods
800 units at $16 a unit............................. 12,800

The following costs were charged to Work in Process — Department 4 during May:

527

Direct materials transferred from Department 3: 2,100 units at
$10.10... $21,210
Direct labor... 7,200
Factory overhead..................................... 5,400

During the month of May, 1,800 units of M-1 were completed and 1,600 units were sold. Inventories on May 31 were as follows;

Work in process — Department 4: 800 units 3/4 completed
Finished Goods: 1,000 units

Instructions:

(1) Determine the following, presenting the computations in good order:
  (a) Equivalent units of production for Department 4 during May.
  (b) Unit processing cost for Department 4 for May.
  (c) Total and unit cost of Product M-1 started in a prior period and finished in May.
  (d) Total and unit cost of Product M-1 started and finished in May.
  (e) Total cost of goods transferred to finished goods.
  (f) Work in process inventory for Department 4, May 31.
  (g) Cost of goods sold (indicate number of units and unit costs).
  (h) Finished goods inventory, May 31.
(2) Prepare a cost of production report for Department 4 for May.

20-5A. Logan Company manufactures joint product X and Y which it sells for $8 and $10 per unit respectively. During the current year ended December 31, 20,000 units of X and 10,000 units of Y were manufactured and sold.

Production costs totaled $195,000 and there was no inventory of goods in process at either the beginning or the end of the year.

The sales and costs have been relatively stable over the past few years, and they are expected to remain so for the foreseeable future. A proposal has been made to put Product Y through an additional process at an additional cost of $2.50 per unit. The end product, Product Z, can be sold for $12 per unit.

Instructions:

(1) Determine the unit production cost for Product X and Product Y produced during the current year using the sales value method of allocating joint costs.

(2) Prepare a schedule indicating the amount of gross profit on sales per unit of Product X and Product Y for the current year.

(3) Prepare an income statement through gross profit on sales for the current year.

(4) The Company decided to put Product Y through the additional process. The decision was based upon the expectation that all of the Product Z could be sold and that the information presented below was reliable.

Unit sales price, Product Z......................		$12.00
Less: Unit cost price, Product Y..................	$7.50	
Unit cost for additional processing...........	2.50	10.00
Unit gross profit on sales........................		$ 2.00

Do you agree with the decision? Briefly explain.

20-6A. Baker Products manufactures joint products A and B. Materials are placed in production in Department 1 and after processing are transferred to Department 2, where more materials are added. The finished products emerge from Department 2. There are two service departments, Factory Office and Maintenance and Repair.

There were no inventories of work in process at either the beginning or the end of June. Finished goods inventories at June 1 were as follows:

Finished Goods — Product A, 600 units..................	$10,980
Finished Goods — Product B, 800 units..................	9,760

Transactions related to manufacturing operations for the month of June in summary form are as follows:

(a) Materials purchased on account, $12,750.

(b) Miscellaneous costs and expenses incurred on account: Department 1, $180; Department 2, $300; Factory Office, $250; and Maintenance and Repair, $325.

(c) Materials requisitioned for use: Department 1, $4,625 ($4,400 entered directly into the products); Department 2, $10,975 ($10,700 entered directly into the products); Maintenance and Repair, $950.

(d) Labor costs incurred: Department 1, $5,475 ($5,000 entered directly into the products); Department 2, $6,525 ($6,000 entered directly into the products); Factory Office, $900; Maintenance and Repair, $1,600.

(e) Depreciation charged on plant assets: Department 1, $300; Department 2, $700; Factory Office $100; and Maintenance and Repair, $150.

(f) Expiration of various prepaid expenses: Department 1, $50; Department 2, $70; Factory Office, $50; and Maintenance and Repair, $75.

(g) Factory office costs allocated on the basis of man-hours worked: Department 1, 1,000 hours; Department 2, 1,200 hours; Maintenance and Repair, 400 hours.

(h) Maintenance and repair costs allocated on the basis of services rendered: Department 1, 40%; Department 2, 60%.

(i) Factory overhead applied to production at the predetermined rates: 60% and 75% of direct labor cost for Departments 1 and 2 respectively.

(j) Output of Department 1: 1,000 units.

(k) Output of Department 2: 1,200 units of Product A and 1,000 units of Product B. Unit selling price is $30 for Product A and $20 for Product B.

(l) Sales on account: 1,300 units of Product A at $30 and 1,200 units of Product B at $20. Credits to the finished goods accounts are to be priced in accordance with the first-in, first-out method.

Instructions:

Prepare entries in general journal form to record the transactions. Include as an explanation for entry (k) the computations for the allocation of the production costs for Department 2 to the joint products, and as an explanation for entry (l) the units and the unit costs for each product sold.

20-7A. A process cost system is used to record the costs of manufacturing Product P, which requires a series of five processes. The inventory of Work in Process — Department 5 on June 1 and debits to the account during June were as follows:

Balance, 1,200 units, 1/3 completed	$ 4,160
From Department 4, 5,000 units	15,000
Direct labor	6,500
Factory overhead	3,900

529

During June the 1,200 units in process on June 1 were completed, and of the 5,000 units entering the department, all were completed except 900 units, which were 1/3 completed.

Charges to Work in Process — Department 5 for the month of July were as follows:

From Department 4, 6,000 units	$17,400
Direct labor	6,300
Factory overhead	3,780

During July the units in process at the beginning of the month were completed, and of the 6,000 units entering the department, all were completed except 1,200 units, which were 1/6 completed.

Instructions:

(1) Set up an account for Work in Process — Department 5. Enter the balance as of June 1 and the debits and the credits to the account in June. Present computations for determination of (a) equivalent units of production, (b) unit processing cost, (c) cost of goods finished, differentiating between units started in the prior period and units started and finished in June, and (d) work in process inventory.

(2) Bring down the balance of the account as of July 1 and enter the transactions for July. Present the computations listed in instruction (1).

(3) Determine the difference in unit cost between the product started and completed in June and the product started and completed in July. Determine also the amount of the difference attributable collectively to operations in Departments 1 through 4 and the amount attributable to operations in Department 5.

21

Job order cost systems

Job order and process costs distinguished

A process cost accounting system is best suited to manufacturing situations where the processes are continuous and the products are homogeneous. A job order cost accounting system is most appropriate where the product is made to customers' orders or specifications and the identity of each job or order is kept separate. It is also appropriate when standard products are manufactured in batches rather than on a continuous basis. The most significant difference between the job order cost system and the process cost system is that the job order cost system requires the identification of the costs incurred by individual jobs within the manufacturing processes.

The basic concepts of the job order cost system will be illustrated in this chapter. To simplify the illustration, a nondepartmentalized operation will be assumed. In factories with departmentalized operations, costs are accumulated in factory overhead and work in process accounts maintained for each department.

The discussion of the job order cost system directs considerable attention to the source documents that serve as the basis for the entries in the cost system and to the managerial uses of cost accounting in planning and controlling business operations. In many instances, methods, procedures, and managerial applications described in terms of a job order cost system also apply to a process cost system. For example, the system described in this chapter for the acquisition, storage, and issuance of materials applies also to the process cost system.

Materials

Procedures employed in the procurement and issuance of materials vary considerably among manufacturers and even among departments of a particular manufacturer. The discussion that follows is confined to the basic principles, however, and will disregard possible variations and minor details.

Some time in advance of the date that production of a particular commodity is to begin, the department responsible for scheduling informs the purchasing department of the materials that will be needed by means of *purchase requisitions*. The purchasing department then orders appropriate quantities of materials not already in stock by issuing *purchase orders* to suppliers. After the goods have been received and inspected, the receiving department personnel prepare a *receiving report* indicating the quantity received and their condition. Quantities, unit costs, and total costs of the goods billed, as reported on the supplier's invoice, are then compared with the purchase order and the receiving report to make sure that the amounts billed agree with the materials ordered and received. After such verifications the invoice is recorded in the voucher register or purchases journal as a debit to Materials and a credit to Accounts Payable.

The account Materials in the general ledger is a controlling account. An individual account for each type of material is maintained in a subsidiary ledger called the *materials ledger*. Details as to quantity and cost of materials received are recorded in the materials ledger on the basis of the receiving reports or purchase invoices. A typical form of materials ledger account is illustrated below.

Material No. *23*										Reorder Point	*1,000*
Received			Issued			Balance					
Rec. Report No.	Quantity	Amount	Mat. Req. No.	Quantity	Amount	Date		Quantity	Amount		Unit Price
						19— Jan.	1	1,200	600	00	50
			672	500	250 00		4	700	350	00	50
196	3,000	1,620 00					8	{ 700 / 3,000	350 00 / 1,620 00		50 / 54
			704	{ 700 / 100	350 00 / 54 00		18	2,900	1,566 00		54

Materials ledger account

The accounts in the materials ledger may also be used as an aid in maintaining appropriate inventory quantities of stock items. Frequent comparisons of quantity balances with predetermined reorder points enable management to avoid costly idle time caused by lack of materials. The subsidiary ledger form may also include columns for recording quantities ordered and dates of the purchase orders.

Materials are transferred from the storeroom to the factory in response to *materials requisitions*, which may be issued by the manufacturing department concerned or by a central scheduling department. A typical materials requisition is illustrated below. Storeroom personnel record the issuances on the requisition by inserting the physical quantity data. Transfer of responsibility for the materials is evidenced by the signature or initials of the storeroom and factory personnel concerned. The materials requisition is then routed to the materials ledger clerk who inserts unit prices and amounts.

Materials Requisition				
Job No. 62		Requisition No. 704		
Authorized by J. W. Adams		Date January 17, 19 – –		
Description	Quantity Authorized	Quantity Issued	Unit Price	Amount
Material No. 23	800	700 100	$.50 .54	$350 54
				$404
Total issued				
Issued by L. P.		Received by P. P.		

Materials requisition

The completed requisition serves as the basis for posting quantities and dollar data to the materials ledger accounts. In the illustration the first-in, first-out pricing method was employed. A summary of the materials requisitions completed during the month serves as the basis for transferring the cost of materials from the controlling account in the general ledger to the controlling accounts for work in process and factory overhead. The flow of materials into production is illustrated by the entry shown at the top of the next page.

Work in Process...............................	6,500	
Factory Overhead.............................	420	
Materials....................................		6,920

The perpetual inventory system for materials has three important advantages: (1) it provides for prompt and accurate charging of materials to jobs and factory overhead, (2) it permits the work of inventory-taking to be spread out rather than concentrated at the end of a fiscal period, and (3) it facilitates the disclosure of inventory shortages or other irregularities. As physical quantities of the various materials are determined, the actual inventories are compared with the balances of the respective subsidiary ledger accounts. The causes of significant discrepancies between the two should be determined and the responsibility therefor assigned to specific individuals. Remedial action can then be taken.

Factory labor

Unlike materials, factory labor is not tangible, nor is it acquired and stored in advance of its use; hence, there is no perpetual inventory account for labor. The two principal objectives in accounting for labor are (1) determination of the correct amount to be paid each employee for each payroll period, and (2) appropriate allocation of labor costs to factory overhead and individual job orders.

The amount of time spent by an employee in the factory is ordinarily recorded on *clock cards*, which are also referred to as *in-and-out cards*. The amount of time spent by each employee and the labor cost incurred for each individual job, or for factory overhead, are recorded on *time tickets*. A typical time ticket form is illustrated on the next page.

533

The total time reported on each employee's time tickets for a payroll period is compared with the time reported on his clock cards as an internal check on the accuracy of payroll disbursements. A summary of the time tickets at the end of each month serves as the basis for recording the labor costs incurred. The flow of labor costs into production is illustrated by the following entry:

Work in Process...............................	5,000	
Factory Overhead.............................	1,100	
Wages Payable...............................		6,100

Factory overhead

Although it is possible to allocate the actual factory overhead costs among the various jobs, the difficulties and disadvantages of so doing are comparable to those discussed in connection with process cost systems. The use of a predetermined factory overhead rate is helpful to management in preparing bids on contract work and in quoting firm prices on

TIME TICKET

Employee Name____John Kane____   No. 4521

Employee No._____240_____   Date __January 18, 19— —_____

Description of work____Finishing____   Job No. ____62____

Time Started	Time Stopped	Hours Worked	Hourly Rate	Cost
10:00	12:00	2	$4.50	$9.00
1:00	2:00	1	4.50	4.50
Total cost				$13.50

Approved by_____A. C._____

Time ticket

special jobs. Such price determinations are especially important for job order manufacturers if many of their products are manufactured to individual specifications. In addition, the use of a predetermined factory overhead rate permits determination of the total cost of a job shortly after the job is completed. Timely reporting enables management to make whatever adjustments seem necessary in pricing and manufacturing to achieve the best combination of revenue and cost on future jobs.

Amounts of factory overhead applied to work in process are recorded periodically. The flow of factory overhead (80% of direct labor cost) into production is illustrated in the following entry:

Work in Process................................ 4,000
    Factory Overhead............................   4,000

Work in process

Costs incurred for the various jobs are debited to Work in Process. The charges to the account that were illustrated in the three preceding sections may be summarized as follows:

> Direct Materials, $6,500 — Work in Process debited and Materials credited; data obtained from summary of materials requisitions.
>
> Direct Labor, $5,000 — Work in Process debited and Wages Payable credited; data obtained from summary of time tickets.

Factory Overhead, $4,000 — Work in Process debited and Factory Overhead credited; data obtained by applying overhead rate to direct labor cost (80% of $5,000).

Ordinarily a number of jobs are in various stages of production at all times. The work in process account is a controlling account that contains summary information only. The details concerning the costs incurred on each job order are accumulated in a subsidiary ledger known as the *cost ledger*. Each account in the cost ledger, called a *job cost sheet*, has spaces for recording all direct materials and direct labor chargeable to the job and for the application of factory overhead at the predetermined rate. Postings to the job cost sheets are made from materials requisitions and time tickets or from summaries of these documents.

Upon completion of a job, the data on the related job cost sheet are summarized, the unit cost of the finished product is computed, and the sheet is removed from the cost ledger. A summary of the job cost sheets completed during the month provides the basis for an entry debiting Finished Goods and crediting Work in Process.

A work in process account and a summary of the four cost sheets in the related subsidiary ledger are presented below.

WORK IN PROCESS

DATE		ITEM	DEBIT	CREDIT	BALANCE DEBIT	BALANCE CREDIT
19--						
May	1	Balance			1,500	
	31	Direct materials	6,500		8,000	
	31	Direct labor	5,000		13,000	
	31	Factory overhead	4,000		17,000	
	31	Jobs completed		15,960	1,040	

535

COST LEDGER

Job No. 71 (Summary)

Balance......................	1,500
Direct Materials...............	1,000
Direct Labor..................	1,200
Factory Overhead............	960
	4,660

Job No. 73 (Summary)

Direct Materials...............	3,000
Direct Labor..................	2,000
Factory Overhead............	1,600
	6,600

Job No. 72 (Summary)

Direct Materials...............	2,000
Direct Labor..................	1,500
Factory Overhead............	1,200
	4,700

Job No. 74 (Summary)

Direct Materials...............	500
Direct Labor..................	300
Factory Overhead............	240
	1,040

The relationship between the work in process controlling account and the subsidiary cost ledger may be observed in the following tabulation of the data from the accounts illustrated on the preceding page.

WORK IN PROCESS (Controlling)		COST LEDGER (Subsidiary)	
Opening balance............	$1,500 ⟷	Opening balance Job No. 71.............	$1,500
Direet materials............	$6,500 ⟷	Direct materials Job No. 71............. Job No. 72............. Job No. 73............. Job No. 74.............	$1,000 2,000 3,000 500 $6,500
Direct labor...............	$5,000 ⟷	Direct labor Job No. 71............. Job No. 72............. Job No. 73............. Job No. 74.............	$1,200 1,500 2,000 300 $5,000

WORK IN PROCESS (Controlling)		COST LEDGER (Subsidiary)	
Factory overhead...........	$4,000 ⟷	Factory overhead Job No. 71............. Job No. 72............. Job No. 73............. Job No. 74.............	$ 960 1,200 1,600 240 $4,000
Jobs completed............	$15,960 ⟷	Jobs completed Job No. 71............. Job No. 72............. Job No. 73.............	$ 4,660 4,700 6,600 $15,960
Closing balance............	$ 1,040 ⟷	Closing balance Job No. 74.............	$ 1,040

The data in the foregoing cost ledger were presented in summary fashion for illustrative purposes. A form of job cost sheet providing for the current accumulation of cost elements entering into a job order and for a summary at the time the job is completed is presented on the next page for Job No. 72.

When Job No. 72 was completed, the direct materials costs and the direct labor costs were totaled and entered in the Summary column. Factory overhead was added at the predetermined rate of 80% of the direct labor cost, and the total cost of the job was determined. The total cost of the job, $4,700, divided by the number of units produced, 5,000, yielded a unit cost of $.94 for the Type C Containers produced.

536

Job No. __72__   Date _____ May 7, 19—

Item __5,000 Type C Containers__   Date wanted __May 23, 19—__

For __Stock__   Date completed __May 21, 19—__

Direct Materials		Direct Labor				Summary	
Mat. Req. No.	Amount	Time Summary No.	Amount	Time Summary No.	Amount	Item	Amount
834	400.00	2202	83.60	2248	22.50	Direct	
838	500.00	2204	108.40	2250	87.30	materials	2,000.00
841	700.00	2205	67.00	2253	55.40	Direct labor	1,500.00
864	400.00	2210	129.00			Factory	
		2211	98.30		1,500.00	overhead	
	2,000.00	2213	107.20			(80% of	
		2216	110.00			direct	
		2222	77.60			labor cost)	1,200.00
		2224	217.40				
		2225	106.30			Total cost	4,700.00
		2231	53.20				
		2234	45.20			No. of units	
		2237	70.00			finished	5,000
		2242	61.60			Cost per unit	.94

Job cost sheet

Upon the completion of Job No. 72, the job cost sheet was removed from the cost ledger and filed for future reference. At the end of the accounting period, the sum of the total costs on all cost sheets completed during the period is determined and the following entry is made:

Finished Goods... 15,960
   Work in Process 15,960

The remaining balance in the work in process account represents the total costs charged to the uncompleted job cost sheets.

Finished goods and cost of goods sold

The finished goods account is a controlling account. The related subsidiary ledger, which has an account for each kind of commodity produced, is called the *finished goods ledger* or *stock ledger*. Each account in the subsidiary finished goods ledger provides columns for recording the quantity and the cost of goods manufactured, the quantity and the cost of goods shipped, and the quantity, the total cost, and the unit cost of goods on hand. An account in the finished goods ledger is illustrated on the next page.

Just as there are various methods of pricing materials entering into production, there are various methods of determining the cost of the

Item: Type C Container									
MANUFACTURED			SHIPPED			BALANCE			
JOB ORDER No.	QUAN-TITY	AMOUNT	SHIP. ORDER No.	QUAN-TITY	AMOUNT	DATE	QUAN-TITY	AMOUNT	UNIT PRICE
						19 -- May 1	2,000	1,960 00	98
			643	2,000	1,960 00	8	—	—	--
72	5,000	4,700 00				21	5,000	4,700 00	94
			646	2,000	1,880 00	23	3,000	2,820 00	94

Finished goods ledger account

finished goods sold. In the illustration, the first-in, first-out method is used. The quantities shipped are posted to the finished goods ledger from a copy of the shipping order or other memorandum. The finished goods ledger clerk then records on the shipping order the unit price and the total amount of the commodity sold. A summary of the cost data on these shipping orders becomes the basis for the following entry:

```
Cost of Goods Sold.....................................    15,084
        Finished Goods......................................            15,084
```

If goods are returned by a buyer and put back in stock, it is necessary to debit Finished Goods and credit Cost of Goods Sold for the cost.

Sales

For each sale of finished goods it is necessary to maintain a record of both the cost price and the selling price of the goods sold. As indicated above, the cost data may be recorded on the shipping orders. The sales journal may be expanded by the addition of a column for recording the total cost of the goods billed, the total of the column being posted at the end of the month as a debit to Cost of Goods Sold and a credit to Finished Goods. The total of the sales price column is posted at the end of the month as a debit to Accounts Receivable and a credit to Sales.

Summary illustration of job order cost accounting

To illustrate further the procedures described, the following facts are assumed: The Rockford Manufacturing Co. employs a job order cost accounting system. The trial balance of the general ledger on January 1, the first day of the fiscal year, is given on the following page.

Rockford Manufacturing Co.
Trial Balance
January 1, 19--

Cash.	85,000	
Accounts Receivable.	73,000	
Finished Goods.	40,000	
Work in Process.	20,000	
Materials.	30,000	
Prepaid Expenses.	2,000	
Plant Assets.	850,000	
Accumulated Depreciation — Plant Assets.		473,000
Accounts Payable.		70,000
Wages Payable.		15,000
Common Stock.		500,000
Retained Earnings.		42,000
	1,100,000	1,100,000

A summary of the transactions and the adjustments for the month of January, followed in each case by the related entry in general journal form, is presented below. In practice the transactions would be recorded from day to day in various journals.

(a) Materials purchased and prepaid expenses incurred on account.
Summary of receiving reports:

Material A.	$ 20,000
Material B.	17,000
Material C.	12,000
Material D.	13,000
Total.	$ 62,000

Entry: Materials. 62,000
       Prepaid Expenses. 1,000
          Accounts Payable. 63,000

(b) Materials requisitioned for use.
Summary of requisitions:

BY USE

Job No. 1001.	$ 12,000	
Job No. 1002.	26,000	
Job No. 1003.	22,000	$ 60,000
Factory Overhead.		3,000
Total.		$ 63,000

BY TYPES

Material A.	$ 16,000
Material B.	18,000
Material C.	15,000
Material D.	14,000
Total.	$ 63,000

Entry: Work in Process. 60,000
       Factory Overhead. 3,000
          Materials. 63,000

(c) Factory labor used.
Summary of time tickets:

Job No. 1001.........	$ 60,000	
Job No. 1002.........	30,000	
Job No. 1003.........	10,000	$100,000
Factory Overhead......		20,000
Total...............		$120,000

Entry: Work in Process............................. 100,000
     Factory Overhead............................. 20,000
       Wages Payable..............................   120,000

(d) Costs and expenses incurred on account for the factory and by the sales and administrative divisions.

Entry: Factory Overhead............................ 56,000
     Selling Expenses............................. 25,000
     General Expenses............................ 10,000
       Accounts Payable..........................   91,000

(e) Expiration of prepaid expenses chargeable to factory and to the sales and administrative divisions.

Entry: Factory Overhead............................ 1,000
     Selling Expenses............................. 100
     General Expenses............................ 100
       Prepaid Expenses..........................   1,200

540

(f) Depreciation chargeable to factory and to sales and administrative divisions.

Entry: Factory Overhead............................ 7,000
     Selling Expenses............................. 200
     General Expenses............................ 100
       Accumulated Depreciation — Plant Assets......   7,300

(g) Application of factory overhead costs to jobs at the rate of 90% of direct labor cost. See transaction (c).
Summary of factory overhead applied:

Job No. 1001 (90% of $60,000).	$ 54,000
Job No. 1002 (90% of $30,000).	27,000
Job No. 1003 (90% of $10,000).	9,000
Total.....................	$ 90,000

Entry: Work in Process............................. 90,000
       Factory Overhead..........................   90,000

(h) Jobs completed.
Summary of completed job cost sheets:

Job No. 1001...............	$146,000
Job No. 1002...............	83,000
Total.....................	$229,000

Entry: Finished Goods............................. 229,000
       Work in Process...........................   229,000

(i) Sales on account and cost of goods sold.
   Summary of sales invoices and shipping orders:

	SALES PRICE	COST PRICE
Product X.........	$ 19,600	$ 15,000
Product Y.........	165,100	125,000
Product Z.........	105,300	80,000
Total............	$290,000	$220,000

Entry: Accounts Receivable............................ 290,000
   Sales....................................... 290,000

Entry: Cost of Goods Sold............................ 220,000
   Finished Goods............................. 220,000

(j) Cash received and disbursed.

Entry: Cash.. 300,000
   Accounts Receivable........................ 300,000

Entry: Accounts Payable............................ 190,000
   Wages Payable.............................. 125,000
   Cash...................................... 315,000

The flow of costs through the manufacturing accounts, together with summary details of the subsidiary ledgers, is illustrated on the following page. Entries in the accounts are identified by letters to facilitate comparisons with the foregoing summary journal entries.

The trial balance taken from the general ledger of the Rockford Manufacturing Co. on January 31 is as follows:

Rockford Manufacturing Co.
Trial Balance
January 31, 19 --

Cash...	70,000	
Accounts Receivable..........................	63,000	
Finished Goods...............................	49,000	
Work in Process..............................	41,000	
Materials....................................	29,000	
Prepaid Expenses.............................	1,800	
Plant Assets.................................	850,000	
Accumulated Depreciation — Plant Assets......		480,300
Accounts Payable.............................		34,000
Wages Payable................................		10,000
Common Stock.................................		500,000
Retained Earnings............................		42,000
Sales..		290,000
Cost of Goods Sold...........................	220,000	
Factory Overhead.............................		3,000
Selling Expenses.............................	25,300	
General Expenses.............................	10,200	
	1,359,300	1,359,300

The balances of the three inventory accounts, Materials, Work in Process, and Finished Goods, represent the respective inventories on

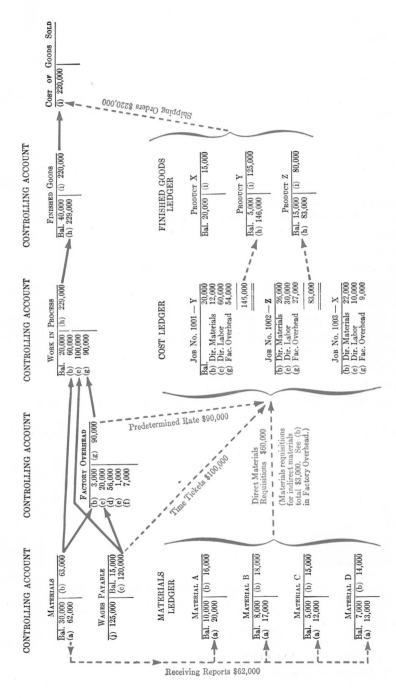

Flow of costs through job order cost accounts

January 31. Each account controls a subsidiary ledger. A comparison of the balances of the general ledger accounts with their respective subsidiary ledgers reveals the following:

Controlling Accounts		Subsidiary Ledgers	
ACCOUNT	BALANCE	ACCOUNT	BALANCE
Materials...............	$29,000	Material A..........	$14,000
		Material B..........	7,000
		Material C..........	2,000
		Material D.........	6,000 $29,000
Work in Process............	$41,000	Job No. 1003...............	$41,000
Finished Goods.............	$49,000	Product X...........	$ 5,000
		Product Y...........	26,000
		Product Z...........	18,000 $49,000

In order to simplify the illustration, only one work in process account and one factory overhead account have been used. Ordinarily a manufacturing business has several processing departments, each requiring separate work in process and factory overhead accounts. In the foregoing illustration, one predetermined rate was used in applying the factory overhead to jobs. In a factory with a number of processing departments, a single factory overhead rate may not provide accurate product costs and effective cost control. A single rate for the entire factory cannot take into consideration such factors as differences among departments in the nature of their operations and in amounts of factory overhead incurred. In such cases, each factory department should have a separate factory overhead rate. For example, in a factory with twenty distinct operating departments, one department might have an overhead rate of 110% of direct labor cost, another a rate of $4 per direct labor hour, another a rate of $3.50 per machine hour, and so on.

543

QUESTIONS

1. Which type of cost system, process or job order, would be best suited for each of the following: (a) soap manufacturer, (b) shipbuilder, (c) flour-milling company, (d) printing shop, (e) automobile manufacturer? Give reasons for your answers.

2. What purpose is served by (a) the purchase requisition and (b) the purchase order?

3. Briefly discuss how the purchase order, purchase invoice, and receiving report can be used to assist in controlling cash disbursements made for materials acquired.

4. What document is the source for (a) debiting the accounts in the materials ledger, and (b) crediting the accounts in the materials ledger?

5. Briefly discuss how the materials requisition is used to help control the issuance of materials from the storeroom.

6. The beginning balance, a purchase, and an issuance to production of a particular type of material are described below in chronological sequence. What is (a) the cost of the materials issued to production and (b) the cost of the inventory after the issuance, determined by (1) the first-in, first-out method and (2) the last-in, first-out method?

> Beginning balance . . . . 300 pounds at $1.00 per pound
> Purchase . . . . 200 pounds at $ .95 per pound
> Issued to production . . . . 100 pounds

7. Discuss the major advantages of a perpetual inventory system over a periodic system for materials.

8. If a perpetual inventory system is used, is it necessary to take a physical inventory? Discuss.

9. Differentiate between the clock card and the time ticket.

10. Discuss how the predetermined factory overhead rate can be used in job order cost accounting to assist management in pricing jobs.

11. Describe the source of the data for debiting Work in Process for (a) direct materials, (b) direct labor, and (c) factory overhead.

12. What document serves as the basis for posting to (a) the direct materials section of the job cost sheet and (b) the direct labor section of the job cost sheet?

13. What account is the controlling account for (a) the materials ledger, (b) the cost ledger, and (c) the finished goods ledger or stock ledger?

14. In a factory with several processing departments, a separate factory overhead rate is often determined for each department. Why is a single factory overhead rate often inadequate in such circumstances?

EXERCISES

21-1. The balance of Material M on June 1 and the receipts and issuances during June are presented below.

Balance, June 1, 200 units at $10

Received during June:
June   3, 400 units at $10.00
June 10, 200 units at $10.50
June 24, 300 units at $11.00

Issued during June:
June   5, 300 units for Job No. 712
June 18, 200 units for Job No. 715
June 27, 300 units for Job No. 716

Determine the cost of each of the three issuances using (a) the first-in, first-out method and (b) the last-in, first-out method.

21-2. The issuances of materials for the current month are presented below.

Requisition No.	Material	Job No.	Amount
217	C	162	$3,700
218	A	163	2,490
219	F	General factory use	700
220	C	159	1,450
221	D	162	3,100

Present the general journal entry to record the issuances of materials.

21-3. A summary of the time tickets for the month of January follows:

Job No.	Amount	Job No.	Amount
1120	$ 820	1125	$3,410
1122	2,250	1126	795
1124	1,775	Indirect labor	1,210

Present the general journal entry to record the factory labor costs incurred.

21-4. The Manning Manufacturing Company applies factory overhead to jobs on the basis of direct labor dollars for work performed in Department 1 and on the basis of machine hours for work performed in Department 2. Estimated factory overhead costs, direct labor costs, and machine hours for the year, and actual factory overhead costs, direct labor costs, and machine hours for January are presented below:

	Department 1	Department 2
Estimated factory overhead costs for year....	$33,750	$37,500
Estimated direct labor costs for year........	$45,000	
Estimated machine hours for year...........		30,000 hrs.
Actual factory overhead costs for January....	$ 2,970	$ 3,150
Actual direct labor costs for January........	$ 3,900	
Actual machine hours for January..........		2,500 hrs.

545

Departmental accounts are not maintained for work in process and factory overhead. (a) What is the factory overhead rate for Department 1? (b) What is the factory overhead rate for Department 2? (c) Prepare the general journal entry to apply factory overhead to production for January. (d) What is the balance of the factory overhead account on January 31? (e) Was factory overhead overapplied or underapplied on January 31?

21-5. The following account appears in the ledger after only part of the postings have been completed for the month of June:

WORK IN PROCESS

Balance, June 1............	8,500
Direct Materials...........	26,750
Direct Labor..............	41,000
Factory Overhead.........	32,800

Jobs finished during June are summarized below.

Job No. 317........	$28,500	Job No. 322........	29,750
Job No. 320........	24,375	Job No. 323........	14,425

(a) Prepare the general journal entry to record the jobs completed and (b) determine the cost of the unfinished jobs at June 30.

21-6. Champion Products began manufacturing operations on March 1. The cost sheets for the four jobs entering production during the month are presented below, in summary form. Jobs Nos. 1 and 2 were completed during the month, and all costs applicable to them were recorded on the related cost sheets. Jobs Nos. 3 and 4 are still in process at the end of the month, and all applicable costs except factory overhead have been recorded on the related cost sheets. In addition to the materials and labor charged directly to the jobs, $325 of indirect materials and $1,100 of indirect labor were used during the month.

Job No. 1		Job No. 2	
Direct Material...........	5,250	Direct Material...........	8,500
Direct Labor.............	4,000	Direct Labor.............	5,300
Factory Overhead........	3,600	Factory Overhead........	4,770
Total.................	12,850	Total.................	18,570

Job No. 3		Job No. 4	
Direct Material...........	7,000	Direct Material...........	2,100
Direct Labor.............	4,700	Direct Labor.............	1,500
Factory Overhead........	4,230	Factory Overhead........	1350

Prepare an entry, in general journal form, to record each of the following operations for the month (one entry for each operation):

(a) Direct and indirect materials used.
(b) Direct and indirect labor used.
(c) Factory overhead to be applied (a single overhead rate is used, based on direct labor cost).
(d) Jobs Nos. 1 and 2 completed.

546

PROBLEMS

The following additional problems for this chapter are located in Appendix C: 21-1B, 21-2B, 21-5B.

21-1A. Beck Custom Products uses a job order cost system. The following data summarize the operations related to production for September, the first month of operations.

(a) Materials purchased on account, $20,500.
(b) Materials requisitioned and factory labor used:

	Materials	Factory Labor
Job No. 1................	$1,720	$ 800
Job No. 2................	2,550	1,350
Job No. 3...	2,800	1,440
Job No. 4................	3,920	1,880
Job No. 5....	1,230	300
Job No. 6	1,400 13620	450 6220
For general factory use....	450 14070	925 7145

(c) Factory overhead costs incurred on account, $4,200.
(d) Depreciation of machinery and equipment, $1,900.
(e) The factory overhead rate is 120% of direct labor cost.

(f) Jobs completed: Nos. 1, 2, 3, and 4.

(g) Jobs Nos. 1, 2, and 4 were shipped and customers were billed for $5,100, $8,250, and $11,150 respectively.   *total 24,500*

Instructions:

(1) Prepare entries in general journal form to record the foregoing summarized operations.

(2) Set up T accounts for Work in Process and Finished Goods. Post to these accounts, using the identifying letters as dates. Bring down the end-of-the-month balances.

(3) Prepare a schedule of unfinished jobs to support the balance in the work in process account.

(4) Prepare a schedule of completed jobs on hand to support the balance in the finished goods account.

If the working papers correlating with the textbook are not used, omit Problem 21-2A.

21-2A. Reliable Furniture repairs, refinishes, and reupholsters furniture. A job order cost system was installed recently to assist in determining the prices to quote to prospective customers, in determining the actual costs incurred on each job, and in reducing costs.

When a prospective customer requests an estimate of the price for a job, the estimated cost data are entered on an unnumbered job order cost sheet. If the customer accepts the estimate, a number is assigned to the job and the costs incurred are recorded in the usual manner on the job order cost sheet. When the job is completed, an explanation for any differences between the estimated and actual costs is entered on the sheet to assist management in evaluating the efficiency of operations and in pricing future jobs.

On June 15, an estimate of $260 for reupholstering a couch was given to William Hale. The estimate was based upon the following data:

Estimated direct materials:	
12 yards at $11 per yard..........................	$132
Estimated direct labor:	
8 hours at $5 per hour..............................	40
Estimated factory overhead: $3.50 per direct labor hour..	28
Total estimated costs.............................	$200
Markup (30% of production costs).....................	60
Total estimate.....................................	$260

On June 20, the couch was picked up from the residence of William Hale with the promise that it would be returned on June 30. The job was completed on June 27. The materials requisitions and time tickets pertaining to the job are summarized below:

Materials Requisition No.	Description	Amount
119	12 yards at $11	$132.00
125	1½ yards at $11	16.50

Time Ticket No.	Description	Amount
241	6 hours at $5	$30.00
242	1½ hours at $5	7.50

Instructions:

(1) Complete that portion of the job order cost sheet that would be completed when the estimate is given to the customer, William Hale.

(2) Assign number 31 to the job, record the costs incurred, and complete the job order cost sheet. In commenting upon the variances between actual costs and estimated costs, assume that 1½ yards of material was spoiled and that the factory overhead rate has been proven to be satisfactory.

21-3A. The trial balance of the general ledger of James Manufacturing Corporation as of July 31, the end of the first month of the current fiscal year, is as follows:

James Manufacturing Corporation
Trial Balance
July 31, 19--

Cash.	87,400	
Accounts Receivable.	81,700	
Finished Goods	44,900	
Work in Process.	10,800	
Materials.	26,650	
Plant Assets	180,000	
Accumulated Depreciation — Plant Assets.		70,000
Accounts Payable		33,500
Wages Payable		8,400
Capital Stock.		200,000
Retained Earnings.		110,350
Sales		82,500
Cost of Goods Sold.	61,000	
Factory Overhead.		200
Selling and General Expenses.	12,500	
	504,950	504,950

As of the same date, balances in the accounts of selected subsidiary ledgers are as follows:

Finished goods ledger:
Commodity A, 700 units, $7,700; Commodity B, 1,500 units, $30,000; Commodity C, 900 units, $7,200.

Cost ledger:
Job No. 810, $10,800.

Materials ledger:
Material M, $17,500; Material N, $8,400; Material O, $750.

The transactions completed during August are summarized as follows:

(a) Materials were purchased on account as follows:

Material M	$14,400
Material N.	7,250
Material O.	600

(b) Materials were requisitioned from stores as follows:

Job No. 810, Material M, $4,100; Material N, $2,500.	$ 6,600
Job No. 812, Material M, $7,500; Material N, $5,700.	13,200
Job No. 813, Material M, $3,400; Material N, $1,800.	5,200
For general factory use; Material O.	550

(c) Time tickets for the month were chargeable as follows:

Job No. 810.	$ 8,000	Job No. 813.	$4,800
Job No. 812.	12,500	Indirect labor.	3,200

(d) Various factory overhead charges of $15,220 were incurred on account.
(e) Selling and general expenses of $12,900 were incurred on account.
(f) Factory payroll checks for $31,400 were issued.
(g) Payments on account were $52,000.
(h) Depreciation on factory plant and equipment of $1,500 was recorded.
(i) Factory overhead was applied to jobs at the rate of 80% of direct labor cost.
(j) Jobs completed during the month were as follows: Job No. 810 produced 3,000 units of Commodity A; Job No. 812 produced 1,700 units of Commodity B.
(k) Total sales on account were $94,500. The goods sold were as follows (use first-in, first-out method): 2,500 units of Commodity A; 1,800 units of Commodity B; 400 units of Commodity C.
(l) Cash of $99,000 was received on accounts receivable.

Instructions:

(1) Open T accounts for the general ledger, the finished goods ledger, the cost ledger, and the materials ledger. Record directly in these accounts the balances as of July 31, identifying them as "Bal." Record the quantities as well as the dollar amounts in the finished goods ledger.
(2) Prepare entries in general journal form to record the August transactions. After recording each transaction, post to the T accounts, using the identifying letters as dates. When posting to the finished goods ledger, record quantities as well as dollar amounts.
(3) Take a trial balance.
(4) Prove the subsidiary ledgers with the general ledger controlling accounts.
(5) Prepare an income statement for the two months ended August 31.

21-4A. The trial balance of Perkins Company at the end of the eleventh month of the current year is presented on the following page.

Transactions completed during June and adjustments required on June 30 are summarized as follows:

(a) Purchased materials on account................		$25,100
(b) Factory labor costs incurred:		
Direct.....................................	$10,500	
Indirect....................................	1,200	11,700
(c) Materials requisitioned for factory use:		
Direct.....................................	$22,000	
Indirect....................................	320	22,320
(d) Incurred following costs and expenses on account:		
Factory overhead..........................	$ 5,900	
Selling expenses...........................	5,750	
General expenses..........................	2,100	13,750
(e) Cash disbursed:		
Accounts payable..........................	$40,150	
Wages payable............................	13,100	
Dividends payable.........................	3,000	56,250
(f) Factory overhead at a predetermined rate: 90% of direct labor cost		
(g) Total cost of jobs completed..................		43,150
(h) Sales, all on account:		
Selling price..............................		69,500
Cost price................................		51,630

Perkins Company
Trial Balance
May 31, 19--

Cash..	76,400	
Accounts Receivable...........................	58,000	
Allowance for Doubtful Accounts...................		2,210
Finished Goods...............................	87,750	
Work in Process..............................	24,600	
Materials.....................................	36,200	
Prepaid Insurance.............................	3,900	
Factory Equipment............................	180,000	
Accumulated Depreciation — Factory Equipment....		43,000
Office Equipment..............................	30,000	
Accumulated Depreciation — Office Equipment......		5,700
Accounts Payable..............................		40,600
Income Tax Payable...........................		11,700
Cash Dividends Payable........................		3,000
Wages Payable................................		2,200
Interest Payable...............................		
Mortgage Note Payable (due 1980)...............		100,000
Common Stock ($100 par)......................		200,000
Retained Earnings............................		58,865
Expense and Revenue Summary..................		
Sales...		641,000
Cost of Goods Sold............................	502,200	
Factory Overhead.............................	550	
Selling Expenses..............................	62,725	
General Expenses.............................	23,850	
Interest Expense..............................	5,400	
Income Tax..................................	16,700	
	1,108,275	1,108,275

(i)	Cash received on account.....................		64,700
(j)	Depreciation charged:		
	Factory equipment.........................		1,000
	Office equipment..........................		190
(k)	Insurance expired:		
	Chargeable to factory......................	$ 150	
	Chargeable to selling expenses...............	25	
	Chargeable to general expenses..............	20	195
(l)	Uncollectible accounts receivable written off......		800
(m)	Recorded additional income tax...............		4,800
(n)	Recorded interest accrued on mortgage note payable......................................		600
(o)	Added to allowance for doubtful accounts based on analysis of accounts in customers ledger, which indicated doubtful accounts of $1,950.		
(p)	Closed balance in Factory Overhead to Cost of Goods Sold.		

550

Instructions:

(1) Open T accounts and record the initial balances indicated in the May 31 trial balance, identifying each as "Bal."

(2) Record the transactions and the adjustments directly in the accounts, using the identifying letters in place of dates.

(3) Record the necessary year-end closing entries directly in the accounts, using a capital "C" to designate these entries.

(4) Prepare an income statement for the year ended June 30, 19--.

(5) Prepare a balance sheet as of June 30, 19--.

21-5A. Selected accounts for Hamilton Products are presented below. For the purposes of this problem, some of the debits and credits have been omitted.

ACCOUNTS RECEIVABLE

June 1 Balance............... 43,500	June 30 Collections........... 51,400
30 Sales.................. (A)	

MATERIALS

June 1 Balance............... 8,900	June 30 Requisitions.......... (B)
30 Purchases.............. 11,700	

WORK IN PROCESS

June 1 Balance............... 7,200	June 30 Goods finished........ (E)
30 Direct materials.......... (C)	
30 Direct labor............. 18,000	
30 Factory overhead........ (D)	

FINISHED GOODS

June 1 Balance............... 15,500	June 30 Cost of goods sold...... (G)
30 Goods finished........... (F)	

FACTORY OVERHEAD

June 1 Balance................ 180	June 30 Applied (80% of direct
1–30 Costs incurred........... 14,150	labor cost)......... (H)

COST OF GOODS SOLD

June 30 (I)	

SALES

	June 30 (J)

Selected balances at June 30:

Accounts receivable.........	$39,600
Finished goods..............	16,800
Work in process............	7,500
Materials..................	5,700

Materials requisitions for June included $450 of materials issued for general factory use. All sales are made on account, terms n/30.

Instructions:

(1) Determine the amounts represented by the letters (A) through (J), presenting your computations.

(2) Is factory overhead overapplied or underapplied at June 30? By how much?

22

Budgetary control and standard cost systems

Accounting aids to management

The individuals charged with the responsibility of organizing and directing the operations of a business enterprise are often referred to collectively as the "management." The basic functions of management are frequently classified as (1) planning and (2) control. *Planning* is the process of selecting realistically attainable business objectives and formulating the general policies and the specific directions needed to achieve such objectives. *Control* encompasses the procedures designed to assure the conformity of actual operations with management's plans.

Effective planning and control are requisites of good business management and successful operations. When the owner of a business can personally supervise every phase of operations, he can perform the basic functions of management with minimum recourse to accounting data. Direct supervision of all phases of operations by a single individual is seldom possible, however, and it is necessary to establish a chain of management command from the chief executive down to department foremen. Under such circumstances, accounting data are indispensable in providing each management level with the financial and operating data needed to achieve sound planning and effective control.

Various uses of accounting data by management have been described in earlier chapters. The value of financial statements in appraising past operations and planning for the future has been emphasized. Attention has been directed to the principles of internal control designed to safeguard assets, assure accurate accounting data, encourage adherence to management policies, and increase efficiency. The role of cost accounting in planning production and controlling costs has been described. This chapter is devoted to budgeting and standard costs, two additional accounting tools designed to assist management in planning and controlling operations.

Nature and objectives of budgeting

The essentials of *budgeting* are (1) the establishment of specific goals for future operations and (2) the periodic comparison of actual results with these goals. Although budgeting is commonly associated with profit-making enterprises, its wide applicability in other areas should be noted. For example, budgeting plays an important role in operating most instrumentalities of government, ranging from rural school districts and small villages to gigantic agencies of the federal government. It is also an integral part of the operations of churches, hospitals, and other nonprofit institutions. Individuals and family units frequently employ budgeting techniques as an aid to careful management of resources.

A *budget* is a formal written statement of management's plans for the future, expressed in financial terms. A budget charts the course of future action. Thus, it serves management in the same manner that the architect's blueprints assist the builder and the navigator's flight plan aids the pilot. A budget, like a blueprint and a flight plan, should contain sound, attainable objectives.

Budgeting and management

Each of management's primary functions is directly served by budgeting. If the budget is to contain sound, attainable goals, planning must be based on careful study, investigation, and research. Reliance by management on data thus obtained lessens the role of hunches and intuition in managing a business enterprise.

In order to be effective, managerial planning must be accompanied by control. The control feature of budgeting lies in periodic comparisons as disclosed by *budget performance reports* between planned objectives and actual performance. Variations between the budget and actual performance reveal the areas that need corrective action. The role of accounting is to assist management in the investigation phase of budget preparation, to translate management's plans into financial terms, and to prepare budget performance reports and related analyses.

Budgeting procedures

The preparation of budgets is ordinarily assigned to a committee composed of the budget director and such high-level executives as the controller, treasurer, production manager, and sales manager. The process is initiated by requesting estimates of sales, production, and other operating data from the various administrative units concerned. It is important that intermediate and lower levels in the chain of accountability participate in the preparation and submission of budget estimates. The involvement of all supervisory personnel engenders cooperation both within and among departments, and also heightens awareness of each department's importance in the overall processes of the company. All levels of management are thus encouraged to establish goals and to control operations in a manner that strengthens the possibilities of achieving the goals.

The various estimates received by the budget committee are revised, reviewed, coordinated, cross-referenced, and finally assembled to form the *master budget*. The estimates submitted should not be substantially revised by the committee without first giving the originator an opportunity to defend his proposals. After agreement has been reached and the master budget has been adopted by the budget committee, copies of the pertinent sections are distributed to appropriate personnel in the chain of accountability. Periodic reports comparing actual results with the budget should likewise be distributed to all supervisory personnel.

Systems of budgetary control

The details of budgeting systems vary among enterprises; they are affected by the type and degree of complexity of the particular company, the volume of its revenues, the relative importance of its various divisions, and many other factors. Budget procedures employed by a large manufacturer of automobiles would obviously differ in many respects from a system designed for a small manufacturer of paper products. The differences between a system designed for factory operations of any type and a financial enterprise such as a bank would be even more marked.

As a framework for describing and illustrating budgeting, a small manufacturing enterprise will be assumed. The principal components of its master budget are as follows:

Budgeted income statement
    Sales budget
    Cost of goods sold budget
        Production budget
        Direct materials purchases budget
        Direct labor cost budget
        Factory overhead cost budget
    Operating expenses budget

Budgeted balance sheet
    Capital expenditures budget
    Cash budget

Budget period

Budgets of operating activities ordinarily encompass the fiscal year of an enterprise. To achieve any effective degree of control the annual budgets must be subdivided into shorter time periods such as quarters of the year, months, or weeks. It is also necessary to review the budgets from time to time and make such revisions as are necessitated by unforeseen changes in business conditions, in the particular industry, or in the individual enterprise.

A frequent variant of fiscal year budgeting, sometimes called *continuous budgeting*, is to maintain at all times a twelve-month projection into the future. At the end of each time interval employed, the twelve-month budget is revised by removing the data for the currently elapsed period and adding the newly estimated budget data for the same period a year hence.

Sales budget

The first budget to be prepared is customarily the sales budget. The amount of revenue expected from sales will, of course, have a material effect on all elements entering into the determination of net income from operations. For use as a part of the master budget and also as the basis for the development of the other budgets, the sales budget ordinarily indicates the quantity of each product expected to be sold. The quantity estimates are based on an analysis of past sales and on forecasts of business conditions generally and for the specific industry. The anticipated sales revenue is then determined by multiplying the volume of forecasted sales by the expected unit sales price. A sales budget is illustrated below.

Dean Company
Sales Budget
For Year Ending December 31, 1970

PRODUCT	UNIT SALES VOLUME	UNIT SELLING PRICE	TOTAL SALES
X	132,000	$ 6.60	$ 871,200
Y	70,000	11.00	770,000
Total.....			$1,641,200

Sales budget

Production budget

The number of units of each commodity expected to be manufactured to meet budgeted sales and inventory requirements is set forth in the production budget. The expected volume of production is determined by subtracting the estimated inventory at the beginning of the period from the sum of the units expected to be sold and the desired inventory at the end of the period. A production budget is illustrated at the top of the next page.

Dean Company
Production Budget
For Year Ending December 31, 1970

	UNITS	
	PRODUCT X	PRODUCT Y
Sales	132,000	70,000
Desired inventory, December 31, 1970.........	20,000	15,000
Total.....................................	152,000	85,000
Less estimated inventory, January 1, 1970......	22,000	12,000
Total production...........................	130,000	73,000

Production budget

The production requirements must be carefully coordinated with the sales budget to assure that production and sales are kept in balance during the period. Ideally, manufacturing operations should be maintained at normal capacity, with no idle time or overtime; nor should there be excessive inventories or inventories insufficient to fill sales orders.

Direct materials purchases budget

The production requirements as set forth in the production budget together with the materials required to manufacture the products provide the data for the direct materials purchases budget. The direct materials purchases necessary to meet production requirements is determined by subtracting the quantity of materials on hand at the beginning of the period from the sum of the units expected to be needed to meet production requirements and the number of units desired in the inventory at the end of the period. The quantities of direct materials required are multiplied by the expected unit purchase price to arrive at the total cost of direct materials purchases.

Dean Company
Direct Materials Purchases Budget
For Year Ending December 31, 1970

	DIRECT MATERIALS		
	A	B	C
Units required for production:			
Product X.........................	195,000	——	260,000
Product Y.........................	73,000	146,000	146,000
Desired inventory, December 31, 1970.....	40,000	20,000	60,000
Total..............................	308,000	166,000	466,000
Less estimated inventory, January 1, 1970.	51,500	22,000	56,000
Total units to be purchased.............	256,500	144,000	410,000
Unit price............................	$ .20	$ .55	$ .35
Total direct materials purchases...........	$51,300	$79,200	$143,500

Direct materials purchases budget

In the direct materials purchases budget illustrated on the preceding page, materials A and C are required for Product X and materials A, B, and C are required for Product Y.

The timing of the direct materials purchases requires close coordination between the purchasing and production departments so that inventory levels can be maintained within reasonable limits.

Direct labor cost budget

The production requirements as set forth in the production budget provide the starting point for the preparation of the direct labor cost budget. The direct labor hours necessary to meet production requirements multiplied by the estimated hourly rate yields the total direct labor cost. It was assumed for the direct labor cost budget illustrated below that manufacturing operations for Products X and Y are performed in two production departments.

Dean Company
Direct Labor Cost Budget
For Year Ending December 31, 1970

	DEPARTMENT 1	DEPARTMENT 2
Hours required for production:		
Product X........................	32,500	26,000
Product Y........................	18,250	29,200
Total........................	50,750	55,200
Hourly rate......................	$4	$5
Total direct labor cost..............	$203,000	$276,000

557

Direct labor cost budget

Factory overhead cost budget

The estimated factory overhead cost that will be necessary to meet production requirements is set forth in the factory overhead cost budget. For use as a part of the master budget, the factory overhead cost budget ordinarily presents the total estimated cost for each item of factory overhead. Supplemental schedules are often prepared to present the factory overhead cost for each individual department. Such schedules enable each department foreman to confine his attention to those costs for which he is responsible. They also aid the production manager in evaluating performance in each department. A factory overhead cost budget is illustrated at the top of the next page.

Cost of goods sold budget

The budget for the cost of goods sold is prepared by combining the relevant estimates of quantities and costs presented in the direct materials purchases, direct labor cost, and factory overhead cost budgets, and

Dean Company
Factory Overhead Cost Budget
For Year Ending December 31, 1970

Indirect factory wages..	$120,500
Supervisory salaries..	65,000
Power and light...	56,000
Depreciation of plant and equipment..................................	50,000
Indirect materials..	32,500
Maintenance..	24,000
Insurance and property taxes...	11,250
Total factory overhead cost..	$359,250

Factory overhead cost budget

Dean Company
Cost of Goods Sold Budget
For Year Ending December 31, 1970

Finished goods inventory, January 1, 1970.......			$ 186,400
Work in process inventory, January 1, 1970......		$ 11,100	
Direct materials:			
Direct materials inventory, January 1, 1970....	$ 43,700		
Direct materials purchases..................	274,000		
Cost of direct materials available for use.......	$317,700		
Less direct materials inventory, December 31, 1970.................................	40,000		
Cost of direct materials placed in production..	$277,700		
Direct labor...............................	479,000		
Factory overhead...........................	359,250		
Total manufacturing costs....................		1,115,950	
Total work in process during period............		$1,127,050	
Less work in process inventory, December 31, 1970		11,000	
Cost of goods manufactured..................			1,116,050
Cost of finished goods available for sale........			$1,302,450
Less finished goods inventory, December 31, 1970.			198,750
Cost of goods sold..........................			$1,103,700

Cost of goods sold budget

adding data on estimated inventories. A cost of goods sold budget is
illustrated above.

Operating expenses budget

The estimated selling and general expenses are set forth in the operating expenses budget, in a format similar to the factory overhead cost budget illustrated earlier. Where feasible, detailed schedules based on departmental responsibility should be prepared for all major items in the budget. The advertising expense schedule, for example, should include such details as advertising media to be used (newspaper, direct-mail, etc.), quantities (column inches, number of pieces, etc.), cost per unit, frequency of use, and sectional totals. It is only through careful attention to details that a realistic budget can be produced, and through assignment of responsibility to departmental supervisors that effective controls can be achieved.

Budgeted income statement

A budgeted income statement can ordinarily be prepared from the data presented in the budgets for sales, cost of goods sold, and operating expenses, with the addition of data on other income, other expense, and income tax. It brings together in condensed form the projection of all profit-making phases of operations. It need not differ in form and arrangement from an income statement based on actual data in the accounts and hence is not illustrated. If the budgeted net income, in relationship to sales or to stockholders' equity, is disappointingly low, an additional review of all causative factors should be undertaken in an attempt to improve the plans.

Capital expenditures budget

The capital expenditures budget summarizes future plans for acquisition of plant facilities and equipment. Substantial expenditures may be required to replace machinery and other plant assets as they wear out, become obsolete, or for other reasons fall below minimum standards of efficiency. In addition, an expansion of plant facilities may be planned to keep pace with increasing demand for a company's product.

It is evident that the magnitude of capital expenditures is likely to vary considerably from year to year. The customary practice, therefore, is to project the plans for a number of years into the future.

The expected amount of depreciation on new equipment to be acquired in the current year must be taken into consideration when preparing the budgets for factory overhead and operating expenses. The manner in which the proposed expenditures are to be financed will also affect the cash budget. A five-year capital expenditures budget is illustrated below.

Dean Company
Capital Expenditures Budget
For Five Years Ending December 31, 1974

ITEM	1970	1971	1972	1973	1974
Machinery — Department 1.......	$50,000			$ 70,000	$60,000
Machinery — Department 2.......	45,000	$65,000	$40,000	50,000	
Office equipment................		22,500			15,000
Total....................	$95,000	$87,500	$40,000	$120,000	$75,000

Capital expenditures budget

Cash budget

The cash budget presents the expected inflow and outflow of cash for a day, week, month, or longer period. Receipts are classified by source and disbursements by purpose. The expected cash balance at the end of the period is then compared with the amount established as the minimum balance and the difference is the anticipated excess or deficiency for the period.

The minimum cash balance represents a safety buffer for miscalculations in cash planning and for unforeseen contingencies. However, the amount designated as the minimum balance need not remain fixed; it should perhaps be larger during periods of "peak" business activity than during the "slow" season.

The interrelationship of the cash budget with other budgets may be observed from the illustration below. Data from the sales budget, the various budgets for manufacturing costs and operating expenses, and the capital expenditures budget affect the cash budget. Consideration must also be given to dividend policies, plans for equity or long-term debt financing, and other projected plans that will affect cash.

Dean Company
Cash Budget
For Three Months Ending March 31, 1970

	JANUARY	FEBRUARY	MARCH
Estimated cash receipts from:			
Cash sales....................................	$ 28,000	$ 30,000	$ 25,000
Collections of accounts receivable..............	116,500	119,500	91,500
Other sources (issuance of securities, interest, etc.).	——	——	1,500
Total cash receipts.......................	$144,500	$149,500	$118,000
Estimated cash disbursements for:			
Manufacturing costs.........................	$ 90,200	$ 92,700	$ 84,000
Operating expenses..........................	25,300	25,300	23,400
Capital expenditures.........................	——	27,000	18,500
Other purposes (notes, income tax, etc.).........	7,500	3,000	31,500
Total cash disbursements...................	$123,000	$148,000	$157,400
Cash increase or decrease*......................	$ 21,500	$ 1,500	$ 39,400*
Cash balance at beginning of month..............	78,000	99,500	101,000
Cash balance at end of month...................	$ 99,500	$101,000	$ 61,600
Minimum cash balance........................	75,000	75,000	75,000
Excess or deficiency*.........................	$ 24,500	$ 26,000	$ 13,400*

Cash budget

The importance of accurate cash budgeting can scarcely be overemphasized. An unanticipated lack of cash can result in loss of discounts, unfavorable borrowing terms on loans, and damage to the credit rating. On the other hand, an excess amount of idle cash is also indicative of poor management. When the budget indicates periods of excess cash, such funds should be used to reduce loans or they should be invested in readily marketable income-producing securities. Reference to the illustration on the preceding page indicates excess cash during January and February, and a deficiency during March.

Budgeted balance sheet

The budgeted balance sheet presents estimated details of financial condition at the end of a budget period, assuming that all budgeted operating and financing plans are fulfilled. It need not differ in form and arrangement from a balance sheet based on actual data in the accounts and hence is not illustrated. If the projection reveals weaknesses in financial planning, such as an abnormally large amount of current liabilities in relation to current assets, or excessive long-term debt in comparison to stockholders' equity, an additional examination should be made of all relevant factors.

Budget performance reports

A budget performance report comparing actual results with the budgeted figures should be prepared periodically for each budget. All significant variations should be investigated immediately to determine their cause and to seek means of preventing their recurrence. If corrective action cannot be taken because of changed conditions that have occurred since the budget was prepared, future budget figures should be revised accordingly. A budget performance report is illustrated below.

Dean Company
Budget Performance Report — Factory Overhead Cost, Department 1
For Month Ended June 30, 1970

	BUDGET	ACTUAL	OVER	UNDER
Indirect factory wages..............	$ 5,050	$ 5,065	$ 15	
Supervisory salaries.................	2,600	2,600		
Power and light....................	2,375	2,355		$20
Depreciation of plant and equipment...	2,000	2,000		
Indirect materials..................	1,250	1,375	125	
Maintenance.......................	1,000	990		10
Insurance and property taxes.........	525	525		
	$14,800	$14,910	$140	$30

Budget performance report

The budget column figures are determined from supplemental schedules accompanying the master budget. The actual column indicates the costs actually incurred during June. The last two columns indicate the amounts by which actual costs exceeded or were below budgeted figures. As indicated in the illustration, variations between the actual and budgeted amounts exist for several items; an investigation should be made to determine the cause of the variation for indirect materials and to find means of possible corrective action.

Flexible budgets

Implicit in the discussion of budget systems has been the assumption that the volume of sales and manufacturing activity achieved during a period approximated the goals established in the budgets. When substantial changes in expectations occur during a budget period, the budgets should be revised to give effect to such changes. Otherwise they will be of questionable value as incentives and instruments for controlling costs and expenses.

The effect of fluctuations in volume of activity can be "built-in" to the system by what are termed *flexible budgets*. Particularly useful in estimating and controlling factory overhead costs and operating expenses, a flexible budget is in reality a series of budgets for varying rates of activity. To illustrate, assume that because of extreme variations in demand and other uncontrollable factors the output of a particular manufacturing enterprise fluctuates widely from month to month. In such circumstances the total factory overhead costs incurred during periods of high activity are certain to be greater than during periods of low activity. It is equally certain, however, that fluctuations in total factory overhead costs will not be exactly proportionate to the volume of production. For example, if $100,000 of factory overhead costs are ordinarily incurred during a month in which production totals 10,000 units, the factory overhead for a month in which only 5,000 units are produced would unquestionably be more than $50,000.

Items of factory cost and operating expense that tend to remain constant in amount regardless of variations in volume of activity may be said to be *fixed*. Real estate taxes, property insurance, and depreciation expense on buildings are examples of fixed costs; the amounts incurred are substantially independent of the level of operations. Costs and expenses which tend to fluctuate in amount in accordance with variations in volume of activity are designated *variable*. Supplies and indirect materials used and salesmen's commissions are examples of variable costs and expenses. The degree of variability is not the same for all variable items; few, if any, vary in exact proportion to sales or production. The terms *semivariable* or *semifixed* are sometimes applied to items that have both fixed and variable characteristics to a significant degree. An example is electric power, for which there is often an initial flat fee, for example $500 for the first 10,000 kw-hrs consumed during a month and a lower rate, such as $.03 per kw-hr for additional usage.

A flexible budget for factory overhead cost is illustrated on the next page. A single manufacturing department and a single product are assumed, with budgeted costs stated at three different levels of production. In practice, the number of production levels and the interval between levels will vary with the range of production volume. For example, instead of budgeting for 8,000, 9,000, and 10,000 units of product, it might be necessary to provide for levels, at intervals of 500, from 6,000 to 12,000 units. Alternative factors may also be used in measuring volume of activity, such as hours of departmental operation or direct labor man hours.

W. Mann and Company
Monthly Factory Overhead Cost Budget

Units of product...................	8,000	9,000	10,000
Variable cost:			
Indirect factory wages..............	$ 32,000	$ 36,000	$ 40,000
Electric power.....................	24,000	27,000	30,000
Indirect materials..................	12,000	13,500	15,000
Total variable cost..............	$ 68,000	$ 76,500	$ 85,000
Fixed cost:			
Supervisory salaries.................	$ 40,000	$ 40,000	$ 40,000
Depreciation of plant and equipment..	25,000	25,000	25,000
Property taxes.....................	15,000	15,000	15,000
Insurance........................	12,000	12,000	12,000
Electric power.....................	10,000	10,000	10,000
Total fixed cost..................	$102,000	$102,000	$102,000
Total factory overhead cost............	$170,000	$178,500	$187,000

Flexible budget for factory overhead cost

Standard costs

The determination of the unit cost of products manufactured is fundamental to cost accounting. The process cost and job order cost systems discussed in the preceding chapters were designed to determine *actual* or *historical* unit costs. The aim of both systems is to provide timely data on actual manufacturing costs and to facilitate cost control and profit maximization.

The use of budgetary control procedures is often extended to the point of unit cost projections for each commodity produced. Cost systems employing detailed estimates of each element of manufacturing cost entering into the finished product are sometimes referred to as *standard cost systems*. The use of such estimates enables management to determine how much a product should cost (standard), how much it does cost (actual), and the cause of any differences (variances) between the two. Standard costs thus serve as a measuring device for determination of efficiency. If the standard cost of a product is $5 per unit and its current actual cost is $5.50 per unit, the factors responsible for the excess cost can be determined and remedial measures taken. Thus supervisors have a device for controlling costs, and employees become more cost-conscious.

Standard costs may be used in either the job order type of production or the process type of production. For most effective control, standard costs should be used for each department or cost center in the factory. It is possible, however, to use standard costs in some departments and actual costs in others.

The establishment of standards requires exhaustive research. Motion and time studies are made of each operation, and the work force is trained to use the most efficient methods. Direct materials and productive equipment are subjected to detailed study and tests in an effort to achieve maximum productivity at minimum cost. A wide variety of management skills are needed in setting standards. This requires the joint effort of accounting, engineering, personnel administration, and other managerial areas.

Variances from standards

Production management's goal is the attainment of properly determined standards. Differences between the standard cost of a department or product and the actual costs incurred are termed *variances*. If actual cost incurred is less than standard cost, the variance is favorable; if actual cost exceeds standard cost, the variance is unfavorable. When actual costs are compared with standard costs, only the "exceptions" or variances are reported to the individual responsible for cost control. This reporting by the "principle of exceptions" enables the one responsible for cost control to concentrate on the cause and on the correction of the variances.

The total variance for a particular period is ordinarily a composite of a number of variances, some of which may be favorable and some unfavorable. There may be variances from standards in direct materials costs, in direct labor costs, and in factory overhead costs. The remainder of the chapter is devoted to illustrations and analyses of these variances for a hypothetical manufacturing enterprise. In actual practice a wide variety of direct materials might be used, there could be a substantial number of processing departments, and two or more classes of commodities would probably be produced. For illustrative purposes, however, it is assumed that only one type of direct material is used, that there is a single processing department, and that Product X is the only commodity manufactured.

Direct materials cost variance

Two principal factors enter into the determination of standards for direct materials cost: (1) the quantity (usage) standard and (2) the price standard. If actual quantity of direct materials used in producing a commodity differs from the standard quantity, there is a *quantity variance;* if the actual unit price of the materials differs from the standard price, there is a *price variance*. To illustrate, assume that the standard direct materials cost of producing 10,000 units of Product X and the direct materials cost actually incurred during the entire month of June were as follows:

$$\text{Standard: 20,000 pounds at \$.50} \quad \$10,000$$
$$\text{Actual:} \quad \text{20,600 pounds at \$.52} \quad 10,712$$

It is readily apparent that the unfavorable variance of $712 resulted in part from an excess usage of 600 pounds of direct materials and in part from an excess cost of $.02 per pound. The analysis of the materials cost variance is as follows:

QUANTITY VARIANCE:
Actual quantity............20,600 pounds
Standard quantity..........20,000 pounds

    Variance — unfavorable...   600 pounds × standard price, $.50........$300

PRICE VARIANCE:
Actual price............... $.52 per pound
Standard price.............   .50 per pound

    Variance — unfavorable... $.02 per pound × actual quantity, 20,600.. 412

TOTAL DIRECT MATERIALS COST VARIANCE — unfavorable...................$712

Direct materials cost variance

The physical quantity and the dollar amount of the quantity variance should be reported to the factory superintendent and other personnel responsible for production. If excessive amounts of direct materials were used because of the malfunction of equipment or some other failure within the production department, those responsible should correct the situation. However, an unfavorable direct materials quantity variance is not necessarily the result of inefficiency within the production department. If the excess usage of 600 pounds in the example above had been caused by inferior materials, the purchasing department should be held responsible.

The unit price and the total amount of the materials price variance should be reported to the purchasing department, which may or may not be able to control this variance. If the materials could have been purchased from another supplier at the standard price, the variance was controllable. On the other hand, if the variance resulted from a market-wide price increase, the variance was not subject to control.

Direct labor cost variance

As in the case of direct materials, two principal factors enter into the determination of standards for direct labor cost: (1) the time (usage or efficiency) standard, and (2) the rate (price or wage) standard. If the actual direct labor hours spent producing a product differ from the standard hours, there is a *time variance;* if the wage rate paid differs from the standard rate, there is a *rate variance.* The standard cost and the actual cost of direct labor in the production of 10,000 units of Product X during June are assumed to be as shown at the top of the next page.

```
Standard:  8,000 hours at $2.00..........  $16,000
Actual:    7,900 hours at  2.10..........   16,590
```

The unfavorable direct labor variance of $590 is a composite of a favorable time variance and an unfavorable rate variance, as indicated below.

TIME VARIANCE:
   Standard time..............8,000 hours
   Actual time................7,900 hours
      Variance — favorable...... 100 hours × standard rate, $2.............$200
RATE VARIANCE:
   Actual rate.................$2.10 per hour
   Standard rate............... 2.00 per hour
      Variance — unfavorable...$ .10 per hour × actual time, 7,900 hours.... 790
TOTAL DIRECT LABOR COST VARIANCE — unfavorable.....................$590

Direct labor cost variance

The control of direct labor cost is often in the hands of production foremen. To assist them in the control of direct labor costs, daily or weekly reports analyzing the cause of any direct labor variance are often prepared. A comparison of standard direct labor hours and actual direct labor hours will provide the basis for an investigation into the efficiency of direct labor (time variance). A comparison of the rates paid for direct labor with the standard rates highlights the efficiency of the foremen or personnel department in selecting the proper grade of direct labor for production (rate variance).

Establishing standards for factory overhead cost

Some of the difficulties encountered in allocating factory overhead costs among products manufactured have been considered in earlier chapters. These difficulties stem from the great variety of costs that are included in factory overhead and their nature as indirect costs. For the same reasons, the procedures employed in determining standards and variances for factory overhead cost are more complex than those used for direct materials cost and direct labor cost.

A flexible budget is employed to establish the standard factory overhead rate and to assist in determining subsequent variations from standard. The standard rate is determined by dividing what the factory overhead costs should be by the standard amount of productive activity, generally expressed in direct labor hours, direct labor cost, or machine hours. A flexible budget indicating the standard factory overhead rate for June is presented at the top of the next page.

The standard factory overhead cost rate is determined on the basis of the projected factory overhead costs at 100% of normal productive capacity, where this level of capacity represents the general expectation

566

Nelson Manufacturing Company
Factory Overhead Cost Budget
For Month Ending June 30, 1970

Percent of normal productive capacity..	80%	90%	100%	110%
Direct labor hours....................	8,000	9,000	10,000	11.000
Budgeted factory overhead:				
Variable cost:				
Indirect factory wages............	$ 6,400	$ 7,200	$ 8,000	$ 8,800
Power and light.................	2,800	3,150	3,500	3,850
Indirect materials...............	1,600	1,800	2,000	2,200
Maintenance.....................	1,200	1,350	1,500	1,650
Total variable cost............	$12,000	$13,500	$15,000	$16,500
Fixed cost:	1,50	1.50	1,50	1.50
Supervisory salaries.............	$ 2,250	$ 2,250	$ 2,250	$ 2,250
Depreciation of plant and equipment	2,750	2,750	2,750	2,750
Insurance and property taxes......	1,000	1,000	1,000	1,000
Total fixed cost................	$ 6,000	$ 6,000	$ 6,000	$ 6,000
Total factory overhead cost...........	$18,000	$19,500	$21,000	$22,500

Factory overhead rate per direct labor hour ($21,000 ÷ 10,000)... $2.10

Factory overhead cost budget indicating standard factory overhead rate

of business activity under normal operating conditions. In the above illustration, the standard factory overhead rate is $2.10 per direct labor hour. This rate can be subdivided into $1.50 per hour for variable factory overhead ($15,000 ÷ 10,000 hours) and $.60 per hour for fixed factory overhead ($6,000 ÷ 10,000 hours).

567

Factory overhead cost variance

Variances from standard for factory overhead cost result (1) from operating at a level above or below 100% of normal capacity, which is called the *volume variance*; and (2) from incurring a total amount of factory overhead cost greater or less than the amount budgeted for the level of operations achieved, which is called the *controllable variance*. To illustrate, assume that the standard cost and the actual cost of factory overhead for the production of 10,000 units of Product X during June were as follows:

Standard: 8,000 hours at $2.10.............		$16,800
Actual: Variable factory overhead........	$12,300	
Fixed factory overhead..........	6,000	18,300

The unfavorable factory overhead cost variance of $1,500 is composed of a volume variance and a controllable variance as indicated in the tabulation presented at the top of the next page.

Ch. 22 • Budgetary control and standard cost systems

VOLUME VARIANCE:

Normal productive capacity of 100%....................	10,000	hours
Standard for product produced........................	8,000	hours
Productive capacity not used.........................	2,000	hours
Standard fixed factory overhead cost rate...............	× $.60	
Variance — unfavorable........................		$1,200

CONTROLLABLE VARIANCE:

Actual factory overhead cost incurred..................	$18,300	
Budgeted factory overhead for standard product produced..	18,000	
Variance — unfavorable.......................		300
TOTAL FACTORY OVERHEAD COST VARIANCE — unfavorable..............		$1,500

Factory overhead cost variance

Volume variance. The volume variance is a measure of the penalty of operating at less than 100% of normal productive capacity or the benefit from operating at a level above 100% of normal productive capacity. In determining the amount of the variance, the productive capacity not used (or the productive capacity used in excess of 100% of capacity) is multiplied by the standard fixed factory overhead cost rate. In the illustration, the 2,000 hours of idle productive capacity was multiplied by $.60, the standard fixed factory overhead cost rate. It should be noted that the variable portion of the factory overhead cost rate was ignored in determining the volume variance. Variable factory overhead costs vary with the level of production; thus, a curtailment of production should be accompanied by a comparable reduction of such costs. On the other hand, the fixed factory overhead costs are not affected by fluctuations in the volume of production. The fixed factory overhead costs therefore represent the costs of providing the capacity for production and the volume variance measures the amount of the fixed factory overhead cost attributed to the variance between capacity used and 100% of capacity. In the illustration the volume variance was unfavorable. This unfavorable volume variance of $1,200 can be viewed as the cost of the available but unused production capacity.

The idle time may be due to such factors as failure to maintain an even flow of work, machine breakdowns or repairs causing work stoppages, and failure to obtain enough sales orders to keep the factory operating at full capacity. Management should then ascertain the causes of the idle time and should take corrective action. A volume variance caused by failure of foremen to maintain an even flow of work, for example, can be remedied. Volume variances caused by lack of sales orders may be corrected through increased advertising or other sales effort, or it may be advisable to develop other means of utilizing the excess plant capacity.

Controllable variance. The controllable variance is the difference between the actual amount of factory overhead incurred and the amount

568

of factory overhead budgeted for the level of production achieved during the period. In the illustration, the standard direct labor hours for the product manufactured during June was 8,000, which represents 80% of normal productive capacity. According to the flexible budget on page 567, the factory overhead budgeted at this level of production is $18,000. The excess of the $18,300 of factory overhead costs actually incurred over the $18,000 budgeted yields the unfavorable controllable variance of $300.

The amount and the direction of the controllable variance indicate the degree of efficiency in keeping the factory overhead costs within the limits established by the budget. Most of the controllable variance is related to the cost of the variable factory overhead items because generally there is little or no variation in the costs incurred for the fixed factory overhead items. Therefore, responsibility for the control of this variance generally rests with department foremen.

Reporting factory overhead cost variance. The most effective means of presenting standard factory overhead cost variance data is through a factory overhead cost variance report. Such a report, illustrated below, can present both the controllable variance and the volume variance in a format that pinpoints the causes of the variance and facilitates placing the responsibility for control.

Nelson Manufacturing Company
Factory Overhead Cost Variance Report
For Month Ended June 30, 1970

			VARIANCES	
Normal production capacity for the month........................			10,000 hours	
Actual production for the month..................................			8,000 hours	
	BUDGET	ACTUAL	FAVORABLE	UNFAVORABLE
Variable cost:				
Indirect factory wages.............	$ 6,400	$ 6,510		$ 110
Power and light..................	2,800	2,790	$10	
Indirect materials................	1,600	1,800		200
Maintenance.....................	1,200	1,200		
Total variable cost.............	$12,000	$12,300		
Fixed cost:				
Supervisory salaries..............	$ 2,250	$ 2,250		
Depreciation of plant and equipment	2,750	2,750		
Insurance and property taxes.......	1,000	1,000		
Total fixed cost................	$ 6,000	$ 6,000		
Total factory overhead cost.........	$18,000	$18,300		
Total controllable variances.........			$10	$ 310
Net controllable variance — unfavorable......................				$ 300
Volume variance — unfavorable:				
Idle hours at the standard rate for fixed factory overhead—2,000 × $.60				1,200
Total factory overhead cost variance — unfavorable.................				$1,500

Factory overhead cost variance report

The variance in many of the individual cost items in factory overhead can be subdivided into quantity and price variances, as were the variances in direct materials and direct labor. For example, the indirect factory wages variance may include both time and rate variances and the indirect materials variance may be composed of both a quantity variance and a price variance.

The foregoing brief introduction to analysis of factory overhead cost variance suggests the many ramifications and complexities that may be encountered in actual practice. The rapid increase of automation in factory operations has been accompanied by increased attention to factory overhead costs. The use of predetermined standards, and the analysis of variances from such standards, provides management with the best possible means of establishing responsibility and controlling factory overhead costs.

Standards in the accounts

Although standard costs can be employed solely as a statistical device apart from the ledger, it is generally considered preferable to incorporate them in the accounts. When this plan is adopted, the work in process account is debited for the actual costs of direct materials, direct labor, and factory overhead entering into production. The same account is credited for the standard cost of the product completed and transferred to the finished goods account. The balance remaining in the work in process account is then a composite of the ending inventory of work in process and the variances of actual cost from standard cost. In the illustrative accounts presented below there is assumed to be no ending inventory of work in process, hence the balance in the account is the sum of the variances (unfavorable) between standard and actual costs.

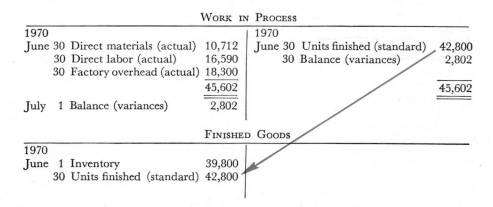

WORK IN PROCESS

1970			1970		
June 30 Direct materials (actual)	10,712		June 30 Units finished (standard)	42,800
30 Direct labor (actual)	16,590		30 Balance (variances)	2,802
30 Factory overhead (actual)	18,300			
	45,602			45,602
July 1 Balance (variances)	2,802			

FINISHED GOODS

1970		
June 1 Inventory	39,800
30 Units finished (standard)	42,800

Variances from standard costs are ordinarily not reported to stockholders and others outside the management group. However, it is customary to disclose the variances on income statements prepared for management. An interim monthly income statement prepared for internal use is illustrated below.

Nelson Manufacturing Company
Income Statement
For Month Ended June 30, 1970

	FAVORABLE	UNFAVORABLE	
Sales..			$77,900
Cost of goods sold—at standard..............			40,700
Gross profit on sales—at standard............			$37,200
Less variances from standard cost:			
Direct materials quantity................		$ 300	
Direct materials price...................		412	
Direct labor time.......................	$200		
Direct labor rate.......................		790	
Factory overhead volume................		1,200	
Factory overhead controllable...........		300	2,802
Gross profit on sales.....................	———		$34,398
Operating expenses:			
Selling expenses........................		$14,500	
General expenses.......................		9,125	23,625
Income before income tax................			$10,773

At the end of the fiscal year, the variances from standard are usually transferred to the cost of goods sold account. However, if the variances are significant or if many of the products manufactured are still on hand, the variances should be allocated to the work in process, finished goods, and cost of goods sold accounts. The result of such an allocation is to convert these account balances from standard cost to actual cost.

QUESTIONS

1. Name the two basic functions of management.

2. What is a budget?

3. How does a budget aid management in the discharge of its basic functions?

4. What is a budget performance report?

5. Why should all levels of management participate in the preparation and submission of budget estimates?

6. What is meant by *continuous* budgeting?

7. Why should the production requirements as set forth in the production budget be carefully coordinated with the sales budget?

8. What is a capital expenditures budget?

9. Discuss the purpose of the cash budget.

10. What is a flexible budget?

11. Which of the following costs incurred by a manufacturing enterprise tend to be fixed and which tend to be variable? (a) insurance on factory building; (b) direct labor; (c) property taxes on factory building; (d) electric power (purchased) to operate manufacturing machinery; (e) cost of steel tubing entering into finished product; (f) salary of factory superintendent; (g) depreciation of factory building.

12. The Eastern Corporation uses flexible budgets. For each of the following variable operating expenses, indicate whether there has been a saving or an excess of expenditures, assuming actual sales were $500,000.

Expense Item	Actual Amount	Budget Allowance Based on Sales
Store supplies expense	$10,200	2%
Uncollectible accounts expense	4,650	1%

13. What are the basic objectives in the use of standard costs?

14. As the term is used in reference to standard costs, what is a *variance*?

15. (a) What are the two types of variances between actual cost and standard cost for direct materials? (b) Discuss some possible causes of these variances.

16. (a) What are the two types of variances between actual cost and standard cost for direct labor? (b) Who generally has control over the direct labor cost?

17. Describe the two variances between actual costs and standard costs for factory overhead.

18. Where do the variances for direct materials, direct labor, and factory overhead appear on interim income statements prepared for management?

EXERCISES

22-1. The Barker Company manufactures two models of adding machines, A and B. Based on the following production and sales data for the month of June of the current year, prepare (a) a sales budget and (b) a production budget.

	A	B
Estimated inventory (units), June 1	4,500	2,250
Desired inventory (units), June 30 .	4,000	2,500
Expected sales volume (units)	7,500	5,000
Unit sales price	$75	$120

22-2. Foster Company uses flexible budgets. Prepare a flexible operating expenses budget for July of the current year for sales volumes of $200,000, $225,000, and $250,000, based upon the following data:

Salesmen's commissions.	10% of sales
Advertising expense	$10,000 for $200,000 of sales
	$10,700 for $225,000 of sales
	$11,200 for $250,000 of sales
Miscellaneous selling expense .	$ 1,000 + 1% of sales
Office salaries	$ 7,000
Office supplies expense.	½ of 1% of sales
Miscellaneous general expense.	$750 + ½ of 1% of sales

22-3. The operating expenses incurred during July of the current year by Foster Company were as follows:

Salesmen's commissions.......	$22,500
Advertising expense..........	10,450
Miscellaneous selling expense..	3,150
Office salaries..............	7,000
Office supplies expense.......	1,500
Miscellaneous general expense.	2,000

Assuming that the total sales for July were $225,000, prepare a budget performance report for operating expenses on the basis of the data presented above and in Exercise 22-2.

22-4. The following data relating to direct materials cost are taken from the records of Jacobs Manufacturing Company for the month of August of the current year:

Quantity of direct materials used................	20,000 lbs.
Unit cost of direct materials.....................	$2 per lb.
Units of finished product manufactured............	9,800 units
Standard direct materials per unit of finished product.	2 lbs.
Direct materials quantity variance — unfavorable....	$1,000
Direct materials price variance — favorable........	$10,000

Determine the standard direct materials cost per unit of finished product, assuming that there was no inventory of work in process at either the beginning or the end of the month. Present your computations.

22-5. Standard costs and actual costs for direct materials, direct labor, and factory overhead incurred for the manufacture of 2,000 units of product were as follows:

	Standard Costs	Actual Costs
Direct materials....	10,000 units at $1.50	9,900 units at $1.55
Direct labor.......	5,000 hours at $2.50	5,150 hours at $2.40
Factory overhead...	Rates per direct labor hour, based on normal capacity of 6,000 labor hours:	
	Variable cost, $1.00	$5,400 variable cost
	Fixed cost, $.50	$3,000 fixed cost

Determine (a) the quantity variance, price variance, and total direct materials cost variance; (b) the time variance, rate variance, and total direct labor cost variance; and (c) the volume variance, controllable variance, and total factory overhead cost variance.

22-6. The Elder Manufacturing Company prepared the factory overhead cost budget for Department 1 for May of the current year shown at the top of the next page. The company expected to operate the department at normal capacity of 20,000 direct labor hours.

During May the department was operated for 19,000 direct labor hours, and the factory overhead costs incurred were: indirect factory wages, $5,280; power and light, $1,870; indirect materials, $1,450; supervisory salaries, $4,000; depreciation of plant and equipment, $1,800; and insurance and property taxes, $1,200.

573

Variable cost:
Indirect factory wages.............	$5,400	
Power and light....................	2,000	
Indirect materials.................	1,500	
Total variable cost..............		$ 8,900
Fixed cost:		
Supervisory salaries................	$4,000	
Depreciation of plant and equipment.	1,800	
Insurance and property taxes........	1,200	
Total fixed cost..................		7,000
Total factory overhead cost............		$15,900

Prepare a standard factory overhead variance report for May. To be useful for cost control, the budgeted amounts should be based on 19,000 direct labor hours.

22-7. Prepare an income statement for presentation to management from the following data taken from the records of Higgins Manufacturing Company for the month of January of the current year:

Cost of goods sold (at standard).....................	$115,000
Direct materials quantity variance — favorable........	1,200
Direct materials price variance — unfavorable........	950
Direct labor time variance — favorable.............	750
Direct labor rate variance — unfavorable............	500
Factory overhead volume variance — unfavorable.....	2,000
Factory overhead controllable variance — unfavorable.	500
Selling expenses...................................	32,500
General expenses...................................	27,800
Sales..	210,750

574

PROBLEMS

The following additional problems for this chapter are located in Appendix C: 22-1B, 22-3B, 22-4B.

22-1A. Castle Company prepared the following factory overhead cost budget for the Finishing Department for April of the current year:

Castle Company
Factory Overhead Cost Budget — Finishing Department
For Month Ending April 30, 19—

Direct labor hours:		
Normal productive capacity...........		10,000
Hours budgeted......................		9,000
Variable cost:		
Indirect factory wages...............	$4,500	
Indirect materials....................	3,600	
Power and light.....................	1,800	
Total variable cost.................		$ 9,900

Fixed cost:

Supervisory salaries	$7,200	
Indirect factory wages	4,150	
Depreciation of plant and equipment	3,125	
Insurance	1,125	
Power and light	1,100	
Property taxes	1,000	
Total fixed cost		17,700
Total factory overhead cost		$27,600

Instructions:

(1) Prepare a flexible budget for the month of May indicating capacities of 8,000, 9,000, 10,000, and 11,000 direct labor hours and the determination of a standard factory overhead rate per direct labor hour.

(2) Prepare a standard factory overhead cost variance report for May. The department was operated for 8,000 direct labor hours and the following factory overhead costs were incurred:

Indirect factory wages	$ 8,400
Supervisory salaries	7,200
Indirect materials	3,375
Depreciation of plant and equipment	3,125
Power and light	2,550
Insurance	1,125
Property taxes	1,000
Total factory overhead costs incurred	$26,775

22-2A. The budget director of Cooper Company requests estimates of sales, production and other operating data from the various administrative units every month. Selected information submitted for the month of May of the current year concerning sales and production are summarized as follows:

(a) Estimated sales for May:
   Product A: 5,000 units at $50 per unit
   Product B: 2,000 units at $75 per unit

(b) Estimated inventories at May 1:
   Direct materials:
      Material M: 7,500 lbs.
      Material N: 2,100 lbs.
      Material O: 2,250 lbs.
      Material P: 950 lbs.
   Finished products:
      Product A: 2,750 units
      Product B: 850 units

(c) Desired inventories at May 31:
   Direct materials:
      Material M: 8,000 lbs.
      Material N: 2,000 lbs.
      Material O: 2,500 lbs.
      Material P: 1,000 lbs.
   Finished products:
      Product A: 3,000 units
      Product B: 1,000 units

(d) Direct materials used in production:
    In manufacture of Product A:
      Material M: 2 lbs. per unit of product
      Material N: .5 lb. per unit of product
      Material O: 1 lb. per unit of product
    In manufacture of Product B:
      Material M: 2 lbs. per unit of product
      Material N: .5 lb. per unit of product
      Material P: 1 lb. per unit of product
(e) Anticipated purchase price for direct materials:
    Material M: $1.00 per lb.
    Material N: $5.00 per lb.
    Material O: $2.50 per lb.
    Material P: $6.00 per lb.
(f) Direct labor requirements:
    Product A:
      Department 1: 1 hour at $3 per hour
      Department 2: 2 hours at $5 per hour
    Product B:
      Department 1: 1 hour at $3 per hour
      Department 3: 3 hours at $6 per hour

Instructions:

(1) Prepare a sales budget for May.
(2) Prepare a production budget for May.
(3) Prepare a direct materials purchases budget for May.
(4) Prepare a direct labor cost budget for May.

22-3A. Mercer Manufacturing, Inc. maintains perpetual inventory accounts for materials, work in process, and finished goods and uses a standard cost system based upon the following data:

	Standard Cost Per Unit	
	Quantity	Price
Direct materials........	4 lbs. @ $1 per lb.	$ 4.00
Direct labor............	2 hours @ $4 per hr.	8.00
Factory overhead.......	$1.25 per direct labor hour	2.50
Total.....................		$14.50

There was no inventory of work in process at the beginning or end of July, the first month of the current year. The transactions relating to production completed during July are summarized as follows:

(a) Materials purchased on account, $20,600.
(b) Direct materials used, $17,480. This represented 18,400 pounds at $.95 per pound.
(c) Direct labor paid $38,180. This represented 9,200 hours at $4.15 per hour. There were no accruals at either the beginning or the end of the period.
(d) Factory overhead incurred during the month was composed of indirect labor, $5,100; depreciation on plant and equipment, $4,000; insurance, $600; and miscellaneous factory costs, $1,200. The indirect labor and miscellaneous factory costs were paid during the period, and the insurance represents an expiration of prepaid insurance. Of the total factory overhead of $10,900, fixed costs amounted to $6,000 and variable costs were $4,900.
(e) Goods finished during the period, 4,500 units.

Instructions:

(1) Prepare entries in general journal form to record the transactions, assuming that the work in process account is debited for actual production costs and credited with standard costs for goods finished.

(2) Prepare a T account for Work in Process and post to the account, using the identifying letters as dates. Balance and rule the account.

(3) Prepare schedules of variances for direct materials cost, direct labor cost, and factory overhead cost. Normal productive capacity for the plant is 10,000 direct labor hours.

(4) Total the amounts of the standard cost variances and compare this total with the balance of the work in process account.

22-4A. The treasurer of Long and Company instructs you to prepare a monthly cash budget for the next three months. He presents you with the following budget information:

	April	May	June
Sales.....................	$720,000	$900,000	$800,000
Manufacturing costs......	470,000	560,000	515,000
Operating expenses......	186,000	201,000	192,000
Capital expenditures.....	100,000	—	—

The company expects to sell about 25% of its merchandise for cash. Of sales on account, 80% are expected to be collected in full in the month following the sale and the remainder the next following month. Depreciation, insurance, and property taxes represent $20,000 of the estimated monthly manufacturing costs and $6,000 of the probable monthly operating expenses. Insurance and property taxes are paid in January and July respectively. Of the remainder of the manufacturing costs and operating expenses, two thirds are expected to be paid in the month in which they are incurred and the balance in the following month. Current assets as of April 1 are composed of cash of $179,800, marketable securities of $100,000, and accounts receivable of $630,000 ($520,000 from March sales and $110,000 from February sales). Current liabilities as of April 1 are composed of a non-interest-bearing note payable of $125,000, due May 15, accounts payable of $150,000 incurred in March for manufacturing costs, and accrued liabilities of $58,000 incurred in March for operating expenses.

It is expected that $2,200 in dividends will be received in April. An estimated income tax payment of $50,000 will be made in April. Long and Company's regular quarterly dividend of $7,500 is expected to be declared in April and paid in May. Management desires to maintain a minimum cash balance of $100,000.

Instructions:

(1) Prepare a monthly cash budget for April, May, and June.

(2) On the basis of the cash budget prepared in (1), what recommendation should be made to the treasurer?

22-5A. As a preliminary to requesting budget estimates of sales, costs, and expenses for the fiscal year beginning January 1, 1970, the following tentative trial balance as of December 31 of the preceding year is prepared by the accounting department of Ellis Manufacturing Company:

Cash..	$ 27,500	
Accounts Receivable.............................	81,500	
Finished Goods..................................	67,200	
Work in Process.................................	31,400	
Materials..	15,000	
Prepaid Expenses................................	3,400	
Plant and Equipment............................	550,000	
Accumulated Depreciation — Plant and Equipment.		$190,000
Accounts Payable................................		51,750
Income Tax Payable.............................		25,500
Common Stock, $10 par..........................		300,000
Retained Earnings...............................		208,750
	$776,000	$776,000

Factory output and sales for 1970 are expected to total 100,000 units of product, which are to be sold at $10 per unit. The quantities and costs of the inventories (lifo method) at December 31, 1970 are expected to remain unchanged from the balances at the beginning of the year.

Budget estimates of manufacturing costs and operating expenses for the year are summarized as follows:

	Estimated Costs and Expenses	
	Fixed (Total for Year)	Variable (Per Unit Sold)
Cost of goods manufactured and sold:		
Direct materials.....................	—	$1.50
Direct labor.......................	—	2.50
Factory overhead:		
Depreciation of plant and equipment	$40,000	—
Other factory overhead............	95,000	.75
Selling expenses:		
Sales commissions...................	15,000	.50
Advertising........................	22,000	—
Miscellaneous selling expense........	7,500	.20
General expenses:		
Office and officers' salaries..........	75,000	.10
Supplies...........................	1,100	.05
Miscellaneous general expense........	8,500	.10

Balances of accounts receivable, prepaid expenses, and accounts payable at the end of the year are expected to differ from the beginning balances by only inconsequential amounts. The liability for income tax listed in the tentative trial balance is due on March 15, 1970.

For purposes of the problem, assume federal income tax liability of $75,000 on taxable income of 1970 of which $42,000 will be payable during the year in four installments, and the remainder on March 15, 1971. Regular quarterly cash dividends of 50¢ a share are expected to be declared and paid in February, May, August, and November. It is anticipated that plant and equipment will be purchased for $50,000 cash in December.

Instructions:
(1) Prepare a budgeted income statement for 1970.
(2) Prepare a budgeted balance sheet as of December 31, 1970.

23

Income taxes
and their effect on
business decisions

Nature of income taxes

Income taxes are assessed against *taxable income*, which, in general, is gross income less various exclusions and deductions specified by the statutes and administrative regulations. The principal economic entities against which a tax on annual income is levied are individuals, corporations, estates, and trusts. The federal government and approximately three fourths of the states levy an income tax. Some states permit enactment of an income tax by municipalities or other political subdivisions.

The data required for the determination of income tax liability is supplied by the taxpayer on official forms and supporting schedules that are referred to collectively as a *tax return*. Failure to receive the forms from the governmental agency or failure to maintain adequate records does not relieve taxpayers of their legal obligation to file an annual tax return and pay the amount due. Willful failure to comply with the income tax laws may result in the imposition of severe penalties, both civil and criminal.

A common characteristic of income taxes, particularly those assessed against individuals, is the provision for a graduated series of tax rates, successively higher rates being applied to successive segments of income. It is because of this progression of rates that an income tax is sometimes termed a *progressive* tax.

Relationship to accounting

Because of the intricacies of income determination, it is inevitable that accounting and income taxes should be closely interrelated. An understanding of any but the simplest aspects of income taxes is almost impossible without some knowledge of accounting concepts.

One of the major concerns of tax accountants is tax minimization. Managers of business enterprises make few decisions about proposals for new ventures or about significant changes in business practices without first giving careful consideration to the tax consequences.

There are many situations in which an enterprise or an individual taxpayer may choose from among two or more optional accounting methods. Examples of such situations described in earlier chapters are cost-flow assumptions for inventories (first-in, first-out; last-in, first-out; etc.), depreciation methods (straight-line, declining-balance, etc.), and revenue recognition practices (point of sale, installment method, etc.). The particular method elected may have a substantial effect on the amount of income tax, not only in the year in which the election is made but also in subsequent years.

Prerequisite to a meaningful discussion of the impact of income taxes on business decisions is an acquaintance with the basic structure of the federal income tax. The explanations and illustrations of the federal system presented in this chapter are of necessity brief and relatively free of the many complexities encountered in actual practice.

Federal income tax system

The present system of federal income tax originated with the Revenue Act of 1913, which was enacted soon after the ratification of the Sixteenth Amendment to the Constitution. All current income tax statutes, as well as other federal tax laws, are now codified in the Internal Revenue Code (IRC).

The executive branch of the government charged with responsibility in tax matters is the Treasury Department. The branch of the Department concerned specifically with enforcement and collection of the income tax is the Internal Revenue Service (IRS), headed by the Commissioner of Internal Revenue. Interpretations of the law and directives formulated in accordance with express provisions of the IRC are issued in various forms. The most important and comprehensive are the "Regulations" which occupy over two thousand printed pages.

Taxpayers alleged by the IRS to be deficient in reporting or paying their tax may, if they disagree with the determination, present their case in informal conferences at district and regional levels. Unresolved disputes may be taken to the federal courts for adjudication. The taxpayer may seek relief in the Tax Court or he may pay the disputed amount and sue to recover it, either in the appropriate District Court or the Court of Claims. Either party may appeal an adverse decision to the Court of Appeals of the appropriate circuit, and thence to the Supreme Court.

The income tax is not imposed upon business units as such, but upon taxable entities. Business enterprises organized as sole proprietorships are not taxable entities. The net income or the net loss of a sole proprietorship is reported by the owner as an individual, together with his income from other sources, his allowable deductions, and his personal exemptions. Partnerships are not taxable entities but are required to report in an informational return the details of their revenues, expenses, and allocations to partners. Each partner then reports in his individual return the amount of net income and other special items allocated to him on the partnership return.

Corporations engaged in business for profit are generally treated as distinct taxable entities. However, it is possible for two or more corporations with common ownership to join in filing a consolidated return. Subchapter S of the IRC also permits a closely held corporation that conforms to specified requirements to elect to be treated as a partnership. The effect of the election is to tax the individual stockholders on their respective distributive shares of the corporation's net income. The corporation itself is not taxed and, of course, distributions of once-taxed earnings in the form of dividends are tax-free to the shareholders.

Accounting methods

Although neither the IRC nor the Regulations provide uniform systems of accounting for use by all taxpayers, detailed procedures are prescribed in specified situations. In addition the IRS has the authority to prescribe accounting methods where those employed by a taxpayer fail to yield a fair determination of taxable income. In general, taxpayers have the option of using either the cash basis or the accrual basis.

Cash basis. Because of its greater simplicity, the cash method of determining taxable income is usually adopted by individuals whose sources of income are limited to salary, dividends, and interest. Employers are required to use the cash basis in determining the salary amounts which they report to their employees and also to the IRS in connection with the withholding of income tax. Payments of interest and dividends by business enterprises are also required to be reported in accordance with the cash method. Copies of such notifications, supplemented by check stubs, sales tickets, and other memorandums, frequently provide all of the information needed by an individual to determine his tax base.

Professional enterprises and businesses engaged in selling services also ordinarily employ the cash basis of determining net income. An advantage is that the amounts charged to clients or customers are not considered to be earned until payment is received. There is also no need to determine uncollectible accounts expense by either the allowance or the direct write-off method. Receivables that become uncollectible represent a reduction in anticipated revenue rather than an expense. Liabilities incurred for rent, electricity, supplies, and other items of expense also need not be given formal recognition in the accounts, the expenses being recorded only at the time of cash payment. It is not permissible, of course, to treat the entire cost of long-lived assets as wholly expense of the period in which the cash payment is made. Deductions for depreciation on equipment and buildings used for business purposes may be claimed in the same manner as under the accrual basis, regardless of when payment is made. Similarly, when advance payments for insurance premiums or rentals on business property exceed a period of one year, the total cost must be prorated over the life of the contract.

Recognition of revenue in accordance with the cash method is not always contingent upon the actual receipt of cash. When gross income becomes available to the taxpayer without restrictions, it is said to be *constructively* received. For example, a check received late in December of a taxable year as payment for services performed in December represents income of such taxable year even though the check is not cashed until the following January. Other examples of constructive receipt are the maturing of bond interest coupons and the crediting of interest to a savings account.

Accrual basis. For businesses in which production or trading in commodities is a material factor, purchases and sales must be accounted for on the accrual basis. Thus, revenues from sales must be reported as such in the year in which the goods are sold, regardless of when the cash is received. Similarly, the cost of commodities purchased must be reported in the year in which the liabilities are incurred, regardless of when payment is made. The usual adjustments must also be made for beginning and ending inventories in order to determine the cost of goods sold and the gross profit on sales. However, manufacturing and mercantile enterprises are not required to extend the accrual basis to all other phases of their operations. A considerable degree of hybridization of accounting methods is allowed, provided they are used consistently and the results are reasonable.

Methods of accounting in general, as well as many of the regulations affecting the determination of net business or professional income, are not affected by the legal nature or the organizational structure of the taxpayer. On the other hand, the tax base and the rate structure for individuals differ markedly from those applicable to corporations.

Tax base of individuals

The tax base to which tax rates for individuals are applied is identified by the IRC as *taxable income*. The starting point in the computation is the determination of the amount of *gross income* to be reported. Amounts subtracted from gross income are divided into two principal categories. The first category is composed of expenses of operating a business or profession and certain other expenses related to the earning of revenues. Subtraction of these *deductions from gross income* yields an intermediate balance identified as *adjusted gross income*. The second category is subdivided into (1) so-called *nonbusiness* expenses and specified expenses that are primarily of a personal nature, and (2) arbitrary allowances known as *exemptions*. The procedures are summarized in the following computations:

Gross income...............................		$27,600
Deductions from gross income:		
Expenses (related to business or specified revenue)..		13,200
Adjusted gross income........................		$14,400
Deductions from adjusted gross income:		
Expenses (nonbusiness and personal)[1]...........	$1,140	
Exemptions..............................	1,200	2,340
Taxable income............................		$12,060

Gross income and filing requirements

Gross income is defined in Section 61(a) of the Internal Revenue Code as follows:

> Except as otherwise provided in this subtitle, gross income means all income from whatever source derived, including (but not limited to) the following items: (1) compensation for services, including fees, commissions, and similar items; (2) gross income derived from business; (3) gains derived from dealings in property; (4) interest; (5) rents; (6) royalties; (7) dividends; (8) alimony and separate maintenance payments; (9) annuities; (10) income from life insurance and endowment contracts; (11) pensions; (12) income from discharge of indebtedness; (13) distributive share of partnership gross income; (14) income in respect of a decedent; and (15) income from an interest in an estate or trust.

---

[1]Instead of itemizing these deductions, an alternative *standard deduction* may be elected. The alternative is described later in the chapter.

Statutory items of gross income are sometimes referred to as *taxable gross income* or *includable gross income*. Exceptions to the general rule provided elsewhere in the IRC are frequently termed *nontaxable gross income* or *excludable gross income*. Examples of common items of gross income inclusions and exclusions are presented below. They are illustrative only and should not be considered to be exhaustive lists.

Includable in Gross Income of Individuals	Excludable from Gross Income of Individuals
Wages and other remuneration from employer.	Federal and state old-age pensions.
Tips and gratuities for services rendered.	State unemployment benefits.
Interest on United States obligations.	Value of property received as a gift.
Interest on commercial and industrial obligations.	Value of property received by bequest, devise, or inheritance.
Dividends on stock in excess of $100.	Dividends on stock of $100 or less.[2]
Portion of pensions, annuities, and endowments representing income.	Life insurance proceeds received because of death of insured.
Rents and royalties.	Interest on obligations of a state or political subdivision.
Gross profit from a business.	Undergraduate scholarships for which no services are required.
Taxable gains from the sale of real estate, securities, and other property.	Portion of pensions, annuities, and endowments representing return of capital invested.
Distributive share of partnership income.	Compensation for injuries or for damages related to personal or family rights.
Income from an estate or trust.	Workmen's compensation insurance for sickness or injury.
Prizes won in contests.	Limited sick pay benefits.
Gains from wagering.	

584

Wholly excludable items of gross income, such as interest on state bonds, are not reported on the tax return. Partly excludable items, such as dividends on corporation stocks and annuity benefits, are reported in their entirety and the excludable portion is then deducted.

Partnerships and corporations organized for profit are required to file annual income tax returns regardless of the amount of their income. Individuals under 65 years of age as of the last day of the taxable year must file a return if their gross income for the year is $600 or more. Those who are 65 or older are required to file if their gross income is $1,200 or more.

Deductions from gross income

Business expenses and other expenses connected with earning certain types of revenue are deducted from gross income to yield adjusted gross income. The categories of such expenses that are of general applicability are described in the following paragraphs.

---

[2] In a joint return of husband and wife the exclusion is $200. However, neither may use any part of the other's exclusion.

Business expenses other than as an employee. Ordinary and necessary expenses incurred by the taxpayer in the operation of his own unincorporated business or profession are deductible from gross income. The tax forms provide spaces for reporting sales, cost of goods sold, gross profit, salaries, taxes, depreciation, and other business expenses, and finally net income, which is the adjusted gross income derived from the business.

Business expenses of an employee. The types of expenses that an employee may deduct from salary and similar remuneration are circumscribed by the statutes and regulations. The broad term "ordinary and necessary expense" used in the preceding paragraph does not apply to employees. The types of employment-related expenses that an employee may deduct from his salary or wages in determining adjusted gross income are briefly described below.

Transportation expenses, which include the costs of public transportation and the cost of operating an employee-owned automobile. The cost of commuting from home to the place of employment is not deductible.

Travel expenses, which in addition to transportation expenses include the cost of meals and lodging if incurred when away from home overnight or when rest and recuperation are required during the day.

Outside salesmen's expenses, which include expenses incurred in soliciting business away from the employer's establishment, such as telephone, secretarial help, meals for customers, and entertainment.

585

Moving expenses, which include costs incurred by an employee in changing his place of residence in connection with beginning work in a new location. Minimum requirements are specified for the distance of the move and the number of weeks employed at the new location.

Reimbursed expenses, which include all employment-connected expenses incurred by the employee for which he receives reimbursement from the employer. (If the amount of the reimbursement exceeds the expenses incurred, the excess must be included in gross income.)

Expenses attributable to rents and royalties. Expenses that are directly connected with earning rent or royalty income are allowable as deductions from gross income in determining adjusted gross income. Expenses commonly incurred in connection with rental properties include depreciation, taxes, repairs, wages of custodian, and interest on indebtedness incurred to purchase the income-producing property.

Losses from sale or exchange of property. Losses from the sale or the exchange of property are deductible from gross income provided the property was acquired or held for the production of income. Thus, losses from the sale of rental property or of investments in stocks and bonds are deductible; losses from the sale of the taxpayer's residence or of his family automobile are not deductible.

Adjusted gross income

Each category of expenses described in the preceding section is deducted from the amount of related gross income to yield adjusted gross income. If the adjusted gross income from a particular source is a negative amount, such as a net loss from business operations or from property rentals, it is deducted from the positive amounts in the other categories. The system of assembling data for each type of gross income and its related deductions is illustrated by the following summary for a hypothetical taxpayer:

SUMMARY OF GROSS INCOME AND RELATED DEDUCTIONS		ADJUSTED GROSS INCOME
Salary from employment	$12,600	
Deductions	700	$11,900
Rental income	$ 1,500	
Deductions	1,700	(200)
Dividends from corporation stocks	$ 820	
Exclusion	100	720
Interest on savings deposits		300
Total adjusted gross income		$12,720

Deductions from adjusted gross income

Certain specified expenditures and arbitrary allowances are deducted from adjusted gross income to yield taxable income, the base against which the tax rates are applied. These allowable deductions may be classified as follows:

1. Specified expenditures and losses.
   A. Nonbusiness expenses.
   B. Charitable contributions, and certain specified expenses and losses of a personal nature that are wholly unrelated to income-producing activities.

2. Exemptions.

The deductions from adjusted gross income that are of general applicability are described in the paragraphs that follow.

Nonbusiness expenses. This term is applied to expenses related to gainful pursuits that are not deductible from gross income in determining adjusted gross income. Specifically, nonbusiness expenses are expenses attributable (1) to the production or collection of income, (2) to the maintenance or management of income-producing property, or (3) to the determination, collection, or refund of any tax, except for such expenses that qualify as deductions from gross income. For example, labor union dues are deductible from *adjusted gross income* as a nonbusiness expense, but travel expenses of an employee are deductible from *gross income*. Both expenses are attributable to the "production of income," but only the latter qualifies as a deduction from gross income. Other examples of nonbusiness expenses are fees paid for the preparation of a personal income tax return, the cost of investment advisory services, and the cost of uniforms not suitable for street wear.

Charitable contributions. Contributions made by an individual to domestic organizations created exclusively for religious, charitable, scientific, literary, or educational purposes, or for the prevention of cruelty to children or animals, are deductible provided the organization is nonprofit and does not devote a substantial part of its activities to influencing legislation. Contributions to domestic governmental units and to organizations of war veterans are also deductible.

Contributions in the form of property are deductible to the extent of the fair market value of the property at the date of the donation. The difference between the fair market value and the donor's cost basis is not recognized as a gain or loss. For example, if a taxpayer contributes to a qualified organization listed securities worth $5,000 that he had acquired earlier for $1,000, the amount of the contributions deduction is $5,000 and the $4,000 appreciation is not recognized as a gain. In a similar fashion, if appreciated property is sold to a qualified organization for the amount of the donor's cost basis, the appreciation in value is deductible as a contribution.

587

The total amount of the deduction for charitable contributions may in general not exceed 20% of adjusted gross income. However, there is an additional allowance of 10% of adjusted gross income for charitable contributions to organizations that are publicly supported, or to domestic governments for exclusively public purposes.

Interest expense. Interest expense of an entirely personal nature, such as on indebtedness incurred to buy a home, household appliances, or an automobile, is deductible.

Taxes. Some state and local taxes of a personal or nonbusiness nature are deductible from adjusted gross income. Federal excise taxes may qualify as deductions only when the expense to which they relate is deductible as a nonbusiness expense. Taxes of general applicability are listed in the table at the top of the following page, classified according to their status.

DEDUCTIBLE	NOT DEDUCTIBLE
State and Local	*State and Local*
Real estate taxes.	Gift, inheritance, and estate taxes.
Personal property taxes.	Auto licenses and drivers' licenses.
Income taxes.	Cigarette and alcoholic beverage taxes.
General sales taxes.	Admission taxes.
Gasoline taxes.	
	Federal
Federal	Gift and estate taxes.
Excise taxes on items of deductible *non-business* expense.	Employees FICA taxes.
	Income taxes.
	Excise taxes on *personal* expenditures.

Medical expenses. One half of the premiums paid for medical care insurance, but not in excess of $150 a year, is deductible from adjusted gross income. The remaining amount of such premiums is combined with other medical expenses, which are deductible to the extent that they exceed 3% of adjusted gross income. Amounts paid for medicines and drugs may be included in medical expenses only to the extent that they exceed 1% of adjusted gross income. An example of the computations required to determine the medical expense deduction is presented below, assuming that the taxpayer's adjusted gross income is $11,000 and his expenses include a medical care insurance premium of $170.

One half of medical care insurance premium.............			$ 85
Total cost of medicines and drugs.....................	$120		
Less 1% of adjusted gross income of $11,000...........	110	$ 10	
Other medical expenses (including $85 insurance premium).		380	
Total......................................		$390	
Less 3% of adjusted gross income of $11,000.............		330	60
Medical expense deduction...........................			$145

Casualty and theft losses. Property losses in excess of $100 resulting from fire, storm, automobile accident or other casualty, or theft are deductible to the extent not compensated for by insurance. The $100 limitation applies to each occurrence rather than to total losses for the year. It should be noted that only a loss of taxpayer's own property is deductible; there is no deduction for payments to another person for property damage or personal injury caused by the taxpayer.

Child care expenses. Widows, widowers, and certain married persons who, in order to earn a living, incur expenses for the care of dependents are allowed a limited deduction for such expenses. The expenses must be incurred for the care of a child or children under the age of 13, or other dependent, regardless of age, who is physically or mentally incapable of caring for himself. The maximum deduction is $600 a year if there is only one qualifying dependent or $900 if there are two or more qualifying dependents. There are additional limitations on the amount that may be deducted by married taxpayers.

Standard deduction. Instead of itemizing the deductions from adjusted gross income, taxpayers may elect to claim a so-called *standard deduction*, which is the larger of (1) the 10% standard or (2) the minimum standard. For single taxpayers and married taxpayers filing a joint return,[3] with adjusted gross income of $5,000 or more, the *10% standard* is equal to 10% of the adjusted gross income but not more than $1,000. The *minimum standard* is equal to $200 plus $100 for each of their exemptions, but also not more than $1,000. The following examples illustrate the application of these provisions:

EXAMPLE	ADJUSTED GROSS INCOME	NUMBER OF EXEMPTIONS	10% STANDARD	MINIMUM STANDARD	ALLOWABLE STANDARD DEDUCTION
A	$ 6,000	3	$ 600	$ 500	$ 600
B	6,000	5	600	700	700
C	9,000	4	900	600	900
D	9,000	10	900	1,000	1,000
E	12,000	6	1,000	800	1,000

Taxpayers with adjusted gross income of less than $5,000 who elect the standard deduction use an optional tax table that provides for variable amounts of adjusted gross income (under $5,000) and a variable number of exemptions.

589

Exemptions. In addition to the allowable deductions from adjusted gross income described above, every individual taxpayer is entitled to a *personal* exemption of $600 for himself plus an additional exemption of the same amount for each *dependent*.

In general, a dependent is a person who satisfies all of the following requirements: (1) is closely related to the taxpayer, (2) received over one half of his support from the taxpayer during the year, (3) had less than $600 of gross income during the year, and (4) if married, does not file a joint return with his or her spouse. However, the $600 limitation on gross income does not apply to a child of the taxpayer who is either under 19 years of age at the close of the taxable year or who has been a full-time student at an educational institution during each of five months of the year.

An additional exemption is allowed to a taxpayer who is 65 years of age or older on the last day of the taxable year. An additional exemption is also allowed to a taxpayer who is blind at the close of the taxable year.

---

[3]Married persons usually file joint returns. For this reason the special rules applicable to separate returns of married persons are not described.

Computing the income tax

Taxpayers with adjusted gross income of less than $5,000 who itemize their deductions therefrom must compute the amount of their income tax. Taxpayers with adjusted gross income of $5,000 or more must also compute their tax regardless of whether they claim their actual deductions from adjusted gross income or elect the standard deduction.

The tax is computed by applying the appropriate schedule of rates to the amount of taxable income reported on the tax return. There are three tax rate schedules for individuals, classified as follows: (1) for single persons and married persons filing a separate return, (2) for married persons filing a joint return, and (3) for heads of household. The first two schedules are presented on page 591. Although the rate structure is amended from time to time, the progressive characteristic is a permanent feature of the income tax system. The manner in which a rate schedule is used may be illustrated as follows, assuming taxable income of $15,300 for a single person:

Tax on $14,000........	$3,550
Tax on $ 1,300 at 39%.	507
Total income tax......	$4,057

The rate schedule for married persons filing a joint return is designed to attribute half of their combined taxable income to each spouse. This characteristic of joint returns is sometimes referred to as the *split-income* feature. As can be noted from the two rate schedules, both have the same progressive percentage rates but the amount of taxable income in each bracket of the joint return schedule is twice that of the schedule applicable to single persons. For purposes of filing a tax return, marital status is determined as of the last day of the taxable year or at the date of death if one spouse dies during the year.

If only one spouse has income, or if the difference between the amounts of their individual incomes is substantial, it is ordinarily advantageous for married couples to file a joint return. However, it is possible for the advantages of the joint return rate schedule to be outweighed by the availability of greater deductions for medical expenses or for certain specified losses when separate returns are filed.

For the two years following the year in which a married person dies, the surviving spouse may continue to use the joint return rate schedule, provided the surviving spouse (1) maintains as his or her home a household in which a dependent son or daughter resides and (2) does not remarry.

The schedule of tax rates applicable to heads of household (not illustrated) provides for approximately half of the split-income advantage of the joint return. To qualify as a head of household, an individual must

SINGLE TAXPAYERS			
If the taxable income is:		The tax is:	
Not over $500................14% of taxable income			
Over	But not over		of excess over
$ 500 — $ 1,000..$		70, plus 15% — $	500
1,000 —	1,500..	145, plus 16% —	1,000
1,500 —	2,000..	225, plus 17% —	1,500
2,000 —	4,000..	310, plus 19% —	2,000
4,000 —	6,000..	690, plus 22% —	4,000
6,000 —	8,000..	1,130, plus 25% —	6,000
8,000 —	10,000..	1,630, plus 28% —	8,000
10,000 —	12,000..	2,190, plus 32% —	10,000
12,000 —	14,000..	2,830, plus 36% —	12,000
14,000 —	16,000..	3,550, plus 39% —	14,000
16,000 —	18,000..	4,330, plus 42% —	16,000
18,000 —	20,000..	5,170, plus 45% —	18,000
20,000 —	22,000..	6,070, plus 48% —	20,000
22,000 —	26,000..	7,030, plus 50% —	22,000
26,000 —	32,000..	9,030, plus 53% —	26,000
32,000 —	38,000..	12,210, plus 55% —	32,000
38,000 —	44,000..	15,510, plus 58% —	38,000
44,000 —	50,000..	18,990, plus 60% —	44,000
50,000 —	60,000..	22,590, plus 62% —	50,000
60,000 —	70,000..	28,790, plus 64% —	60,000
70,000 —	80,000..	35,190, plus 66% —	70,000
80,000 —	90,000..	41,790, plus 68% —	80,000
90,000 —	100,000..	48,590, plus 69% —	90,000
100,000 —	....	55,490, plus 70% —	100,000

MARRIED TAXPAYERS — JOINT RETURN			
If the taxable income is:		The tax is:	
Not over $1,000................14% of taxable income			
Over	But not over		of excess over
$ 1,000 — $ 2,000..$		140, plus 15% — $	1,000
2,000 —	3,000..	290, plus 16% —	2,000
3,000 —	4,000..	450, plus 17% —	3,000
4,000 —	8,000..	620, plus 19% —	4,000
8,000 —	12,000..	1,380, plus 22% —	8,000
12,000 —	16,000..	2,260, plus 25% —	12,000
16,000 —	20,000..	3,260, plus 28% —	16,000
20,000 —	24,000..	4,380, plus 32% —	20,000
24,000 —	28,000..	5,660, plus 36% —	24,000
28,000 —	32,000..	7,100, plus 39% —	28,000
32,000 —	36,000..	8,660, plus 42% —	32,000
36,000 —	40,000..	10,340, plus 45% —	36,000
40,000 —	44,000..	12,140, plus 48% —	40,000
44,000 —	52,000..	14,060, plus 50% —	44,000
52,000 —	64,000..	18,060, plus 53% —	52,000
64,000 —	76,000..	24,420, plus 55% —	64,000
76,000 —	88,000..	31,020, plus 58% —	76,000
88,000 —	100,000..	37,980, plus 60% —	88,000
100,000 —	120,000..	45,180, plus 62% —	100,000
120,000 —	140,000..	57,580, plus 64% —	120,000
140,000 —	160,000..	70,380, plus 66% —	140,000
160,000 —	180,000..	83,580, plus 68% —	160,000
180,000 —	200,000..	97,180, plus 69% —	180,000
200,000 —	....	110,980, plus 70% —	200,000

Income tax rate schedules

be unmarried at the close of the taxable year and must, in general, maintain as his home a household in which at least one of the following persons lives: (1) an unmarried son, daughter, or descendent, (2) a married son, daughter, or descendent who qualifies as a dependent of the taxpayer, or (3) any other close relative who qualifies as a dependent of the taxpayer. The head of household status may also be claimed by an unmarried taxpayer who maintains his dependent mother or father in a separate household.

591

Capital gains and losses

Gains and losses of individuals resulting from the sale or the exchange of certain types of assets, called *capital assets*, are accorded special treatment for income tax purposes. Capital assets most commonly owned by taxpayers are stocks and bonds. Under certain conditions, land, buildings, and equipment used in business may also be treated as capital assets.

The gains and losses from the sale or exchange of capital assets held for six months or less are classified as *short-term*. Gains and losses from those held for more than six months are classified as *long-term*. The aggregate of all short-term gains and losses during a taxable year is called a *net short-term capital gain* or a *net short-term capital loss* and the aggregate of all long-term gains and losses is similarly identified as a *net long-term capital gain* or a *net long-term capital loss*.

After determining the net short-term and the net long-term results, the two amounts are combined to yield *net capital gain* or *net capital loss*. If there is a net capital loss, it can be deducted from gross income to the extent of $1,000 only; however, any excess may be carried forward and used in future years.

A net capital gain is reported as a part of gross income. To the extent that the net capital gain is composed of an excess of net long-term gain over net short-term loss (if any), the taxpayer is allowed to deduct 50% of such excess from gross income.

The application of these provisions may be demonstrated by the following examples:

	A	B	C
Net short-term capital gain (loss).........	($2,000)	$8,000	$3,000
Net long-term capital gain (loss).........	8,000	(2,000)	3,000
Net capital gain — gross income..........	$6,000	$6,000	$6,000
Long-term capital gain deduction........	3,000	—	1,500
Adjusted gross income from capital gain.	$3,000	$6,000	$4,500

In addition to the long-term capital gain deduction allowed to individuals, the IRC limits the amount of tax on the taxable portion of the net long-term gain to a maximum of 50%. This ceiling limitation is of benefit only to taxpayers with sufficient taxable income to place them above the 50% tax bracket.

Payment of tax; filing returns

The income tax withheld from an employee's earnings by his employer represents current payments on account. An individual whose income is not subject to withholding, or only partially so, or an individual whose income is fairly large must estimate his income tax in advance and file a tax form known as a *Declaration of Estimated Income Tax*. The estimated tax for the year, after deducting the estimated amount to be withheld and any credit for overpayment from prior years, must be paid currently, usually in four installments.

Annual income tax returns must be filed within 3½ months following the end of the taxpayer's taxable year. Any balance owed must accompany the return. If the return indicates an overpayment, the taxpayer may direct (1) that it be credited to his estimated tax for the following year, (2) that it be applied to the purchase of United States savings bonds, with the excess over the purchase price refunded, or (3) that the entire amount be refunded.

Determination of income tax of individuals

The method of assembling income tax information and determining the tax liability may be illustrated with data taken from the records of John D. Long and his wife, Ruth T., who file a joint return. John owns and operates a retail mercantile enterprise; Ruth owns a building with four apartments and is also employed as a part-time secretary. In addition to one personal exemption for each of them, they are entitled to two additional exemptions for dependent children. Sources and amounts of includable gross income, itemized deductions, exemptions, and other data are presented in condensed form below. In practice, the data would be reported in considerably greater detail on official tax forms.

John D. and Ruth T. Long
Summary of Federal Income Tax Data
For Calendar Year 19——

Gross income and deductions from gross income:			
Salary....................................			$ 2,500
Dividends on corporation stocks:			
Owned by husband......................	$470		
Owned by wife.........................	80	$ 550	
Exclusion ($100 for husband, $80 for wife).		180	370
Rents:			
Gross income.........................		$ 6,800	
Expenses.............................		3,700	3,100
Business:			
Sales.................................		$126,000	
Cost of merchandise sold.................		83,000	
Gross profit...........................		$ 43,000	
Expenses..............................		22,600	20,400
Capital gains and losses:			
Net long-term capital gain...............		$ 4,000	
Net short-term capital loss...............		1,000	
Net capital gain.......................		$ 3,000	
Long-term capital gain deduction.........		1,500	1,500
Adjusted gross income.....................			$27,870
Deductions from adjusted gross income:			
Charitable contributions...................	$730		
Interest on residence mortgage note..........	640		
Real estate tax on residence.................	539		
State sales tax............................	220		
State gasoline tax.........................	30		
Safe-deposit box rental....................	11	$ 2,170	
Exemptions (4 × $600).....................		2,400	4,570
Taxable income...........................			$23,300
Income tax liability:			
On $20,000.............................		$ 4,380	
On $ 3,300 at 32%......................		1,056	
Total tax................................			$ 5,436
Advance payments:			
Tax withheld from salary..................		$ 260	
Payments of estimated tax.................		4,800	
Total payments...........................			5,060
Balance due.............................			$ 376

Federal income tax data summary

Taxable income of corporations

Certain classes of corporations are accorded special treatment because the sources and nature of their income differ from that of general business corporations. Included in the special categories are insurance companies, mutual savings banks, regulated investment companies, farm cooperatives, and corporations specifically exempt by statute.

Excluding the special classes from consideration, the taxable income of a corporation is determined, in general, by deducting its ordinary business expenses from the total amount of its includable gross income. Of the numerous variations from this general procedure there are three of broad applicability that merit brief consideration.

Dividends received deduction. All dividends received on shares of stock in other corporations are includable in gross income. However, 85% of such dividends is ordinarily allowed as a special deduction from gross income. Certain small corporations may deduct the entire amount of dividends received.

Charitable contributions. The deduction for charitable contributions is limited to 5% of taxable income, computed without regard to the contributions and the special deduction for dividends received. Contributions in excess of the 5% limitation may be carried forward to the five succeeding years, deductions in the succeeding years also being subject to the 5% maximum.

Capital gains and losses. As in the case of individuals, capital gains and losses of corporations are classified as short-term (assets held for six months or less) and long-term (assets held for more than six months). The excess of a net long-term capital gain over a net short-term capital loss is included in its entirety in taxable income. However, the tax thereon is limited to a maximum of 25%. No part of a net capital loss may be deducted from ordinary income but it may be carried forward and deducted from capital gains realized during the succeeding five years.

Corporation income tax

Corporations in general are subject to a *normal tax* on the amount of their taxable income and to a *surtax* on taxable income in excess of $25,000. Procedures for determining taxable income and the income tax are summarized in the tabulation at the top of the next page, assuming a normal tax rate of 22% and a surtax rate of 26%.

There are two additional taxes designed to limit the use of the corporate form as a means of avoiding income tax on individuals. Although the statutes which provide for these "loophole closing" taxes are too

Gross income (including dividends of $20,000)		$200,000
Deductions		90,000
Taxable income before special deduction		$110,000
Special deduction for dividends received, 85% of $20,000.		17,000
Taxable income		$ 93,000
Normal tax, 22% of $93,000	$20,460	
Surtax, 26% of ($93,000 − $25,000)	17,680	
Total income tax		$ 38,140
Payments of estimated tax		31,000
Balance due		$ 7,140

voluminous for detailed explanations, their basic nature merits brief consideration.

Accumulated earnings tax. An additional income tax may be assessed against corporations that accumulate earnings with intent to avoid the income tax that would be levied on shareholders if such earnings were distributed as dividends. Accumulated earnings of up to $100,000 are exempt from this tax; additional accumulations are subject to the additional tax unless it can be proved by a preponderance of evidence that they are not in excess of the reasonable needs of the business. The tax rate is 27.5% of the first $100,000 of accumulated taxable income and 38.5% of the excess over $100,000.

Personal holding company tax. The statutory definition of a personal holding company is quite technical. In general, the special tax is designed to discourage individuals from transferring their investment properties to a corporation in exchange for its stock, or to "incorporate" their personal talents or services. The additional tax, which is levied at the rate of 70% of the undistributed personal holding company income, is an effective deterrent to the use of this device for the accumulation of "tax-sheltered" income.

Minimizing income taxes

There are various means of minimizing or reducing federal income taxes, some of which are of broader applicability than others. Much depends upon the volume and the sources of a taxpayer's gross income, the nature of his expenses and other deductions, and the accounting methods employed.

The amount of income tax that may be saved by any particular proposal can be determined by estimating the total tax assuming that the proposal is to be adopted, and comparing that amount with the estimated tax according to the alternative proposals under consideration. In many cases it is possible to determine the tax effect of a proposal by merely computing the tax at the *marginal* rate on the amount of taxable income differential. To illustrate the latter procedure, assume that a married couple filing a joint return will report taxable income of $42,000 if they claim the standard deduction of $1,000. According to the applicable rate schedule on page 591 their marginal tax rate, which is the rate for the segment of taxable income in the $40,000 to $44,000 bracket, is 48%. If an analysis of their check stubs and other records should reveal actual deductions of $1,900, there would be a tax saving of $432 (48% of $900) in itemizing their deductions instead of electing the standard deduction.

It should be noted that the effect of a tax saving is greater than additional taxable earnings of an equivalent amount. If instead of saving $432 of income tax in the foregoing example the taxpayer had earned additional taxable income of $432, there would have been additional income tax on the additional income. The $432 saving is the equivalent of approximately $830 ($432 ÷ [100% − 48%]) of additional earnings.

Form of business organization

One of the most important considerations in selecting the form of organization to use in operating a business enterprise is the impact of the federal income tax. If the business is a sole proprietorship, the owner must report the income on his personal income tax returns. In a partnership each individual partner is taxed on his distributive share of the business income in much the same manner as a sole proprietor. If the business is incorporated, the corporation must pay an income tax on its earnings, and the remaining earnings are again taxed to the owners (shareholders) when they are distributed in the form of dividends.

The double taxation feature of the corporate form might seem to outweigh any possible advantages of employing it for a family enterprise or other closely held business. This is not necessarily the case, however. For most business enterprises there are likely to be both advantages and disadvantages in the corporate form. Among the many factors that need to be considered are the following: (1) magnitude of net income, (2) fluctuations in net income from year to year, (3) disposition of after-tax income (withdrawn from the enterprise or used for expansion), (4) method of financing, (5) number of owners and shares of ownership, and (6) income of owners from other sources.

The type of analysis required to appraise the relative merits of alternative forms of organization is illustrated on the next page. Assume that Philip G. Parker and his wife are considering the incorporation of a business enterprise which they have operated for several years as a partnership. The business has been yielding taxable income of $65,000, their ownership of various investments in real estate and corporation securities yield an additional $15,000 of taxable income, their nonbusiness and personal deductions from adjusted gross income total approximately

$4,000, they have three dependent children, and they file a joint return. Their withdrawals of $2,500 a month would become a salary expense if the enterprise is incorporated. The federal income tax consequences under the two forms of organization are presented below, using the tax rates presented in this chapter.

PARTNERSHIP FORM

Tax on individuals:			
Business income			$65,000
Other income			15,000
Adjusted gross income			$80,000
Deductions:			
Nonbusiness and personal		$4,000	
Exemptions (5)		3,000	7,000
Taxable income			$73,000
Income tax liability:			
On $64,000			$24,420
On $ 9,000 at 55%			4,950
Total income tax — partnership form			**$29,370**

CORPORATION FORM

Tax on corporation:			
Taxable income, $65,000 − ($2,500 monthly salary × 12)			$35,000
Income tax liability:			
Normal tax, 22% of $35,000		$ 7,700	
Surtax, 26% of ($35,000 − $25,000)		2,600	$10,300
Tax on individuals:			
Salary			$30,000
Other income			15,000
Adjusted gross income			$45,000
Deductions:			
Nonbusiness and personal		$4,000	
Exemptions (5)		3,000	7,000
Taxable income			$38,000
Income tax liability:			
On $36,000			$10,340
On $ 2,000 at 45%			900	11,240
Total income tax — corporation form			**$21,540**

597

Comparison of the two tax liabilities indicates that an annual tax saving of approximately $8,000 ($29,370 − $21,540) could be effected by adopting the corporate form. However, the possible distribution of the corporation's net income as dividends was not taken into consideration. If the corporation's after-tax net income of $24,700 were to be paid to the Parkers as dividends, their taxable income would total $62,700 instead of $38,000. The resulting increase in their personal income tax amounting to approximately $12,500 would convert the expected $8,000 advantage of the corporate form to a $4,500 disadvantage.

Earnings accumulated by the corporation in the foregoing example might at some future time become available to the stockholders through sale of their stock. They would thus be converted into long-term capital gains subject to a maximum tax of 25% (50% of half of the gain). However, retention of earnings beyond the $100,000 exemption could result in imposition of the accumulated earnings tax. If additional accumulations were beyond the reasonable needs of the business, the shareholders might then elect partnership treatment under Subchapter S and thus avoid the double tax on corporate earnings. Additional information about the intentions of the Parkers and prospects for the future would be needed to explore additional ramifications of the problem.

It is readily apparent that the best form of organization, from the standpoint of the federal income tax, can be determined only by a careful detailed analysis of the particular situation. Generalizations are likely to be of little benefit and may even be misleading. The impact of state and local taxes also varies according to the form of business organization, and the importance of such nontax factors as limited liability and transferability of ownership should be weighed.

Timing of transactions and reporting

"Timing" is an important element in the effect of management's decisions on liability for income tax. The selection of the fiscal year, the choice of accounting methods, and acceleration or deferment of gross income or expense are some of the time factors that need to be considered. Applications of timing considerations to relatively common situations are described in the paragraphs that follow.

Cash basis v. accrual basis. Corporations that regularly have taxable income in excess of the $25,000 surtax exemption are unlikely to be greatly affected by their choice of the cash or accrual basis of accounting. A small corporation whose taxable income tends to fluctuate above and below the $25,000 amount from year to year may be better able to control the fluctuation if the cash basis is used. For example, near the close of a taxable year in which taxable income is likely to exceed $25,000, some of the excess, which will be subject to the surtax (26%) may be shifted to the succeeding year. It may be possible to postpone the receipt of gross income by delayed billings for services, or expenses may be increased by payment of outstanding bills prior to the end of the year. The timing of expenditures and payment for such expenses as redecorating, repairs, and advertising may also be readily subject to control.

Unincorporated businesses may also be able to reduce fluctuations in net income, with a consequent lowering of the marginal tax rate of the owners. Even individual taxpayers whose income is primarily from salary may have opportunities to save a modest amount by careful planning of payment of deductible items. For example, if a substantial amount of medical expense is incurred near the end of the year, it would be preferable to pay all such bills before the end of the year if by so doing the medical expense deduction and other itemized deductions will exceed the standard deduction. Conversely, if early payment would not yield a reduction in taxes for the current year, postponement of payment to the following year might be beneficial.

A closely related technique is to alternate from year to year between electing the standard deduction and claiming actual deductions. Because of differences between the taxable year of the individual, which is usually the calendar year, and the fiscal year of charitable organizations and local taxing authorities, it is often possible to pay two fiscal-year amounts in a single calendar year. To illustrate, assume that a married couple with average annual adjusted gross income of $15,000 has average annual deductions of $900 exclusive of exemptions. By electing the standard deduction of $1,000, they benefit to the extent of the tax on $100 computed at their marginal tax rate. If they were able to alternate $700 of their deductions from year to year, they could then alternate between claiming actual deductions of $1,600 ($900 + $700) and the standard deduction of $1,000. By this means a saving equivalent to the tax on $600 at their marginal rate could be effected in alternate years.

Installment method. The installment method of determining gross income from sales of merchandise on the installment plan, which was described in Chapter 14, is widely used for income tax purposes. The method may also be employed in reporting the net gain from a sale of real estate or from a casual sale of personal property at a price in excess of $1,000, provided the payments received in the year of sale do not exceed 30% of the selling price.

To illustrate the potential tax advantage of the installment method, assume that a taxpayer sells his controlling interest in a closely held corporation for $100,000, with payment to be spread evenly over six years, on which he realizes a gain of $60,000. Assume further that he files jointly with his wife and that their ordinary annual taxable income is expected to remain at $22,000. Reporting the entire $60,000 gain in the year of sale would increase their total taxable income by $30,000 ($60,000 less the 50% long-term capital gain deduction). Alternatively, if they elect installment reporting, their total taxable income for the year of sale and each of the succeeding five years would be increased by $5,000 (1/6 of $30,000). The tax liabilities resulting from each of the alternatives, based on the schedule of rates on page 591, is presented at the top of the next page. The analysis reveals that installment reporting would yield an overall tax saving of $2,720 ($43,160 − $40,440). The spreading of tax payments evenly over the six years would also be advantageous.

	LUMP-SUM REPORTING		INSTALLMENT REPORTING	
YEAR	TAXABLE INCOME	INCOME TAX	TAXABLE INCOME	INCOME TAX
First.........	$ 52,000	$18,060	$ 27,000	$ 6,740
Second.......	22,000	5,020	27,000	6,740
Third........	22,000	5,020	27,000	6,740
Fourth.......	22,000	5,020	27,000	6,740
Fifth.........	22,000	5,020	27,000	6,740
Sixth........	22,000	5,020	27,000	6,740
Total........	$162,000	$43,160	$162,000	$40,440

Capital gains and losses. The timing of capital gains and losses is ordinarily subject to a high degree of control because the taxpayer is able to sell capital assets or to refrain from selling them, as he chooses. Postponement of a sale by only a single day can result in a substantial tax saving. To illustrate, assume that an individual sells listed stocks that he has owned exactly six months, realizing a gain of $4,000. The gain would be classified as a short-term capital gain and taxed as ordinary income. Assuming that the taxpayer's marginal tax rate is 60%, the tax on the $4,000 gain would be $2,400. Alternatively, if the individual had held the securities at least one additional day before selling them, the $4,000 gain (assuming no change in selling price) would have qualified as a long-term capital gain, of which only half would be subject to tax at a rate not higher than 50%. Thus, if the sale were postponed by at least one day, the tax would have been $1,000 (50% of $2,000) instead of $2,400.

The analysis of the illustrative transaction would be somewhat different for a corporation. If the corporation's taxable income, including the $4,000 capital gain, does not exceed $25,000, the entire amount would be taxed at the assumed normal tax rate of 22%, regardless of whether the gain was short-term or long-term. On the other hand, if the total taxable income of the corporation were $29,000 or more, the $4,000 would be taxed, based on the rates given on page 594, at 48% if a short-term gain and at 25% if a long-term gain.

When a taxpayer owns various lots of an identical security that were acquired at different dates and at different prices, it may be possible to choose between realizing a gain and realizing a loss, and perhaps to a limited extent to govern the amount realized. For example, a taxpayer who has realized gains from the sale of securities may wish to offset them, in whole or in part, by losses from the sale of other securities. To illustrate, assume that a taxpayer who owns three 100-share lots of a particular listed common stock purchased at $40, $50, and $60 a share respectively wishes to sell 100 shares at the current market price of $55 a share. He will realize a gain of $1,500, a gain of $500, or a loss of $500, depending on the particular 100-share lot sold. If the particular lot sold is not determinable from the taxpayer's records, the first-in, first-out cost flow assumption must be employed; averaging the cost of different lots is not permissible.

Accelerated depreciation. The declining-balance and sum-of-the-years-digits methods of computing depreciation were described and illustrated in Chapter 10. The use of these methods of accelerating depreciation expense are specifically authorized in the IRC for new items of plant and equipment having a useful life of at least three years. Taxpayers may also elect to deduct additional first-year depreciation of 20% on up to $10,000 ($20,000 on a joint return) of tangible personal property having a useful life of at least six years.

The 20% "extra" depreciation is computed without regard to the period of time the asset has been held during the year or to the residual value. Taxpayers electing to claim the additional deduction must identify the specific assets to which it is applied, and they must deduct the extra depreciation from the asset cost before computing the "regular" depreciation. To illustrate the application of this provision, the extra and regular depreciation on a $10,000 item of equipment is computed below. The asset is expected to have a useful life of six years; it was acquired near the end of the third month of the taxable year; and the declining-balance method, at twice the straight-line rate, is elected.

601

Extra depreciation, 20% of $10,000...................................	$2,000
Declining-balance depreciation on $10,000 − $2,000, 9/12 of (33⅓% of $8,000)...................................	2,000
Total depreciation...................................	$4,000

The accelerated write-off of depreciable assets does not, of course, effect a long-run net saving in income tax. The tax reduction of the early years of use is offset by higher taxes as the annual depreciation expense diminishes. The ever-present possibility of changes in tax rates in future years adds to the uncertainty of the real merits of accelerated depreciation. Nevertheless, the additional funds made available by current tax savings are usually considered to be sufficiently advantageous to justify the election of accelerated depreciation.

Equalization among taxable entities

In some situations a saving in income taxes may be effected by transfers of income-producing properties among members of a family group or by the use of multiple corporations in operating business enterprises. For example, a taxpayer who is accustomed to making substantial cash gifts to members of his family might consider the alternative of gifts of shares of stock or other income-producing property. The income from the gift property would then be taxed to the donee, whose marginal tax rate is presumably well below that of the donor.

When the corporate form of organization is employed for a business enterprise owned by a family or other relatively small group of individuals, a tax saving may be effected through the use of multiple corporations. The first $25,000 of taxable income of each corporation would be exempt from surtax. However, there is an additional normal tax of 6% on the first $25,000 of taxable income earned by group-controlled corporations. The net tax savings, assuming a surtax rate of 26%, would be 26% − 6%, or 20%, of annual taxable income up to $25,000. This means of tax minimization is available only in bona fide situations in which there is a good business reason for the separate units; if tax reduction is the sole purpose, only one surtax exemption will be allowed for the group.

Impact of income taxes generally

The foregoing description of the federal income tax system and discussion of tax minimization, together with explanations in other chapters, demonstrates the importance of income taxes to business enterprises. The most important factor influencing a business decision is often the federal income tax. Many accountants, in both private and public practice, devote their entire attention to tax planning for their employers or their clients. The statutes and the administrative regulations, which change frequently, must be studied continuously by anyone who engages in this phase of accounting.

602

QUESTIONS

1. Who initially determines the amount of a taxpayer's *taxable income*?

2. Does the failure to maintain adequate records qualify as a legitimate means of tax avoidance? Discuss.

3. A particular individual owns three unincorporated business enterprises, maintaining a separate accounting system for each. (a) Is a separate income tax return required for each enterprise? (b) May the owner elect to file a separate return and determine the tax on each enterprise separately?

4. Describe briefly the system employed in subjecting the income of partnerships to the federal income tax.

5. The adjusted gross income of a sole proprietorship for the year was $30,000, of which the owner withdrew $20,000. What amount of income from the business enterprise must the owner report in his income tax return?

6. Do corporations electing partnership treatment (Subchapter S) pay federal income tax? Discuss.

7. Which of the two methods of accounting, cash or accrual, is more commonly used by individual taxpayers?

8. During the year an attorney who uses the cash basis of determining taxable income spends $300 for a new office desk and determines that a $200 fee billed to a client during the year is uncollectible. Discuss the status of these two items as allowable deductions.

9. Describe *constructive* receipt of gross income, as it applies to (a) salary check received from employer, (b) interest credited to a savings account, and (c) bond interest coupons.

10. Arrange the following in their proper sequence for the determination of the income tax base of an individual:

(a) Personal exemptions.
(b) Expenses (related to business or specified revenue).
(c) Taxable income.
(d) Gross income.
(e) Expenses (nonbusiness and personal).
(f) Adjusted gross income.

11. Identify the following items as (a) includable or (b) excludable by an individual in determining his taxable income.

(1) Interest on municipal bonds.
(2) Wages received for farm labor.
(3) Receipts from rental of room in taxpayer's home.
(4) Shares of corporation stocks received as a gift.
(5) Dividends in excess of $100 on stock acquired in (4).
(6) Scholarship received from State University by a sophomore.
(7) Insurance proceeds received by beneficiary because of death of insured.
(8) Cash received from a friend in repayment of a non-interest-bearing loan.

12. Which of the following are required to file an income tax return?

(a) Unmarried man, 70 years old; gross income of $1,100.
(b) Child, 14 years old; gross income of $915 from investments.
(c) Married man, 45 years old; gross income of $15,000.
(d) Wife of man in (c), 40 years old; gross income of $300.
(e) Corporation; net loss of $6,000.
(f) College student, 20 years old, supported by father; gross income of $650.

603

13. Identify the following items as (a) deductible from gross income in determining adjusted gross income, (b) deductible from adjusted gross income in determining taxable income, or (c) not deductible. (Ignore any possible limitations on the amount of the deduction.)

(1) Storm damage to family residence, not covered by insurance.
(2) State license tax on family automobile.
(3) Property taxes on apartment building held as an investment.
(4) Fire insurance on taxpayer's residence.
(5) Federal excise tax on commodities purchased for family use.
(6) State sales taxes on commodities purchased for family use.
(7) Loss incurred by architect on sale of corporation securities.
(8) Transportation expenses incurred by employee for employer.
(9) Interest on money borrowed for use in unincorporated business.
(10) Contribution to State University by unincorporated business enterprise.

14. Determine the allowable standard deduction for the following taxpayers, assuming that each is under 65 and is not blind, and that the married couples file a joint return.

(a) Single person, 2 dependents, adjusted gross income of $8,000.
(b) Single person, 3 dependents, adjusted gross income of $5,900.
(c) Married couple, 4 dependents, adjusted gross income of $7,000.
(d) Married couple, 1 dependent, adjusted gross income of $7,500.
(e) Married couple, no dependents, adjusted gross income of $14,000.

15. An acquaintance plans to decline an opportunity to earn an additional thousand dollars before the end of the year because he would be subjected to a higher tax bracket. How should you advise him?

16. An unmarried son of the taxpayer, 22 years of age, was a full-time student at a university until his graduation in August; his gross income for the year was $1,800. (a) What requirement must be met to enable the taxpayer to claim the son as a dependent? (b) If the son was married during the year, would there be an additional requirement? Discuss.

17. According to the tax rate schedule for single taxpayers appearing in this chapter, the tax on taxable income of $20,000 is $6,070. (a) What is the approximate average tax rate at this level of taxable income? (b) What is the marginal tax rate at this level of taxable income?

18. A single taxpayer had a net long-term capital gain of $12,000 and a net short-term capital loss of $2,000 during the year. (a) What is the amount of his adjusted gross income from net capital gain? (b) Assuming that the taxpayer's taxable income, exclusive of capital gains and losses, is $120,000 (marginal tax rate of 70%), what is the amount of income tax on the net capital gain?

19. A corporation had a net long-term capital gain of $4,000 during the year (no short-term capital gains or losses). Determine the amount of income tax on the $4,000, assuming the tax rates stated in this chapter, if the ordinary taxable income (exclusive of the $4,000) for the year is (a) $20,000, (b) $100,000.

20. The president and major stockholder of X Corporation receives in salary and income from other investments an amount which places him in the 64% income tax bracket. (a) Which corporate policy would be more advantageous to him, retention of earnings or distribution in dividends? (b) Describe the deterrent to retention of earnings provided by the IRC.

21. Describe the general limitations and carry-over features applicable to a net capital loss incurred by (a) individuals, (b) corporations.

22. What terms are applied to the two basic income tax rates levied against corporations?

EXERCISES

23-1. An employee who is not an outside salesman received a salary of $15,000 during the year and incurred the following unreimbursed expenses related to his employment: (a) transportation, $300, and lunches, $150, while not away from home overnight; (b) travel while away from home overnight, $700; and (c) customer entertainment, $350. Determine his adjusted gross income from salary.

23-2. Determine the adjusted gross income from salary of employees A, B, and C, assuming that none of them is an outside salesman and that no travel expenses were incurred.

	A	B	C
Salary....................	$11,000	$12,000	$10,000
Reimbursement from employer for entertainment expenses........	720	900	500
Entertainment expenses incurred.	600	1,000	500

23-3. Taxpayer husband and wife, each entitled to one exemption, with two dependent children, have adjusted gross income of $12,000 for the year. Amounts paid for medical expenses during the year were as follows: medical care insurance premiums, $320; medicines and drugs, $165; other medical expenses, $420. (a) Determine the amount of their allowable deduction for medical expenses. (b) What is the maximum amount that they may deduct for charitable contributions? (c) What is the amount of their minimum standard deduction? (d) What is the maximum amount that they may claim as a standard deduction? (e) Assuming that they claim the standard deduction, determine their income tax, applying the appropriate schedule of rates appearing in this chapter.

23-4. The capital gains and losses of an individual taxpayer during the year are listed below. Losses are identified by parentheses.

Short-term: $4,000, $1,000, ($3,000)
Long-term: $6,000, ($2,000), $5,000

Determine the following: (a) net short-term capital gain or loss; (b) net long-term capital gain or loss; (c) net capital gain or loss; (d) long-term capital gain deduction, if any; (e) adjusted gross income from net capital gain or loss; and (f) amount subject to the tax rate limitation of 50%.

23-5. Taxpayer husband and wife, entitled to one exemption each and three additional exemptions for dependents, file a joint return. Other summary data related to their income tax return are as follows:

Includable gross income	$25,000
Allowable deductions from gross income	2,000
Allowable itemized deductions from adjusted gross income	970
Tax withheld from salary	3,200
Payments of estimated tax	600

Determine the following: (a) adjusted gross income; (b) taxable income; (c) income tax liability, using the appropriate schedule of rates appearing in this chapter; and (d) balance due.

23-6. The data required for the determination of a particular corporation's income tax for the current year are summarized below.

Dividends received from other corporations	$ 30,000
Net short-term capital loss	4,000
Net long-term capital gain	20,000
Includable gross income from ordinary operations (i.e., in addition to the three items listed above)	160,000
Allowable deductions, exclusive of special deduction for dividends received	70,000

Determine the corporation's total income tax for the year, using the rates appearing in this chapter (assume an 85% dividends received deduction).

23-7. An unmarried taxpayer whose taxable income for the year will exceed $130,000 (marginal income tax rate of 70%) is considering the immediate sale of a highly speculative security (capital asset) which he has held for four months. His cost basis is $10,000 and the current market price is $25,000. (a) Determine the amount of cash, after allowing for the effect of the federal income tax, that the sale of the security in the usual manner would yield. Ignore possible broker's commission. (b) Determine the amount of cash, after allowing for the effect of the federal income tax, that the sale of the security to his church for $10,000 would yield. His total contributions will not exceed the percentage limitations.

PROBLEMS

The following additional problems for this chapter are located in Appendix C: 23-1B, 23-2B, 23-4B, 23-5B.

23-1A. R. L. Foster owns a small office building from which he receives rental income. He uses the cash method of determining income, depositing all rents received from tenants in a special bank account. All disbursements related to the building, as well as occasional unrelated disbursements, are paid by checks drawn on the same account. During the current taxable year ending December 31, he deposited $31,000 of rent receipts in the special account.

Disbursements from the special bank account during the current year are summarized as follows:

Wages of custodian (gross earnings $4,680):	
Withheld for FICA tax and paid to IRS.................	$ 234
Withheld for income tax and paid to IRS................	458
Paid to custodian.......................................	3,988
Real estate tax...	2,110
Payments of personal income tax:	
Applicable to preceding year...........................	1,200
Applicable to current year.............................	4,000
Interest on mortgage note payable on land and office building.	1,400
Installment payments of principal on mortgage note payable..	3,000
Utilities expense.......................................	780
Air-conditioning units installed in two offices not previously air-conditioned.......................................	1,860
Repainting interior of two offices.........................	620
Premium on a three-year insurance policy on the building, effective July 1.......................................	480
Repairs to heating and plumbing equipment...............	340
Payroll tax expense.....................................	234
Contributions:	
United Fund..	250
State University......................................	400
Political party.......................................	100
Miscellaneous expenses incurred in earning rentals...........	537
Purchases of various stocks..............................	6,140

In addition to the foregoing data, you determine from other records and the tax return for the preceding year that the allowable deduction for depreciation expense is $3,800 and that current expirations of insurance premiums paid in earlier years total $275.

Instructions:

Prepare a statement of adjusted gross income from rents, identifying each of the allowable deductions from gross income.

23-2A. James B. Roth, unmarried and entitled to one exemption for himself, is engaged in the practice of architecture. He uses the cash method of determining taxable income and reports on the calendar-year basis. A summary of his record of cash receipts and disbursements for the current calendar year is presented at the top of the next page.

The automobile was used 60% of the time for professional purposes. It is to be depreciated by the declining-balance method at twice the straight-line rate, assuming an estimated life of 3 years. Allocate 60% of the depreciation and other automobile expenses to professional purposes.

Cash Receipts

Professional fees..	$51,200
Borrowed from bank (professional purposes)................	4,000
Inheritance from uncle's estate...........................	3,000
Dividends on corporation stocks.........................	422

Cash Disbursements

Wages of draftsmen and typist:	
Taxes withheld and paid to IRS.....................	$ 1,960
Paid to employees....................................	10,450
Payroll taxes.......................................	817
Fees to collaborating engineers..........................	4,250
Office rent...	3,000
Telephone expense (office)...........................	290
Electricity (office).................................	310
Blueprints..	520
Office supplies expense............................	173
Insurance on office equipment (3-year policy, dated January 1)	123
Partial repayment of bank loan (see receipts)............	1,500
Interest on bank loan...............................	205
Charitable contributions............................	650
Payment on principal of residence mortgage note..........	1,500
Interest on residence mortgage note....................	820
Personal property tax on office equipment................	52
Real estate tax on home.............................	735
State sales tax on purchases for personal use.............	174
State inheritance tax................................	90
New automobile (purchased January 10).................	4,950
Office equipment (purchased at various times)............	900
Automobile operating expenses (exclusive of depreciation)...	610
Purchase of 50 shares of Jackson Corporation stock........	1,720
Payments of estimated income tax for current year........	7,200

The cost of the office equipment owned at the beginning of the year was $2,600, the additions made during the year are indicated above, and none of the equipment was disposed of during the year. Use a composite depreciation rate of 10%, based on the average of the beginning and ending balances.

Instructions:

Prepare a summary of federal income tax data for Roth, applying the appropriate schedule of tax rates presented in this chapter.

23-3A. The preliminary income statement of B. T. Gordon's Hilltop Record Shop appearing at the top of page 608 was prepared as of the close of the calendar year in which the business was established. You are engaged to examine the statement, review the business records, revise the accounting system to the extent necessary, and determine the adjusted gross income.

You obtained the following information during your examination:

(a) The preliminary income statement is a summary of cash receipts and disbursements. Sales to customers on account are not recorded until cash is received; in the meantime they are evidenced only by duplicate sales tickets. Similarly, invoices for merchandise and other purchases are not recorded until payment is made; in the meantime they are filed in an unpaid file.

Sales.................		$89,367
Purchases.............		70,415
Gross profit on sales.		$18,952

Operating expenses:

Salaries..........	$14,460	
Rent............	2,250	
Store equipment..	6,200	
Insurance........	480	
Utilities........	390	
Fuel.............	410	
Advertising......	572	
Taxes...........	796	
Donations........	118	
Miscellaneous....	621	26,297
Net loss..........		$ 7,345

(b) Uncollected sales to customers on account at December 31 amount to $1,984.

(c) Unpaid invoices at December 31 for expenditures of the past year are summarized as follows:

Merchandise............	$6,718
Utilities..............	53
Fuel...................	58

(d) The inventory of merchandise on hand at December 31 amounted to $19,627.

(e) Withdrawals of $5,200 by the owner of the enterprise were included in the amount reported as Salaries.

(f) The agreement with the three part-time salesclerks provides for a bonus equal to 1% of cash collected on sales during the year, payable in January of the following year. (Figure to nearest dollar.)

(g) The rent for January of the following year ($250) was paid and recorded in December.

(h) The store equipment reported in the preliminary income statement was installed on April 5. It has an estimated life of 10 years and no residual value. Depreciation is to be claimed for 9 months, using the declining-balance method at twice the straight-line rate.

(i) A total of $210 of insurance premiums was unexpired at December 31.

(j) Taxes paid are composed of $470 of payroll taxes and $326 of federal income tax of the owner for the preceding year. Accrued payroll taxes and property taxes on the equipment and inventory as of the end of the year total $361.

(k) Payments classified as Donations were contributions to charitable, religious, and educational organizations.

(l) Payments classified as Miscellaneous included $192 of personal expenses of the owner.

Instructions:

Prepare a statement of adjusted gross income from the business for submission with the income tax return of B. T. Gordon, the owner, employing the accrual method of accounting.

23-4A. H. A. Fleming is negotiating the sale of a tract of unimproved land to Desert Estates, Inc. The sales price of the property is to be $90,000, payable in 5 equal annual installments, with the first installment payable during the current year. The property, which was acquired by Fleming as an inheritance a number of years ago, has a cost basis of $10,000.

Mr. and Mrs. Fleming expect to have approximately $12,000 of ordinary taxable income (adjusted gross income less itemized deductions and exemptions) for the current year and for each of the following 4 years, exclusive of the gain on the sale of the land, which qualifies as a long-term capital gain.

Instructions:

(1) Assuming the accuracy of the estimate of future income and no changes in the Internal Revenue Code, determine the Flemings' total estimated federal income tax (joint return) for 5 years, beginning with the current year, based on (a) reporting the entire gain this year and (b) reporting the gain by the installment method. Apply the appropriate schedule of tax rates appearing in this chapter.

(2) What is the amount of federal income tax saved by electing the installment method?

(3) Could the installment method have been elected if the terms had provided for a down payment of one third of the sales price?

23-5A. Late in December, the last month of the current taxable year, Arthur B. Osborn and his wife Helen engage you to prepare their income tax return and to advise them concerning other matters that may affect the amount of their tax liability. They are entitled to a total of five exemptions for themselves and their dependent children. They have been using the cash method of determining taxable income and expect to file a joint return.

Mr. Osborn is employed at a salary of $24,000 for the current year and has been notified that he will receive an increase of $300 per month, effective in January. He has no deductible expenses connected with his employment. Income from dividends for the current year will amount to $900 for Mr. Osborn and $400 for Mrs. Osborn, with a 50% increase expected for the following year.

During the current year Mr. Osborn sold A Company stock at a loss of $1,000. He proposes to sell his holdings of B Company stock before the end of the year. They were acquired three years ago at a cost of $2,000, and the market price, which has been relatively stable, is currently $3,000. He plans to use the funds to pay amounts pledged to his church, $500 for the operating budget and $2,500 for the building fund, both due by the following March 31. He also suggests that it might be advantageous to use the $1,000 loss on the sale of A Company stock as an offset to the gain on B Company stock.

Miscellaneous payments for the current year to date that would qualify as deductions from gross income total $400. In addition, real estate taxes of $350 for the first half of the year have been paid. Unpaid real estate taxes of $350 for the second half of the year are due on December 31 but may be paid as late as January 10 without penalty.

Miscellaneous deductions of $550 are anticipated for the following year; real estate taxes are expected to amount to $1,000 for the following year, and an additional $650 will be pledged to the church for its fiscal year beginning on April 1 of the following year.

Instructions:

(1) Advise the Osborns concerning the contemplated sale of Company B stock and the timing of deductions from adjusted gross income. Consideration is to be given only to the current taxable year and to the following taxable year. The Internal Revenue Code and

regulations, as well as the taxpayers' exemptions, are assumed to remain unchanged during the period, and the estimates for the succeeding years are assumed to be accurate.

(2) Prepare a summary of estimated federal income tax data for the Osborns (a) for the current taxable year and (b) for the following taxable year, assuming that they follow your advice and that the actual amount of income and deductions agrees exactly with the estimates. The itemized deductions from adjusted gross income may be classified as follows: Contributions to church, Real estate taxes, and Miscellaneous. Apply the appropriate schedule of tax rates presented in this chapter.

23-6A. Three married individuals, designated as W, X, and Y, who are engaged in related types of businesses as sole proprietors, plan to combine their enterprises to form Zed Co. They have discussed the relative merits of the partnership and the corporation form of organization, exclusive of the effect of the federal income tax. You are engaged to assemble and analyze the relevant data and to determine the immediate income tax consequences to each of them of the two forms of organization. The consolidation is planned to take effect as of next January 1, the beginning of the company's fiscal year.

The annual net income of the three separate enterprises has typically totaled $100,000. It is anticipated that economies of operation and other advantages of the consolidation will have the immediate effect of increasing annual net income by $20,000, making a total of $120,000 before considering owners' salaries.

Each of the owners is to be assigned managerial duties as a partner, or alternatively, to be designated an officer of the corporation. In either event, each is to be paid an annual salary, which is to be treated as an operating expense of the enterprise. In addition, they plan to distribute $10,000 of earnings annually, which are to be allocated among them in accordance with their original investments. It is anticipated that the remaining earnings will be retained for use in expanding operations. The agreed capital investments, salaries, and distributions of earnings are to be as follows:

	W	X	Y	Total
Capital investment........	$120,000	$200,000	$80,000	$400,000
Salary...................	25,000	15,000	20,000	60,000
Distribution of earnings....	3,000	5,000	2,000	10,000

The estimated adjusted gross income from sources other than Zed Co., for each individual and his wife, and other pertinent data are reported below. The amount of income reported for each includes dividends on corporation stocks in excess of the allowable exclusion, and each files a joint return for the calendar year prepared in accordance with the cash method.

	W	X	Y
Ordinary adjusted gross income, exclusive of salary and net income of Zed Co.....	$26,000	$2,000	$24,000
Allowable deductions from adjusted gross income, including exemptions.........	5,000	3,000	6,000

Instructions:

(1) Present the following reports of estimated results of the first year of operations, based on the assumption that Zed Co. is to be organized as a partnership: (a) Estimated capital statement of the

partners of Zed Co. (b) Statement of estimated federal income tax of W, X, and Y, applying the appropriate schedule of tax rates presented in this chapter.

(2) Present the following reports of estimated results of the first year of operations, based on the assumption that Zed Co. is to be organized as a corporation: (a) Statement of estimated federal income tax of Zed Co., applying the corporation tax rates presented in this chapter. (b) Estimated statement of stockholders' equity of each of the stockholders in Zed Co., allocating each increase and decrease in the manner employed in (1a) above. (c) Estimated federal income tax of W, X, and Y, applying the appropriate schedule of tax rates presented in this chapter.

(3) Present a report comparing the estimated federal income tax effects of the two methods of organization on each of the three individuals. For purposes of this report, the income tax on the corporation should be allocated among the individuals, as in (2b) above.

23-7 A. James and Lois Morton, each of whom is entitled to one exemption, have 2 dependent children. The older child, 18 years of age, earned $850 during the year, and the younger child earned $210. Mr. Morton also contributed more than half of the cost of supporting his mother, who received gross income of $675 during the year. During the current year ended December 31, Mr. Morton realized a net short-term capital gain of $1,800 and Mrs. Morton incurred a net long-term capital loss of $600. Other details of their receipts and disbursements during the year are presented below.

Cash Receipts

James Morton:

Salary as sales manager of Astrasonic Co.	$31,310
(Earnings, $48,000. Withholding: income tax $12,300; FICA tax, $390; purchases of Astrasonic stock, $4,000)	
Interest on bonds of City of Fresno.	480
Dividends on corporation stocks.	710

Lois Morton:

Withdrawals of net income from Lang & Associates, a partnership in which she is a partner (distributive share of the net income for the year, $9,800).	4,800
Rent from property owned.	8,000
Insurance proceeds (death of father).	15,000
Dividends on corporation stocks.	92
Interest on short-term U.S. Treasury bills.	631

Cash Disbursements

James Morton:

Charitable contributions.	2,410
Interest on mortgage on residence.	792
Automobile license fees (family cars).	42
Real estate tax on residence.	1,136
State sales tax on items purchased for personal or family use.	297
State gasoline tax (family cars).	102
Federal gasoline tax (family cars).	67
Damages for accidental injury suffered by visitor, not compensated by insurance.	2,000
Payments of estimated income tax for current year.	4,800

Lois Morton:
    Rental property:
        Real estate tax.................................... 624
        Insurance (one-year policies)...................... 106
        Painting and repairs.............................. 875
    Mortgage note payments:
        Principal... 3,000
        Interest.. 1,256
            (Building was acquired several years ago at a cost of
            $60,000 and is being depreciated at the rate of 4%)
    Charitable contributions............................. 443

Instructions:

Prepare a summary of federal income tax data for the Mortons, applying the appropriate schedule of tax rates presented in this chapter.

612

24

Cost and revenue
relationships
for management

Alternative concepts of cost and revenue

One of the primary objectives of accounting is the determination of net income. For this purpose costs are classified as either assets or expenses. The costs of properties or services acquired that are on hand at any particular time represent assets. As the assets are sold or consumed they become expenses. This concept of cost has been explored in detail in earlier chapters. Various criteria for determining when revenues should be recognized and reported in the income statement were also described and discussed.

Another important objective of accounting is to provide data that will be useful to management in analyzing and resolving current problems and making plans for the future. For any particular business problem there may be a variety of possible solutions, only one of which can be selected. Much of the analysis involved in consideration of alternatives is concerned with costs and revenues. Useful data on past costs and revenues may be available in the ledger, but there are some situations, particularly those related to proposed new projects, in which relevant data cannot be found there. In any case, the record of past events alone is seldom an adequate basis for a decision affecting the future. The more important cost and revenue concepts and relationships, and their application to decision making, are described in this chapter.

Historical cost and replacement cost

As used in a broad generic sense, the term "cost" means the amount of money or other property expended, or liability or other obligation incurred, for goods or services purchased. References to the amount of property expended or liability incurred for goods or services may be expressed by the shorter phrase "cash or equivalent." The element of time is important in discussions of cost, often necessitating the use of the adjective "historical" or "replacement."

Historical cost is the cash or equivalent outlay for goods or services actually acquired. *Actual cost* is sometimes used to mean the same thing, particularly if comparisons are being made with estimates or standards. Historical costs are recorded in the ledgers and other basic accounting records; the expired portions are reported as expenses in the income statement and the unexpired portions are reported as assets in the balance sheet. Historical costs are relevant in the determination of periodic net income and current financial status. They may be of only slight consequence or entirely irrelevant, however, in planning for the future.

Replacement cost is the cost of replacing an asset at current market prices. In many planning situations the cost of replacing an asset is of greater significance than its historical cost. To illustrate, assume that an offer is received for goods to be manufactured at a specific price. Assume also that there is a sufficient quantity of unprocessed materials in stock that were acquired at a considerably higher cost than current market prices. In deciding whether to accept the offer, it is the replacement cost of the materials that is significant. It might be advisable to accept the offer even though, on the basis of historical costs, a loss is likely to result.

Replacement cost analysis is useful in planning the replacement of worn-out or obsolete plant assets. Because of technological improvements and other changes in physical characteristics, new equipment is rarely identical with the asset it replaces. The cost of the replacement asset is also likely to differ from the cost of the original asset, in part because of changes in price levels. A variant of this type of analysis is to compare annual depreciation expense based on historical cost with depreciation based on estimated replacement cost. The difference between the two represents the estimated amount of net income that should be retained in order to maintain the productive capacity of the physical plant. If, for example, depreciation expense recorded for the year is $120,000 and depreciation based on estimated replacement cost is $200,000, it may be prudent for the board of directors to authorize an $80,000 appropriation of retained earnings for "replacement of facilities." In any event there should be a realization by management that if the replacement of facilities is not to be financed in part by earnings, it may be necessary to issue more stock or debt obligations.

The significance of replacement cost, adjusted for depreciation, in the admission or the withdrawal of a partner was considered in an earlier chapter. Similar analyses play a significant role in negotiations for the purchase and the sale of a going business, in the merging of two separate enterprises, and in weighing the consequences of liquidating an enterprise. The values finally placed on plant assets in such situations are greatly influenced by the bargaining process, but consideration of replacement cost is often the starting point.

Absorption costing and variable costing

The cost of manufactured products is customarily considered to be composed of direct materials, direct labor, and factory overhead. All such costs ultimately become a part of the finished goods inventory and remain there as an asset until the goods are sold. This is the conventional treatment of manufacturing costs. It is sometimes referred to as *absorption costing* because of all costs being "absorbed" into finished goods. Although the concept is indispensable in the determination of historical cost and taxable net income, another costing concept may be more useful to management in making decisions.

The concept of *variable costing*, which is also termed *direct costing*, considers the cost of products manufactured to be composed only of those manufacturing costs that increase or decrease as the volume of production rises or falls. According to this point of view, the cost of finished goods includes, in addition to direct materials and direct labor, only those factory overhead costs which vary with the rate of production. The remaining overhead costs, which are the nonvariable or fixed items, are related to the productive capacity of the manufacturing plant and are not affected by changes in the quantity of product manufactured. Accordingly, the nonvariable overhead does not become a part of the costs of finished goods but is considered to be an expense of the period.

Variable costing and the income statement

The arrangement of data in the variable costing income statement differs considerably from the format of the conventional income statement. Variable costs and expenses are presented as separate categories from fixed costs and expenses, with significant summarizing amounts inserted at intermediate points. The differences between the two forms may be observed by comparing two income statements prepared from the same basic information. To illustrate, assume an enterprise engaged in manufacturing a single product. During the first month of operations it produced 15,000 units, of which 12,000 were sold for $120,000 and 3,000 units remained in the inventory. Costs and expenses for the month, identified as to variable and fixed, are given on the next page.

615

	TOTAL COST OR EXPENSE	NUMBER OF UNITS	UNIT COST
Manufacturing costs:			
Variable...............	$ 75,000	15,000	$5
Fixed.................	30,000	15,000	2
Total...............	$105,000		$7
Selling and general expenses:			
Variable...............	$ 12,000		
Fixed.................	10,000		
Total...............	$ 22,000		

The two income statements are presented below. Memorandum data are inserted parenthetically as an aid to understanding the computed amounts.

ABSORPTION COSTING INCOME STATEMENT

Sales..		$120,000
Cost of goods sold:		
Cost of goods manufactured (15,000 × $7).................	$105,000	
Less ending inventory (3,000 × $7)......................	21,000	
Cost of goods sold.....................................		84,000
Gross profit on sales....................................		$ 36,000
Selling and general expenses ($12,000 + $10,000).............		22,000
Net income from operations...............................		$ 14,000

VARIABLE COSTING INCOME STATEMENT

Sales..		$120,000
Variable cost of goods sold:		
Variable cost of goods manufactured (15,000 × $5)..........	$ 75,000	
Less ending inventory (3,000 × $5)......................	15,000	
Variable cost of goods sold............................		60,000
Manufacturing margin.....................................		$ 60,000
Variable selling and general expenses.......................		12,000
Marginal income..		$ 48,000
Fixed costs and expenses:		
Fixed manufacturing costs..............................	$ 30,000	
Fixed selling and general expenses......................	10,000	40,000
Net income from operations...............................		$ 8,000

Comparison of absorption costing and variable costing income statements

In the absorption costing income statement, both fixed and variable manufacturing costs are included in cost of goods sold, and the excess of sales over cost of goods sold is identified as gross profit on sales. In the variable costing income statement, only the variable manufacturing costs are included in cost of goods sold; the excess of sales over the variable cost of goods sold is termed *manufacturing margin*. Deduction of the variable selling and general expenses from manufacturing margin yields *marginal income*, which is the remaining amount of revenue available for fixed manufacturing costs, fixed expenses, and net income. The fixed costs and expenses are then deducted from marginal income to yield net income from operations.

When the level of inventory fluctuates from period to period, the net income reported under absorption costing differs from that reported under variable costing. The difference in net income arises because absorption costing, by including the fixed factory overhead as a part of the cost of the product produced, defers to another period that portion of the fixed factory overhead included in inventory on hand, whereas variable costing includes all the fixed factory overhead costs incurred during the period as expenses of the period. In a period in which the level of inventory increases, such as in the illustration above, the net income reported by absorption costing will be larger than the net income reported by variable costing. In the illustration this difference of $6,000 ($14,000 − $8,000) is composed of the $2 unit cost of fixed factory overhead multiplied by the 3,000 units of product remaining in the inventory. When inventory decreases, the effect is reversed; that is, a smaller net income will be reported if absorption costing is used.

Variable costing as a managerial aid

Many concepts of cost and revenue are useful to management in making decisions. Some of these concepts, however, are not acceptable for published financial statements which report the results of operations and financial condition to stockholders, creditors, and others outside the management group. Variable costing is one such concept.[1] Although it cannot be used for published financial statements or generally for federal income tax purposes, variable costing can be very useful to management in making decisions relating to cost control, product pricing, production planning, and other management functions.

Variable costing as an aid in cost control

All costs are controllable by someone within the firm, but they are not all controllable at the same level of management. For example, a plant foreman has control over the use of materials in his department, but he cannot control the cost of insurance on the building that houses his department. For a specific level of management, *controllable costs* are costs that it controls directly, and *uncontrollable costs* are costs that another level of management controls. This distinction, as applied to specific levels of management, is useful in fixing the responsibility for incurrence

617

---

[1] *Accounting Research and Terminology Bulletins,* "No. 43, Restatement and Revision of Accounting Research Bulletins" (New York: American Institute of Certified Public Accountants, 1961), pp. 28–29.

of costs and then for reporting the cost data to those responsible for cost control. The term sometimes applied to this concept is *responsibility accounting*.

Variable manufacturing costs are responsive to the control of the operating level of management because they vary with changes in production. By including only the variable manufacturing costs in the cost of the product, variable costing provides a product cost figure that is subject to control by operating management. The fixed factory overhead costs are ordinarily the responsibility of a higher echelon of management. When the fixed factory overhead costs are reported as a separate item in the variable costing income statement, they are easier to identify and control than when they are spread among units of product as in absorption costing.

As is the case with the fixed and variable manufacturing costs, the control of the variable and fixed operating expenses are ordinarily the responsibility of different echelons of management. Under variable costing, the variable selling and general expenses are reported in a separate category from the fixed selling and general expenses. Because they are reported in this manner, both types of operating expenses are easier to identify and control than is the case under absorption costing where they are not reported separately.

Variable costing as an aid in pricing

Many factors enter into the determination of the selling price of a product. The cost of making the product is obviously a significant factor. Microeconomic theory deduces, from a set of restrictive assumptions, that income is maximized by expanding output to the volume where the revenue realized by the sale of the final unit (marginal revenue) is equaled by the cost of that unit (marginal cost). Since the exact information assumed in economic theory is rarely available, a firm can seldom make the precise adjustments in selling price that are necessary to maximize income. Nevertheless, the concepts of marginal revenue and marginal cost can be used in pricing decisions.

In the short run, the firm is committed to the existing capacity of its manufacturing facilities, and the pricing decision should be based upon making the best use of such capacity. The fixed costs and expenses cannot be avoided, but the variable costs and expenses can be eliminated if the company does not manufacture the product. The selling price of a product therefore should not be less than the variable costs and expenses of making and selling it. Any revenue resulting from a selling price in excess of variable costs and expenses contributes toward covering fixed costs and expenses and providing net income. Variable costing procedures yield data which emphasize these relationships.

In the long run, plant capacity can be increased or decreased, and if an enterprise is to continue in business, the selling prices of its products must be sufficient to cover all costs and expenses and provide a reasonable net income. Hence, in establishing pricing policies for the long run, information provided by absorption costing procedures is needed. There are no simple solutions to most pricing problems; consideration must be given to many factors of varying importance. Accounting can contribute by preparing analyses of various pricing plans for both the short run and the long run.

Variable costing as an aid in production planning

Production planning has both short-run and long-run implications. In the short run, production is limited to existing capacity, and operating decisions must be made promptly before opportunities are lost. For example, a company manufacturing products with a seasonal demand may have an opportunity to obtain an off-season order that will not compete with regular products. The relevant factors for such a short-run decision are the revenues and the variable costs and expenses. If the revenues from the special order will provide marginal income, the order should be accepted because it will add to the company's net income.

In production planning, then, variable costing, by including only the variable costs in product cost and by separating the variable operating expenses from the fixed operating expenses, supplies the cost data in a format especially useful for short-run decision making. For long-run planning, management must also consider the fixed costs and expenses.

619

Applications of variable costing

To control and plan operations, management needs information on the profitability of the various segments of its business, such as types of products, sales territories, and methods of distributing the products. Variable costing makes a significant contribution to management decision making in providing data for effective profit planning in such areas. Two aspects of profit planning are (1) determination of the most profitable sales mix of a company's products and (2) determination of the contribution being made by each sales territory.

Sales mix studies

Sales mix is generally defined as the relative distribution of sales among the various products. Ordinarily some lines are more profitable than others, and management should concentrate its sales efforts on those products that will provide the maximum total net income. The marginal income and the amount of production facilities required to produce each product are two important factors for management to consider in selecting the products that should be emphasized in sales promotion.

The illustrative statement presented below is an example of the type of data needed for an evaluation of sales mix. The hypothetical enterprise, which manufactures two products and is operating at full capacity, is considering the advisability of changing the emphasis of its advertising and other promotional efforts.

Marginal Income by Unit of Product
April 15, 19--

	PRODUCT A	PRODUCT B
Sales price...	$6.00	$8.50
Variable cost of goods sold......................	3.50	5.50
Manufacturing margin.............................	$2.50	$3.00
Variable selling and general expenses..........	1.00	1.00
Marginal income..................................	$1.50	$2.00

Marginal income statement — unit of product

The statement indicates that Product B yields a greater amount of marginal income per unit than Product A and hence provides the larger contribution to the recovery of fixed costs and expenses and the realization of net income. If the amount of productive facilities devoted to each product is assumed to be equal, it is obvious that it would be desirable to increase the sales of Product B. However, if it is assumed that Product B requires double the amount of production facilities that are devoted to Product A, the conclusion would be different. Under the latter assumption, the production of one additional unit of Product B would require a decrease of two units of Product A. The effect on marginal income would be an increase of $2 (Product B) and a decrease of $3 (Product A), or a net decrease of $1. Under such circumstances, a change in sales mix designed to increase sales of Product A would be desirable.

Sales mix studies are based on assumptions, such as the ability to sell one product in place of another and the ability to convert production facilities to accommodate manufacture of one product instead of another. Research relating to sales mix studies indicates that they often affect only small segments of a company's total operations. In such cases, changes in sales mix can often be made within the limits of existing capacity, and the presentation of cost and revenue data in the variable costing form is useful in achieving the most profitable sales mix.

Contribution of sales territories

An income statement presenting the marginal income by sales territories is often useful to management in appraising past performance and in directing operations. An income statement prepared in such a format is illustrated below in abbreviated form.

Marginal Income Statement by Sales Territory
For Month Ended July 31, 19--

	TERRITORY A	TERRITORY B	TOTAL
Sales.....................................	$210,000	$335,000	$545,000
Less variable costs and expenses..........	126,000	167,500	293,500
Marginal income.......................	$ 84,000	$167,500	$251,500
Less fixed costs and expenses.............			198,000
Net income from operations.............			$ 53,500

Marginal income statement — sales territories

In addition to sales volume and marginal income, the marginal income ratio for each territory is of importance to management. For Territory A the ratio is 40% ($84,000 ÷ $210,000), and for Territory B it is 50% ($167,000 ÷ $335,000). The marginal income ratio is useful in comparing sales territories, evaluating performance, and directing operations toward more profitable activities.

Differential analysis

Planning for future operations is chiefly decision making. For some decisions, revenue and cost information drawn from the general ledger and other basic accounting records is very useful. For example, historical cost data in the absorption costing format are helpful in setting pricing policies for the long run, and historical cost data in the variable costing format are useful for pricing decisions affecting the short run. However, the revenue and cost data needed to evaluate courses of future operations or to choose among competing alternatives are often not available in the basic accounting records.

The relevant revenue and cost data in the analysis of future possibilities are the differences between the alternatives under consideration. The amounts of such differences are called *differentials* and the area of accounting concerned with the effect of alternative courses of action on revenues and costs is called *differential analysis.*

Differential revenue is the amount of increase or decrease in revenue expected from a particular course of action as compared with an alternative. To illustrate, assume that an enterprise is considering the manufacture and sale of Product X as compared with the manufacture and sale of Product Y. Analysis of the market indicates probable monthly revenue of $50,000 from sales of Product X as compared with probable monthly revenue of $75,000 from sales of Product Y. The anticipated differential revenue from the latter course of action would be $25,000.

Differential cost is the amount of increase or decrease in cost that is expected from a particular course of action as compared with an alternative. For example, if an increase in advertising expenditures from $100,000 to $150,000 is contemplated, the differential cost of the undertaking would be $50,000.

Accountants often use the term *sunk costs* to refer to costs that will not be affected by subsequent decisions. Because sunk costs cannot be changed, they should be ignored in differential analysis. To illustrate, assume that alternative uses are being considered for a plant asset that was acquired for $100,000. The $100,000 cost is a sunk cost and can be ignored in evaluating the proposals for its use. If the choice is between using the asset to manufacture Product X or Product Y, the factors to be considered are the differential revenue and the differential cost associated with the two products; the cost of the plant asset is irrelevant.

Use of differential analysis

Differential analyses can be used advantageously by management in arriving at decisions on a variety of alternatives, such as (1) whether equipment should be leased or sold, (2) whether or not to obtain additional business at a special price, (3) whether to discontinue an unprofitable endeavor, (4) whether to manufacture or purchase a needed part, (5) whether to replace usable plant assets, (6) whether to expand or contract production capacity, and (7) whether to introduce new products or abandon old products. The remainder of the chapter is devoted to the use of differential analysis in analyzing some of these alternatives.

Lease or sell

The principal advantage of differential analysis, as illustrated in this first example, is its selection of relevant revenues and costs related to alternate courses of action. Differential analysis reports emphasize the significant factors of a problem, help to clarify the issues, and conserve the time of the reader.

Assume that an enterprise is considering the disposal of an item of equipment that is no longer needed in the business. Its original cost is $100,000 and accumulated depreciation to date totals $60,000. It is believed that it can be sold through a broker for $50,000 less a 6% commission. A tentative offer has been received to lease the machine for a number of years for a total of $80,000, after which the machine would be sold as scrap for a negligible amount. The repair, insurance, and property tax expenses during the period of the lease are estimated at $17,500. The decision to be made is whether the equipment should be leased or sold. The report of the analysis is presented at the top of the next page.

Proposal to Lease or Sell Equipment
June 22, 19—

Differential revenue from alternatives:

Revenue from lease	$80,000	
Proceeds from sale	50,000	
Differential revenue from lease		$30,000

Differential cost of alternatives:

Estimated repair, insurance, and property tax expenses during lease	$17,500	
Commission expense on sale	3,000	
Differential cost of lease		14,500

Net advantage of lease alternative	$15,500

Differential analysis report — lease or sell

It should be noted that it was not necessary to consider the $40,000 book value ($100,000 − $60,000) of the equipment. As a sunk cost it had no bearing on the decision. Only those alternative revenues and costs associated with future transactions were relevant. The validity of the above report can be verified by the following conventional analysis:

Lease alternative:

Revenue from lease		$80,000	
Depreciation expense	$40,000		
Estimated repair, insurance, and property tax expense	17,500	57,500	
Net gain			$22,500

Sell alternative:

Sale price		$50,000	
Book value of equipment	$40,000		
Commission expense	3,000	43,000	
Net gain			7,000

Net advantage of lease alternative	$15,500

The alternatives presented in the illustration were relatively uncomplicated. Regardless of the number and complexity of the additional factors that may be involved, the approach to differential analysis remains basically the same. Two factors that frequently need to be considered are (1) the differential revenue from investing the funds generated by the alternatives and (2) the income tax differential. In the example above there would undoubtedly be a differential advantage to the immediate investment of the $47,000 net proceeds from the sale over the investment of the net proceeds from the lease arrangement, which would become available over a period of years. The income tax differential would be that related to the differences in timing of the income from the alternatives and the differences in the amount of investment income.

Acceptance of business at a special price

In considering the advisability of accepting additional business at a special price, management must consider the differential revenue that would be provided and the differential cost that would be incurred. If the company is operating at full capacity, the additional production will increase both fixed and variable production costs; but if the normal production of the company is below full capacity, additional business may be undertaken without increasing fixed production costs. In the latter case, the variable costs will be the differential cost of the additional production; they are the only costs pertinent in making a decision to accept or reject the order. If the operating expenses are subject to change, these differentials must also be considered.

To illustrate, assume that the usual monthly production of an enterprise is 10,000 units of a particular commodity. At this level of operation, which is well below capacity, the manufacturing cost is $6.50 per unit, composed of variable costs of $4 and fixed costs of $2.50. The selling price of the product in the domestic market is $10. The manufacturer receives an offer from an exporter for 5,000 units of the product at $6 each. Production can be spread over a three-month period without interfering with normal production or incurring overtime costs. Pricing policies in the domestic market will also not be affected. Comparison of a sales price of $6 with the present unit cost of $6.50 would indicate the advisability of rejecting the offer. However, if attention is confined to the differential cost, which in this case is composed of the variable costs and expenses, the conclusion is quite different. The essentials of the analysis can be presented in the following brief report:

Proposal to Sell to Exporter
March 10, 19--

Differential revenue from acceptance of offer:	
Revenue from sale of 5,000 additional units at $6.....................	$30,000
Differential cost of acceptance of offer:	
Variable costs and expenses of 5,000 additional units at $4..............	20,000
Gain from acceptance of offer.......................................	$10,000

Differential analysis report — sale at special price

Proposals to sell an increased output in the domestic market at a reduced price may necessitate additional considerations of a complex nature. It would clearly be inadvisable to increase sales volume in one territory by means of a price reduction if sales volume would thereby be jeopardized in other areas. Manufacturers must also exercise care to avoid violations of the Robinson-Patman Act, which prohibits price discrimination within the United States unless the difference in price can be justified by a difference in the cost of serving different customers.

Discontinuance of an unprofitable endeavor

If a department, branch, territory, or other segment of an enterprise is operating at a loss, management may be faced with the decision of whether or not to eliminate the unprofitable endeavor. It might be assumed that the net income of the enterprise as a whole will be increased by discontinuing the unsuccessful activity. Discontinuance of the losing venture will eliminate the variable costs and expenses of the activity. However, if the losing venture represents a relatively minor segment of the enterprise, the fixed costs and expenses such as depreciation, property taxes, and insurance will continue even though the operation is terminated. It is entirely possible in this situation for the total net income of a company to be reduced rather than increased by eliminating an unprofitable endeavor. As a basis for illustrating this type of situation, an income statement for the year just ended, which was a normal year, is presented below. For purposes of the illustration it is assumed that discontinuance of Product C, on which losses are incurred annually, will have no effect on the aggregate fixed costs and expenses.

Condensed Income Statement
For Year Ended August 31, 19--

	PRODUCT			
	A	B	C	TOTAL
Sales.....................	$400,000	$500,000	$100,000	$1,000,000
Cost of goods sold:				
Variable costs..............	$200,000	$220,000	$ 60,000	$ 480,000
Fixed costs...............	80,000	120,000	20,000	220,000
Total cost of goods sold.........	$280,000	$340,000	$ 80,000	$ 700,000
Gross profit on sales.............	$120,000	$160,000	$ 20,000	$ 300,000
Operating expenses:				
Variable expenses.............	$ 60,000	$ 95,000	$ 25,000	$ 180,000
Fixed expenses...............	20,000	25,000	6,000	51,000
Total operating expenses........	$ 80,000	$120,000	$ 31,000	$ 231,000
Net income (loss) from operations......	$ 40,000	$ 40,000	$(11,000)	$ 69,000

Data on the estimated differential revenue and differential cost associated with discontinuing Product C, which had a net loss of $11,000 for the past year, may be assembled in a report as shown below.

Proposal to Discontinue Product C
September 29, 19--

Differential revenue from annual sales of product:		
Revenue from sales.....................................		$100,000
Differential cost of annual sales of product:		
Variable cost of goods sold............................	$60,000	
Variable operating expenses...........................	25,000	85,000
Net annual gain from sales of Product C.................		$ 15,000

Differential analysis report — discontinuance of unprofitable endeavor

Instead of an increase in annual net income to $80,000 (Product A, $40,000; Product B, $40,000) that might seem to be indicated by the income statement, the discontinuance of Product C would reduce net income to an estimated $54,000 ($69,000 — $15,000). If plant capacity made available by discontinuance of a losing operation can be utilized in some other manner or if plant capacity can be reduced with a consequent reduction in fixed costs and expenses, additional analysis would, of course, be required.

In decisions involving the elimination of an unprofitable endeavor, management must also consider such other factors as the effect of such a decision on employees and customers. If a segment of the business is discontinued, some employees may have to be discharged and others may have to be relocated and retrained. Also important is the possible loss of customers who may be attracted to the firm by that segment of the business.

Make or buy

A substantial element of manufacturing operations is often the assembly of numerous parts. Many of the large factory complexes of automobile manufacturers are specifically designated as assembly plants. Some of the components of the finished automobile, such as the motor, are produced by the automobile manufacturer, while other parts, such as tires, are often purchased from other manufacturers. Even in manufacturing the motors, such items as spark plugs, nuts and bolts, and other items may be acquired from suppliers in their finished state. When parts or components are purchased, it is generally because management has evaluated the question of "make or buy" and has concluded that a savings in cost results from buying the part rather than manufacturing it. However, "make or buy" options are likely to arise anew when a manufacturer has excess productive capacity with attendant unused equipment, space, and labor.

As a basis for illustrating make or buy alternatives, assume that a manufacturer has been purchasing a component, Part X, for $5 a unit. The factory is currently operating at 80% of capacity and no significant increase in production is anticipated in the near future. The cost of manufacturing Part X, determined by absorption costing methods, is estimated at $1 for direct materials, $2 for direct labor, and $3 for factory overhead (at the predetermined rate of 150% of direct labor cost), or a total of $6. The decision based on a simple comparison of a "make" price of $6 with a "buy" price of $5 is obvious. However, to the extent that unused capacity could be used in manufacturing the part, there would be no increase in the total amount of fixed factory overhead costs; hence only the variable factory overhead costs need to be considered. Variable factory overhead costs such as power, lubricants, and maintenance are determined to amount to approximately 65% of direct labor cost. The cost factors to be considered are summarized in the report below.

Proposal to Manufacture Part X
February 15, 19--

Purchase price of part....................................		$5.00
Estimated cost to manufacture part:		
Direct materials..	$1.00	
Direct labor...	2.00	
Variable factory overhead..............................	1.30	4.30
Cost reduction from manufacturing Part X...................		$ .70

Differential analysis report — make or buy

Other possible effects of a change in policy should also be considered, such as the possibility of a future increase in volume of production that would necessitate the use of the presently idle capacity of 20%. The possible effect of the alternatives on employees and on future business relations with the supplier of the part, who may be providing other essential components, are additional factors that might require study.

Equipment replacement

The usefulness of plant assets may be impaired long before they are considered to be "worn out." Equipment may be not ideally adequate for the purpose for which it is used, but on the other hand it may not have reached the point of complete inadequacy. Similarly, the point in time when equipment becomes obsolete may be difficult to determine. Decisions to replace usable plant assets should be based on studies of relevant costs rather than on caprice or subjective opinions. The costs to be considered are the alternative future costs of retention as opposed to replacement. Sunk costs are irrelevant.

To illustrate some of the factors involved in replacement decisions, assume that an enterprise is contemplating the disposal for $25,000 of several identical machines having a total book value of $100,000 and an estimated remaining life of five years. The old equipment would be replaced by a single high-speed machine at a cost of $250,000, with an estimated useful life of five years and negligible residual value. Analysis of the specifications of the new machine and of accompanying changes in manufacturing methods indicate an estimated annual reduction in variable manufacturing costs from $225,000 to $150,000. No other changes in the manufacturing costs or the operating expenses are expected. The basic data to be considered may be summarized in a report similar to that illustrated at the top of the next page.

Annual variable costs associated with present equipment.......	$225,000	
Annual variable costs associated with proposed new equipment..	150,000	
Annual reduction in variable costs.........................	$ 75,000	
Number of years applicable................................	× 5	
Cost reduction attributable to difference in variable costs.......	$375,000	
Proceeds from sale of present equipment....................	25,000	$400,000
Cost of new equipment....................................		250,000
Net cost reduction anticipated from replacement, 5-year total...		$150,000
Annual cost reduction anticipated.........................		$ 30,000

Differential analysis report — equipment replacement

Complicating features could be added to the foregoing illustration, such as a disparity between the remaining useful life of the old equipment and the estimated life of the new equipment, or possible improvement in the product attributable to the new machine, with consequent increase in selling price or volume of sales. Another factor that should be considered is the importance of alternative uses for the cash outlay necessary to acquire the new equipment. The increase in net income that would result from the best available alternative to the proposed use of resources is sometimes called *opportunity cost*. If, for example, it is assumed that the use of the $225,000 of additional funds required to replace the equipment would yield a 10% return, the opportunity cost of the replacement proposal would be $22,500.

It should be noted that the term "opportunity cost" introduces a new concept of "cost." In reality it is not a cost in any usual sense of the word; instead it represents the foregoing of possible income. The term is unquestionably useful nevertheless.

628

QUESTIONS

1. (a) Differentiate between historical cost and replacement cost. (b) Why would replacement costs be more useful than historical costs in preparing a capital expenditures budget?

2. What is the basic difference between absorption costing and variable costing?

3. If the variable costing concept is followed, which of the following costs would be included as part of the cost of product manufactured: (a) depreciation on plant, (b) direct labor, (c) direct materials, (d) property taxes on plant, (e) insurance on plant, and (f) electricity purchased to operate machinery.

4. How are the fixed factory overhead (fixed manufacturing) costs reported on the variable costing income statement?

5. How is *manufacturing margin* determined on the variable costing income statement?

6. How is *marginal income* determined on the variable costing income statement?

7. What types of costs and expenses are included in the fixed costs and expenses category on income statements prepared on the basis of variable costing?

8. For the period in which the level of inventory increases, would the net income reported by absorption costing be larger or smaller than the net income reported by variable costing? Explain.

9. Is variable costing generally acceptable for use in (a) published financial statements and (b) federal income tax returns?

10. Inasmuch as all costs of operating a business are controllable, what is the significance of the term *uncontrollable cost?*

11. What is meant by *responsibility accounting?*

12. Discuss how the use of financial data prepared on the basis of variable costing can assist management in the development of short-run pricing policies.

13. Explain the meaning of (a) *differential revenue* and (b) *differential cost.*

14. Thompson Lumber Co., which currently sells its lumber in "rough-cut" form at $70 per thousand board feet, is considering the possibility of extending the processing operations to a point where the lumber can be sold at $80 per thousand board feet. The current cost of processing is $15 per thousand board feet, and it is estimated that if the processing is extended the total processing cost will increase to $23 per thousand board feet. What is the amount of (a) the differential revenue and (b) the differential cost to be considered in arriving at a decision?

15. (a) What is meant by *sunk costs?* (b) A company is contemplating replacing an old piece of machinery, which cost $25,000 and has accumulated depreciation to date of $20,000, with a new machine costing $40,000. What is the sunk cost in this situation?

16. Franklin Company manufactures three products. The income statement for the current year is presented below.

| | Product | | | |
	A	B	C	Total
Sales....................	$420,000	$65,000	$325,000	$810,000
Less variable costs and expenses..	255,000	45,000	205,000	505,000
Marginal income.............	$165,000	$20,000	$120,000	$305,000
Less fixed costs and expenses.....	135,500	25,500	94,000	255,000
Net income or (loss)...........	$ 29,500	$ (5,500)	$ 26,000	$ 50,000

Management anticipates no significant change in the sales volume or the variable costs and expenses associated with the production and sale of Product B and proposes that it be dropped from the product line. If Product B is discontinued, the fixed costs and expenses will not be materially affected. Do you agree with management's proposal? Explain.

17. (a) What is meant by *opportunity cost?* **(b)** Hillcrest Company is currently earning 5% on $100,000 invested in marketable securities. It proposes to use the $100,000 to acquire plant facilities to manufacture a new product that is expected to add $7,500 to net income. What is the opportunity cost involved in the decision to produce the new product?

EXERCISES

24-1. Matson Company is contemplating purchasing the net assets of Owens Lumber Company. Owens Lumber Company has lumber on hand that cost $95,000 and is included in its accounts at that figure. Its replacement cost is $110,000. **(a)** At what figure should the inventory of lumber be included on the balance sheet of Owens Lumber Company? Briefly explain the reason for your answer. **(b)** How much might Matson Company be expected to pay for the inventory if it purchases the net assets of Owens Lumber Company? Briefly explain the reason for your answer.

24-2. On March 1, Doyle Company began operations and operated at 100% of capacity during the month. The following data summarizes the results for March:

Sales (15,000 units)		$112,750
Production costs (20,000 units):		
Direct materials..................	$50,000	
Direct labor.....................	30,000	
Variable factory overhead..........	20,000	
Fixed factory overhead............	12,000	112,000
Selling and general expenses:		
Variable selling and general expenses.	$ 7,500	
Fixed selling and general expenses....	6,750	14,250

630

(a) Prepare an income statement in accordance with the absorption costing concept. **(b)** Prepare an income statement in accordance with the variable costing concept. **(c)** What is the reason for the difference in the amount of net income reported in (a) and (b)?

24-3. Gilbert Company normally operates at 90% of productive capacity, producing 4,500 grinders per month. The total manufacturing costs for a normal month are typically as follows:

Direct materials............	$135,000
Direct labor...............	112,500
Variable factory overhead....	67,500
Fixed factory overhead......	90,000
Total manufacturing costs..	$405,000

The company has been invited by a governmental agency to submit a bid for 200 grinders to be delivered within a month. If the contract is obtained, it is anticipated that the additional activity will not interfere with normal production or increase the selling or general expenses. **(a)** What is the present unit product cost on an absorption costing basis? **(b)** What is the present unit product cost on a variable costing basis? **(c)** What is the unit cost below which the Gilbert Company should not go in bidding on the government contract? **(d)** Is a unit cost figure based on absorption costing or one based on variable costing more useful in arriving at a bid on this contract? Explain.

24-4. Osborn Manufacturing Company has a plant capacity of 200,000 units, but production currently is 175,000 units. Fixed costs and expenses are $262,500 and variable costs and expenses are $5 per unit. The present selling price is $7.50 per unit. On October 15 the company received an offer from Beck Company for 15,000 units of the product at $7 each. The Beck Company will market the units in Canada under its own brand name. The additional business is not expected to affect the regular selling price or quantity of sales of Osborn Manufacturing Company. (a) Prepare a differential analysis report for the proposed sale to Beck Company. (b) Briefly explain the reason why the acceptance of this additional business will increase net income. (c) What is the minimum price per unit that would produce marginal income?

24-5. An income statement by product line for Root Manufacturing Company indicated a net loss for Product A of $20,000 for the past year. Because of this net loss, management is giving consideration to the elimination of the unprofitable endeavor. The net loss resulted from sales of $200,000, cost of goods sold of $130,000, and operating expenses of $90,000. It is estimated that 25% of cost of goods sold represents fixed factory overhead costs and that 40% of operating expenses is fixed. Since Product A is only one of many products, the fixed costs and expenses will not be materially affected if the product is discontinued. (a) Prepare a differential analysis report dated January 30 of the current year for the proposed discontinuance of Product A. (b) Should Product A be retained? Explain.

24-6. Neff Company has been purchasing carrying cases for its portable typewriters at a delivered cost of $8 per unit. The company, which is currently operating below full capacity, charges factory overhead to production at the rate of 120% of direct labor cost. The direct materials and direct labor costs per unit to produce comparable carrying cases are expected to be $3 and $2.50 respectively. If the carrying cases are made, fixed factory overhead costs will not increase and variable factory overhead costs associated with the manufacture of the cases are expected to be 80% of direct labor costs. (a) Prepare a differential analysis report dated May 12 of the current year for the make or buy decision. (b) On the basis of the data presented, would it be advisable to make or to continue buying the carrying cases? Explain.

24-7. Tipton Company produces a commodity by application of direct labor and a shaping machine. The original cost of the machine was $50,000, the accumulated depreciation now amounts to $30,000, the remaining useful life of the machine is 4 years, and its present salvage value is negligible. On April 7, a proposal was made to replace the present manufacturing procedure with a fully automatic machine that will cost $125,000. The automatic machine has an estimated useful life of 4 years and no significant scrap value. For use in evaluating the proposal, the accountant accumulated the additional data at the top of the next page covering operations for the past year and yearly expected operations if the automatic machine is acquired. The volume of operations is not expected to change significantly over the next 4 years.

(a) Prepare a differential analysis report for the proposal to replace the machine. Include in the analysis both the net reduction in costs and expenses anticipated over the 4 years and the annual reduction in costs and expenses anticipated. (b) Based only on the data presented, should the proposal be accepted? (c) Before a final decision is made, what are some other factors that should be considered?

	Present Operations	Proposed Operations
Sales.......................	$125,000	$125,000
Direct materials............	55,800	55,800
Direct labor................	40,250	——
Power and maintenance.......	4,500	6,000
Taxes, insurance, etc........	2,700	3,200
Selling and general expenses..	15,000	15,000

24-8. On September 20 of the current year, Mason Company is considering leasing a building and purchasing the necessary equipment to operate a public warehouse. The project would be financed by selling $100,000 of 5% U.S. Treasury bonds that mature in 10 years. The bonds had been purchased at face value and are currently selling at face value. The following data have been assembled:

Cost of equipment....................	$100,000
Life of equipment....................	10 years
Estimated residual value of equipment..	$ 2,500
Yearly costs to operate the warehouse..	$ 24,000
Yearly expected revenues—first 3 years..	$ 30,000
Yearly expected revenues—next 7 years.	$ 50,000

(a) Prepare a differential analysis report presenting the differential revenue and the differential cost associated with the proposed operation of the warehouse for the 10 years compared with present conditions. (b) Based upon the results disclosed by the differential analysis, should the proposal be accepted? (c) If the proposal is accepted, what is the total estimated net income from operation of the warehouse for the 10 years?

PROBLEMS

The following additional problems for this chapter are located in Appendix C: 24-1B, 24-2B, 24-4B.

24-1A. Allied Chemical Company refines Product A in batches of 25,000 gallons, which it sells for $.25 per gallon. The associated unit costs and expenses are currently as follows:

	Per Gallon
Direct materials....................	$.100
Direct labor.......................	.035
Variable factory overhead..........	.030
Fixed factory overhead.............	.030
Salesmen's commissions............	.010
Fixed selling and general expenses...	.015

The company is presently considering a proposal to put Product A through several additional processes to yield Products A and B. Until recently, the company found such further processing unwise, but new processing methods have reopened this question. Existing facilities can be used for this processing; but inasmuch as additional machine time would be required and the plant is operating at full eight-hour-day capacity, the processing would have to be performed at night. Additional costs of processing would be $500 per batch and there would be an evaporation loss of 10%, with 40% of the processed material evolving as Product A and 50% as Product B. Selling price of Product B is $.40 per gallon. Salesmen's commissions are a uniform percentage based on the sales price.

Instructions:

(1) Prepare a differential analysis report as of October 7, presenting the differential revenue and the differential cost per batch associated with the processing to produce Products A and B compared with processing to produce Product A only.
(2) Briefly report your recommendation.

24-2A. Universal Press purchased a machine costing $120,000 on July 8, 1968. The company's manufacturing costs for a normal year, exclusive of depreciation, total $200,000, operating expenses are $90,000 yearly, and revenues total $360,000 yearly. The annual depreciation for this machine is $20,000 based on a 6-year useful life and no residual value.

Early in July, 1970 a new type of machine priced at $250,000 becomes available. It has an estimated life of 4 years, with no salvage value, and its use is expected to reduce the company's manufacturing costs, exclusive of depreciation, to $125,000 yearly. The old machine can be sold for only $15,000. Revenues and operating expenses will not be affected by the use of either machine.

Instructions:

(1) Prepare a differential analysis report comparing operations with the proposed acquisition with operations using the present equipment. The analysis should indicate the net cost reduction or net cost increase that would result over the 4-year period if the new machine is acquired.
(2) List other factors that should be considered before a final decision is reached.

24-3A. Farrel Company is planning a one-month campaign for May to promote sales of one of its two products. A total of $300,000 has been budgeted for advertising, contests, redeemable coupons, and other promotional activities. The following data have been assembled for their possible usefulness in deciding which of the products to select for the campaign.

	Product M	Product N
Unit selling price..............	$100	$150
Unit production costs:		
Direct materials..............	$20	$35
Direct labor.................	15	20
Fixed factory overhead.........	10	25
Variable factory overhead......	20	20
Total unit production costs.....	65	100
Unit variable operating expenses..	15	30
Unit fixed operating expenses.....	5	10
Total unit costs and expenses...	$ 85	$140
Net income per unit...........	$ 15	$ 10

No increase in facilities would be necessary to produce and sell the increased output. It is anticipated that 25,000 additional units of Product M or 20,000 additional units of Product N could be sold without changing the unit selling price.

Instructions:

(1) Prepare a differential analysis report as of April 5 of the current year presenting the additional revenue and additional costs and expenses anticipated from the promotion of (a) Product M and (b) Product N.

(2) The sales manager had tentatively decided to promote Product M, because by so doing net income would be increased by $75,000 ($15 net income per unit for 25,000 units, less promotion expenses of $300,000). He also believed that the selection of Product N would decrease net income by $100,000 ($10 net income per unit for 20,000 units, less promotion expenses of $300,000). State briefly your reasons for supporting or opposing the tentative decision.

24-4A. Product P is one of numerous products manufactured by Emery Company. The demand for Product P has dropped sharply because of recent competition from a similar product. The company's chemists are currently completing tests of various new formulas, and it is anticipated that the manufacture of a superior product can be started on May 1, one month hence. No changes will be needed in the present production facilities to manufacture the new product because only the mixture of the various materials will be changed.

The controller has been asked by the president of the company for advice on whether to continue production during April or to suspend the manufacture of Product P until May 1. The controller has assembled the following pertinent data:

Emery Company
Estimated Income Statement — Product P
For Month Ending March 31, 19--

Sales (50,000 units).............	$100,000
Less cost of goods sold..........	75,000
Gross profit on sales............	$ 25,000
Less selling and general expenses..	35,000
Net loss......................	$ 10,000

The estimated production costs and selling and general expenses based on a production of 50,000 units are as follows:

Direct materials..................	$.50 per unit
Direct labor.....................	.40 per unit
Variable factory overhead.........	.25 per unit
Fixed factory overhead............	.35 per unit
Variable selling and general expenses.	.40 per unit
Fixed selling and general expenses...	$15,000 for March

Sales for April are expected to drop about 40% below those of the preceding month. No significant changes are anticipated in the production costs or operating expenses. No extra costs will be incurred in discontinuing operations in the portion of the plant associated with Product P. The inventory of Product P at the beginning and end of April is expected to be inconsequential.

Instructions:

(1) Prepare an estimated income statement in absorption costing form for April for Product P, assuming that production continues during the month.

(2) Prepare an estimated income statement in variable costing form for April for Product P, assuming that production continues during the month.

(3) State the estimated amount of net loss arising from the activities associated with Product P for April if production is temporarily suspended.

(4) Prepare a brief statement of the advice you think the controller should give.

24-5A. The Decker Company manufactures three styles of folding chairs, A, B, and C. The income statement has consistently indicated a net loss for Style A and management is considering three proposals: (1) continue Style A, (2) discontinue Style A and reduce total output accordingly, or (3) discontinue Style A and conduct an advertising campaign to expand the sales of Style C so that the entire plant capacity can continue to be used. The sales, costs, and expenses have been relatively stable over the past few years and they are expected to remain so for the foreseeable future. The income statement for the past year is:

	Style			
	A	B	C 20%	Total
Sales.....................	$100,000	$300,000	$500,000	$900,000
Cost of goods sold:				
Variable costs..............	$ 70,000	$180,000	$250,000	$500,000
Fixed costs.................	20,000	55,000	125,000	200,000
Total cost of goods sold.......	$ 90,000	$235,000	$375,000	$700,000
Gross profit on sales...........	$ 10,000	$ 65,000	$125,000	$200,000
Less operating expenses:				
Variable expenses...........	$ 10,000	$ 30,000	$ 50,000	$ 90,000
Fixed expenses.............	7,500	17,500	35,000	60,000
Total operating expenses......	$ 17,500	$ 47,500	$ 85,000	$150,000
Net income or (loss)...........	$ (7,500)	$ 17,500	$ 40,000	$ 50,000

635

If Style A is discontinued and production curtailed, the annual fixed production costs and fixed operating expenses could be reduced by $5,000 and $2,000 respectively. It is anticipated that an additional expenditure of $15,000 for advertising Style C would yield an increase of 20% in its sales volume; also that the increased production of Style C would make use of the plant facilities released by the discontinuance of Style A.

Instructions:

(1) Prepare an income statement in the variable costing format, indicating the projected annual net income under each of the three proposals.

(2) Why would total net income be reduced below its present level if Proposal 2 is accepted?

(3) Why would total net income increase above its present level if Proposal 3 is accepted?

25

Management reports and special analyses

Purpose of management reports and special analyses

A basic function of accounting is to provide the data needed to report the results of the economic activities of an enterprise to all interested parties. One group making extensive use of accounting data is operating management. The manager of even a very small business needs factual data to assist him in making decisions. As the size and the complexity of businesses increase, the importance of accounting as a tool in directing operations becomes more apparent.

In assisting management, the accountant relies upon a variety of methods of analysis. The use of cost accounting and of cost relationships as they affect planning and controlling operations was discussed in earlier chapters. In this chapter additional reports and analyses for the use of management will be explained and illustrated.

The term *management reports* is applied generally to various statements, schedules, and summaries prepared solely for the use of management. There are no standardized patterns for such reports. They may be devoted to a very small segment of the activities of the enterprise or to special problems confronting management. They often contain forecasts rather than historical data, and timeliness is more important than complete accuracy.

Reports prepared for the top echelon of management should ordinarily be broad in scope, presenting summaries of data rather than minute details. They should be departmentalized to the extent necessary to assign responsibility. Reports for personnel at the lower end of the managerial range should ordinarily be narrow in scope and contain detailed data. To illustrate, assume that a manufacturer records direct labor idle time and classifies it according to such causes as machine breakdown, inferior materials, absenteeism, and accidents. Such data are of little if any value unless reported to the responsible persons with authority to take action. The report to the executive vice president or other appropriate officer should summarize the data by departments and causes so that he can identify the persons responsible. The superintendent of maintenance is not concerned with absenteeism or faulty materials, but he needs to know the details of machine breakdowns. It is equally evident that the foremen of the various factory departments should be supplied with detailed data on idle time within the departments for which they are held responsible.

Rate of return on assets

The rate of return on assets is a useful measure of the relative efficiency of assets employed in earning income. It can be computed for an enterprise as a single unit, but its usefulness is enhanced if segments of income can be identified with specific groups of assets. This basic determination may be difficult or it may be fairly simple, as in computing the rate of return on the stocks and bonds owned by a business enterprise. For example, if the total cost of an investment portfolio is $100,000 and the dividends and interest earned for the year amount to $4,700, the rate of return on the assets is 4.7% ($4,700 ÷ $100,000).

Even in such relatively clear-cut situations as the foregoing, complicating factors may be introduced. The amount of administrative expense that should be allocated to the investment earnings is not subject to exact determination. The portion of the income tax allocable to the earnings could also be deducted in order to yield the net rate of return. There may also be alternatives in selecting the asset value to be used in the computation. There was an unstated assumption in the illustration that the composition of the investments remained unchanged during the year. Any material fluctuations in the amount invested should be taken into consideration and an average computed. In addition, it could be argued that the rate of return should be computed on the basis of the current market value of the investments rather than on their cost.

The rate of return on assets is often computed on a departmental basis for the purpose of measuring relative operating performance. For such computations the interest on borrowed funds and income taxes are ordinarily not taken into consideration. In evaluating a segment of a business, such nonoperating items as interest on borrowed funds should not be considered because the return on assets is basically a measure of the efficiency with which the assets have been used. The nonoperating items are not relevant to the evaluation of divisional management efficiency because such items are beyond the control of the division managers.

To illustrate, assume that for the past year the two operating divisions of a business had about the same volume of sales and approximately the same amount of operating income. Assume also that there was a substantial difference in the amounts of assets employed by each division. The following report points out the significance of this disparity.

Rate of Return on Assets
For Year Ended December 31, 19—

	DIVISION A	DIVISION B
Sales................................	$400,000	$435,000
Operating expenses..................	350,000	380,000
Net income from operations...........	$ 50,000	$ 55,000
Average assets employed..............	$500,000	$300,000
Rate of return on assets..............	10%	18.3%

Rate of return on assets report

Information such as that presented in the report above would alert management to the far greater effectiveness of Division B in the employment of assets. It would indicate the need for a careful study of the operating policies of the two divisions and the causes of the variation in rate of return.

The rate of return on assets can also be used as a control device by the establishment of a minimum rate of return and then by comparison of rates actually achieved with this minimum. The measure can be used in new product pricing by making it possible to determine the price necessary to earn a certain rate of return on the assets employed. It is also useful in profit planning and in evaluating proposed purchases of machinery and equipment and other capital expenditures.

Analysis of proposed capital expenditures

With the accelerated growth of American industry in recent years, increasing attention has been given to accounting analyses designed to evaluate plans requiring substantial outlays for plant replacement, improvement, and expansion. Three types of analysis commonly employed in evaluating proposals for major capital expenditures are described.

Average rate of return. The expected *average rate of return* is a measure of the anticipated profitability of an investment in plant assets. The amount of net income expected to be earned from the investment is stated as an annual average over the number of years the asset is to be used. The amount of the investment may be considered to be the original cost of the plant assets, or recognition may be given to the effect of depreciation on the amount of the investment. According to the latter view, the investment gradually declines from the original cost to the estimated residual value at the end of its useful life. Assuming straight-line depreciation and no residual value, the average investment would be equal to one half of the original expenditure.

To illustrate, assume that management is considering the acquisition of a particular machine at a cost of $50,000, that it is expected to have a useful life of 4 years with negligible residual value, and that its use during the 4 years is expected to yield total net income of $20,000. The expected average annual net income is therefore $5,000 ($20,000 ÷ 4) and the average investment is $25,000 ($50,000 ÷ 2). Accordingly, the expected average rate of return on the average investment is 20%, computed as follows:

$$\frac{\$20,000 \div 4}{\$50,000 \div 2} = 20\% \text{ average rate of return}$$

Comparison of this expected rate of return with the rate established by management as the minimum reward for the risks involved will indicate the comparative attractiveness of the proposed expenditure. If the foregoing analysis had been based on original cost of the equipment instead of the average investment, the rate of return would have been computed as 10% ($5,000 ÷ $50,000) instead of 20% ($5,000 ÷ $25,000).

A significant objection to the use of this measure is its disregard of the effect (1) of the timing of the expected recovery of the amount invested in plant assets, or (2) of the timing of the net income that such investment is expected to produce. Funds derived from the recovery of the cost of a capital expenditure and from the net income that it generates can be reinvested in other income-producing activities. Therefore, a project that recovers a high proportion of its investment and yields high income early in its life is more desirable than a project with the same average rate of return but with lower cost recovery and income in the earlier years.

Cash payback period. The expected period of time that will elapse between the date of a capital expenditure and a complete recoupment in cash or equivalent is called the *cash payback period*. To simplify the analysis, the revenues and the out-of-pocket operating expenses expected to be associated with the operation of the plant assets are assumed to be entirely in the form of cash. The excess of the cash flowing in from revenue over the cash flowing out for expenses is termed *net cash flow*.

The time required for the net cash flow to equal the initial outlay for the plant asset is the payback period.

For purposes of illustration, assume that the proposed expenditure for a plant asset with an 8-year life is $200,000 and that the annual net cash flow is expected to be $40,000. The estimated cash payback period for the expenditure is 5 years, computed as follows:

$$\frac{\$200,000}{\$40,000} = \text{5-year cash payback period}$$

The cash payback concept is widely used in evaluating proposals for expansion and for investment in new projects. A relatively short payback period is desirable, because the sooner the cash is recovered the sooner it becomes available for reinvestment in other projects. In addition, there is likely to be less possibility of loss from changes in economic conditions and other unavoidable risks when the commitment is short-term. The cash payback concept is also of interest to bankers and other creditors who may be dependent upon net cash flow for the repayment of claims associated with the initial capital expenditure.

The principal limitation of the cash payback period as a basis for decisions is its failure to take into consideration the expected profitability of a proposal. A project with a very short payback period coupled with relatively poor profitability would be less desirable than one for which the investment was committed for a longer period but with satisfactory profitability.

Discounted cash flow. An expenditure for plant and equipment may be looked upon as the acquisition of a series of future net cash flows composed of two elements: (1) recovery of the initial expenditure and (2) net income. Both the absolute and the relative amounts of these two elements are obviously important. The period of time over which the net cash flows will be received is also important. Any specified amount of cash that is to be received at some date in the future is not the equivalent of the same amount of cash held at an earlier date. Cash on hand can be immediately employed. The income that can be earned by earlier investment may be an important factor to consider. This element of timing is given recognition in *discounted cash flow* analysis. The expected future net cash flows originating from proposed present capital expenditures are reduced to their present values.

The concept of present value of future payments was noted in an earlier chapter in connection with discounting promissory notes. Application of the concept of discounted cash flow analysis may be illustrated by computing the amount to be deposited at a given rate of interest that will yield a specified sum at a later date. If the rate of interest is 6% and the sum to be accumulated in one year is $1,000, the amount to be invested is $943.40 ($1,000 ÷ 1.06). If the funds were to be invested a year earlier, with the interest compounded at the end of the first year, the amount of the deposit would be $890.00 ($943.40 ÷ 1.06).

Instead of determining the present value of future sums by a series of divisions in the manner just illustrated, it is customary to find the present value of 1 from a table of present values and to multiply it by the amount of the future sum. A partial table is presented below. Multiplication of .890, the present value of $1 two years hence at 6%, by $1,000 yields the same amount that was determined by the two successive divisions in the preceding paragraph. The rounding of the values in the table at three decimal places would not be sufficiently accurate for some purposes, but any greater exactitude is not necessary for our analysis.

YEARS	6%	10%	15%	20%
1	.943	.909	.870	.833
2	.890	.826	.756	.694
3	.840	.751	.658	.579
4	.792	.683	.572	.482
5	.747	.621	.497	.402
6	.705	.564	.432	.335
7	.665	.513	.376	.279
8	.627	.467	.327	.233
9	.592	.424	.284	.194
10	.558	.386	.247	.162

Present value of 1 at compound interest

The particular rate of return selected in discounted cash flow analysis is affected by the nature of the business enterprise and its relative profitability, the purpose of the capital expenditure, and other related factors. If the present value of the net cash flow expected from a proposed expenditure, at the selected rate, equals or exceeds the amount of the expenditure, the proposal is desirable. For purposes of illustration, assume a proposal for the acquisition of $200,000 of equipment with an expected useful life of 5 years, and a minimum desired rate of return of 10%. The anticipated net cash flow for each of the 5 years and the analysis of the proposal are presented on the following page. The report indicates that the proposal is expected to recover the investment and provide more than the minimum rate of return.

Each of the three methods of analyzing proposals for capital expenditures has both advantages and limitations. It is often advisable to employ a combination of methods in evaluating the various economic aspects of major projects. It is obvious, of course, that estimates play a substantial role in all analyses of future expectations. Such factors as product pricing, improvements in products, availability and training of personnel, marketing procedures, and severity of competition must also be given consideration in arriving at decisions.

Analysis of Proposal to Acquire Equipment
June 30, 19—

YEAR	PRESENT VALUE OF 1 AT 10%	NET CASH FLOW	PRESENT VALUE OF NET CASH FLOW
1	.909	$ 70,000	$ 63,630
2	.826	60,000	49,560
3	.751	50,000	37,550
4	.683	40,000	27,320
5	.621	40,000	24,840
Total		$260,000	$202,900

Amount to be invested in equipment............ 200,000

Excess of present value over amount to be invested. $ 2,900

Discounted cash flow analysis report — equipment acquisition

Gross profit analysis

Gross profit on sales is frequently considered to be the most significant intermédiate figure in the income statement. It is customary to determine its percentage relationship to sales and to make comparisons with prior periods. However, the mere knowledge of the percentages and the degree and direction of change from prior periods is insufficient; management needs information about the underlying factors. The procedure employed in developing such information is termed *gross profit analysis.*

Inasmuch as gross profit is the excess of sales over the cost of goods sold, it follows that a change in the amount of gross profit can be caused by (1) an increase or decrease in amount of sales and (2) an increase or decrease in the amount of cost of goods sold. An increase or decrease in either element may in turn be attributable to (1) a change in the number of units sold and (2) a change in the unit price. The effect of these two factors on either sales or cost of goods sold may be expressed as follows:

1. *Quantity factor.* The effect of a change in the number of units sold, assuming no change in unit price.
2. *Price factor.* The effect of a change in unit price on the number of units sold.

The data to be used as the basis for illustrating gross profit analysis are presented below. For the sake of simplicity, a single commodity will

	1970	1969	INCREASE DECREASE*
Sales......................	$225,000	$200,000	$ 25,000
Cost of goods sold...........	162,500	140,000	22,500
Gross profit on sales.........	$ 62,500	$ 60,000	$ 2,500
Number of units sold........	125,000	100,000	25,000
Unit sales price.............	$1.80	$2.00	$.20*
Unit cost price..............	$1.30	$1.40	$.10*

642

be assumed. The amount of detail entering into the analysis would be greater if a number of different commodities were sold, but the basic principles would not be affected.

The analysis of the foregoing data is presented below. The report indicates that the favorable increase in the number of units sold was partially offset by a decrease in unit selling price, and that the increase in the cost of goods sold attributable to increased quantity was partially offset by a decrease in unit cost.

Analysis of Increase in Gross Profit
For Year Ended December 31, 1970

Increase in amount of sales attributed to:			
Quantity factor:			
Increase in number of units sold in 1970.........	25,000		
Unit sales price in 1969......................	× $2	$50,000	
Price factor:			
Decrease in unit sales price in 1970.............	$.20		
Number of units sold in 1970.................	×125,000	25,000	
Net increase in amount of sales.................			$25,000
Increase in amount of cost of goods sold attributed to:			
Quantity factor:			
Increase in number of units sold in 1970.........	25,000		
Unit cost price in 1969.......................	× $1.40	$35,000	
Price factor:			
Decrease in unit cost price in 1970.............	$.10		
Number of units sold in 1970.................	×125,000	12,500	
Net increase in amount of cost of goods sold.......			22,500
Increase in gross profit on sales.................			$ 2,500

Gross profit analysis report

The data presented in the report may be useful both in evaluating past performance and in planning for the future. The importance of the cost reduction of $.10 a unit is quite evident. If the unit cost had remained unchanged from the preceding year, the net increase in amount of sales ($25,000) would have been more than offset by the increase in cost of goods sold ($35,000), causing a decrease in gross profit of $10,000. The $2,500 increase in gross profit actually attained was made possible, therefore, by the ability of management to reduce the unit cost.

The means by which the reduction in the unit cost of the commodity was accomplished is also significant. If it was attributable to the spreading of fixed factory overhead costs over the larger number of units produced, the decision to reduce the sales price in order to achieve a larger volume was probably wise. On the other hand, if the $.10 reduction in unit cost was attributable to operating efficiencies entirely unrelated to the increased production, the $.20 reduction in the unit sales price was ill-advised. The accuracy of the conclusion is demonstrated by the

643

following analysis, which indicates the possible loss of an opportunity to have realized an additional gross profit of $7,500 ($70,000 − $62,500):

	ACTUAL		HYPOTHETICAL	
Number of units sold.........	125,000		100,000	
Unit sales price.............	$1.80		$2.00	
Sales......................		$225,000		$200,000
Unit cost price.............	$1.30		$1.30	
Cost of goods sold...........		162,500		130,000
Gross profit on sales.........		$ 62,500		$ 70,000

If the reduction in unit cost had been achieved by a combination of the two means, the approximate effects of each could be determined by additional analyses. The methods employed in gross profit analysis may also be extended, with some modifications, to the analysis of changes in selling and general expenses.

Cost-volume-profit relationships

The determination of the selling price of a product is a complex matter that is often affected by forces partially or entirely beyond the control of management. Nevertheless, management must formulate pricing policies within the bounds permitted by the market place. Accounting can play an important role in the development of policy by supplying management with special reports on the relative profitability of its various products, the probable effects of contemplated changes in selling price, and other cost-volume-profit relationships.

The unit cost of producing a commodity is affected by such factors as the inherent nature of the product, the efficiency of operations, and the volume of production. An increase in the quantity produced is ordinarily accompanied by a decrease in unit cost, provided the volume attained remains within the reasonable limits of plant capacity.

Quantitative data relating to the effect on net income of changes in unit selling price, sales volume, production volume, production costs, and operating expenses enable management to improve the relationship among these variables. If a change in selling price appears to be desirable or, because of competitive pressure, unavoidable, the possible effect of the change on sales volume and product cost needs to be studied. Inquiry into the likely effect on net income of a promotional sales campaign is another example of special studies that may be undertaken.

A requisite of cost-volume-profit analysis is that all costs and expenses be subdivided into two categories: (1) fixed and (2) variable. Analyses of this type are facilitated by the use of variable costing procedures, which require that costs and expenses be so classified. When conventional absorption costing systems are employed, it is necessary as a preliminary procedure to first divide the relevant cost data between the fixed and variable categories. Types of analyses employed in appraising the interactions of selling price, sales and production volume, variable cost and expense, fixed cost and expense, and net income are described and illustrated in the next three sections.

Break-even analysis

The point in the operations of an enterprise at which revenues and expired costs are exactly equal is called the *break-even point*. At this level of operations an enterprise will neither realize a net income nor incur a net loss. Break-even analysis can be applied to past periods, but it is most useful when applied to future periods as a guide to business planning, particularly if either an expansion or a curtailment of operations is anticipated. In such cases it is concerned with future prospects and future operations and hence relies upon estimates. Obviously the reliability of the analysis is greatly influenced by the accuracy of the estimates.

The break-even point can be computed by means of a mathematical formula or it can be ascertained from a graphic presentation of the relationship between revenue, costs, and volume of productive capacity. In either case the data required are (1) total estimated fixed costs and expenses for a future period, such as a year, and (2) the total estimated variable costs and expenses for the same period, stated as a percent of net sales. To illustrate, assume that fixed costs and expenses are estimated at $90,000 and that variable costs and expenses are expected to amount to 60% of sales. The break-even point is $225,000 of sales revenue, computed as follows:

$$\text{Break-Even Sales (in \$)} = \text{Fixed Costs (in \$)} + \text{Variable Costs (as \% of Sales)}$$
$$S = \$90,000 + 60\%S$$
$$40\%\,S = \$90,000$$
$$S = \$225,000$$

Break-even analysis may also be employed in estimating the sales volume required to yield a specified amount of net income. The formula stated above can be modified for use in this computation by the addition at the end of the equation of the desired amount of net income. For example, the sales volume required to yield net income of $40,000 for the enterprise assumed above would be $325,000, computed as follows:

$$\text{Sales} = \text{Fixed Costs} + \text{Variable Costs} + \text{Net Income}$$
$$S = \$90,000 + 60\%S + \$40,000$$
$$40\%\,S = \$130,000$$
$$S = \$325,000$$

A break-even chart, based on the foregoing data, is illustrated on the following page. It is constructed in the following manner:

1. Percentages of productive capacity of the enterprise are spread along the horizontal axis, and dollar amounts representing operating data are spread along the vertical axis. The outside limits of the chart represent 100% of productive capacity and the maximum sales potential at that level of production.

2. A diagonal line representing sales is drawn from the lower left corner to the upper right corner.

3. A point representing fixed costs is plotted on the vertical axis at the left and a point representing total costs at maximum capacity is plotted at the right edge of the chart. A diagonal line representing total costs at various percentages of capacity is then drawn connecting these two points. In the illustration, the fixed costs are $90,000 and the total costs at maximum capacity amount to $330,000 ($90,000 plus variable costs of 60% of $400,000).

4. Horizontal and vertical lines are drawn at the point of intersection of the sales and cost lines, which is the break-even point, and the areas representing net income and net loss are identified.

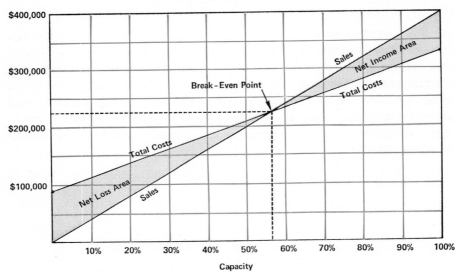

Projected Break-Even Chart
For Year Ending December 31, 19−−

Break-even chart

Presentation of break-even analysis in the chart form is frequently preferred over the equation form. From such a chart the approximate net income or net loss associated with any given sales volume or percentage of capacity can be readily determined.

Relying as it does on rigid assumptions concerning the behavior of sales and costs, break-even analysis should be employed with caution. If the selling price of a product is increased or decreased or if the amount of cost changes, the analysis prepared prior to such action will no longer be valid. In addition, the assumptions underlying the classification of costs as fixed or variable must be recognized. Among these is the assumption of relatively stable use of plant facilities. For example, in the foregoing illustration it is quite possible that at 80% and 100% of capacity the fixed costs would be $90,000, while if production were only 10% of capacity the fixed costs would be less than $90,000. Under conditions of substantial change in the use of plant facilities, very few costs would be fixed. Since substantial changes in the use of plant facilities are relatively rare in practice, break-even analysis can often be used quite effectively in decision making.

It should also be noted that a break-even chart for an enterprise selling two or more products must be based on a specified "product-mix." Changes in the mix would necessitate additional analysis and construction of a new chart. Recognition of the inherent assumptions and the limitations of break-even analysis is essential to the effective use of studies of this type in management planning.

Margin of safety

Business enterprises do not adopt the break-even point as their goal for future operations. Rather, they seek to achieve the largest possible volume of sales above the break-even point. The difference between the current sales revenue and the sales at the break-even point is called the *margin of safety*. It represents the possible decrease in sales revenue that may occur before a net loss results, and it may be expressed either in terms of dollars or as a percentage of sales. For example, if the volume of sales is $250,000 and sales at the break-even point amount to $200,000, the margin of safety is $50,000 or 20% as indicated by the following computation:

$$\text{Margin of Safety} = \frac{\text{Sales} - \text{Sales at Break-Even Point}}{\text{Sales}}$$

$$\text{Margin of Safety} = \frac{\$250,000 - \$200,000}{\$250,000} = 20\%$$

The margin of safety is useful in evaluating past operations and as a guide to business planning. For example, if the margin of safety is low, management should carefully evaluate forecasts of future sales revenue because even a small decline in sales revenue will result in a net loss.

Marginal income ratio

Another relationship between costs, volume, and profits that is especially useful in business planning because it gives an insight into the profit potential of a firm is the *marginal income ratio*, sometimes referred to as the *profit-volume ratio*. This ratio indicates the percentage of each sales dollar available to cover the fixed expenses and to provide net income. For example, if the volume of sales is $250,000 and variable expenses amount to $175,000, the marginal income ratio is 30% as indicated by the following calculation:

$$\text{Marginal Income Ratio} = \frac{\text{Sales} - \text{Variable Expenses}}{\text{Sales}}$$

$$\text{Marginal Income Ratio} = \frac{\$250,000 - \$175,000}{\$250,000} = 30\%$$

The marginal income ratio permits the quick determination of the effect on net income of an increase or a decrease in sales volume. To illustrate, assume that the management of a firm with a marginal income ratio of 30% is evaluating the effect on net income of the addition of $25,000 in sales orders. Multiplying the ratio (30%) by the change in sales volume ($25,000) indicates an increase in net income of $7,500 if the additional orders are obtained. In employing the analysis in such a situation, factors other than sales volume, such as the amount of fixed expenses, the percentage of variable expenses to sales, and the unit sales price, are assumed to remain constant. If these factors are not constant, the effect of any change in these factors must be considered in applying the analysis.

The marginal income ratio is also useful in setting business policy. For example, if the marginal income ratio of a firm is large and production is at a level below 100% capacity, a comparatively large increase in net income can be expected from an increase in sales volume. Conversely, a comparatively large decrease in net income can be expected from a decline in sales volume. A firm in such a position might decide to devote considerable effort to additional sales promotion because of the substantial change in net income that will result from changes in sales volume. On the other hand, a firm with a small marginal income ratio will probably want to devote considerable attention to reducing costs and expenses before concentrating large efforts on additional sales promotion.

Operations research

Each of the previously discussed uses of accounting data in planning and controlling business operations has been concerned with a restricted number of objectives or variables. In recent years a framework of analytical methods known as *operations research* has been developed in which the skills of engineers, mathematicians, economists, accountants, and sociologists are combined in solving problems for business enterprises. Mathematical models encompassing a large number of interdependent variables are often employed.

One of the areas for which operations research is often utilized is inventory control. For each category of materials in the inventory it is important to know the ideal quantity to be purchased in a single order and the minimum and maximum quantities to be on hand at any time. Such factors as economies of large-scale buying, storage costs, work interruption due to shortages, and seasonal and cyclical variations in production schedules need to be considered.

The use of linear programming in solving a simplified problem related to purchasing is presented. In practice, linear programming, which is basically a technique for selecting the most favorable course of action from among many feasible alternatives, has been used in solving complex business problems. Although the use of complex algebraic expressions is common in such situations, the following illustration demonstrates the essentials of the technique without the use of algebraic expressions.

The Dow Company needs to purchase Part P for use at both its West Coast and East Coast plants. Part P is available in limited quantities from two suppliers. The total unit cost price varies considerably for parts acquired from the two suppliers principally because of differences in transportation charges. The relevant data bearing upon the decision as to the most economical purchase arrangement are summarized in the diagram below.

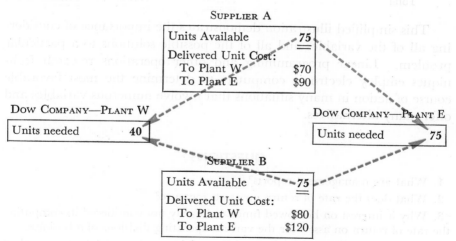

On the surface, it appears that the most economical policy would be to purchase as many units as needed by Plant W at $70 per unit from Supplier A because this is the lowest unit cost. Then the units needed by Plant E would be purchased at the lowest possible cost which would be 35 units from Supplier A (the remainder of his supply) at $90 per unit and 40 units from Supplier B at $120 per unit. The total cost of purchases that would result from following this course is $10,750 as indicated on the following page.

	COST OF PURCHASES		
	FOR PLANT W	FOR PLANT E	TOTAL
From Supplier A:			
40 units at $70..........	$2,800		$ 2,800
35 units at $90..........		$3,150	3,150
From Supplier B:			
40 units at $120.........		4,800	4,800
Total..................	$2,800	$7,950	$10,750

Although many possible combinations of purchases are feasible, the most economical purchase arrangement would be achieved by purchasing for Plant E the entire number of units needed from Supplier A or 75 units at $90 per unit. Then the units needed at Plant W would be purchased from Supplier B. The total cost from such a purchase procedure would be $9,950, even though no units were purchased at the lowest unit cost, as illustrated below:

	COST OF PURCHASES		
	FOR PLANT W	FOR PLANT E	TOTAL
From Supplier A:			
75 units at $90..........		$6,750	$6,750
From Supplier B:			
40 units at $80..........	$3,200		3,200
Total..................	$3,200	$6,750	$9,950

650 This simplified illustration demonstrates the importance of considering all of the variables and all of the possible solutions to a particular problem. Linear programming and other operations research techniques employ electronic computers to determine the most favorable course of action in many situations that involve numerous variables and offer many alternatives.

QUESTIONS

1. What are management reports?

2. What does the rate of return on assets measure?

3. Why is interest on borrowed funds ordinarily not considered in computing the rate of return on assets for the various operating divisions of a business?

4. What is a significant objection to the use of the average rate of return method in evaluating capital expenditure proposals?

5. (a) As used in analysis of proposed capital expenditures, what is the cash payback period? (b) Discuss the principal limitation of this method for evaluating capital expenditure proposals.

6. Which method of evaluating capital expenditure proposals reduces the expected future net cash flows originating from the proposals to their present values?

7. Discuss the two factors affecting both sales and cost of goods sold to which a change in gross profit can be attributed.

8. The gross profit of the Caldwell Company increased by $12,500 over the preceding year. Discuss possible unfavorable occurrences that might have accompanied the increase.

9. The analysis of increase in gross profit report for Thompson Company includes the effect that an increase in quantity of goods sold has had on sales. How is this figure determined?

10. (a) What is the break-even point? (b) How can the break-even point be determined?

11. (a) If fixed costs and expenses are $500,000 and variable costs and expenses are 50% of sales, what is the break-even point? (b) What sales are required to realize net income of $100,000 under the conditions described in (a)?

12. Both the Allen Company and the Walker Company had the same sales, total costs and expenses, and net income for the current fiscal year, yet the Allen Company had a lower break-even point than the Walker Company. Explain the reason for this difference in break-even points.

13. What is the advantage of presenting break-even analysis in the chart form over the equation form?

14. (a) What is meant by the term "margin of safety"? (b) If sales are $200,000, net income $20,000, and sales at the break-even point $150,000, what is the margin of safety?

15. What ratio indicates the percentage of each sales dollar that is available to cover fixed costs and expenses and to provide a profit?

16. An examination of the accounting records of Klein Company disclosed a high marginal income ratio and production at a level below maximum capacity. Based on this information, suggest a likely means of improving net income. Explain.

17. What is operations research?

EXERCISES

25-1. The sales, net income, and asset investments of two companies in the same industry are as follows:

	Company A	Company B
Sales	$400,000	$300,000
Net income	40,000	30,000
Assets	800,000	200,000

(a) What is the percentage of net income to sales for each company?
(b) What is the rate of return on assets for each company?
(c) As far as the data permit, comment on the relative performance of these two companies.

25-2. A. J. Greenwood Company is considering the acquisition of machinery at a cost of $20,000. The machinery has an estimated life of 4 years and no salvage value. It is expected to provide yearly net income of $3,000 and yearly net cash flows of $8,000. The company's minimum desired rate of return for discounted cash flow analysis is 15%. Compute the following:

(a) The average rate of return, giving effect to depreciation on investment.
(b) The cash payback period.
(c) The excess or deficiency of present value over the amount to be invested as determined by the discounted cash flow method. Use the table of present values appearing in this chapter.

25-3. From the following data for the Bailey Company, prepare an analysis of the decrease in gross profit for the year ended December 31, 1970.

	1970		1969	
Sales.................	50,000 units @ $6	$300,000	60,000 units @ $5.50	$330,000
Cost of goods sold......	50,000 units @ $4	200,000	60,000 units @ $3.75	225,000
Gross profit on sales....		$100,000		$105,000

25-4. Fowler Company anticipates for the coming year fixed costs and expenses of $150,000 and variable costs and expenses equal to 40% of sales.
  (a) Compute the anticipated break-even point.
  (b) Compute the sales required to realize net income of $30,000.
  (c) Construct a break-even chart, assuming sales of $400,000 at full capacity.
  (d) Determine the probable net income if sales total $340,000.

25-5. Miller Company operated at full capacity during the past year. Fixed costs and expenses were $220,000, variable costs and expenses were 45% of sales, and sales totaled $500,000. Management proposed to expand plant capacity by 50%, which will increase fixed costs and expenses by $110,000 yearly but will not affect the ratio of variable costs and expenses to sales.
  (a) Compute the net income under present conditions.
  (b) Compute the break-even point under present and proposed conditions.
  (c) Compute the sales necessary under proposed conditions to reach current net income.
  (d) Compute the maximum net income under proposed conditions.

25-6. (a) If Franklin Company, with a break-even point at $400,000 of sales, has actual sales of $500,000, what is the margin of safety expressed (1) in dollars and (2) as a percentage of sales?

  (b) If the margin of safety for Barker Company was 20%, fixed costs and expenses were $130,000, and variable costs and expenses were 35% of sales, what was the amount of actual sales?

25-7. (a) If Carson Company has actual sales of $400,000, fixed costs and expenses of $175,000, and variable costs and expenses of $120,000, what is the marginal income ratio?

  (b) If the marginal income ratio for Garner Company is 60%, sales were $800,000, and fixed costs and expenses were $375,000, what was the net income?

25-8. For the past year Myers Company had sales of $600,000, a margin of safety of 30%, and a marginal income ratio of 40%. Compute:
  (a) The break-even point.
  (b) The variable costs and expenses.
  (c) The fixed costs and expenses.
  (d) The net income.

25-9. For 1969 Cooper Company had sales of $2,000,000, fixed costs and expenses of $630,000, a margin of safety of 30%, and a marginal income ratio of 45%. During 1970 the variable costs and expenses were 55% of sales, the fixed costs and expenses did not change from the previous year, and the margin of safety was 20%.
  (a) What was the net income for 1969?
  (b) What was the break-even point for 1970?
  (c) What was the amount of sales for 1970?
  (d) What was the net income for 1970?

PROBLEMS

The following additional problems for this chapter are located in Appendix C: 25-1B, 25-3B, 25-4B, 25-6B.

25-1A. Roth Manufacturing Company is considering the addition of a new product to its line. For 1969, production was at 80% of capacity, the assets employed were $5,000,000 (original cost), and the income statement showed a net operating income of $475,000 computed as follows:

Sales....................		$4,000,000
Less: Cost of goods sold.....	$2,100,000	
Selling expenses......	950,000	
General expenses.....	475,000	3,525,000
Net operating income.......		$ 475,000

If the new product is added, market research indicates that 20,000 units can be sold in 1970 at an estimated selling price of $50 per unit. The idle capacity will be utilized to produce the product, but an additional $500,000 in plant assets will be required. The cost data per unit for the new product are as follows:

Direct materials.........................	$18.50
Direct labor.............................	12.50
Factory overhead (includes depreciation on additional investment)..................	8.75
Selling expenses........................	5.50
General expenses.......................	1.75
	$47.00

Instructions:

(1) Prepare an estimated income statement for 1970 for the new product.

(2) Prepare a schedule indicating the rate of return on assets under present conditions and for the new product. Use the original cost of the assets in your computations.

(3) Would you recommend addition of the new product? Would you require other data before you make your decision? If so, what data would you require?

25-2A. The chief accountant of Powell Company prepares weekly reports of idleness of direct labor employees for the plant superintendent. These reports classify the idle time by departments. Idle time data for the week ended April 21 of the current year are as follows:

Department	Standard Hours	Productive Hours
A	1,000	880
B	1,200	1,140
C	800	800
D	1,500	1,320

The hourly direct labor rates are $4.50, $3.75, $4.25, and $5.00 respectively for Departments A through D. The idleness was caused by a shortage of materials in Department A, a lack of sales orders in Department B, and a machine breakdown in Department D.

653

Instructions:

Prepare an idle time report classified by departments for the week ended April 21 for the plant superintendent. Use the following columnar headings for the report:

| Dept. | Production | | | Idle Time | | Remarks |
	Standard Hours	Actual Hours	Percentage of Standard	Hours	Cost of Idle Time	

25-3A. The capital expenditures budget committee is considering two projects. The estimated net income and net cash flows from each project are presented below:

| Year | Project A | | Project B | |
	Net Income	Net Cash Flow	Net Income	Net Cash Flow
1	$ 4,000	$ 9,000	$ 8,000	$13,000
2	4,000	9,000	7,000	12,000
3	5,000	10,000	6,000	11,000
4	6,000	11,000	4,000	9,000
5	8,000	13,000	2,000	7,000
	$27,000	$52,000	$27,000	$52,000

Each project requires an investment of $25,000 with no salvage value expected. The committee has selected a rate of 20% for purposes of the discounted cash flow analysis.

Instructions:

(1) Compute the following:
  (a) The average rate of return for each project, giving effect to depreciation on the investment.
  (b) The excess or deficiency of present value over amount to be invested as determined by the discounted cash flow method for each project. Use the present value table appearing in this chapter.
(2) Prepare a brief report for the budget committee advising it on the relative merits of the two projects.

25-4A. Shaw Company expects to maintain the same inventories at the end of 1970 as at the beginning of the year. The total of all production costs for the year is therefore assumed to be equal to the cost of goods sold. With this in mind, the various department heads were asked to submit estimates of the expenses for their departments during 1970. A summary report of these estimates is presented at the top of the next page.

It is expected that 90,000 units will be sold at a selling price of $12 a unit. Capacity output is 100,000 units.

Instructions:

(1) Determine the break-even point in (a) dollars of sales, (b) units, and (c) terms of capacity.
(2) Prepare an estimated income statement for 1970.
(3) Construct a break-even chart, indicating the break-even point in dollars of sales.
(4) What is the expected margin of safety?
(5) What is the expected marginal income ratio?

	Estimated Fixed Expense	Estimated Variable Expense (per unit sold)
Production costs:		
Direct materials.............	$ —	$3.00
Direct labor................	—	2.75
Factory overhead............	200,000	.75
Selling expenses:		
Sales salaries and commissions..	25,000	.35
Advertising................	30,000	—
Travel.....................	12,500	—
Miscellaneous selling expenses..	8,500	.15
General expenses:		
Office and officers' salaries.....	75,000	.10
Supplies...................	3,500	.05
Miscellaneous general expenses..	5,500	.05
	$360,000	$7.20

25-5A. Verner Company manufactures only one product. In 1969 the plant operated at full capacity. At a meeting of the board of directors on December 3, 1969, it was decided to raise the price of this product from its price of $8, which had prevailed for the past few years, to $9, effective January 1, 1970. Although the cost price was expected to rise about $.40 per unit in 1970 because of a direct labor wage increase, the increase in selling price was expected to cover this increase and also add to net operating income. The comparative income statement for 1969 and 1970 is presented below.

	1970		1969	
Sales.......................		$360,000		$400,000
Cost of goods sold — variable....	$112,000		$120,000	
fixed.......	100,000	212,000	100,000	220,000
Gross profit on sales...........		$148,000		$180,000
Operating expenses — variable...	$ 54,000		$ 60,000	
fixed......	70,000	124,000	70,000	130,000
Net operating income..........		$ 24,000		$ 50,000

Instructions:

(1) Prepare a gross profit analysis report for the year 1970.

(2) At a meeting of the board of directors on February 12, 1971, the president, after reading the gross profit analysis report, made the following comment:

"It looks as if the increase in unit cost price was $.90 and not the anticipated $.40. The failure of operating management to keep these costs within the bounds of those in 1969, except for the anticipated $.40 increase in direct labor cost, was a major factor in the decrease in gross profit."

Do you agree with this analysis of the increase in unit cost price? Explain.

25-6A. W. J. Scott and Company operated at full capacity during 1969. Its income statement appears below.

Sales............................		$750,000
Cost of goods sold..............		450,000
Gross profit on sales...........		$300,000
Operating expenses:		
Selling expenses.............	$150,000	
General expenses.............	75,000	
Total operating expenses...		225,000
Net operating income...........		$ 75,000

An analysis of costs and expenses reveals the following division of costs and expenses between fixed and variable.

	Fixed	Variable
Cost of goods sold..............	40%	60%
Selling expenses................	50%	50%
General expenses...............	60%	40%

The management of W. J. Scott and Company is considering a plant expansion program that will permit an increase of $350,000 in yearly sales. The expansion will increase fixed costs and expenses by $100,000 but will not affect the relationship between sales and variable costs and expenses.

Instructions:

(1) Determine for present capacity (a) the total fixed costs and expenses and (b) the total variable costs and expenses.

(2) Determine the percentage of total variable costs and expenses to sales.

(3) Compute the break-even point under present conditions.

(4) Compute the break-even point under the proposed program.

(5) Determine the amount of sales that would be necessary under the proposed program to realize the $75,000 of net operating income that was earned in 1969.

(6) Determine the maximum net operating income possible with the expanded plant.

(7) If the proposal is accepted and sales remain at the 1969 level, what will the net operating income be for 1970?

(8) Based upon the data given, would you recommend accepting the proposal? Explain.

656

26

Funds statement
and cash flow

Concepts of funds

In accounting and financial usage the term "fund" has a variety of meanings. It was first used in this book to denote segregations of cash for a special purpose, as in "change fund" and "petty cash fund." Later it was employed to designate the amount of cash and marketable investments segregated in a "sinking fund" for the purpose of liquidating bonds or other long-term obligations at maturity. When used in the plural form, "funds" is often a synonym for cash, as in the phrase associated with dishonor of a check, "not sufficient funds."

The concepts of "funds" that will be employed in this chapter are those associated with the principal subject matter of the chapter, "funds statements" and "cash flow." In this context the term has three different but not wholly unrelated meanings. They range from the broad concept of "all financial resources," through the intermediate concept of "working capital," to the narrow concept of "cash." Attention will first be directed to the intermediate concept.

Working capital concept of funds

The amount by which the total current assets of an enterprise exceed its total current liabilities is called *working capital* or *net current assets*. Both of the amounts used in the computation must, of course, be as of the same moment of time, such as at a balance sheet date. If, for example, the balance sheet of an enterprise lists current assets of $500,000 and current liabilities of $260,000, the amount of its working capital at that time would be $240,000 ($500,000 − $260,000). The principal categories of current assets and current liabilities that usually appear on a balance sheet are presented in the schedule below. In addition to containing detailed data and the amount of working capital for two successive balance sheet dates, the changes in each item are shown.

	DECEMBER 31 1970	DECEMBER 31 1969	INCREASE DECREASE*
Current assets:			
Cash............................	$ 30,000	$ 35,000	$ 5,000*
Marketable securities...............	60,000	40,000	20,000
Receivables (net)...................	100,000	115,000	15,000*
Inventories.......................	350,000	295,000	55,000
Prepaid expenses..................	10,000	15,000	5,000*
Total.........................	$550,000	$500,000	$50,000
Current liabilities:			
Notes payable.....................	$ 55,000	$ 50,000	$ 5,000
Accounts payable..................	120,000	145,000	25,000*
Income tax payable................	30,000	40,000	10,000*
Dividends payable.................	25,000	25,000	——
Total.........................	$230,000	$260,000	$30,000*
Working capital (net current assets)...	$320,000	$240,000	$80,000

According to the schedule above, the current assets at the later date totaled $550,000 and current liabilities totaled $230,000, yielding working capital of $320,000. The combined effect of the increase of $50,000 in current assets and the decrease of $30,000 in current liabilities was to increase working capital by $80,000. It should be observed that working capital is a "net" concept; it cannot be identified with any specific asset or liability nor solely with total current assets or total current liabilities.

The amounts of most current assets and current liabilities change between balance sheet dates. Many of the items, such as cash, inventories, and accounts receivable and payable, fluctuate continually. Prepaid expenses are used up, direct materials progress through work in process to finished goods, finished goods are sold to customers on account, and accounts receivable are collected in cash. Cash flowing in is used to prepay expenses, to pay wages and other current expenses, to purchase additional materials, and to liquidate notes payable, accounts

658

payable, and other liabilities. An understanding of this continuous cycle of interplay among the various current assets and current liabilities is essential to an understanding of the concept of working capital and analyses related to it. In the illustration, for example, the fact that the amount of dividends payable at both the beginning and the end of the period was $25,000 is not an indication that the account balance remained unchanged throughout the year. If dividends were paid quarterly, four separate liabilities would have been created and four would have been liquidated during the period. It may also be noted that the amount of working capital is neither increased nor decreased by a transaction that affects (1) only current assets (such as a purchase of marketable securities for cash), (2) only current liabilities (such as issuance of a short-term note to a creditor on account), or (3) only current assets and current liabilities (such as payment of an account payable).

Information about significant fluctuations in working capital is important to managers, owners, and creditors because the success of a business enterprise is often materially affected by the relationship between current assets and current liabilities. The financial statement designed to impart this information is variously termed *funds statement, statement of source and application of funds, statement of resources provided and applied*, and *statement of changes in working capital*. Because of its brevity, "funds statement" will be used for discussion purposes; but the formal statement will be identified by the more descriptive title "statement of source and application of funds."

The period of time encompassed by a funds statement may be as short as a single month or as long as the entire period of a company's existence. The time period assumed in the discussion and the illustrations that follow will be a fiscal year.

Funds-flow analysis

Both the purpose and the nature of funds-flow analysis have changed over the years. Originally the information was assembled almost exclusively for the use of management. The more recent trend is to present a formal funds statement as a part of the annual financial report to stockholders. Although the funds statement is not as basic as the income statement or the balance sheet, its increasing importance is evidenced by a trend toward its inclusion in the opinions (certificates) rendered by independent public accountants.

Just as there are a variety of titles for the statement and many variations in the nature of funds-flow analysis, there continues to be a considerable amount of experimentation in the form of the funds statement.[1] One widely used basic form will be discussed in this chapter.

---

[1]Specimen funds statements are presented in Appendix B.

Funds statements are divided into two major sections. The first section is devoted to the funds that have flowed into an enterprise, classified as to source. The second section contains details concerning the outflow of funds classified according to the manner of their use or application. Ordinarily the total of the amounts reported in each section are not exactly equal. If the inflow (sources) has exceeded the outflow (applications), the excess is the amount of the increase in working capital. When the reverse situation occurs, the excess of outflow is a measure of the amount by which working capital has decreased. Accordingly, the difference between the total of the sources and the applications sections of the funds statement is identified as an increase or a decrease in working capital. The details of this balancing amount are frequently presented in a subsidiary section of the statement or in a separate supporting schedule.

Some of the funds-flow data needed in preparing a funds statement, such as the balances of current asset and current liability accounts, can be obtained from the balance sheet. Information regarding net income, the amount of dividends declared, and other transactions affecting stockholders' equity accounts may be obtained from the income and retained earnings statements. However, the principal financial statements do not reveal the particulars of every fund source and application. For example, a comparative balance sheet will not necessarily disclose the amount of funds provided by the issuance of bonds nor the amount applied to the purchase of plant assets. Some of the relevant data must be obtained from accounts in the general ledger or from the initial entries in one of the journals.

Although funds may be affected by many different kinds of transactions, consideration will be confined to the most common sources and applications. As a matter of convenience in the discussion that follows, all asset and liability accounts other than current assets and current liabilities will be referred to as "noncurrent" accounts.

Sources of funds

Transactions that bring working capital into an enterprise are sources of funds. It is not necessary to review the journals or source documents and classify every transaction that occurred during the year to determine these sources. It is also unnecessary to determine the individual effects of a number of transactions of a similar nature. For purposes of discussion, the transactions which provide funds are classified in terms of their effect on noncurrent accounts, as follows:

1. Transactions that decrease noncurrent assets.
2. Transactions that increase noncurrent liabilities.
3. Transactions that increase stockholders' equity.

Decreases in noncurrent assets. The sale of long-term investments, equipment, buildings, land, patents, or other noncurrent assets represents sources of funds. However, the amount of funds provided by the sale of a noncurrent asset is not necessarily the same as the amount of the reduction in the account. For example, if a patent with a book value of $20,000 was sold during the year for $50,000, the funds provided by the sale amounted to $50,000 but the patents account decreased by only $20,000. Similarly, if long-term investments carried in the ledger at $100,000 at the beginning of the year were sold for $75,000, the transaction was a source of funds amounting to $75,000 rather than $100,000.

Increases in noncurrent liabilities. The issuance of bonds or long-term notes is a common source of funds. For example, if during the year bonds with a face value of $500,000 are sold at 100 for cash, the amount of funds provided by the transaction would be indicated by a $500,000 increase in the bonds payable account. If the bonds were issued at a price above or below 100, it would be necessary to refer to the bond premium or discount account, in addition to the bonds payable account, in order to determine the amount of funds provided by the transaction. For example, if the $500,000 of bonds had been issued at 90 instead of 100, the funds provided would have been $450,000 instead of $500,000.

Increases in stockholders' equity. Often the largest and most frequently recurring source of funds is profitable operations. Revenues realized from the sale of commodities or services are accompanied by increases in working capital. On the other hand, many of the expenses incurred are accompanied by decreases in working capital. Inasmuch as the significant details of revenues and expenses appear in the income statement, they need not be repeated in the funds statement. However, the amount of net income reported on the income statement is not necessarily equivalent to the funds provided by operations. Such expenses as depreciation of plant assets and amortization of patents decrease net income but they do not affect current assets or current liabilities. Hence they have no effect on funds. Similarly, an entry to amortize discount on bond investments increases net income, but it affects noncurrent accounts instead of current accounts. The amount reported as net income on the income statement must therefore be adjusted upward or downward to determine the amount of funds provided by operations.

If capital stock is sold during the period, the amount of funds provided will not necessarily be equal to the increase in the capital stock account; consideration must also be given to accompanying debits or credits to other paid-in capital accounts. A stock dividend or a stock split affects only stockholders' equity accounts and has no effect whatsoever on funds.

661

Applications of funds

As in the case of fund sources, it is convenient to classify the applications of funds according to their effects on noncurrent accounts. Transactions affecting the outflow or applications of funds may be described as follows:

1. Transactions that increase noncurrent assets.
2. Transactions that decrease noncurrent liabilities.
3. Transactions that decrease stockholders' equity.

Increases in noncurrent assets. Funds may be applied to the purchase of equipment, buildings, land, long-term investments, patents, or other noncurrent assets. However, the amount of funds used for such purposes is not necessarily indicated by the net increases in the related accounts. For example, if the debits to the equipment account for acquisitions during the year totaled $100,000 and the credits to the same account for disposals amounted to $25,000, the net change in the account would be $75,000. Such facts can be determined only by reviewing the details in the account.

Decreases in noncurrent liabilities. The liquidation of bonds or long-term notes represents an application of funds. The amount of funds applied would be indicated by the decrease in the balance of the liability account if the face value was paid at maturity. If the obligations were redeemed prior to maturity, it would be necessary to consider any unamortized premium or discount and any gain or loss on the transaction.

Decreases in stockholders' equity. Probably the most frequent application of funds in reduction of stockholders' equity results from the declaration of cash dividends. Funds may also be applied to the redemption of preferred stock or the purchase of treasury stock. Appropriations of retained earnings or other transfers among stockholders' equity accounts have no effect on funds.

Assembling data for the funds statement

Much of the information on funds flow is obtained by the accountant in the process of preparing the balance sheet, the income statement, and the retained earnings statement. Working papers designed for the purpose may be employed in assembling the data but they are not essential. Because of their complexity and procedural involvements they tend to obscure the basic concepts of funds analysis. It is for this reason that special working papers will not be used here in assembling the data needed for the funds statement.

In the illustration that follows, the information will be obtained from (1) a comparative balance sheet and (2) ledger accounts for noncurrent assets, noncurrent liabilities, and stockholders' equity. The comparative balance sheet in simplified form appears below; ledger accounts will be presented contemporaneously with the discussion of the related data. Descriptive notations have been inserted in the accounts to facilitate the explanations; otherwise it would be necessary to refer to relevant journal entries to ascertain the complete effect of some of the transactions.

Glendale Corporation
Comparative Balance Sheet
December 31, 1970 and 1969

	1970	1969	INCREASE DECREASE*
Assets			
Cash.....................................	$ 48,000	$ 22,000	$26,000
Trade receivables (net).........................	68,000	65,000	3,000
Inventories..................................	171,000	180,000	9,000*
Prepaid expenses.............................	2,000	3,000	1,000*
Equipment..................................	107,000	88,000	19,000
Accumulated depreciation — equipment............	(41,000)	(40,000)	(1,000)
Building...................................	100,000	100,000	——
Accumulated depreciation — building.............	(34,000)	(30,000)	(4,000)
Land.......................................	4,000	10,000	6,000*
Total assets.............................	$425,000	$398,000	$27,000
Liabilities			
Accounts payable (merchandise creditors)...........	$ 41,000	$ 31,000	$10,000
Dividends payable............................	5,000	3,000	2,000
Bonds payable...............................	80,000	100,000	20,000*
Total liabilities...........................	$126,000	$134,000	$ 8,000*
Stockholders' Equity			
Common stock...............................	$200,000	$200,000	——
Retained earnings............................	99,000	64,000	$35,000
Total stockholders' equity...................	$299,000	$264,000	$35,000
Total liabilities and stockholders' equity............	$425,000	$398,000	$27,000

Inasmuch as only the noncurrent accounts reveal sources and applications of funds, it is not necessary to examine the current asset or the current liability accounts. The first of the noncurrent accounts listed on the comparative balance sheet of the Glendale Corporation is Equipment.

Equipment. The comparative balance sheet indicates that the cost of equipment increased $19,000. The equipment account and the accumulated depreciation account illustrated on the following page reveal that the net change of $19,000 was the result of two separate transactions, the discarding of equipment that had cost $8,000 and the purchase of equipment for $27,000. The equipment discarded had been fully depreciated, as indicated by the debit of $8,000 in the accumulated depreciation account, and no salvage was realized from its disposal. Hence the transaction had no effect on working capital and is not reported on the funds statement. The effect on funds of the purchase of equipment for $27,000 was as follows:

> Application of funds:
> Purchase of equipment..................... $27,000

The credit in the accumulated depreciation account had the effect of reducing the investment in equipment by $9,000 but caused no change in working capital. Further attention will be given to depreciation in a later paragraph.

EQUIPMENT

DATE		ITEM	DEBIT	CREDIT	BALANCE DEBIT	BALANCE CREDIT
1970						
Jan.	1	Balance			88,000	
May	9	Discarded, no salvage		8,000		
July	7	Purchased for cash	27,000		107,000	

ACCUMULATED DEPRECIATION — EQUIPMENT

DATE		ITEM	DEBIT	CREDIT	BALANCE DEBIT	BALANCE CREDIT
1970						
Jan.	1	Balance				40,000
May	9	Discarded, no salvage	8,000			
Dec.	31	Depreciation for year		9,000		41,000

Building. According to the comparative balance sheet there was no change in the $100,000 balance between the beginning and end of the year. Reference to the building account in the ledger confirms the absence of entries during the year and hence the account is not shown here. Although the credit in the accumulated depreciation account reduced the investment in building, working capital was not affected.

ACCUMULATED DEPRECIATION — BUILDING

DATE		ITEM	DEBIT	CREDIT	BALANCE DEBIT	BALANCE CREDIT
1970						
Jan.	1	Balance				30,000
Dec.	31	Depreciation for year.........		4,000		34,000

Land. The comparative balance sheet indicates that land decreased by $6,000 during the year. The notation in the account reveals that the land was sold for $18,000. Although further attention to the $12,000 gain on the sale will be required, the significant aspect of the sale is its effect on working capital. The notation is therefore as follows:

> Source of funds:
> Sale of land.............................. $18,000

LAND

| DATE | | ITEM | DEBIT | CREDIT | BALANCE | |
					DEBIT	CREDIT
1970						
Jan.	1	Balance			10,000	
Apr.	10	Sold for $18,000 cash		6,000	4,000	

Bonds payable. The next noncurrent item listed on the balance sheet, bonds payable, decreased $20,000 during the year. Examination of the bonds payable account, which appears below, indicates that $20,000 of bonds payable were purchased at face value, requiring the expenditure of working capital. The effect on funds is noted as follows:

> Application of funds:
> Retirement of bonds payable.............. $20,000

BONDS PAYABLE

| DATE | | ITEM | DEBIT | CREDIT | BALANCE | |
					DEBIT	CREDIT
1970						
Jan.	1	Balance				100,000
June	30	Purchased for cash at face	20,000			80,000

Common stock. The amount listed for common stock at both balance sheet dates is $200,000. Reference to the account in the ledger confirms the absence of entries during the year.

665

Retained earnings. According to the comparative balance sheet, retained earnings increased by $35,000 during the year. Examination of the ledger account, reproduced on the next page, reveals two debits of $5,000 each and a credit of $45,000. The effect on working capital of the declaration of cash dividends of $10,000 was as follows:

> Application of funds:
> Declaration of cash dividends.............. $10,000

Although the $45,000 credit to the retained earnings account is identified as net income, it is not necessarily the measure of funds so provided. In the examination of the land account it was observed that land costing $6,000 was sold at a gain of $12,000. In the memorandum notation the amount recorded as funds from this source was the entire $18,000 proceeds. Hence the $12,000 gain on the sale of the land must be excluded from the funds provided by net income, leaving a remainder of $33,000 ($45,000 − $12,000).

Unlike most expenses, depreciation expense does not require an outlay of cash, an incurrence of a current liability, or otherwise decrease working capital. Deduction of depreciation expense from revenues, though proper in the determination of net income, causes the amount so determined to be incorrect as a measure of funds provided by operations. It is therefore necessary to add back to net income the depreciation expense on equipment and building, which amounted to $13,000 ($9,000 + $4,000).

After giving effect to the foregoing adjustments to reported net income, the funds provided by operations may be noted as follows:

Source of funds:
    Operations:
        Net income, exclusive of $12,000 gain on sale of land . . $33,000
        Depreciation on equipment and building. 13,000 $46,000

RETAINED EARNINGS

DATE		ITEM	DEBIT	CREDIT	BALANCE DEBIT	BALANCE CREDIT
1970						
Jan.	1	Balance				64,000
June	30	Cash dividend	5,000			
Dec.	31	Cash dividend	5,000			
	31	Net income		45,000		99,000

Form of the funds statement

Although there are many possible variations in the form and the content of the funds statement, it is customary to present the source of funds first and to present net income as the first item in the section. The other data are generally listed in the order of importance as indicated by the magnitude of the amounts. It is also common practice to present comparative data for the preceding year or for a series of years. A funds statement for the Glendale Corporation is illustrated below.

Glendale Corporation
Statement of Source and Application of Funds
For Year Ended December 31, 1970

Source of funds:			
Operations:			
Net income, exclusive of $12,000 gain on			
sale of land.	$ 33,000		
Add expenses not requiring funds:			
Depreciation on equipment and			
building	13,000	$ 46,000	
Sale of land.		18,000	$64,000
Application of funds:			
Purchase of equipment.	$ 27,000		
Retirement of bonds payable.	20,000		
Declaration of cash dividends.	10,000	57,000	
Increase in working capital.			$ 7,000

Funds statement (*continued*)

Schedule of changes in working capital:

	December 31 1970	December 31 1969	Working Capital Increase or Decrease*
Cash........................	$ 48,000	$ 22,000	$26,000
Trade receivables (net)...............	68,000	65,000	3,000
Inventories.........................	171,000	180,000	9,000*
Prepaid expenses....................	2,000	3,000	1,000*
Accounts payable...................	41,000	31,000	10,000*
Dividends payable..................	5,000	3,000	2,000*
Increase in working capital..............			$ 7,000

Funds statement *(concluded)*

Changes in working capital. The difference between the totals of the source section and the application section of the funds statement is identified as the increase or the decrease in working capital. The statement may conclude with this final amount, or the change in working capital may be supported by a schedule such as that appearing in the illustration. The two amounts reported as the increase or the decrease in working capital obviously must agree. Data for the schedule of changes are easily obtained from the comparative balance sheet.

All financial resources concept of funds

Instead of strict adherence to the working capital concept of funds there is substantial support for the somewhat broader concept of *all financial resources*.[2] Adherence to this concept requires that the funds statement report the financial aspects of all significant transactions between the enterprise and outsiders, regardless of whether they affect working capital. Transactions of this type which are of most frequent occurrence may be classified as follows:

1. Issuance of noncurrent liabilities or capital stock in exchange for non-current assets.
2. Issuance of capital stock in exchange for noncurrent liabilities.

Noncurrent liabilities or capital stock for noncurrent assets. Bonds, or other long-term liabilities, or capital stock of an enterprise are sometimes issued in exchange for buildings, land, patents, or other noncurrent assets. Such a transaction affects only noncurrent accounts; there is no change in the amount of working capital. However, it is a financial transaction that would ordinarily be significant. The transaction can be reported on the funds statement as two separate transactions: (1) as though funds were provided by issuance of the noncurrent liability or capital stock and (2) as though such funds were used to purchase the

667

---

[2]*Opinions of the Accounting Principles Board, No. 3,* "The Statement of Source and Application of Funds" (New York: American Institute of Certified Public Accountants, 1963).

noncurrent assets. To illustrate, assume that $50,000 of common stock is issued in exchange for patents valued at the same amount. The effects on funds may be noted as follows:

Source of funds:
    Issuance of common stock at par............ $50,000

Application of funds:
    Acquisition of patents..................... $50,000

Capital stock for noncurrent liabilities. Common stock of an enterprise is sometimes issued in exchange for some or all of its outstanding bonds or other noncurrent liabilities. Although such a transaction affects only noncurrent accounts, it may be reported on the funds statement both as a source of funds and as an application of funds. For example, the issuance of $100,000 of common stock in exchange for $100,000 of outstanding bonds could be reported on the funds statement as follows:

Source of funds:
    Issuance of common stock at par........... $100,000

Application of funds:
    Retirement of bonds payable.............. $100,000

Cash concept of funds

When *cash* is employed as the concept of funds, the analysis is devoted to the movement of cash rather than to the inflow and outflow of working capital. Data for a cash-flow statement could be developed from an analysis of the receipts and disbursements recorded in the cash account, employing detailed classifications for each source of receipts and each purpose of disbursements. The usual practice, however, is to combine such items as cash sales, receipts from customers on account, cash purchases, payments to creditors on account, and payment of expenses into the single category of "cash from operations." Other sources of cash are then presented on the cash-flow statement, followed by the various applications of cash.

Cash-flow analysis

There is much experimentation in the methodology of cash-flow analysis and the form of the cash-flow statement. The approach that will be employed here is patterned after the procedures used in the preceding discussion and illustrations. Although the two concepts of funds discussed earlier are more commonly used, particularly in preparing funds statements for reports to stockholders, the cash concept is useful in evaluating financial policies and current cash position. It is especially useful to management in preparing cash budgets.

The format of a funds statement based on the cash concept may be quite similar to the form illustrated on pages 666 and 667. Cash-flow

668

statements are divided into two principal sections, sources of cash and applications of cash. The difference between the totals of the two sections is the cash increase or cash decrease for the period. The principal parts of the report may be followed by a listing of the cash balance at the beginning of the period, the end of the period, and the net change. A variant is to begin the statement with the beginning cash balance, add the total of the sources section, subtract the total of the applications section, and conclude with the cash balance at the end of the period.

Assembling data for the cash-flow statement

Much of the cash-flow data is assembled in the manner illustrated earlier in assembling data for the funds statement. The comparative balance sheet on page 663 and the related financial data presented on succeeding pages will be used as the basis for illustration.

The following items of sources and applications of funds assembled earlier for Glendale Corporation were cash transactions:

Source of cash:
Sale of land............................. $18,000

Application of cash:
Purchase of equipment..................... $27,000
Retirement of bonds payable............... 20,000

The amount of cash provided by operations is ordinarily not identical with the amount of working capital so provided. The treatment of dividends may also differ if the rate has changed during the year.

Flow of cash from operations. As was explained earlier, the amount reported on the income statement as net income for the period is not a true measure of the inflow of working capital from operations. In the illustrative funds statement on page 666, the ordinary net income of $33,000 was increased by depreciation expense of $13,000, which had had no effect on working capital. It is equally evident that the same depreciation adjustment is required in the determination of cash-flow from operations. In addition, it is necessary to recognize the effect of the accrual method of accounting in its relationship to cash.

Not all of the costs and expenses (in addition to depreciation expense) reported on the income statement require an equivalent disbursement of cash. For some items, such as insurance and supplies, cash may be paid in advance of the time the benefits of the expenditure are converted to expense. For others, such as wages and taxes, the accrual of the expense may occur in the period preceding payment. Reference to the comparative balance sheet on page 663 indicates that the changes in the balances of accounts payable, inventories, and prepaid expenses necessitate adjustments to net income as a measure of cash inflow.

According to the comparative balance sheet, accounts payable (merchandise creditors) increased by $10,000 during the year. Inasmuch as accounts payable are composed solely of obligations arising from merchandise purchases, it is evident that the amount of cash disbursed was less, by $10,000, than the amount reported as purchases on the income statement. Consequently, $10,000 must be added to net income in determining the amount of cash provided by operations. In a similar manner the $9,000 decrease in inventories, which resulted from an excess of cost of goods sold over purchases, must be added back to net income. Finally, the decrease in prepaid expenses, as reported on the comparative balance sheet, indicates that the amount consumed during the year exceeded, by $1,000, the amount acquired. Although the $1,000 is unquestionably deductible from revenue as an expense of the period, it required no cash outlay during the period.

The amount of revenues during a period, determined by the accrual method of accounting, is seldom the exact equivalent of the cash received from revenue sources. According to the comparative balance sheet of Glendale Corporation, net trade receivables increased from $65,000 at the beginning of the year to $68,000 at the end. Revenue from sales was accordingly $3,000 greater than the amount of cash collected from customers, with the consequence that this amount must be deducted from net income in determining the amount of cash inflow from operations.

After giving effect to the adjustments described above, the details of the cash-provided-by-operations category may be noted as follows:

Source of cash:

Operations:		
Net income, exclusive of $12,000 gain on sale of land.		$33,000
Add: Depreciation on equipment and building.....	$13,000	
Increase in accounts payable...............	10,000	
Decrease in inventories....................	9,000	
Decrease in prepaid expenses..............	1,000	33,000
		$66,000
Deduct increase in trade receivables.............		3,000 $63,000

It should be evident that if any of the changes in the balances of the current asset or current liability accounts described had been in the opposite direction, the effect of the related adjustments to the reported net income would also have been reversed.

Cash applied to payment of dividends. As noted earlier in the analysis of funds-flow for Glendale Corporation, two semiannual cash dividends of $5,000 were declared during the year. The effect of the declaration was a $10,000 application of funds. If the balance of dividends payable had been $5,000 at both the beginning and end of the year there would have been a corresponding cash application of $10,000. However, the balance of the account increased from $3,000 to $5,000, indicating that the dividends declared during the year had exceeded the amount paid by $2,000. The effect of the dividend payments on cash flow may therefore be noted as follows:

Application of cash:		
Cash dividends declared..............	$10,000	
Deduct increase in dividends payable.....	2,000	$8,000

Form of the cash-flow statement

There are numerous variations in the format and terminology employed in statements of cash flow. The illustrative statement presented below is comparable in form to the funds statement illustrated earlier. The statement may conclude with the amount of increase or decrease in cash or it may be supported by a reconciliation such as that appearing in the illustration.

Glendale Corporation
Statement of Cash Flow
For Year Ended December 31, 1970

Source of cash:			
Operations:			
Net income, exclusive of $12,000 gain on sale of land........................		$33,000	
Add: Depreciation on equipment and building......................	$13,000		
Increase in accounts payable.....	10,000		
Decrease in inventories...........	9,000		
Decrease in prepaid expenses......	1,000	33,000	
		$66,000	
Deduct increase in trade receivables......		3,000	$63,000
Sale of land........................			18,000 $81,000
Application of cash:			
Purchase of equipment.................		$27,000	
Retirement of bonds payable............		20,000	
Payment of dividends:			
Cash dividends declared..............	$10,000		
Deduct increase in dividends payable.....	2,000	8,000	55,000
Increase in cash........................			$26,000
Schedule of change in cash:			
Cash balance, December 31, 1970..........			$48,000
Cash balance, December 31, 1969.........			22,000
Increase in cash........................			$26,000

Statement of cash flow

The information that is conveyed in a statement of cash flow is generally considered to be less significant than the data included in a funds statement. Accordingly, statements of source and application of funds are more often presented in financial reports to stockholders. Both types of statements might well be useful for managerial purposes but only one would ordinarily be presented in published reports.

Cash flow from operations

The term *cash flow* is sometimes encountered in reports to stockholders. It may be mentioned in a company president's letter to stockholders, in operating summaries, or elsewhere in the report. Although there are variations in the method of determination, cash flow is approximately equivalent to net income plus depreciation, depletion, or other expenses that had no effect on working capital. Thus, as the term is often used, it corresponds to *flow of funds from operations*, as reported on the funds statement. Synonyms sometimes employed for cash flow from operations are "cash income," "cash earnings," and "cash throw-off."

The amount of cash flow from operations for a period may be useful to internal financial management in considering the possibility of retiring long-term debt, in planning replacement of plant facilities, or in formulating dividend policies. However, when it is presented without reference to the funds statement and its importance stressed in reporting operations to stockholders, it is likely to be misunderstood. There may be a tendency for the reader to substitute cash flow for net income in appraising operating results. Ordinarily the magnitude of cash flow is larger than net income; even an enterprise with negative net income (loss) might well have a positive cash flow from operations.

Certified public accountants are substantially in agreement with the following recommendation:

> .... No generalization or conclusion can be drawn as to the significance of the "cash flow" without reference to the entire flow of funds as reflected in the complete statement of source and application of funds. . . .
>
> The amount of funds derived from operations cannot be considered as a substitute for or an improvement upon properly determined net income as a measure of results of operations and the consequent effect on financial position. Misleading implications can result from isolated statistics in annual reports of "cash flow" which are not placed in proper perspective to net income figures and to a complete analysis of source and application of funds. "Cash flow" and related terms should not be used in annual reports in such a way that the significance of net income is impaired, and "cash earnings" or other terms with a similar connotation should be avoided. The Board regards computations of "cash flow per share" as misleading since they ignore the impact of cash expenditures for renewal and replacement of facilities and tend to downgrade the significant economic statistic of "earnings per share."[3]

---

[3]*Ibid.*, pp. 17–18.

QUESTIONS

1. The word *fund* may be used to mean (a) cash or (b) a combination of cash and investments. Give an example of each usage.

2. What meanings are attached to *funds* as the term is employed in financial reports known as funds statements and cash flow statements?

3. (a) What is meant by *working capital*? (b) Name another term, other than "funds," that has the same meaning.

4. State the effect of each of the following transactions, considered individually, on working capital:

    (a) Purchased $3,000 of merchandise on account, terms 2/10, n/30.
    (b) Sold for $500 cash merchandise that had cost $325.
    (c) Borrowed $10,000 cash, issuing a 60-day, 6% note.
    (d) Issued a $5,000, 30-day note to a creditor in temporary settlement of an account payable.
    (e) Received $250 from a customer in payment of his account.
    (f) Purchased office equipment for $1,000 on account.
    (g) Issued 1,000 shares of common stock for $50 a share, receiving cash.

5. What is the effect on working capital of writing off $1,500 of uncollectible accounts against Allowance for Doubtful Accounts?

6. Give examples of (a) "noncurrent" asset accounts and (b) "noncurrent" liability accounts.

7. A corporation issued $1,000,000 of 10-year bonds for cash at 95. Was this a source or an application of funds and what was the amount?

8. Machinery with a cost of $15,000 and accumulated depreciation of $13,300 was sold for $2,000 cash. (a) What was the gain or loss on the sale? (b) What was the effect of the transaction on working capital? (c) How would the transaction be reported in the funds statement?

9. Fully depreciated office equipment costing $1,200 was discarded and no salvage was realized. What was the effect of the transaction on working capital?

10. The board of directors declared a cash dividend in December of the fiscal year ending December 31, payable on January 15. (a) What was the effect of the declaration on working capital? (b) Did the declaration represent a source or an application of funds, assuming funds are defined as working capital? (c) Did the payment of the dividend in January affect working capital, and, if so, how?

11. (a) What is the effect on working capital of the declaration and issuance of a stock dividend? (b) Assuming that funds are considered to be working capital, does the stock dividend represent a source or an application of funds?

12. A company reported a net loss on its income statement and an increase in working capital on its funds statement, both for the current year. Explain how the working capital could have increased in spite of the fact that during the period there were no sales of noncurrent assets and no issuances of noncurrent liabilities or capital stock.

13. The income statement reports a net loss of $10,000. The only revenue or expense item not affecting working capital was $6,000 of depreciation expense for the year. Will "operations" appear in the source section or the application section of the funds statement, and at what amount?

14. Why is depreciation expense for the year added to reported net income in arriving at the amount of funds provided by operations?

15. What is the effect on working capital of an appropriation of retained earnings for plant expansion?

16. When the "all financial resources" concept of funds is adopted, what two common types of transactions, other than transactions affecting working capital, would be reported on the funds statement?

17. How would the acquisition of $25,000 of equipment in exchange for a long-term note be reported on the funds statement, if funds are defined as: (a) working capital, (b) all financial resources?

18. An enterprise employing the accrual method of accounting owed merchandise creditors $11,000 at the beginning of the year and $6,000 at the end of the year. What adjustment for the $5,000 decrease must be made to net income in determining the amount of cash provided by operations? Explain.

19. If revenue from sales amounted to $570,000 for the year and trade receivables totaled $50,000 and $30,000 at the beginning and end of the year respectively, what was the amount of cash received from customers during the year?

20. The board of directors declared cash dividends totaling $120,000 during the year. The comparative balance sheet indicates dividends payable of $25,000 at the beginning of the year and $40,000 at the end of the year. What was the amount of cash disbursed to stockholders during the year?

EXERCISES

26-1. On the basis of the current assets and current liabilities of Finley Corporation listed below, prepare the section of the funds statement devoted to changes in working capital.

| | December 31 | |
	1970	1969
Cash.	$ 32,500	$ 35,000
Accounts receivable (net). . .	57,000	53,000
Notes receivable.	10,000	6,000
Inventories.	151,000	147,500
Prepaid expenses.	2,200	2,500
Accounts payable.	45,000	41,200
Salaries payable.	6,700	10,500

26-2. The net income reported on the income statement of Horton Corporation for the current year was $70,200. Adjustments to be made to net income to determine the amount of funds provided by operations, as well as some other data used for the year-end adjusting entries, are described below. Employing the working capital concept of funds, prepare the source of funds provided by operations section of the funds statement.

(a) Depreciation expense, $18,250.

(b) Uncollectible accounts expense, $2,400.

(c) Amortization of patents, $1,500.

(d) Interest accrued on notes receivable, $500.

(e) Income tax payable, $15,600.

(f) Wages accrued but not paid, $2,600.

26-3. On the basis of the details of the stockholders' equity accounts presented at the top of the next page, assemble in memorandum form the data needed to prepare a funds statement. (Ignore net income as a source.)

COMMON STOCK, $10 PAR

DATE		ITEM	DEBIT	CREDIT	BALANCE DEBIT	BALANCE CREDIT
19—						
Jan.	1	Balance, 25,000 shares				250,000
July	1	5,000 shares issued for cash		50,000		300,000
Dec.	31	1,500 share stock dividend		15,000		315,000

PREMIUM ON COMMON STOCK

DATE		ITEM	DEBIT	CREDIT	BALANCE DEBIT	BALANCE CREDIT
19—						
Jan.	1	Balance				90,000
July	1	5,000 shares issued		50,000		140,000
Dec.	31	Stock dividend		17,500		157,500

RETAINED EARNINGS

DATE		ITEM	DEBIT	CREDIT	BALANCE DEBIT	BALANCE CREDIT
19—						
Jan.	1	Balance				195,000
June	30	Cash dividend	12,500			182,500
Dec.	31	Cash dividend	15,000			167,500
	31	Stock dividend	32,500			135,000
	31	Net income		80,000		215,000

675

26-4. On the basis of the following data for Hoover Company, prepare a funds statement, omitting the schedule of changes in working capital. Assume that no items of equipment were disposed of during the year, that the stock was issued for cash, and that the only entries in the retained earnings account were for net income of $40,000 and cash dividends of $25,000.

	June 30 1970	June 30 1969	
Cash	$ 45,000	$ 30,000	15
Trade receivables (net)	60,000	50,000	10
Inventories	81,000	63,000	18
Equipment	155,000	115,000	40
Accumulated depreciation	(55,000)	(40,000)	(15)
Land	45,000	30,000	15
	$331,000	$248,000	83
Accounts payable (merchandise creditors)	$ 60,000	$ 52,000	8
Common stock, $25 par	200,000	150,000	50
Premium on common stock	10,000	—	10
Retained earnings	61,000	46,000	15
	$331,000	$248,000	83

26-5. From the data presented in Exercise 26-4, prepare a statement of cash flow, omitting the schedule of change in cash.

26-6. On the basis of the details of the plant asset account presented below, assemble in memorandum form the data needed to prepare a funds statement, employing the all financial resources concept of funds.

LAND

DATE		ITEM	DEBIT	CREDIT	BALANCE DEBIT	BALANCE CREDIT
19—						
Jan.	1	Balance			100,000	
May	6	Sold for $50,000 cash		30,000	70,000	
June	20	Purchased for cash	25,000		95,000	
Dec.	10	Purchased with long-term mortgage note	75,000		170,000	

26-7. The net income reported on the income statement of Dodson Company for the current year was $25,000. Depreciation recorded on equipment and building for the year amounted to $15,000. Balances of the current asset and current liability accounts at the end and beginning of the year are listed below. Prepare the cash provided by operations section of a statement of cash flow.

	End	Beginning
Trade receivables......................	$38,000	$30,000
Inventories..........................	45,000	35,000
Prepaid expenses......................	3,000	2,200
Accounts payable (merchandise creditors)...	36,500	41,500
Salaries payable.......................	4,550	3,500

PROBLEMS

The following additional problems for this chapter are located in Appendix C: 26-1B, 26-2B, 26-3B.

26-1A. The comparative balance sheet of the Carter Corporation at June 30, 1970 and 1969, appears below in condensed form.

Assets	1970	1969
Cash.....................................	$ 19,900	$ 28,100
Accounts receivable (net)................	21,200	30,700
Merchandise inventory....................	89,600	94,500
Prepaid expenses........................	2,600	2,950
Plant assets............................	198,000	150,000
Accumulated depreciation — plant assets ...	(44,000)	(64,000)
	$287,300	$242,250

Liabilities and Stockholders' Equity		
Accounts payable.......................	$ 45,800	$ 27,900
Mortgage note payable..................	—	50,000
Common stock, $10 par.................	150,000	100,000
Premium on common stock..............	10,000	—
Retained earnings.....................	81,500	64,350
	$287,300	$242,250

Additional data obtained from the income statement and from an examination of the noncurrent asset, noncurrent liability, and stockholders' equity accounts in the ledger are as follows:

(a) Net income for the year, $29,150.
(b) Depreciation expense for the year, $10,000.
(c) Cash dividends declared during the year, $12,000.
(d) The mortgage note payable was due in 1975, but the terms permitted earlier payment without penalty.
(e) An addition to the building was constructed during the year at a cost of $78,000, and fully depreciated equipment costing $30,000 was discarded, no salvage being realized.
(f) During the year 5,000 shares of common stock were issued for cash at $12.

Instructions:

(1) On the basis of the comparative balance sheet and the other information, assemble in memorandum form the data needed to prepare a funds statement (working capital concept) for the year ended June 30, 1970.
(2) Prepare a statement of source and application of funds, including a schedule of changes in working capital.

26-2A. The comparative balance sheet of the Lane Corporation at December 31, 1970 and 1969, appears below in condensed form.

Assets	1970	1969
Cash	$ 34,900	$ 23,500
Marketable securities	30,300	28,300
Accounts receivable	48,600	41,400
Inventories	29,100	24,200
Prepaid expenses	2,700	2,200
Buildings	160,400	110,400
Accumulated depreciation—buildings	(40,100)	(36,900)
Machinery and equipment	75,000	75,000
Accumulated depreciation—machinery and equipment	(27,000)	(15,000)
Land	30,000	30,000
Patents	48,000	51,000
	$391,900	$334,100

Liabilities and Stockholders' Equity		
Accounts payable	$ 25,300	$ 33,000
Salaries payable	15,700	12,900
Mortgage note payable	50,000	——
Bonds payable	10,000	60,000
Common stock, $10 par	230,000	180,000
Premium on common stock	23,000	23,000
Retained earnings	37,900	25,200
	$391,900	$334,100

An examination of the income statement and the accounting records revealed the following additional information:

(a) Net income for the year, $28,700.
(b) Cash dividends declared during the year, $16,000.

(c) Depreciation expense for the year: buildings, $3,200; machinery and equipment, $12,000.

(d) Patent amortization for the year, $3,000.

(e) A mortgage note due in 1974 was issued in payment of the purchase of a building costing $50,000.

(f) 5,000 shares of common stock were issued in exchange for $50,000 of bonds payable.

Instructions:

(1) On the basis of the information presented above, assemble in memorandum form the data needed to prepare a funds statement (all financial resources concept) for the year ended December 31, 1970.

(2) Prepare a statement of source and application of funds, including a schedule of changes in working capital.

26-3A. Condensed versions of the comparative balance sheet and income statement of Oxford Company are presented below and at the top of the next page.

Comparative Balance Sheet
December 31, 1970 and 1969

Assets	1970	1969
Cash..................................	$ 46,000	$ 28,900
Trade receivables (net).................	41,000	45,000
Inventories..........................	48,000	51,000
Prepaid expenses......................	4,100	3,700
Machinery...........................	330,000	310,000
Accumulated depreciation — machinery....	(131,000)	(185,000)
Buildings............................	580,000	475,000
Accumulated depreciation — buildings.....	(225,000)	(215,000)
Land................................	60,000	50,000
	$753,100	$563,600

Liabilities and Stockholders' Equity

	1970	1969
Accounts payable (merchandise creditors)...	$ 32,500	$ 37,000
Wages payable	4,500	7,500
Income tax payable....................	7,000	5,000
Mortgage note payable, due 1980.........	100,000	——
Common stock, $20 par.................	400,000	350,000
Premium on common stock..............	55,000	45,000
Retained earnings.....................	154,100	119,100
	$753,100	$563,600

Additional data obtained from an examination of the ledger are as follows:

(a) Dividends of $40,000 were declared during the year.

(b) Machinery with an original cost of $80,000 and accumulated depreciation of $74,000 was sold during the year for $6,000 cash. New machinery was also purchased for $100,000 cash.

(c) Land and buildings were acquired during the year at a cost of $115,000. In addition to a down payment of $15,000, a ten-year, 6% mortgage note for $100,000 was issued to the seller.

(d) Common stock with a par of $50,000 was issued for $60,000 cash.

Income Statement
For Year Ended December 31, 1970

Sales....................................		$810,000
Cost of goods sold......................		460,000
Gross profit on sales....................		$350,000
Operating expenses:		
Depreciation expense — machinery......	$ 20,000	
Depreciation expense — buildings.......	10,000	
Other operating expenses.............	175,500	205,500
Income before income tax................		$144,500
Income tax..............................		69,500
Net income		$ 75,000

Instructions:

Prepare a statement of cash flow including a schedule of change in cash.

26-4A. The comparative balance sheet of Davis, Inc. at December 31, 1970 and 1969, in condensed form, and the noncurrent asset accounts, the noncurrent liability accounts, and the stockholders' equity accounts for 1970 are presented below and on pages 680 and 681.

Assets	1970	1969
Cash....................................	$ 73,650	$ 48,500
Accounts receivable (net)..............	84,200	67,300
Inventories............................	235,820	245,350
Prepaid expenses......................	6,250	5,350
Equipment.............................	445,500	375,500
Accumulated depreciation — equipment..	(86,000)	(75,000)
Buildings..............................	380,750	241,000
Accumulated depreciation — buildings....	(31,100)	(22,750)
Land...................................	50,000	90,000
Discount on bonds payable.............	9,500	——
	$1,168,570	$975,250

Liabilities and Stockholders' Equity	1970	1969
Accounts payable......................	$ 37,250	$ 90,030
Income tax payable....................	14,600	15,500
Bonds payable.........................	200,000	——
Common stock.........................	618,000	600,000
Premium on common stock.............	48,000	45,000
Appropriation for contingencies.........	50,000	30,000
Retained earnings.....................	200,720	194,720
	$1,168,570	$975,250

EQUIPMENT

DATE		ITEM	DEBIT	CREDIT	BALANCE	
					DEBIT	CREDIT
1970						
Jan.	1	Balance			375,500	
Apr.	12	Discarded, no salvage		25,000		
July	17	Purchased for cash	60,000			
Nov.	18	Purchased for cash	35,000		445,500	

ACCUMULATED DEPRECIATION — EQUIPMENT

DATE		ITEM	DEBIT	CREDIT	BALANCE DEBIT	BALANCE CREDIT
1970						
Jan.	1	Balance				75,000
Apr.	12	Equipment discarded	25,000			
Dec.	31	Depreciation for year		36,000		86,000

BUILDINGS

DATE		ITEM	DEBIT	CREDIT	BALANCE DEBIT	BALANCE CREDIT
1970						
Jan.	1	Balance			241,000	
July	9	Purchased for cash	139,750		380,750	

ACCUMULATED DEPRECIATION — BUILDINGS

DATE		ITEM	DEBIT	CREDIT	BALANCE DEBIT	BALANCE CREDIT
1970						
Jan.	1	Balance				22,750
Dec.	31	Depreciation for year		8,350		31,100

LAND

DATE		ITEM	DEBIT	CREDIT	BALANCE DEBIT	BALANCE CREDIT
1970						
Jan.	1	Balance			90,000	
Nov.	17	Sold for $45,000 cash		40,000	50,000	

DISCOUNT ON BONDS PAYABLE

DATE		ITEM	DEBIT	CREDIT	BALANCE DEBIT	BALANCE CREDIT
1970						
July	1	Bonds issued	10,000		10,000	
Dec.	31	Amortization		500	9,500	

BONDS PAYABLE

DATE		ITEM	DEBIT	CREDIT	BALANCE DEBIT	BALANCE CREDIT
1970						
July	1	Issued 10-year bonds		200,000		200,000

COMMON STOCK, $25 PAR

DATE		ITEM	DEBIT	CREDIT	BALANCE DEBIT	BALANCE CREDIT
1970						
Jan.	1	Balance				600,000
Dec.	10	Stock dividend		18,000		618,000

DATE		ITEM	DEBIT	CREDIT	BALANCE DEBIT	BALANCE CREDIT
1970						
Jan.	1	Balance				45,000
Dec.	10	Stock dividend		3,000		48,000

APPROPRIATION FOR CONTINGENCIES

DATE		ITEM	DEBIT	CREDIT	BALANCE DEBIT	BALANCE CREDIT
1970						
Jan.	1	Balance				30,000
Dec.	31	Appropriation		20,000		50,000

RETAINED EARNINGS

DATE		ITEM	DEBIT	CREDIT	BALANCE DEBIT	BALANCE CREDIT
1970						
Jan.	1	Balance				194,720
Apr.	10	Cash dividend	9,000			
Oct.	10	Cash dividend	9,000			
Dec.	10	Stock dividend	21,000			
	31	Appropriated	20,000			
	31	Net income		65,000		200,720

Instructions:

(1) On the basis of the comparative balance sheet and the accounts of Davis, Inc., assemble in memorandum form the data needed to prepare a funds statement (working capital concept) for the year ended December 31, 1970. (Exclude from operating income the gain on the sale of land.)

(2) Prepare a statement of source and application of funds, including a schedule of changes in working capital.

26-5A. The comparative balance sheet of Powers Company at December 31, 1970 and 1969 and a condensed income statement for the year ended December 31, 1970 are presented below and at the top of the following page.

Comparative Balance Sheet

Assets	1970	1969
Cash....................................	$ 47,500	$ 22,500
Marketable securities....................	12,500	7,500
Trade receivables (net).................	69,900	75,600
Inventories.............................	90,000	76,400
Prepaid expenses........................	2,000	1,750
Equipment...............................	287,500	260,000
Accumulated depreciation — equipment....	(105,400)	(80,750)
Buildings...............................	230,000	190,000
Accumulated depreciation — buildings.....	(60,500)	(53,000)
Land....................................	40,000	30,000
	$613,500	$530,000

Liabilities and Stockholders' Equity

Accounts payable (merchandise creditors)...	$ 34,000	$ 37,500
Income tax payable....................	12,000	11,000
Dividends payable.....................	15,000	10,000
Mortgage note payable.................	50,000	——
Bonds payable........................	100,000	100,000
Common stock........................	260,000	250,000
Premium on common stock.............	39,000	35,000
Retained earnings....................	103,500	86,500
	$613,500	$530,000

Income Statement

Sales.....................................	$945,000
Cost of goods sold.........................	667,500
Gross profit on sales......................	$277,500
Operating expenses (including depreciation of $32,150).	187,000
Net income from operations.................	$ 90,500
Interest income...........................	400
	$ 90,900
Interest expense...........................	6,900
Income before income tax..................	$ 84,000
Income tax................................	37,000
Net income................................	$ 47,000

682 Additional information obtained from an examination of the ledger is as follows:

(a) Marketable securities were purchased for $5,000 cash during the year.
(b) A five-year, 6% mortgage note payable for $50,000 was issued in payment of additional land and buildings acquired during the year.
(c) Equipment was purchased for $27,500 cash during the year.
(d) During the year, 1,000 shares of common stock were issued for cash at $14.
(e) Cash dividends of $30,000 were declared during the year.

Instructions:

(1) Prepare a statement of source and application of funds (including a schedule of changes in working capital) employing the all financial resources concept of funds.

(2) Prepare a statement of cash flow including a schedule of change in cash.

27

Consolidated statements and other statements

The history of business organization in the United States has been characterized by continuous growth in the size of business entities and the combining of separate enterprises to form even larger operating units. The trend toward combining individual businesses engaged either in similar types of activity or in wholly dissimilar pursuits has been influenced by such objectives as efficiencies of large-scale production, broadening of markets and sales volume, reduction of competition, diversification of product lines, and savings in income taxes.

The methods and procedures employed in combining separate corporations into larger operating units are varied and complex. The discussion that follows is intended to be only of an introductory nature, with particular emphasis on the financial statements of business combinations. Combinations may be effected through a fusion of two or more corporations to form a single unit or through common control of two or more corporations by means of stock ownership.

Mergers and consolidations

When one corporation acquires the properties of another corporation and the latter then dissolves, the fusion of the two enterprises is called a *merger*. Ordinarily all of the assets of the acquired company, as well as its liabilities, are taken over by the acquiring company, which continues its operations as a single unit. Payment may be in the form of cash, obligations, or capital stock of the acquiring corporation, or there may be a combination of several types of consideration. In any event the consideration received by the dissolving corporation is distributed to its stockholders in final liquidation.

When two or more corporations transfer their assets and liabilities to a corporation which has been created for purposes of the take-over, the combination is called a *consolidation*. The new corporation ordinarily issues its own securities in exchange for the properties acquired, and the original corporations are dissolved.

There are many legal, financial, managerial, and accounting problems associated with mergers and consolidations. Perhaps the most crucial matter is the determination of the class and amount of securities to be issued to the owners of the dissolving corporations. The resolution of this problem is based on the relative value of the net assets contributed and on the relative earning capacities of the respective units. The relative bargaining ability of the negotiators is also likely to affect the final outcome to a significant degree.

The assets acquired by the continuing corporation in a merger or consolidation may be recorded at their agreed values, in a comparable manner to that described earlier in connection with organizing a partnership or admitting new partners. Value in excess of the total amount assigned to specific assets on the basis of appraisals may be associated with excess earning capacity and identified as goodwill.

Parent and subsidiary corporations

In addition to effecting a business combination through the fusion of two or more corporations, similar objectives may be achieved through ownership by one corporation of a controlling interest in one or more other corporations. When this method is employed in combining corporate enterprises, none of the participants dissolves; all continue as separate legal entities. The corporation owning all or a majority of the voting stock of another corporation is known as the *parent* company and the corporation that is controlled is known as the *subsidiary* company. A corporation that controls a number of subsidiaries and confines its activities primarily to their management is sometimes called a *holding* company. Although each corporation maintains its separate legal identity, the relationship between parent and subsidiary is somewhat like that between the home office of an enterprise and one of its branch offices. Two or more corporations closely related through stock ownership are sometimes referred to as *affiliated* or *associated* companies.

The amount of the parent company's investment in the stock of its subsidiary is reported on the parent company's balance sheet as a long-term investment. The parent company's share of the net income of the subsidiary, as determined by its proportionate stock ownership, is reported on the parent's income statement. Retention of earnings by the subsidiary increases the amount of its stockholders' equity and hence the amount of the parent's investment. Payment of dividends by the subsidiary has the opposite effect, reducing its stockholders' equity and the amount of the parent's investment. Other intercorporate transactions with a reciprocal effect on the financial statements include acquisition, by one of the corporations, of bonds payable or other obligations of the other, and by the purchase and sale of commodities and services between them.

Because of the control of a subsidiary by its parent company, and the intertwining of their transactions, it is often considered desirable to combine their financial statements as though they were a single unit. Such statements are likely to be more useful than separate statements for each corporation, except for a subsidiary engaged in business operations wholly unlike those of the parent. An example of the exceptional situation would be an automobile manufacturer owning all of the stock in a subsidiary corporation engaged in purchasing and servicing installment finance contracts obtained from the parent's retail agencies.

Composite financial reports of a parent corporation and one or more subsidiaries are referred to generally as *consolidated* statements. Specifically, they may be identified by adding "and subsidiary" to the name of the parent company or by modifying the title of the respective statements, as in *consolidated balance sheet* or *consolidated income statement*.[1]

Basic principles of consolidation

The basic principles applicable to the consolidation of the statements of a parent corporation and its subsidiaries are similar to those described earlier for combining the statements of a home office and its branch offices. The ties of relationship between the separate corporations are evidenced by the reciprocal accounts appearing in their respective ledgers and financial statements. It is necessary to eliminate these reciprocals from the statements that are to be consolidated. The remaining items on the subsidiary's financial statements are then combined with the like items on the financial statements of the parent.

The complexity of the problems encountered in determining the eliminations varies greatly, being influenced by the manner in which the parent-subsidiary relationship was created, the extent of the parent corporation's ownership of the subsidiary, and the nature of their continuing transactions with each other. If the parent corporation creates the subsidiary, holds all of its stock, and does not buy commodities or services from or sell them to the subsidiary, their financial statements can be consolidated with a minimum of difficulty. On the other hand,

[1]Examples of consolidated statements are presented in Appendix B.

if the parent corporation acquires control of an already existing company by purchasing less than 100% of its stock and engages in profit-making activities with the subsidiary, the consolidation of their statements may present intricate problems.

Consolidated balance sheet

The stock of a subsidiary acquired by the parent is recorded in an investment account in the parent company's ledger. The reciprocal of the investment account in the subsidiary's ledger at the date of acquisition is the composite of all of its stockholders' equity accounts. Attention will first be directed to consolidating the balance sheets immediately after the relationship of parent and subsidiary has been established. The illustrative companies will be identified merely as Parent and Subsidiary.

Consolidation at time of acquisition. In order to direct attention more effectively to the basic concepts, most of the data appearing in financial statements will be omitted from the illustrations and the term "net assets" will be used as a substitute for the specific assets and liabilities that appear on the balance sheet. Explanations will also be simplified by using the term "book value" in referring to the amount of the stockholders' equity of the subsidiary acquired by the parent.

Wholly owned subsidiary acquired at a cost equal to book value. Assume that Parent creates Subsidiary, transferring to it $120,000 of assets and $20,000 of liabilities, and taking in exchange 1,000 shares of $100 par common stock of Subsidiary. The effect of the transaction on Parent is to replace net assets of $100,000 with a single item: Investment in Subsidiary, $100,000. This effect on the balance sheet of Parent, together with the balance sheet of Subsidiary prepared immediately after the transaction, is depicted below.

	Assets	Capital
Parent:		
Investment in subsidiary, 1,000 shares...............	$100,000	
Subsidiary:		
Net assets...	$100,000	
Common stock, 1,000 shares........................		$100,000

In consolidating the balance sheets of the two corporations, the reciprocal accounts Investment in Subsidiary and Common Stock are offset against each other, or eliminated. The individual assets (Cash, Equipment, etc.) and the individual liabilities (Accounts payable, etc.) comprising the $100,000 of net assets on the balance sheet of Subsidiary are then added to the corresponding items on the balance sheet of Parent. The consolidated balance sheet is completed by listing Parent's capital stock and other paid-in capital balances, and retained earnings.

Wholly owned subsidiary acquired at a cost above book value. Instead of organizing a subsidiary corporation, a corporation may acquire an established business by purchasing the stock of an existing company. In such cases the cost of the stock to the parent company ordinarily differs from the book value of the stock. To illustrate, assume that Parent acquires for $180,000 all of the outstanding stock of Subsidiary, a going concern, from Subsidiary's stockholders. Assume further that the capital, or stockholders' equity, of Subsidiary is composed of 1,000 shares of $100 par common stock and retained earnings of $50,000. Parent records the investment at its cost of $180,000, regardless of the amount of book value of Subsidiary. It should also be noted that the $180,000 paid to stockholders has no effect on the assets, liabilities, or capital of Subsidiary. The situation immediately after the transaction may be presented as follows:

	ASSETS	CAPITAL
Parent:		
Investment in subsidiary, 1,000 shares...	$180,000	
Subsidiary:		
Net assets...	$150,000	
Common stock, 1,000 shares...		$100,000
Retained earnings...		50,000

It is readily apparent that the reciprocal items on the separate balance sheets are unequal by the amount of $30,000. If the reciprocals are eliminated, as in the preceding illustration, and are replaced on the consolidated balance sheet solely by the $150,000 of net assets of Subsidiary, the total assets reported will be less, by $30,000, than the combined total of liabilities and capital. There are several alternative methods of reporting the $30,000 excess of cost over book value, depending on the attendant circumstances.

If the assets of Subsidiary are determined to be undervalued because of excessive depreciation or amortization recorded in earlier years or because of changing price levels, the $30,000 could be absorbed by upward adjustments to such assets. Alternatively, part of the price paid for the stock might be in recognition of Subsidiary's favorable earning capacity, in which case the $30,000 would be reported on the consolidated balance sheet as "goodwill." In many instances the amount of research required to authenticate the nature of the balancing amount would be prohibitive, or it might be impossible to obtain verifiable objective evidence. A common practice, which will be followed in this chapter, is to describe the item as "Excess of cost over book value of subsidiary interest." It is reported in the assets section of the consolidated balance sheet, frequently as the last item.

Wholly owned subsidiary acquired at a cost below book value. When all of the stock of a corporation is acquired from its stockholders at a cost which is less than book value, the situation is the reverse of that described in the preceding section. For purposes of illustration, assume that the stock in Subsidiary is acquired for $130,000 and that the capital of Subsidiary is composed of 1,000 shares of $100 par common stock and retained earnings of $50,000. Parent records the investment at its cost of $130,000. The situation immediately after the transaction is as follows:

	ASSETS	CAPITAL
Parent:		
Investment in subsidiary, 1,000 shares...............	$130,000	
Subsidiary:		
Net assets..	$150,000	
Common stock, 1,000 shares........................		$100,000
Retained earnings.................................		50,000

Elimination of the reciprocal accounts and reporting the $150,000 of net assets of Subsidiary on the consolidated balance sheet creates an imbalance of $20,000. The possible explanations for the "bargain" purchase would be somewhat the reverse of those given in support of acquisition at a price higher than book value. In the absence of satisfactory substantiating evidence, the balancing item, in this case $20,000, would be reported on the consolidated balance sheet, usually as the last item in the liabilities section. It is identified as "Excess of book value of subsidiary interest over cost" or a variant with similar meaning.

688   *Partially owned subsidiary acquired at a cost above or below book value.* When one corporation seeks to achieve control over another by purchase of its stock, it is not necessary and often not feasible to acquire all of the stock. To illustrate this situation, assume that Parent acquires 80% of the 1,000 shares of $100 par common stock of Subsidiary, whose total stockholders' equity is $180,000. The 800 shares are purchased from the stockholders of Subsidiary at a total cost of $190,000. The relevant data immediately after the acquisition of the stock are presented below.

	ASSETS	CAPITAL
Parent:		
Investment in subsidiary, 800 shares.................	$190,000	
Subsidiary:		
Net assets..	$180,000	
Common stock, 1,000 shares........................		$100,000
Retained earnings.................................		80,000

The explanation of the $10,000 imbalance in the reciprocal items is less apparent than in the preceding two illustrations. Parent acquired 800 shares, or 80%, of the 1,000 outstanding shares of Subsidiary, hence only 80% of the stockholders' equity accounts of Subsidiary can be eliminated. The remaining 20% of the stock is owned by outsiders, who are referred to collectively as *minority interest*. Subsidiary's common stock and retained earnings allocable to the minority interest are reported on the consolidated balance sheet, ordinarily preceding the stockholders' equity accounts of Parent. The partial elimination of Subsidiary's common stock and retained earnings and the determination of the amount of the minority interest are computed as follows:

Subsidiary:

Common stock.....................................	$100,000	
Eliminate 80% of Subsidiary stock.................	80,000	$ 20,000
Retained earnings.................................	$ 80,000	
Eliminate 80% of Subsidiary retained earnings......	64,000	16,000
Minority interest.................................		$ 36,000

The difference between the $190,000 paid by Parent for the stock of Subsidiary and the book value acquired is determined as follows:

Parent:

Investment in subsidiary...........................	$190,000	
Eliminate 80% of Subsidiary stock.................	$ 80,000	
Eliminate 80% of Subsidiary retained earnings......	64,000	
Excess of cost over book value of subsidiary interest........		$ 46,000

It should be noted that the two eliminations from the stockholders' equity accounts of Subsidiary ($80,000 and $64,000) are exactly matched by the two eliminations from Parent's investment account.

Consolidation subsequent to acquisition. The net income of a subsidiary corporation earned subsequent to its acquisition effects an increase in the parent company's investment. The parent's share of such earnings may be recorded periodically by debiting the account Investment in Subsidiary and crediting Income of Subsidiary. The credit to Income of Subsidiary is transferred to the parent's retained earnings account through the periodic closing of accounts. A dividend received by the parent corporation from its subsidiary reduces the amount of its investment; it is recorded by a debit to Cash and a credit to Investment in Subsidiary.

In preparing consolidated balance sheets subsequent to acquisition, the amount eliminated from Investment in Subsidiary on the parent's balance sheet and from the stockholders' equity accounts on the subsidiary's balance sheet will change each year, keeping pace with the changes in the balance of the subsidiary's retained earnings. The amount originally determined as the difference between the parent's cost of the investment and the related book value of the subsidiary will, of course, remain unchanged.

To illustrate the analysis required subsequent to acquisition, assume that Subsidiary in the preceding illustration earns net income of $50,000 and pays dividends of $20,000 during the year subsequent to Parent's acquisition of 80% of its stock. The net effect on Subsidiary is thus

689

an increase of $30,000 ($50,000 − $20,000) in net assets and in its retained earnings account. The effect of Subsidiary's operations on Parent's investment account is an increase of $24,000 (80% of $30,000), as indicated by the following illustrative entries by Parent:

Investment in Subsidiary..........................	40,000	
Income of Subsidiary...........................		40,000
Cash......................................	16,000	
Investment in Subsidiary.......................		16,000

Continuing with the illustration, the balance in Subsidiary's retained earnings account has increased from $80,000 at date of acquisition to $110,000 ($80,000 + $50,000 − $20,000) at the later date. Correspondingly, the balance in Investment in Subsidiary, in Parent's ledger, has increased from the original cost of $190,000 to $214,000 ($190,000 + $40,000 − $16,000). Eliminations from the partially reciprocal accounts and determination of the amounts to be reported on the consolidated balance sheet are as follows:

Subsidiary:		
Common stock.....................................	$100,000	
Eliminate 80% of Subsidiary stock................	80,000	$ 20,000
Retained earnings....................................	$110,000	
Eliminate 80% of Subsidiary retained earnings......	88,000	22,000
Minority interest.....................................		$ 42,000
Parent:		
Investment in subsidiary............................	$214,000	
Eliminate 80% of Subsidiary stock.................	$ 80,000	
Eliminate 80% of Subsidiary retained earnings......	88,000	
Excess of cost over book value of Subsidiary interest........		$ 46,000

In comparing the above computations with the analysis as of the date of acquisition (page 689), note (1) that the minority interest increased by $6,000 ($36,000 to $42,000) which is equivalent to 20% of the $30,000 net increase in Subsidiary's retained earnings and (2) that the excess of cost over book value of the subsidiary interest remained unchanged at $46,000.

Consolidated income statement and other statements

The consolidation of the income statement and other statements of affiliated companies usually presents fewer complexities than are encountered in balance sheet consolidations. The difference is largely because of the inherent nature of the statements. The balance sheet reports cumulative effects of all transactions from the very beginning of an enterprise to a current date, whereas the income statement, the retained earnings statement, and the funds statement are restricted to

690

selected transactions only and are for a limited period of time, usually a year.

In consolidating the income statements of a parent and its wholly or partly owned subsidiary, the amount of sales, purchases, interest income, interest expense, management fee revenue, management fee expense, and all similar operating data resulting from intercompany transactions should be fully eliminated. It may also be necessary to eliminate intercompany gross profit from beginning and ending inventories in determining consolidated gross profit. The eliminations required in consolidating the retained earnings statement and any other statements are based largely on data assembled in consolidating the balance sheet and the income statement.

Pooling of interests

The combinations discussed thus far have been viewed as the purchase of one business enterprise by another business enterprise. Differences between the purchase price of the stock or assets acquired and their related book value or basis were given recognition through revaluation of specific assets, by reporting goodwill, or by reporting the "excess" as a single item on the consolidated balance sheet.

An alternative accounting treatment of business combinations which has been employed increasingly during the past two decades is called *pooling of interests*. When a combination is effected through exchanges of stock between corporations and substantially all of the original ownership is continued, the combination may be said to be a pooling of interests. It is as though the corporations join forces, with the original stockholders of the constituent companies continuing in control. The corporations may maintain their separate legal entities or, through cancellation of shares, one may be merged into the other. It should be noted that the exact criteria for differentiating between a combination characterized as a purchase and one that qualifies as a pooling of interests are still a subject of debate in the accounting profession.

When a combination is deemed to be a pooling of interests, there is no new basis of accountability. The assets of the constituent companies are carried forward in the combination without changes in value. The retained earnings of the separate companies may also be combined and reported as a single item on the balance sheet of the combined corporations. To illustrate the procedure for consolidating the balance sheets of two corporations deemed to have pooled their interests, the basic data assumed for the illustration on page 687 will be reexamined under slightly different conditions.

The net assets of Subsidiary remain unchanged at $150,000, as in the earlier illustration. It is also assumed that both corporations agree, as

691

before, that the net assets are worth $180,000. Instead of purchasing the 1,000 outstanding shares of Subsidiary stock for $180,000, Parent is to issue its own $5 par common stock in exchange. The number of shares to be issued is to be based on its current market value of $9 a share. Basic balance sheet data for Parent prior to the acquisition are as follows:

	ASSETS	CAPITAL
Parent:		
Net assets......................................	$230,000	
Common stock, 20,000 shares.......................		$100,000
Retained earnings................................		130,000

The number of Parent Corporation shares to be issued in exchange for Subsidiary's outstanding stock is 20,000 ($180,000 [value of Subsidiary net assets] ÷ $9 [market value of Parent stock]). Parent records the investment at $100,000, which is equivalent to the par of its 20,000 shares issued in exchange. Basic balance sheet data of the two corporations after the exchange of stock are as follows:

	ASSETS	CAPITAL
Parent:		
Investment in subsidiary, 1,000 shares................	$100,000	
Other net assets....................................	230,000	
Common stock, 40,000 shares.......................		$200,000
Retained earnings..................................		130,000
Subsidiary:		
Net assets....................,....................	$150,000	
Common stock, 1,000 shares.......................		$100,000
Retained earnings		50,000

In consolidating the balance sheets of the two companies in accordance with the pooling of interests concept, Parent's investment account and Subsidiary's common stock account are eliminated. The net assets of the two companies ($230,000 and $150,000) are then combined without changes in valuation, and the amounts of their retained earnings ($130,000 + $50,000) are also combined for presentation on the consolidated balance sheet.

In preparing the consolidated balance sheet when the amount recorded in the parent corporation's investment account at the time of acquisition exceeds the balance of the subsidiary's capital stock account, the excess is deducted from other paid-in capital accounts until such accounts are eliminated. Any remaining excess is deducted from retained earnings. If the reverse situation applies, the excess of the subsidiary's capital stock account over the parent's investment account is reported on the consolidated balance sheet as additional paid-in capital.

Purchase accounting versus pooling of interests

As indicated earlier, the criteria for differentiating between the purchase of one corporation by another, and the pooling of interests of two corporations are not well defined. As a result, accounting practice permits the selection of either alternative accounting method in many cases. Continuing innovation in methods of effecting business combinations and in types of securities employed have also tended to hinder an acceptable resolution of the problem.

Numerous articles devoted to the accounting for business combinations continue to appear in professional periodicals and the financial press. The publication of two research studies sponsored by the AICPA is indicative of the complexities of the problem and the continuing search for a consensus.[2] In interpreting the financial statements of corporations that have been affected significantly by combinations, particularly the so-called "multi-industry" or "conglomerate" concerns, an understanding of the accounting methods employed is essential.

Alternative forms of principal financial statements[3]

Conventional forms of the principal financial statements have been described and illustrated in earlier chapters. There are many possible variations in the general format of such statements as well as differences in terminology employed and the extent to which details are presented. Some of the variations in the form of published statements are described and illustrated in the sections that follow.

Financial position form of balance sheet. The arrangement of assets on the left-hand side of the statement, with the liabilities and stockholders' equity on the right-hand side, is the traditional and still the customary form of the balance sheet. If the entire statement is confined to a single page, it is customary to present the three sections in a downward sequence with the total of the assets section equaling the combined totals of the other two sections. Two variations from the customary forms are encountered with sufficient frequency to justify brief consideration. Both are sometimes referred to as the *financial position* or *financial condition* form of the balance sheet. In one of the variations the total of the liabilities section is subtracted from the total of the assets section to yield stockholders' equity. The other variant emphasizes the working capital position of an enterprise by deducting current liabilities from current assets. The illustration on the next page was severely condensed to focus attention on its principal features. Such condensation is not an essential characteristic of the form.

693

---

[2]Arthur R. Wyatt, *A Critical Study of Accounting for Business Combinations,* Accounting Research Study No. 5 (New York: American Institute of Certified Public Accountants, 1963), 146 pages.

George R. Catlett and Norman O. Olson, *Accounting for Goodwill,* Accounting Research Study No. 10 (New York: American Institute of Certified Public Accountants, 1968), 180 pages.

[3]Examples of some of the alternative forms described in this section are presented in Appendix B.

Electronic Products, Inc.
Statement of Financial Position
September 30, 19—

Current assets................................		$420,600
Deduct:		
Current liabilities..........................		180,400
Working capital............................		$240,200
Add:		
Investments................................	$150,000	
Plant assets (net)..........................	522,300	672,300
Total assets less current liabilities..............		$912,500
Deduct:		
Long-term liabilities........................		200,000
Net assets.................................		$712,500
Stockholders' equity:		
Common stock, $10 par.....................		$400,000
Retained earnings..........................		312,500
Total stockholders' equity...................		$712,500

Financial position form of balance sheet

In addition to the specific disclosure of the amount of working capital, the financial position form presents the amount of the excess of total assets over current liabilities and the amount of the excess of total assets over total liabilities. The balancing amounts in the statement are thus the net assets and the total stockholders' equity. The principal advantage claimed for this form is its emphasis on working capital, which is a significant factor in judging financial stability. A major criticism is its failure to present the total of the assets and the total of the liabilities.

Single-step form of income statement. The *single-step* form of income statement derives its name from the fact that the total of all expenses is deducted from the total of all revenues. This is in contrast to the multiple-step form, which contains conventional groupings of items, with intermediate balances, before concluding with the net income balance. A single-step form of income statement, severely condensed, is illustrated at the top of the next page.

The use of the single-step form, in many cases varying slightly from the illustration, has steadily increased during the past two decades. It has the advantage of simplicity and also emphasizes total revenues and total expenses as the determinants of net income. The most common variation from the form illustrated is to present income tax as a separate deduction from income. If there are extraordinary items to be reported, they should also be shown in a separate last section. The arrangement of the additional sections may be identical to the format illustrated on page 426 for a multiple-step statement. An objection to the single-step form is that such relationships as gross profit to sales and net operating

Electronic Products, Inc.
Income Statement
For Year Ended September 30, 19--

Revenues:		
Sales...		$940,000
Interest income.............................		27,500
Total revenues		$967,500
Expenses:		
Cost of merchandise sold......................	$530,000	
Selling expenses.............................	146,800	
General expenses.............................	120,400	
Interest expense.............................	10,500	
Income tax...................................	70,200	
Total expenses........................		877,900
Net income (per share, $2.24)................		$ 89,600

Single-step form of income statement

income to sales are not as readily determinable as when the conventional groupings and intermediate balances are shown.

Combined income and retained earnings statement. It is not unusual to add the analysis of retained earnings at the bottom of the income statement to form a *combined* income and retained earnings statement. The income statement portion of the combined statement may be presented either in multiple-step form or in a single-step form, as in the illustration below.

695

Electronic Products, Inc.
Income and Retained Earnings Statement
For Year Ended September 30, 19--

Revenues:		
Sales...		$940,000
Interest income		27,500
Total revenues		$967,500
Expenses:		
Cost of merchandise sold......................	$530,000	
Selling expenses.............................	146,800	
General expenses.............................	120,400	
Interest expense.............................	10,500	
Income tax...................................	70,200	
Total expenses........................		877,900
Net income (per share, $2.24)................		$ 89,600
Retained earnings, October 1, 19--...........		262,900
		$352,500
Deduct dividends		40,000
Retained earnings, September 30, 19--........		$312,500

Combined income and retained earnings statement

The combined statement form emphasizes net income as the connecting link between the income statement and the retained earnings portion of the stockholders' equity and thus facilitates understanding by the reader. A possible criticism of the combined statement is the fact that net income, a very significant figure, is buried in the body of the statement. If a portion of retained earnings is appropriated for various purposes, or if there have been other increases or decreases of an unusual nature, separate statements may be preferable.

Money as a unit of measurement

The effects of business transactions are recorded in the accounts of an enterprise in terms of money. Because of the homogeneity of money and its use as a standard of value, it is the only practicable medium for recording and reporting financial data. A balance sheet containing detailed descriptions in nonmonetary terms of inventories and plant assets would impart information of scant usefulness. Furthermore, such statements would be lacking in qualities of comparability, either between different points in time or between different enterprises.

It was noted in an earlier chapter that as a means of measurement money lacks the stability of the standards used in measuring time and the weight, dimensions, and other physical properties of matter. The dollar is an abstraction that has relevance only when related to a particular level of prices. The long-run movement of price levels has been upward, but there have been occasional severe and protracted reversals of the inflationary trend.

An early attempt to recognize the effects of inflation in the accounts proved to be unacceptable. During the inflationary period 1920–29 many corporations revised their plant asset accounts to bring them up to their appraised value. There was no question as to the effects of inflation on the cost of replacing the assets; the hazard was in departing from the objectively verifiable evidence of original cost. The offsetting credits for the write-up were identified by such titles as "Appraisal Capital" or "Revaluation Capital." Most of the upward revisions in the accounts were reversed in the severe deflationary period that followed.

The problems created by increasing price levels in planning for the replacement of inventories and plant assets have been described in earlier chapters. The use of the lifo method of inventory determination and of accelerated depreciation methods provide some relief, particularly through income tax reductions. The accompanying increase in the amount of funds available to an enterprise is advantageous, but such devices are only partial measures. They do not resolve the financial reporting problems.

Effect of changes in price level

Changes in the general price level do not affect all assets and liabilities in the same manner. For discussion purposes it is helpful to classify all balance sheet items as either (1) monetary or (2) nonmonetary. Monetary items are composed of cash and claims which are to be settled in cash, such as accounts receivable, notes receivable, investments in bonds, and all liabilities. Monetary items are fixed by law or contract, and consequently remain fixed in terms of dollars regardless of changes in the price level. Nonmonetary items are all other items. Nonmonetary items change with a change in the price level. The discussion and illustrations that follow are inflation oriented; the effects and conclusions indicated would be reversed, of course, if a deflationary period were assumed.

Nonmonetary items. To illustrate the effect on a nonmonetary asset of a change in the price level, assume that a plot of unimproved land was purchased ten years ago for $10,000. Assume also that during the period the general price level has increased by 50%. The cost of the land in terms of current dollars is therefore no longer $10,000 but $15,000 (150% of $10,000). This does not mean that the land is worth $15,000, in the usual sense of "worth," nor that it can be sold for $15,000. The general price level is an average of many prices; the prices of some types of assets included in the average would have increased by more than 50%, others by less than 50%, and some prices might even have declined over the ten-year period. Thus the particular plot of land, influenced by local real estate developments, by population growth, by economic conditions of the area, etc., might be appraised by an expert at far more than $15,000 or far less than $10,000. The price at which the land could be sold currently is irrelevant in terms of price level changes. It should also be noted that the $5,000 increase from the original cost of $10,000 to the present equivalent cost of $15,000 is not in any sense a profit. To generalize from the illustration, conversion of the cost of nonmonetary assets from original dollars to current dollars gives recognition to the changing value of the dollar, without recognition of gain or loss.

697

Monetary items. An individual bond will be used to illustrate the effect of an increase in general price level on monetary items, first as a bond investment and then as a bond payable. Assume that a ten-year, $10,000 bond was purchased at face value ten years ago. The bond matures currently and the holder receives $10,000 from the obligor corporation. Although the number of dollars received is exactly the same as the number originally invested, the investor is restored to his original position only if there has been no change in the price level. Assuming an increase in price level of 50%, as in the preceding illustration, it is evident that the investor has incurred a purchasing-power loss of $5,000 during the period. The loss is measured by the difference between $15,000 (150% of $10,000), the amount needed to maintain the original purchasing power, and $10,000, the actual amount of money available from the transaction.

It is evident that the effect of the issuance and redemption of the bond by the obligor corporation would be the reverse of the effect on the investor. During the ten-year period the purchasing power of the $10,000 originally received for the bond had increased to $15,000, but only $10,000 was needed to satisfy the obligation, hence a purchasing-power gain of $5,000 was realized.

Generalizations that may be derived from the foregoing illustrations are as follows, assuming an inflationary trend:

1. A purchasing-power loss results from holding monetary assets.
2. A purchasing-power gain results from maintaining liabilities.

Price level indexes

A price level index is a ratio of the total price of a group of commodities prevailing at a particular time to the total price of an identical group of commodities at a selected base period. The prices at the base period time are assigned a value of 100 and the indexes for all other items or periods are expressed as a ratio to 100. For example, if the composite of commodity prices totaled $2,000 for the base period and $2,200 for a later period, the index for the base period would be 100 and for the later period it would be 110.

Price level data are systematically collected by governmental agencies and converted into price level indexes. The differing opinions as to which of several such indexes most accurately measures the movement of the general price level need not concern us here. The manner in which a price level index is used to convert the cost of nonmonetary assets from original dollars to dollars of another time is demonstrated below, based on the following hypothetical index:

YEAR	INDEX
19X1	100
19X2	103
19X8	140
19X9	143
19X10	150

The $10,000 cost of the land in the earlier example can be converted to dollars of a later period by use of a multiplier in which the index for the later period is the numerator and the index at the time of the transaction is the denominator. If the land had been acquired in 19X1,

the monetary equivalent in 19X8 dollars would be $14,000 (140/100 ×
$10,000). Conversion of the original dollars to 19X10 dollars could be
made in a similar manner by applying the multiplier, 150/100, to the
original $10,000, or the 19X8 amount could be converted by applying
the multiplier, 150/140, to the $14,000 obtained earlier.

Reporting effect of price level changes in financial statements

As indicated by articles in professional journals and more especially
by publication of the results of research sponsored by accounting organizations, the attitude of accountants toward reporting the effects of price
level changes in financial statements has changed over the years. In 1953
a committee of the AICPA considered the possibility of introducing
partial adjustments in financial statements in recognition of the effect
of price level changes on plant assets. As the following excerpt from
their report indicates, the idea was rejected.

> . . . The committee on accounting procedure has reached the conclusion
> that no basic change in the accounting treatment of depreciation of plant
> and equipment is practicable or desirable under present conditions to meet
> the problem created by the decline in the purchasing power of the dollar.

> . . . While there are differences of opinion, the prevailing sentiment . . .
> is against any basic change in present accounting procedures. The com-
> mittee believes that such a change would confuse readers of financial state-
> ments and nullify many of the gains that have been made toward clearer
> presentation of corporate finances.

> . . . Should inflation proceed so far that original dollar costs lose their
> practical significance, it might become necessary to restate all assets in terms
> of the depreciated currency, as has been done in some countries. But it does
> not seem to the committee that such action should be recommended now
> if financial statements are to have maximum usefulness to the greatest
> number of users.[4]

The more recent viewpoint in support of reporting the effect of
price level changes would not limit the scope to plant assets nor substitute current dollar costs for historical costs in the financial statements.
Instead, the recommendations are directed toward supplementing the
conventional statements by using parallel columns for the converted
data, by preparing completely separate statements, or by presenting
detailed supporting schedules or charts. Restatement by means of price
indexes would also be extended to all data to be reported in the balance
sheet, the income statement, and the retained earnings statement.

Although the nature of the problems involved in constructing supplementary statements have been identified and the necessary procedures

---

[4]*Accounting Research and Terminology Bulletins*, "No. 43, Restatement and Revision
of Accounting Research Bulletins" (New York: American Institute of Certified Public
Accountants, 1961), pp. 68–69.

devised, little use has been made of them. Relatively few companies in the United States have thus far seen fit to include in their published reports details of the effects of inflation on operations and financial position.[5] Of the annual reports of 600 industrial and commercial corporations included in a recent survey, none reported the effects of inflation on their financial statements.[6]

The discussion of the merits and techniques of reporting the effect of price level changes on financial statements is likely to continue as long as inflation is a material factor in management decisions and government policies. Whether presenting readers of financial statements with additional complexities in the form of supplemental statements would be helpful or only increase their perplexities is also subject to debate.

QUESTIONS

1. What is the term applied to a business combination effected by forming a corporation to acquire the assets and assume the liabilities of two other corporations, followed by dissolution of the latter?

2. If Corporation A acquires the assets and assumes the liabilities of Corporation B and the latter is then dissolved, is the combination termed a *merger* or a *consolidation?*

3. What is the term applied to a corporation that owns the controlling stock interest in two or more companies and confines its activities primarily to their management?

4. Parent Corporation transferred $2,000,000 of net assets to its newly created subsidiary, receiving shares of common stock in return. The effect of the transaction on the books of Subsidiary Corporation, expressed as a general journal entry, was as follows:

Assets	2,100,000	
Liabilities		100,000
Common Stock, $10 par		1,600,000
Premium on Common Stock . . .		400,000

What reciprocal items should be eliminated in preparing a consolidated balance sheet immediately after the transaction?

5. Are entries recorded in the respective ledgers of the parent corporation or the subsidiary corporation for the eliminations that are made in the process of preparing the consolidated statements?

6. Parent purchased from stockholders the entire outstanding stock of Subsidiary for a total of $2,600,000 in cash. At the date of acquisition Subsidiary had $300,000 of liabilities and total stockholders' equity of $2,200,000. (a) As of the same date what was the total amount of Subsidiary's assets? (b) As of the same date what was the amount of Subsidiary's *net assets?* (c) What is the

[5] *Reporting the Financial Effects of Price-Level Changes,* Accounting Research Study No. 6 (New York: American Institute of Certified Public Accountants, 1963), pp. 169–219.

[6] *Accounting Trends and Techniques, 1968* (New York: American Institute of Certified Public Accountants, 1968), p. 19.

amount of difference between the investment account and the book value of subsidiary interest acquired? (d) Give three possible dispositions of the difference determined in (c) in preparing a consolidated balance sheet as of the date of acquisition.

7. If a parent corporation owns 90% of the outstanding stock of a subsidiary, what term is applied to the owners of the remaining 10%?

8. Is the amount reported on a consolidated balance sheet as the difference between the cost of the investment and the book value of the stock purchased affected by earnings retained by the subsidiary subsequent to acquisition?

9. At the time Parker Corporation purchases 90% of the stock of Shaw Corporation for $300,000, the stockholders' equity accounts of the latter are composed of common stock of $100,000 and retained earnings of $100,000. (a) Assuming that the excess of the price paid over the book value is attributable to earning capacity, what is the amount of goodwill from consolidation at the date of acquisition? (b) What is the amount of the minority interest at the date of acquisition?

10. Shaw Corporation (in Question 9) earned $50,000 and paid cash dividends of $20,000 from the date of acquisition by Parker to the end of the fiscal period. (a) Give Parker's entry to record its share of Shaw's earnings. (b) Give Parker's entry to record the receipt of Shaw's dividends. (c) How much of the $20,000 of dividends was paid to the minority shareholders? (d) What is the amount of the minority interest at the end of this fiscal period? (e) What is the amount of goodwill from consolidation at the end of this fiscal period?

11. At the close of the fiscal year the amount of notes receivable and notes payable reported on the respective balance sheets of a parent and its wholly owned subsidiary are as follows:

	Parent	Subsidiary
Notes Receivable.....	$120,000	$50,000
Notes Payable.......	60,000	30,000

If $40,000 of Subsidiary's notes receivable are owed by Parent, determine the amount of notes receivable and notes payable to be reported on the consolidated balance sheet.

12. Sales and purchases of merchandise by a parent corporation and its wholly owned subsidiary during the year were as follows:

	Parent	Subsidiary
Sales.............	$2,000,000	$500,000
Purchases.........	1,200,000	300,000

If $200,000 of the sales of Parent were made to Subsidiary, determine the amount of sales and purchases to be reported on the consolidated income statement.

13. At the end of the year the cost of the merchandise inventory purchased by a wholly owned subsidiary from its parent company during the year amounts to $100,000. (a) If the parent company's rate of gross profit on sales is 35%, what is the amount of unrealized gross profit to be eliminated from the merchandise inventory in preparing the consolidated balance sheet? (b) What other item must be reduced by the same elimination in preparing the consolidated balance sheet?

14. Which of the following procedures for consolidating the balance sheet of a parent and wholly owned subsidiary are characteristic of acquisition of control by purchase and which are characteristic of a pooling of interests? (a) Assets are not revalued. (b) Retained earnings of subsidiary at date of acquisition are eliminated. (c) Goodwill may be recognized. (d) Retained earnings of subsidiary at date of acquisition are combined with retained earnings of parent.

15. What two financial statements are frequently combined and presented as a single statement?

16. Describe the general format of a single-step income statement.

17. What effect does a general increase in the price level have on the purchasing power of the dollar?

18. During a period of inflation, does a purchasing-power gain result from holding cash and receivables or from maintaining liabilities?

19. Is an investment in common stock classified as a monetary item or as a nonmonetary item?

20. Assume that the price level index was 100 at the beginning of a period and 106 at the end of the period. (a) Would an enterprise holding $11,000 in cash at both the beginning and end of the period incur a purchasing-power gain or a purchasing-power loss, and if so, how much? (b) Would an enterprise with $20,000 of various non-interest-bearing liabilities outstanding at both the beginning and end of the period incur a purchasing-power gain or a purchasing-power loss, and if so, how much?

21. Six hundred shares of common stock of ABC Corporation were purchased for $40,000 at a time when the price level index was 100. Six years later the price level index is 125 and the market price of the six hundred shares is $55,000. (a) What is the amount of the owner's purchasing-power gain or loss, if any, during the period? (b) How much of the increase in market value can be attributed to the change in price level? (c) If the stock is sold for $55,000, how much gain would be considered to be realized, according to conventional accounting?

702

EXERCISES

27-1. On the last day of the fiscal year, Penn Company purchased 80% of the common stock of Scott Company for $408,000, at which time Scott Company reported the following on its balance sheet: assets, $720,000; liabilities, $170,000; common stock, $10 par, $360,000; retained earnings, $190,000.

   (a) In preparing a consolidated balance sheet as of the date of acquisition, where and in what amounts will the following be reported:
   (1) Difference between cost and book value of subsidiary interest.
   (2) Minority interest.
   (b) During the following year Penn Company realized net income of $750,000, exclusive of the income of the subsidiary, and Scott Company realized net income of $150,000. In preparing a consolidated income statement for the year, in what amounts would the following be reported:
   (1) Minority interest's share of net income.
   (2) Consolidated net income.

27-2. On December 31 of the current year, Percy Corporation purchased 90% of the stock of Salter Corporation. The data reported on their separate balance sheets immediately after the acquisition are reported below. Prepare a consolidated balance sheet as of that date, in report form, omitting captions for current assets, plant assets, etc.

Assets	Percy Corporation	Salter Corporation
Cash....................................	$ 22,000	$ 8,000
Accounts receivable (net).................	35,000	24,000
Inventories.............................	143,000	56,000
Investment in Salter Corporation...........	220,000	——
Equipment (net)........................	380,000	162,000
	$800,000	$250,000

Liabilities and Stockholders' Equity		
Accounts payable.......................	$ 41,000	$ 13,000
Common stock, $10 par..................	460,000	150,000
Retained earnings......................	299,000	87,000
	$800,000	$250,000

27-3. The Alpha Company exchanged 10,000 shares of $10 par common stock for 1,000 shares of Beta Company common stock held by Beta stockholders on December 31. The separate balance sheets of the two companies immediately after the exchange of shares are shown below. Prepare a consolidated balance sheet in accordance with the pooling of interests concept.

Assets	Alpha Company	Beta Company
Current assets............................	$ 40,000	$ 15,000
Investment in Beta Company (1,000 shares)..	100,000	——
Other assets............................	500,000	160,000
	$640,000	$175,000

Liabilities and Stockholders' Equity		
Liabilities.............................	$ 20,000	$ 8,000
Common stock (50,000 shares and 1,000 shares)	500,000	100,000
Retained earnings.......................	120,000	67,000
	$640,000	$175,000

27-4. Alpha Company purchased 1,000 shares of Beta Company stock on December 31 for $100,000 cash. The individual balance sheets of the two corporations immediately after the purchase are as presented in Exercise 27-3. Prepare a consolidated balance sheet, using purchase accounting procedures.

27-5. Summary financial data for the Taylor Corporation at December 31 of the current year are as follows: common stock, no-par, $220,000; current assets, $280,000; current liabilities, $110,000; investments, $45,000; long-term liabilities, $60,000; plant assets (net) $195,000; and retained earnings, $130,000. Prepare a financial position form of balance sheet, disclosing the amount of working capital.

27-6. Summary operating data for the A. B. Carlson Company during the current year ending December 31 are as follows: cost of goods sold, $530,000; general expenses, $72,000; income tax, $35,000; interest expense, $8,000; rent income, $25,000; sales, $780,000; and selling expenses, $120,000. At December 31, there were 20,000 shares of $25 par common stock outstanding. Prepare a single-step income statement, listing income tax as an item in the expenses section.

27-7. Convert the account balances listed below to current purchasing-power equivalents according to each of the following assumptions:

(a) The price level index at the time the assets were acquired was 90 and currently it is 120.
(b) The price level index at the time the assets were acquired was 120 and currently it is 90.

Account Balances

Investments in common stock......	$12,000
Building......	60,000
Accumulated depreciation........	15,000
Land......	7,200

PROBLEMS

The following additional problems for this chapter are located in Appendix C: 27-1B, 27-3B, 27-4B, 27-5B.

27-1A. Porter Corporation purchased 90% of the outstanding stock of Swift Company for $350,000. Balance sheet data for the two corporations immediately after the transaction, which occurred on June 30 of the current year, are presented below. The interest receivable reported on Swift Co. balance sheet is the accrual on the bond investment.

Assets	Porter Corp.	Swift Co.
Cash and marketable securities....	$ 85,000	$ 39,300
Accounts receivable....	70,000	50,300
Allowance for doubtful accounts....	(3,000)	(2,000)
Interest receivable....	——	2,700
Inventories....	325,500	132,500
Investment in Swift Company stock, 36,000 shares...	350,000	——
Investment in Porter Corporation bonds, face value...	——	90,000
Equipment....	724,800	239,400
Accumulated depreciation....	(173,300)	(74,200)
	$1,379,000	$478,000

Liabilities and Stockholders' Equity		
Accounts payable....	$ 134,300	$ 79,200
Income tax payable....	80,600	35,800
Interest payable....	9,000	——
Bonds payable (due in 1980)....	300,000	——
Common stock, $10 par....	600,000	——
Common stock, $5 par....	——	200,000
Retained earnings....	255,100	163,000
	$1,379,000	$478,000

Instructions:

(1) Prepare in report form a detailed consolidated balance sheet as of June 30 of the current year.

(2) Assuming that Swift Company earns net income of $90,000 and pays dividends of $40,000 during the fiscal year and that Porter Corporation records its share of the earnings and dividends, determine the following as of the end of the year:

   (a) The amount at which the investment in Swift Company will appear on Porter Corporation's balance sheet.

   (b) The amount of the difference between the cost and the book value of the subsidiary interest owned by the parent corporation.

   (c) The amount of the minority interest.

27-2A. Power Company purchased 9,000 of the 10,000 outstanding shares of stock of Stable Corporation on November 30 two years ago for $155,200, at which time total capital of the latter was $218,400. Since the date of acquisition, Power Company has debited the investment account for its share of the subsidiary's earnings and has credited the account for dividends declared. Balance sheet data for the two corporations as of November 30 of the current year appear below. Stable Corporation holds $30,000 of short-term notes of Power Company, on which there is accrued interest of $1,800. Stable Corporation owes Power Co. $10,000 for a management advisory fee for the second half of the year. It has been recorded by both corporations in their respective accounts payable and accounts receivable accounts.

Assets	Power Co.	Stable Corp.
Cash.	$ 74,000	$ 26,000
Notes receivable.	15,000	30,000
Accounts receivable.	137,500	34,300
Interest receivable.	1,700	1,800
Dividends receivable.	4,500	—
Prepaid expenses.	3,600	2,000
Inventories.	230,000	93,200
Investment in Stable Corp. stock, 9,000 shares . . .	173,200	—
Equipment.	480,000	165,000
Accumulated depreciation.	(141,000)	(40,000)
	$978,500	$312,300

Liabilities and Stockholders' Equity		
Notes payable.	$ 35,000	—
Accounts payable.	82,400	$ 40,700
Income tax payable.	75,000	28,200
Dividends payable.	10,000	5,000
Interest payable	2,100	—
Common stock, $25 par.	400,000	—
Common stock, $10 par.	—	100,000
Premium on common stock.	—	50,000
Retained earnings.	374,000	88,400
	$978,500	$312,300

Instructions:

(1) Prepare in report form a detailed consolidated balance sheet as of November 30 of the current year.

(2) What was the amount of the excess of book value of the subsidiary interest over cost at the date of acquisition?

(3) What was the amount of the minority interest at the date of acquisition?

27-3A. On March 31 of the current year Major Corporation exchanged 16,000 shares of its common stock for the 10,000 outstanding shares of Minor Corporation common stock. Balance sheet data of the two corporations immediately before the exchange occurred are presented below. The par of Major Corporation's stock is to be used by Major Corporation as the basis for recording the investment.

Assets	Major Corporation	Minor Corporation
Cash.	$ 50,000	$ 10,000
Accounts receivable	60,000	20,000
Inventories.	120,000	40,000
Plant assets (net).	270,000	80,000
	$500,000	$150,000

Liabilities and Stockholders' Equity		
Notes payable	$ 10,000	$ 3,000
Accounts payable	30,000	17,000
Common stock, $10 par.	250,000	—
Common stock, $5 par.	—	50,000
Premium on common stock.	90,000	—
Retained earnings.	120,000	80,000
	$500,000	$150,000

706

Instructions:

(1) Present the journal entry to record the investment by Major Corporation.

(2) As a preliminary to preparing a consolidated balance sheet immediately after the exchange of stock, determine the amount of the various stockholders' equity items to be eliminated, employing pooling of interests procedures.

(3) Prepare a consolidated balance sheet immediately after the exchange. Sectional captions for current assets, current liabilities, etc. may be omitted.

27-4A. The balances in the accounts of Burton's, Inc. after adjustment at November 30, the close of the current fiscal year, are as follows:

Accounts Payable.		78,200
Accounts Receivable.	62,500	
Accumulated Depreciation — Buildings		17,900
Accumulated Depreciation — Equipment. . .		36,700
Allowance for Doubtful Accounts.		3,800
Bond Sinking Fund.	45,600	
Bonds Payable (due 1982).		90,000
Buildings.	76,200	
Cash in Bank.	52,100	
Common Stock, $5 par		150,000
Cost of Goods Sold.	254,800	
Dividends Payable.		10,000

Equipment.................................	157,200	
General Expenses.........................	44,140	
Income Tax...............................	47,000	
Income Tax Payable.......................		17,000
Interest Expense..........................	5,400	
Interest Income...........................		3,300
Inventories...............................	134,800	
Land......................................	45,200	
Prepaid Insurance.........................	3,900	
Retained Earnings........................		106,740
Sales.....................................		469,200
Salaries Payable..........................		2,700
Selling Expenses..........................	56,700	
	985,540	985,540

Dividends debited to Retained Earnings during the year totaled $40,000; there were no other debits or credits to the account during the year. The number of shares of stock outstanding remained unchanged during the year.

Instructions:

(1) Prepare a combined income and retained earnings statement using the single-step form, listing income tax as an item in the expenses section. Insert the earnings per share as a parenthetical notation on the same line with net income.

(2) Prepare a detailed balance sheet in financial position form, disclosing the amount of working capital.

27-5A. The balances of selected ledger accounts of an enterprise as of the end of the year are listed below. The price level index at the beginning of the year was 120 and at the end of the year it was 130. Merchandise inventory is stated at cost, employing the fifo flow assumption. It is assumed to have been acquired when the price level index was 125, midway between the beginning and end of the year. The marketable securities, which are stated at cost, are common stocks purchased at the beginning of the year. The equipment was acquired a number of years ago, at which time the price level index was 90.

Account Title	Account Balance
Cash.........................	$10,800
Accounts Receivable...........	25,200
Marketable Securities..........	19,440
Merchandise Inventory.........	30,000
Equipment....................	74,250
Accumulated Depreciation......	35,730
Accounts Payable.............	48,000

Instructions:

(1) Convert the account balances to current purchasing-power equivalents as of the end of the period, presenting the details indicated by the following captions:

Account Title	Account Balance	Conversion Multiplier	Converted Balance

(2) Determine the purchasing-power gain or loss during the year on each of the monetary items, assuming that the account balances were the same at the beginning and end of the year.

28

Financial statement analysis

Need for analysis

The financial condition and the results of operations of business enterprises are of interest to various groups, including owners, managers, creditors, governmental agencies, employees, and prospective owners and creditors. The principal statements, together with supplementary statements and schedules, present much of the basic information needed to form opinions and to make decisions regarding the business.

Most of the items in these statements are of limited significance when considered individually. Users of financial statements often gain a clearer picture through studying relationships and comparisons between items. The selection and the preparation of analytical aids are a part of the work of the accountant.

It will be readily recognized that particular aspects of financial condition or of operations are of greater significance to some interested groups than to others. In general, all groups are interested in the ability of a business to pay its debts as they come due and to earn a reasonable amount of income. These two aspects of the status of an enterprise are sometimes referred to as factors of *solvency* and *profitability* respectively. An enterprise that cannot meet its obligations to its creditors on a timely basis is likely to experience difficulty in obtaining credit, which may lead to a diminution in its profitability. Similarly, an enterprise whose earnings are comparatively less than those of its competitors is likely to be at a disadvantage in obtaining credit or new capital from stockholders. In addition to keeping in mind this interrelationship between solvency and profitability, it is important to recognize that analysis of historical data is useful in assessing both the past performance of an enterprise and in forecasting its future performance.

Earlier chapters have included references to several types of financial analysis. For example, break-even analysis, gross profit analysis, and the funds statement were all forms of analysis. In this chapter, additional types of financial analysis will be discussed.

Basic analytical procedures

The analytical measures obtained from financial statements are usually expressed as ratios or percentages. For example, the relationship of \$150,000 to \$100,000 (\$150,000/\$100,000 or \$150,000:\$100,000) may be expressed as 1.5, 1.5:1, or 150%.

Analytical procedures may be used to compare the amount of specific items on a current statement with the corresponding amounts on earlier statements. For example, in comparing cash of \$150,000 on the current balance sheet with cash of \$100,000 on the balance sheet of a year earlier, the current amount may be expressed as 1.5 or 150% of the earlier amount. The relationship may also be expressed in terms of change, that is, the increase of \$50,000 may be stated as a 50% increase.

Analytical procedures are also widely used to indicate relationships of individual items to each other and of individual items to totals on a single statement. To illustrate, assume that included in the total of \$1,000,000 of assets on a balance sheet are cash appearing at \$50,000 and inventories at \$250,000. In relative terms, the cash balance is 5% of total assets and the inventories represent 25% of total assets. Individual items in the current asset group could also be related to total current assets. Assuming that the total of current assets in the example is \$500,000, cash represents 10% of the total and inventories represent 50% of the total.

There is no standard rule governing the rounding of computed ratios and percentages. Ordinarily, however, there is no need to carry calculations beyond one decimal point; the ratio 2.46:1, for example, may well be stated as 2.5:1 and 14.33% may be stated as 14.3%.

It should be noted that increases or decreases in items may be expressed in percentage terms only when the base figure is positive. If the base figure is zero or a negative value, the amount of change cannot be expressed as a percentage. For example, if comparative balance sheets indicate no liability for notes payable on the first, or base, date and a liability of \$10,000 on the later date, the increase of \$10,000 cannot be stated as a percent of zero. Similarly, if a net loss of \$10,000 in a particular year is followed by a net income of \$5,000 in the succeeding year, the increase of \$15,000 cannot be stated as a percent of the loss of the base year.

In the discussion and the illustrations of analytical procedures that follow, the basic significance of the various measures will be emphasized. It should be borne in mind that the measures developed are not ends in themselves; they are only guides to the evaluation of financial and operating data. Many other factors, such as trends in the industry, changes in price levels, and general economic conditions and prospects may also need consideration in arriving at sound conclusions.

Horizontal analysis

The percentage analysis of increases and decreases in corresponding items in comparative financial statements is sometimes referred to as *horizontal analysis*. The amount of each item on the most recent statement is compared with the corresponding item on one or more earlier statements. The increase or the decrease in the amount of the item is then listed, together with the percent of increase or decrease. When the comparison is made between two statements, the earlier statement is used as the base. If the analysis includes three or more statements, there are two alternatives in the selection of the base: the earliest date or period may be used as the basis for comparing all subsequent dates or periods, or each statement may be compared with the immediately preceding statement. The two alternatives are illustrated below.

BASE: EARLIEST YEAR

				INCREASE OR DECREASE*			
				1968–69		1968–70	
ITEM	1968	1969	1970	AMOUNT	PERCENT	AMOUNT	PERCENT
A	$100,000	$150,000	$200,000	$ 50,000	50%	$100,000	100%
B	100,000	200,000	150,000	100,000	100%	50,000	50%

BASE: PRECEDING YEAR

				INCREASE OR DECREASE*			
				1968–69		1969–70	
ITEM	1968	1969	1970	AMOUNT	PERCENT	AMOUNT	PERCENT
A	$100,000	$150,000	$200,000	$ 50,000	50%	$ 50,000	33%
B	100,000	200,000	150,000	100,000	100%	50,000*	25%*

Comparison of the amounts in the last two columns of the first analysis with the amounts in the corresponding columns of the second analysis reveals the effect of the base year on the direction of change and the amount and percent of change.

A condensed comparative balance sheet for two years, with horizontal analysis, is presented at the top of the next page.

The significance of the various increases and decreases cannot be fully determined without additional information. Although total assets at the end of 1970 were $91,000 (7.4%) less than at the beginning of

Martin Company
Comparative Balance Sheet
December 31, 1970 and 1969

	1970	1969	INCREASE OR DECREASE*	
			AMOUNT	PERCENT
Assets				
Current assets...............	$ 550,000	$ 533,000	$ 17,000	3.2%
Long-term investments........	95,000	177,500	82,500*	46.5%*
Plant assets (net).............	444,500	470,000	25,500*	5.4%*
Intangible assets.............	50,000	50,000	————	
Total assets.................	$1,139,500	$1,230,500	$ 91,000*	7.4%*
Liabilities				
Current liabilities............	$ 210,000	$ 243,000	$ 33,000*	13.6%*
Long-term liabilities..........	100,000	200,000	100,000*	50.0%*
Total liabilities..............	$ 310,000	$ 443,000	$133,000*	30.0%*
Stockholders' Equity				
Preferred 6% stock, $100 par. .	$ 150,000	$ 150,000	————	————
Common stock, $10 par.......	500,000	500,000	————	————
Retained earnings............	179,500	137,500	$ 42,000	30.5%
Total stockholders' equity......	$ 829,500	$ 787,500	$ 42,000	5.3%
Total liab. & stockholders' equity	$1,139,500	$1,230,500	$ 91,000*	7.4%*

the year, liabilities were reduced by $133,000 (30%) and capital increased $42,000 (5.3%). It would appear that the reduction of $100,000 in long-term liabilities was accomplished, for the most part, through the sale of long-term investments. A funds statement would, of course, provide more definite information about the changes in the composition of the balance sheet items.

The foregoing balance sheet may be expanded to include the details of the various categories of assets and liabilities, or the details may be presented on separate schedules. Opinions differ as to which method presents the clearer picture. The form of supporting schedules is illustrated by the following comparative schedule of current assets with horizontal analysis:

Martin Company
Comparative Schedule of Current Assets
December 31, 1970 and 1969

	1970	1969	INCREASE OR DECREASE*	
			AMOUNT	PERCENT
Cash.......................	$ 90,500	$ 49,700	$ 40,800	82.1%
Marketable securities.........	75,000	75,000	————	
Accounts receivable (net)......	115,000	120,000	5,000*	4.2%*
Merchandise inventory........	264,000	283,000	19,000*	6.7%*
Prepaid expenses.............	5,500	5,300	200	3.8%
Total current assets..........	$550,000	$533,000	$ 17,000	3.2%

The changes in the composition of the current assets would appear to be favorable, particularly in view of the increase in sales shown on the income statement below. The reduction in accounts receivable may have come about through changes in credit terms or improved collection policies. Similarly, a reduction in the merchandise inventory during a period of increased sales probably indicates an improvement in management of inventory.

The comparative income statement and the comparative retained earnings statement for Martin Company, with horizontal analysis, appear on this and the following page. Examination of the income statement reveals an increase of 24.8% in net sales. An increase in sales, considered alone, is not necessarily favorable. The increase in sales was accompanied by a somewhat greater percentage increase in the cost of merchandise sold, which indicates a narrowing of the gross profit margin. Selling expenses increased markedly and general expenses increased slightly, making an overall increase in operating expenses of 20.7% as contrasted with a 19.7% increase in gross profit.

Martin Company
Comparative Income Statement
For Years Ended December 31, 1970 and 1969

	1970	1969	INCREASE OR DECREASE*	
			AMOUNT	PERCENT
Sales.....................	$ 1,530,500	$ 1,234,000	$ 296,500	24.0%
Sales returns and allowances....	32,500	34,000	1,500*	4.4%*
Net sales...................	$ 1,498,000	$ 1,200,000	$ 298,000	24.8%
Cost of merchandise sold.......	1,043,000	820,000	223,000	27.2%
Gross profit on sales..........	$ 455,000	$ 380,000	$ 75,000	19.7%
Selling expense..............	$ 191,000	$ 147,000	$ 44,000	29.9%
General expense.............	104,000	97,400	6,600	6.8%
Total operating expense.......	$ 295,000	$ 244,400	$ 50,600	20.7%
Net operating income.........	$ 160,000	$ 135,600	$ 24,400	18.0%
Other income...............	8,500	11,000	2,500*	22.7%*
	$ 168,500	$ 146,600	$ 21,900	14.9%
Other expense...............	6,000	12,000	6,000*	50.0%*
Income before income tax......	$ 162,500	$ 134,600	$ 27,900	20.7%
Income tax.................	71,500	58,100	13,400	23.1%
Net income.................	$ 91,000	$ 76,500	$ 14,500	19.0%

Obviously, the increase in net operating income and in the final net income figure is favorable. It would be erroneous for the management to conclude, however, that its operations were at maximum efficiency. A study of fixed and variable expenses and additional analysis and comparisons of individual expense accounts should be made.

Martin Company
Comparative Retained Earnings Statement
For Years Ended December 31, 1970 and 1969

	1970	1969	INCREASE OR DECREASE* Amount	Percent
Retained earnings, Jan. 1......	$ 137,500	$ 100,000	$ 37,500	37.5%
Net income for year..........	91,000	76,500	14,500	19.0%
Total.....................	$ 228,500	$ 176,500	$ 52,000	29.5%
Dividends:				
On preferred stock..	$ 9,000	$ 9,000	———	———
On common stock.........	40,000	30,000	$ 10,000	33.3%
Total...................	$ 49,000	$ 39,000	$ 10,000	25.6%
Retained earnings, Dec. 31.....	$ 179,500	$ 137,500	$ 42,000	30.5%

The income statement illustrated is in condensed form. Such a condensed statement ordinarily provides sufficient information for all interested groups except management. If desired, the statement may be expanded or supplemental schedules may be prepared to present details of the cost of merchandise sold, selling expenses, general expenses, other income, and other expenses. The comparative schedule of cost of merchandise sold presented below is illustrative.

Martin Company
Comparative Schedule of Cost of Merchandise Sold
For Years Ended December 31, 1970 and 1969

	1970	1969	INCREASE OR DECREASE* Amount	Percent
Merchandise inventory, Jan. 1..	$ 283,000	$ 311,000	$ 28,000*	9.0%*
Purchases.................	1,024,000	792,000	232,000	29.3%
Merchandise available for sale..	$1,307,000	$1,103,000	$204,000	18.5%
Merchandise inventory, Dec. 31.	264,000	283,000	19,000*	6.7%*
Cost of merchandise sold.......	$1,043,000	$ 820,000	$223,000	27.2%

Vertical analysis

Percentage analysis may also be used to show the relationship of the component parts to the total in a single statement. This type of analysis is sometimes called *vertical analysis*. As in horizontal analysis, the statements may be prepared in either detailed or condensed form. In the latter case, additional details may be presented in supporting schedules. Although the analysis is confined within each individual statement, the significance of both the amounts and the percents is increased by preparing comparative statements. The condensed comparative balance sheet of Martin Company, with vertical analysis, is presented below.

Martin Company
Comparative Balance Sheet
December 31, 1970 and 1969

	1970		1969	
	AMOUNT	PERCENT	AMOUNT	PERCENT
Assets				
Current assets...............	$ 550,000	48.3%	$ 533,000	43.3%
Long-term investments........	95,000	8.3	177,500	14.4
Plant assets (net)............	444,500	39.0	470,000	38.2
Intangible assets.............	50,000	4.4	50,000	4.1
Total assets.................	$ 1,139,500	100.0%	$ 1,230,500	100.0%
Liabilities				
Current liabilities............	$ 210,000	18.4%	$ 243,000	19.7%
Long-term liabilities..........	100,000	8.8	200,000	16.3
Total liabilities..............	$ 310,000	27.2%	$ 443,000	36.0%
Stockholders' Equity				
Preferred 6% stock............	$ 150,000	13.2%	$ 150,000	12.2%
Common stock...............	500,000	43.9	500,000	40.6
Retained earnings............	179,500	15.7	137,500	11.2
Total stockholders' equity......	$ 829,500	72.8%	$ 787,500	64.0%
Total liab. & stockholders' equity	$ 1,139,500	100.0%	$ 1,230,500	100.0%

Each asset item is stated as a percent of total assets, and each liability and stockholders' equity item is stated as a percent of total liabilities and stockholders' equity. The major relative changes in assets were in the current asset and long-term investment groups. In the lower half of the balance sheet the greatest relative change was in long-term liabilities and retained earnings. Stockholders' equity increased from 64% of total liabilities and stockholders' equity at the close of 1969 to 72.8% at the close of 1970, with a corresponding decrease in the claims of creditors. Supporting schedules may be prepared to provide additional details of the changes in the various categories. If supporting schedules are prepared, the percentage analysis may be based on either the total of the schedule or the balance sheet total.

In vertical analysis of the income statement, each item is stated as a percent of net sales. The condensed comparative income statement of Martin Company, with vertical analysis, appears on the next page.

Care must be used in judging the significance of differences between percentages for the two years. For example, the decline of the gross profit rate from 31.7% in 1969 to 30.4% in 1970 is only 1.3%. In terms of dollars of potential gross profit, however, it represents a decline of approximately $19,000 (1.3% × $1,498,000).

Martin Company
Comparative Income Statement
For Years Ended December 31, 1970 and 1969

	1970		1969	
	AMOUNT	PERCENT	AMOUNT	PERCENT
Sales....................	$ 1,530,500	102.2%	$ 1,234,000	102.8%
Sales returns and allowances....	32,500	2.2	34,000	2.8
Net sales.................	$ 1,498,000	100.0%	$ 1,200,000	100.0%
Cost of merchandise sold........	1,043,000	69.6	820,000	68.3
Gross profit on sales...........	$ 455,000	30.4%	$ 380,000	31.7%
Selling expense..............	$ 191,000	12.8%	$ 147,000	12.3%
General expense.............	104,000	6.9	97,400	8.1
Total operating expense.......	$ 295,000	19.7%	$ 244,400	20.4%
Net operating income.........	$ 160,000	10.7%	$ 135,600	11.3%
Other income...............	8,500	.6	11,000	.9
	$ 168,500	11.3%	$ 146,600	12.2%
Other expense...............	6,000	.4	12,000	1.0
Income before income tax......	$ 162,500	10.9%	$ 134,600	11.2%
Income tax..................	71,500	4.8	58,100	4.8
Net income..................	$ 91,000	6.1%	$ 76,500	6.4%

Common-size statements

Horizontal and vertical analyses with both dollar and percentage figures are helpful in disclosing relationships and trends in financial condition and operations of individual enterprises. Vertical analysis with both dollar and percentage figures is also useful in comparing one company with another or with industry averages. Such comparisons may be facilitated by the use of *common-size* statements, in which all items are expressed only in relative terms (percentages of a common base).

Common-size statements may be prepared to compare percentages of a current date or period with past dates or periods, to compare individual businesses, or to compare one business with industry percentages published by trade associations and financial information services. A common-size income statement for Martin Company and Grant Corporation is presented on the next page.

Examination of the common-size income statement on the next page reveals that although Martin Company has a slightly higher rate of gross profit than Grant Corporation, the advantage is more than offset by its higher percentage of both selling and general expenses. As a consequence the net operating income of Martin Company is 10.7% of net sales as compared with 14.4% for the other company, an unfavorable difference of 3.7%.

Martin Company and Grant Corporation
Condensed Common-Size Income Statement
For Year Ended December 31, 1970

	MARTIN COMPANY	GRANT CORPORATION
Sales..	102.2%	102.3%
Sales returns and allowances....................	2.2	2.3
Net sales..................................	100.0%	100.0%
Cost of merchandise sold......................	69.6	70.0
Gross profit on sales........................	30.4%	30.0%
Selling expense.............................	12.8%	11.5%
General expense............................	6.9	4.1
Total operating expense......................	19.7%	15.6%
Net operating income.......................	10.7%	14.4%
Other income..............................	.6	.6
	11.3%	15.0%
Other expense.............................	.4	.5
Income before income tax....................	10.9%	14.5%
Income tax................................	4.8	5.5
Net income................................	6.1%	9.0%

Other analytical measures

In addition to the percentage analyses discussed above, there are a number of additional relationships that may be expressed in ratios and percentages. The items used in the measures are taken from the accounting statements of the current period and hence are a further development of vertical analysis. Comparison of the items with corresponding measures of earlier periods constitutes an extension of horizontal analysis.

Some of the most significant and commonly used ratios will be discussed in the sections that follow. The examples will be based on the statements of Martin Company presented above. In a few instances items from the company's earlier statements are also used.

Current position analysis

To be useful, ratios must express significant relationships. One such relationship is the expression of the company's ability to meet its currently maturing debts. This expression or analysis is referred to as *current position* analysis. This analysis is of particular interest to short-term creditors.

Working capital. The excess of the current assets of an enterprise over its current liabilities at a particular moment of time is referred to as *working capital.* The absolute amount of working capital and the flow of working capital during a period of time as reported by a funds statement are often used in evaluating a company's ability to meet currently maturing obligations. Although useful for making intraperiod comparisons for a company, these absolute amounts are difficult to use for comparing companies of different sizes or for comparing such amounts with industry figures. For example, working capital of $100,000 may be very adequate for a small building contractor specializing in residential construction, but it may be completely inadequate for a large building contractor specializing in industrial and commercial construction.

Current ratio. Another means of expressing the relationship between current assets and current liabilities is through the *current ratio*, sometimes referred to as the *working capital ratio* or *bankers' ratio*. The ratio is computed by dividing the total of current assets by the total of current liabilities.

The working capital and the current ratio of Martin Company at December 31, 1970 and 1969, are shown below, together with the underlying data:

	1970	1969
Current assets.	$550,000	$533,000
Current liabilities.	210,000	243,000
Working capital.	$340,000	$290,000
Current ratio.	2.6:1	2.2:1

The current ratio is a more dependable indication of solvency than is working capital. To illustrate, assume that Scott Corporation lists current assets of $2,000,000 and current liabilities of $1,540,000 on its balance sheet for December 31, 1970. The working capital of the corporation is $460,000 and the current ratio is 1.3:1. In comparison with Martin Company, Scott Corporation has a larger amount of working capital ($460,000 compared to $340,000) but a lower current ratio (1.3:1 compared to 2.6:1). Considering these facts alone, a bank is more likely to grant short-term loans to Martin Company than to Scott Corporation.

Acid-test ratio. The amount of working capital and the current ratio are two indicators of a company's ability to meet currently maturing obligations. However, these two measures do not take into account the distribution of the various items making up the current assets; a distribution that may be very significant. To illustrate, assume the current position data for Albert Corporation and Bailey Company as shown at the top of the next page.

Both companies have working capital of $650,000 and a current ratio of 2 to 1. But the ability of the two companies respectively to meet their currently maturing debts is vastly different. Albert Corporation has a large portion of its current assets in inventories, which must be sold and

	ALBERT CORPORATION	BAILEY COMPANY
Current assets		
Cash...	$ 200,000	$ 550,000
Marketable securities..............................	100,000	100,000
Receivables (net)....................................	200,000	200,000
Inventories..	800,000	450,000
Total current assets.............................	$1,300,000	$1,300,000
Current liabilities..................................	650,000	650,000
Working capital......................................	$ 650,000	$ 650,000
Current ratio...	2:1	2:1

the receivables collected before the current liabilities can be paid in full. A considerable amount of time may be required to convert these inventories into cash in the normal operating processes. Declines in market prices and a reduction in demand could also impair the ability to pay current liabilities. Bailey Company has almost enough cash on hand to meet its current liabilities.

A ratio that measures the "instant" debt-paying ability of a company is the *acid-test ratio*, sometimes referred to as the *quick ratio*. It is the ratio of the sum of cash, receivables, and marketable securities, which are sometimes called *quick assets*, to current liabilities. The computation of the acid-test ratio of Martin Company is presented below.

	1970	1969
Quick assets		
Cash...	$ 90,500	$ 51,000
Marketable securities..............................	75,000	75,000
Receivables (net)....................................	115,000	120,000
Total..	$280,500	$246,000
Current liabilities..................................	$210,000	$243,000
Acid-test ratio	1.3:1	1.0:1

A thorough analysis of a firm's current position would include the determination of the amount of working capital, the current ratio, and the acid-test ratio. These ratios are most useful when viewed together and when compared with similar ratios for previous periods and with those of other firms in the industry.

Accounts receivable analysis

The magnitude and composition of accounts receivable change continually during business operations. The amount is increased by sales on account and reduced by collections. Firms that grant long credit terms tend to have relatively greater amounts tied up in accounts receivable than those granting short terms. Increases or decreases in the volume of sales also affect the amount of outstanding accounts.

Accounts receivable yield no revenue, hence it is desirable to keep the amount invested in them at a minimum. The cash made available by prompt collection of receivables may be employed to reduce bank loans and thus yield a saving of interest, to purchase merchandise in larger quantities at a lower price, to pay dividends, or for other purposes. Prompt collection also reduces the risk of loss from uncollectible accounts.

Accounts receivable turnover. The relationship between credit sales and accounts receivable may be stated as the *accounts receivable turnover.* It is computed by dividing net sales on account by the average accounts receivable. The average of the monthly balances of accounts receivable should be used in the computation, as it takes seasonal fluctuations into account. When such data are not available, it is necessary to use the average of the balances at the beginning and the end of the year. If there are trade notes receivable as well as accounts, the two should be combined.

The accounts receivable turnover of Martin Company is computed below. All sales were made on account.

	1970	1969
Net sales on account..........................	$1,498,000	$1,200,000
Accounts receivable (net):		
Beginning of year............................	$ 120,000	$ 140,000
End of year.................................	115,000	120,000
Total......................................	$ 235,000	$ 260,000
Average....................................	$ 117,500	$ 130,000
Accounts receivable turnover....................	12.7	9.2

719

The increase in the accounts receivable turnover for Martin Company for 1970 indicates that there has been an acceleration in the collection of receivables, due perhaps to improvement in either credit or collection practices, or both.

Number of days' sales in receivables. Another means of expressing the relationship between credit sales and accounts receivable is the *number of days' sales in receivables.* This measure is determined by dividing the accounts receivable at the end of the year by the average daily sales on account (net sales on account divided by 365).

The determination of the number of days' sales in receivables for Martin Company, together with the data from which the measures are computed, are presented below.

	1970	1969
Accounts receivable, end of year................	$ 115,000	$ 120,000
Net sales on account..........................	$1,498,000	$1,200,000
Average daily sales on account.................	$ 4,104	$ 3,288
Number of days' sales in receivables............	28.0	36.5

The number of days' sales in receivables gives a rough measure of the length of time the accounts receivable have been outstanding. A comparison of this measure with the credit terms, with figures for comparable firms in the same industry, and with figures of Martin Company for prior years will help reveal the efficiency in collecting receivables and the trends in the management of credit.

Merchandise inventory analysis

Although an enterprise must maintain sufficient inventory quantities to meet the demands for its merchandise, it is desirable to keep the amount invested in inventory to a minimum. Inventories in excess of the needs of the business tie up funds that could be used in other ways to better advantage and may cause increases in the amount of insurance, property taxes, storage, and other expenses. There is also added risk of loss through price declines and deterioration or obsolescence of the merchandise.

Merchandise inventory turnover. The relationship between the volume of merchandise sold and merchandise inventory may be stated as the *merchandise inventory turnover*. It is computed by dividing the cost of merchandise sold by the average inventory. If monthly data are not available, it is necessary to use the average of the inventories at the beginning and the end of the year. Given monthly figures for purchases and sales, the interim monthly inventories can be estimated by the gross profit method described in Chapter 8. The computation of the merchandise inventory turnover for Martin Company is presented below.

	1970	1969
Cost of merchandise sold..........................	$1,043,000	$820,000
Merchandise inventory:		
Beginning of year.............................	$ 283,000	$311,000
End of year..................................	264,000	283,000
Total..	$ 547,000	$594,000
Average......................................	$ 273,500	$297,000
Merchandise inventory turnover.................	3.8	2.8

The improvement in the turnover resulted from an increase in the cost of merchandise sold, combined with a decrease in average inventory. The variation in types of merchandise is too great to permit any broad generalizations as to what constitutes a satisfactory turnover. For example, a firm selling food should have a higher turnover than one selling furniture or jewelry, and the perishable foods department of a supermarket should have a higher turnover than the soaps and cleaners department. However, for each business or each department within a business there is a reasonable turnover rate. A turnover below this rate means that the company or the department is incurring extra expenses such as those for administration and storage, increasing its risk of loss because of obsolescence and adverse price changes, and incurring interest charges in excess of those considered necessary or failing to free funds for other uses.

Number of days' sales in merchandise inventory. Another means of expressing the relationship between the cost of merchandise sold and merchandise inventory is the *number of days' sales in merchandise inventory.* This measure is determined by dividing the merchandise inventory at the end of the year by the average daily cost of merchandise sold (cost of merchandise sold divided by 365). The determination of the number of days' sales in merchandise inventory for Martin Company is illustrated below.

	1970	1969
Merchandise inventory, end of year	$ 264,000	$283,000
Cost of merchandise sold	$1,043,000	$820,000
Average daily cost of merchandise sold	$ 2,858	$ 2,274
Number of days' sales in inventory	92.4	124.5

The number of days' sales in inventory gives a rough measure of the length of time it takes to acquire, sell, and then replace the average merchandise inventory. The trend for Martin Company is favorable although a comparison with prior years' figures and with figures for comparable firms in the same industry would be necessary before reaching a final conclusion as to the effectiveness of inventory control.

As with many attempts to analyze financial data, it is possible to determine more than one measure to express the relationship between the cost of merchandise sold and merchandise inventory. Both the merchandise inventory turnover and number of days' sales in merchandise inventory are financial indicators useful for evaluating the efficiency in the management of inventory. Whether both measures are used or whether one measure is preferred over the other, is a matter for the individual analyst to decide.

Ratio of stockholders' equity to liabilities

Claims against the total assets of an enterprise are divided into two basic groups, those of the creditors and those of the owners. The relationship between the total claims of the two groups provides an indication of the margin of safety of the creditors and the ability of the enterprise to withstand adverse business conditions. If the claims of the creditors are large in proportion to the equity of the stockholders, there are likely to be substantial charges for interest payments. If earnings decline to the point of inability to meet interest payments, control of the business may pass to the creditors.

The relationship between stockholder and creditor equity is shown in the vertical analysis of the balance sheet. For example, the balance sheet of Martin Company presented on page 714 indicates that on December 31, 1970, stockholders' equity represented 72.8% and liabilities represented 27.2% of the sum of the liabilities and stockholders' equity (100.0%). Instead of expressing each item as a percent of the total, the relationship may be expressed as a ratio of one to the other, as illustrated below.

	1970	1969
Total stockholders' equity........................	$829,500	$787,500
Total liabilities................................	$310,000	$443,000
Ratio of stockholders' equity to liabilities...........	2.7:1	1.8:1

By reference to the balance sheet of Martin Company it may be seen that the principal factor affecting the change in the ratio was the $100,000 reduction in long-term liabilities during 1970. The ratio at both dates indicates a substantial margin of safety for the creditors.

722

Ratio of plant assets to long-term liabilities

Long-term notes and bonds are frequently secured by mortgages on plant assets. The ratio of total plant assets to long-term liabilities provides a measure of the margin of safety of the noteholders or bondholders. It also gives an indication of the potential ability of the enterprise to borrow additional funds on a long-term basis. The ratio of plant assets to long-term liabilities of Martin Company is computed as follows:

	1970	1969
Plant assets (net)...............................	$444,500	$470,000
Long-term liabilities............................	$100,000	$200,000
Ratio of plant assets to long-term liabilities.........	4.4:1	2.4:1

Ratio of net sales to assets

The ratio of net sales to assets is a measure of the effectiveness of the utilization of assets. Assume that two competing enterprises have equal amounts of assets but that the amount of the sales of one is double the amount of the sales of the other. Obviously, the former is making better use of its assets. In computing the ratio, any long-term investments should be excluded from total assets as they are wholly unrelated to sales of commodities or services. Assets used in determining the ratio may be the total at the end of the year, the average at the beginning and the end of the year, or the average of the monthly totals.

The computation of the ratio of net sales to assets for Martin Company is as follows:

	1970	1969
Net sales......................................	$1,498,000	$1,200,000
Total assets (excluding long-term investments):		
Beginning of year............................	$1,053,000	$1,010,000
End of year..................................	1,044,500	1,053,000
Total.......................................	$2,097,500	$2,063,000
Average.....................................	$1,048,750	$1,031,500
Ratio of net sales to assets	1.4:1	1.2:1

Rate earned on total assets

The rate earned on total assets is a measure of the productivity of the assets, without regard to the equity of creditors and stockholders in the assets. The rate is therefore not affected by differences in methods of financing an enterprise.

The rate earned on total assets is derived by adding interest expense to net income and dividing this sum by total assets. By adding interest expense to net income, the productivity of the assets is determined without considering the means of financing the acquisition of the assets. The computation of the rate earned by Martin Company on total assets appears below.

	1970	1969
Net income.....................................	$ 91,000	$ 76,500
Plus interest expense............................	6,000	12,000
Total.......................................	$ 97,000	$ 88,500
Total assets:		
Beginning of year............................	$1,230,500	$1,187,500
End of year..................................	1,139,500	1,230,500
Total.......................................	$2,370,000	$2,418,000
Average.....................................	$1,185,000	$1,209,000
Rate earned on total assets	8.2%	7.3%

It is sometimes considered preferable to determine the rate of net operating income (net income before nonoperating income, nonoperating expense, and income tax) to total assets. If nonoperating income is excluded from consideration, the investments yielding such income should be excluded from the assets. The use of net income before income tax eliminates the effect of changes in the tax structure on the rate of earnings. When considering published data on rates earned on assets, it is obviously important that the reader take note of the exact nature of the measure.

Rate earned on stockholders' equity

Another relative measure of earnings is obtained by dividing net income by the total stockholders' equity. In contrast to the rate earned on total assets, this measure emphasizes the income yield in relationship to the amount invested by the stockholders.

The amount of the total stockholders' equity varies throughout the year; additional stock may be issued, a class of stock may be retired, dividends may be paid, and net income accrues gradually. If monthly figures are not available, the average of the stockholders' equity at the beginning and the end of the year is used. The computation for Martin Company follows:

	1970	1969
Net income...................................	$ 91,000	$ 76,500
Stockholders' equity:		
Beginning of year.........................	$ 787,500	$ 750,000
End of year..............................	829,500	787,500
Total.................................	$1,617,000	$1,537,500
Average..................................	$ 808,500	$ 768,750
Rate earned on stockholders' equity	11.3%	10.0%

The rate earned by a thriving enterprise on the equity of its stockholders is ordinarily higher than the rate earned on total assets. The reason for the variance is that the amount earned on assets equivalent in amount to the total claims of creditors exceeds the interest charges on such claims. This tendency of the rate on stockholders' equity to vary disproportionately from the rate on total assets is sometimes referred to as *leverage*. The Martin Company rate of 11.3% for 1970, shown above, compares favorably with the rate of 8.2% earned on total assets, as reported on the preceding page. The leverage factor of 3.1% (11.3% − 8.2%) for 1970 also compares favorably with the 2.7% (10.0% − 7.3%) differential for the preceding year.

Rate earned on common stockholders' equity

When a corporation has both preferred and common stock outstanding, the holders of the common stock have the residual claim on earnings. The net income for the period, reduced by the preferred dividend requirements, may be stated as a percent of the average equity of the common stockholders.

Martin Company has $150,000 of preferred 6% nonparticipating stock outstanding at both balance sheet dates, hence annual preferred dividends amount to $9,000. The common stockholders' equity is the total stockholders' equity reduced by the par of the preferred stock ($150,000). The computation is presented at the top of the next page.

	1970	1969
Net income....................................	$ 91,000	$ 76,500
Preferred dividends.............................	9,000	9,000
Remainder — identified with common stock.........	$ 82,000	$ 67,500
Common stockholders' equity:		
Beginning of year.............................	$ 637,500	$ 600,000
End of year..................................	679,500	637,500
Total.....................................	$1,317,000	$1,237,500
Average.....................................	$ 658,500	$ 618,750
Rate earned on common stockholders' equity	12.5%	10.9%

Earnings per share on common stock

One of the financial measures most commonly quoted in the financial press and included in the income statement in corporate annual reports is earnings per share on common stock. If there is only one class of stock, the earnings per share are determined by dividing net income by the number of shares outstanding. If there are both preferred and common stock outstanding, the net income must be reduced first by the amount necessary to meet the preferred dividend requirements.

Any changes in the number of shares outstanding during the year, such as would result from stock dividends or stock splits, should be disclosed in quoting earnings per share on common stock. Also if net income includes extraordinary items, the per share amounts should be presented for (1) net income before extraordinary items, (2) extraordinary items (less applicable income tax), and (3) net income.

The computation of the earnings per share of common stock of Martin Company is as follows:

	1970	1969
Net income.......................................	$91,000	$76,500
Preferred dividends...............................	9,000	9,000
Remainder — identified with common stock..............	$82,000	$67,500
Shares of common stock outstanding....................	50,000	50,000
Earnings per share on common stock	$1.64	$1.35

Earnings per share on common stock is commonly used by the investor or prospective investor in evaluating past operating performance of a business enterprise, in attempting to project its future potential, and in weighing the merits of one investment opportunity in comparison with those of others.

Selection of analytical measures

The analytical measures that have been discussed and illustrated are representative of many that can be developed for a medium-size mer-

725

chandising enterprise. Some of them might well be omitted in analyzing a specific firm or additional measures could be developed. The type of business activity, the capital structure, and the size of the enterprise usually affect the measures employed. For example, in analyzing railroads, public utilities, and other corporations with a high ratio of debt to stockholders' equity, it is customary to express the relative risk of the bondholders in terms of the number of times the interest charges are earned during the year. The higher the ratio, the greater the assurance of continued interest payments in the event of decreased earnings. The measure also provides an indication of general financial strength, which is of concern to stockholders and employees, as well as to creditors.

In the data for a hypothetical corporation presented below, it should be noted that the amount available to meet interest charges is not affected by taxes on net income.

	1970	1969
Income before income tax	$ 900,000	$ 800,000
Add interest charges	300,000	250,000
Amount available to meet interest charges	$1,200,000	$1,050,000
Number of times interest charges earned	4	4.2

Analyses similar to the above can be applied to dividends on preferred and common stock. The number of times preferred dividends are earned indicates the relative assurance of continued dividend payments to preferred stockholders. For corporations with a policy of regular dividends on common stock, the number of times the common dividend is earned provides a similar measure for the common stockholders. In addition, it is a measure of the extent to which the corporation is retaining its earnings for use in the business.

Percentage analyses, ratios, turnovers, and other measures of financial position and operating results are useful analytical devices. They are helpful in appraising the present performance of an enterprise and in forecasting its future. They are not, however, a substitute for sound judgment nor do they provide definitive guides to action. In selecting and interpreting analytical indexes, appropriate consideration should be given to any conditions peculiar to the particular enterprise or to the industry of which the enterprise is a part. The possible influence of the general economic and business environment should also be weighed.

The interrelationship of the measures employed in appraising a particular enterprise should be carefully studied, as should comparable indexes of earlier fiscal periods, to ascertain trends. Data from competing enterprises may also be helpful in determining the relative efficiency of the firm being analyzed. In making such comparisons, however, it is important to consider the effect of any significant differences in their accounting methods.

726

QUESTIONS

1. In analysis of the status of an enterprise, what is meant by *solvency?*

2. Bennett Company and Wallace, Inc. are both department stores. For the current year, they reported net income (after income tax) of $300,000 and $600,000 respectively. Is Wallace, Inc. a more profitable company than Bennett Company? Discuss.

3. Illustrate (a) horizontal analysis and (b) vertical analysis, using the following data taken from a comparative balance sheet:

	Current Year	Preceding Year
Inventories.................	$ 300,000	$200,000
Total current assets..........	1,000,000	800,000

4. What is the advantage of using comparative statements for financial analysis rather than statements for a single date or period?

5. The current year's amount of net income (after income tax) is 10% larger than that of the preceding year. Does this indicate an improved operating performance? Discuss.

6. What are common-size financial statements?

7. (a) Name three measures or ratios that are useful in the analysis of a firm's current position. (b) Why is the analysis of current position of particular interest to short-term creditors?

8. Company C and Company S have working capital of $100,000 and $200,000 respectively. Does this mean that Company S has a higher current ratio than Company C? Explain.

9. The working capital for Downey Company at December 31, 1970 exceeds the working capital at December 31, 1969, by $25,000 as reported below. Does this mean that the current position at the end of 1970 is stronger than at the end of 1969? Explain.

	1970	1969
Current assets:		
Cash, marketable securities, and accounts receivable..	$ 75,000	$ 75,000
Merchandise inventory.........................	150,000	50,000
Total current assets........................	$225,000	$125,000
Current liabilities..........................	150,000	75,000
Working capital............................	$ 75,000	$ 50,000

10. Name two measures that are useful in the analysis of accounts receivable.

11. A company that grants terms of n/30 on all sales has an accounts receivable turnover for the year, based on monthly averages, of 6. Is this a satisfactory turnover? Discuss.

12. What does a decrease in the accounts receivable turnover ordinarily indicate about the credit and collection policy of the firm?

13. (a) Why is it advantageous to have a high merchandise inventory turnover? (b) Is it possible for a merchandise inventory turnover to be too high? Discuss.

14. In determining the rate earned on total assets, why is interest expense added to net income before dividing by total assets?

15. Explain why the rate earned on stockholders' equity by a thriving enterprise is ordinarily higher than the rate earned on total assets?

16. The net income (after income tax) of Parker Company was $2.50 per common share in the latest year and $4 per common share for the preceding year. At the beginning of the latest year, the number of shares outstanding was doubled by a stock split. There were no other changes in the amount of stock outstanding. What were the earnings per share in the preceding year, adjusted to place them on a comparable basis with the latest year?

17. Favorable business conditions may bring about certain seemingly unfavorable ratios, and unfavorable business operations may result in apparently favorable ratios. For example, Franklin Company has increased sales and net income substantially for the current year, yet the current ratio at the end of the year is lower than at the beginning of the year. Discuss some possible causes of the apparent weakening of the current position while sales and net income have increased substantially.

EXERCISES

28-1. Revenue and expense data for Norton Company are presented below:

	1970	1969
Sales	$ 600,000	$ 500,000
Cost of merchandise sold	366,000	300,000
Selling expense	120,000	75,000
General expense	54,000	50,000
Income tax	24,000	30,000

(a) Prepare an income statement in comparative form stating each item for both 1970 and 1969 as a percent of sales.
(b) Comment upon the significant changes disclosed by the comparative income statement.

28-2. The following data were abstracted from the balance sheet of Nance Company:

Cash	$ 85,000
Marketable securities	40,000
Accounts and notes receivable (net)	115,000
Merchandise inventory	152,500
Prepaid expenses	7,500
Accounts and notes payable (short term) . .	160,000
Accrued liabilities	40,000

(a) Determine (1) working capital, (2) current ratio, and (3) acid-test ratio. (Present figures used in your computations.)
(b) What conclusions can be drawn from these data as to the company's ability to meet its currently maturing debts?

28-3. The following data are from the financial statements for Bradford Company:

	1970	1969
Accounts receivable, end of year	$ 260,000	$ 290,000
Monthly average accounts receivable (net) .	250,000	275,000
Net sales on account	2,000,000	1,925,000

Terms of all sales are 1/10, n/60.

(a) Determine for each year (1) the accounts receivable turnover and (2) the number of days' sales in receivables.

(b) What conclusions can be drawn from these data concerning the composition of accounts receivable?

28-4. The following data are from the income statements of Mason Corporation:

	1970	1969
Sales.....	$1,900,000	$2,350,000
Beginning inventory...	290,000	270,000
Purchases....	1,020,000	1,220,000
Ending inventory....	310,000	290,000

(a) Determine for each year (1) the merchandise inventory turnover and (2) the number of days' sales in merchandise inventory.

(b) What conclusions can be drawn from these data concerning the composition of the merchandise inventory?

28-5. The data presented below were taken from the financial statements of J. W. Lewis and Co. for the current fiscal year.

Plant assets (net)			$ 625,000
Liabilities:			
Current liabilities....			$ 150,000
Mortgage note payable, 5%, due 1986...			250,000
Total liabilities....			$ 400,000
Stockholders' equity:			
Preferred 7% stock, $100 par, cumulative, nonparticipating (no change during year)			$ 100,000
Common stock, $10 par (no change during year)			400,000
Retained earnings:			
Balance, beginning of year....	$233,100		
Net income....	97,900	$331,000	
Preferred dividends....	$ 7,000		
Common dividends....	24,000	31,000	
Balance, end of year			300,000
Total stockholders' equity....			$ 800,000
Net sales.....			$1,320,000
Interest expense....			12,500

729

Determine the following, presenting figures used in your computations: (a) ratio of stockholders' equity to liabilities, (b) ratio of plant assets to long-term liabilities, (c) ratio of net sales to assets, (d) rate earned on total assets, (e) rate earned on stockholders' equity, (f) rate earned on common stockholders' equity.

28-6. The net income reported on the income statement of Richmond Products, Inc. was $2,500,000. There were 500,000 shares of $10 par common stock and 50,000 shares of $100 par 5% preferred stock outstanding throughout the year. The income statement included a gain on the sale of long-term investments of $1,000,000 and a fire loss of $500,000, both after applicable income tax. Determine the per share figures for common stock for (a) net income before extraordinary items, (b) extraordinary items (less applicable income tax), and (c) net income.

28-7. The balance sheet for Kelley Corporation at the end of the current fiscal year indicated the following:

Total current liabilities (non-interest bearing).....	$250,000
Bonds payable, 5% (issued in 1960, due in 1980).	500,000
Preferred 6% stock, $100 par....................	200,000
Common stock, $10 par........................	400,000
Premium on common stock.....................	100,000
Retained earnings............................	350,000

Income before income tax was $150,000 and income taxes were $65,000 for the current year. Determine each of the following: (a) rate earned on total assets, (b) rate earned on stockholders' equity, (c) rate earned on common stockholders' equity, (d) number of times bond interest charges were earned, (e) number of times preferred dividends were earned, (f) earnings per share on common stock.

PROBLEMS

The following additional problems for this chapter are located in Appendix C: 28-1B, 28-3B, 28-4B.

28-1A. Data pertaining to the current position of C. D. Adler and Company are presented below.

Cash.........................	$110,000
Marketable securities.............	50,000
Accounts and notes receivable (net).	200,000
Merchandise inventory............	228,000
Prepaid expenses................	12,000
Accounts payable................	175,000
Notes payable (short-term).........	40,000
Accrued liabilities...............	25,000

Instructions:

(1) Compute (a) working capital, (b) current ratio, and (c) acid-test ratio.
(2) Consider each of the following transactions separately and assume that only that transaction affects the data given above.

(a) Paid notes payable, $40,000.
(b) Purchased merchandise on account, $75,000.
(c) Paid accounts payable, $100,000.
(d) Received cash on account, $125,000.
(e) Declared a common stock dividend on common stock, $50,000.
(f) Declared a cash dividend, $25,000.
(g) Borrowed cash from bank on a long-term note, $100,000.
(h) Issued additional shares of stock for cash, $100,000.
(i) Paid cash for store supplies, $2,000.
(j) Sold marketable securities, $25,000.

State the effect of each transaction (increase, decrease, or no effect) on working capital, current ratio, and acid-test ratio. Use the following column headings for recording your answers:

	Effect on		
Item	Working Capital	Current Ratio	Acid-Test Ratio

28-2A. Presented below for the current calendar year are revenue and expense data for Carr Paper Company and for the paper industry. The Carr Paper Company data are expressed in dollars; the paper industry averages are expressed in percentages.

	Carr Paper Company	Paper Industry Average
Sales....................	$3,030,000	100.5%
Sales returns and allowances.	30,000	.5%
Cost of merchandise sold.....	2,130,000	69.0%
Selling expense.............	243,000	9.8%
General expense.............	210,000	8.2%
Other income...............	18,000	.5%
Other expense..............	42,000	1.5%
Income tax.................	180,000	5.5%

Instructions:

(1) Prepare a common-size income statement comparing the results of operations for Carr Paper Company with the industry average.
(2) As far as the data permit, comment on significant relationships revealed by the comparisons.

28-3A. For 1970, Powell Company initiated an extensive sales promotion campaign that included the expenditure of an additional $100,000 for advertising. At the end of the year, Charles Powell, the president, is presented with the following condensed comparative income statement:

Powell Company
Comparative Income Statement
For Years Ended December 31, 1970 and 1969

	1970	1969
Sales.....................	$927,000	$714,000
Sales returns and allowances..	27,000	14,000
Net sales..................	$900,000	$700,000
Cost of merchandise sold.....	477,000	350,000
Gross profit on sales.........	$423,000	$350,000
Selling expense.............	$279,000	$140,000
General expense............	116,000	105,000
Total operating expense......	$395,000	$245,000
Net operating income........	$ 28,000	$105,000
Other income...............	3,600	3,500
Income before income tax....	$ 31,600	$108,500
Income tax.................	9,000	49,000
Net income................	$ 22,600	$ 59,500

Instructions:

(1) Prepare a comparative income statement for the two-year period, presenting an analysis of each item in relationship to net sales for each of the years.
(2) To the extent the data permit, comment on the significant relationships revealed by the vertical analysis prepared in (1).

Ch. 28 • Financial statement analysis

28-4A. The financial statements of W. L. Stevens and Co. are presented below and on page 733.

W. L. Stevens and Co.
Balance Sheet
December 31, 1970

Assets

Current assets:
Cash	$ 108,000	
Marketable securities	60,000	
Accounts receivable (net)	340,000	
Merchandise inventory	480,000	
Prepaid expenses	12,000	
Total current assets		$1,000,000
Long-term investments:		
Investment in affiliated company		200,000
Plant assets:		
Equipment (net)	$ 650,000	
Buildings (net)	1,225,000	
Land	125,000	
Total plant assets		2,000,000
Total assets		$3,200,000

Liabilities

Current liabilities:		
Accounts payable		$ 620,000
Long-term liabilities:		
Mortgage note payable, due 1985	$ 200,000	
Bonds payable, 5%, due 1990	600,000	
Total long-term liabilities		800,000
Total liabilities		$1,420,000

Stockholders' Equity

Preferred 6% stock, cumulative, nonparticipating,		
$100 par	$ 500,000	
Common stock, $20 par	500,000	
Retained earnings	780,000	
Total stockholders' equity		1,780,000
Total liabilities and stockholders' equity		$3,200,000

Additional data, taken from the balance sheet at December 31, 1969, are as follows:

Accounts receivable (net)	$ 210,000
Long-term investments	175,000
Total assets	2,800,000
Total stockholders' equity (preferred and common stock outstanding same as in 1970)	1,700,000

W. L. Stevens and Co.
Income Statement
For Year Ended December 31, 1970

Sales...	$3,090,000	
Sales returns and allowances.......................	90,000	
Net sales......................................		$3,000,000
Cost of merchandise sold:		
Merchandise inventory, January 1, 1970.........	$ 360,000	
Purchases (net)...............................	2,220,000	
Merchandise available for sale.................	$2,580,000	
Merchandise inventory, December 31, 1970......	480,000	
Cost of merchandise sold...................		2,100,000
Gross profit on sales............................		$ 900,000
Operating expenses:		
Selling expenses..............................	$ 450,000	
General expenses.............................	140,000	
Total operating expenses...................		590,000
Net operating income..........................		$ 310,000
Other income..................................		9,000
		$ 319,000
Other expense (interest).......................		40,000
Income before income tax......................		$ 279,000
Income tax....................................		133,000
Net income...................................		$ 146,000

W. L. Stevens and Co.
Retained Earnings Statement
For Year Ended December 31, 1970

Retained earnings, January 1, 1970..............		$ 700,000
Add net income for year.......................		146,000
Total..		$ 846,000
Deduct dividends:		
On preferred stock...........................	$ 30,000	
On common stock............................	36,000	66,000
Retained earnings, December 31, 1970............		$ 780,000

Instructions:

Determine for 1970 the ratios, turnovers, and other measures listed below and on the next page, presenting the figures used in your computations:

(1) Working capital.
(2) Current ratio.
(3) Acid-test ratio.
(4) Accounts receivable turnover.
(5) Number of days' sales in receivables.
(6) Merchandise inventory turnover.
(7) Number of days' sales in merchandise inventory.

(8) Ratio of plant assets to long-term liabilities.
(9) Ratio of stockholders' equity to liabilities.
(10) Rate earned on total assets.
(11) Rate earned on stockholders' equity.
(12) Rate earned on common stockholders' equity.
(13) Ratio of net sales to assets.
(14) Earnings per share on common stock.

28-5A. Edward Thomas is considering making a substantial investment in W. L. Stevens and Co. The company's financial statements for 1970 were given in Problem 28-4A. To assist in the evaluation of the company, Mr. Thomas secured their financial statements for the preceding year, which are presented below and on the next page.

W. L. Stevens and Co.
Balance Sheet
December 31, 1969

Assets

Current assets:		
Cash....................................	$135,000	
Marketable securities.....................	75,000	
Accounts receivable (net).................	210,000	
Merchandise inventory....................	360,000	
Prepaid expenses........................	20,000	
Total current assets.....................		$ 800,000
Long-term investments:		
Investment in affiliated company..........		175,000
Plant assets:		
Equipment (net)........................	$ 700,000	
Buildings (net).........................	950,000	
Land.................................	150,000	
Total plant assets......................		1,800,000
Intangible assets:		
Patents...............................		25,000
Total assets...........................		$2,800,000

Liabilities

Current liabilities:		
Accounts payable.......................		$ 500,000
Long-term liabilities:		
Bonds payable, 5%, due 1990.............		600,000
Total liabilities........................		$1,100,000

Stockholders' Equity

Preferred 6% stock, cumulative, nonparticipating, $100 par..............................	$ 500,000	
Common stock, $20 par...................	500,000	
Retained earnings.......................	700,000	
Total stockholders' equity................		1,700,000
Total liabilities and stockholders' equity...........		$2,800,000

W. L. Stevens and Co.
Income Statement
For Year Ended December 31, 1969

Sales....................................	$2,657,200	
Sales returns and allowances..............	57,200	
Net sales................................		$2,600,000
Cost of merchandise sold:		
Merchandise inventory, January 1, 1969........	$ 300,000	
Purchases (net).......................	1,765,000	
Merchandise available for sale..............	$2,065,000	
Merchandise inventory, December 31, 1969......	360,000	
Cost of merchandise sold....................		1,705,000
Gross profit on sales......................		$ 895,000
Operating expenses:		
Selling expenses.........................	$ 416,000	
General expenses........................	150,800	
Total operating expenses....................		566,800
Net operating income......................		$ 328,200
Other income.............................		8,400
		$ 336,600
Other expense (interest)...................		30,000
Income before income tax..................		$ 306,600
Income tax...............................		146,600
Net income...............................		$ 160,000

W. L. Stevens and Co.
Retained Earnings Statement
For Year Ended December 31, 1969

Retained earnings, January 1, 1969..............		$ 595,000
Add net income for year.......................		160,000
Total......................................		$ 755,000
Deduct dividends:		
On preferred stock.........................	$ 30,000	
On common stock..........................	25,000	55,000
Retained earnings, December 31, 1969...........		$ 700,000

Additional data taken from the balance sheet at December 31, 1968, are as follows:

Accounts receivable (net).....................	$ 190,000
Long-term investments.......................	150,000
Total assets................................	2,700,000
Total stockholders' equity (preferred and common stock outstanding same as in 1969)	1,595,000

Instructions:

Prepare a report for Mr. Thomas based on an analysis of the financial data presented above. In preparing your report, include all ratios and other data that will be useful in arriving at a decision regarding the investment.

part **Eleven** | Appendixes

Alternative method of recording merchandise inventories

Difference in methods

The recording of adjusting entries for merchandise inventory at the end of the accounting period is described and illustrated in Chapter 6. The alternative method presented here classifies the entries for the beginning and the ending merchandise inventories as *closing* entries instead of *adjusting* entries. The difference in viewpoint has a minor effect on the work sheet, the sequence of entries in the journal, and the expense and revenue summary account in the ledger. It does not affect the overall results, nor does it alter the financial statements in any way.

Work sheet

The merchandise inventory at the beginning of the period is to be reported on the income statement as a part of the cost of merchandise sold. On the work sheet it is therefore extended from the Trial Balance Dr. column to the Income Statement Dr. column.

The inventory at the end of the period is to be reported on the balance sheet as an asset and on the income statement as a deduction from the cost of merchandise available for sale. The ending inventory is therefore entered on the work sheet as a debit in the Balance Sheet Dr. column and as a credit in the Income Statement Cr. column. Both the debit and the credit amounts are placed on the same line as that used for the beginning merchandise inventory.

Preston Electric Supplies
Work Sheet
For Year Ended December 31, 1969

	ACCOUNT TITLE	TRIAL BALANCE DR.	CR.	ADJUSTMENTS DR.	CR.	INCOME STATEMENT DR.	CR.	BALANCE SHEET DR.	CR.	
1	Cash.........................	8,590						8,590		1
2	Accounts Receivable..........	6,880						6,880		2
3	Merchandise Inventory........	19,700				19,700	22,150	22,150		3
4	Store Supplies...............	970			(a) 420			550		4
5	Office Supplies..............	480			(b) 200			280		5
6	Prepaid Insurance............	1,560			(c) 910			650		6
7	Store Equipment..............	10,200						10,200		7
8	Accumulated Depr. — Store Equip........		4,600		(d) 1,100				5,700	8
9	Office Equipment.............	5,570						5,570		9
10	Accumulated Depr. — Office Equip........		2,230		(e) 490				2,720	10
11	Building.....................	41,000						41,000		11
12	Accumulated Depr. — Building..........		9,400		(f) 1,500				10,900	12
13	Land........................	3,000						3,000		13
14	Accounts Payable.............		7,420						7,420	14
15	Salaries Payable.............				(g) 296				296	15
16	Mortgage Note Payable........		9,000						9,000	16
17	T. J. Preston, Capital.......		48,256						48,256	17
18	T. J. Preston, Drawing.......	12,000						12,000		18
19	Sales.......................		162,736				162,736			19
20	Sales Returns and Allowances...........	2,140				2,140				20
21	Sales Discount...............	1,822				1,822				21
22	Purchases....................	105,280				105,280				22
23	Purchases Discount...........		1,525				1,525			23
24	Sales Salaries...............	15,820		(g) 224		16,044				24
25	Advertising Expense..........	3,460				3,460				25
26	Depreciation Expense — Store Equip.......			(d) 1,100		1,100				26
27	Insurance Expense — Selling..............			(c) 580		580				27
28	Store Supplies Expense..................			(a) 420		420				28
29	Miscellaneous Selling Expense............	230				230				29
30	Office Salaries..........................	4,960		(g) 72		5,032				30
31	Taxes Expense..........................	1,810				1,810				31
32	Depreciation Expense — Building........			(f) 1,500		1,500				32
33	Depreciation Expense — Office Equip......			(e) 490		490				33
34	Insurance Expense — General............			(c) 330		330				34
35	Office Supplies Expense.................			(b) 200		200				35
36	Miscellaneous General Expense...........	310				310				36
37	Rent Income............................		1,200				1,200			37
38	Interest Expense.......................	585				585				38
39		246,367	246,367	4,916	4,916	161,033	187,611	110,870	84,292	39
40	Net Income...........................					26,578			26,578	40
41						187,611	187,611	110,870	110,870	41

Work sheet

All adjustments are recorded in the Adjustments columns of the work sheet in the same manner as was illustrated on pages 142 and 143 except that by this method no entries are required in the Adjustments columns for merchandise inventory. The balances are then extended to the Income Statement and Balance Sheet columns, and the work sheet is completed. A work sheet employing this alternative procedure is illustrated on the preceding page. Note that the totals of the Income Statement and Balance Sheet columns and the amount of net income shown on this work sheet are the same as those on the work sheet on page 143.

Adjusting entries

The adjusting entries made from the alternative work sheet are illustrated below. They are exactly the same as those illustrated on page 150 except for the exclusion of adjustments for inventory.

1969		Adjusting Entries				
Dec.	31	Store Supplies Expense....................	615	420		
		Store Supplies.........................	115		420	
	31	Office Supplies Expense..................	716	200		
		Office Supplies........................	116		200	
	31	Insurance Expense — Selling.............	614	580		
		Insurance Expense — General............	715	330		
		Prepaid Insurance.....................	117		910	
	31	Depreciation Expense — Store Equip........	613	1,100		
		Accumulated Depreciation — Store Equip.	122		1,100	
	31	Depreciation Expense — Office Equip........	714	490		
		Accumulated Depreciation — Office Equip.	124		490	
	31	Depreciation Expense — Building..........	713	1,500		
		Accumulated Depreciation — Building....	126		1,500	
	31	Sales Salaries...........................	611	224		
		Office Salaries..........................	711	72		
		Salaries Payable.......................	213		296	

739

Adjusting entries

Closing entries

All items in the Income Statement Cr. column of the work sheet are closed in one compound entry to the credit of Expense and Revenue Summary. All items in the Income Statement Dr. column are closed in one compound entry to the debit of Expense and Revenue Summary. Expense and Revenue Summary and the drawing account are then closed to the capital account with the same entries as the last two illustrated on page 151. All of the closing entries for the alternative procedure are presented on the next page.

1969							
Dec.	31	*Closing Entries*					
		Merchandise Inventory......................	114	22,150		
		Sales..	411	162,736		
		Purchases Discount.........................	512	1,525		
		Rent Income................................	812	1,200		
		Expense and Revenue Summary...........	313		187,611	
	31	Expense and Revenue Summary.............	313	161,033		
		Merchandise Inventory....................	114		19,700	
		Sales Returns and Allowances.............	412		2,140	
		Sales Discount...........................	413		1,822	
		Purchases...............................	511		105,280	
		Sales Salaries...........................	611		16,044	
		Advertising Expense......................	612		3,460	
		Depreciation Expense — Store Equip........	613		1,100	
		Insurance Expense — Selling...............	614		580	
		Store Supplies Expense....................	615		420	
		Miscellaneous Selling Expense..............	619		230	
		Office Salaries...........................	711		5,032	
		Taxes Expense...........................	712		1,810	
		Depreciation Expense — Building...........	713		1,500	
		Depreciation Expense — Office Equip........	714		490	
		Insurance Expense — General..............	715		330	
		Office Supplies Expense...................	716		200	
		Miscellaneous General Expense.............	719		310	
		Interest Expense.........................	911		585	
	31	Expense and Revenue Summary.............	313	26,578		
		T. J. Preston, Capital....................	311		26,578	
	31	T. J. Preston, Capital......................	311	12,000		
		T. J. Preston, Drawing....................	312		12,000	

740   Closing entries

Expense and revenue summary account

The difference between the debit and the credit posted to the expense
and revenue summary account from the compound closing entries represents the net income or the net loss for the period. The posting of the
entry transferring the net income or the net loss to the capital account
closes Expense and Revenue Summary. The account is illustrated below.

	EXPENSE AND REVENUE SUMMARY				ACCOUNT No. 313		
DATE	ITEM	POST. REF.	DEBIT	CREDIT	BALANCE		
					DEBIT	CREDIT	
1969							
Dec. 31		J29		187,611		187,611	
31		J29	161,033			26,578	
31		J29	26,578		—	—	

Expense and revenue summary account

B

Specimen corporation statements

Deere & Company

Statement of Consolidated Income and Earned Surplus

	Year Ended 31 October	
	1968	1967
Sales and Other Income:		
Net sales	$1,030,539,000	$1,086,379,000
Interest and miscellaneous income	23,764,000	17,233,000
Net income of credit company subsidiaries	4,607,000	4,360,000
Total sales and other income	1,058,910,000	1,107,972,000
Less:		
Cost of goods sold	799,072,000	819,711,000
Selling, administrative and general expenses	126,848,000	117,889,000
Provision for income taxes (1968 includes deferred taxes of $24,000,000)	49,998,000	68,808,000
Interest	35,744,000	33,204,000
Foreign exchange losses	493,000	5,930,000
Miscellaneous charges	4,133,000	4,820,000
Total deductions	1,016,288,000	1,050,362,000
Net Income for the Year	$ 42,622,000	$ 57,610,000
Earnings per share based on average number of shares outstanding	$2.88	$3.90
Earned Surplus at Beginning of Year	499,163,000	468,902,000
Total	541,785,000	526,512,000
Less Cash Dividends Declared		
1968 - $2.00 a share, 1967 - $1.85 a share	29,588,000	27,349,000
Earned Surplus at End of Year (Note 3)	$ 512,197,000	$ 499,163,000

The notes to the consolidated financial statements on page 26, the explanation of pensions on page 13, and the financial review on pages 20 through 22 are an integral part of this statement.

Assets   1968

Current Assets:

Cash ....$ 216,838,060

Marketable securities, valued at lower of cost or market. 1,609,086,088

Notes and accounts receivable...less reserve:

    $22,445,133......................... 1,201,466,663

Inventories, valued at lower of average cost or market.. 226,286,172

Prepaid insurance, taxes, etc...................... 47,394,211

                 $ 3,301,071,194

Other Investments and Sundry Assets 27,320,779

Plant, Rental Machines and Other Property...at cost:

Land 112,633,018

Buildings 663,655,612

Factory, laboratory and office equipment............ 1,132,448,170

             1,908,736,800

Less: Accumulated depreciation................... 889,007,180

             1,019,729,620

Rental machines and parts....................... 5,088,453,536

Less: Accumulated depreciation................... 2,693,143,969

             2,395,309,567

                 3,415,039,187

Patents and Goodwill............................ 1

                 $ 6,743,431,161

The notes on pages 50 to 55 are an integral part of this statement.

Note: The comparative data included in the report to stockholders has been omitted because of space limitations.

Sheet at December 31:

Liabilities and Capital	1968
Current Liabilities:	
U.S. Federal and foreign income taxes...estimated....$	567,631,316
Accounts payable and accruals.....................	899,033,842
Loans payable.................................	64,336,040
	$ 1,531,001,198
Deferred Income Taxes...........................	51,896,220
Reserves for Employees' Indemnities and Retirement Plans...........................	46,303,055
Long-Term Indebtedness........................	545,090,514
Capital Stock...Par Value $5.00 Per Share 2,095,614,836	
Authorized: 120,000,000 shares	
Issued and outstanding: 112,968,369 shares	
Retained Earnings 2,473,525,338	
	4,569,140,174
	$ 6,743,431,161

743

R.H.Macy & Co., Inc. AND CONSOLIDATED SUBSIDIARIES

Consolidated Statement of Financial Condition

Assets

Current Assets:	August 3, 1968	July 29, 1967
Cash	$ 20,354,850	$ 22,332,533
Marketable securities, at amortized cost (approximate market)	41,956,151	18,013,532
Customers' accounts receivable, per statement on page 14	62,060,029	53,124,359
Other receivables	8,358,950	8,017,935
Merchandise inventories (Note 1 — page 16)	105,530,176	104,282,268
Prepaid expenses and supplies	7,905,847	6,805,603
Total current assets	$246,166,003	$212,576,230

Other Assets:		
Investment in Macy Credit Corp., at equity, per statement on page 18	$ 21,354,066	$ 19,599,877
Miscellaneous, including unamortized deferred charges of $3,418,256 and $4,951,961	9,614,187	11,614,371
	$ 30,968,253	$ 31,214,248

Property and Equipment:		
Land	$ 36,415,329	$ 33,377,687
Buildings and improvements on owned properties	93,277,634	80,630,872
Buildings and improvements on leased properties and leaseholds	57,780,964	47,102,697
Fixtures and equipment	93,829,874	74,036,753
Construction in progress	12,666,779	30,622,185
	$293,970,580	$265,770,194
Accumulated depreciation and amortization	72,664,483	65,154,965
	$221,306,097	$200,615,229

Goodwill and Other Intangible Assets — at cost, less accumulated amortization of $2,036,365 and $1,952,106	$ 654,945	$ 739,204
	$499,095,298	$445,144,911

* As restated from previously published figures.
See notes to financial statements on pages 16 and 17.

part eleven • Appendixes

Liabilities and Investment of Shareholders

	August 3, 1968	July 29, 1967
Current Liabilities:		
Accounts payable and accrued liabilities	$ 81,008,816	$ 72,363,948*
Federal income taxes (Note 2 — page 16) —		
Current	4,647,143	6,704,908
Deferred	28,735,739	25,778,047
Long-term debt due within one year	4,661,114	5,229,699
Total current liabilities	$119,052,812	$110,076,602
Deferred Credits:		
Deferred Federal and state taxes (Note 2 — page 16)	$ 26,428,859	$ 23,552,083*
Deferred investment credit ($4,401,074 and $3,174,211) and unamortized capital gains on sales and leasebacks	7,599,978	6,474,127
Deferred contingent compensation and pension funding, less estimated Federal income tax effect	2,337,182	2,479,356
	$ 36,366,019	$ 32,505,566
Long-Term Debt, due after one year, per statement on page 14:		
R. H. Macy & Co., Inc.	$ 57,644,783	$ 40,473,631
Real estate subsidiaries	85,939,687	77,226,182
	$143,584,470	$117,699,813
Investment of Shareholders, represented by:		
Cumulative preferred shares, 500,000 authorized; par value $100 each —		
4¼% Series A — 165,600 shares issued; 5,990 in treasury; 159,610 outstanding, callable at $107.50 each	$ 15,961,000	$ 15,961,000
4% Series B — 100,000 shares issued and outstanding	10,000,000	10,000,000
Preference shares, $5.00 par value per share — 1,000,000 shares authorized and unissued	—	—
Common shares, $0.25 par value, assigned value $3.75 per share — 20,000,000 authorized; 9,132,291 and 8,946,608 issued; 15,756 in treasury; leaving 9,116,535 and 8,930,852 outstanding (Notes 3 and 4 — page 16) . .	34,187,006	33,490,695
Additional paid-in capital, per statement on page 15	23,766,350	22,254,042
Earnings reinvested in the business, per statement on page 11; at August 3, 1968, $74,200,000 is not distributable to common shareholders under terms of long-term debt agreements	116,177,641	103,157,193
Total investment of shareholders	$200,091,997	$184,862,930
	$499,095,298	$445,144,911

745

Westinghouse Electric Corporation
Consolidated Balance Sheet

Assets	December 31	
	1968	1967
Current Assets		
Cash..	$ **80,114,347**	$ 71,354,624
Marketable securities – at cost which approximates market..........	**7,760,896**	14,858,308
Customer receivables (less allowance for doubtful accounts 1968 – $4,235,212)......................................	**688,841,402**	564,724,566
Inventories – valued principally on last-in, first-out method..........	**623,252,933**	689,048,626
Recoverable engineering and development costs (Government contracts)..	**55,792,631**	61,644,221
Long term contracts in process..............................	**242,823,997**	219,965,016
Progress payments to sub-contractors.........................	**132,241,206**	60,238,381
Prepaid expense...	**17,861,552**	15,541,368
Miscellaneous..	**67,385,907**	31,060,850
	1,916,074,871	1,728,435,960
Less: Progress billing on contracts...........................	**563,165,592**	403,893,084
Total Current Assets...............................	**1,352,909,279**	1,324,542,876
Investments		
Wholly and majority owned companies not consolidated............	**133,356,116**	115,078,160
Other securities – at cost or less, not in excess of market...........	**19,212,314**	20,482,349
	152,568,430	135,560,509
Plant and Equipment		
Land and buildings.......................................	**420,789,323**	378,993,889
Machinery and equipment..................................	**841,786,645**	744,229,281
Construction in progress...................................	**102,392,994**	71,585,121
	1,364,968,962	1,194,808,291
Less: Accumulated depreciation.............................	**728,886,061**	695,336,488
	636,082,901	499,471,803
Other Assets		
Purchase price of going businesses acquired in excess of their net tangible assets..	**47,030,283**	46,975,695
Non-current customer receivables (less allowance for doubtful accounts 1968 – $4,088,330)......................................	**45,778,289**	37,009,218
Mortgages receivable.....................................	**15,403,071**	13,801,739
Miscellaneous..	**21,639,113**	17,916,448
	129,850,756	115,703,100
Total Assets......................................	**$2,271,411,366**	$2,075,278,288

746

Liabilities and Stockholders' Equity

	December 31	
	1968	1967
Current Liabilities		
Short term bank loans and current maturities of long term debt......	$ **149,749,341**	$ 66,045,095
Accounts payable – trade.....................................	**131,090,296**	126,920,711
Accrued payrolls and payroll deductions payable to others..........	**110,800,695**	95,110,037
Federal and foreign income taxes.............................	**22,239,000**	30,306,000
Deferred Federal income taxes...............................	**36,200,000**	13,722,000
Other taxes...	**18,988,742**	18,798,783
Product guarantees..	**22,159,000**	18,839,000
Other current liabilities....................................	**96,555,374**	89,541,386
Total Current Liabilities............................	**587,782,448**	459,283,012
Deferred Federal Income Taxes – Non-Current..............	**2,646,000**	
Long Term Debt		
Debentures 2⅝% – Due September 1, 1971.....................	**6,810,000**	6,810,000
Debentures 3½% – Due December 15, 1981....................	**180,000,000**	195,000,000
Debentures 5⅝% – Due April 1, 1992........................	**200,000,000**	200,000,000
Debentures 6¼% – Coral Ridge Properties, Inc....................	**4,566,000**	4,567,200
Mortgages and notes payable – Coral Ridge Properties, Inc..........	**13,032,930**	20,209,210
	404,408,930	426,586,410
Total Liabilities.....................................	**994,837,378**	885,869,422
Stockholders' Equity		
Preferred stock, cumulative, par value $100, authorized 409,851 shares; 3.80% Series B, issued and outstanding (339,825 shares at December 31, 1968).....................................	**33,982,500**	39,233,500
Cumulative preference stock, without par value; authorized 10,000,000 shares, none issued....................................		
Common stock, par value $6.25 per share; authorized 50,000,000 shares, issued (38,673,293 shares at December 31, 1968).............	**241,708,081**	238,647,525
Capital surplus – principally amount paid the Corporation for capital stock in excess of par value...............................	**243,559,129**	220,017,657
Retained earnings.......................................	**765,145,573**	699,182,899
	1,284,395,283	1,197,081,581
Less: Cost of common stock held in treasury (164,188 shares at December 31, 1968).....................................	**7,821,295**	7,672,715
Total Stockholders' Equity............................	**1,276,573,988**	1,189,408,866
Total Liabilities and Stockholders' Equity................	**$2,271,411,366**	$2,075,278,288

747

The accompanying Financial Review on pages 21, 22 and 23 is an integral part of these financial statements.

Consolidated balance sheet

December 31	1968	1967
Assets		
Current assets		
Cash	$ 12,622,000	$ 10,623,000
Marketable securities, at cost which		
approximates market value	1,793,000	1,142,000
Accounts receivable, less reserve:		
1968, $778,000; 1967, $616,000	52,873,000	38,313,000
Inventories	47,461,000	43,410,000
Other current assets and prepayments	6,729,000	3,114,000
Total current assets	121,478,000	96,602,000
Capital assets	82,194,000	73,928,000
Patents and goodwill, less amortization	2,207,000	2,763,000
Other assets	2,225,000	1,713,000
Total assets	$208,104,000	$175,006,000
Liabilities and stockholders' equity		
Current liabilities		
Accounts payable	$ 24,973,000	$ 18,828,000
Income taxes payable	7,498,000	886,000
Notes payable and current portion of long-term debt	6,210,000	15,116,000
Advance billings	17,876,000	15,842,000
Total current liabilities	56,557,000	50,672,000
Deferred taxes on income	5,344,000	6,156,000
Long-term debt	34,453,000	15,724,000
Total liabilities	96,354,000	72,552,000
Stockholders' equity		
4% convertible cumulative preferred stock,		
$50 par value	12,000,000	12,000,000
Common stock, $2 par value	11,973,000	11,922,000
Capital in excess of par value	19,743,000	18,517,000
Retained earnings	68,034,000	60,015,000
Total stockholders' equity	111,750,000	102,454,000
Total liabilities and stockholders' equity	$208,104,000	$175,006,000

748

See notes, page 28

Pitney-Bowes, Inc.
and subsidiaries

AMERACE·ESNA

amerace esna corporation and subsidiaries
Statement of Consolidated Financial Position
december 31, 1968 with comparative figures for 1967

	1968	1967 (Note A)
Current assets		
Cash	$ 3,248,000	$ 3,819,000
Marketable securities—at cost plus accrued interest (approximate market) . . .	2,795,000	2,808,000
Receivables, less allowances 1968—$406,000; 1967—$640,000	20,930,000	21,869,000
Inventories—Note B	29,921,000	31,021,000
Prepaid expenses	1,650,000	1,794,000
Total Current Assets	58,544,000	61,311,000
Current liabilities		
Accounts payable and accrued expenses	13,793,000	13,431,000
Notes payable and portion of long-term debt due within one year—Note E . . .	10,202,000	3,171,000
Federal and Canadian income taxes—Note C	160,000	3,318,000
Dividends payable	1,313,000	960,000
Total Current Liabilities	25,468,000	20,880,000
Working Capital	33,076,000	40,431,000
Investment in and advances to foreign companies—at cost—Note A	2,199,000	2,137,000
Property, plant and equipment—net—Note D	48,002,000	37,141,000
Trade-marks, formulae and other intangibles—at cost	1,708,000	1,729,000
Other assets	1,577,000	1,264,000
Cost of investments in excess of net assets of businesses acquired	6,741,000	6,895,000
	60,227,000	49,166,000
	93,303,000	89,597,000
5% Convertible Subordinated Debentures—Note E	14,995,000	15,000,000
Long-term debt less current portion—Note E	2,825,000	2,624,000
Deferred Federal income taxes	1,332,000	1,093,000
Unamortized investment credits—Note C	926,000	520,000
	20,078,000	19,237,000
Total Stockholders' Equity	$73,225,000	$70,360,000
Source of Stockholders' equity		
Preferred Stock, $10 par value—authorized 2,000,000 shares; Series A, issued and outstanding 1968—887,379 shares; 1967—918,906 shares (liquidation preference $57,680,000)—Note A	$ 8,874,000	$ 9,189,000
Common Stock, $5 par value—authorized 10,000,000 shares; issued 1968—2,474,412 shares; 1967—2,417,503 shares—Notes A and F	12,372,000	12,088,000
Additional paid-in capital	17,398,000	17,698,000
Retained earnings—Note E	35,316,000	31,535,000
	73,960,000	70,510,000
Less Common Stock in treasury—at cost; 1968—20,863 shares; 1967—5,563 shares	735,000	150,000
Total Stockholders' Equity	$73,225,000	$70,360,000

See notes to consolidated financial statements.

749

Standard Oil Company (New Jersey)

Consolidated statement of financial position, December 31, 1968–1967

Assets	1968	1967 (Restated)
Current assets		
Cash	$ 462,673,000	$ 419,395,000
Marketable securities, at lower of cost or market	904,189,000	952,933,000
Notes and accounts receivable, less estimated doubtful amounts	2,545,995,000	2,361,677,000
Inventories		
Crude oil, products, and merchandise	1,193,282,000	1,068,527,000
Materials and supplies	174,159,000	165,150,000
Prepaid taxes and other expenses	243,849,000	245,493,000
Total current assets	5,524,147,000	5,213,175,000
Investments and advances	936,709,000	904,174,000
Property, plant, and equipment, at cost, less depreciation and depletion	10,077,164,000	9,074,867,000
Deferred charges and other assets	248,343,000	180,454,000
Total assets	16,786,363,000	15,372,670,000

Liabilities	1968	1967
Current liabilities		
Notes and loans payable	975,571,000	960,574,000
Accounts payable and accrued liabilities	1,804,668,000	1,605,330,000
Income taxes payable	652,502,000	637,916,000
Total current liabilities	3,432,741,000	3,203,820,000
Long-term debt	2,082,721,000	1,500,415,000
Annuity, insurance, and other reserves	465,021,000	437,335,000
Deferred income tax credits	431,755,000	337,046,000
Other deferred credits	85,777,000	96,921,000
Equity of minority shareholders in affiliated companies	432,552,000	421,784,000
Total liabilities	6,930,567,000	5,997,321,000

Shareholders' equity		
Capital	2,233,146,000	2,244,241,000
Earnings reinvested	7,622,650,000	7,131,108,000
Total shareholders' equity	$ 9,855,796,000	$ 9,375,349,000

The financial information on pages 27, 28, 29, and 30 is an integral part of these statements.

Standard Oil Company (New Jersey)

Consolidated statement of income for the years 1968 and 1967

	1968	1967
		(Restated)
Revenue		
Sales and other operating revenue	$15,473,909,000	$14,409,369,000
Dividends, interest, and other revenue	399,397,000	335,129,000
	15,873,306,000	14,744,498,000
Costs and other deductions		
Crude oil, products, materials, and services	6,668,899,000	6,304,760,000
Taxes and other payments to governments	5,607,094,000	5,177,269,000
Wages, salaries, and employee benefits	1,246,387,000	1,186,176,000
Depreciation and depletion	849,163,000	762,619,000
Interest and other financial charges	177,961,000	117,883,000
Income applicable to minority interests	47,121,000	40,763,000
	14,596,625,000	13,589,470,000
Income before extraordinary item	1,276,681,000	1,155,028,000
Estimated recoveries on claims for World War II losses		40,000,000
Net income	$ 1,276,681,000	$ 1,195,028,000
Per share		
Income before extraordinary item	$5.94	$5.36
Net income	$5.94	$5.54

751

Consolidated statement of changes in working capital for the years 1968 and 1967

	1968	1967
		(Restated)
Sources		
Net income accruing to Jersey shareholders	$1,276,681,000	$1,195,028,000
Net income accruing to minority interests	47,121,000	40,763,000
Depreciation and depletion	849,163,000	762,619,000
Sales of property, plant, and equipment	71,870,000	58,796,000
Net increase in long-term debt	582,306,000	463,812,000
Net increase in deferred income tax credits	94,709,000	52,660,000
	2,921,850,000	2,573,678,000
Uses		
Additions to property, plant, and equipment	1,944,067,000	1,618,574,000
Additions to investments and advances	32,535,000	59,378,000
Cash dividends to Jersey shareholders	785,139,000	743,037,000
Cash dividends to minority interests	39,430,000	36,207,000
Cost of shares reacquired, less proceeds from shares sold	11,095,000	17,394,000
Other—net	27,533,000	(14,961,000)
	2,839,799,000	2,459,629,000
Net increase	$ 82,051,000	$ 114,049,000

The financial information on pages 27, 28, 29, and 30 is an integral part of these statements.

TRW

Consolidated Balance Sheet

ASSETS

December 31	1968	1967	
		As Adjusted For Poolings of Interests	As Shown In Annual Report
CURRENT ASSETS			
Cash	$ 63,836,119	$ 41,094,922	$ 29,580,357
Marketable securities—at cost (approximate market) .	13,255,263	25,264,775	6,661,063
Accounts receivable	162,534,107	171,165,994	133,775,403
Reimbursable costs, fees and claims to be billed under contracts	42,555,003	28,464,919	28,464,919
Inventories—Note B	237,432,506	231,183,798	158,749,438
Prepaid expenses	13,682,070	8,266,820	6,341,490
TOTAL CURRENT ASSETS	533,295,068	505,441,228	363,572,670
PROPERTY, PLANT AND EQUIPMENT—on the basis of cost			
Land	14,348,794	11,545,911	7,218,188
Buildings	165,131,981	152,790,205	119,414,698
Machinery and equipment	413,019,793	362,385,727	271,444,700
	592,500,568	526,721,843	398,077,586
Less allowances for depreciation and amortization. .	315,071,695	274,048,907	215,231,593
TOTAL PROPERTY, PLANT AND EQUIPMENT—net	277,428,873	252,672,936	182,845,993
COST OF ACQUIRED BUSINESSES IN EXCESS OF RECORDED NET ASSETS AT ACQUISITION DATES . .	49,797,115	47,678,099	41,656,612
OTHER ASSETS—Note C	21,100,648	16,397,328	13,528,958
	$881,621,704	$822,189,591	$601,604,233

752

LIABILITIES AND SHAREHOLDERS' INVESTMENT

December 31	1968	1967	
		As Adjusted For Poolings of Interests	As Shown In Annual Report
CURRENT LIABILITIES			
Notes payable	$ 15,860,383	$ 21,874,549	$ 18,080,319
Trade accounts payable	48,681,665	51,108,121	41,181,355
Accrued expenses and other liabilities	90,957,863	88,762,302	59,674,852
Dividends payable	10,459,446	4,657,928	4,561,010
Federal and foreign income taxes	34,047,566	25,756,231	14,475,377
Current portion of long-term debt	5,198,426	3,040,594	2,297,594
TOTAL CURRENT LIABILITIES	205,205,349	195,199,725	140,270,507
LONG-TERM DEBT—excluding current portion—Note D	200,976,783	182,139,948	164,199,217
MINORITY INTERESTS IN SUBSIDIARIES	2,698,067	2,989,111	2,223,361
SHAREHOLDERS' INVESTMENT— Notes D, E and F			
4% Cumulative Preferred Stock, $100 par value	1,988,700	6,120,800	6,120,800
Serial Preference Stock, without par value	29,279,800	37,403,800	37,403,800
Serial Preference Stock II, without par value (aggregate involuntary liquidation price $265,741,168)	10,500,550	10,424,133	—0—
Common Stock, $1.25 par value	30,181,545	29,408,280	26,303,298
Other capital	79,475,661	68,375,082	44,775,781
Retained earnings	321,315,249	290,128,712	180,307,469
TOTAL SHAREHOLDERS' INVESTMENT	472,741,505	441,860,807	294,911,148
LONG-TERM LEASE COMMITMENTS AND CONTINGENT LIABILITIES—Notes C and G	—	—	—
	$881,621,704	$822,189,591	$601,604,233

See notes to financial statements.

753

MESTA MACHINE COMPANY

Statement of Financial Position

	December 31	
	1968	**1967***
	(In thousands of dollars)	
CURRENT ASSETS		
Cash	$ 488	$ 582
Marketable securities, at cost which approximates market	13,361	6,172
Accounts receivable	12,634	18,480
Inventories (Note 1)	39,773	25,553
Less—progress billings	(32,412)	(15,314)
Estimated future tax benefits—net (Note 4).....	1,211	1,329
Other	701	163
	35,756	36,965
LESS—CURRENT LIABILITIES		
Accounts payable and accrued liabilities	8,857	9,210
Mortgage installment payable	395	395
Taxes on income (Note 4)	725	2,155
Estimated replacements on sales	1,118	1,012
	11,095	12,772
WORKING CAPITAL	24,661	24,193
LONG-TERM RECEIVABLES AND INVESTMENTS, at cost	457	1,134
PROPERTY, PLANT AND EQUIPMENT, at cost less accumulated depreciation and amortization (Note 2)	19,911	20,048
	45,029	45,375
3% MORTGAGE, payable in annual installments, due 1976	2,407	3,029
	$42,622	$42,346
SHAREHOLDERS' EQUITY		
Common stock—authorized 1,400,000 shares of $5.00 par value—issued 1,000,000 shares ...	$ 5,000	$ 5,000
Retained earnings	37,690	37,414
Less—12,021 treasury shares	(68)	(68)
	$42,622	$42,346

Restated (see Note 4) and reclassified on a basis of classifications adopted in 1968.

SCM CORPORATION STATEMENT OF CONSOLIDATED INCOME

	Years Ended	
	June 30, 1968	June 30, 1967
Net Sales	$744,758,000	$705,160,000
Costs and expenses:		
Cost of sales	532,291,000	499,132,000
Selling, administrative, and research expenses	169,828,000	156,656,000
Interest expense—net	11,819,000	5,746,000
	713,938,000	661,534,000
Income before income taxes	30,820,000	43,626,000
United States and foreign income taxes	13,061,000	18,550,000
Income before extraordinary items	17,759,000	25,076,000
Extraordinary items	4,700,000	
Net Income	$ 13,059,000	$ 25,076,000
Earnings per share:		
Income before extraordinary items	$2.22	$3.01
Extraordinary items	.57	
Net income	$1.65	$3.01

755

SCM CORPORATION STATEMENT OF CONSOLIDATED SOURCE AND APPLICATION OF FUNDS

Source of funds:		
Net income	$ 13,059,000	$ 25,076,000
Depreciation and depletion	17,807,000	15,384,000
Provision for deferred income taxes	383,000	2,703,000
Amortization of deferred charges and intangibles	236,000	431,000
Cash flow from operations	31,485,000	43,594,000
Net increase from issuance of long-term debt	3,512,000	40,667,000
Sale of common stock	23,834,000	993,000
Stock issued for net assets of companies acquired		5,578,000
Total	$ 58,831,000	$ 90,832,000
Application of funds:		
Net capital expenditures	$ 27,818,000	$ 36,116,000
Reduction of long-term debt	8,437,000	4,382,000
Cash dividends	4,763,000	8,782,000
Other applications, net	3,163,000	1,140,000
Increase in working capital	14,650,000	40,412,000
Total	$ 58,831,000	$ 90,832,000

See accompanying notes to financial statements.

The Procter & Gamble Company and Subsidiary Companies

CONSOLIDATED STATEMENT OF SOURCE AND USE OF FUNDS
Year ended June 30, 1968

SOURCE OF FUNDS

Earnings from operations	$182,623,000
Extraordinary profit on sale of Clorox shares	19,403,000
Depreciation and depletion	41,754,000
Net increase in borrowing — International	41,373,000
Deferred income taxes — net increase	5,228,000
	290,381,000

USE OF FUNDS

Capital expenditures	163,166,000
Dividends to shareholders	97,644,000
Net change in inventories, receivables, and payables	20,217,000
Accelerated payment of federal income taxes	24,347,000
Net decrease in borrowing — U.S.	19,021,000
Other items — net	84,000
	324,479,000

DECREASE IN CASH AND MARKETABLE SECURITIES	$ 34,098,000

Report of Independent Auditors

HASKINS & SELLS
CERTIFIED PUBLIC ACCOUNTANTS

ONE EAST FOURTH STREET
CINCINNATI 45202

To the Board of Directors of
The Procter & Gamble Company

We have examined the consolidated balance sheet of The Procter & Gamble Company and subsidiary companies as of June 30, 1968 and the related consolidated statements of earnings and source and use of funds for the year then ended. Our examination was made in accordance with generally accepted auditing standards, and accordingly included such tests of the accounting records and such other auditing procedures as we considered necessary in the circumstances.

In our opinion, such financial statements present fairly the financial position of the companies at June 30, 1968 and the results of their operations and source and use of their funds for the year then ended, in conformity with generally accepted accounting principles applied on a basis consistent with that of the preceding year.

August 2, 1968

Haskins & Sells

Consolidated Statement of Funds

	Year Ending December 31,	
	1968	1967
SOURCE OF FUNDS:		
Net income from consolidated income statement......	$148,262,340	$127,065,887
Expenses not requiring a current outlay of funds—		
principally depreciation and deferred taxes.........	107,296,260	92,297,285
Total from operations........................	255,558,600	219,363,172
Proceeds from long term debt....................	92,621,300	41,831,700
Sale of common stock under Employes'		
Stock Option Plans	2,111,753	1,803,841
Property disposals, etc.	6,100,551	1,498,627
	356,392,204	264,497,340
APPLICATION OF FUNDS:		
Expenditures for:		
Properties and plants..........................	234,510,511	174,407,736
Miscellaneous investments, etc.	4,728,456	3,215,008
Payment of cash dividends.......................	50,924,823	48,106,998
Funds held by trustee for plant construction..........	975,707	45,378,775
	291,139,497	271,108,517
INCREASE (DECREASE) IN WORKING CAPITAL.........	$ 65,252,707	$ (6,611,177)

757

Opinion of Independent Accountants

TO THE BOARD OF DIRECTORS AND SHAREHOLDERS OF THE GOODYEAR TIRE & RUBBER COMPANY:

In our opinion, the accompanying Consolidated Balance Sheet and Consolidated Statements of Income, Retained
Earnings, Capital Surplus and Funds present fairly the consolidated financial position of The Goodyear Tire & Rubber
Company and its domestic and foreign subsidiary companies at December 31, 1968 and the consolidated
results of their operations and supplementary information on funds for the year then ended, in conformity
with generally accepted accounting principles applied on a basis consistent with that of the preceding year.
Our examination was made in accordance with generally accepted auditing standards, and accordingly included such
tests of the accounting records and such other auditing procedures as we considered necessary in the circumstances.

Cleveland, Ohio
February 5, 1969

Price Waterhouse & Co.

STATEMENT OF CONSOLIDATED INCOME

	1968	1967	Increase Decrease
	(In Thousands)		
Net Sales..	$1,792,938	$1,637,482	$155,456
Cost of Goods Sold......................................	1,324,595	1,214,561	110,034
Gross Profit..	468,343	422,921	45,422
Less:			
Selling and administrative expenses....................	179,611	162,779	16,832
Research, development, patent and engineering expenses................................	86,281	84,224	2,057
	265,892	247,003	18,889
Operating Profit..	202,451	175,918	26,533
Income Charges—Net....................................	11,519	10,445	1,074
Income Before Income Taxes............................	190,932	165,473	25,459
Provision for Income Taxes:			
Current...	83,908	70,238	13,670
Deferred (credit)......................................	(1,801)	(3,462)	1,661
	82,107	66,776	15,331
Income Before Extraordinary Item......................	108,825	98,697	10,128
Extraordinary Gain on Sale of Investment, Less Applicable Income Tax of $2,131,000............		6,394	*6,394*
Net Income...	$ 108,825	$ 105,091	$ 3,734
Earnings a Common Share [(1)]:			
Before extraordinary item.............................	$3.30	$3.00	$.30
Including extraordinary item...........................	3.30	3.19	.11

(1) Based on shares outstanding at end of year— 33,008,920 in 1968 and 32,962,005 in 1967.
The above statement should be read in conjunction with pages 17, 18 and 19 of this report.

758

STATEMENTS OF CONSOLIDATED PAID-IN SURPLUS AND RETAINED EARNINGS

	1968	1967
	(In Thousands)	
PAID-IN SURPLUS		
Balance at Beginning of Year:		
As previously reported..	$580,533	$550,842
Adjustment—see note on page 17..	601	601
As restated...	581,134	551,443
Additions:		
Excess of approximate market value of common capital stock distributed as a stock dividend over the par value thereof..........................		29,440
Excess of amounts received over the par value of common capital stock issued under stock option plans......................................	1,636	251
	582,770	581,134
Deduction:		
Pro-rata portion of excess of cost over par value of 199,412 shares of common capital stock in treasury, issued to effect the acquisition, in pooling of interests transactions, of equities in two subsidiary companies (see Retained Earnings below).....................................	3,466	
Balance at End of Year...	$579,304	$581,134
RETAINED EARNINGS		
Balance at Beginning of Year:		
As previously reported..	$428,408	$406,134
Adjustment—See note on page 17..	3,210	2,477
As restated...	431,618	408,611
Addition—Net Income for the Year......................................	108,825	105,091
	540,443	513,702
Deductions:		
Dividends on capital stock of parent company:		
Cash—$1.65 a share in 1968 and $1.60 a share in 1967..............	54,032	51,347
Stock—2%..		30,732
	54,032	82,079
Dividend of subsidiary prior to acquisition...............................		5
Pro-rata portion of excess of cost over par value of 199,412 shares of common capital stock in treasury, issued to effect the acquisition, in pooling of interests transactions, of equities in two subsidiary companies (see Paid-in Surplus above)...	5,929	
	59,961	82,084
Balance at End of Year...	$480,482	$431,618

759

The above statements should be read in conjunction with pages 17, 18 and 19 of this report.

Ayrshire Collieries Corporation AND SUBSIDIARIES

Consolidated Balance Sheets

Assets

	June 30	
	1968	**1967**
CURRENT ASSETS:		
Cash	$ 4,902,284	$ 3,827,307
Marketable securities (including U. S. Government securities of $3,000,000 and $5,857,615, respectively), at cost	3,481,634	9,970,553
Accounts receivable (less reserves of $100,799 and $95,799, respectively)	8,194,234	7,801,148
Coal and other products, at market or less	916,378	417,344
Federal income tax effect from production payment (Note 4)	1,512,000	960,000
	19,006,530	22,976,352
PROPERTY, PLANT AND EQUIPMENT, at cost (Note 5):		
Plant and equipment (including leased equipment of $5,083,242 in 1968)	71,184,018	60,990,853
Less—Accumulated depreciation	34,390,973	31,310,602
	36,793,045	29,680,251
Coal lands and rights (less accumulated depletion of $5,027,228 and $4,594,944, respectively) (Note 4)	34,539,181	30,850,753
Construction in progress	6,224,206	4,900,889
	77,556,432	65,431,893
INVESTMENTS:		
Investments in nonconsolidated companies, at cost plus equity in undistributed income	4,994,209	4,099,517
Cash surrender value of life insurance	90,723	176,291
Other	186,178	158,379
	5,271,110	4,434,187
PREPAID EXPENSES AND DEFERRED CHARGES:		
Repair parts and supplies	3,602,407	3,337,736
Other	1,150,918	876,168
	4,753,325	4,213,904
	$106,587,397	$ 97,056,336

The accompanying notes to consolidated financial statements are an integral part of these statements.

760

Liabilities and Shareholders' Equity

	June 30	
	1968	**1967**
CURRENT LIABILITIES:		
Accounts payable and accrued expenses	$ 5,314,402	$ 4,815,782
Federal income taxes	1,398,351	1,126,564
Current requirements on long-term obligations	5,263,515	2,917,197
Proceeds from production payment	3,000,000	2,000,000
	14,976,268	10,859,543
LONG-TERM OBLIGATIONS:		
5% unsecured note, due serially to 1975	15,000,000	16,875,000
5% equipment note, due serially to 1974	2,500,000	2,875,000
Royalty and land purchase contracts, due serially to 2012	7,276,661	7,395,172
Equipment purchase contracts	155,425	2,199,629
6% lease obligation, due quarterly to 1980	4,694,950	—
Other	—	31,420
	29,627,036	29,376,221
RESERVES AND DEFERRED ITEMS:		
Work stoppage expense	—	300,000
Reclamation expense	498,000	—
Deferred Federal income taxes (Note 4)	4,901,831	4,006,831
Unamortized investment tax credit (Note 4)	607,897	419,299
	6,007,728	4,726,130
CONTINGENT LIABILITY (Note 7)		
SHAREHOLDERS' EQUITY:		
Common stock, par value $3 per share, authorized 800,000 shares;		
issued and outstanding 790,145 shares	2,370,435	2,370,435
Paid-in surplus (no change during the year)	8,687,816	8,687,816
Capital maintained by recognition of price-level depreciation (Note 1)	4,609,546	4,242,629
Earned surplus	40,308,568	36,793,562
	55,976,365	52,094,442
	$106,587,397	$ 97,056,336

761

Ayrshire Collieries Corporation AND SUBSIDIARIES

Statements of Consolidated Income

	Year Ended June 30	
REVENUES:	1968	1967
Sales of coal and coke	$59,684,111	$62,008,842
Income from other products, royalties, interest, rentals, etc.	1,474,863	1,180,785
Equity in net income of nonconsolidated companies (Note 5)	884,560	647,780
	62,043,534	63,837,407
EXPENSES:		
Cost of products sold and other operating charges, exclusive of items listed below	47,711,790	49,919,638
Depreciation and depletion (Notes 4 and 5)	3,112,837	3,545,058
Selling, administrative and general expenses	4,043,491	3,940,821
Interest expense	1,098,118	1,213,163
	55,966,236	58,618,680
INCOME BEFORE FEDERAL INCOME TAXES AND EXTRAORDINARY ITEMS	6,077,298	5,218,727
PROVISION FOR FEDERAL INCOME TAXES (Note 4):		
Current	411,402	842,300
Deferred	895,000	248,630
Investment tax credit (net)	188,598	106,070
	1,495,000	1,197,000
INCOME BEFORE EXTRAORDINARY ITEMS	4,582,298	4,021,727
EXTRAORDINARY ITEMS, net of income taxes (Note 3) (per share: 1968—$.11) ..	87,710	—
NET INCOME (conventional net income before deducting provision for price-level depreciation expense)	4,670,008	4,021,727
Provision for price-level depreciation (Notes 1 and 5)	366,917	352,274
NET INCOME, after deducting provision for price-level depreciation (per share: 1968—$5.45; 1967—$4.64)	$ 4,303,091	$ 3,669,453

Statements of Consolidated Earned Surplus

	Year Ended June 30	
	1968	1967
BALANCE, at beginning of year	$36,793,562	$33,912,194
Net income, after deducting provision for price-level depreciation	4,303,091	3,669,453
	41,096,653	37,581,647
Cash dividends, $1.00 per share	788,085	788,085
BALANCE, at end of year	$40,308,568	$36,793,562

The accompanying notes to consolidated financial statements are an integral part of these statements.

762

C
Series B problems

Numbers assigned to the problems in this appendix correspond to the numbers of the comparable problems presented at the end of the chapters, with the substitution of the letter "B" for the letter "A." For example, Problem 1-2B presented below is the alternate for Problem 1-2A presented on page 25. The working papers correlating with the textbook are designed for use either for the series A problems at the end of the chapters or for the series B problems in this appendix.

Chapter 1

1-2B. On January 1, the beginning of the current fiscal year, the amount of R. H. Jackson's capital in Jackson Co. was $35,870. During the year he made weekly cash withdrawals of $275 (total of $14,300). The amounts of the enterprise's assets and liabilities at December 31, the close of the current fiscal year, and of its revenue and expense for the year ended on that date are listed below.

Accounts payable....................	$ 4,280
Accounts receivable..................	7,010
Advertising expense..................	2,460
Building............................	43,800
Accumulated depreciation — building ...	20,300
Cash...............................	7,720
Depreciation expense — building........	830
Depreciation expense — equipment......	1,560
Equipment.........................	18,270
Accumulated depreciation — equipment.	8,230
Insurance expense....................	770
Land..............................	5,000
Miscellaneous expense................	1,810
Prepaid insurance....................	2,320
Sales..............................	68,800
Salaries payable.....................	160
Salary expense......................	23,500
Supplies............................	1,830
Supplies expense.....................	1,880
Taxes expense.......................	3,510
Taxes payable.......................	1,170
Utilities expense.....................	2,240

Instructions:

(1) Prepare an income statement for the current fiscal year ending December 31, exercising care to include each item of expense listed.
(2) Prepare a capital statement for the current fiscal year ending December 31.
(3) Prepare a balance sheet as of December 31 of the current fiscal year.

1-3B. R. L. Logan operates a business known as Century Dry Cleaners. The actual work of dry cleaning is done by another company at wholesale rates. The assets and the liabilities of the business on November 1 of the current year are as follows: Cash, $1,500; Accounts Receivable, $200; Supplies, $90; Equipment, $4,800; Accumulated Depreciation, $900; Accounts Payable, $1,120. Business transactions during November are summarized below.

(a) Paid rent for the month, $150.
(b) Purchased supplies on account, $60.
(c) Paid creditors on account, $930.
(d) Received cash from cash customers for dry cleaning sales, $1,270.
(e) Charged customers for dry cleaning sales on account, $560.
(f) Received monthly invoice for dry cleaning expense for November (to be paid on December 10), $890.
(g) Received cash from customers on account, $530.
(h) Reimbursed a customer $20 for a garment lost by the cleaning company, which agreed to deduct the amount from the invoice received in transaction (f).
(i) Paid the following: wages expense, $160; truck expense, $50; utilities expense, $30; miscellaneous expense, $20.
(j) Purchased an item of equipment on account, $110.
(k) Paid personal expenses by checks drawn on the business, $310, and withdrew $50 in cash for personal use.
(l) Determined by taking an inventory the cost of supplies used during the month, $30.
(m) Estimated depreciation of truck and other equipment for the month, $110.

Instructions:

(1) State the assets, liabilities, and capital as of November 1 in equation form similar to that shown in this chapter.
(2) Record, in tabular form below the equation, the increases and decreases resulting from each transaction, indicating the new balances after each transaction. Explain the nature of each increase and decrease in capital by an appropriate notation at the right of the amount.
(3) Prepare an income statement, a capital statement, and a balance sheet.

Chapter 2

2-1B. James A. Sloan established an enterprise to be known as Sloan Decorators, on April 16 of the current year. During the remainder of the month he completed the following business transactions.

April 16. Sloan transferred cash from a personal bank account to an account to be used for the business, $3,600.
16. Purchased supplies on account, $320.
16. Paid rent for period of April 16 to end of month, $110.
17. Purchased equipment on account, $480.

17. Purchased a truck for $4,200, paying $1,000 cash and giving a note payable for the remainder.
19. Received cash for job completed, $210.
22. Purchased supplies for cash, $120.
23. Paid wages of employees, $620.
26. Paid creditor for equipment purchased on April 17, $480.
27. Recorded sales on account and sent invoices to customers, $3,070.
28. Received cash for job completed, $163. This sale had not been recorded previously.
29. Paid premiums on property and casualty insurance, $396.
29. Received an invoice for truck expenses, to be paid in May, $57.
29. Paid utilities expense, $23.
29. Paid miscellaneous expenses, $41.
30. Received cash from customers on account, $1,960.
30. Paid wages of employees, $650.
30. Withdrew cash for personal use, $490.

Instructions:

(1) Prepare a ledger for Sloan Decorators, using the following titles and account numbers: Cash, 11; Accounts Receivable, 12; Supplies, 13; Prepaid Insurance, 14; Truck, 16; Equipment, 18; Notes Payable, 21; Accounts Payable, 22; James A. Sloan, Capital, 31; James A. Sloan, Drawing, 32; Sales, 41; Wages Expense, 51; Rent Expense, 53; Truck Expense, 54; Utilities Expense, 55; Miscellaneous Expense, 59.
(2) Record each transaction in a two-column journal, referring to the above list of accounts or to the ledger in selecting appropriate account titles. (Do *not* insert the account numbers in the journal at this time.)
(3) Post the journal to the ledger, inserting appropriate posting references as each item is posted.
(4) Insert pencil footings and balances in the accounts where appropriate, and prepare a trial balance as of April 30.

765

If the working papers correlating with the textbook are not used, omit Problem 2-3B.

2-3B. The following records of Speedy TV Service are presented in the working papers:

> Two-column journal for the month of January
> Ledger as of January 31
> Preliminary trial balance as of January 31

Locate the errors, supply the information requested, and prepare a corrected trial balance, proceeding in accordance with the detailed instructions presented at the top of the next page. The balances recorded in the accounts as of January 1 and the entries in the journal are correctly stated. If it is necessary to correct any posted amounts in the ledger, a line should be drawn through the erroneous figure and the correct amount inserted above. Although corrections to memorandum pencil footings and balances are ordinarily accomplished through erasures, any such errors discovered may be corrected by crossing out the erroneous amount and substituting the correct figure. Corrections or other notations may be inserted on the preliminary trial balance in any manner desired. It is not necessary to complete all of the instructions if equal trial balance totals can be obtained earlier. However, the requirements of instructions (9) and (10) should be completed in any event.

Instructions:

(1) Verify the totals of the preliminary trial balance, inserting the amounts obtained in the schedule provided.

(2) Compute the difference between the trial balance totals.

(3) Determine whether the amount obtained in (2) is evenly divisible by 9.

(4) If the amount obtained in (2) is an even number, determine half the amount.

(5) Scan the amounts in the ledger to determine whether a posting has been omitted or erroneously posted to the wrong side of an account.

(6) Compare the listings in the trial balance with the balances shown in the ledger.

(7) Verify the accuracy of the memorandum footings and balances in the ledger.

(8) Trace the postings in the ledger back to the journal, using small check marks to identify items traced. (Correct any memorandum amounts in the ledger that may be necessitated by errors in posting.)

(9) Journalize as of January 31 the issuance of a note payable of $500 and a payment of $100, for the purchase of an item of equipment for $600. The transaction had occurred on January 31 but was inadvertently omitted from the journal. Post to the ledger. (Revise any memorandum amounts necessitated by the posting.)

(10) Prepare a new trial balance.

2-4B. The following business transactions were completed by James C. Hunt during September of the current year:

Sept. 3. Deposited $19,000 in a bank account for use in acquiring and operating Sunset Drive-In Theatre.

4. Purchased the Sunset Drive-In Theatre for $31,000, allocated as follows: equipment, $6,000; buildings, $12,000; land, $13,000. Paid $11,000 in cash and gave a mortgage note for the remainder.

5. Paid premiums for property and casualty insurance policies, $1,310.

7. Paid for September billboard and newspaper advertising, $410.

8. Purchased supplies, $245, and equipment, $1,250, on account.

9. Cash received from admissions for the week, $1,525.

11. Paid miscellaneous expense, $80.

15. Paid semimonthly wages, $1,600.

16. Cash received from admissions for the week, $2,110.

16. Entered into a contract for the operation of the refreshment stand at a rental of 10% of the concessionaire's sales, with a monthly minimum of $250, payable in advance. Received cash of $125 as the advance payment for the period September 16, the effective date of the contract, to September 30.

18. Purchased supplies for cash, $30.

20. Paid cash to owner for his personal use, $945.

23. Cash received from admissions for the week, $2,280.

24. Paid miscellaneous expenses, $55.

25. Paid for advertising leaflets for September, $45.

27. Returned portion of equipment purchased on September 8 to the supplier, receiving full credit for its cost, $225.

28. Recorded invoice of $1,940 for rental of film for September. Payment is due on October 5.

28. Paid cash to creditors on account, $1,270.

29. Paid electricity and water bills, $280.

30. Paid semimonthly wages, $1,900.

30. Cash received from admissions for remainder of the month, $2,810.

30. Recorded additional amount owed by the concessionaire for September, whose sales for September 16–30 totaled $2,000. Rental charges in excess of the advance payment are not due and payable until the tenth of the following month.

Instructions:

(1) Prepare a ledger for Sunset Drive-In Theatre, using the following account titles and numbers: Cash, 11; Accounts Receivable, 12; Prepaid Insurance, 13; Supplies, 14; Equipment, 17; Buildings, 18; Land, 19; Accounts Payable, 21; Mortgage Note Payable, 24; James C. Hunt, Capital, 31; James C. Hunt, Drawing, 32; Admissions Income, 41; Concession Income, 42; Wages Expense, 51; Film Rental Expense, 52; Advertising Expense, 53; Electricity & Water Expense, 54; Miscellaneous Expense, 59.

(2) Record the transactions in a two-column journal.

(3) Post the journal to the ledger.

(4) Prepare a trial balance as of September 30.

(5) Determine the following:

    (a) Amount of total revenue recorded in the ledger.

    (b) Amount of total expenses recorded in the ledger.

    (c) Amount of net income for September, assuming that additional unrecorded expenses were as follows: Supplies expense, $30; Insurance expense, $40; Depreciation expense — equipment, $60; Depreciation expense — buildings, $70; Interest expense (on mortgage note), $95.

    (d) Based on the assumptions in (c), the amount of increase or decrease in capital subsequent to the initial investment on September 3.

    (e) Based on the assumptions in (c), the amount of capital as of September 30.

    (f) The understatement or overstatement of net income for September that would have resulted from failure to record the invoice for film rental until it was paid in October. (See transaction of September 28.)

    (g) The understatement or overstatement of liabilities as of September 30 that would have resulted from failure to record the invoice for film rental in September.

2-6B. The following trial balance for Best Household Services as of March 31 of the current year does not balance because of a number of errors.

Cash	2,110	
Accounts Receivable	2,430	
Supplies	1,420	
Prepaid Insurance	234	
Equipment	8,160	
Notes Payable		1,600
Accounts Payable		870
Richard Foster, Capital		6,240
Richard Foster, Drawing	600	
Sales		9,900
Wages Expense	2,200	
Rent Expense	490	
Advertising Expense	23	
Gas, Electricity, and Water Expense	84	
	17,751	18,610

In the process of comparing the amounts in the trial balance with the ledger, recomputing the balances of the accounts, and comparing the postings with the journal entries, the following errors were discovered:

(a) The pencil footing of the credits to Cash was understated by $200.
(b) A cash receipt of $340 was posted as a debit to Cash of $430.
(c) A debit of $60 to Accounts Receivable was not posted.
(d) A return of $10 of defective supplies was erroneously posted as a $100 credit to Supplies.
(e) An insurance policy acquired at a cost of $56 was posted as a credit to Prepaid Insurance.
(f) A debit of $250 in Notes Payable was overlooked when determining the balance of the account.
(g) The pencil footings of $1,720 debit and $2,690 credit in Accounts Payable were correct but the balance was computed incorrectly.
(h) A debit of $200 for a withdrawal by the owner was posted as a credit to the capital account.
(i) The balance of $230 in Advertising Expense was entered as $23 in the trial balance.
(j) Miscellaneous Expense, with a balance of $130, was omitted from the trial balance.

Instructions:

Prepare a corrected trial balance as of March 31 of the current year.

Chapter 3

3-1B. The trial balance of Walton Laundromat at March 31, the end of the current fiscal year, and data needed for year-end adjustments are presented below.

Walton Laundromat
Trial Balance
March 31, 19—

Cash	1,230	
Laundry Supplies	2,010	
Prepaid Insurance	498	
Laundry Equipment.......	21,350	
Accumulated Depreciation.		5,200
Accounts Payable		366
Jane Carson, Capital......		11,984
Jane Carson, Drawing.....	4,900	
Laundry Revenue.........		22,060
Wages Expense	7,070	
Rent Expense	1,250	
Utilities Expense.........	962	
Miscellaneous Expense.....	340	
	39,610	39,610

Adjustment data:
(a) Laundry supplies on hand at March 31. $ 210
(b) Insurance expired during the year...... 250
(c) Depreciation for the year............. 1,720
(d) Wages accrued at March 31........... 75

Instructions:
(1) Record the trial balance on an eight-column work sheet.
(2) Complete the work sheet.
(3) Prepare an income statement, a capital statement
    (no additional investments were made during the year),
    and a balance sheet in report form.
(4) Record the adjusting entries in a two-column journal.
(5) Record the closing entries in a two-column journal.
(6) Compute the following:
    (a) Percent of net income to sales.
    (b) Percent of net income to capital balance at the beginning of year.

3-2B. As of November 30, the end of the current fiscal year, the accountant for Morrow Company prepared a trial balance, journalized and posted the adjusting entries, prepared an adjusted trial balance, prepared the statements, and completed the other procedures required at the end of the accounting cycle. The two trial balances as of November 30, one before adjustments and the other after adjustments, are presented below.

Morrow Company
Trial Balance
November 30, 19—

	Unadjusted		Adjusted	
Cash..................................	1,790		1,790	
Supplies.............................	2,475		550	
Prepaid Rent........................	3,595		1,580	
Prepaid Insurance...................	435		260	
Automobile..........................	5,250		5,250	
Accumulated Depreciation — Automobile.		825		1,900
Equipment..........................	12,600		12,600	
Accumulated Depreciation — Equipment..		3,950		5,300
Accounts Payable....................		470		550
Salaries Payable.....................		—		125
Taxes Payable.......................		—		45
Edward Morrow, Capital..............		11,090		11,090
Edward Morrow, Drawing.............	10,000		10,000	
Service Fees Earned..................		35,955		35,955
Salaries Expense.....................	14,740		14,865	
Rent Expense.......................	—		2,015	
Supplies Expense....................	—		1,925	
Depreciation Expense — Equipment......	—		1,350	
Depreciation Expense — Automobile.....	—		1,075	
Utilities Expense....................	570		650	
Taxes Expense......................	425		470	
Insurance Expense...................	—		175	
Miscellaneous Expense................	410		410	
	52,290	52,290	54,965	54,965

Instructions:
(1) Present the eight journal entries that were required to adjust the accounts at November 30. None of the accounts was affected by more than one adjusting entry.
(2) Present the journal entries required to close the books at November 30.
(3) Prepare a capital statement for the fiscal year ended November 30. There were no additional investments during the year.

C • Series B problems

If the working papers correlating with the textbook are not used, omit Problem 3-3B.

3-3B. The ledger of Scott Machine Repairs as of October 31, the end of the first month of its current fiscal year, is presented in the working papers. The books had been closed on September 30.

Instructions:

(1) Prepare a trial balance of the ledger, listing only the accounts with balances, on an eight-column work sheet.
(2) Complete the eight-column work sheet. Data for the adjustments are as follows:

Supplies on hand at October 31.......	$285.00
Insurance expired during the month...	32.50
Truck depreciation for the month......	140.00
Equipment depreciation for the month.	70.00
Wages accrued at October 31.........	146.00

(3) Prepare an income statement, a capital statement, and a balance sheet.
(4) Record the adjusting entries in a two-column journal and post.
(5) Record the closing entries in a two-column journal and post.
(6) Rule the closed accounts and balance and rule the remaining accounts that contain more than one entry.
(7) Prepare a post-closing trial balance.

Chapter 4

4-1B. Farrell Trading Co. was established in May of the current year. Its sales of merchandise on account and related returns and allowances during the remainder of the month are described below. Terms of all sales were n/30, FOB destination.

May 17. Sold merchandise on account to Barrett Corp., Invoice No. 1, $630.
    18. Sold merchandise on account to Doyle & Ellis, Invoice No. 2, $810.
    20. Sold merchandise on account to Richards & Co., Invoice No. 3, $990.
    22. Issued Credit Memorandum No. 1 for $50 to Doyle & Ellis for merchandise returned.
    22. Sold merchandise on account to B. A. Rowe Co., Invoice No. 4, $420.
    25. Sold merchandise on account to R. G. Holmes, Inc., Invoice No. 5, $1,030.
    26. Issued Credit Memorandum No. 2 for $90 to Barrett Corp. for merchandise returned.
    27. Sold merchandise on account to Doyle & Ellis, Invoice No. 6, $1,350.
    28. Issued Credit Memorandum No. 3 for $30 to B. A. Rowe Co. for damages to merchandise caused by faulty packing.
    30. Sold merchandise on account to Richards & Co., Invoice No. 7, $220.

Instructions:

(1) Open the following accounts in the general ledger, using the account numbers indicated: Accounts Receivable, 113; Sales, 411; Sales Returns and Allowances, 412.
(2) Open the following accounts in the accounts receivable ledger: Barrett Corp.; Doyle & Ellis; R. G. Holmes, Inc.; Richards & Co.; B. A. Rowe Co.
(3) Record the transactions for May, posting to the customers' accounts in the accounts receivable ledger *immediately* after recording each

entry. Use a sales journal similar to the one illustrated on page 94 and a two-column general journal.

(4) Post the general journal and the sales journal to the three accounts in the general ledger, inserting the account balances only after the last posting.

(5) (a) What is the sum of the balances of the accounts in the subsidiary ledger?

(b) What is the balance of the controlling account?

If the working papers correlating with the textbook are not used, omit Problem 4-2B.

4-2B. Three journals, the accounts receivable ledger, and portions of the general ledger of Randall Company are presented in the working papers. Sales invoices and credit memorandums were entered in the journals by an assistant. Terms of sales on account are 2/10, n/30, FOB shipping point. Transactions in which cash and notes receivable were received during June of the current year are as follows:

June 1. Received $1,029 cash from George Ives & Co. in payment of May 22 invoice, less discount.

  2. Received $2,040 cash in payment of a $2,000 note receivable and interest of $40.

  Post transactions of June 1, 3, and 4 to customers' accounts.

  8. Received $686 cash from Paul M. Vincent in payment of May 29 invoice, less discount.

  9. Received $1,600 cash from John T. Porter Corp. in payment of May 9 invoice, no discount.

  Post transactions of June 8, 9, 10, 12, and 15 to customers' accounts.

  15. Cash sales for first half of June totaled $8,019.

  17. Received $360 cash refund for return of defective equipment purchased for cash in May.

  19. Received $1,323 cash from George Ives & Co. in payment of balance due on June 10 invoice, less discount.

  22. Received $735 cash from John T. Porter Corp. in payment of June 12 invoice, less discount.

  Post transactions of June 18, 19, 22, 23, 24, 25, and 26 to customers' accounts.

  29. Received $13 cash for sale of store supplies at cost, as an accommodation.

  30. Received $359 cash and a $500 note receivable from R. J. Cole, Inc. in settlement of the balance due on the invoice of May 3, no discount. (Record receipt of note in the general journal.)

  30. Cash sales for second half of June totaled $8,413.

  Post transactions of June 30 to the customer's account.

Instructions:

(1) Record the cash and notes received in June and post all three journals to the customers' accounts, in date sequence, at the points indicated in the narrative of transactions.

(2) Post the appropriate individual entries from the cash receipts journal and the general journal to the general ledger.

(3) Add the columns of the sales journal and the cash receipts journal and post the appropriate totals to the general ledger. Insert the balance of each account after the last posting.

(4) Prepare a schedule of accounts receivable and compare the total with the balance of the controlling account.

771

4-3B. Transactions related to sales and cash receipts completed by Stark Company during January of the current year are described below. The terms of all sales on account are 2/10, n/30, FOB shipping point. All delivery charges are prepaid and charged to the customer.

Jan. 2. Issued Invoice No. 362 to Henry Morrow Co., $1,200; delivery, $24; total, $1,224.
    3. Received cash from Allen & Beeler for the balance due on its account, no discount.
    6. Received cash from Stone & Co. for the balance due on their account, less discount.

Post all journals to the accounts receivable ledger.

    8. Issued Invoice No. 363 to Henry Morrow Co., $1,700; delivery, $33; total, $1,733.
   11. Issued Invoice No. 364 to R. M. Hart, $1,414; delivery, $29; total, $1,443.
   12. Received cash from Henry Morrow Co. for invoice of January 2, less discount.
   13. Received cash refund for return of office supplies, $21.

Post all journals to the accounts receivable ledger.

   16. Recorded cash sales for first half of the month, $5,170.
   17. Received cash from R. M. Hart for the balance owed on January 1; no discount.
   17. Issued Invoice No. 365 to Stone & Co., $2,239; delivery, $40; total, $2,279.
   18. Received cash from Henry Morrow Co. for invoice of January 8, less discount.
   24. Issued Credit Memo No. 41 to Stone & Co., $9.

Post all journals to the accounts receivable ledger.

   24. Issued Invoice No. 366 to Allen & Beeler, $2,400; delivery, $55; total, $2,455.
   26. Received $909 cash in payment of a $900 note receivable and interest of $9.
   27. Received cash from Stone & Co. for the balance due on invoice of January 17, less credit memo of January 24, less discount.
   29. Issued Invoice No. 367 to Henry Morrow Co., $1,166; delivery, $22; total, $1,188.
   31. Recorded cash sales for the second half of the month, $4,810.
   31. Issued Credit Memo No. 42 to Allen & Beeler, $52.

Post all journals to the accounts receivable ledger.

Instructions:

(1) Open the following accounts in the general ledger, inserting the balances indicated, as of January 1:

111	Cash........................	$2,437
112	Notes Receivable............	1,900
113	Accounts Receivable.........	3,668
115	Office Supplies..............	174
411	Sales.......................	————
412	Sales Returns and Allowances.	————
413	Sales Discount..............	————
615	Delivery Expense............	————
811	Interest Income.............	————

(2) Open the following accounts in the accounts receivable ledger, inserting the balances indicated, as of January 1:
Allen & Beeler, $1,193, including a delivery charge of $43;

R. M. Hart, $1,651, including a delivery charge of $51;
Henry Morrow Co.; Stone & Co., $824, including a delivery charge
of $24. Make a notation of the amount of the delivery charges
in the item section of each account.

(3) Record the transactions for the month in a sales journal similar
to the one illustrated on page 107, a sales returns and allowances
journal similar to the one illustrated on page 99, and a cash
receipts journal similar to the one illustrated on page 101.
Post to the accounts receivable ledger at the points
indicated in the narrative of transactions.

(4) Add the columns of the journals and post the individual
entries and totals to the general ledger. Insert the account
balances after the last posting.

(5) Determine that the subsidiary ledger agrees with the
controlling account.

4-4B. The statutes of the state in which Peterson Markets Co. is located
require that retailers collect a sales tax of 3% on all sales to consumers except
on certain items, such as seeds and fertilizers, and on sales to governmental
units, such as public schools, cities, and counties. They provide further that
in the event the amount charged to customers is less than 3% of net taxable
sales, the deficiency must be borne by the retailer. Payments for each calendar
quarter are payable by the end of the month following the quarter.

The balances in certain accounts of Peterson Markets Co. as of March 31,
after adjustments had been made for the additional tax liability for the period
January 1–March 31, and balances of the same accounts as of June 30, before
adjustments for the additional tax liability for the period April 1–June 30, are
presented below. The company closes its books on December 31.

	March 31	June 30
Sales Tax Payable	3,674.07	4,453.18
Sales	127,326.10	283,789.30
Sales Returns and Allowances	1,622.04	3,618.70
Sales Tax Expense	27.63	27.63

Supplementary records indicate that sales for the period April 1 through
June 30 included nontaxable sales of $5,282.05 and that returns and allowances
on nontaxable sales for the same period amounted to $348.95.

Instructions:

(1) Determine the amount of the total liability for sales tax for
the period April 1–June 30, identifying all figures and
presenting them in good order.

(2) Determine the sales tax expense (deficiency in amount of tax
charged to customers) for the period April 1–June 30.

(3) Present the entry as of June 30 to record the sales tax expense
and the additional liability for sales taxes for
the period April 1–June 30.

(4) On the basis of the ledger information presented above, determine
the amount of the net taxable sales for the
first quarter of the year.

Chapter 5

5-2B. Hillside Men's Wear was established in July of the current year. Transactions related to purchases, returns and allowances, and cash payments during the remainder of the month are described below.

July 16. Issued Check No. 1 in payment of store supplies, $52, and office supplies, $37.

16. Purchased store equipment on account from Reed Supply Corp., $7,850.

16. Issued Check No. 2 in payment of rent for July, $290.

17. Purchased merchandise on account from Smart Clothes, Inc., $2,250.

19. Purchased merchandise on account from Norris Clothing Co., $2,048.

20. Purchased merchandise on account from Damon & Co., $1,450.

21. Received a credit memorandum from Norris Clothing Co. for returned merchandise, $98.

Post the journals to the accounts payable ledger.

23. Received a credit memorandum from Damon & Co. for defective merchandise, $42.

24. Issued Check No. 3 to Reed Supply Corp. in payment of invoice of $7,850.

26. Issued Check No. 4 to Smart Clothes, Inc., in payment of invoice of $2,250, less 2% discount.

27. Issued Check No. 5 to a cash customer for merchandise returned, $23.

28. Issued Check No. 6 to Norris Clothing Co. in payment of the balance owed, less 2% discount.

28. Purchased merchandise on account from Damon & Co., $2,321.

Post the journals to the accounts payable ledger.

29. Purchased the following from Reed Supply Corp. on account: store supplies, $26; office supplies, $63; office equipment, $750.

30. Issued Check No. 7 to Damon & Co. in payment of the invoice of $1,450 less the credit of $42.

30. Purchased merchandise on account from Smart Clothes, Inc., $1,990.

31. Issued Check No. 8 in payment of incoming transportation charges on merchandise delivered during July, $128.

31. Issued Check No. 9 in payment of sales salaries, $885.

31. Received a credit memorandum from Reed Supply Corp. for defect in office equipment, $20.

Post the journals to the accounts payable ledger.

Instructions:

(1) Open the following accounts in the general ledger, using the account numbers indicated.

111	Cash	
116	Store Supplies	
117	Office Supplies	
121	Store Equipment	
122	Office Equipment	
211	Accounts Payable	

412 Sales Returns and Allowances
511 Purchases
512 Purchases Discount
611 Sales Salaries
712 Rent Expense

(2) Open the following accounts in the accounts payable ledger: Damon & Co.; Norris Clothing Co.; Reed Supply Corp.; Smart Clothes, Inc.

(3) Record the transactions for July, using a purchases journal similar to the one illustrated on pages 118 and 119, a cash payments journal

similar to the one illustrated on page 126, and a two-column general journal. Post to the *accounts payable ledger* at the points indicated in the narrative of transactions.

(4) Post the appropriate individual entries to the *general ledger*.

(5) Add the columns of the purchases journal and the cash payments journal, and post the appropriate totals to the general ledger. (Because of omission from the problem of transactions related to cash receipts, the cash account in the ledger will have a credit balance.)

(6) Prepare a schedule of accounts payable.

If the working papers correlating with the textbook are not used, omit Problem 5-3B.

5-3B. Guardian Specialty Co. uses carbon copies of its sales invoices as a sales journal, posting to the accounts receivable ledger directly from the invoices. At the end of the month the invoices are totaled and the appropriate entry is recorded in the general journal. Purchases on account are recorded in a similar manner, the invoices being used as a purchases journal. Sales and purchases on account during May of the current year were as follows:

Sales

May 4.	James Oliver Corp....................	$2,100
6.	Vincent & Yost......................	830
10.	Howard Alden & Co..................	1,340
16.	C. A. Harris........................	1,170
17.	Howard Alden & Co..................	2,486
22.	Vincent & Yost	1,970

Purchases

May 2.	M. J. Barton & Co.: store supplies, $87; office supplies, $33	$ 120
3.	Lee Corp., merchandise	2,630
11.	Fisher-Jordan, Inc., merchandise	2,400
18.	Potter Manufacturing Co., store equipment..	1,800
19.	R. B. Warren, Inc., merchandise..........	896
29.	M. J. Barton & Co., store supplies.........	31
31.	Fisher-Jordan, Inc., merchandise..........	563

775

Other transactions completed during the month were recorded in a 4-column general journal, a cash receipts journal, and a cash payments journal, all of which are presented in the working papers. The subsidiary ledgers and the general ledger accounts affected by transactions of the month are also presented in the working papers.

Instructions:

(1) Summarize the sales invoices and the purchases invoices listed above and record the appropriate entries in the 4-column general journal.

(2) Post all items affecting the *subsidiary ledgers*, in the following order: (a) sales invoices, (b) purchases invoices, (c) general journal, (d) cash receipts journal, (e) cash payments journal. When postings are made daily, which is the usual practice, the entries in customers' and creditors' accounts will appear in chronological order. The fact that in this problem postings to some of the accounts will not be in perfect date sequence is immaterial.

(3) Post all items recorded in the Sundry Accounts Dr. and Sundry Accounts Cr. columns of the journals, in the following order:

(a) general journal, (b) cash receipts journal, (c) cash payments journal.
(4) Add the columns of the general journal. Post the appropriate columnar totals of the journals in the following order: (a) general journal, (b) cash receipts journal, (c) cash payments journal.
(5) Prepare a trial balance.
(6) Determine the sum of the balances in the:
  (a) Accounts receivable ledger (compare with balance of controlling account).
  (b) Accounts payable ledger (compare with balance of controlling account).

5-4B. The transactions completed by Trump's during September, the first month of the current fiscal year, were as follows:

Sept. 1. Issued Check No. 497 for September rent, $475.
 2. Purchased merchandise on account from Sloan-Wiley Corp., $2,170.
 3. Purchased equipment on account from Foster Supply Corp., $1,550.
 3. Issued Invoice No. 721 to S. R. Riggs, Inc., $1,010.
 5. Received check for $2,772 from Ames & Marlowe in payment of $2,800 invoice, less discount.
 5. Issued Check No. 498 in payment of miscellaneous selling expense, $93.
 5. Received credit memorandum from Sloan-Wiley Corp. for merchandise returned to them, $70.
 8. Issued Invoice No. 722 to West & Co., $1,925.
 9. Issued Check No. 499 for $3,663 to Beck Manufacturing Co. in payment of $3,700 balance, less 1% discount.
 9. Received check from James Hoyt Corp. on account, $950, no discount.
 10. Issued Check No. 500 to L. A. Mitchell & Co. in payment of invoice of $631, no discount.

Post all journals to the accounts receivable ledger and accounts payable ledger.

 10. Issued Invoice No. 723 to Ames & Marlowe, $2,510.
 11. Issued Check No. 501 to W. J. Zimmer, Inc. in payment of account, $1,273, no discount.
 12. Received check from S. R. Riggs, Inc. on account, $776, no discount.
 14. Issued credit memorandum to Ames & Marlowe for damaged merchandise, $110.
 15. Issued Check No. 502 for $2,079 to Sloan-Wiley Corp. in payment of $2,100 balance, less 1% discount.
 15. Issued Check No. 503 for $525 for cash purchase of merchandise.
 15. Cash sales for September 1–15, $3,685.
 17. Purchased merchandise on account from L. A. Mitchell & Co., $2,590.
 18. Received check for return of merchandise that had been purchased for cash, $31.
 18. Issued Check No. 504 in payment of miscellaneous general expense, $179.
 22. Purchased the following on account from Foster Supply Corp.: store supplies, $22; office supplies, $38.
 22. Issued Check No. 505 in payment of advertising expense, $375.

Post all journals to the accounts receivable ledger and accounts payable ledger.

 23. Issued Invoice No. 724 to James Hoyt Corp., $2,496.

24. Purchased the following on account from Beck Manufacturing Co.: merchandise, $880; store supplies, $23.
25. Issued Invoice No. 725 to West & Co., $1,920.
25. Received check for $2,376 from Ames & Marlowe in payment of $2,400 balance, less discount.
26. Issued Check No. 506 to Foster Supply Corp. in payment of invoice of September 3, $1,550, no discount.
29. Issued Check No. 507 to David Trump as a personal withdrawal, $800.
30. Issued Check No. 508 for monthly salaries as follows: sales salaries, $1,300; office salaries, $600.
30. Cash sales for September 16–30, $4,495.
30. Issued Check No. 509 for transportation on commodities purchased during the month as follows: merchandise, $126; equipment, $31.

Post all journals to the accounts receivable ledger and accounts payable ledger.

Instructions:

(1) Open the following accounts in the general ledger, entering the balances indicated as of September 1:

111	Cash..................	$ 6,370	411 Sales
113	Accounts Receivable.....	4,526	412 Sales Returns and Allowances
114	Merchandise Inventory...	24,720	413 Sales Discount
115	Store Supplies...........	280	511 Purchases
116	Office Supplies..........	165	512 Purchases Discount
117	Prepaid Insurance.......	839	611 Sales Salaries
121	Equipment.............	16,417	612 Advertising Expense
121.1	Accumulated Depreciation	4,680	619 Miscellaneous Selling Expense
211	Accounts Payable........	5,604	711 Office Salaries
311	David Trump, Capital...	43,033	712 Rent Expense
312	David Trump, Drawing..		719 Miscellaneous General Expense

(2) Open the following accounts in the accounts receivable ledger, entering the balances as of September 1 in the balance columns: Ames & Marlowe, $2,800; James Hoyt Corp., $950; S. R. Riggs, Inc. $776; West & Co.

(3) Open the following accounts in the accounts payable ledger, entering the balances as of September 1 in the balance columns: Beck Manufacturing Co., $3,700; Foster Supply Corp.; L. A. Mitchell & Co., $631; Sloan-Wiley Corp.; W. J. Zimmer, Inc., $1,273.

(4) Record the transactions for September, using a sales journal (as on page 94), a purchases journal (as on pages 118 and 119), a cash receipts journal (as on page 101), a cash payments journal (as on page 126), and a 2-column general journal. The terms of all sales on account are FOB shipping point, 1/15, n/60. Post to the subsidiary ledgers at the points indicated in the narrative of transactions.

(5) Post the appropriate individual entries to the *general ledger*.

(6) Add the columns of the special journals and post the appropriate totals to the general ledger.

(7) Prepare a trial balance.

(8) Prepare a schedule of accounts receivable and a schedule of accounts payable. (Compare totals with balances of related controlling accounts.)

C • Series B problems

6-1B. The accounts in the ledger of the Newman Company, with the balances on March 31, the end of the current fiscal year, are as follows:

Cash.....................	$ 4,150	Sales...................	$164,000
Accounts Receivable.......	10,780	Purchases...............	98,200
Merchandise Inventory.....	39,900	Sales Salaries...........	17,750
Store Supplies............	470	Advertising Expense.......	2,290
Prepaid Insurance........	1,910	Depreciation Expense —	
Store Equipment..........	20,500	Store Equipment.......	——
Accumulated Depreciation—		Delivery Expense........	1,330
Store Equipment........	1,800	Store Supplies Expense....	——
Accounts Payable..........	6,200	Rent Expense............	8,000
Salaries Payable...........	——	Insurance Expense........	——
Henry Newman, Capital....	50,310	Misc. General Expense....	1,910
Henry Newman, Drawing...	15,000	Loss on Disposal of Equip..	120
Expense and Revenue Sum..	——		

The data needed for year-ended adjustments on March 31 are as follows:

Merchandise inventory on March 31 ...	$33,100
Store supplies inventory on March 31...	140
Insurance expired during the year......	710
Depreciation for the current year.......	2,000
Accrued salaries on March 31	170

Instructions:

(1) Prepare an eight-column work sheet for the fiscal year ended March 31, listing all of the accounts in the order given.
(2) Prepare an income statement.
(3) Prepare a capital statement. There were no additional investments during the year.
(4) Prepare a balance sheet.
(5) Compute the following:

(a) Percent of net income from operations to sales.
(b) Percent of net income to the capital balance at the beginning of the year.

If the working papers correlating with this textbook are not used, omit Problem 6-2B.

6-2B. A. R. Hoyt owns and operates Hoyt Appliances. The general ledger balances at the beginning of the twelfth month and the journals for the twelfth month of the current fiscal year are presented in the working papers.

Instructions:

(1) Post the journals to the general ledger accounts, following the order indicated below. Balances need not be inserted in the balance columns of the accounts until all journals have been posted. Assume that entries to the subsidiary ledgers have been posted by an assistant.

POSTING ORDER

Individual items in Sundry Accounts columns:
  General Journal, Purchases Journal, Cash Receipts Journal, Cash Payments Journal.
Column totals:
  Sales Journal, Purchases Journal, Cash Receipts Journal, Cash Payments Journal.

(2) Take a trial balance at December 31 on an eight-column work sheet, listing all of the accounts in the ledger.

(3) Complete the work sheet. Adjustment data are:

Merchandise inventory at December 31.	$22,015.00
Supplies on hand at December 31	111.20
Insurance expired during the year........	498.00
Depreciation for the current year on:	
Store equipment...................	1,150.00
Office equipment....................	185.00
Accrued taxes at December 31	170.00

(4) Prepare an income statement, a capital statement, and a balance sheet. There were no additional investments of capital by the owner during the year.

(5) Journalize and post the adjusting entries.

(6) Journalize and post the closing entries. Indicate closed accounts by inserting a line in both balance columns, as illustrated in the salary expense account on page 155.

(7) Prepare a post-closing trial balance.

(8) Journalize and post the reversing entry or entries as of January 1.

6-3B. A portion of the work sheet of Palmer & Co. for the current year ending June 30 is presented below.

Account Title	Income Statement Debit	Income Statement Credit	Balance Sheet Debit	Balance Sheet Credit
Cash.....................................			13,260	
Accounts Receivable.....................			46,930	
Merchandise Inventory....................			53,750	
Supplies................................			267	
Prepaid Rent............................			1,950	
Prepaid Insurance.......................			1,860	
Store Equipment........................			20,200	
Accumulated Depr. — Store Equip...........				5,800
Office Equipment.......................			4,113	
Accumulated Depr. — Office Equip.........				1,620
Accounts Payable.......................				32,900
Sales Salaries Payable.....................				230
Mortgage Note Payable...................				15,000
H. B. Palmer, Capital.....................				69,150
H. B. Palmer, Drawing...................			14,000	
Expense and Revenue Summary.............	49,500	53,750		
Sales....................................		318,000		
Sales Returns and Allowances..............	10,300			
Purchases...............................	222,000			
Purchases Discount.......................		2,650		
Sales Salaries...........................	23,100			
Delivery Expense.........................	10,950			
Supplies Expense........................	1,865			
Depreciation Expense — Store Equip.........	1,350			
Miscellaneous Selling Expense..............	760			
Office Salaries...........................	11,900			
Rent Expense............................	7,650			
Insurance Expense........................	2,200			
Depreciation Expense — Office Equip.........	275			
Miscellaneous General Expense..............	1,220			
Interest Income..........................		300		
	343,070	374,700	156,330	124,700

Instructions:

(1) From the partial work sheet presented on the preceding page, determine the entries that appeared in the adjustments columns and present them in general journal form. The only accounts affected by more than a single adjusting entry were Merchandise Inventory and Expense and Revenue Summary. The balance in Prepaid Rent before adjustment was $9,600, representing a prepayment for the first three months of the past year at $600 a month and for the next twelve months at $650 a month.

(2) Determine the following:

(a) Amount of net income for the year.

(b) Amount of the owner's capital at the end of the year.

Chapter 7

7-1B. The following were selected from among the transactions completed by Lindsey Co. during the current year:

Jan. 10. Purchased merchandise on account from J. E. McFall Co., $950.
     20. Paid J. E. McFall Co. for the invoice of January 10, less 2% discount.
Feb. 11. Purchased merchandise on account from Pryor & Co., $1,200.
Mar. 13. Issued a 30-day, 5% note for $1,200 to Pryor & Co. on account.
Apr. 12. Paid Pryor & Co. the amount owed on the note of March 13.
May 23. Issued a 60-day, non-interest-bearing note for $6,000 to Valley National Bank. The bank discounted the note at the rate of 6%.
July 22. Paid Valley National Bank the amount due on the note of May 23.
Aug. 5. Borrowed $4,000 from First National Bank, issuing a 60-day, 7% note for that amount.
Oct. 4. Paid First National Bank the interest due on the note of August 5 and renewed the loan by issuing a new 30-day, 7% note for $4,000. (Record both the debit and the credit to the notes payable account.)
Nov. 3. Paid First National Bank the amount due on the note of October 4.
Dec. 1. Purchased office equipment from Barr Corp. for $5,400, paying $400 and issuing a series of ten 6% notes for $500 each, coming due at 30-day intervals.
    31. Paid the amount due Barr Corp. on the first note in the series issued on December 1.

Instructions:

(1) Record the transactions in general journal form.

(2) Determine the total amount of interest accrued as of December 31 on the nine notes owed to Barr Corp.

(3) Assume that a single note for $5,000 had been issued on December 1 instead of the series of ten notes, and that its terms required principal payments of $500 each 30 days, with interest at 6% on the balance. Determine the amount that would have been due and payable on December 31.

7-2B. The following were selected from among the transactions completed by Ratterman & Co. during the current year:

Jan. 8. Sold merchandise on account to Clark & Foley, $960.
    18. Accepted a 30-day, 6% note for $960 from Clark & Foley on account.
Feb. 17. Received from Clark & Foley the amount due on the note of January 18.

Mar. 18. Sold merchandise on account to Keller Corp., $1,500, charging an additional $35 for prepaid transportation costs.

28. Received from Keller Corp. the amount due on the invoice of March 18, less 2% discount.

Apr. 6. Loaned $900 cash to James Mitchell, receiving a 30-day, 6% note.

May 6. Received the interest due from James Mitchell and a new 60-day, 6% note as a renewal of the loan. (Record both the debit and the credit to the notes receivable account.)

July 5. Received from James Mitchell the amount due on his note.

Aug. 19. Sold merchandise on account to L. B. Ames, Inc., $2,400.

Sept. 17. Accepted a 60-day, 8% note for $2,400 from L. B. Ames, Inc. on account.

Oct. 7. Discounted the note from L. B. Ames, Inc. at the Citizens National Bank at 6½%.

Nov. 16. Received notice from Citizens National Bank that L. B. Ames, Inc. had dishonored its note. Paid the bank the maturity value of the note.

Dec. 16. Received from L. B. Ames, Inc. the amount owed on the dishonored note, plus interest computed on the maturity value of the note at 8% for the additional 30 days.

Instructions:

Record the transactions in general journal form.

7-3B. The transactions, adjusting entries, and closing entries described below are related to uncollectible accounts. All were completed during the current fiscal year ended December 31.

Jan. 29. Wrote off the $1,012 balance owed by Graham Corp., which has no assets.

May 2. Received $245 from Ronald Meyer in payment of his account, which had been written off in the preceding year. (Reinstate the account.)

June 28. Received 20% of the $600 balance owed by Norris & Co., a bankrupt, and wrote off the remainder as uncollectible.

Nov. 3. Received $150 from William Coleman in payment of his account, which had been written off two years earlier. (Reinstate the account.)

Dec. 28. Wrote off the following accounts as uncollectible (compound entry): Arthur Finch, $110; Shaw & Thompson, $320; Hartley & Co., $578; Edward D. Cross, Inc., $490.

31. On the basis of an analysis of the $93,240 of accounts receivable, it was estimated that $2,960 will be uncollectible. Recorded the adjusting entry.

31. Recorded the entry to close the appropriate account to Expense and Revenue Summary.

Instructions:

(1) Open the following selected accounts, recording the credit balance indicated as of January 1 of the current fiscal year:

114.1	Allowance for Doubtful Accounts....	$2,325
313	Expense and Revenue Summary.....	——
718	Uncollectible Accounts Expense.....	——

(2) Record in general journal form the transactions and the adjusting and closing entries described above. After each entry, post to the three selected accounts affected and extend the new balances.

(3) Determine the expected realizable value of the accounts receivable as of December 31.

(continued)

(4) Assuming that, instead of basing the provision for uncollectible accounts on an analysis of receivables, the adjusting entry on December 31 had been based on an estimated loss of $\frac{3}{4}$ of 1% of net sales for the year of $360,000, determine the following:

(a) Uncollectible accounts expense for the year.

(b) Balance in the allowance account after the adjustment of December 31.

(c) Expected realizable value of the accounts receivable on December 31.

If the working papers correlating with the textbook are not used, omit Problem 7-4B.

7-4B. The following transactions, all of which are related to receivables and payables, were selected from among the transactions completed by Powell Corp. during the current fiscal year.

Jan. 7. Received from Farrow Co. a 90-day, non-interest-bearing note for $6,500, dated January 6, on account.

21. Issued to Bowen & Son a 2-month, 6% note for $5,500, on account.

Feb. 20. Discounted at First Citizens Bank at 6% the note received from Farrow Co., dated January 6.

Mar. 14. Received from R. A. Singer the amount due on a March 4 invoice for $1,850, less 2% discount.

21. Issued Check No. 414 to Bowen & Son in payment of the note issued on January 21.

Apr. 10. Wrote off against the allowance account the $260 owed by D. R. Yoder.

25. Borrowed $5,000 from First Citizens Bank, issuing a 7%, 90-day note.

May 6. Received from P. Riley a 90-day, 6% note for $3,000, dated May 4, on account.

18. Purchased land for a building site from Progressive Development Co. for $50,000, issuing Check No. 457 for $10,000 and a 7% mortgage note for the balance. The contract provides for payments of $4,000 of principal plus accrued interest at intervals of six months.

June 20. Discounted at First National Bank at 6% the note received from P. Riley dated May 4.

July 10. Received from Fleming Corp. on account a 30-day, 6% note for $1,800, dated July 10.

24. Issued Check No. 537 to First Citizens Bank for the amount due on the note dated April 25.

Aug. 3. Received notice from First National Bank that P. Riley had dishonored the note due on August 2. Issued Check No. 586 for the amount due on the note, plus a protest fee of $3.

9. Fleming Corp. dishonored its note dated July 10. Charged the dishonored note to its account.

Sept. 8. Received from Fleming Corp. the amount due on the note dishonored on August 9, including interest at 6% for 30 days on the maturity value of the note.

15. Reinstated the account of Donald West that had been written off against the allowance account in the preceding year, and received cash in full payment, $145.

Nov. 1. Received from P. Riley the amount due on the note dishonored on August 2, including interest at 6% from August 2 to October 31 on the amount charged to his account on August 3.

18. Issued Check No. 699 for principal and interest due on the mortgage note issued on May 18.

Instructions:

(1) Record the selected entries in the three journals provided in the working papers: Cash Receipts, Cash Payments, and a general journal. No posting is required.

(2) At the end of the year, Accounts Receivable has a debit balance of $106,000. The distribution of the accounts, by age intervals, is presented in the working papers, together with the percent of each class estimated to be uncollectible. Determine the amount of the accounts estimated to be uncollectible.

(3) Prior to adjustment at the end of the year, Allowance for Doubtful Accounts has a credit balance of $757. Record the adjusting entry in the general journal as of December 31.

(4) Present the data on accounts receivable as they will appear in the balance sheet as of December 31.

Chapter 8

8-1B. Benton Television Co. employs the periodic inventory system. Details regarding their inventory of television sets at January 1, purchase invoices during the year, and the inventory count at December 31 are summarized below.

Model	Inventory Jan. 1	Purchase Invoices 1st	Purchase Invoices 2nd	Purchase Invoices 3rd	Inventory Count Dec. 31
97	5 at $114	7 at $120	6 at $128	———	4
101	6 at 56	9 at 60	4 at 53	7 at $ 60	9
176	7 at 149	4 at 160	3 at 164	1 at 180	4
222	3 at 242	3 at 257	10 at 258	5 at 264	6
352	3 at 189	5 at 202	5 at 212	4 at 195	4
401	———	2 at 410	7 at 415	4 at 398	3
500	5 at 313	5 at 305	5 at 300	———	6

783

Instructions:

(1) Determine the cost of the inventory on December 31 by the first-in, first-out method. Present data in columnar form, using the columnar headings indicated below. If the inventory of a particular model is composed of an entire lot plus a portion of another lot acquired at a different unit price, use a separate line for each lot.

Model	Quantity	Unit Cost	Total Cost

(2) Determine the cost of the inventory on December 31 by the last-in, first-out method, following the procedures described in instruction (1).

(3) Determine the cost of the inventory on December 31 by the weighted average method, using the columnar headings described in instruction (1).

8-2B. The beginning inventory of Commodity 238Y and data on purchases and sales for a three-month period are presented below.

April	1.	Inventory.......	6 units at $32	$192
	13.	Purchase........	12 units at 35	420
	17.	Sale...........	9 units at 48	432
	26.	Sale...........	5 units at 48	240

May	1.	Purchase........12 units at 36	432
	7.	Sale............ 4 units at 49	196
	11.	Sale............ 6 units at 50	300
	19.	Purchase........12 units at 37	444
June	3.	Sale............ 7 units at 52	364
	10.	Sale............ 4 units at 53	212
	17.	Purchase........12 units at 38	456
	29.	Sale............ 8 units at 54	432

Instructions:

(1) Record the inventory, purchase, and cost of merchandise sold data in a perpetual inventory record similar to the one illustrated on page 201, using the first-in, first-out method.

(2) Determine the total sales and the total cost of Commodity 238Y sold for the period, and express their effect on the general ledger by two entries in general journal form. Assume that all sales were on account.

(3) Determine the gross profit from sales of Commodity 238Y for the period.

(4) Determine the cost of the inventory at June 30, assuming that the periodic system of inventory had been employed and that the inventory cost had been determined by the last-in, first-out method.

8-3B. Selected data on merchandise inventory, purchases, and sales for the Fresno Co. and the Sacramento Co. are presented below.

Fresno Co.

	Cost	Retail
Merchandise inventory, May 1......	$451,762	$722,500
Transactions during May:		
Purchases......................	142,320	221,500
Purchases discount..............	1,250	
Sales..........................		441,200
Sales returns and allowances......		5,700

Sacramento Co.

Merchandise inventory, June 1..............	$120,300
Transactions during June and July:	
Purchases................................	152,500
Purchases discount.......................	1,500
Sales....................................	220,000
Sales returns and allowances..............	2,100
Estimated gross profit rate................	35%

Instructions:

(1) Determine the estimated cost of the merchandise inventory of the Fresno Co. on May 31 by the retail method, presenting details of the computations.

(2) Estimate the cost of the merchandise inventory of the Sacramento Co. on July 31 by the gross profit method, presenting details of the computations.

If the working papers correlating with the textbook are not used, omit Problem 8-4B.

8-4B. Data on the physical inventory of Mercer & Co. as of September 30, the close of the current fiscal year, are presented in the working papers. The quantity of each commodity on hand has been determined and recorded on the inventory sheet; unit market prices have also been determined as of September 30 and recorded on the sheet. The inventory is to be determined at cost and also at the lower of cost or market, using the first-in, first-out method. Quantity and cost data from the last purchase invoice of the year and the next-to-the-last purchase invoice are summarized below.

Description	Last Purchase Invoice		Next-to-the-Last Purchase Invoice	
	Quantity Purchased	Unit Cost	Quantity Purchased	Unit Cost
1839B	75	$ 17	50	$ 16
FC566	65	80	115	80
OPL14	30	205	20	210
JM482	10	240	30	242
1642A	10	43	20	42
1945D	55	96	30	92
SL416	300	11	400	10
269LB	200	25	200	29
MJ630	300	5	600	4
653ND	400	10	900	9
WD87	90	13	200	14
31VW	50	39	100	43
AAA17	60	51	100	53
666RS	150	8	100	9
E3B1Y	300	16	400	13
CB111	72	19	288	21
XXX75	220	7	200	6
BC243	240	5	480	4

Instructions:

Record the appropriate unit costs on the inventory sheet and complete the pricing of the inventory. When there are two different unit costs applicable to a commodity, proceed as follows:

(1) Draw a line through the quantity and insert the quantity and unit cost of the last purchase.

(2) On the following line insert the quantity and unit cost of the next-to-the-last purchase. The first item on the inventory sheet has been completed as an example.

8-5B. The preliminary income statement of Powell & Co. presented at the top of the following page was prepared before the accounts were adjusted or closed at the end of the fiscal year. The company uses the periodic inventory system.

The following errors in the ledger and on inventory sheets were discovered by the independent accountant retained to conduct the annual audit:

(a) A number of errors were discovered in pricing inventory items, in extending amounts, and in footing inventory sheets. The net effect of the corrections, exclusive of those described below, was to increase by $1,800 the amount stated as ending inventory on the income statement.

(b) A purchase invoice for merchandise of $400, dated June 28, had been received and correctly recorded, but the merchandise was not received

Powell & Co.
Income Statement
For Year Ended June 30, 19--

Sales (net)		$134,300
Cost of merchandise sold:		
Merchandise inventory, July 1, 19—.	$ 24,250	
Purchases (net)	91,420	
Merchandise available for sale	$115,670	
Less merchandise inventory, June 30, 19—. . .	23,330	
Cost of merchandise sold		92,340
Gross profit on sales		$ 41,960
Operating expenses		24,310
Net income		$ 17,650

until July 3 and had not been included in the June 30 inventory. Title had passed to Powell & Co. on June 28.

(c) A purchase invoice for merchandise of $350, dated June 27, was not received until July 1 and had not been recorded by June 30. However, the merchandise, to which title had passed, had arrived and had been included in the June 30 inventory.

(d) A sales order for $900, dated June 30, had been recorded as a sale on that date but title did not pass to the purchaser until shipment was made on July 2. The merchandise, which had cost $525, was excluded from the June 30 inventory.

(e) An item of office equipment, received on June 30, was erroneously included in the June 30 merchandise inventory at its cost of $830. The invoice had been recorded correctly.

(f) A sales invoice for $1,600, dated June 30, had not been recorded. The merchandise was shipped on June 30, FOB shipping point, and its cost, $1,000, was excluded from the June 30 inventory.

Instructions:

(1) Journalize the entries necessary to correct the general ledger accounts as of June 30, inserting the identifying letters in the date column. All purchases and sales were made on account.

(2) Determine the correct inventory for June 30, beginning your analysis with the $23,330 shown on the preliminary income statement. Assemble the corrections in two groupings, "Additions" and "Deductions," allowing six lines for each group. Identify each correction by the appropriate letter.

(3) Prepare a revised income statement.

Chapter 9

9-1B. The accounts listed at the top of the next page appear in the ledger of Mountainview Realty at December 31, the end of the current fiscal year. None of the year-end adjustments has been recorded.

The following information relating to adjustments at December 31 is obtained from physical inventories, supplementary records, and other sources:

(a) Interest accrued on notes receivable at December 31, $52.
(b) Inventory of supplies at December 31, $78.

786

113 Interest Receivable......	——	411 Rental Income........	$65,400
114 Supplies..............	$250	511 Salary and Commissions	
115 Prepaid Insurance.......	870	Expense.............	13,200
116 Prepaid Advertising.....	——	513 Advertising Expense....	2,100
117 Prepaid Interest........	——	514 Insurance Expense.....	——
213 Salaries and Commis-		515 Supplies Expense.......	——
sions Payable........	——	611 Interest Income........	275
215 Unearned Rent.........	——	711 Interest Expense.......	710
313 Expense and Revenue			
Summary............	——		

(c) The insurance record indicates that $518 of insurance has expired during the year.

(d) Of a prepayment of $600 for advertising space in a local newspaper, 60% has not been used, but will be used in the following year.

(e) A short-term non-interest-bearing note payable was discounted at a bank in December. The amount of the total discount of $150 applicable to the next year is $60.

(f) Salaries and commissions accrued at December 31, $990.

(g) Rent collected in advance that will not be earned until the following year, $3,750.

Instructions:

(1) Open the accounts listed and record the balances in the appropriate balance columns, as of December 31.

(2) Journalize the adjusting entries and post to the appropriate accounts after each entry, extending the balances. Identify the postings by writing "Adjusting" in the item columns.

(3) Prepare a compound journal entry to close the revenue accounts and another compound entry to close the expense accounts.

(4) Post the closing entries, inserting a short line in both balance columns of accounts that are closed. Identify the postings by writing "Closing" in the item columns.

(5) Prepare the reversing journal entries that should be made on January 1 and post to the appropriate accounts after each entry, inserting a short line in both balance columns of accounts that are now in balance. Write "Reversing" in the item columns.

787

9-2B. McDaniel Co. closes its accounts annually as of December 31, the end of the fiscal year. All relevant data regarding notes payable and related interest from November 15 through February 13 of the following year are presented below. (All notes are dated as of the day they are issued.)

Nov. 15. Issued an $18,000, 7%, 90-day note on account.
Dec. 11. Issued a $5,400, 7%, 60-day note on account.
    14. Borrowed $9,000 from Second National Bank, issuing an 8%, 60-day note.
    22. Paid principal, $8,000, and interest, $140, on note payable due today.
    31. Recorded an adjusting entry for the interest accrued on the notes dated November 15, December 11, and December 14. There are no other notes outstanding on this date.
    31. Recorded the entry to close the interest expense account.
Jan. 1. Recorded a reversing entry for the accrued interest.
    11. Issued a $7,200, 7%, 30-day note on account.
Feb. 9. Paid $5,463 on the note issued on December 11.
    10. Paid $7,242 on the note issued on January 11.

12. Paid $9,120 on the note issued on December 14.
13. Paid $18,315 on the note issued on November 15.

Instructions:

(1) Open accounts for Interest Payable (Account No. 214) and Interest Expense (Account No. 711), and record a debit balance of $996 in the latter account as of November 15 of the current year.
(2) Present entries in general journal form to record the transactions and other data described above, posting to the two accounts after each entry affecting them.
(3) If the reversing entry had not been recorded as of January 1, indicate how each interest payment in January and February should be allocated. Submit the data in the following form:

Note (face amount)	Total Interest Paid	Dr. Interest Payable	Dr. Interest Expense
$ 5,400	$	$	$
7,200			
9,000			
18,000			
Total	$	$	$

(4) Do the February 13 balances of Interest Payable and Interest Expense obtained by use of the reversing entry technique correspond to the balances that would have been obtained by the more laborious process of analyzing each payment?

788

If the working papers correlating with the textbook are not used, omit Problem 9-3B.

9-3B. The Gibson Company prepares interim financial statements at the end of each month and closes its books annually on December 31. Its income statement for the two-month period, January and February of the current year, is presented in the working papers. In addition, the trial balance of the ledger as of one month later is presented on an eight-column work sheet in the working papers. Data needed for adjusting entries at March 31, the end of the three-month period, are as follows:

(a) Uncollectible accounts expense is estimated at $\frac{1}{2}$ of 1% of net sales for the three-month period.
(b) Estimated merchandise inventory at March 31, $59,440.
(c) Insurance expired during the three-month period:
   Allocable as selling expense, $220.
   Allocable as general expense, $92.
(d) Estimated inventory of store supplies at March 31, $215.
(e) Depreciation for the three-month period:
   Store equipment, $450.
   Office equipment, $130.
(f) Estimated property tax of $132 a month for January and February was recorded in the accounts. The tax statement, which was received in March, indicates a liability of $1,656 for the calendar year.
(g) Salaries accrued at March 31:
   Sales salaries, $310.
   Office salaries, $75.

(h) The notes payable balance of $14,000 is composed of the following:
$10,000, 90-day, non-interest-bearing note discounted at Merchants Trust Co. on March 1. The $150 discount was debited to Interest Expense. (Record adjustment in work sheet before considering the other note.)
$4,000, 6-month, 6% note dated December 1 of the preceding year. (Accrue interest for 4 months.)

Instructions:

(1) Complete the eight-column work sheet for the three-month period ended March 31 of the current year.

(2) Prepare an income statement for the three-month period, using the last three-column group of the nine-column form in the working papers.

(3) Prepare an income statement for the month of March, using the middle three-column group of the nine-column form in the working papers.

(4) Prepare a capital statement for the three-month period. There were no additional investments during the period.

(5) Prepare a balance sheet as of March 31.

(6) Determine the amount of interest expense on each note allocable to the month of March and compare the total with the amount reported as interest expense in the income statement for March.

9-4B. The Dawson Co. prepares interim statements at the end of each month and closes its accounts annually on December 31. Property taxes are assessed for fiscal years beginning on July 1 and ending on June 30. Selected transactions and property tax allocations for the period July 1 to December 31 of one year and of January 1 to June 30 of the following year are presented below.

July 31. Property tax allocation for July based on estimated property tax of $6,996 for the taxing authority's fiscal year beginning July 1.
Oct. 31. Property tax allocation for October, based on tax statement dated October 20 indicating a tax assessment of $7,152.
Nov. 15. Paid first half of tax assessment, $3,576.
30. Property tax allocation for November.
Dec. 31. Property tax allocation for December.
Jan. 31. Property tax allocation for January.
Apr. 15. Paid second half of tax assessment, $3,576.
May 31. Property tax allocation for May.
June 30. Property tax allocation for June.

Instructions:

(1) Present in general journal form the entries to record the selected tax allocations and payments, assuming in all cases that appropriate entries have been recorded in the accounts for all intervening months.

(2) Indicate the amount of prepaid property tax and property tax payable that would be reported on the balance sheets prepared as of (a) September 30, (b) December 31, and (c) May 31. In each case list the section in which the item would appear (Current asset, etc.), the account title (Prepaid Property Tax, etc.), and the amount.

9-7B. Selected accounts from the ledger of Londonderry Co., with the account balances before and after adjustment, at the close of the fiscal year are presented at the top of the following page.

	Unadjusted Balance	Adjusted Balance		Unadjusted Balance	Adjusted Balance
Interest Receivable	$———	$ 50	Rent Income.....	$ 5,200	$ 4,800
Supplies.........	510	235	Wages Expense...	14,290	14,600
Prepaid Insurance.	———	450	Supplies Expense..	———	275
Prepaid Prop. Tax.	195	———	Property Tax Exp.	2,025	2,220
Prepaid Interest...	———	50	Insurance Expense.	690	240
Wages Payable....	———	310	Interest Income...	420	470
Interest Payable...	———	15	Interest Expense..	210	175
Unearned Rent...	———	400			

Instructions:

(1) Journalize the adjusting entries that were posted to the ledger at the close of the fiscal year.

(2) Insert the letter "R" in the date column opposite each adjusting entry that should be reversed as of the first day of the following fiscal year.

Chapter 10

10-1B. The following expenditures and receipts are related to land, land improvements, and buildings acquired for use in a business enterprise. The receipts are identified by an asterisk.

(a) Cost of real estate acquired as a plant site: Land.........	$ 35,000
Building......	40,000
(b) Delinquent real estate taxes on property, assumed by purchaser......	3,000
(c) Fee paid to attorney for title search....................	500
(d) Cost of razing and removing the building...............	4,200
(e) Architect's and engineer's fees for plans and supervision ...	31,000
(f) Cost of land fill and grading.......................	6,000
(g) Premium on 1-year insurance policy during construction..	5,000
(h) Money borrowed to pay building contractor............	400,000*
(i) Paid to building contractor for new building............	590,000
(j) Cost of repairing windstorm damage during construction ..	2,100
(k) Cost of trees and shrubbery, planted..................	900
(l) Cost of paving parking lot to be used by customers.......	2,000
(m) Real estate taxes accrued during construction..........	2,300
(n) Special assessment paid to city for extension of water main to the property...................................	800
(o) Proceeds from sale of salvage materials from old building ..	500*
(p) Cost of repairing vandalism damage during construction..	250
(q) Interest accrued on building loan during construction	28,000
(r) Proceeds from insurance company for windstorm damage.	1,800*
(s) Cost of floodlights on parking lot, installed.............	1,200
(t) Refund of premium on insurance policy (g) canceled after 11 months......................................	250*
	$349,700

Instructions:

(1) Assign each expenditure and receipt (indicate receipts by an asterisk) to Land, Land Improvements, Building or "Other Accounts." Identify each item by letter and list the amounts in columnar form, as follows:

Item	Land	Land Improvements	Building	Other Accounts
	$	$	$	$

(2) Total the amount columns.

10-2B. An item of new equipment acquired at a cost of $60,000 at the beginning of a fiscal year has an estimated life of 5 years and an estimated trade-in value of $6,000. The manager requested information (details given in Instruction 1) regarding the effect of alternative methods on the amount of depreciation expense deductible each year for federal income tax purposes.

Upon the basis of the data presented to the manager in accordance with Instruction 1, the sum-of-the-years-digits method was elected. In the first week of the fourth year the equipment was traded in for similar equipment priced at $80,000. The trade-in allowance on the old equipment was $15,000, cash of $10,000 was paid, and a note payable was issued for the balance.

Instructions:

(1) Determine the annual depreciation for each of the estimated 5 years of use, the accumulated depreciation at the end of each year, and the book value of the equipment at the end of each year by (a) the straight-line method, (b) the declining-balance method (at twice the straight-line rate), and (c) the sum-of-the-years-digits method. The following columnar headings are suggested for each schedule:

Year	Depreciation Expense	Accumulated Depreciation End of Year	Book Value End of Year

(2) Present the debits and credits required, in general journal form, to record the exchange at the beginning of the fourth year, assuming that the gain or loss on the disposal is to be recognized.

(3) Present the debits and credits required, in general journal form, to record the exchange at the beginning of the fourth year, assuming that the gain or loss on the disposal is not to be recognized.

(4) What is the cost basis of the new equipment, for purposes of computing the amount of depreciation allowable for income tax purposes?

(5) Assuming that the trade-in allowance had been $20,000 instead of $15,000, determine the cost basis of the new equipment, for purposes of computing the amount of depreciation allowable for income tax purposes, solving by two methods.

If the working papers correlating with the textbook are not used, omit Problem 10-3B.

10-3B. Modern Printing Co. maintains a subsidiary equipment ledger for the printing equipment and accumulated depreciation accounts in the general ledger. A small portion of the subsidiary ledger, the two controlling accounts, and a general journal are presented in the working papers. The company computes depreciation on each individual item of equipment. Transactions and adjusting entries affecting the printing equipment are as follows:

1969
Oct. 4. Purchased a power cutter (Giant Model, Serial No. 5484) from Olympia Typograph Co. on account for $6,120. The estimated life of the asset is 9 years, it is expected to have no residual value,

and the straight-line method of depreciation is to be used. (This is the only transaction of the year that directly affected the printing equipment account.)

Dec. 31. Entered depreciation for the year in subsidiary accounts 125-81 to 125-83, and inserted the new balances. (It is assumed that an assistant enters the depreciation and the new balances in accounts 125-1 to 125-80.)

31. Journalized and posted the annual adjusting entry for depreciation on printing equipment. The depreciation for the year entered in subsidiary accounts 125-1 to 125-80 totals $16,240, to which must be added the depreciation entered in accounts 125-81 to 125-83.

1970

May 8. Purchased a Model X9 rotary press from Parker Press Co., priced at $27,210, giving the Model 16 flatbed press (Account No. 125-81) in exchange plus $7,210 cash and a series of ten $1,000 notes payable, maturing at 6-month intervals. (Record depreciation to date in 1970 on item traded in; gain or loss on the disposal is not to be recognized.)

Instructions:

(1) Record in general journal form the transaction of October 4. Post to Printing Equipment in the general ledger and to Account No. 125-83 in the subsidiary ledger.

(2) Record the adjusting entries required on December 31 and post to Accumulated Depreciation — Printing Equipment in the general ledger.

(3) Record in general journal form the entries required by the purchase of printing equipment on May 8. Post to Printing Equipment and to Accumulated Depreciation — Printing Equipment.

(4) Assuming that the rotary press purchased on May 8 has an estimated residual value of $2,500 and an estimated life of 8 years, determine the depreciation on this press by the declining-balance method, at twice the straight-line rate, for the fiscal years ending (a) December 31, 1970 and (b) December 31, 1971.

10-4B. The following transactions, adjusting entries, and closing entries were completed by Murray Furniture Co. during a 3-year period. All are related to the use of delivery equipment.

1969

Feb. 24. Purchased a used delivery truck for $2,400, paying cash.

26. Paid $330 for major repairs to the truck.

Nov. 21. Paid garage $45 for miscellaneous repairs to the truck.

Dec. 31. Recorded depreciation on the truck for the fiscal year. The estimated life of the truck is 3 years, with a trade-in value of $300. The straight-line method of depreciation is used.

31. Closed the appropriate accounts to Expense and Revenue Summary.

1970

Sept. 10. Traded in the used truck on a new truck priced at $4,970, receiving a trade-in allowance of $1,085 and paying the balance in cash. (Record depreciation to date in 1970; gain or loss on exchange is not to be recognized.)

Dec. 5. Paid garage $62 for repairs to the truck.

31. Recorded depreciation on the truck. It has an estimated trade-in value of $800 and an estimated life of 5 years. The declining-balance method (twice the straight-line rate) of depreciation is used.

31. Closed the appropriate accounts to Expense and Revenue Summary.

1971

Aug. 28. Purchased a new truck for $5,700, paying cash.

Oct. 29. Sold the truck purchased in 1970 for $2,600 cash. (Record depreciation.)

Dec. 31. Recorded depreciation on the remaining truck. It has an estimated trade-in value of $900 and an estimated life of 4 years. The declining-balance method (twice the straight-line rate) of depreciation is used.

31. Closed the appropriate accounts to Expense and Revenue Summary.

Instructions:

(1) Open the following accounts in the ledger:

     121   Delivery Equipment
     121.1 Accumulated Depreciation — Delivery Equipment
     614   Depreciation Expense — Delivery Equipment
     615   Truck Repair Expense
     912   Loss on Disposal of Plant Assets

(2) Record the transactions and the adjusting and closing entries in general journal form. Post to the accounts and extend the balances after each posting.

10-6B. The trial balance of Ventura Markets at the end of the current fiscal year, before adjustments, is as follows:

Ventura Markets
Trial Balance
March 31,19 --

Cash	10,200	
Merchandise Inventory	108,000	
Prepaid Expenses	5,600	
Delivery Equipment	17,800	
Accumulated Depreciation — Delivery Equipment		8,000
Store Equipment	26,500	
Accumulated Depreciation — Store Equipment		15,800
Office Equipment	1,400	
Accumulated Depreciation — Office Equipment		270
Buildings	26,800	
Accumulated Depreciation — Buildings		12,800
Land	3,000	
Notes Payable (short term)		2,000
Accounts Payable		4,600
H. G. Nichols, Capital		112,780
H. G. Nichols, Drawing	16,000	
Sales (net)		430,000
Purchases (net)	310,000	
Operating Expenses (control account)	60,750	
Interest Expense	200	
	586,250	586,250

Data needed for year-end adjustments:

(a) Merchandise inventory at March 31, $105,640.

(b) Insurance and other prepaid operating expenses expired during the year, $1,860.

(c) Depreciation is computed at composite rates on the average of the beginning and the ending balances of the plant asset accounts. The beginning balances and rates are as follows:

Delivery equipment, $15,400; 25%   Office equipment, $1,000; 8%
Store equipment, $23,500; 9%   Buildings, $26,800; 2½%

(d) Accrued liabilities at the end of the year, $620, of which $45 is for interest on the notes and $575 is for wages and other operating expenses.

Instructions:

(1) Prepare an income statement for the current year.

(2) Prepare a balance sheet in report form, presenting the plant assets in the manner illustrated in this chapter.

Chapter 11

11-1B. The cash in bank account for Morrow Company at March 31 of the current year indicated a balance of $8,415.40 after both the cash receipts journal and the check register for March had been posted. The bank statement indicated a balance of $12,819.65 on March 31. Comparison of the bank statement and the accompanying canceled checks and memorandums with the records revealed the following reconciling items:

(a) A deposit of $1,502.15 representing receipts of March 31 had been made too late to appear on the bank statement.

(b) Checks outstanding totaled $5,790.30.

(c) A check for $10 had been erroneously charged by the bank to Morrow Company's account as $100.

(d) A check for $83 returned with the statement had been recorded in the check register as $38. The check was for the payment of an obligation to Logan Equipment Company on account for the purchase of office equipment.

(e) The bank had collected for Morrow Company $255 on an interest-bearing note left for collection. The face of the note was $250.

(f) Bank service charges for March amounted to $3.90.

Instructions:

(1) Prepare a bank reconciliation.

(2) Journalize the necessary entries. The accounts have not been closed. The voucher system is used.

11-2B. Lang Company had the following vouchers in its unpaid voucher file at June 30 of the current year:

Due Date	Voucher No.	Creditor	Date of Invoice	Amount	Terms
July 5	690	Cross Co.	June 25	$1,000	2/10, n/30
13	677	Peterson and Son	June 13	510	n/30
23	689	Fisher Co.	June 23	485	n/30

The vouchers prepared and the checks issued during the month of July were as shown on the next page.

VOUCHERS

Date	Voucher No.	Payee	Amount	Terms	Distribution
July 2	693	Brown Co.	$ 90	cash	Store supplies
3	694	Nelson and Son	700	1/10, n/30	Purchases
6	695	Adler Co.	1,200	2/10, n/30	Purchases
6	696	Neff Co.	350	n/30	Office equipment
10	697	Green Supply	800	1/10, n/30	Purchases
10	698	Price, Inc.	75	cash	Office supplies
16	699	Morton Trust Co.	1,020		Note pay., $1,000 Interest, $20
20	700	Lake Bros.	1,250	2/10, n/30	Purchases
21	701	Olson Co.	1,500	1/10, n/30	Purchases
21	702	Green Supply	425	n/30	Office equipment
22	703	Davis Co.	3,500	2/10, n/30	Purchases
27	704	News Gazette	80	cash	Advertising exp.
29	705	Petty Cash	77		Store supplies, $23 Office sup., $20 Delivery exp., $8 Misc. selling exp., $17 Misc. gen. exp., $9

CHECKS

Date	Check No.	Payee	Voucher Paid	Amount
July 2	916	Brown Co.	693	$ 90
5	917	Cross Co.	690	980
10	918	Price, Inc.	698	75
13	919	Nelson and Son	694	693
13	920	Peterson and Son	677	510
16	921	Morton Trust Co.	699	1,020
16	922	Adler Co.	695	1,176
20	923	Green Supply	697	792
23	924	Fisher Co.	689	485
27	925	News Gazette	704	80
29	926	Petty Cash	705	77
30	927	Lake Bros.	700	1,225
31	928	Olson Co.	701	1,485

795

Instructions:

(1) Set up a four-column account for Accounts Payable, Account No. 211, and record the balance of $1,995 as of July 1.

(2) Record the July vouchers in a voucher register similar to the one illustrated in this chapter, with the following amount columns: Accounts Payable Cr., Purchases Dr., Store Supplies Dr., Office Supplies Dr., and Sundry Accounts Dr. Purchases invoices are recorded at the gross amount.

(3) Record the July checks in a check register similar to the one illustrated in this chapter, but omit the Bank Deposits and Balance columns. As each check is recorded in the check register, the check number should be inserted in the appropriate place in the Check No. column of the voucher register. Assume that appropriate notations

are made in the Paid column of the voucher register when the June vouchers are paid.

(4) Total and rule the registers and post to the accounts payable account.

(5) Prepare a schedule of unpaid vouchers.

If the working papers correlating with the textbook are not used, omit Problem 11-3B.

11-3B. Portions of the following accounting records of J. W. Gates Co. are presented in the working papers:

Voucher Register	General ledger accounts:
Check Register	Prepaid Insurance
General Journal	Notes Payable
Insurance Register	Accounts Payable
Notes Payable Register	

Expenditures, cash disbursements, and other selected transactions completed during the period March 25–31 of the current year are described below.

Mar. 25. Issued a 90-day, 6% note (No. 44), dated today to Sloan Co. in settlement of Voucher No. 797, $5,000. The note is payable at Citizens National Bank.

26. Recorded Voucher No. 817 payable to Parker Co. for merchandise, $3,000, terms 2/10, n/30. (Purchases invoices are recorded at the gross amount.)

26. Issued Check No. 912 to Brown Co. in payment of Voucher No. 811 for $4,500.

27. Recorded Voucher No. 818 payable to Urbana County Bank for note payable (No. 43), $12,500.

27. Issued Check No. 913 in payment of Voucher No. 818.

28. Recorded Voucher No. 819 payable to Dixon Automobile Insurance Co. for the following insurance policy, dated today: No. 172AC, automobiles, 1 year, $1,230.

28. Issued Check No. 914 in payment of Voucher No. 819.

28. Recorded Voucher No. 820 payable to Hill Co. for merchandise, $2,750, terms 1/10, n/30.

28. Recorded Voucher No. 821 payable to *Danville Courier* for advertising, $375.

28. Issued Check No. 915 in payment of Voucher No. 821.

29. Recorded Voucher No. 822 payable to Petty Cash for $125.60, distributed as follows: Office Supplies, $30.15; Advertising Expense, $13.40; Delivery Expense, $11.85; Miscellaneous Selling Expense, $41.30; Miscellaneous General Expense, $28.90.

29. Issued Check No. 916 in payment of Voucher No. 822.

30. Recorded Voucher No. 823 payable to Hanover Insurance Co. for the following insurance policy, dated today: No. 2977, Building, $600,000, 3 years, $7,995.60.

30. Issued Check No. 917 in payment of Voucher No. 823.

31. Issued Check No. 918 to Brook Co. in payment of Voucher No. 816 for $1,250 less cash discount of 1%.

After the journals are posted at the end of the month, the cash in bank account has a debit balance of $14,796.90.

The bank statement indicates a March 31 balance of $24,481.90. Comparison of paid checks returned by the bank with the check register reveals that

Nos. 915, 917, and 918 are outstanding. Check No. 888 for $172, which appeared on the February reconciliation as outstanding, is still outstanding. A debit memorandum accompanying the bank statement indicates a charge of $95.10 for a check drawn by J. C. Carter, a customer, which was returned because of insufficient funds.

Instructions:

(1) Record the transactions for March 25–31 in the appropriate journals. Immediately after recording a transaction, post individual items, where appropriate, to the three general ledger accounts given.

(2) Enter the necessary notations in the notes payable register and the insurance register, rounding insurance expirations to the nearest month.

(3) Total and rule the voucher register and the check register, and post totals to the accounts payable account.

(4) Complete the schedule of unpaid vouchers. (Compare the total with the balance of the accounts payable account as of March 31.)

(5) Prepare a bank reconciliation and journalize any necessary entries.

(6) Total the Expired Premium column for March in the insurance register, journalize the adjusting entry, and post to the prepaid insurance account. (Determine the balance of prepaid insurance as of March 31 from the columns in the insurance register and compare it with the balance of the prepaid insurance account as of the same date.)

(7) Determine the amount of interest accrued as of March 31 on notes payable (Nos. 42 and 44). (Assume 28 days in February.)

(8) Determine the amount of interest prepaid as of March 31 on notes payable (No. 40). (The non-interest-bearing note was discounted by the bank.)

797

11-5B. Wyman Company employs the voucher system in controlling expenditures and disbursements. All cash receipts are deposited in a night depository after banking hours each Wednesday and Friday. The data required to reconcile their bank statement as of June 30 of the current year have been abstracted from various documents and records and are reproduced below. To facilitate identification the sources of the data are printed in capital letters.

CASH IN BANK ACCOUNT
Balance as of June 1...................................... $4,882.61

CASH RECEIPTS JOURNAL
Total of Cash in Bank Debit column for month of June 6,121.64

DUPLICATE DEPOSIT TICKETS
Date and amount of each deposit in June:

Date	Amount	Date	Amount	Date	Amount
June 2	$711.20	June 14	$877.70	June 23	$499.77
7	620.72	16	527.50	28	602.40
9	901.50	21	661.25	30	719.60

C • Series B problems

CHECK REGISTER
Number and amount of each check issued in June:

Check No.	Amount	Check No.	Amount	Check No.	Amount
890	$440.37	897	$215.71	904	$ 247.67
891	90.22	898	297.80	905	607.05
892	127.60	899	311.77	906	Void
893	318.90	900	85.60	907	749.67
894	441.95	901	179.52	908	463.46
895	29.50	902	133.39	909	710.62
896	117.65	903	760.50	910	376.30

Total checks issued for June................................ $6,705.25

BANK STATEMENT FOR JUNE
Balance as of June 1.................................... $5,153.13
Date and amount of each deposit in June:

Date	Amount	Date	Amount	Date	Amount
June 1	$571.15	June 10	$901.50	June 22	$661.25
3	711.20	15	877.70	24	499.77
8	620.72	17	527.50	29	602.40

Balance as of June 30.................................... $6,063.19

CHECKS ACCOMPANYING BANK STATEMENT FOR JUNE
Number and amount of each check, rearranged in numerical sequence:

Check No.	Amount	Check No.	Amount	Check No.	Amount
809	$117.65	894	$441.95	901	$179.52
888	94.52	895	29.50	902	133.39
889	331.80	896	117.65	903	760.50
890	440.37	897	215.71	905	607.05
891	90.22	898	297.80	907	749.67
892	172.60	899	311.77	908	463.46
893	318.90	900	85.60		

BANK MEMORANDUMS ACCOMPANYING BANK STATEMENT FOR JUNE
Date, description, and amount of each memorandum:

Date	Description	Amount
June 19	Bank credit memo for note collected:	
	Principal.....................................	$1,000.00
	Interest......................................	10.00
28	Bank debit memo for check returned because of insufficient funds.............................	110.40
30	Bank debit memo for service charges.............	3.10

BANK RECONCILIATION FOR PRECEDING MONTH
(See the top of the next page.)

Instructions:

(1) Prepare a bank reconciliation as of June 30. If errors in recording deposits or checks are discovered, assume that the errors were made by the company.

(2) Journalize the necessary entries. The accounts have not been closed.

(3) What is the amount of Cash in Bank that should appear on the balance sheet as of June 30?

Wyman Company
Bank Reconciliation
May 31, 19--

Balance per bank statement...................		$5,153.13
Add: Deposit of May 31, not recorded by bank..		571.15
		$5,724.28
Deduct: Outstanding checks:		
No. 809....................	$117.65	
884....................	297.70	
888....................	94.52	
889....................	331.80	841.67
Adjusted balance............................		$4,882.61
Balance per books...........................		$4,885.41
Deduct: Service charges.....................		2.80
Adjusted balance...........................		$4,882.61

Chapter 12

12-1B. The Rexart Corporation has nine employees. They are paid on an hourly basis, receiving time-and-one-half pay for all hours worked in excess of 40 a week. The record of time worked for the week ended December 12, of the current year, together with other relevant information, is summarized below:

Name	Total Hours	Hourly Rate	Income Tax Withheld	Bond Deductions	Cumulative Earnings, December 5
A	40	$3.00	$17.60	$1.50	$5,880
B	42	2.50	9.70	1.75	2,155
C	35	2.80	14.70	———	4,852
D	48	2.20	8.10	———	2,940
E	45	3.80	30.60	7.50	8,410
F	40	2.75	15.70	2.00	6,346
G	44	2.40	20.60	1.75	5,824
H	35	3.10	14.80	———	2,937
I	43	4.00	25.10	5.00	7,760

In addition to withholdings for income tax, FICA tax, and bond purchases, $22 is to be withheld from B for partial payment of his account receivable.

C and H are office employees; the others are salesmen. The following tax rates and limitations are assumed: FICA, 5% on maximum of $7,800; state unemployment (employer only), 2.2% on maximum of $3,000; federal unemployment, .4% on maximum of $3,000.

Instructions:
(1) Prepare the payroll register for the week, using a form like the one illustrated on pages 306 and 307.
(2) Journalize the entry to record the payroll for the week.
(3) The company uses a voucher system and pays by regular check. Give the necessary entries in *general journal form* to record the payroll voucher and the issuance of the checks.

(continued)

(4) Complete the payroll register by inserting the check numbers, beginning with No. 946.

(5) Journalize the entry to record the employer's payroll taxes for the week.

12-2B. The following accounts, with the balances indicated, appear in the ledger of M. Larkin and Co. on December 1 of the current year:

214	Salaries Payable....................	——
215.1	FICA Tax Payable................	$ 376.40
215.2	Employees Income Tax Payable.....	843.70
215.3	State Unemployment Tax Payable...	107.64
215.4	Federal Unemployment Tax Payable.	248.38
216.1	Bond Deductions Payable...........	327.50
216.2	Medical Insurance Payable.........	525.00
611	Sales Salary Expense...............	91,632.60
711	Officers Salary Expense.............	37,800.00
712	Office Salary Expense..............	8,690.30
719	Payroll Tax Expense...............	6,118.24

The following transactions relating to payroll, payroll deductions, and payroll taxes occurred during December:

Dec. 1. Prepared Voucher No. 722, payable to First National Bank, for $187.50 to purchase United States savings bonds for employees.

2. Issued Check No. 829 in payment of Voucher No. 722.

10. Prepared Voucher No. 743 for $1,220.10, payable to First National Bank, for the amount of employees income tax and FICA tax due on December 15.

10. Issued Check No. 848 in payment of Voucher No. 743.

14. Prepared a general journal entry to record the biweekly payroll. A summary of the payroll record follows:

Deductions: FICA tax, $96.10; income taxes withheld, $624.60; bond deductions, $86.75; medical insurance deductions, $90.

Salary distribution: sales, $4,130; officers, $1,685; office, $740. Net amount: $5,657.55.

14. Prepared Voucher No. 751, payable to Payroll Bank Account, for the net amount of the biweekly payroll.

14. Issued Check No. 858 in payment of Voucher No. 751.

16. Prepared Voucher No. 754, payable to Reliable Insurance Co., for $525, the semiannual premium on the group medical insurance policy.

17. Issued Check No. 861 in payment of Voucher No. 754.

28. Prepared a general journal entry to record the biweekly payroll. A summary of the payroll record follows:

Deductions: FICA tax, $61.47; income taxes withheld, $568.90; bond deductions, $81.25.

Salary distribution: sales, $3,827; officers, $1,685; office, $740. Net amount: $5,540.38.

28. Prepared Voucher No. 786, payable to Payroll Bank Account, for the net amount of the biweekly payroll.

29. Issued Check No. 894 in payment of Voucher No. 786.

30. Prepared Voucher No. 787, payable to First National Bank, for $112.50 to purchase United States savings bonds for employees.

30. Issued Check No. 896 in payment of Voucher No. 787.

31. Prepared a general journal entry to record the employer's payroll taxes on earnings paid in December. Taxable earnings for the two payrolls, according to the payroll records, are as follows: subject to FICA tax, $3,151.40; subject to unemployment compensation tax, $819.20. Assume the following tax rates: FICA, 5% ; state unemployment, 2.2%; federal unemployment, .4%.

Instructions:

(1) Open the accounts listed and enter the account balances as of December 1.

(2) Record the transactions, using a voucher register, a check register, and a general journal. The only amount columns needed in the voucher register are Accounts Payable Cr. and Sundry Accounts Dr. (subdivided into Account, Post. Ref., and Amount). The only amount columns needed in the check register are Accounts Payable Dr. and Cash in Bank Cr. After each entry, post to the accounts opened in the ledger and extend the new balances to the appropriate balance column.

(3) Journalize the adjusting entry on December 31 to record salaries for the incomplete payroll period. Salaries accrued are as follows: sales salaries, $520; officers salaries, $240; office salaries, $100. Post to the accounts.

(4) Journalize the entry to close the salary expense and payroll tax expense accounts to Expense and Revenue Summary and post to the accounts.

(5) Journalize the entry on January 1 to reverse the adjustment of December 31 and post to the accounts.

12-3B. The following information relative to the payroll for the week ended December 30 was abstracted from the payroll register and other records of Neptune Transportation, Inc.:

Salaries:

Sales salaries........	$29,560
Warehouse salaries..	7,020
Office salaries	4,310
	$40,890

Deductions:

Income tax withheld .	$3,840
U.S. savings bonds...	320
Group insurance.....	150

FICA tax withheld is assumed to total the same amount as the employer's tax.

Tax rates assumed:
FICA, 5%
State unemployment (employer only), 2%
Federal unemployment, .4%

Instructions:

(1) Assuming that the payroll for the last week of the year is to be paid on December 31, present the following entries:

(a) December 30, to record the payroll. Of the total payroll for the last week of the year, $20,710 is subject to FICA tax and $2,630 is subject to unemployment compensation taxes.

(b) December 30, to record the employer's payroll taxes on the payroll to be paid on December 31.

(2) Assuming that the payroll for the last week of the year is to be paid on January 2 of the following fiscal year, present the following entries:

(a) December 31, to record the payroll.

(b) January 2, to record the employer's payroll taxes on the payroll to be paid on January 2.

12-5B. Universal Company began business on January 2 of last year. Salaries were paid to employees on the last day of each month and both FICA tax and federal income tax were withheld in the required amounts. All required payroll tax reports were filed and the correct amount of payroll taxes was remitted by the company for the calendar year. Before the Wage and Tax Statements (Form W-2) could be prepared for distribution to employees and filing with the Internal Revenue Service, the employees' earnings records were inadvertently destroyed.

Data on dates of employment, salary rates, and employees' income taxes withheld, which are summarized below, were obtained from personnel records and payroll registers. None of the employees resigned or were discharged during the year and there were no changes in salary rates. The FICA tax was withheld at the rate of 5% on the first $7,800 of salary.

Employee	Date First Employed	Monthly Salary	Monthly Income Tax Withheld
A	Jan. 2	$ 600	$ 82.30
B	Mar. 1	540	91.20
C	Jan. 2	820	136.80
D	Oct. 16	560	61.70
E	Jan. 2	1,000	137.70
F	Feb. 1	460	72.70
G	July 1	720	106.40

Instructions:

(1) Determine the amounts to be reported on each employee's Wage and Tax Statement (Form W-2) for the year, arranging the data in the following form:

Employee	Gross Earnings	Federal Income Tax Withheld	Earnings Subject to FICA Tax	FICA Tax Withheld

(2) Determine the total FICA tax withheld from employees during the year.

(3) Determine the following payroll taxes for the year paid by the employer: (a) FICA; (b) state unemployment compensation at 1.8% on first $3,000; (c) federal unemployment compensation at .4% on first $3,000; (d) total.

(4) In a manner similar to the illustrations in this chapter, develop four algorithms to describe the computations required to determine the four amounts in part (1), using the following symbols:

$$n = \text{Number of payroll periods}$$
$$g = \text{Monthly gross earnings}$$
$$f = \text{Monthly federal income tax withheld}$$
$$G = \text{Total gross earnings}$$
$$F = \text{Total federal income tax withheld}$$
$$T = \text{Total earnings subject to FICA tax}$$
$$S = \text{Total FICA tax withheld}$$

13-1B. Jewel Markets is a newly organized enterprise. The list of asset, liability, and capital accounts to be opened in the general ledger is presented below, arranged in alphabetical order. The accounts are to be arranged in balance sheet order and account numbers assigned. Each account number is to be composed of three digits; the first digit is to indicate the major classification ("1" for assets, etc.), the second digit is to indicate the subclassification ("11" for current assets, etc.), and the third digit is to identify the specific account ("111" for Cash in Bank, etc.).

Accounts Payable
Accounts Receivable
Accumulated Depr. — Building
Accumulated Depr. — Del. Equip.
Accu. Depr. — Office Equip.
Accu. Depr. — Store Equip.
Allowance for Doubtful Accounts
Building
Cash in Bank
Delivery Equipment
J. H. Hunt, Capital
J. H. Hunt, Drawing
Interest Payable

Land
Merchandise Inventory
Mortgage Note Payable (long-term)
Notes Payable (short-term)
Office Equipment
Office Supplies
Petty Cash
Prepaid Insurance
Salaries Payable
Store Equipment
Store Supplies
Taxes Payable

Instructions:
Construct a chart of accounts for the accounts listed.

13-2B. Southern Illinois Water Co. employs an automated system for billing customers for water. There are two rate structures, residential and industrial. A master file of customers is maintained on punched cards, with name, address, and appropriate rate structure indicated. At the end of each billing period the meter readers are given prepunched and printed cards containing the name, address, and last meter reading for each customer on their route. The current meter readings are recorded on the cards by the meter readers with a special pencil. The reproducer converts the pencil markings to holes in the card and the cards are then matched by the collator against the master file to assure that a current billing card has been prepared for each customer. The current billing cards are then processed by an electronic computer that computes the amount of the billing and prints the sales journal. The journal is then subjected to clerical review before processing is continued.

Instructions:
Construct a flow chart of the following computer operations:
read a current billing card; compute the amount of billing, including
provision to employ the appropriate rate structure; print an entry
in the sales journal; and continue the processing until the last
current billing card has been processed.

If the working papers correlating with the textbook are not used, omit Problem 13-4B.

13-4B. Martin Supply Company employs punched card machines in processing much of its accounting data. This problem requires the manual processing of a portion of the data normally processed by the machines.

(1) Remove from the working papers and separate the 15 punched cards. Note that the cards numbered 1–3 represent customers' account balances at June 30, the cards numbered 4–6 represent receipts on account from customers at various dates during July, and the cards numbered 7–15 represent sales made to customers on account at various dates in July. Record on the top line of the cards numbered 13–15 the following additional sales data:

	Customer No.	Date	Salesman No.	Invoice No.	Com- modity No.	Quantity Sold	Unit Sales Price	Amount
13.	110	7/20	1	17189	212	20	5.00	100.00
14.	114	7/25	3	17190	202	200	.75	150.00
15.	117	7/30	3	17191	208	300	1.25	375.00

(2) Sort the cards into numerical order according to customer number.
(3) Sort the cards for each customer according to date, placing the earliest date on top.
(4) Using the data recorded on the cards, prepare the three customers' statements of account.
(5) Resort cards numbered 7–15 into numerical order according to salesman number. Prepare for the sales manager a report of sales by salesmen during July.
(6) Resort cards numbered 7–15 into numerical order by commodity number. Prepare for the store manager, who also acts as buyer, a report of the quantity of each commodity sold during July.

804

Chapter 14

14-1B. You are engaged to review the accounting records of Spruce Company prior to closing of the expense and revenue accounts as of December 31, the end of the current fiscal year. The following information comes to your attention during the review:

(a) Accounts receivable include $900 owed by H. L. Jacobs, a bankrupt. There is no prospect of collecting any part of the amount owed. The allowance method of accounting for receivables is employed.
(b) Merchandise inventory on hand at December 31 of the current year has been recorded in the accounts at cost, $43,750. Current market price of the inventory is $47,000.
(c) No interest has been accrued on a $30,000, 6%, 60-day note receivable, dated December 11 of the current year.
(d) The store supplies account has a balance of $1,700. The cost of the store supplies on hand at December 31, as determined by a physical count, was $450.
(e) Since net income for the current year is expected to be considerably less than it was for the preceding year, depreciation on equipment has not been recorded. Depreciation for the year on equipment, determined in a manner consistent with the preceding year, amounts to $19,000.
(f) Land, recorded in the accounts at a cost of $35,000, was appraised at $50,000 by two expert appraisers.
(g) The company is being sued for $50,000 by a customer who is claiming damages for personal injury apparently caused by a defective product.

Company attorneys feel extremely confident that the company will have no liability for damages resulting from this case.

Instructions:

Journalize any entries required to adjust or correct the accounts, identifying each entry by letter.

14-3B. Shapland Construction Company began construction on three contracts during 1969. Contract A was completed in 1970 and Contract B in 1971. The contract prices, estimated total costs, and costs incurred are as follows:

	Contract Price	Estimated Cost	1969 Costs	1970 Costs	1971 Costs
Contract A	$3,000,000	$2,400,000	$1,600,000	$ 825,000	——
Contract B	2,500,000	2,000,000	400,000	1,200,000	$ 432,500
Contract C	4,500,000	3,600,000	360,000	1,080,000	1,440,000

Instructions:

Determine the amount of revenue and the net income to be recognized for each of the following years: 1969, 1970, and 1971. Assume that the recognition of revenue is to be spread over the life of the contract and that the estimated percentage of completion is determined by comparing incurred costs with the estimated total cost. Present computations in good order.

14-4B. Becker Company was organized on January 1, 1968. During its first three years of operations, the company determined uncollectible accounts expense by the direct write-off method, the cost of the merchandise inventory at the end of the period by the last-in, first-out method, and depreciation expense by the straight-line method. The amounts of net income reported and the amounts of the foregoing items for each of the three years were as follows:

	First Year	Second Year	Third Year
Net income reported	$15,000	$22,500	$31,750
Uncollectible accounts expense .	300	850	1,800
Ending merchandise inventory .	27,500	32,000	40,000
Depreciation expense.	7,000	8,000	8,500

The firm is considering the possibility of changing to the following methods in determining net income for the fourth and subsequent years: provision for doubtful accounts through the use of an allowance account, first-in, first-out inventory, and declining-balance depreciation at twice the straight-line rate. In order to consider the probable future effect of these changes on the determination of net income, the management requests that net income of the past three years be recomputed on the basis of the proposed methods. The uncollectible accounts expense, ending inventory, and depreciation expense, for the past three years, computed in accordance with the proposed methods, are as follows:

	First Year	Second Year	Third Year
Uncollectible accounts expense .	$ 750	$ 1,200	$ 1,600
Ending merchandise inventory .	29,000	35,000	43,500
Depreciation expense.	14,000	13,500	12,700

Instructions:

Recompute the net income for each of the three years, presenting the figures in an orderly manner.

14-6B. Frank Allen owns and manages Allen Sporting Goods on a full-time basis. He also maintains the accounting records. At the close of the first year of operations, he prepared the following income statement and balance sheet.

Allen Sporting Goods
Income Statement
For Year Ended December 31, 19--

Sales.		$67,500
Purchases.		60,300
Gross profit on sales.		$ 7,200
Operating expenses:		
Salary expense.	$8,300	
Rent expense.	5,200	
Utilities expense	1,750	
Miscellaneous expense	1,250	
Total operating expenses. .		16,500
Net loss.		$ 9,300

Allen Sporting Goods
Balance Sheet
December 31, 19--

Cash.	$ 4,200
Equipment.	4,000
Frank Allen.	$ 8,200

Because of the large net loss reported by the income statement, Allen is considering discontinuing operations. Before making a decision, he asks you to review the accounting methods employed and, if material errors are found, to prepare revised statements. The following information is elicited during the course of the review:

(a) The only transactions recorded have been those in which cash was received or disbursed.
(b) The accounts have not been closed for the year.
(c) The business was established on January 10 by an investment of $15,000 in cash by the owner. An additional investment of $2,500 was made in cash on July 1.
(d) Accounts receivable from customers at December 31 total $2,200.
(e) Uncollectible accounts are estimated at $200.
(f) The merchandise inventory at December 31, as nearly as can be determined, has a cost of $12,500.
(g) Insurance premiums of $750 were debited to Miscellaneous Expense during the year. The unexpired portion at December 31 is $500.
(h) The equipment listed on the balance sheet at $4,000 was purchased for cash on January 11. Equipment purchased July 1 for $2,000 in cash was debited to Purchases. Equipment purchased on December 30 for $1,000, for which a 60-day non-interest-bearing note was issued, was not recorded.

(i) Depreciation on equipment has not been recorded. The equipment is estimated to have a useful life of 10 years and a salvage value of 10% of its original cost. (Use straight-line method.)

(j) A total of $3,600 is owed to merchandise creditors on account at December 31.

(k) Salaries owed but not paid on December 31 total $350.

(l) Rent Expense includes an advance payment of $400 for the month of January in the subsequent year.

(m) Supplies of $900 purchased during the year were debited to Purchases. An estimated $325 of supplies were on hand at December 31.

(n) The classification of operating expenses as "selling" and "general" is not considered to be sufficiently important to justify the cost of the analysis.

(o) The proprietor made no withdrawals during the year.

Instructions:

(1) On the basis of the financial statements presented above, prepare an unadjusted trial balance as of December 31, on an eight-column work sheet.

(2) Record the adjustments and the corrections in the Adjustments columns and complete the work sheet.

(3) Prepare an income statement, a capital statement, and a balance sheet.

(4) On the basis of the revised financial statements, evaluate the effectiveness of the first year of operations.

Chapter 15

15-1B. Robert Black and James Cole have decided to form a partnership. They have agreed that Black is to invest $20,000 and that Cole is to invest $30,000. Black is to devote full time to the business and Cole is to devote one-half time. The following plans for the division of income are considered:

(a) Equal division.

(b) In the ratio of original investments.

(c) In the ratio of time devoted to the business.

(d) Interest of 6% on original investments and the remainder in the ratio of 2:1.

(e) Interest of 6% on original investments, salaries of $8,000 to Black and $4,000 to Cole, and the remainder equally.

(f) Plan (e), except that Black is also to be allowed a bonus equal to 10% of the amount by which net income exceeds the salary allowances.

Instructions:

Determine the division of net income under each of the following assumptions: net income of $30,000 and net income of $12,000. Present the data in tabular form, using the following columnar headings:

Plan	$30,000		$12,000	
	Black	Cole	Black	Cole

15-2B. On July 1 of the current year F. K. Doyle and B. A. Evans form a partnership.

Doyle invests certain business assets at valuations agreed upon, transfers business liabilities, and contributes sufficient cash to bring his total capital to $20,000. Details regarding the book values of the business assets and liabilities, and the agreed valuations, follow.

	Doyle's Ledger Balance	Agreed Valuation
Accounts Receivable....................	$ 8,800	$ 8,800
Allowance for Doubtful Accounts..........	600	500
Merchandise Inventory.................	10,500	11,900
Equipment............................	15,000⎫	7,000
Accumulated Depreciation — Equipment..	9,500⎭	
Accounts Payable......................	4,200	4,200
Notes Payable........................	5,000	5,000

Evans agrees to invest merchandise inventory priced at $12,500 and $2,500 in cash.

The articles of copartnership include the following provisions regarding the division of net income: interest on original investment at 6%, salary allowances of $7,000 and $5,000 respectively, and the remainder in the ratio of 2:3.

Instructions:

(1) Give the entries, in general journal form, to record the investments of Doyle and Evans in the partnership accounts.

(2) Prepare a balance sheet as of July 1, the date of formation of the partnership.

(3) After adjustments and the closing of revenue and expense accounts at June 30, the end of the first full year of operations, the expense and revenue summary account has a credit balance of $19,100 and the drawing accounts have debit balances of $7,500 (Doyle) and $4,500 (Evans). Present the journal entries to close the expense and revenue summary account and the drawing accounts at June 30.

15-5B. Feld, Gray, and Hill decide to discontinue business operations as of May 31 and liquidate their partnership. The firm's post-closing trial balance at that date appears below.

Feld, Gray, and Hill
Post-Closing Trial Balance
May 31, 19--

Cash.....................................	11,250	
Accounts Receivable....................	10,100	
Allowance for Doubtful Accounts........		800
Notes Receivable......................	5,000	
Merchandise Inventory.................	22,500	
Prepaid Insurance.....................	450	
Supplies..............................	250	
Equipment............................	10,750	
Accumulated Depreciation — Equipment .		4,250
Buildings.............................	40,000	
Accumulated Depreciation — Buildings...		22,000
Land.................................	8,000	
Accounts Payable......................		8,600
Mortgage Note Payable................		25,000
Albert Feld, Capital...................		13,050
Robert Gray, Capital..................		23,500
John Hill, Capital....................		11,100
	108,300	108,300

The partners share net income and losses in the ratio 1:2:1. The realization and liquidation transactions are summarized as follows:

(a) Collected $9,050 of accounts receivable; the remainder are worthless.
(b) Collected $5,000 on notes receivable.
(c) Sold the merchandise for $21,750 cash.
(d) Realized $350 cash from cancellation of the insurance policies.
(e) Sold the supplies for $200 cash.
(f) Sold the equipment for $7,500.
(g) Sold the land and buildings for $35,000, purchaser paying $10,000 cash and assuming the mortgage note. The mortgage holder released the partners from further liability.
(h) Paid miscellaneous expenses in connection with the sale of the assets, $450. (Charge to Loss and Gain on Realization.)
(i) Distributed the gain on realization to the partners' capital accounts.
(j) Paid the accounts payable in full.
(k) Distributed remaining cash to the partners.

Instructions:
(1) Set up T accounts for Cash, Loss and Gain on Realization, and the capital accounts.
(2) Record the May 31 balances in the T accounts.
(3) Present entries, in general journal form, to record the liquidation; post to the T accounts as appropriate; rule the accounts.
(4) Assuming that there had been a net loss of $44,400, instead of the amount determined above, prepare a complete summary of the liquidation in the form illustrated in the chapter. No entries are required.
(5) Assuming that there had been a net loss of $46,800, instead of the amount determined above, prepare a complete summary of the liquidation in the form illustrated in the chapter. No entries are required.

Chapter 16

16-2B. The annual dividends declared by Mitchell Company during a six-year period are presented in the table below. During the entire period the outstanding stock of the company was composed of 1,000 shares of cumulative, participating, 6% preferred stock, $100 par, and 20,000 shares of common stock, $20 par. The preferred stock contract provides that the preferred stock shall participate in distributions of additional dividends after allowance of a $2 dividend per share on the common stock, the additional dividends to be divided among common and preferred shares on the basis of the total par of the stock outstanding.

Year	Total Dividends	Preferred Dividends Total	Preferred Dividends Per Share	Common Dividends Total	Common Dividends Per Share
1966	$21,000				
1967	3,000				
1968	14,000				
1969	61,000				
1970	26,000				
1971	46,000				

Instructions:
(1) Determine the total dividends and the per share dividends declared on each class of stock for each of the six years, using the headings

presented on the preceding page. There were no dividends in arrears on January 1, 1966.

(2) Determine the average annual dividend per share for each class of stock for the six-year period.

(3) Assuming that the preferred stock was sold at 105 and the common stock was sold at par at the beginning of the six-year period, determine the percentage return on initial shareholders' investment based on the average annual dividend per share (a) for preferred stock, and (b) for common stock.

16-3B. Selected data from the balance sheets of six corporations, identified by letter, are presented below:

A. Common stock, $20 par...... $2,000,000
   Premium on common stock... 100,000
   Deficit.................... 60,000

B. Preferred 7% stock, $100 par . $1,000,000
   Premium on preferred stock... 100,000
   Common stock, $10 par...... 1,000,000
   Discount on common stock ... 50,000
   Deficit.................... 100,000

   Preferred stock has prior claim to assets on liquidation to the extent of par.

C. Preferred 6% stock, $50 par .. $ 500,000
   Common stock, $25 par...... 1,000,000
   Premium on common stock... 40,000
   Retained earnings.......... 200,000

   Preferred stock has prior claim to assets on liquidation to the extent of par.

D. Preferred 6% stock, $100 par . $1,000,000
   Premium on preferred stock .. 50,000
   Common stock, $50 par...... 4,000,000
   Deficit.................... 230,000

   Preferred stock has prior claim to assets on liquidation to extent of 110% of par.

E. Preferred 7% stock, $100 par . $1,000,000
   Common stock, $5 par....... 1,250,000
   Premium on common stock... 50,000
   Retained earnings.......... 100,000

   Dividends on preferred stock are in arrears for 3 years including the dividend passed during the current year. Preferred stock is entitled to par plus unpaid cumulative dividends upon liquidation to the extent of retained earnings.

F. Preferred 6% stock, $50 par .. $ 500,000
   Discount on preferred stock... 30,000
   Common stock, $10 par...... 1,000,000
   Retained earnings.......... 50,000

   Dividends on preferred stock are in arrears for 2 years including the dividend passed during the current year. Preferred stock is entitled to par plus unpaid cumulative dividends upon liquidation, regardless of the availability of retained earnings.

Instructions:

Determine for each corporation the equity per share of each class of stock, presenting the total stockholders' equity allocated to the class and the number of shares outstanding.

16-5B. The stockholders' equity and related accounts appearing in the ledger of Heath Corporation on July 1, the beginning of the current fiscal year, are listed below.

Preferred 7% Stock Subscriptions Receivable..	$ 105,000
Preferred 7% Stock, $100 par (15,000 shares authorized, 8,000 shares issued)...........	800,000
Preferred 7% Stock Subscribed (2,000 shares).	200,000
Premium on Preferred Stock................	50,000
Common Stock, $10 par (500,000 shares authorized, 300,000 shares issued).........	3,000,000
Premium on Common Stock................	1,600,000
Retained Earnings.......................	1,500,000

During the year the corporation completed a number of transactions affecting the stockholders' equity. They are summarized below.

(a) Received balance due on preferred stock subscribed and issued the certificates.
(b) Purchased 5,000 shares of treasury common for $75,000.
(c) Sold 2,000 shares of treasury common for $36,000.
(d) Received subscriptions to 1,000 shares of preferred 7% stock at $105, collecting 40% of subscription price.
(e) Issued 25,000 shares of common stock at $20, receiving cash.
(f) Sold 1,000 shares of treasury common for $19,000.

811

Instructions:

(1) Prepare entries in general journal form to record the transactions listed above. (Use of T accounts for the stockholders' equity accounts is suggested for accumulating balances needed to record particular transactions and for use in remainder of problem.)
(2) Prepare the stockholders' equity section of the balance sheet as of June 30. Net income for the year amounted to $745,000. Dividends charged to Retained Earnings during the year totaled $400,000.

Chapter 17

17-1B. Selected transactions completed by the Adler Company during the current fiscal year are as follows:

Feb.   6. Discovered that a receipt of $350 cash on account from J. W. Miller had been posted in error to the account of J. N. Hiller. The transaction was recorded correctly in the cash receipts journal.
      20. Purchased 1,000 shares of own common stock at $75, recording the stock at cost. (Prior to the purchase there were 20,000 shares of $20 par common stock outstanding.)
Apr. 15. Declared a semiannual dividend of $3 on the 10,000 shares of preferred stock and a $2 dividend on the common stock to stockholders of record on April 25, payable on May 10.

May 10. Paid the cash dividends.

July 8. Sold 500 shares of treasury stock at $70, receiving cash.

Oct. 15. Declared semiannual dividends of $3 on the preferred stock and $2 on the common stock. In addition, a 5% common stock dividend was declared on the common stock outstanding. The fair market value of the common stock to be issued is estimated at $72.

Nov. 10. Paid the cash dividends and issued the certificates for the common stock dividend.

Dec. 31. Recorded $95,000 of additional federal income tax allocable to net income for the year. Of this amount, $82,500 is a current liability and $12,500 is deferred.

31. The board of directors authorized the appropriation necessitated by the holdings of treasury stock.

Instructions:

Record the transactions above in general journal form.

17-3B. The following data were selected from the records of W. L. Gregory Company for the current fiscal year ended June 30:

Merchandise inventory (July 1)	99,400
Merchandise inventory (June 30)	88,000
Sales	985,000
Sales salaries	75,500
Sales commissions	49,250
Purchases	630,000
Rent expense	20,000
Office salaries	24,250
Delivery expense	4,850
Store supplies expense	2,100
Advertising expense	18,500
Depreciation expense — store equipment	6,000
Office supplies expense	850
Insurance expense	3,500
Depreciation expense — office equipment	900
Interest expense	2,800
Miscellaneous selling expense	2,900
Miscellaneous general expense	1,700
Uninsured flood loss	22,000
Gain on sale of investments	34,000
Income tax:	
Net of amount applicable to extraordinary items	59,000
Applicable to uninsured flood loss	9,000
Applicable to gain on sale of investments	8,500
Common stock, $10 par	500,000

Instructions:

Prepare an income statement with earnings per share shown parenthetically for "net income before extraordinary items," "extraordinary items (less applicable income tax)," and "net income."

17-4B. The stockholders' equity accounts of International Products Incorporated with balances on January 1 of the current fiscal year are as follows:

Common Stock, stated value $5 (100,000 shares authorized, 75,000 shares issued)	$375,000
Paid-in Capital in Excess of Stated Value	300,000
Appropriation for Contingencies	50,000

Appropriation for Treasury Stock.	60,000	
Retained Earnings.	170,000	
Treasury Stock (5,000 shares, at cost).	60,000	

The following selected transactions occurred during the year:

Jan. 10. Paid cash dividends of 30¢ per share on the common stock. The dividend had been properly recorded when declared on December 10 of the preceding fiscal year.

Apr. 10. Sold all of the treasury stock for $75,000 cash.

10. Issued 5,000 shares of common stock for $75,000 cash.

May 16. Received land with an estimated market price of $20,000 from the Melrose Industrial Park Council as a donation.

June 10. Declared a 4% stock dividend on common stock. The market price of the stock to be issued is $16 a share.

July 9. Issued the certificates for the dividend declared on June 10.

Nov. 5. Purchased 2,000 shares of treasury stock for $34,000.

Dec. 18. Declared a 30¢ per share dividend on common stock.

18. The board of directors authorized the increase of the appropriation for contingencies by $25,000.

18. Decreased the appropriation for treasury stock to $34,000.

31. Closed the credit balance of the expense and revenue summary account, $95,750.

Instructions:

(1) Set up T accounts for the stockholders' equity accounts and enter the balances as of January 1.

(2) Prepare entries in general journal form to record the selected transactions and post to the stockholders' equity accounts. Set up additional stockholders' equity accounts as needed.

(3) Prepare the stockholders' equity section of the balance sheet as of December 31 of the current fiscal year.

813

Chapter 18

18-1B. The following transactions were completed by Ferris Co.:

1969

Oct. 31. Issued $1,000,000 of 10-year, 6% bonds dated October 31, 1969 at 103. Interest is payable semiannually on October 31 and April 30.

Dec. 31. Recorded the adjusting entry for interest payable.

31. Recorded amortization of premium on bonds.

31. Closed the interest expense account.

1970

Jan. 1. Reversed the adjusting entry for interest payable.

Apr. 30. Paid the semiannual interest on the bonds.

Oct. 31. Paid the semiannual interest on the bonds.

Dec. 31. Recorded the adjusting entry for interest payable.

31. Recorded amortization of premium on bonds.

31. Closed the interest expense account.

Instructions:

(1) Record the foregoing transactions in general journal form.

(2) State the amount of the interest expense in (a) 1969 and (b) 1970.

(3) What is the effective rate of interest expressed as a percentage of the face value of the bonds?

18-2B. The board of directors of W. W. Lane Company is planning an expansion of plant facilities expected to cost $1,000,000. The board is undecided about the method of financing this expansion and is considering two plans:

Plan 1. Issue an additional 25,000 shares of no-par common stock at $40 per share.

Plan 2. Issue $1,000,000 of 20-year, 6% bonds at face value.

The condensed balance sheet of W. W. Lane Company at the end of the most recent fiscal year is presented below.

W. W. Lane Company
Balance Sheet
December 31, 19--

Assets		Liabilities and Capital	
Current assets.........	$ 850,000	Current liabilities.........	$ 720,000
Plant assets...........	3,150,000	Common stock (100,000	
		shares issued)..........	2,500,000
		Retained earnings........	780,000
Total assets...........	$4,000,000	Total liabilities and capital.	$4,000,000

Net income has remained relatively constant over the past several years. The expansion program is expected to increase yearly income before tax (and before bond interest) from $400,000 to $550,000. Assume a tax rate of 50%.

Instructions:

(1) Prepare a tabulation indicating the expected earnings per share on common stock under each plan.

(2) List factors other than earnings per share that the board should consider in evaluating the two plans.

(3) Which plan offers the greater benefit to the present stockholders? Give reasons for your opinion.

18-3B. During 1969 and 1970 Wallace Company completed the following transactions relating to its $5,000,000 issue of 20-year, 6% bonds dated April 30, 1969. Interest is payable on April 30 and October 31. The corporation's fiscal year is the calendar year.

1969
Apr. 30. Sold the bond issue for $4,970,000.
Oct. 31. Paid the semiannual interest on the bonds.
Dec. 31. Recorded the adjusting entry for interest payable.
  31. Recorded amortization of bond discount.
  31. Deposited $88,000 in a bond sinking fund.
  31. Appropriated $160,000 of retained earnings for bonded indebtedness.
  31. Closed the interest expense account.

1970
Jan. 1. Reversed the adjustment for interest payable.
  7. Purchased various securities with sinking fund cash at a cost of $87,225.
Apr. 30. Paid the semiannual interest on the bonds.
Oct. 31. Paid the semiannual interest on the bonds.
Dec. 31. Recorded the receipt of $4,375 of income on sinking fund securities, depositing the cash in the sinking fund.
  31. Recorded the adjusting entry for interest payable.
  31. Recorded amortization of bond discount.

31. Deposited $132,000 cash in the sinking fund.
31. Appropriated $240,000 of retained earnings for bonded indebtedness.
31. Closed the interest expense account.

Instructions:

(1) Record the foregoing transactions in general journal form.
(2) Prepare a columnar table, using the headings presented below, and include the information for each of the two years.

Account Balances at End of Year

Year	Bond Interest Expense for Year	Sinking Fund Income for Year	Bonds Payable	Discount on Bonds	Sinking Fund Cash	Sinking Fund Investments	Appropriation for Bonded Indebtedness

18-5B. The following transactions relate to certain securities acquired by Gleason Company:

1967
June 1. Purchased $100,000 of Barker Company 10-year, 6% coupon bonds dated March 1, 1967 directly from the issuing company for $101,755 plus accrued interest. Barker is an important customer of Gleason Company and it is expected that the bonds will be held as a long-term investment.
July 20. Purchased as a long-term investment 200 common shares of Roland Corporation at 79¼ plus commission and other costs of $110.
Sept. 1. Deposited the coupons for semiannual interest on Barker Company bonds.
10. Received the semiannual dividend of $2.50 per share on Roland Corporation stock.
Dec. 31. Recorded the adjustment for interest receivable on the Barker Company bonds.
31. Recorded the amortization of premium on the Barker Company bonds.

(Assume that all intervening transactions and adjustments have been recorded properly, and that the amount of bonds and shares of stocks have not changed from December 31, 1967 to December 31, 1969.)

1970
Jan. 1. Reversed the adjustment for interest receivable.
Mar. 1. Deposited coupons for semiannual interest on the Barker Company bonds.
12. Received the semiannual dividend of $2.50 per share and a 5% stock dividend on the Roland Corporation stock.
Apr. 1. Sold the Barker Company bonds at 102½ plus accrued interest. The broker deducted $250 for commission and taxes, remitting the balance. The amortization of the premium for the year to date was also recorded.
Sept. 15. Received the semiannual dividend of $2.50 per share on the Roland Corporation stock.
Oct. 22. Sold 100 shares of Roland Corporation stock at 70. The broker deducted commission and other costs of $46, remitting the balance.

Instructions:

Record the foregoing transactions in general journal form.

19-1B. Rodgers and Co. operates two sales departments: Department A for men's clothing and Department B for women's clothing. The following trial balance was prepared at the end of the current fiscal year after all adjustments, including the adjustments for merchandise inventory, were recorded and posted:

Rodgers and Co.
Trial Balance
July 31, 19--

Cash...	77,600	
Accounts Receivable......................	96,500	
Merchandise Inventory — Department A......	29,500	
Merchandise Inventory — Department B......	34,250	
Prepaid Insurance.........................	1,900	
Store Supplies............................	850	
Store Equipment..........................	41,500	
Accumulated Depreciation — Store Equipment.		26,500
Accounts Payable.........................		33,400
Income Tax Payable.......................		6,300
Common Stock............................		100,000
Retained Earnings.........................		82,800
Expense and Revenue Summary..............	56,250	63,750
Sales — Department A.....................		300,000
Sales — Department B.....................		450,000
Sales Returns and Allowances — Department A.	2,100	
Sales Returns and Allowances — Department B.	7,050	
Purchases — Department A..................	253,700	
Purchases — Department B.................	365,100	
Sales Salaries............................	34,250	
Advertising Expense.......................	8,500	
Depreciation Expense — Store Equipment.....	8,000	
Miscellaneous Selling Expense..............	1,000	
Office Salaries............................	10,000	
Rent Expense.............................	9,600	
Heating and Lighting Expense..............	3,000	
Property Tax Expense......................	2,000	
Insurance Expense.........................	1,100	
Store Supplies Expense....................	1,100	
Uncollectible Accounts Expense.............	900	
Miscellaneous General Expense.............	600	
Interest Income...........................		600
Income Tax...............................	17,000	
	1,063,350	1,063,350

Merchandise inventories at the beginning of the year were: Department A, $26,500; Department B, $29,750.

The bases to be used in apportioning expenses, together with other essential information, are as follows:

Sales salaries — payroll records: Department A, $14,500; Department B, $19,750.

Advertising expense — usage: Department A, $3,000; Department B, $5,500.

Depreciation expense — average cost of equipment. Balances at beginning of year: Department A, $18,000; Department B, $20,500. Balances at end of year: Department A, $18,000; Department B, $23,500.

Office salaries — Department A, 40%; Department B, 60%.

Rent expense and heating and lighting expense — floor space: Department A, 1,800 sq. ft.; Department B, 2,700 sq. ft.

Property tax expense and insurance expense — average cost of equipment plus average cost of merchandise inventory.

Store supplies expense — requisitions: Department A, $450; Department B, $650.

Uncollectible accounts expense, miscellaneous selling expense, and miscellaneous general expense — volume of gross sales.

Instructions:

Prepare an income statement departmentalized through net income from operations.

19-2B. Gordon's, a department store, has 18 departments. Those with the least sales volume are Department F and Department H, which were established about a year ago on a trial basis. The board of directors feels that it is now time to consider the retention or the termination of these two departments. The adjusted trial balance, severely condensed, as of January 31, the end of the first month of the current fiscal year, is presented below. January is considered to be a typical month. The income tax accrual has no bearing on the problem and is excluded from consideration.

Gordon's
Trial Balance
January 31, 19 ——

Current Assets.............................	480,125	
Plant Assets................................	340,000	
Accumulated Depreciation—Plant Assets......		180,000
Current Liabilities..........................		155,000
Common Stock..............................		300,000
Retained Earnings..........................		107,125
Sales—Department F.........................		12,100
Sales—Department H.........................		17,850
Sales—Other Departments....................		795,000
Cost of Merchandise Sold—Department F......	9,050	
Cost of Merchandise Sold—Department H.....	12,925	
Cost of Merchandise Sold—Other Departments.	547,500	
Direct Expenses—Department F..............	3,750	
Direct Expenses—Department H..............	3,925	
Direct Expenses—Other Departments.........	111,200	
Indirect Expenses..........................	53,600	
Interest Expense...........................	5,000	
	1,567,075	1,567,075

Instructions:

(1) Prepare an income statement for January departmentalized through departmental margin.

(2) State your recommendations concerning the retention of Departments F and H, giving reasons.

19-4B. Fisher's opened a branch office in Hamilton on May 1 of the current year. Summaries of transactions, adjustments, and year-end closing for branch operations of the current year ended December 31 are described below.

(a) Received cash advance, $25,000, and merchandise (billed at cost), $95,000, from the home office.
(b) Purchased equipment on account, $20,000.
(c) Purchased merchandise on account, $100,000.
(d) Sales on account, $110,000; cash sales, $65,000.
(e) Received cash from customers on account, $95,000.
(f) Paid operating expenses, $19,200 (all expenses are charged to Operating Expenses, a controlling account).
(g) Paid creditors on account, $105,000.
(h) Sent $35,000 cash to home office.
(i) Recorded accumulated depreciation, $500, and allowance for doubtful accounts, $350.
(j) Merchandise inventory at December 31, $62,750.
(k) Closed revenue and expense accounts.

Instructions:
(1) Present, in general journal form, the entries on the branch books to record the foregoing. Post to the following T accounts: Cash, Accounts Receivable, Allowance for Doubtful Accounts, Merchandise Inventory, Equipment, Accumulated Depreciation, Accounts Payable, Home Office, Expense and Revenue Summary, Sales, Shipments from Home Office, Purchases, and Operating Expenses.
(2) Prepare an income statement for the year and a balance sheet as of December 31 for the branch.
(3) Present, in general journal form, the entries required on the home office books. Post to a T account entitled Hamilton Branch.

Chapter 20

If the working papers correlating with the textbook are not used, omit Problem 20-1B.

20-1B. The work sheet for Jenkins Manufacturing Co. for the current year ended December 31 is presented in the working papers. Data concerning account titles, trial balance amounts, and selected adjustments have been entered on the work sheet.

Instructions:
(1) Enter the six adjustments required for the inventories on the work sheet. Additional adjustment data are:

Finished goods inventory at December 31	$47,900
Work in process inventory at December 31	37,750
Direct materials inventory at December 31	34,000

(2) Complete the work sheet.
(3) Prepare a statement of cost of goods manufactured.
(4) Prepare an income statement.

20-2B. Arnold Company manufactures Product A. Material M is placed in process in Department 1 where it is ground and partially refined. The output of Department 1 is transferred to Department 2, where Material N is added at the beginning of the process and the refiring is completed. On June 1, Arnold Company had the following inventories:

Finished goods (2,000 units)...	$60,000
Work in process—Department 1...	——
Work in process—Department 2 (1,000 units, ¼ completed).	24,025
Materials...	14,500

Departmental accounts are maintained for factory overhead and there is one service department, factory office. Manufacturing operations for the month of June are summarized as follows:

(a) Materials purchased on account... $22,400

(b) Materials requisitioned for use:

Material M...	$15,000
Material N...	6,000
Indirect materials—Department 1...	750
Indirect materials—Department 2...	550

(c) Labor used:

Direct labor—Department 1...	$30,C00
Direct labor—Department 2...	15,750
Indirect labor—Department 1...	1,750
Indirect labor—Department 2...	900
Factory office...	400

(d) Miscellaneous costs incurred on account:

Department 1...	$ 3,100
Department 2...	2,050
Factory office...	1,160

(e) Expiration of prepaid expenses:

Department 1...	$ 490
Department 2...	320
Factory office...	90

(f) Depreciation charged on plant assets:

Department 1...	$ 5,250
Department 2...	2,900
Factory office...	350

(g) Distribution of factory office costs:

Department 1 ...	60% of total factory office costs
Department 2...	40% of total factory office costs

(h) Application of factory overhead costs:

Department 1...	40% of direct labor cost
Department 2...	50% of direct labor cost

(i) Production costs transferred from Department 1 to Department 2: 3,000 units were fully processed and there was no inventory of work in process in Department 1 at June 30.

(j) Production costs transferred from Department 2 to finished goods: 2,800 units were fully processed including the inventory at June 1. 1,200 units were ½ completed at June 30.

(k) Cost of goods sold during June: 2,800 units (use the first-in, first-out method in crediting the finished goods account).

Instructions:

Prepare entries in general journal form to record the foregoing operations.

20-4B. Kane Company manufactures Product P by a series of four processes, all materials being introduced in Department 1. From Department 1 the materials pass through Departments 2, 3, and 4, emerging as finished Product P. All inventories are priced at cost by the first-in, first-out method.

The balances in the accounts Work in Process — Department 4 and Finished Goods were as follows on March 1:

Work in Process — Department 4
    600 units, ⅔ completed.................................... $11,800
Finished Goods
    1,000 units at $21 a unit................................ 21,000

The following costs were charged to Work in Process—Department 4 during March:

Direct materials transferred from Department 3: 2,300 units at
    $15.50.. $35,650
Direct labor... 9,625
Factory overhead.. 5,775

During the month of March, 2,000 units of P were completed and 2,200 units were sold. Inventories on March 31 were as follows:

Work in process — Department 4: 900 units ⅔ completed
Finished Goods: 800 units

Instructions:
(1) Determine the following, presenting the computations in good order:
    (a) Equivalent units of production for Department 4 during March.
    (b) Unit processing cost for Department 4 for March.
    (c) Total and unit cost of Product P started in a prior period and finished in March.
    (d) Total and unit cost of Product P started and finished in March.
    (e) Total cost of goods transferred to finished goods.
    (f) Work in process inventory for Department 4, March 31.
    (g) Cost of goods sold (indicate number of units and unit costs).
    (h) Finished goods inventory, March 31.
(2) Prepare a cost of production report for Department 4 for March.

20-6B. Kinney Products manufactures joint products X and Y. Materials are placed in production in Department 1 and after processing are transferred to Department 2, where more materials are added. The finished products emerge from Department 2. There are two service departments, Factory Office and Maintenance and Repair.

There were no inventories of work in process at either the beginning or the end of July. Finished goods inventories at July 1 were as follows:

Finished Goods — Product X, 500 units... $ 3,750
Finished Goods — Product Y, 900 units... 11,250

Transactions related to manufacturing operations for the month of July in summary form are as follows:

(a) Materials purchased on account, $14,500.
(b) Miscellaneous costs and expenses incurred on account: Department 1, $500; Department 2, $350; Factory Office, $275; and Maintenance and Repair, $450.
(c) Materials requisitioned for use: Department 1, $8,725 ($8,250 entered

directly into the products); Department 2, $4,300 ($4,000 entered
directly into the products); Maintenance and Repair, $550.

(d) Labor costs incurred: Department 1, $7,350 ($6,250 entered directly
into the products); Department 2, $5,800 ($5,000 entered directly into
the products); Factory Office, $550; Maintenance and Repair, $1,700.

(e) Expiration of various prepaid expenses: Department 1, $75; Department 2, $50; Factory Office, $75; and Maintenance and Repair, $50.

(f) Depreciation charged on plant assets: Department 1, $500; Department 2, $300; Factory Office, $100; and Maintenance and Repair, $150.

(g) Factory office costs allocated on the basis of man-hours worked: Department 1, 1,000 hours; Department 2, 800 hours; Maintenance and
Repair, 200 hours.

(h) Maintenance and repair costs allocated on the basis of services rendered:
Department 1, 60%, Department 2, 40%.

(i) Factory overhead applied to production at the predetermined rates:
80% and 70% of direct labor cost for Departments 1 and 2 respectively.

(j) Output of Department 1: 3,000 units.

(k) Output of Department 2: 1,000 units of Product X and 2,000 units of
Product Y. Unit selling price is $15 for Product X and $22.50 for
Product Y.

(l) Sales on account: 1,200 units of Product X at $15 and 1,900 units of
Product Y at $22.50. Credits to the finished goods accounts are to be
priced in accordance with the first-in, first-out method.

Instructions:

Prepare entries in general journal form to record the transactions.
Include as an explanation for entry (k) the computations for the
allocation of the production costs for Department 2 to the joint
products, and as an explanation for entry (l) the units and the unit
costs for each product sold.

821

Chapter 21

21-1B. Cook Products uses a job order cost system. The following data
summarize the operations related to production for June, the first month of
operations.

(a) Materials purchased on account, $18,750.
(b) Materials requisitioned and factory labor used:

	Materials	Factory Labor
Job No. 1	$ 800	$ 400
Job No. 2	1,250	700
Job No. 3	3,750	1,900
Job No. 4	2,100	1,150
Job No. 5	2,800	1,450
Job No. 6	900	500
For general factory use	350	775

(c) Factory overhead costs incurred on account, $3,300.
(d) Depreciation of machinery and equipment, $1,250.
(e) The factory overhead rate is 90% of direct labor cost.
(f) Jobs completed: Nos. 1, 2, 4, and 5.
(g) Jobs Nos. 1, 2, and 4 were shipped and customers were billed for $2,400,
$3,950, and $6,500 respectively.

Instructions:

(1) Prepare entries in general journal form to record the foregoing summarized operations.

(2) Set up T accounts for Work in Process and Finished Goods. Post to these accounts, using the identifying letters as dates. Bring down the end-of-the-month balances.

(3) Prepare a schedule of unfinished jobs to support the balance in the work in process account.

(4) Prepare a schedule of completed jobs on hand to support the balance in the finished goods account.

If the working papers correlating with the textbook are not used, omit Problem 21-2B.

21-2B. Keck Furniture Company repairs, refinishes, and reupholsters furniture. A job order cost system was installed recently to assist in determining the prices to quote to prospective customers, in determining the actual costs incurred on each job, and in reducing costs.

When a prospective customer requests an estimate of the price for a job, the estimated cost data are entered on an unnumbered job order cost sheet. If the customer accepts the estimate, a number is assigned to the job and the costs incurred are recorded in the usual manner on the job order cost sheet. When the job is completed, an explanation for any differences between the estimated and actual costs is entered on the sheet to assist management in evaluating the efficiency of operations and in pricing future jobs.

On May 4, an estimate of $225 for reupholstering a couch was given to James Wilson. The estimate was based upon the following data:

Estimated direct materials:	
10 yards at $9 per yard..........................	$ 90
Estimated direct labor:	
12 hours at $5 per hour...........................	60
Estimated factory overhead (50% of direct labor cost).	30
Total estimated costs.............................	$180
Markup (25% of production costs)..................	45
Total estimate...................................	$225

On May 10, the couch was picked up from the residence of James Wilson with the promise that it would be returned on May 30. The job was completed on May 26.

The materials requisition and time tickets pertaining to the job are summarized below:

Materials Requisition No.	Description	Amount
152	10 yards at $9	$90
153	1 yard at $9	9

Time Ticket No.	Description	Amount
287	6 hours at $5	$30
288	7 hours at $5	35

Instructions:

(1) Complete that portion of the job order cost sheet that would be completed when the estimate is given to the customer, James Wilson.

(2) Assign number 60 to the job, record the costs incurred, and complete the job order cost sheet. In commenting upon the variances between actual costs and estimated costs, assume that 1 yard of material was spoiled and that the factory overhead rate has been proven to be satisfactory.

21-5B. Selected accounts for Collins Company are presented below. For the purposes of this problem, some of the debits and credits have been omitted.

ACCOUNTS RECEIVABLE

May 1 Balance............32,400	May 31 Collections..........40,600
31 Sales............... (A)	

MATERIALS

May 1 Balance............ 7,500	May 31 Requisitions......... (B)
31 Purchases...........12,200	

WORK IN PROCESS

May 1 Balance............ 6,900	May 31 Goods finished....... (E)
31 Direct materials...... (C)	
31 Direct labor.........20,000	
31 Factory overhead..... (D)	

FINISHED GOODS

May 1 Balance............18,200	May 31 Cost of goods sold..... (G)
31 Goods finished....... (F)	

FACTORY OVERHEAD

May 1 Balance............ 150	May 31 Applied (70% of direct
1–31 Costs incurred.......13,950	labor cost)........... (H)

COST OF GOODS SOLD

May 31 .... (I)	

SALES

	May 31 .... (J)

Selected balances at May 31:

Accounts receivable..	$27,500
Finished goods......	16,600
Work in process.....	7,275
Materials..........	6,100

Materials requisitions for May included $325 of materials issued for general factory use. All sales are made on account, terms n/30.

Instructions:
(1) Determine the amounts represented by the letters (A) through (J), presenting your computations.
(2) Is factory overhead overapplied or underapplied at May 31? By how much?

Chapter 22

22-1B. Monroe Company prepared the following factory overhead cost budget for the Sanding Department for July of the current year:

Monroe Company
Factory Overhead Cost Budget — Sanding Department
For Month Ending July 31, 19--

Direct labor hours:		
Normal productive capacity.........		10,000
Hours budgeted....................		8,000
Variable cost:		
Indirect factory wages..............	$5,600	
Indirect materials.................	3,600	
Power and light....................	2,400	
Total variable cost...............		$11,600
Fixed cost:		
Supervisory salaries................	$7,200	
Indirect factory wages	4,000	
Depreciation of plant and equipment..	3,200	
Insurance........................	1,100	
Power and light....................	1,020	
Property taxes.....................	980	
Total fixed cost..................		17,500
Total factory overhead cost............		$29,100

Instructions:
(1) Prepare a flexible budget for the month of August indicating capacities of 8,000, 9,000, 10,000, and 11,000 direct labor hours and the determination of a standard factory overhead rate per direct labor hour.
(2) Prepare a standard factory overhead cost variance report for August. The Sanding Department was operated for 9,000 direct labor hours and the following factory overhead costs were incurred:

Indirect factory wages...............	$10,150
Supervisory salaries.................	7,200
Indirect materials...................	4,100
Power and light.....................	3,870
Depreciation of plant and equipment...	3,200
Insurance...........................	1,100
Property taxes.......................	980
Total factory overhead costs incurred.	$30,600

22-3B. Conner Manufacturing, Inc. maintains perpetual inventory accounts for materials, work in process, and finished goods and uses a standard cost system based upon the following data:

	Standard Cost Per Unit	
	Quantity	Price
Direct materials..........	2 lbs. @ $1.50 per lb.....	$ 3
Direct labor	2 hours @ $5 per hr.......	10
Factory overhead........	$2 per direct labor hour..	4
Total.....		$17

There was no inventory of work in process at the beginning or end of July, the first month of the current year. The transactions relating to production completed during July are summarized as follows:

(a) Materials purchased on account, $14,700.
(b) Direct materials used, $13,630. This represented 9,400 pounds at $1.45 per pound.
(c) Direct labor paid, $44,880. This represented 8,800 hours at $5.10 per hour. There were no accruals at either the beginning or the end of the period.
(d) Factory overhead incurred during the month was composed of indirect labor, $9,600; depreciation on plant and equipment, $6,300; insurance, $900; and miscellaneous factory costs, $1,450. The indirect labor and miscellaneous factory costs were paid during the period, and the insurance represents an expiration of prepaid insurance. Of the total factory overhead of $18,250, fixed costs amounted to $7,500 and variable costs were $10,750.
(e) Goods finished during the period, 4,500 units.

Instructions:
(1) Prepare entries in general journal form to record the transactions, assuming that the work in process account is debited for actual production costs and credited with standard costs for goods finished.
(2) Prepare a T account for Work in Process and post to the account, using the identifying letters as dates. Balance and rule the account.
(3) Prepare schedules of variances for direct materials cost, direct labor cost, and factory overhead cost. Normal productive capacity for the plant is 10,000 direct labor hours.
(4) Total the amounts of the standard cost variances and compare this total with the balance of the work in process account.

22-4B. The treasurer of Morton Company instructs you to prepare a monthly cash budget for the next three months. He presents you with the following budget information:

	March	April	May
Sales....	$600,000	$560,000	$700,000
Manufacturing costs......	345,000	321,000	411,000
Operating expenses......	209,000	200,000	239,000
Capital expenditures.....	——	50,000	——

The company expects to sell about 20% of its merchandise for cash. Of sales on account, 75% are expected to be collected in full in the month following the

825

sale and the remainder the next following month. Depreciation, insurance, and property taxes represent $15,000 of the estimated monthly manufacturing costs and $5,000 of the probable monthly operating expenses. Insurance and property taxes are paid in January and July respectively. Of the remainder of the manufacturing costs and operating expenses, two thirds are expected to be paid in the month in which they are incurred and the balance in the following month.

Current assets of March 1 are composed of cash of $147,000, marketable securities of $75,000, and accounts receivable of $540,000 ($400,000 from February sales and $140,000 from January sales). Current liabilities as of March 1 are composed of a $100,000, 6%, 60-day note payable due March 15, $110,000 of accounts payable incurred in February for manufacturing costs, and accrued liabilities of $60,000 incurred in February for operating expenses.

It is expected that $750 in dividends will be received in April. An estimated income tax payment of $32,500 will be made in April. Morton Company's regular semiannual dividend of $50,000 is expected to be declared in April and paid in May. Management desires to maintain a minimum cash balance of $75,000.

Instructions:
(1) Prepare a monthly cash budget for March, April, and May.
(2) On the basis of the cash budget prepared in (1), what recommendation should be made to the treasurer?

Chapter 23

23-1B. Howard G. Emery owns a small business building from which he receives rental income. He uses the cash method of determining income, depositing all rents received from tenants in a special bank account. All disbursements related to the building, as well as occasional unrelated disbursements, are paid by checks drawn on the same account. During the current taxable year ending December 31, he deposited $35,000 of rent receipts in the special account.

Disbursements from the special bank account during the current year are summarized as follows:

Wages of custodian (gross earnings $5,240):	
Withheld for FICA tax and paid to IRS	$ 262
Withheld for income tax and paid to IRS	576
Paid to custodian	4,402
Real estate tax	2,480
Payments of personal income tax:	
Applicable to preceding year	1,300
Applicable to current year	4,200
Interest on mortgage note payable on land and office building	1,640
Installment payments of principal on mortgage note payable	3,300
Utilities expense	920
Air-conditioning units installed in two offices not previously air-conditioned	1,780
Repainting interior of two offices	730
Premium on a three-year insurance policy on the building, effective April 1	540
Repairs to heating and plumbing equipment	365
Payroll tax expense	262

Contributions:

United Fund	150
Community Church	500
Salvation Army	50
Miscellaneous expenses incurred in earning rentals	498
Purchases of various stocks	5,210

In addition to the foregoing data, you determine from other records and the tax return for the preceding year that the allowable deduction for depreciation expense is $4,200 and that current expirations of insurance premiums paid in earlier years total $245.

Instructions:

> Prepare a statement of adjusted gross income from rents, identifying each of the allowable deductions from gross income.

23-2B Eric Larson, unmarried and entitled to one exemption for himself, is engaged in the practice of architecture. He uses the cash method of determining taxable income and reports on the calendar-year basis. A summary of his record of cash receipts and disbursements for the current calendar year is presented below.

Cash Receipts

Professional fees	$64,600
Borrowed from bank (professional purposes)	3,000
Inheritance from uncle's estate	5,000
Dividends on corporation stocks	518

Cash Disbursements

Wages of draftsmen and typist:	
FICA and income taxes withheld and paid to IRS	$ 2,773
Paid to employees	12,307
Payroll taxes	1,014
Fees to collaborating engineers	6,610
Office rent	3,600
Telephone expense (office)	490
Electricity (office)	370
Blueprints	510
Office supplies expense	96
Insurance on office equipment (3-year policy, dated January 1)	162
Partial repayment of bank loan (see receipts)	1,500
Interest on bank loan	120
Charitable contributions	850
Payment on principal of residence mortgage note	1,200
Interest on residence mortgage note	640
Personal property tax on office equipment	64
Real estate tax on home	770
State sales tax on purchases for personal use	202
State inheritance tax	150
New automobile (purchased January 6)	4,800
Office equipment (purchased at various times)	800
Automobile operating expenses (exclusive of depreciation)	720
Purchase of 50 shares of Bowen Corporation stock	1,580
Payments of estimated income tax for current year	12,000

The automobile was used 40% of the time for professional purposes. It is to be depreciated by the declining-balance method at twice the straight-line rate, assuming an estimated life of 4 years. Allocate 40% of the depreciation and other automobile expenses to professional purposes.

The cost of the office equipment owned at the beginning of the year was $2,800, the additions made during the year are indicated above, and none of the equipment was disposed of during the year. Use a composite depreciation rate of 10%, based on the average of the beginning and ending balances.

Instructions:

Prepare a summary of federal income tax data for Larson, applying the appropriate schedule of tax rates presented in this chapter.

23-4B. J. B. West is negotiating the sale of a tract of unimproved land to Emerald Hills Estates, Inc. The sales price of the property is to be $108,000, payable in 6 equal annual installments, with the first installment payable during the current year. The property, which was acquired by West as an inheritance a number of years ago, has a cost basis of $12,000.

Mr. & Mrs. West expect to have approximately $10,000 of ordinary taxable income (adjusted gross income less itemized deductions and exemptions) for the current year and for each of the following 5 years, exclusive of the gain on the sale of the land, which qualifies as a long-term capital gain.

Instructions:

(1) Assuming the accuracy of the estimate of future income and no changes in the Internal Revenue Code, determine the Wests' total estimated federal income tax (joint return) for 6 years, beginning with the current year, based on (a) reporting the entire gain this year and (b) reporting the gain by the installment method. Apply the appropriate schedule of tax rates appearing in this chapter.

(2) What is the amount of federal income tax saved by electing the installment method?

(3) Could the installment method have been elected if the terms had provided for a down payment of $33,000 in the current year and annual payments of $15,000 for the remaining 5 years?

23-5B. Late in December, the last month of the current taxable year, Philip H. Ballard and his wife Sue engage you to prepare their income tax return and to advise them concerning other matters that may affect the amount of their tax liability. They are entitled to a total of five exemptions for themselves and their dependent children. They have been using the cash method of determining taxable income and expect to file a joint return.

Mr. Ballard is employed at a salary of $26,400 for the current year and has been notified that he will receive an increase of $250 per month, effective in January. He has no deductible expenses connected with his employment. Income from dividends for the current year will amount to $1,100 for Mr. Ballard and $400 for Mrs. Ballard, with a 40% increase expected for the following year.

During the current year Mrs. Ballard sold X Company stock at a loss of $1,000. Mr. Ballard proposes to sell his holdings of Y Company stock before the end of the year. He acquired the stock two years ago at a cost of $2,200, and the market price, which has been relatively stable, is currently $3,200. He plans to use the funds to pay amounts pledged to his church, $500 for the operating budget and $2,700 for the building fund, both due by the following March 31.

He also suggests that it might be advantageous to use Mrs. Ballard's $1,000 loss on the sale of X Company stock as an offset to his gain on Y Company stock.

Miscellaneous payments for the current year to date that would qualify as deductions from gross income total $300. In addition, real estate taxes of $400 for the first half of the year have been paid. Unpaid real estate taxes of $400 for the second half of the year are due on December 31 but may be paid as late as January 10 without penalty.

Miscellaneous deductions of $500 are anticipated for the following year, real estate taxes are expected to amount to $900 for the following year, and an additional $700 will be pledged to the church for its fiscal year beginning on April 1 of the following year.

Instructions:
(1) Advise the Ballards concerning the contemplated sale of Company Y stock and the timing of deductions from adjusted gross income. Consideration is to be given only to the current taxable year and to the following taxable year. The Internal Revenue Code and regulations, as well as the taxpayers' exemptions, are assumed to remain unchanged during the period, and the estimates for the succeeding year are assumed to be accurate.
(2) Prepare a summary of estimated federal income tax data for the Ballards (a) for the current taxable year and (b) for the following taxable year, assuming that they follow your advice and that the actual amount of income and deductions agree exactly with the estimates. The itemized deductions from adjusted gross income may be classified as follows: Contributions to church, Real estate taxes, and Miscellaneous. Apply the appropriate schedule of tax rates presented in this chapter.

829

Chapter 24

24-1B. Kelley Chemical Company refines Product P in batches of 10,000 gallons, which it sells for $.20 per gallon. The associated unit costs and expenses are currently as follows:

	Per Gallon
Direct materials.	$.090
Direct labor	.030
Variable factory overhead	.025
Fixed factory overhead.	.020
Salesmen's commissions	.010
Fixed selling and general expenses . . .	.005

The company is presently considering a proposal to put Product P through several additional processes to yield Products P and Q. Until recently, the company found such further processing unwise, but new processing methods have reopened this question. Existing facilities can be used for this processing; but inasmuch as additional machine time would be required and the plant is operating at full eight-hour-day capacity, the processing would have to be performed at night. Additional costs of processing would be $250 per batch and there would be an evaporation loss of 10%, with 50% of the processed material evolving as Product P and 40% as Product Q. Selling price of Product Q is $.35 per gallon. Salesmen's commissions are a uniform percentage based on the sales price.

Instructions:

(1) Prepare a differential analysis report as of November 17 presenting the differential revenue and the differential cost per batch associated with the processing to produce Products P and Q compared with processing to produce Product P only.

(2) Briefly report your recommendation.

24-2B. Midwest Press purchased a machine at a cost of $200,000 on June 29, 1968. The company's manufacturing costs for a normal year, exclusive of depreciation, total $450,000, operating expenses are $195,000 yearly, and revenues total $750,000 yearly. The annual depreciation for this machine is $25,000 based on an 8-year useful life and no residual value.

Early in July, 1970 a new type of machine priced at $400,000 becomes available. It has an estimated life of 6 years, with no salvage value, and its use is expected to reduce the company's manufacturing costs, exclusive of depreciation, to $380,000 yearly. The old machine can be sold for only $50,000. Revenues and operating expenses will not be affected by the use of either machine.

Instructions:

(1) Prepare a differential analysis report comparing operations with the proposed acquisition with operations using the present equipment. The analysis should indicate the net cost reduction or net cost increase that would result over the 6-year period if the new machine is acquired.

(2) List other factors that should be considered before a final decision is reached.

24-4B. Product A is one of numerous products manufactured by Avery Company. The demand for Product A has dropped sharply because of recent competition from a similar product. The company's chemists are currently completing tests of various new formulas, and it is anticipated that the manufacture of a superior product can be started on July 1, one month hence. No changes will be needed in the present production facilities to manufacture the new product because only the mixture of the various materials will be changed.

The controller has been asked by the president of the company for advice on whether to continue production during June or to suspend the manufacture of Product A until July 1. The controller has assembled the following pertinent data:

Avery Company
Estimated Income Statement — Product A
For Month Ending May 31, 19--

Sales (10,000 units)........................	$200,000
Less cost of goods sold	150,000
Gross profit on sales......................	$ 50,000
Less selling and general expenses........	70,000
Net loss................................	$ 20,000

The estimated production costs and selling and general expenses based on a production of 10,000 units are as follows:

Direct materials.........................	$5.50 per unit
Direct labor............................	4.00 per unit

Variable factory overhead.		2.00 per unit
Fixed factory overhead.		3.50 per unit
Variable selling and general expenses . . .		4.00 per unit
Fixed selling and general expenses.		$30,000 for May

Sales for June are expected to drop about 30% below those of the preceding month. No significant changes are anticipated in the production costs or operating expenses. No extra costs will be incurred in discontinuing operations in the portion of the plant associated with Product A. The inventory of Product A at the beginning and end of June is expected to be inconsequential.

Instructions:

(1) Prepare an estimated income statement in absorption costing form for June for Product A, assuming that production continues during the month.

(2) Prepare an estimated income statement in variable costing form for June for Product A, assuming that production continues during the month.

(3) State the estimated amount of net loss arising from the activities associated with Product A for June if production is temporarily suspended.

(4) Prepare a brief statement of the advice you think the controller should give.

Chapter 25

25-1B. Bowers Manufacturing Company is considering the addition of a new product to its line. For 1970, production was at 90% of capacity, the assets employed were $4,000,000 (original cost), and the income statement showed a net operating income of $400,000, computed as follows:

Sales		$4,500,000
Less: Cost of goods sold.	$3,275,000	
Selling expenses	575,000	
General expenses	250,000	4,100,000
Net operating income.		$ 400,000

If the new product is added, market research indicates that 10,000 units can be sold in 1971 at an estimated selling price of $50 per unit. The idle capacity will be utilized to produce the product, but an additional $500,000 in plant assets will be required. The cost data per unit for the new product are as follows:

Direct materials.	$19.00
Direct labor.	10.00
Factory overhead (includes depreciation on additional investment).	8.00
Selling expenses.	5.25
General expenses.	2.25
	$44.50

Instructions:

(1) Prepare an estimated income statement for 1971 for the new product.
(2) Prepare a schedule indicating the rate of return on assets under present conditions and for the new product. Use the original cost of the assets in your computations.
(3) Would you recommend addition of the new product? Would you require other data before you make your decision? If so, what data would you require?

25-3B. The capital expenditures budget committee is considering two projects. The estimated net income and net cash flows from each project are presented below:

Year	Project A Net Income	Project A Net Cash Flow	Project B Net Income	Project B Net Cash Flow
1	$ 8,000	$18,000	$ 4,000	$14,000
2	7,000	17,000	5,000	15,000
3	5,000	15,000	6,000	16,000
4	3,000	13,000	6,000	16,000
5	2,000	12,000	4,000	14,000
	$25,000	$75,000	$25,000	$75,000

Each project requires an investment of $50,000 with no salvage value expected. The committee has selected a rate of 15% for purposes of the discounted cash flow analysis.

Instructions:

(1) Compute the following:
   (a) The average rate of return for each project, giving effect to depreciation on the investment.
   (b) The excess or deficiency of present value over amount to be invested as determined by the discounted cash flow method for each project. Use the present value table appearing in this chapter.
(2) Prepare a brief report for the budget committee advising it on the relative merits of the two projects.

25-4B. Clay Company expects to maintain the same inventories at the end of 1970 as at the beginning of the year. The total of all production costs for the year is therefore assumed to be equal to the cost of goods sold. With this in mind, the various department heads were asked to submit estimates of the expenses for their departments during 1970. A summary report of these estimates is presented at the top of the next page.

It is expected that 72,000 units will be sold at a selling price of $15 a unit. Capacity output is 80,000 units.

Instructions:

(1) Determine the break-even point (a) in dollars of sales, (b) in units, and (c) in terms of capacity.
(2) Prepare an estimated income statement for 1970.
(3) Construct a break-even chart, indicating the break-even point in dollars of sales.
(4) What is the expected margin of safety?
(5) What is the expected marginal income ratio?

	Estimated Fixed Expense	Estimated Variable Expense (per unit sold)
Production costs:		
Direct materials...............	$ ——	$4.00
Direct labor..................	——	3.50
Factory overhead.............	150,000	.80
Selling expenses:		
Sales salaries and commissions...	45,000	.30
Advertising..................	35,000	——
Travel......................	17,500	——
Miscellaneous selling expenses...	9,000	.20
General expenses:		
Office and officers' salaries......	90,000	.10
Supplies.....................	6,000	.05
Miscellaneous general expenses..	7,500	.05
	$360,000	$9.00

25-6B. Davidson Company operated at full capacity during 1969. Its income statement appears below.

Sales		$800,000
Cost of goods sold...........		500,000
Gross profit on sales.........		$300,000
Operating expenses:		
Selling expenses...........	$160,000	
General expenses..........	65,000	
Total operating expenses.		225,000
Net operating income........		$ 75,000

An analysis of costs and expenses reveals the following division of costs and expenses between fixed and variable.

	Fixed	Variable
Cost of goods sold............	30%	70%
Selling expenses..............	35%	65%
General expenses.............	60%	40%

The management of Davidson Company is considering a plant expansion program that will permit an increase of $300,000 in yearly sales. The expansion will increase fixed costs and expenses by $60,000 but will not affect the relationship between sales and variable costs and expenses.

Instructions:

(1) Determine for present capacity (a) the total fixed costs and expenses and (b) the total variable costs and expenses.
(2) Determine the percentage of total variable costs and expenses to sales.
(3) Compute the break-even point under present conditions.
(4) Compute the break-even point under the proposed program.
(5) Determine the amount of sales that would be necessary under the proposed program to realize the $75,000 of net operating income that was earned in 1969.

(continued)

(6) Determine the maximum net operating income possible with the expanded plant.

(7) If the proposal is accepted and sales remain at the 1969 level, what will the net operating income be for 1970?

(8) Based upon the data given, would you recommend accepting the proposal? Explain.

Chapter 26

26-1B. The comparative balance sheet of the Klein Corporation at June 30, 1970 and 1969, appears below in condensed form.

Assets	1970	1969
Cash.	$ 28,200	$ 20,000
Accounts receivable (net)	40,700	24,000
Merchandise inventory.	91,400	93,400
Prepaid expenses.	2,800	2,600
Plant assets.	180,000	155,000
Accumulated depreciation — plant assets . . .	(61,000)	(84,000)
	$282,100	$211,000

Liabilities and Stockholders' Equity		
Accounts payable	$ 29,000	$ 24,500
Mortgage note payable	25,000	———
Common stock, $10 par.	175,000	150,000
Premium on common stock.	5,000	———
Retained earnings.	48,100	36,500
	$282,100	$211,000

Additional data obtained from the income statement and from an examination of the noncurrent asset, noncurrent liability, and stockholders' equity accounts in the ledger are as follows:

(a) Net income for the year, $21,600.

(b) Depreciation expense for the year, $12,000.

(c) Cash dividends declared during the year, $10,000.

(d) The mortgage note payable is due in 1975.

(e) An addition to the building was constructed during the year at a cost of $60,000, and fully depreciated equipment costing $35,000 was discarded, no salvage being realized.

(f) During the year 2,500 shares of common stock were issued for cash at $12.

Instructions:

(1) On the basis of the comparative balance sheet and the other information, assemble in memorandum form the data needed to prepare a funds statement (working capital concept) for the year ended June 30, 1970.

(2) Prepare a statement of source and application of funds, including a schedule of changes in working capital.

26-2B. The comparative balance sheet of the Campfield Corporation at December 31, 1970 and 1969, appears below in condensed form.

Assets	1970	1969
Cash..	$ 24,800	$ 30,500
Marketable securities.........................	15,000	25,000
Accounts receivable..........................	49,700	42,200
Inventories...................................	80,000	55,800
Prepaid expenses............................	2,300	2,900
Buildings....................................	165,400	125,400
Accumulated depreciation — buildings.........	(42,400)	(39,400)
Machinery and equipment....................	65,000	65,000
Accumulated depreciation—machinery and equipment.	(35,000)	(24,000)
Land..	25,000	25,000
Patents......................................	40,000	45,000
	$389,800	$353,400

Liabilities and Stockholders' Equity		
Accounts payable............................	$ 22,100	$ 29,700
Salaries payable.............................	8,400	11,200
Mortgage note payable.......................	40,000	——
Bonds payable	——	50,000
Common stock, $10 par	250,000	200,000
Premium on common stock	10,000	10,000
Retained earnings...........................	59,300	52,500
	$389,800	$353,400

835

An examination of the income statement and the accounting records revealed the following additional information:

(a) Net income for the year, $16,800.

(b) Cash dividends declared during the year, $10,000.

(c) Depreciation expense for the year: buildings, $3,000; machinery and equipment, $11,000.

(d) Patent amortization for the year, $5,000.

(e) A mortgage note due in 1974 was issued in payment of the purchase of a building costing $40,000.

(f) 5,000 shares of common stock were issued in exchange for $50,000 of bonds.

Instructions:

(1) On the basis of the information presented above, assemble in memorandum form the data needed to prepare a funds statement (all financial resources concept) for the year ended December 31, 1970.

(2) Prepare a statement of source and application of funds, including a schedule of changes in working capital.

26-3B. Condensed versions of the income statement and comparative balance sheet of Rockford Company are presented at the top of the following page.

Income Statement
For Year Ended December 31, 1970

Sales.		$900,000
Cost of goods sold		510,000
Gross profit on sales		$390,000
Operating expenses:		
Depreciation expense — machinery	$ 23,000	
Depreciation expense — buildings	12,000	
Other operating expenses	200,500	235,500
Income before income tax		$154,500
Income tax		74,500
Net income		$ 80,000

Comparative Balance Sheet
December 31, 1970 and 1969

Assets	1970	1969
Cash.	$ 45,000	$ 39,500
Trade receivables (net)	70,000	57,000
Inventories	95,500	80,000
Prepaid expenses	3,700	3,100
Machinery	310,000	290,000
Accumulated depreciation — machinery	(143,000)	(155,000)
Buildings	535,000	450,000
Accumulated depreciation — buildings	(212,000)	(200,000)
Land	65,000	50,000
	$769,200	$614,600

Liabilities and Stockholders' Equity

	1970	1969
Accounts payable (merchandise creditors)	$ 43,600	$ 64,000
Wages payable	8,500	6,000
Income tax payable	5,000	7,500
Mortgage note payable, due 1980	80,000	——
Common stock, $10 par	450,000	400,000
Premium on common stock	45,000	40,000
Retained earnings	137,100	97,100
	$769,200	$614,600

Additional data obtained from an examination of the ledger are as follows:

(a) Dividends of $40,000 were declared during the year.

(b) Machinery with an original cost of $40,000 and accumulated depreciation of $35,000 was sold during the year for $5,000 cash. New machinery was also purchased for $60,000 cash.

(c) Land and buildings were acquired during the year at a cost of $100,000. In addition to a down payment of $20,000, a ten-year, 6% mortgage note for $80,000 was issued to the seller.

(d) Common stock with a par of $50,000 was issued for $55,000.

Instructions:

Prepare a statement of cash flow including a schedule of change in cash.

27-1B. Patton Corporation purchased 16,000 shares of the outstanding stock of Sharp Company at $20 a share. Balance sheet data for the two corporations immediately after the transaction, which occurred on September 30 of the current year, are presented below. The interest receivable reported on Sharp Co. balance sheet is the accrual on the bond investment.

Assets	Patton Corp.	Sharp Co.
Cash and marketable securities...............	$ 95,000	$ 35,200
Accounts receivable......................	78,000	47,300
Allowance for doubtful accounts............	(3,500)	(2,200)
Interest receivable.........................	—	1,300
Inventories...............................	270,000	116,400
Investment in Sharp Company stock, 16,000 shares.....................................	320,000	—
Investment in Patton Corporation bonds, face value.......................................	—	50,000
Equipment................................	914,600	219,200
Accumulated depreciation..................	(192,200)	(56,700)
	$1,481,900	$410,500

Liabilities and Stockholders' Equity		
Accounts payable.........................	$ 127,400	$ 47,600
Income tax payable.......................	35,200	21,900
Interest payable..........................	9,100	—
Bonds payable (due in 1982)..............	350,000	—
Common stock, $5 par....................	700,000	—
Common stock, $10 par...................	—	200,000
Retained earnings........................	260,200	141,000
	$1,481,900	$410,500

837

Instructions:

(1) Prepare in report form a detailed consolidated balance sheet as of September 30 of the current year.

(2) Assuming that Sharp Company earns net income of $90,000 and pays dividends of $50,000 during the fiscal year and that Patton Corporation records its share of the earnings and dividends, determine the following as of the end of the year:

(a) The amount at which the investment in Sharp Company will appear on Patton Corporation's balance sheet.

(b) The amount of the difference between the cost and the book value of the subsidiary interest owned by the parent corporation.

(c) The amount of the minority interest.

27-3B. On May 31 of the current year Pearce Corporation exchanged 40,000 shares of its common stock for the 10,000 outstanding shares of Sloan Company common stock. Balance sheet data of the two corporations immediately before the exchange occurred are presented at the top of the following page.

Assets	Pearce Corp.	Sloan Co.
Cash....................................	$ 60,000	$ 15,000
Accounts receivable......................	75,000	30,000
Inventories.............................	140,000	70,000
Plant assets (net).......................	310,000	90,000
	$585,000	$205,000

Liabilities and Stockholders' Equity		
Notes payable...........................	$ 25,000	$ 8,000
Accounts payable........................	40,000	21,000
Common stock, $5 par....................	300,000	—
Common stock, $10 par...................	—	100,000
Premium on common stock.................	70,000	—
Retained earnings.......................	150,000	76,000
	$585,000	$205,000

Instructions:

(1) Present Pearce Corporation's journal entry to record the investment, based on the total par of the 40,000 shares issued in the exchange.

(2) As a preliminary to preparing a consolidated balance sheet immediately after the exchange of stock, determine the amount of the various stockholders' equity items to be eliminated, employing pooling of interests procedures.

(3) Prepare a consolidated balance sheet immediately after the exchange. Sectional captions for current assets, current liabilities, etc. may be omitted.

27-4B. The balances in the accounts of Arnold's, Inc. after adjustment at January 31, the close of the current fiscal year, are as follows:

Accounts Payable.......................		58,300
Accounts Receivable....................	63,900	
Accumulated Depreciation — Buildings...		21,700
Accumulated Depreciation — Equipment..		39,300
Allowance for Doubtful Accounts........		3,600
Bond Sinking Fund.....................	48,700	
Bonds Payable (due 1981)...............		100,000
Buildings.............................	104,100	
Cash in Bank..........................	31,800	
Common Stock, $10 par.................		200,000
Cost of Goods Sold....................	268,700	
Dividends Payable.....................		12,500
Equipment............................	178,400	
General Expenses......................	46,720	
Income Tax...........................	51,300	
Income Tax Payable....................		16,900
Interest Expense......................	6,500	
Interest Income.......................		5,200
Inventories...........................	173,200	
Land.................................	27,200	
Prepaid Expenses......................	4,400	
Retained Earnings.....................		109,120
Sales.................................		496,300

Salaries Payable.........................		3,200
Selling Expenses........................	61,200	
	1,066,120	1,066,120

Dividends debited to Retained Earnings during the year totaled $50,000; there were no other debits or credits to the account during the year. The number of shares of common stock outstanding remained unchanged during the year.

Instructions:

(1) Prepare a combined income and retained earnings statement using the single-step form, listing income tax as an item in the expenses section. Insert the earnings per share as a parenthetical notation on the line reporting net income.

(2) Prepare a detailed balance sheet in financial position form, disclosing the amount of working capital.

27-5B. The balances of selected ledger accounts of an enterprise as of the end of the year are listed below. The price level index at the beginning of the year was 120 and at the end of the year it was 130. Merchandise inventory is stated at cost, employing the fifo flow assumption. It is assumed to have been acquired when the price level index was 125, midway between the beginning and end of the year. The marketable securities, which are stated at cost, are common stocks purchased at the beginning of the year. The equipment was acquired a number of years ago, at which time the price level index was 80.

Account Title	Account Balance
Cash.............................	$15,600
Accounts Receivable...............	48,900
Marketable Securities..............	29,160
Merchandise Inventory.............	60,000
Equipment........................	99,000
Accumulated Depreciation..........	31,760
Accounts Payable..................	39,000

839

Instructions:

(1) Convert the account balances to current purchasing-power equivalents as of the end of the period, presenting the details indicated by the following captions:

Account Title	Account Balance	Conversion Multiplier	Converted Balance

(2) Determine the purchasing-power gain or loss during the year on each of the monetary items, assuming that the account balances were the same at the beginning and end of the year.

Chapter 28

28-1B. Data pertaining to the current position of Clark Company are presented below and on the following page.

Cash................................	$ 70,000
Marketable securities................	40,000
Accounts and notes receivable (net)...	121,000

Merchandise inventory...............	179,000
Prepaid expenses...................	10,000
Accounts payable..................	145,000
Notes payable (short-term)...........	50,000
Accrued liabilities..................	15,000

Instructions:

(1) Compute (a) working capital, (b) current ratio, and (c) acid-test ratio.

(2) Consider each of the following transactions separately and assume that only that transaction affects the data given above.

(a) Paid accounts payable, $75,000.
(b) Purchased merchandise on account, $35,000.
(c) Paid notes payable, $50,000.
(d) Received cash on account, $61,000.
(e) Declared a cash dividend, $20,000.
(f) Declared a common stock dividend on common stock, $25,000.
(g) Issued additional shares of stock for cash $200,000.
(h) Borrowed cash from bank on a long-term note, $100,000.
(i) Paid cash for office supplies, $1,500.
(j) Sold marketable securities, $20,000.

State the effect of each transaction (increase, decrease, or no effect) on working capital, current ratio, and acid-test ratio. Use the following column headings for recording your answers:

	Effect on	
Item	Working Capital	Current Ratio	Acid-Test Ratio

840

28-3B. For 1970, Mahan Company initiated an extensive sales promotion campaign that included the expenditure of an additional $50,000 for advertising. At the end of the year, Edward Mahan, the president, is presented with the following condensed comparative income statement:

Mahan Company
Comparative Income Statement
For Years Ended December 31, 1970 and 1969

	1970	1969
Sales.......................	$663,000	$505,000
Sales returns and allowances....	13,000	5,000
Net sales....................	$650,000	$500,000
Cost of merchandise sold.......	403,000	300,000
Gross profit on sales...........	$247,000	$200,000
Selling expense...............	$130,000	$ 75,000
General expense..............	31,200	25,000
Total operating expense........	$161,200	$100,000
Net operating income..........	$ 85,800	$100,000
Other income	2,600	2,500
Income before income tax......	$ 88,400	$102,500
Income tax..................	39,000	46,000
Net income..................	$ 49,400	$ 56,500

Instructions:

(1) Prepare a comparative income statement for the two-year period, presenting an analysis of each item in relationship to net sales for each of the years.

(2) To the extent the data permit, comment on the significant relationships revealed by the vertical analysis prepared in (1).

28-4B. The financial statements of H. K. Palmer Company are presented below and on the following page.

H. K. Palmer Company
Balance Sheet
December 31, 1970

Assets

Current assets:

Cash......................................	$ 95,000	
Marketable securities.....................	50,000	
Accounts receivable (net).................	395,000	
Merchandise inventory.....................	353,000	
Prepaid expenses..........................	7,000	
Total current assets......................		$ 900,000

Long-term investments:

Investment in affiliated company...........		200,000

Plant assets:

Equipment (net)...........................	$ 720,000	
Buildings (net)...........................	1,080,000	
Land......................................	100,000	
Total plant assets........................		1,900,000
Total assets..............................		$3,000,000

Liabilities

Current liabilities:

Accounts payable..........................		$ 600,000

Long-term liabilities:

Mortgage note payable, due 1980..............	$ 260,000	
Bonds payable, 6%, due 1990..................	500,000	
Total long-term liabilities..................		760,000
Total liabilities...........................		$1,360,000

Stockholders' Equity

Preferred 6% stock, cumulative, nonparticipating, $100 par......	$ 500,000	
Common stock, $10 par.......................	500,000	
Retained earnings...........................	640,000	
Total stockholders' equity..................		1,640,000
Total liabilities and stockholders' equity..........		$3,000,000

841

H. K. Palmer Company
Income Statement
For Year Ended December 31, 1970

Sales	$3,577,000	
Sales returns and allowances.	77,000	
Net sales.		$3,500,000
Cost of merchandise sold:		
Merchandise inventory, January 1, 1970.	$ 327,000	
Purchases (net)	2,406,000	
Merchandise available for sale	$2,733,000	
Merchandise inventory, December 31, 1970.	353,000	
Cost of merchandise sold.		2,380,000
Gross profit on sales.		$1,120,000
Operating expenses:		
Selling expenses.	$ 531,500	
General expenses.	302,000	
Total operating expenses.		833,500
Net operating income.		$ 286,500
Other income		13,500
		$ 300,000
Other expense (interest)		43,000
Income before income tax.		$ 257,000
Income tax.		122,000
Net income.		$ 135,000

842

H. K. Palmer Company
Retained Earnings Statement
For Year Ended December 31, 1970

Retained earnings, January 1, 1970.		$ 560,000
Add net income.		135,000
Total.		$ 695,000
Deduct dividends:		
On preferred stock	$30,000	
On common stock.	25,000	55,000
Retained earnings, December 31, 1970.		$ 640,000

Additional data, taken from the balance sheet at December 31, 1969, are as follows:

Accounts receivable (net).	$ 365,000
Long-term investments.	200,000
Total assets	2,800,000
Total stockholders' equity (preferred and common stock outstanding same as in 1970).	1,560,000

Instructions:

Determine for 1970 the ratios, turnovers, and other measures listed below and on the next page, presenting the figures used in your computations:

  (1) Working capital.

  (2) Current ratio.

(3) Acid-test ratio.

(4) Accounts receivable turnover.

(5) Number of days' sales in receivables.

(6) Merchandise inventory turnover.

(7) Number of days' sales in merchandise inventory.

(8) Ratio of plant assets to long-term liabilities.

(9) Ratio of stockholders' equity to liabilities.

(10) Rate earned on total assets.

(11) Rate earned on stockholders' equity.

(12) Rate earned on common stockholders' equity.

(13) Ratio of net sales to assets.

(14) Earnings per share on common stock.

843

a

b

c

c

d

847

e

e

f

848

g•h

i

i

Input media, 328, 329
Installment method, 352; and income tax, 423, 599
Insurance expense, 474
Insurance premium, 287
Insurance policy, 287
Insurance register, 286; *illustrated*, 286, 287
Intangible assets, 257
Intangible property, 226
Integrated data processing (IDP), 337
Interest, determining, 167
Interest-bearing note, 167, 172; *illustrated*, 166
Interest expense, 167; and notes payable, 169; deductible from adjusted gross income, 587
Interest income, 33, 167; and notes receivable, 171
Interim monthly income statement,

illustrated, 571
Interim statements, 78
Internal auditors, 5
Internal check, 268
Internal control, 268; assignment of responsibility, 268; for payroll systems, 311; independent review, 270; of cash payments, 277; of cash receipts, 275; over cash, 270; proofs and security measures, 269; rotation of duties, 268; separation of operations and accounting, 269; separation of responsibility, 269
Internal Revenue Code (IRC), 580; gross income defined, 583
Internal Revenue Service (IRS), 580
Internal transactions, 10
Inventory, 189, 501; determining actual quantities, 192; determin-

ing the cost of, 193; gross profit method of estimating, 203; importance of, 189; of partially processed materials, 511; valuation at lower of cost or market, 197
Inventory costing, 193; comparison of methods, 196; first-in, first-out method (fifo), 194; last-in, first-out method (lifo), 195; retail method, 199; weighted average method, 195
Inventory systems, 191
Investments, in stocks and bonds, 452; income from bonds, 455; income from stocks, 454; long-term, 454; recording in partnership, 370; sale of, 456; temporary, 453
Invoice, purchase, 117; sales, 92, 117

j•k

Job cost sheet, 535; *illustrated*, 537
Job order cost accounting, 530; flow of costs through, 542; summary illustration of, 538
Job order cost systems, 505; distinguished from process cost systems, 530

Joint costs, 513
Joint products, 513
Joint return, split-income feature, 590
Journal, business documents as, 99; cash payments, 125; cash receipts, 101; general, 90; pur-

chases, 118; purchases invoices as, 124; sales, 94, 107; special, 88; two-column, *illustrated*, 36
Journal entry, 30; compound, 31
Journalizing, 37; adjusting entries, 70
Key punch, 331

l

849

Land, 664
Last-in, first-out method (lifo), 195
Lease or sell, 622
Ledger, 28; accounts payable at end of month, *illustrated*, 128; accounts receivable at end of month, 105; after accounts are adjusted, closed, ruled, and balanced, *illustrated*, 74; customers, 93; flow of data from sales journal to, *illustrated*, 93; for a service enterprise, *illustrated*, 45; general, 93; subsidiary, 92; see also Gen-

eral ledger accounts
Legal capital, 396
Leverage, 724
Liabilities, 11, 32; accrued, 63, 213, 222; contingent, 356; current, 32; fixed, 32; long-term, 32; plant assets to long-term, 722; ratio of stockholders' equity to, 721
Liability accounts, ruling and balancing, 73
Limited life, of partnership, 369
Liquidating dividend, 429

Liquidation of partnership, 379
List price, 91
Listed securities, 452
Long-term capital gains and losses, 591
Long-term investments, 454; income from, 454; on balance sheet, 454; sale of, 456
Long-term liabilities, 32
Losses from sale or exchange of property, 585

m

Machine language, 333
Magnetic ink, 330
Magnetic ink character processors, 330
Magnetic tape, 330
Make or buy, 626
Maker, of note, 166
Management, accounting aides to, 552; and budgeting, 553
Management accounting, 5
Management reports, 636; and special analyses, 636; purpose of, 636
Management services, 6
Manufacturing expenses, 500
Manufacturing margin, 616
Manufacturing operations, 500; general accounting for, 502
Margin of safety, 647
Marginal income, 617; ratio, 647; statement by sales territories, *illustrated*, 621; statement by unit of product, *illustrated*, 620

Marginal tax rate, 595
Market price, of stock, 409
Market value method of allocation of joint costs, 515
Marketable securities, 453
Matching revenue and expired costs, 350
Materiality, 356
Materials, 501, 531; ledger, 531; ledger account, *illustrated*, 531
Materials requisition, *illustrated*, 532
Medical expenses, deductible from adjusted gross income, 588
Memory unit, of computer, 332
Merchandise inventory, 189; adjustments at end of period, 139, 141; analysis, 720; number of days' sales in, 721; presentation on balance sheet, 202; turnover, 720
Merchandising, 89

Mergers, 683; and consolidations, 683
Minimizing income taxes, 595
Minimum standard deduction, 589
Minority interest, 688
Miscellaneous general expense, 475
Miscellaneous selling expense, 475
Mixed accounts, 60
Monetary amounts, and business transactions, 11
Monetary items, 697
Monetary unit, stability of, 349
Money, as a unit of measurement, 696
Mortgage notes payable, 32
Mortgage payable, 32
Moving average, 202
Moving expenses, 585
Multiple-step form of income statement, 145

850

p

Promissory notes, 166
Property, 240; intangible, 226; personal, 226; real, 226; tangible, 226; types of, 226
Property tax expense, 474
Property taxes, 226; accounting for, 227; payment of, 227
Proprietorship, 12, 32
Protest fee, 174
Public accounting, 4
Public corporation, 393
Punched card machines, 331

Punched cards, 330
Punched paper tape, 330
Purchase accounting, versus pooling of interests, 692
Purchase invoice, 117; *illustrated*, 117
Purchase orders, 531
Purchase requisitions, 531
Purchased treasury stock, 405
Purchases, on account, 13
Purchases discount, 100, 283
Purchases invoices, used as a

journal, 124
Purchases journal, 118; *illustrated*, 118–119; posting the, 120; relationship with ledgers, *illustrated*, 122; using purchases invoices as, 124
Purchases returns and allowances 121; general journal entries for, *illustrated*, 123
Purchasing procedures, 116

q•r

Quick assets, 718
Quick ratio, 718
Quantity variance, 564
Rate earned, on common stockholders' equity, 724; on stockholders' equity, 724; on total assets, 723
Rate of return on assets, 637; report, *illustrated*, 638
Rate schedules, for income tax, 591
Rate variance, 565
Ratio, of net sales to assets, 722; of plant assets to long-term liabilities, 722; of stockholders' equity to liabilities, 721
Real accounts, 35
Real estate, 226
Real property, 226
Realization, 379; gain on, 380; loss on, with capital deficiency, 382; loss on, with no capital deficiencies, 381
Realty, 226
Receivables, aging the, 178; classification of, 165; numbers of days'

sales in, 719; presentation on balance sheet, 165; trade, 165
Receiving report, 118, 531
Reciprocal accounts, 482; in consolidation, 686
Redemption of bonds, 451
Registered bonds, 445
Reimbursed expenses, 585
Remittance advice, 271
Remuneration, types of, 300
Rent earned, 14
Rent expense, 474
Replacement cost, 614
Report, auditor's, 457
Report form, of balance sheet, 17; *illustrated*, 18, 69
Reports, scope of, 349
Reproducer, for punched cards, 331
Reserve, 427; method, 174
Residual value, 243
Responsibility accounting, 618
Retail inventory method, 199
Retail merchandising, 90
Retained earnings, 396, 665; appropriation of, 427; on balance sheet, 428

Retained earnings statement, 434; combined with income statement, *illustrated*, 695; comparative, *illustrated*, 713; *illustrated*, 435; with horizontal analysis, *illustrated*, 713; see also Appendix B
Returns and allowances, purchases, 121; sales, 96
Revaluation of assets, 377
Revenue, 14, 32; accounts, 34; accrued, 214; degree of contract completion method of recognizing, 352; differential, 621; expenditures, 247, 248; from sales, on income statement, 147; installment method of recognizing, 352; matching with expired costs, 350; received in advance, 213; recognition of, 351
Reversing entries, 153; for accrued interest, 225; for accrued salaries, 222; for prepaid interest, 216; for unearned rent, 220; *illustrated*, 156
Ruling and balancing accounts, 73

851

s

Salaries payable, adjustment on work sheet, 144
Salary, 300
Sale, point of, 351
Sales, 14, 33; cash, 91; in merchandising business, 90; of finished goods in manufacturing company, 91; on account, 14, 91; ratio of net to assets, 722
Sales account, after posting sales journal, *illustrated*, 96
Sales allowance, 96
Sales budget, 555; *illustrated*, 555
Sales discounts, 100
Sales invoice, 92, 117; *illustrated*, 92, 117; posted directly to customer's account, 99
Sales journal, 94; after posting, *illustrated*, 94; designed for charging prepaid transportation costs, *illustrated*, 107; posting the, 94; relationship with ledgers, *illustrated*, 93; using invoices as, 99
Sales mix, 619
Sales returns, 96; general journal entries for, *illustrated*, 97
Sales returns and allowances, 96; journal, *illustrated*, 99; posting of, *illustrated*, 98
Sales salaries, 473
Sales taxes, 108; collection of, 109
Sales territories, contribution of, 620
Sales ticket, 91
Sales value, method of allocation of joint costs, 515

Salvage value, 243
Schedule of accounts payable, *illustrated*, 129, 149
Schedule of accounts receivable, *illustrated*, 106,148
Scrap value, 243
Secured bond, 446
Securities, listed, 452; marketable, 453; unlisted, 452
Selling expenses, 147
Semifixed costs, 562
Semivariable costs, 562
Separate legal existence, of corporation, 394
Serial bonds, 446
Service departments, and process costs, 506
Shareholders, 394
Shareholders' equity, 395; reporting discount and premium on stock and a deficit, *illustrated*, 401
Shareholders' investment, 395; paid-in capital section of balance sheet, *illustrated*, 421
Shares of stock, 394
Shipments to branch, 483; billed at selling price, 488
Short-term capital gains and losses, 591
Signature card, 270
Single-step form, of income statement, 145, 694; *illustrated*, 695
Sinking fund, 449; on balance sheet, 450; trustee, 449
Slides, 48
Sole proprietorship, defined, 8
Solvency, 708

Sorter, 331
Sources of funds, 660
Special journals, 88
Split-income feature, of joint return, 590
Stability of monetary unit, 349
Standard cost systems, 563
Standard costs, 563; incorporated in the accounts, 570; variances from, 564
Standard deduction, 589
Standard form, two column account, *illustrated*, 37; two column journal, *illustrated*, 36
State unemployment compensation tax, 314
Stated value, of stock, 396
Statement, of cash flow, *illustrated*, 671; of changes in working capital, 659; of cost of goods manufactured, 502; of cost of goods manufactured, *illustrated*, 503; of resources provided and applied, 659; of retained earnings, 434; of source and application of funds, 659; of source and application of funds, *illustrated*, 666, 667
Statements, accounting methods disclosed on, 356; analysis of, 708; combined for home office and branch, 487; common-size, 715; events subsequent to date of, 356; for a partnership, 374; preparation of, 145; *see also* Financial statements
Stock, authorized, 396; book value,

Index

852

Index

853